The Big Red Book of AMERICAN LUTHERIE

Volume Five, 1997–1999

Guild of American Luthiers
8222 South Park Avenue
Tacoma, Washington 98408
253-472-7853
www.luth.org

The Big Red Book of AMERICAN LUTHERIE

Volume Five, 1997–1999

Edited by Tim Olsen

Guild of American Luthiers
8222 South Park Avenue, Tacoma, Washington 98408 USA

ISBN 978-0-9626447-7-1

First printing February 2008

The following GAL staff members and consultants
made significant contributions to the production of this book:

Cyndy Burton: Editing, proofreading

Deb Olsen: Proofreading and correction

Jon Peterson: Digital photo preparation, proofreading

Dale Phillips: Copy preparation, digital graphics preparation

Drawings have been redrawn by Guild staff members Bon Henderson and Tim Olsen
based on sketches provided by the authors of the individual articles, unless otherwise credited.

Dust jacket photo shows a classical guitar soundboard by Jeffrey Elliott.
Photo by Jeffrey Elliott, 1998.

Printed in USA by Thomson-Shore on acid-free paper.

Foreword

Since the early days of the Golden Age of American Lutherie, the Guild of American Luthiers has provided a forum for the free exchange of information about the construction, repair, and restoration of all types of stringed instruments. The GAL is a nonprofit educational organization supported entirely by our members and by publication sales. We now have over thirty-five hundred members in about forty countries and publish what we feel to be the world's foremost magazine on the subject, *American Lutherie*.

For thirteen years after the Guild's beginnings in 1972, our publications consisted of a small-format quarterly journal with technical articles enclosed as separate data sheets. We adopted the present format of *American Lutherie* magazine in 1985. Much of the material we published before 1985 is available in our two-volume *Resource Book* series: *Lutherie Tools,* and *Lutherie Woods and Steel String Guitars.*

The Guild is an information-sharing system. We believe that the material we publish is of lasting and cumulative value, and we see it as part of our ongoing mission to keep that material in print. By the end of 2007, *American Lutherie* magazine has grown to ninety-two issues, an impractical number to keep in print.

The purpose of the *Big Red Book of American Lutherie* series is to present, in compact, economical, lasting, and convenient form the content of past years of *American Lutherie* magazine. This volume, the fifth in the series, encompasses *American Lutherie #49* through *#60,* originally published in 1997, 1998, and 1999. Advertisements and matters of minor or temporary interest have been excluded. Future volumes in the *Big Red Book of American Lutherie* series are planned for publication on a regular basis, making it easier to procure and access the wealth of lutherie information generated over the years by the Guild's membership.

The organization of this volume is roughly chronological. Note that the original publication information is given at the top of every article. The Guild is not, of itself, an authority. An important part of the GAL's publications is the highly individual style and approach of our many authors as they offer the wisdom they have gained for the benefit of their fellows. We make no representation that the information published in this book is unassailable, only that the author has found it useful and has freely offered it for your consideration. As time marches on, new discoveries are made and new insights are gained; the reader will find it useful to note the year of publication of each article and of the updates offered at the end of some articles.

There are about ninety articles in this book, plus dozens of consolidated column entries. Since they are not grouped by topic, we felt a table of contents would be of little use. Instead, we have prepared two indexes. The first lists all authors alphabetically, followed by the titles of their articles in page order. The second lists topics alphabetically, followed by the article titles and author names in page order. The list of topics corresponds to the list of keywords in our searchable abstracts document, available on our website. These two indexes, combined with the roughly chronological order of the material, should allow one to find any particular article easily.

Speaking of our searchable abstracts document, remember that you can search online for any topic keyword (or any word) that appears in our abstracts of all our publications. This way you can quickly locate information on any topic in any of our magazines or books. This can be helpful for finding updates to material that you read in this present volume. In fact, it can be a very effective way to find information within this book itself. Go to www.luth.org and click on "searchable abstracts."

A generation of American luthiers has grown up with the Guild. Thousands of members and hundreds of authors have supported our experiment in information exchange. This book, as well as all the Guild's other publications, is evidence that the experiment is working. This is our thirty-seventh year of service to the instrument making community. We are proud of, and grateful for, the successes the Guild has achieved, and firmly believe our greatest accomplishments are yet ahead of us.

Tim Olsen
Founder/Editor

Originally published in *American Lutherie #49*, 1997

Meet the Maker: René Baarslag

by Woodley White

IMAGINE IF YOU WILL a second-story workshop washed with morning light and supplied with well-honed chisels and other fine hand tools. Picture this workshop nestled on the side of a mountain on a piece of arid Spanish property. Around the house are fields filled with aromatic fruit trees. And now picture the whole scene on the outskirts of cobble-stoned Granada, a mere fifteen miles from the azure coast of the Mediterranean.

Cigarette smoke and flamenco music float in the air of this workshop of René Baarslag. Born in Holland, the master guitar maker has created an environment here in Spain that suits his personality. René symbolizes a melding of Northern European and Spanish cultures which is reflected also in the instruments he makes.

It was Wednesday on a hot July evening at the American School of Lutherie, the midpoint of the week in which René Baarslag was teaching his class called "Guitarmaking in Granada" when I had the good fortune to sit down and speak to this gifted man. René is a charming and sensitive person as well as a master guitar builder. I interviewed René after a full day of guitar construction to get to know him better and to ask him some questions about some of the differences between guitars made in Granada and guitars made in Madrid. Charles Fox was present and asked some of the questions for the interview.

René, tell us a little bit about your background.

Here is my history. I hope it doesn't contradict other histories. I was born in Heerlen, Holland, September 4, 1948. I am the oldest child with two brothers and one sister. I studied mechanical engineering at the university.

I went to Spain to study flamenco about twenty years ago. I had one car, one guitar, and one toothbrush. When I got there I just wanted to stay with some people for three days. I ended staying more than fifteen years. So watch out when you come to visit Granada.

For recreation, I like to work the land. My hobby is planting trees including fruit trees on my property. I also like to run, downhill only. It feels a little bit like flying. Our home is on the side of a mountain which slopes down to the Mediterranean about fifteen miles away.

You speak five languages fluently. When you say that English is your worst, it is hard for those of us attending your class to believe you. Your English is terrific!

ALL COURTESY RENE BAARSLAG

I learned English as I was learning the guitar and wanted to understand the lyrics. There were a lot of songs that I wanted to learn and the words were in English. I also learned some English in school as a boy. There are many visitors who come to Granada, so knowing English is a real asset. When I moved to Spain I was in my later twenties. I did not have a job in Holland.

Did you know much Spanish when you moved there?

Not one word. The idea I had was to go to Spain to learn more flamenco. I had some interest in guitar building. I went into a shop in Holland to buy some wood for a dulcimer and the shop owner almost threw me out. Nobody was going to pay you for sitting down and playing the guitar.

I developed a friendship with Antonio Marin. I purchased one of his guitars. When it needed some repair, I turned to the maker. After getting to know him, I said to Antonio, "I think I would like to make one." Antonio responded, "Well, what can I do about it?" So I began to set up my own shop, and when I needed advice, I turned to Antonio for instruction. That was twenty years ago. The first four guitars I built for sale were cypress. I sold them as flamenco guitars because nobody would buy them as classical instruments. I traveled around Europe selling them and then I took the money and bought some more material and made some more. I moved at that point into rosewood and more traditional materials.

Antonio is kind of a center in Granada, a school of guitar making. He's kind of the godfather of the Granada scene. Antonio was open to teaching me. Usually at that time it was kind of a secret. The sound thing, that was for you to figure out. This school run by Charles Fox is totally opposite to anything I have known in the past. Now days there is a lot more information about the guitar; if you are not stupid, you can pick it up. Back then it was much more likely to be exclusive information. For many generations, a guitar maker might pass his trade on only to his son or to his brother's son. No one else would be taught the art. I had to learn the hard way. But there are some new makers in Granada with me, and we share information with each other.

And here you are teaching with students pouring all over your work with dial calipers.

Yes, but I am sure that they still did not see 70% of what I am doing, because I know what I know by experience. It took me five or ten years of doing it to learn it.

Charles: *In that sense this experience has been more of a European experience. Not much lecture, just experiential learning.*

Woodley: *René, what about the passion for your art? Where does it come from?*

The first seven or eight years it was a holiday for me. I wasn't working. If the sun comes in the room where you are working in the morning, it is heaven. And then you get paid for it as well. When you get to the point and start to look at the instrument as a dollar sign, you begin to lose interest, it changes. It should be fun to do it. I think it is a beautiful profession.

Antonio Marin

Are you to the point where you have enough orders that you can relax?

At the moment, yes, but I have stopped worrying about it. From the beginning I didn't care. I had my last $10 and still I said, "Let's spend it today." I think if you are that way in life, things come to you. The same is true with the guitar. If you have joy, you can hear it. Otherwise, you don't hear it. I am eclectic in my musical tastes. I get bored easily. I don't want a whole day of jazz or a whole day of classical music. Right now I'm listening to a bit of Arabic music. I am a person who gets things by listening to them. I can read some poetry and not understand a word, but then someone sings it and suddenly I get it and it moves me.

A little while ago you described your studio in ways that make it sound so beautiful.

It is possible to create an environment that is aesthetically pleasing. After all it is the place where you are most of your waking hours.

René, what are your goals?

I am looking for a certain development year by year.

Is there a particular sound you are looking for?

Yes, a sound you can influence a lot. Not too clean a sound. Good for all kinds of music. Not too typical a guitar sound. Very few cedar guitars can produce this sound, and yet, Madrid keeps making cedar. When you begin this craft you probably have this fantasy that you are the one to make the best guitar.

Charles: *I am impressed that in your line of work you have not strayed or been too radical.*

You need a long time just to know the wood. To know the spruce. To know the rosewood. Only after you have a lot of experience should you begin to vary from it. To the young builder, I would say, "Try to make a good Hauser or a good Torres guitar." That would not be a bad start. If you do it well, you will be as good as Hauser or Torres.

Charles: *What I admire about you is your respect for simplicity, the simplicity of your design. I know it will have lasting effect on me.*

My wife, Ann, started building about a year ago. She started with a Torres model. She got a guitar out of it. People come in and say, "I want one like hers." We should not respect what is old just because it is old. An old person can be just as stupid as a young one. But if they have wisdom, you show respect. The master builders of the past deserve respect.

Charles: *What this school is all about — teaching contemporary methods of guitar building — means that we need to be that much more committed to the standards and to learning from people like you. It is a matter of combining the contemporary with the tried and true and looking for what runs through all of it.*

Woodley: *Tell me about your connection with Robert Bouchet.*

*(See **Baarslag** on page 11)*

Originally published in *American Lutherie #49*, 1997

Passport to Spain

from René Baarslag's American School of Lutherie workshop

by Woodley White

THE AMERICAN School of Lutherie had the vision to bring the unique talent of René Baarslag to the Napa Valley for a one-week workshop on guitar building this last July. But no matter how far René is from the orchards and ocean breezes of his home near Granada, he wears the magic of his existence like a mantle.

Also magic is the skill by which he creates instruments that allow other artists to speak the universal language of music. Music, like guitar building, has at least a dual nature. Not only does it speak this universal language, but it also takes on the quality of local geography and culture. Therefore it unites people all around the planet just as it enhances indigenous expression.

Granada is one of the most vital creative centers of Spanish guitar building. René Baarslag developed his own style there as he learned his craft from the great Antonio Marin, the father of the Granada school of guitar building. This article is a summary of the building process with construction details elaborating some of the stylistic and acoustic design considerations that are distinctive of René's guitars.

Watching René was almost like seeing time-lapse photography as he assembled an instrument in only five days. He came to the States with the neck partially completed, the plates joined and the rosette inlaid, the soundhole reinforced, and the sides bent. The rest of the construction process was done in the presence of the class. Unfortunately, much of what he taught the class cannot be articulated, just as one struggles to describe a great performance of music.

The goal of the class was to build an instrument in a week, to prepare the French polish, sand, fill the pores, to polish, and as the instrument was constructed, to answer any questions the students had.

Materials

René began the class by emphasizing the importance of wood selection. German spruce is his material of choice for the top. In order to find the best wood, he indicates that Germany is the best place to buy it. He says that he looks for an "equal grain," not a "close grain," and makes certain that the cross grain has a quality of stiffness that pleases him. Further, none but split materials will do for a good top.

He does not listen for tap tones in selection of top material, because when he buys it, it is still wet and it has hairs on it from sawing. He chooses the hardest tops. Appearance, to René, is of secondary importance and he currently pays about 50–100 marks per top (roughly $75) at the mill. To check for proper stiffness, back in his shop, he measures deflection of the plates. Then he adjusts the thickness of the top according to

ALL BY WOODLEY WHITE

René Baarslag teaching at the American School of Lutherie in the summer of 1996. Here he checks the height after trimming back braces to a uniform height using a plane with an curved sole, creating in them an arch which matches the curvature of the back.

how the wood flexes. If the top has adequate stiffness, he sands it down as thin as 2.5MM.

There is a wide range of variety and quality of woods at the mill: "Some you can roll up like a newspaper, some you can't bend at all, some you want to dump in the trash can. For example, Engelmann is now plentiful, German spruce is scarce." And René indicates that much of the supply used to come from Yugoslavia, but with the war, that is impossible now.

For this artisan, spruce is the most important wood in material selection. The second most important is the rosewood, and René uses mostly Indian rosewood. "It is still possible to get a very fine quality of the Indian," René says with a wry smile, "but Brazilian is not such a high quality any more. I think they are cutting the roots. I use cedar for the neck. The ebony should be as straight as possible. I always make the bridge from Brazilian rosewood. And I select dark Brazilian for the purfling."

The rosettes he makes from mahogany, rosewood, and sycamore. He uses a router to cut for the rosette inlay. And he prefers a high-speed steel router bit because he feels it is so much sharper than carbide.

Glue, of course, for any European craftsman is one of the more important elements. René prefers warm hide glue in the basic construction of the instrument including the rosette. "I warm my workboard by placing it behind the oven. I also heat the top. Then you cannot answer the telephone or anything. Otherwise you end up with huge differences in the size of the tiles. You try to keep your inconsistencies consistent."

After the inlay is completed, he covers the rosette with superglue. He says he doesn't like the stuff, but he appreciates what it's good for: quick adhesion and permanence. At this point, he is ready to start reducing the top to its final dimension.

Plate Thickness

Often, guitar makers construct the instrument and then thickness the top to achieve a certain tone. Not René. He understands that the sound is related to the tensile strength of the plate. So he measures deflection and thickness and achieves a uniformity of tone by virtue of consistent, careful, measurements.

"Normally, I take my tops down to 2.7MM on the sanding machine then I begin scraping. By the time I assemble them they are 2.0MM–2.4MM. You should always sand the top to a uniform thickness. I go a little thinner on the edges. I don't tune the individual instruments. I make the changes in the beginning, then I know I will achieve that difference in the guitar. It is a process of making more guitars while always aiming for consistency. I want to change only one variable at a time.

"After I thickness the top plate to 2.7MM I measure the deflection of the top with a weight. I suspend it across two blocks, located about equal with the bridge, and supporting the top only on the edge. With 380G placed about where the bridge will be, the deflection should be 9MM–10MM. The extremes for deflection are 8MM–11MM."

The soundhole has approximately an 88MM diameter. René had applied the soundhole-reinforcement donut prior to coming to California. The grain was parallel with the grain of the top. I would guess that he glued it on prior to cutting the soundhole because the inside edges were flush in the soundhole circle. He had shaped the donut so that a cross section would look something like the cross section of an airplane wing. We didn't get to see how he did this. I am pretty sure that it is made of excess top material.

Bracing the Back

For attaching braces René uses the hide glue mentioned above, because it has certain qualities he has learned to trust over the years. He begins by heating the braces so the hide glue will stick to both the plate and the braces. And the braces themselves are an art form all their own.

"The back plate is thicknessed to about 2.0MM or 2.1MM. The back strip is made of rosewood. The braces for the back are made of Spanish cedar, and are about 8MM thick. The brace across the lower bout is 17MM high, the one across the waist is 14MM high, and the brace across the upper bout is 13MM high. I rough them out a little taller than that. These braces are quite arched — at least 5MM. I cut the arch with a router, duplicating off a brace template. The middle brace is the strongest, I think."

René glues the arched side of the braces to the back. The go-bar system presses the braces to the plates on top of the solera. After a brace is clamped in place he uses water to take excess glue off before drying it with cotton. René lets the glue dry from a half to one-and-a-half hours before proceeding to the next step. He usually constructs two instruments at a time, so that while one is drying he can duplicate the same step on guitar number two.

The go-bar deck seen in the photos was constructed especially for this class. The one René uses in his shop at home has a light on the bottom surface of the upper deck for maximum visibility.

When the glue has dried he shapes the tops of the braces to follow a curve that is parallel to the arch of the back. He does this scalloping with a plane that has an arched bottom. Then with a small plane he rounds over the top edge of the brace. The ends of the braces are then scalloped to 8MM to fit into the linings. To carve these scallops on the end of each brace, he has a template which he holds along side the brace and carves the matching shape.

Top: René uses a go-bar deck to glue bracing to tops and backs. Here he is carefully cleaning glue squeeze-out before it has a chance to dry. A solera supports the back.
Bottom: A completed back with shaped braces and center strip.

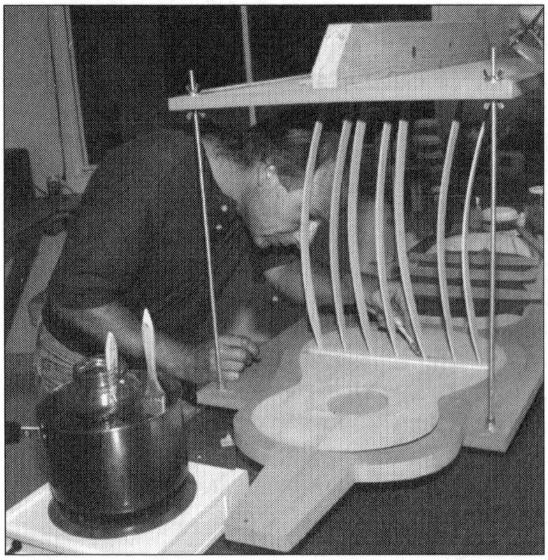
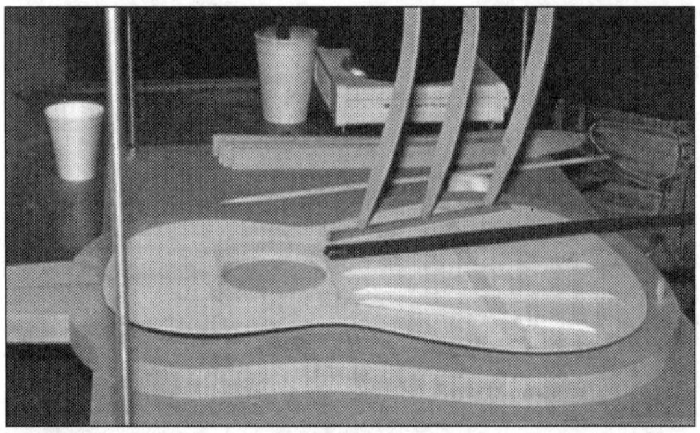
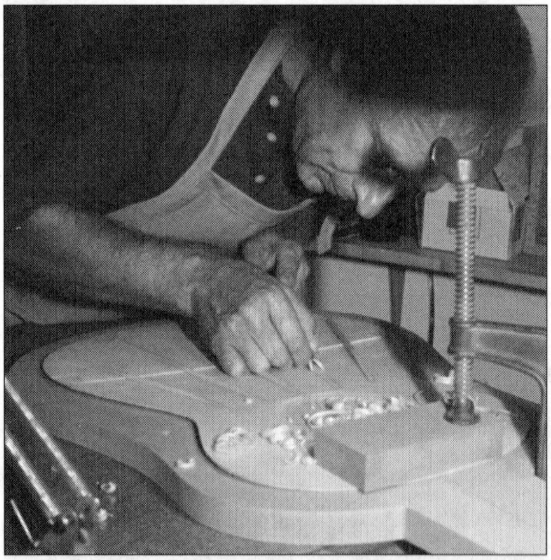
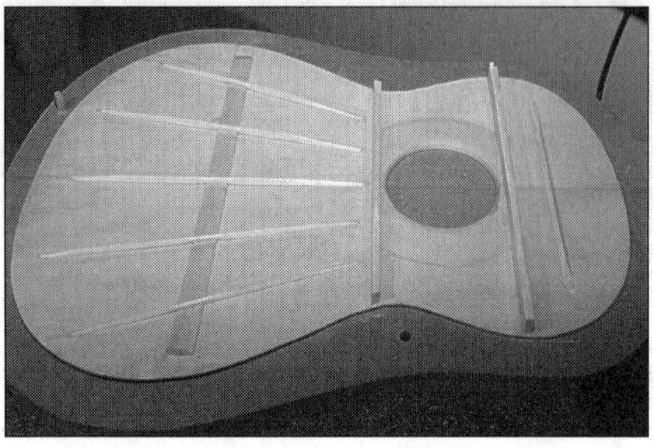

Bracing the Top

René says, "I make the guitar top asymmetrically to avoid the preference of one tone." The bridge patch René uses is typical of Granada-made guitars, and is influenced by the Bouchet design. (About ten years ago Robert Bouchet more or less chose Antonio Marin to go on with his work and thus bequeathed the Northern European influence to Spain. Bouchet's bridge bar goes over the fan braces.) The material is vertical-grain spruce. The grain runs lengthwise, cross grain to the top. After it is glued to the top René uses a plane to taper the bridge patch from 1.5MM on the treble side to just under 1MM on the bass side. He finishes it by beveling the ends down to nothing.

René uses five fan braces with no barrier bar, which is typical of Granada-made guitars. It is also common to use struts that are lower and wider. René's vary from bass to treble with the following measurements: 4MM×5MM; 4.5MM×5.5MM; 6MM×6MM; 5.5MM×6.5MM; 6MM×7MM. He says if the top is too thick or too heavily braced the sound becomes "too round," and if the top is too thin it goes to "the flamenco sound." René designs the layout of the fan braces by aiming them toward the center of the 12th fret. Before he attaches the fan braces to the guitar top he arches the surface of each brace that contacts the top by 1MM–2MM at each end, and he notches the braces for the bridge patch with a chisel.

The cauls for gluing the fan bracing to the top are concave and fit squarely on top of each brace. They are about the size of a fan brace. There is a groove on one edge so that they fit snugly over the fan braces. Before gluing, both the top and the brace are preheated. To heat the top René heats up a piece of metal bar slightly larger than the brace and lays that in position on the top to transfer its warmth. Meanwhile, the brace itself is warming on a heating element.

After the fan braces have been glued in place René trims them to their final shape. The cross section of a brace would be roughly triangular, except where it is notched over the bridge patch.

The transverse braces for the top taper slightly in width, with the treble end slightly wider and the bass end slightly thinner. The bass end also needs to be slightly higher than the treble end. The brace above the soundhole is 6.5MM–7.5MM wide and 16MM–18MM high. The brace below the soundhole is 5.5MM–6.5MM high and 14MM–15MM wide.

The small transverse bar under the fretboard is not tapered. It functions mainly to prevent cracking.

After these braces are in place, only the sanding is left in the preparation of the top and back. René works from 80-, to 180-, to 240-grit paper. To sand along the sides of the brace, René cuts a slight arch on one edge of the sandpaper, so that it will not dig in to the back plate as he sands. After 240-grit paper, he uses steel wool on the back. Then he wipes it all down with a cotton cloth.

René is meticulous about his tools, even about his sanding blocks. He glues a little pad of cork on the sanding block to get just the right touch in finish sanding. He carefully finishes the braces and bridge patch with his custom sanding block and thus provides a clean appearance for the inside of the instrument.

Top: Gluing the bridge patch in place in a go-bar deck. Second from top: Gluing fan braces in place using shaped cauls. The dark metal bar has been heated and is warming the position where the next brace will be glued. The brace is also preheated. Preheating helps keep hide glue thin and workable until pressure is applied. Third from top: Shaping the braces with a chisel. Bottom: A fully braced top.

Assembly

René finishes the heel section of the neck that will be inside the guitar — first with a little shellac, then with a little "benguin" (gum benzoin, a finish that is available from the violin shop) which smells a little bit like chocolate and gives the inside of his instruments a particular aroma. He also seals inside the edges of the soundhole with superglue to keep the ebony dust from getting into the wood pores during assembly.

The neck, tail block, and back bracing are all made of cedar. That is the material of preference in Granada. Antonio Marin has used mahogany when he couldn't get cedar. René thinks it funny that we Americans call this wood Spanish cedar, because it is from the *Cedrella* family and it comes from the Caribbean, not Spain.

In chiseling the step recess for the top to fit to the neck, he establishes a slight angle (a slight V shape) which will determine the neck/body angle and the proper bridge height after the body is completed. The solera which René uses for construction has a corresponding bevel at the neck/body joint to establish the correct neck/body angle. To check this angle, after the guitar sides, neck, and top are together, prior to installation of the back, René places a straightedge on the guitar top with one end resting at the nut and the other at the point where the saddle will be. The gap between the straightedge and the guitar at the 12th fret should be the thickness of one U.S. quarter. He teases that a nickel or a dime will not do.

René arches the tail block both inside and outside on the surface which contacts the sides with a jig and a power sander. To clamp it in place he uses C-shaped clamps which he made by cutting up some chair springs.

The sides are glued to the top with individual cedar blocks rather than a kerfed lining. He makes these blocks on his table saw. First, he surfaces all four sides of the material on a drum sander, and slices it diagonally. Then he places the V-shaped material in a cradle which allows him to run this stock through the drum sander to surface the diagonal face, after which he glues many of these diagonal strips back together by applying glue across the ends. Then each crosscut will produce about twenty little blocks. "All the makers in Granada use these blocks," he says. After these blocks and the support blocks for the transverse braces are in place, the back is fit to the sides.

The back linings are 6mm × 17mm and are kerfed on the back side. In other words, the kerfed edge is the edge that is pressed against the side. This is opposite from the way most people install their linings, but it has the advantage of adding a great deal of strength to the side. They are applied to the side after it has been bent but prior to assembly. René leaves his linings protruding higher than the side so that he can hold the back in position and accurately mark where to cut the notches for the back braces. The gluing surface of the lining is pretty close to flush with the edge of the sides at the upper bout and the lower bout, but it extends up 4mm–5mm at the waist. The lining thus determines the proper depth of the guitar box rather than the side accomplishing this task. The side is shaped to allow the linings to stick up. Of course, the protrusion must be less than the height of the binding.

The gluing surface of the heel is carefully trimmed to fit the back. René reaches through the soundhole and marks where the back reinforcement strip will be cut to butt up against the heel. The reinforcement strip will then help the neck maintain the correct angle to the guitar top.

This was one thing that really surprised me. I had not seen anyone carve the heel of the neck after the sides, top, neck, and back had been joined. René carves the heel with a sharp chisel, very carefully aiming it away from the sides. He was able to create a beautifully shaped heel without one nick in the sides.

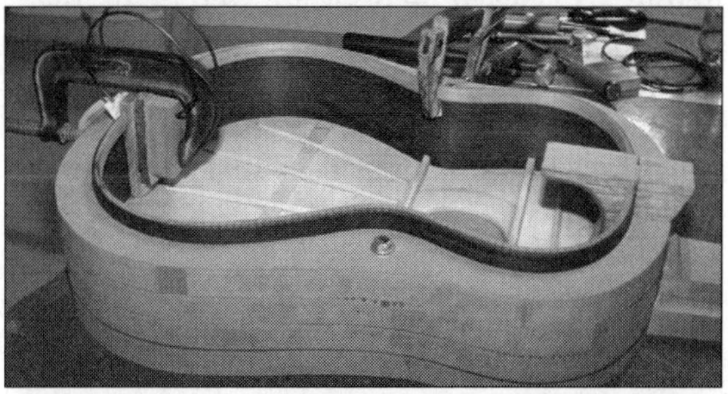

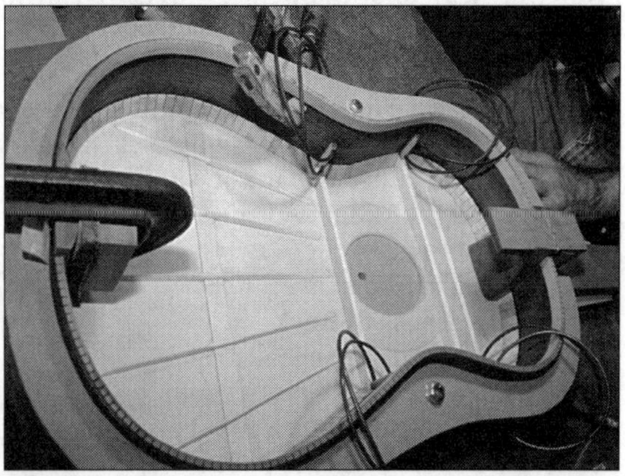

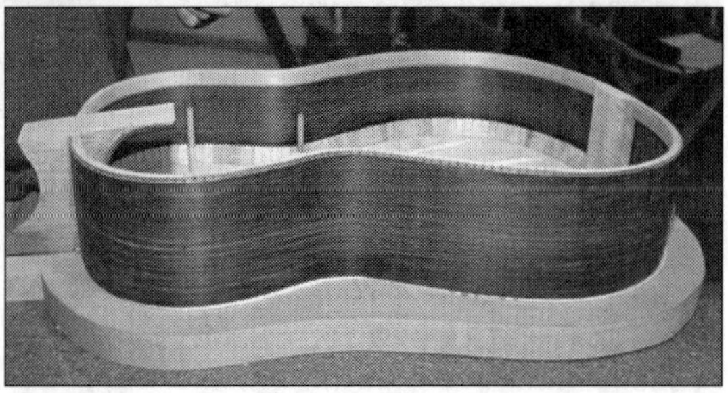

Top: Checking the pitch of the neck with a straightedge. Second from top: The tail block is glued to the sides using a C-clamp and clamps made from chair springs. Third from top: Individual cedar blocks are used to attach the top to the sides, and support blocks are glued over the transverse braces. Note that the kerfed lining of the back has been glued on with the slots toward the sides. This makes for a more rigid construction than gluing the unkerfed surface to the sides. Bottom: The guitar is ready for the back to be fit.

Purfling and Bindings

René cuts the inlay strip at the tail of the guitar with a hand saw after first scoring the sides with a knife on either side of the inlay.

To cut the notch for the bindings, René uses a laminate trimmer with a wooden base which has a slightly beveled bottom. This bevel compensates for the arch of the top and back, keeping the mortising bit parallel with the side.

He ropes the purfling and binding in place and interweaves the purfling strips, making each a different length so the seams are invisible. The binding is the one portion of the guitar where René uses Titebond glue. After binding the top, he begins carving the heel and then he cuts the rabbets for the back bindings.

After the bindings are on, René finishes them with a scraper. Then he seals the bindings with a coat of superglue. The purfling is made of a highly figured maple. He says if he does not seal them, the rosewood will bleed into the grain of the maple. The purfling strips are .4mm, .6mm, .8mm, and .12mm thick. René cuts his own. The white strips are curly maple which was violin stock. They just shimmer.

The Fretboard

The guitar constructed in this class has a 65mm scale length. He has heard scale lengths as long as 67mm by Ramírez but 65mm is the standard in Granada. René has made two that were shorter, 63.5mm, but feels that the bass wasn't as good and that they were actually harder to play.

He glues the preslotted fretboard in place, and then begins shaping the neck with a chisel and a rasp. With a rasp he cuts close to the shape at each end of the neck and then removes the material in-between these two points with a spoke shave. The finished thickness of neck plus fretboard is 21mm at the 1st fret and 23mm at the 9th.

He only sands the neck to 80 grit because when he does the pore filling on the body, the rosewood stains the neck, so he does finish sanding of the neck after the pores are filled on the body.

René first planes the fretboard so that it is a flat surface. Then he takes a little more off so that has a slight relief from the nut to the 7th fret. A straightedge placed on top of the fretboard will show a very

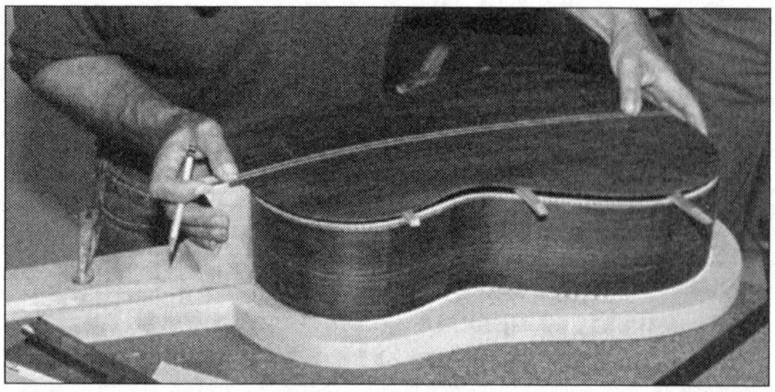

From top: René positions the back to mark where to cut the notches for the back braces in the lining. The heel is carefully trimmed to fit the back first with a chisel, and then with a plane. Brace notches are cut in the lining, and the body is ready to receive the back. Glue is applied, and the back is clamped to the sides using cord. Inset: René carves the heel after the back has been glued in place.

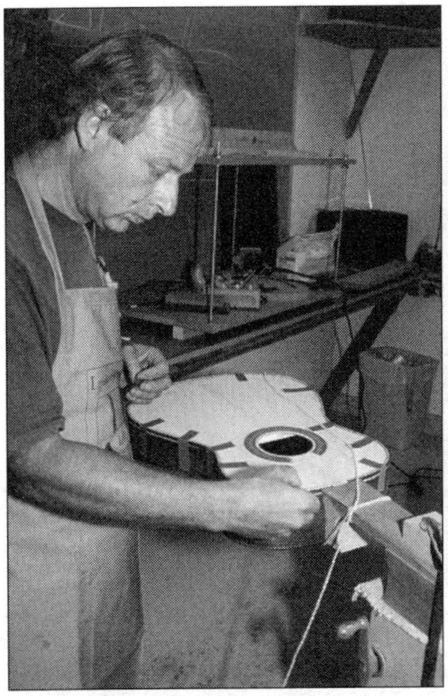

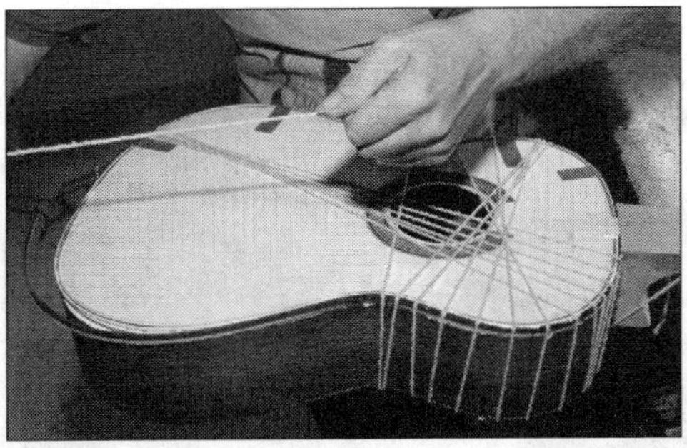

Above: Fitting the top binding using tape.
Center top: Half of the tape and binding are removed from the top, glue is applied, and that half of the binding is clamped in place with a cord.

Center bottom: The procedure is the same for installing the back binding.
Right: Cleaning up and leveling the binding with a scraper.

slight gap at the 7th fret (a few thousandths). This is done to eliminate any fret buzz at the 4th fret. Then he takes off a little more material on the bass side from the 12th fret to the soundhole. After planing, he surfaces the fretboard with a sanding block. He also slightly arches the fingerboard.

Next, he rescrapes the bindings to remove the superglue which is on the surface.

One of the interesting aspects of René's guitars is his use of the zero fret. Rather than a bone nut, he uses a slightly larger metal fret in order to make the fingered notes and the open string sound more similar in tone.

René has what is probably an old-school method for applying the bridge to the top. He wraps the same cord that was used for binding around the lower bout several times and around the waist several times. He then wedges two pieces of wood under these two bands in order to apply downward pressure on the bridge.

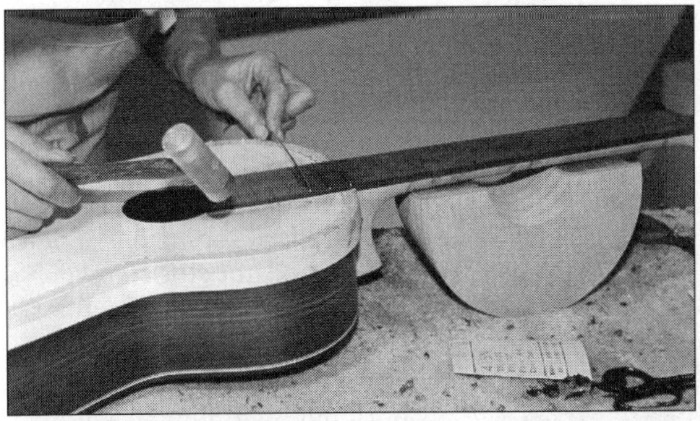

Top left: Installing frets.
Right: The area around the bridge is taped off, and cord is wrapped around the body in preparation for gluing on the bridge.

Bottom left: Two sticks are wedged under wrappings of cord to put pressure on the bridge while the glue dries.

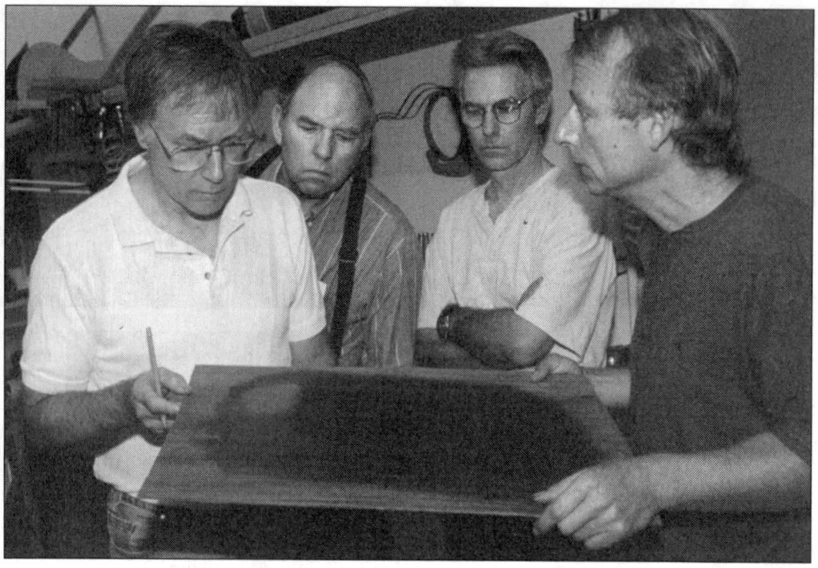

Sanding the Plates

To finish the plates, René scrapes them with a cabinet scraper until all of the major scratches are out. Then he sands with 180-, then 240-grit sandpaper. Then he wets the plates with a moist rag to raise the grain. Finish sanding is accomplished with 300- or 360-grit sandpaper.

Charles Fox provided a joined but unfinished guitar back for the students to work on and a cabinet scraper so that each class participant would have the opportunity to learn how to prepare and apply the French polish. During spare time throughout the week, they would move to work benches to scrape, sand, polish, and the results of their work were very impressive.

French Polish

After the surfacing of the instrument has been accomplished with finish sanding, René wipes down the instrument with water that has a small amount of hide glue in it — approximately 4 or 5 parts of water to 1 part glue. This is done for two purposes: 1) To seal the bindings; 2) To raise the grain so that a final sanding will leave the instrument entirely smooth.

Top left: René explains pore filling with pumice.
Top right: Rod Hanson, Brian Burns, Kenny Hill, and René examine a test back.
Above: René applies finishing touches to his guitar.

"I do finishing in two basic steps: First I fill the pores, then I build up the finish. Pore filling with pumice is now about one hour of work for me. You fill the guitar with pumice, then you wait until the next day. If you have a blemish in the finish, you don't try to sand it off. Rather you rub it with alcohol to take it back off. In filling you use more alcohol than shellac. With a cotton ball (a handful of cotton) dip it only one time into the dish with the polish in it. Then load the cotton with alcohol. Dab seven or eight shakes of the pumice powder on the rosewood and polish until the pores seem saturated and the white residue just begins to show. Then switch to the other side of the cotton and use alcohol only to remove any residue. If the residue dries without being removed, it will be possible to sand off later."

In doing finishing, René prefers morning light. He believes that the light in your workshop is one of the most important elements. He says that to do good work you surely need daylight. The rising sun allows you to see all of the imperfections. "They just light up," he says. "Take the best hours of the day for the most difficult tasks. I always sand cross grain until the very end. I also put my hand in the soundhole to support the area where I am sanding."

Completion and Listening

As Friday evening approached, the students were eager to listen to René's guitar. In order to accommodate them, René cut his finishing process short, put the tuning machines on the peghead, and tied on the strings. Kenny Hill took the new instrument in his arms and helped it to take its first breath. The sound was very distinctive, sweet, and articulate, with that Spanish throatiness that is the sound of a guitar made by a master's hand. The class applauded and then began to pack their belongings for their journeys home, somewhat weary from a week of intensive guitar making, but extremely grateful for the firsthand experience of watching this fine craftsman at work. ——

*(**Baarslag** from page 3)*

I was in France, riding my bicycle, when someone told me that a famous guitar maker named Antonio was coming to Paris. I said to him, "No, this cannot be!" So, I got to meet Bouchet through this connection. Bouchet and Antonio built some guitars together. This ultimately influenced both Antonio and the other builders. Bouchet's system means a large strap under the bridge. Most Granada builders today use five fan braces like I do.

Was your being a foreigner a hindrance to your career?

No. Germany has a guild system for teaching guitar building where the apprentice must be paid, so no one wants an apprentice. In Spain, they would take their son or nephew as an apprentice, no one else. I think my knowing English was an advantage. I could speak to customers for Antonio and tell him what they wanted.

Are you the only foreign builder in Granada?

No, Jonathan Hinves is English, and Bernd Martin is German. They are the only other foreigners in Granada.

How many guitar makers are there in Granada?

Probably seven to nine good ones. There are probably twenty makers, but these are the ones doing quality work.

Is there a sense of competition among the builders?

Yes, but it's healthy. If you work with the principle, "How do I get better than him?" it drives you to better quality. There is no sense that the builders are trying to undercut one another.

Are people making shorter scale lengths?

You can get them, but 65MM is standard.

What are the main markets?

America, Japan, Europe, all over. It is a good thing that I have a fax machine. It allows me to communicate with buyers all over the world. Like Japan, for instance. The average price for a guitar is $3,000. Not much more. People come to Granada to buy a guitar. It works in Granada because you get a lot for your money. The price is relatively cheap. I have made 250–300 guitars over my twenty-year career. That would average out to about fifteen per year or one and a half or two a month.

It has been interesting to see how you use hand tools where I would use a power tool and vice versa.

In Granada, there is a great skill in using hand tools and at the same time we are power tool freaks. I guess you would say tradition plus new technology.

How would you characterize the guitars built in Granada as opposed to those constructed in Madrid?

The guitar from Granada is smaller. It has the European classical influence as well as the Spanish influence. The voicing is different. It is lighter and more articulate. In Madrid they build larger, heavier guitars, and they use mostly cedar for the tops. Antonio Marin's correspondence with Bouchet was a collaboration on design, an openness and mutual respect for one another. Still, the Granada instrument is very much built in the Spanish style. We care about this because over time the instrument evolves and we ask, what has it been? What is it becoming? And how does it fit into the niche required by contemporary players?

With that statement, we concluded our interview. Upon reflecting about the man and the talent of René Baarslag, one thing becomes more and more obvious: that his talent and the act of building are all one. It takes courage for such a man to spend his last penny on wood or to venture off to an unknown country in pursuit of a dream. But this is not an idle dream. This is the dream of one who has an unshakable belief in the nature of things and his place in the scheme. And this, more than guitar building, is what René teaches. His inborn belief that the impossible is possible translates itself from the very tissue of his body to everything he does. This is the lesson of René Baarslag. I was fortunate to have been a witness, and now a disciple.

I don't know about you, but I think I hear Spain calling. ——

A view of René's home from his orchard. This property is located on the side of a mountain which slopes down to the Mediterranean Sea, fifteen miles away.

Originally published in *American Lutherie #49*, 1997

Stage Acoustic Guitars

by John Calkin

IF YOU'RE OF THE OPINION that the ideal acoustic/electric guitar is a state-of-the-art pickup loaded into a fine but otherwise normal flattop, I doubt if I'll be able to convince you otherwise. But for musicians who have decided that their acoustic sound is not as vital as the electric signal to their PA system, there are many good reasons to pursue an alternate kind of guitar.

The instruments described here are crafted from a solid block of wood. In the first examples, the side units are sawn from a thick blank, much as Orville Gibson was said to have done, and the top and back plates are then glued in place. This method is wasteful of wood, and I only use it under special circumstances. More commonly, I hollow the body from the top, leaving the sides, back, and head and tail blocks as one unit, and then glue on a top plate much as a conventional guitar is made. Such guitars have been around for years, and a stroll through a good guitar store might turn up examples produced by Gibson, Guild, Giannini, Carvin, and others.

I'd like to call these guitars "stage acoustics." They should have two main qualities. They should sound wonderful when plugged in, and they should be loud enough unplugged to make practice a pleasure. They should be rugged enough to withstand the rigors of a heavy travel schedule, but within that setting I don't see why you shouldn't push for as much tone and volume as a little box can produce.

My stage acoustics look very much like electric guitars, and not like thin-body dreadnoughts, though this is a choice you can make for yourself. Many guitarists who adopt stage acoustics come from an electric-guitar background, and the compactness of an electric, along with a rock-and-roll appearance, appeals to them. Since the body is small, design concessions have to be made to get the balance right, for it's easy to make a neck-heavy instrument. To add weight, the back can be left especially thick, sometimes on the order of 3⁄8″. A Telecaster shape might fall into this category, depending on the body wood you choose. The guitar can be made lighter if a design is chosen that shifts the center of gravity toward the body of the guitar while the guitar is worn on a strap, as a Stratocaster does. However, maximum comfort is achieved when the body/neck-weight proportions are in synch. I always use mini machine heads, and if the budget can stand it, I replace the metal buttons with knobs of ebony, turtleoid, or fake mother-of-pearl. This saves several ounces out there where it counts. Working with standardized shapes is almost inevitable if you hope to sell your work. If you are braver, or building for yourself, the sky is the limit, since the piezo pickups don't care what shape body they are sitting on, or even if the body is hollow. As you build more pieces you may morph the standard shapes a bit in a manner that satisfies your sense of creativity and independence along with the needs of the marketplace.

I've talked to many avid GAL members who plan to build guitars but have yet to approach their first instrument. What I'd like to do is eliminate their last reason for not diving in. The first design has nothing to do with excellence in guitar design, and everything to do with finally having an instrument of your own manufacture to play. No stationary machinery is needed, though of course it helps. If you have a jigsaw and a router you can get by. A sanding drum in an electric drill will be a big help. You can make the neck or buy the neck, since it bolts on. You can even buy the bridge if you are out for the least challenge. The material for the sides I scrounged from a construction site. The wood for the top and back was also free, taken from a lauan grand piano packing crate a music store was happy to be rid of. Get the picture? Anything goes here.

Make a heavy plywood template of your body shape. Stacked plywood is used for the sides. Plan on leaving the sides about 3⁄8″–1⁄2″. Leave plenty of wood at the neck joint for a pocket to mount the neck in, just like an electric guitar. Leave extra material where the strap buttons screw in and where the jack will be placed. Since I have a bandsaw, I glue up the stacks and then cut out the sides. With a jigsaw you may wish to cut the layers to shape and then glue up the stack. Glue on the top and back. Any form of 1⁄4″ plywood will do, though a smooth surface will take a lot of distress out of the finish process. If you wish, tack your template in place where the neck will go and where the bridge mounts, and then run around the edge with a pattern-maker's bit in the router to refine the final shape (a pattern-maker's bit is a flush trim bit with the guide bearing mounted on the bit shaft). Remove the pattern and drill for the hardware and rout the neck pocket. Mount the neck and find the exact spot for the bridge, then glue it in place. I'm assuming here that you have other reference works to guide you through neck and bridge construction.

These guitars are tanks. If your budget is small you can string up without a pickup, but I promise you the acoustic sound will not thrill you. Eventually you can add a Martin Thinline or some such, and later an Active Jack to boost the gain and completely resurrect your sound. A completely reasonable alternative would be to use a No. 2 cedar top and light spruce braces, which will punch up your acoustic tone greatly and give you practice you're going to need anyhow. After you get flush and build your confidence, you can recycle the neck, hardware, and electronics into a nicer instrument.

The process of building with sides that are separate from the back is worth keeping in mind. With it, you get a body cavity the full depth of the sides. The Tobias-shaped body pictured has sides of poplar and a top and back of sappy bubinga. I introduced some arch into the top and back by rubbing the side unit in a sanding form with a 15′ cylindrical radius. The top and back plates were thin enough to conform to the arch when I glued them on. The arching looks foxy, feels good, and (with proper bracing) permits the use of a Mike Christian pickup. This pickup is mounted in a Schaller Tune-O-Matic-style bridge which might cause a flat top to buckle. Think in terms of a jazz-guitar design rather than a flattop. The pickup sounds warm, even without a preamp; is adjustable for height and intonation; and looks sharp with your choice of tailpieces. Be aware, though, that when the sides are cut from a solid board they are extremely fragile until they are glued to the plates, especially in the areas of the cutaways and the tail block. Again, cut out the sides with enough wood in which to mount the neck.

If possible, the best place to buy body wood is a sawmill. Normal 8⁄4 lumber is planed to 1¾″, even if it would have been clean at 2″. That ¼″ is meaningful to the body capacity of a guitar when the body is so small to begin with.

You can mill the wood flat and clean yourself, even if all you have is a router. Build a frame of wood that is slightly deeper than your body blank, and just large enough to contain it. (I'm assuming a one-piece body, or a multi-piece blank that is already glued up. Get a one-piece blank if you can find it.) I normally usc 1×4 softwood stock for the frame. The body blank is plopped into the frame and held there by screws that enter from the outside edge of the frame and pierce the blank somewhere near the center of its edge. Use three screws per side, on opposite sides of the frame. In the picture, one screw has missed the laid-up blank. It doesn't matter. You needn't predrill the blank for the screws, just run them in tight. By the time you adjust the blank to even out any warp it may be suspended in the air by the screws. That's fine.

Now you have to make a new router base that's big enough to ride on top of the frame. The base I currently use is 9″×30″, cut from ¾″ plywood. The router is let into the base ½″ and two hardwood stiffeners run the length of the base. Use a ⅝″ or ¾″ bit, or bigger if your router is a real brute. Don't cut more than ⅛″ at a pass. Rout the whole surface until your body template can sit on clean, flat wood. Flip the blank over, and if necessary use blocks to bring the blank close to the top of the frame, then rout the second face. Wear safety goggles. You'll be looking into a real dust storm, and even at that it's so hard to see under the router base that you'll be working blind most of the time. Just work carefully and don't slam the router around. It's not hard to bend a ¼″ shaft on a ¾″ bit. This is one of the dustiest of guitar-making operations. Don't try it in the kitchen unless you live alone. Or want to. Your last pass on each side should just touch the wood, and even then you'll get router tracks that will have to be scrubbed off with 80-grit sandpaper. Unless the ultimate in portability is your goal, I suggest you leave the blank as thick as it will let you.

If your router is of the cheesy variety you might be totally bummed at this point. One summer long ago I burned up three Sears 1 h.p. routers preparing body blanks, and I haven't bought a motorized tool from Sears since. The safe minimum is probably 1½ horses. If the prospect of hollowing your guitar with a router has you on the ropes, go ahead and build a solidbody electric. I'll never tell.

If you have a drill press there is an easier way to prepare the blank. Adjust it in the frame so the wood sits *above* the frame, then run the whole unit under a rotary planer. When one side is clean, remove the

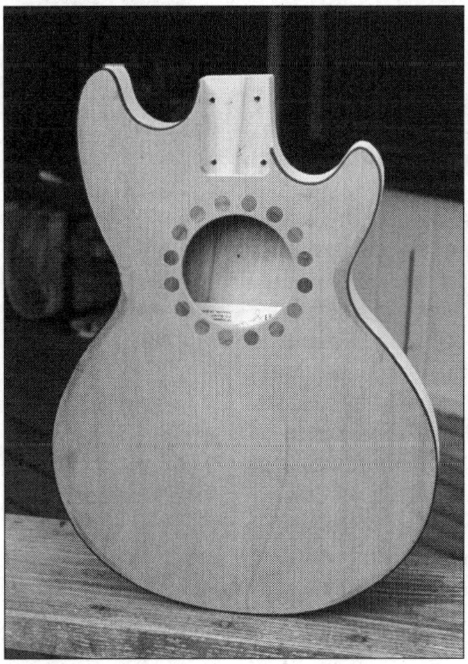
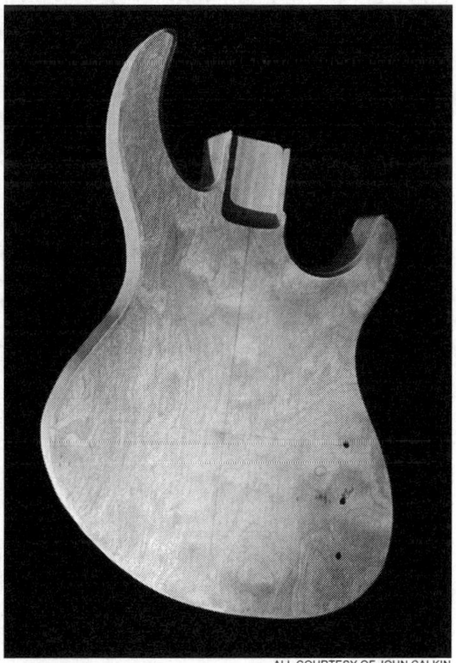

ALL COURTESY OF JOHN CALKIN

Left: Existing designs can easily be modified to suit individual needs. This body of sycamore and red cedar is a Les Paul copy with a second horn added to shift the balance back toward the body.
Right: This futuristic design is straight from a Tobias bass. The ribs are poplar, and the top and back are sappy bubinga. Both plates are brace-arched into a 15′ radius. Either a standard flattop bridge or a Mike Christian Schaller-style piezo bridge can be used on this body, though the neck pitch will be different for each bridge. The three holes are for mounting the controls from a disassembled Fishman belt-pack preamp unit.

Top: An extended router base is necessary for hollowing the body blanks. This one is 9″x30″, made of 3/4″ plywood and stiffened with walnut braces. The router is let into the base 1/2″. The plywood rides on top of the frame. Middle: A mahogany body blank in a hastily made routing frame. If the frame were maple instead of pine the sides would only have to be one layer thick. The blank is suspended from the screw points.

blank from the frame and plane the second side. This is much faster than routing and produces more chips than dust. Because of the limited space between the rotary plane and my drill press support column, this method leaves a small rectangle of unplaned wood in the middle of the blank. A more efficient frame might cure the problem, but life is short, and my block plane is sharp.

Remove the blank from the frame and bandsaw the body to shape. If you're using poplar or basswood you can get away with a portable jigsaw, but it's no fun.

Make another template out of 3/4″ plywood, this time with both the external and internal dimensions. The sides should be no thinner than 1/4″, and 3/8″ is a reasonable outer limit. Once more, make sure there is enough wood left for the neck pocket. I always leave extra wood in the tips of the horns and at the butt of the guitar. Think about things for awhile. If you are building with hard maple (you brave soul) you can make the sides and back thinner and still have the strength and weight you need. Poplar should be left much beefier. Walnut or mahogany fall somewhere in-between. If the guitar will have one of the jack-mounted preamps it will need a side thickness that will support it, but not so thick that the nut won't go onto the jack (think about the dimensions of an acoustic guitar tail block). That same preamp will need access to a battery. Where will it go?

Take your bandsawn blank to the drill press and dress it to the pencil lines with a drum sander. To speed up production I've turned to a $30 gizmo called a Robo-Sander (Woodworkers Supply #860-372, www.woodworker.com, also available from other common catalog companies), and it has altered life in my shop forever, or until I can afford a pin router. The Robo-Sander is a 3″ sanding drum with a bearing on the bottom of it, much like a standard flush-trim router bit. Tack the template to the sides with 1″ brads and push the blank into the sander, template down. The bearing reads the template, and good clean work comes off the table with no mistakes or hassles. I gave up on fixed-sleeve drums years ago because, typically, the used sleeves seize to the drum and won't come off, and new ones struggle not to go on. The Robo's sleeves present no such difficulty, and the coarse grits last a long time. Rather than worry about exact fits, I cut my templates to be a skosh oversize, so that final sanding brings the wood down to the mark. The bearing is not a wonder of high technology, and multiple passes may be needed to bring a piece to final dimensions. But a run of six neck blanks

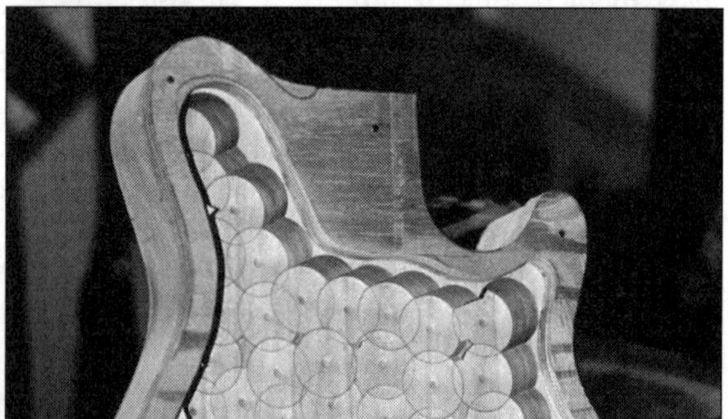

This body has the inside template tacked in place. It has been hollowed with a 1 1/2″ Forstner bit in the drill press, and is ready for routing.

measured ±.005″ at the 1st fret after profiling, and all six were done faster than I could have finished one by hand. Plenty accurate, I think. The only hassle occurs when changing sleeves, since a different tension on the drum bolt can cause the sleeve to cut a different dimension than the original setup when the template was made. Differences are normally slight, however, and another turn of the bolt or a layer of tape on the bearing normally corrects everything. As long as I work with woods with low oil content the sleeves seem to last for several weeks, which minimizes the problem. A rubber drum can never be as precise as a steel cutter, but at this point I'd hate to work without the silly thing.

The Robo-Sander won't fit into the cutaways. I get in there with my Singley drums.

Another form is handy for routing out the interior of the guitar, especially if you don't own a router mat. It prevents the body from skating around as you work. Using any available construction material, cut out the shape of the body. The exterior piece is what you are after, and precision isn't necessary as long as the body drops into the void. With the hollowing body template tacked to the top of the sides, drop the body into the sheet face up. Hold the sheet to the table with clamps that won't interfere with the movement of the router base and go to it with your big pattern maker's bit. Serious chips are going to fly. I built a fold-down table on an outside wall of my shop for this. In bad weather I work in the shop inside a plastic tent to prevent the mass contamination of my little world.

A drill press can save your bacon once again. I use a 1½″ Forstner bit to clean out 90% of the waste before I even begin routing. One body makes about four gallons of chips, and by the time a run of five or six bodies was finished I'd be calf-deep in chips. That was the old days. Now I work with one hand on the drill press crank while the other shifts the work and holds a vacuum hose. Nearly all the chips get captured, and the 16 gallon vac fills up in no time. The spur of the Forstner bit leaves a hole that ought to be routed away, so plan for that when you set the depth of the drill cut. After drilling, the initial routing only touches the sides, and goes very quickly. When the router depth adjustment runs out, remove the template and run the bit bearing on the part of the sides already trimmed. You may eventually have to extend the bit to the limit of its shaft or switch to a bit with a longer cutting surface to reach final depth.

Once the body is hollowed you're back on familiar terrain, and there are a number of references to guide you through to the end. You may still have to innovate, though. I built a pair of stage guitars around the Ernie Ball EVH model. At 13″ wide the body proved too squat to permit X bracing. I used ladder bracing and everything was fine, but I still wanted to use an X pattern. I enlarged the body using an opaque projector, but it looked funny as it got bigger. Finally, I left the upper half of the body at its 13″ size, and began morphing the lower bouts freehand. At 14⁷⁄₁₆″ wide everything jelled. I was crazy about the shape, and the X bracing fit in nicely. When using fancy hardwoods for tops the style of bracing is relatively unimportant, but when you return to spruce or cedar with the hope of pulling out all the tone a body can offer, it's nice to be able to utilize all the possibilities within the scope of your knowledge.

I use a 24⅝″ scale on the 13″ guitars and a 25½″ scale on the larger version. By far, most of the stage guitars I've built have been patterned after the Stratocaster. In fact, I used to call them Stratocoustics. I feel that a bolt-on neck may prove to be important to the life of the guitar, since the small body may — in the long run — torque out of shape more than a normal acoustic. A bolt-on neck can be reset in minutes.

Normally, an electric guitar neck is set ⅝″ into the neck pocket. You may find that this isn't deep enough, and that your bridge requires an impossibly high saddle to get the action right. Check for this before you finish the neck or glue on the bridge. It will probably prove easier to thin the neck ¹⁄₁₆″ or so than to recut the neck pocket. Support the neck, frets down, on the same block used to radius the fingerboard. Carefully pass the neck under the rotary planer in the drill press. A bit of neck reshaping will likely be in order, too, to deal with the new flat that extends out past the pocket.

I put a heel on my necks, even though they are bolt-ons. I think it adds a lot in appearance and costs little in extra time. If such a neck needs to be thinned at the body joint, use the same procedure and run the rotary planer right up against the heel to remove as much stock as possible (on my planer the cutters don't quite extend out as far as the body of the planer). Remove the remaining waste with a sharp chisel.

The neck heel itself presents its own slight problems. I fit the neck blank to the body, then glue on the heel with two or three paper spacers between the heel and the body. If the heel itself takes the brunt of the string tension (which I would like, actually), the stress on the glue joint may force the glue to creep. The heel may pop right off, which is pretty embarrassing. The paper spacers leave a gap that isn't noticeable, but leaves the heel stress-free. If the neck has to be thinned to correct the action, the little stub of neck wood in the heel will take the stress (it says right here in fine print). But if the neck is ever pitched back (shimmed), the heel may come into contact again. Perhaps a switch to an epoxy glue joint will alleviate this little worry.

I'd also like to show you my bridge-making jigs that utilize the Robo-Sander. With these simple jigs I can make eight bridges in the time it used to take me to make one. For the jigs to function smoothly, all bridge blanks should be of uniform size and thickness. There are four jigs, and each one is simply a block of plywood with a shelf built in that automatically indexes the bridge blank for a specific operation. The first jig traps the blank by horizontal tension while preset rails guide a laminate trimming router as it cuts the saddle slot. The rails and the end stops are only nailed in position, and changing the specifications of the slot can be done in minutes. The idea, though, is to get it right and never change it again. However, cutting the slot this way is so

I add a heel to my bolt-on necks for the sake of appearance. Though an integral heel would be stronger, it is wasteful of wood and hard to justify for a guitar meant to sell in the $1,000 bracket.

convenient that I often alter the setup to make a custom bridge for a repair job. Switching back is not a problem.

The second jig is the simplest. The blank is placed on its shelf. A blank-sized piece of wood is placed over it in proper orientation. Six 1⁄16″ holes representing the bridge pin holes are drilled into this piece, and brads are set into the holes. Six taps with a small hammer mark the bridge-pin positions, which are then drilled out with a brad point 3⁄16″ drill bit in the drill press. Brads are not precision made at the nail factory. Snip off the heads, then file them round while they spin in the drill press, then reverse them and file a new point on-center.

The third jig has a shelf with the exact top profile of the finished bridge. The blank is placed on the shelf and the profile drawn on it, after which the blank is placed flat on the bandsaw table and roughly cut to the lines. Then the blank is placed back on the shelf and run against the Robo-Sander.

The last jig has a shelf outlining the thickness profile of the bridge and functions the same way as the previous jig. Slap the blank in place and trace the shape, then thin the wings on the bandsaw. Put the blank back in place and hold everything against the Robo-Sander.

The top edges of the bridge are rounded on a belt sander, then the entire unit is sanded by hand with 120 grit, followed by a 320-grit sanding with a drum sander in the drill press. Hand sanding with 400 grit finishes the work until the time comes to glue the bridge to the guitar top. Eventually I'd like to have three Robo-Sanders. The first would have a 60-grit sleeve and three layers of tape around the bearing. The second would have a 100-grit sleeve and one layer of tape around its bearing. The third would have the finest sleeve available and no tape on the bearing. Each step would leave just enough wood for the next grit to clean up, and by the time the wood was smooth it would be down to the proper tolerances.

Using oily tropical woods I can process eight bridges an hour. My True Companion travel guitars use a smaller bridge of walnut, and I can whip out almost twenty bridges per hour. Plus sanding (damn it).

I haven't mentioned neck making, other than adding a heel. Nothing I do is very unconventional. I love two-way truss rods. They are a snap to put in. If gluing on the fingerboard causes any warping it can be adjusted out before the board is radiused. The profiles of my necks are also finished with the Robo-Sander. I like to make up necks in batches and store them for the future, but even for a neck with custom dimensions I find that it's faster to make up templates for the Robo-Sander than to cut the profiles by hand. I have settled on walnut necks for my stage guitars because it is strong enough, lighter than maple, easy to work, and I have a lot of it. I've used mahogany and koa, but on a neck with sixteen frets clear of the body I find their strength is marginal, all those Les Pauls not withstanding.

I'm no expert on piezo pickups. I've installed tons of Barcus-Berrys, and I don't like them. They are poorly made, fragile, hard to balance, and cost as much as all the others. The Martin Thinline and its Fishman counterpart, and the EMG are good units. I've always thought that a 1⁄8″ piezo puts out a stronger signal than a 3⁄32″ model, but it could be my imagination at play. Piezos without preamps sound pretty fair through a guitar amp but

The Guitar from Deadwood. The back/sides are spalted sycamore, and the top is spalted maple. Spalting is a fungus infection in wet wood that leaves a crazy pattern of black lines and eventually (if left wet) will destroy the wood. The binding is comprised of red veneer and 1″ lengths of ivoroid, just one way to use up those left-over lengths of plastic. Note battery box in the back. This design evolved from the Ernie Ball EVH electric guitar. It sounded as good acoustically as any of the others in this series, and much better than the Ruffian Brothers.

may not put out enough signal to feed a PA board. The preamped pickups by Fishman and EMG are wonderful, though I use the Fishman if my customer has no preference. The plain Martin Thinline with an active jack is a shade cheaper and has a sound all its own. I like it. I've installed Baggs pickups, but have never lived with one. The built-in saddle insures a good string-to-string balance, but I'm more comfortable with a separate saddle. The Kramer Ferrington guitars used a preamped Shadow pickup which always sounded harsh and brittle to my ears. As mentioned before, the Christian pickup is a fine one, especially if you enjoy an untraditional, high-tech appearance. It requires a separate tailpiece.

I prefer not to put any controls on the guitar, though they don't look out of place on a body that emulates an electric instrument. If a customer insists, I'll run the signal through a 1MΩ volume pot before it goes to the preamp. Most controls meant to go into a normal acoustic guitar won't fit into a stage guitar. However, the Fishman belt pack control unit can be removed from its box and installed in a thin body, though you'll have to add a control cavity cover to the back of the guitar. It has preamp circuitry and separate knobs for volume, bass, and treble.

Bridge jig #1. The caul and spring clamps hold the bridge blank by lateral tension while the minirouter cuts the saddle slot in accordance with preset guide rails.

Bridge jig #2. The slotted bridge blank is merely indexed by the jig while a wooden plate pierced by six brads is placed over it. Six taps with the hammer locate the bridge pin holes, which are then drilled out on a drill press.

Any pickup utilizing a preamp requires a 9v battery to drive it. It's hard to hide a battery from sight and still have access to it through the soundhole on a thin-body instrument. External access is much handier. Stewart-MacDonald sells two battery cases meant to be mounted in electric or standard acoustic guitars. The electric guitar version installs well in the back of a stage guitar. You may find that your guitar is deep enough to use the acoustic version (which is easier to mount), but the thick back typical of these guitars prevents its use. Instead, the case must be screwed to a small block of wood glued to the inside top of the guitar. I attach the case in the upper bout next to the neck pocket, a relatively dead portion of the top.

Stage guitars offer a good learning experience matched with a good market potential. I wish you luck with them. ——

Bridge jig #3. The blank is indexed by the jig shelf. The finished outline of the bridge is traced on the blank, then is roughed out on the bandsaw. The blank is placed back on the jig and run against the Robo-Sander. The bearing on the sanding drum reads the jig and the drum duplicates that shape on the blank.

Bridge jig #4. The edge contours are traced from the jig onto the blank, which is then roughly bandsawn. The blank then goes back onto the jig and is Robo-Sanded to shape. Edge shaping is completed on the belt sander, then finer hand and drum sanding complete the bridge until it is glued in place.

Originally published in *American Lutherie #49*, 1997

Meet the Maker: Fred Carlson

by Tim Olsen

ALL COURTESY FRED CARLSON EXCEPT AS NOTED

FRED CARLSON: a luthier for whom the word unique is far too small, and whose stature, while diminutive, is too great to be appreciated by the present generation. To me, Fred is the very personification of the sheer joy of discovery and creation on which the current Golden Age of Lutherie is built. Who among us can judge whether he represents what the American luthier has been, or what we may yet become?

Fred, I suspect that you were a child once. Did you make yogurt-tub ukes or perform other youthful pranks which might have presaged your future slide into lutherie?

Tim, you're one of the first to make the assumption that I'm no longer a child! No, I had a lutherie-deprived childhood. My grandmother used to say I was the only one in the family that could carry a tune. I don't recall thinking about building instruments until I was fifteen, although I did get a guitar lesson when I was nine. (I had intended to get off on a tangent about how my grandmother had gangrene when I was six, and I painted her toes with Merthiolate every night to stimulate circulation, and once I accidently stepped on her foot and one of her toes came off... but I can see I'm heading in a different direction).

When I was fourteen and living with my brother Barney and our wild mother in a commune we had started, I asked for a guitar. The members of the community shared all income. I had no personal money. I saw a guitar at Dude and Harry Thompson's junk shop in Lower Cabot, Vermont. It was a Tokai steel string and Harry wanted $40. I brought my request before "The Group" at a weekly meeting where we hashed out dishwashing chores and relationship problems. Little Freddy asks if he can spend forty big ones on a Japanese guitar. The group said yes (my mom was an income earner!) and soon I was attempting to learn Bob Dylan songs. Then a woman moved in who had an old frailing banjo. I was enchanted.

My mom had kicked my dad out of the house years before, so I latched onto various surrogate father figures at the commune, mostly young carpenters. At some point I made the connection between my affinity with woodworking and my desire to learn about music, especially the banjo. At age fifteen I enrolled myself in an alternative high school. It was up to me. My mom was pretty much out the door by then, off to save the world. I asked the director, a guitarist and banjoist himself, if he could find someone to teach me to build a banjo. That was a pivotal point in my life, although not as immediately terrifying as "the Toe Incident."

You learned lutherie in high school?

A-yup. A teacher was found, someone who was making dulcimers. We started with a "class" of sorts, meeting twice a week. The two other students must have not stuck with it, because the experience became one-on-one pretty quickly.

Ken Riportella, our teacher, was no ordinary backwoods craftsman. He was a wild young hippie artist, who had gotten involved in instruments through Dennis Murphy, who would later be another of my mentors. Dennis was half the music faculty at Goddard College in Plainfield. He made the first Javanese Gamelan orchestra ever built outside of Indonesia, and Ken welded the big gongs. Ken had a serious fine arts background: his grandfather was a respected oil painter, his father a restorer of famous masters' paintings. Ken's goal was to "beat his father into the Met" (have his work exhibited in the Metropolitan Museum of Art before dad did), and he achieved this goal.

Ken got into musical sculpture and made little welded steel creatures with rods sticking out called "gong-a-longs." You hit on their various parts with various striking devices and got cool sounds. He got into lap dulcimers, which he was exploring when I began studying with him. He had very little technical knowledge about instruments, woods, tools, or machinery, but had amazing artistic intuition. He worked mostly with scrap "doorskin," which was 1/8″ plywood, and salvaged packing crates from Bevins Speed & Cycle. He bent all his plywood sides by kerfing them on the inside with a table saw, and I learned to do that too. Somehow, this wild, lawless artist (who was living off his student loan while he created the most psychedelic dulcimers you could imagine) took a liking to me and instilled in me an excitement for creating musical things that still goes strong. I knew then, at sixteen, that this was my life's work.

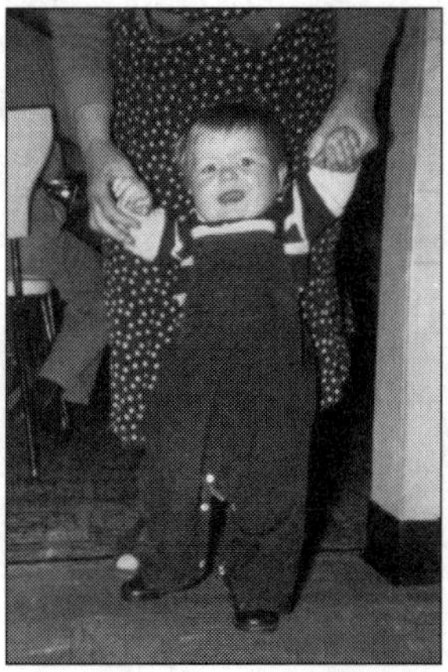

Working with Ken, I made a rather clunky dulcimer, and I did get to make that banjo, too. Ken had helped a friend make a little plywood-topped, open-backed, rectangular banjo. It had the sweetest sound, like crickets singing on a summer night. I made myself something similar, with carved wooden tuning pegs and a round peghead that made the whole thing look like a giant thermometer. I sewed a case out of a rummage sale raincoat, and carried it everywhere with me for a couple years, playing hours a day.

I was also building stuff on my own in the cooperative wood shop at the commune. I made dulcimers and a lot of little wooden banjos: square, octagonal, even round. We started using more solid woods, almost entirely mail-ordered from Craftsman Wood Service. I hadn't used skin heads for banjos until we butchered a couple of baby goats at the commune, and I tried to tan the skins into banjo heads. I made unplayable mini-banjos for a couple kids at our place, with hair still on around the edges.

Once, a young unknown banjo player by the name of Tony Trishka stayed at our place after a local concert, and left the next day with one of my octagonal banjos with a hand-shaped peghead. He had given me $75 for it, which I proudly put into the communal coffers. That was certainly one of my first sales, and pretty darned exciting.

In 1973 Ken had a friend, Betty Magbie, who had an old farm in Calais. She wasn't the farming type. She let Ken camp out in the field and set up a workshop in the barn. It was small and smelled like the cows of days gone by. We made fine workbenches up against the stanchions, right over the manure cleanout troughs. I remember first looking at a beat-up copy of Sloane's classic guitar building book, right there among the ghosts of Guernseys.

Ken set up camp in an overgrown pasture that was coming back in scrubby pines and poplars, with wild raspberries everywhere. In a moment of exemplary brilliance, Ken decided to see how much of the summer he could get through without wearing any clothes. After all, no one else was around but me, Betty Magbie, her kid, and their dog Zeke. I remember my first visit to Ken's camp. I arrived to find him stark naked on the hillside, eating raspberries. We spent hot, lazy summer afternoons in the driveway outside the barn, sanding away at our current projects, getting wood dust on our birthday suits.

Ken and I rented a place together for several months that winter. I remember Ken's dog eating the couch, which got us in trouble, and Ken eating Tiger's Milk bars and ice cream every day for breakfast. He developed a condition which the local health clinic termed "pregnant woman syndrome," describing the general shape such a diet fostered. I made a pretty cool dulcimer there that Ken sold to somebody for $200 without asking me. I was upset that he charged so much. I thought money was immoral, and through association with it one became equally immoral. After twenty-some years of doing this professionally, pricing and selling my work is still a difficult thing for me.

I know you studied with Charles Fox at a point that was early in both your career and his. I'll bet that was something of a change from the free-form methods of Ken Riportella. How did you find Charles, and was he wearing flowers in his hair?

In 1975 I got a flyer for Charles Fox's little residential guitar building program, then called Earthworks. This was the old days, even before the fabled "GRD" (Guitar Research and Design), which Earthworks soon became. I think the cost was $800 for six weeks. I was still income sharing at the commune, and $800 was way out of our price range for Fred's education. I must have mentioned it to my dad, who I hadn't lived with since age twelve, and who didn't have much money himself. He allowed as how he'd saved up a couple thousand dollars that he'd intended to let me spend on college education; if guitar building was my chosen field of study, he was willing to go with it. So starting in November of 1975, I spent what were to be six of the most influential weeks of my life learning to build my first guitar.

Facing page: Fred Carlson in his workshop, 1985.
This page, top: Watch your feet, Gramma! Here comes Freddie, 1957.
Above: Members of the Vermont Musical Instrument Builders Co-op, 1981: Ken Riportella, Suzy Norris, Fred Carlson, Sam Shaffer, and Elliot Burch.

Charles, these days, often alludes to how "we were all hippies back then." I don't remember flowers in his hair, but he and his family did live in a big log house he'd built, filled with artwork and guitars. The six students lived in yurts. Charles was bearded, high-powered, gracious, a fine guitar builder, and most importantly, a truly gifted teacher. He was well organized, thoughtful, and supportive of his students in every way. I was probably an ideal student for him since I'd been at it for several years already. All I needed was to be shown the rules and techniques. He was the perfect complement to the sculptural approach of Ken Riportella. Plus, he knew how to sharpen chisels. Ken did most of his luthing with heavy-grit sandpaper on a electric drill sanding disk.

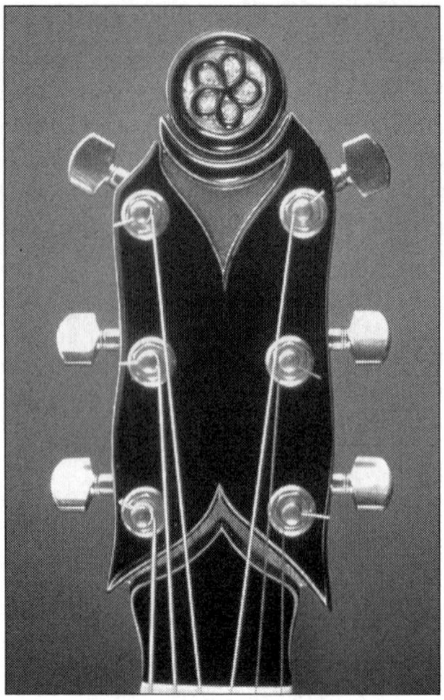

One of my great delights was bringing together these two mentors of mine. Each brilliant in his own way, they had interesting areas of conflict and confluence. Charles also had a serious art background, and still refers to himself as a frustrated painter. One afternoon, after my session at Earthworks had ended, I drove down with Ken to visit Charles. Charles made us sandwiches in the kitchen in his grand log house. Ken fixed his eye on a debilitated Land Rover in Charles' yard and negotiated a deal. He felt he'd pulled off a major coup, and Charles was probably happy to see it go. I listened to them ramble on about the world of fine art and enjoyed watching the interaction between these two teacher/father-figure friends of mine. At nineteen, I was getting my college education from these guys; no degree, but what experience!

At one point, Charles offered to take me on as a working apprentice to help teach the course while he focused more time on setting up a production shop. I went so far as to apply for government funding. The CETA representative looked at me in my ripped, dust-covered clothes and ratty hair, and lectured me about how they didn't want to fund people who only wanted to make $2000 a year and live like hippies. They wanted to create valuable citizens who earned $10,000 a year! I'll tell you, $2000 would have been a king's wages for me. I still have never made anywhere near $10,000 in a year! CETA grudgingly accepted me. I was a textbook example of who they were supposed to be helping: no high school diploma, poor, and all that. But I basically chickened out.

I set up a shop at Iron Bridge Woodworkers. These were mostly guys who lived at the commune and had a collective carpentry/cabinetry business. They had basic machinery, and I spent the rest of my dad's "college" gift on a set of chisels, a couple planes, a drill, workboard materials, and some wood. These basic tools got me started, and have remained mostly what I use to this day.

Somewhere around that time I did get a CETA job, one of the two "real" jobs I ever had. It lasted two weeks and involved typing, which I still can't do. Because it was CETA funded, I was assigned a social worker. She was an artist herself, and I showed her one of my guitars. She was appalled that someone with such a talent should be pretending to type for lousy pay. She convinced the local Arts Council to hire me for a pilot project sending artists into institutions to work with "special populations." This was much cooler than typing, and I got to play banjo at all sorts of odd places, and make instruments out of found materials. After about three months I was invited to go on a nationwide tour with Bread and Puppet Theater, one of Vermont's great treasures of performance art. So ended my entire experience with gainful employment; I was back on the streets as a hippie musician/artist.

In the summer of 1977 Ken and I travelled to the First Annual New England Artists Festival and Showcase, down near Boston. We exhibited instruments and I won first prize in the woodworking category. On that trip I met another young guitar builder, Michael Millard, who called his business Froggy Bottom Guitars. I also paid a visit to a classical builder named Alan Chapman. He was cranking out instruments in his bedroom and garage, which seemed pretty upscale to me.

Ken got info on an exhibit the Smithsonian was mounting in their Renwick Gallery; they were looking for work from contemporary instrument builders. He was applying, and thought I should, too. Now there's a presumptuous notion! Little Freddie, all of 21 at the time (I think I'd just gotten my driver's license) sending his home-taken photos off to

Washington, DC! We both passed the first screening, and I got a letter saying they wanted to see an instrument in person! It happened that the Bread and Puppet tour was performing in DC, and I brought along a guitar and dropped it off, just left it there with all these official, grown-up strangers who knew about Art. A couple months later, when the tour was rounding the West Coast, I got word that I'd been accepted. I chronicled the opening of that exhibit for the *GAL Quarterly.* It was quite a thrill for me, and when the tour ended in late spring of '78, I was hot to get back in the shop and build guitars.

How did you and Big Blue Harold come to be at our 1978 National Convention in Winfield, Kansas? And what did you think of that, your first GAL meeting?

I'd heard of the GAL through Charles Fox in 1975, and I became a member. I'd been doing theater with my brother Barney for years, and I had the notion of presenting a theater piece at the convention. We decided to make a "cranky," or paper movie, basically a roll of wide paper with pictures painted on it which is scrolled with a crank. Turn the crank and the pictures roll by. We painted the pictures the night before I left for Winfield and I wrote the text on the train to Kansas.

I was carrying a 12-string guitar and a tenor viol, each in a huge homemade case, along with camping gear and all my food for a week. I hadn't traveled enough to know that they had food in other parts of the country. I couldn't have afforded it anyway. I also had the "cranky" and Big Blue Harold. Big Blue was a mask character, a full-size, larger-than-life head with a suit coat, originally created to be a mutant protester at antinuclear demonstrations. He quickly found his true calling as a performer of impromptu blues songs. I had to take the bus to Springfield, Massachusetts, then get the Amtrak train at the station some blocks away. Somehow I managed to carry instruments, food, sleeping bag, tent, Harold, cranky, and various sundries, all the way to the train station. Then I noticed a large greasy stain coloring the outside of the old laundry bag that was crammed full of my food, clothing, and camping supplies. Oh no, the almond butter! I did make the train, and smelled nice and nutty for the rest of the week. I was chagrined to discover when I got off the train that I was not exactly in Winfield. I started trudging to the bus station with my burden, and I must have looked nearly as bad as I felt, because it wasn't long before a car pulled up, and a nice young couple offered me a ride. The bus station was closed, and they said they'd take me to the convention site. None of us knew where the place was, but my saviors had a CB radio, and they talked to truckers until someone came up with directions. I arrived, alive and trembling with excitement, or else in allergic reaction to skin contact with so much almond butter!

Facing page, top: Detail of the 1978 guitar which was exhibited in the Smithsonian's Renwick Gallery. Facing page, bottom: Fred's first guitar, built at Chales Fox's Earthworks in 1975.
This page: Fred in his workshop, 1993.

People who have only attended our national conventions in the 1990s might not remember the days when folks who are now the Old Masters would hitchhike into town or arrive in a packed VW van and camp out for the duration. The only thing mightier that a luthier's poverty in those days was the desire to actually meet another luthier!

It was a very exciting event for me. Highlights included trying out a guitar by the young, dashing R.E. Bruné. I don't think I'd ever laid hands on a decent classical guitar; his seemed transcendent. And I met Richard Schneider. I had no notion who he was. Someone got excited about my 12-string with a face carved in the heel-cap. They brought Richard by to see it. He told me my prices were too low. That was our only communication.

I presented the cranky *A Guitar Is Born* and at least several people saw it. I know Big Blue made a lasting impression on some folks. Remember that amazing tornado and hailstorm? And I took my pack apart to get a piece of wire from the frame to unlock Don Bradley's truck, in which he had locked his keys.

All right, now we know Big Blue Harold. But who is Beonardo da Chintzi?

We all went down to the 1979 Boston GAL Convention in Ken's ancient blue Ford Falcon, The Blue Dream. That was where I met Suzy Norris, still my sweet buddy after all these years. My bro and I wanted to do another theater piece, so I, as Frederique de la Carlson, and Barney, as Beonardo da Chintzy, performed a hot little script called *The History of Early, Late, and Mid Evil*

Instruments with some fine jokes about Liars, Viles, and other Evil instruments. I had made a couple of papier-mâché guitars. These had no backs, so you could look inside at the broken eggshells glued there: this was the cracked "eggs-bracing" that proved these to be "ba-roke" guitars. Also, there were buckwheat groats glued to the bridges, my first attempt at a real "kasha" bridge. And on like that. Ken was there, and we all exhibited right next to another young feller by the name of Steve Klein. I remember being petrified with embarrassment when Ken asked Steve Klein if he was on cocaine.

Tell us about Suzy.

Suz had apprenticed with Paul Shuback in Portland, Oregon around the same time I was learning guitar building, then had moved to Vermont. It turned out she was living in another nearby commune, Quarry Hill. I had never been to Quarry Hill, or met anyone who had, but the rumor was that Quarry Hill was a Wild Place. You know, sex, drugs, the kind of stuff you were supposed to do at communes. It's odd that people living in one commune would have those stereotypical notions about folks in another commune. We were all just people, like everyone else, trying to get by. Suzy was trying to get by making fiddles outdoors on a woodpile at Quarry Hill, having no shop. We had just finished setting up our new cooperative shop on our land in Plainfield, and things were relatively swanky there. I was very shy, but Ken talked a lot with Suzy, and I remember jamming at an after-hours party with her and some other musicians.

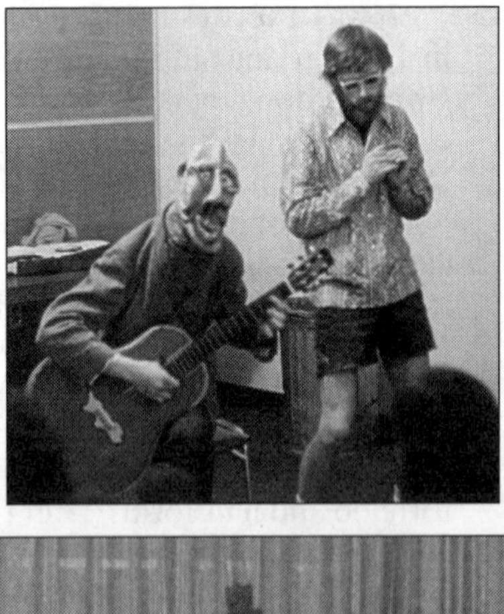

Yeah, I remember taking photos of that jam session. I didn't know it was so momentous!

After the convention, Ken met up with her again and brought her by the shop. She saw an opportunity to rise beyond her woodpile, moved to Plainfield, and was soon making fiddles in our shop. She was thrilled to discover people doing nontraditional shapes, and jumped right in making some rather un-Stradivarioid creations. We started playing music together one night a week, and that was the beginning of our courtship. By the early '80s Suzy and I were "a thing," and spent most of our time making and playing instruments together.

In 1981 or thereabouts, Suz invented the Suzalyne, her violin/viola with sympathetic strings, inspired by the Hardanger fiddle and the viola d'amore. This was a turning point for both of us. Suzy started getting orders for Suzalynes, and I decided to make a guitar with sympathetic strings. Thus began about ten years of experimentation; Suz refining the Suzalyne, me inventing and developing the Sympitar. It was pretty wonderful to have a spouse-type partner who was also a work partner and a music partner. It's still wonderful, although we seem to be moving in slightly different directions these days. Suz is studying healing, and has had to put lutherie on the back burner while she crams for eventual licensing to practice herbal medicine.

This is getting confusing. Let's see if I have it so far. You were born in a cow barn, where a little dog ate your swaddling clothes. Your brother, Charles Fox, luthed naked until Ken Riportella cancelled his government grant and towed away his log house. Big Blue Harold had saved up to send you to college, but decided that the GAL convention was close enough. You met Suzy at a no nukes riot, where you admired the way she broke into Don Bradley's car. You moved from Vermont to California carrying all your worldly belongings and enough food for the trip on your back. You passed Grand Coulee Dam and wrote the well known anthem "Roll On Columbia." You now live on the Skywalker Ranch were you are teaching George Lucas to make environmentally responsible paper movies. And you like to bathe in a healing potion of almond butter.

ALL THIS PAGE BY TIM OLSEN

Top: Frederique de la Carlson and Beonardo da Chintzy lecture on the various evil instruments at the Guild's 1979 Boston convention. Torres made a guitar with a papier-mâché back. Fred went one better: a papier-mâché guitar with no back!
Middle: Big Blue Harold makes his second annual appearance.
Bottom: The after-hours jam session, featuring (left to right) Dick Deneve, Paul Lathrop, Doug Ecker, Suzy Norris, Fred Carlson, Alphonso Mysterioso, Nicholas Clarke, and Don Bradley. And a lady with braids.

Actually, I wasn't a personal associate of George Lucas until at least 1985, although most of the material for the *Star Wars* trilogy did come from my teenage diary.

So everything was cool at the co-op. Do you mean to say that the commune had built this nice shop?

It was a fine shop, and also sported a host of other woodworkers and some potters. The shop's main users shared the costs of utilities, maintenance, and property taxes with a monthly payment of about $35 each. The carpenters had some impressive machinery, including a bright orange Boak 18″ jointer. They also had a big ol' table saw, a great drill press, a bandsaw, and various routers and drills. We got to use these treasures for the crippling rate of $1 per hour. One day the bookkeeper came up to me and said, "Will you guys please stop charging yourselves to use the machines!? It's screwing up the books!" After that, Suzy and I had use of all those toys for free.

Top: Fred and Suzy in the New Hamburger co-op workshop, 1981.
Middle: Singin' up a storm with Sympitar and Suzalyn, 1990.
Bottom: Ain't they sweet? Fred and Suzy in 1996.

So how do you leave a commune? Do you have to buy out the value you have added?

There were a lot of problems associated with income sharing, mostly revolving around the fact that some people had incomes and some did not. Over the years income sharing got replaced by a system of monthly taxation. Initially this had some tie to an individual's income, but eventually we began to think of our monthly payments as simply rent; we all paid the same amount and those who were "full members" were equal owners of the land and all its buildings.

You have used some interesting company names over the years. Can you give us some insight as to what significance they may have?

"New Hamburger" was and is the name of the commune in Vermont. Rumor is that I thought of it at age fourteen. It had to do with a cow skull that was nailed to the door of the Big House. We had been calling the skull "the Old Hamburger" and I reasoned that our commune should be called the New Hamburger. Somehow this stuck, and there were later formed a lot of socio-political justifications for it.

"Sacred Fire/Frogs Delight" was my guitar shop name for a while. It was preceded by "Tooth and Snail Musical Instruments," which came from a preguitar period when I was building instruments with snail shells glued on the pegheads – a cheap way to make a scroll!

We had a little non-organization called the Vermont Musical Instrument Builders Society that was basically Ken, Suzy, and myself. That eventually became the Vermont Musical Instrument Builders' Cooperative, which was four or five people who worked in our shop.

We got a couple of magazine articles written on us, including one in, of all places, the Travel section of the *New York Times.*

"Beyond the Trees" is our current shop, and has been since the mid-'80s or so. We wanted a name to share, I think to kind of formalize our working together. Ironically, directions to get here tend to include that it's the "first driveway on the left, beyond the trees." We had originally thought of it as something a little more metaphorical.

Speaking of Beyond the Trees, how did you two come to move west?

Suz and I each had our reasons. I'd lived at the commune for twenty years since my mother basically abandoned me there. Wonderful as it was, I had felt trapped, but terrified to leave. Leaving there was the hardest, saddest thing I've ever done, and the most liberating. At least I think it has been. But I'm still dealing with the sadness.

Suzy had reasons involving her health and the very cold winters. I leapt at Suzy's need as an excuse to get myself unstuck. We decided to find a new place to call home: someplace still rural but with greater proximity to metropolitan areas. Someplace with mountains, trees, ocean nearby, lots of music, and a place to garden. We had no intention of ending up in Santa Cruz on Suzy's parents' ranch. In fact, Suzy was adamant in our discussions that it was the one place we wouldn't end up. We toured California for three months with a couple of buddies from Vermont, playing music for contra dances and at coffee houses. We saw some interesting sights, but we had just come from an amazing place, and we weren't about to settle for much less.

After the tour was over we were moping around Suzy's folks' beautiful ranch in the hills outside Santa Cruz. The offer was made for us to stay there "temporarily." Suzy's dad said they had a store room that could be turned into a shop, and we could do some instrument building to get grounded. Boy, that sounded good! So we settled in, and yup, we're still here. It's a nice place. Heck, it's an amazingly gorgeous place! And this summer, after nearly six years of sort of camping out in a spare bedroom and our converted storeroom/shop, work has begun on a new shop and house for us on an adjoining piece of property overlooking the Monterey Bay. We're both more than a little humbled by this amazing good fortune. We're also not sure that Santa Cruz is our ultimate home. But, we're going with the flow, and right now things are flowing all over the place!

So let's talk about Fred, the famous luthier. Both you and Suzy have had pretty good exposure in the music press lately. A picture in Acoustic Guitar *of Alex de Grassi playing a Sympitar can't hurt, and that Darol Anger thing in* Strings *mag a while back was a real big vote for the Suzalyne. Maybe you and Breedlove kind of pave the way for each other aesthetically. Is it possible that your stuff may be catching on?*

I've decided to let you in on my secret to success. Space Aliens! There, the cat is out of the bag. The thing that allows me to complete these orders in a timely fashion, so that my fame and fortune continue to skyrocket, is that I utilize the incredibly cheap labor on other planets! I first learned of this business strategy in a talk by Chris Martin in 1985. Mr. Martin asserted that the future of guitar building was in Korea and other countries where labor could be had for next to nothing. It was a small stretch for me to apply this wisdom beyond the confines of our planet. Why, on Mars they prize wood dust beyond almost any other material! But they are not so good at following instructions, and I end up with some unusual products, which I try to capitalize on as "design innovations."

Seriously, it does seem like I'm finally getting some recognition as a luthier, and it has not come easily. I don't have a lot of trouble impressing people with my unusual design ideas, but it has taken a long time for people to start taking me seriously as a builder of fine musical instruments. The same has been true for Suzy. The lutherie world is governed by tradition and market, neither of which we build for. Although we have much love for the traditions our craft springs from, we are both artists at heart, and believe in following our own passions as the way to create the best that we as individuals can. And neither of us has any real desire to build for "the market." We're trying to make instruments that are exceptional in both form and function, and I think we do that. We hope that our instruments will become increasingly accepted and appreciated. And we are very grateful to the individuals who have believed in us and supported us over the years: the musicians, our teachers, family, and friends.

I think Breedlove makes one of the most interesting production guitars around. Aesthetically, they are doing some really nice stuff. And I have to admit, there's a certain similarity in some of their designs to my early-'80s "Starchaser" guitar. I think it's true that the work of more mainstream innovators like Breedlove lends more credibility to people like me; I hope it works both ways!

The lutherie-boom generation has changed quite a bit since the 1978 GAL Convention. Many builders these days are highly jigged and moving toward higher production of standard models. Some luthiers now even have decent cars and go places on airplanes! Coincidence? You seem to have kept closer to your experimental and custom roots.

Yeah, there seems to be a trend in luthing to become practical, efficient, and perhaps profitable. In theory, it doesn't sound half bad. Make some jigs, get your process figured out, crank out a few more of those OM-dreadnought-cutaway-flat-top wonders with the prewar sound and the onboard preamp, and heck, maybe even pay off that rust bucket before you get the next one! Unquestionably, you can improve aspects of work and product by doing those things. I've tried a few times to whip myself into that kind of submission, most recently with my odd little Dreadnautilus guitars. What I invariably find is that for me the life goes out of the work when it stops being new, when I'm not trying to stretch myself and make a work of art rather than just a more cost-effective and consistent version of the last thing I made. I'm really trying with these Dreadnautili, and they're great little instruments, but I look at them, and at myself, and I have to face the fact that building them is not doing what I do best. I'm not using my true gift, that of designing and creating one-of-a-kind, humorous, beautiful, instrument sculptures that work exquisitely as musical tools and are unique individuals. We all have our gifts, our talents, things that we excel at. To not follow the path that using those gifts leads us on is, in my opinion, to not do that thing which will be best for us individually, and for the world as a whole. I'm truly glad that there are people who do the production thing well. I try my best to learn from these people, and often find them inspiring. I hope, in some small way, that I teach and inspire some of them as well.

For the future, who knows? There will be much potential in our new shop for greater efficiency, and even enough room to have some jigs, if I get it together to make some. Of course, there will also be room for building sculpted papier-mâché creature/guitars, tree violins, humanitars, smilophones, jomamas, and whatever else grabs us. My mission, should I decide to accept it, is to attempt to remain open to the forces that carry those inspirations, and to somehow keep body and soul together enough to get around to realizing some of them. I don't intend to stop building recognizable instruments, perhaps occasionally even traditional ones. But I know I can't stop doing the other. ——

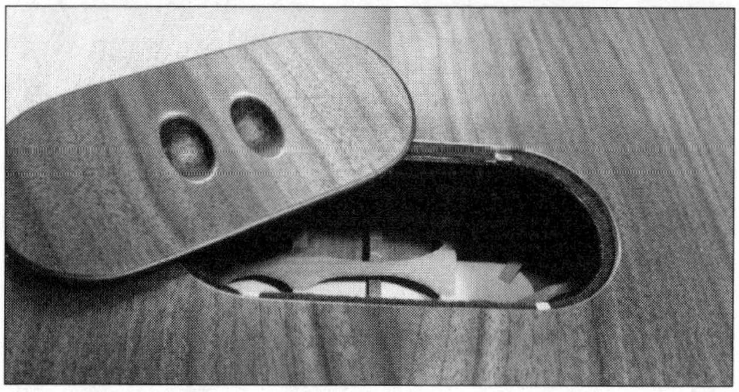

Facing page: Fred in his Santa Cruz workshop, 1996. A Simpitar is in progress on the bench. What's this? The back has a "sound" hole! This page: Fred calls his headless travel guitar the "Dreadnautilus." The top photo shows the bracing pattern and "internal tailpiece." In the middle photo we see how the banjo 5th-string pegs mount through the top. The bottom photo shows another of those holes in the back. The cover for this one is held in place with magnets.

Originally published in *American Lutherie #49*, 1997

Time is the Enemy

Richard Beck shares two of his time-saving fixtures with Jonathon Peterson

WHEN I STARTED BUILDING, it quickly became apparent that there were certain procedures that took way too long to do "by hand," and more importantly, the accuracy of those procedures was inconsistent. If you are just going to build one or two guitars you don't really need many jigs or fixtures, but with my assistant, Tim Fox, I build about twelve guitars a year, and we fit that work in with repairing hundreds of instruments. Time is the enemy, and jigs and fixtures are part of the solution. I've got two here that I would like to share with you.

Richard, before we take a look at these jigs I'd like to get a little background. I know that you have been a repairman for a lot longer than you have been a builder. How did you get started with that?

When I first picked up a guitar, over thirty years ago, nobody told me which way to hold it, so I started playing left-handed. Or was I playing backwards? I soon learned if my playing was to progress like the rest of my friends, playing *Pipeline* and *Louie Louie,* I'd have to have my guitars set up "the other way," with the action left-handed, not just backwards. But, finding someone who actually worked on guitars was another story. I searched every music store in and around my town, but no skilled guitar repairman was to be found. I emphasize the word skilled. Oh sure, there were people who said they understood the repairs and modifications I requested. I even had a "Big Name Repair Guy" fix (read butcher) one of my beloved guitars. Bear in mind that by this time I owned a '59 dot-neck ES-335, mint, a '62 block-neck, mint, a killer Brazilian D-21, and a Brazilian 00-28. I had some nice axes, and I didn't want them screwed up. There were so few good repair people in '64. I suspect that's because the guitar itself hadn't been taken seriously, and the financial incentive for woodworkers to venture into this "new field" didn't exist.

The lutherie world was pretty small in those days. The lutherie community that we know today didn't exist, and neither did the market for their work.

Broken guitars were considered junk, and vintage was a term applied to wine. A steady flow of Gibsons, Martins, and Gretschs could be found at swap meets and junk dealers. I can clearly recall buying a D-18 with a cracked neck for $39 (still, a serious amount of cash for a sixteen-year-old kid in '67). I also bought many Gibson mandolins without bridges dirt cheep, and a '50s Tele that someone had taken completely apart and couldn't put back together for $25.

I would buy this stuff, fix what was broken, sell it to local kids at bargain prices, then take the money and start the whole thing over again. Soon, my friends were

ALL BY RICHARD BECK

Two of Richard's guitars. On the left is a J-M-1 of flame maple and spruce. Right is an all koa J-EX-K with paua-shell purfling and rosette.

bringing me their guitars for work, and every year there were more refrets, bridge resets, nut replacements, broken braces — the work that is the bread and butter of a guitar fixer. By '75 I had secured my first professional full-time gig as a repairman in a local shop. Titebond in hand, the world was my oyster.

Even though you guys are repairing like mad, your main interest these days seems to be in building acoustic instruments.

One thing that really changed my direction was the year I spent in Puyallup, Washington working with the venerable solidbody luthier Ken Warmoth. Warmoth Guitar Products makes a ton of excellent electric guitar necks and bodies. Their production machines, custom jigs, and shaping fixtures are designed to make identically shaped parts which fit and match other precision parts. I'd been through a Gibson authorization training class years earlier in Kalamazoo and had seen the degree of "automation" they applied to their production, but Ken's operation was another thing.

Another big influence was getting my hands on some of the amazing handmade guitars built by John Greven of Bloomington, Indiana. They would occasionally pass through my shop for repairs or resale. When I first saw one of John's highly flamed maple jumbos it was obvious that the look, the feel, and the sound were miles above most of the production instruments I'd seen. I searched inside for a label (a fine piece of art in itself), gave him a ring, and introduced myself. Little did I know that once I actually started building, twenty years later, I would be calling him for long-distance tutorials on many subjects. Thank you, John.

So working at Warmoth showed me how, and John gave me the direction and inspiration to build.

The kind of machinery and fixtures that they use at Warmoth (see "Inside Warmoth Guitar Products," *American Lutherie #26,* or *Big Red Book of American Lutherie Volume Three*, p. 60) *is really ideally suited to building bolt-on-neck electrics. After all, Leo Fender was a machinist, so that's the heritage of that kind of design. There are certainly many applications for that type of approach in the building of acoustic instruments* (see "A Walk Through Gibson West," *AL#26,* or *BRBAL3,* p. 244; "A Talk with Bob Taylor," *AL#28,* or *BRBAL3,* p. 126; and "The Great White (and Hot Pink) North," *AL#13,* or *BRBAL2,* p. 12), *but a lot of the tooling that the factories use these days is quite expensive.*

Well, of course, not everybody can afford a CNC. It's a question of your mind set, how you look at things and how you approach them. Most of my fixtures are pretty low tech. For instance, before I go to the trouble of making a jig in metal I always do it in plexiglas first. Plexi is strong as hell, you can make alterations easily or repair it if damaged, it's dimensionally stable, and you don't have to hire a machinist to fabricate it. That lets you work the bugs out, believe me. Of the jigs I am showing you here, the headstock fixtures can be built from laminated plexiglas, and the jig for arching braces uses a 2″×¾″×32″ piece of plexi for the master template. If you get to the point where you want to have a more permanent metal version of a jig, I definitely recommend that you find a machinist who has a strong interest in guitars so that you can barter or trade services. I made a habit of asking my customers what they did for a living, and I eventually turned up my tool maker, Dave Hawkins of Dave's Custom Tools.

Tell me about your headstock jig and then show me how you use it.

Much of my production work is done with a shaper. I don't have a real shaper yet, so I use a heavy-duty router on a shop-made router table. The router is a 3 h.p. Porter Cable I bought from Woodcraft (part #24A63). For cutting out the shape of my headstocks I set it up with a 1⅛″ diameter two-flute cutter with a cutting length of 1½″, a ½″ shank, and a shank-mounted, flush-trim bearing guide (**Photo 1**). It's a big motha.

Here is the headstock-shaping template next to a headstock (**Photo 2**). As I said before, I started out by making plexi templates so I could play with the shape and the tuning gear placement until they were right, and then made this one made out of ½″ aluminum. I scribed centerlines on it so I could position it properly on the necks. It's secured to the neck with heavy-duty 3M double-stick tape. Unquestionably a vacuum system would be cooler for production work, but if you have flat surfaces double-stick tape works fine.

The headstock is cut out with the router on a shaper table (**Photo 3**). I have a foot switch hooked up to my router so that I can get a firm hold on my work before the cutter starts spinning, and I can stop the router before I let go. Always be aware of the direction

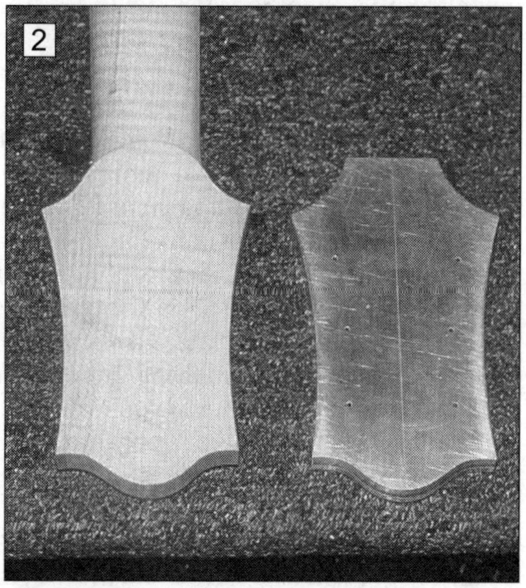

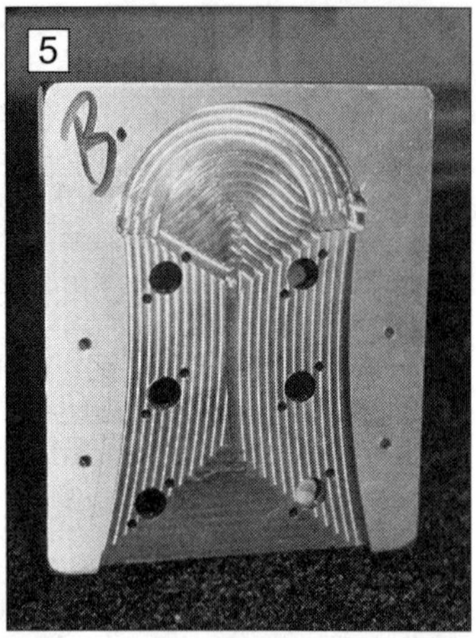

of the cutterhead (note the arrows on the table), and always feed into the direction of the cut. With the power of this router and the size of the cutterhead, I was surprised just how easily and quickly I was able to shape headstocks. It's like butter. For the sake of clarity this picture was taken after the routing had been done. The bearing on the bottom of the cutterhead rides against the template so one headstock will be identical to the next (taking into consideration the basic minimal wear on the cutting blades and the amount of material they lose when they are resharpened). This precision is important in the next operation.

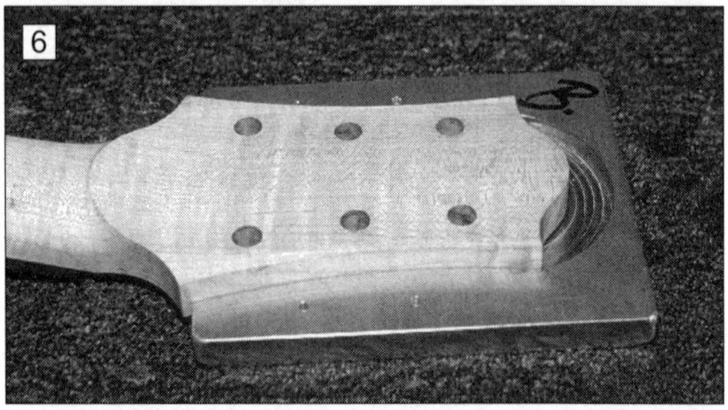

The jig for drilling the tuning-gear holes has two parts. Plate A (**Photo 4**), which bolts to the drill press table, is $5\frac{1}{2}'' \times 7\frac{1}{2}'' \times \frac{1}{4}''$ thick and is made from aluminum. Approximately in its center is a $\frac{25}{64}''$ hole, which is what you want for the Schaller Mini M-6 tuning gears I always use. There are two press-fit locating pins made from $\frac{1}{8}''$ steel rod sticking up $\frac{1}{4}''$ from the surface of the aluminum plate, one on either side of the hole. Plate B has a recess cut into it which accepts the previously shaped headstock exactly (**Photos 5 and 6**). This is a little more difficult to make out of aluminum, but my first one was made of laminated plexi, and it worked quite well. The surface of Plate B that mates to Plate A has holes drilled in it (**Photo 7**) to accept the locating pins in Plate A. At this point you'll see the obvious. Plate A is aligned on the drill press so the bit goes through the hole. Plate B is then placed on Plate A with the alignment pins in the alignment pin holes, and the headstock is held snug as you drill the first tuning-gear hole (**Photo 8**). Then simply move Plate B to another position, and repeat.

If you're thinking, "What's the big deal? Just cut that sucker out and drill some holes" — easier said than done. Any of you who have done this will know what a time consumer laying out and trying to drill without blowout in your nice ebony face cap can be. If your headstock shape varies from piece to piece you have to adjust your tuning gear placement slightly each time. Worse yet is having your drill bit wander off your original marks. With this setup I can shape a headstock with practically no need for sanding and drill the holes for the tuning keys exactly where I intended them to be in about five minutes with no face cap splintering or blow out.

That's pretty cool! Most people want their headstocks to be uniform anyway, so you are not really losing anything in terms of creativity. And man, what a time saver! What is the other fixture you were going to show us?

I arched the top and back braces on several of my first guitars by hand — just me, my belt sander, and my

best ten-year-old spruce. They came out OK, but this is quicker and more consistent, and I know that the gluing surface is going to be perfect. Using this jig I can cut the braces for a dozen guitars in about an hour. It's so easy to make and use.

The plexiglas template (**Photo 9**) started as a scrap about 36″×2½″×¾″. I made a few test tops and backs, then I made a template to match the arches I liked. One edge of the plexi stock got the arch for the top braces, and the other edge got the arch for the back braces. Upon checking I found the top arch is about a 35′ radius, and the back is about a 20′ radius, both of which are a little more rounded than Martin's or Taylor's.

The base for this jig is 32″×11″×½″ MDF. To that I screwed and glued a piece of oak 1⅝″×⅝″×32″. This strip was set back 1⅛″ from a side, creating a ledge on which to set the brace stock. The DE-STA-CO clamps are mounted on ¾″ thick blocks of mahogany, and are positioned to exert fairly even pressure on the template.

On my table saw I rip the spruce for braces into two sizes: ⅝″×1½″ for the braces under the fretboard and the back braces, and 5⁄16″×1½″ for the X braces and the tone bars.

Here you can see the jig, with two pieces of brace stock and the plexi template lying beside it on my shaper table (**Photo 10**). The two pieces of brace stock get stacked on the ledge and pushed up against the oak brace alignment stop, and the template gets placed on top of the brace stock and pushed up against positioning blocks which are screwed to the top of the brace alignment stop (**Photo 11 and Diagram**). Then I crank down the clamps. The roundish rubber feet on the clamps index to depressions drilled into the template.

The router bit for this operation is a flush trim, two-fluted, ½″-diameter, ½″-shank unit with a bottom-mounted bearing (**Photo 12**), bought from Woodcraft. Note that the bearing for the headstock shaping rode on a template underneath the work, while on the brace jig the bearing rides on a template on top of the work.

Always be extra careful around routers and shapers. They can ruin work, or catch and throw it, and they don't care whether they are cutting wood or flesh. Good luck from Arizona. ——

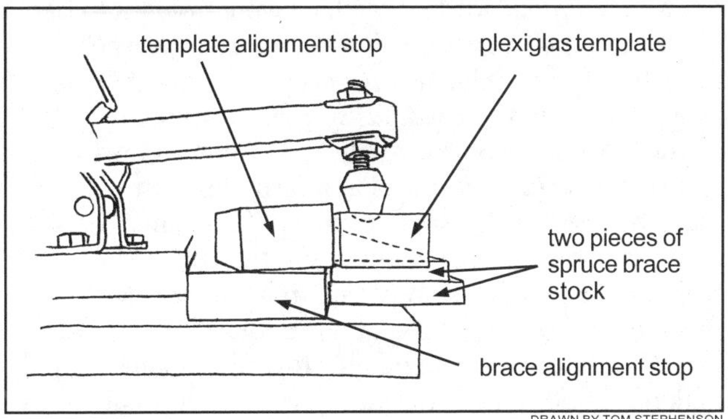

DRAWN BY TOM STEPHENSON

Originally published in *American Lutherie #49*, 1997

Wood Identification for Luthiers

by Nicholas Von Robison

THERE HAS BEEN little scientific identification of the woods used in early instruments, and for the average maker/repairperson, the techniques and resources to do any valid identification on their own has, until recently, been pretty much insurmountable for someone not wishing to acquire specialized academic training. But to those who study, restore, repair, or make reproduction copies, the exact identification of original woods is important. The intent of this article is to point out some of the resources available today for anyone who wants to venture into the world of scientific wood identification.

It is unfortunate that many who have worked with musical instruments at the scholarly level have not had much detailed knowledge of wood even though wood science is a very old and well-developed discipline. Standard works of music history may repeat earlier works verbatim, or frequently avoid the issue altogether of what woods were used by early makers, stating (with much legitimacy) that the historical distinctions are vague between the common names pine, spruce, and fir. "Spruce-pine," "whitewood," and "white deal" are obviously ambiguous to us today as far as the exact wood talked about. Statements from old manuscripts like "This is the wood of the silver fir (*Pinus picea*)..." are awkward and outdated to a contemporary botanist since this is not a valid binomial, though the music researcher or scholar might insist that this was European spruce (*Picea abies*) but not have any botanical proof. While the historical names of wood may be indistinct from different times and places, the botanical distinctions between different woods have usually been quite clearly defined.

Of the little scientific identification done on woods used in early instruments, the results have been instructive. A number of samples taken from 17th- and 18th-century keyboard instruments at the Smithsonian were sent to the Forest Products Laboratory in Madison, Wisconsin for analysis. The primary case wood of French and Flemish harpsichords is usually described in the literature to be linden (*Tilia sp.*), but all the samples were identified as poplar (*Populus sp.*). Some samples of French harpsichord jacks which were thought to be the traditional pearwood (*Pyrus communis*) turned out to be Norway maple (*Acer platanoides*), mountain ash (*Sorbus sp.*), or apple (*Malus sp.*). Dr. John Koster, conservator of the Shrine to Music Museum (now the National Music Museum), has microscopically identified over 1,000 samples from European and American keyboard instruments in the Boston collection and has also reported many surprises along this line, including the use of more imported tropical woods by late 18th- and early 19th-century keyboard makers. Whether the deviation from traditional materials was the result of experimentation and innovation, or if the old makers had as much or more trouble than we do locating suitable traditional woods and supply, is not certain. It is no doubt indicative of a more highly developed global trade in these exotics.

Many woods that are similar in appearance, such as beech and oak, have distinctive rays and pores and can easily be separated by the naked eye or a hand lens, even under a stain or varnish. However, many other woods are so similar that making an identification by gross, superficial features is unacceptable for most purposes, as witness the linden and pear examples above. This is doubly true for instruments that have surfaces that are dirty, faded, darkened by UV exposure, or covered with stain or varnish. In most cases, it is advisable to examine the cellular structure microscopically to get a valid identification. Anything else is pretty much guesswork.

Wood is a complex material and wood anatomy can be intimidating. Anatomical terms such as vasicentric tracheids, fusiform parenchyma cell, scalariform perforation plate, and fibril angle seem incomprehensible and "hard." But are they any harder than thermonuclear, polyunsaturated, Cartesian coordinates, frequency modulation, or cyanoacrylate — terms I randomly picked from literature on my bookshelf? The thought of using a microscope might seem forbidding to some, but the techniques are really quite simple and the equipment needed is minimal; even a $125 student 'scope is adequate. Throw in a $5 hand lens, some razor blades, microscope slides and covers, and a few other small items, and that's all you need.

All except for some instruction on methodology and basic wood anatomy, that is. In the past, you'd have to take some college wood science courses to learn the techniques of sectioning (taking a small sliver of wood for slide mounting) and anatomy basics. For the past few years, R. Bruce Hoadley, Professor of Wood Technology at the University of Massachusetts in Amherst, has introduced hundreds of craftspeople from all fields to the science of wood identification in annual week-long sessions at Amherst. Recently, the International Wood Collectors Society has experimented with a small wood identification workshop and I hope they continue and expand it.

Reference Materials

One of the best things to happen to wood craftspeople interested in wood ID was the publication of Dr. Hoadley's book *Identifying Wood: Accurate Results With Simple Tools;* Taunton Press, Newtown, CT; 1990; ISBN 0-942391-04-7; $39.95. Profusely illustrated and in language accessible to anyone, it will guide you through botanical systems of nomenclature and classification, and the cellular variations of wood. How samples are taken and prepared, as well as microscope and hand lens techniques, are explained in good detail and the separation (i.e., identification) of wood done in a practical and unique way. This book should provide you with the basic information and techniques to get you started on your way (see my review of this in *American Lutherie #29,* or *Big Red Book of American Lutherie Volume Three, p. 467*). However, its range of species covered is understandably limited to the major trade woods used in the USA and a handful of the more common imported exotics. For more broad-based work in identifying world woods, it is necessary to have on hand, or have accessible, reference works that cover world woods with high resolution photomicrographs.

My old, dog-eared college text is *Textbook of Wood Technology: Structure, Identification, Properties, and Uses of the Commercial Woods of the United States and Canada;* Panshin and de Zeeuw; 3rd edition; McGraw-Hill, 1970; 4th edition, 1980, ISBN 0-07-048441-4. This covers more species than the Hoadley book and has a lot more photomicrographs as well as dichotomous keys. It's dry reading, as college texts usually are, but a valuable resource for U.S. and Canadian woods.

Photomicrographs of World Woods; Anne Miles; Her Majesty's Stationery Office, London; 1978. This is a nontext atlas of world woods with some 1,400 photomicrographs covering over 450 species.

Anatomie Europäischer Holzer/Anatomy of European Woods; Fritz Han Schweingruber; Verlag Paul Haupt, Berne; 1990. This is a massive atlas of 600 European species with over 3,000 photomicrographs, dichotomous keys, and brief descriptions in German and English.

Die Holzer Mitteleuropas; Dietger Grosser; Springer-Verlag, Berlin; 1977. This book is unfamiliar to me but John Koster says it is indispensable. The text is in German and the technical descriptions are supposed to be very clear. Covers about 70 common central-European species.

If wading through technical German doesn't sound like much fun, get the *Multilingual Glossary of Terms Used in Wood Anatomy;* Committee on Nomenclature; International Association of Wood Anatomists; Heidelberglaan 2, 3584 CS Utrecht, The Netherlands; 1964; $10US. Covers English, French, German, Italian, Portuguese, Spanish, and Serbo-Croatian.

CSIRO Atlas of Hardwoods; Jugo Ilec; Crawford House Press, NSW Australia; 1991. This atlas, also textless, covers about 1,750 species in close to 8,000 photographs.

Fichas de Caracteristicas das Madeiras Brasileiras; Mainieri and Chimelo; Instituto de Pesquisas Tecnologicas, São Paulo; 1989. Covers 200 Brazilian species with 600 photomicrographs. Text is in Portuguese except for the properties tables which are in English and Portuguese. This fine addition to my library was made possible by the donation of this hard-to-find book to the 1995 GAL auction by Brazilian luthier Roberto Gomes.

Atlas d'Identification des Bois de l'Amazonie et des Régions Voisines; Détienne and Jacquet; Centre Technique Forestier Tropical, Nogent-sur-Marne; 1983. This atlas covers about 540 species in more than 1,600 photomicrographs of one of the principal regions of sources of tropical woods. Text in French.

There is no reason to obtain all of these resource books unless you are interested in wood identification in a major way. The first two (Hoadley, and Panshin and de Zeeuw) will generally suffice in the beginning and you can add Miles' and Schweingrubers' later. Many of the others can usually be accessed at major city libraries, regional botanical gardens, and xylariorums (to find an institutional wood collection near you get *Index Xylariorum – 3;* William Stern; International Association of Wood Anatomists; Utrecht, The Netherlands). Normally, the woods you need to identify will be pretty common woods. Occasionally, you'll need to thumb through one of the offbeat atlases to find your unknown. Sometimes the unknown wood will be so uncommon that these methods will not be adequate so you'll have to resort to other means.

One way is to resort to dichotomous keys (as in Panshin and de Zeeuw's, and Schweingruber's, cited above). A key takes the form, in a most simplistic way as:

1.....Wood is whitish......go to 2
1.....Wood is dark..........go to 18
  2.....Wood has odor.............go to 3
  2.....Wood has no odor.........go to 37

Each step of the way you make a choice between two variables. The idea is that sooner or later you will finally eliminate all extraneous features and it will end with the identification of the unknown, everything else being eliminated. More often than not, you take a wrong turn somewhere in determining more and more complex features, or can't find a feature the key calls for, and wind up in a dead end morass after a lengthy process.

Computer packages for wood identification have been in use for more than a decade and have surpassed manual procedures such as written descriptions, dichotomous keys, and edge-clipped cards. The programs allow a large amount of anatomical information to be entered at one sitting and the search is practically instantaneous. One easy-to-use and inexpensive program ($40?) is *GUESS* (General Unknown Entry Search System) developed by Dr. Elisabeth A. Wheeler and associates at the Department of Wood and Paper Science at North Carolina State University in Raleigh, NC. It's available for PC and MAC and has a reference manual that provides illustrations and descriptions of the various anatomical features supported. Spoiled MAC and Windows users may not like the bare-bones look of the screen displays, but it is user friendly and one database contains more than 5,200 entries.

In *GUESS,* if you've isolated eight anatomical features in your unknown sample and the program supports them, they are entered in coded form and the search begins. Normally, a listing of several taxa are the result (be suspicious if only one or two come back with these few features entered) and then you'll have to resort back to the literature for detailed descriptions and to compare photomicrographs. I don't use *GUESS* very often since conventional techniques are usually sufficient to get a viable result, but for very difficult woods it is a marvelous tool.

Another computer tool that shows great promise is *Woods of the World* database put together by Tree Talk, Inc., a nonprofit educational organization focused on wood and forest issues. It has up to eighty-five categories of data on wood (common names, uses, texture, odor, specific gravity, bending strength, environmental status, etc.) including low-magnification cell photomicrographs of several hundred wood species. This is still relatively new, but has great potential in coming years though it is not a search tool in itself. *(Available through various wood dealers, Amazon.com and so forth.)*

Illustrative Stories

▸ **Case History:** I had a guitar brought to me for repair by the maker's great-grandson. Great-grandpa had built a couple of instruments to wile away the long Midwest winter evenings, and though this one was crude and boxy, it had sentimental value to the owner. Back and sides were walnut, soundboard of white pine, and the binding, a portion of which had been damaged in a collision with a table, was a brilliant orange which I assumed was dyed holly. Upon cutting out the damaged portion of binding, I discovered it was not a dyed wood. I thought of the satinwoods and scoured wood literature to find out what other wood it might possibly be. When the owner called to see how the repair was going, I told him of my problem in identifying that wood and he gave me the hint that the old farmer had probably used local woods found in central Ohio. That narrowed it down some, but I could find no reference to any orange wood that grew in the Midwest. Totally stumped, I prepared a small sliver of the wood, put it on a microscope slide, and looked through various wood atlases. Finally resorting to a *GUESS* computer search, I determined that the wood was that of the smoketree (*Cotinus obovatus*) — actually a large shrub. I had a nasty time trying to locate some of this wood for the repair but was finally successful. To resort to dyeing a light colored wood and hope to get a suitable match in color and refraction index would have been chancy, and I went into the red badly on this due to all the time I had spent for a simple binding repair, but it was instructive and turned out well.

▸ **Case History:** In 1992 at the GAL Convention exhibition I stopped by R. E. Bruné's table for a chat. He had one of his superb guitars with him and a couple of tops that looked like western red cedar. He told me the soundboards were Japanese spruce. I probably looked incredulous because he said, "at least that's what they said they were; maybe they were wrong." Intrigued, I later obtained some samples from him and with ten minutes of work had determined that they were indeed a spruce (*Picea sp.)*. I need to point out here that because of the simple cellular structure of softwoods, it is not possible to take identification down to the species level for the most part, but a softwood's cellular structure at the genus level is quite distinct from any other genera. Even consulting *Identification of Living Gymnosperms on the Basis of Xylotomy (*Pal Greguss; Akadémiai Kaidó, Budapest; 1955), a comprehensive volume that embraces virtually every important softwood species in the world, yielded nothing on the species. This dark-colored spruce is still a mystery at the species level.

▸ **Case History:** In 1993 during an ongoing e-mail discussion with a luthier in New York, he mentioned that he had been rescuing white spruce from a lumberyard near the USA/Canada border. He said he took great pains to select the best quartersawn boards but that once he got them reduced to rough soundboards, tops from one board would be great and tops from another would be lousy. Neither of us could figure out how careful initial selection could end in such widespread results. Curious, I asked him to send me some samples of good and bad. Doing twenty minutes of sectioning and microscope work showed me that the bad wood was balsam fir (*Abies balsamea*) and the good was indeed white spruce (*Picea glauca*). We later found out that because white spruce and balsam fir overlap in their ranges and are quite similar in appearance, the two get lumped together sometimes, intentionally or otherwise, in a lumberyard, but have different tonal, stiffness, strength, weight, and shrinkage properties. I sent him a small bottle of bromo-phenol blue, a pH indicator, and with this he could weed out the balsam fir on-site. A drop on fir will turn red, while a drop on spruce remains blue.

Is It Really European?

Veteran lutherie woodcutter Bruce Harvie once showed me his method of determining Sitka spruce from the other spruces. Dragging a fingernail over a rough wood hunk he said, "Did you hear that?" "Uh, yeah, I guess," I nodded dumbly. No doubt Bruce heard (or felt) something determining in that rasping glissando, but it was lost on us bystanders. That's not to say that his method of separating Sitka from the other spruces is invalid. Over years of working with wood we all develop a repertoire of tiny insights into identifying favorite woods based on color, texture, weight, taste, dryness, and so on. The problem is that it doesn't go far enough. For one thing, it can't be taught to someone else as it's based on an individual's unique senses. My quick-and-dirty method for determining fir is to put a piece in my mouth and suck on it for a minute. If it's rich in calcium oxalate crystals, which it usually is, I get a distinctive, really lousy taste. You might try it and say it's just "woody" or "tastes like Cheerios." All of us are different. The other problem is that these gross methods of identification are not provable by themselves since they are so subjective and require something more substantive.

"Proving" a wood requires a bit more discipline and some knowledge of wood anatomy, and sometimes even cellular structure. You have a hunk of wood there which you believe to be mahogany, but don't know for sure if it's American (*Swietenia sp.*) or African (*Khaya sp.*)? With a sharp knife and a $5 hand lens, you can isolate enough anatomical features to have your case "stand up in court" so to speak. But don't be surprised if your mahogany turns out to be sapele (*Entandrophragma cylindrican*) or another mahogany look-alike. If you're dealing with wood on an existing instrument and don't have good access to cross, radial, and tangential sections of the unknown, then that's a bit more problematic and beyond the scope of this article.

There's a funny thing about wood: the hardwoods are very anatomically complex which makes them fairly easy to differentiate since you have so many features to work with and they can usually be seen at the hand lens level. The rub is that there are very, very many world hardwoods. On the other hand, softwoods evolved on earth before the hardwoods and retain a relatively primitive cell structure within a few hundred genera. This simplicity means that there are fewer distinguishing features to separate one softwood from another, particularly on the macroscopic level, but fewer woods to wade through. To prove a softwood, you usually have to resort to the microscopic level to find enough features to get a true genus, but you may not be able to determine the species at all.

The latter sentence has irksome implications for those who have hoped that the current level of wood technology would, or *should*, be able to differentiate between European spruces and our domestics. Without getting into any of the brouhaha on whether the Europeans sell back to us U.S. or Canadian woods, I flatly state that it is impossible to prove it by current scientific anatomical methods. Only Sitka spruce displays enough consistent, distinguishing features (macro and micro) to reliably separate it from the other spruces. The other spruces are our continental species (red, white, black, blue, and Engelmann), the Northern and Central European species, the Romanian/Slavic species, and the Asian/Siberian species, all of which are indistinguishable from each other on a species level. That's the way it is.

One hope for the future is with the expanding field of chemotaxonomy, the science of separating woods based on their heartwood chemicals. To date, very few softwoods have been found to contain unique extractives or essential oils which provide identification, and as it turns out, those species can usually be readily separated by conventional microscopic techniques anyway. Even a rigorous study of world spruces using scanning electron microscopy may not turn up any consistent, unique, identifying features of the various *Picea spp.*, but at any rate, no research of this is ongoing at this time to my knowledge. Oh, there is one way to determine European spruce from our domestics, and that is by looking at the bark and needles from the tree which the wood came from. Vouchered botanical material is as good as gold in this case. Barring that, the question remains — is it really European spruce? ——

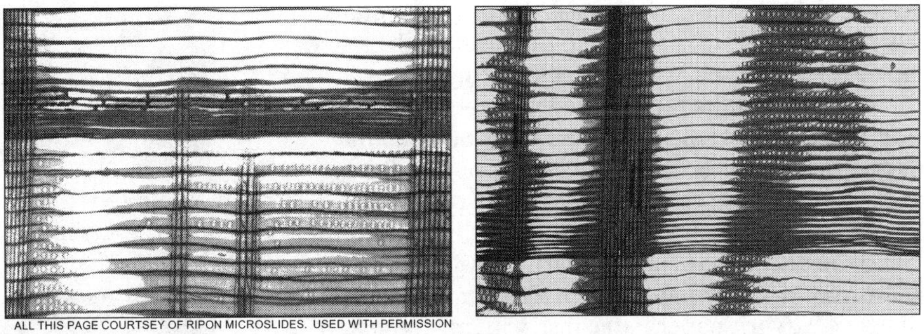

ALL THIS PAGE COURTSEY OF RIPON MICROSLIDES. USED WITH PERMISSION

*Talk about persnickety! The photomicrographs to the right are Sitka (*Picea sitchensis*), while those on the left are various other tonewoods. Note in the views of radial sections above that Sitka has a coarser texture than the Douglas fir (*Pseudotsuga menziesii*) and exhibits doubled pit pairs (lower left in photo).*

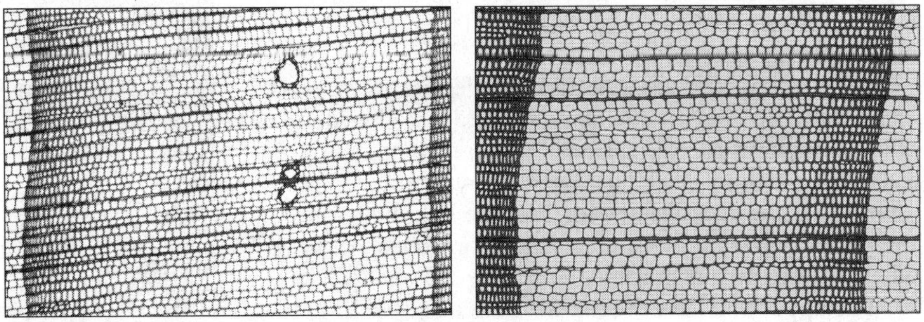

*In these cross-section views, the Sitka again shows a coarser texture and a more abrupt transition from earlywood to latewood than the other spruce (red spruce, *Picea rubens*). If our Sitka sample had resin cells, we would see that they are larger than the red spruce, and that the inner, epithelial cells, are much thicker.*

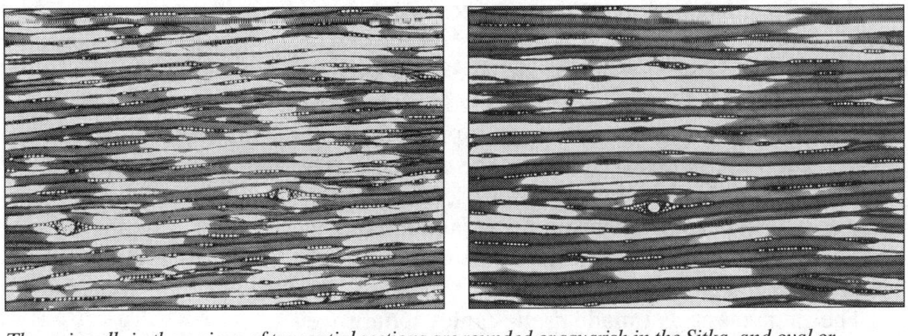

*The resin cells in these views of tangential sections are rounded or squarish in the Sitka, and oval or elongated in the other spruce (white spruce, *Picea glauca*). It's hard to see in these two samples, but ideally many more samples would be available for comparison.*

Originally published in *American Lutherie #49*, 1997

Soundboard Doming

by Brent Benfield

AS A CABINET MAKER and builder of speaker cabinets, I like to build very solidly. The key is good fitting, tight joinery. As a guitar maker, I consider tight joinery even more important. After scanning all the guitar literature available to me, it became apparent that a domed soundboard was the way to go to ensure the best tone production and the strongest box. However, no source seemed to offer a method of attaining consistently tight joints between the ribs and the domed top.

I wanted the entire top of my classical guitars to be domed, so I ordered Finnish birch spherically-dished workboards from Luthiers Mercantile International. After staring at them for some time, I began to realize how I might best use them. I use the fixture to arch every piece that will be glued to the top, and then glue up the entire top right in the workboard.

Assume that the top is joined, thicknessed, the rosette is in place, the soundhole is cut out, and the layout of all parts is traced on the underside. I cut a piece of flat board the same size as the soundhole reinforcement patch, then tape the patch to the board. Sand the patch on the 25′ radius of the workboard until its surface makes complete contact. I simply hold a sheet of 220-grit paper in the dish with my free hand during this operation. Then I place the top on the workboard and glue the patch in position while it's still taped to the board. Afterward, the extraneous wood is chiseled from the patch and it is sanded with 220-, 320-, and 400-grit paper.

I store the joined top and back in a dehumidifying chamber when they are not being worked on. I learned about this while attending Dave Freeman's Timeless Instrument School, and it has proven invaluable. The chamber is dehumidified with a simple light bulb, and the plates reside in the chamber at all times except for when gluing on and shaping the braces.

The upper and lower harmonic bars, all seven fan braces, and the bottom V struts are all placed in their turn on the dished workboard. The radius is marked on them, and all the parts are roughed to shape on the bandsaw or with a plane. Then each piece is held in position and rubbed over 220-grit paper on the workboard until its entire gluing surface touches the fixture without any pressure. While sanding I use the same area of the workboard that will support the brace during glue-up, holding the brace at the angle it will be on the top (**Fig. 1**). The brace tops are left flat until after glue-up. The upper harmonic bar and fan braces are glued on and chiseled to shape, then the lower harmonic bar and V struts are added.

The first classicals I made used Stanley Doubtfire's book, *Make Your Own Classical Guitar*, as a guide. He uses a Bouchet bar under the bridge. I adapted this feature to my domed-top construction method by sanding its gluing surface to the radius of the workboard, and gluing it to the top on the workboard, as was done with the other bars and braces. The Bouchet bar is the last piece glued to the top, and is attached after the final shaping has been done to the fan braces.

ALL BY BRENT BENFIELD

A fan brace before being sanded in the dished form. Fan braces are not carved to their final shape until after they have been glued to the top.

The soundboard is in the spherical jig and a prefitted fan brace is being glued in place. Other braces have already been glued and chiseled to shape.

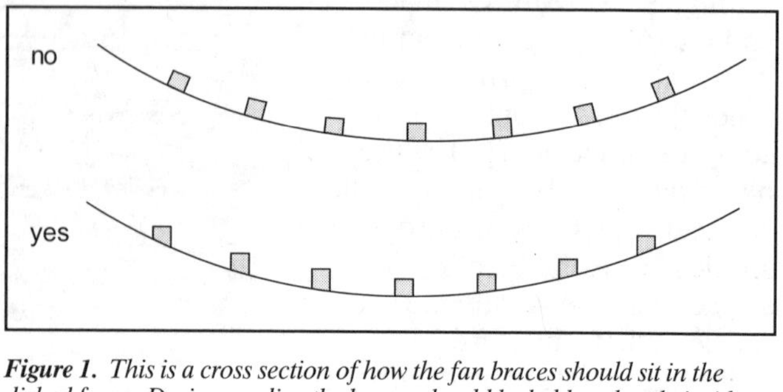

Figure 1. *This is a cross section of how the fan braces should sit in the dished form. During sanding the braces should be held so that their sides are straight up and down. The glue surface of each brace must be sanded over the same spot on the form which will support it when it is glued up.*

The bent sides are glued to the tail block and into slots in the neck block (**Fig. 2**), which gives me a freestanding unit. The top edge of the sides can be quickly planed to nestle roughly into the workboard, then the kerfed lining is glued on standing 1MM proud of the sides.

Place the neck/side unit onto the workboard upside-down, with the neck/body joint resting at the edge of the fixture. The peghead end of the neck is supported by a separate block. Though the neck angle was set when the slots were cut in the neck block, slight adjustments can be made by changing the height of the headstock support block (**Fig. 3**). If the support block is the same height as the rim of the dished workboard, a negative neck angle will automatically result. Since the workboard is wider than the guitar body is long, the butt of the guitar will "fall into" the dish just slightly.

A jig is used to hold the waist of the guitar at its proper width, and also holds the sides securely at 90° to the plane of the fretboard and parallel to each other. It's simply a wooden bar with two 90° extensions (sort of like a square wooden horseshoe) that squeeze the waist to its proper dimension. When working on the top edges, the waist jig is applied from the back of the instrument, and vice versa.

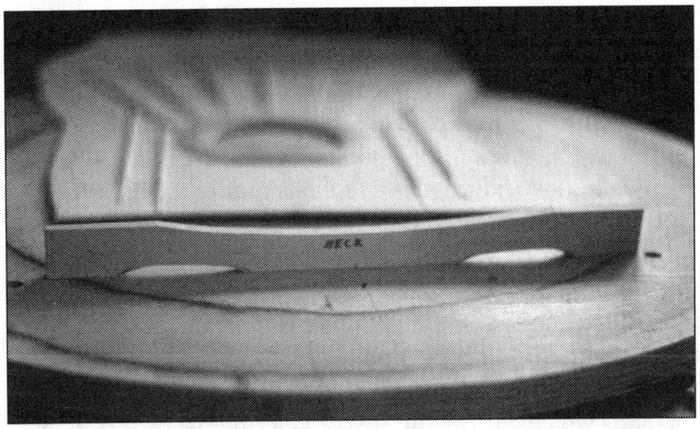

Upper harmonic bar is fitted to the jig. The long scallop saves a bit of weight. The two smaller scallops create a clearance for longitudinal braces that run through the upper bout.

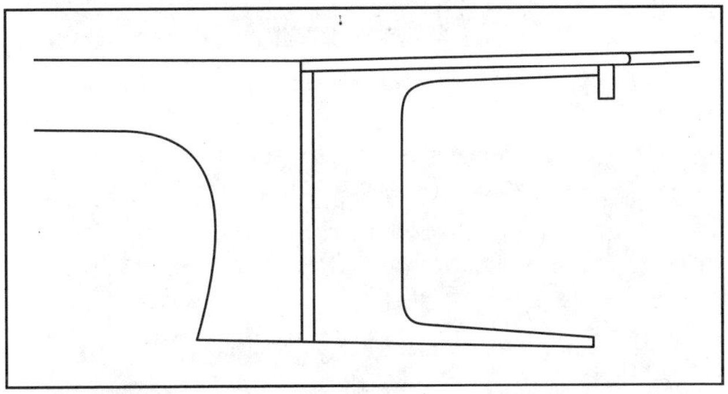

***Figure 2.** Benfield's neck construction follows standard Spanish practice of fitting the sides into slots in the neck block. He extends the block all the way to the upper harmonic bar for structural reasons. The glue surfaces of the neck block are fully contoured to the spherical arch of the top at the same time as the sides are sanded to mate with the top.*

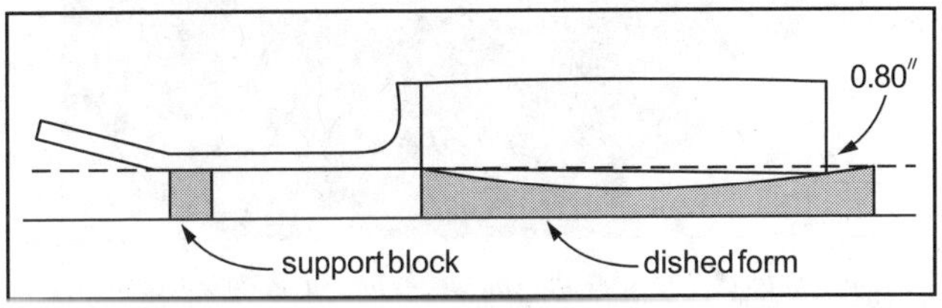

***Figure 3.** The 12th-fret area of the guitar rests at the edge of the dished form when the soundboard is glued on. If the peghead is supported at the same height as the 12th fret, a negative neck angle will automatically result. Since the body is shorter than the width of the form, the tail block "falls into" the dish, creating the negative angle. As wood is removed from the neck block during the fitting process, creating a relief so that the surface of the soundboard can end up flush with the surface of the neck, this neck angle will flatten out. However, the angle can be controlled by adjusting the height of the neck support block. Brent builds with a slightly negative neck angle.*

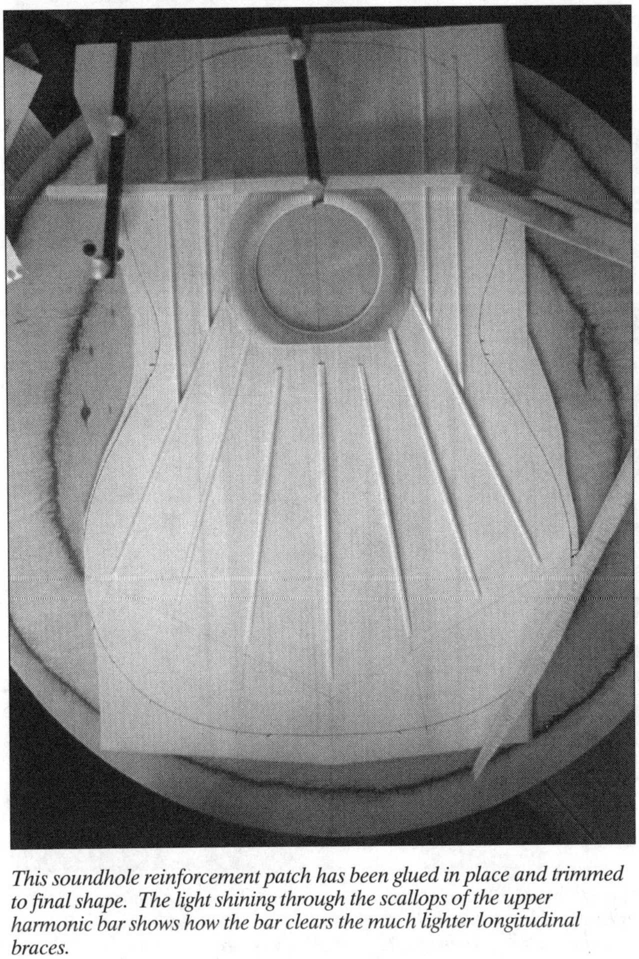

This soundhole reinforcement patch has been glued in place and trimmed to final shape. The light shining through the scallops of the upper harmonic bar shows how the bar clears the much lighter longitudinal braces.

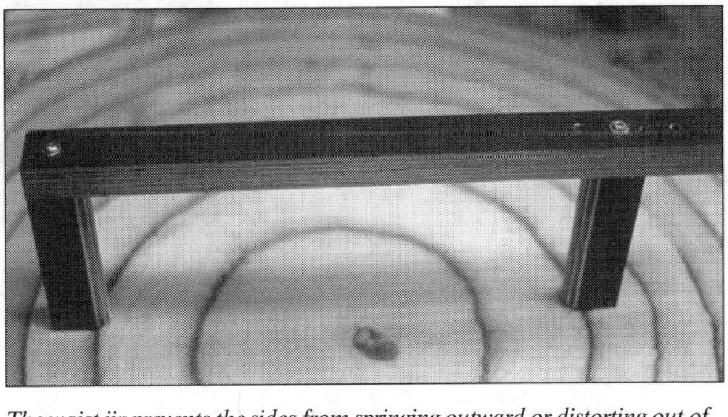

The waist jig prevents the sides from springing outward or distorting out of shape, keeping them parallel once they have been glued to the neck block and tail block. It remains in place during all sanding and gluing operations while the sides are being fitted to the arch of the plates. The inside edges of the vertical members of the jig are rounded to protect the sides and to limit the bars to one point of contact.

Details of neck block and soundhole reinforcement patch. Harmonic bar pillarets are not in place yet.

Waist jig in place. The sides and end blocks have already been mated to the top. In this instance, the arched back braces are being glued to the sides first, rather than to the back plate. This permits a more accurate fitting of the brace support pillarets.

With the neck supported at its proper angle and the waist jig in place, slide a sheet of 220-grit paper under the guitar, abrasive side up. Pull the paper out with one hand while pushing down on the sides gently with the other. Work carefully around the body until the radius of the workboard is transferred to the rib edges and blocks. The soundboard support of the neck block can be roughly chiseled before sanding begins, but leave enough stock so the radius will be formed on the entire support surface. At the 12th fret the support is sanded the full thickness of the soundboard so that it can lend its full support to the soundboard's arch as it reaches into the body. The end result is a neck/side unit that is sanded to a 25′ radius at every point where it will contact the soundboard.

The kerfed portion of the lining is trimmed away to permit a drop-in fit of the harmonic bars **(Fig. 5)**. The ends of the harmonic bars are supported by pillarets which are glued to the sides.

The dished workboard is used as a gluing fixture when the soundboard is attached to the ribs and blocks. To maintain the proper neck angle, the height of the peghead support block has to be increased by the exact thickness of the top. Use clamps or weights to close the joint. The waist jig should be used at this time, also.

Much the same procedure is used to make and attach the back as was used for the top. I've come to prefer a 25′ radius for the back, the same as the top. Others use a 15′ radius. The three back bars are sanded on the workboard and glued to the dehumidified back plate. I don't sand a curve into the back-seam reinforcing strip. The waist jig is applied from the top, then the sides are placed on the workboard, and the back radius sanded in, just as was done on the top. Be careful to maintain the proper neck angle. On two guitars I've glued the back braces to the ribs, sitting them proud, then sanded the radius into them along with the rest of the side assembly (I got this idea from José

*(See **Doming** on page 43)*

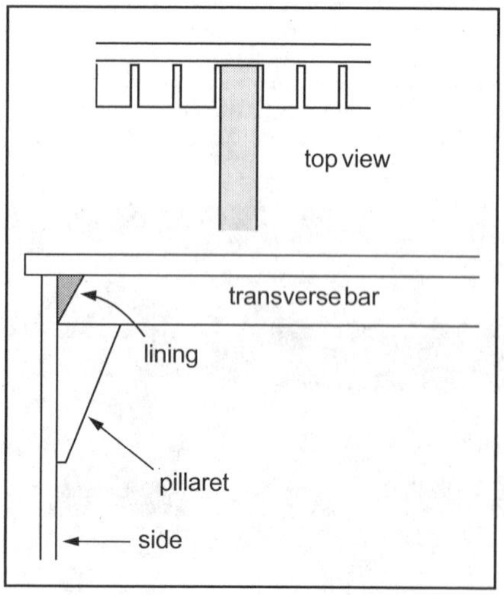

Figure 5. *The author does not run the ends of any cross braces directly onto the sides. The kerfed portion of the lining is trimmed away and the ends of the braces are carefully fitted for length. Pillarets are glued to the sides to support the ends of the braces.*

The goal is to create a perfectly and completely domed plate that fits to the ribs with as little stress as possible. Here the body nestles comfortably onto the dished form with complete contact at all points of the soundboard. The back braces have already been glued to the side assembly.

IN MEMORIAM

Originally published in *American Lutherie* #49, 1997

Richard L. Schneider

March 5, 1936 – January 31, 1997

IVAN-ROGER SITA

I first met Richard in 1964 while accompanying a long-time friend on a chance visit to his Detroit workshop. The three of us spent an enjoyable afternoon taking turns playing his guitars, and I fondly remember Richard's Mexican folk songs. That afternoon changed my life. My friend left knowing he would have a new guitar, and I left *knowing* I had to make them.

Fate smiled and eventually Richard accepted me as an apprentice, fulfilling my dreams. Many months later Richard began my friend's guitar. One day Richard asked if I'd like to work on it. I was surprised and delighted with the prospect of contributing to the realization of my friend's instrument. This thoughtful gesture is typical of the generosity, trust, consideration, and a sense of the poetic that was Richard's.

I was the first of many who Richard taught over his thirty-five years of guitar making. He was a great teacher, and his enthusiasm was infectious and inspiring. His work exemplified his standard of fine craft and aesthetic harmony combined with imagination and the eternal search for the ideal sound. He was one of the most innovative people I have ever known, and his contribution to guitar making will continue to influence generation after generation of luthiers.

Via con Dios, Richard, you will be missed.

——— *Jeff Elliott*

Originally published in *American Lutherie #50*, 1997

Meet the Maker: Kent Everett

by John Calkin

KENT EVERETT builds steel string guitars in Atlanta, Georgia. He used to build a variety of guitars before he decided to focus on acoustics. In fact, he used to be a full-time repairman who built guitars at night. From the time in his college years when he learned that there were such things as independent guitar makers, he set his sights on joining that fraternity.

The mid-'70s found him in British Columbia. Since he was an avid guitarist, and since the opportunity was in front of him, he apprenticed himself to a luthier.

"I really don't want to name any names, especially since he's not in the business anymore," says Everett. "It was a three-month apprenticeship. I paid to be there. The project felt so good, and we worked up such a head of enthusiasm, that I stayed for a year."

RON HIPP

The apprenticeship happened in Victoria, BC, home of the Larrivée guitar shop. Kent wandered down to Larrivée's to look for work, and was immediately struck by the efficiency and skill of the staff there. It was readily apparent that his training had not prepared him to step into a job as a professional.

"Jean was laying off help. It was the dark days of disco. He offered to hire me when the guitar scene turned around, but after a year I couldn't keep telling myself that good things were going to happen to me in Canada."

While waiting for a break with Larrivée, Kent worked at a cabinet shop to pay the bills. He also built four guitars while he was there.

"Jean was tickled when I showed him each new piece. He's extremely supportive of new builders. Much of the Canadian lutherie scene springs from him. He was streamlining his staff at the same time that he was planning to boost production, and here was this guy hanging out and building guitars just up the street in his spare time. I was trying hard, but I'm sure he could see that my apprenticeship had been largely a waste of effort."

Kent "hung out" until he was stretched too thin, then high-tailed it back to Georgia. He hired on at the Atlanta Guitar Works as a repairman.

"It was a very rude awakening. I thought I was prepared to be a professional, but first I had to unlearn everything I was taught as an apprentice. They gave me a fret job to do, and about halfway through it they came over to see how I was making out. They took that guitar away and started me on an intensive learning process. For a while all I did was pull frets. It's not necessarily an obvious procedure. When I could do that cleanly I learned how to prep the fingerboard, which is also more complicated than you might think. You have to consider the different kinds of wood, the problems introduced by having to preserve inlays, work through various forms of neck distortion, and maybe even rotted wood. Most of the big time repair people agree that to get a new man up and running efficiently and independently is about a five-year process."

Everett credits Devon Bogue with setting him straight as a repairman.

"Devon was an anal-retentive type — I think they make the best teachers. He'd drive all over Atlanta looking for the perfect color to touch up a sunburst. He's really responsible for showing me proper repair technique."

The shop plugged into a heavy repair scene during the '80s rock boom. The Atlanta Guitar Works developed a reputation for good work at a price that undercut the luthiers in many of the nation's metropolitan centers, and bands shipped in their guitars from all over the country.

"We made our money on fret jobs," said Kent. "We did everything else, too, but all the other work was pretty much to help bring in the fretwork."

The whole staff put in fifty-hour weeks. The money was good, but personal problems among the staff introduced a certain frustration.

"I almost took a job in graphics design. A friend was willing to start me as an apprentice for better pay than I was making as a luthier. But I just couldn't turn my back on guitars."

At night Kent went back to work. Building just wouldn't leave him alone. He made six to ten instruments a year — flattops, semisolid archtop electrics, acoustic archtops, solidbody electrics, and a few mandolins. There were also twenty or so prototypes for a patented electric guitar design that no manufacturers were willing to pick up.

One by one, their personal problems caused the other members of the staff to drop out. By the late 1980s Everett owned the shop.

"It was sort of an organic process. I was the one left with the most experience, and I inherited the bills."

Everett's self-discipline and organization took over the store, and it did better than ever. He had a lot of well-known musicians in his clientele, and he'd sold an acoustic guitar to Amy Ray of the Indigo Girls. The word spread around Atlanta that he made a good guitar. He also noticed a turn in the acoustic guitar market, and decided that perhaps the time was right to shift his emphasis.

"I was making good money in repair, but I didn't want to do that anymore. I had enough savings stashed away to support a move into full-time building."

In 1991 he closed Atlanta Guitar Works and walked away from the repair business. Everett Guitars was born.

"It was a tough go. Atlanta's a pretty big city, but the market base for high-end acoustic guitars is only a small percentage of the guitar-playing population, and it's especially tough when you have to hang your guitars next to instruments by Taylor, Santa Cruz, and Collings. Seems like the hardest blow was realizing that the quality wasn't quite there in my guitars. They played and sounded fine, but there was always some little thing that was not quite right with each one, and sophisticated guitarists can spot those things."

The answer, he decided, was to refine his entire construction process.

"It had already become apparent to me that the process is as important as the finished guitar, and as long as I was repairing I never had time to work on the process. Most guys aim toward a killer guitar. I decided to shoot for a killer process, and figured the killer guitars would naturally follow. It requires a lot of thought but the results are worth it. I found that I was not only making guitars better, but faster, and that the increased experience with each step compounded the progress. It seemed like the faster I was able to work, the better the guitars got. Everybody stumbles over some part of the guitar, whether it's the binding, or the finish work, or whatever. Whatever it is, once you beat it, it becomes a pleasure every time you come back to it. The work becomes more satisfying," he said.

It also became apparent that the only way to make higher production pay was to sell through dealers.

"The idea of giving 40% of each guitar to a dealer was hard to face, but it seemed like the only way to get my guitars in front of a substantial playing public."

Everett sat down with a calculator and decided he had to make six guitars a month to make the proposition pay, and he set out to do it.

"I did it, too, and it about killed me. But after building six a month for awhile, dropping back to five a month was a piece of cake."

It was a very tough go, despite the reward of watching the quality of his guitars improve. Orders came in just fast enough to keep him hanging on, and all the while his savings were trickling away. Kent refined his production techniques, went to trade shows, built his dealer base, began to ship more guitars.

"After about three years I went up in the Georgia mountains with my girlfriend. She turned to me and said, 'There *is* a light at the end of this struggle. It's really going to happen,' and I knew it was true. Now it's four years later, and the sky is just beginning to look blue. In 1997 I should make as much money as I did during my last year as a repairman."

What happened to the calculations that dictated the necessity of building six guitars a month?

"It's amazing how you can sit down and recalculate things when you have to," Everett said with a smile.

Kent's long suit may be his ability to organize his mind and his shop. He keeps his entire building process laid out on a color-coded, four-week wall chart that never leaves his next move in doubt. The work just seems to flow with no breaks. His description made me think of a spiral galaxy — as he moved methodically around the arms of the galaxy different guitar parts and assemblies trickled toward the middle. Five guitars popped magically out of the center, and right behind them were more necks and bodies flowing toward completion.

"When everything is going just right it really is like a dance. It's great. And every so often you get a month with five weeks in it, and I use it to catch up on odds and ends like finishing a fancy set of inlays, making a special rosette, stuff like that. And if a particular batch of guitars is giving me trouble I rely on that fifth week to maintain my schedule."

Though the cycle repeats itself every four weeks, it actually takes eight weeks to process each batch of five guitars. The schedule runs like this:

▸ Week 1: Build five bodies. With luck, two or three of them will get bound. On Saturday the previous batch of five guitars have their lacquer wet sanded with 600 grit, then they are left to hang for a week.

▸ Week 2: If any of the current guitars have shell purfling, that would have been done over the weekend. Monday and Tuesday, finish the binding and prep the neck blanks for fitting to the bodies. Wednesday, fit necks to bodies and glue on fingerboards, normally a ten-hour day. Thursday and Friday, run the necks over the shaper, finish the headstocks, and carve the heels. On Saturday the previous batch gets

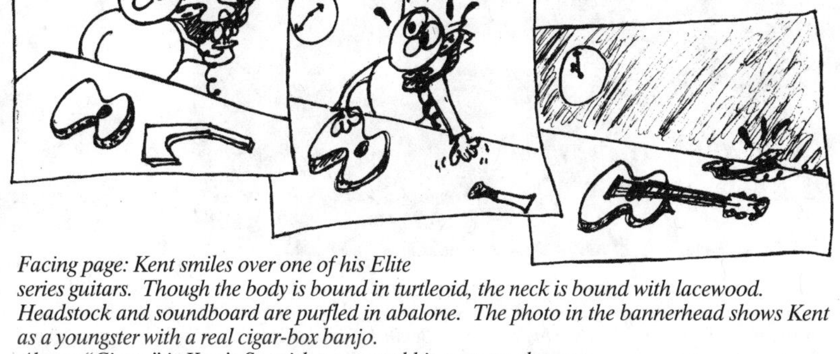

Facing page: Kent smiles over one of his Elite series guitars. Though the body is bound in turtleoid, the neck is bound with lacewood. Headstock and soundboard are purfled in abalone. The photo in the bannerhead shows Kent as a youngster with a real cigar-box banjo.
Above: "Ciento" is Kent's Spanish name and his cartoon alter-ego.

any lacquer drop-fills that may be necessary, and is then sanded to 1000 grit.

▸ Week 3: Early in the week the previous batch is sanded to 1500 grit and buffed; necks are attached to bodies of the current batch, bridges are glued in place; the previously assembled guitars are strung to pitch and left to hang in a climate-controlled room for a week. They are now each within 2–2½ hours of completion. Thursday and Friday, the current batch of five is sanded, pore filler is applied, spray prepping is completed, and the guitars get a wash coat of finish.

▸ Week 4: Early in the week the current batch is lacquered. Later, the previous batch is unstrung, buffed, and waxed; the frets are dressed and the saddles, nuts, and truss rods are adjusted as necessary. If everything runs smoothly, two sets of sides will be bent and kerfed to get a jump on the following week, which begins the cycle all over again. On Saturday five guitars of the previous batch are boxed, and on Monday of the new Week 1, UPS takes them away.

After five solid months of guitar building, the actual assembly process stops for four weeks while he makes the parts that will become the next twenty-five instruments. Tops and backs are joined and thickness sanded, bridges and binding made up, fingerboards slotted and tapered, braces cut and shaped, all the usual chores. Once production begins again it's just a matter of reaching for the right parts. All the shelves and bins are full and ready. Twice a year Kent works in the time to revamp the shop and his building process. The evolution never really stops.

"I reorganize the shop, build new jigs, or rebuild old ones. I keep notes about what could or should be improved upon, then I take the time to do it. I love the refining and the inventing. Remember Rube Goldberg? I joke with my girlfriend that my real goal is to show up for work and crank a big set of weights way up in the air, and then just sit back all day while these weights slowly descend and drive the whole shop. The weights clank down one link of chain at a time, and at the other end finished guitars flow off a belt for the UPS driver."

The near distance for Kent includes an expansion of his line of Elite flattops, a gussied-up guitar which at this point is available only on special order directly from Everett Guitars. The Elites should be available from dealers soon.

"I'm working up other special models, mostly using different kinds of trim and fancier inlay patterns. And there's a classical guitar in the works, too."

The future seems rosier after talking to Kent Everett; he's that kind of optimist. But it's also apparent that the machinery that builds a better day is lubed with a good dose of elbow grease. ——

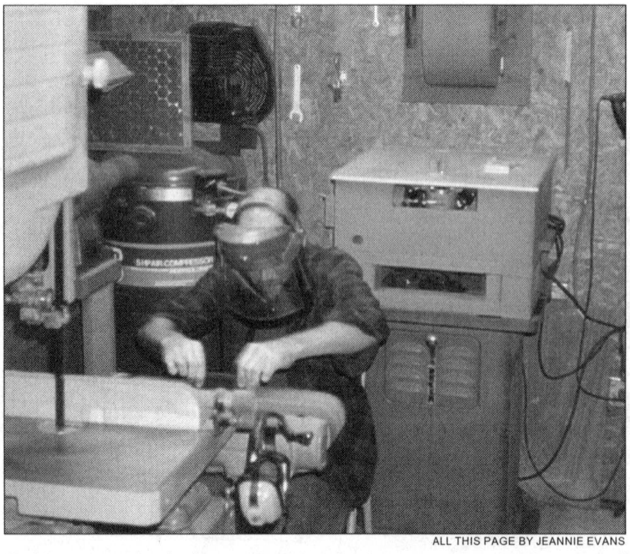

ALL THIS PAGE BY JEANNIE EVANS

Perhaps one aid to higher production is having separate rooms for many of the construction operations. Here Kent power sands an ebony bridge in the "dirt room." All millwork is done in this room. Behind him is a table-mounted router and squirrel-cage exhaust fan.

Five guitars per month adds up to a lot of sanding. Note holes in the body for the neck attachment bolts and truss rod access.

This is the front room. It is kept clean, and housing the final setup of every guitar is one of its primary functions.

Kent inside the climate control room. Note the stack of spruce behind him. Work in progress is shuttled into other rooms while under construction, then hustled back to this room as quickly as possible. All guitars spend a week under string tension in this room while the lacquer goes through final curing.

Originally published in *American Lutherie #50*, 1997

Understanding Nitrocellulose Lacquer

from his 1996 Healdsburg Guitar Festival talk

by Michael Hornick

UNDERSTANDING the way lacquer works is the key to working successfully with it. You can never establish a set routine for applying lacquer. Conditions change daily and you have to be able to change your mix and techniques in response.

Nitrocellulose lacquer is a solvent-based finish. It is literally dissolved plant fiber, and the solids are suspended in an enormous amount of liquid. Most of each coat will evaporate, leaving the thinnest layer of finish. Getting the thinners out quickly and thoroughly is the key to cycling the spray work through the shop in good order.

These solvents do nasty things to your body if you breathe them in or touch them with your bare skin. Be very careful with them. Breathing the fumes is bad enough, but getting your bare hands in the stuff puts a full dose of poisons straight into your blood stream.

Lacquer can be brushed on if the material is mixed differently. I've seen wonderful guitars finished in brushed lacquer. But we're all working under a tight time frame, and spraying will accomplish the job much faster. Spraying is what I am most familiar with.

Lacquer sticks to itself better than it sticks to wood, and this can give rise to finish lifting. Any place the lacquer is put under pressure, such as around the washers of the machine heads, the finish is prone to lift and leave little white lines. So I use a vinyl sealer on the bare wood. Vinyl sealer sticks to wood tenaciously, and lacquer sticks tenaciously to the vinyl. It's also important that the finish products be absolutely compatible, so I get them from the same company, McFadden. They've been making lacquer for Guild Guitars for umpteen years, and they understand that furniture, piano, and guitar lacquers need different amounts of plasticizers. Companies that make only one blend don't take this into account. For maximum compatibility I also use McFadden's vinyl sealer. If you're happy with another brand of lacquer, fine. But if you're going to switch to a vinyl sealer, make sure it's compatible with your top coat.

Once the guitar is sealed, a pore filler is used on the open-grain woods. Before I begin the filling process I tape off all the binding and purfling. I bind my guitars with ebony, and if the brown filler gets into the pores it looks lousy, and is a pain to clean it out with a needle.

I reduce McFadden's filler with naphtha to the consistency of light cream, and apply it with a wad of burlap. Burlap has a loose enough weave to hold lots of filler, and I try to smoosh it into every pore. I let it haze over, then rub it off across the grain with clean burlap. Occasionally I'll have to do this twice to a guitar. After filling I'll rub a shine back onto the sealer with some clean burlap, and then with paper towels, which makes it easier to see that no filler is left sitting on top of the wood. You'll never get a 100% fill at this stage. If all the pores are 80% filled you can move on to the next stage.

McFadden filler is available in different tints, but I use mahogany for all my guitars. Using the same color filler on the neck and body lends a color consistency to the guitar that I like, even though the body may be rosewood and the neck mahogany. Walnut filler is much darker than mahogany, and seems like it ought to be the choice for rosewoods, but it looks grayish to my eyes. I use mahogany filler on mahogany, rosewood, koa, and any other wood that requires filling.

Recently I've tried the microbead acrylic paste filler from Luthiers Mercantile. My tests look good, but before I commit to changing my guitars I will need to be very sure of what I'm doing.

Just before I begin spraying I scuff the surface of the guitar with 320-grit paper to provide some tooth for the lacquer and to be doubly sure that there's no filler left on top of the wood. If you use any color treatment on the wood itself you must be extraordinarily careful not to cut through it with the 320 grit.

I finish bodies and necks separately and use different guns for each. For bodies I use a large production gun, an Astro AS-8. I have a small cup for spraying vinyl sealer. I also have a Sharps gun that I sometimes use. These are Taiwanese guns, inexpensive but adequate. They've been rejetted; that is, fitted with smaller tips and the packings and such that make those tips work efficiently. For necks I use my old DeVilbis EGA Series 502 door jamb gun. I think that keeping your guns scrupulously clean is more important than which gun you use. I never shoot anything but sealer and clear nitrocellulose through my guns, and if I had to, I think I'd go buy another cheap gun for the colors.

You'll find that there is no one perfect pressure for spraying. I run from 33psi–34psi all the way up to 50 psi, depending on the lacquer mix and atmospheric conditions. In the summer you can cut back on pressure somewhat. I've tried heating the lacquer, but decided it wasn't worth the trouble and the potential hazard.

The thinners you cut your lacquer with have to be of a high quality. Too many people overlook this. Good lacquer thinner does cost more, but more care is taken to keep it uncontaminated.

The amount of thinners in your mix will have to be adjusted all the time. If you're brushing the lacquer it has to be thin enough to flow out or you'll get thick and thin spots. If you're spraying lacquer that's too thick you'll likely get areas of major orange peel, a very pebbly surface. If the lacquer is too thin it will run, and if you spray light enough to control the running you'll have to spray too many coats to get a useful build.

Getting a handle on how much retarder to use is also a matter of experience. Retarder slows down the flash time, or drying time. More retarder is called for if you're brushing, so your overlaps will flow together. Spraying requires less retarder, but you may have to adjust it for daily conditions. Warm, dry air calls for more retarder to keep the finish from flashing off between passes of the spray gun. Cold or moist air calls for less retarder or the finish can sag and run before it flashes off. You'll develop your own style with a spray gun, and you'll have to mix your finish to suit your style. But if you know what mixtures cause what problems, you won't be baffled when they occur, you can simply adjust for them.

When you do it right, lacquering is like welding. Each new coat melts into the last, and there is no remnant of individual coats.

When I prep a body I put a block of foam into the soundhole, then a layer of cardboard, and finally a piece of inner-tube rubber. The foam and cardboard keep the rubber pressed against the inside of the top to seal off the soundhole. The day after spraying I can remove the rubber, heat it with a hair dryer, peel off the lacquer, and get an accurate measurement. I know that with one gun I'm going to get a build of .0015″ after four or five coats, which is one day's spraying, and with my other gun I'll get a build of about .002″. What I'm after is a finished build of between .0035″ and .005″. Putting on less than .0035″ is just begging to get rubbed through when you level the surface. Anything over .005″ will increase the probability of cold checking and may begin to smother the guitar. It costs more in time and materials, too.

I spray necks and bodies separately, so after spraying I have to strip the finish beneath the fingerboard and bridge. I measure that finish to see what the final thickness turned out to be, and it's never as much as the sum of all the coats. The finish keeps losing solvents and getting thinner with time, and this will continue throughout the life of the guitar.

The barrel of the neck needs a lot more finish than the body, since it receives a lot of wear. I'll usually shoot a total of twelve coats on the back of the neck. The heel doesn't need so much finish, nor does the back of the headstock. If you use rosewood to cap the headstock it may require more lacquer to be sure of a good fill, but don't use more than necessary.

I was having problems with finish sinking back into the pores. I noticed Collings guitars didn't exhibit this problem, so I called Bill up. What a wonderful guy he can be! He told me about a process called gassing that he learned in the automobile finishing trade. When I tried it, it just turned my life around.

Here's how it works. On day one of finishing I shoot three to five coats, depending on conditions. On the morning of day two I sand the lacquer with 180-grit Tri-M-ite paper, just to cut the surface. I make no attempt to level the surface. I cut the surface tension of the finish, opening it up to let out the maximum amount of solvents. That's gassing. I let the work gas for two days, during which no spraying is done. On day four I shoot another three to five coats.

On day five I open the finish with 220 grit, but now I also begin to sand for flatness. Not completely flat, because I don't want to go through, but as much as I feel can safely be done. If a spot is going to give me real problems I'll get a brush and treat the area with Cell-U-Solve to open up or restore some solvent content to the lacquer, then brush on a bit of lacquer to build up that area. The work is allowed to gas for two days.

On day seven I'll spray again, but not so many coats, just what I think is called for, and then I'll try to let the work rest for three to five days before I go back to it. There will be a tremendous amount of sinking of the finish. At that point I'll wet sand for flatness with 800 grit. I put liquid Wol-wax in the water instead of dish soap. It's a Star Chemical product that helps prevent the paper from loading up. When the paper loads up it actually scratches the surface, puts in a new groove.

I find that 600 grit leaves too coarse a surface for me. I've heard that 3M makes all their papers up through 600 grit in the same room, which can let stray grits from coarser papers sneak in there. But 800-grit paper and finer is made in a special room. The 800 is made specially for the automotive industry. It leaves a smoother surface than 600, yet it cuts faster.

Don't go for a totally flat surface with 800. I keep dropping down through 1200, 1500, 2000, and finally 2500 grit, each time taking out some dimples as well as the scratches from the previous grit. Wet sanding leaves the guitar with a wonderful surface in which I can read the label of the light bulb in the reflection. I change the direction of my strokes with each grit, so I know when the scratches of the previous grit have been eliminated.

If I have to do drop fills on a few pores that didn't take enough filler, I level the hardened drop with a fine file on which the end is taped off to prevent digging. Sanding or scraping the filled area produces a wave in the finish that I can't live with. If a larger area is touched up I level it with a steel scraper. I file the end of the scraper flat, but I don't raise a bevel on it. Once these areas are filed or scraped they are wet sanded with a flat block to blend them with the rest of the guitar.

Because I wet sand to such a fine surface, I only have to use one grade of polish on my buffing wheel to bring up a good shine. The abrasive is from Menzerna-werk, a German company. I used to buy it as Glanz wax. LMI stocks it now. I use a single 16″ buffing wheel of Canton flannel, which is a double-sided flannel. The fabric itself can't scratch the lacquer. I used to gang these buffs into a 4″ or 5″ wide wheel until I realized I was just creating heat on the lacquer surface. Heat drives out the solvents, which makes the lacquer shrink into the pores again, destroying the flat surface I just created. Too much heat can even move the lacquer, cause it to bunch up in spots, and form a texture you can feel. So I use just one wheel, and I keep it moving over a large surface to keep the heat down.

Good buffing requires the same patience as wet sanding. You're not going to skate over the guitar one time and get this killer rub. You have to keep spinning the body as you go to keep the wheel in proper alignment with the edges of the instrument. Don't buff into any edges, always away from the edges. At the soundhole you've got to turn the body quickly to keep the wheel spinning into the hole. Not only can the wheel burn the finish off an edge before you know it, but it can grab the guitar and whip it right out of your hands. I had an apprentice who fed an edge into the buffing wheel, and it grabbed hold and smashed his guitar onto the floor.

My buffer spins at 1400rpm–1800 rpm, but 700 rpm–1000 rpm is better, much more user friendly. Almost all of the big shops I know of have gone to the slower buffers.

The wheel always leaves a residue on my guitars. I do a final clean and polish by hand with Novus #2, a plastic polish. I continue to keep the guitars cleaned and polished with the Novus polish for as long as they are in my possession.

I always bind my fretboards with ebony. I hate the way an unbound board chips out at the fret slots, especially during refretting. Before spraying I mask the fretboard to the very edge of its surface. A tiny ridge of lacquer normally builds at the edge of the tape. Once the finish has seasoned, I file away the ridge with a 3″ mill bastard file, *before* I pull the tape, to prevent any chipping. Go to the surplus store and buy a toothbrush with brass bristles, they're great for cleaning little files. They sell them with nylon bristles, too, and they're good for cleaning clogged paper while you're wet sanding.

To keep machine-head washers from blistering the headstock finish, I fit the machines tightly. The hole for Schaller machines is 25⁄64″, but the holes get lacquer in them during spraying. I clean them out with a size-W bit, which leaves a hole that's a shade smaller than 25⁄64″. Push the machines in from the back, don't crank them in by tightening the nut. I also bevel the holes for the machines from both sides to prevent any chipping while I'm doing this work. I haven't had any headstock blistering problems on my last fifty or sixty guitars. The thinnest possible finish that leaves the surface you want will also help.

When doing touchup work on old guitars it's important to revitalize the old finish with a product such as Cell-U-Solve Acetate or Behlen's Renew. This stuff is just a form of lacquer retarder that restores some life to the old lacquer, enabling the touch-up coats to melt into the old surface. Without the Cell-U-Solve you can see the two layers at the feather edge after rubbing them out. It looks bad. The Cell-U-Solve can be brushed onto small areas or sprayed over a large repair. Keep in mind, though, that the crazing process is a natural part of the life of a lacquer finish, and it makes the guitar sound better. When the lacquer on the top of a guitar crazes, it breaks the surface tension of the finish, allowing the spruce to vibrate more freely. I believe this is one of the reasons why old guitars sound better. It's also one of the reasons why I don't switch to one of the modern synthetic finishes. They are production friendly, and they look great, but what you get today is what you're going to have tomorrow. They don't improve with age. ——

(**Doming** *from page 36*)

Romanillos' book, *Antonio de Torres, Guitar Maker — His Life & Work*). It worked nicely.

Before the back is glued on, a bridge clamping caul is fitted to clear the fan braces and radiused in the dish to fit the soundboard.

The underside of the bridge must be arched to properly mate to the domed top. A piece of board 4½″×7″ is sanded to the 25′ radius of the workboard, then sandpaper is placed over its convex surface. The bridge is rubbed over this sanding block until its underside evenly matches the 25′ radius of the top.

The guitar top is marked with the exact outline of the fingerboard, and this area is made perfectly flat with a sanding block. The amount of wood removed probably adds up to no more than .010″–.015″. Some wood must be removed from the underside of the fingerboard, from the 12th fret to the end of the fingerboard, to compensate for the pitch of the neck.

Most references suggest that the soundboard arch should extend from the tail block to the lower harmonic bar, leaving the upper bout flat. This makes it easier to fit the neck block and fingerboard. However, I can't help thinking that arching the entire top produces a stiffer, more resonant soundboard, and I don't see why a fully radiused top shouldn't work for any bracing design. ——

Update

Since writing this article, I have made a few changes to my system. I now join the top to the sides with tentellones. I use the 15′ radius for backs, and glue the braces to the back before gluing the back to the sides.

—— *Brent Benfield (2006)*

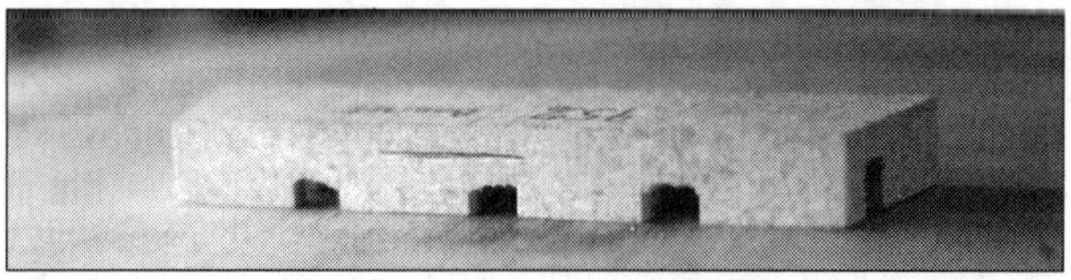

The interior bridge clamping caul sitting in the dished form. The notches clear the fan braces and the Bouchet bar. The contact surface is carefully mated to the arch of the top plate.

Here the back is being glued to the ribs using weights instead of clamps. Note the even line of glue squeeze-out. The dished form is on the bottom of the pile.

Originally published in *American Lutherie #49*, 1997

Resetting a Neck with Jeff Traugott

from his 1996 American School of Lutherie workshop

by Colin Kaminski

I HAVE OFTEN WONDERED what it takes to make a living in our profession. I had never met Jeff Traugott until the 1996 series of repair lectures at the American School of Lutherie, and I had secretly wondered how he was able to come from nowhere and get that now-infamous spread in *Acoustic Guitar* magazine and the ad for D'Addario Strings.

In the course of talking to Jeff I found that he had been working for Santa Cruz Guitar Co. for years. That gave him the chance to learn their production techniques (and develop some for them), and it also gave him the opportunity to meet all of their dealer network. But as I spoke with him I found there was more to it than that. Jeff is one of the friendliest, kindest, and most helpful people I have ever met.

During the ASL class we got to see Jeff do a complete neck reset. If you have ever done one, you know it can be a tricky operation. Jeff instructed and answered all of our questions while he worked. We were able to distract him enough that he got the neck set to such an angle that the E strings were out of alignment with the edges of the fingerboard by a few thousandths of an inch. He asked us to be quiet and in a few minutes, with no sign of frustration on his face, all was well and he was ready to proceed. Seeing how calm he remained while things were going wrong on a customer's expensive instrument was very instructive in itself.

I have reset about forty necks in my repair career, but Jeff's method is safer than the method I had used. Always looking to make my life easier, I figured I would give it a try. Since attending the class, I have had a chance to use his techniques, as carefully as I could follow his instructions, on three guitars. What follows is his method tempered with some warnings from my experience with his and my own methods.

If you have never done a neck reset before, *practice on an inexpensive instrument.* This is not easy and can be frustrating until you understand the geometry of the dovetail completely.

There are a few tools and supplies that are needed which are out of the realm of normal repairs.

- A small burner to heat the pressure cooker.
- A small pressure cooker with a hose to a basketball needle with the end cut off so as to let the steam go straight out and not to the side.
- A sharp $\frac{1}{4}''$ chisel. Working end grain requires a very sharp chisel.
- A jig that holds the body and presses the heel of the neck straight out (more on that later).
- A way of heating the fingerboard extension (more on that later).

Examine the guitar. What is the string height? What is the height of the saddle? Is the saddle glued in? Are the strings lined up with the edges of the fingerboard? Are all of the soundboard braces glued in place? A loose brace can cause the top to bow and make the action high. Is the bridge plate warped? Is the bridge glued down? If all of these things are taken care of and the string height is still too great, it is time to reset the neck.

We also need to establish goals for a well-set neck. A well set neck has the saddle about $\frac{1}{8}''$ above the bridge with the action, measured above the 12th fret, set to where the player is comfortable. Unless the player is playing bluegrass, very hard, I like to set the action to $\frac{6}{64}''$ on the bass side and $\frac{5}{64}''$ on the treble side above the 12th fret. The neck should not have any gaps where it meets the body, including at the heel cap. The neck should hang on for many decades. The fingerboard should have no gaps to the body especially at the 14th fret above the binding. The fingerboard should be perfectly playable to the 20th fret.

With all of this in mind, it is time to remove the neck. Put the strings, saddle, bridge pins, and the nut (if it is loose) in a plastic bag and put it in the case. Check the tuning key grommets; if they are loose put them in the bag as well. The first task is to unglue the fingerboard extension. To do that we have to heat it up until the glue softens. The best way, and the way Jeff uses, is to use a silicon blanket with no thermostat. An alternate way is to make a block of steel or aluminum the size of the extension and heat it in the oven to about 300°F and clamp it to the fingerboard extension. The worst way is to use a heat lamp over the extension. This will often crack the fingerboard and can damage the finish of the top even under a caul.

Once the fingerboard is hot, insert a $2''$ palette knife from the soundhole end of the fingerboard and loosen the fingerboard up to the 15th fret (13th fret on twelve-fret models). Don't worry about the area on the sides of the dovetail on the face of the guitar between the 14th and 15th fret. If these are still glued down it will help keep the steam from damaging the finish. If the fingerboard is hot enough the knife will slide easily in. If you have to force it you are probably lifting some of the spruce with it. You should be able to lift the fingerboard extension without lifting any spruce whatsoever. Patience helps.

If you are refretting, now is the time to remove all of the frets on the fingerboard extension. The heat will help prevent chipping. Jeff always refrets when he is doing a reset. It is the only way to make the neck to body transition on the fingerboard perfect. Otherwise when we kick the neck back, the end of the fingerboard will fall off the string line and make the action high above the body. The other options are to fit a shim under the fingerboard extension or leave it alone and mill the frets.

Remove the 15th fret (13th fret on twelve-fret models). Use a pair of flush-ground end nippers so the fingerboard does not chip. Drill a 5⁄64″ hole in the 15th fret slot about 3⁄8″ off center (to miss the truss rod). The dovetail gap is usually 5⁄8″ from the neck body joint (on a Martin) so you may have to angle the drill one way or the other. Test the hole you have drilled by inserting a guitar string as deep as it will go. It should go almost all the way to the back.

Clamp the body into the neck-press jig. Jeff's neck-press jig is just a workboard with three adjustable positioning stops for the guitar body (two at the waist and one at the tail block end), a couple of pieces of bungee cord to hold the guitar down, and a short block on which the heel cap rests, holding the upper back of the guitar slightly off of the workboard. When the shoulders of the guitar are clamped toward the workboard, the block presses against the heel and, if the glue has been softened sufficiently, pushes the dovetail joint apart. I use one I made from a picture from the Brian Galloup article in *American Lutherie #40*. (See *Big Red Book of American Lutherie Volume Four*, p. 116.)

ALL BY COLIN KAMINSKI EXCEPT AS NOTED

Warm up your pressure cooker and insert the needle into the hole you just drilled. Put a small amount of pressure on the neck-press jig. Be careful here. If you try to use the neck press jig to push out the neck before the glue is soft it will collapse the sides!

As the steam oozes out, keep a paper towel handy to wipe up any water droplets. Any standing water will tend to turn the finish white, especially in a French polish finish. If the finish turns white you can usually polish it by hand and heat it up enough to release the trapped water.

If all goes well the neck will pop off all by itself. If one side of the dovetail releases before the other, it may be necessary to hold the neck with a little pressure to close the free side in order to force the steam to the other side. Do not rock the neck back and forth to try to release the glue. This can result in a cracked heel block. As this process goes on, you will be able to see where the neck has released by gently flexing the neck in relation to the body and looking at the gap between the heel and body.

The neck is off! This usually takes me about twenty minutes from the time I open the case until the neck is in my hand. Turn off the steam generator. Clean off all the glue while it is still hot. Use a chisel for the large glue pieces, then switch to a terry-cloth wash rag. If necessary you can use a little steam to clean it further. It will be much easier now than after the glue has rehardened.

Top left: Jeff installs a guitar in his neck-press jig. Bungee cords and adjustable stops at the waist and end hold the instrument in position.
Middle left: Heating the upper end of the fretboard prior to working it loose.
Bottom left: The heel rests on a block on the neck-press jig while clamps press the body towards the padded workboard.
Bottom right: Jeff keeps an eye on things as steam is applied through a small hole in a fret slot to soften the glue in the neck joint.

JEFF TRAUGOTT

Let the neck and body dry before proceeding. I like to give them a week. I am rarely in a hurry, since I always quote at least a month for a neck reset. One day in low humidity is probably enough.

We need to prepare the neck for fitting. But first a little dovetail theory. The dovetail itself holds the neck on the body. The end grain does nothing other than hide the dovetail from view. Therefore, it is only important to have the edge of the heel touching the body. Take your *sharp* chisel and cut a relief channel around the dovetail leaving about 1/8″ ledge on the edge. This will make fitting the heel much easier.

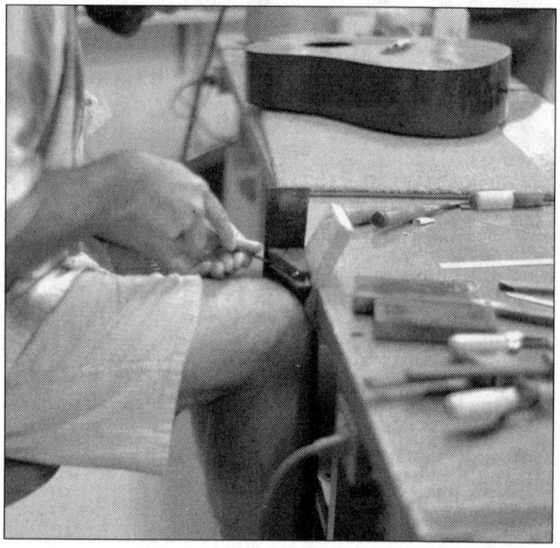

Check to make sure the face of the dovetail does not contact the heel block inside the dovetail slot. If it does it will hold the heel from contacting the body. Also check to be sure only the 1/8″ ledge contacts the body of the guitar.

Put the neck back onto the body. Holding a straightedge on the top of the frets, tilt the neck back until the straightedge goes just above the bridge (or about 1/32″ over on guitars with a lot of give). Measure the gap between the neck and the body at the top of the neck. This is how much you will have to take off the heel at the bottom to give the desired change.

Do not put too much neck angle on the guitar! Fixing this problem shortens the neck, throwing out the intonation. Then you will have to move the saddle.

Cover the sides around the dovetail with premask. Don't try this technique without it. Premask is a very thin masking tape about 6 1/4″ wide with the gentlest adhesive I have ever found. It is more gentle than Post-it notes. It serves to protect the finish from the grit that falls loose from the sandpaper.

Now we need to change the neck angle. I have always used a chisel and files to do this. This takes a lot of skill and practice or the lacquer chips out. It also requires that you are always sure where the neck is creating a gap. Not always an easy thing to figure out.

Jeff's brilliant method (learned at Santa Cruz) is to place the neck in the body, hold the heel firmly against the body, and pull a piece of 120-grit Tri-M-ite sandpaper through the joint to carefully remove material from the heel.

Cut the paper into 1″ strips, 8″ long. Put a strip into the neck-body joint on one side and put pressure on the heel, with more pressure on the heel cap end of the neck. Firmly pull the piece of sandpaper out of the joint and under the heel cap five times on each side. Be careful not to pull the sandpaper in a manner that rounds the heel cap up, making a larger gap at the heel cap.

After five pulls, change to the other end of the paper and pull five more times. Check the neck angle. It probably hasn't moved very much but check often, as you don't want to go too far. Look at your 1/8″ ledge and make sure it has not widened. If so, use your chisel and deepen the trough. Also check to be sure the heel cap is not forming a little nub in the center keeping the neck from sitting down to the body. If this is a problem, pull the sandpaper from the center of the neck a few times. Pulling the paper correctly can eliminate this problem.

Top: The neck is off. Clean off the old glue while it is still soft.
Middle: Jeff cuts a relief into the surface of the neck which will touch the sides to reduce the contact area.
Bottom: After masking off the sides, Jeff inserts sandpaper between the body and the neck and pulls it through while exerting pressure on the area where material must be removed.

When you are getting close to having the neck angle about right (this is often eighty pulls on each side), start checking to make sure the E strings line up properly with the fingerboard. If you need to make an angle change on this axis, try five pulls on one side only.

When everything is right, take off the mask and check the neck angle and fit of the heel. This is your last chance to make any changes, so make sure it is perfect.

Now that we have the right angle on the neck, the dovetail does not fit anymore. Glue some mahogany shims on the sides of the dovetail. They should be about full length and about .025″ thick. Jeff uses some cauls that are cut to the dovetail angles to make clamping easier. I like to let these dry overnight so they don't shrink after they are fit.

Put a piece of carbon paper on each side of the dovetail and assemble the neck-to-body joint. Jeff recommends "thin blue articulating paper" from a dental supply house. At this point the neck should not go all the way into the body. If it does then you needed thicker shims and you need to remove the ones you glued on and start over. Only one shim per side please. I tap the fingerboard with a small dead-blow hammer to mark the dovetail. Disassemble the dovetail; using a sharp file, remove the areas that have carbon on them.

Repeat this process until there is good contact on the shims and the neck seats all the way down to the body. The most important place to have contact is the bottom of the dovetail. This is the place that has the most force on it and is also the place that gives way first.

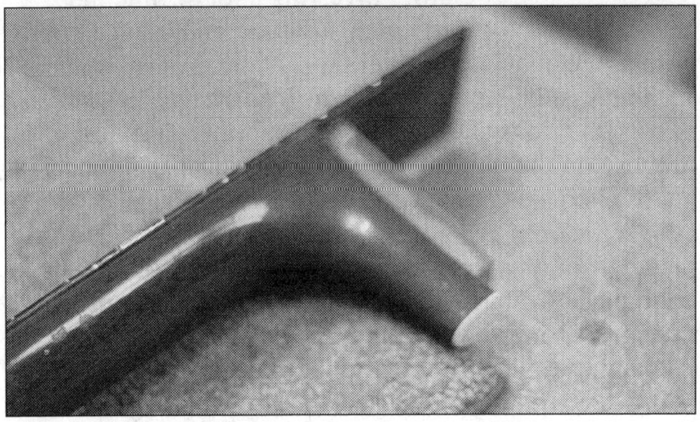

Top: Shims are glued to both sides of the dovetail.
Bottom: The neck is pressed into the heel block with carbon paper positioned on the shims, ink side in. When the neck is removed, ink deposits indicate where material must be trimmed. This process is repeated until there is good contact the full length of the shims, especially at the dovetail's narrow end.

Now, string up the guitar. What did he say? Yes, string up the guitar! If everything has been done right you can string up the guitar and play it before gluing on the neck. This is your chance to make sure the heel cap does not pull away from the body and you like the neck angle. When you are happy, and only then, it is time to glue on the neck.

Sand or scrape the under side of the fingerboard and the soundboard under the fingerboard to assure a good glue joint. Put a little lacquer thinner on the edge of the lacquer on the heel to soften it and make it look more acceptable.

Put glue on the sides of the dovetail. Put glue on the fingerboard extension. Jeff only puts glue on the edges of the fingerboard extension (as do many builders, including Taylor). Clamp the neck into the body. I always use a piece of wax paper against the back to keep my clamp from sticking to the lacquer.

Clamp the fingerboard extension down. Use a caul that puts pressure on the edges of the extension to keep the fingerboard from curling up. Clean up all excess glue. I use wet Q-tips.

Did you notice that we put no glue on the end grain? End grain does not provide any gluing strength. Since the dovetail holds the neck on without glue, the glue is only to hold the neck in place. If you use hide glue, the neck will come off easier for the next repairman who resets the neck fifty years down the road.

If there are slight gaps, less than the thickness of paper, force a little yellow glue into them as a filler. Jeff says it will even look good against a white heel cap.

With practice this process should have the instrument on your bench for about two hours. Don't be surprised if this takes eight hours or more on your first try. I don't refret guitars during this repair and charge about $290 depending on how bad the repairman ahead of me was. This price includes a shim under the fingerboard, any necessary fret milling, and a new saddle. If you are refretting this adds another hour or so.

Pat yourself on the butt! You have just completed one of the most challenging repairs on an acoustic guitar. ——

Sources

Heat blankets
Length 5″, Volts 120, Watts 50
Code number 020050C1
Ash Equipment Co.
www.ashequipment.com

Thin Blue Articulating Paper, .0035″ thick
Henry Schein Dental
www.henryschein.com

Originally published in *American Lutherie #50*, 1997

A Feast for the Eye

from Larry Robinson's 1996 American School of Lutherie workshop

by Kalia Kliban

LAST SUMMER I attended an inlay workshop that was part of the American School of Lutherie's Guitar Maker's Summer Institute in Healdsburg, California. Attendees included instrument builders (ranging from "haven't given up my day job" to "this is my day job"), repair people, at least one graphic artist, and miscellaneous woodworkers. There were workshops on Spanish and contemporary guitar building techniques, a three-day repair intensive, and workshops on finishing and jigs and fixtures, all capped off by Richard Schneider's Lost Mountain Seminar on Kasha/Schneider guitar design and the Healdsburg Guitar Festival.

Our presenter was Larry Robinson, one of the foremost artists in the inlay business. He got his start in the trade by accident when he was building guitars for Alembic, Inc. in 1975. Convinced that building solidbody instruments would be a breeze after the demands of acoustic guitar construction, he managed "to drill completely through two $2,000 basses while installing pickups." His boss, Rick Turner (himself no slouch in the inlay business), simply taught Larry how to cover the mistakes with inlay. "We can call it custom and charge more for it." It's over twenty years later and Larry Robinson is still cutting inlay, except now he does it intentionally. He has recently released a book describing the tools, materials, and techniques of the craft, called *The Art of Inlay* (Miller Freeman Books, 1994. See review in *American Lutherie #41, Big Red Book of American Lutherie Volume Four,* p. 464). It's clear, well-written, concise, beautifully illustrated, and covers the process in detail from start to finish. I highly recommend this book to anyone interested in experimenting with inlay. He has also released two videos, one for beginners and one intermediate level, which are very helpful.

ALL BY RICHARD LLOYD EXCEPT AS NOTED

Larry at work. Note cutting table and working position.

The workshop was set up like a television cooking show in that Larry had an assortment of projects in varying stages of completion, and would run us through just enough of each process to explain and demonstrate how it worked. Once all we students were clear on the basic principles of the inlay equivalent of, say, white sauce, he would produce an assembled casserole and explain the next step. The truly astonishing thing is how such an essentially simple process — you cut a shape, you cut a hole, you put the shape in the hole — can be manipulated with such subtlety and to such spectacular effect.

Larry stressed that the design is the most important part of an inlay job, and it's crucial to get it right before you ever pick up the saw. The best technique in the world won't make up for an awkward or ugly initial drawing, and it's a lot easier to make adjustments on paper than in a piece of pearl shell. Since the drawing you produce is the guide for your saw cuts, the lines should be as fine as possible. A pencil with a 9H lead, kept needle sharp, can produce a hair-thin line. Curves should be fair and clean, no lumps, and straight lines should be straight. Your hand and wrist are well suited to drawing smooth, freehand curves, and it's possible to scale your initial drawings to take advantage of that.

Though French curves and flexible rulers can be a help with long, wiggly elements like vines, it helps to step back and look at the overall effect. Often you can spot awkward transitions that aren't obvious close up. If you just can't get the lines fine enough, do your drawing at 200% then shrink it to full size.

Most designs spring from a client or dealer request of some kind — a particular image or motif that they are fond of, or a general look they are trying to achieve. These requests can often be somewhat vague: "I want a sort of vine thing on the fretboard" or, "My wife really loves bugs, so I want her guitar to have bugs all over it." These will give you a lot of room for interpretation, and it is very possible that you and the client will have quite different images in mind. Before investing a lot of time in a particular direction, make sure you both agree on what the client wants.

The vast library of copyright-free images available in clip art books (Dover Press has about ten thousand of these on the market, on every conceivable subject) is an excellent resource for general artistic styles as well as specific images. Even if your final design will be a piece of your own original art, books of clip art can be a good place to start with the client who really wants that special something but can't quite describe it.

Images can be found in other places as well. Some people take photos of models to avoid hunting through mountains of books for just the right pose. A video camera with a freeze frame can be useful, too. If you give the client a set of images to look at and choose from, you will often get a clearer response than if you merely ask them to describe the desired effect without any visual reference. Once you have established the basic concept, make tracings of all the images that you are likely to need in the composition process and pack them onto a few pages. Make a pile of copies of these pages in about 10% size increments to cover the size range you think you'll need.

A note about copiers: If you do as much inlay and design work as Larry, you may find it makes sense to buy your own copy machine, as he did. It can be difficult to maintain your concentration on a project if you have to run into town every half hour for "just one more reduction of that page with the frogs on it." Balanced against the cost of driving (walking, kayaking, whatever) to the copy place over and over, owning your own machine can be pretty economical.

You will also need an accurate, full-scale drawing or blueprint of the item that will be receiving the inlay. Beware of working from your client's dimensional drawings ("I'm really sure about the resonator size this time, honest") unless your client is actually building the item in question, in which case you can just use the client's blueprint. Faxes can also distort quite a bit, so while they can be used for rough sketching, they should not be used as a framework for the final drawings. Make a few reduced copies and tracings on which to work out your rough composition, and at least one full-sized accurate tracing for final composition. Cut apart your pages of source material and arrange them under the tracing until you've got them where you want them. You may want to make clean copies of several different compositions so that you and the client have something to choose from. Once the design is complete, you will need two final, full-sized drawings. One of them should be just outlines, with each piece of the inlay pattern numbered. This will be your cutting drawing. The other will include outlines plus any engraving details.

The tools you need for cutting and setting inlay are mostly quite simple and inexpensive. Jeweler's saws are available in both 4″ and 6″ throat depth, and the 4″ should suffice for all but the very largest jobs. Blades come in a wide range of sizes, but 000 blades will work well for most inlay materials, and will produce a fine cut without being too fragile (though you will break a lot of blades). The cutting block, the surface that supports the inlay material as you cut, can be easily made from a block of scrap wood and can be fitted with an integral vacuum port to draw away cutting dust. This is important, especially when working with pearl, which, in dust form, can be very irritating to the lungs. Many people put a screen over the dust port to avoid losing tiny pieces into the vacuum. You should arrange your seating so that you have your feet comfortably on the ground, your face about 8″ above the work surface, and your lighting should be bright and adjustable. For cutting patterns and for scribing around assembled inlays, an X-acto knife with #11 blades (you'll break or dull a lot of these, too, so buy a large box) is indispensable, and a small set of needle files (medium-cut half-round, rat-tail, square, and wedge-shaped) will be useful when your saw blade has gone awry. A tool that Larry refers to as "my best friend in the inlay business" is his pair of sheet-metal vise grips with the jaws ground down to about 1″ wide, which he uses to hold inlay pieces that need filing or tweaking. Just make sure when you're shopping to pick a set whose jaws meet evenly across the front edge. The router for cutting the inlay cavities is the only expensive item in the tool kit. Dremel and Foredom flex-shaft tools work well, as do miniature hand-held routers. Make sure your router can take 1/16″ shaft bits, and you will need to build or buy a router-style flat base with which you can adjust the bit depth.

Superglue figures largely in the inlay process, and Larry favors 3Bond, mostly for the delicate nozzles that come on

LARRY ROBINSON

Three examples of Larry's inlay work. Other examples are shown throughout this article.

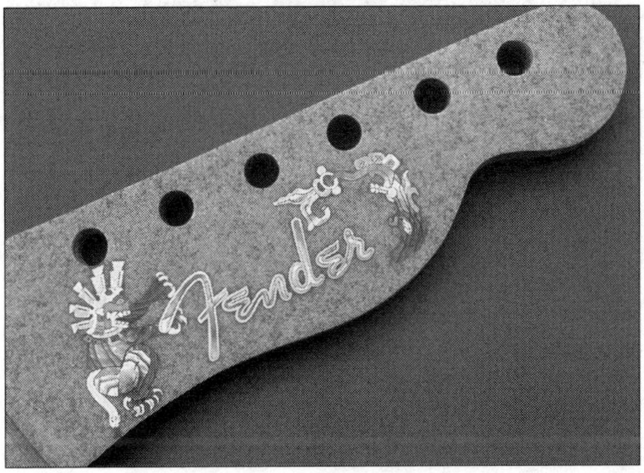

its bottles (it's a small thing, but important). We had a brief discussion of the relative merits of various brands of cyanoacrylate glue, with the upshot that they're pretty much the same except for Zap, which was, according to Colin Kaminsky, universally disliked by other glue manufacturers. Nobody was quite sure if that was in its favor or otherwise. There is a black cyanoacrylate glue available from Locktite that can be useful in certain jobs, but it is a bit rubbery when dry, and very expensive. Though they can be tinted, 24-hour epoxies often swell over time and may lift or buckle delicate inlay, which is why Larry uses them only when he needs the extra working time for a delicate or intricate clamping job. (You should avoid 5-minute epoxy if you want the finished piece to survive for a while.) Epoxy and superglue fumes can cause unpleasant allergic reactions, so you should always ventilate your work space and wear a mask when working with them.

There is a huge variety of inlay materials available, all of which have subtly different working characteristics. From the brittle and unforgiving pearl shells to the cheap and adaptable plastics, the inlay artist has a wide palette to choose from.

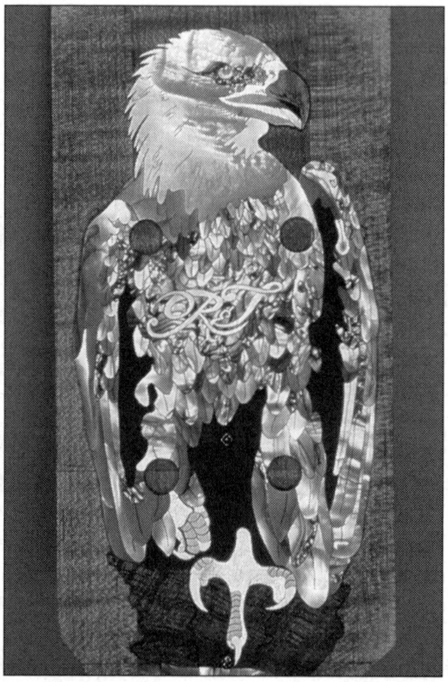

The flash and shimmer of pearl shell can be manipulated by the skilled artist to produce effects ranging from a subtle ripple of color to a brilliant blast. Though there are thousands of kinds of decorative shells, there are only a few different animals that produce the bulk of the pearl shell available today. California red abalone is a major staple in the shell industry. The shells are thick and gently curved, producing a high yield of usable pearl, and the color tends to be a swirl of greens and pinks. The center section of the shell, where the abalone is attached, is called the "heart," and is extremely highly figured. In this area, the decorative layer is thick enough that it is occasionally possible to bookmatch sections. The sections around the air holes can also produce interesting visual effects, usually a sort of bull's-eye. The green and black abalones are much rarer and (no surprise here) more expensive. These two shells are thinner than red abalone, so the yield is necessarily smaller; however the colors can be much purer and more intense than those of the red abalone, often including brilliant green and a sort of smoky opal color. Paua is a small, thin-shelled abalone from New Zealand with an almost startling, iridescent blue-green color, but the shape of the shell prevents it from being cut into large usable pieces. Apparently most of the really good stuff stays in the New Zealand jewelry industry, but it is possible to buy whole shells here and slab them yourself.

Mother-of-pearl is a large, flat bivalve shaped like a cross between a scallop and a mitten. It is a very thick, high-yield shell and is commercially available in several different colors. Standard mother-of-pearl ranges from snowy, pearly white with green and pink overtones to the more expensive golden color. Black mother-of-pearl, found in Tahiti, runs to either smoky iridescent black or purplish brown.

Freshwater mussel from Mississippi is newly available in inlay slices from Len Wood. Since its shells are very small, the resultant pinkish-white material is relatively expensive, though apparently quite attractive.

A completely new product available from Chuck Erikson (www.dukeofpearl.com) is a laminate of epoxy and extremely thin slices of pearl shell or abalone. Although the lines where the pieces of shell join together are visible in some cases, careful cutting and design can make them almost, or completely, invisible in the final product. The laminates, called "veneer sheets," are reasonably easy to work and their large size (about $5\frac{1}{2}'' \times 9''$, as I recall) is a real blessing for the inlay artist.

A historically important inlay material, but one which is finally (and not a minute too soon) falling out of favor, is ivory. Ivory is the teeth or tusks of walrus, hippo, whale, narwhal, elephant, boar, or mastodon. The use of all but the last two is severely restricted by the CITES treaty banning trade in products made from endangered species. Elephant ivory imported by certain dealers before 1976 is still legal, but the paperwork and government stamps are crucial, and international sales of items you make that contain this ivory are likely to be complicated. (Tortoise shell is similarly restricted, and state laws may differ, so check with your local Fish and Game Department before using it.) Legal restrictions can result in seizure by customs officials of any item containing the prohibited types of ivory, and the emotional cost is also very high. Despite all the points to the negative, ivory is lovely to work with and quite beautiful.

There are alternatives to using endangered species, and they should be utilized. Fossil mastodon is a completely legal and nonreprehensible alternative to elephant ivory, and can be distinguished by the subtle differences in its internal grain structure and the gray or brown cast to its color. The customs agents who check these things out can tell the difference by the way, so don't mess with them. Boar tusks are very available, relatively cheap, excellent to work, and have the advantage of coming from a species that has been designated as a serious pest in certain parts of this country (I have heard that there is a strict hunting limit of no more than one per day during the season). I am not sure about the legal ramifications of using domestically obtained boar tusk in items that will be shipped internationally. Antler and bone, though interesting for other uses, are difficult as inlay materials due, respectively, to their porous internal structure and stringy texture. They can be useful for special effects, however.

Synthetic ivories, or "ivoroids," are getting more and more convincing, but can still be difficult to obtain. People seem to guard their sources jealously, since supplies seem somewhat limited. Tagua nuts, often called vegetable ivory, are useful for small pieces, but are a bit of a pain in the neck to take apart because of the void in the middle of each nut. Their color and texture are very similar to certain types of animal ivory, and they are increasingly widely available.

Plastics provide a wide range of colors and textures without the emotional burden that can come with the use of animal products. They are also, relative to the more traditional inlay materials, incredibly cheap. Corian (and presumably the related kitchen countertop materials like Avonite) is good for engraving, easy to cut and resaw, comes in many colors, and can be gotten in enormous pieces from your local sink installer. Colorcore formica is also useful, and conveniently comes in thin sheets. If you are buddies with any contractors who do a lot of kitchens, see if they are willing to save you some scraps. Plexiglas is not as easy to work as the countertop materials, but comes transparent, translucent, opaque, and in some truly hallucinatory colors. CDs might work as a recycler's alternative to pearl shell, and it could be truly satisfying to run a terrible recording through your bandsaw. Bear in mind that many plastics are susceptible to acetone, which you may be using to remove glue during the inlay process. Metals are another of the traditional inlay materials, and are easy to obtain and work. Unfortunately, with the exception of gold and platinum, metals will dull or tarnish over time, even under protective finishes. Gold and silver sheet (12- to 14 gauge metal is about the same thickness as .060″ shell, pearl, or ivory) can be bought in small amounts for a particular job, but aluminum, copper, brass, and Dixgold (a brass alloy) are cheap enough to buy in square-foot sheets. Metal dust can also be used by packing it into the recess and flooding it with superglue.

Wood can provide a vast range of colors and patterns, but you should be aware that many woods won't hold their color for long. Purpleheart, for example, is notorious for fading to the exciting color of mud after exposure to sunlight, though bloodwood seems to keep its color. Make sure to test your materials for susceptibility to fading. If you are inlaying something that will see a lot of wear and handling (a fingerboard for example), make sure that the woods you use as inlays won't wear down. If you are using commercial veneers, most of which are either 1/28″ or 1/40″, you will need to build them up several plies thick to make a workable piece that isn't too thin or fragile. If you are cutting your own veneers, remember to leave them thicker than your other inlay materials. Thicker wood inlay is relatively easy to sand down at the end of the job, and not as likely to break during cutting or handling. When asked what his favorite woods were, Larry replied, "Ebony. It covers a lot of mistakes."

Stones and jewels can also be used in inlay, but must be treated with particular attention. Transparent or translucent materials will disappear unless backed with a reflective coating such as gold leaf, foil, or paint. Amber backed with gold leaf is said to be quite spectacular. Opaque stones can be cut and set like other inlay materials, but they are often extremely fragile and must be worked quite thick, which makes the sanding process very slow. After the finish has been applied and buffed out, faceted stones can be glued into shallow recesses that leave most of the stone proud of the surface to catch the light.

The cutting process is a combination of focus and relaxation. Larry referred to it as "meditative" and said it was his favorite part of the job. As you cut, keep your arm and shoulder loose, your hand relaxed on the saw handle, and let the weight of the saw do some of the work for you. Even tiny, almost subconscious body movements will affect the smoothness of the lines you cut, so pushing the blade gently to the side, leaning a

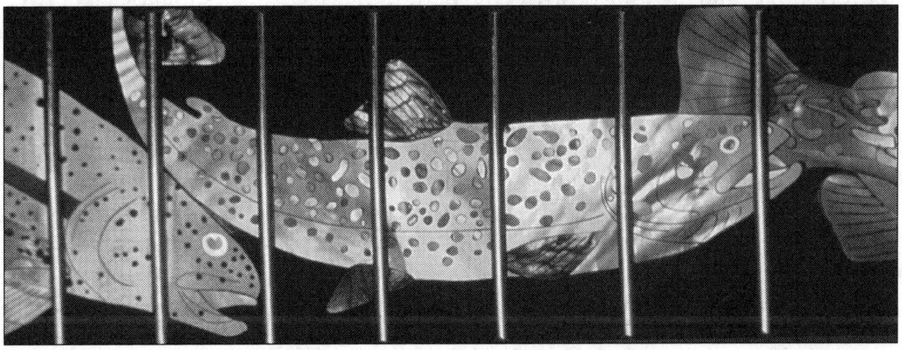

COLIN KAMINSKI

tiny bit (though the blade should be mostly straight up and down), or making minute adjustments in the pressure of your fingers around the handle may enable you to cut more cleanly. If you're sure you're doing everything right and the blade still seems to be wandering off on its own, check the blade tension — it may be too loose. The blade should go "ping" when plucked. If the tension is fine but the tracking is still bad, you may have a dull blade, though usually they don't last long enough to get dull.

To start the cutting process, you will need several copies of your cutting drawing (the one with all the pieces numbered.) The more complex your design, the more copies you need. One copy should be taped to a flat metal or glass plate with a layer of waxed paper taped securely over the top of it. As each piece is cut, you can superglue it to the previous pieces in position over the drawing. When everything has been cut and glued together, you should be able to peel the entire assembled inlay off of the waxed paper. In a complex project, this technique allows you to keep track of what might be several hundred small pieces of inlay, and to make sure that everything is fitting together properly as you go. The other copies of the cutting drawing will be cannibalized, bit by bit, for cutting patterns.

With an X-acto knife, cut one of the numbered pieces out of one of the copies, leaving a little extra paper around the outside of the line, then superglue the paper onto the appropriate inlay material. Cutting the pattern out of the drawing destroys the pattern pieces immediately next to it, which is why you'll need several copies of your cutting drawing in order to get an intact pattern for every piece.

If the pattern piece you are about to cut is right against the edge of the inlay material and you will be starting your cut at a shallow angle, it can be difficult to get the blade to bite. By gently wedging the saw blade between the material and the edge of the cutting block, you create a scissors effect that forces the blade to bite and gives you a great deal of control when starting a cut. Make very sure, before you cut, that you are securely holding the piece to be cut. If your grip is loose you could lose control on the upstroke (result: broken blade) or on the downstroke (result: broken blade or inlay, or sliced finger). The blades, once broken, can easily and deeply puncture a finger or a knuckle, "and they're just like fishhooks when they're in there." For better control, it's good to keep the pressure of your fingers and the movement of the saw blade as close to the supporting edge of the block as possible. Align the inside edge of the blade with the inside edge of the line so that as you cut, the line is just barely eliminated. The thinner and more accurate your pencil lines, and the more careful your cutting, the better the fit of your final inlay assembly.

Undercutting ever so slightly will also help you to butt the pieces together tightly. If you cut inside the line, toss the piece and start over. To correct a bulge while you're cutting, back up to where the bulge starts, twist the saw teeth gently toward the bulge and saw back to where you left off. The pressure of the blade sideways in the slot should act like a file to grind the bulge away.

Two problem spots tend to be the beginning and the end of a cut around a smoothly curved object like a disk. Instead of spiraling into a curved cut, sneaking up on it as it were, Larry prefers to cut directly toward the edge of the curve then make a sharp turn at the line. This avoids having an ever-weaker remainder to finish the cut in. At the end of a cut the material often breaks or separates just before the last bit is sawn through, which leaves a little nub that needs to be filed off later. To avoid this, during the last few strokes apply gentle pressure to the back of the blade with the finger that is holding the piece down. This pressure, and a firm grip on both the inlay material and the piece you are cutting out of it, should keep the piece from "jumping" and breaking off at the end of the cut.

Itty-bitty pieces are always difficult to control. Larry is quite unusual in being a lefty who plays guitar right handed. This gives him lovely, long fingernails on his right hand to use as clamps while he's sawing with his left/dominant hand. Those of us who pick or frail with our dominant hand are out of luck in this regard and will simply have to come up with another solution (fingerpicks, maybe?). When you've finished making the cut around a tiny piece, back the saw blade out or unstring it, then slide the inlay piece toward you off of the tapered edge of the cutting block and pinch the small piece between your fingers until you can grab it with tweezers. This keeps the tiny bits from getting sucked into the vacuum.

An exercise that was included in the book and in our workshop is a star/circle/pentagon figure. This exercise contains straight lines, curves, and both inside and outside versions of acute and obtuse angles. The different kinds of corners require slightly different treatments for clean results. Outside corners can be cleanly cut by overshooting the corner just a hair then sawing in place while rotating the saw to the new angle. When cutting an inside corner, saw all the way into the corner, then back the saw out just a bit, sawing in place until the new angle is reached. At this point you can back the saw into the corner and cut from there. Long, straight cuts can often benefit from being touched up with a wide flat file after cutting. On gradual curves, keep the saw in one place and move the piece into it. Right-handed people will tend to cut around the outside of a shape in a counterclockwise direction, and around the inside of a shape in a clockwise direction, since it is easiest to see the cutting line and to hold the work in this position. Looking along the line a bit ahead of where you're cutting can help you track more accurately, as can anticipating curves and changes in direction.

COLIN KAMINSKI

Cutting a shape out of the interior of another solid shape is known as "piercing." In this procedure, you drill a small hole in the material and thread the saw blade through the hole, then make the cut. If you are making a shape that is pierced very heavily, especially if the material is brittle like shell (a zebra head was the example in class), it helps to cut just one hole, then cut the shape that fits it and glue them together before proceeding with the next hole. This preserves the structural integrity of the larger piece as you work. If you are cutting a lot of small pieces out of one chunk of inlay material, you will have an easier time of it if you start in the middle and work your way to the edges, which will leave you with something solid to hang on to as you go.

Larry was explaining all of this as he sawed out the pieces of the exercise. When he was done he tried fitting the pieces together, then did about two minutes of filing to adjust the fit. He clicked the pieces together and handed them around while he went on with the discussion. There was virtually no light visible between the edges of the pieces, and the fit was incredibly tight and clean. There was some mumbling from people in the class who had the book and had already tried the exercise, to the effect that theirs hadn't come out quite so well. The mumbling increased when Larry mentioned that his daughter had done the exercise when she was seven years old.

So, you have assembled your leaping salmon, or team of huskies, or railway map of the British Isles, and it is sitting on the waxed paper waiting for the next step. The surface it is going to be set into should be sanded to 220 grit. Peel your inlay off the waxed paper and glue it into position on the receiving piece with a few small dabs of Duco cement or other airplane glue. You only need enough glue to hold the inlay in place while you scribe around it. When the glue is completely dry, scribe around the outside of the piece with an X-acto knife. A needle or scratch awl will tear the wood fibers instead of cutting them cleanly, and the line quality will not be as good. Cut deeply enough to cleanly score the grain, but not so deeply that your blade digs into and follows the grain lines. You should turn the work as often as necessary to work comfortably, and in deep inside corners, like between wing feathers, turn the blade so that the point points into the corner and cut out from there. Because of the thickness of the X-acto blade, you may want to tilt the knife just a hair so that the scribed line accurately reflects the outline of the inlay, but try to avoid applying too much sideways pressure to the knife. You could easily break the blade or dislodge the inlay.

To remove the inlay, slip a very thin palette knife, spatula, or razor blade under the inlay and gently cut through the glue spots. If the inlay is especially delicate, you may want to apply a little acetone with a syringe to help soften the glue. Bear in mind that acetone, useful though it is, has been listed as a carcinogen, so treat it with due care. You should not apply acetone around inlays containing susceptible plastics, or you will end up with a melted mess. Once you have removed the inlay assembly, you can clean any remaining glue residue off the surface with more acetone.

The scribe lines can be accented by sprinkling in a little colored or white chalk then rubbing it in gently with a cloth. Waxy pigments like colored pencil dust should be avoided as they could cause problems down the line with gluing or finishing.

You can do almost any inlay routing job with only two or three bits. For hogging out the bulk of the

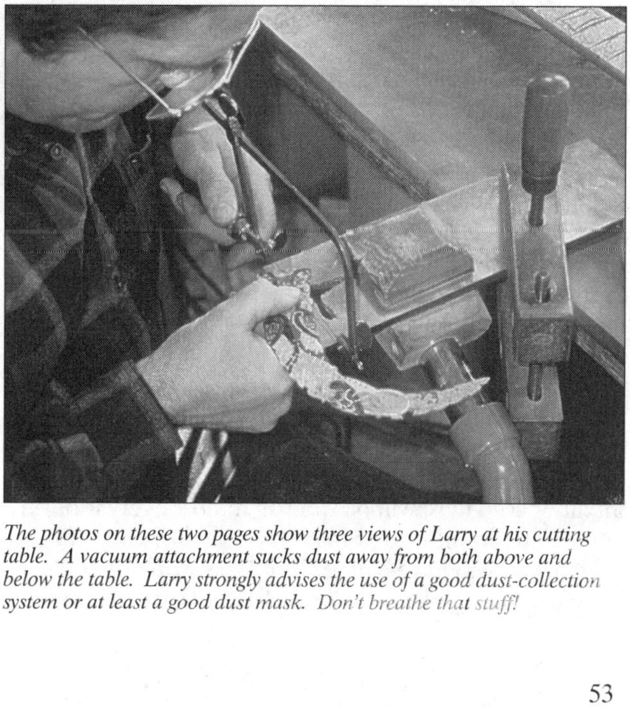

The photos on these two pages show three views of Larry at his cutting table. A vacuum attachment sucks dust away from both above and below the table. Larry strongly advises the use of a good dust-collection system or at least a good dust mask. Don't breathe that stuff!

material in the inlay recess, you will need a ⅛″ straight bit. Larry uses a high-speed steel, two-flute bit for this part of the job. For detailing, 1/16″–1/32″ carbide bits work best. If you're having trouble with the edges of your cut "fuzzing" and curling up as you approach your scribed line, try a left-hand spiral bit. Slightly used carbide bits can often be gotten from dentists, who are required to throw them away after one use.

To set the depth of your bit, use your thinnest inlay material as a depth gauge. You want the inlay to sit almost flush when you've finished the routing, to minimize the amount of sanding you'll have to do.

If you work from the center of the recess toward the edges, you'll always have a solid surface to slide the router base on. Securing the work piece to the table or to a larger workboard with double-face tape may help you keep it under control. Even if the edges of the recess are straight lines, don't go all the way to the edge with the large bit; the smaller bits are easier to control and will do less damage if they get away from you. Anytime you lose sight of your line under shavings and dust, you stand a chance of cutting past it without noticing, so keep your path clean. Larry keeps the snorkel of his shop-vac tucked under his arm while he routs to clear shavings and dust from the workpiece. When you start to approach the line with the smaller bits, try not to remove too much material at one time, as the bit could grab and pull itself outside the line. Nibble gently away at the small amount of material left inside the lines. The score lines, if deep enough, should shear away when you get to them, leaving a clean, incised line around the edge of the recess and a slight amount of visible chalk. In case of disaster, you may be able to modify your inlay by adding another feather (or petal or tentacle) to cover the mistake so that it looks intentional. There will be spots in almost every job where, due to the size of the bits or the intricacy of the design, you will have a little slop. This won't be such an issue if you are inlaying into dark woods, but lighter woods can make mistakes painfully obvious. Hence the prevalence of inlay in rosewood and ebony.

Above: Scribing around inlay pieces to define areas where inlay recesses will be cut. Below: Routing for a fingerboard inlay using a flexible-shaft tool with a router-base attachment.

Larry's biggest hint of the day was, "Don't tell anyone where the mistakes are." Early on in his career in inlay he caught himself pointing out all the mistakes and goobers in a job to someone and realized he should just keep his mouth shut. It's a strange tendency we have to want to make sure everyone knows just exactly how we've screwed up, but if we could just keep a cork in it, most of the mistakes would go unnoticed, or at least unremarked.

When you've finished the routing, check the fit and make any necessary adjustments with the router or with a tiny, sharp chisel. Make sure that the entire inlay sits flat on the bottom of the recess.

Your gluing method will differ slightly depending on whether you are using superglue or epoxy, but in both cases you should be wearing a filter mask and have good ventilation in your work area.

You can use superglue anytime you are sure of the fit of your inlay (check it without glue first) and you don't need to clamp. This would probably be the case for any small-to-medium-sized inlay in a flattish surface. Cover the bottom of the recess with glue and press the inlay into place, making sure it hits bottom all the way around. Then run a line of glue around the edge of the recess until it stops sucking down into the gap and beads up a little higher than the surface. Let the glue dry, then fill the perimeter again, to make up for the shrinkage of the first batch of glue. Don't rush the drying time.

If your inlay is large or unwieldy, or you are setting it into a complex, curved surface like the back of a banjo resonator, you will want the added working time afforded by 24-hour epoxy. Epoxy is thick enough that if you cover the bottom and edges of the recess, as well as the bottom of the inlay, you should get the proper amount of squeeze-out with light clamping pressure, thus eliminating the need to fill the glue line from the top. If you are using any kind of particulate fill such as a dust/epoxy combination to fill gaps, you may have trouble pressing your inlay all the way down to the bottom. Clamping pressure can come from spring clamps, wooden cam clamps, a go-bar deck, or even sandbags, though anytime you have a clamp surface in contact with your inlay there should be a layer of waxed paper between the two. For more information on clamps, see *The Art of Inlay* or the GAL's *Lutherie Tools.* When you are inlaying into ebony, you can tint epoxy with carbon-based ink or ebony dust to minimize the visual impact of the glue line, though tinting or dust-fill won't be very effective in lighter woods. Again, make absolutely sure that you have given your glue enough time to dry before proceeding.

Sanding is Larry's least favorite part of the inlay process. As with routing, you will want to vacuum as you go, and constantly watch to make sure you don't sand divots into soft materials that are next to hard inlay (or vice versa). Make yourself a hardwood sanding block (Larry's is 1½″×4″, and about 2″ tall, so he can efficiently use ⅛ sheets of sandpaper) to ensure that the surface gets leveled, not just smoothed, and start sanding with 80-grit silicon-carbide paper. When the surface of the inlay is just flush with the surrounding material, switch to 100 grit, then 220. If you are sanding over metal inlay, check the temperature from time to time with the inside of your wrist. If it feels uncomfortably hot, stop and let it cool so the surrounding glue doesn't melt. After you have sanded to 220 and vacuumed away the dust, check your glue lines for pits and bubbles. These should all be filled (you may need to puncture the bubbles to fill them) with dabs of superglue or epoxy, depending on what you used, then the surface should be releveled. Avoid using any kind of sanding lubricant (water, oil, or alcohol) unless there are no even remotely porous materials in the project. Sanding slurry can work its way into wood grain, pores, and crevices and be almost impossible to remove. Finish sanding with 400-grit paper, vacuum out all the dust, and wipe everything down. Now is your chance to catch any problems such as bubbles or inlay that have been sanded through.

Above: Pressing an inlay into place, making sure it hits the bottom of the recess all of the way around. Below: Larry applies ink to engraved lines to define the feathers in the wings of this owl inlay.

BOTH THIS PAGE BY COLIN KAMINSKI

Although there are hundreds of specialty tools on the market for engravers, there are really only a few that you will need to get through most inlay jobs. The three cutters that Larry uses most often are the knife, square, and liner tools, along with a small chasing hammer for engraving metal.

Lines in wood can easily be cut with a razor knife or heavy X-acto blade. A diamond-point scribe used to scratch lines can work well in bone, shell, and ivory. Start by drawing your engraving lines lightly on the surface of the inlay with a sharp pencil. Work gently and slowly, and start the cuts shallow, deepening as you go. Your workpiece should be secured to the table with clamps or tape — you will want both hands and most of your attention on the tool, not on whether your piece is going to slither off the table. Bone and ivory tend to flake at the edges of heavy cuts, which can be disastrous when you are trying to produce delicate facial detail. Work lightly.

When you have the details where you want them, fill the lines with colored ink (such as Dr. Martin's Concentrated Watercolors) using a fine, small brush to apply the color into the lines. A 000 watercolor brush would work well for this. Before you apply ink to engraving lines in wood, you should seal the surface with a thin coat of lacquer to avoid color seepage. Any excess color left on the surface can be buffed off with 400- or 600-grit sandpaper after the ink is dry. The engraving lines can then be filled by flooding them with superglue and leveling with 400-grit paper, or you could just proceed with your normal finish.

To say that this workshop was inspirational would be something of an understatement. I cannot speak for the others who attended, but I have been itching to work some inlay into the jobs that come through my shop. I hear my jeweler's saw calling me everytime I discuss a new project with a client, but sadly there's not a lot of call for inlaid bookshelves and kitchen backsplashes in my neighborhood. While I'm waiting, I'll keep trying to get that little star to fit in its star-shaped hole. ——

Originally published in *American Lutherie #50*, 1997

Meet the Maker: Arul Dominic Xavier

by Jonathon Peterson

THE 1996 HEALDSBURG GUITAR Festival attracted builders from all over the map, but none traveled as far to get there as Arul Dominic Xavier, the only Guild member who lives in India. He is also a career civil servant whose work helps to improve the lives of people throughout his country.

Tell me a little about where you grew up.

Actually, it's a little bit complicated because India, like the USA, is a very big country. I was born in a place called Gola Goldfields. It's in the Carnataka State, Gola district, in the south. There are mountains. It's a quiet town, a mining town. It's not even a town really, because when we would go for a haircut or something like that, you would say we are going to the town, so where we lived was more of a village, I suppose. It was a very quiet place.

Was it forested?

No, it was not forested, but there were trees, many trees. We had huge houses, huge compounds, and we paid very little rent as it was provided by the mining company. That's where my father worked. He was a superintendent in the mines.

So it was a big mining center, and everybody that lived there worked for the mine?

Yes, pretty much. Of course there were a certain number of businesses, and shops, and schools. There were missionary schools and just a few private schools. I went to a good school.

What started your interest in woodworking?

My father had a lathe. He was very interested in wood turning, and he made a lot of furniture and things for the house. He even made these, what do you call them, tops? With the string, you spin them. All these things he used to make, turn them out of wood on his lathe. I used to help him.

We never had a motor in those days. We had a huge wheel like a cartwheel with a belt fitted from it to the pulley on the lathe, and somebody would have to turn the wheel to make the lathe work.

Were you the designated motor sometimes?

Yes, sometimes, but I was too small, and my father wouldn't let me do that alone because the handle sometimes would catch hold of a shirt or something, and it had thrown some people around.

ALL BY JONATHON PETERSON EXCEPT AS NOTED

That must have been a heavy flywheel!

Yes, so he never made me do that, but I used to hold it on the opposite and pull it anti-clockwise, when some elders were doing it from the other side.

I was always observing him. I was his helper, so when he said that he wants a ½″ chisel, I would have to hand it to him, and I would have to give him the handle first. These are the ways he taught me. That's how I began woodworking, right from childhood.

Finally he did manage to buy a motor. It was very difficult for him to buy it. That was his life's ambition, to get a motor and electrify the lathe. And when he bought the motor, he put down a concrete base, and bolted it down, and tried it. And then he said that starting tomorrow we'll work at it. That night he died.

Wow! How old was he?

He was 53, and he'd had a couple of heart attacks. I was about thirteen at that time. I was in the 7th standard in school. Thereafter, with studies and all that, somehow I got through.

Would that be what we call 7th grade?

Yes; 10th standard would mean I would pass out of high school. After that we go to junior college, and we call that the 11th and 12th standards — our preuniversity course. We call it P.U.C., and there you start off in different directions, either science, or commerce, or arts.

But I decided that college was not for me, because at that time things were difficult. We were five children in the family, and only my eldest brother was working at that time, so I thought that going to college would not be a good thing for me in the sense that it would be trouble for somebody else. Early in life I realized that I didn't want to be a source of burden to anyone.

I thought I would learn a trade instead, so I went to learn repairing motorcycles. I was there for one year, but many of the customers felt that I should go to college because I didn't really fit into that kind of place, in their opinion. So many people said that I was capable of going to college that I decided I would. I got an admission to a college. I didn't finish college directly. I did some competitive examinations part way through, and I got a job in the government of India in 1977. I continued my graduation studies as a part-time course until I finished. I am a commerce graduate — business, accounting, and economics. Then again I did examinations, and now I'm a section officer in the government of India, in the Ministry of Rural Areas and Development.

What do your duties entail?

The entire ministry takes care of all the rural development activities. That includes rural employment, the training of women and children in rural areas, rural housing, water supply, and sanitation. I am in the water supply and sanitation sector. I monitor all the water-supply projects in rural India.

For your district?

No. I represent the central government.

Would that be like a national public utilities department?

Yes, it is called the National Drinking Water Mission. We work in a mission mode. First we identify a problem. For instance, in some places there is arsenic in the water, in some places there is fluoride in the water, there's iron, brackishness, and so many things. We discuss how the problem is to be solved, what kind of project is suitable for that area and situation, and we develop a plan. I'm a section officer. I manage the administrative section. That's where all the papers come, where all the action is initiated. We also have a technical wing, where they are all civil engineers and water technologists. We get proposals for projects from the state governments, and we put these proposals forth to the technical group. They analyze the project and make a feasibility report, and then we place it before a screening committee which has been empowered to sanction projects. They may sanction it, or they may reduce the cost, or they may break up the project into phases, and they may set a time schedule for achieving each of these phases. Once they do that we have a conference with the finance division, and we release the funds. Thereafter we monitor the progress of the project. Sometimes, if we are not able to solve a problem, we give it out as a research project to certain institutions. They tell us what to do and what not to do, and according to that we try to improve the situation. All these things I am suppose to be monitoring.

We also get funds from UNICEF, from the World Health Organization, from the World Bank, and from other countries and agencies which have pilot projects. We are dealing with them all, and that is also my responsibility.

To go through school, and various jobs and situations, and to get into such a position of authority and responsibility — one that is so important to so many — most people would consider that to be pretty much their life work, but you're doing lutherie besides.

Yes, and that is a thing, you know? I'm not considered normal in my country, or in my family, or amongst my friends. It's an obsession. Right from the beginning I've been making bats for children and things for around the house. I've made speaker cabinets, shelves, tables. I never throw away anything. Whatever is broken, I repair it and make it better, or hopefully, not make it worse. *(laughs)* Basically, from the time that my father couldn't run that motor because he died, I've felt that I should restart that activity. So that's been an obsession with me.

How did that feeling develop into an interest in lutherie?

It did not start right from that time, because I was not in a position to do that. I was only fourteen. I was not mature enough to understand many things. The older I grow the more fond I am of my father, in retrospect, you know? At that time I never felt of woodworking as a great thing. You see, in India these kinds of occupations are considered somewhat lower in status, and I didn't have the respect for work and other things that you understand only later on in life. Besides that, I didn't have the money nor did I have a place to work. I was staying alone, I was about 2,000KM away from home, and I was hardly twenty. At twenty in India, you are still considered a kid, part of the family. I had moved out and I was staying in a lodge, but even there I made two guitars in my room.

While you were going to school?

In my school days I made my first electric guitar. That was, I think in somewhere around '72, '73. I made a solidbody electric guitar. We used to plan during the holidays what shall we do. Somebody would repaint a cycle or something. I made a guitar, and it worked. From then on I've been trying to make good guitars.

Was it hard to get parts?

Local parts are never hard to get, and they're very cheap. But the thing is you don't get the quality, nor do you get that look on the guitar. It functions, yes.

Do you still have that guitar?

I still have it, but I converted it into a bass guitar. Somebody asked me to play bass with them, and I didn't have a bass guitar. You see, bass guitars were never used in Indian music. I just pulled out the neck and I put in another longer neck. I calculated the fret positions and all that from a book, *Complete Guitar Repair*, by Hideo Kamimoto. I worked two days and I made my guitar into a bass guitar. I played that night, and thereafter the guitar was dismantled because the pickup belonged to somebody else. *(laughs)* The neck is still not polished.

After that you just continued to make instruments?

Yes, I made a few more when I was working in Nashpur. I was staying alone. I just had a saw and one chisel, and I used to borrow a hammer. I never had a rasp, or a file, or anything like that. I use to file with the saw held sideways. I don't know what all I did, but I made three guitars there.

I use to play in some bands. It was sort of a one-horse town. There were very few guitar players, but there were a lot of Christians, and where there are Christians, there is some Western music. There were a lot of people from the State of Goa in that area, and some of them were excellent guitar players. I think a couple of them even got admission in some school of music. They had to pass auditions and do other things to get selected, so that shows that they were good; they could read music. In Goan homes in those days everybody learned music formally. They played the piano, and there was that music tradition.

Did you play Western music too?

Yes, all Western music. We never played anything Indian. We were bands like any other bands. We played for dances, and jam sessions, and Christmas. We played songs like *Pussycat,* and some John Denver songs, and Lobo songs. Lobo and John Denver were my favorite, but nobody liked them because they wanted something fast to dance to. You see, those who knew how to dance didn't need fast music, but those who did not know how to dance needed fast music to dance. There was a mixed audience, and normally the Goans are good dancers. They would enjoy a fox trot, or a waltz, or whatever. But the others could only just jump around, so you had to play something fast. So we would take some song and double the speed, and they would like that. *(laughs)*

Pussycat *at double speed! (laughs)*

Yeah, or *Smile,* and all that. *(laughs)* But really, we wouldn't do such songs as that. We would see that it was adaptable, then we would really speed it up, to like a 33 rpm record at 78 rpm.

You showed me some pictures of your shop. How long have you been in there?

In that shop, about a year and a half. Earlier I had another room that I rented for about four or five years, but I gave that up.

I have been working for the government for nineteen years and my job is very demanding. Office hours are 9:00 to 5:30, but I generally work until 7:00 or 8:00 in the evening, sometimes even 9:00 or 10:00. I often go to the office on Saturday and Sundays also. When I go to the office my workshop is closed. If I work late and then go to the shop I sometimes have no energy to put things away and clean up, so I just lock up and push off. Then it might be a while before I have the time to get into the shop again, so next time I come in I don't know what's what and where it is, and it takes me a day to clean up. Once I went in and found that a cat had littered some kittens. So it was a lot of money that I was just paying for a shop that I was not using very much, and sometimes I don't have the money.

Any kind of a project requires a certain amount of investment. For example, if you want to cut a soundhole you can do it in many ways. You can just drill a ½″ hole and make it a soundhole by filing it, or you can cut away the wood with a knife or a chisel. But I want to do it right, so I need a circle cutter. I either have to make a tool or I have to buy one. I'll keep that job back until I can get a circle cutter. If I want to cut lining strips I have to build a table saw. Otherwise I cannot cut them evenly the way I want to. That means cutting that lining would take me another whole month, because first I would have to find the money and the materials to build a table saw. I would have to wait until I get a bonus, or a cost-of-living allowance, or some other lump sum that is not already assigned to other expenses. A 1 h.p. motor costs about 800 rupees. If I get a 700 rupee bonus I will put in another 100 rupees and get the motor. Next time I can afford it I will get some 1½″ angle iron, or a steel plate, or some nuts and bolts, or some bearings.

It's not an option to just go and buy the tools? Are they not available, or do they just cost too much?

India is a country where everything is available, but do you have the resources to buy it? That goes in any country for that matter. If you have the money you can have it, but when you make it yourself it costs you half the price. Also, sometimes in guitar making you want certain modifications that are not available in the tools you can buy. I want just a bare tool. Whatever I have to do, I will just set up for that. For instance, my table saw has no adjustments to make the blade or the table go up and down. To adjust the height of the saw blade I have cut pieces of plywood, and I stack them up and make the setup for cutting linings, and I don't change that setup until I've made all the linings I need. That's the way I've been working.

COURTESY DOMINIC XAVIER

Above: Dominic, left, and his friend Mr. Khatri, who has been very encouraging and generous in supporting the GAL's only member in India by providing him rent-free working space in his factory.

Did you bring any of your work with you?

I just have a couple of small pieces that I was using to practice my inlay.

What is the darker wood called?

This is called shisham *(Bucida buceras)*.

Is it a kind of rosewood?

Yes, it is a kind of rosewood, but it's more reddish, not as purple as Indian rosewood. It is another good wood for backs and sides.

This other wood that the rosette ring is in is called deodar *(Cedrus deodara),* and they use it for pattern making in India. It's very stable, very light. It grows in the hilly areas, the mountain ranges. It's a fast growing wood.

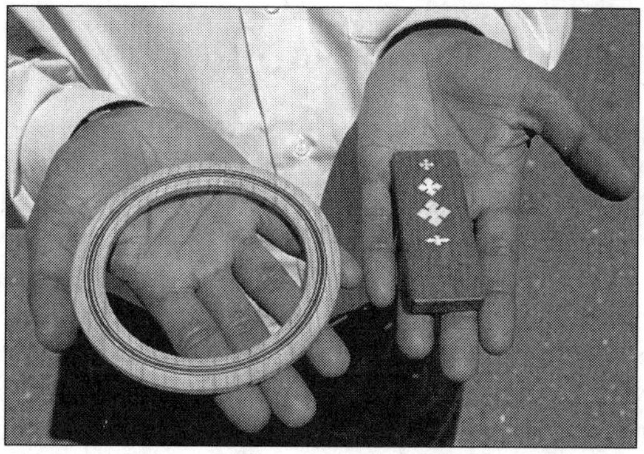

Dominic holds two of his practice inlay pieces. The woods in which the inlays were done are native to India.

How did you hear about the Guild?

I had written to Ken Warmoth of Warmoth guitars to ask him for an apprenticeship. He sent me his catalog, and he suggested that I write to the Guild and to ASIA. You responded very quickly, but the subscription was too high for us. That $46 would have meant about 2,000 rupees. I can't imagine buying one issue of *American Lutherie* for about 500 rupees.

How long does it take you to earn 2,000 rupees?.

My total salary is about 6,500 rupees per month, but that is not take-home salary. That is the gross. After insurance, deductions, and all those things I get around 4,000. That means paying half of one month's take-home salary for membership in the Guild.

Wow! That's not really optional.

It's not optional, but I want to build guitars, so I've been writing to a lot of people trying to get a job while I am in the USA where I can learn about building guitars. Now, I have to rethink my strategy, because I find that I was under an illusion that in the USA people are selling guitars as fast as they can make them, and it would be easy to get a job. I've spoken to many prominent builders who honestly told me that they cannot afford to pay me. I didn't know it would be so difficult.

How much longer are you going to be in the States?

I'll be here for three months. I have a visa for three months and return ticket for four and a half months. If I get an extension for another one month or so I'll try to hang on rather than just go back.

Can you tell me about your family? How long have you been married?

I've been married now thirteen years. My wife's name is Sophia, and we have one son named Arul. He'll be ten in November. Arul was my father's name. Arulnathen is his full name, but I just call him Arul. He's a good boy. He's learning guitar. I am teaching him. He's learning tabla. I teach him tennis, football, cricket, hockey. I bought him a computer a month back, so he's meddling with that now. I want to give him a different kind of life, because there are many things that I missed on the way. All the facilities that I didn't have I want to provide to him. Maybe if I had these things I would have had other opportunities professionally. You see, I have studied commerce, but here I am monitoring water supply projects. I wanted to either be in a bank, or in some financial institution, or in some accountancy, but situations were not always convenient to pursue such things, and building guitars professionally has not been an option. But, in September of '97 I will complete twenty years of service to the government of India and be eligible for early retirement. If I take early retirement I will get a pension, certain gratuities, and things like that. I want to learn as much as I can, and to be able to take early retirement and build guitars.

Some time after returning home from the Healdsburg Guitar Festival, where this interview was conducted, I received a letter from Dominic updating me on his American adventures. It read, in part:

"After Healdsburg, I went to Petrolia on the California coast with Craig Carter, and learned about hand-splitting and resawing soundboards. I am learning classical guitar building from Steve Newberry. I go to Ralph Novak's shop once a week to do repair work. I am nearing completion of a steel string acoustic. I took it to the NCAL meeting to show and tell. I felt ecstatic. I visited Santa Cruz Guitars, Fred Campbell, Hideo Kamimoto, Tim McCoy, and Brian Burns."

I spoke with Steve Newberry shortly before this issue was published, and he told me that in his final days in the USA Dominic sustained a severe injury to his left hand in a shop accident. We hope and pray that he has a speedy and successful recovery, and send our best wishes to him and his family. ——

Update

Dominic recovered from his injury, and went on to study with Kenny Hill. He is now building guitars full-time in India. See his website at www.arulguitars.com. His son Arul passed away in 2004 at the age of seventeen.

(2007)

Originally published in *American Lutherie #50*, 1997

How Frank Frets

from his 1995 GAL Convention workshop

by Frank Ford

TODAY I will present a fret job from start to finish, just the way I normally work. I think it's instructive to watch other people work, just doing what they do. I'll talk you through it so you can understand what you're seeing.

The first thing that I do is evaluate the guitar, in this case a 1973 Martin D-12-20. It needs frets because there's some wear, and because they're a little loose. Looking down the neck I can see a nasty little hump in the fretboard where it goes up onto the body that will need to be dealt with.

I'll need to take the frets out, so I'll plug in my soldering iron. While it's heating I'll snip the strings off with some diagonal cutters (**Photo 1**). I use the same cutters to pull the bridge pins, not biting them with the jaws, only lifting. It saves time using the same tool for both these operations, so I do that rather than picking up and putting down different tools. The old strings go in the trash.

The next thing is to pull out the nut. On Martin guitars the nut is glued in, and it's a little wider at the bottom than it is at the top, so it's sort of wedged under the head veneer. I like to use a small saw (.010″ kerf) to cut a relief just behind the nut (**Photo 2**). This is the thinnest-kerfed saw that I have, and the gap it leaves is so small that it usually doesn't need to be filled when the nut is installed again. I'm trying to cut into the nut just a little bit, and into the veneer a little bit. Once I've cut that relief I'll take a block of wood and tap the nut out.

Next I'm going to oil the tuners (**Photo 3**). This is probably more oil than they've gotten in their whole life. Players almost never oil their gears. I'm using a little Tri-flow from the bike shop, but any oil will work. I'll also take a couple rubber bands and wrap them around the tuner knobs to keep the vibration down. Sometimes I hit on these necks pretty hard as I'm pounding frets, and parts can rattle loose. If the tuners had bushings I'd wind rubber bands around the shafts to keep the bushings from falling out. I'm also going to take a second to check the screws on the tuning gears. Open gears have little screws that can sometimes work loose under the vibration of the hammering, so I like to check to see that they are okay. It just takes a second. I hate hunting for little screws or bushings.

By now the fret-removing soldering iron is getting hot. I'm going to put just a little bit of water on the fretboard. I don't really know why I do this. *(laughter)* The best reason I can come up with is that I like to hear the sizzle when I heat them. *(laughter)* Wipe the excess off. I use a little bit of detergent in the water with the idea that it sort of oozes under the frets. I guess it does, and maybe it helps lubricate them as they come out.

I use this wide, low-tack masking tape to protect the soundboard on either side of the upper end of the fretboard while I'm working. It's called premask application tape (available through sign-maker supply shops, or from Stew-Mac), and it has a very gentle adhesive. Previous to getting this I used lots of strips of regular masking tape, and that works, but this is easier and it's safer for the finish. It's very minimal protection, actually. If I make any big mistakes here with all you guys watching, you'll just have to take it on faith that I usually don't.

***Audience:** How many watts is your iron?*

I don't know. I'll use any soldering iron I can get my hands on. I have several. This is one Weller makes for stained-glass work, and it's my favorite for this job. I took the tip out and threw it away, then I put a piece of brass rod in there and filed it to a chisel point. If you

1

2

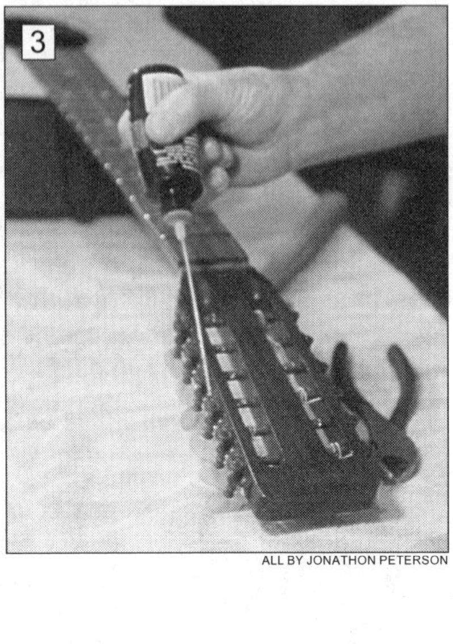

3

ALL BY JONATHON PETERSON

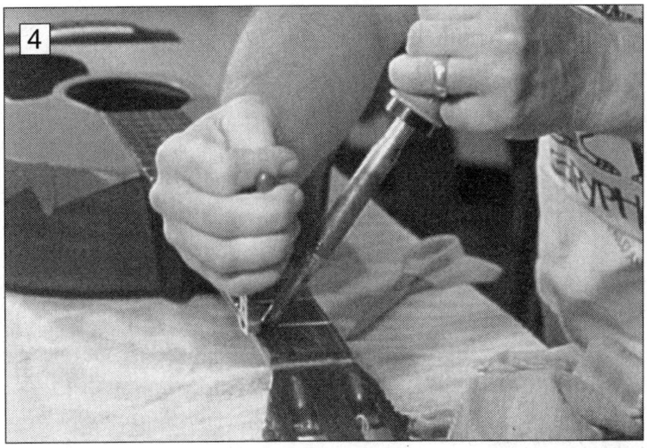

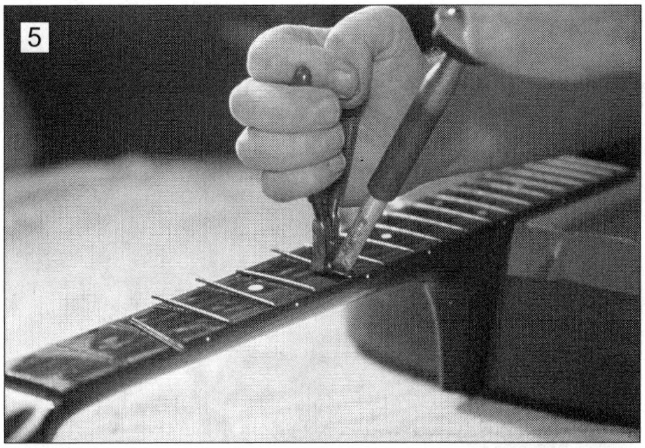

look at it carefully, you'll see that the point has a little V groove in it so that when I put it on the top of a fret it doesn't slide off. If it falls off, of course, it burns the fretboard. If you're up over the body and it falls onto the guitar top, in no time at all it's right through the finish and you've got a big problem. The tape gives you an extra instant to react, but as I said, it's not much protection. I usually add a layer of .005″ steel shim stock on top of the tape for extra protection, but I forgot to bring it. You have to be careful in any case.

My fret nippers are the same ones that Stewart-MacDonald's sells. Just about everybody uses nippers similar to this. They're just regular end nippers ground down on the end to cut flush.

I heat each fret by pulling the hot iron along its top with one hand, and as I do that I'm walking the end nippers along just behind it (**Photos 4 and 5**). I'm simply biting underneath the frets with the nippers, not lifting at all, and the frets pop right out. The tool wedges underneath the bead of the fret, and as it pulls the fret up it also pushes down on the fretboard to help keep it from chipping. This is an Indian rosewood fingerboard, and I can work very quickly. If it were ebony I'd be going slower, or if a fret felt like it was grabbing I would be going slower.

Why would it be slower?

Because I would have to heat it more. Here it's not even getting to the point where the water is sizzling too much. We'll have the frets out in no time at this rate. As you can see, they're coming out very neatly with no chips at all, and that's ideal. If a fretboard is a little bit older and drier you would need more heat.

Have you ever oiled the fingerboard before you pulled the frets to help keep it from chipping?

No, I haven't. I don't know of any reason to put oil on a fingerboard other than to make it look prettier, which in itself is a really good thing to do, but this isn't the time for that.

I'm up over the body now, and I'm finding I have a little trouble gripping this one. In fact I'm having a lot of trouble gripping it. It's not uncommon on Martin guitars, and others as well, to find that they have used a little bit of glue in the fret slots over the body. It's also not uncommon to encounter slots that have been sized differently. If this had been refretted a half-dozen times you could find that it had three or four different sizes of slots in the fretboard, especially if some of the fret jobs were partial — big wide slots near the nut from banging in lots of frets (maybe even the wrong-sized frets), and real mucky ones up over the body from having frets glued in. I chose to use a guitar for this demonstration without those kinds of problems.

I've got them all out now, so I'm unplugging the soldering iron. The old frets go in the proper receptacle. I make a lot of trash when I work.

Is there anyplace you can recycle old frets?

There probably is, but I tried saving the stuff up and after four years I had a gallon, and I threw it away. That's a lot of fret jobs, but it just isn't that much material.

At this point I'm going to take a look at the fingerboard, briefly. I see I have a slight reverse curve in the whole neck, which I basically like. At least that's what it looks like. It's not a bad idea to stick a ruler on there to check what you think you see. When I do that I can see that the reverse curve is actually pretty slight. This neck's really just about flat. The fretboard drops off over the body, and I like the looks of that too, but I really don't like the looks of where the drop-off starts. If I put a straightedge on here you will see that it rocks on this spot just before where the neck joins the body, and the fretboard drops off toward the upper end. That means that under tension the neck will bend gradually through the lower part, and there will be a hump where it joins the body. That's the hump that I told you I saw before I took the strings off. If you don't get rid of that hump and you try to set the action low, it's going to be buzz city right in the middle of the neck. That's exactly what people don't want, so we're going to level the fingerboard.

This is the only leveling tool that I've ever used. It's a metal jack-plane body that I got at a garage sale, and I use it as a sanding block. I just tear up sandpaper and fold it to fit.

That hump is pretty nasty, so I'm going to be fairly aggressive with my sanding to level that area. I'll start with 100-grit sandpaper. It's significant where you hold the neck while you are sanding the fretboard. I like to

work freehand, and I hold it so that the part of the neck that is being sanded with one hand is being supported with my other hand (**Photos 6 and 7**). If I support the neck out near the peghead, the neck is going to flex as I press down on it, and I'm going to end up removing material from the nut end of the fingerboard disproportionately. You can see how I am holding the guitar and the sanding block, and you can hear it bump as I go across the hump, but what you can't do is feel what I'm feeling. Your sense of touch is very important in all of this. I can feel that somebody has oiled the fingerboard, and my sandpaper is clogging and not biting, so I know it's time to put on a fresh piece.

I work with a vacuum cleaner right at hand, and I keep the slots cleaned out to keep the sawdust from getting packed in there.

I'm going to keep doing this until I have a sense that I've got a pretty level surface. I no longer feel a bump as I go back and forth over where it was. As I do this I'm rotating my plane body slightly from side to side along its long axis so that I maintain the arch in the fingerboard. I am varying where I am putting pressure all of the time, trying not to disturb the radius significantly.

I'll clean the slots out again now, and begin going over it with 120 grit. I watch where the dust collects in the slots, because that is an indicator where you are cutting. As I sand, the slots fill in and I can see exactly where I've cut.

I've sanded to 120, and I'm going to go to 150 now. On a rosewood fingerboard I will frequently stop at 150, but I'm going to go to 180 here. It's gliding along very easily. I can feel it cutting nicely, and I see a good cutting pattern.

Now when I put a straightedge on the fretboard it lies a little differently. In fact, I can feel that it's touching practically all along its length. It still pivots just a little, so the hump is still there just a little. I am working on it without any string tension or tension simulating device, but everything flexes under tension, and because of where the neck flexes I can tell that it's going to give me trouble when this neck is under string tension. The bulk of my experience is with this sort of instrument, and this is a condition that develops consistently in flattop steel string guitars. This neck is going to pull forward under the load of the strings. Away from the body is where the neck is most flexible, and that's also the point of greatest leverage, so that's where it's going to move the most. A little hump where the fretboard goes onto the body that is barely noticeable when there is no string tension, can become a problem when string tension is applied. You need to make sure that when it pulls up it doesn't cause an uphill hump in that area. That is really rather easy to prevent, and I think it's a significant difference between a good fret job and a not-so-good fret job.

I want to move the point where the fretboard starts to drop off back down the neck towards the nut a little bit, and this is how I do it. This is regular masking tape, and I'll put on four layers of it on the fretboard right around the 5th fret (**Photo 8**). I'm going to use a piece of sandpaper that's only half as long as what I've been using to level the fretboard. I'll wrap it around one end of the plane body, and I'm going to use those pieces of tape to support the other end of the plane body as I sand on the high spot (**Photo 9**). I might position the tape differently depending on the guitar, but it's usually somewhere between the 5th and the 7th frets. I do this on every regular flattop steel string guitar because of their natural tendency to create a hump next to the body. This fretboard already drops off over the body. If you looked closely you could see I haven't even sanded it up there. There is really no point in taking material off where it's too low already. I'm just trying to move the point where it starts to drop off away from the body a little bit. I'm sanding with the grain, working back and forth across the board. If you look in the slots you can see exactly where I've been sanding. You can't miss it. If I were really worried about it I'd put pencil marks on the fretboard to make sure that I wasn't cutting beyond a certain point.

I'm going to roll through the same grits that I used when I was leveling so the surface will look the same. I'm being pretty aggressive with the sanding here. Air conditioning and all, I'm still managing to work up a sweat. This is a 12-string, and it has an Indian rosewood fingerboard, which is fairly soft. Those are factors I'm taking into consideration as I think about how much the neck is going to pull up.

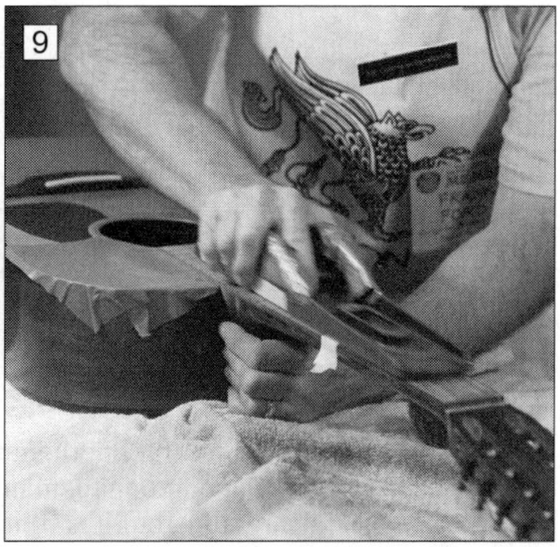

If I check the fretboard now I can see it's straight right to the 10th fret, and from there it gradually drops off to a few thousandths lower at the very end of the fingerboard (**Photo 10**). That's how I like it. On a fourteen-fret guitar the drop-off point would be at about the 12th fret.

Doesn't that make the action a little higher than it would need to be on the upper end of the board?

Theoretically, yes, but I'm not that interested in specific measurements. I just want to make sure it will play cleanly. Most players can have the action increase a little up there without it causing them any problems.

At this point we've theoretically got all the sanding done. If I were back at the shop I'd walk outside and blast it with compressed air to get rid of all the dust in the slots.

Next thing is to just clean the bottom of the fret slots. Lately I've been using this Japanese saw (**Photo 11**). It's not particularly a given size that's important to me, I just want to clean that packed-down dust out.

These Japanese saws cut on the pull stroke. I like that because when I'm working at the end of the fingerboard over the face of the guitar I can see how close I am to the protective tape so that I'm not cutting into the tape or into the guitar. I'm also less likely to pull or push chips out. I elevate the back end of the saw quite a bit, and I'm only cutting halfway across. When I was using an American saw, I had a habit of sawing guitars in half. Cutting the guitar in half is a bad thing.

For the most part I am just clearing dust, not cutting the slots deeper. The 13th-fret slot was full of glue, so I actually had to saw into it. You probably couldn't hear it, but I could hear the saw noise suddenly muffle as I was cutting, and I could feel the gumminess. Except for problem spots like that I'm cutting downwards very little because I don't want to make the slots any deeper.

Everything looks pretty level and smooth. I can see a couple of little spots where I didn't actually sand the surface at all, so I am going to take another piece of paper and hit those spots very lightly so the board has a clean, uniform look and it's ready for frets.

I like to back up the neck when I'm pounding frets in it, so I have a very high-tech tool here — a block of wood with some leather on it for padding.

Jim Dunlop's #6240 happens to be my current favorite fretwire. It seems to do well on Martin refrets. I'm going to try that first. It comes in rolls, and I usually just hold the roll up and check the curve of the wire against the arch in the fretboard. I want the curve of the fretwire to have a tighter radius than the fretboard so that I know it's going to go down cleanly at the ends. That's really significant. If the fretwire is too flat, I have a fret bender that I got from Stewart-MacDonald, and I just crank the wire to a tighter radius than the fingerboard.

I've got some bath towels here that I like to throw over the soundboard when I am hammering frets. It kind of quiets the guitar down.

To test the fit of the fretwire I pick a slot, usually not the first one, and I tap in a fret to see how it goes in. This is fitting rather well. In fact I like it quite a lot, so that's the right fretwire for this job.

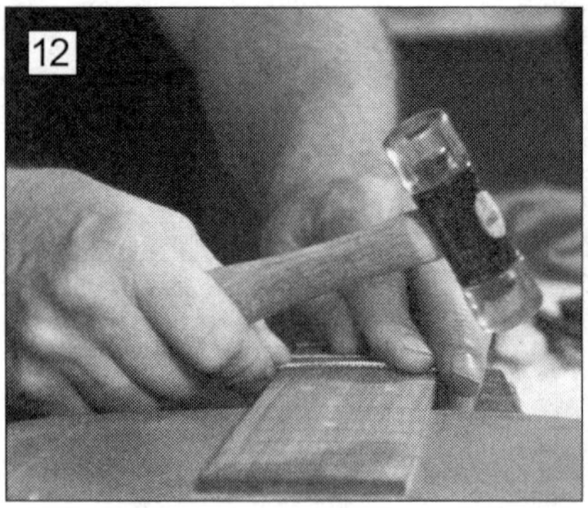
12

13

14

I like to cut a set of frets and put them in my little fret holder before I start pounding them in. The holder is not really a significant tool, but it is something I like to use. I'll cut these about ⅜″ over long. For that I use a set of diagonal cutters that I've ground to cut flush. They are Sears Craftsman brand, so when they get all chewed up I can take them back and get free replacements. *(laughter)* They are quite worn in one spot and won't cut all the way through the wire, so I can get away with cutting a whole bunch of these to length without having them fall apart, then I just break them off and stick them in the holder. Anytime I have a chance to save time on an operation, I do it. Installing frets involves about twenty identical operations, and I think a fret job simply comes out neater if you do all twenty operations the same way. On this guitar we've actually got nineteen frets.

I like fret hammers with plastic heads for a variety of reasons. One is that I have a phobia about denting the tops of frets. I go absolutely nuts if I dent the top of a fret. Another is that I hate denting the fingerboard, and if I bump the fingerboard with a plastic hammer I'm not going to damage it. I have a couple of hammers that I use. This is a Stanley.

I place the fret tang in the slot (**Photo 12**), and begin by tapping the fret in gently at the ends (**Photo 13**). It's important how you hold the hammer. Pounding frets in takes a fairly gentle motion, we hope, and I find that if I hold the hammer with the handle parallel to the fret, it really gains me a lot of control. I can rock the hammer back and forth as I work along the length of the fret, and I won't catch the fret with a corner of the hammer. If you hit the fret with the corner of your hammer and get a little ripple in it, that fret is gone. You can never recover it.

I use as many taps as needed, slowly increasing the force, until I've tapped it nice and tightly all the way across (**Photo 14**). I can usually hear it seat itself.

Before I install the frets over the body I am going to quickly trim the excess material off the ends of the frets that are in, using the same flush-cut diagonal cutters I mentioned before (**Photo 15**). You have to watch out when you are doing this because if a loose fret end winds up on your bench pad it has a habit of embedding itself into the back of the guitar. You only have to do that three or four times before you catch on and come up with some method of avoiding it. *(laughter)*

I'll take a quick look down the neck to see how things are shaping up (**Photo 16**). It looks good so far. People like to look down the necks of their guitars. They really want to know what it is that other guys are seeing. I don't think that most people are actually aware of what they are supposed to be seeing, but they are really interested in doing it. *(laughter)*

On a Martin guitar the first two frets over the body are supported by the neck block, so I can hammer those right in. From there up the fretboard is only supported by the guitar top. You're basically hammering on an eggshell, so they have to be handled a bit differently.

For the frets over the soundboard I use this lead weight to support the area I am hammering (**Photo 17**). It's not a particularly significant piece of lead, but it's the one I use. It's got a big handle so I don't lose it.

I hold the weight directly under the fret I'm pounding, whether or not that happens to be on a brace

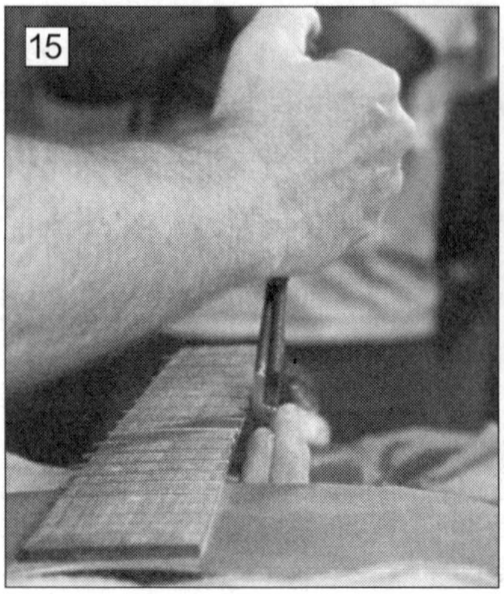
15

16

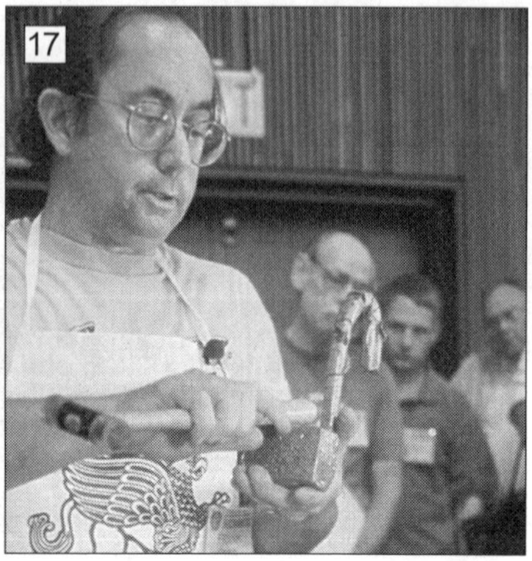
17

(**Photo 18**). In one case I was beyond the brace, in another case it was right on the brace. I want as much support directly under that fret as precisely as possible. With proper support I can hit the frets as hard as I want without hurting anything.

How do you guard against driving the frets in too far and having the ends spring up?

Experience has a lot to do with all of this, of course. The biggest insurance I have against that is my plastic hammer. With this it's almost impossible to drive a fret too hard. In fact, I think it is impossible to drive one too hard into ebony. In Brazilian rosewood it would really be a trick. With Indian rosewood it's still pretty safe. You can slug away.

I have a way of looking down necks that works for me when I'm working with the frets like this. I'm not looking at it the way I would be if it had strings on it. In that case I would be trying to sight down the corners of the frets. In this case what I'm looking at is the surface of the frets and how the light reflects off of them. I'm trying to find highlights or dark spots. If it's bright it might be too high, and if it's dark it might be too low. It could also just be dirty or shiny, but it's typically a problem in height. When I catch one with my eye it's kind of hard to tell exactly which one it is, so I hold my finger up between the light source and the fret so it casts a shadow on the fret, then I let my finger follow the shadow to the fret in question. I can then test it to see if it is driven in well enough, or I can plop a straightedge on it to see what's going on.

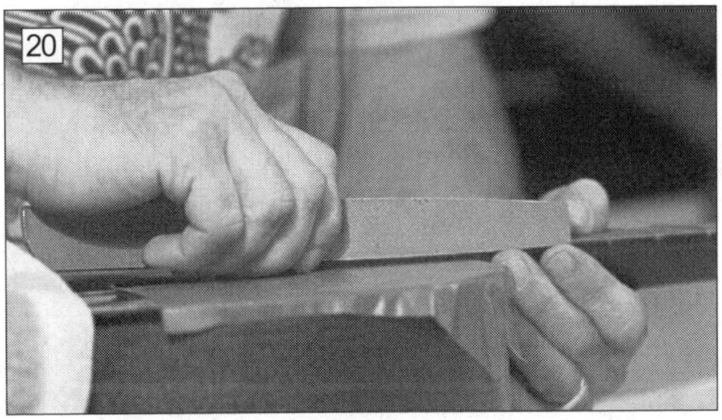

How level are the frets when they go in? It's important. On this guitar the frets over the body are dropping off a little. The action will naturally be higher up there, so there's not to much that needs to be done in that area. But down the neck where the musician will be playing most of the time, it's critical that they're exactly level. I never hit a fret with a steel hammer, but I have a little piece of steel plate about 3⁄32″ thick and long enough to span several frets that I will place it over the frets and hammer on with a steel hammer (**Photo 19**). I can hit it as hard as I want, and I never scratch it or dent the frets. If the frets were a little out of level this might iron them down and seat them evenly.

I'm going to trim the ends of the upper frets flush with the fingerboard, and then I'm going to file the ends of the frets, and I have a very high tech tool for that. It's a 10″ mill bastard file. I chose this kind of file for this job because I can buy them cheap by the box. I broke the tang off and touched it on a grinder so it isn't sharp. I've given up using safe-edged files for this operation because they cost more, and I don't find that particular feature is significant to me right now.

I'll start up over the body. I'm holding the file so that it's not grazing my tape, holding it up with my fingers, and I'm using the fingers of my left hand to keep the front end from diving down and cutting the top binding (**Photos 20 and 21**). I'm going to file along the edge until I feel and hear that I'm down to the wood.

I'm holding the file at a slight angle from vertical. You can hear it as it gets down and just starts to touch the wood.

I have a file holder for doing my fret ends that keeps the file at a constant 30° angle. Do you ever use something like that?

No, I just hold it. I've got plenty of control, and just using my hands gives me a more direct feel for what is going on, and more flexibility.

Now I've got them trimmed, I've slowly rotated the file around towards vertical, and I don't feel the tangs sticking out anymore. Now I'm going to roll it back and cut the facets on the ends (**Photo 22**). I go somewhere between 45° and 60° depending on the look I'm after. I like to be able to vary the angle of the fret ends depending on the job. Sometimes the owner is going to want the playing surface of the frets to extend way out towards the edge of the fretboard because the string spacing is wider, or because they do a lot of bending. Some people will want to have them rounded over more so that they feel smoother.

I try to talk to people about what it is that they like. I think it's highly important for me to be the guy who talks to the customer. The more I know about what he wants, the better I can accommodate him. Ultimately he's my boss, and he's the one I want to keep happy.

Do frets ever come loose during filing?

That's not too unusual, and I can hear when they do. I hear one now, as a matter of fact. Do you hear that little high-pitched chirp as I file over it? I don't think it's loose enough to move around and cause problems, though. If the frets are too loose I will glue them in. I prop up the peghead so the neck is at a 30° angle and place a little superglue on the front edge of the fret. It is impossible to not leave some residue on the fingerboard so I clean it up with acetone as I go.

I now have the fret tangs filed flush with the neck, and the bevels filed about the way I like them. To fill the fret ends I use a Q-tip to apply a little accelerator to each fret end. Then I place a single drop of superglue on each fret end. My goal here is to not let any run in, I just want to fill-in that spot.

What about deep gouges in the fingerboard?

If you look at it closely you'll notice that there are still some divots here from fingernails. If I had more time and if the customer requested it, I'd fill those with cyanoacrylate and some of this sanding dust, or sometimes I'll try to sand through them when I'm leveling the fretboard, depending on how deep they are. I might also just leave them alone, depending on the owner's tastes and needs. In this case, obviously, I'm going to be leaving them alone. I try to tell people who are making those gouges that they are going to do it again, and they ought to just get used to it.

Now I'm going to take a smaller, finer version of that same file, and touch up the bevels one last time with a machinist's technique called draw filing. Normally, a file cut is made by pushing the file lengthwise

22

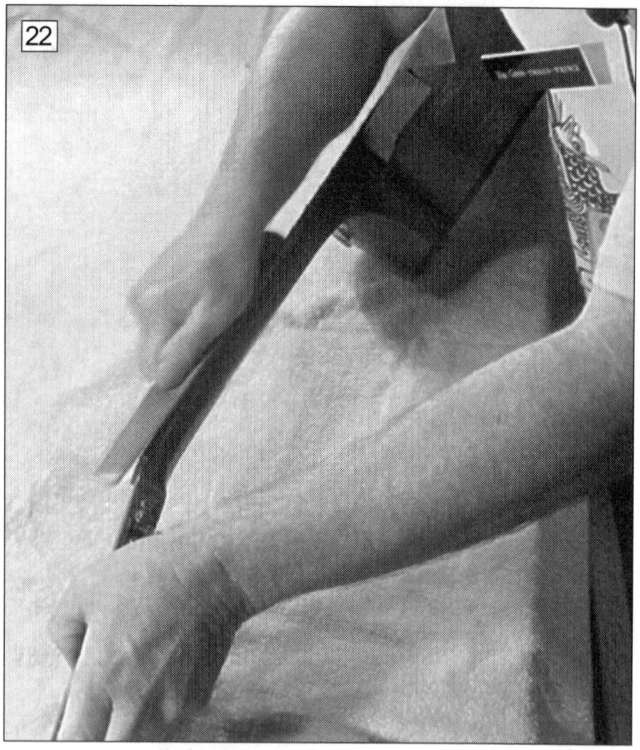

across a surface. Draw filing is done with the file held sideways to the direction of the cut, which puts the teeth at a very low cutting angle, resulting in a sheering action which creates a very smooth surface that helps to knock off any little file chatter marks that the first filing might have left. Hold the file perpendicular to the face of the fingerboard and lightly draw file the fret ends until you just start to scuff the finish. You are only trying to remove the little nubs of superglue and the tiniest amount of fret material, so go easy. Of course, because of the orientation of the file, draw filing can only be done on the ends of the neck frets, not the body frets. Make sure all of the excess superglue is gone, and that all the fret-slot ends are filled.

I have a little routine for finishing the ends of the frets so that they don't feel rough to the player's hand. I begin by creating a little facet, a little bevel, on either side of each end of each fret. As I file these I try to keep my body positioned about the same, and I try to hold the file and my arm the same way for each stroke. A lot of fret work is visual. It looks nice if all the little facets on the ends line up and look the same. On the frets over the body it's kind of tight because the file is coming down at an angle, and if I'm not careful I could scar the top. The rest of the neck doesn't give you that problem. The file I use for this has a safe edge ground on each corner. It's called a cant-saw file, and it's more or less triangular. To make the bevel I slide the safe corner of the file right against the corner of the fingerboard, and cut the corner of the end of the fret in one motion using the weight of my arm to push it (**Photo 23**).

Even though the file is rubbing up against the fingerboard it's not making any marks?

Take a look. There's no mark at all, but don't forget, I'm holding the end of the file up so the file is at an angle, and it's only contacting the fretboard on the very corner.

You can get a real rhythm going — same grip, same stroke, same angle, same cut — so it doesn't take a lot of time. That gives you a series of identical facets that look nice. They are sharp as hell, though.

The next step is to round the corners of those facets. I'm going to use the same file, but this time I'm holding it so that the cutting surface is more vertical (**Photo 24**), and my action is going to be a little different. It's going to be a rounding cut rather than a facet cut. It's not as significant over the body because you don't grip the neck the same way up there, but I do touch each one to give it that little highlight so they look uniform.

Where do you get your files?

There is a huge hardware store in our area called Orchard Supply Hardware that has about every file in the world in stock. This one is made by Nicholson.

Now they actually feel fairly good. They are still a little sharp, but that will get smoothed out later. At this point I will go back to my plane body and sandpaper, and level the tops of all the frets. This is Klingspor 600-grit waterproof sandpaper (available from www.sandingcatalog.com). It's great stuff. I fold it around my sanding block.

The problem with using a sanding block on frets is that the leading edge of the paper can curl up and snag on the frets, so instead of working along the neck I'm going to go across it sideways, and I'm going work in little circles. I support the neck with my hand at the center of the neck.

The block is perfectly flat, and the sandpaper will obviously only cut the frets where it touches them. I'll cut narrow shiny facets along the length of the tops of all of the frets. Obviously, you're going to cut more off some than others, or this step wouldn't be necessary.

Now I will give it an eyeball test to see how everybody looks. I can see little flat spots across all the frets, so I'm going to give it one more pass to make all those little flat spots have their sanding scratches in the same direction. The reason I do that is that it's easier for me to see them as I look down the fingerboard if they are uniform. It looks pretty darn good.

What I would normally do at this point is take what's left of the grit on my sandpaper and go back over my ends of the frets and the edges of the fingerboard. Backing the sandpaper with my hands only, I'll buff the tops of the frets rounding them sufficiently to give them a good feel. I'll also sand the ends of the frets just a little bit with my fingers, just bumping up and down to round those babies off a little bit. At the same time I'm sanding the finish a tiny bit at the edges and smoothing out any fret-slot fill that might be left on the surface.

Do you ever use steel wool or Scotchbrite?

I like a steel-wool finish on frets. I've never used Scotchbrite. The steel wool that I like best comes out of the Netherlands . LMI carries it. It's oil free, and it comes in a 2 KG roll about 2″ wide. It's very, very fine and it produces a good polish. Some of the finishing places sell it. It's so much better than any other steel wool I have used.

What grade is it?

The finest that I can get. It's a European product, and they don't use the same grade-numbering system we do, but it's something like 0000.

How about buffing with a polishing compound?

The problem with that is that it leaves compound everywhere, and I don't want to take the time to clean that stuff off the fingerboard if I don't really have to.

The frets are in, they're level, rounded, and they're finished more finely than frets on a new Martin guitar would be, so I would say it reaches that quality of good enough. If I were going to be a little slicker about it, I would use Micro-mesh. You can go through the grits to polish up the finish on the edge of the fingerboard so it looks nice and shiny. I might also use the buffer for that, depending on the situation and the time. But, as I said, at this point on this instrument the work is good enough, so the fingerboard would get a little bit of lemon oil from the supermarket to give it a nice clean look. It's time to string it up and send it home. ——

23

24

Originally published in *American Lutherie #50*, 1997

Meet the Maker: Michael Hornick

by Tim Olsen

Here we are at the 1997 Healdsburg Guitar Festival, reminiscing about the 1986 Guild Convention in Tacoma. You brought your first instruments there, didn't you? As I remember they were pretty nice looking guitars.

I had the audacity to put "luthier" on my business card! I'm still proud of those three instruments. In fact this is the first show that I've done in a long time where that first guitar isn't on display and played. It's a great sounding guitar, but I don't worry all about the dents and dings anymore.

How did you get into guitar making?

Richard Hoover is really the responsible person. I had a friend who sold a Martin and another guitar to get a Santa Cruz in 1977. He brought it over to my house. I listened to this guitar and went "Wow!" I called Santa Cruz and asked if I could come over on a Saturday, and they said sure. I went over there and bought a guitar.

ALL COURTESY MICHAEL HORNICK

That helps make a luthier friendly!

I walked into their shop and I thought, "I've got better tools than this. I've got a better shop. How can they do this magic?" That visit started a friendship with Richard. He is my best friend in the business, as well as my mentor. I avoided a lot of mistakes by the great good fortune of having somebody like Richard Hoover. We had a great connection. He gave me time and I didn't feel like I was taking advantage of him. Which is the same thing that I do now, in reverse, for other people. He gave me all the material for that first guitar, and it was good quality wood. But it wasn't until '84 that I finally tried to build it. That took a year. I loved the whole process, and I really was knocked out when I strung it up. I said, "This is it."

I've been working wood all my life, always knowing it was what I wanted to do, but always hating everything that I did. I was making custom furniture. It was really a Catch-22. I got excited, I got a job, I did all the design; but once I started building, it was drudgery. The guitar wasn't that way. I didn't mind the building at all, I enjoyed it. To me musical instruments are the ultimate for woodworkers. They're alive. They are an entity on their own. It makes a big difference.

This was what I'd been looking for. I don't make a great living at it, but I'm still doing it and that's the real issue for me. Just being able to do it well enough and make enough doing it that I don't have to quit and go back to doing work that is just a job about money.

Are you still chasing a sound? How close do you think you've gotten to what you were after?

I'm truly happy with the sound of every instrument I've built. There aren't any I wish I could burn. But there's constant experimentation that goes on to see if I can get more of this or more of that. My sound is constantly expanding. I used to compare everything to my first instrument. It's ten years old, so it is very much broken in, but it can't hold its own against my new ones. So I know I'm getting more tone, better separation, and better clarity. The sound I'm getting is consistent enough that very seldom does something jump out. It's all what I call tone sculpting. The goal is to achieve the sound I'm after in a particular genre rather than to compare it to this guitar over here. How successful have I been at dialing in a particular quality of tone and feel for the player? Is it what he or she wants?

My one complaint is that I'm so busy I don't get to go crazy and experiment. I would love to. I can't wait to use some of the stuff I learned today listening to Richard Schneider and Tim White. A lot of it was reinforcing scientifically what I do intuitively, but some of it was like, "Ah ha!" I understand what's going on when you relieve the ends of the braces and what it's doing to tone, to some degree. But I never dreamed of making a brace taper from side to side. Now I have another tool to play with.

Have you changed a lot things over the ten years?

Yeah. It's always small things but they add up to big stuff. Interlocking braces all the way through has to do with structure as well as tone. My bridge plates are laminated. I'll never have a broken bridge plate and bridge now. In experimenting with woods for bridge plates and what they do to tone, I have added that lamination. It takes more time but I think it's a better product.

Speaking of time, do you find the voicing process to be very time consuming?

It's just a start-to-finish process. I think it was Richard Hoover who said that from the moment he's choosing wood for the instrument until he's finally putting finish on it, the voicing procedure is happening. I'm paying attention to what I'm hearing all the time. Intuition is what makes it all work, but now I also have enough experience to know what leads to the sound I want. With intuition alone, I might want to change it but not know why. Experience has given me decision-making abilities about those things that are not intuitive.

You explained in your talk today that you vary the thickness of the top. Have you done that with woods other than spruce?

Spruce, red cedar, and koa are the top woods I use. The same principles that apply to spruce also apply to koa, but it has to be worked thinner. Koa has more density, and it takes more energy to excite. I'm trying to get one piece of wood to make bass tones, midrange tones, and treble tones. I'm trying to get that piece of wood to have sustain but also have power in the note. I'm still asking it to do everything but I'm choosing the woods based on the tone I want. If a fingerstyle player really loves the woody, earthy sound, I'm going to want to do an all-koa guitar for them. I'm not going to want to do a spruce guitar, because it's not going to have that bright thing. Those choices are a part of the voicing right from the beginning, but you have to work each individual piece differently. For example, I have cut two tops from the same billet and put them on two guitars of the same shape and size. In order to make them feel right and ultimately to make them work right I had to work the plates to different thicknesses. And that is as close to the same pieces of wood as you can get.

When you made your first guitar, did you think much about top thickness and graduation?

Yes, right from the beginning. Part of that was the blessing of having become friends with Richard and

Bruce Ross at Santa Cruz Guitars. I knew they used a tapered plate, so I ended up with just a straight taper on my first guitar, thicker on the treble and thinner on the bass. Now I graduate in both directions. I want the thickest part of the plate under the bridge rather than on the treble side.

I think that having the ability to work the top in different ways is one of the real keys. I don't think you can do it by block sanding afterwards with anywhere near the efficiency. I think the old masters did it, but it would be a very time consuming process to do all the thicknessing from the exterior. For me, it's really about the way that it feels. I've got to get it to feel right and still have enough wood left to be able to use it.

I keep an accurate record, but I thickness according to feel, not dimensions. I do have a parameter. I won't go below 2MM on the bass side on a full-size steel string. I don't have that open playground of building on spec. I'm afraid to use things that my intuition tells me not to because I'm going for a specific sound on a custom order. If I didn't have orders I could build what I wanted and then whoever liked the way it sounded would buy it.

Do you think that you will use any other soundboard materials?

I will always want to keep experimenting with that, particularly with woods that will be planet friendly. European silver spruce is simply not going to be available at the rate we are building instruments. That's all there is to it. Adirondack spruce is already way too scarce.

Engelmann I don't like. It looks beautiful, it has a great tap tone, but I haven't played an Engelmann instrument that turned me on yet from any builder. I haven't built one, so I should reserve judgement until I compare it to what I'm doing. I know players who think it is *the* sound. So if I had a customer that clearly had an ear for Engelmann, I'd see what I could do with it. I do have some really nice Engelmann sets. But it doesn't seem to have the headroom; you can't drive Engelmann the way you can German or red spruce or even Sitka for that matter.

And then there's cedar. Cedar is a marvelous wood, but I much prefer it for fingerpicking over flatpicking. James Taylor uses a cedar-topped guitar. He's got a bunch of them now from Olson. When he's fingerpicking that guitar, it's just awesome. It works OK for flatpicking, but not like the spruces. Cedar enhances that initial explosion of tone. Then the explosion decays without the sustain decaying. Classical guitar playing is the ultimate fingerstyle, and I think that's why cedar is a real staple for classical builders. It's also very reforestable and renewable, assuming everyone doesn't think they have to have 400-year-old, old-growth wood.

What about brace wood?

Oh man. I am *really* into red spruce. I had been using Sitka for all my braces, and I tried red spruce as an experiment. I was just blown away. I hate to put Sitka on anything now. I don't know what it is about the red spruce, but stuff is happening clearer, cleaner, and quicker. Plus I love the feel of working with it.

So would you use it to brace all kinds of top wood?

That's what I'm moving toward.

Have you done much experimentation with brace patterns?

Always the X brace. I've changed the angle of the X, location of tone bars coming off the X, position of the X on the centerline. But I never change more than one thing at a time. If I do something that seems to make a difference, I'll do it a bunch more times to see if it is really there. I don't know how good an understanding I'm developing, but I'm getting more and more tools to work with. I have more ways to deal with treble, bass, midrange, balance, volume, sustain, and all these different criteria. Every little detail counts if you want the highest result. I think the key is learning how the little things add up so you can have that as a playground.

You brought your first instruments to the Guild convention in 1986, and you had only been building for two years. What was your impression at that convention of how you were fitting in?

That's a loaded question. Trying not to sound too egotistical, I was amazed that I was clearly on the right track. I knew that I was doing what I wanted to be doing and that I was going to be able to do it at a higher level than average.

That's one way of looking at the difference in quality of this show versus that Guild convention ten years ago. The people here who are showing their first, second, and third instruments are every bit at the same kind of place I was in 1986. But in 1986 there were a lot of people who were on their on their tenth and twentieth instruments that weren't getting it. I really believe that we have made that progress because we are sharing. I'm sharing all my information, and more builders are getting better because of that. More players are playing better instruments, so that's bringing more builders into the circle. It's definitely a snowball effect.

I don't think the craft was even on the same planet ten years ago. At that convention there were a few makers that really stood out for me. There was Steve Grimes, Steve Klein, Somogyi, and especially Jeffrey Elliott, wow! That was the only time I had met him and seen his instruments before this show. There was a guitar listening session, and there was no contest between Jeffrey's classic guitar and the others. The sound matched the quality of the workmanship. But what was really cool was that the personality of the maker was the same as the beauty in the sound. There were some builders there I highly respected that had too much ego for me to want to hang with. Jeffrey was a little bit overwhelmed, but more than anything he wanted to empower other people. He said something to me that I haven't done yet, although I have really valued the thought. He said that if you want to learn sensitivity, make classics. What that meant to me was, make sure you're being as sensitive as you can when you are building steel string guitars; just because you've got more string tension doesn't mean that it will work. He was talking about sensitivity to the instrument, not about a formula.

I think Jeff has done that for a lot of people. He has shown them another level that they can achieve.

By example, and by caring.

What do you think of the work at this show?

I am just knocked over. There's hardly anything out there that isn't completely stunning. Right on down the line to the beginning instruments, there's a whole new understanding of what's available and a willingness to go for it. This is truly a Big Daddy show here; we really are talking some of the best in North America.

I see a really big step across these ten years. It really is amazing to me. And it's pleasing, because our whole thing is sharing information. It does in fact work. We now have scientific proof! I think information sharing is the whole issue, and the Guild started it. It's not about holding your secrets and being better than the other guy. There are no secrets.

I would have learned to make guitars whether Richard Hoover had helped me or not. If you're going to get it, you're going to get it. Why not help the guy get it right now? That makes me more, rather than less.

Don't we want the field that we work in to be better? If you don't help other people, the field that you work in is going to be less. We want it to be more.

Exactly. Thanks to people like James Taylor and Alex de Grassi, the players are not afraid of ordering a handmade guitar anymore. Many of them have had good experiences with a lot of individual luthiers. They can see that we are working at a very high level and that we are offering them a whole new gamut of qualities.

Michael Hornick and his first three guitars at his display table during the 1986 GAL Convention in Tacoma, Washington

Assuming that the national economy stays stable, where do you think the field will be in another ten years?

That's a good question. I think there will be more people doing it, and more of the people doing it will be making a real living. We have started something that isn't going to quit. People are starting to realize that there is value in hand craftsmanship. I think this is going to help every aspect of our society.

I have a real big button about the way government has tried to kill the artistic side of people in order to control them. Our present government gives ten times the money to the navy and army bands than for all the arts things that get any federal money. I have been real disappointed about that. Then I finally woke up to the fact that 3,000,000 new stringed instruments a year are being sold worldwide. There are an unbelievable number of people playing music which is totally artistic and creative. We fooled them! They haven't figured out yet that we're doing it to them with music. We are out here just playing music and having a ball and laughing at them. This is the way our society, and our planet, is going to maintain its soul. Music is the key.

Twenty years ago the difference between an instrument by an experienced maker like Eugene Clark and a beginning luthier would have been enormous. A typical first instrument in those days was definitely a homemade job, and it looked like it. The range of quality in handcrafted guitars twenty years ago ran from A to Z. Nowadays the general level of the craft is way up there. How much farther can it go?

I don't think the craft can jump as far as it has in this past ten years. We probably won't see as much radical change in the looks or the function of the design, but we'll see a continued improvement. Sometimes you make an instrument that really stands out. It just has more of everything. I think we're going to see a more consistent level of those instruments. That is a very small difference, but it's really a huge difference.

I don't think visual quality is going to move a whole lot more and I don't think tone is going to move a whole lot more except that they are going to take that extra step. It's going to have the Steve Klein quality of craftsmanship where it's just flat impeccable. And that will bring the focus back even more to tone. We had to get the craftsmanship up. Let's keep that and improve it, but now let's work on what it's really all about, which is tone.

The competition is going to be a lot greater, and it's going to weed out those who are not in it for the right reasons. People who are in it because they think they're smarter at it or they can market more won't still be doing it. I don't think the market will carry them. Right now it's expanding so fast everybody is having a good time. It will weed itself back out. Everything goes through those cycles.

The really great craftsmen that have the tone are going to be the ones that last. And the big boys like Larrivée, Taylor, Collings, Santa Cruz, Mossman, and Gallagher are going to make it regardless, because of what they brought and what they will continue to bring. But on the individual level it's going to be a fight for tone. It's going to be a fight for who gets the most out of the instrument.

Nowadays we are offering guitars that have more than the players can get out of them. They can grow into them. A lot of these instruments nobody could ever outgrow, unless they are not being honest with themselves.

Now it's really about the performer. We did our job, now they get to do theirs. ——

Originally published in *American Lutherie #50*, 1997

The Concert Zither

by John Roeder

WHEN ONE HEARS the word "zither" it evokes some confusion as to what really is a zither: is it an autoharp or a dulcimer? But if we say "concert zither" there should be little doubt. Unfortunately, the concert zither is all but forgotten in America. It was popular in the 19th century and into the early 20th century, having been brought from its native Southern Germany and Austria by immigrants. American builders in the 19th century included Washburn, C.F. Martin (until the 1880s), and the most famous of all, Franz Schwarzer in Washington, Missouri. Today it is only commercially built in parts of Germany, notably in Bavaria and in Saxony, in Markneukirchen.

The concert zither is a flat asymmetrical soundbox over which there is a fretboard of five metallic strings and twenty-nine frets, and twenty to forty open metal-and-nylon strings stretched across two bridges. As shown in **Photo 1,** the fretted melody strings are stopped with the left-hand fingers and plucked with a narrow, hard metallic thumbpick or, more properly, a *zitherring,* in a forward and downward motion of the right thumb. At the same time, the chords and rhythm strings, three octaves of bass clef, are plucked by the right-hand fingers in a squeezing action toward the player. It is a self-contained instrument in that both treble and bass clefs are played like a piano score. In fact, zither sheet music resembles a piano or modern accordion score.

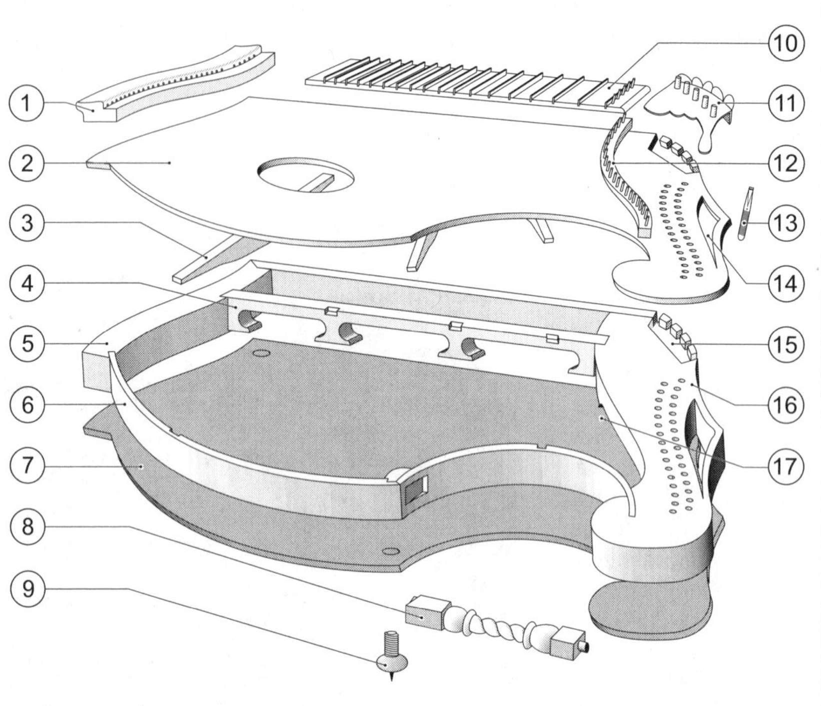

Figure 1. *Exploded diagram of the concert zither. 1: Right handrest or saddle and right bridge. 2: Top or soundboard. 3: Braces. 4: Fretboard brace. 5: Right end block. 6: Curved ribs. 7: Bottom or back. 8: Ornamental column. 9: Feet. 10: Fretboard. 11: Tuning machine. 12: Left bridge. 13: Tuning pin. 14: Hole for air resonance. 15: Recess for German tuning machine. 16: Tuning block. 17: Air resonance cutout on bottom of tuning block.*

ALL COURTESY OF JOHN ROEDER

The basic design and concept of the concert zither is at first puzzling: how do we get the sound and resonance of the melody strings over to the soundhole when the fretboard lies over a hollow, braced cavity that is parallel to all the open strings? Refer to the diagram in **Fig. 1**. The top quartersawn spruce panel (with veneer covering) and the bottom panel of either spruce or rosewood, are both much thicker than guitar tops and backs. The straight and bent ribs of either mahogany or maple are also thicker than guitar ribs. The end blocks for the string posts and tuning pins seem massive at first, made out of hard maple, mahogany, or beechwood. The spruce internal braces are also more massive than those of an acoustic guitar. On the left side there is a curved wooden bridge for the open strings, usually of pearwood (or rosewood in my model). On the right-hand side there is a more massive wooden bridge and handrest that holds all the strings. It is called a saddle, and can be rosewood (or cocobolo in my model), or some combination of rosewood and maple or pearwood.

The goal of the zither builder is to make all parts of the soundbox, bridges, and fretboard work together to insure that the fret strings will sound louder than, but not drown out, the open accompaniment strings. One needs to understand that the zither produces bright but "throaty" tones on the fretboard, which are somewhat darker and heavier than a mandolin in the high octaves. In the lower octaves on the wound G and C strings, the lower tones are darker and mellower than a flattop guitar, but still brighter and more resonant than an archtop guitar. The open stings have a quality that is more harplike in the first thirteen strings or upper register, and the lower bass and contrabass strings have a dark, acoustic, slightly metallic character.

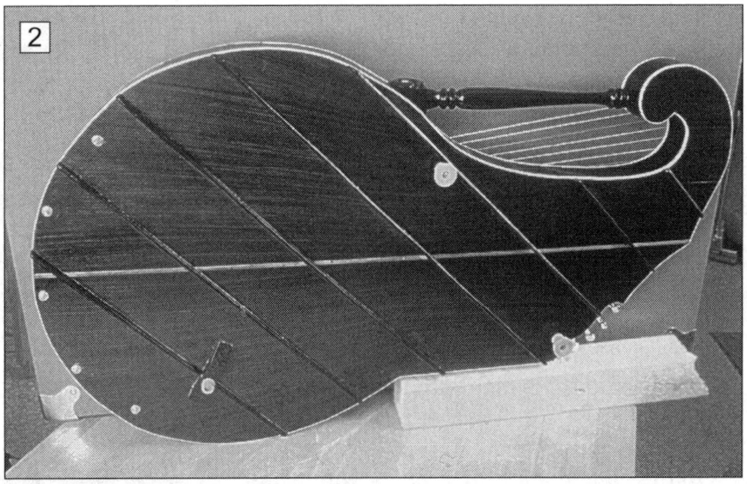

2

Facing page: The zitherring, or thumbpick, is used to pluck the fretted strings, while the fingers of the right hand pluck the thirty-two open strings.

This page: These two photos show the author's Arion II model zither, an enlaged version of the Mittenwald harp zither, or Arion model. The external back braces are peculiar to this type of zither; concert zithers have no back braces. The tailpiece, another feature found only on harp zithers, allows bringing the bridge out from the end block to increase tone.

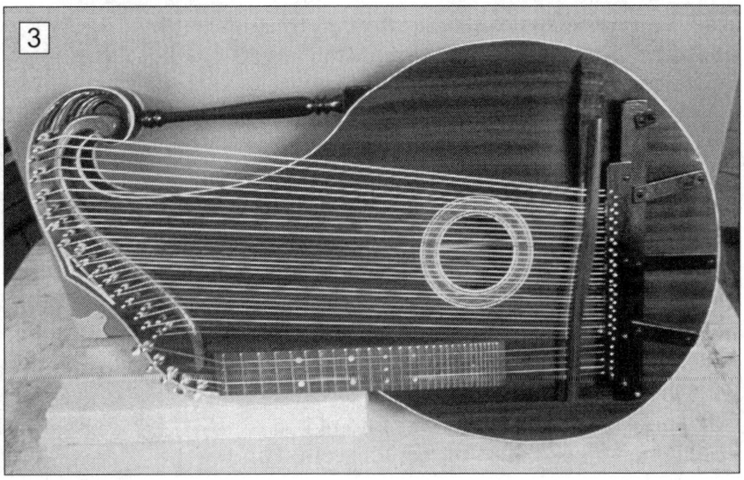

3

Designs

The drawings in **Figs. 2, 3, 4, and 5** (p. 79) show the basic proportions and most popular designs of zither soundboxes over the last 130 years in the USA. Soundboxes ranged in depth from 3/4″ up to 1 3/4″. The instrument plan in this issue is based on the standard modern concert zither. **Fig. 6** (p. 79) shows my own design, the *Arion II* Mittenwald-harp style, which is the instrument shown in most of the detail photos.

Basic loudness and good resonance depends upon the selective thinning and tap-tuning of the top or sound table underside. I've shown the basic thicknesses in the plan, and the areas to be tuned (above, below, and to the left of the soundhole) are indicated. Notice that all three areas have been thinned considerably, down to about .09″. All three should be within 1/8 step of the same pitch when tapped with a finger. If hearing the pitches is difficult, rely on the thickness gauge for equality. Planing and tap tuning is done prior to veneering the table or cutting the soundhole.

The table consists of two bookmatched, quartersawn spruce panels, grain running lengthwise. The stock should be about 3/16″ thick. If it is too thin to start with, the sound will be too bright; if too thick, it will mute or excessively darken the tone quality. That same principle applies to the ribs (about 1/8″– 3/16″ thick) and to the braces (at a width of 1/3″– 3/8″). The bottom is also 3/16″ thick if spruce is used, but I used a rosewood bottom that is thinner (about 3/32″–1/8″) with diagonal maple cross braces on the outside (**Photo 2**). The outside bottom cross braces enhance the loudness and were based upon a design called the "piano bottom" by Franz Schwarzer in the 1890s. **Photo 2** also shows the three rubber feet upon which the zither sits. The older models use tiny ivoroid balls, about 3/8″ in diameter, that contain metal tack-like pins that sink into a table when played. **Photo 3** shows a front view of the same *Arion II* zither.

Braces

The three main braces carry the resonance out from under the fretboard across the table on either side of the soundhole. Each brace starts at a notch in the rib, under the 1st fretted string. How the braces are spaced from each other is determined by the Golden Section (.618 or 61.8 %). The mathematical multiples of the fret scale length, when multiplied by .618 yields the pearl dot positions on the fretboard. Fretboards are usually made of pearwood in Germany, but I find a good rosewood to be sufficient. Using those pearl dots, the middle brace begins at the 12th fret at the three small dots, which is also the octave center of the scale length. The other two braces are placed at about 3rd fret on the left and at the right end of the fretboard. Each of those positions is equally distant from the center brace and is a fraction of the scale length using the Golden Section. Each brace is carefully scalloped down before it meets the ribs and before it intersects the fretboard bridge.

The fretboard bridge is the spruce brace that runs parallel to and just under the upper edge of the fretboard just beyond the fretted C string. In the plan front side view we see that this special bridge notches into both end blocks but only touches the bottom panel at three specially scalloped "feet" directly under each cross brace. If these special feet were too massive, as in the case of smaller 19th-century "Prime" zithers, the resulting fret tones are too shallow and lose too much brightness. **Photos 4, 5, and 6** show the braces and the fretboard bridge with its feet.

Blocks

In the plan, the left block is the tuning pin and tuning-machine holder. The right block holds the anchoring pins for all the strings. But in my Arion II zither, owing to its round box, the strings are held by a steel and aluminum tailpiece. A massive beechwood brace, as seen in **Photos 4 and 5**, acts as the 3rd, right-hand cross brace. This special brace vibrates with the saddle above it, thus producing greater resonance across the large semicircular half of the soundbox.

The graceful curve of the beechwood tuning block is seen in **Photos 4, 5, and 6** and in closeup in **Photo 7** showing its underside. Notice the smoothed curved section that does not touch the bottom panel. This is the bottom of the tuning pin section. In **Photo 6** on the right, this section appears to have a wide tunnel-like opening at the bottom.

That little "tunnel" goes from the main section of the soundbox out to the three-sided hole in the top at the very end of the beechwood block. Thus the center section of the block mass is freer to vibrate along with the adjacent table and braces. This entire design feature is called the *Luftresonance* (air resonance) by the Germans. In **Photo 3** of the finished zither, it appears as the section over which most of the tuning pins are installed at the far left just above the chrome tuners for the fret strings. The whole purpose of this *Luftresonance* is to keep both that section of the tuning block and the adjacent section of the table in a looser, or more resonant form. In this manner, the table and block and the portion of the two braces from the fretboard outward all now vibrate more freely than if the entire length of the tuning block were completely glued to the bottom panel. This design innovation was invented around 1900 and gave the zither greater loudness and fuller tone from its fret strings.

But what about the little holes drilled into the tuning pin block at top and bottom ends in **Photos 6 and 7**? They are a way to

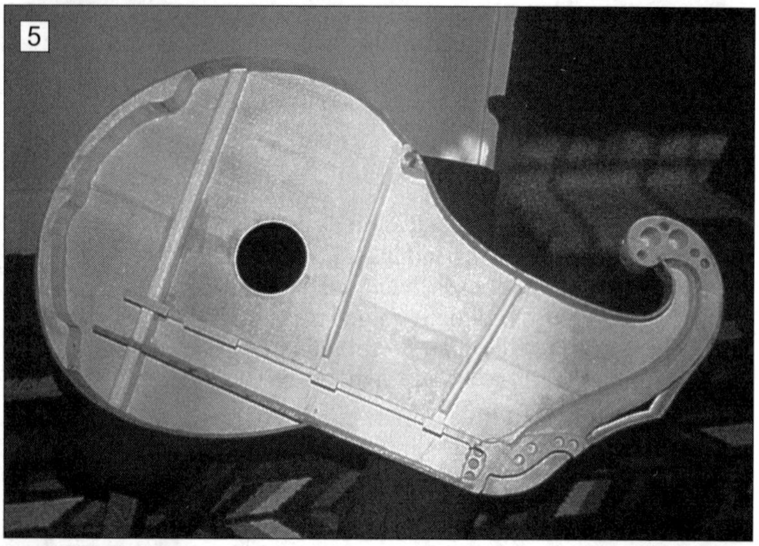

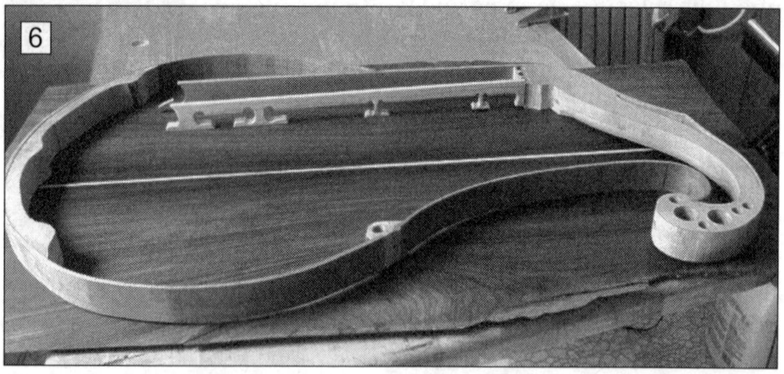

These interior shots of the Arion II zither show the spruce fretboard bridge and its feet in relation to the top braces. Also note the contoured cutaway on the left end block which, when the back is in place, forms a sort of tunnel leading to the "air resonance" hole behind the tuning pins. The recess at the player's end of the left end block will be fitted with standard steel string guitar tuners to avoid the need for a specialized German five-in-one tuning mechanism.

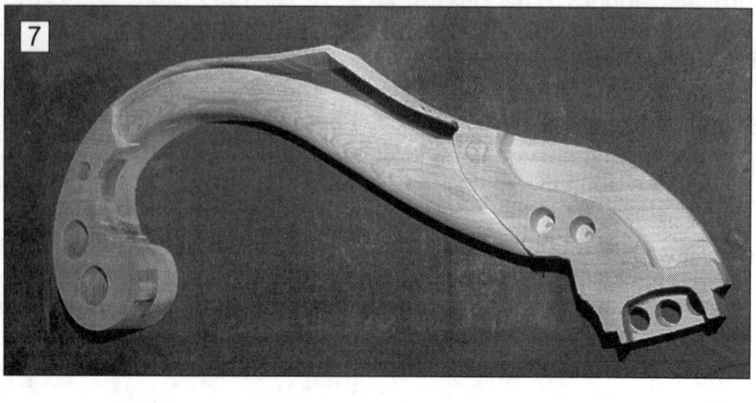

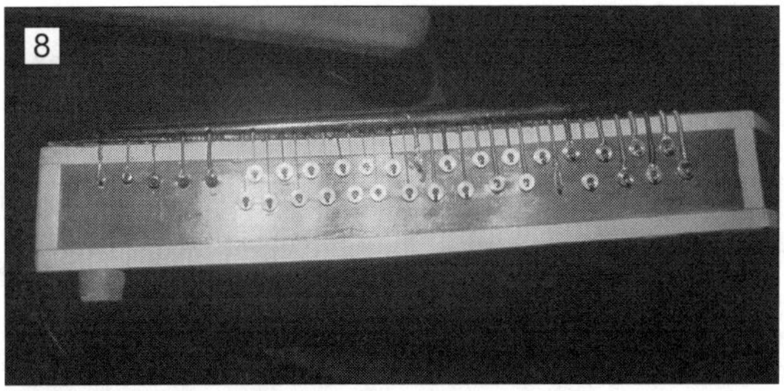

lighten the overall beechwood mass by removing wood. The lighter mass now will resonate more freely along with the rest of the ribs, table, bracing, and overall soundbox and thus add greater brightness to both fretted- and open-string tones. Having stated all of this, the plan and design in **Photos 4 and 5** should make more sense.

In those two photos you will also see the large hard maple crescent-shaped piece that lines the inside of the huge curved end. This maple piece gives extra strength and is the base on which the steel and aluminum tailpiece is bolted, as seen in **Photo 3**. A fully tuned zither exerts over 900 lbs. of tension from bridge to bridge. In the plan the strings are anchored at the hitch pins, and are made of hard steel music wire sections (closeup in **Photo 8**) at the right-hand end block. That is the modern conventional design that won out while the old Arion or Mittenwald rounded-box-and-tailpiece design died out around World War One.

Tuning Machines

Photos 9 and 10 show the top and inside of a typical German-built tuning machine or *Mechanik*. When one of those gears jams, all five strings must be loosened and the entire plate unscrewed from the tuning block as shown. My design, however, uses five Gotoh minis installed from the bottom in **Photo 11**. If one machine malfunctions, only one string has to be disturbed.

This design, also shown in the plan and on its underside in **Photo 5**, incorporates a series of holes and three little holes directly under the beginning of the fretboard. Once again, the holes lighten the wood mass and permit the fretboard greater resonance freedom. Look again at **Photo 9** and notice that the routed channel or well in the German tuning block also lightens that section but from the top instead. The channel ends at the starting end of the fretboard, thus giving the fretted section the same resonance freedom.

I have gone one step further by shifting the design of the tuning block farther to the left of the fretboard (see **Photo 3**). The serpentine bridge, the tuning pins, and the tuning gears are all farther to the left in the *Arion II* than they are in the instrument plan. This shift is one further way to give the table, braces, and fretboard greater resonance freedom. Older 19th-century zithers had their open-string bridges and tuning blocks starting immediately at the starting edge of the fretboard. When I played on such an old model, the fretted tones sounded sadly shallower and darker, especially on the wound G and C strings.

Above left: Strings are anchored on pins driven into the right end block. Above: An elegant German Mechanik *or combined tuner. Also note the traditional use of a tall "zero" fret and pins in place of a slotted nut. Below: Guitar tuners can be used if the zither is designed for them.*

Photo 12 is a closeup of the Arion II's left end showing the pins, the serpentine bridge for the open strings, the black lacquered sides, and the harp column. The serpentine bridge is cut from one piece of rosewood, not heat bent. The column defines the "harpzither" design. It is there for strength and is notched into the soundbox at both ends. It is never to be used as a handle for picking up the instrument! I know of no one "right" wood for the column.

Photo 13 shows the unstrung bridge and fretboard from the opposite side. One important point: the left-hand bridge must be somewhat lower than the right-hand bridge-and-handrest assembly where the metal bridge wire lies. This is for all the open strings. In **Photo 14** is the closeup of the cocobolo saddle and bridge surface for both fret and open strings as well as the unpainted tailpiece assembly. One small steel pin is shown in the tailpiece to illustrate how each string loop or eyelet is secured. The saddle is drilled with holes for each string. An alternate design uses slots cut down into the top surface with a string lying in each slot.

Fret Strings and Action

Looking at the fretboard, the bottom two strings are tuned open to middle concert a and are steel with a diameter of .016″ to .018″. The center string is tuned to middle d and is usually solid bronze. It could also be wound bronze over steel, or solid steel, and would usually have a diameter of .020″ up to .028″. The 4th string is tuned to open bass G and is a steel string with nickel or bronze winding. German-made sets can even use a steel core covered with nylon floss and then wound with a very small diameter winding to cut down on string squeak, as in the lines of "Bergfee" (Maxima) or Pyramid. German strings are about .034″ but I have used strings up to .038″. The top string is tuned to open bass C in similar wound materials with diameters from .044″ to .048″. All strings are tuned to concert pitch.

The steel a strings clear fret 5 at .042″ and at the final fret 29 at .100″ inside clearance. The d string clears fret 5 at .042″ and fret 29 at .075″. The G is .042″ at fret 5 and .075″ at fret 29. The C string is .044″ at fret 5 and .082″ at fret 29.

The unusual profiling of the fretboard wood is a key factor. The board is planed slightly thinner from left to right and on a diagonal from the lower left corner to the upper corner at the right end. This proportion can be stated at the right end, upper corner as being about 63% of the height at the left side and the lower right-hand corner as being 70% of the left side's height. The surface of the wood is flat and not rounded as on a guitar fretboard. While I used old-style nickel bar stock for my frets, standard or high guitar frets can be used provided that the right-hand bridge is chiseled lower to keep the string action low. Traditional German zither frets are of very high, narrow, nickel-alloy stock.

In the old days, zithers were custom measured for the person's hand size. Larger hands meant wider string spacings, fretboard, and a wider soundbox. My hands are small but I measured my spacings as follows: spread the right hand over the plan just on top of the right-hand handrest or saddle so that all fingers are spread out and the middle finger points to the left and is parallel to the fret strings. The lower tip of the thumbnail should touch the 1st fret string and the edge of the little fingernail will touch where the open contrabass C string 29 will be placed. Note that open strings are numbered starting with string 1 as the $e^{\flat}$, just above the fretted C string. This string 1 should be about $\frac{1}{2}''$ away from the fretted C string. The fretted strings are not numbered.

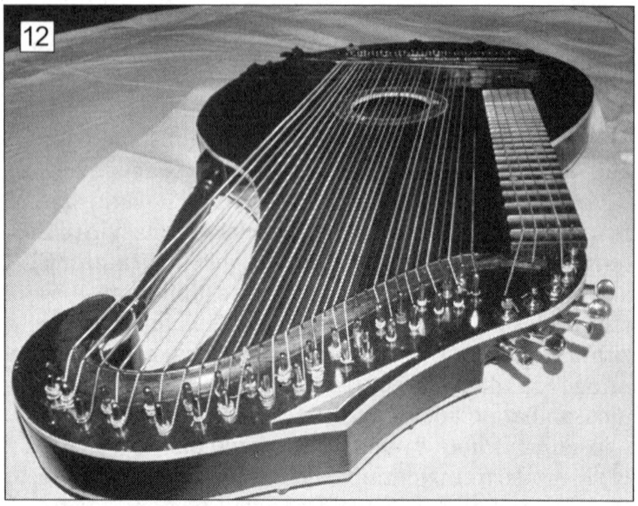

Above: Views of the zither's left end, showing tuning pins, serpentine bridge, and air resonance hole.
Below: Details of the Arion II bridge and tailpiece. While a concert zither does not use a tailpiece, the scheme of the combination bridge and handrest is similar.

Low action is preferred. For the two steel a strings: .036″ clearance at fret 5 up to .10″ clearance at fret 29. For the d string: .042″ at fret 5 and .074″ at fret 29. For the G string: .042″ at fret 5 and .075″ at fret 29. For the C string: .044″ at fret 5 and .082″ at fret 29.

One note of caution: if conventional or high guitar fretwire is used, the wooden bridge surface at the saddle side will have to be chiseled lower to allow the above action clearances.

Open Strings

These strings are set up in two circles of fifths followed at the top by contrabass strings in a descending chromatic scale. **Table 1** shows the standard or "Munich" tuning that is predominant today. There is a lesser-used serpentine tuning called "Vienna," which I can give you on request. It is, however, confusing to most beginners.

Imported German strings by Maxima (Bergfee) and Pyramid are available from the Zither Newsletter in Chicago and from Mr. Leonard Zapf in Philadelphia. I experimented with different types of guitar strings, but cannot find the equivalent that matches the tuning length and sound quality of German strings. There is one so-called "zither" string line made by La Bella, but I tried them with poor and very tinny-sounding results. Even the string positions marked on each envelope did not match the musical pitch of a modern zither.

German open strings run from .034″ to .050″ in strings 1–13, and from .060″ to .070″ in strings 14–32. Lower-tension sets use a nylon floss core with fine bronze winding in the first circle of fifths, and a steel core wrapped with nylon floss and overwound with small-diameter bronze for the second. Higher-tension sets use similar windings, but a steel core and nylon floss in the first circle of fifths, and steel core with silk floss in the second. Contrabass string construction is similar to the second circle of fifths in each case, except that contrabass strings are double wound.

Note that the spacing of the open strings is equal between the strings. The center-to-center distance increases with string gauge.

Closing Thoughts

The concert zithers and harp-style concert zithers have bravely survived in 20th-century America among the few remaining zither clubs, soloists, and collectors. In this modern, hi-tech era, there is no real market for them in the USA. Most zitherists own German imports or well-reconditioned older models, often from the old shop of Franz Schwarzer. Although he died in 1904, his shop in Washington, Missouri held on until the last worker closed it in the 1950s. Some models were built in the 1920s and 1930s by Tony Godetz. In the 1960s and 1970s Rudy Wacek built a handful of hollow-body electric zithers with built-in magnetic pickups under the strings.

My large, 37″×20″×2.75″ *Arion II* model is a throwback to the old early-19th-century Bavarian or Mittenwald design concept of an almost symmetrical pear-shaped box with a tailpiece. Its loudness and tone quality are as good as any modern German model. Today, the modern harpzither is the usual model of choice by the accomplished soloist.

I still hope that there will be a renewed interest in playing zithers in this country. In southern Germany, there was a zither renaissance among the younger folks in the 1980s, much to the instrument's benefit! In the USA, Alissa Pesavento of Fredonia, Pennsylvania, recently wrote a massive, well-illustrated master's thesis on the concert zither in America. Copies of this work are available from her and are a must for the historian. In my own public solo repertoire, when I perform in Columbus, Ohio, I play both German- and old Viennese-cafe-style pieces as well as light classics. ——

Fretted Strings		
1	a′	
2	a′	
3	d	
4	G	
5	C	
Open Strings		
1	e^b	
2	b^b	
3	f	red
4	c	
5	g	
6	d	
7	a	red
8	e	
9	b	
10	$f^\#$	
11	$c^\#$	red
12	$g^\#$	
13	E^b	
14	B^b	
15	F	red
16	C	
17	G	
18	D	
19	A	red
20	E	
21	B	
22	$F^\#$	
23	$C^\#$	red
24	$G^\#$	
Contrabass strings		
25	F	red
26	E	
27	E^b	
28	D	
29	$C^\#$	red
30	C	
31	B	
	(and so on)	

Table 1. *Concert zither tuning chart.*

Concert Zither

GAL Instrument Plan #41

by John Roeder

This instrument plan is available as a full-size blueprint from the GAL.

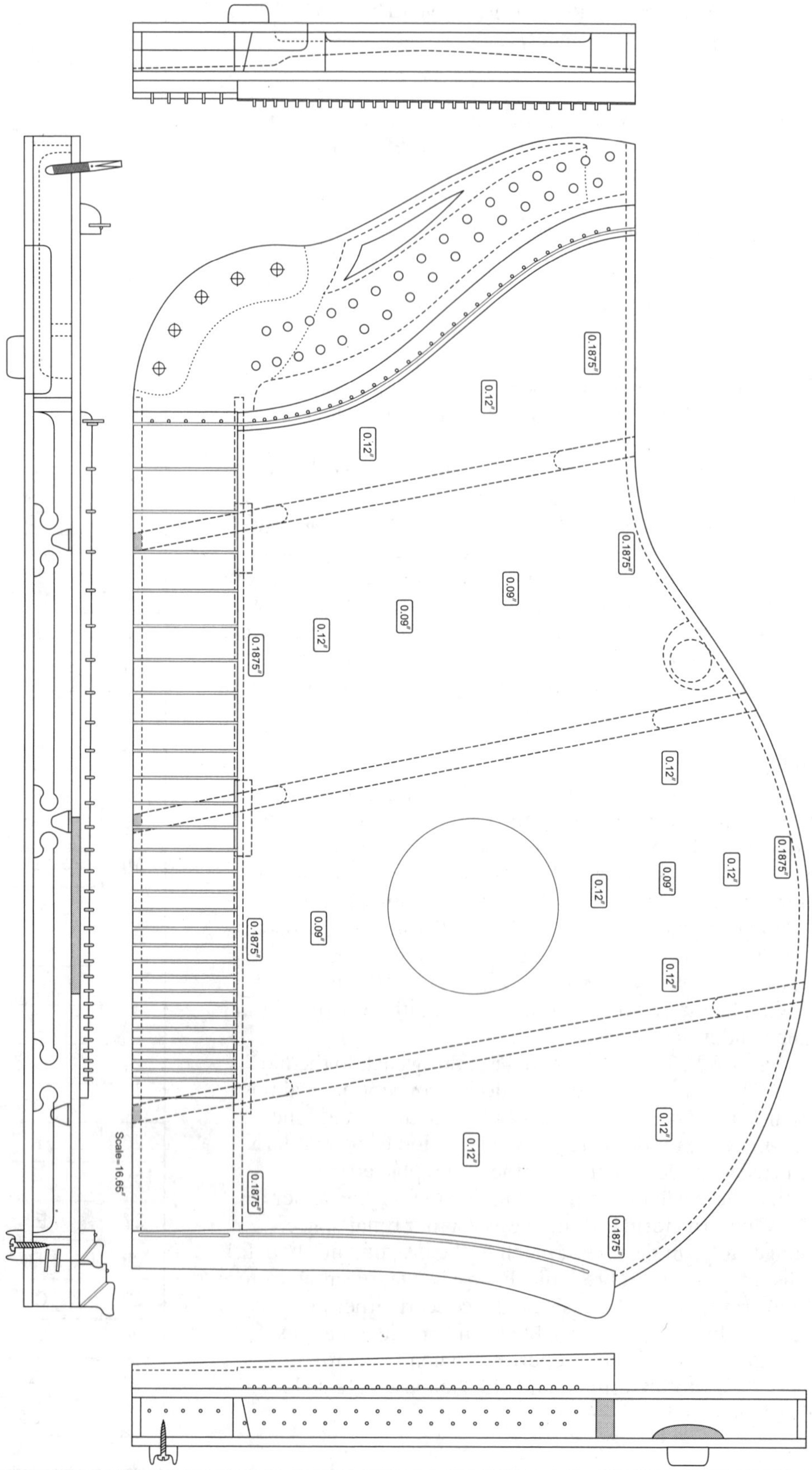

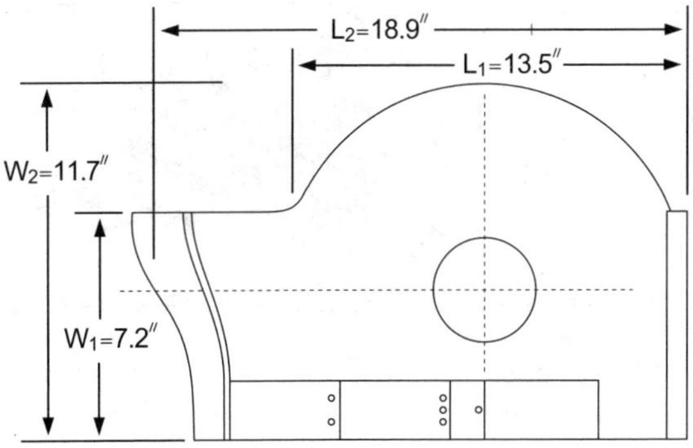

Figure 2. *1860s prime zither*

L_1:L_2=.71	W_2:scale=.75
W_1:W_2=.62	hole:scale=.226
W_2:L_2=.62	scale=15.5″

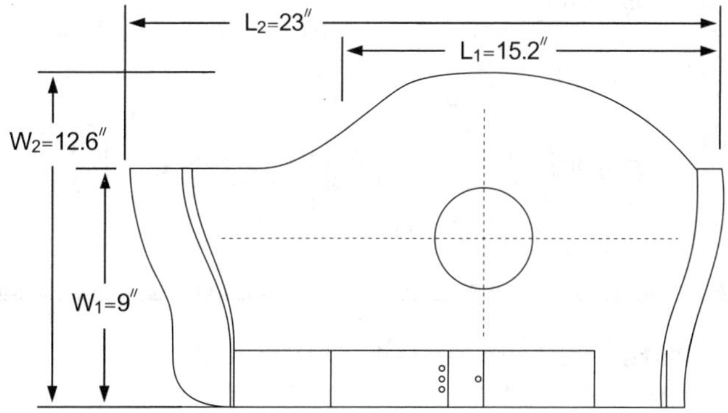

Figure 3. *Modern concert zither*

L_1:L_2=.66	W_2:scale=.75
W_1:W_2=.71	hole:scale=.223
W_2:L_2=.55	scale=16.8″

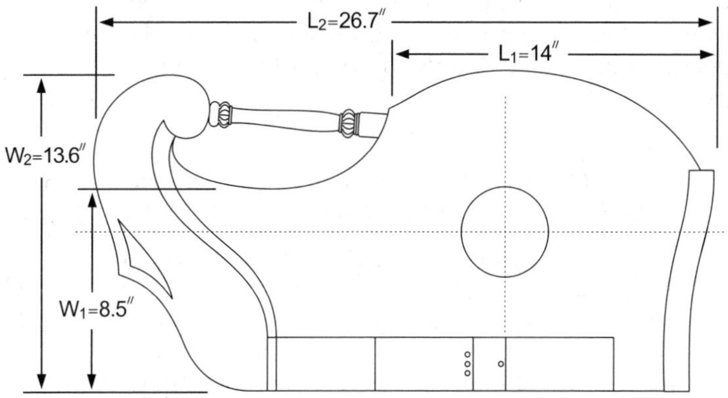

Figure 4. *Modern harp zither*

L_1:L_2=.52	W_2:scale=.79
W_1:W_2=.63	hole:scale=.217
W_2:L_2=.50	scale=17.25″

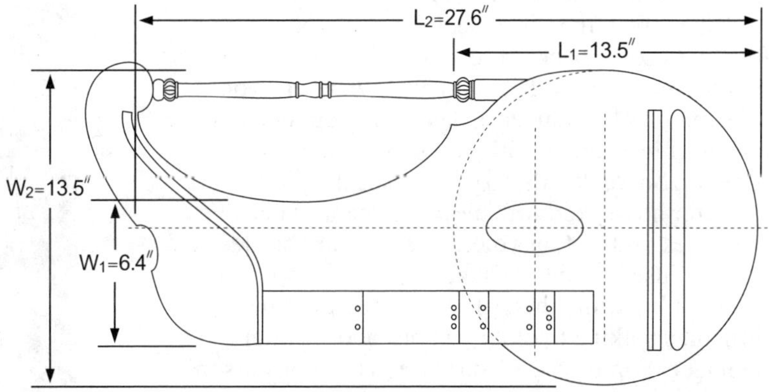

Figure 5. *Mittenwald harp zither*

L_1:L_2=.49	W_2:scale=.79
W_1:W_2=.47	scale=17.1875″
W_2:L_2=.49	

(historical scale was16.75″)

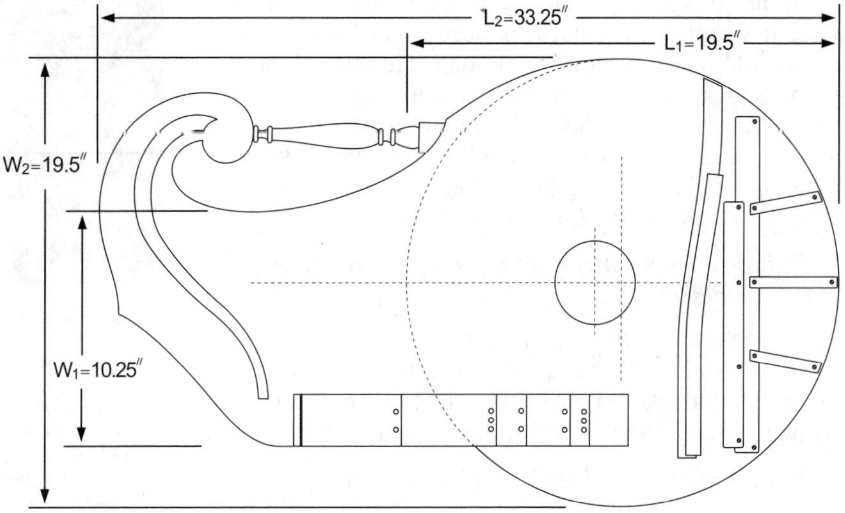

Figure 6. *Arion II zither (author's design)*

L_1:L_2=.59
W_1:W_2=.53
W_2:L_2=.59

Originally published in *American Lutherie #51*, 1997

Meet the Maker: Hermann Hauser III

by Armin Kelly

I SPOKE with Hermann Hauser, III in Amherst, Massachusetts in the summer of 1994 when he and his family were visiting the United States for the first time. To say our common language was English is an exaggeration. A mutual friend kindly helped translate when neither of us was able to quite understand. My deepest thanks go to Cyndy Burton for her valuable assistance.

I wanted to first ask you about your training — formal and informal. How did you learn to make instruments?

I first started guitar making when I was sixteen. My father said, "Hermann, you must go to another workshop to see how to make an instrument." I went to a workshop of one of his friends for about two and a-half years. I was attending a vocational school studying carpentry at that time. After that I attended Mittenwald, the department for string instruments, which includes guitar, lute, violin, and so on.

When my father became ill, he said, "Now it's time for you to come back." I returned home on weekends to practise in the workshop with my father. He would say, "Hermann, what you learn there is not enough to make a Hauser instrument. It's necessary that we work together on weekends, so you can see the difference."

After he worked with me some years he became more sick and lost his voice. It was a very hard time for me, because I was very young and I had to speak for my father. I knew the things I spoke about, but it was difficult speaking to older persons about guitars — a teenager. Some people don't accept a young person's knowledge.

In the last years I said to my father, "You worked so much in your life, maybe it's not necessary now, because you are ill." He kept working, though. He showed me all the things to do, wrote them down on paper so we could communicate. Then a short illness came and he couldn't see well enough. He died in 1988, so I make the shop alone. My grandfather died in 1952, October. Since I was born in 1958, I never knew him.

Did you continue in the same tradition as your father and grandfather?

My ideas are in the tradition. I think maybe a person who starts fresh has it much easier, because he can do what he likes. I have always had the tradition in my head. So maybe in some things I'm not so free.

Did your father work alone or with assistants?

One. He has been with the Hausers for over thirty years, a long, long time. His name is Hasie (Franz Hasenfratz) and he is also a very nice person. He is not only an assistant; he helped me in hard times, not only as a worker and friend. He's like a surrogate father. Recently he broke his leg, so he is not working with me right now.

When Hasie was helping, what kind of work would he be doing?

He doesn't make the tops or any construction on the body. He does finish and fingerboard work.

My older brother Eric also works some with me. (He also attended Mittenwald and won a gold medal in guitar making.) He works with me when he has free time. Normally he works for BMW in their carpet department. He comes and helps me out a little bit

ALL BY DAVID RIGGS EXCEPT AS NOTED

Hermann III with his mother in their parlor/reception room/family museum in their home in Reisbach. The Hauser's collection includes guitars by all three Hausers, Torres, Stauffer, and lots of other fine instruments, mostly by German and Austrian builders.

Facing page: HHIII holding a partially completed HHI guitar. The body had a couple cracks, the head was never put on, and it's been hanging around since the family moved to Reisbach from Munich just after WWII. The Munich house got bombed and was roofless. Hermann Hauser Sr. built the Reisbach house, where this picture was taken.

with finishing, because time is short; I have only two hands and sometimes I need six.

What kind of finish do you use?

The standard is to French polish the top and use nitrocellulose lacquer on the rest. Nitro has improved a lot since the '60s. It used to be too hard and it always cracked. I like it better than shellac in some ways. It needs not so much time to dry as French polish. You can sand it two or three days after spraying it. It saves money. The price of a high-quality classical guitar is so high, and shellac (French polishing) makes it higher. We have found that shellac is not better than lacquer for sound, but some players like it better — some like the feel of it. It's hard to explain the difference. If you have to compromise, making the top shellac and the body nitrocellulose is good. Maybe it's old thinking that a classical guitar of high quality must be shellac. It is not so bad to think about new things. For example, instrument makers have problems getting Rio (Brazilian) rosewood. So it's necessary to try alternative woods.

Let's talk about woods for a minute. Do you have a plentiful supply of what you need?

I have a lot of wood in stock. Some tops are between eighteen and a hundred years old, and Indian and Rio rosewood sixty years old. I also have cocobolo and some bubinga.

Have you made any guitars of cedar or Sitka spruce?

Yes, cedar when I have an order for it. I don't like Sitka. For the sound of the guitar I prefer spruce from the Bavarian Mountains or the Alps. And I like Indian rosewood very much, although the future may show the same scarcity with Indian as we have now with Rio. I have very old wood from my grandfather and father.

As you use this wood are you purchasing wood for future generations?

It's necessary to take wood now to replace what I use so I can hand it to my children who may like to make instruments one day.

Did your father teach you about what to look for in trees?

Yes. We often went to the forest on weekends when I was a boy. He taught me to look at the kind of tree, what conditions a tree must have, and its age. I found it very interesting. I now take my children in the forest, in the Alps and Bavarian Mountains. In the summer when it is not so cold we look for mushrooms, for eating. And we look for trees, too. It's very hard to find the right tree.

Is there a problem with acid rain?

Yes. The quality of the wood is not the same. I can say this because I have the old wood and I see the difference in the new woods. If you find a good tree, you must cut it in the winter time, and it's very difficult.

And it must be treated right or it will turn blue inside, which will ruin it.

Have you ever tried African blackwood?

Do you mean for fingerboards?

No, for the box.

No.

What about maple?

I have a lot of maple. Of course maple has been used traditionally for lutes and violins. But sometimes the white wood doesn't look so pretty. Maple guitars have a brilliant treble, a warm go-to-the-heart sound. Maybe it's not so bad as people think. For Spanish music it may need a little bit harder sound like Indian rosewood produces. You can experiment with it; make it thicker and get the same quality of sound as rosewood. But people don't accept it.

Because of the color or the sound?

More the color, I think.

The dream guitar you showed me last night was Brazilian rosewood with maple in the center of the back. Could you tell me more about that?

I wanted to make a point to guitarists about the scarcity of Brazilian rosewood, the destruction in the rainforests. The Brazilian pieces are no longer big enough to make two-piece backs. Also a guitar made with Rio rosewood has a very hard sound in the treble, much harder than one made with Indian rosewood. If you don't like it so hard, the combination with the maple can cut the top off the hardness.

In other words, you're blending the sound by introducing another wood; you're shaping the quality of sound that comes out of the instrument. You've done this with Brazilian and maple, have you tried mixing other woods?

Yes. This is a very good idea to make experiments to find out the characteristics of sound. Maybe this is a way we can look to the future more than now.

What other kinds of experiments have you been doing on your instruments? Have you tried different box sizes and depths?

Yes, it is necessary. I very often think about instruments in a new way. I'm not a man who is saying, "This is tradition. Only this is good." I already know the results of the many experiments my grandfather and father did. I know what they tested so it's easier for me to make a special line of testing. If my grandfather tried something and found it not very good, it is not necessary for me to make the same experiment again.

Do you make more than one instrument at a time?

I work in a period of a year. It can be that I make eight instruments one year and fifteen the next. It is not always the same. My father and grandfather worked in the same style.

Do you have any idea how many guitars your father and grandfather made?

In a life a guitar maker can make without an assistant maybe 500 or 600 or as many as 800. My grandfather made also zithers, Vienna construction guitars, violins, and viola d'amores. He didn't number his instruments, but I know he must have made 150–200 classical guitars. My father kept numbers. He started with the number 500 and ended with about 1150.

Can you tell us more about your process?

First I select the wood for ten or fifteen instruments. Then I make the bodies and begin the finishing. Finishing takes a lot of time, so I may not finish the instrument the same year. Sometimes a body is glued two years before it is finished. A new instrument ready to be sold can have a label that is three years old.

Is that the case with the guitar you showed me for Julian Bream?

This is meant as a test model for Julian. I have also made a second one. I will show him the first when it is finished, and find out if it is good or not. The instrument with the experiment I do not sell. I keep it for myself to see how it changes over time. How stable is the top? How do the neck and back change? It is necessary to control an instrument a minimum of five or six years after an experiment. An experiment needs time. Some people may think an experiment is for the moment. You test the model and say, "OK, this model is good," and make it every year, always this one. You have no control instrument.

So you have a collection of some of your experimental instruments?

Yes, but I have sold some if they pass the test of time. For example, #12 in 1978 I sold because I have seen that the construction is good, the result was good. I sold it because I know the quality is perfect, so I can put my name in it and say to the guitarist, "This is a guitar I built and I stand behind it with my name."

You mentioned last night that you have a collection of your father's and grandfather's instruments. That means you can compare them all. That sounds like a great resource.

I can see how my father's and grandfather's guitars developed. It is very interesting for me to see where they changed construction a little bit.

Do you use different scale lengths and body sizes?

Yes. If a guitarist has long fingers he needs a bigger measurement, and a smaller person may need a smaller measurement. The anatomy of people is different so the instrument must be different. But you must not lose sound quality if you make different sizes and different bodies. My standard model is the Segovia Model with a 65cm scale, although I will make scales as short as 63cm or as long as 66cm. An instrument is always a compromise. I tell the guitarist the same thing. It has to do with ease of play, string height off the fingerboard and off the top, and so on. The compromise starts with the

GAL member David Riggs (left) was in the U.S. Army stationed in Germany for a time in the mid-1990s. While there he visited the Hausers. Here he and Hermann III heft a Brazilian rosewood log that Hermann Sr. bought in the '30s. They've never milled it because it's kind of small, and they've got lots. The big bandsaw came from Hermann I's shop in Munich. David says HHIII's hobby is target shooting with fancy tournament air rifles, and that he is a crack shot.

wood selection. You must find for example the top and back which will be the perfect compromise. (You must make a lot of experiments and think before you select the wood.) The better the compromise, the better the instrument after finishing.

For me the separation of voices is important. Even very good guitarists cannot always hear the clarity, cannot always hear the difference. I am very happy to work with people who give me inspiration, for example Julian Bream and the Romero family. I also build for longevity. It's a tradition of the instruments made by our family to last. Guitars built in 1915 or 1920 can still be played without a problem.

Do you have one ideal sound that you're looking for?

This may be a thing which one is always changing. It may be best if a guitarist doesn't know exactly what he (or she) likes. Then the best compromise is the standard Segovia Model.

Is it like the '37 Segovia Hauser at the Metropolitan Museum of Art?

There are small differences; it's not exactly the same.

Do you find a smaller-bodied instrument sounds smaller or projects better?

It's only thinking in the head of the guitarist. A smaller body can have as much sound as a bigger one. The treble strings for example are much better with a smaller body. The best is a good compromise. You must find a balance between a big one and a small one for each person.

Body depth is also very important. You need to understand the effects of deeper and shallower boxes. To explain this would take a long, long time. The best is the compromise.

We've talked a bit about your dream guitar, but I'm wondering what are your dreams for guitar making in general? Are there instruments you want to make?

I'm always looking to find a new way but without forgetting the tradition of 200 years, maybe longer. You always have one note which is not so clear, not so perfect on an instrument. One is C and another is C#, for example. One wants a balanced fingerboard. My dream is to make an instrument one day that has no bad sounding notes.

Sometimes I'll make an instrument I'm very pleased with, but it's very hard to make another just like it. You must remember that wood is a living thing, so not every part is the same. I made twin instruments one time — same rosewood, same top wood (made from sister cuts which I alternated). It's very hard to make two instruments exactly alike even then. If you are experienced enough you know what you are doing, and you will get the result you like. If I experiment, sometimes the result can be a surprise.

I understand zithers are very popular in Germany. Do you make these also?

Sometimes. They are very popular in Bavaria, Austria, and Switzerland. Now there's interest in Japan and in the United States. My great grandfather wrote zither music and my father and grandfather also made them. My grandfather bought a zither firm which was founded in 1835.

What do you see for the future of the classical guitar?

At the moment it's in a small hole, but I think the guitar will have a renaissance. I think it will become more popular again. I think that Julian Bream and the Romeros will push the guitar up again after Segovia.

It is necessary to be sure that the typical characteristic sound of the classical guitar does not get lost. For example the zither has lost its typical character and sounds like a cembalo or spinet now. The electric guitar is a special guitar for special music and has nothing to do with classical concert guitars, because the sound is very different.

Is there anything you would like to tell the readers of American Lutherie? *Any ideas or thoughts you'd like to share that I haven't asked you about?*

Yes. I feel a person who makes instruments must go his own way. He must find the product he likes for himself and also for the people. If he goes his way he will have success. If he only makes copies, he will not arrive at this point. You have to have the courage to discover your own way. ——

BOTH THIS PAGE BY ARMIN KELLY

Top: Philip de Fremery, on the left, plays a Hauser III guitar as Hermann looks on expectantly. Philip is a fine guitarist who teaches at several colleges and universities in central Massachusetts.
Bottom: Hermann Hauser III playing his own guitar.

Originally published in *American Lutherie #51*, 1997

Rocky Mountain Tonewood Alternatives

by Don Musser

JOSEPH LOVATO

Don Musser, in regulation logging duds, standing beside a big blue spruce log.

WHILE SEARCHING OUT Engelmann logs for top wood at various New Mexico and Colorado saw mills, I've come across a few other softwood species that have tonewood potential. The trees are two varieties of fir — white fir (*Abies concolor*) and subalpine fir (*Abies lasiocarpa*) and two species of spruce — Colorado blue spruce (*Picea pungens*) and another as yet unidentified (by me) spruce variety.

White fir here in the Rockies can grow as a very large fine-grained tree, 3′–4′ feet at the base. I've been tempted by a few logs that were limb free ("slick" in logger jargon) for the full 33′ length. A standard log is 33′ long, and is commonly cut into two 16′ 6″ lengths for sawing. White fir is a true fir tree. The wood is a little harder and denser than spruce, and it can be very white and even in color.

I have yet to take a chance on a white fir tree. One of the log scalers at a mill here in Colorado tells me that while the color can be flawlessly even and white, the tree can also be very unpredictably discolored with yellow and reddish sections.

Several builders I know have been interested in trying Douglas fir for top wood. I have even sawn up a few sets, but it is a very harsh-feeling wood which splinters and cracks easily. The white fir boards that I've examined don't have that harsh, splintery feel. I think they have possibilities as instrument-grade wood. The way to investigate further would be to look for some clean, quartered planks in the output of a mill that is sawing white fir logs. That way the risks involved in buying a whole log can be avoided.

The second interesting fir tree is the subalpine fir, also known as silver fir and sometimes piss fir. The old mill workers say it has a smell similar to horse urine — hence, piss fir. These trees generally grow in spruce stands and are usually a little smaller than Engelmann, ranging from 2′–2½′ at the butt end.

I have bought a log of subalpine fir and sawn up some top wood. The wood has some unique properties. It can be fine grained and pure white in color and it is the least dense species of softwood that I have run across. A cut top just feels incredibly light in your hands but at the same time, when perfectly quartered, it has an exceptional cross-grain stiffness. I've sold this wood to several builders who felt it would be well suited for flamenco guitars due to the lightness and stiffness.

The most exciting top wood alternative that I've found is the Colorado blue spruce (*Picea pungens*). It grows only in the Rocky Mountain range and can be found side by side with Engelmann as well as in pure stands. It is also commonly used as a decorative tree because of the attractive bluish tinge to its foliage. The trees can be up to 4′ in diameter at the butt end and can be relatively limb free for the full 33′ length. The wood is superb — straight, even, fine grain with flawless white coloration.

To describe blue spruce more fully, a few comparisons with Engelmann spruce can be made. Firstly, the Engelmann here in Colorado and New Mexico can be nicely colored — even and white — but usually not throughout the whole log. Often the percentage of the top-grade, flawlessly colored wood in an Engelmann tree is very low, less than 5% of the total yield. Most of the tree is unevenly colored by pink and tan streaking. With blue spruce it is much easier to find a log that is relatively free of streaking.

Secondly, the bark on Engelmann trees is very thin. The blue spruce bark is quite a bit thicker. Though I am not a biologist, I suspect the extra bark thickness serves as a buffer to moisture loss by the blue spruce tree and results in a more even growth and grain spacing. This is one of the first things that caught my eye about the blue spruce: on an end cut, the logs generally have a more even grain spacing than Engelmann.

Also, the medullary-ray structure in blue spruce tends to be consistent and frequently strongly defined. With Engelmann, I've processed quite a few logs that have weak or even no medullary rays. The same thing holds true for late growth (winter growth) definition. The blue spruce seems to have consistently better-defined winter growth than does the Engelmann spruce tree.

The one negative to blue spruce is that occasionally it will appear to be fairly limb free and yet when it is cut up you will find a lot of fine little branches that show up as pin knots. There must be something about the local environment of individual trees that elicits the growth of those fine little branches. When a blue spruce does show pin knots, the yield is diminished quite a bit. Engelmann does not typically have as many of those fine branches.

I have built several guitars with the blue spruce including two classicals and four steel strings, and I am totally pleased with the results. The instruments are responsive to a light touch and yet do not fall short when played aggressively. The cosmetics are excellent: even white color with strong medullary rays from center joint to the lower bout edge.

There is another spruce tree here in the Rockies that I've been unable to correctly identify. It has characteristics of both Engelmann and blue spruce. The bark is thicker than Engelmann but not as thick as the blue spruce, and its color is very similar to that of an Engelmann tree: sort of a rust-brownish color. The wood itself is also sort of intermediate — it isn't as evenly colored as the blue, but it is not as colorful as Engelmann either. A couple of mill owners, when questioned about one of these trees, have suggested that it may be a hybrid species. Nicholas Von Robison has suggested that it may be another variety of blue spruce. More investigation is required.

The fir trees — white and subalpine fir — will probably never be much more than specialty top woods for a few unique purposes. The unidentified spruce is an excellent versatile tonewood, but the quantity of trees that I've seen is limited. The blue spruce, however, is abundant enough and the quality of the wood is high enough for top-wood purposes that I suspect it will become increasingly in demand as it gains exposure to the instrument-building community. ——

ALL THIS PAGE BY DON MUSSER

Top left and right: End views of the same blue spruce log Don is pictured beside on the facing page. This section of the tree is 16′ long, about 30″ in diameter at the freshly cut narrow end, and about 45″ in diameter at the butt end. Note the thick bark.
Bottom: An unidentified spruce log 30″ in diameter and 8′ long. Don says this wood has characteristics somewhere in-between those of Engelmann and blue spruce. He has been told that it may be a hybrid or a blue-spruce variant.

Originally published in *American Lutherie #51*, 1997

Scale Length and Tone

from his 1995 GAL Convention lecture
by Ralph Novak

WHEN WE CHOOSE the parameters for constructing an instrument on a tonal basis, such as woods, thicknesses, or bracing, for example, we may exercise what I call an intuitive familiarity with the tonal effects of our various choices on the finished instrument. I'd like us all to be able to exercise the same intuitive familiarity with regard to our scale length choices so that we can more precisely model our tonal goal.

One of the fascinating things about this craft is that there is not just one way of doing things. New methods, and even completely revolutionary ideas, are being injected into the craft continually, enhancing its refinement and growth. It is inspiring and stimulating to see a new approach that is also well executed. Results matter.

During today's instrument exhibition, besides checking out some fine work and great design ideas, I took an informal poll to see how different makers thought about scale length. Most builders shared the big picture of what they were looking at when they were building their guitars and how scale length fit into that picture. I got many different answers to my question:

▸ Some said they were looking specifically at *size*. A short scale was appropriate for a small instrument.

▸ Some said they were adhering to *tradition*. The type of instrument they were making had always used that scale.

▸ Some said *tension*, relative to either "feel" when played or structural stress.

▸ Some said *tooling*. They use commercially available jigs or the Ibex Fret Rule.

▸ Some said *tone*. They liked the sound of that scale length with their instrument design.

These are all good reasons to use a particular scale length, and many aspects of your design could take precedence over scale length considerations for your instruments. But if we are building primarily to achieve a particular tonal ideal, then we must consider scale length *first*, and the other parameters must follow. Scale lengths do have distinct harmonic voices, and this aspect of scale length should be of utmost importance to us as builders.

When we build an instrument, we pay critical attention to the components that go into it. We manipulate materials and structure for aesthetics, longevity, strength, and tone. Scale length fits directly into these considerations and may dictate some of the parameters. Scale length comes first because the harmonic content of the final tone produced by the instrument begins with the string. Factors such as structure and materials can only act as "filters" to tone — they can't add anything, they only modify input. Therefore, if the harmonic structure is not present in the string tone, it won't exist in the final tone. Woods, bracing, thickness, pickups, and electronics: these are *controlling* factors. The string is the *originating* factor, and therefore, parameters that control string harmonic output have utmost bearing on tone.

The familiar example might be the "Strat vs. Les Paul" comparison: as stock instruments they have distinctly different voices. We could put the Les Paul pickups in the Strat and vice versa, then take the screws out of the Strat neck and glue it in, and break out the Les Paul neck and screw it back in. *Voilà!* The Strat still maintains much of its clear, cutting quality, although a bit "fatter," and the Les Paul still has a round attack and mushy bass, although "thinner." We've discovered that the pickups and construction can't override the tonal effects of scale length. The upper partials present in the harmonic structure of the longer-scale Strat string tone give it a cutting clarity that distinguish it from the sweet, round, lower partials that dominate the shorter-scale Les Paul string tone.

The tone of an instrument originates with the string, and the primary factor that controls string tone (except for defective strings) is scale length. And since scale length affects tension and structural stresses, it may control other factors of our design, such as dimension and material choices. Therefore, when we get that vision of our ideal tone dancing in our heads, we must

ALL BY ROBERT DESMOND

Ralph Novak, right, explains two of his multiple-scale guitars to Jeremy Moldovan-Trujillo at the 1995 GAL Convention. The solidbody is his own design, and the flattop is a modified Harmony Soveriegn.

begin by selecting the scale length that complements our tonal recipe.

We probably are all familiar with the three basic laws of string vibration, if not exactly, then intuitively. These laws were described by Pythagoras, and set down by the French mathematician Mersenne in 1636.

1) If the mass and tension stay the same and the length is changed, the pitch changes. This change in pitch is proportional to the length. For example, halving the string length doubles the frequency (raises the pitch one octave).

2) If the mass and length stay the same, a change in tension results in a change in pitch proportional to the square root of the tension. For example, four times the tension results in a pitch change of one octave (double the frequency).

3) If the length and tension are constant, the change in pitch is inversely proportional to the square root of the mass of the string. For example, four times the mass results in a pitch change of one octave (half the frequency).

Theory is fine, but we're building guitars. Let's confine ourselves to concrete reality. Certain string gauges (mass) are commonly used, certain tunings (tension) are commonly used, and certain scale lengths are practical and common.

I'd like to share my way of understanding how string tension, string gauge, and string length relate to each other. In **Fig. 1**, scale length becomes the fulcrum of a balance between string gauge (mass) and string tension (tuning). If we move toward the left — shorter scale length — to keep the gauge in balance with the tension, we must increase the gauge or decrease the tension. The opposite is true if we increase the scale length. Given the technology of string making and the availability of commonly gauged string sets, we really don't have a very wide range of choices for a given scale length and tuning, so it is relatively easy to develop an intuitive familiarity with the harmonic voices of different scale lengths for the particular instruments we make.

An example of how we can use this relationship in practical terms might be the case of a guitarist who likes to use the dropped-D tuning, where the low E string is lowered in pitch one whole step. If the player is using a Martin D-18 with light gauge strings, he may possibly get an acceptable tone from the slackened .054 gauge string. The experienced player knows that a bit heavier string sounds better when tuned down this way. The increased tension of the heavier string improves brightness and definition, and the increased mass improves volume. So, the player reasons, if the .058 sounds good, how about a .065? Here's where we cross the line: the stiffness of a .065 string at the D-18 scale length is too great. The string can't divide up into enough harmonic nodes to render a pleasing tone, or a precise, sustained pitch. Yet, that same string on a 34″ scale bass sounds great. One of the laws of string vibration relates to stiffness: stiffness implies a certain limit to the number of divisions a vibrating string can accommodate.

At this point, I'd like us to turn our attention to solidbody electric guitars, although this may stimulate an allergic reaction in some of you. The solidbody electric guitar is a nearly ideal tool to examine scale-length tone, because it can display dramatically the tonal effects of different scale lengths. Its solid construction introduces fewer resonances to color the tone. Also, it doesn't dissipate energy from the string as quickly as a diaphragm, so the voice of the string is clearer and more sustained. Modern electric guitar players and builders generally recognize two commonly used scale lengths: the "Gibson" scale, at 24⅝″ (not 24¾″) and the "Fender" scale at 25½″. Interestingly, Fender used the scale that Epiphone used at the time for most of its models. Archtop players began to demand instruments with more power and top end to cut through the band when playing ensemble, and this led the Epiphone company to adopt the longer scale. Gibson actually makes instruments with several different scale lengths, some of their archtop models also having a 25½″ scale length. Most solidbody players, however, will know the 24⅝″ scale length because Gibson uses it for almost all of their solidbody line. There is an emerging awareness of the subtle differences in a third scale length, the 25″ scale, as used by Danelectro (Silvertone) and Paul Reed Smith, among others. Players seem to recognize it as a distinctive tone, not a compromise between "Gibson" and "Fender."

The following spectrum-analyses charts were made with a monochord. This solidbody instrument has a single string, a fixed bridge with a piezo transducer under the saddle, and a moveable nut. Further, I made a mechanical picker to consistently pluck the string, as altering picking intensity alters harmonic content. It was also adjustable to pluck at a determined fraction of the string length for each scale length.

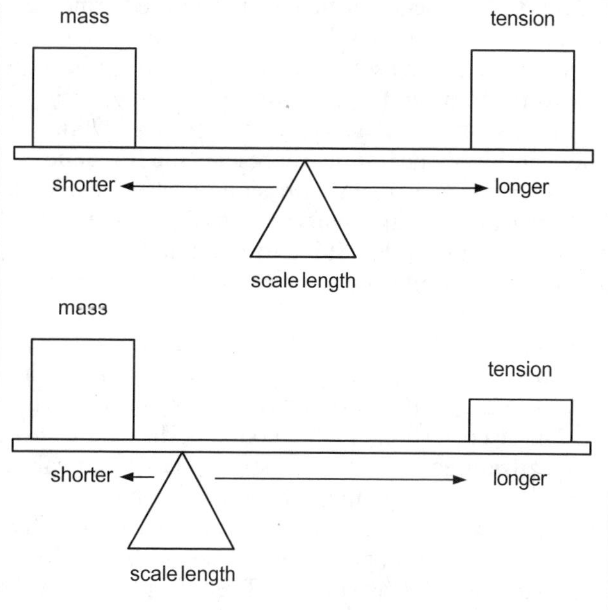

Figure 1. *The dynamic relationship of string mass, tension, and scale length.*

Principal to these tests was Bill Bartolini, who put considerable time and energy into this project. Most of you know Bill's great guitar and bass pickups, but few of you know of his passion for guitar making or his extensive research into classical guitar construction.

"Experimental Studies of the Acoustics of Classic and Flamenco Guitars," by W. Bartolini and P.A. Bartolini, published in the *Journal of Guitar Acoustics*, is a landmark work and I recommend it as required reading. Bill's interest in all aspects of guitar design is what allowed me to tempt him with this project, coinciding neatly with his acquisition of some new computerized test equipment.

A program that analyses the harmonic content of a tone over a specified time period captures a sample and "transforms" the sound into a spectral analysis of the harmonic components and their relative intensity. The graphic output is called a Fourier transform, and is *not* a waveform such as you might see with an oscilloscope. This is not attack, sustain, and decay. It is a graphic analysis of the harmonic content of a tone with the "spikes" representing the most intense frequencies. Attack, sustain, and decay do figure in some aspects of scale length tone, but we're focusing on harmonic content.

I don't mean to imply that this is the final word on the subject. While we did everything possible to maintain consistency and accuracy, these are only results that we got under these conditions and with this equipment. I do, however, believe that the general conclusions obtained by these tests are reasonably accurate and give us some guidelines that we can use.

In addition, before I show you the first transform, I must invoke Helmholtz, who tells us that no two sounds of different quality can correspond to the same mode of vibration; many different modes of vibration can give rise to a sound of only one quality. What this means relative to our spectrum analysis is that the harmonic content and magnitudes that comprise a tone are unique to that tone. It can't sound the same and look different, or look the same and sound different.

Fig. 2 shows a .010 gauge high E string at 330Hz. The scale along the bottom represents the frequencies from 0KHz–5KHz, with each division representing 500Hz. The vertical scale represents magnitude, or intensity, measured in millivolts. It is sort of an arbitrary number for our purposes, but it gives us a good relative comparison.

Observe that there are peaks of intensity (spikes) that correspond to the frequencies 330Hz, 660Hz, 990Hz, and 1320Hz, and at a lower intensity, 1650Hz, 1980Hz, etc. These correspond to the "textbook" harmonic series attributed to a vibrating string. The first peak, at 330Hz, is the fundamental. Then, the first partial (or harmonic) which is the second peak at 660Hz. Here the string is "dividing" in half — one node in the middle — and sounding an octave higher. The second harmonic is the third peak, at 990Hz, which shows the string "dividing" into thirds — two nodes — and sounding an octave and a fifth above the fundamental. The third harmonic is the fourth peak, at 1320Hz, with three nodes, and sounding two octaves above the fundamental (four times the frequency). We can continue, but I think we're all up to speed on this.

Did someone say textbook? While we're in an academic frame of mind, let's recall some of the principles of the vibrating string and see how they apply to our transform. One point we've mentioned already is that the louder intensity harmonics contribute more of their voice to the tone. Relative to this, it is also generally accepted that harmonics with an intensity of less than about 20% of the magnitude of the harmonic of greatest intensity contribute insignificantly to the tone. I'd like to extrapolate this to point out that *absence* of harmonic frequencies can also significantly color tone.

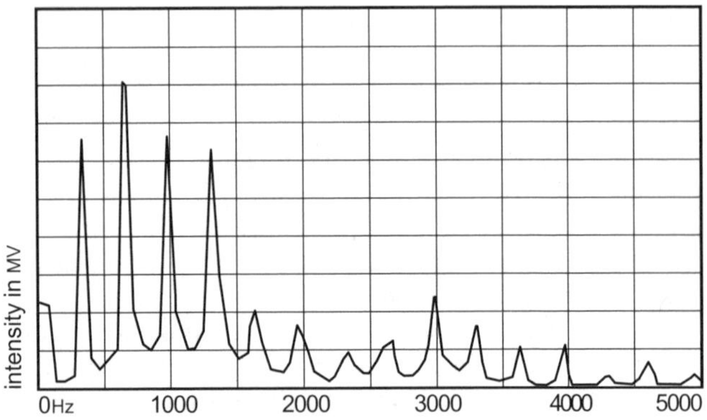

Figure 2. *$24\frac{5}{8}''$ scale .010 string at 330Hz*

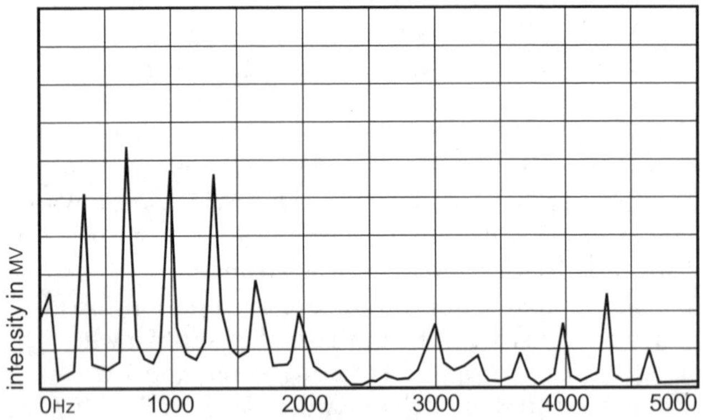

Figure 3. *$25\frac{1}{2}''$ scale .010 string at 330Hz*

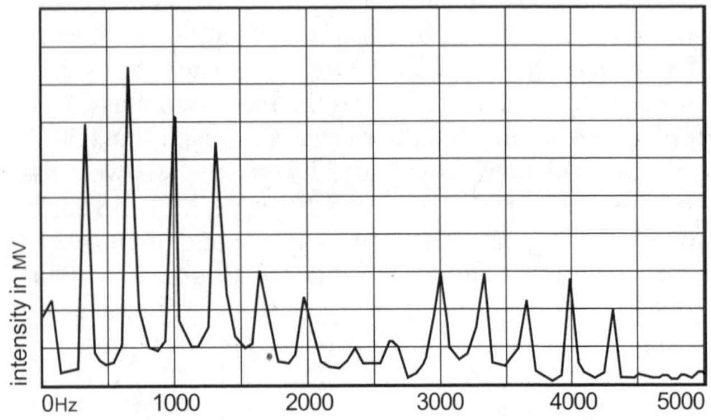

Figure 4. *$25''$ scale .010 string at 330Hz*

In addition, a plucked string differs significantly from a struck string. A struck string favors formation of higher partials because all partials have (in an ideal model) a potential for the same intensity. The plucked string, however, favors partials inversely to the square of their ordinal number: the fundamental has a potential of 1, the octave has a potential of ¼, the second harmonic has a potential of 1/9, etc. While these facts contrast a piano string versus a guitar string, they can be significant for bassists who play certain styles. Percussive string attack is an increasingly common stylistic approach for guitar as well.

Another "law" applying to the formation of harmonics of the vibrating string is that the first six partials are generally agreed to be harmonious. We can add the eighth, tenth, twelfth, fifteenth, and sixteenth without impairing the consonance of the tone. Due to natural string division, the seventh, eleventh, thirteenth, and fourteenth are discordant. They are mathematical multiples, but they do not belong to the musical scale; therefore they impair the consonance of the tone.

One final point concerning the plucked string is that the picking point can suppress the formation of harmonics. Guitarists avail themselves of this principle all the time. Strumming or picking closer to the bridge suppresses the lower partials and makes the tone brighter. Strumming or picking closer to the neck suppresses the higher partials and sounds fuller and warmer. The picking point in these tests was carefully controlled to be at an exact fraction of the string length, rather than a consistent distance from the bridge.

Now, let's view some of these spectrum analyses in greater detail. The first three (**Fig. 2, 3, and 4**) will compare a .010 gauge string tuned to 330Hz, a high E on the guitar, at three common scale lengths. I'll also state for the record that we did literally dozens of tests to ensure that we got consistent results. Let's look at the 25½″ scale (**Fig. 3**). The strongest component, the first four partials, are fairly smooth (up to 1320Hz). The fifth, ninth, and thirteenth contribute significantly, about 30%–40% intensity (that's 1650Hz, 1980Hz, and 4290Hz). Remember that the thirteenth sounds discordant, and note that we see almost no activity at the seventh and eighth, and tenth and eleventh. There's a big "valley" between 2200Hz and 2800Hz — very interesting — an absence of a wide band in the upper midrange.

Let's compare this to the 25″ scale (**Fig 4**). The strongest component, the first four partials, are not very smooth. The first harmonic, the octave, is about 20% stronger than the others. We're also getting a significant contribution from the fifth, ninth, tenth, and twelfth, (1650Hz, 2970Hz, 3300Hz, and 3960Hz), at about 36% intensity, and the sixth, eleventh, and thirteenth are also contributing at about 25%. Note that the eleventh and thirteenth are discordant, and again there is a little activity at the seventh and eighth. This may be explained by the plucking point that I chose: ⅛ of the scale length, approximately where a guitarist would commonly pluck.

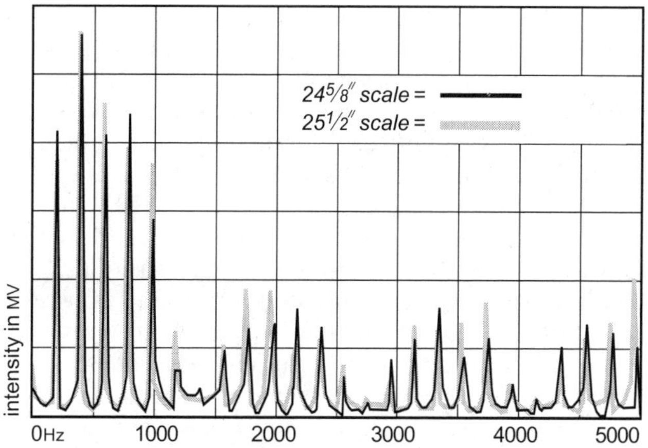

Figure 5. .024 string at 196Hz

If we examine the 24⅝″ scale in **Fig. 2** (⅞″ shorter than the 25½″ scale) we see that the first four partials are also not smooth, rather like the 25″ scale with a strong second (octave) harmonic. We can also see that the higher partials contribute little to the tone, as the fifth is about 25% and the ninth is at about 30%, and all others are insignificant. There isn't much top-end "sizzle" in the shorter scale length.

None of this should be surprising to seasoned builders and players. These tests bear out what our ears tell us. We can conclude that the 25½″ scale offers the "smoothest" harmonic response with good presence of the first six partials (the most harmonious), and a bit of the thirteenth for "character" or "edginess." The 25″ scale has a less smooth harmonic content with a bit more upper mids. It's also fairly strong in the number of discordant partials (eleventh and thirteenth). The 24⅝″ scale has the strongest character in the first four partials, with relatively little above the first four. There is an absence of discordant partials, possibly because the shorter length and decreased tension won't allow the string to divide easily into higher partials.

Fig. 5 shows the spectrum analysis of a wound string, a .024 gauge nickel wound, tuned to G at 196Hz. We'll compare the 24⅝″scale (shown in black) and the 25½″ scale (shown in grey).

Both scales exhibit strong first-octave components, with the fundamental, third, and fourth partials about equal, but only about 60% of the strength of the second partial. The fifth partial (two octaves plus a third), is relatively strong at between 40% and 60% of the octave, and the ninth and tenth partials between 20% and 25% the strength of the octave. There's a "scoop" between 1100Hz and 1700Hz — an absence of upper midrange. Although texts claim that harmonics with less than 20% contribution are tonally insignificant, I find it interesting that there is almost *no* activity at the sixth harmonic, 1372Hz, for the longer 25½″ scale, while the shorter scale shows twice the activity. (Still tonally insignificant?)

The 25½″ scale, represented by the grey line, has a minutely (about 10%) stronger third partial, the fifth partial is about 14% stronger, and the eighth and ninth partials are again about 33% stronger than the 24⅝″ scale, but still only about 25% of the second partial.

The slight increase in upper partial intensity of the 25½″ scale is not as dramatic as we saw with the plain string, but it is evident, with 2, 4, 5, 8, and 9 stronger for 25½″. These tests graphically demonstrate, to some extent, what we intuitively know about scale length and the harmonic voices of the scales.

Something that has me particularly excited is the "clang tone" concept. The clang tone is the result of the *elasticity* of the vibrating string. It is the tone of the string stretching and relaxing as it performs its transverse vibrations, and is referred to as longitudinal vibration.

A taut string actually vibrates in three modes: transverse, which we are most concerned with; longitudinal, which is usually the concern of piano builders, because the struck string has greater potential for excitation of higher harmonics; and torsional, or twisting of the string, which has no musical value, only mathematical value.

Some interesting points about the clang tone:

▸ It is almost completely unaffected by tension! Altering the tuning of the string by changing the tension does not change the clang tone by more than a "comma" over the entire range of tension of the string.

▸ It is minimally affected by mass or weight.

▸ It is primarily affected by length.

Modern guitarists often use percussive techniques, and bassists rely heavily on percussive styles. Acoustically, modern instruments are more sensitive to the subtleties of string vibration, and electronic advances have made electric instruments more accurate reproducers, so the clang tone deserves some examination. Interestingly, piano soundboard construction has been revolutionized by modern technology, making the clang tone accessible to piano builders. Traditional piano construction has been dramatically altered since a 1969 patent outlining deliberate manipulation of string lengths to avoid the inharmonicity of clang tones.

Where does the clang tone "live?" One source states that in a piano it can be found at about three octaves and a fifth to about four octaves and a third above the fundamental. Another source says that it is at least ten times the frequency of the fundamental.

I'd like to demonstrate a clang tone for you. I have a guitar, some rosin, and a rag. First, we'll produce the tone with the string tuned to pitch. I'll rub some rosin on the rag and glide it along the string. *EEEEK!* Sounds like someone learning to play the violin! Now I'll lower the tension of the string and compare the clang tone. *EEEEK!* Sounds the same, doesn't it? Just to be sure, I'll tune it up again. *EEEEK!* That's a horrible sound, but it's amazing that the pitch doesn't change when the string is retensioned.

We can view the clang tone in **Fig. 6** and spare our hearing. This is a .010 string, tuned to E at 330Hz at the 24⅝″ scale (black) and the 25½″ scale (grey). We find the clang for the 24⅝″ scale at 3850Hz, and the clang for the 25½″ scale at 3500Hz. It definitely changes with the scale length. Just to show the consistent relationship, we also tested for the clang tone at the octave (**Fig. 7**). The 24⅝″ scale clang shows clearly at 3850Hz and the octave (12th fret, or 12 5/16″) clang at 7700Hz. The magnitude of the octave clang is, coincidentally, about half the magnitude of the full-scale clang, and a bit stronger than the octaves of the full-scale clang.

The clang-tone concept has me excited because it may explain the comments that players make when they hear a "fanned-fret" guitar compared to a single-scale length guitar. Consistently they say the sound is more "focused," more "alive," and more "in tune." This has been such a consistent response from so many different players that I've been seeking to discover the reason. Perhaps the clang-tone effect is strong enough in the guitar to be a factor. Since the string tension and weight won't affect the clang tone much, single-scale-length guitars have essentially the same clang tone for all strings! My multiple-scale-length guitars ("fanned-frets") have a different clang tone for each string, possibly smoothing out the harmonic "holes" or changing the phase relationships between the actual tuning frequency and the clang frequency, similar to the way piano tone is improved by manipulating clang tones.

To review:

▸ We must consider scale length when we are building to satisfy a tonal parameter. The scale length we choose may dictate certain other parameters of our construction, so we must consider scale length first.

▸ The voice of the scale length will determine the harmonic "input" that the woods and electronics will have available to filter, resulting in the sound of the completed instrument.

Ralph Novak uses a bit of rosined rag to demonstrate the rather unpleasant clang tone of a guitar string.

▸ Since all parts of the instrument interact — act upon the other parts as they themselves are acted upon — we can't quantify the relationship of scale length to the other parameters of instrument construction. We can, however, form an "intuitive familiarity" with how scale length affects the tone of our completed instruments.

▸ The scale-length voice is clearly made up of peaks of harmonic intensity that will vary with the length chosen. Remember that the lack of intensity at particular peaks also colors the voice of a particular scale.

Audience: *I'd like to know if the patterns you showed us were mathematically developed or measured in an actual sound environment.*

Using the monochord I described earlier, we carefully controlled the string tension and length, as well as picking point and pressure. We did dozens of tests, discarding ones that had serious problems, and Bill's watchful analytical eye was always looking for inconsistencies and artifacts. The ones you're seeing here tonight are repeatable and representative of the total samples.

I also have many more questions myself. If this equipment were at my disposal to use at anytime, I'd explore the clang-phase relationships in detail, especially as notes are fretted, and compare the various scale lengths. This may account for Marc Silber's comment to the 1992 GAL Convention that "some scales just don't tune" which from a purely Pythagorean point of view seems improbable, but in practice may point up problematic clang-phase relationships with certain scale lengths.

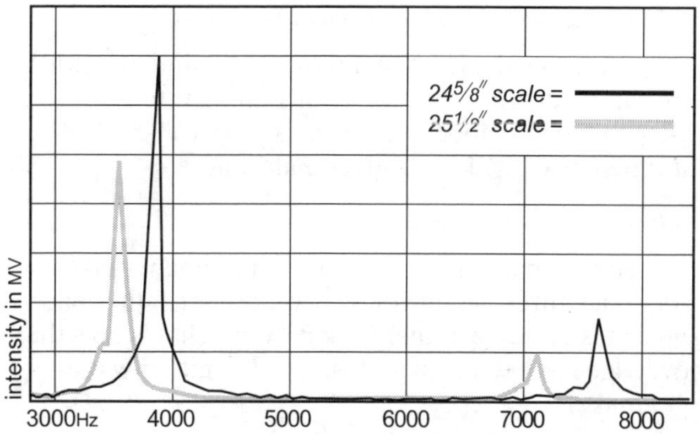

Figure 6. *.010 string at 330Hz*

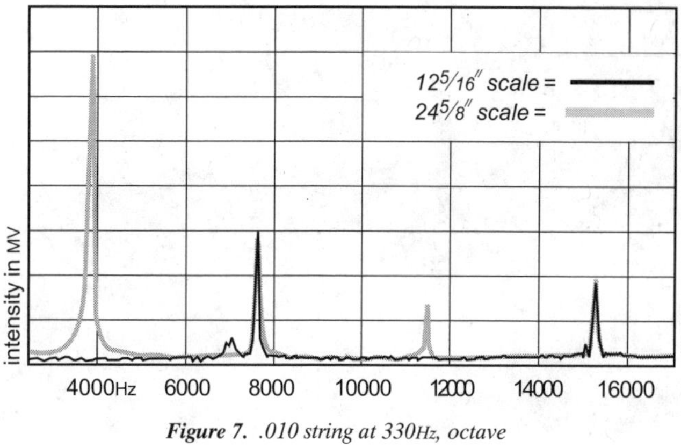

Figure 7. *.010 string at 330Hz, octave*

Does compensation in the individual strings of a single-scale-length guitar introduce clang-phase-relationship problems or beat frequencies? This is another question that needs further investigation.

What is your time frame?

Since this is a spectrum analysis and not a wave form, the sample is limited to a fraction of a second immediately after the pluck, when the harmonics are richest, and the vibrations have stabilized.

Earlier, you produced the clang tone on a string that was already up to tension. How about a slack string?

We can try that right here. The clang tone changes almost imperceptibly with tension, but since we're discussing vibrating strings, we will need a little bit of tension. By the way, from what I've read, the string is most elastic up to 70% of its breaking strength. When that 70% point is exceeded, the string loses elasticity rapidly. There, is that loose enough? *(String sounds "boinnggg." Audience agrees it is loose enough.)* I'll put a bit of rosin on the cloth and... *EEEEK!* Now I'll tune it back up arbitrarily *(string sounds "twanngg"),* and rub it... *EEEEK!* Sound like the same pitch? *(Audience agrees.)* I think we don't want to build a lot of that into our sound!

When you compared the short and long scales, did you try keeping the tension the same and testing both scales?

As we remember from Mersenne, that would result in different pitches, so the harmonic peaks wouldn't align. If we tested at 196Hz and 188Hz, how could we compare the harmonics? Perhaps we could vary the weight of the string to maintain tension at different scale lengths, but that also changes the way the string vibrates because it changes its elasticity, so we'd be comparing apples to oranges.

When you finger a chord, aren't you creating a number of different scale lengths?

Yes, that's exactly what you're doing. You're fingering a chord, which will have its own pattern, based on the contributing tones; the scale length vs. string size vs. tuning relationships for each note of that chord. So, while the concept of scale length may seem nebulous when applied to the complexities of actually playing the guitar, we can see that when broken down to the individual string tone, it is vital in determining that tone, and a particular scale length will color the tone of chords built from notes generated by that scale length.

These graphs can only show us that a relationship exists. The exact parameters for our instruments will vary, but I believe that the general relationships will remain consistent. It is my hope that this information will broaden your understanding of guitar making, will be useful to you immediately, and may help you to achieve something elusive that you've been seeking. ——

Originally published in *American Lutherie #51*, 1997

Meet the Maker: Boaz Elkayam

by Jonathon Peterson

JONATHON PETERSON

ALL COURTESY OF BOAZ ELKAYAM EXCEPT AS NOTED

Top: Boaz at the '96 Healdsburg Guitar Festival. Other views of this guitar with Baroque-style ornamentation can be seen on p. 99. Above: Boaz' bar mitzvah in Jerusalem. He's the kid in the t-shirt. His father, who was also a luthier, is the second from the left. Right: A teenage Boaz working in his father's shop.

BOAZ ELKAYAM wheeled most of Europe and Central and South America on a journey that mixed personal adventure and lutherie before he showed up at the 1996 Healdsburg Guitar Festival where I met him. Here is an amazing story about an amazing guy.

My name is Boaz Elkayam. It's hard to pronounce, I know. I grew up in the north of Israel, just above Galilee.

You said yesterday your family was originally from Spain.

Not exactly. My mother and father are Sephardic. At home they speak Ladino, a very old form of Spanish. Now originally, yeah, their ancestors came from Spain from the time of the Inquisition. The Jews that fled Spain and went along the Mediterranean to the south of Italy, Greece, Turkey, and North Africa — they're Sephardic Jews. They kept the language, the traditions, everything. The other main branch of Judaism is the Ashkenaz Jews. They are more associated with Eastern Europe and Yiddish. For Americans that is a more familiar Jewish tradition.

How long has your family lived in Israel?

My father's side, ten generations. My mother's side is there three generations. Her family immigrated from Turkey to Israel before '48, before Israel was Israel. At that time it was British-occupied Palestine.

How did you become a luthier?

I come from a family of stringed instrument makers. It goes back three generations. My mother's father had the business, and my father took it over. That is how the knowledge has been passed this way. My father was a violin maker.

So you studied instrument building with your father?

I never really studied, you know, just worked with him. I helped him here, helped him there. He was mostly occupied at the time with violins, mandolins, and here and there a balalaika for the Russian immigrants. As a young boy I didn't like violins. I thought that cool guys don't play the violin, and I focused more interest on the guitar. My father was smart enough to tell me that if you want to build a good guitar you should learn how to play it, and that's where it starts. Besides building, I actually put a lot of time and energy into playing and developing technique.

What brought you to the United States?

It's kind of a long story. In 1982 I entered the Israeli military, the same year the Lebanon war started. In 1985 I finished my military responsibility. In 1985 the Lebanon war stopped. I won't tell you it was horrible, because it's part of the system. You just do it, but I knew I needed to relax after that, to pay myself back the time that I gave away. I just wanted to travel, and I did for eight years.

Where did you go?

I left home with a round-trip ticket to Holland, and when I got there I bought a motorcycle. I went to Germany, Denmark, Sweden, Norway, Finland, and then back to Holland. I stayed there for two months, then I went to Italy, Switzerland, Greece, and Turkey. I spent three months in Turkey, then went back to Holland. Then I went through Belgium, France, to the south of Spain, Portugal, and again back to Holland. I went home to visit my family in Israel, and it was already over two years later. I took two months off of traveling to finish a guitar, because I had no money. There were people waiting for my instruments, people crazy enough to wait until I came back home who were willing to pay Boaz' price .

So you had a local reputation before your military service?

Something like that. I was no big shot, but those looking for the real thing knew that I could do it. My father didn't have the energy, especially for a guitar.

When I had made some money I had my motorcycle shipped to Brazil, and I flew to New York City. I spent two weeks in New York, and then went to Carniváll in Brazil. After Carnival I spent a year and a half travelling on my motorcycle in South America. Of course, every place I went I visited guitar stores, luthiers. Most of them are not well known, but I tried to pick up whatever I could. Always I had the interest. It's a disease that you carry with you as a luthier, you know? I believe everyone at this event would know what I mean.

I went to Paraguay, where I spent three weeks in the Chako desert. I visited with a master luthier in Uruguay, then went to Argentina. I went as far south as roads will take you, which is a small village called Oshuwiya in Tierra del Fuego, at the southern tip of South America. Then I turned north and went up the Carratera Ostral, which is a beautiful road that goes the length of Chile, to San Diego de Chile, and to Cusco, Peru for the Fiesta de Sol. It's an ancient Indian holy day, and people come from all over South America. In the old days they probably sacrificed people, but today it's just a big happening. From Peru to Bolivia, Equador, Colombia, and Venezuela, where I sold my motorcycle and went back to New York City. I just had a feeling I wanted to be there.

In New York I had no interest in making guitars or in playing the guitar. I had no interest doing anything but just changing fields, changing atmosphere, doing something different. What happened was that my roommate was also a guy named Boaz. He was quite successful in the makeup industry in New York, and I had studied makeup and hair dressing in Israel. When I arrived, he left. So people would call and I'd pick up the phone and say, "Yeah, I'm Boaz," and I took his job. Actually, I took his reputation and built it up. I had the knowledge. I was a hair dresser and makeup artist there for three years. The shop was called Boaz' Salon, on 8th Avenue, near St. Mark's.

Top of page: Not much shade here. Boaz and his BMW in a Mexican desert.
Above: With friends in an ice cave in Tierra del Fuego.

Then my father died, and that day I flew to Israel. I stayed for a month, as a good Jew — you know, to show respect for the family and the tradition. Then I went back to New York, sold my salon. I bought a new top-of-the-line GS100 BMW Paris-Dakar, and I took my girlfriend to travel Central America for one year. At one point we stopped in Paracho, Mexico, which is a guitar-making center, and I said, "Oh, that's interesting. I'll be back." Then off to Guatemala, El Salvador, Honduras, Nicaragua, Costa Rica, and Panama.

How were you supporting yourself during all of your travels?

The answer is very simple. My tools are in one box. I got orders from Israel, and my mother would send me the tools, the wood, the binding. When I was done I would send it home for finishing and putting in the label. In Holland, I built a couple of guitars. I built guitars in Guatemala, and in Brazil. It didn't matter where. That's how I managed.

In my years of traveling I've learned so much by stopping to visit guitar builders, with an attitude that I don't know anything, with an attitude that this is very exciting, just picking up tips. You have to understand that in Europe it's much more difficult because they're more secretive, in Spain especially. They're afraid that if you build guitars you will take business from them, or something. I don't know what they think. I'm not putting down Spanish luthiers or their guitars. Don't get me wrong. But I think the concept of keeping your methods a secret is self-destructive. You must understand that I come from a family that has done the same thing — no one comes into the workshop, you don't show what you are doing. That doesn't work for me. And that's the beauty of this craft in America. You share the knowledge and you create a better instrument. They keep the knowledge and slowly, slowly they're going downhill. Not downhill, really, but they are staying in the same place while builders over here are moving forward. In Spain today you don't find the Kasha construction of Richard Schneider, you don't find builders like Tom Humphrey and John Gilbert. There are so many I admire here. And look at all of the amazing work at this show!

I am thirsty for knowledge. I arrived in Paracho in Michoacan, Mexico, where you can buy a guitar for $30, and I told them, "I don't know anything and I want to learn." I paid a guy $30 for a guitar, then gave him $200 more and said, "Build me a guitar, and let me watch you." I sat there, and I learned so much. Before that

Top, right: Boaz did the hair and makeup for these models for a show of Harry Winston jewelry in the Waldorf Astoria in New York. Each model is wearing in excess of $1,000,000 worth of jewelry.
Above: Boaz and Richard Schneider at the Luthiers Mercantile open house following the 1996 Healdsburg Guitar Festival.

Above: Repairing a pump organ at the Rainbow Cafe, Antigua, Guatemala. Facing page: A steel string travel guitar with a two-piece bridge (the saddle portion floats on the soundboard). The prototype for this and other Boaz travel guitars was built on a table at the Rainbow Cafe in Antigua, Guatemala, using only a Swiss Army knife, just for fun and to prove it could be done. The interest it generated led to so many orders that Boaz ended up building sixty in one year all by himself.

I worked with a chisel, like they do in Spain. Now I use a knife for more things, like they do in Paracho. Tomorrow I start learning about the Kasha design with Richard Schneider. It's like starting again. I'm telling you right now, my guitars are going to be completely different when I'm back home. That's it. His concepts just make sense to me, and he's willing to share. Yes, you have to pay. You have to pay because he has to eat, and because it took him thirty years to pick up this knowledge. I'm here to take his course and learn. I think that as a luthier you need this knowledge. You don't have to build this way or that way, but you need the knowledge. You know, Albert Einstein said that God is in details, and just from reading about Richard's work and from listening to his lecture yesterday you can tell that he is involved with the details.

At what point did you take up guitar building again?

On the way back up to the United States from my Central America trip in 1993 I stopped in Antigua, Guatemala. While I was there I hung out at this place called The Rainbow Cafe, which was owned by an American guy named Ted. He was a guitar player, and the cafe was a really happening place. It had a big open area with a fire pit in the middle. People would gather there, and he would have poetry nights, and music sometimes. He had a pump organ that was about 120 years old that he got for free, but it was badly damaged. I stayed to fix it for him with whatever tools were there. I also made a concert-quality guitar at one of the tables in the cafe, and I made a travel guitar, with small body, using only a Swiss Army knife, just for fun and to prove it was possible. It's still there as far as I know. While I was building it people were saying, "Hey, build me one." This was a place where people who were traveling would gather, and I got eight orders for a ridiculous price, so I thought that maybe it's a good idea and I should make them. I didn't have the tools or the workshop, so I decided I would go to Paracho to do the production. I thought I was going to have help from experienced luthiers that live there, but I was completely wrong. I wouldn't put my name on an instrument if I wasn't satisfied perfectly with the details, and so I ended up working all alone. It was a hard four months for me, finishing these instruments people were waiting for, yet I had a wonderful time there.

When I got back to New York I found that I just couldn't do the hair dressing anymore. I just didn't feel like it. My girlfriend showed one of the travel guitars that I built in Paracho to Beverly Maher at the Guitar Salon and she says, "Oh, Boaz, this is wonderful! It's so small, but sounds so big. Let's do it." She put an ad in *Acoustic Guitar* magazine, I got plenty of orders, and the instruments were pretty successful. *Acoustic Guitar* featured one on the cover of their magazine (April 1996). They reviewed several travel guitars and said mine was one of the best-sounding. My price was high compared to the others they reviewed, but that's because I used all solid woods, put in a real rosette, used a high-gloss finish, and that kind of thing.

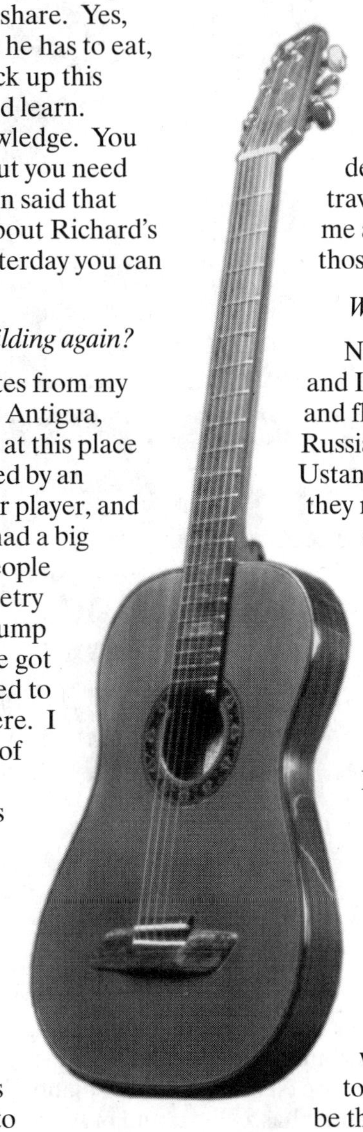

I couldn't afford to rent shop space in New York, so I went back to Paracho, where you could get a room for $30 per month. I ended up building sixty travel guitars that year, working all by myself. When I had filled all of the orders, I decided I was not going to make any more travel guitars because it was the same work for me as building a regular guitar, but building those got me back into lutherie again.

Where are you living now?

Now I am in Los Angeles. I have a workshop, and I'm filling orders. I'm booked for classicals and flamencos. Most of my guitars are going to Russia, Austria, and places like that. Vladimir Ustanov and all of his students have them, and they really love the instruments. So now I'm completely into it again, full gas.

With all of your travelling and not having a steady shop location for so long, how do you get orders from people so far away?

I mostly work through guitar salons. The benefit of guitar salons is amazing. You go to someone like Armin Kelly, Beverly Maher, Dan Zeff, the Guitar Salon in San Francisco, or the Guitar Salon in Los Angeles and you can see all these classical instruments right in front of you. You actually have a José Ramírez in your hand, and at the same time you have a Fleta, or maybe something from a new builder. You get to see and hear a traditional guitar, or a graphite guitar, or whatever you want! It's all in front of you to compare! It's a very fair thing. It used to be that you would go into a music store and there would be a few electrics, a few acoustics (mostly made from plywood), and if you were lucky, one classic from Spain made by I don't know who. Today the situation is completely different. I think it's an amazing concept. I don't know if there are salons like these in other parts of the world, but it's definitely big time in the U.S. That's the key of this beautiful land — go big time!

Is LA just another stop in your travels, or are you going to settle down for awhile?

LA is just another stop. I am trying to do the best I can showing my instruments and developing my craft. One day it's back home. Recently, I bought land in Israel. I have to go back soon because my mother is alone since my father died. I have brothers and sisters, but it's kind of important to the family that I am there.

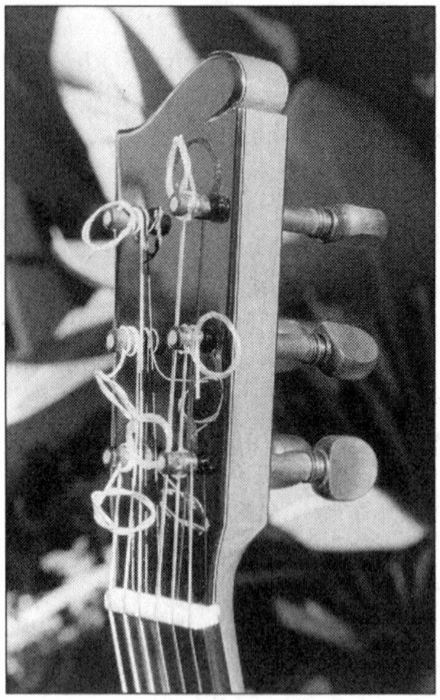

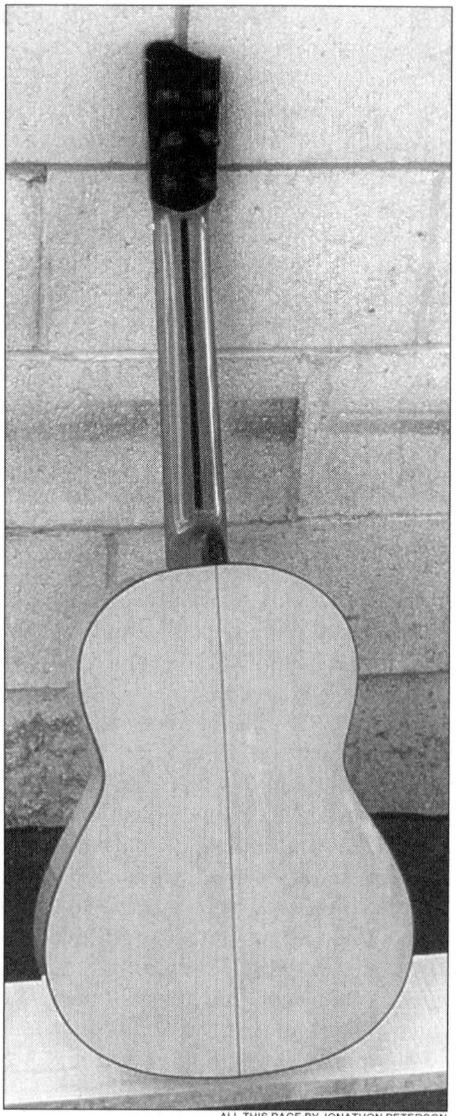

ALL THIS PAGE BY JONATHON PETERSON

Why don't you show me some of your instruments. Start out with this flamenco.

This is typical of my more traditional instruments. The back and sides are Monterey cypress, the top is Engelmann, the bridge is Indian rosewood, and it has a 65CM scale length. I also made the pegs.

Where did you come up with the idea for this double-fretboard instrument?

I was seventeen, and I was trying to figure out a way to make the instrument more versatile. The problem with any instrument almost, except the piano and the guitar, is that you cannot do chords. You cannot do chords on a flute, or on a clarinet, or sax. But you can do chords on a piano and on a guitar. On a guitar you only have six strings, so that's six notes at once, and only the ones you can fret or play open with your left hand in one position, so you are limited not only in the number of notes you can play at one time, but also in which ones you can play. With this you can play two hands, if your coordination is good enough. You can play both fretboards at the same time and the sound will come together. You can use the thumb of the right hand to play the guitar neck while you play the second fretboard with the fingers, or you can just lift your hand and play regular classic guitar technique. The two hands can play like a piano. I find it fascinating. It takes a lot of skill and practice. It's a new concept. Of course, I didn't build the first one like this. I just put another fretboard on a beat-up guitar to see if it would work. Every time you make a new one you have to improve it. This is the latest one.

Do you tap on the second fingerboard?

No, you don't tap. People like Stanley Jordan who play with a tapping technique use electric guitars because hitting the strings doesn't create much vibration, but the pickup will detect it so you can amplify it. You could tap on this guitar, but there's no point if you want to completely control the sound. When you tap, you don't control it. One hit, that's it. You can tap harder or softer, but it doesn't matter — you get one sound. When you pluck you can completely control the sound. If you play with a tapping technique on a classic guitar people will throw tomatoes at you.

It's not real. You have to play a classic guitar with the fingers, not a pick, or by hammering, or whatever. You have to play what the instrument is.

With this you pluck the strings for the second fretboard with the little finger(s) of your right hand while you are fretting with the other fingers of the same hand. The six strings on the second fingerboard are tuned normally, but the scale is slightly shorter, which makes the strings slightly loose so you can grab them easier. Of course, technically it's a thousand times harder to play this way, and it's a pity no one else actually follows this idea. I tried to interest people during my travels, and I put a lot of time and effort into developing a two-handed playing technique, but no one else is willing to work at it, and so far I am the only one who plays it.

Above: Boaz in concert in New York playing his double-fretboard guitar. Check out that right hand! The little finger is plucking while the others bend and fret.
Below: A double-fretboard guitar. Tuners for the second-fretboard strings are around back at the tail end.
Facing page: Several views of a 1996 Boaz flamenco guitar. The bone tieblocks behind the bridge serve to increase string breakover angle by eliminating the traditional knot which pulls up on the string behind the saddle.

JONATHON PETERSON

It was important for me to record with it. I had to prove that it works, it functions, and that it can sound beautiful. I actually give tapes away because I want people to listen. You never know. Joe Schmoe in the middle of nowhere might hear it and say, "Wow, it makes sense. I want one." I'll be happy to build it for him, not because I make extra money, but because another guy is going carry on with this idea.

Isn't it risky business to build an instrument which requires players to develop a difficult new technique?

Well, as I said, most of my orders are for more traditional classicals and flamencos, but here and there I am very happy to stop and work on a new project, a new thing. That always fascinates me. For instance, I just finished a guitar with forty-nine frets, and it is designed so that you can actually change its tone — not the tune of the strings, but the sound and response of the instrument.

How is that?

There is a peg in the end that turns a cam inside the instrument which puts pressure on the bracing, and that stretches the soundboard. By adjusting the amount of pressure you can actually change the sound of the instrument.

Was it a commission, or did you build it on spec?

It was built for a Swiss guitar player named Yussi Wagner. He said that he wanted a guitar that sounds like this, and sounds like that. I thought that he was confused, but then I said to myself, "Wait! The guy wants a guitar that sounds like this, and sounds like that. I should make it! Sure! You can make it sound any way you want." I came up with this solution.

Here's a picture of that guitar (p. 98). It's a 12-string with six nylon and six steel strings. The front part of the bridge floats, so you can adjust its position to correct the intonation. It has an ebony neck, so it doesn't need finish, and your fingers don't stick to it.

Wow! I've never seen anything like that! With twelve tuning machines and an ebony neck, did you have to do any counterweighting to keep it from being too neck heavy?

That's a good question. The neck was hollowed out, and I put soft wood in to lighten it.

The back of the Yussi's guitar is arched-in. The top is domed slightly as is normal, but the depth of the sides is much shallower at the waist, and the back is bent to conform to their shape. The lowest point is beneath the soundhole. The gluing surfaces of the back braces have a slight negative arch as well. It's something new. I do this on some of my concert classics.

Lutes have a slight scoop to their soundboards in front of the bridge. Bending a plate in that way really adds structure and stability. Was that your idea?

I did it for the sound, to see how it changes, to see how I can improve it. I won't build a guitar this way if no one orders it. On classic guitars especially, people want to see a classic look. They don't want anything that looks too different.

Here you can see the door that hides the peg which adjusts the cam. The cam has nine different settings for different sounds. Change the setting and you can immediately hear the difference.

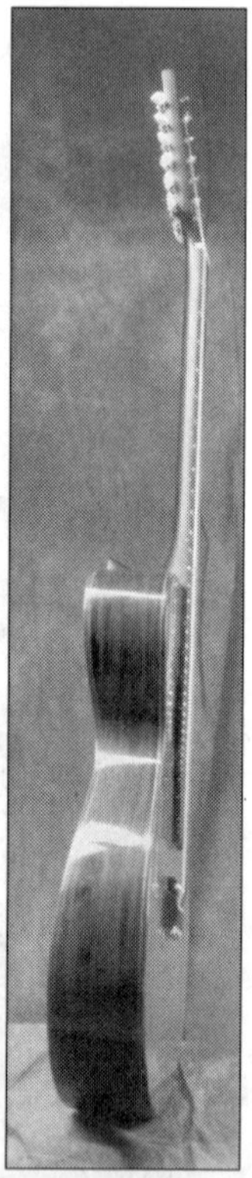

Does having that wheel restrict the movement of the bracing affect the sustain of the instrument?

When it is very tight, yes, but it taught me something about how that affects the sound, and I can apply that knowledge to other instruments whether I build them with this design or not. In this way I have learned something about how much flexibility I want in my classical guitars. It was an opportunity for me to experiment on someone else's account. He gets the guitar he wants, and I learn something that can improve all of my instruments.

I've got orders now for two ornately inlaid mandolins that use the same concept. A guy comes to me and says, "I want a mandolin that sounds like this," and he gave me tapes of twenty different mandolins!

Will these be archtop, or Neapolitan, or Flatiron style?

They will be carved archtops, but I'm going to use a Star-of-David shaped bracing, like on Yussi's guitar. That's a pattern I am working with lately. The braces jump over each other so they don't touch, which gives the top more freedom to move in certain ways.

Do you find it hard to come to firm conclusions about the effects of the things that you've done when you are making more than one change at a time? For instance, on one instrument you have Star-of-David bracing, you have the cam that presses on the top, you've got the ebony neck with forty-eight frets, and twelve strings with both nylon and steel, and a floating bridge. Each one of those is a pretty radical change, and they are all in one instrument.

I know what you are saying, and I don't have any really solid answers for you right now. It's based on instincts. When I built one of my first guitars my father said,

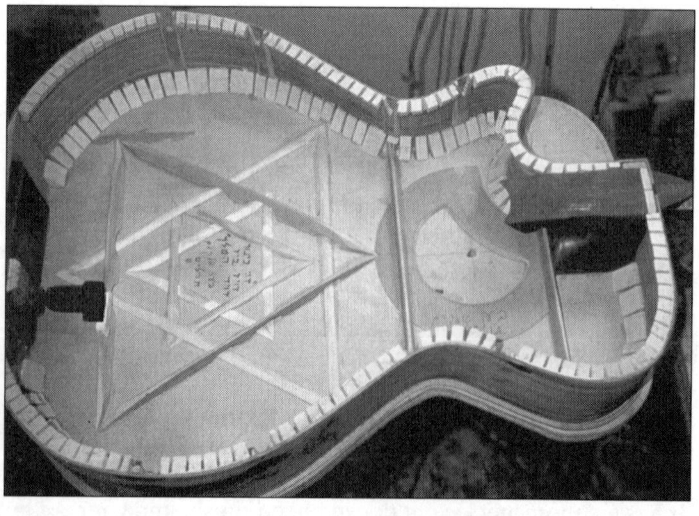

Four views of a 12-string, forty-nine-fret guitar built for Yussi Wagner. Each brace triangle has arches for the braces below it to pass through, allowing more freedom of movement than interlocking braces would. The dial behind the door panel in the lower left photo turns a cam which exerts variable pressure on a brace, tensioning the soundboard and changing the guitar's sound. Boaz said that because the upper frets are so close to the bridge, their positions had to be individually determined by testing pitch rather than by relying on a scale formula.

"Wow! This sounds good. What did you do here?" I told him that I didn't know. I braced it however I felt like doing it. I didn't know if I was right or wrong, I just did it. He said, "Boaz, if I throw a ball, will you catch it?" I said, "Yeah, I will catch it." Then he said, "Can you build a robot that will catch a ball?" I said, "No." He said, "So look how developed the instincts are. To make a robot to catch a ball, how complicated would the mechanics have to be, how involved would the mathematical program have to be, and just to catch a ball? It's such a simple thing to do! So, trust your instincts." Since then that's what I do. I just trust my instincts, and I go for it. When a client pays for an experimental guitar, I trust my instincts. It will be fine — nothing to worry about. I don't have to build a prototype. I just go right into the instrument. Right into it.

Do you use the same working methods in your shop as you did when you were working out of your toolbox?

If you visit my workshop you won't even see a drill with a motor. I still use a manual hand drill. It's slow, it's sure. It's all hand tools, not that I make a big deal out of it. For me it's just more practical, especially with the kinds of guitars I make and the number I produce. I have nothing against power tools. Sometimes they can do the job even better, but in order for someone else to cut a channel for the binding they have to get out a router, put a jig on it, try it on a piece of wood, and measure the cut, and adjust the depth, and maybe build an elaborate setup to hold the guitar while they are doing it. I just take a hand tool, scratch the wood, then use my knife and cut it out. For one guitar it's almost the same time as using machines and jigs. If you are going to build six, seven, or eight of the same guitar, there is no doubt the power tools will do it faster, and be accurate, and no sweat.

I don't use molds. I bend sides on a tube, and I do a fine job. People don't understand how I bend sides so evenly on a tube, but there is nothing to understand. Just take your time, and do it right — three hours, four hours, whatever. Do it slowly, and do it right, and don't practice on scrap. Practice on the real thing, then you will do it right. On scrap, of course you will rush. What do you care? It cost you $5. It's from the garbage. You pay $400 for some rosewood, I guarantee you will take care and do it right the first time. If you don't you are crazy, because you worked hard for those $400. Find another business.

So you believe if you are careful you should be able to get good results the first time?

Many people come to me with their first guitar and say, "What do you think?" And I truly think that it is a beautiful instrument, but I don't think it is a big deal to build the first guitar very good. You just fell into something you had talent for and found yourself. Super! That's your place. You have it. Build guitars.

That's my philosophy on one leg. It's not difficult to build a good first guitar. It's difficult to build all of them good. That's it. ——

BOTH THIS PAGE BY JONATHON PETERSON

Two views of an eye-popping Boaz Baroque-style guitar which never fails to attract attention. Boaz is pictured holding this guitar on p. 92.

Originally published in *American Lutherie #51*, 1997

Of Sympitars and Suzalynes

by Fred Carlson

I THINK IT WAS IN 1984 that I first began developing the Sympitar, my acoustic guitar with sympathetic resonating strings that run inside the neck and body. My inspiration in this madness came from my violin-building sweetie, Suzy Norris, when we worked in our cooperative shop in rural Vermont. She had a vision one day, while out walking in the beautiful rolling hills around our place, which resulted in her inventing the Suzalyne. This is a 5-string fiddle that has five sympathetic strings which were initially set up like the Norwegian Hardanger fiddle, with all the strings running over separate locations on the same bridge. It sounded incredible, and Suz began getting orders for them. The whole thing took a big leap forward after a rather unusual set of circumstances led us to become familiar with the Indian method of setting up sympathetic strings.

COURTESY FRED CARLSON

Above: Suzy with an early Suzalyne, and Fred with the very first Sympitar, performing at the Champlain Valley Folk Festival, circa 1984. Below: A 16-string Suzalyne (eleven sympathetics). Facing page: 1992 "Moon" Sympitar.

At a festival in the early '80s we met a harmonica player who was a follower of Sri Chinmoy, the Indian guru. Some months later the harp player called, reminded us of our meeting, and explained that "The Guru" was interested in the Suzalyne. Would we play it for the Guru over the phone? We asked him to call again in about ten minutes, since Suzy had to run back to the house for an instrument. She ran back and forth through a couple of feet of good old Vermont snow, wondering all the while what to play for a guru over the phone. Would Chinmoy appreciate a lilting Irish piece? She gave it a try. Sri Chinmoy never actually talked to us on the phone himself. Our harmonica-playing contact came back on the line and said, "The Guru wants you to play on only one string, please. The Guru only plays on one string." So Suzy played him a simple one-string melody. Came the reply, "The Guru would like to see your instrument. The Guru would like you to come today." The Guru happened to be 300 miles away in New York City, but he offered to pay for Suzy's plane fare. She arrived in New York late at night, was met by the harmonica man, and the next day Sri Chinmoy had a go at the Suzalyne. He wasn't a violinist, so unfortunately his attempts at playing the instrument were not completely satisfying (he didn't end up commissioning one). But Suzy did get taken on a tour of the Guru's property, a solid block of New York real estate. Among other holdings was a music shop that sold Indian instruments. For the first time she got a close look at the way Indians deal with sympathetic strings. They run them over a wide, nearly flat bridge that makes them buzz.

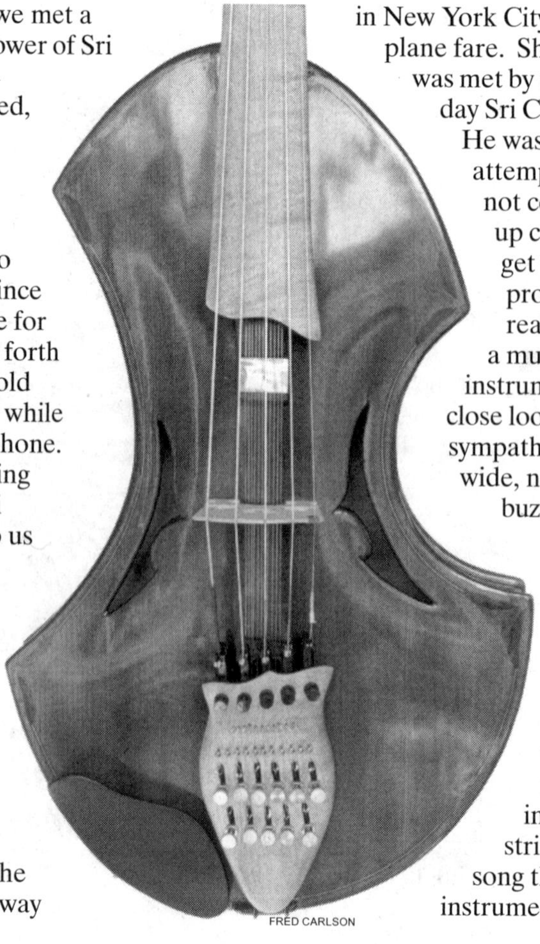

FRED CARLSON

Suzy didn't come home as a devotee of Sri Chinmoy, but she was plenty excited about this new way of dealing with sympathetic strings. The Hardanger fiddle and the European viola d'amore both run the sympathetics through the neck. They then pass through holes in the main bridge, below the bowed strings, transferring their sympathetic song through that bridge to the top of the instrument. This yields a very ringy sound, but with little distinct speaking of the sympathetics. They just sort of blend in with the swirl of tone. Once a Suzalyne was made with a separate wide and flattish bridge for the sympathetics, the difference was quite striking. Now the sympathetics had a voice of their own. Not only was the ringy, echoey effect pronounced, but the sympathetics could be heard as voices separate from the bowed strings.

My reaction was, "Wow!" I want to do that on a guitar, I want those angel voices singing along inside. It took about a year of spare-time work to make the prototype, which had six sympathetic strings along with the normal six fretted strings. I ran the sympathetics through a channel in the neck, similar to the Hardanger setup. But this was on a flattop guitar, which meant that the sympathetic strings ended up running along the underside of the top, going over their separate "buzzy bridge" *inside* the instrument, and eventually coming up through holes in the main bridge to anchor (**Fig. 2**, p. 103). The geometry of the string path and its relation to neck channel, guitar top, and bridge had to be planned out very precisely. The first Sympitar utilized a ½″ OD square steel tube in the neck to house the extra strings. This reinforced the neck like anything, but in combination with the extra tuners proved to be a bit heavy.

The braces also had to be redesigned, since the sympathetics had to run close to the underside of the top unobstructed. I build primarily in the Spanish style, with an integral neck/heel/foot/shelf that is attached to the top before the sides and back are glued in place. This let me mock up the sympathetic strings before gluing on the back, to be sure I had the geometry and clearances right. There's not a lot of room for error. The sympathetics have a window of about ⅛″ between the bottom of the channel and the tops of a couple of pared-down braces on the instrument's top. Amazingly, after some fussing with the contour of the buzzing surface of the sympathetic bridge, it worked! The sympathetic strings sounded great.

However, adjusting the sympathetic-string bridge through the soundhole proved to be a gruesome amount of work, since all the strings had to be slacked so I could get my hand inside, then all had to be brought back to pitch to test the change I had made. On the second Sympitar I added a pickup to this bridge, which compounded the grief, and when I went to a battery-powered unit I found that I couldn't reach the battery without slacking all the strings. As the instrument evolved I also reduced the size of the soundhole and extended the fingerboard over it to get twenty-four frets. Setting up and maintaining the instrument became a form of self-torture. After about a half-dozen Sympitars I decided to build in a trap door that would give me direct access to the bridge area of the guitar. At some point, I had an Ovation guitar, a repair job, come through the shop; it was a model with a trap door in the middle of the molded back. Having experimented with this guitar to see how the opening in the back affected the sound, I was expecting that the trap door would always be closed during playing, to maintain proper bass response. My first Sympitar that included a trap door surprised me when played without the panel, since not only was the change in tone subtle, it was also rather pleasing. It was a big-bodied, bassy guitar made of Indian rosewood. Removing the door caused a slight loss of "woof" in the bass, something almost felt more than heard, and added a corresponding sparkle to the midrange. So I not only had terrific access to the inside of the box, I had additional tone control as well. Cool! The most recent Sympitar (the one in the photos) has a trap door with tiny magnets in it, which proves to be a very classy way to hold it in place. It's a smaller guitar of soft flamed maple and redwood, and doesn't exhibit any noticeable change in tone color when the door is removed. I'm now thinking that with a trap door, having a soundhole in the top is less important, as long as it's large enough to permit tuning of the sympathetic strings. The next step may be to shrink the hole in the top to a minimum and add a soundhole in the side of the guitar, with a cone to project sound frontward and to tune the body.

The trap door is just the latest in a series of improvements since the original prototype was made. Guitarist Alex De Grassi borrowed the first one about eight years ago and suggested numerous improvements. Over the years Alex has been my great supporter in this

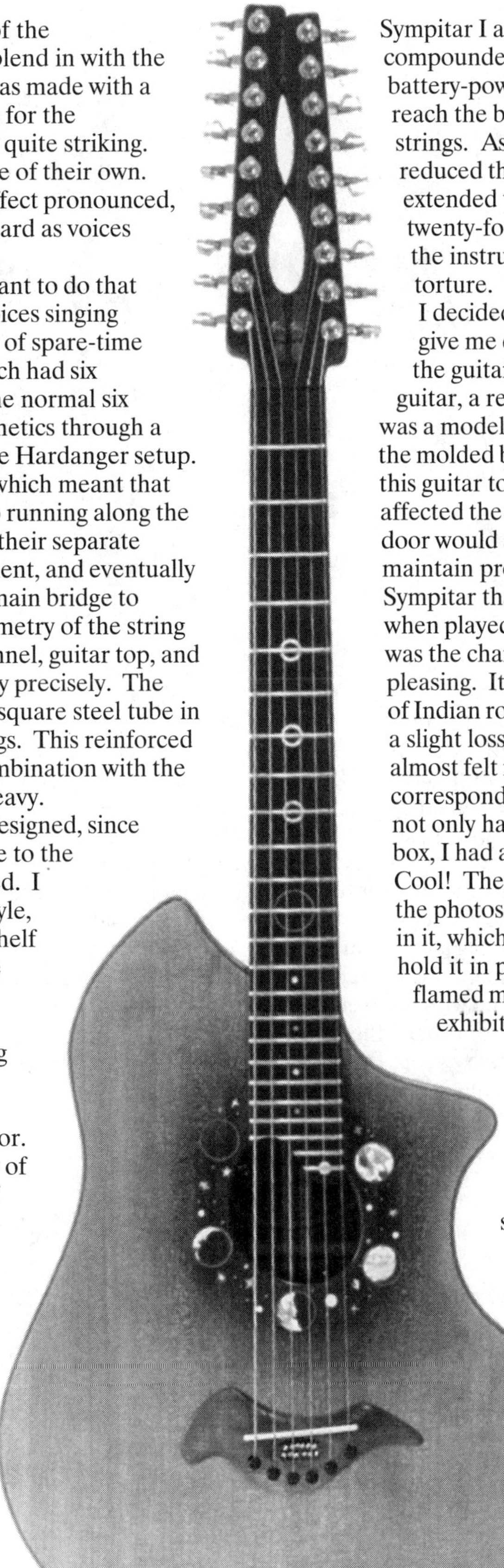

FRED CARLSON

ALL THIS PAGE BY TIM OLSEN

experiment, and I am tremendously grateful to him. The "gearshift lever," a little knob at the upper left of the soundhole that operates a string-dampening mechanism that turns off the sympathetic strings, was a De Grassi innovation. The channel through the neck for the sympathetic strings is now reinforced by a hollow beam I make up from epoxy graphite bar stock, which is very light and stiff.

The counter-tension that the sympathetics exert on the top seems to have little effect on the guitar. I've been able to make great sounding, structurally sound guitars with all those extra strings just doing their thing in there.

There have been other guitars made with nonfretted strings, but sympathetic vibration is not usually the main point. I'm familiar with some cases where the extra strings were intended for sympathetic response, but that response was rather subtle. There are two general rules that have worked well for me, though I have no knowledge of scientific justification for them. Sympathetic response seems greater if the sympathetic string has a long vibrating length; that is, strings that have both ends attached to the body of the instrument aren't long enough to respond well. Sympathetic response also seems to be greater in a string that runs parallel to the plucked strings.

I met a guy a while back who had made a beautiful archtop guitar with the open-style fretwork of a sitar and sympathetic strings running under the frets in the manner of that Indian instrument. Although in some ways that instrument was eerily close to what I've been doing, I have yet to see another instrument quite like the Sympitar. ——

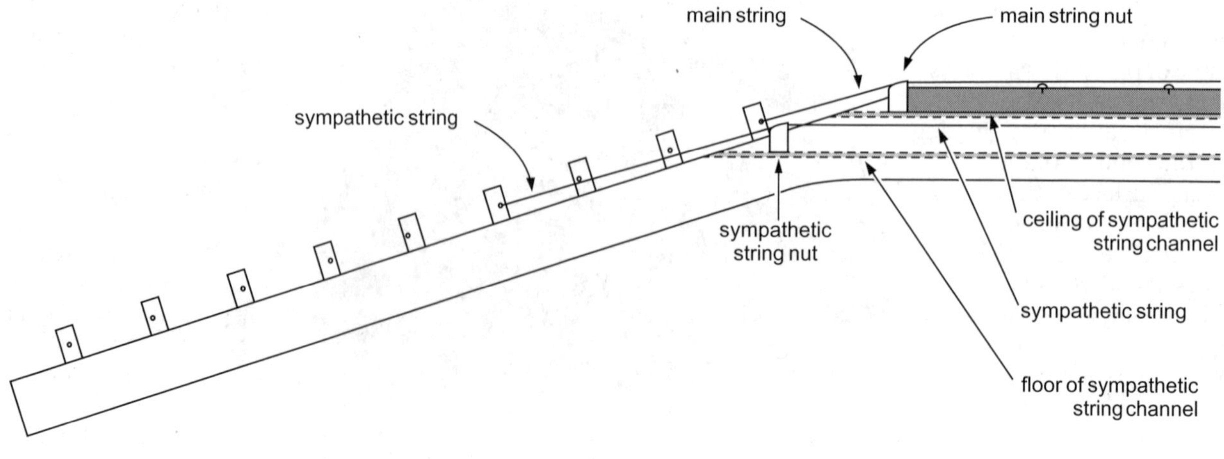

Figure 1. Cross section of Sympitar peghead

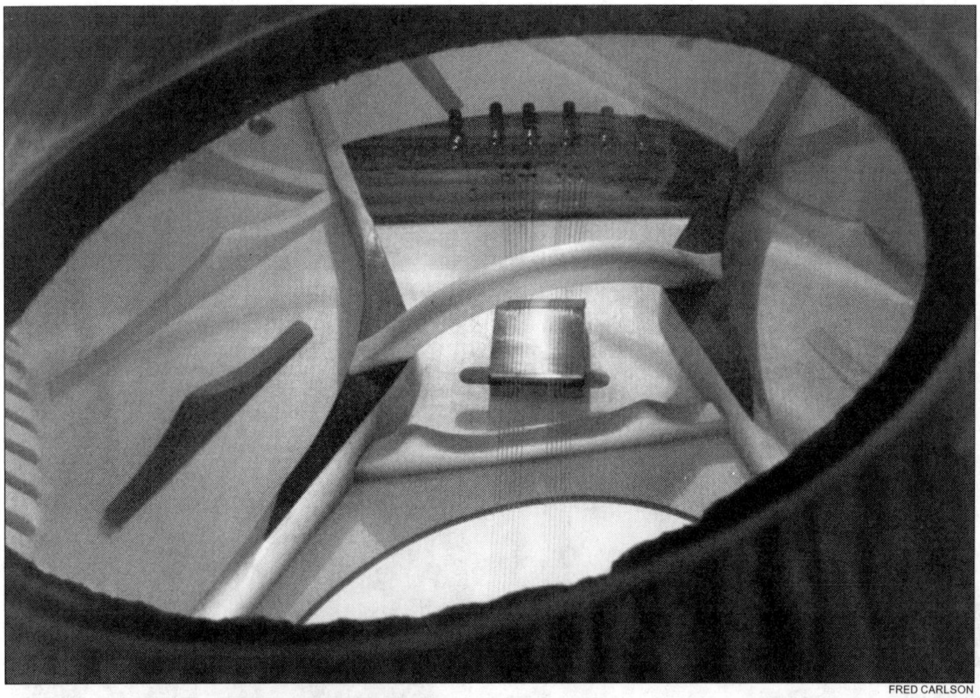

FRED CARLSON

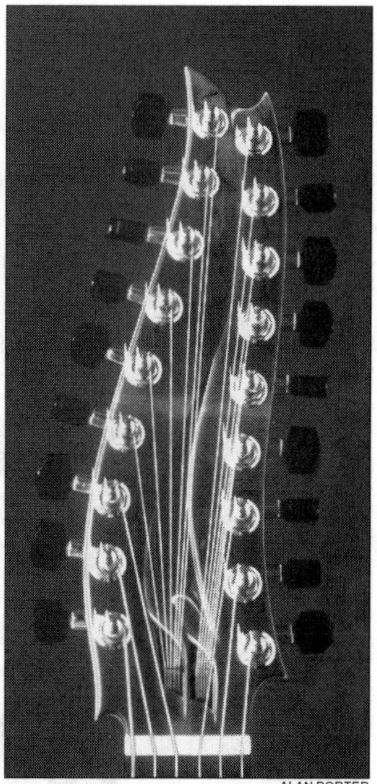

ALAN PORTER

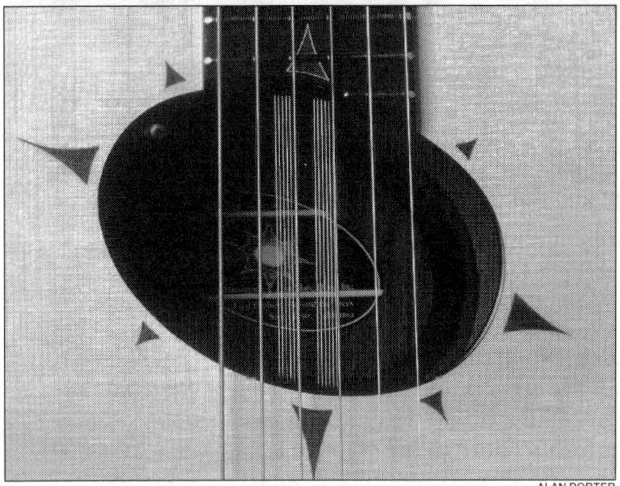

ALAN PORTER

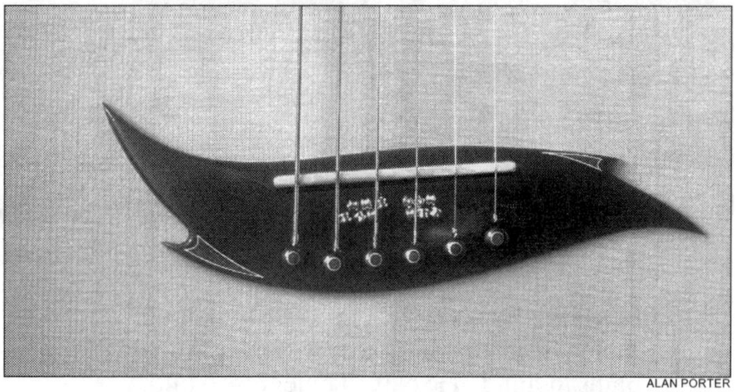

ALAN PORTER

This page, clockwise from upper left: View of top bracing and sympathetic-string bridge as seen through trap door in back of Sympitar; Sympitar peghead showing through-the-neck routing of sympathetic strings; bridge detail showing mounting of eighteen strings; soundhole detail showing sympathetic strings. Facing page: Three views of a Sympitar trap door.

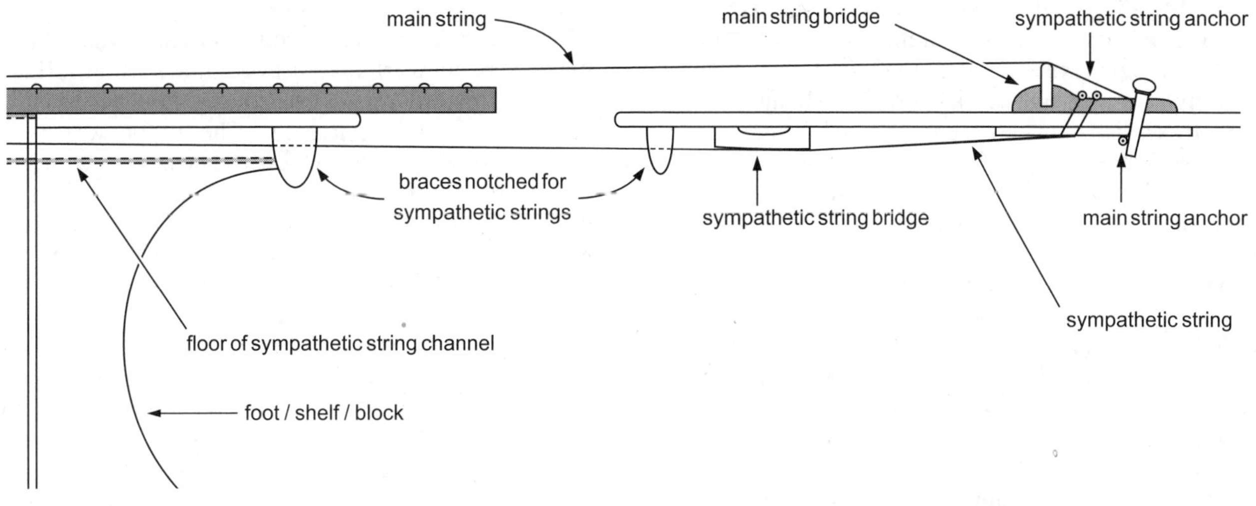

***Figure 2.** Cross section of Sympitar bridge*

Originally published in *American Lutherie #51*, 1997

Meet the Makers:
Jeffrey Huss and Mark Dalton
by John Calkin

ALL BY JOHN CALKIN

Left to right: Jeff Huss, Mark Dalton, and Luke Bair in their shop in Stuarts Draft, Virginia.

JEFF HUSS blew into Virginia's Shenandoah Valley from North Dakota with no particular plans in mind. He played bluegrass banjo. When he heard that Geoff Stelling had recently relocated to the Rockfish Valley, just over the Blue Ridge, and was looking for banjo makers, he thought he'd give it a shot. He began doing inlays and roughing out necks, laid up resonators, then learned to mill frets. After nine years he began to realize that what he truly wanted was his own shop, and he wanted to make guitars.

Mark Dalton was hired by Stelling to replace Huss, but Dalton's eight years in an auto body shop proved too useful to waste, and Mark became the banjo company's finish man. Huss and Dalton became good friends who stayed in touch after Jeff finally left Stelling's. Jeff built a 900 sq. ft. shop onto his house (thinly disguised as a garage) and went into the guitar business.

Jeff built a guitar for Mark. Mark was impressed. He was also looking for a satisfying career move that would give him more control over his own life. Jeff, it turned out, was soon looking for a way to escape the eight-guitars-a-year syndrome that many lone luthiers get locked into. After dropping hints in front of each other for several months it all boiled down to three truths: they got along really well; Jeff had a business; Mark had his life savings of $25,000 to invest. They became partners.

For four months they designed and made jigs and fixtures, acquired machinery, and rebuilt the shop. They also drew salaries from their start-up capital.

"We were prudent with our money, but it was frightening to watch it drain away. We bought a Performax double-drum thickness sander for $3,000. We couldn't work without it, but it was scary to watch the money go," said Jeff.

"Not only did we plot a start-up schedule for ourselves, we were able to stick to it. But unless you've been in a similar situation you can't know what a relief it was to begin work on our first guitar," said Mark.

Their immediate goal was four guitars per month, and it wasn't too hard to meet. The company wasn't without growing pains, however. The new machinery needed tweaking. Some of their fixtures weren't as efficient as others and had to be redesigned. When a jig Mark made for shaping the headstock was improved, it threw off all the jigs that Jeff had made for completing the necks.

"The path to smoother production is hardly ever a straight line," drawled Mark. "We spend a fair amount of time scratching our heads and talking things through before we're satisfied that we've got it right. We call it 'floppin' on the dock'."

"In the long run these are little things," said Jeff, "but the short-term effect can be painful. A company like Martin has an engineering staff to keep the plant evolving while doing as little damage to the production flow as possible. We not only do our own design work, we have to take time from production to build the fixtures, and when the fixtures don't work as planned, it really hurts."

"Yeah, it doesn't add up to two periods of down time, but possibly four, since the jigs have to be newly created and tested in production. But we're almost up to speed now. When we hired Luke, our production jumped to six guitars a month, and we should be up to seven shortly. On the whole, we are way ahead of our initial plans. We thought we'd spend two or three years in the garage, but when we saw how smoothly everything ran we pushed it up to maybe five years. We've kept or beaten every schedule we ever set for ourselves," said Mark.

"But we kept our eyes open for another building all the time. We looked at three places before our current facility came along, and when we saw it we knew we couldn't let it pass," added Jeff.

The new shop is part of a business complex in downtown Stuarts Draft. The building is sound, well insulated, bright, and their six rooms and cubbyholes add up to a spacious 1900 square feet.

"Partly because of the larger shop, we were able to hire our first employee years before we thought we'd reach that point," said Jeff.

The company started with a wonderful cushion. Two or three guitars per month go to another manufacturer who's name goes on those guitars. Though all the guitars come from the same dreadnought molds, they are not identical. All Huss & Dalton guitars have a spherically arched top. The other brand is made with arched braces, but the top is glued on flat in the vintage Martin style. It was a wonderful opportunity to compare the tonal differences of the two designs.

"The actual sound of the notes is pretty similar, but the string-to-string balance is different," said Mark. "The domed top makes a guitar with an equal volume from all the strings. The traditional design is bass heavy, real good for bluegrass

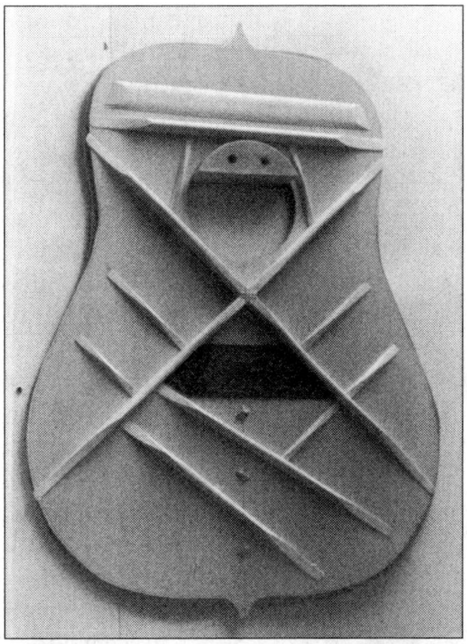

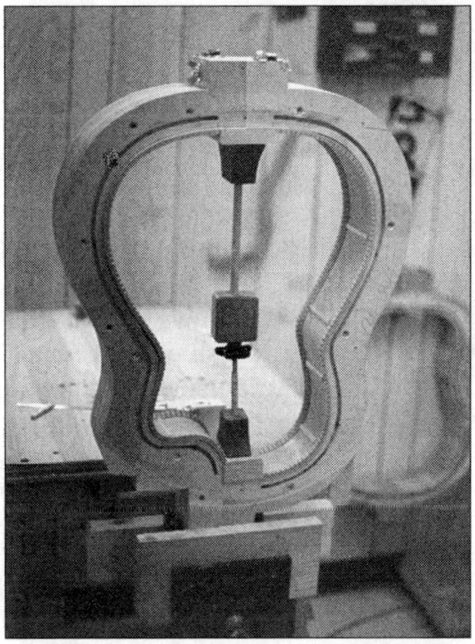

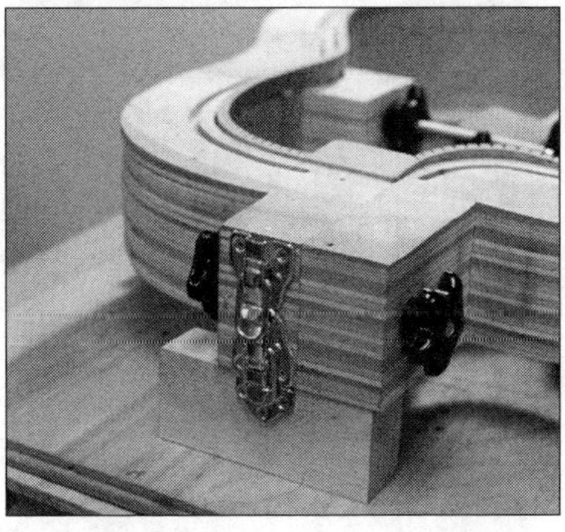

Top: Tops are braced in a conventional manner, but with an extra finger brace between the X and the first tone bar, which helps prevent top distortion behind the bass side of the bridge. Holes in the tabs at the ends of the center seam are used to pin the plates to the mold during glue-up.
Middle: A set of sides in an H&D cutaway mold.
Bottom: Molds are held off the bench by small blocks and are secured with suitcase latches.

backup work. The chief advantage of the domed top is stability. I haven't noticed any soundhole sinking on our guitars, but I see it on some other brands even when they're new."

The Huss & Dalton brace pattern is a standard scalloped X brace with two tone bars. However, they have added a finger brace inside the X, just behind the bridge plate on the bass side. Sometimes an X-braced top will show a crease at the bass end of the bridge after it is strung up. The new finger brace eliminates the crease without changing the tone of the guitar.

The division of labor between the partners fell into a natural pattern. "Jeff told me I had to learn all the steps he disliked," Mark joked. They began building bodies as a team, since that was the most efficient way to assemble and test their jigs, after which Mark took over the body shop. He also does the setup work on completed instruments. Jeff makes the necks, fits them to the bodies, does the inlay work, and fits the bridges. Their finish work is done by Luke Bair, a Roberto-Venn School of Lutherie graduate who came to Huss & Dalton after a string of repairman jobs. Luke also does the rough milling work and draws all their original inlay patterns.

All of their guitars are of traditional dreadnought design except their cutaway model. They resaw much of their own wood, which gives them access to varieties not normally stocked by tonewood suppliers.

"We stick largely to traditional woods, though. We got a good deal on Honduras rosewood from a local guy. We have some Brazilian. Tone-wise, I don't hear much difference among the rosewoods. We've been selling a lot of guitars made from a curly Philippine mahogany. I don't know what we'll do when we use up those boards."

All bracewood is red spruce. Dreadnoughts come stock with a Sitka spruce top. Cutaways come with Engelmann tops. A red spruce top is an option on any guitar. Fingerboards and bridges are ebony, as are the bridge pins. They make an

Above: In a production situation, jig making is an on-going affair. Jeff Huss shows off the shaper and a wall full of specialized jigs. Below: At this bench the bodies are routed for binding and purfling. By changing the shoe on the far router, different depths can be cut for binding. Different widths of purfling are accommodated by changing the bearings on the near router.

advertising point of not using plastic for any part of their guitars. All bindings and purflings are wood. All nuts and saddles are bone.

A Fox bender is used for the sides, and they designed their own addition to the machine for bending cutaways. "It's pretty clumsy, actually. When it's all assembled the machine looks like a magnet dragged through a bucket of bolts. I have a whole stack of second-rate mahogany sides that I abused while learning to bend cutaways. I'm investigating other ways to get the job done, but this way is dependable now that I've gotten used to it," said Mark.

The edge contours of the sides are cut with a shaper before bending. Once the end blocks have been glued in place, the edges are trued using a motorized spherically dished form with 60-grit abrasive glued to it. The machine is driven by a 2 h.p. motor that used to drive Jeff's shop-made thickness sander. A series of pulleys gear its rotation way down. The dish is supported with outfeed rollers intended for use with saws. When activated, the machine sounds like a wooden cart trundling quickly down a rocky road, but it works perfectly. The dust made by the coarse paper is so heavy that it is trapped in the box, and mechanical dust collection is unnecessary .

Backs and tops are left with little tabs at the ends of the center joints. Holes are drilled through the tabs, and the holes are used to pin the plates in place on the mold during glue-up, so they can't slide off center.

Binding and purfling channels are cut on a pair of horizontally mounted Porter-Cable routers. A pair of bearings is attached to an extension on each router base for the sides to roll on. The routers themselves are never adjusted. To change the depth of the cut for a binding or purfling channel, a shoe of a different thickness is screwed to the base. To change the width of the cut, bearings of a different diameter are used. To make a cut, the guitar is moved against the fixed router base's shoe and its bearings. Jeff said, "I found that if I tried to eyeball it, I had a tendency to rock the guitar on the rollers, so now I look away and do it by feel, and the job comes out much cleaner. I'm sure this isn't the last rig we'll have for this job, but it's a lot faster than running a router with a special base around the body, and making a different adjustment for each pass. Cutting the channels that way used to take two and a half hours per guitar, but this way I can do six in an hour."

Necks are bolted to the bodies using threaded inserts. A maple dowel is set into the full length of the heel beneath the heel cap, and the inserts are screwed into the maple, since threading into the end grain of the mahogany neck is usually the weak link in this system. Jeff also made a jig for locating three steel pins in the heel and body. "Initially the pins were just to index the major parts, but it's amazing how much stiffer the joint becomes when using them. The neck will actually stay in place using just the pins," he said.

Most parts are roughed out in batches on the table saw, shaper, or table router. Necks are roughed out on the shaper, and headstocks are brought to finished dimensions there. The bridge-making jigs were a real trick to build, since finished bridges have no flat surfaces. Bridge plates are arched on the shaper and are held in the jig by a vacuum clamp while being machined. A vacuum box is used to glue braces to the plates. Their vacuum system is the pump available from Luthiers Mercantile International (part #SPVAC). It's a compact unit that can be readily moved from station to station, and is powered by an air compressor. H&D even made a body vise that utilizes the vacuum pump. Its simply a deck of plywood that can be clamped to a bench. The pump attaches to the top rear of the unit, and an air channel exits from the middle of the vertical deck. Rings of foam surround the air vent. Though special foam is available, Jeff reports that standard weather stripping does a pretty fair job. The body is held against the foam while the air exhaust on the pump is opened, and the body is sucked to the deck. A small shelf is provided to support the body, just in case. Some woods are so porous that they won't stick in the vise. But after the pores are filled they usually work all right, says Jeff.

All guitars are finished in Fullerplast, a catalyzed varnish. Open-pored wood is filled after sealing, and perhaps a second time after the first heavy coat of finish is sprayed. Did Mark find his body shop experience to be an advantage in guitar finishing?

"The spray work in a body shop is about a thousand times more sophisticated than in most guitar shops, but finishing wood is a lot different than metal, and I had to learn all that. Mostly, the body shop taught me how to work hard. A strong work ethic is crucial to running your own business. But I have to admit that I'm happy to let Luke run the finishing department."

"Our shop is just about up to speed, and we were happy with our guitars right from the start. We've expanded our dealer base, though we're always looking for more dealers," said Jeff. "Life is good." ——

Top: Mark Dalton, left, and Jeff Huss posing at a body-assembly station. Bottom: H&D neck attachment system utilizes two bolts and three steel pins that hold everything in perfect alignment. A maple dowel set into the heel beneath the heel cap provides the neck-bolt inserts with a secure seat. The plexiglas jig on the right is used to drill the holes for the neck pins. Hardened steel bushings are mounted in the plastic for long life.

Three views of H&D's vacuum vise. Vacuum pressure holds an H&D cutaway body on the vacuum vise, making it a piece of cake to scrape or sand the sides. Vacuum also holds the vise fast to a mounting plate screwed to the side of the bench. By remounting the vise on a bench top, the top or back of a body can be worked. Standard weather stripping is used to create the seal. A venturi-effect vacuum unit provides the suction.

Originally published in *American Lutherie #52–#54*, 1997–1998

Crazy Like Charles Fox:
Guitar Making Jigs for the 21st Century
by John Calkin

WHY ARE ACOUSTIC GUITARS so hard to build? OK, that's a loaded question. Perhaps, for any given skill level, guitars are no more difficult than violins, or carved-top mandolins. Maybe guitars are easier, I don't know. If you've built a flattop and it came out OK, you may be wondering why I pose the question. But I'm talking about a guitar that could be placed with no apologies along side any other guitar in the world, a guitar that not only sounds good but is right in all the dozens of little details that comprise a fine instrument.

I've only completed four or five conventional acoustics, and I'm quick to admit that that's part of the problem. Each kind of instrument I've tackled has taught me that the mind, hands, and eyes don't get fully coordinated until approximately the twentieth attempt. Somewhere in that time scheme, a mysterious organic process jells. Things begin to go right without such an horrendous amount of coaxing. Is there a shortcut to the same end? Maybe.

1
CYNDY BURTON

I don't think I've ever admired a display of handmade instruments without wishing I could get some detailed advice from the able luthier who created them. As it turned out, I had just such an opportunity, and I'd like to report on the experience. It was in every sense a good one.

Charles Fox has a long history of training guitar makers. His first lutherie school was the School of Guitar Research and Design in Vermont. Opening in 1973, it was the first school for guitar builders in North America. After a protracted absence from the craft, he is back. Fox's American School of Lutherie opened its doors three years ago in Healdsburg, California. The class I attended contained twelve pupils with an age span of about forty years. Some of us had yet to complete an instrument. A few had attended other schools and had several instruments under their belts. I rounded out the pack with sixteen years of professional experience as a builder/repairman and a history of mountain dulcimer madness before that. Each of us brought different expectations to the school, as well as a unique background from which we could contribute to the class. Charles has been teaching for a long time, and where people are concerned he is a quick study. He expects to learn from each group, as well as to instruct them, and he worked to pull from us useful ideas. Ours was his largest ASL class to date, and while it made the daily routine a bit slower and perhaps more cumbersome for Charles, he made it clear that the broth of our commingling was especially rich. In a smaller class you may find that you have Charles more to yourself, and that can certainly be valuable, too. Class size seems to be a win/win situation.

2
ALL BY JOHN CALKIN EXCEPT AS NOTED

I've agonized for some time about how to organize this article. Charting our day-to-day routine seemed promising. Charles has his schedules well thought out. The flow is not at all haphazard. However, I don't want to create a set of expectations in your mind. Some of Charles' building techniques date back two decades and haven't changed because he hasn't encountered anything more accurate, faster, or more satisfying. But it's also obvious from the first day that his methods are always evolving, and that what he recommends today may not be what he teaches a year from now. Between school sessions Fox is a luthier on the trail of higher quality and increased output within the parameters of the one-man shop. Where this may lead him is part of this story and the reason why I hesitate to predict what you may find at the school in the future. It's probable that each successive class will be a richer and deeper experience.

The class isn't so much about guitars as about building them. Charles has built or overseen the production of hundreds of steel string and solidbody electric guitars. At the moment his personal focus is on classical guitars for the high-end market. But there is a larger reason for using the classical guitar in the classroom, and the market place has little to do with it. Fox's overview is more generic than specific. Classical and flattop guitars are far more alike than they are different. Though the top bracing and headstocks are obviously dissimilar, other differences are more subtle. The knowledge needed to build the two styles is largely the same. Charles likes to use the classical guitar as an example because it comes from a tradition of small shops and hand building. No mass-produced classical guitar has ever won high regard. The steel string, however, evolved in a factory situation that was perhaps too willing to sacrifice maximum performance for instrument longevity. Fox considers the typical flattop guitar to be overbuilt. All this isn't to say that Charles won't be building steel string guitars when you get to the school. The classical guitar was the primary interest of only one or two students in my class, but none of us steel stringers felt short changed.

Charles points out early in the first session that the bulk of the guitars in the world are actually guitar-shaped objects that function sort of in a musical fashion. As luthiers we have to know about them, but they are in no sense models to be emulated. Luthiers must be guided by only the best examples and aim for the highest plateaus of performance. Even if we don't take it as a moral obligation to the craft, it's the only way to stay afloat in the guitar business as it exists today.

The school is set up to teach several methods of reaching the same goal. If you wish to work from a small bench with a select clutch of hand tools, Charles can help you. If you'd like to set up a minifactory Charles can really help you. Fox considers two guitars a month to be a reasonable output for an individual luthier, while twice that many is feasible for a highly organized one-man shop. But he insists that there be no emphasis on numbers until the quality is there. If you are already an experienced builder, Charles will help increase your production very quickly.

Two books may prove helpful. Charles recommends that students be familiar with Cumpiano and Natelson's *Guitarmaking: Tradition and Technology*, but mostly to keep beginners from walking in cold and becoming instantly befuddled. Jim Williams' *A Guitar Maker's Manual,* first published in 1986, bears a resemblance to parts of Fox's course. Williams attended the Fox school in Vermont, and much of his book stems directly from that experience. Parts of the course have not changed greatly since then, especially the handtool segments. The illustrations in the book are better than the sketches you'll be able to whip out during class. Charles recommends the book, even though what you'll witness in class has moved beyond the bounds of the old school. At no time does Charles ask you to crack a book and follow along. Lectures are combined with demonstration, and the lectures themselves include nonstop dialog. If you come with specific guitar-building problems, Charles wants to know about them. If you have insights to offer, you are invited to share them with the class.

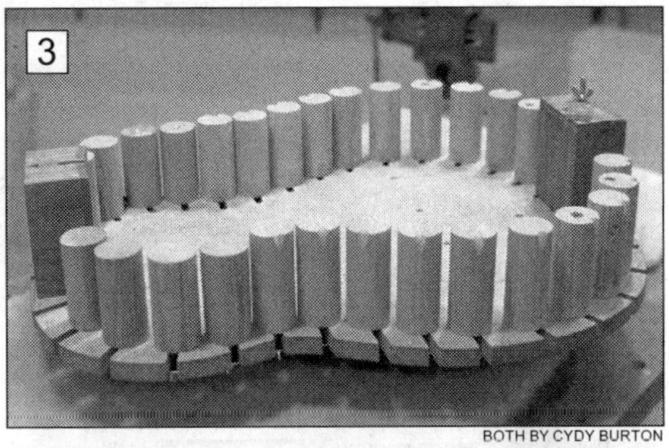

BOTH BY CYDY BURTON

The main workbench is the focus of perhaps 80% of the class time. It is sturdy, and has a generous work surface. Threaded inserts are set into top of the bench to accept clamps that Charles made and pop-up dogs prevent work from shooting off the bench while being planed or scraped (though Charles often prefers to clamp a stop to the edge of the bench top). On one corner of the bench is a Versa-Vise. At the opposite end is a shop-made vise large enough to encompass any guitar body (**Photo 1**). The jaws of the vise are curved to put all their pressure on the edges of the body, and carpeted to prevent scarring. Screws meant for a veneer press (a catalog item) allow independent adjustment of each end of the vise. An addition not seen here, though recommended by Fox, is a fabric sling to catch the guitar should it fall through the jaws.

Three different molds show up in class. One is very similar to the rigid molds most of us make, a simple framework that suits only one body shape. Its chief function is to support the sides and hold them in shape as the guitar progresses. The second mold is adjustable within a wide range of body shapes and sizes. The third mold is an elaborate version of the first, and offers many conveniences that make construction faster and more accurate. Mold #1 comes in two varieties. The steel string version (**Photo 2**) is a fully enclosed frame of heavy construction.

The classical version has a gate at the heel-block region to accommodate Spanish-style construction, which utilizes a heel block that is integral with the neck. Charles points out that either construction works equally well for either style of guitar. A steel string made with a Spanish foot makes a wonderful guitar, the only problem being that at some point down the road the neck will likely have to be reset, and the Spanish foot is notoriously difficult to disassemble. Likewise, a classical guitar with a dovetailed or bolted-on neck can be the equal of a guitar made with a Spanish foot, but that market is not prepared to accept a bolted-on neck. As we'll see later, both problems can be addressed during construction.

Mold #2 is especially useful to the custom builder who doesn't offer a set line of guitars, but might build a differently shaped guitar for each customer. The chief components of the mold are a guitar-shaped workboard and thirty-four thick wooden dowels, each about $3\frac{1}{2}''$ long (**Photos 3 and 4**). Each dowel (made of $1\frac{1}{4}''$ closet-pole stock) has a length of threaded rod extending from the center of one end to which a washer and wing nut is attached. The workboard is cut by thirty-four radial slots extending from the edge toward the centerline of the board. The dowel bolts fit into the slots, and the dowels create the mold of the guitar. The workboard should be as large as the largest anticipated guitar, and the slots in it should extend inward to form the mold for the smallest anticipated guitar. A cross of heavy wooden beams supports the board from the back.

Mold #3 (**Photo 5**) is the most useful, most elaborate, and hardest to build. It's a good example of a strong ASL theme: hours spent making accurate fixtures result in days of saved labor, and more accurate work. The emphasis placed on reproducing one model of guitar also reflects one of the Fox principles: "Know your box." At the present time, all of Charles' guitars come out of the same mold. He believes that the advantage of knowing one body style intimately outweighs the marketing possibilities of offering a full line of guitars.

The guitar begins life face down. The rim-supporting segments of mold #3 are mated to a flat board, even though the top will eventually have an arch. The rim supports are 3/4″ shy of the full depth of the sides. The back will be made with a spherical contour, and this same contour is built into the upper surface of the mold. A spreader bar made of a turnbuckle and guitar-shaped blocks of MDF holds the rim firmly to the mold at the waist, and a second one provides clamping pressure on the end blocks, holding the rim unit firmly within the mold.

A guitar-sized panel is used as a clamping caul for the back, and should be considered an integral part of the mold. This panel is dished with the same spherical contour as the back. Dense foam runs around the outline of the back, over the footed heel block, and also provides for gluing up a guitar with a cutaway (**Photo 6**).

A pair of clamps bolt to the mold at the end blocks (**Photo 7**). Their function is to hold down the rims and blocks during glue-up.

A closer look at mold #3 requires an explanation of a detail in Charles' classical guitar. Fox doesn't build in the Spanish style, but his classical guitars look that way once completed. His heel block is footed. In fact, a second foot, or shelf, supports the soundboard beneath the fingerboard, though it's not visible from the soundhole. The back of the heel block is cut with a vertical mortise. A matching mortise is machined into the neck. Later, after the neck is fitted to the body, a 1/4″ spline is glued into the neck and becomes a tenon for the mortise in the heel block. The mold is also cut

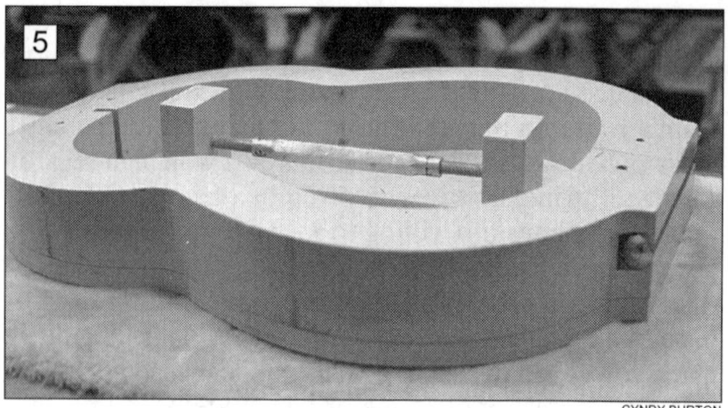

CYNDY BURTON

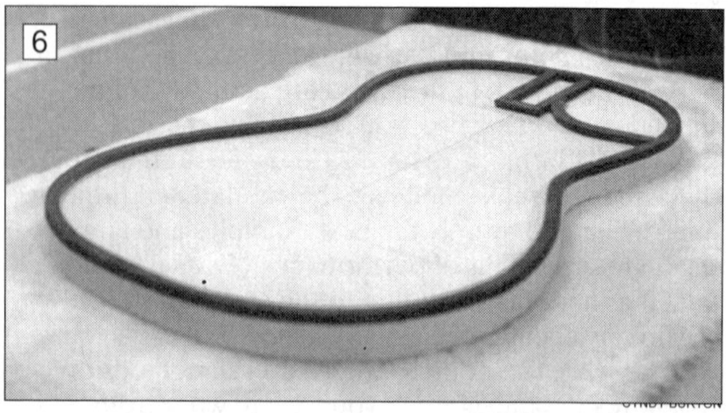

with this mortise. When the block is glued to the ribs, a key holds it in proper alignment, which simplifies fitting the neck later on.

No doubt you're getting an idea of the time and thought that went into mold #3. It is finished to last indefinitely. Charles coated it with multiple coats of epoxy boat finish, then painted it with refrigerator white enamel. Titebond doesn't stick to it. If other glues adhere to the paint it's a simple matter to sand them off and touch up the enamel.

Nicely finished jigs and fixtures are a Fox trademark. Complex construction is not. Most of his creations are made of medium density fiberboard (MDF) and standard hardware-store items. Because Charles designs his tooling to be easily reproduced by his students, he seldom uses specialized industrial components.

10

11

Another workboard is sort of a tray into which the body fits snugly (**Photos 8 and 9**). The body lives in this tray from the time it is removed from the mold until the time the neck is affixed. Notice that in **Photo 9** there is yet another workboard already clamped in the Versa-Vise behind Charles. The tray will be clamped to the board in the vise while the guitar is routed for binding.

Photo 10 shows a belt-sander fixture as well as a jig meant to be used with it. The fixture is simply a small plank of MDF with a length of angle aluminum set into it. Beneath the plank is a runner that slides into the miter slot of the sander table. The aluminum angle is parallel to the sanding belt. The jig in the picture shapes a tail block to the contour of the butt of the guitar. The tail block stock must be thick enough to extend out over the aluminum rail. The base of the jig is curved to match the body contour. The aluminum rail reads the jig base, and the sanding belt transfers the shape to the tail block. **Photo 11** shows the fixture and jig in use. The same concept is used for fitting many different parts, including the heel block and the arched braces.

Not all fixtures need to be so elaborate. **Photo 12** shows a dedicated table-saw fence for cutting truss-rod slots. (Yes, Charles places a graphite reinforcement beam in his classical guitar necks. More later.) The fixture is just an MDF board with a runner underneath it that fits into the miter slot of the saw table. The distance from the edge of the fixture to the 6″ dado set is the only critical measurement, and to make it work all neck blanks must be the same width. When this fixture is mounted in the opposite miter slot, its other edge becomes a fence for ripping neck blanks to a 3″ width.

A similar fixture is used for tapering long edges. A miter slot runner is fixed to an MDF board with the board overlapping the saw blade. The runner is dropped into its slot, then the board is run through the saw. Any stock lined up to overlap that edge can then be quickly trimmed on the saw. Charles added a set of hold-down clamps made of aluminum bar stock and T-nuts, and a pair of door handles for a good grip. **Photo 13** shows a side about to be tapered. Fingerboards are tapered on the same fixture.

Charles also utilizes a more elaborate version of this jig that serves a slightly different purpose. A much larger carrier table is fixed with a miter slot runner and its edge is trimmed, same as above. But this time a full-length clamp is added right at the blade edge. The wooden piece that does the actual clamping is held between two walls. Downward pressure is created by three wooden cams that

12

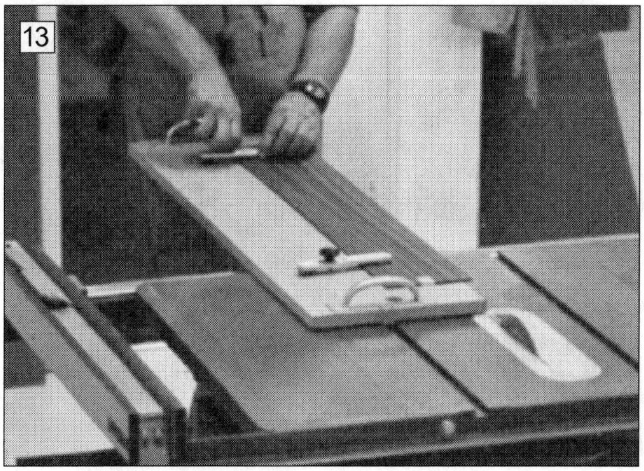
13

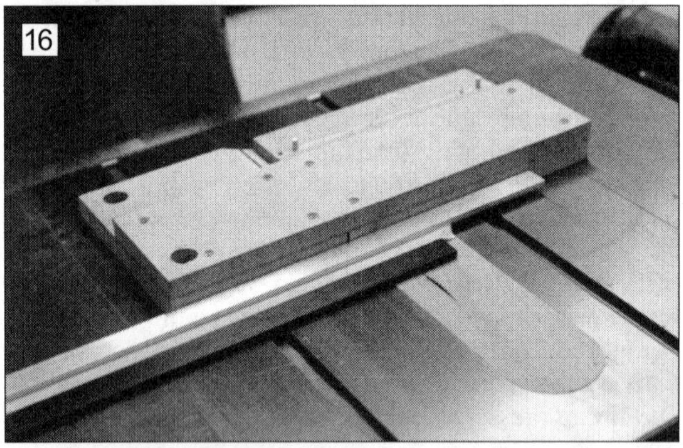

are also pinned between the walls. **Photo 14** shows this rig set up to trim the joint edge of a soundboard set. Note that the set is taped together for alignment purposes.

A very similar jig is shown in **Photo 15**, where the top set is run against a table router to form the actual glue joint (the overhead router is for binding, and is not in use here). The base of the jig includes a ¼″ thick steel straightedge that has been machined true, and a bearing on the bit shaft reads this straightedge. All router bits leave a microscopic series of dips along the machined edge, and the large bit minimizes them. This is pretty heavy equipment for a light-duty job.

The table saw doesn't have much to offer the luthier until he begins to jig up his operation, and then it comes into its own. The jig in **Photo 16** serves two functions according to how it is loaded onto the saw. Two runners guide the jig for extra stability. In the photo, fret slots are about to be cut in an ebony fingerboard. An aluminum fret stick, scribed with the proper fret locations, is taped to the fingerboard. The dark line on the side of the jig is a clearance cut for the jig's other function. The true index line is much harder to see, but shows up well in **Photo 17**, as do the fret location marks on the fret stick. The fingerboard is slid along the wall of the jig until the guides line up, then is pushed through the saw blade, a 6″ blade that cuts a slot .028″ wide used in conjunction with 5″ blade stiffeners (the set is available from Luthiers Mercantile International).

During its alternate function, the fret slotting jig is used to trim the headstock face lamination square to the neck blank and the nut slot. The truss rod slot drops over the ¼″ pins protruding from the table of the jig. The neck is indexed lengthwise by eye. The saw blade height is adjusted to cut flush with the upper surface of the jig, then the cut is made across the neck (**Photo 18**). Note that the fret-slotting blade has been replaced with the 10″, thin-kerf, 80-tooth carbide combination blade Charles uses for virtually all other table saw operations.

Another table saw jig serves double duty once the mahogany block that will form the heel has been glued

to the neck shaft (remember, Charles isn't using the Spanish style neck on his classical guitars). This jig uses a $3\frac{1}{2}''$ MDF wall screwed to an MDF platform (**Photo 19**). Pins in the wall index in the truss rod slot. Since the neck is now tapered, it can't simply be laid on the table top. The jig is held true to the saw blade by runners in the miter slots. Hand pressure holds the neck to the jig as the body end is sawn square.

Guide lines for the mortise in the heel are then drawn, and the width of the heel cap is marked on the heel. The neck is placed back on the jig, and the saw blade is lowered to match the bottom edge of the heel cap (**Photo 20**). In the photo the contour of the heel is drawn on to match the radius of the blade. The depth of the cut is adjusted and set with a stop block, and the excess material is nibbled from the heel one pass at a time (**Photo 21**). When the final pass is completed, the neck is flipped over and the other side of the heel is shaped. Charles gleaned this operation from Arthur Overholtzer's classical guitar book. The heel comes off the saw looking lean and racy. This really simplifies the job of shaping the heel symmetrically.

One last table-saw jig is peculiar to Charles' unique guitar design, and it is used to cut the slot for the spline that becomes the tenon that fits into the mortise in the heel block. Again, runners in the miter slots hold the jig square to the saw. Index pins in the vertical portion of the jig position the truss rod slot (**Photo 22**). The height of the dado set is adjusted, then the neck is held upside down in the jig and passed over the blade. Instant mortise.

If any of these jigs are in your future, your first step should be the creation of many feet of runner stock. If the slot in your belt sander table is a different size, make some runner stock for that and stash it away. Same thing for your bandsaw table. Although all the jigs require careful construction, the runners are often the only components that demand tight tolerances, and having the stock on hand will go a long way toward putting you in the mood for jig making.

Charles makes no bones about the fact that some of his methods may be too complex for some beginners. Mt. Everest shouldn't be your first target when you decide to take up mountain climbing. He also recognizes that many people who take up lutherie as a hobby find in simple tools and hand work a purity that is lost when the machinery and higher production goals enter the scene. Indeed, traditional construction methods are taught at ASL, and we'll get closer to them when we take a more detailed look at actual guitar construction. Admittedly, so far this report has been machine heavy and production biased, partly because Charles does it so well and partly because that was my chief interest when I got there. But don't be put off if it suddenly seems that your shop is under equipped. "Let your guitars pay for your equipment," is another Fox aphorism. You don't have to hock the kids to buy everything at once.

If you don't already receive a flock of tool and machinery catalogs you must be in the federal witness-protection program. Get a woodworking magazine and send for all the catalogs. Charles keeps an eye on the scene and reports that imported machinery is getting better and cheaper all the time. Heavy-duty equipment isn't required to make guitars. Table-top style $10''$ table

CYNDY BURTON

saws can be had for less than $200. The same is true for drill presses, 6″×48″ belt sanders, and bandsaws. Fox plans to set up two or three such table saws as dedicated equipment. When I was there, his immediate future included buying a case of laminate trimmer routers, each of them to be dedicated to a specific task and never changed. By the time your guitars are selling in the $5,000 range, you'll be able to think big, too.

Charles buys mahogany in 3″ thick planks and rips neck blanks off them. He then severs the headstock at an angle, flips it over, and glues it back on. The simple

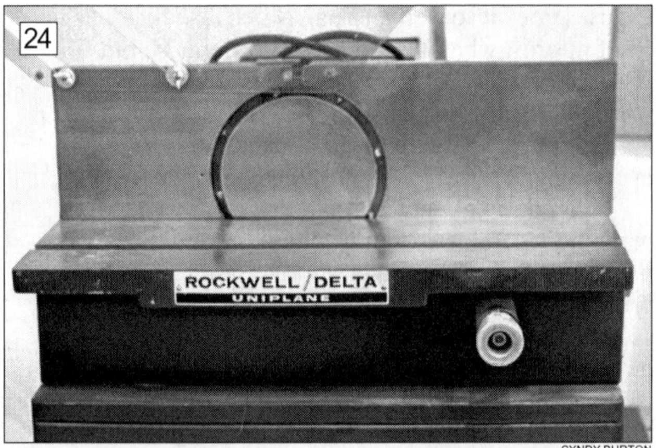

CYNDY BURTON

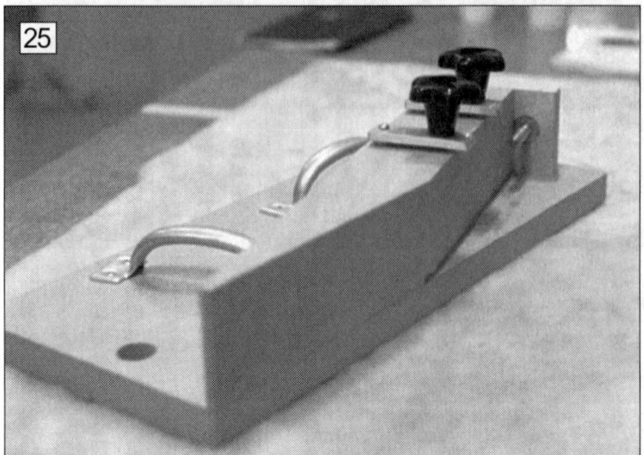

CYNDY BURTON

bandsaw jig shown in **Photo 23** is used for the decapitation. The jig feeds straight into the blade, the neck blank rests along the angled beam, and the bolt near Charles' hand acts as a stop to adjust the length of the cut-off portion.

Since the gluing surface of the headstock is now rough with saw marks, it must be accurately trued. Charles does this on a Rockwell Uniplane (**Photo 24**). The jig for this is shown in **Photo 25**. The headstock blank is held by the clamps on the angled beam. The cutting head of the Uniplane is mounted vertically, and the glue surface of the headstock is trimmed clean as it is passed by the cutter. The pieces are rejoined using a clamping box that holds the parts in alignment while clamping pressure is applied by a veneer press screw (**Photo 26**).

Charles tapers the arm and thins the headstock (front-to-back dimension) by bandsawing slices off the front. One jig is used for both operations (**Photo 27**). **Photo 28** shows how it's done. The fixture mounted to the back of the table is a reversible fence that is bolted in place. When the neck blank is mounted on the jig, it overhangs the edges by the amount that needs to be amputated. A long taper of mahogany is cut from what will be the fingerboard surface, and an even slice of wood is removed from the headstock.

The rough surfaces are then cleaned and trued on the Uniplane. Charles is quick to admit that this is overkill for most shops, but that he always wanted a Uniplane, which is no longer manufactured. It may be hard to find, but it certainly leaves a lovely surface on the mahogany. Again, two similar jigs are necessary to true the neck, one for the headstock and one for the neck arm. In **Photo 29** the neck surface is being planed to receive the fingerboard.

27

28

CYNDY BURTON

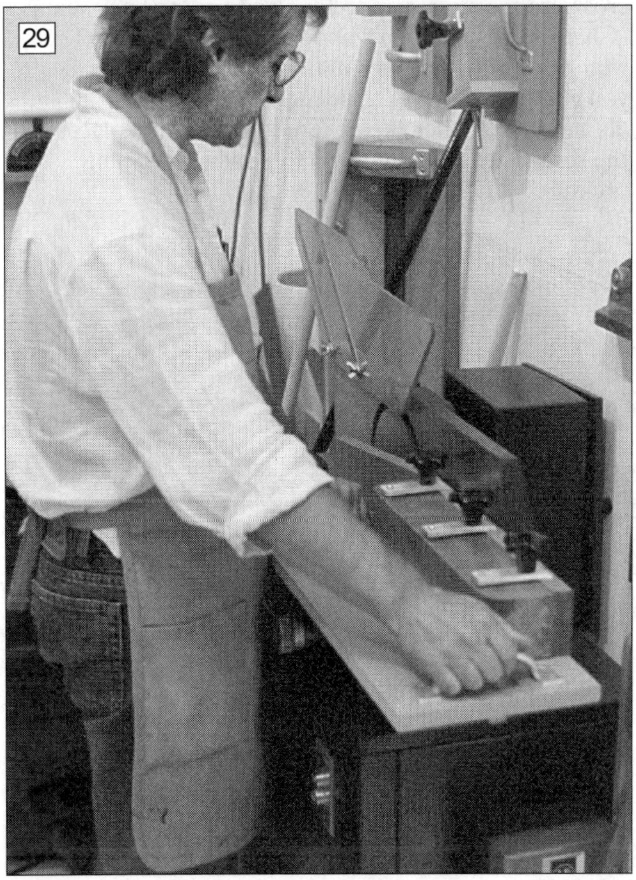
29

The peghead's face plate is separated from the headstock by a couple contrasting veneers, and yet another press is used to laminate them (**Photo 30**). The cams mounted on the main block hold the layers in alignment while pressure is applied with the veneer clamp. (Are you sensing a few repetitive themes at work here? When something works for you the easiest thing is to keep using it.)

The unit for which Charles is best known is the Fox Universal Sidebender. During his absence from the guitar scene, Luthier's Mercantile asked Charles if they could market a set of blueprints along with a hardware kit. Luthiers all over the world have since made their own sidebenders, and many larger guitar companies have installed them for specialized work. Most GAL members already know how this machine works, even if they haven't built one yet. Three 200w light bulbs inside the machine, or a dedicated heat blanket, are used to preheat a pair of stainless steel sheets. The moistened guitar side is sandwiched between the hot metal sheets, a veneer press screw presses the side/sheet-metal sandwich into the waist portion of the jig, and spring-loaded hold downs are used to pull the ends tight to the shape of the upper and lower bouts. The side is cooked between the metal sheets for fifteen minutes, then left to cool. As a bonus, a set of wood bindings can be bent simultaneously with each side. The machine is as close to foolproof as is possible, is no harder to put together than a guitar, and new guitar shaped-forms can be built as the need arises. In **Photo 31** Charles is holding an accessory part that bends a cutaway, again using a veneer press screw as the clamping force. Charles still does some hand bending for every guitar. The bending machine doesn't leave the sides quite perfect enough to suit him, so they are touched up on a hot copper pipe.

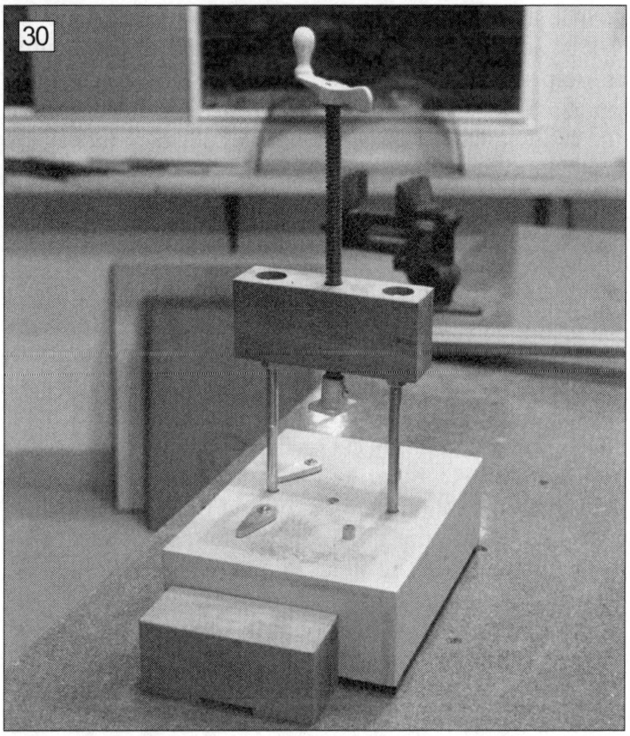
30

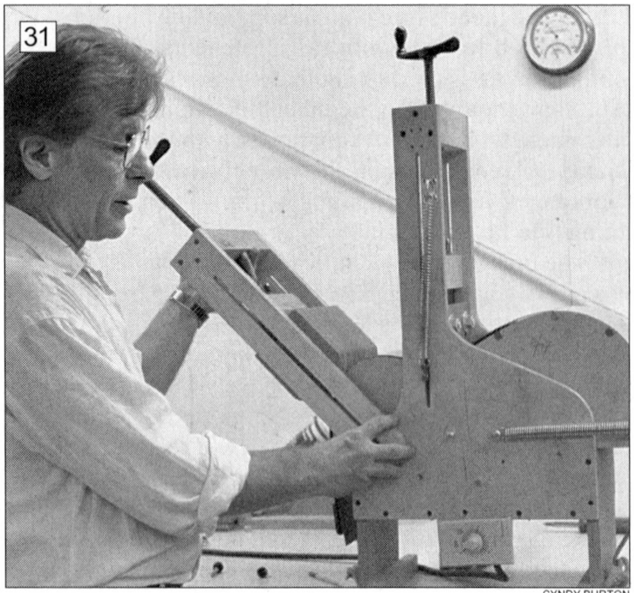

31

CYNDY BURTON

A clever pair of router jigs are used for two very similar functions. The principle behind the jigs is the same. **Photo 32** shows the jig that is used for routing the slot in the guitar back to accept a decorative seam strip. The back is clamped to the jig base using threaded inserts, bolts with knob heads, and aluminum bar stock to do the clamping. Fixed bolts with wing nuts protrude through slots in the moveable router guides. Note that each guide is made of two parts, a base and a fence. During construction the fence is glued to the base with too much of the base projecting under the router, then a pass from the router leaves the base exactly the right dimension to clear the router bit. Both guides are made this way. In use, the back is clamped to the jig's workboard, the center strip is positioned over the seam, then the router guides are brought into contact with the strip and bolted down. The strip is removed and the slot is routed. If the jig is accurately made, the procedure is foolproof, and no measuring is necessary to set up the operation other than the depth of cut. The bevels on the inside edges of the router guides permit a more accurate view of the final setup.

A very similar jig is shown in use in **Photo 33**. The guitar body, barely visible in the padded bench vise, is clamped in the rails of the jig. Charles is preparing to rout the slot for the trim that covers the butt seam of the sides. The jig is centered on the seam and the wing nuts on the jig rails are carefully tightened. The butt strip is held in place while the router guides are brought in to embrace it, after which the guides are locked in place. Set the depth of cut on the router and go.

Photo 34 is a picture of the auxiliary table on the ASL drill press. The unit is bolted to the iron drill-press table with the pin in the white table insert centered beneath the chuck. Interchangeable table inserts change the function of the table. The relief under the auxiliary surface permits the work piece to be clamped firmly in place.

The tour is winding down. We've already seen the more elaborate of Charles' shop creations. However,

32

CYNDY BURTON

33

CYNDY BURTON

the fact that other fixtures are smaller or easier to build does not make them less useful or elegant in design.

Photo 35 is a picture of a fixture used for gluing the cross-grain center strip to the inside of the back seam (Charles calls this thin wooden ribbon a "web"). The web stock is not in place in the illustration, but I'm sure you get the picture. The seam is aligned under the aluminum bar, the glue-covered web is put in place, and the screws are brought down to provide clamping pressure. Piece of cake.

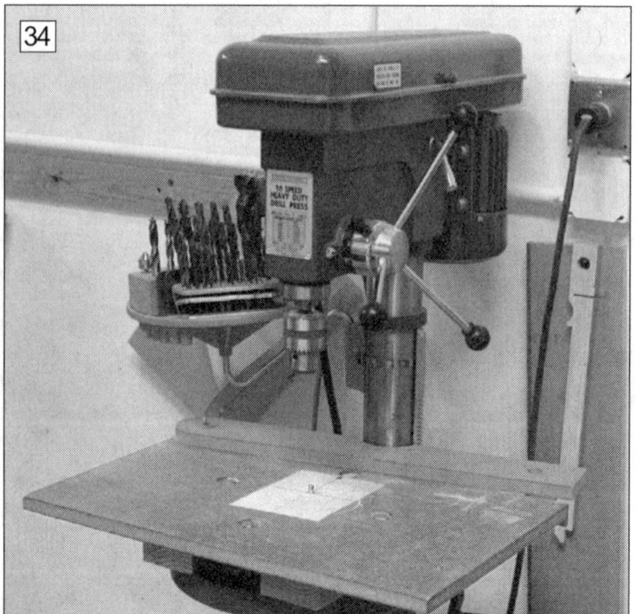

34

The fixture used to support the neck during hand shaping is the object of **Photo 36**. The headstock and fingerboard are clamped to the fixture, leaving the heel and the neck shaft unencumbered. Note the feet that hold the fixture upright on the workbench when not in the vise.

The concept of spherically arched guitar plates came into general acceptance while Charles was on hiatus. He was quick to embrace the spherically arched back, and the dished forms for this work figure prominently in the ASL program. The dish in **Photo 37** has pins inset that position the back braces while they are glued in place. Hold-down clamps for the back are threaded into the dish. After the glue is dry, the back unit has been moved to a portion of a dish that has been cut into a rectangle for the sake of easy access, and it's here that the braces are shaped with chisels and sandpaper.

The radiused dishes are available from Luthiers Mercantile, but Charles needed so many of them that he went down to the Mojave Desert and cut a deal with the man who makes them for LMI. You probably won't be able to do that. A couple students in the class had already made their own using a radiused cradle for their router that spanned the board to be dished. The round board was indexed on a center pin. When routing began the board tended to spin of its own accord. Multiple passes are necessary to cut the full dish, and some materials are more conducive to success than others. MDF may tend to warp as the dish deepens. Shallow relief cuts on the back (which make the board look like a target) help minimize the warping. The LMI boards are made from $1''$ MDF, rather than $\frac{3}{4}''$ stock, which minimizes warping.

Currently, the tops of the Fox guitars are not arched spherically, but cylindrically. Charles makes his own forms for laying up the arched tops using thick and thin workboards, forcing the thin board into a cylindrical

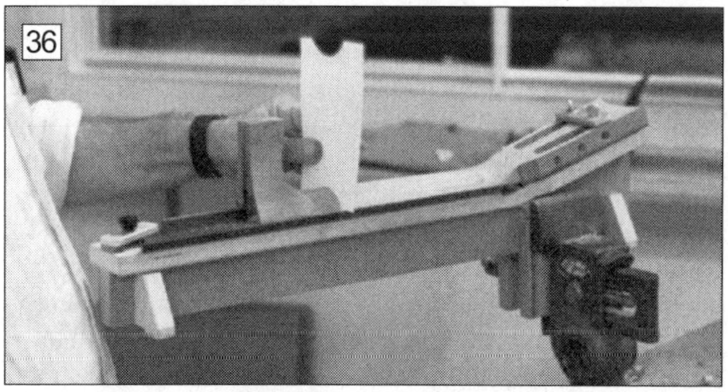

CYNDY BURTON

arch with equal stacks of posterboard between the boards. The first board was made by trial and error, and took some time. By counting the number of posterboard layers, and the graduated width of the stack, subsequent arched boards were easy to make. The edges are taped to keep the completed board secure, clean, and pretty.

Two methods of rough shaping the headstock on the bandsaw are shown. The first (**Photo 38**) uses a riser block on a workboard bolted to the iron table of the saw. Charles has drilled and tapped several holes in his bandsaw table for such uses. The second method uses a jig to which the neck is clamped. A round block mounted on yet another workboard acts as a bearing guide for the jig. As the jig is run against the bearing, the headstock is automatically cut to the shape of the jig (**Photo 39**). After the tuner holes are bored, a $\frac{1}{4}''$ aluminum template is fixed to the peghead and a router with a bearing mounted on the bit shaft is used to rout the peghead slots and clean the profile of the headstock.

Binding guitars was a bugaboo for most members of the class I attended. Charles explained about six ways

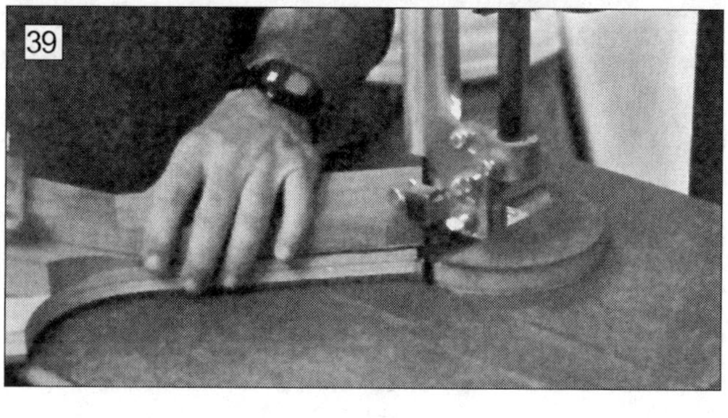

to do it. **Photo 40** shows a router base for cutting binding rabbets. If guitar plates were flat, binding would be easy to install. The trouble is that binding must be installed square to the sides, not square to the curved plates. This router base has an extended foot that reads the sides of the guitar, while the tiny portion of the base that actually rests on the plate is too small to be affected by the curvature. **Photo 41** shows this base mounted on a router. Charles maintains that the weight of a medium-size router is helpful in stabilizing the process.

By the way, Charles is highly enthusiastic about the Shopsmith combination machine. It uses one drive to power a table saw, drill press, disk sander, and so on. You name it, Shopsmith probably makes an accessory for it. It is not a heavy-duty machine, but a luthier's shop doesn't require powerful equipment. Most of the Fox school in Vermont was constructed with a Shopsmith, and when it closed, the Shopsmith was the one piece of equipment Charles was certain to store away. When he decided to start ASL, the Shopsmith was hauled out of retirement and used to build the new shop. His advice is worth repeating: begin small and let your guitars pay for more elaborate machinery. Even after you are fully equipped, if you still have the Shopsmith, you'll have two of everything. That can be *very* helpful during the production of many parts.

CYNDY BURTON

Shopsmiths are often available used for truly reasonable prices, often as low as $600 for a fully equipped machine. Keep an eye on the classifieds of your local papers. Charles even bought a second Shopsmith to use for parts on his original.

It's worth repeating that the main function of custom tooling is to make the work more accurate. Increased production rate is a welcome by-product. Not only does the actual work progress more rapidly, but much of the hesitation between steps is removed because you create a set plan of attack that eliminates all the variables you once had to consider. In many cases the next step comes as easily as loading the jig and turning on the proper machine. There is no down time while you sip coffee and build your courage for the approaching test of your abilities.

Before I arrived at ASL I already had an idea of what characteristics were embodied in a master luthier. The confidence instilled by years of experience and the construction of dozens or hundreds of instruments is a huge factor in precise and speedy work and manifests itself in every procedure. To pick a simple example, a beginner is likely to cut wide of his layout lines to allow for a fudge factor, then expend a large amount of time working down to dimensions that were correct to begin with. The master cuts right to the line, then goes on to the next operation. Experience has made the master's hands deft and has removed all the mystery from the building process. Everything is done with direct intention. Good luthiers develop the same effortless concentration as good musicians. I'm not sure these factors can be learned, but they can be earned; at some point they just come to you.

There's also no denying that talent has an individual, perhaps even genetic quotient that is out of our control. Builders also have an individual outlook that makes their guitars unique. Some luthiers build wonderful guitars but never worry about pushing their woodworking skills to the highest possible level. When their intuition tells them to quit, they quit. The difference never shows up in the music. But Charles' advice is that we always strive to get better.

Many of the characteristics of Fox guitars are driven by the market place. For instance, since the market is willing to pay a premium for a rosewood guitar, rosewood is the obvious choice of materials. Charles isn't inclined to try alternative woods simply to indulge his curiosity. His guitars will always have a decorative strip down the back seam because that is what is expected in the best guitars. And though a personalized rosette on his classicals seemed superfluous in light of the fine rosettes that can be bought, he was willing to concede that he would likely have to come up with a design of his own, if only to be more recognizable in the stores. There will always be a compromise between creativity and practicality.

We'll get to the design factors Charles incorporates as we examine how he creates a guitar, but first I'd like to address a few general considerations as well as his work habits.

Charles is very particular about the visual aspects of his guitars. His shop is next door to Luthier's Mercantile International, which gives him access to one of the largest supplies of tonewood in the country. He's able to select wood for appearance, then go back and grade it for stiffness and other physical characteristics. This may seem an unfair advantage, but as Charles says, "I don't see why any guitar maker would live any place other than Healdsburg." Immediate access to wood also spares him the necessity of stockpiling large quantities. Once purchased, each top and back is mated for the most perfect mirror image in the book match. Each side set is trimmed for the best match at the butt seam.

Fox uses four kinds of glue for each guitar. Titebond is used for general construction. Titebond II is used for special purposes. For example, because it is more heat resistant than regular Titebond, he uses Titebond II on X braces and fan braces, which will help keep them intact should heat ever be used to remove a bridge. Titebond II also reaches leather hardness quicker, which can be an advantage under certain circumstances. The chief disadvantage of Titebond II is that it leaves a visible orange trace along the glue line which makes it unsuitable for many applications. Charles uses thin CA glue for adhering bindings, which are always made of wood. Slow-set epoxy is used to glue the graphite neck reinforcement bar and fingerboard in place.

Charles doesn't enjoy the tedium of building in batches, and sees no need for it in a small-scale production setting. He has created storage space for work in progress, so he is never caught with a full bench while he waits for glue to dry. Although each guitar ties up the mold for an extended period of time, other work (perhaps on another guitar) continues on workboards simultaneously. There are end blocks and braces to be made, not to mention all the neck work. Once the order of events is established, the work flows naturally, nonstop, and when a workboard or the mold is emptied, the work on the next guitar is begun. There is no down time, and never a need to sand six guitars in a row, for instance.

The sequence of events that follows makes editorial sense, but doesn't pretend to follow the order of events that Charles might use in actual practice. Neither is it a representation of the flow of information in class at ASL. And as mentioned before, the information will change as Fox's guitar making evolves.

The most important place to match the grain pattern of the sides is at the butt. Once matched, the sides are taped together and trimmed on the table saw to establish the edge that will be glued to the top. The sides are not trimmed to length at this time. The side bending machine indexes off a line at the waist of the guitar, not off the ends, and isn't absolutely precise.

The Universal Sidebender is closed up just as if a side was in place, and preheated for five minutes. A side is moistened with a spray bottle of water just before the sheet-metal bending forms reach maximum temperature. Charles does not advocate soaking or saturating the sides, since it can cause rippling of the wood, and since luthiers place a premium on well-seasoned wood, it seems foolish to intentionally introduce any more water than necessary.

Two lengths of wood binding can be bent at the same time as a side. The waist area is bent first, then the bouts are bent individually.

Each side is left under full heat in the bender for fifteen minutes to dry, which helps set the wood in its new shape. Nevertheless, it's safest to wait overnight for complete drying. Even when fresh from the bending machine, Charles finds that the sides may not fit the mold perfectly, and that a bit of touchup on a hot pipe is necessary. Fresh sides need not be wetted before they face the pipe. Prebent sides that have waited to be used may have succumbed to a degree of springback that requires a more severe reshaping, and the spritzer bottle is called into service again in such a case. The precise fit isn't made to the mold, but to the template from which the mold was made. Always go back to a primary source.

Once he is happy with the shape of the sides, they are trimmed to length on the bandsaw. These are not finished edges, and any chipping left from the saw will be cleaned up later. The butt seam will receive a decorative graft, and the head seam will be routed away when forming the mortise that will receive the graphite tenon of the neck. At this point the inner sides are scraped clean. Though well sanded to begin with, wetting and bending can raise the grain and force oils to ooze from the rosewood, and light colored woods might be lightly scorched upon occasion. Charles is concerned that the interior of the box must be nicely finished, and that any part of the interior visible through the soundhole must be immaculately dressed.

Creation of Charles' elaborate heel block was not something we witnessed in my class. In **Photo 42,** a heel block for one of his classical guitars sits upon a heel block for a steel string guitar. They are dimensionally similar, since both guitars will come from the same mold. However, the steel string block has holes for the neck-mounting bolts and is dressed a bit differently.

Photo 43 shows the end blocks being glued in place in Charles' elaborate mold #3. Clamps hold the sides down to the built-in workboard while another set of clamps hold the tail block in place from the top. The back of the heel block has a mortise to accept the graphite spline mounted in the neck, and the mold is cut with a matching mortise. A wooden spline fixes the heel block in precise position in the mold. Another turnbuckle spreader bar will apply pressure to the waist area. Note that the sides are substantially taller than the heel block.

Once bent, the sides could have been marked with the paper pattern and trimmed to shape with a coping saw, the method most of us will no doubt use; but Charles' trick mold permits him a much slicker maneuver. Remember that the guitar is being built on its face. The built-in workboard of the mold is flat. However, the top edge of the mold is shaped with the same spherical arch that the back of the guitar will receive. Charles made a router base with the female equivalent of the same arch, then mounted a fly cutter in the router. One trip around the perimeter of the guitar leaves the sides neatly trimmed and with the proper bevel to accept the back. In **Photo 44** it's apparent how much material is being removed.

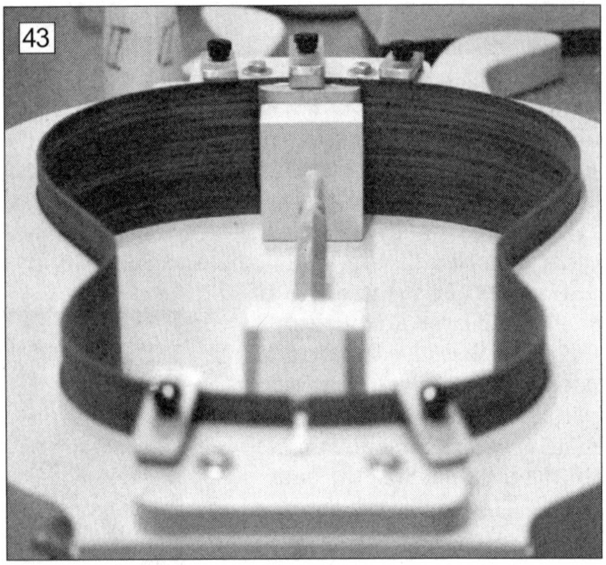
43

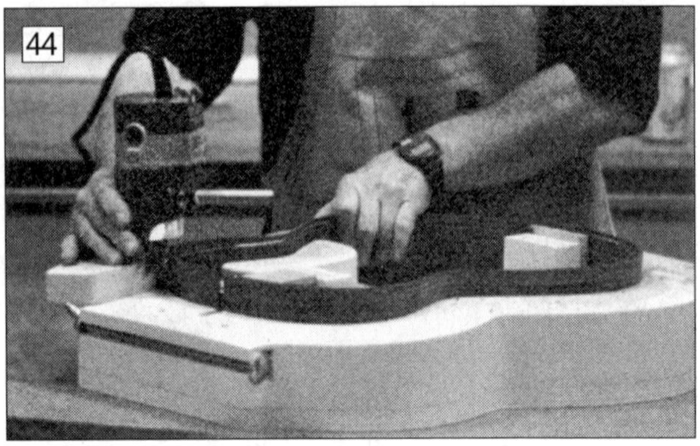
44

Charles was using commercial kerfed lining when I was there. He doesn't consider the choice of lining wood to be a strong factor in the tone production of guitars, but wishes that someone would produce the design of his choice. He has two sets of sides that were put away when he left Vermont. One side has conventional kerfed lining, and it's not only floppy but has deformed over the years. The second set has kerfed linings with the kerfed surface glued to the sides. This set has held its shape and is much more rigid that the first. Stiffer is good. The linings are prebent by hand, then glued in proud of the sides with no attempt made to coerce them to match the topography of the edge. Charles uses clothes pins, just like the rest of us. (In early 1997, Fox began to manufacture his own reversed lining. It is 1″ tall and ¼″ thick, and is finished to a quarter-round on its inside edge.)

When the glue is dry he hauls out the same router and trims the lining to the sides (again, leaving the glue surface with the arch of the back). The router, however, can't reach all the surfaces of the end blocks. A sanding stick of the proper radius can finish the job, or a dished form can be used as a huge sanding block to bring the entire back into uniformity. At this point the side assembly is put aside.

There is an alternate method of fitting the back for those of us who have yet to invest in such an elaborate mold (as probably few of us intend to do). The side-to-side arch of the back can be established either with prearched braces and a spherically dished form, or, more simply, with prearched braces and similarly arched cauls for the other side of the back. Charles is beginning the bracing operation in **Photo 45**. The braces are left overly long to fit between indexing pins in the form which establish the brace positions.

Once the back is lifted from the dish, the fore-and-aft arch is lost. It is restored by the setup in **Photo 46**. A stout straightedge is tied to the back by the center brace. The proper arch is induced with wedges.

45

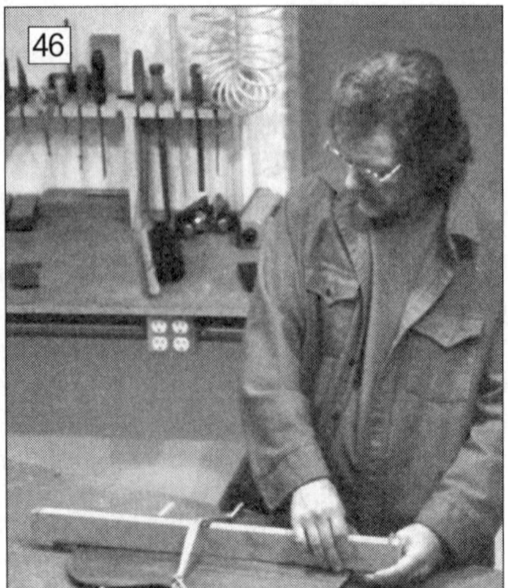
46

The side assembly is put in the adjustable mold (mold #2), and the back, still in its arching harness, is balanced in place over the sides (**Photo 47**). If necessary, wedges are used to even the orientation of the top. A set of dividers with a pencil mounted in one leg is adjusted to the widest gap between the back and the sides, and while one leg rides the back, the pencil transfers the contours to the sides. On dark wood, it helps to tape off the sides with masking tape to make the pencil line more legible. The sides are block planed to the pencil line while holding the plane at an angle steeper than the proper arch, leaving the linings too high. Then the linings and end blocks are dressed down with an arched sanding stick or the dished form lined with sandpaper. As you might guess, the dished form will do a more accurate, faster, and more satisfying job, but a determined luthier without such paraphernalia will eventually learn to do as good a job. After the back is fitted, Charles invited the class to view the assembly close up and from bench height. The sinuous, rolling lines of the dressed edge are quite pleasant to behold.

If the back and sides are perfectly mated they can be glued together using only masking tape for clamping force. Again, Charles has a more elaborate version, and one that can be used without the rest of his fancy mold. He cut a dished form into a caul the shape of his guitar, then lined the pressure points with dense foam. This was shown earlier in **Photo 6**. He secures the back to the sides with a few tabs of tape to keep them registered, then finishes the job with four Klemsia clamps (**Photo 48**).

Let's backtrack, since we've skipped the construction of the back. It's in the nature of instruction that the clearest path doesn't lie in the straightest line, an element that comes into play at ASL as well. Charles uses an interesting and ancient method of joining plates, but it shows up in the section about tops, so jump ahead if you like.

The decorative back seam strip is inlaid with a fixture seen in **Photo 49**, a workboard to which the back is clamped, and over which is mounted two moveable platforms, each one of which has a fence to guide a router with a particular bit. The inside edge of each platform is as far from its fence as the edge of the router base is from the cutting edge of the bit. The strip is laid in place, and the platforms are closed upon it like jaws and locked in place. The strip is removed and a preset, dedicated router is run across platforms. The procedure takes a couple of minutes. Once glued in place, the center strip is scraped level with the back. The master template is used to trace the shape of the guitar on the back, and it is bandsawn to shape.

Charles has a special workboard for gluing the cross-grain spruce strip to the back, which was shown in **Photo 35**, but he is as likely to perform the operation in a go-bar deck. Charles calls this brace a "web," and by the time he finishes shaping it, it's hardly more than that. He contends that overly cautious luthiers pay too large a price in tone by over-bracing their guitars.

Charles moves to the customized dished form for gluing prearched braces to the back, which was shown in **Photo 37**. The back is aligned on center and held firmly by his ubiquitous shop-made aluminum clamps. The braces are held against the pairs of pins and glued to the back in the go-bar deck. The rough braces are first tapered with a chisel. They are tapered so finely on the

ends that even though they reach under the lining, no allowance need be made for them when the back is fitted to the sides (**Photo 50**). Sheet-metal strips are used to protect the back as the braces are block planed to final shape and sanded, then the back is glued to the ribs.

When the glue has dried, the guitar is removed from the mold and the back is dressed even with the sides using a wood file and sanding blocks. It is then returned to the mold, top side up. The flat base of the mold is replaced with a dished form to give the back full and proper support.

When laying out the joint of the back plate, Charles symmetrically balances the figure of the wood. There is no reason to try to hide the joint, since the decorative back strip is going to make it boldly obvious that two pieces of wood are involved. On the top, however, he takes pains to find the one grain line that might best disguise the glue line, and it is to that line the set is trimmed on the table saw using the elaborate fixture that holds the spruce in place with wooden cams. The top set is taped together to maintain proper register. The set is then transferred to a similar fixture where the glue edge is perfected on a table router using a large pattern-maker's bit. The router leaves a cleaner edge for gluing than the saw blade.

Charles' method of edge joining the plates with ropes and wedges goes back to the ancient Egyptians. It can be done entirely with sticks, wedges, and rope, but as he is inclined to do, Charles has made a more elaborate, permanent version. The glue-up hardly takes longer to perform than it does to describe. The support sticks are placed in their slots (**Photo 51**), the top is put in position, and glue is applied (**Photo 52**). A long cord is tied over the top at each brace in a figure-eight

pattern. The cord is snug but not tight, since over-tightening could buckle the joint (**Photo 53**). Wedges are slid under the cord, simultaneously supporting the top and snugging the glue joint (**Photo 54**).

Rosettes are set into the top in a manner familiar to most luthiers. A ¼″ hole is drilled in the top plate dead center where the soundhole will be. A router mounted on a commercial circle-cutting base is indexed through this hole. All layout lines and trial cuts are done near the top of the soundhole where the fingerboard will be glued. The slot for the inner edge is cut just shy of perfect, and micro-adjustments of the router bring the cut to the correct dimension. The rosette is held in place while the outer edge is marked, the router reset (again just shy of the mark). One last micro-correction should bring in a perfect fit once any remaining waste wood is routed away. Perhaps the most important consideration is that Charles finds commercial rosettes to be sliced much thinner than they used to be, and that they must be carefully set to their full depth in the top wood. They are also more inclined to be out of round than in the past, but he finds that there is enough give in the routing setup that a careful worker can force the correct degree of eccentricity without adjusting the router base.

Rather than using a spherically arched form to make his tops, Fox uses a workboard with a cylindrical arch. This is a feature to which he is not totally married, and you may find a different procedure by the time you get to ASL. His classical guitars utilize a traditional seven-fan brace pattern. We asked to see him glue up a steel string top, so Charles made one with a conventional X pattern. However, on his own steel strings he has always used what he refers to as a floating spider pattern. It is similar to the double-X pattern Gibson used to use, with the bridge plate located between the Xs. Charles' version is much lighter, though, and all the braces taper off to almost nothing as they approach the lining, as we saw in his back braces. All his braces are arched on the belt sander using a jig that functions just like the ones that sand the end blocks to fit the sides. When necessary, the braces are mated to the top by rubbing them in the sandpaper-covered cylindrical form.

In **Photo 55** the X braces are being glued to the top in the go-bar deck. The entire assembly is mounted on the cylindrical workboard. Only the speed and convenience of a vacuum-clamping system could dissuade Charles from using the go-bar deck. He is quite enthusiastic about the sculptural beauty of the deck in use. The vacuum system is also demonstrated in class.

The top is moved to a smaller workboard before the braces are shaped. Squeeze-out is cleaned up with a straight chisel. The braces are tapered with a 10″ dogleg pattern maker's chisel (**Photo 56**), then sanded to height using a wide sanding block. The shortest fan brace is 6mm tall, and the fans taper in height until the longest is only 3mm–4mm tall. Final shaping is accomplished with the dogleg chisel and sandpaper. A good two-thirds of the brace stock is removed during shaping.

The method used to mate the top and sides can also be used for the back and sides if you work from an arched workboard. The guitar is removed from the mold. Masking tape is applied to the sides, then the unit is placed face down on the cylindrical workboard. Wedges are used to adjust the sides until the gap at the tail is similar to the gap at the heel block, and dividers are adjusted to that gap (**Photo 57**). Then one leg of the dividers follows the contour of the board, while the pencil draws the contour on the tape. With the guitar returned to the mold, the sides are block planed to the line, again holding the plane at an angle greater than the dome of the top. An arched sanding board is then used to accurately mate the sides to the top. Linings are applied proud of the sides, then planed to the ribs, after which the sanding board is again used to perfect the joint line. Extra strong masking tape is used to clamp the top to the sides during glue-up, while a Pony clamp

58

59

60

holds the top to the heel block (**Photo 58**). Note that the mold and guitar are once again nestled snugly in a dished workboard.

The body is removed from the mold, which can now be loaded with another set of sides. Any overhang of the top is filed and sanded away, then the sides are carefully scraped smooth and clean.

From this point the body lives in a cradle until the neck is attached.

Virtually all the members of my ASL class admitted a dislike for the binding process. Charles begins his explanation with hand cutters and chisels, but it should surprise no one that he has several mechanized variations to offer. Custom router bases are an obvious option. **Photo 59** shows one with a tapered base made to ride the arched plates. A base of another style is shown in **Photo 60**. This base has the advantage of registering on the side of the guitar, rather than the plate. The pad that rests on the plate is too small to be affected by the curve of the plate. Charles was developing a router mounted on a sliding vertical column that should eliminate all the risk and inaccuracy, but it wasn't functioning while I was there.

A certain amount of hand fitting of the binding is usually necessary, a bit of irritation to most of us that

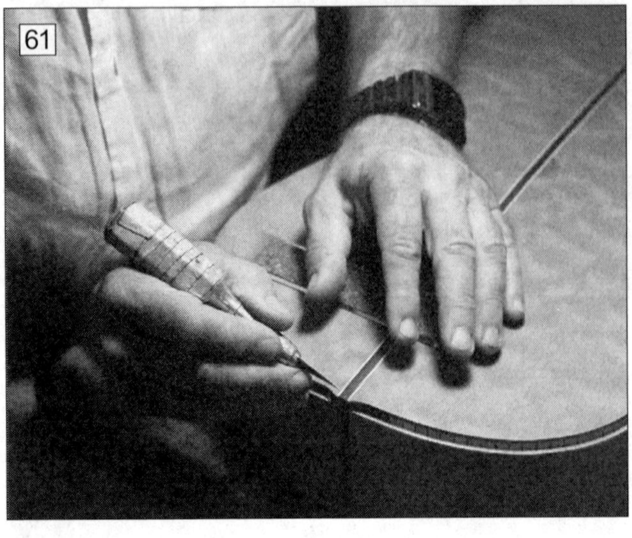

61

Charles takes in stride and deals with matter-of-factly. The back binding must be mitered with the back seam inlay (**Photo 61**). The binding might have to be rebent slightly (dry) on the hot pipe. Charles glues the binding with thin superglue, holding it in place as capillary action draws the glue into the joint, occasionally cleaning the rabbet ahead of him with a chisel. One of his coolest tricks is simply the use of the fingertips cut from a heavy rubber glove. The rubber fingers get stuck to the guitar time and again, but pull free without a struggle. After binding an entire body he had no superglue on his fingers. Slick!

After the neck blank is made on the bandsaw and the uniplane as shown in **Photos 23–29**, a dado set is used to plow the truss rod slot. Steel string necks have a rod that adjusts through the soundhole. Classical necks have a $\frac{1}{4}'' \times \frac{1}{2}''$ graphite bar that extends from the headstock to a slot cut in the heel block to receive it.

The headstock veneers are clamped in place using a special press (**Photo 62**). The box in the foreground holds a variety of veneers.

The headstock is roughed to shape on the bandsaw, and the taper is cut on the shaft of the neck. A template of plexiglas and a router equipped with a pattern maker's bit were used to shape the headstock and cut the tuner slots (**Photo 63**).

Classical machine heads come three on a plate utilizing a standardized post spacing. Charles uses a commercial drilling jig and a hand drill to seat the tuners (**Photo 64**). Masking tape wrapped around the drill bit acts as a depth stop.

The front edge of the headstock veneers have to be cut square to the nut slot they will help create. Charles is jigged up to do this chore on the table saw, but the operation can easily be done with a back saw on the bench (**Photo 65**). A press similar to the one used to glue up the headstock veneers is used to glue the block that will form the heel to the neck.

Preliminary shaping of the heel is done on the table saw using a jig shown in **Photos 19, 20, and 21**).

The fingerboard was slotted and precisely tapered on the table saw, and at this time the graphite bar and the fingerboard are glued in place (**Photo 66**). The

62

63

64

carpenter's level acts as a clamping caul. The C clamps keep the board from slipping sideways, and the Pony clamps provide gluing pressure.

Preliminary shaping begins with a small spokeshave (**Photo 67**). Charles recommends that the neck be laid out in a series of lines running the length of the neck. One line is drawn below the fingerboard and one on either side of the centerline. All the wood between these two lines is removed, leaving a facet. Other lines can be drawn and new, narrower, facets cut, until the neck becomes gradually round. Altering the position of the lines changes the shape of the neck. It's an accurate

65

66

and predictable way to carve a neck. (A more elaborate description of this shaping process can be found in *American Lutherie #33.* See *Big Red Book of American Lutherie Volume Three,* p. 306.)

After the spokeshave a series of rasps and files are used to shape the neck. A template is used to insure neck-to-neck consistency (**Photo 68**).

A final shoeshine with 80-grit paper removes all flat spots and makes any remaining rasp marks obvious (**Photo 69**).

The heel is shaped separately (**Photo 70**), but the same faceting system can be used. Preshaping the heel on the table saw helps a lot toward a symmetrical shape.

A careful scraping leaves the neck ready to fit to the body. A complete demonstration of fretting and instrument finishing is not part of the ASL agenda, but Charles freely discusses both. Seventy hours just isn't enough time to cover all there is to say about guitar

67

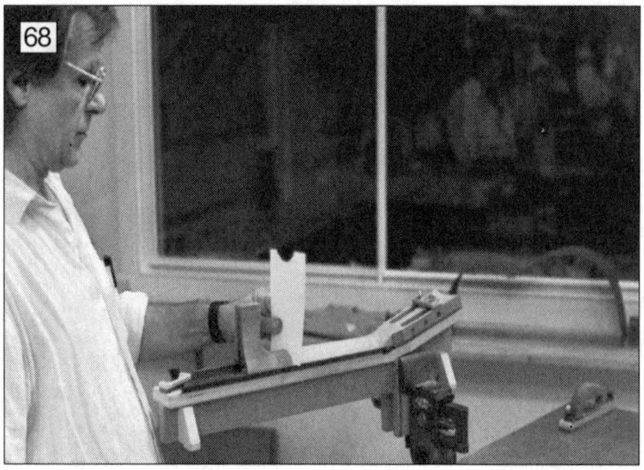

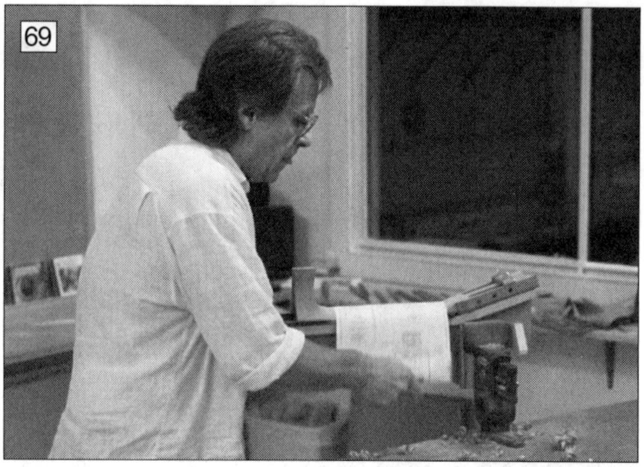

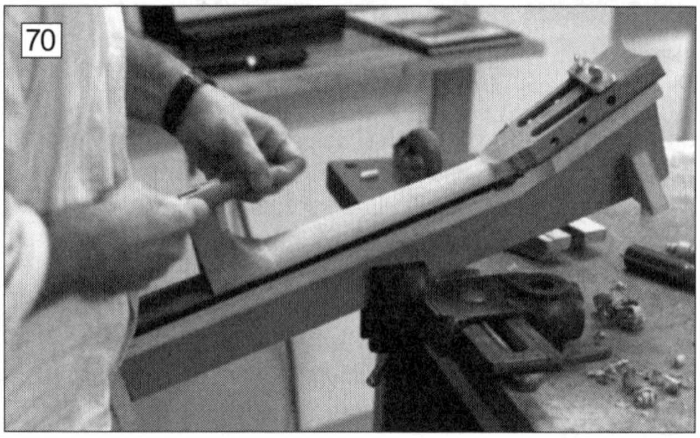

construction. However, there are usually a couple periods of time where Charles has to do repetitive work in order to move the guitar toward the next step, and while he works, the class is encouraged to watch professional videos about fretting and finishing. They may also watch him work if they prefer.

There is still the little matter of fitting the neck to the body. After all the jiggery, the fit should be pretty close as is. A template is used to find the proper relationship of neck to body. An insert mounted in the end of the template represents the height of the bridge. The neck is tipped until the insert touches the top, and a small C clamp fastened to the fingerboard through the soundhole holds it in position. Posterboard shims are stacked along the heel until they equal the largest gap between body and heel (while the guitar is held upright in the vise), then a line is scribed on the heel across the top of the stack. The heel is trimmed back to the scribed line, and the fit should be perfect.

Photo 71 shows a view of the template setup. Note how obvious the arch of the top is. It's imperative that this arch be incorporated into the bottom of the bridge or the top will certainly be cracked when clamps are applied.

Once the neck is fitted to the body and a heel cap is installed, you've pretty much got a guitar. ——

Update

Since I attended ASL Charles has equipped his fancy mold with a vacuum system that sucks the ribs to the mold and the plates to their contoured clamping cauls.

——*John Calkin (2006)*

Originally published in *American Lutherie #54*, 1998

After the Fox:

How Charles Changed my Lutherie Life

by John Calkin

WHEN I SET UP my lutherie shop in 1980 I had no intention of ever making acoustic guitars. Three things happened in fairly rapid succession that clinched my resolve.

First of all, good guitars were everywhere. There was an especially rich deposit of '60s Guilds knocking around, and as they passed through my shop for repairs I couldn't imagine why anyone would invest in a custom flattop when they could pick up, for cheap, a decent guitar that already had character.

Secondly, I helped a friend run the sound system at a charity folk gathering, an event that drew good talent armed with beautiful high-end guitars, but they were all blown off the stage by a plywood Yamaha. At first strum it seemed like God had joined us in the dimly lit church basement, the difference in tone was that dramatic. If a cheapo instrument could do that, what was the point of investing my life in the creation of guitars that might never measure up?

To top things off, I bought a copy of David Russell Young's *The Acoustic Guitar*, and was introduced to the theory of domed plates. It made complete sense, but gearing up to make such guitars seemed like too much work. I went back to my electric guitars and dulcimers.

Well, times change. At the same time that the high-end acoustic market began to expand, the custom electric market was co-opted by factory custom shops. The supply of good used Yamahas and Guilds was replaced by a pool of not-so-satisfactory Yamahas, Sigmas, and Takamines. I began to piddle around with flattops. They came out OK, but were never wholly pleasing to the critical eye.

It's fair to say that Charles Fox and his American School of Lutherie not only resurrected my interest in the flattop but gave me the keys to build them on a whole other level. Charles would be dismayed to know that I left the school with reservations about the program, but upon looking back, I believe that it was my exhaustion doing the thinking. I think we were a dozen brain-dead guitar junkies as the class headed home. I don't know about the others, but it took me weeks to recover. But as I began to revamp my shop according to what I had learned at ASL, an all-new enthusiasm began to brew inside me, and it grew with each new piece of gear I put together. When I actually began to build guitars, my enthusiasm blossomed into a hunger. I couldn't wait to get out to the shop each morning, and I couldn't believe how fast the guitars went together. My past production had been less than a guitar a year, and it was certainly the frustration factor that kept me from trying to work faster. In no time at all I had five new bodies awaiting binding, and all of them were better made than anything I had done in the past. And that's not to mention the ukes and mandos I assembled at the same time with the same equipment.

I hasten to add that all this was done on a severe budget. Moving to a remote neighborhood in Virginia virtually put me out of the lutherie business, and reinvesting in my shop in any major way seemed like a foolish endeavor. I've put less than $350 into new gear since ASL, and that's counting a silicone heating blanket for $110. My largest expense for the complete shop revitalization has been medium-density fiberboard, mounting hardware, and glue. So far I've used five sheets of MDF, with two more quartered sheets waiting in the wings. None of the jigs or fixtures is especially time-intensive to create, it's just that there's so many of them. Don't be put off by this. Just approach them one at a time and they'll fall like dominoes.

I hope this will seem like more than a regurgitation of the jigs and fixtures we examined in an earlier ASL article, but I'm not sure I can capture the enthusiasm for the guitar that I got from Charles Fox. I take the guitar far more seriously now, not only because it deserves it, but because I finally feel qualified to approach it with a competence and confidence I didn't have before. I may not launch back into the industry, but I certainly won't have to make excuses for my personal guitars. It will also be obvious that I have collected ideas from sources other than ASL. Charles would be the first to acknowledge that no one person has all the answers. Keep scouting the terrain, there are plenty of good ideas out there.

Medium-density fiberboard is a very useful material, though it has some shortcomings. Low expense and stability are MDF's key virtues, though it will swell a bit during high humidity the same as any other material made of wood. It's not terribly strong, however. Running nails or screws into its edges is always risky, since the material flakes apart easily. Tape will pull chunks from the surface of MDF, especially double-sided tape. Large jigs and workboards that are dropped on the floor are easily mutilated, and their glue joints might pop apart in a ragged fashion. Plates of unsupported ¾″ MDF warp readily when placed under stress. The material machines beautifully, but the dust particles created are so fine that they pack cuts solidly. I normally use a hole saw to cut sheet stock scraps into rounds for spool clamps, but the first time I tried this with MDF, smoke poured off the work and the saw dust compressed itself into coals that glowed a bright red. If such coals were unknowingly sucked into a dust collector, a fire might easily be the result. I have formed the habit of bandsawing scrap MDF into the largest possible rectangular pieces. They have proven so useful for building small jigs and clamping cauls, that after using up three full sheets all my little leftovers dropped into a shoe box.

The first order of the day was the creation of dished workboards. A board with a $25'$ radius has become standard for guitar tops, and a $15'$-radius board is usually used for the back. I also wanted boards with much tighter radii. Commercial boards cost at least \$65 each, plus shipping, and only the two common measurements are offered. My boards came out to \$8 apiece and have proven wholly satisfactory. The usual method of construction is to rout the radius into $1''$ MDF using a large router mounted on a radiused carrier, but the ordeal sounded too time consuming and messy. I opted to make multipart workboards using MDF as the foundation and $\frac{1}{4}''$ tempered masonite for the dish. The two sheets are separated by spokes of MDF that bear the proper radius **(Photo 1)**. A jig was made up to assure the uniformity of the spokes **(Photo 2)**, which are finished on the drill press using a Robo-Sander, a sanding drum with a bearing guide bolted to its bottom. The dished boards were initially assembled using twelve spokes, but the edge of the masonite proved too floppy. Eleven more spokes were inserted between the original dozen, and the problem was solved.

It has by no means been conclusively proven that a domed top plate sounds superior to a flat top. The mechanical advantages seem obvious, however. A flat plate is normally deformed by the tension of the strings. It becomes arched, but not evenly so. Arching the plate by means of curved braces creates a stronger top unit that offers the string tension a shape that should deform to a much smaller degree over time. A domed top also has some give when subjected to low humidity. It can flatten out, whereas a flat plate can only crack. All this is largely theoretical, but it makes too much sense to ignore. Fitting domed or arched plates to the ribs used to be one of the most frustrating aspects of guitar making since a poor fit can introduce stresses that may crack the plates before the guitar is even strung up, but the dished workboards make accurate assembly a given, and the time involved is minimal. Fitting a back used to take me as long as half a day. A quarter hour is more like it now. The shallower arch of the top makes it even easier to fit, and is often accomplished during the span of one song on the radio.

I made my dished workboards $22''$ in diameter, which is just large enough to conveniently build a standard dreadnought. In the future I'll make them $24''$ across like the commercial versions. Initially I thought I'd need a few boards in each radius, but one in each size has sufficed. I covered them with 80-grit abrasive from 6×48 sanding belts using rubber cement. After eight instruments the paper looks a little ragged, but it's hanging in there. I'm afraid that a more aggressive glue might damage the boards when the worn abrasive is peeled off.

I also made a set of cylindrical workboards **(Photo 3)**. They are curved across their width but are straight in length, and I had mandolins in mind when I made them up. Charles was using such a board for guitar tops, and I had used them myself in the past for the same job. I've made cylindrical workboards as tight as $3'$. My first radii templates were made in the Cumpiano fashion of bending a $\frac{3}{16}''$ steel rod between three brads. See *Guitarmaking: Tradition and Technology* for his exact specs. This method produces a fair curve, but not necessarily the radius of a circle. It worked quite well for $15'$ and $25'$, but tighter curves didn't come out as a radius. Tighter templates were made by nailing a $9'$ length of molding to the floor

The foundation of the shop-made dished workboards is a disk of $\frac{3}{4}''$ MDF and a generous set of spokes that bear the proper radius. A disk of $\frac{1}{4}''$ masonite will be glued to the spokes to form the working surface. The hole in the center is for a bolt that will keep the pieces aligned while the glue sets and assist the clamping process during assembly.

Jigs were made to help create uniform spokes for the dished workboards. This jig is standing on its edge. In use, a rough spoke is placed in the jig, then the curved portion of the jig is run against the guide bearing of the Robo-Sander drum. This board will have a $9'$ radius when completed.

When this board is finished it will have a cylindrical curve with a $3'$ radius. Pegboard or $\frac{1}{8}''$ masonite must be used for the work surface, since $\frac{1}{4}''$ stock won't bend to the curves of such tight spokes without undue stress.

after slotting it at various distances from the nail for the blade of a utility knife. Swinging the blade on the pivot created crisp templates in posterboard which were then made into MDF spokes for the workboards. Masonite wouldn't bend into the tight curves I needed without undue stress, so I used pegboard for the radical cylindrical boards and it has worked quite well.

I built a Fox Universal Sidebender years before attending ASL. Using it proved to be one of those watershed events that changes shop life forever. I never enjoyed hand bending, and was never especially good at it. The same set of steel slats has been used for at least six sizes and shapes of guitar, and at this point they produce a side that is sort of generic. That is, not an especially good fit to any of my molds. This wouldn't upset Charles a great deal, since he expects to set up a hot pipe for some precision bending for every guitar, but that's a step I'd like to avoid. The obvious answer seemed to be a huskier mold with a stronger clamping system that would force the sides into an accurate fit, but this was never a satisfactory solution. The unobvious solution proved to be a variation in the recommended use of the side bender. Normal usage calls for the side to be left for ten minutes at full heat to be followed by a cool down period during which the side takes a set. By removing the side from the bender immediately after its ten minutes of cooking, the pliable, steaming wood can be clamped into the mold with large spring clamps, and a perfect shape results.

To avoid the complexity of adding a device to the machine for bending cutaways, I decided to pursue the Florentine cutaway. This involves bending the cutaway from a separate piece of wood, yielding a three-piece set of sides, but it can be executed in a manner that yields a round horn as easily as a pointed horn **(Photo 4)**. I cap the horn with contrasting wood and shape the cap to whatever profile the guitar or customer suggests. Bending the cutaway section over a hot pipe was never a difficult proposition, but the acquisition of a silicone heating blanket has made it even easier. I use the full-size blanket intended for side bending for all building and repair work except bridge plate removal, which requires a special blanket. I enjoy building mandolins, citterns,

(continued on following page)

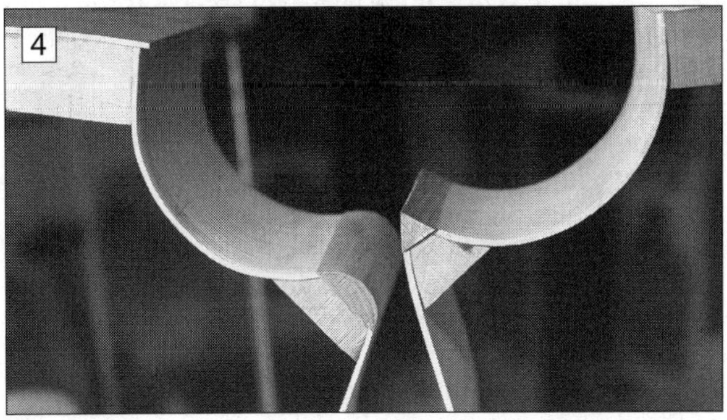

Florentine cutaways normally come to a sharp point, but by adding a block of wood to form the horn, almost any shape can be had. These guitars of oak and buttonwood demonstrate the principle.

Originally published in *American Lutherie #49 and #50*, 1997

QUESTIONS

EDITED BY CYNDY BURTON

■ ***Dave Hajicek from Minnetonka, MN** asks:*

A friend recently made the mistake of exposing his guitar to a Minnesota winter with the predictable results that the lacquer finish crazed extensively. Is there a reliable method of repairing this finish? If I were to guess, I would think that padding lacquer might work. But since I have only one shot at it, I would like to hear how others have successfully made this repair.

***Fred Campbell from San José, CA** responds:*

To repair finish checking, shoot a light mist of 10% lacquer, 70% thinner, and 20% retarder. Shoot fairly dry on the first pass. Wait about thirty minutes and repeat, shooting a little wetter. Wait one hour and shoot a medium-wet coat of 50/50 lacquer/thinner. Allow it to gas off a minimum of 72 hours. Block and buff *lightly*. This will not completely eliminate the checking, but will rebond the dried, broken lacquer lines. To completely remove all crazing, simply apply several more coats of lacquer before blocking, and allow sufficient time for gassing off.

***Dave Hajicek from Minnetonka, MN** tells us how he solved his problem another way*:

My solution is simple, but a little more aggressive than I would have desired. First clean the guitar well with denatured alcohol (assumes a lacquer finish) to get rid of polish and silicone in the craze lines.

To "amalgamate" the surface, brush on or spray on pure MEK (methyl ethyl keytone). This will penetrate the fine cracks and redissolve the lacquer. (If you try just fresh lacquer, it probably will not penetrate well enough.) If you do this rapidly, it has minimal effect on the surface smoothness. You will see minor blemishes from material in the cracks, but most seem to disappear after a second application and fresh lacquer if necessary. (Straight lacquer thinner did not work as it was not aggressive enough but that could be the cut of lacquer thinner I used.) However, problems occurred with the rosewood body because of what appear to have been voids in the rosewood pores caused by filler and lacquer shrinkage over the years. Two things happened. First, the lacquer settled into the pores making them very visible. Second, some voids surfaced as bubbles over the pores as the trapped air rose to the surface. This obviously requires extra work and time to deal with. A dryer spray is undoubtedly safer, especially on woods with large pores.

Mohawk makes a product called Amalgamator *for this purpose (www.mohawk-finishing.com).* ——

mountain dulcimers, and ukuleles, none of which fit under the Fox bender. The silicone blanket dished up the same sense of liberation for these instruments as the Fox bender did for the guitar. Michael Keller wrote a fine article about side bending with the blanket in *American Lutherie #25* (see *Big Red Book of American Lutherie Volume Three,* p. 30), but in the end I found his bending forms to be needlessly elaborate **(Photo 5)**. I make them out of MDF using Titebond II, and find that they function just as well when not covered with sheet aluminum. It's more convenient to adapt the forms for use with cam or spring clamps than to build clamping devices into the form **(Photo 6)**. All of my later forms are 5¾″ wide to support the full width of the blanket, regardless of the width of the side I might be bending. On smaller instruments both sides can be bent at the same time. Excess blanket length is allowed to dangle over the edge of the workbench.

The one hitch to the Fox side bender is the difficulty involved in indexing the side between the steel slats before bending. If the sides are left generously oversize this never becomes an issue. However, there are huge advantages to accurately indexing the sides before bending, since the top and back contours can be machined into them while they are still flat, which saves a bunch of time. (Try to see the Jeff Traugott portion of the Stew-Mac video *Trade Secrets On the Road, Part 1* for an eye-opening explanation of this.) Precision indexing is easy with the heating blanket, since the side(s) can be clamped at one end before the blanket is even plugged in.

The actual bending process with the blanket is easy. Spritz the side(s) liberally with water. Clamp one end in place and plug in the blanket. Heat comes up very quickly. Bend from one end to the other, applying as many clamps as necessary to get the wood to conform to the bending form. An accurately made caul is necessary for the waist. Leave the heat on until you first notice a trace of smoke, then unplug. When the wood is cool you can start to build — the side will be dry. So far I haven't scorched any wood. I did crack a quilted maple uke side once, but it was fixable. Thermostats and timers are available, but the process happens so quickly that I can't imagine walking away while the heat is on.

These bending forms are modeled after those described by Michael Keller in AL#25 (see BRBAL3), but they turned out to be fancier than necessary. A set of sides and the electric heating blanket are still mounted in the dulcimer form. Sides are bent on the ukulele form using the same blanket.

This simplified bending form is easier to use. Fiddle sides are being bent while the excess blanket dangles off the workbench. The wet sides are clamped at one end, then the blanket is plugged in. Bending progresses from one end to the other.

I used the blanket to bend solid cedar linings for one of my mandos and it worked quite well.

The first guitar made with dished workboards may be time consuming and may not come out precisely to the side dimensions you had in mind. Don't worry about it. Once you've achieved the proper side contour you can slide a length of posterboard between a side and the mold and trace the outline of the contour. With this template the proper contour can be traced onto subsequent sets of bent sides (before the end blocks are glued in place) and the depth will come out exactly as you wish. I use a coping saw and the finest blades I can find to cut the contour on the bent sides. The same procedure could be used for the top contours, but I prefer to leave them square until it's time to fit the top. Sanding in the top contour using the dished workboard only takes five minutes or less at that time. Keep in mind that the end blocks need to be slightly taller than the sides since their finished shape must follow the contour of the plates, which rise toward the middle of the guitar.

The Fox jigs used for fitting end blocks to the sides are another Godsend **(Photo 7)**. The blocks are fitted to the ribs using the belt sander with an auxiliary table that has an aluminum angle let into it. As the jig rubs the aluminum fence, the proper shape is ground into the end block. I tried to shortcut the jig making process by making a .090″ stack of posterboard to represent the sides, rubber cementing the posterboard in place on the mold, then casting the nose of the jig in Bondo body filler. Sometimes it works perfectly, but often the curve comes out too tight, necessitating some hand fitting. Cutting down the stack of posterboard seems like an obvious fix, but I haven't tried it yet. Once the nose is accurately fitted, the rest of the jig can be made. If you like, predrill a few holes in the nose of the MDF and insert brads to support the Bondo. Dan Erlewine first made the Bondo/guitar connection, and he's got dozens of Bondo stunts in his bag of tricks.

Molds and forms are as interesting to make as guitars, and more fun since they don't have to be sanded

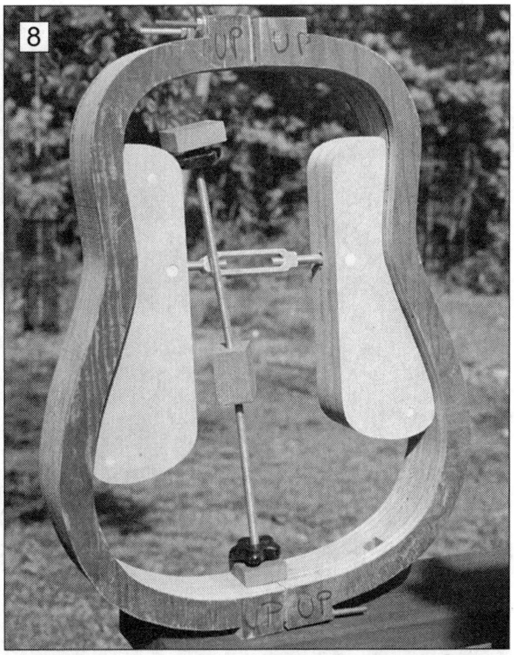

Photo 7. *Pictures of this jig's proper use were shown in earlier segments of this series. Here it's shown that some jigs can do double duty. Instead of making dreadnought tail blocks on the belt sander, this one is being used to fit a support block to the inside of a Florentine cutaway. The work is guided by eye, of course.*
Photo 8. *This heavy-duty clamping system was initially used to force ill-fitting sides to the mold. Not a recommended process. It does a fine job of stabilizing the ribs in the mold as construction progresses.*
Photo 9. *Jeff Traugott uses this method of clamping end blocks and stabilizing the ribs in the mold. The real advantage is that everything can be left in place during construction, then removed through the soundhole.*
Photo 10. *If the ribs are a good fit to the mold, this system of clamping them is perfectly adequate and is very light.*

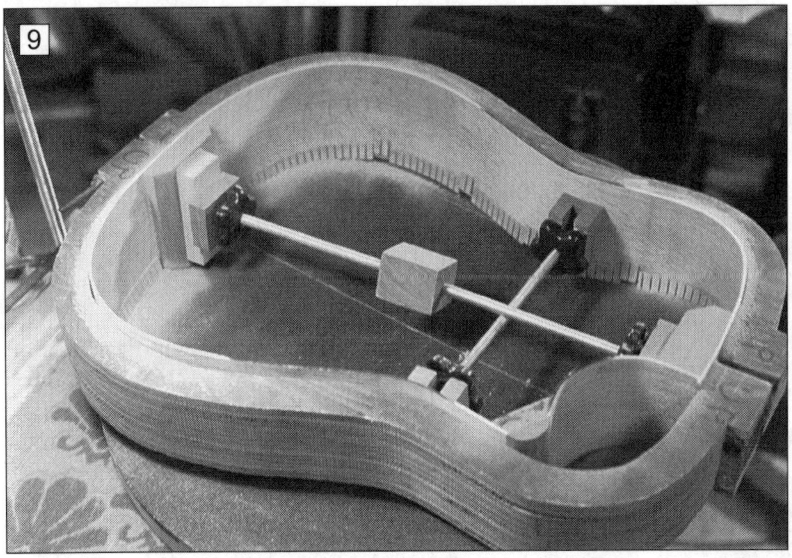

or lacquered. As cool as Charles' molds are, I decided in the end to stick with the conventional outside molds that I've always used. I copied his clamping system **(Photo 8)** in order to force the sides to the mold until I discovered the trick of mounting the hot ribs directly in the mold. Charles' ribs fit the mold perfectly, so he uses such a sturdy system to keep the sides from vibrating while they are worked on, and it performs that duty well. Jeff Traugott's system of wood blocks, threaded rod, and plastic knobs **(Photo 9)** braces the ribs at the end blocks and waist, and can be left in place through the entire construction process and then removed through the soundhole, which is a nice touch. If the sides are a tight fit in the mold, it's often enough to brace them temporarily with lengths of bowed lath, which leaves the assembly almost feather light **(Photo 10)**. Anything will do as long as the ribs remain in position while they are sanded with the dished workboard. I like to color the edges to be sanded with a black marker. It's fun to watch the color disappear and easier to know if the sides are coming down evenly. After the lining is glued in place and trimmed with a block plane, the edges are sanded again. I color the edges of the ribs again, not the linings. Even when the ribs are clamped sturdily in the mold I often find that the fit is disturbed when the linings are added. When the color is sanded off everywhere else the waist area remains black. I don't know why. It's important to keep sanding until all the marker is removed, however.

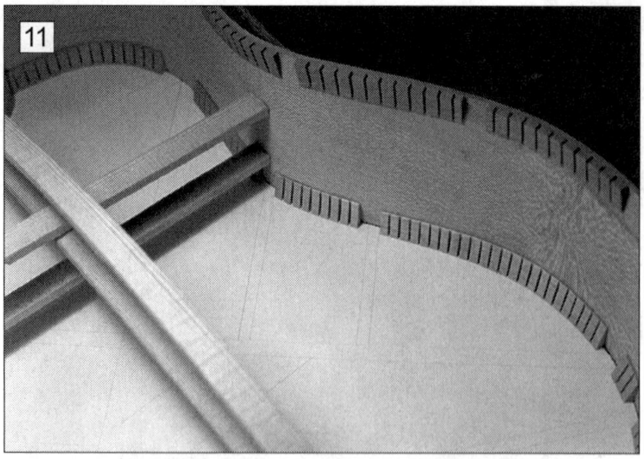

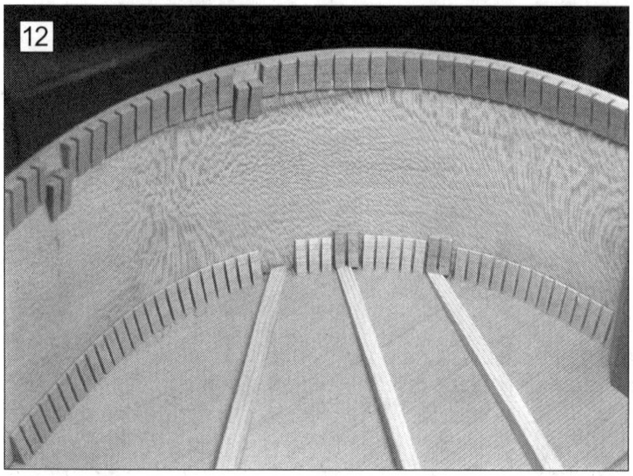

Photo 11. The side assembly sits on a plan of the top bracing, which sits on the dished workboard. No lining is glued to the spots intersected by braces. Lining has been fitted for the back in the same manner.
Photo 12. The plates are placed in the dished workboard then covered with the sides (still in the mold). Bits of lining are glued to the sides to support the brace ends, but are not glued to the braces until both plates are fitted and simultaneously glued to the assembly. The wood shown here is buttonwood.
Photo 13. A workboard was made up to join guitar plates. The round stops are moveable, the same as the wedges. The wedging action is used to drive the pieces of the plate together. This is a re-creation using a back of ziricote and maple. If the operation were real, there would be wax paper under the glue seams. Having this board always ready saves a good bit of time. A similar board mounts a dulcimer plate or two mandolin plates.

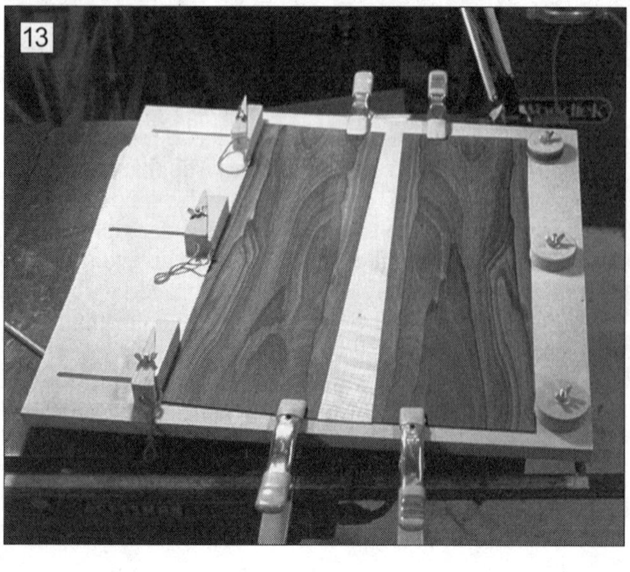

The Fox method of fitting the plate braces into the lining is exciting and even a bit scary the first time out. The braces are tapered almost to nothing. They are shaved so thin at the end that no allowance need be made for them when the plates are glued on. A more traditional approach is to leave the braces thicker and let them into the lining all at once, which strikes me as shooting in the dark. Stew-Mac's Don MacRostie files the ends of the braces to .100″ and then cuts a slot of that exact depth through both the lining and the side (see it in the video *Building a Herringbone Style Acoustic Guitar*). I tried this on a mandolin back and thought it was an elegant way to go. However, I ended up using a method I first saw on Augie LoPrinzi's guitars twenty-five years ago. Augie lined the back in the normal way, then completely removed bits of lining where the braces intersected it. After the back was glued in place short lengths of lining were butted against the brace ends. No attempt was made to make the binding the same height around the perimeter, and it had an intriguing cityscape look to it when viewed through the soundhole. The top braces had to be let into the lining since the interior of the guitar was no longer accessible once the back was in place.

Using the dished workboards, however, both plates can be prefitted before either is glued on. I place the rib assembly on a drawing of the back-brace layout and mark where the braces will end. No lining is glued on these spaces **(Photo 11)**. The lined sides are sanded with the dished workboard, then the side assembly is placed over the braced plate, which in turn rests in the dished workboard. Bits of lining are butted against the brace ends using thick superglue. Glue is only applied between the lining and the rib **(Photo 12)**. Then the back is set aside and the top lining is fitted in the same manner, first to a drawing of the braces and then to the braced top. Both plates can then be glued to the ribs at the same time and all braces that reach the linings end up fully supported. The innards of the guitar end up clean and unmarred, since no cutting or chiseling has to be done once assembly is begun.

In the middle of all this I realized I had to finish the plates before I could finish the side assembly, though this would have been out of sequence in my old order of events. As fascinated as I was by Charles' method of joining plates, I decided to stick to my old ways. It's true — old habits die hard. I used to simply mount the plate on a workboard and drive the halves together with brads that were angled under the outside edges. That no longer seemed like a neat enough solution, so I made up a set of dedicated workboards. Along one edge is mounted adjustable stops, and to the other an adjustable set of wedges that apply the clamping pressure. One board will glue up a guitar plate, the other will handle a dulcimer plate or two mandolin plates **(Photo 13)**.

When I began bracing the guitar plates I suddenly realized that none of my clamps would reach into the center of the dished workboards. A go-bar deck was hastily made up using 24″×24″ pieces of MDF and ½″ threaded rod. I had seen René Baarslag's deck in

Photo 14. *The overhanging plate material can be safely and quickly trimmed away using the Robo-Sander.*
Photo 15. *This portable version of the Fox guitar vise is mounted outside in good weather for dirty operations. The screws mount to nuts that are driven into countersunk holes in the back layer of MDF. More durable hubs and handle knobs are next on the list for this unit.*
Photo 16. *After returning home, I realized that I hadn't documented how Charles Fox built this jig used for routing the butt wedge of the guitar. This version works, but such details shouldn't get away from you if you attend such a seminar.*

AL#49 (see p. 4), so rather than buy a passel of dowels, I cut dozens of laths out of a scrap cedar board, then thickness-sanded them in the drill press to the right degree of flexibility. Cutting them to the right length was an uncertain process since a dished workboard with a 15′ radius is significantly deeper in the center than at the edges. To add to the problem, the MDF flexes enough that after seven or eight laths were in place, the first ones began to fall down, even though I had a 2×4 clamped across the top of the deck. Longer, more flexible laths proved to be the solution. The go-bar deck is wonderful. I should have built one eons ago.

Once the body is assembled, any plate material that overhangs the ribs can be eliminated quickly using the drill press and the Robo-Sander (**Photo 14**). Care is required, but the procedure is safe enough, and much faster than trimming the plates by hand with a file and sanding blocks.

A copy of Charles' guitar vise was next on the agenda. I do virtually all my work on an auxiliary table mounted upon my table saw, so I made a portable version of the vise that could be installed or removed quickly with two bolts. As a bonus, I found that I could mount the vise on an outdoor table for sanding and other messy operations (**Photo 15**). The body of the vise is 100% MDF. The veneer-press screws that Fox uses to operate the jaws are very elegant, but the first price I found was $60 per screw, so I stopped looking. I used ½″ threaded rod instead. The thread pitch is too fine for absolute convenience, but it's bearable. I even used MDF for the handle hubs, though I knew it would give me problems. I've split one hub three times by pressing against the handle as I work, and eventually I'll have to turn a set of nice hardwood hubs. My wife Jan gave me a braided throw rug for lining the jaws, and a double layer glued to each jaw has worked well. Make sure the curve of the jaws is greater than the arch of any instrument you intend to load into it.

When I went to build the jig Charles uses to fit the decorative butt wedge I realized that I had pictures of the jig in use but none of how it was constructed. Don't let these things get away from you if you attend a seminar. I came up with a functioning jig, but I'm not sure it's as finely made as Charles' (**Photo 16**). The jig clamps to the butt of the guitar, then sliding tables close on the butt wedge as it's held firmly in position by the fingers. The fence on each table guides the router to cut exactly where the edge rests, so a wedge-sized piece of the guitar is cleanly removed. I wasn't able to make one jig work for both guitars and mandolins, so for now I'm still inlaying the wedge in smaller instruments by hand.

I still haven't been able to make binding into a fun proposition. Arched plates turn binding into an ordeal. None of the binding rigs I saw at ASL would work for me, because I wanted one setup that I could use to bind all the various instruments I build. A hand-held rig that registers on the side of a guitar won't work on the much-narrower side of a mandolin. When I interviewed Jeff Huss and Mark Dalton for *American Lutherie* I was quite taken by their binding setup, though I knew it was too elaborate for my shop. They mount their routers horizontally. Attached to the router base is a bearing-laden guide shaft on which the guitar side is rested. Rather than adjust the router for different bindings and purflings, they change the setup mechanically by switching pilot bearings or the guide foot attached to the router bases. I made up a much simplified portable version of the Huss & Dalton rig using all MDF and masonite **(Photo 17)**. It worked OK, though multiple passes were needed, and any rocking of the guitar resulted in a little moon cut wide of the binding line. I had to purfle a couple guitars that I had only intended to bind, to cover the moons. A trip back to H&D turned up the problem. The foot of the router base against which the side is held has to have a carefully adjusted flat surface. If the guitar is rocked the flat surface forces the edge away from, rather than into, the router bit, eliminating the moons. Jeff's routers are also mounted a foot or so below benchtop level, and my rig sat high on a benchtop **(Photo 18)**. Mounted low, the operator can press the guitar firmly onto the guide shaft. Jeff admitted that multiple passes were usually necessary, but he can still cut the binding and purfling channels in fifteen minutes and they come out perfectly. I haven't worked out the last details yet, but this system is the way to go for me. In his book *Steel-String Guitar Construction,* Irving Sloane shows Jimmy D'Aquisto at work on another sort of horizontal binding rig, though not many details can be gleaned from the shot.

Many of the Fox fixtures rely on runners that fit into either the table saw, bandsaw, or belt sander table slots. There's an easy way to fit the runners accurately to the fixture. Make the runners so they fit slightly low in the slot, then cover their top sides with double-sticky tape. Place the fixture in its exact relationship to the blade or belt, then carefully pry up the runners until the tape makes contact. Gingerly slide the fixture off the table, pressing the tape joint tight as it becomes accessible. Once free of the table, flip it over and tack down the runners with long brads. Trim off any excess length.

I decided to forego most of Charles's neck-making jigs. Again, old habits die hard. I've made at least two hundred necks using my simpler system and I trust it completely. Both methods involve slicing off the headstock portion of the neck **(Photo 19)**, flipping it, then gluing it back where it came from. I've always put the joint under the 1st fret area, as found on Ibanez electric guitars, for instance. It was the consensus of the class (and Charles) that the joint should be moved back into the headstock where it's less visible. On a deluxe job where the front and back of the headstock are capped, the joint virtually disappears, and I like that. If the headstock is left plain the joint remains visible, in which case I'd rather have it in the neck shaft where the fingerboard will help support it. Good joinery is a joy to behold and needn't be hidden, as far as I'm concerned, but it makes sense to give in to the demands of the marketplace where one way is as easy as the other.

I did build the jig used for squaring and shaping the heel. Charles indexes his necks on the jig with 1/4″ pins

Photo 17. This is the binding unit the author came up with. The ribs are slid along the protruding shaft while the plate rubs against the squiggly lines of the guide foot. An adjustable foot would be an advantage. The goal was to build a machine for binding all instruments, not just guitars. It works, but it's hardly the last word in such a machine.

Photo 18. The binding machine at work. Since the router bit can't be seen, the work has to be done by feel. Mounting it somewhat lower turned out to be a big help. This guitar is made of cedar and bubinga sapwood.

Photo 19. This simple jig is used to cut the headstock from the rest of the neck. The joint can be placed under the1st fret or in the headstock, though of course different measurements must be made. For most acoustic instruments, the heel would be stacked using a matching piece of wood.
Photo 20. *Pins mounted in blocks that are temporarily wedged into the truss rod slot guide the neck along this jig while the face of the heel is squared and the heel is contoured.*
Photo 21. *If this work were actually in progress, a vacuum hose would be fixed to the saw table. The stacked heel is obvious here. Contouring the neck this way is a huge aid in quickly producing symmetry in a piece of work.*

that protrude from the vertical portion of the jig into the slot in his necks that houses the reinforcement equipment (either a graphite bar or a truss rod, depending on the type of guitar). I wanted my jig to be generic and useful for any of the necked instruments I build. I cut a series of horizontal slots in the wall of the jig. Pins are fitted into the truss rod slots (**Photo 20**), or right into the neck in the case of ukes. The pins fit into the slots, and the neck can be slid along the jig without changing its angle of orientation (**Photo 21**). Charles' method is less complicated if all you build is guitars.

Don't assume that your necks should be a 90° fit to the body until you've had a chance to fiddle with a real neck, fingerboard, body, and bridge. You don't want to be surprised after the fretboard is already glued to the neck. In fact, I found that none of my necks fit a body with a domed top at a 90° angle, but I came up with a formula for fitting them using the table-saw jig. A fake fingerboard must be clamped to the top of the neck. The thickness should be correct, but it should only extend $\frac{1}{4}''$ or so onto the body. Put a fret at each end of it if you want to get really exact. With the extension resting on the body, rock the neck back until the tops of the frets line up with the top of the bridge (yup, you have to tape a dummy bridge to the guitar, too). A gap will open up under the fingerboard between the neck and the body. Measure that gap to the nearest $\frac{1}{64}''$. Strip the neck and place it in the same jig used to square and shape the heel. Place a shim under the nut area of the neck that is twice as thick as the gap was wide, and run the heel through the saw blade. I use business cards to make the shim, and one guitar needed a stack of twenty cards to make the heel angle correct. You may find that the geometry of your guitars requires a different ratio of gap-to-shim size, but I bet that an accurate ratio can be found. It makes life much easier once you know it. As it happened, the first two guitars I finished had necks that were a bit over set. A thicker bridge was used to make up the difference. In light of this, it's safer to initially under set the neck since increasing the set is a simple matter later on. Use the same sandpaper method described in past *American Lutherie* articles to reset guitar necks. It's much more time consuming to correct a neck that is over set than under set. Once you discover the correct ratio of gap-to-shim, the problem should disappear.

All my guitar necks bolt on. The threaded brass inserts used for joining the neck to the body should be suitably countersunk, though carbide router bits will cut the brass if you guess wrong. Charles recommends that the holes for the threaded inserts simply be drilled by hand. As a matter of fact, the inserts wobble quite a bit as they go in, which can upset any amount of precision you use to drill the holes. Nevertheless, I made a simple drill press jig (**Photo 22,** next page). It holds the face of the heel square to the drill bit while the truss rod slot is guided true by a couple tabs of wood. Nothing to it. To get the neck under my drill press I had to swivel the power unit on its column, though.

None of my body designs is flat in the heel block region, so the center portion of the neck that butts against the body must be relieved for a proper fit. The relieved area doesn't have to be a perfect fit as long as the contact edges of the heel are right. I made a guide for my laminate trimmer so that I could quickly make a relief cut in the middle of the contacting surface of the heel. This reduces the amount of material which must be removed in the final fitting, which speeds the process dramatically. My guide leaves an ⅛″ rim around the edges of the heel **(Photo 23)**. Any adjusts in the fit of the neck to the body are made on this rim.

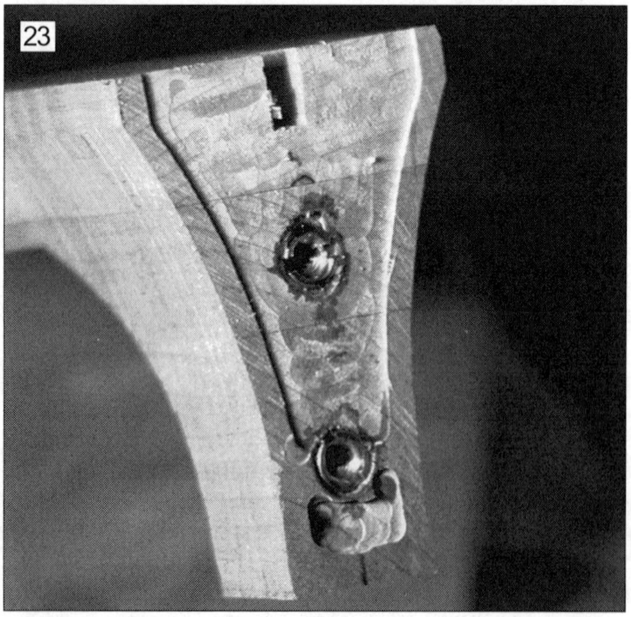

Photo 22. *This jig assures accuracy when drilling the pilot holes for the threaded inserts used for attaching the neck. A spur bit drill is used. Blocks that fit into the truss rod slot hold the neck vertical.*
Photo 23. *Just squaring the neck won't provide a very good fit to most guitar bodies. Relieving the center of the heel speeds up the fitting process dramatically. This work was guided by a simple wooden shoe fitted to the bottom of a laminate trimmer.*

The neck is mated to the body by butting the neck in place while the centerline of the fretboard is clamped true to the center seam of the top. Sandpaper is dragged between the parts. The neck is unclamped, scooted forward, then clamped and sanded again. A very good fit should be the result. The long-term solution is to refine your jigs until a good fit can be taken for granted. While the entire process of refitting your shop is in progress, it makes sense to stick to one design of guitar. I wish I had been smart enough to realize that. My first batch included guitars of three sizes and shapes, two scale lengths, and both 12- and 14-fret necks. Jigs for one model didn't carry over to any others. Jigging up for ukes and mandos was as complicated as for guitars. If you are new to building, you definitely want to cut yourself as much slack as possible.

The segment of the fingerboard from the 14th fret up must be tapered in thickness a bit due to the dome of the top. Small discrepancies can be corrected when the top of the board is leveled. I've been doing this freehand on the belt sander, but my final solution may be to go back to cylindrically arched top plates, rather than spherically arched plates. The advantages should remain, but some of the pain will be taken from the building process.

Normally I build all winter and finish all summer, but this year summer overtook me with more than twenty instruments in progress. When the rising level of humidity was about to shut me down I built a cabinet in which to store guitars and parts in a controlled environment **(Photo 24)**. It's pretty large and mounted on wheels. It will hold three assembled guitars or enough parts for four or five guitars and a slew of smaller instruments. The door has a slot at the bottom to let in room air, and the back has a slot at the top to let the moisture out. Heat is provided by two light bulbs. Changing the wattage of the bulbs and/or adjusting the top slot controls the interior humidity. A hygrometer is a nice touch, but not necessary. If arched plates begin to flatten, the cabinet is too warm. Parts are never removed from the cabinet for longer than it takes to complete the next step. This system proved viable for a long summer of work, and over the winter the unheated cabinet should prove to be the safest sanctuary for work-in-progress that I've ever had. Charles uses a similar stationary cabinet in his shop, though in Northern California it doesn't get used all that often.

That about wraps it up. **Photo 25** shows the proof of the pudding, though from the picture you can't tell these are the tightest guitars I've ever made. They are roughly single-0 size, and both have walnut necks and bodies and a peculiar tic-tac-toe bracing scheme. The one with the Engelmann top sings very nicely. The walnut-topped guy is more subdued, but I love to play it. Both were initially disappointing, but after being strung (and not played much) for three weeks they suddenly came to life. Larger, more conventional guitars should

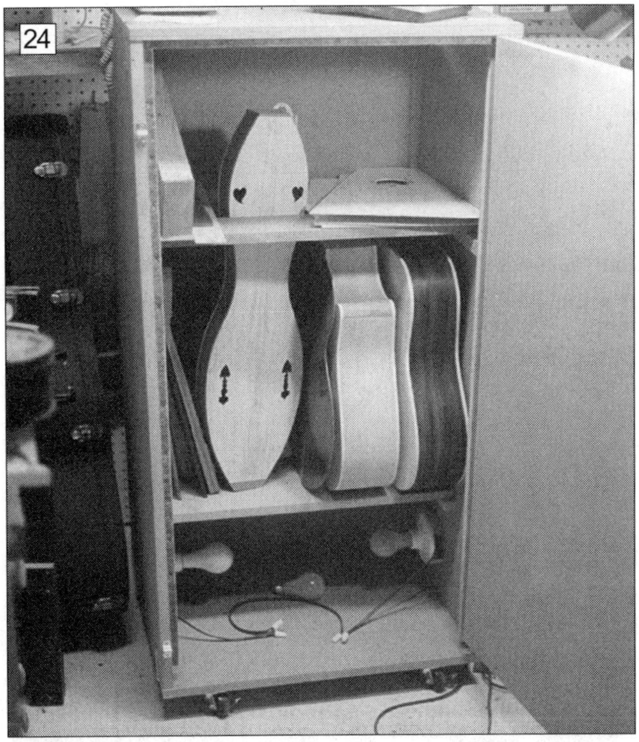

Without climate control in the shop, a cabinet of some sort to store work in progress is a must at certain times of the year. Humidity is controlled by changing the wattage of the light bulbs. A certain amount of air interchange with the shop is necessary to carry off excess moisture. Judging the humidity is easy. If arched plates go flat, it's too dry in there.

follow shortly. It's been a long journey which is by no means over. Efficiency is the name of the game. Jigs, procedures, and instruments can always be improved upon. My evolution as a guitar maker has only just begun. But thanks in large part to Charles Fox, I don't feel like the last of the Neanderthal luthiers any more. ——

Originally published in *American Lutherie #50 and #52*, 1997

QUESTIONS

EDITED BY CYNDY BURTON

■ ***Al Carruth of Dedham, MA** asks:*

Does anyone know what C.F. Martin used for finish before they went to nitro? When did they switch?

***Mike Longworth of Bell Buckle, TN** responds:*

When I was writing my book (*Martin & Co., a History,* originally published 1975) I talked to old Mr. Martin about that. Before 1900 most Martin guitars were French polished. In fact shellac finishes were used into the '20s. Roughly between 1919–1922 a semigloss finish was available. This was also shellac, but it was dulled by oil sanding.

For awhile a satin finish was offered which had a clear varnish coat on the body over the shellac. The neck was still just shellac. Although Mr. Martin specified 1923 as the date for this compound finish, I'm fairly certain it was used on some instruments in the teens as well. The use of nitrocellulose lacquer was begun 1926 on the Hawaiian 0-17H guitar, and by 1929 it was the standard finish.

If there were additives in the shellac to make it more durable, I am unaware of what they were, and I doubt that there's anyone still around who would know. I remember lots of milky looking shellac, though, where moisture had gotten under the finish. I also remember burnt umber being used as a coloring agent in some of those orange-looking shellac finishes.

Martin's old records are not as complete as many imagine. For guitars sold between 1898 and 1924 there were three 600-page ledgers which gave the serial number, who the instrument was sold to, and when it was sold (not when it was made). Many of those were sold to stores. No record was made of the finish used.

***Michael Darnton of Chicago, IL** adds:*

Orange shellac, when it ages and oxidizes, becomes insoluble and resistant to almost everything. The Hills used it for retouching violins around the turn of the century, until they got smart. You can recognize those jobs by the glazing layer of varnish in places where it has no right to be, for instance the edges, which usually wear a lot. It is very hard for the modern restorer to redo one of those old jobs. The original finish under the shellac will come off, taking the shellac with it, which is positively not the right order of things.

***Cyndy Burton of Portland, OR** adds:*

Eugene Clark in his French polishing class at the American School of Lutherie (Aug. '97), said the same thing, except that he believes that Martin used bleached blond or white shellac, which also will attain extreme hardness over time. Eugene points out that the process is polymerization, not oxidation. ——

Originally published in *American Lutherie #52*, 1997

Meet the Maker: Augustino LoPrinzi

by Jonathon Peterson

AUGIE LOPRINZI began instrument work during a time when, if you were a luthier in the United States, you were almost certainly self-taught. His natural curiosity, ingenuity, hard work, and determination took him from the back room of a barber shop to ownership of two guitar companies, landed him consulting jobs with some of the biggest guitar making companies in the country, and made him a major figure in American guitar making. It also put him through the grinder. Today he has come full circle and is working in a small shop, building about 120 classical and flamenco guitars a year with help from his daughter and a part-time retiree, enjoying the craft like he did in the beginning.

JONATHON PETERSON

Augie LoPrinzi with one of his recent classical guitars outside the exhibition hall at the 1996 Healdsburg Guitar Festival.

Tell us, how did you get into lutherie?

I started violin lessons at school when I was twelve. I started tinkering with my violins, taking them apart and putting them back together. Just curious. I missed a few lessons because I couldn't get my violin back together in time for class. The word spread through my relatives that I could fix fiddles, and they began to bring them to me. I'd already done a little woodcarving and stuff. Until I was eighteen the only instruments I worked on were violins.

Where was this?

In Flemington, New Jersey. In the very early '50s its population was only about 3,000. My father had a barbershop, and he used to let me use the back room as a shop. No one else in the area worked on instruments, so I had no idea how to go about it formally. When I turned eighteen, I got my Master's license as a barber. The rule was that you had to have your license for two years before you could open up your own shop, so I decided to wait out my two years in the army. I didn't want to get drafted after I opened my barbershop, you see. That was in 1956. In 1958 I opened a barbershop, but I made sure it had enough room in the back to work on instruments, and that's when I switched from violins to classical guitars. As the barber business grew, I hired other barbers, and soon I was making guitars all week and cutting hair just on Saturdays. Then I opened a guitar studio next door and hired two classical guitar teachers. For ten years I built classical and flamenco guitars in the barbershop.

How long was it before you met another luthier?

Never, during that period. Gibson, Guild, and Martin owned the market. I'd heard of Michael Gurian and a couple others who were hand building guitars, but I didn't meet any of them until later. There was a little book from England by a man named Sharpe about how to build a classical guitar, just a ten-page pamphlet really, but I'd already been building for three or four years when I found it.

Did you study other guitars that you took in to repair?

No, I didn't do any repair work at that time. I was definitely flying by the seat of my pants. I only had three tools to make my first guitar. I had a rasp. I cut out necks with a bow saw meant for pruning trees. For close work I reworked a paring knife that my mother gave me. I had those, and I had sanding blocks.

I didn't know any procedures. I knew what the parts were from looking into guitars, but I had no idea what to make first, or when to glue which things together. I just kept doing it until it made sense. "Oh, if I would have glued this piece first it would have made the next three steps easier."

But you know, right from the beginning I was production minded. I wanted to make the operation easier, which in turn made it faster. I had more fun making jigs and fixtures than making guitar parts, and that's how I made the connection to other makers.

How's that?

In the mid-'60s I was featured in some newspapers, and then an educational TV station made an hour-long show about me making guitars. C.F. Martin saw that show, and the company called me up. I went in to help them revamp their line of classical guitars, to help them set up new equipment and modernize the shop. But it never happened, because they wouldn't change the shape of their guitars. They didn't want to make all new molds. So that project really came to nothing, but I was associated with them for years.

Were there other things that you saw them doing that could have been done more efficiently?

They were tying on their binding one-quarter of a guitar at a time, and I showed them how to bind a whole guitar nonstop by using tape. They gave it a try, but the guys in the shop were too set in their ways to change, and they raised a big stink. The company didn't try to force them. They also dovetailed their heel blocks before gluing them into the guitar. I tried to show them that if you completed the body and then cut the dovetail it would be much easier to maintain the centerline of the guitar. But they wouldn't do it. Their thinking was too fossilized. I did help them with their side bending machines, though. They were getting up to 20% breakage. They used a two-part electric mold, male and female of the finished side shape that you put the side between, but the wood wouldn't always slide in the mold, especially oily woods. I had a machine made for myself where three hinged pieces pressed the side onto a form. The center came down to form the waist, then each bout was bent separately. Breakage was never a problem. I invited Martin down to see it and that's what they went with.

Working alone probably helped me in the long run. If I had seen how other people or companies did things I might have stopped there and never figured out a better method for myself. I went on to help several other companies set up production. When Al Dronge owned Guild, I designed and helped jig up for the Mark IV. I made all the fixtures, jigs, and machinery setups for Funn Guitars down in Texas, but they never went into production. When Kramer moved to Neptune, New Jersey, I helped them with a lot of things.

How did your barber business turn into a full-time guitar shop?

In 1969 I stopped cutting hair to make guitars full time. I was a one-man shop until 1972, when I started the LoPrinzi Guitar Company. Up to that point I'd made 526 instruments — classical guitars, flamencos, lutes, and violins, but mostly classical guitars. I had only dabbled in steel strings, but I knew the classical market couldn't support a company of the size I was thinking about. When it got rolling I had 30 employees and we made 80 guitars a month.

Holy cow! That's a lot of guitars! How do you start a company? Did you start small and work up?

You know, if I had known what I was in for I'd probably still be cutting hair. My brother was my first employee. He was tired of barbering, so I invited him into the business. I taught a lot of others as the business expanded. Roger Sadowsky learned guitar making in my shop. I knew I'd have to stay one step ahead of the growth, so I took a minicourse in marketing. Running a guitar company may sound romantic, but every business sits on the same foundation of necessary evils like marketing, paperwork, running an office staff, handling salesmen and reps. I wanted to spend my time building instruments, but I knew I'd have a much bigger show to run than just the woodworking. I expanded the business, and then I sold stock. I sold a block of shares to AMF *(Editor's note: Famous for their bowling alleys.)* and spent most of the money on new machinery, which really expanded the business. Soon I wasn't working on guitars at all. I had a staff of thirteen salesmen to contend with, plus a full office staff. I had to redesign the shop fixtures as the production came up, because suddenly something wasn't fast enough anymore and was creating a bottleneck. I redesigned all the tooling and fixtures several times, and each time I had to retrain the staff to use them. By the end of November in 1975 I'd had enough. I sold controlling interest in the LoPrinzi Guitar Co. to AMF and left the company.

Did they keep the LoPrinzi name?

Yes. My brother Tom stayed with the company. He became the president, and he signed all the labels. I immediately started Augustino Guitar Company (Augustino is my first name). I learned a lot during those three years at LoPrinzi. I knew I didn't need half the machinery they had, and the staff was way too large. I was sure I could run an assembly line with a smaller crew. But the crucial element was limiting the production. I decided to shoot for thirty guitars a month, which was a big drop, but at LoPrinzi a staff of thirty made eighty guitars a month. At Augustino I made thirty guitars with a staff of five, so the profit was much better, and I didn't have all these different personalities to contend with.

Did you get to do some woodwork, too?

I had five helpers to make the parts. I did almost all of the actual construction. I already had all my business contacts in place. When I left LoPrinzi, the five key guys I had taught came with me, so the shop was set. I decided to go without a rep, because I knew the dealer network myself. In two hours on the phone I had enough orders for the first month. In two weeks I designed a line of eight steel string guitars and made all the fixtures to produce them.

In two weeks?

For two weeks that's all we did. I knew exactly what I wanted, but more importantly, I knew what I didn't need. I learned my lessons with AMF. They had put almost a million dollars into machinery, and they were convinced that machinery was the key. They couldn't see the importance of training the staff to use the machines correctly, or to do the necessary hand work. You can't just pour in money and churn out good acoustic guitars. It doesn't work like that, but AMF was intractable. We were going to lose the company. I could see it in the future, and I didn't want to hang around for that. Instrument quality was slipping away from them. They lasted about two years after I left, then they folded. I learned how to run a guitar company at AMF's expense.

A lot of dealers who had always dealt with Augie LoPrinzi didn't like doing business with AMF, and it didn't phase them that I was Augustino Guitars now, and not LoPrinzi Guitars. I took them away from AMF.

Where did you set up shop when you left AMF?

Right next door! Literally, right next door to the old factory. Boy, it bugged the heck out of them, too! They wanted their lawyers to come into my shop and check out our operation, but I told them, "Your lawyers may walk in on their own two feet, but they'll leave with broken legs." What got to them most was that I still owned stock in LoPrinzi Guitars, so I could read the stock report and know exactly what they were doing, but they had no idea what I was doing. They harassed me for a year, trying to make sure I didn't sign my name to my guitars.

Because AMF still owned your last name?

Right, but I ended up getting it back. AMF owned Harley Davidson, too, and they ran that company into the ground. So there was a hostile takeover of AMF. I waited a year for the dust to settle before I called them. It took me that long to work up my courage. I said that I wanted the name back in the family. I didn't want them to think it was really worth something to me. This was years after they closed their guitar division, and I was hoping that no one would remember me. They gave me the run around and said they'd get back to me. Another year went by. They finally called to say they had no interest in building guitars or in the name, that I could have it back. About three months later the new owner of AMF happened to be vacationing in Florida. He came into my shop and said he was there to make the name change official. "But it's going to cost you," he said. I laughed a little, because I figured if it was going to cost me I didn't want it back, I was doing fine with Augustino.

"Well, what's it going to cost me?" I asked.

He pulls out an instrument case and he says, "Well, I'm a banjo player, and the binding on my neck is starting to come off." So I fixed his binding and he gave me back my name.

I didn't know what to do with it at the time, or whether it was good or bad to use it. Later on I decided to build strictly classical guitars again, and I thought that that was the time to resurrect the LoPrinzi name. My brochures say Augustino at the top, and LoPrinzi at the bottom. I'm trying to tie the two together in people's minds. I've answered to Augustino like it was my last name for a long time. It doesn't hurt, but now I'm switching back to LoPrinzi as the name gets out there.

You told me yesterday that after moving to Florida you went through lutherie burnout. When was that, and how did you recover?

I moved to Florida in 1978 when Augustino Guitars was three years old. About 1988 I let everybody go. It was a dark time. I felt like the business had swallowed my life and not left me with very much. I cut off my dealers, everything. I made steel strings by myself. I was making a living as a one-man shop, but I was seriously unhappy, and had been for a few years.

Then I sold my personal classical guitar. I had studied classical guitar. I never played steel string music. One of the good teachers in the area bugged me for six months to sell him my guitar, and finally I did. I'd had that guitar for a long time (though I forget just when I built it), and it was really nice. I was left with a couple junky guitars to play on, and they took all the joy out of playing. A few months went by before I decided to build myself another classical guitar, and building it was almost magical. It was fun. When it was done I decided I would only build classicals, and I didn't care if they sold or not. I'd only build what I wanted to make.

After that, things kind of fell into place. I studied the market to see which slice I could fit into and decided how many I could make and what my price structure had to be. I wanted to offer a good deal on an all-solid-wood classical. Some stores sell my guitars for more than my list price, so I know they're a good buy. In the first month I took sixty orders. Actually, I was pretty surprised.

Are you still working alone?

My daughter works with me, and I have a helper who works part time. He's a seventy-year-old man.

Has your approach to jigs and fixtures changed much since you've switched to a lower production mode? Can a small shop be over jigged?

I don't think so. A part has to be a certain way, and the guitar doesn't care if that part was made slowly by a man with a knife or rapped out in one blow by a three-ton machine. The part is the same. The jigs allow me the time to do the critical hand work and help me knock out the hard work without tiring myself. For me they make guitar making even more enjoyable. I've learned to make a lot of parts on the drill press using a rotary planer. The job is safer and faster than using a shaper, and the parts come out cleaner, but the procedure is so unorthodox that people see it happen and they don't believe it. All the jigs are keyed to specific machines. There's no measuring and no elaborate setup, just load in the wood and turn on the machine. It removes most of the tedium. Life is pleasant again. ——

Originally published in *American Lutherie #52,* 1997

Hangin' with Augie

by John Calkin

I **WISH I COULD SAY** Augie LoPrinzi used to cut my hair, just to augment my hometown credentials, but I don't remember that he ever did. And though I developed a serious interest in music during college, that didn't evolve into an interest in guitars for another decade. Nonetheless, I knew Augie by reputation. I was bookish and socially maladjusted, but the other guys on my construction crew lived for a game called pool, and every one of them knew of Augie LoPrinzi. He was simply the best local talent anybody could remember. It's twenty years since Augie left Flemington, and longer than that since he had time for pool, but it's not too hard to find men who will fondly recall a night when he took their money and shattered their egos.

After college I fell under the sway of a suave banjo-picking ne'r-do-well of a gunsmith named Hank Baer, who lived with my sister Dar. He'd been everywhere, done everything, and knew everybody, so of course he knew Augie. I had built a few mountain dulcimers and was in love with the instrument. After seeing Hank's walnut Ode I wanted to build banjos, too. I was learning to play guitar, but had no interest in building one. Hank offered to take me out to Augie's, but I turned him down. (I was socially screwed up, remember?)

A year later, about 1976, my roofing crew was laid off for the winter. I was drawing unemployment. We had to turn in a fresh list of jobs we had sought every two weeks, and I was running out of places to apply to. I was also making more dulcimers, and I thought that a peek into a professional shop could only do me good. I decided to stop in at Augie's place and kill both birds at once.

Augie had split from the big factory that he owned with AMF, and had already moved out of his next shop in Hopewell. I found him one bright winter day at the Cane Farm in Rosemont, New Jersey. The Cane Farm had once housed chickens. The poultry was long gone, and it had become a community of craftsmen and small businesses. Next to Augie's was a maker of electronic-effects pedals that I recognized from ads in *Guitar Player.*

Augustino Guitars was chilly and damp. The staff looked up, then went back to work. The oldest man kept his eyes on me. He was short, very Italian looking. "What?" he said. Augie wasn't one to waste words.

"I'm looking for work," I said.

"Sorry," said Augie. "What do you do?" he added as I turned to leave.

I fetched a dulcimer from my jeep, a fancy curly maple hourglass piece I was making as a gift for my sister-in-law. Augie was pretty amused.

"That's the kind of work I'd be doing if I didn't have to make a living at it," he said. He smiled kind of funny. Sometimes it was hard to tell when Augie was putting you on. We talked, and he mentioned that maybe I could come hang out when I had the time. "No pay, though."

I decided to stay until he threw me out. Every day for weeks (much to my wife's amazement and disgust), I drove the twenty miles to Augie's just like it was a job. Augie liked company. His crew did the rough work, and he did all the real building in his own little cubicle. He'd made so many guitars that it was no problem for him to tell stories and build too. He wiped glue off his fingers onto the bottom of his maple workbench, and stalactites of Titebond were oozing toward the floor. He was cranking out twenty-four guitars a month, and had his sights fixed on thirty. That's a lot of gluing.

Augie fixed my attitude toward instrument collectors early on. He had once made a run of guitars with a line of blue plastic in the purfling and around the soundhole. These "blue stripers" were already being traded for more than their retail value had been, and Augie felt cheated.

"You know how you deal with that?" he asked. "Every time you start a new line you start the serial numbers with ten. Then, if they get hot later on, you can make the first nine and cash in." Like I said, it was sometimes hard to tell when he was putting you on.

One day Augie surprised me with a car story. Flemington was still a sleepy little burg of about 7,000 people, but there was a dirt track at the fairgrounds that drew stock car racers from all over the Northeast. Bobby Pickle was a local hero, and sometimes a drive down South Main would turn up a view of his car carrier. It was a Cadillac with the body amputated behind the front seats, behind which a flatbed had been added to carry his stock car. It was as cherry as any custom car ever made. Augie flipped open a copy of the Hunterdon County Democrat and pointed to a picture of the strange beast.

"That used to be my car," he said. "One night my wife and I were stopped on Route 12 waiting for a chance to turn left into a driveway. I looked into the rear view mirror and saw a set of headlights come screaming toward us. I just had time to turn to my wife and say, "Sit straight, put your head back," when the guy creamed us. I don't think he even hit his brakes. My wife was hurt pretty bad. Bobby Pickle got my Cadillac from the junk yard and rebuilt it."

At one point Augie decided to build bluegrass banjos, and he asked me to make up a set of inlays. For days I doodled, trying to come up with shapes that were attractive, distinctive, and nonderivative. I had already made up a set for my own future banjo. They were heavy blocks with curlicues, somewhat Ome-ish. I had cut them into sheet copper, and one morning I dropped the stack on Augie's bench.

"Any of these suit you?" I asked.

Augie shuffled the stack for less than a minute and picked out the ones he wanted, then quickly laid out a pattern onto a sheet of thin black plastic that had his headstock design drawn on it.

"Cut that out and we'll see how it looks."

When I brought it back he slid one of his decals across the top of the plastic.

"Looks good," he said, and went back to work. He never made a banjo that I know of, but I still have the headstock template.

One morning Augie put a coarse sanding block in my hand and put me with the rest of the crew thickness sanding rosewood backs. An hour of that was enough.

"Ever try an electric sander?" I asked.

"A wood block is faster."

He gave me a speed block sander and told me to find out for myself. He was right, but I wanted nothing more to do with the operation.

"If you want me to do this kind of grunt work you have to put me on the payroll," I told him. He gave me that funny little smile, like maybe I was smarter than I looked. Later on he cobbled together a thickness sander, and Hank Baer came in to turn the wooden drum for him.

Augie was full of tricks and jigs. He was tired of hiring wannabe guitar makers and having them leave after picking his brains. A couple had even set up shop within a territory that Augie considered his. His goal was to be so jigged up he could hire men with no talent or ambition to produce all his parts, but it wasn't an easy plan to inaugurate.

"Know what happened with AMF?" he asked. "I made a precise piece for each work station, and they were to trace that piece and copy it. But the template piece would get glued into a guitar, and they'd grab a new piece and trace it. Then the new template would get stuffed into a guitar, and they'd pick a new one as a template. Every time they changed templates the pieces got a pencil line bigger, and after awhile you could feel it in the guitars. They weighed a ton. Never let a bowling-alley company make your guitars. They screwed up Harley Davidson, too."

Eventually I got called back to work to sandblast cement trucks for the rest of the winter, and when the weather broke, it was back to roofing. Augie moved his shop to Baptistown, New Jersey. It was a nicer, airier shop, but I didn't have time to hang out. Hank Baer initiated a Thursday night bluegrass jam session at Augie's. Since my guitar playing was still weak, my contribution was a new, strange beer every week. Iron City, Pearl, Lone Star, Buffalo, Robin Hood — it was a time of new beer labels. When the music was good Augie was content to work through the evening, but when things were slow he acted as host/entertainer. He was a magician and card trickster, and pretty good at both. My favorite Augie memory was a night when he dealt three-card monte and I couldn't lose the queen. I felt touched by the Tao or something, but no matter how fast he moved, Augie couldn't lose me. He became quite frustrated. I traded seats with one of the others, thinking that the light was just perfect at my seat and he would be able to pick the queen. But he couldn't, and neither could I after I moved. The moment was gone.

Despite the increasing guitar production, I think money was always tight for Augustino Guitars. Rumor had it that a new distributor had taken thirty guitars and never paid for them. One of the staff mentioned that Augie had offered to make up his back wages in guitars. A music shop owner told me that the local stores were miffed at Augie for selling guitars out the back door of his shop. I bought one myself that way, the last New Jersey DR-11, the Augustino version of a 000 Martin.

Augie moved to Clearwater, Florida. And I got divorced. For the next eighteen months I lived in my van, and the DR-11 was good company. In 1980 I opened my own repair shop, and that's when I really began to learn about Augie's guitars. About ten years later a pre-AMF LoPrinzi from 1972 came into my shop for a neck reset. It was made of Brazilian rosewood, and the whole guitar was collapsing on itself. The top and back were both cracked, and the action was ½″ high. I'd been to two of Augie's shops, and neither had climate control. There were a lot of cracked Augies around, and I thought of them all as summer guitars, made when the wood was swollen with humidity. I couldn't find the dovetail on this particular guitar, so I sawed off the fretboard at the 14th fret and cooked it free of the guitar top. There was no sign of joinery. I talked the customer into a new bridge and a thick fingerboard that tapered toward the nut. He didn't want to invest in having the cracks fixed. Unbeknownst to me, the merry minstrel took the guitar to Florida, where Augie might have fixed it in person. But one night after playing in a bar, he happened to sell the guitar to a stranger who was on vacation from Lambertville, New Jersey, a town about ten minutes from my shop. The stranger not only brought the guitar home to New Jersey, he brought it to a repairman he didn't know to have it worked on. Me. Another sign from the Tao, I figured. I was meant to work on this beast until I got it right. I tracked down Augie's number in Clearwater and called him. He didn't remember who I was, but he remembered the guitar.

"It's built in the Spanish style. The neck and block are one piece, and the sides are let into the block."

"So how would you reset the neck?" I asked.

"Easy! Pry the back off the heel block, pull back on the head, and reglue the back to the sides and the block."

It was an old trick usually called slipping the block. I'd never done it because it was thought of as a half-assed repair method, and it's about as complex an operation as steaming the neck out of a dovetail when done to a nice guitar. It came out great, and the guitar played like butter. And something had happened to it. It was easily, spookily, the best sounding guitar I've ever heard. I kept it for two weeks after the operation, telling myself that I wanted to be sure it would hold its adjustment. I finally had to admit that I was stalling, and that I just wanted to play it. I called my customer, who was overjoyed with the way it came out.

"If you ever want to sell it, call me first," I told him.

He looked at me as if he had suddenly realized that I was out of my mind.

"I don't think I'll be selling it," he said, clutching the Augie to his chest. ———

Originally published in *American Lutherie #51*, 1997

Finger Planes, the Cheap and Easy Way

By Nathan D. Missel

I HAVE MADE SEVERAL well-balanced and inexpensive hollowing planes of copper for archtop-guitar and violin-plate carving. I hope these prove as useful to you as they have to me.

To make these planes, I purchased a 1¼″ copper pipe coupling from my local hardware store. The average price is around 40¢. I also bought a 1″×4″ piece of ⅛″ copper plate, a roll of lead-free solder, a tube of flux, and several 8×32 knurled-head brass thumbscrews. Everything else needed was found lying around the shop.

The pipe coupling serves as the body of the plane. When one buys the coupling it is usually about 1½″ long, so it must be cut down. Take the copper coupling and cut it in half. Select one of the pieces and press it in a vise while heating with a propane torch, turning the circular opening into a symmetrical oval opening. The heat limits the amount of distortion in the bend.

Take the pressed sleeve and position it on the copper plate. Trace the inside of the oval with a sharp pencil, leaving a line on the copper plate. Cut this out carefully on the bandsaw, and fit it precisely into the sleeve.

From one end of the plate mark 7⁄16″, then a further ⅛″. Cut on these marks to produce three pieces. The small piece is scrap. Now bevel the straight edge of the largest piece to the proper angle of the plane blade.

Place the two cut pieces in the sleeve so as to leave a slot where the third piece would have been. This ⅛″ square slot is where the blade will protrude from the plane body. Clamp the two pieces in the desired position and solder them in with a standard propane torch. It is best to clamp both pieces in place, then solder them in the sleeve at the same time. Use flux as necessary. **Fig. 1** shows the assembled plane body.

Round the bottom of the plane on a belt sander. The average radius of the sole curvature should be around 12″ lengthwise and 1⅞″ in width. Be careful not to grind through the sole.

Find a piece of 1⁄16″ high-quality oil-hardening steel blade stock. An old file can be modified to work well. Grind the teeth off both sides with a belt sander (preferably) or grinder. These blades usually retain an HRC (Rockwell hardness, scale C) of around 60–65, meaning they take a very fine edge and retain it. The blade should be almost as wide as the maximum width of the slot, or just under ⅞″. It can be cut short, to about 1¼″, and rounded off. Or, it can be left long and a wooden ball slotted to fit over the end. This would provide a pushing point that would fit into the palm of your hand.

The angle of the blade is determined mostly by the height of the walls, that is, the length of the original coupler. To lower the blade angle it may be necessary to notch the walls a bit where the edges of the blade dig in. This also helps to stabilize the blade's position.

Cut a piece of copper from the remaining plate to serve as the blade cap. A hole should be drilled and threaded to accommodate the tensioning thumbscrew, and a groove should be filed in the cap. **Fig. 2** shows top and side views of the cap.

When the blade sits in the body at the proper angle and can slide smoothly into the slot, hold the blade in place and mark a line representing the top surface of the blade on the inside of the body. Acquire a piece of 3⁄32″ diameter steel rod, perhaps a nail that has been hardened. This will serve as a retaining rod. Allowing for the thickness of the cap, drill a 3⁄32″ hole through both sides of the plane body about halfway along the length of the blade and insert the rod. Slip the cap under the rod and tighten the thumbscrew to lock the blade in position. **Fig. 3** shows the assembled plane. ——

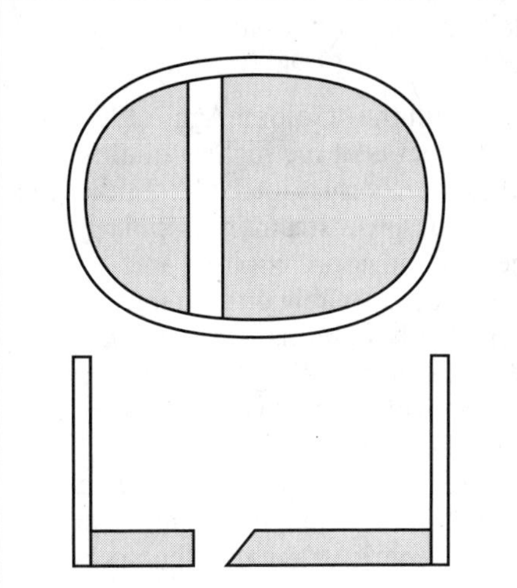

Figure 1. *The plane body*

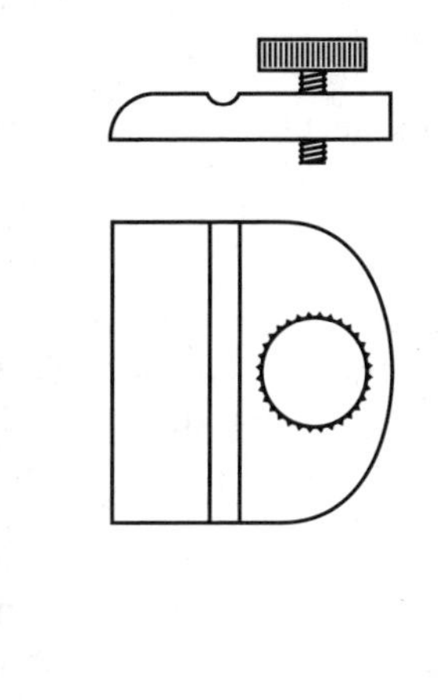

Figure 2. *The blade cap*

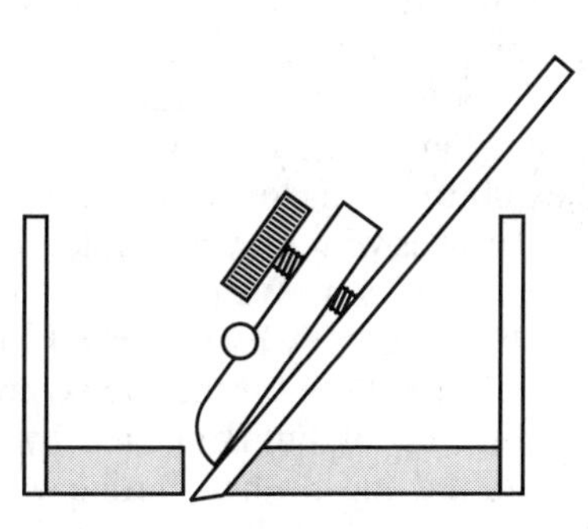

Figure 3. *The assembled plane*

Originally published in *American Lutherie #52,* 1997

Meet the Maker: R.E. Brunè

by Tim Olsen

RICHARD E. BRUNÉ, or "Broony" as we affectionately call him, began his self-taught lutherie endeavors thirty-one years ago at age seventeen, when he made a flamenco guitar from an old dining table. The experience was a positive one, and from there it was a matter of, as he puts it, "crawling into the funnel from the little end." Bruné toured as a flamenco performer (another of his self-taught skills) before moving from his home town of Dayton, Ohio, to Chicago in 1972 to open a guitar shop in the back room of a music store. A year later he moved to his present location, which he then rented but now owns. About that same time he was having discussions with Jerrold Beall about the need for an organization to encourage information exchange between instrument makers. Jerry was then a maker of dulcimers and harpsichords, but is now better known as the maker of the Beall wood threader. A classified ad in *Guitar Player* placed by Beall led to the formation of the Guild of American Luthiers.

COURTESY R.E. BRUNE

The Guild's first meeting was an afternoon picnic at Beall's shop in Newark, Ohio, plus a similar meeting in Tacoma, in the summer of 1974. At that meeting, Bruné was elected President of the Guild, which meant that he made all the decisions until the next meeting, at which time the assembled members would elect a new chump. (Sorry. Make that "champ.") He decided to host the 1975 GAL Convention in Chicago, and managed to present a show that, while on a modest scale, had all the features of a modern Guild meeting.

The American lutherie-boom generation was young in 1975. I know I was! When you are a twenty-two-year-old self-taught luthier, someone with an extra three years of age and experience has a great deal of seniority. I considered Bruné to be a real leader in the American lutherie movement, and that opinion has surely proven out with time.

This past summer, Deb and I, along with our sons Isaac and Sam, visited this stalwart Guild author, lecturer, and exhibitor in his lovely home in Wilmette, Illinois, where he lives with his wife Pauletta and their son Marshall, thirteen. We then took the short drive over to his shop in nearby Evanston, which we had not seen since we were there for the 1975 convention. The shop has changed a lot, but Bruné hardly at all. He appears a bit better fed and clothed, but he was a bachelor in those days. Look at the pictures. Does he look twenty-two years older? One reason may be his excellent attitude toward lutherie and life. Lutherie is a part of life, not life itself. Richard's exemplary scholarship and excellent craft spring from delight, not obsession. As he said in a 1985 interview, "In the big picture, lutherie means nothing. Nothing! It is not worth risking your family and the other truly important things for." That should be framed and hung in every luthier's workshop.

I interviewed Bruné by fax.

You have been calling this the "Golden Age of American Lutherie" for quite some time. It must be platinum and jewel-encrusted by now!

For players this is still the "Golden Age" of lutherie. There are more instruments of the highest quality than ever before, and prices are very affordable. I think this holds true for just about any instrument popularly played today. One can find good repairers and restorers who will work reasonably on valuable collector instruments, although this is still much more difficult to find than someone willing to build a new instrument which will rival the best vintage instruments for a fraction of their cost.

I'm not exaggerating when I say there is as much interest in making guitars as in playing them. The Guitar Foundation of America has a membership of about 2,000 classical guitarists, and attracts about 200 participants to their annual festival. The GAL has

ALL BY TIM OLSEN EXCEPT AS NOTED

about 3,000 members and we attract well over 500 participants to our convention.

The current lutherie situation in America is a gravy train compared to the '70s and '80s. How long can it last?

I think the good ride ended about five years ago. Curiously, we are in a situation not unlike what happened in the 16th–18th centuries to the area of Füssen in the Tyrol. For various reasons, far more luthiers were trained than there was demand. The solution was simple: they exported luthiers to other parts of Europe. Various schools of lutherie sprang up overnight, most with connections to Füssen and their instrument-making guild. Today, this solution cannot be considered, as luthiers are already found in all parts of the civilized world.

Following the natural laws of economics, the ultimate outcome of continued production by luthiers whose collective capacity far exceeds the demand will be a lowering of prices. I expect this will have more effect on those who are just trying to get established than it will on those with long waiting lists and considerable pent up demand.

Most luthiers today are making light bulbs that don't burn out, so we all compete with our own used merchandise, as C.F. Martin learned in the '70s. My philosophy has been to do everything possible to make my new instruments more appealing than my old ones. The last thing I want to hear is some buzz about how my guitars from the '??s (plug in your pet date here) were the ones "from his golden period."

As for dealing in instruments, which historically has always been an integral part of being a luthier, the same situation is occurring at an even more accelerated pace. Musicians whose careers have not panned out have taken up dealing in instruments, despite the fact that most are not qualified to really identify, authenticate, and accurately describe for sale the guitars they are dealing in. This has been lost on most players however, whose knowledge on the subject is even more deficient, and so they are frequently swayed by "sizzle" and price. Later, when they learn of "problems" their expensive "vintage" guitar has with authorship, condition, originality, etc., they often feel compelled to "shoot the messenger." Stuck with merchandise of questionable value, they are forced to seek devious outlets to get out from under their mistake or risk loosing considerable equity.

The ease with which anyone can become a dealer and set up in their home with a "web page" and a few consigned instruments does not serve the musician well. The in-house capability of repair/restoration, adjustment, and expertise in identification *is essential,* and none outside the world of lutherie have this capacity. In my opinion this has been one of the worst eras for classical guitar dealing, although I'm sure few guitarists share this opinion. Over the years, I have tried to convey a smattering of my knowledge on the subject via numerous articles in hopes that this will eventually trickle down to the buyers of these instruments, who will make more intelligent purchases based on accurate historical information. Frankly, this has been an uphill battle, as I'm afraid many "collectors" (whatever that means) are more concerned with how much an instrument is worth, and how much it may go up in value, rather than what the instruments themselves represent: The best musical tools of their respective eras.

You started as a one-man shop, but by the mid-'80s you had two employees, I believe. Now you are back to working alone. What did you learn from your experiment with employees?

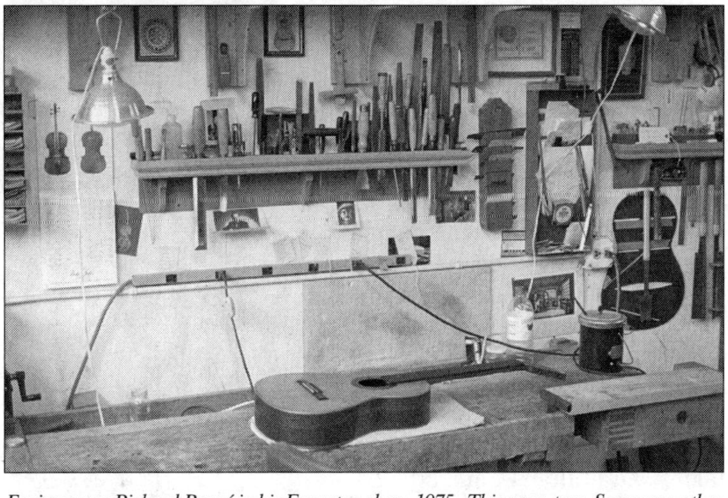

Facing page: Richard Bruné in his Evanston shop, 1975. This page, top: Same guy, other end of the same room, 1997. The flamenco guitar he is playing is an interesting experiment. Bruné built it with a domed top and no fan braces. It sounds great and the bridge has not twisted. Above: The straightforward workbench is a reflection of the man.

Bruné's neck attachment system is similar to the process he observed at the Asturias workshop in Japan, and which he described in American Lutherie #15*. (See* Big Red Book of American Lutherie Volume Two*, p. 86.) Both the body and the neck are routed with a slot which will tightly accept a spline. Then the body and neck are accurately held in the proper relationship to each other while a sanding belt is passed between them. The body becomes the pattern to which the neck is fitted. The spline is glued in, completing the operation. This method allows for minute and simple adjustment of neck angle.*

Above: Bruné developed a number of jigs and dedicated tools during the time that he had employees in his shop. These were designed to be accurate and mindless. The high initial cost of this dedicated peghead boring machine was thought to be effective in that it allowed the operation to be performed by the less-skilled employee. Now that the employees are gone, Bruné uses it because it is quick.

I was a one-man operation until around 1975, at which time my friend Howard Levy, now a world renowned musician, helped me part-time with some harpsichord jack assembly. He was already in considerable demand as a musician, but he enjoyed being around the shop and participating in something exotic like harpsichord making.

In 1983 I took on Kurt Bjorling to assist with preparing parts for my guitars, and he stayed with me until about 1990. Kurt plays clarinet in the Klezmer group Brave Old World. Recently he has been flying to New York to coach Itzak Perlman on Klezmer music. Kurt is a talented luthier in his own right. He is making cymbaloms now, and he stops by the shop from time to time to show me his latest work.

San Sun, a Cambodian refugee, also worked for me in those years doing materials preparation. He is a highly talented traditional Cambodian musician and also makes Cambodian instruments such as the *takhe* and *tro u*. San wisely left to train in the violin

Richard Bruné poses with a small part of his guitar collection. He holds a "cross-eyed" 1929 Francisco Simplicio, one of only nine examples of this style made. On the wall behind him is his guitar #418, which he made in 1986 and sold to Andrés Segovia. The first instrument to his right is a 1934 Santos Hernández flamenco. The next case is for the Simplicio, and the next one holds a 1918 Enrique Garcia. Out of the photo but on the same wall are a 1936 Domingo Esteso and a 1912 Manuel Ramírez, which is the sister instrument of the Ramírez instrument used by Segovia and now on display at the Metropolitan Museum of Art.

shops of William Harris Lee and Ken Stein here in Chicago, the premier violin making/repairing city in the world today.

Several others also worked in my shop for brief periods. The idea was to free up my time to work on the difficult tasks that are the bottlenecks of production. Eventually I faced the choice of either becoming the GM of guitar makers or remaining an artist. For me there was no choice. But I have no regrets about my brief foray into the industrial world. It helped me organize in my mind what was important and what was superfluous to the essence of being a luthier and to the making of a world-class instrument. I have always said that how you arrive at an instrument is not as important as the instrument itself.

Today I do get help from Pauletta, who does the office and bookkeeping work, including the ordering and shipping. And Marshall does some repair work in the shop, as well.

So where do you go from here?

I'll continue to do what I do best and hope that it will continue to work for me as it has for the past thirty-odd years. Unless a luthier just starting out only wants to build new instruments (which I believe is now unrealistic), it will be imperative that they become established and trained with a well-known luthier who routinely handles rare and exotic instruments. Because of the high values these instruments are commanding today, no owner in their right mind is going to entrust the repair, restoration, or even adjustment of one of these instruments to someone whose major qualification to do the work is a glitzy web page that their cousin designed for them. This has been the rule in the violin world, and it will be the new rule in the vintage guitar world. I don't think it would be realistic today for a luthier to come up self-taught, the way I did. Since the traditional "apprentice" system has been dead for centuries, aspiring luthiers should view the acquisition of their basic knowledge and experience no differently than any college level degree, and they should expect their compensation to be commensurate with the level of their knowledge. In order to run a successful shop, one needs the equivalent of a PhD, along with excellent references.

You appear to be a successful guitar builder, collector, scholar, restorer, importer, exporter, and author. You also play flamenco quite well and have a beautiful home where you do not appear to be a stranger. All this is done without employees. How do you do it?

I do what I love, and love what I do. I'm blessed with my wife Pauletta, who understood when she married me that being a self-employed luthier is living life on the edge without a safety net. She has permitted (no, *encouraged*) me to be the best I can be, wisely knowing that our income depends entirely on my success in that goal. My son Marshall has never known any other life. I try my best to convey to him that there is no room for "pretty good" in this world I inhabit, on the chance he may someday decide to follow a similar path. ——

Originally published in *American Lutherie #53*, 1998

QUESTIONS

EDITED BY CYNDY BURTON

■ ***John Calkin of Greenville, VA asks:***

In the last "Sources" column you described a method of using 5-minute epoxy as a filler for rosewood under shellac. Will it work under lacquer?

***Cyndy Burton of Portland, OR** answers:*

Yes, I believe so. I know two people who have done it. Anyone else care to comment?

***Christopher Luck of N. Vassalboro, ME** responds:*

I've used both water-based and nitrocellulose lacquer in this setting without any problems, although I do scuff sand the epoxy with 220-grit paper first.

***Fred Campbell of San José, CA** responds:*

In my experience, it is *not* really advisable to use 5-minute epoxy as a filler under lacquer. The greatest problem arises several months after the instrument is completed. The pores become cloudy or chalky in appearance. Also, due to the nature of the volatiles used in both materials (i.e., ketones, toluene, and so on), sinkage is not significantly minimized over the long term. With the added labor involved in the application of the epoxy figured in, the detriments seem to outweigh the benefits.

*And **Douglas Somervell of Brasstown, NC** responds:*

I first spray a sealer coat of shellac and allow ample time for it to dry. I like the 20-minute, finish-cure epoxy from Bob Smith Industries. It allows enough working time to do the entire instrument at once. And although it takes eight hours to completely cure, it then sands away nicely with 320 (I like the yellow 3M paper from the auto parts store). The shellac doesn't sand so well and so acts almost as a stop.

I work the epoxy into the pores with old credit cards, and I include the rosette and perimeter purflings and bindings of the top. Be certain to sand away all traces of the epoxy from the surface, leaving it only in the pores and pits. Now it is important that another coat of shellac be applied. If you fail to do this, any area where you may have sanded to the wood will appear blotchy in the finished instrument. If necessary, repeat where the pores didn't fill, then apply top coats. I used Behlen's Musical Instrument Lacquer on my last instrument, and I am very impressed with it. In the past I've used a couple different brands of nitrocellulose and a precatalyzed lacquer and they all worked well with the epoxy pore fill. ——

Originally published in *American Lutherie* #52, 1997

ALL BY R.E. BRUNE EXCEPT AS NOTED

The Restoration of Agustín Barrios' Francisco Simplicio

by R.E. Bruné

Author's note: Agustín Barrios Mangoré (1885–1944) was one of the most notable and illustrious player/composers of the early 20th century. Though despised by Segovia for using metal strings and appearing in concerts dressed as an Indian, his music has survived the test of time very well, and is probably more popular now than ever before. He owned and used many different guitars during his career, this guitar being the best preserved of those surviving today. His recorded legacy is now widely available, as is his biography Six Silver Moonbeams *by Richard Stover.*

TIM OLSEN

Above: Richard Bruné holding the restored 1927 Francisco Simplicio, Ex Barrios. Top of page: Front view, after restoration; back view, before restoration.

SEVERAL YEARS AGO I purchased a 1927 Francisco Simplicio guitar (No. 156) which was reputed to have been used by Barrios. It had been in the possession of Aida Borda y Pagola de Pío Bano of Maldonado, Uruguay[1] who said that Barrios had used this guitar extensively. The fingerboard showed obvious signs of the guitar having been mounted with a steel 1st string, and having been played by a guitarist who utilized the entire fretboard, as the ebony was worn with pits right up to the 16th fret (**Photo 1**). It was also obvious that the person who had been playing this guitar sweated profusely, as not only was the varnish caked with enormous sweat stains on the back and sides, but the purflings where the right arm rests were worn away to the linings from the acid erosion of the sweat[2] (**Photo 2**).

Although I had little else to confirm that this was Barrios' guitar,[3] I decided that its condition warranted restoring to playing condition. Doing so would involve removal and replacement of the original fingerboard and restoration of the eroded purflings and varnish. This past spring I undertook this project, and upon removal of the fingerboard,[4] I discovered written in pencil on the neck, the name "Borda Pagola" (**Photo 3**). Martín Borda y Pagola was the patron of Agustín Barrios and provided Barrios with significant financial support during his career. He was also a patron of Francisco Simplicio, from whom he must have ordered this guitar. In the Prat *Diccionario de Guitarristas y Guitarreros* written in 1934, Prat specifically mentions that Borda y Pagola was a collector of fine guitars.[5] I am familiar with other instruments known to

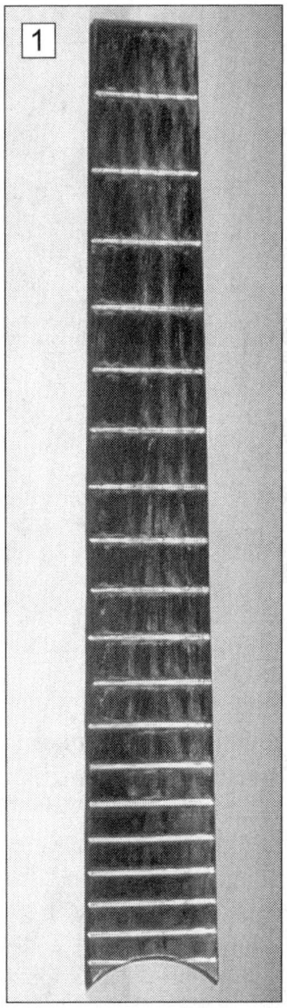

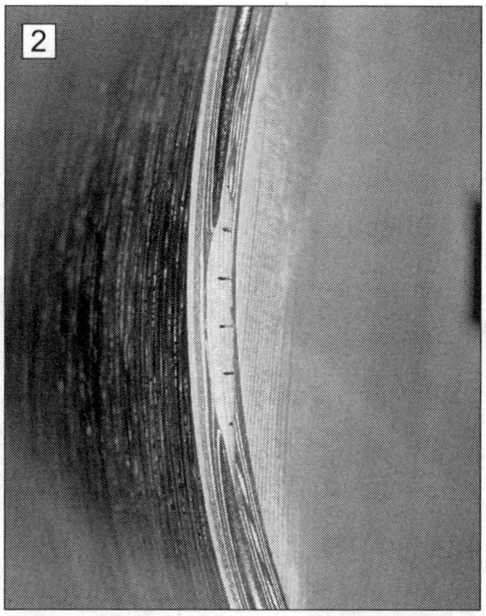

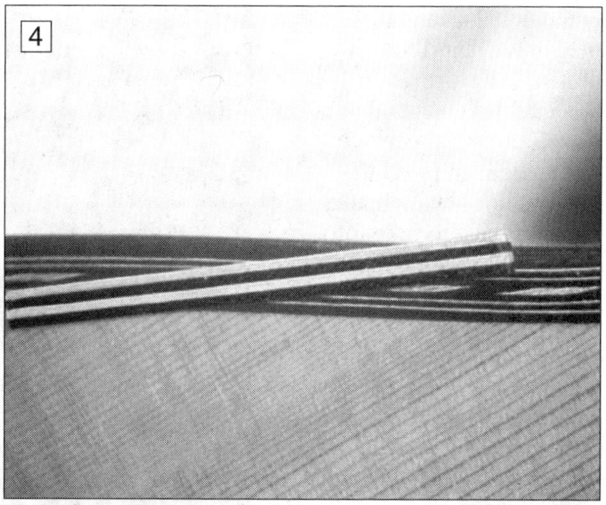

have been owned by Borda y Pagola, yet this is the only one which shows such extensive musical wear. As it was not played after Borda y Pagola's death, remaining in the family as an heirloom, that leaves only Barrios as the probable source for the heavy wear exhibited by the instrument.

Restoring the purflings proved to be an interesting project. The main difficulty was in getting the little black-white-green-white angled pieces of "rope" exactly right, and in rhythm, as they had to enter and exit the *falseta* of the inlay exactly in *compas*. Using my eye to estimate thicknesses and color hues, I made up a sandwich of what I thought to be the right stuff, and cut off some strips, which I laid down on the straight part of the waist to check the rhythm and angles **(Photo 4)**. Actually, the first sample was not up to snuff, so I made a second batch, correcting the previous mistakes and got it just right.

I then laid up the strips exactly in the correct angle by gluing them down on a scrap pine board **(Photo 5)**. After this was dry, I used my plane to dress the edge "along the grain" of the angled pieces, and I made a final check of the size and color. Using my 14″ bandsaw with a 3⁄8″ bandsaw blade .014″ thick[6] (from which I meticulously removed the kerf by hammering with a ball-peen hammer over an anvil), I clamped a custom rip fence over a plywood subtable and set it to cut the .5mm wide rope material I needed **(Photo 6)**.

The purfling lines were a simpler matter, which only required making exact duplicates of the size, species,

and dye colors of the originals. If you haven't done this before, even this may take several batches to get the look right. Bear in mind that black is not always black, and you have to take into account the effect of the varnish after it is applied over the repaired area, and the subsequent color shifts that will occur when a colored French polish is used. In this case, the reddishness of the French polish that duplicated Simplicio's original would cause the greens to shift to grey, which meant that underneath the varnish the greens had to actually appear more bluish than greenish. I was able to anticipate this by looking at the color of the matching inlays of the rosette that were under the original fingerboard, where they had not faded by exposure to light.

Since you should use the same species of wood as the original for this type of inlay restoration, naturally this means dyeing your own veneer in small lots, which is not as difficult nor cumbersome as it sounds. Water soluble dyes cooked into the already thinned veneers with a small pressure cooker will work just fine, and this method will allow you to control their intensity so you can duplicate the effects of fading and age. The closer you get it here, before assembling the restored components on the guitar, the better, as you don't want to be trying to artificially age a brand-new looking section that is immediately adjacent an original section.

Using the knife, I recut the purfling channel and made long scarf joints that were staggered for each separate component (white-black-white, or rope, etc.). Working from the soundboard out using only hot hide glue, I installed each separate component one by one, and let each dry thoroughly before proceeding. When I got to the rope, I took extra care to make sure that the width, angle, and repetitive rhythm exactly blended in with the original, as any slight deviation will show up from across the room. Finally, I finished off the outer components and outside banding/purfling, which was also installed with staggered long scarf joints **(Photo 7)**. I had to remake this outside banding a second time because what I originally had thought was cypress wood purfling turned out to be lemonwood (*dégame*), which is much more exotic. Fortunately I had several planks of the stuff with just the right grain.

Touching up the varnish was a breeze after taking so much care to get the foundation right, and this was done by French polish **(Photos 8 and 9)**. The back of the neck was rutted beyond belief and devoid of any semblance of original varnish, so after installing the new fingerboard, I decided the best solution was to gently recut the neck contours. Fortunately, like so many early 20th-century Spanish instruments, the original contours were generous in wood, so this was feasible. True to the original finishing technique used by Simplicio, I used thinned hot glue to size the recut neck, and filled with a water-based pore filler which dries quickly. I sized a second coat of thinned glue over the filled area to prevent it from darkening when the varnish was applied. Using some dry fresco colors mixed in with the French polish, I was able to match perfectly the original brownish-red-tinted opaque varnish which Simplicio frequently used on his necks **(Photo 10)**.

Finally, using French polish I touched up the areas on the top and the rest of the instrument where finger wear and erosion had worn them to bare wood **(Photo 11)**. Where the top was deeply discolored from oxidation of the exposed raw wood, I left it as it was rather than try to bleach (or even worse, sand back to fresher wood) the discolored areas. As this instrument still retained nearly all of its original French polish, the thicknesses of the plates had never been violated, so it fortunately still has a firm, brilliant, strong sound, which was further enhanced by using the Hannabach Carbon trebles, with medium tension 728 Hannabach basses. This setup is a compromise between the nylon strings favored today, and the harsh steel 1st that Barrios strung this guitar with.

Today, this guitar is just as playable and viable as a musical instrument for the most demanding concert player as it was seventy years ago when Barrios played it. In terms of time, this restoration took about thirty-five hours, which is about how long it probably took Simplicio to build the guitar in 1927. On the average he was making thirteen to fifteen instruments per year, a pace that seems surprising today when one considers that all of this very precise inlay material was made by Simplicio in house without any electrically powered equipment. ——

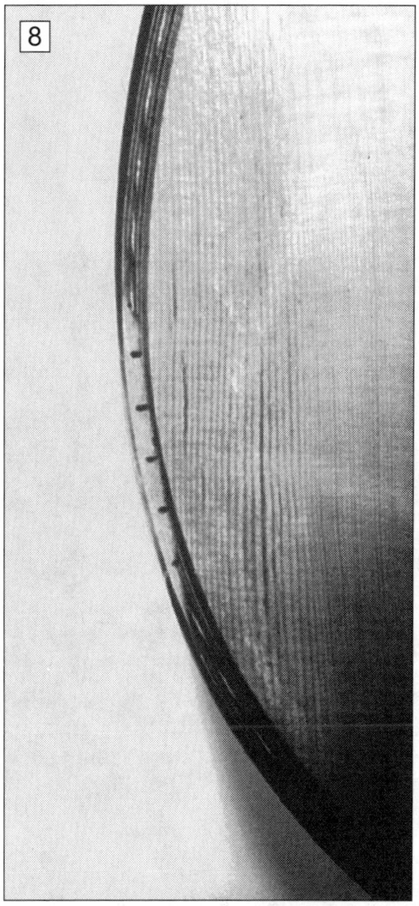

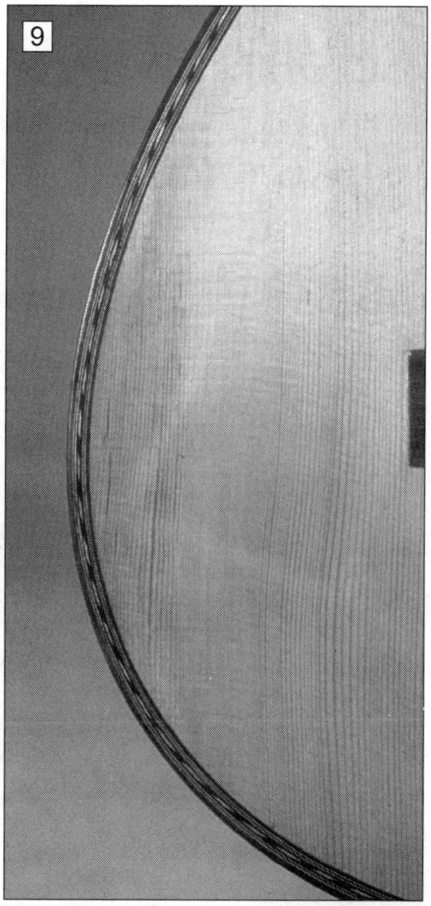

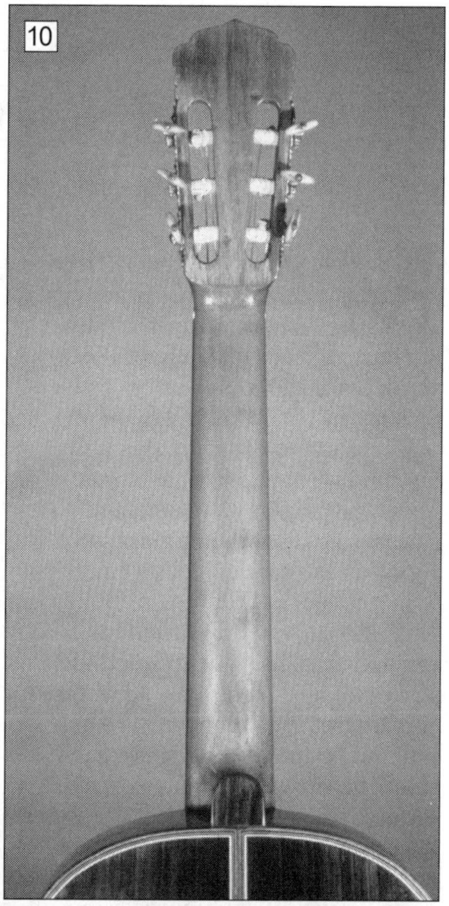

TIM OLSEN

Notes

1. Aida Borda y Pagola is the daughter of Martín Borda y Pagola, and it is from her that we have the legend that this guitar was given to Barrios by her father.
2. Stover relates in his book that Barrios sweated profusely, which may have been part of the reason that he used steel for his stringing, the cost and poor quality of gut being a strong second factor.
3. The photograph on p. 175 of Richard Stover's biography of Barrios, *Six Silver Moonbeams,* shows Barrios holding what is thought to be this same guitar.
4. Fingerboards are best removed by using heat to soften the glue line, and a blunt table knife to gradually and gracefully separate the joint starting at the nut and working down toward the soundhole. I use a simple clothes iron set on "cotton" to provide the heat and work in sections shorter than the iron is long. Over the soundboard, I use a cardboard insulating shield with a separate galvanized sheet-metal reflective shield on top of the cardboard to protect the delicate French polish (and other types of varnishes) which are heat sensitive. Done properly, this operation should leave the varnish of the neck and soundboard perfectly intact right up to the glue line of the fingerboard.
5. Domingo Prat. *Diccionario de Guitarristas y Guitarreros.* Buenos Aires: Romero y Fernandez, 1934, p. 61.
6. This blade is available from Olson Saw Company, Bethel, CT, www.olsonsaw.com.

Originally published in *American Lutherie #52,* 1997

Scroll Carving

from his 1995 GAL Convention workshop

by Guy Rabut

MOST OF THE SCROLLS that I carve are based on historical models. The one I'm carving today is based on a scroll from a golden-period Stradivari, 1714–1715. I had the opportunity to examine this instrument, so the outline of the scroll and pegbox was developed from a tracing of the original scroll. I took all the crucial measurements with a caliper at that time as well.

ALL BY JONATHON PETERSON EXCEPT AS NOTED

Guy Rabut at work during his scroll carving presentation at the 1995 GAL Convention. Facing page: A scroll by Guy Rabut.

I also had the opportunity to take photographs. It is always good to have a lot of pictures around while you are carving so that you can get into the aesthetic mind-set of each scroll, because each model has a different look or concept.

I usually shoot left, right, front, and back views. Other views are useful as well. The top view is one of my favorites because it shows the transition between the front view and the back. The turns as seen from the back are often convex, while from the front they are usually concave, so you have to figure out how to go from round to hollow. For the duck tail on the back of a scroll or the turns in the volute, a three-quarter view like this is helpful. This is a scroll from one of my instruments, a Guarneri model. A three-quarter view is also good for seeing the sculpting behind the ears. If you particularly like some detail, extreme closeups are helpful.

Just a note on photography. I prefer to shoot slides. I shoot Ektachrome tungsten film, EPY-64. I use tungsten lights, and a medium-grey background. I use a 105MM macro lens, and I don't bracket shots. I put the camera on automatic, and I just shoot. Last year we went to L.A. and shot something like 5,000 exposures, and there were only about three duds — somebody bumped the camera. It's fail-safe. You can make prints for reference, you have slides if you want to go to reproduction, and if you are into the modern technology you can scan them onto a CD, put them into your computer, and use that as a base for drawing and design work. It is a very practical and convenient format.

If you can't personally examine the instruments you are copying there are a lot of good books with nice pictures, so reference material is not that difficult to get.

A plaster cast of a scroll from a real Italian instrument is a nice thing to have, too. They are safe in the workshop — you're not going to ruin somebody's varnish. I happen to have a couple that I received as gifts. They show you the three-dimensional aspects of the sculpting — how deep a cut is, how it plunges in, the alignment of the ears, whether they are straight through, whether they are undercut — things like that. These have been obtained through various colleagues in the trade. As far as I know there is no commercial source for casts. The process to create such a cast is extremely risky and should only be attempted if you are working with someone who has previous experience working with very valuable and fragile instruments.

***Audience:** When you are working from a certain model, do you ever try to reproduce the original asymmetries and irregularities?*

Some people do. If I were making a scroll from one of the makers that was more asymmetrical and freestyle, I might very well try to reproduce that. A certain amount of flexibility and asymmetry comes just with the working, unless you are so amazingly gifted that you just can't help but make it perfect. I don't have that problem.

I like a scroll to be beautiful and have graceful curves. To me a scroll is a piece of sculpture. It's the one part of the violin where you are working totally with sculpture and line. It has no acoustic bearing. Some people think that something hacked out and crooked is very beautiful, and that is certainly a valid opinion. I prefer something a little more elegant and refined, particularly if I am working off of one of the models whose foundation is about elegance and

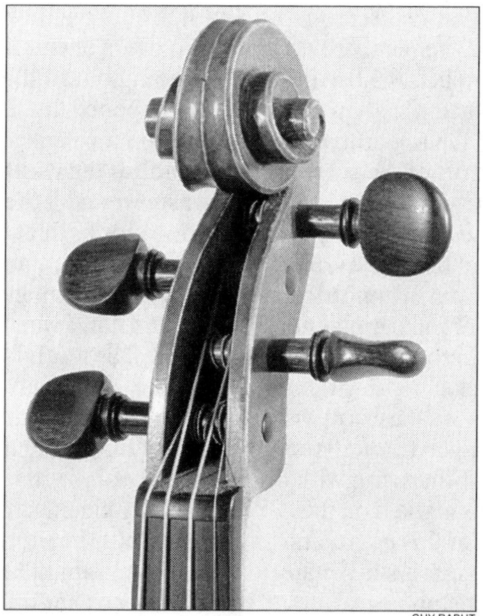
GUY RABUT

refinement such as an Amati, a Stradivari, or the better versions of del Gesù. I have a middle-period del Gesù casting, from the few years that he was working carefully, and it is reasonably well executed. It flows pretty well. There are a couple of lumps and bumps. When I am making that scroll I will take those out and make my own lumps and bumps. (*audience laughs*)

Carving a scroll from a pattern is, for me, a more natural process than just imitating every little lump and bump. If you were trying to copy someone's signature and laboring over each turn it wouldn't have a natural flow. When you write it has a natural flow, and when you work I think it should have a nice, natural flow. It's sculpture, it's my personal statement, but I am keeping it in line with tradition. If I am working from a Stradivari or Guarneri model, certainly no one would mistake my scroll for a Strad or Guarneri, though they would recognize where it came from.

With any given pattern, you can create scrolls with different attitudes, whether it's one with a circular feel, or a droopy one, or one that points up in the air. Look at different Strads. Strad is relatively consistent, but you'll see each one has a little different attitude. Some have a diagonal axis, some a more horizontal axis, some are fairly centered. You want to give your scroll an attitude, to make it your own.

Tools for scroll carving are very basic stuff. Most of the gouges in my set were made by Dastra in Germany. I'm not in love with them, but they're OK. I bought them years ago and I haven't found anything better. Some people use long gouges, some people use short ones. These were long ones that I cut off. I'm not sure why I cut them off, but that was when I was in school twenty years ago. They are a #6 sweep, and they vary from 6mm to 30mm wide. The 30mm is for one cut on the back of a cello scroll, and I use it once a year for that one cut. I like the soft, gentle #6 sweep. A #7 sweep is too round for me. It cuts too much at one time and doesn't have as much flexibility. I can't adjust and work with the shape of the tool as much. I also have a few #3 sweeps: a 14mm, an 18mm, a skinny one that's maybe 8mm or 9mm, and a fairly wide one, about 25mm, which I like. They are very flat. I also use a few flat chisels. These happen to be Japanese chisels because I like them, but any flat chisels will work. I use one double-beveled skew chisel for up inside the pegbox, but we won't get to that today.

I also use a few files and sanding sticks. The sanding sticks I make are shaped like little curved paddles, and I use them for evening the turns of the scroll after I finish my carving. Lately I have been using a metal-sandpaper product from Sandvik, called Sandplate, on my sanding sticks. It lasts a lot longer than sandpaper and leaves a nicer surface. It comes in strips, and they sell holders for the strips, but you can also just glue it onto a piece of wood. I know one guy who glues them on pieces of plexiglas.

I brought a four-ended Japanese mill file, which is wonderful. The Japanese call them plastics files. You can get them in hobby shops in Tokyo, so if you have a friend going there you should ask them to get you a few. They are very sharp and very aggressive for a mill file. I also use a Nicholson Handy File sometimes, and various rasps — whatever works.

So, I've got my pictures and castings here for when I need a quick reference, I've got a list of measurements, and I've got all of my tools laid out in a row in order. I try to keep them that way so I can find what I need quickly. Let's begin.

Before you start carving there are a couple of things you need to do. First, you need to square up the block. The top is flat, the top being the fingerboard surface. Often a cello-scroll block is wedge shaped because they cut them from the tree quartered in a wedge to conserve wood. In that case I usually glue wood on either side to help me square it up. On a violin that's not usually a problem. Simply square up what you have. In this case it was big enough to make the sides perfectly square with the top to the width of the ears. (I call them ears. Some people call them eyes.) In this case it was about 41mm. Most Strad scrolls are between 39mm and 42mm. You choose the look that you like.

The second step is to trace the pattern onto the sides of the scroll. This is a pattern for the scroll as seen from the side, and I have another pattern that wraps around the end and gives me the lines for the width of center section on the front, top, and back, and the shape of the duck tail. They are just outlines. The side template is punched with a series of small holes which are used to transfer the spiral pattern to the wood. I connect the little pin pricks with a pencil line so I can see them better. It really gives me a good idea of exactly what I want to do and helps me to visualize the shape. It also gives me a chance to change or correct the shape if I don't like where it's going.

I make templates from 10-mil frosted acetate, which should be available at your art supply store. Working with acetate to create a pattern is quite simple. Trace the pattern off of a drawing, cut it with a knife and break it out, and file and sand it to shape. If you don't like a spot, cut it off, tape on a new piece of acetate in its place, and correct it until you get what you want. You can make any layout or placement indicators right on the template.

For instance, I've made a little note on my cello scroll template that says "set back 3.0mm," so I remember that when I lay it on the block the front should be set 3.0mm behind the line of the fingerboard surface. That gives a little margin which allows me to plane the fingerboard gluing surface without taking the nose off of the scroll. On a violin the setback is about 1.5mm.

You want to make sure that the side pattern is positioned and traced symmetrically on both sides of the scroll so that you will at least start out symmetrical. To position the template, make a square indicating line at the upper edge of the nut that goes across the top and continues down both sides of the scroll block. Using those lines as a reference, I secure the pattern to the wood with two push pins, mark the outline, and punch through the holes to mark the points in the turns of the scroll with a needle. I also have my peg hole positions marked on the template. I mark them onto the wood at this point, and I drill them with a drill press while the block is still square. That avoids having problems later lining up pegs.

Next I cut the outside shape of the scroll on the bandsaw, and I refine it until the profile as seen from the side is finished exactly. This is finished. The peak of the bevel of the finished scroll is on this surface.

Once the final profile is established I scribe a centerline down the middle of the whole block. There is evidence that Strad did it on some of the scrolls that are in less-worn condition. He also used a divider to mark the widths, and those marks are still visible. I use a plastic pattern wrapped around the end to lay out the lines from under the chin, up over the top, and down to the duck tail. Then I cut the waste away from the sides of the neck and the pegbox up to where the turns start. That's where I am now, and we can start carving.

When you carve you need to support your work. You can just use the edge of your bench, or you can make some kind of an apparatus. I use a support fixture that a friend came up with that's sort of clever. He calls it the "scroll-o-matic." The scroll fits into the curves many different ways to support your work as you are cutting. I put a piece of masonite on the bottom of it so I can clamp it to the bench.

Chisel in such a way that you're supporting whatever you're doing. You're always supporting your tool and your work so you can't slip. Don't just put pressure against a piece of wood with no support. It could let go and you'll either make a mistake or cut yourself.

Do you generally find yourself holding the work with one hand, or do you ever clamp work down so you can stabilize it better?

I have friends who clamp their work down, and every time I see them do it, it seems like a great idea. (*laughter*) I should try to clamp my work more often, but I generally hold it. For a violin scroll freehand carving works well, but for certain procedures I do clamp the work down so I can hold my tool with two hands. If you can clamp it down, hold the tool with two hands, and have better control, all the better.

As I carve the scroll I'm basically going to be making two kinds of cuts beginning from the pegbox and working out to the ear. First I'm making cuts into this spiral pencil line at 90° to the side of the pegbox, then I'm coming back and making perpendicular cuts to establish the width of the scroll and to remove the waste wood all the way around. I often use the same gouge for both cuts. The first cut, the one that goes in from the side, should be deeper than the second cut, so that you end up having a clean face on the turn. On the second cut, I want the chips created by the first cut to just fall away. I don't want to have to carve them away. You try not to have too many gouge cuts into the sides of the turns, because that surface is a finished surface. Every time you have a finished surface, you want to preserve it so that it will be nice. It's just a matter of working cleanly. Inevitably there will be marks on the sides, but the more care you take the better off you'll be.

The grain in the scroll block is always slightly off one way or another, so there's usually an easy side and a hard side to cut. One side may cut in nicely, and on the other you may have to go at it a little differently. The easy side is usually the one that comes out nicer. On any scroll there's always one better side, even on Strads.

When I am carving a scroll I try to end each step with a finished surface so I'm not noodling back and forth. So often one step depends on the previous step. Particularly in the scroll, if you go back and forth you lose your continuity, and the reference points are constantly being cut away because of the nature of the process.

Do you reestablish your lines as you cut them away?

Once you've used a pencil line to get where you want to go you don't need it anymore. Then you make another pencil line for your next step. I don't need to put it back. If you work back and forth, then yes, you'll need to redraw lines. I recommend trying to cut right to the line. Finish what you are doing before you move on. Leaving a lot unfinished is a mistake.

For instance, ordinarily I start by making saw cuts to remove waste wood, so I will make a line to guide the saw and once I cut to that line I don't need it anymore.

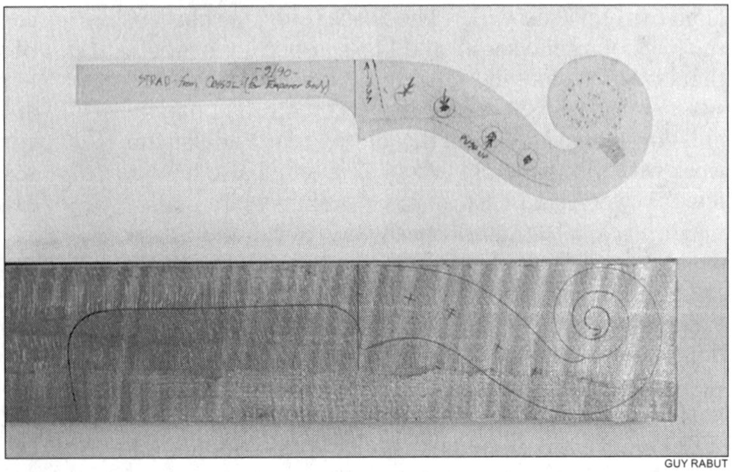

GUY RABUT

A Strad scroll template and a neck blank on which the pattern which it produces has been marked.

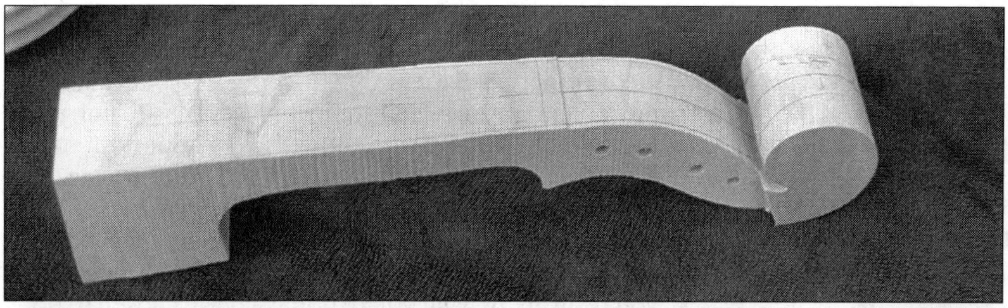

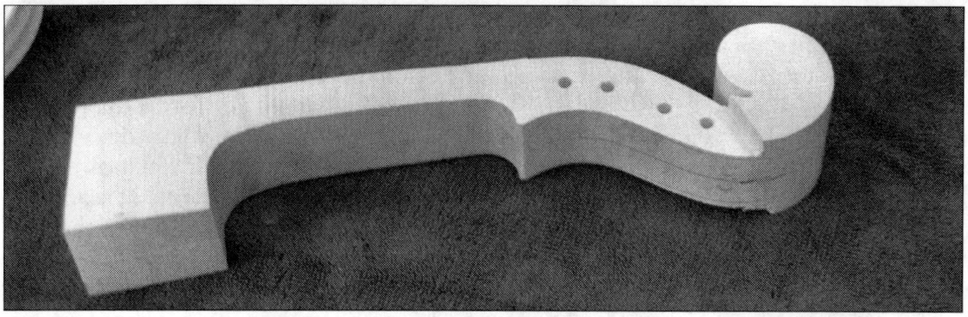

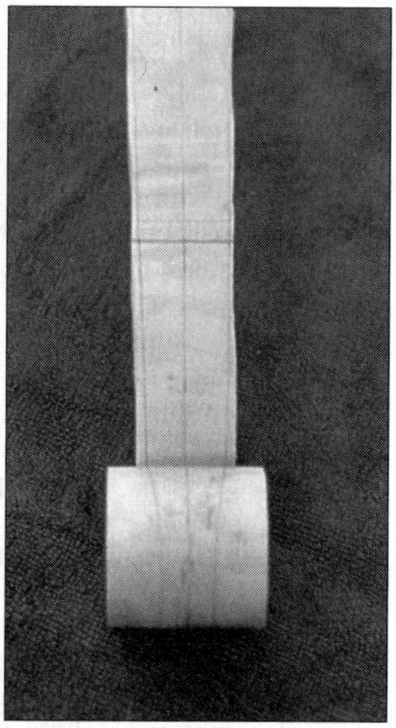

As I am working my way out towards the ear, I need a line on the surface exposed by the 90° cuts so I can see the slope of the spiral as it comes around. Just in front of my work, I need that line. As soon as I create a surface, another surface will present itself, and I will continue that line to show where I need to go next.

You are always turning your work, rolling it around to see what is developing, looking for any irregularities.

I got going trying to make the turns so you could see some of that, but I should finish the sides of the pegbox now. I usually do that before I start carving the turns. I don't take it to a completely finished surface at this point, but I establish the surface so I know where it's going to end up. For that I use these little fingerplanes, and then I use a rasp, and I clean up with a file or scraper.

I cast these planes from some that my teacher had. They are both the same, but one has a curved sole, and the other has been flattened on the bottom. Just a word on using a finger plane. A little plane like this is used as an extension of your arm. My teacher said, "Hold it like a pencil." That was his admonition. And I said, "What do you mean like a pencil?" And, of course, he said again, "Hold it like a pencil." Eventually we determined that, in fact, you hold it like a pencil. The two fingers in the back are guiding it, the front one is exerting the pressure, and you're riding on your knuckles. You're not pinching it. You keep your elbows in. It's a nice, natural process, and you can plane all day that way.

After I've planed, I file it a little bit. You want to get it down close to the line. I usually use a rasp, but I didn't bring mine, so I'll use this Sandvik Sand plate. It's fairly aggressive and leaves a nice surface.

I take it pretty much down to the line. The line is just an indicator of where I want to go, then I use my caliper to measure it. I like the plastic dial-indicator calipers for scrolls because they have nonmarring jaws, they're cheap, and they're plenty accurate for woodworking.

The surface you're working on now, the side of the pegbox — do you leave that flat?

I was just discussing this with a friend the other day. He makes a slightly rounded pegbox. I draw a straight line, and I work from that. It rounds off a little as it comes into the neck to blend smoothly, but I make it reasonably flat. All the old ones would have had neck grafts pushed up into them, and that affects the lower end, but I think they were reasonably flat as well.

Is the pegbox wider at the back than the front at the nut?

It depends on the width of your duck tail in back. Some of them are wider than others, but generally they taper just a little. I probably have about 25MM in the

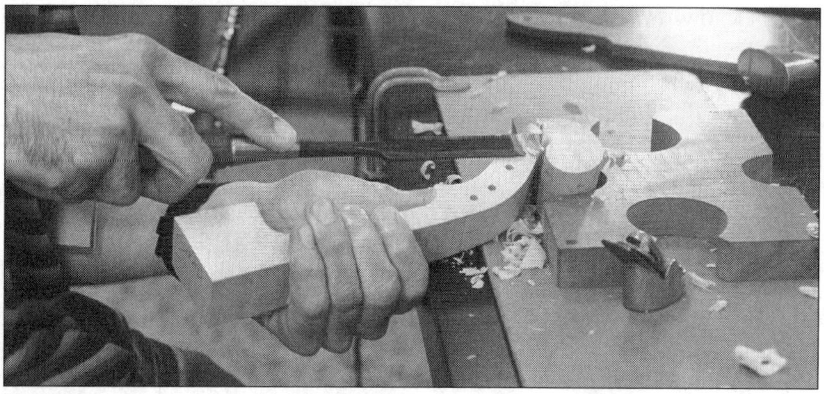

Top of page: Three views of the neck blank Guy brought to work on during his demonstration. Above: The carving is begun by using a flat chisel to remove waste material from the side of the pegbox up to the point where the turns will start. The photos on the following pages show Guy's scroll-carving procedure and are presented in the order in which they were shot. Note the sequence of the cuts, how the tools and the work are handled, and how the work is supported.

back, and I'm going to have 24.5MM at the nut. It could be 25.5MM on the back, again, depending on what look you like. Strads usually flare slightly toward the back.

I'll do the little round part where the back of the scroll meets the neck with a knife. I often hold my tool hand in place with my other hand just for stability. All the pressure is from my thumb in this case. My right hand is just holding the knife. This thumb is applying all the pressure. It's amazing the amount of power you have with that thumb.

If you can, always slice with the knife as you're pushing it. As you know, if you try to cut a tomato, even with a sharp knife, and you just push it straight into the tomato it ends up all over the place. You have to use a slicing motion.

I'll cut down the neck to where I've made a stop cut. A little stop cut gives you control, so you're not flying off into the air. If you give yourself something to go up against you're always safer. I'll leave the rest of the neck until later.

Just an aside on tool handling: Whenever you are cutting with a knife or a chisel you always want to brace yourself and your work in some way. The worst thing you can do is to be holding your work, with one foot up, watching TV. It is just bad form. When you play tennis, there's a certain way you grip the racket, or in golf you spend hours practicing your swing and holding the club right. There's a reason you do that. There's a physical, mechanical way of doing something which is efficient, safe, doesn't get you tired, and will help you avoid hurting yourself. The same is true for tool handling. The French always tell you to keep your elbows at your side — *"coudes au corps,"* (elbows to body) is the expression. They'll shout it out if they see you working with your elbows out. They want your elbows down. Maybe it's because they forgot to shower, I don't know. (*laughter*)

My elbows are braced against my body, the work is braced, the hand that is holding the tool is being braced by the other hand, so nothing is loose. You have more power and control when you're braced. You're not going to slip or be flying all around. It's very important to keep yourself clear of the edges of the tools, because hopefully these things are sharp. (*laughter*)

I do find myself, sometimes, letting my arm come out a little, but I try to keep it in control. As long as you're aware of what you're doing, you've chosen to do something, it's perfectly all right. But if you find yourself doing something that is not efficient and safe, then stop. Quite often there's a premonition. I don't know what it is. You think, "This seems like a really bad idea..." and then it happens. If you look at my hands there are plenty of scars from cuts, but not many of them are recent.

It's time to check the widths with a caliper to see where I am in terms of final widths of the pegbox. I'm sure it's very close to my template, but I'll check one more time just to make sure that it's what I intended.

I like to make the duck tail to describe a section of a circle. It's not pointed, not square, and not square cornered. It could be a slightly squat circle. In other words, the diameter of the circle that describes the curve could be a little wider than the width of the scroll. You can stick a compass in on the centerline and swing an arc, which is what that little compass-point mark is that you see in the middle of the duck tail. I don't mind leaving those little marks. They are part of the construction of the violin and give you a sense of the process. Sometimes these marks can be useful. For instance, I mark the bridge position on my tops. Working from a point in the middle, I mark with a divider where I want the outside of the two bridge feet to be. When the

instrument is varnished, the finish sinks into those two pin pricks. I can always place my bridge using those marks. I don't have to measure or mark it with tape. Anybody putting the bridge back will see them.

We have the outside of the pegbox close to completion, and I'll go back to cutting the scroll. I use a saw to remove the waste wood. The more wood you remove with your saw, the less you have to chisel. Once you make the saw cuts, you have square corners, and you can cut the corners away with a gouge. It's just a process of cutting squares and making them round. Try not to undercut with the saw. If you are going to undercut, do it intentionally, and do it with the gouge.

This scroll-o-matic is pretty handy for sawing. I just hold the neck in one hand with the scroll braced in one of these recesses. It's completely solid, and I don't have to clamp it in. My other hand is free to make the saw cuts.

I normally use a little Japanese backsaw, but I didn't bring mine. It is very sharp and precise, and I like the fact that it cuts on the pull stroke. I find it easier to hold the scroll steady while cutting towards myself.

As I begin to define the spirals of the scroll, a strong light will help by creating a contrasting shadow. If you get the light right, you'll get a shadow on the turns that helps you see what you're doing. Up to this point I have basically been following my line, but once I start finalizing it, I want to take a good look and get rid of any little bumps and lumps.

It's close enough so that I can now draw my line on the front surface. You really need to keep your surfaces perpendicular and square as you go. It just keeps the whole thing in line.

I keep the sculpting somewhat generous in the beginning and develop my final concept as I proceed. It's a connect-the-dots process. You begin with the points you know, such as measurements of existing scrolls, photographs, and drawings, and it's just a matter of blending all of these aspects together. It's not as scary or mysterious as you might think.

I've just drawn around again, and I'm going to make a few more cuts. Before I cut my line away I see one more spot I want to fix. Once you lose that line, you've erased all the evidence of any layout work

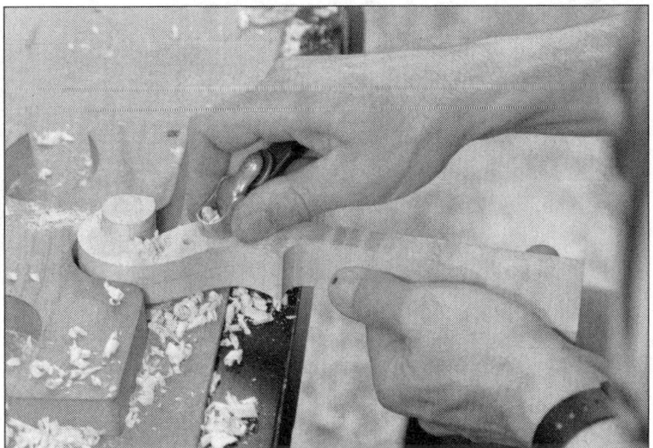

you have done. You can opt to leave the line if you want to leave the extra wood. On the side of the scroll you want to cut right through the middle of the pin pricks, not cut them away completely. As you cut through each pin prick you will see half of the pin-prick mark left on the side and on the corner. You might find it hard to see those little pin pricks at this point. That's why I draw the line through the marks to make the spiral more visible.

Ordinarily when I am working I have two lights, and I'll push one out of the way and pull the other one in, and alternate them so I get light from both sides at different angles. As I said before, you need good light. A window is nice. Figure out what works best for you.

Do you leave a round button at the end of the ear?

It's relatively round. I think when I designed it, I pretty much made a circle. There's some variation, but I try to keep the circular concept.

As you are carving are you keeping the shoulders square?

Yes, the faces of the turn are flat and square. There's no sculpting yet. I am establishing the nature of the spiral and the nature of the curves. When those two things are defined I will draw lines to show where the edges of the bevel on the corners will be and do the sculpting, but we won't get that far today.

For the most part I do the sculpting by eye. I will refer to some of my photos or a plaster cast, but most of the sculpting of the turns is done by eye, from experience.

Where do you generally start the undercut?

The undercut sculpting of the sides of the scroll usually begins just above the upper peg hole. It goes in fairly quickly to the deepest point towards the front of the scroll and then it becomes shallower around the back in the second turn. It becomes deeper once again as it proceeds to the front and remains fairly deep as it finishes up by the "comma" of the ear. I like to create a lot of dynamic energy by varying the depth of the sculpting at the spiral turns. One should always look for ways to keep the viewer's eye engaged by creating a dynamic interplay of sculptural forms. The three-quarter front and back views of a scroll are very useful to observe the depth and finish of the sculpting of any given scroll.

Could you comment on the types of wood you like to use for a neck and scroll?

I choose a neck block which is dense, even a bit heavy. I look for fine grain and mild, shallow flames. If you select deeply flamed wood for a neck, you will find that it is more difficult to carve and it has a tendency to warp. If you look at the scrolls of the great makers, you will see, for the most part, wood with fairly mild flames. Often the maple on the back would be more highly figured than that of the neck.

Do you use European woods exclusively?

Mostly. I don't really care where the wood is from as long as the wood has the qualities that I like. If it looks like a good piece of wood, I'll use it. Most of my wood is European because I bought most of it there. The maple in this neck I bought in Germany. It looks European to me.

Does the cost of wood affect the price of your instruments?

The cost of the wood is negligible in terms of the cost of the instrument, except for cello wood, which is getting rather expensive. But still, in terms of the cost of the instrument, it's maybe 10%. I don't always buy

the most expensive wood. Some of the wood that I like the best is not necessarily the most expensive.

Have you used any of the domestic maples?

I've used some domestic big leaf maple. Big leaf maple is not generally as hard, so it can be tougher to scrape, and it's not quite as strong, but it's OK. I haven't yet used any of the maple coming out of Minnesota or Michigan. I believe it's what they call red maple, or soft maple, but it's not necessarily soft. My experience with North American maples other than big leaf maple is that they are a little heavier, a little harder, a little more rubbery. In the neck it's not a big issue, really, as long as you can carve it. I don't want a soft, punky maple for a neck. Your pegs are going to split it, and the neck is going to warp. Definitely, I go for the harder and closer-grained wood.

Have you ever tried any alternative woods?

I made a viola with elm ribs recently. Elm has a tendency to split, though. I don't think it's that good. It looks pretty. Some of the Amatis have some sort of chestnut or ash for the ribs. I've never used it. I've used poplar and willow for backs for cello and viola, with good results.

Do you use any power tools in scroll carving?

Only for a couple of steps. I cut the pattern on the bandsaw, and then use the drum sander to go around the profile just because it's quick, but you can file it and rasp it by hand. I drill the peg holes on a drill press. Later I drill my pegbox to remove most of the waste wood with a Forstner bit. Other than that, it's all hand tools.

Could you say something about sharpening?

All my gouges are hollow ground, because it makes sharpening easy. I have an angled tool rest I made out of a piece of wood that I use with my grinding wheel to regulate the hollow-ground bevel. I also shape the ends of my gouges so that the cutting edges aren't straight like a flat chisel, but are slightly curved. Some people say that the curve of the sweep should be the same as the curve of the end. I just round the ends slightly to make it work for me.

To hone a hollow-ground gouge you rock it on a sharpening stone until you find the flat of the bevel, and then just slide it back and forth with a rocking motion. I use the artificial Japanese stones. When I discovered them I wrapped up my oil stones and put them away. I also use a small Belgian stone I found at a flea market.

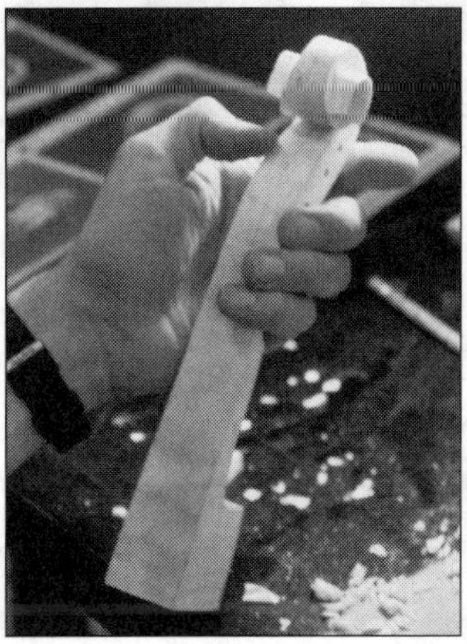

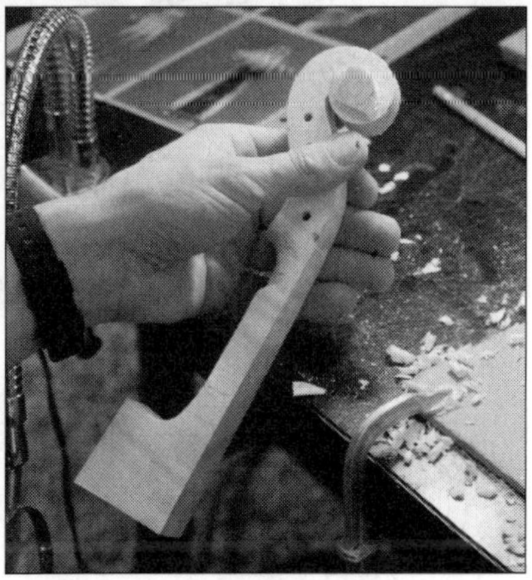

I don't know where to get them anymore. I heard that the mine in Belgium is finished. They used to be common, and were used for razor sharpening, and they're wonderful. This one is reasonably soft, and I like that. I just rounded the end of it a little bit so I could use it as a slipstone on the inside of the gouges. I have a leather strop with one rounded side that I use for the gouges. Most of my tools I don't strop because it rounds them over too much. With the scroll gouges, it's not as crucial. In fact, you're not really using the flat of the tool quite as much. These gouges are soft enough so they strop very easily.

I sharpen my gouges fairly often during scroll carving, partly because the steel is so soft, but also because I want a clean cut. What you see on the side of the scroll is the cut from the gouge. If your gouge's edge has little teeth or nicks, then of course it will leave tracks.

How long does it take you to carve a scroll?

For a violin scroll, if I don't get interruptions, a couple of eight- to nine-hour days, a day being from when you come into the workshop to when you leave. Who works an eight-hour day? (*laughter*) The phone rings, people come by, and all that.

What do you do if you make a mistake and break off a corner or tear out some grain while you are carving?

If you chip something off, just get your Elmer's glue out and glue it back on. Do it right away. It's not the end of the world. It'll be fine if it's not structural.

What if the scroll block is not wide enough?

If you are making a cello and the wood for your scroll is a little too narrow, you can take a piece out from right in front of the head, split it in half, open it up, slide it out and glue it on to extend the ear. You can get another 3MM–4MM that way. Once you've blended it in and cut it you'll see a very faint line, but it blends in beautifully. Many of the old Italians glued on ears. It's perfectly acceptable.

Is the scroll a Baroque design, or is it taken from other earlier instruments, or was it created for violin?

I think it's a universal Baroque shape. If you look at furniture or architecture, it's just a way of finishing

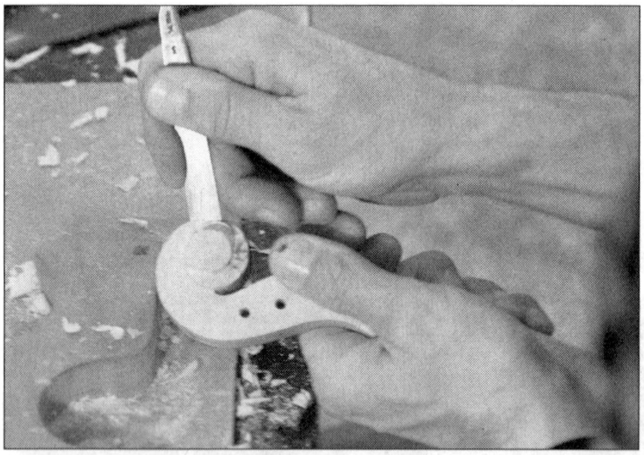

something. Even the Romans used scroll shapes for decoration. It would have been natural to finish the violin neck with it. Carved heads or crests were used on some of the instruments, but 99% were scrolls. It is traditional, and it's a nice shape to work with.

Where the flutes end underneath the front, are you knifing or gouging that?

I gouge it around to the front of the scroll, and then I knife the underside with a long, thin knife. You start at the front and work your way all the way back in. I leave the knife cuts. There's no scraping or anything. I scrape the back, top, and front lightly, but I stop scraping as I proceed under the chin which is just cut with the knife. You'll see little facets in there.

Do you like tool marks on the scrolls?

Yes, some of them. Strad is so clean that there are not a lot of tool marks. There are some on Guarneri scrolls.

Why do you suppose there is so much variation in del Gesù's work, with regards to the scrolls? It's almost as though he didn't have any awareness of the earlier work. It's almost as if there were two different people.

Some people have suggested that. I don't know why there's so much variation. It's a tough one, because there are some very organized scrolls, very neat, but those late ones are really out there, and it happens in a short span of twenty years. I've been doing this for almost twenty years and I've evolved and changed, but

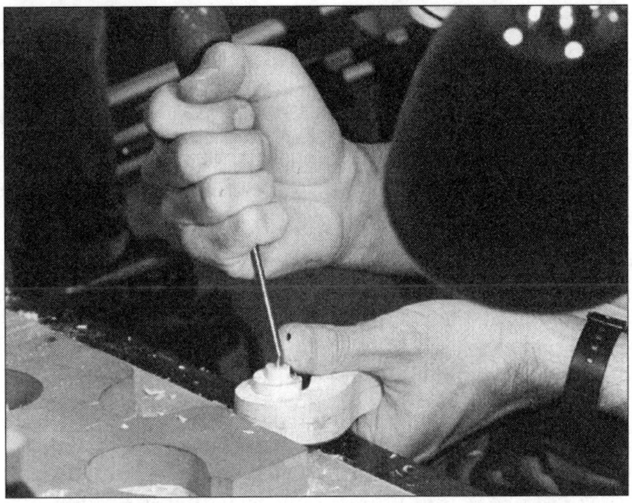

not like that. So, who knows what happened? Strad worked until he was ninety-three, and his scrolls are very consistent.

How much documentation follows these instruments, as far as who has owned them and who has worked on them?

Some instruments are very well documented, but many lack such documentation. If an instrument was owned by a famous musician or important royalty there is often a great deal of information. In more recent times many of the important violin dealers have collected and kept good records on instruments that they have handled. As to the work that has been done on any

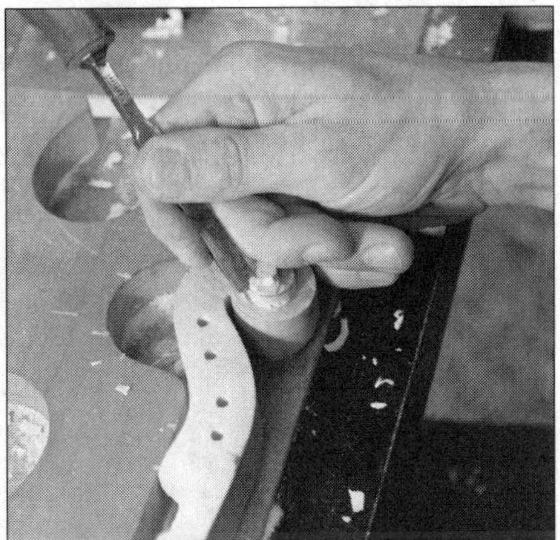

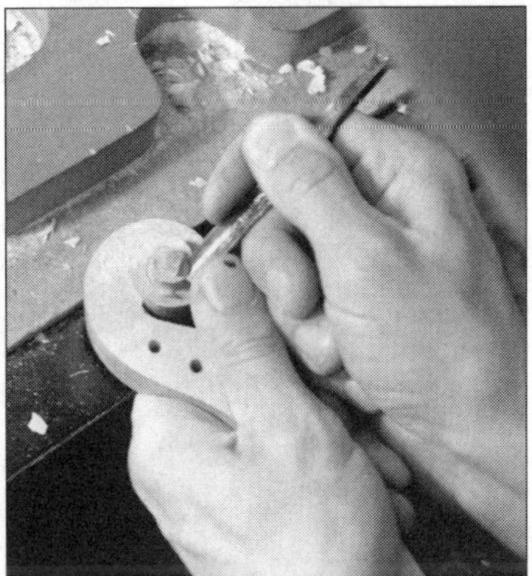

instrument, there is usually some oral history passed on to each owner, but most of the specifics get lost.

When you create the round surfaces on those faces, are you using the shape of the gouge to define that curve, or is the gouge not as tight as the curve you are cutting?

The gouge is just slightly flatter than the curve, so the corners of the gouge are clearing the surface. This allows me to shape more easily. I want more control over how these curves are blending, because at any given point it's not just a #6 or a #7 sweep. There are sets of gouges which supposedly, if you match them end to end, create a perfect scroll, but what's a perfect scroll? They are all a little different. I want a little more flexibility.

Do you use gouges with increasingly tighter curves as the turns on the scroll get tighter?

I don't. My approach is to go to smaller gouges with the same #6 sweep. The widths in this set are 4MM, 6MM, 7MM, 9MM, 10MM, 12MM, 14MM, 18MM, 20MM, 22MM, 25MM, and 30MM. You can get by without so many. Depending on the model I'm making, I use fewer gouges. If I want to leave more chisel marks I use a flatter #3 sweep gouge and just leave the big bold chisel marks there. It gives you a very nice faceted look. Strad's work didn't have that faceted look, so I won't do that here. Some of the del Gesù scrolls have more tool marks, which is nice.

There's not that much wood to remove when you're carving a scroll, when you really get down to it, particularly in a violin. It goes reasonably quickly. A few cuts and you're there. And a few more cuts and you've gone too far. (*laughter*)

Could you quickly review the whole process, especially the final steps that you didn't get to today? For instance, are you beveling the corners before you start hollowing the faces? What's the order?

Some people like to work both sides of the scroll at the same time. Some people like to work one side and turn it around. Working both sides the same time is going to help you with your symmetry in some ways. It's a personal preference. I generally work both sides at the same time to the same level of finish.

First I get it to the point where the spirals are defined — they are kind of square spirals — then I refine those lines and shapes. After I finish the turns completely I finish the side, and I do the pegbox next. Then I flute the back, and I do the bevel very last. I have a friend who keeps a bevel going the whole time, sort of a working bevel. He learned that way. It's a different style of working.

For the bevel I make a little line 1MM–1.5MM out from either side of the corner defining the layout of the bevel, then I do the sculpting using the line as an indicator of where the bevel will be. Once I've done all of the carving and scraping I put the bevel everywhere. For that I have a little Nicholson mill file which I've rounded on all the ends and the corners. I ground it, polished it, and buffed it so that the nose of the file doesn't tear up the inside of the turning if it hits it. It works very well. I use it for one purpose only.

Do you ever burnish the bevels?

No, I just file them. I even avoid scraping the bevels as a scraper tends to chatter. I don't fuss over any surface. I do it, and leave it, and move on. I like the surface to have some life. I don't want this thing to look as if it was airbrushed. By the time you put on your undercoat and you varnish it, it has been handled so many times that it's finished enough.

Do you do any scraping or sanding at all on the scroll?

I scrape the sides, but not the faces. If you use a nice sharp gouge, it's amazing how good a surface you get. Try to cut as much as you can. Abrading, scraping, and all those things are fine, but cutting is the fastest, leaves the nicest surface, gives you the nicest look, and it's more fun. If you're doing too much sanding and filing, you haven't cut enough. The only places I use sandpaper on the finished surfaces of the instrument are on the neck and on the edges of the body.

Has your approach to violin making changed very much since you started?

I think that I'm always developing new ideas, particularly in the acoustical area. You can't get that in school. You get basic fundamentals, but you have to

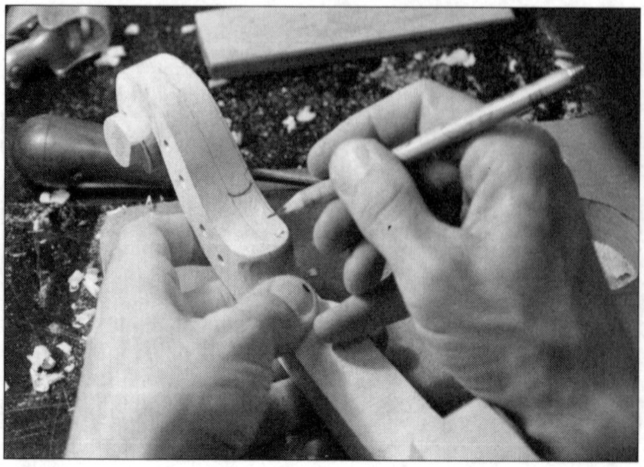

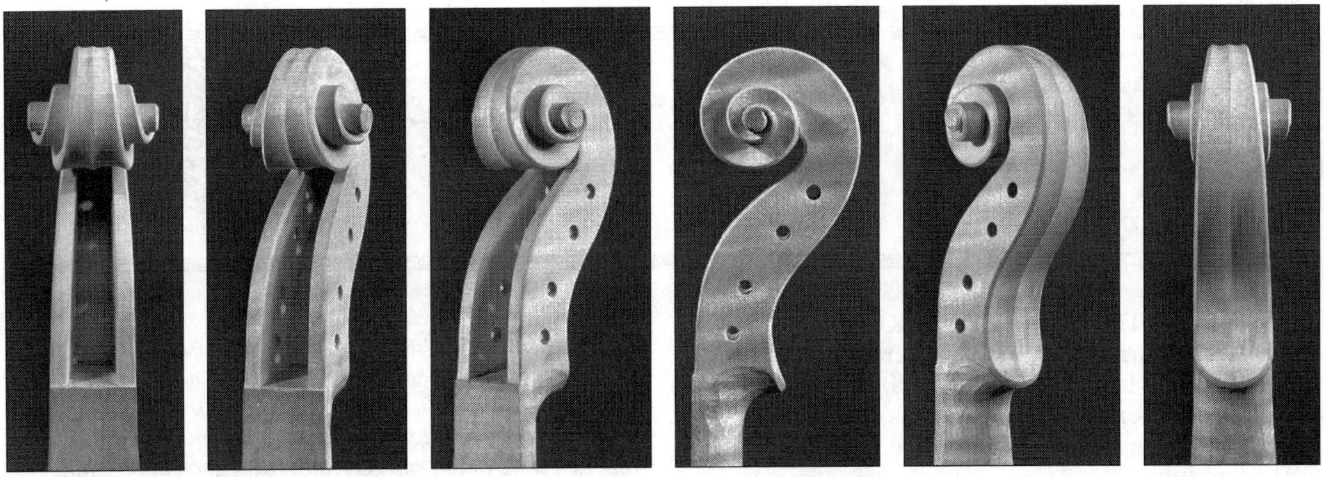

learn and develop your acoustic sense by working with musicians. The other area that only develops with time and exposure is the aesthetic sense. In school you learn one particular aesthetic, which is the way it should be. But after you've looked at a lot of older instruments and have more exposure to other ideas you begin to develop your own personal ideas. There's the odd technique or tool that someone will show me, like this scroll-o-matic. I used to use a bench stop, and I was never very happy with it. This seemed like a good idea, so I made one, and liked it. There're always new things to learn and changes to make to improve what you are doing or how you are doing it. It's fun to figure out new ways of doing things.

Do you stockpile scrolls?

I only make scrolls ahead when I need to take some work with me on a trip away from the shop. Scrolls and the necessary tools travel very conveniently. I never mind having an extra scroll or two ahead.

Are there any successful scroll makers using nontraditional means like carving machines?

There's so little wood to remove that by the time you set up some very clever routing-device carving system I don't know if it would be worth it. I know they do that commercially. There's a fellow in Germany who showed me little 3/4 size lion-head scrolls that he carved all by machine. They were amazing. But I like carving wood. That's why I became a violin maker. (*laughter*) I don't like selling, I don't like running a business, but I actually do like carving wood. Cutting scrolls is great. When the wood is nice, it's a real pleasure. It's one of the most enjoyable parts of violin building.

Where did you get your training?

I went to the school in Salt Lake City. I graduated in '78 and I worked for Jacques Français, a violin dealer, doing repairs and restorations for five years. When I left there I just worked at home making my own instruments and doing restorations and repairs. About five or six years ago I stopped doing a lot of repairs just to concentrate on new instruments. About three years ago I moved my shop out of my living room and into a studio in Carnegie Hall, which I share with a bow maker and an instrument-dealing business. I wanted to separate my business from my home life.

How do you market your instruments, and how many can you make in a year?

I primarily make instruments on commission, and some I make on spec. I sell for the most part directly to musicians who come to my shop. There have been productive years when I have made as many as ten, and other years, like when I was renovating my studio, when there were fewer. It varies each year.

The side of this scroll that I have been working on is pretty well roughed out, and I don't think we have time to go much further. Once it's roughed out, the scroll is about halfway completed. By the end of the day I'm usually pretty well defined in the curves. It's a good point to stop. In the morning you come back and look at it with fresh eyes. You always see a few bumps you didn't see the day before. The second day, I finish it. ——

Update

In the ten-plus years since I gave this presentation I have continued to use the same basic approach to my scroll carving. Here are a few notes to bring the information up to date. "Sandplate" sanding material from Sandvik is no longer made or sold. The scroll holding device continues to evolve. Each new model is designed to be versatile and portable for the purpose of working away from the shop. To the question about the variation in the Guarneri del Gesù scrolls, there has since been published an excellent book (*Guiseppi Guarneri del Gesù* by Carlo Chiesa and Roger Hargrave, published by Peter Biddulph, 1998) with a great deal of good information about del Gesù mentioning that it is now assumed that the different scrolls were made by different members of the family or the workshop including his father who was an excellent scroll carver. Hence the variation in the different periods of his work.

—— *Guy Rabut (2006)*

Originally published in *American Lutherie #53*, 1998

Meet the Maker: Shelley Park

by Cyndy Burton

I SPOKE WITH SHELLEY PARK at the 1997 Healdsburg Guitar Festival where she exhibited her fine Maccaferri-style guitars. We'll get to see as well as hear her and her instruments in the '40s swing group Pearl Django this summer in Tacoma at the 15th GAL Convention.

Shelley, how did you get started building guitars?

I suppose I got started by a music teacher I had. I was given an old Yamaha guitar by my parents for high-school graduation and immediately stopped doing anything productive and started playing guitar all the time. My music teacher had a beautiful Larrivée guitar that I coveted. One day he said, "Why don't you build your own guitar?" There was a *eureka* moment where I thought, "Wow, people build guitars? They don't just appear?" The seed had been planted in my brain. Further down the line, I was working a bad job in a resort town, and one day decided I needed to do something with my life. I went to the town library and found the only Canadian college course on guitar making, which was in New Westminster, British Columbia. I gave a week's notice and disappeared to Vancouver to take the course with Michael Dunn.

ALL BY JONATHON PETERSON EXCEPT AS NOTED

How long ago was that?

About five years ago. My plan was to take this course for a year, work for Michael Dunn, then go off into the real world and work a little bit, then continue my studies with Michael later. But when I went off into the real world I ended up working for Jean Larrivée and actually stayed there for three years and change. In the meantime I was working on my own guitars in my off hours, which I continue to do today. I have a day job working for David Webber, making Webber Guitars, and make my own in the evenings.

It interests me that you worked in a production situation. I haven't seen Larrivée's Vancouver shop, but I did visit him near Victoria some time ago, and he didn't do a lot of cross training back then. Did you learn a lot of different skills or did you get really, really good at one thing?

Both. I started out kerfing frames and I stayed at that station for a few months. Then I moved on to sanding bodies, wet sanding, and a number of other odd jobs. Eventually I spent most of my time in the buffing and setup department. I probably buffed a few thousand Larrivée guitars, so I am fairly confident about this skill. While most of the work I did there was repetitive and at times monotonous, I gained valuable experience which could have taken me fifteen years to accumulate on my own.

How is Webber's shop a different experience?

The obvious difference is in the size of the operation. When I left Larrivée a year ago there were about sixty people on the payroll. At the Webber shop there are only David and myself. The fact that David's operation is so much smaller means we can pay more attention to the details that are often neglected by larger manufacturers. This attention to detail has not slowed David down. We are hoping to build one hundred instruments this year, and we have already reached fifty-three. Even at this pace, I would suggest they are some of the cleanest guitars in the industry.

David has spent most of his life making things. In his previous career as a diver he built bridges and oil rigs and was a hobby boat builder. I think that at some point he began to get tired of being cold and wet all the time, so he started building guitars in a diving-company workshop in his spare time. He built from books early on, but he is largely self-taught using trial and error and his intuition. I think the fact that he has never worked for someone else has been a major influence on the methods he uses today. He is not afraid to dismiss a traditional method in favor of a process that might use unique fixtures and jigs and technology from other industries. The shop is filled with unusual machines and techniques which are crucial in his quest for what he calls "the final 2%" — the 2% which is the difference between a pretty good instrument and one that plays well, sounds great, and is of flawless construction.

It seems like very few people get the opportunity to work in production situations when they are trying to learn to make handmade guitars. And I always have thought it would be a very useful thing to do. When I visited Larrivée he said he really didn't like to hire people who were aspiring to make guitars.

Absolutely. I think Jean found that aspiring guitar makers were too romantic and not focussed enough on the task at hand or the day's quota.

He loved hiring musicians.

I think Jean liked to hire musicians because their romance was with the end product rather than the process. It was also a way for an aspiring musician to stay connected with the music community and even do some networking. Of course, there was also the desire in most of us to one day own one of these gorgeous guitars, and many musicians put in lots of weekends to pay for the cherished instruments.

How has working in production situations influenced your hand building? Has it made you conscious of how you spend every minute?

I have gained a lot of confidence through my experience. At one time I would waste a great deal of time staring at a joint before I applied the glue, or measuring and remeasuring before making a cut. By now I have done most of these processes a multitude of times in my daytime environment. So now very little time is wasted agonizing when I go to work in my own shop.

Production work has also taught me the value of standardizing procedures in the interest of efficiency and consistency. I have narrowed my building focus to basically two models: the D-hole Maccaferri and the oval-hole Selmer. Rather than trying to build one of everything, I am in the process of building the jigs which will help me make these two models efficiently without compromising quality.

You specialize in playing those models too, I understand.

I play with a band based in Tacoma, Washington called Pearl Django, and we play the music of Django Reinhardt, the Gypsy guitarist who was famous in the '30s, '40s, and early '50s. Django was listening to Gypsies playing traditional music in their caravans while also being influenced by radio broadcasts of American jazz legends like Duke Ellington. From these sources he developed his unique sound, and he has remained famous for it. I play rhythm guitar in Pearl Django and there are two other guitar players, both of whom own and play

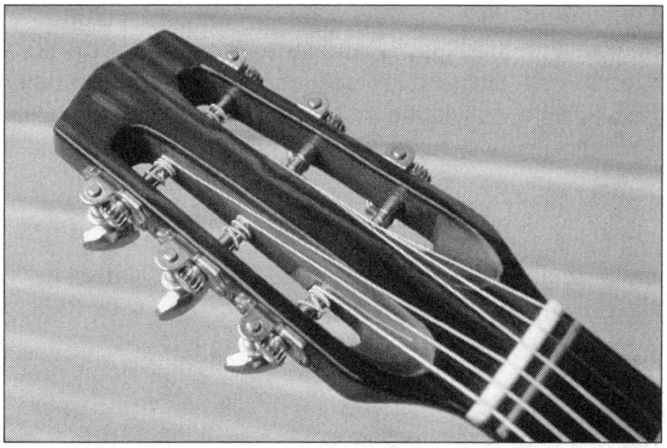

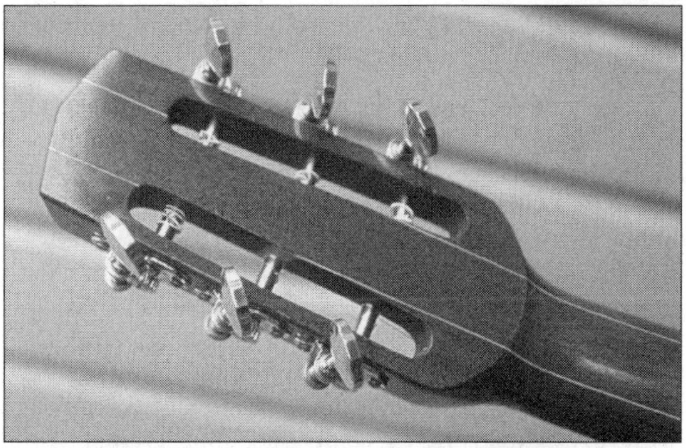

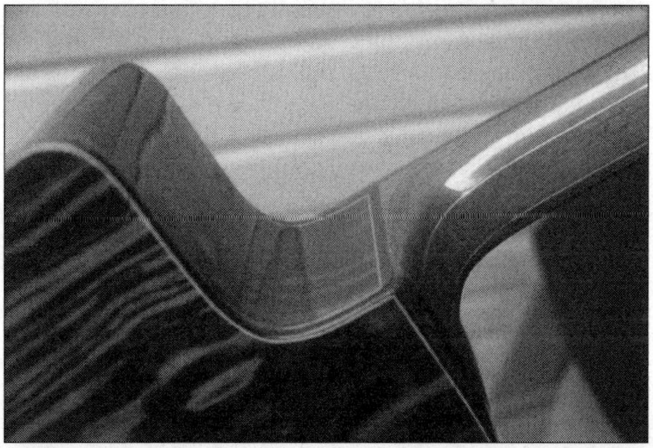

Facing page: Shelley on her way to a Pearl Django gig with one of her Selmer-style guitars. Above: Four views of this same instrument which features a figured Sitka spruce top, Macassar ebony back and sides, and a laminated mahogany neck with a 67CM scale length.

Park guitars. We're a weekend-warrior band, and we play around the Puget Sound area. It's a lot of fun. It's probably my first love, playing music, but guitar making runs an extremely close second. I figure I have the best of both worlds, because I get to do both all the time.

You must be on the road a lot, too.

Yes, I spend way too much time in my car. And unfortunately the band has put a little bit of a dent in the production of my own guitars, because I used to get a lot of work done on the weekends, and now my weekends are gone. That is a bit frustrating, but a good band only comes along once in a while, so I'm going to make the most of this opportunity.

Let's talk about your guitars. I've seen them, but not heard them. What are they like?

They are replicas of the instruments Django would have played. The ones I have here on exhibit are modeled after Selmer guitars from the '40s and '50s. An Italian luthier, Mario Maccaferri was asked by the Selmer Company, which still exists but mostly makes saxophones now, to design a production guitar for them and he came up with the Selmer design. It has a short, fairly wide, cutaway body, with a ladder-braced top, a very small oval soundhole, floating bridge and tailpiece, and quite a long scale length, 67CM ($26^3/_8{}''$). It is strung with very light strings which produce that "Django sound." These guitars really don't function very well in other musical environments because of their unique tone. They have a somewhat nasal voice and a dry sound. Overall I think they bear more resemblance to archtop guitars than flattops.

They are archtops, right?

Sort of. The tops are not carved, but they do have much more arch than typical American flattops. Tops are thicknessed to about 3MM then press-fit onto the braces. When I went to France last year I spoke to many builders, and the consensus was that the top was thicknessed then pressed to the braces. The braces are what is actually arched in them, to about a 15′ radius. It seems to work. So far so good; we'll see in ten years.

What woods are you using?

I prefer Sitka spruce for the top because I like its stiffness. Engelmann is certainly the prettier of the two, but I find it a little less appealing because of its tendency to have serious runout. Also, I have built almost exclusively with Sitka so it is more familiar and predictable to me. Right now there seems to be a bit of a deficit of Sitka in Vancouver. There are piles and piles of Engelmann and very little Sitka, but that will probably turn around. For back and sides, just about anything goes. I've used all the traditional woods and others as well: maple, mahogany, rosewood, koa, Macassar ebony, padauk, purpleheart, so I'm not loyal to any particular combination of woods, aside from really liking Sitka spruce for the top. If it's pretty and it's structurally sound, I'll go with it.

COURTESY SHELLEY PARK

In Todd Taggart's talk on alternate woods here at the Healdsburg Guitar Festival, he didn't talk about purpleheart or padauk, probably because there's not enough demand for them. I get the feeling that the so-called alternate woods are not all that popular. Do you have any feelings about the qualities of some of these woods?

I'm not particularly scientific about the woods I use. I don't carry particular recollections about the sound of the guitar with padauk sides and back as opposed to the Macassar ebony guitar. To me they either worked or they didn't work. If a piece of wood is stiff enough and sounds the right way, I'm happy to build with it. I haven't run into much friction from people saying, "What's wrong with rosewood? I want a rosewood guitar." Usually people say, "Wow. That looks cool and it sounds great."

Maybe your clientele is pretty open minded already. Their coming to a woman builder may indicate that.

Just by virtue of the fact that you're a woman, you attract a different clientele, and they may be a little more open minded to begin with. They're willing to put their faith in you, whereas there are a lot still out there who don't think we can glue things together properly. So that may be why I've had the flexibility to experiment, play with colors, play with materials. The tendency to use alternate woods is one of Michael Dunn's greatest influences on me. Michael will build with anything. He'll combine eighteen different colors on one guitar.

His influence not withstanding, it seems to me, based on what I've observed of all the women exhibiting here, lots of so-called rules are being broken and lots of attention is being paid to aesthetics.

Looking at the women's instruments here, they all are just a little bit different from the rest. You look at Judy Threet's guitars and they're beautiful, elegant instruments, meticulously put together. The whole design package is right for that instrument. And Cyndy, your instruments are gorgeous, stunning. And Linda Manzer's display her great design sense and they are beautifully constructed. The four women represented are all doing stuff that bears their signature.

I agree, and thanks for the compliment. Someone pointed out yesterday that three of the four happen to be Canadian. Why is that?

I don't know. Linda is also a Larrivette. *(laughter)* Judy studied with a fellow named Michael Heidon, who is a mandolin and guitar builder in Vancouver, who used to work in Calgary, where Judy lives. But of course there are others in the States. Still, you'd think there would be more, wouldn't you?

Yes. One would.

Actually there's another handful of women up in Canada, too. I don't know how many are doing it full time. I know of at least two other women in Vancouver who also attended Michael Dunn's course.

I understand his course is no longer being taught.

That's right. It was a ten-month course at a community college outside Vancouver. To complete the course you had to complete three guitars. It was a fantastic opportunity. I didn't realize then what an opportunity it was. Basically you were turned loose in a shop with someone advising you if you wanted it. Every year about fifteen people completed the course. And that went on for ten years, so there are well over one hundred builders who have been through that course, although many of them are no longer involved with guitar making. But there is still a clutch of people in Vancouver and across the country who owe their beginnings to Michael.

What's he doing now?

He's still building. He's finally crashed into the American market with full force. He's working with George Gruhn out of Nashville, the Mandolin Brothers, and so on. He's up to his ears in guitars, selling them as fast as he can make them. He's doing very well, and he deserves to. He's put in a lot of work to get to that point.

Currently I share a workshop with a cabinet maker and canoe restorer. You may know of Ted Turner, former harpsichord maker, now builder and restorer of canvas canoes. He has a couple orders for instruments, so he hasn't left lutherie behind altogether.

One of my favorite subjects is finish. What kind do you use?

I've used a couple different finishes for a couple different reasons. I've done a fair amount of French polishing. I polished Michael Dunn's guitars, about ten or twelve a year, for a couple of years. I started to get reasonably good at it, then got too busy to be working on his instruments. I now finish my instruments with a catalyzed polyester finish, which is what I had worked with at Larrivée's, buffing and so on. Recently I've been doing a little bit of French polishing again. But I've lost my touch, so it's pretty frustrating. I didn't think that would be something that would go away, but I've forgotten an awful lot, unfortunately. But I love shellac finish. It has some drawbacks: it's a bit time consuming, and I'm pushed for time these days; and it's a bit fragile for the first year. But aside from that, I think it's a wonderful finish. Once it's cured, it's hard as nails. And I like the less glossy look. I also like polyester. To someone who's not familiar with handmade instruments, who has hung out in guitar stores and seen Martins and Gibsons, the shiny, flat finish looks familiar. It looks like they think it should look. Plus I like the toughness. Personally, as a player I'm really hard on guitars. I destroy French-polished finishes in a number of ways. I haven't been able to damage the polyester finish yet. Plus I have a lot of experience with the polyester finish, having worked with it at Larrivée's on the buffer for a year and a half. I can buff just about anything out of polyester finish, and I know how it sounds. So I like them both. Both have their benefits and drawbacks.

Once the shellac has really hardened, can you still destroy it?

I don't know. With the style of guitar I play, I have a really wide sweep with the right hand. I end up all over the top, then start chewing through it with a really stiff hard pick. Plus I have a sweaty arm resting on the side of it. And there's the simple fact that I'm kind of mean to my own guitars, because I know there's another one coming. Everybody else treats them very nicely, and I treat other people's guitars very nicely, but I kick my own personal playing guitar around. It's a bad habit.

Have you tried buffing shellac finishes?

Yes. Buffing won't flatten out the texture you leave in the finish from the pad. It will shine up the finish, but make that texture more obvious. I think you'd probably have to sand, then buff. I've never tried that. ——

COURTESY SHELLEY PARK

Facing page: Shelley rubbing finishes for Jean Larrivée, 1995. Above: Shelley is currently sharing shop space with harpsichord, hurdy-gurdy, cabinet, and canoe builder, Ted Turner.

Originally published in *American Lutherie #53,* 1998

D'Aquisto's Design Development

from his 1995 GAL Convention lecture

by Paul Gudelsky

WHEN YOU CONSIDER the emphasis placed on the archtop guitar today, it's amazing to consider that the life span of the traditional version of that instrument can be encompassed by the working lives of two men, John D'Angelico and Jimmy D'Aquisto. D'Angelico is credited by many as having carried the traditional archtop to its zenith, and it's ironic that his pupil, Jimmy D'Aquisto, the man who had the most to gain by maintaining the tradition, was the very luthier who led the parade away from the conventional form and forced the evolution of the instrument. The fact that we've been discussing the possible demise of the traditional archtop suggests the influence D'Aquisto has had.

Jimmy had a hard time in school. He didn't fit in, and he wanted to put all that behind him. He began hanging out at D'Angelico's shop, and in 1952 John put him to work. I think he enjoyed Jimmy, perhaps he saw something of himself in the kid. D'Angelico was at the top of his game, the best there was, but I and many others think that Jimmy went on to surpass the work of his mentor. Though to some dealers and collectors John's work represents the quintessential archtop, Jimmy had a way of moving it to a whole new realm. I place him above Stradivari in importance in his field. Violins by Del Gesù and Nicola Amati were and are considered the equals of Stradivari, but Jimmy had no real equals.

TIM OLSEN

ALL BY ROBERT DESMOND EXCEPT AS NOTED

Top: Jimmy D'Aquisto lectures to the 1978 GAL Convention in Winfield, Kansas. Jimmy also spoke at the 1979 convention in Boston.
Above: Paul Gudelsky lectures to the 1995 convention in Tacoma.

A recent segment of *60 Minutes* alluded to Stradivari's mystical abilities, and how he had taken so many secrets to the grave. Someone said at Jimmy's funeral, "Unfortunately, he takes so many secrets to the grave." But Jimmy would have strongly disagreed. The course he was pursuing was completely evident in his guitars. Most of his innovations were simple in concept, and they mark an investigation into what to many of us are unknown factors.

Most luthiers quickly reach a point where they realize that they have to speed up production to make a living. They jig up as many operations as they can and invest in machinery. Jimmy followed this path too, but he knew the hazards from the beginning. He needed more efficient construction methods because he was sick, and because he only had so much energy, but he never lost sight of the fact that standardized construction techniques can dictate the kind of guitar you can make, and he didn't want that. He wanted the freedom to build in the manner that each piece of wood seemed to indicate. Wood suggested various ideas to him, and he wanted to be free to follow them. Inevitably there was a conflict between the guitars his muses had him build and the guitars that players expected him to make. Musicians aren't always free thinkers where their instruments are concerned, but this was a frustration that Jimmy came to grips with. As he put it, "This is the business, this is guitar making." When you view any of his later models, it's important to keep in mind that Jimmy was the one man who had the most to gain by maintaining the old concepts. His art would not let him do that.

Jimmy was not interested in change for its own sake. He didn't like gimmickry, and he had a grasp of the subtle. This sense of subtlety prevented him from taking on an apprentice. He believed that touching the wood was an intrinsic part of getting the most tone out of it, and that an undeveloped sense of touch and intuition could never produce the kind of guitars he wanted to come out of his shop. One of his famous lines is that "sound is a noise, but tone is a color." Sound could be any kind of noise, but tone referred to the character and quality of sound that the maker pulls from the wood and that the player pulls from the instrument. Increasing the tonal range of the archtop guitar became the heart of his work. Players wanted to take their archtops to a musical place they had never been, and Jimmy's guitars became a reflection of that desire.

Jimmy always used European spruce for his tops, and from long experience he knew how to work each piece of this wood to full advantage. He preferred slightly wider grain than most luthiers, but he learned to use whatever came in each shipment. The wood became his tutor, and nothing was wasted. He might decide that a certain top would be the last of a batch to be used, but he eventually used it and the guitar was inevitably a choice item. He trusted his touch. He bought his brace stock as quartersawn spruce boards, but he didn't worry much about grain lines per inch or that sort of thing. He simply cut the next set of braces off the board and worked them until the tap tones sounded good to his ear. The tone color of the braces had to match the tone colors of the top

European maple was his choice for the body wood. It's very expensive, but he felt that there was no other way to go. At one point he went ten months without building an acoustic archtop guitar because his shipment of maple was delayed. His commitment was such that he couldn't bring himself to use American maple, no matter how pretty it might be. He had honed his skills on European maple, and to use anything else would be a disservice to his customers.

It's worth noting that Jimmy believed that the back of an archtop guitar is as important as the top. When I went to study with him I took with me a collection of tools and an archtop completed in the white and strung up. After watching him voice a couple instruments, I was able to tune the back of my guitar to the point where the power of the instrument was doubled.

Jimmy always preferred ebony for his fingerboards and bridges. There may have been a lot of reasons for that, but I think he just liked the evenness of grain and the simplicity of its visual presentation, its lack of pores. Ebony is also acoustically neutral, it doesn't bring to the guitar a tone color of its own as rosewood can. He eventually went to Macassar ebony for tailpieces and pickguards, but that was a move made necessary by the dwindling supply of good, solid black Gabon ebony.

Though it's often considered a cosmetic addition to the guitar, Jimmy was concerned about the binding he put on his instruments. He may have moved from plastic to wood initially because he wanted to escape from the Art Deco, New Yorker-inspired regime of guitar making, but he came to realize that wood binding became a more intrinsic part of the guitar than plastic. It moved seasonally as the rest of the body moved, it vibrated in a similar fashion, and it didn't shrink and break as time went on. But just as importantly, wood weighs less than plastic, and unnecessary weight only inhibits the sensitivity of an instrument. He worked hard to make each guitar into an entity of the highest sensitivity. Everything had to work together, and there were no unimportant parts.

Toward the end of his career it became important to Jimmy that musicians be able to make all the setup adjustments on his guitars themselves, so he worked to streamline and simplify his designs. But as much as anything else, he wanted players to stop thinking of the archtop as a design that peaked in 1942. He wanted them to realize that the archtop had much more to offer, tonewise, if they would just stop approaching it with preconceived ideas.

Tweaking many of the design considerations can alter the archtop's tone in controlled ways. It involves the exploitation of the body size, including the depth as well as the width, and also the depth of the arch in both plates as well as the shape of the plates. If you consider the entire instrument at once, the geometry, the proportion, and the bracing, you find that there exists a profound ability to control the tone. Many builders start off with an 18″ box with $3\frac{1}{4}''$ ribs, or maybe even $3\frac{3}{8}''$. The problem is that too much depth in the body causes the sound to get lost inside. Jimmy felt that the appropriate depth of the archtop was between $2\frac{7}{8}''$ and $3\frac{1}{8}''$ as a finished dimension, and that the ribs themselves should be from $2\frac{3}{8}''$ to $2\frac{1}{2}''$ wide.

His view of controlling the tone of the instrument was different from many other luthiers. Most archtop makers tune the top plate and maybe the back plate and then glue them in place. Jimmy carved the plates to approximate dimensions that left them far too thick,

Pat Smith tries out the 1982 New Yorker. Paul Gudelsky called this guitar the "beater" of his D'Aquisto collection.

glued them to the ribs, and then tuned the whole instrument by planing and scraping the outside. He considered it futile to fine tune a plate and then have its characteristics change after it was glued in place, and then change again when the second plate was glued on, and then change again after sanding was completed. The addition of the neck might easily cause another change. He built the entire instrument and then he "tuned the box" as he called it. He planed and scraped until the guitar was right for that person, for that purpose. There was a freedom in his construction process that many luthiers never achieve. He'd get an order from one of his longtime customers and he'd say, "I know what this guy wants and I see it all at once, all at once. The neck angle, the arch, all at once and working together." There were no preset design considerations to inhibit the creation of his vision.

There's a well-known photo of Jimmy standing next to a pantograph router, and certainly more than a few unknowing people knock him for using a pantograph. But despite a debilitating illness that sapped his strength, he only removed a fraction of the wood from the plates by pantograph. He did 90% of the work by hand; it was the only way to pursue the guitar on his own terms. Machining the plates to a finished dimension would have left him unable to tune the box.

There are many considerations to take into account when shaping the arches of the top and back. The top must be arched to suit the neck angle and bridge height that is envisioned for the guitar. A lower arch is thought to give a mellower tone, and might improve bass response. A higher arch generally emphasizes the upper register. A flatter plate (in terms of shape and not so much of height) gives a slightly punchier tone. The arch of the back plate is generally used to control the air space inside the box, but Jimmy would often let the wood dictate the back arch as much as any preconceived notions. If he had a particularly thick piece of maple he would carve a higher arch. He was confident that he could control whatever qualities the extra depth brought to the guitar, and it gave him a chance to experiment and learn new things.

Jimmy struggled to escape from some traditional aspects of the archtop and was frustrated by customers who didn't want to let him. Many wanted *f*-hole guitars, and Jimmy was convinced that the points in the center of the *f* break up the sound. He also wanted to enlarge the holes, and simply enlarging a standard *f*-hole looked awkward. Rather than give in, he changed the shape and size of the soundholes as he saw fit. The difference it makes is obvious if you have access to one of his guitars. Cover a soundhole with your hand and strum, then take your hand away. The difference is amazing. But aside from simple considerations of volume, the new soundholes help contribute to a more versatile guitar, a more responsive instrument for those who might need to play softly or play in a fingerstyle. In fact, Jimmy was convinced that the *f*-hole was obsolete on all instruments, and advocated removing them from violins.

The clean lines added by the wooden binding and his handmade ebony tailpieces and pickguards were part of his escape effort. He wanted to leave behind the complex and ostentatious presentation of the Art Deco look. But as much as anything else, he wanted to remove himself from the immense amount of work that goes into elaborate inlays and multiple layers of binding. He had a limited amount of energy, and he wanted to invest it in the guitar where it would make the most difference in tone, not in the cosmetic appeal of the instrument.

Though it would seem that a guitar with a certain scale length and a certain gauge of strings would have a set string tension, on an archtop the tension placed on the guitar is controlled by several variables, and Jimmy tended to make a guitar with very high tension. The height of the top arch, the pitch of the neck, the height of the fingerboard above the neck joint, the angle of the

DALE BLINDHIEM

Paul Gudelsky brought his personal collection of D'Aquisto guitars for a special display at the 1995 GAL Convention. Special handling, mounting, and photography of these instruments was made possible by the Guild's Bob Mattingly Memorial Fund. In the photo at left we see the mounted collection with the 1982 New Yorker (see p. 169) facing us. The 1992 Avant Garde is to the right. In the photo at right we see the other side of the exhibit, with the 1960 D'Angelico and the Fender Elite Prototype facing us. The 25th Anniversary New Yorker surmounts all.

We were fortunate to have the services of a genuine musical instrument museum curator. In the photo at center, Joe Johnson, formerly of the Shrine to Music Museum (now National Music Museum) and currently with the Georgia Music Hall of Fame, polishes the 1970 Excel prior to mounting it.

headstock, and the length of the tailpiece all have an effect on the tension.

The height of the bridge is controlled by the other factors, but the length and width of the bridge become variables that the luthier can use to control the way the downward tension is applied to the top. In effect, the bridge becomes another brace. The evolution of his bridges eventually culminated in the wedge bridge, in which the top portion that supported the strings was separated from the base by a long, protruding wedge of wood. String height was adjusted by sliding the wedge in or out. The variety of wood used in the wedge made a tonal change in the instrument, adding another bit of control to his bag of tricks. The wedge bridge was an elegant answer to a question no one had asked before.

Jimmy felt that the upper bout was too often a neglected component, and that by increasing its size and carving the plates carefully, the upper bout had much to offer the performance of the instrument. He even believed the area of the cutaway was important. The rest of the top had to be carved by an intuitive process, but the area around the cutaway should be left thick.

I once put a light inside one of Jimmy's guitars, and I was amazed how brightly the entire top glowed. It was thin! But it was not necessarily consistent. It might be much thicker in one area than another, according to how he felt the box ought to be tuned on that guitar. But the overall thinness of the top was almost frightening. His backs might be carved just as lightly, though of course no light would shine through. Or one or both plates might be left very thick, depending on the wood and the function of that particular guitar. There are no rules, but if you examine enough of Jimmy's instruments you begin to realize that there is a method. He had advanced to the point where he believed that demands from musicians might hurt the performance of his guitars. He wanted guitarists to tell him what they needed, and he would tell them how their guitars should be built.

Pursuing his vision of the archtop guitar wore Jimmy out. He was an epileptic, and seizures left him so weak that he lost months of work in some years. But he lived to build guitars — it was his passion. He is criticized for running his prices up past the point that musicians could afford, but I think that's a ludicrous complaint. No intelligent man sells a product for less than he knows he can get, and if wealthy nonprofessionals were willing to pursue a D'Aquisto guitar past the point that a working musician could afford, I don't think we can fault Jimmy.

He definitely died too soon. He had just reached a crossroads in his work, and he was about to reinvent himself. There's no telling where he might have taken the archtop guitar had he not burned out in such an untimely fashion. ——

A Strange Story

Jimmy D'Aquisto was always at the top of our wish-list for convention speakers, and he did speak at our 1978 and 1979 meetings. Things didn't work out in the '80s, but Jimmy accepted our invitation to speak at the 1992 convention in Vermillion, South Dakota. He suffered a seizure at the NAMM show just prior to our meeting. We rescheduled for our next convention in July of 1995. Jimmy died in April of 1995, and we asked Paul Gudelsky to fill his lecture slot. He did so, as well as bringing five D'Aquisto guitars for a special display. We were beginning to work on this article when Paul died in May of 1996. So this project was orphaned twice. We thank John Monteleone, Jimmy's long-time friend and "neighbor," for his valuable assistance.

The guitar that Paul Schmidt commissioned from Jimmy was the New Yorker Classic #1183 shown on page 174. Paul sold the instrument to finance a four-year degree program in theology. The current owner of the instrument, Ken Ciuffreda, sent us the photo.

Jimmy's talk at the 1979 convention was transcribed and edited into an article that proved to be one of our most popular ever, but was out of print for years. It is currently available in the GAL book Lutherie Wood and Steel String Guitars. *We presented a detailed photo essay of Jimmy's method of carving a soundboard in* American Lutherie #37. *(See* Big Red Book of American Lutherie Volume Four, *p. 6.) This was one chapter of what was to be a book project which was cut short by Jimmy's untimely death. The new second edition of Paul Schmidt's book* Acquired of the Angels *contains many new photos of D'Aquisto guitars and is a valuable resource for understanding the development of Jimmy's design ideas. Another fine source is* The Chinery Collection – 150 Years of American Guitars *published by Miller Freeman.*

Thanks to Bob Desmond for special photography of the D'Aquisto instruments at the 1995 convention. We particularly thank all contributors to the Bob Mattingly Memorial Fund for your help in bringing this special exhibit of D'Aquisto guitars to fruition.

16″ D'Aquisto Fender Elite Prototype #120 dated 1988

Jimmy worked with the Fender Corporation for many years developing production archtops. This instrument features a straight bracing design and is very powerful for a 16″ guitar.

Originally published in *American Lutherie #53*, 1998

Remembering Jimmy

by Paul Schmidt

I CAME TO JIMMY as a musician seeking an instrument that would do everything the other instruments I'd experienced would not do. I was seeking a sound in my mind's ear that was of the family of those instruments I'd experienced, yet distinctly different. And it worked!

He was exceedingly patient with my questions and equally generous with his time. My questions were about how the instruments functioned musically, and not being a jazz musician, they were somewhat different. Though specific, you might call them abstract. I'd ask, "Jimmy, I want it to sound like the grass looks after a spring rain... I want it to sound like a halo." He'd laugh a little, as you just did, but then he would say, "Yeah, like a piece of art or something." It was clear from our conversations we were speaking the same language. He introduced me to another client of his, the late Carl Patterson, who was a very beautiful soul. Carl lived within a few hours driving time from me. I visited him and played the guitar, a New Yorker, and related to it musically, aesthetically, and emotionally. So, that's how it started.

I was a graduate student at Pacific Lutheran University (near Tacoma, WA) almost twenty years ago, and it was at that time that Tim Olsen and Jon Peterson had gone to New York to do a story on Jimmy for *Guitar Player* magazine. Tim's sister and Jon's wife, (the same person) Ruth Peterson, went to the same church I did. One time while we were visiting a facility for developmentally challenged people, the topic of guitars came up. That was how I came to know Tim and Jon, and they introduced me to Jimmy's name and work. And I want to say to you, Tim and Jon, that I greatly appreciate that introduction to Jimmy — it has been a significant thing in my life. Being here tonight sort of brings things full circle.

Anyway, as Jimmy and I got to know each other and my questions became more refined, we spent a lot of time discussing tone and music and applications of archtops in other-than-jazz mediums. But that changed as well. Certainly we spoke of topically related things when we were working on my book *(Acquired of the Angels: The Lives and Works of John D'Angelico and James L. D'Aquisto)*, and the times I stayed at his house the anecdotes and memories flowed freely. But in the last years when we visited regularly, we spent more time talking about what it was like to be an artist, his work with the guitars and mine with playing and songwriting — the swings of inspiration, how his health affected his work, how the culture fears and marginalizes artists

ALL BY ROBERT DESMOND EXCEPT AS NOTED

Paul Schmidt plays the 1993 D'Aquisto Avant Garde at the GAL's 1995 convention.

17″ D'Angelico Excel #2105 dated 4/5/1960

Guitars from the last period of John D'Angelico's workshop, from about 1959 to 1964, reflect the strong hand of James D'Aquisto. Jimmy was now doing most of the detail work on the pickguards, bridges, truss-rod covers, headstocks, body bindings, and finishing while John was performing the carving and bending tasks. Extra care was given to every purfling and binding joint. They were using beautiful sets of imported maple and spruce for backs, sides, and tops. These are among my favorite examples of D'Angelico guitars.

on the whole, not to mention just visiting about life in general. In fact, the last few years we didn't really talk much about guitars, which was kind of interesting.

When Tim invited me to talk about Jimmy, it was a gift, because I didn't have much closure with him dying. I found out Jimmy died when I was visiting with Steve Forgey (Frog to those who know him) at Stan Werbin's Elderly Instruments in Lansing, Michigan. After a battalion of phone calls to New York, I learned that the funeral was that very day. This is an opportunity for me to get a little more resolution with it all.

I asked myself, "What am I going to bring this interesting group of people? What can I give them? I'm not a maker; I don't know any secrets; I have no insights about carving or finish." Then I thought, "What would Jimmy say?" And I took that one step further and thought, "What would Jimmy say now?" Not meaning if he hadn't died, but now from his rest. I came up with a few simple things.

The first one is, quite simply, "Be yourself." Jimmy was a visionary and an artist, and a great one. Nobody is going to dispute that. But he didn't just have insights

Three Decades of Innovation

Guitars from the collection of Paul Gudelsky
Captions by John Monteleone

18″ D'Aquisto
25th Anniversary Special
New Yorker #1211 made in 1989

It is apparent that Jimmy built this guitar on an original D'Angelico mold. The wide upper bouts are probably the result of opening up the mold more at the top than at the bottom, a rather common practice for Jimmy even on his own forms. Though he was making a vintage replica, he was not about to sacrifice his years of experience with tone and make a slim little bridge. He was too concerned with sound to let it go. He made what would be a sensible bridge of larger proportions.

17″ D'Aquisto Excel #1039
made in 1970 for Joe Pass

This guitar was obviously made in the D'Angelico Excel mold. The side depth is $2\frac{7}{8}''$. The soundholes are typical of Jimmy's first changes. The ebony tailpiece was added a few years later, and an important reason for it was to permit vertical adjustment to vary the downward string pressure on the bridge. The bridge dimensions show an attempt to capture more surface area of the soundboard. Joe Pass sometimes used a pickguard, which is missing from this guitar. It would have looked a lot like the one on the New Yorker Classic model, but with single white binding around it.

18″ D'Aquisto Avant Garde #1240
made in January 1993

Compare this to the earlier version on p. 175 to see the difference that four years can make. The feel of the design is looser and I sense a strong influence from the new Solo model taking shape during the same time frame. This example shows the enlarged version of the elliptical holes. The biggest change is the "acutune" bridge which also debuted earlier in 1992 on the first Solo model. This new sliding-wedge design would be employed in all the rest of his guitars. It is interesting to note that the interior of this particular instument was pictured on the cover of AL #37.

like some sort of savant. It was an acknowledgement of an inclination and a process to act upon discovery. If you're a visionary and an artist, then you are one. If you aren't, you aren't. Either way it's OK. If you are, it will probably be more difficult. Jimmy started out as a craftsperson, replicating what he felt was "the best of the period" (that was his usual line), which is precisely what John D'Angelico did. And he achieved what he did by following his discoveries, talking to players, trying new ideas, and being honest with what worked and what didn't work to make a great musical tool. So though his vision and artistry were a gift, his response to that gift was a major piece of his development.

Let's say you were a craftsperson and your inclination was to take designs that have already been proven and make your refinements to them. If that would be your contribution to the guitar playing/making world, that would be just great. And in the context of that productive career you would probably trip upon a few things that would likely lead to further inquiries and solutions, because it is all about the process and being honest and authentic. Maybe you don't even want to make guitars, maybe you sense that your role is to do repairs and/or restorations, and that is every bit as honorable. Jimmy was a great repair person. As players you know that even though you have a great guitar, it doesn't perform if it's not set up correctly. Doing that well is another generous way to serve. If that's where you are, be where you are. If it leads you somewhere else, follow it. It sounds very simple and very basic, but most simple things aren't easy, and aren't always easy to remember. Don't chase it, let it happen naturally. Be honest and trust your intuition. Be authentic.

I don't believe that anybody has an easy life, and Jimmy was no exception. There have been a lot of stories about Jimmy's temperament, and I have my own experiences; but there are reasons for everything. I don't think Jimmy ever worked through his grief with losing John D'Angelico. I don't know if he ever got over his anger (at himself) and frustration at losing the D'Angelico trademark early on. And it doesn't do much for one's self-esteem to be asked to leave school. I'm sure many of you know Jimmy suffered from epilepsy; it was an epileptic seizure that killed him. When I was working on the book, I sought to learn a little about epilepsy and how it manifests itself. I contacted the Epilepsy Foundation and asked some general questions, which is all my ignorance would allow. One of the first things they asked me was, "Has your friend had any counseling?" It can be a pretty shame-inducing thing to be crumpled up having a seizure in a public place — a visible sign of not being in control, which is viewed by this culture as a weakness. Of course that's insane, but it's a prevalent view nonetheless. I broached the subject of counseling with Jimmy, but he was like a lot of people from that era; he just wasn't going to do that. It was too hard. It would make him too vulnerable. So I think another thing Jimmy would say to you now is this: When you need help, get it. Doing so would have helped him immeasurably. He would tell you that he contributed to some of the things that made his life difficult, and had he been able to deal with some of them in different ways, it might have made it easier for him and impacted his work for the better.

The third thing I believe he might tell you has to do with balance. Now it might sound funny to be talking about balance at a convention where large numbers of people are gathering because they have great enthusiasm for a single topic. But if it is an obsession, then it will impede the way you live your life, which will impede the way you do your art or your craft. If you have a primary relationship, that needs attention. If you have a family, they need you. And you need them. And that is a difficult thing to balance, especially if you have a lot of zeal for your work and you get caught up in that crazy illusion that happens to a lot of people in this culture about getting your identity from your job. I suspect it would be especially difficult if you were promoting your product and your name was on it. It would be easy to get off track and get distracted by the temptation to self-

KEN CIUFFREDA

18″ D'Aquisto New Yorker
Classic #1183
dated 12/17/1985

This guitar, the first of this model, marks the first use of wood purflings and bindings, as well as maple headstock veneer. Plastic is abandoned and the f-holes are now unbound, although cut to full size. The new body outline is more advanced and the upper bouts are widened. The dip in the truss-rod cover was a holdover which fit the pearl scroll inlay on the old New Yorker headstock. The pickguard is offset as on later models. Softened traditional lines and edges perfectly blend old and new. Jimmy is playing with traditional elements without losing sight of the guitar's integrity.

aggrandizement, which is something I don't think ever troubled Jimmy. It is a tough thing to balance and stay grounded. But I think he'd tell you.

I am very thankful I was able to know Jimmy, and I am thankful I got to experience his instruments. There were many times when I would be playing one of his guitars and tears of great joy would just naturally well up. I got many ideas from the guitar he made for me. I wrote many songs on it and recorded four albums with it. Having it was a great thing.

Jimmy's death was very painful for me. I loved him. And I miss him. And if the situation were offered that Jimmy could come back, but the price would be that all of his instruments would be destroyed and his capacity to create any more would be taken away, I'd call it a bargain and have him back. Because I cared a lot more about him than I did his instruments. It didn't start out that way, but it evolved into that. And I am also thankful I had the opportunity to come here and share a little of this with you. Thanks to all of you. ——

Post-Plastic Progression

Captions by John Monteleone

ALL THIS PAGE BY JOSH McCLURE

18″ D'Aquisto Avant Garde #1212 dated 1/20/1989

Jimmy enjoyed his new-found freedom. He always wanted to use all-wood bindings and he employed them for a fine visual effect. The maple purfling lines and headstock veneers are fabricated from his abundant stack of Tyrolean maple. This is the first cutout headstock of his. The soundholes are not new though. He began using these on some of the mid-'70s Excels. The tailpiece shows the growing interest that Jimmy had in the "feel" of the guitar: namely, the string geometry between the bridge and the tailpiece. This example still has the adjustable-wheel two-piece bridge.

17″ D'Aquisto Solo #1232 dated 3/21/1992

This is the prototype of the Solo model. It is recorded as "new model" in the ledger. Jimmy was following his instincts, always keeping in mind the playability of the guitar. The headstock and tailpiece are beautifully styled and the lines flow very well throughout the body and its accessories. While Jimmy was not afraid of the work, he tired of the old traditional methods of guitar making. He discovered his sculpting talents in this exciting design. The end of the fretboard has a line flow into the pickguard, which now becomes a touch plate, a place of registration for the fingers.

17″ D'Aquisto Centura made in 1993

The Centura is a natural step in evolution from the Solo. It is a simplified version which has no body binding but it does have purfling on the top and back and sides which is inset from the edge. The contours of the truss-rod cover and pickguard are softer. The soundholes are well placed and are a natural progression from the Solo. In fact, this model is just about the same guitar in many ways. The "Delux" version of the Centura was known as the 18″ model. It had sandwiched maple and ebony lines in its parts much like the Avant Garde model and its headstock was cut out.

Originally published in *American Lutherie #53,* 1998

D'Aquisto's Design Development: Another View

by John Monteleone

THE GUITAR SHIPPING CARTON I recently received from one of my customers was not unusual, other than having obviously been used before. My address was on the front as one would expect, and the return was properly in its place over the previous addressee's. I didn't notice it until I happened to be walking casually past this large upright cardboard mass, on a mission of other sorts. My eyes lit up as I caught the faint, scratched-out return address of James L. D'Aquisto in Greenport, Long Island. I stood still in my shoes as I looked further to the also faintly legible recipient's address: Paul Gudelsky. A chill went up my spine. The box turned out to be a revealing piece of ironic history as I reasoned that it was indeed the carton in which the 25th Anniversary D'Aquisto New Yorker was delivered to Paul back in 1990. That unique guitar was just one of many very fine examples in Paul's collection of archtop instruments by James D'Aquisto and John D'Angelico. I don't believe it's likely that I will be recycling this particular piece of historical cardboard.

Although Jimmy was not officially making this model in 1989, he was persuaded to build this one, listed in his ledger as a D'Aquisto/D'Angelico 5/90 for Paul, to celebrate Jimmy's solo efforts since 1964. It was not easy for Jimmy to make it at a time when so much energy was focused in a new direction. If it weren't for the love and obvious devotion that he had for John D'Angelico, I'm not sure that this guitar would have ever been built.

Paul Gudelsky was a fine craftsman in his own right who had come to Long Island to spend a summer with Jimmy at his workshop in Greenport, to learn firsthand the ways and whys of making a D'Aquisto archtop guitar. Paul deeply appreciated Jimmy's skills, and dedicated his later career to the memory of D'Aquisto. Paul's efforts to preserve and keep as many of Jimmy's historic tools, patterns, molds, and benches together as possible gave me respect and admiration for him.

I met Paul for the first time, briefly, at Jimmy's funeral. Later I contacted Paul to borrow a few of Jimmy's templates; I was completing one of the two Centura models that had been hanging incomplete in D'Aquisto's spray booth. We shared several rather lengthy but always very interesting phone calls. Paul wanted to purchase the last but unfinished Centura from the family, which he later did, and to complete it. That part never happened.

When reading the transcript of Paul's lecture to the 1995 GAL Convention, it is interesting to notice how keenly perceptive Paul was to D'Aquisto's career. I believe that Paul would have been a valuable historian and curator for us all, gladly handing down the valuable teachings of James L. D'Aquisto. Paul recognized the teachings of Jimmy as a new and different kind of guitar information; much different from the past. Although Jimmy's philosophies were often laced with character and wit, all of his ideas were genuine and born out of strong will and conviction which affected us all in the guitar community. This speech is filled with the passion of archtop guitar making as it was known to Paul and as it was taught to him by Jimmy. I detect a strong sentimental delivery that reflects on the poignant time and very recent passing of his mentor. How ironic this is. I can only try to expound in my own way upon a few of the ideas that he has already presented rather well.

JOHN MONTELEONE

John Monteleone with one of his own fine instruments.

Paul talks about how Jimmy sacrificed his traditional past for the sake of art. Yes, Jimmy had gone too far in his work to look back. He did reflect with fondness on his time with John D'Angelico, but he didn't dwell on it. He didn't rely on it like a crutch. By the time Jimmy had established his own shop on Long Island, he had discovered his own confidence in building guitars in the traditional style.

Until this time, the musicians would only accept and trust traditional guitar designs. The solo guitar maker as a true artist was not well defined or established with D'Angelico and Stromberg. They were independent artisans, yet still bound by tradition. I can only speculate that had these two men been permitted to abandon the use of plastic, they may have been released from the confines of the old school methods and begun to look at the archtop guitar in a new light. However, these makers and the musicians who supported them were creatures of habit. Mother-of-pearl and *plastic* were considered items of luxury. Gibson set the pace for everyone. This is, of course, not to say that D'Angelico and his contemporaries didn't concern themselves with the sound and quality of their instruments, or the musicians who played them. It's just that they weren't allowed to change beyond the boundaries of what was expected from them. Their place and time in history as luthiers of the highest order became the springboard for the emergence of the modern archtop guitar of the present and future.

When new ideas come along to buck traditional schools of thought, great skepticism is to be expected. Jimmy's departure from the D'Angelico style brought strong resistance from D'Angelico fans. At first, out of great respect and admiration, Jimmy made his guitars just like John's. Jimmy had a strong hand in making the D'Angelico guitars between 1960 and 1964, the period just prior to John's death, and you can see a lot of Jimmy's careful and precise detail in them. It is apparent that Jimmy was the driving force during those final years when he tried to excite John into making guitars again after John closed the old workshop and moved into a new one across the street. Jimmy channeled his energy into refining the old D'Angelico templates, and he was proud to take over the responsible assistantship that once belonged to Vincent Diserio. It is also apparent that the carving was being done largely by a another pair of hands, at a time when Jimmy was learning the archings. His sense of carving style can be identified and traced from his last guitars in 1995 all the way back to those early guitars of the 1960s.

A great deal of the information that came from Jimmy had to do with total concepts — you begin with guitar body parts and carve them in a tonal direction according to a preconceived idea of tone for that instrument. This rough and unfinished guitar body often turns out to be the real essence of what the maker is about, "his/her sound." It is an identifiable thread and as such is reflective of the maker's personality.

It is the desire to turn this craft into an art form that becomes a driving force to create it. The art of making a fine instrument is to have absolute control over the materials at hand. As one gains this control, a confidence emerges which allows the luthier to move forward to maturity.

We are fortunate to live in a time in guitar history that bears witness to the popular acceptance of the art of the archtop guitar. Jimmy was also fortunate to have lived long enough to at least see the influence that he had on luthiers. He turned his back on tradition and boldly unlocked the door to archtop guitar freedom for the rest of us to walk through. For this we owe him a debt of gratitude. He gave us his wonderful gift of vision and independence. It is sadly their misfortune and ours that Jimmy and Paul could not have lived long enough to have enjoyed the benefits of their energy.

Jimmy was very conscious of the musicians' subtle needs for a fine-playing and sensitively balanced instrument. He began to focus on each of the parts of the guitar to improve the ways that they interrelated. His experiments and keen intuition led him to abandon the old, reliable, repetitive designs. Using experience and inquisitive skill, he dared to explore new archtop territory, redesigned his old models, and developed the new models to incorporate his new ideas.

Paul mentions the desire for musicians to "take their archtops to a musical place they had never been." Jimmy correctly believed it was possible to satisfy this need. It required starting over and rethinking the entire instrument from the ground up. The acoustic archtop design needed to become more fulfilling and adaptable to a wider variety of different kinds of musical demands and expressions, not restricted by, and to, what is commonly known as jazz. The archtop is capable of a much broader application than that which it has been assigned. It is not for me to say where musical influences should come from, but it is important for me to make it more possible for those ideas to be expressed at will on a musical instrument. These thoughts were also shared by both Jimmy and Paul.

It is difficult to describe the technique of carving spruce tops and backs without being there to actually witness the practice. There is a good deal of empirical judgment used throughout the carving and graduating process, and it is somewhere within this context that if given the same recipe, the soup begins to taste different with every chef. The wood receives constant evaluation as it goes through the carving, scraping, and sanding process. It becomes a constant and reflexive action to flex, twist, and squeeze the plates. These actions are usually read empirically and are only sometimes guided by mechanical measurement. The personality of the maker is thus sculpted into the wood. By habit and experience, the luthier gains consistency in each piece. It may take considerable time and carving experience to rely instinctively on your own intuition to carve and graduate a superior sounding pair of top and back plates.

My own method of carving these plates begins with the pantograph, as it does for many luthiers. Before I had a pantograph, I used to carve the entire blank with mallet and gouge. It was a good way to get a thorough feel for the material. The pantograph is useful for removing the bulk of material. Then I am in the ball park and I can begin to work the material down with hand tools. One of the most joyful experiences in lutherie is this process of liberating an organic piece of raw wood and reducing it into a vibrant and shimmering piece of highly sensitive tone-producing top or back.

Jimmy would finish carving the interior first. After the top and back were glued onto the sides he would begin to carve the rough and thick outside contours down. He apparently didn't remove much material from the outside of the plates on his pantograph. The reason for this was twofold: the master carving machine templates from D'Angelico were not the same modeling and shape that Jimmy had changed to. And he was now experimenting by carving lower and different profiles than those that were used on John's tops and backs.

*(See **Monteleone** on page 181)*

Originally published in *American Lutherie #53,* 1998

Meet the Maker: George Fortune, Jr.

by John Calkin

STAN OLAH was a Virginia State Trooper and a farmer when one of his children died. Besides a truckload of grief, it engendered in him an urgency to live a little harder because life was indeed very short. He took the job of Chief of Police in Wintergreen, Virginia, a small resort town in Nelson County that sits atop the Blue Ridge. Another part of the fallout was the acquisition of a fiddle, and from trying to play he moved on to trying to make fiddles.

Now it happens that Nelson County is chock full of musicians, and it didn't take Olah long to come across the name of George Thomas Fortune, Jr., the Nelson County fiddle man. A lot of the Fortune family make music. The best known is Jimmy Fortune, a member of the Statler Brothers. But most of them play for parties or local dances or at home, and it was in that arena that George Fortune became a violin maker. In the late '50s he bought a basket-case violin bearing a label that proclaimed it to be a Nicoli Amatus, made in Cremona, Italy. Being of a self-reliant nature, Fortune looked over the box of desiccated parts and decided there wasn't anything in the collection that he couldn't make himself. He made some patterns from the broken instrument, and then he made a fiddle of his own. Then he made a few more, and managed to sell one. The hobby became a little business. Word got around, and folks brought him instruments to repair. George was a full-time mason, but he squeezed in the lutherie work as he could. When bypass surgery ended his mason's career he could still carve fiddles, though his output was never prodigious. "I work when I feel like it," he says, not letting his passion for fiddles get in the way of his independence. He's seventy-eight now, and he's been the Fiddle Man for a long time. Just ask anyone in Nelson County.

ALL BY JOHN CALKIN

Fortune has carved virtually all his violins with these two tools. He made the gouge from a flat file in the early '60s, for his first violin. This Workmate has been his workbench from the beginning.

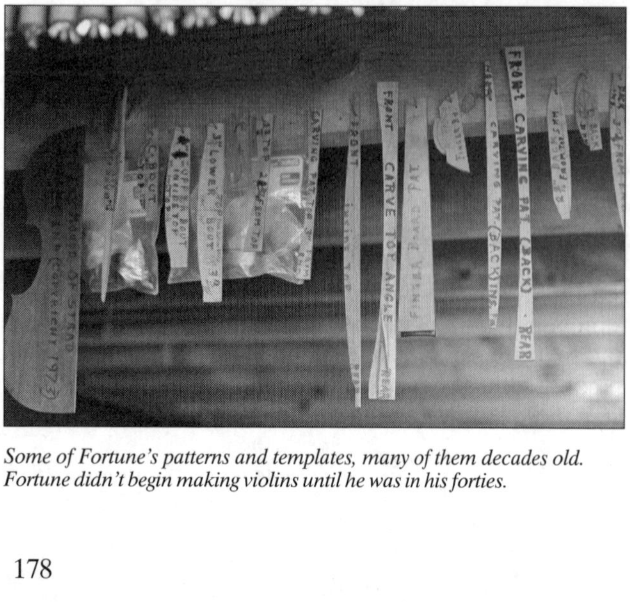

Some of Fortune's patterns and templates, many of them decades old. Fortune didn't begin making violins until he was in his forties.

When Stan Olah first tracked down the old man, Fortune was not receptive.

"I'm not thinking about fiddles today. Today I'm gardening."

Fortune put him off several times, but Olah persisted. He finally showed up at Fortune's door with a half-made fiddle and the old man softened.

"Let's go downstairs and have a look at it," said Fortune, giving up a smile that was partly for Olah and partly for the violin fetus in his hands. Over time the fiddle grew, and session after session the two men forged a strong bond. Stan Olah has become George Fortune's greatest admirer.

"The old boy's incredible. He's completely self-taught, but he makes as good a fiddle as I've heard. I'll be well pleased if some day I'm as good as he is," said Olah.

Down in Fortune's basement the signs of his independent nature hang from the joists. There are rows of homemade templates, forms, molds, and spool clamps made from real spools (Mrs. Fortune sews a lot). Larger spools for cellos dwarf the collection of violin clamps. Commercial tools are scant. There's a small bandsaw, an electric bending iron from Metropolitan Music, and that's about it. When asked to display his carving tools he hauls out a carpenter's chisel and a gouge he ground out of a file.

"That's it?"

"What else do you need?" he smiles. "Oh, there's this," he adds, picking up the rusted head of a garden hoe. "I couldn't figure out how to carve the scoop between the purfling and the beginning of the arch. I was in too much of a hurry to order any tools, so I ground the shape of the trough and the edge of the plate into the hoe and made it into a scraper. It works fine. I've been using it all along."

The Workmate he has always used as a bench sits by the sliding glass doors that illuminate the corner of the basement. The floor is perfectly swept. The shop seems almost barren. Fortune is between fiddles, and his little kit of tools is almost swallowed in the deepening gloom of the room. The only sign of work is a violin suspended from a hook awaiting another coat of varnish. Fortune applies finish with a Badger airbrush powered by a tank of compressed air.

"I've had to pump the tank by hand sometimes, but I'm too old for that now," he admits. "In fact, I thought maybe I could work with some factory parts and save some labor. Didn't work out though." He takes a precarved spruce top out of a drawer and holds it up to the light of the doors. A spot the size of a quarter near the bass *f*-hole glows brightly where too much wood was removed. "Pathetic," he says gently, and you know that it's a comment on the state of the world in general.

Fortune has made thirty-three fiddles and sold twenty of them. A couple were made as gifts. The rest he still has. At the end of the hallway by the bedroom is a built-in display cabinet with room for nine violins. They glow contentedly through the cabinet glass. The stains on the fiddles are wonderful, no two alike. One is finished in white lacquer. They all look creamy, translucent. The finish work is beautiful. A few sport understated bone inlays in the tailpiece.

When asked for a tune, Fortune retreats into the bedroom, where his fiddle *du jour* sits on the dresser. He doesn't test it, he knows it's in tune. He sits to play a hoedown, his foot tapping time firmly. The fiddle sounds husky and full, though he is obviously not leaning into the bow. When finished he smiles shyly, unsure if his audience understands fiddle music. On leaving the room we pass a corner gathering of old and odd instruments awaiting repair.

There's a scrapbook of lutherie work interspersed with family history: shots of the mandolin he made and of a cello once brought to him for repair, clearly a high water mark in his career to judge by the number of snaps. And photos of the fiddles that went out the door, captured for the book like lost family members. One is midnight black with gold sparkle binding, apparently purchased by the leader of a honky-tonk band. Fortune's first fiddle is mounted on the dining room wall in sort of a shrine. The purfling is a bit shaky, but otherwise it looks pretty good.

"You should read the newspaper stuff about me," Fortune offers, then says to his wife, "The write-ups, where's my write-ups?"

He leaves us alone for a moment while he searches. Mrs. Fortune is cuddled in front of the TV for the day, held hostage by a foot ailment. Complimented on her housekeeping, she smiles and confides that when they married back in the early '40s they had thirty-odd cents between them. Her description of life before the Big

Fortune demonstrates the way he forms the lips of his plates. This is bound to end up the most famous hoe in the history of violin making. Made for contouring the edges of violin plates, he has used it for his whole career. Though crude looking, tools like this are right out of lutherie tradition. When something works, it doesn't get replaced.

These are the Fortune violins that have stayed at home. The top violin, second from the right, is finished in white lacquer.

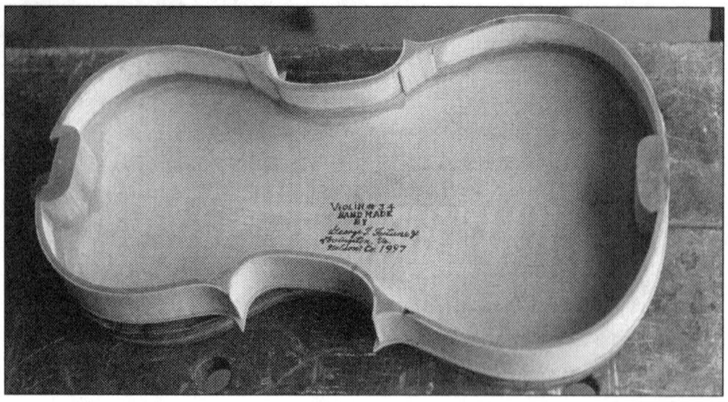

War might almost be from another planet. Back then, rural meant something a lot different than it does today.

Less than half an hour away from the Fortunes is the city of Charlottesville, a prosperous university town that no doubt shelters more violins than fiddles. Folks there are proud of their cultural sophistication, but it comes at a price. Getting a fiddle fixed costs more than fiddles are worth out in the county. Fiddles that don't get fixed go to hell in a hurry. The lucky ones find their way to George Fortune. He's been rescuing them for almost forty years. The others wind up in attics, flea markets, trash bins. Fortune's set of values were established a long time ago, and they give him his own perspective. He gets $1,000 for a new violin. It's a benchmark in his career, and he's proud people will pay that much for them.

Stan Olah grew up in a newer era, but he understands those values. They make sense to him. He's working hard to understand what makes a fiddle tick, but he's not

Top left: Fortune popped the top off #34 so American Lutherie *readers could peek inside. Top right: Fortune has a go at "Old Joe Clark." Above: George Thomas Fortune, Jr. and Stan Olah in Fortune's basement workshop. If Fortune had a fan club, Olah would be its president.*

locked into a set of views. When one set of C bouts proved impossible to bend, he made a set out of mahogany, even though the rest of the ribs were maple.

"Worked just fine. Looked kind of cool, too," he says.

One of his goals is to make a violin of figured walnut. His collection of tools is as expansive as Fortune's is minimalist, but as much as anything it's the mark of growing up in a different, faster time. Olah wants to make progress faster because there's only so much time. For any of us. He's made six fiddles and sold one, so he's on his way. And he knows about Stradivari and those other Italian fiddle cats, but they didn't live in Nelson County. A man's life should somehow reflect his home and vice versa, otherwise the world would all look the same.

Smack on the Blue Ridge Parkway, just a few miles north of Wintergreen, is a visitor's stop with a small historical display dedicated to the hardy souls who farmed the mountains before modern times. In one corner stand dulcimers, banjos, and fiddles collected from the rural South. One or two were captured in their prime, but most seem to have been abandoned, abused, and used up. Perhaps they were once the heart of their community's life, where music and dance gave distant folk an excuse to gather and commingle, but not anymore. No George Fortune was there for them.

Perhaps not in so many words, Stan Olah understands this. It's more a feeling in the blood than an expression in the brain, that people are important to a community in ways not ordinarily considered. He's a cop, and everyone understands what he contributes in that way. But he also wants to be a musician with a heritage to uphold. He's the informal apprentice to George Fortune, a man who learned to fashion instruments out of good wood and perseverance. And he might one day be the Nelson County Fiddle Man. ——

(**Monteleone** *from page 177*)

The arching was now more sweeping and subtle. This is what Paul alludes to when he says, "Machining the plates to a finished dimension would have left him unable to tune the box." So, when Jimmy got his own machine, he had new carving templates made up. By then he was used to carving the rough bulk material off after mounting the top and back onto the sides to get his arching. He discovered that he could bring the plates into better focus visually and sonically as he carved the outside to just the right feel and sound. Constantly tapping, listening, carving, tapping, listening, carving, tapping, listening, scraping, tapping, scraping, listening, scraping, and so on. Thumb pressure is used to feel the resistant flex of the wood. This again is a technique that requires individual feel, and since everyone is different physically and in strength, we will tend to approach the same piece of wood with uniquely different results. The carving process becomes a part of the instrument's DNA. The maker's indelible signature is more than just a name written inside the instrument. It is permanently carved into the parts and pieces of the entire instrument, and it remains there for the life of that instrument unless it is tampered with and destroyed.

I agree with the side depth specifications as being the ideal dimension for better coupling of the top and back. An 18″ body, at 2⅞″, should be slightly shallower than a 17″ body. And a 16″ body should be even higher. An average difference of ⅛″ in height is a good reference.

I am glad to see that Paul talks about Jimmy's bridge and refers to it as another brace. It is, in my opinion, the most important of all the tone bars, and for an archtop it can, according to its shape, mass, and dimension, permit changes to the tonal response. These alterations will affect the tone color, sustain, brilliance, richness, depth, and sensitivity to touch. One of the earliest changes Jimmy made in his bridges was to make the saddle wider to offer a more mellow attack and a tighter chord response, more like a blend of saxes and trumpets.

Some people during the '70s and '80s felt that he was making his bridges too big for his guitars. I feel that he was willing to take that chance to find out just how much is too far. And much to his credit, I believe that he changed the way we now look at a bridge. It's all part of understanding where the parameters are for fine guitar building and good tonal design.

The Accutune sliding-wedge bridge which Jimmy introduced on the first Solo and used for all his subsequent guitars raised a lot of eyebrows. Some people have criticized this concept as being too difficult to adjust and claimed, "it just doesn't work." But if it doesn't work so well, why is it that these later guitars are in the highest-priced and most sought-after category? I believe it shows that Jimmy was thinking. He was using his savvy to deliver the best tone for his guitars that he knew how. This is not to say that this design is going to work for everyone. It is up to the musician to decide if that bridge is working to produce the desired sound. Bridges are not cast in stone and are one of the variables in sound design that Jimmy often talked about.

The section of strings between the bridge and the tailpiece is known as the afterlength. Jimmy and I often discussed this subtle area, and we were in agreement that the feel of the strings is something that relates directly to the feel of the guitar. A shorter distance of afterlength will tighten up the feel. We were also in agreement that the old metal tailpieces were dinosaurs and were, if anything, set up backward. I firmly believe that the slant on the D'Angelico tailpiece is in reverse for an improved feel of the strings. I make the high strings longer to give them a more supple feel and to make them sound fatter. Jimmy had his own distinct ideas on this subject as the tailpieces of the newer models show.

It is interesting to note that the scale lengths on almost all of his acoustic guitars were set at 25¼″. The nut widths were mostly 1¾″, but they tended to increase in the later years to 1⅞″.

Jimmy felt that somehow the quad soundholes of the Solo model were acting like tweeters and woofers, as in a speaker cabinet. I personally don't feel quite the same way about it. I do, however, think that aesthetically it is a magnificent layout. Because the bridge is somewhat tied into the sides as the holes are bisected, there may be an advantage to its unique quality of sound.

Beginning with the New Yorker Classic model, soundholes would no longer be bound on the rest of Jimmy's guitars. This guitar's soundholes were purposely drawn out as if they were going to be bound, but instead he rounded the edges over. This little detail was an important lead-in to the visual looseness and "the look" of his designs that paved the way for other new models to follow.

Although I agree that the larger soundhole openings improve volume and tonal versatility for the archtop guitar, I never understood what Jimmy was talking about when he said that the *f*-hole was obsolete and advocated removing them from violins. I believe that statement to be an over reaction to support his own beliefs in the alternatives to soundhole design. It is important to understand that there can and should be alternatives to what we commonly know and accept as traditional ideas and ideals. This open approach to sound design can allow music and the instruments with which we make our music to grow with it.

I am so glad that I had the opportunity to thank Jimmy personally for his contribution to the guitar community and for giving me the inspiration to be myself. If Paul Gudelsky were alive today I would like to thank him for spreading his knowledge and sharing his enthusiasm with us.

I wish to add that two other very fine luthiers had private study with D'Aquisto: Linda Manzer and Gila Eban. They are experienced, well-qualified makers who are armed with firsthand knowledge of D'Aquisto archtops and how they were made. ——

Originally published in *American Lutherie #54,* 1998

French Polishing with Eugene Clark

from his 1997 American School of Lutherie workshop

by Cyndy Burton

THE PURPOSE OF THE CLASS was "to give you a technical grounding so that you can have predictability in your finishing." To that end, Eugene Clark was prepared with an array of raw materials — shellacs and other resins, oils, pumice — and numerous pages of handwritten notes. He passed out three pages of terms to be defined over the two-day period. His preparation mirrored the depth of the knowledge he gained in the '60s and '70s as a full-time builder of fine classical and flamenco guitars. It also reflected an experimental mind-set that includes a respect for the craft's history and a strong bias against commercial products.

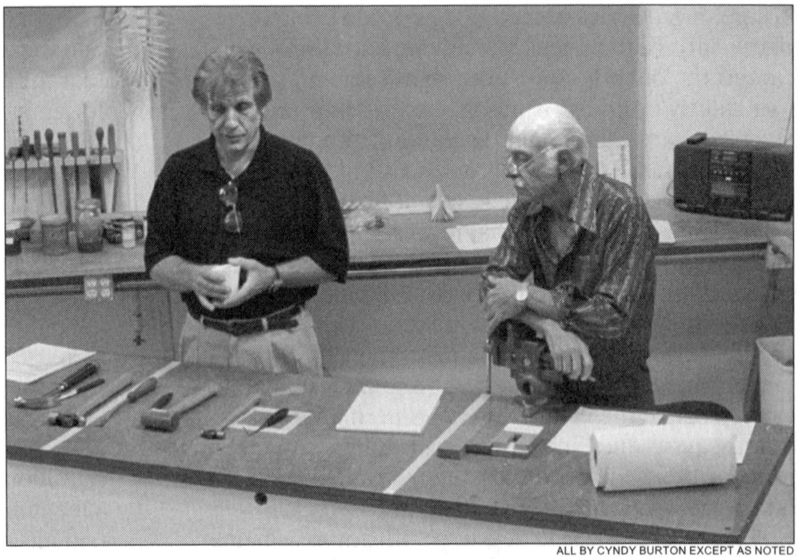

ALL BY CYNDY BURTON EXCEPT AS NOTED

Charles Fox (left) introduces Eugene Clark to the class.

Knowing his subject well, Eugene was able to address the needs and interests of his students with attention to their differing levels. In our class were people who had yet to make or polish a guitar, and a few who had been at it for close to twenty years. Most had made a few guitars and wanted to try French polishing but needed a nudge. Eugene gave us an encyclopedic amount of information over the two days. I cannot reproduce the material in depth here. Eugene has a book "in gradual preparation." We are all looking forward to his published works.

Eugene's appreciation of woods, and of woodworking and finishing, goes back to his childhood. "I was very impressed with the work I saw my grandfather do. I remember as a boy sitting in a stuffed chair that he had made that was covered with leathers of different colors that he had dyed and finished. Next to the chair was a beautiful blonde table, French polished. Standing beside the table was a lamp made of pretty multicolored woods, and it was French polished. I had watched him make that lamp on his lathe. And I remember a humidor that he had made of alternate staves of dark and light woods — walnut and maple. It was also French polished, and I could read the light bulb in it. I looked through its candy-like finish and could see every cell of the wood. I knew that I was looking at something I didn't encounter anywhere else in my environment. I never saw that finish again, until one day as a young man, a little under thirty, I was reading the light bulb through a candy-like finish on my instrument and seeing every cell of the wood. I knew then that I had finally learned enough to perpetuate what my ancestor had been doing."

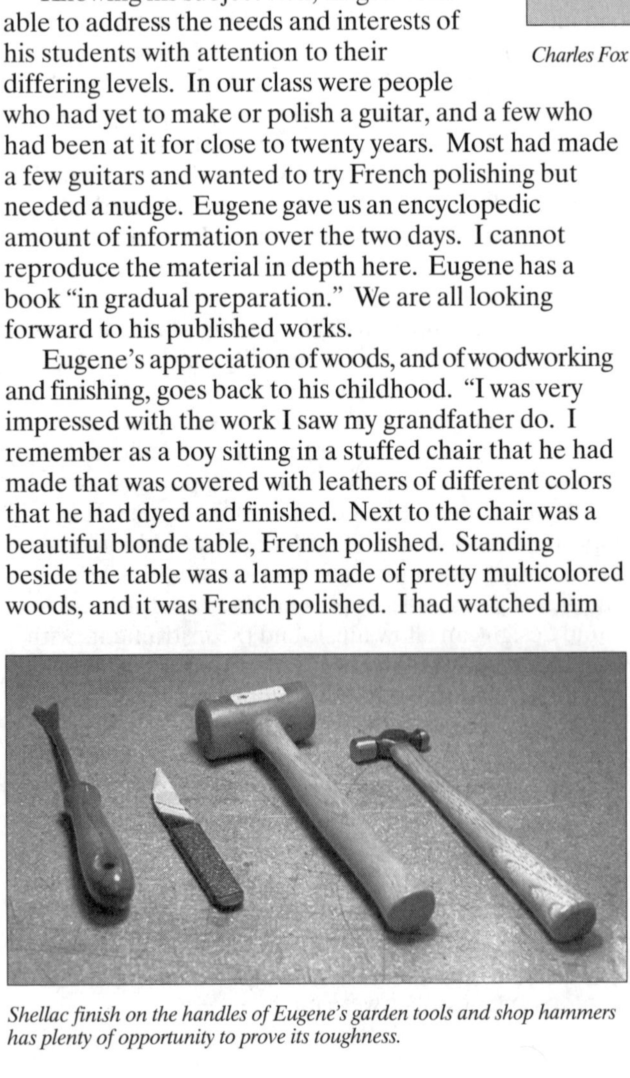

Shellac finish on the handles of Eugene's garden tools and shop hammers has plenty of opportunity to prove its toughness.

Continuing this very old craft is exactly what Eugene set out to do in our class. He began by showing us some garden tools and some hammers from his shop. A leather-handled carpenter's hammer had a very heavy finish of shellac with walnut oil as an additive. It may take a year or two for walnut oil to oxidize and polymerize fully, but once it does this finish is incredibly durable, as it is nearly impervious to alcohol, heat, and almost any other abuse. *Polymerization* was explained to be a process in which a change of properties takes place without any atoms or molecules being added or lost, a rearrangement only. *Oxidation*, on the other hand, involves the acquisition of oxygen molecules.

Another tool handle had an on-the-wood finish of some thickness but of shellac only. Eugene refers to a surface that has a substantial body coat as *varnished*. He says that the wood is *polished* when it has an in-the-wood finish, with traces of shellac shining on the surface. In his own jargon, he might describe what he generally does with a guitar as varnishing over polishing. Another handle had very thick shellac "slopped" or flowed on with a rag. He explained that the flowing of shellac is easy compared with the brushing of shellac. The difference is in the friction that is available with the rag but not with the brush. All of these finishes looked good. Because of clarity, it was hard to tell which ones had thick finish and which didn't. These examples served as introductions to a variety of shellac-based finishes and techniques that Eugene explored in depth over the two days.

When we had examined these tool-handle finishes — I was unable to dent any of them with my thumb nail — Eugene presented a brief history of wood finishing. He assured us that our Stone-Age ancestors certainly had excellent abrasives, and that they were able to grade them by some kind of flotation. Today, a designation of 3F or FFF for a pumice stands for "triple-floated." As an aside, he pointed out that the hard-water deposit that remains on the bottom of a saucepan after the water has boiled away makes an excellent superfine polishing agent. He is clearly an advocate for making your own "products." At the top of his handout, Eugene had printed, "You are the formulator." He stressed that manufacturers of proprietary products have been consistent in their habit of suddenly changing their formulations, causing the finisher to lose control over the end result. This was a theme reiterated throughout the class. He also pointed out that if one were to buy all of the hundreds of cans and bottles that are put up for every special purpose, one would be purchasing pretty much the same ten or twelve common raw materials, in differing colors and scents, all of them quite inexpensive when purchased in bulk.

Eugene demonstrates flattening or shaping with an 80-grit garnet paper wrapped around a cork-faced wooden block.

So, Stone-Age people had fillers and polishing agents, but no distillation technology, therefore no solvents. In ancient Egypt, pitch was melted and spread onto surfaces that were to be protected. Fats, waxes, and the oils pressed from nuts and seeds were all used by early finishers. Over time, the vegetable oils came to be classified as nondrying, semidrying, and drying. Some vegetable oils, such as walnut oil, will dry gradually by oxidation to form a durable and beautiful finish. When a vegetable oil oxidizes and ultimately polymerizes it forms what is called a *linoxyn* — a tough plastic film that has no melting point and no solubility. The ultimate finish. In the history of wood finishing, oil finishes precede the resin-and-solvent finishes that we know as spirit varnishes.

With the advent of distillation, alcohol and turpentine came into use to dissolve various natural resins in the making of a variety of *spirit varnishes*. These same varnishes, with the addition of a drying oil, became known as *oil varnishes*, preferred for their superior resistance to water and weather. In a *cooked oil varnish*, one or more resins are dissolved into a hot drying oil.

What we know as nitrocellulose lacquer (note the root word *lac*) evolved from a simple solution of shellac (shell-lac) and alcohol. Manufacturers began adding pyroxylin, a form of nitrated cellulose, in order to overcome brushing and spraying difficulties. Eventually the shellac was replaced with cheaper products, often a rosin ester or ester gum, which is ordinary pine rosin that has been treated with glycerin. These new materials evolved *not* because they are better, necessarily, as for instance more clear or more beautiful, but in answer to industry's need to provide faster and cheaper finishing. Pyroxylin trades off toughness or wear resistance for hardness. All substitutions for shellac have forced a compromise in permanence and beauty.

Over two days Eugene demonstrated all stages — *sanding, clearing/sealing, filling, bodying,* and *spiriting.* He talked about but did not demonstrate rubbing out. Three or four days would have been a more comfortable time frame to fit the vast amount of information offered.

After we had absorbed a few terms, it was time to get our hands into the finishing. A lecture format was alternated with hands-on demonstrations and our own attempts to duplicate the various processes Eugene demonstrated. We worked on 6″ × 12″ lauan mahogany samples. On the first day we began what Eugene calls *polishing* of the wood, doing a complete finish with no body coat. If he had his way, the term French polishing would refer to this finish, not to wiped-on body coats over some kind of filler. "But," he says, "I accommodate." He feels that French polishing is the clearing, filling, and shining of the wood, with or without body coating. We sanded, sealed, cleared, and filled with a mixture of alcohol, shellac, oil, and pumice. On the second day, if the pores were truly filled, we spirited-off the surface to a shine. That completed the polishing as it was defined, a finish that we could examine on some of the tool samples.

Our preparation of the lauan samples started with sanding. We wrapped small pieces of 80A open-coat garnet paper around cork-faced wooden blocks and were told to sand vigorously *across* the grain until the

This nicely curved felt block also works well for flattening and rubbing out.

Yes, cross grain on the sides, too — use that little felt block!

pieces were level. *Flat — no ripple!* Eugene explained that if you sand only *with* the grain you will not eliminate ripple. He came around to our individual work stations to monitor our progress. Most of us were scratching our heads until he demonstrated with several samples. By sanding across the grain with moderate pressure, the shearing action of a rough grit makes the work go very fast, and it is easy to "read" the surface by feel. Although Eugene was looking for flatness, the sense most engaged was touch. He would say, "Here's a dip. It's not flat here. Feel that?" Dividing sanding into two stages, as he divides all abrading into two stages, Eugene called this sanding process *shaping*. After shaping, a light *smoothing* was done with 320-grit paper, with the grain, but leaving much of the scratching of the coarse garnet paper. What happens to those 80-grit scratches? They get filled with pumice, oil, alcohol, and shellac, just like the grain. And here is where the art comes in. You can enhance the look of some woods with the addition of cross-grain scratches, which "read" in the final finish as medullary rays or figure. I say "art" because it is obvious that you can't leave cross-grain scratches in all woods and expect a superior look at the end. So, the cross-grain sanding has two functions — truly flatting or shaping the wood; and, if scratches are allowed to remain, deliberately brightening the work by adding reflective surfaces.

The two-grit-only exercise, though not suggestive of an ideal schedule for sanding, served to emphasize the point that Eugene was making about not over-working or over-preparing the wood before applying finish. If you sand beyond 320 — and he often sands no finer than 180 — you will be *choking* the wood with sanding dust so that the next step, *clearing*, will be impossible. Eugene washes a guitar with a water-dampened cloth or sponge after sanding, so as to remove as much wood dust as possible, and then resands lightly to flatten the grain if necessary, before clearing and sealing. When sanding, he constantly brushes dust off the surface of the wood to prevent clogging of the sandpaper and choking of the wood. He also uses a small stiff brush to keep the sandpaper clean.

Clearing is a part of the sealing process or wash-coating, and is accomplished by including a little oil into a very thin shellac varnish on the pad. We were each issued one square foot of cheese cloth or gauze that had been purchased at an art supply house, small glass bottles containing alcohol, shellac varnish, olive oil, and a small jar of medium-grit pumice. The alcohol was of hardware store grade, denatured. We were instructed to fold up our cheesecloth to form a pad, mouse, or muñeca about 1½″ square. Sealing and clearing were done with a pad of uncovered cheese cloth charged with a slurp of alcohol, a slurp of oil, and a slurp of shellac varnish of about 2 lb. cut, all taken directly from the bottles in "guesstimates." The oil penetrates just into the surface of the wood, resulting in a "deep" finish, one that you can look into. One of the unique properties of shellac is that it "likes" oil. It combines well with oil, and is adhesive in the presence of oil.

The *clearing/sealing* process was done in seconds with quick, overlapping circular strokes, followed by complete drying of the work. It is important to not keep going over the same area. This first application is only a very thin wash coat. At this point, Eugene suggests locking up the shellac. The tendency that everybody has at this stage, and in the filling stage that follows, is to use way too much shellac. The next step, filling with shellac and pumice, can often be accomplished with no more shellac than is in the pad and on the surface of the wood after sealing. *Using too much shellac makes filling more difficult because the shellac that builds up on the surface will tend to pull out the filling.* A great deal of hard effort on your part may result in little or no filling at all. It is in learning to prevent the buildup of a body coat during the filling that we discover just how willing the shellac is to build. Bodying is clearly the easy part of the French polishing process. In the presence of a little oil, the shellac wants to build.

What about the bleeding of rosewood and of dyed woods? The presence of a little oil "tempers" the solvent action of the alcohol, thus reducing the amount of bleeding. Judicious refolding of the pad should keep wood surfaces clean of free color.

In our class we used only shellac/alcohol varnish. But Eugene talked about adding walnut oil to shellac for the body coats in order to make a somewhat tougher finish, the finish we saw on the leather hammer handle. When the walnut oil is shaken into a shellac varnish it forms a temporary dispersion that is useful because it increases the amount of oil that will combine into the body coats. When asked how much oil he puts into what cut of shellac Eugene replied, "I don't know. The shellac knows how much oil it can hold. The rest will be thrown off, so long as the pad is not saturated with oil." One caveat: If you use walnut oil, be sure to buy a brand that has no additives, and test dry a smear of the oil on a small dish. The once-preferred Hain brand oil is now "improved" with vitamin E, an antioxidant. Spectrum brand oil is still good as of this writing, and is nitrogen sealed for long keeping in the jar (until opened, of course). Find it in health food and gourmet stores. Walnut oil may become rancid rather quickly, so wash or dispose of cloths soon after use, to avoid a heavy and unpleasant odor in the shop.

For clearing, or sealing, the pad is charged with a "slurp" each of shellac, alcohol, and oil.

Where does all the oil go? Much of the oil that is added to the face of the pad becomes part of the body coat. A drying oil will harden eventually, adding serviceability to the body coat. Meanwhile, the body coat will be as if a nondrying oil were used, no different. Walnut oil, if left on the surface of the work, will stiffen in a few days. Removing it could require heavy scrubbing. So, while it is still fresh enough to remove easily, clean it off with a little mineral or vegetable oil, using a cloth, tissue, or paper towel. Spectrum walnut oil stiffens noticeably overnight.

The oil used for the wash coat and filling of our first sample was olive oil, the thick pure greenish kind. Eugene uses the same oil that he likes on his homemade pizza. Olive oil is nondrying, so if it bleeds out onto the surface of the work after your guitar has left the shop, there will be no gummy spotting to be scrubbed off — by your customer! It is possible that the Spectrum oil will dry well enough in the wood and in the pores that bleedout and spotting will not be a problem — as it has been with the Hain oil — but there has been no controlled test.

For lubrication during bodying, Eugene likes raw walnut oil. He feels that walnut oil favors a "buttery" texture and rapid buildup of shellac during the bodying stage. In a discussion of the various drying and nondrying oils, he described the properties and uses of the mineral oils — baby oil, paraffin oil; of castor oil from the castor bean; and of boiled and raw linseed oils. The boiled linseed oil that can be bought in the hardware store contains chemical compounds that serve as driers, usually the metallic salts of cobalt, lead, or manganese. On wood, boiled linseed oil will generally dry enough to be sanded in about 48 hours. The class prepared one lauan sample by filling the pores with boiled linseed oil and nothing but the wood fibers loosened by coarse sanding. We did not have time to verify that those samples would be hard to the touch in about two days.

Eugene warned that raw and boiled linseed oils will bleach the color out of rosettes. Raw linseed oil, hardware store or kitchen grade, will harden eventually, but its use in permanent work is not recommended. Although it is a good padding lubricant, and has good film-forming properties, raw linseed oil has been known to polymerize in a destructive fashion over a number of years, the varnish film eventually turning sticky or gelatinous.

The shellac used in sealing and filling was of about 2-lb. cut, further thinned in the pad. That is, the pad was made pretty wet with alcohol and oil, and a few drops of shellac added so as to make a very dilute solution in the pad. When varnishing, Eugene may have handy several bottles of shellac of different concentrations, from roughly 1-lb. cut to 4- or 5-lb. cut. These numbers are merely estimates, and are for those of us who feel secure when we can quantify things. In reality, he doesn't measure his materials often, except when making up a quantity of shellac varnish for the shelf. For that, a kitchen scale is useful. Eugene also finds uses for a saturated solution he calls "honey" that he makes by using more shellac than will dissolve in alcohol.

Most of us are familiar with the formula for determining "cut." Mixing 1 lb. of dry shellac in 1 gal. of alcohol makes a 1 lb. cut; 2 lbs. in 1 gal. makes a 2-lb. cut. Note that cut is in terms of weight per volume. But we can use a weight-per-weight definition, or "percent solution." Percent solution is the weight of resin as a percentage of total weight of the solution. For example, in a 20% solution, the resin weighs 20% of the total weight of the solution, or ⅕. Therefore, weight of alcohol is ⅘. Think of it as 1 weight of resin in 4 weights of solvent equaling 5 weights in total. To convert alcohol-volume to alcohol-weight, Eugene quotes the adage, "A pint's a pound the world around." For shop purposes, a pint of alcohol can be considered to weigh the same as a pint of water (close enough). A gallon of alcohol, then, weighs about 8 lbs. The following example should clarify things: A 2-lb. cut contains 2 lbs. of resin to 1 gal. of alcohol, which is 2 lbs. of resin to 8 lbs. of alcohol. Total of weights is 10 lbs.

So, the weight of resin is 2⁄10 or 1⁄5 of total weight, or 20%. It is a 20% solution by weight. Another example: A 2.5-lb. cut has 2.5 lbs. of resin in 8 lbs. of solvent. The total weight is 10.5 lbs. Concentration, by percent, is 2.5/10.5, or 0.238. A 2.5-lb. cut is a 24% solution, by weight. Small amounts of shellac varnish can be measured easily in either ounces or grams when a suitable scale is used. It simplifies matters to zero the scale with the jar on it, then add the materials.

The names given to raw lac in its several forms may reflect where and when it was harvested. The trees that play host to the resin-producing insects may be different in India from those found in Thailand or Japan. Over a hundred species of trees and shrubs have been used as hosts, though only a few are commonly used in producing commercial crops of shellac. In India, the Bysaki crop is harvested in the spring. The paler and more desirable Kusmi lac is harvested in December. Fortunately, we do not have to know all the names, places, and hosts to obtain good shellacs. Eugene's article "Shellac and French Polishing" in the LMI Handbook-Catalog *(Editor's note: out of print)* gives an excellent description of how some of the shellacs are derived. A portion is quoted here, with permission of the author and the publisher. I recommend that you read the whole article. Be aware that a few shellac terms are troublesome, because processes have changed over time. And there have been several standards for the naming and grading of shellacs. Definitions do not always serve all situations and all times. And, there is a cost to brevity.

"The term shellac is often used as a generic term for lac in all of its forms. But shellac is only one of the forms in which we encounter the lac. The resin known as *lakh* or *lac* is produced by an insect, the coccus lacca. In the production of lac, a host tree is inoculated with live insects in the form called broodlac. The insects, using their sharp beaks, suck and ingest the sap of the tree, then secrete the resin from pores in their bodies. With the resin, they build habitat for their young in the form of hollow cells. Within these cells, the young insects are protected while they grow to maturity. As with the cocoon of the silk worm and the comb of the honey bee, man has found uses for this insect 'house.'

Lac resin is harvested either by cutting branches from the tree — cut branches are called sticklac — or by climbing the tree and scraping the resin off the branches. Hot knives are used. A measure of bark remains in the resin, to be filtered out later. This lac contains natural waxes amounting to about 4% by weight, on average.

"Once removed from twigs and branches, the lac is crushed, washed, and winnowed to yield the form known as *seedlac*. The seedlac can then be made into *shellac* (shell lac), so named because it is in the form of foil or shell. In the hand making of shellac, seedlac is put into long cloth bags which are heated before a fire and squeezed so that the molten lac can be scraped off and stretched into sheets. This filtering removes most of the debris — insect and bark residues — from the raw lac. The sheets are then cooled and broken into flakes. In this process the flake is produced that we know as orange shellac, the better grades of which are designated as lemon shellac. Flake form permits ready comparison and identification of different grades of lac.

"Button lac is made from seedlacs that are dark in color and which, when molten, are poured, like drop cookies, into what are called buttons. The buttons have often been stamped with a producer's logo. Another product called button shellac, this one a flake, is factory-produced. Generally of a yellow-brown color, though described in earliest literature as ruby red or red-brown, button shellac has a higher than average wax content. Garnet shellac, generally of a red-brown color and having a low wax content, is another factory-produced flake. The residue that remains in the cloth after refining the shellac will contain bug residue and bark, and will have been subjected to the most heat. As refuse lac it may be reclaimed in a factory process. Today there is little hand making of shellacs. Most of the flake on the market is factory-produced by the solvent process. The demand for colored shellacs will remain, but we are likely to see great variability in the products that are offered to meet the need. Increasingly, the terms "button" and "garnet" may come to denote color or hue only."

The old technology for shellac making has been replaced by production methods, and the old way was a highly developed art. The lac artisans were very much like the blacksmiths of old, familiar with their raw materials, and skilled in the application of heat and in hand working their products. Even the very best shellac that we can buy today is lacking in some of the qualities that were inherent in handmade shellacs. Two of them are scent and color. Some handmade shellacs smelled really good, with a spicy pungent odor that filled the room. The color palette has diminished. Also, not much note has been taken of the possibility that heat-process and solvent-process shellacs may have somewhat different properties.

If we want a very light colored shellac, we can purchase granules that have been bleached chemically or flakes that have been decolorized and dewaxed mechanically or by means of charcoal filtration. A typical process for making chemically bleached shellac, or white shellac, is to dissolve the shellac into a boiling soda solution, bleach it with sodium hypochlorite, and precipitate the bleached resin with sulfuric acid. Bleached shellac was used on almost all the early American guitars and on most Spanish guitars until about 1960 or later. Bleached shellac was *the* organic coating material for a long time after its introduction in the early 1800s. Bleached shellac will produce a finish that is very beautiful, but the shelf life of the dry material is limited. LMI's 2 Moons is a granular bleached shellac. Eugene has a sample still dissolving and drying normally after one year, but its self life is unknown.

Dewaxed and decolorized flake shellac (DD) has a shelf life of many years. Eugene knows of more than one stock of DD that is more than twenty-five years old and still behaving as when purchased. These pale shellacs also make beautiful, clear finishes. They can be obtained in a range of values from near water white to medium amber. Colored shellacs can be mixed with each other, or with any pale shellac, to achieve special color effects.

How are we to know if the shellac we have purchased is any good? First of all, buy from a reputable supplier. Eugene told us stories about adulterated shellac, aged shellac, and synthetic shellac sometimes found on the market. Secondly, use your nose. Rub a little shellac solution on your hand like cologne. Wait until the alcohol dries, then smell it. Good shellac smells sweet and pleasant, like something you would not object to eating or wearing. The precipitation test is a more objective way to verify your shellac. In a jar about one-third full of shellac varnish add enough water to fill the jar. Pure shellac will precipitate out almost entirely, in the form of a cohesive curd. The curd can be washed in warm water until nearly free of alcohol. Resembling a not-too-sticky taffy, it can be pulled into long strands, folded, pulled some more. Here also make the smell test. In this state, shellac should have a strong aroma, sweet, free of any kind of harsh or unpleasant chemical odors. This precipitate should not be sticky. It should not cling to your fingers. Recovery of resin through precipitation should be nearly 100%. No significant fraction should remain in the water, which should be only a little milky. In this test, synthetic components are likely to remain dissolved or emulsified in the water, and to not form part of the precipitate. To dry the precipitate, continue pulling and folding, while blotting it. Blotted well, it can be redissolved in alcohol and used immediately. Back where you started! Or, the precipitate can be dried and stored, as if it had never been made into solution in the first place. When using solutions of real shellac, the varnish clings to the fingers and is not so easily removed. If you wash your hands in water, the shellac will tend to harden or set, making it very hard to remove. So, if your "shellac" or "French polish" washes off your hands with water, it fails one of the tests for shellac purity.

It was time to *fill* our samples, which had been cleared and sealed. The wash coat had needed only a few minutes to dry. The pad was charged as before — a tiny amount of shellac varnish, generous amounts of alcohol and oil — and a new ingredient, a "glop" of medium-grit pumice. The pumice was added to the wet pad so that it would get plenty of oil on it in order to clear it. This is particularly important. If the pumice granules don't get coated with oil they may end up as white stuff in the grain, something we have all seen. Just as you clear the wood with oil when you seal it, you clear the pumice with oil to insure its invisibility. In filling, the shellac-pumice mixture is rubbed onto and into the wood with rapid circular motions. Listen for the scratchy sound that tells you that the shellac is not building up on the surface. You are making a slurry that is smeared quickly into the pores, in several brief applications. When you have completed a pass over all

Varifying the quality of the shellac. Water was added to a bottle about one-third full of shellac. The shellac precipitates into a mass in the bottle.

After washing the mass several times, Bob Milburn stretches and pulls it like taffy.

Filling is demonstrated using medium-grit pumice.

surfaces, a little of the slurry should remain on the surface. Too much shellac in the mixture will cause the slurry to be too sticky. In that case, you won't be able to flow it into the grain before it sets up on the surface. Too much shellac in the pores will lead to excessive shrinkage. Aim for a maximum of cleared pumice, and a minimum of shellac. Don't try to fill porous wood in one operation. Don't worry about swirls on the surface. And don't go over the work again for an hour or so. When the initial filling is dry, repeat the process, this

Eugene holds up a hammer handle he has just "flowed" the finish onto. That's one pass with a lot of shellac.

time waiting for about two hours before filling again. Keep doubling the drying time after each application. Three or four fillings are usually needed before the wood is fully *choked*. Filling can be completed in a day, with adequate drying times. Filling of our little lauan samples took three applications, typically. Caution: If you repeatedly go over the filling without letting it dry, you will pull the pumice right back out of the grain. Each of us struggled to do it right the first time, but after messing up a few times we realized that the technique just isn't all that critical. Getting the feel of it — how wet, how much pressure, how much pumice — just takes some practice. In the end, the technique is very forgiving. The wood, when completely filled, should have a smear of varnish and pumice on the surface which can be spirited to a shine —*polished* wood.

When filling and finishing an actual guitar it is important to have both hands free much of the time. Therefore you will want to use a vise and/or clamping arrangement to secure the guitar so that you can work on it in all positions. Eugene likes the Versa-Vise and leather- or cork-covered maple blocks. Some of the work can be done with the instrument unsecured.

Thinned hide glue used directly on the wood, just like any sanding sealer, has been a traditional material for sizing and filling cabinet work and musical instruments. If you look closely at old Spanish guitars you will notice the lack of clarity in the finish caused by the use of glues and inert fillers. But Eugene admonishes that hide glue "likes" moisture, and that it has a low softening point. Around the world, finishers have often used filling methods that Eugene calls "waffle batter." Although we laughed, Eugene was perfectly serious when he said he had no objection to using whatever is available in the kitchen; he has reached for the Bon Ami, both for filler and rubout, but not for the eggs or the wheat flour.

Not a lot of class time was spent on resins other than shellac, but sandarac was mentioned. It dissolves readily in alcohol and has been used as a hardener in shellac finishing. In filling, a little sandarac can serve as a retarder to prevent buildup. However, shellac alone, once cured, is very tough, very plastic, and reasonably resistant to heat. The softening point is about 150°F. Shellac is nontoxic, especially if grain alcohol is used as a solvent. Shellac is edible, being used in the food and drug industry to coat candy, fruit, pills, and a multitude of other things.

We would not have time during the two-day class to build up or body the finish on our samples. However, Eugene demonstrated several techniques for "getting the stuff on." Our current standards and customer expectations require a finish that is thicker, more level, and uniformly more shiny than most of the finishes of the past.

One technique that Eugene called "flowing" uses the cheesecloth pad soaked with plenty of shellac varnish. The varnish can be thin or thick. Although flowing is like brushing, the shellac goes on with much more control and creates a smoother surface. If you have ever brushed shellac, you know how quickly the surface becomes very uneven. Holding a hammer by the head, Eugene slowly pushed the very wet pad of uncovered cheese cloth, loaded wet with shellac, down the handle. He cautioned to always move from dry to wet on the surface that you are padding, in a manner that avoids overlap. On a guitar surface you can pad a stripe of about one to two inches in width, lengthwise; skip an area equal in width; make another stripe; continue striping in that manner until you are all the way across. Let the finish dry, then complete the work by filling in the skipped areas. In this fashion, you can avoid the problems inherent in overlapping sticky applications.

Eugene was able to pass around the hammer after about ten minutes of drying. To accomplish the flowing technique successfully, the pad must hold enough finish to complete a full stroke. It must be wet. You must press the pad to the work just hard enough to feel a considerable drag in order that the varnish will "bite." As with any other skill, this one will take some practice. But, Eugene reassured us, it will be well worth the effort to learn the flowing technique for the time and labor that it can save. A finish bodied in this manner may be a little more brittle or chippy because of the absence of the plasticizing effect of an oil.

Hammer handle with new, smooth, flowed-on finish. It's dry enough to pass around in a few minutes.

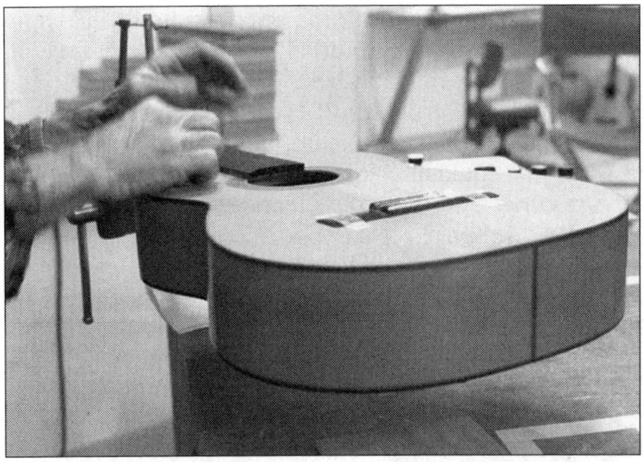

Do the tricky spots beside the fretboard and around the bridge first.

Eugene shows how to get close in when polishing with the bridge on.

Eugene's usual technique for bodying he sometimes describes as "paint and pull over." He applies as much shellac as possible using a long straight stroke followed immediately by a round stroke that "pulls over" the padding marks. Or the reverse, circles are "pulled over" by straight strokes. He starts out with light strokes (the wetter the pad, the faster and lighter the strokes), slowing down and increasing pressure as the pad dries. The figure-8 stroke, he says, is a turnaround stroke used to reverse the direction of the pad without stopping, since stopping would cause a "burn." It is particularly useful at the ends of the bridge and in the curve of the waist. By the way, Eugene may use pumice to help build the body coats faster (even on the top). When he does that, to insure a minimum of clouding of the finish, he combines the pumice with a little of the oil in a shallow dish or saucer, then deposits it onto the pad with a finger.

During bodying and stiffing he monitors his results by reading the light bulb in the finish. He warns that too much of looking at the glare on a shiny surface can cause an uncomfortable eye strain. He is not too much concerned about pad marks or swirls as the body coats go on, as these will be "pulled over" again with alcohol or spiriting solution (alcohol with a small amount of varnish added) toward the end of the finishing process, perhaps with the aid of a powdered abrasive. Seeing is less important than feeling right now. When the finish starts to feel soggy, as if you can't add any more, you are just moving it around and you may notice the surface getting ropy or orange peely — it is time to stiff the surface.

Stiffing is a pressure stroke, completed by stroking with the grain, and with the pad nearly dry, using only traces of oil and alcohol. It is a spiriting operation, with pressure. The bodying pad, with only traces of shellac remaining in it, will serve nicely for stiffing. A suitable amount of alcohol, maybe a single drop, is added to the pad and blotted on a paper towel. Or, a drop of alcohol can be put onto the hand, and a portion of it picked up on the pad. A trace! Go as slowly as possible without stalling, while pressing hard. Maintain a steamy vapor trail behind the pad. Stiff the finish with as much pressure as is practicable until it pulls over smooth, firms up, and suddenly clears. This process is essential for hardening the finish, and permits the addition of more finish right away. Stiffing will compact the resin coat, and will squeeze out excess oil, preventing soft finish and "printing." Be sure the pad is not saturated with oil. The pad can be rinsed out at any time, in a small container of alcohol. Alternate the application of finish with stiffing until you have completed a generous body coat. With as much stiffing as is needed, bodying can sometimes be done in a day.

How do you get into the tough places: the head, around the bridge, the side-heel intersection, the fingerboard-top intersection? Eugene says the Spanish makers have almost always finished their guitars with the bridge on. "You will, too," he says, "once you see how easy it is." The trick is to shape a small pad to fit the situation. Keep the cover loose. Press the pad into corners to achieve fit. Then apply varnish, solvent, and oil in small amounts, sometimes with a finger, *to select portions of the pad — not to the whole pad*. Put the varnish on the pad only where you need it. Blot as necessary. Begin in the corners and work out toward open areas. A spot-finishing technique is used. With the right amount of oil on the surface of the instrument, the shellac will "bite" only when sufficient pressure is applied, and otherwise will glide over the surface without effect. French polishing is a *pressure-feed* technique. The wings of a guitar bridge can often be done in this manner without masking off the top.

For the hard-to-reach places of the head, Eugene has sometimes used a thickened shellac and a "dry-transfer" technique. Or call it "burnishing." On the head scroll, for example, you can "shoe-shine" the shellac with a cloth that is almost dry. Dry means that there will be little or no odor of alcohol on the cloth. The shellac is burnished on and will fill grain. Instead of a pad, an strip of cheese cloth may be used. To get into the area between the saddle slot and the tieblock of the bridge, the cloth can be backed by a slender piece of wood. Any thick shellac will work for this. Eugene even puts finish on his pinky finger and waves it in the air for a moment to dry it a little, then rubs it into the head slots. That technique works well with a waxy shellac that has been thickened to a gel in a water bath.

A gel can be made from any *waxy* shellac using the water bath, which is a setup in which flammable liquids can be heated safely by immersing a container of the flammable liquid in a bath of water that is heated in a pot or saucepan over a heat source. The water bath is extremely dangerous unless all of the following precautions are taken. A capable fire extinguisher should be within reach. The pot or saucepan that serves as the water bath should have a well-fitting lid that can be applied immediately to smother a flameup. Eugene speaks from experience when he says, "You will have a flameup, sooner or later." The inner container that holds the flammable liquid (your shellac solution), usually a small heatproof jar, should be no taller than the sides of the pot so that the pot lid will fit on in a hurry. The water bath pot or saucepan should not have enough water in it to float the container of flammable liquid, or else tipping of the container is inevitable. Use a heavy-bottomed jar, not easily cracked, and small batches of flammable liquid. The jar should rest off the bottom of the pot or saucepan on a wire or wood screen, so that indirect heat is provided. A candy thermometer can be clipped to the side of the pot to monitor water temperature. *Warning — immersion into the hot alcohol solution of any dry chemical or other material or of any sort of stirring rod or other object, can cause a sudden boilover.* It can happen to you! Prepare for it. Many a home chemist has burned the house down making varnishes.

Is it dry yet?

To make a jell, start with a waxy shellac, such as Behlen's Button Shellac or LMI's Lemon I. Heat a shellac solution — a 20% solution works fine — to nearly the boiling point of alcohol, about 70°C or 170°F. Hold it there for a few minutes, stirring cautiously. Then set it aside to cool. When cool, the shellac will have jelled (peptized), and will stay that way. The cut, or concentration, will be unchanged, but the shellac will be thick and buttery.

Back on our samples, we were struggling to see if they were truly filled so that we could experience spiriting them off to a gloss. We had watched Eugene body his, but we were doing the "no-varnish varnish," which is very traditional. Here, the wood is filled completely, then the surface is spirited off. Only a "whisper" of finish remains on the surface. We were doing it that way for the same reason as those French polishers of old, in the interest of time.

Eugene does much of his polishing with uncovered cheese cloth except for final coats, where he covers the pad in order to get better control over the shape of the pad, and a smoother texture. The cover should be of an open-weave material, preferably 100% cotton. Old t-shirt material is probably best. Thin t-shirts, many times laundered, provide ideal covers that are soft, elastic, and porous. Such material does not form corners that could interfere with detail work. Old polo shirt material is a little too stiff, and does not feed as well. Percale bed sheets are poor because the weave is so tight that the cover will glaze over quickly, leaving you very soon with no friction and no feed. The purpose of a cover is to get control over the shape and firmness of the pad; to provide a bigger contact surface; and for a smoother varnish coat. Lacking a good cotton cover, try using a cheese-cloth pad with a cheese-cloth cover. It is not the worst.

Spiriting is for shining. Spiriting can be done with a trace of alcohol or spiriting solution, and a trace of oil. The spiriting solution is nothing but alcohol to which a tiny amount of varnish has been added, just enough to guarantee that the sprirting procedure will *add* a little shellac, rather than to *remove* a little. By using the spiriting solution, a surface that has been fine-sanded or compounded can be spirited smooth. Without the tiny amount of shellac present in the solvent, alcohol alone might not fully remove or "heal" all scratches. Hold the pad to your cheek. It should feel slightly moist and cool. Start with light, fairly quick passes, with the grain. As the pad becomes drier, a slower stroke is possible, as well as more pressure. In French polishing, the distinction between stiffing and spiriting may blur. It is the purposes that are different. To see the effects of your work, read the light bulb as you go. If the finish begins to feel tacky during spiriting, rest it for a half-hour or so, then resume spiriting.

Our samples were quite flat, and did not need to be sanded before spiriting. On a guitar, though, Eugene said he would always level the work toward the end of the varnishing with wet-or-dry paper or tripoli powdered abrasive, using water, or soap and water. This "flatting" or "leveling" can be done just before the final thin coat of varnish, and after bodying. Soak waterproof papers in water before use, so as to soften the backing. In the final spiriting you will be applying only enough shellac, if any, to eliminate scratches that were put there in leveling the surface. After spiriting and after drying, a rubout of some kind is generally necessary if you are looking for perfection.

How soon can you rub it out? The time will vary depending on the thickness of the body coat, and the amounts of drying time given to the bodying applications. But four or five days after the spiriting, the new surface should be firm enough to be brought to a perfect shine, and be ready for service. Eugene likes to finish the guitar off with a rub of diatomaceous earth, and has used water, soap and water, oils, and waxes for this rubout. He has rubbed guitars out using Meguiar's MGH10 (nonabrasive) as a medium. Experiment with your methods for achieving a final surface. Tripoli and diatomaceous earth are both progressive abrasives — that is, they break down as you rub with them. Pumice, being volcanic glass, does not break down so well. Even very fine pumice is coarser than tripoli, but it is not more aggressive. Tripoli is a fine powder from rock or mineral sources. Diatomaceous earth is the fossil remains of single-celled marine or fresh water algae. You can buy it at nurseries or through mail-order garden and farm supply houses. It may be available as a swimming pool filtering agent. In nurseries diatomaceous earth is sold as slug bait. Make sure no pesticides have been added. With powdered abrasives, Eugene rubs, wipes off, rubs, and wipes off, so that the surface has ever less of the abrasive. With continued rubbing, and by repeatedly decreasing the amount of abrasive remaining, the surface polishes out ever more brilliant. Two abrasives, tripoli and diatomaceous earth, will accomplish all the cutting and polishing from medium coarse to ultra fine.

JONATHON PETERSON

After his lecture on finishing at the '96 Healdsburg Guitar Festival, Eugene shows a French-polished Clark 8-string to a group of admirers.

Eugene polishes with a piece of well-worn Turkish towel, a square of about 4″×4″, wrapped around a hard felt block or folded into a pad. He is very particular about the toweling. His cloth is light in weight, with a short nap — something lighter than a fancy bath towel, and heavier than a flimsy one. He uses the same square many times over, washing well as often as needed. Keeping abrasive powders wetted in a little water will help keep them out of your lungs, where the same sharp edges that make your finish shine so nicely can lodge and cause damage (silicosis). Eugene calls diatomaceous earth the Micro-mesh® of powdered abrasives. It is a component of some commercially available products. Novus II is said to contain diatomaceous earth.

Eugene sometimes brings a guitar to a final sheen with a favorite piece of the ubiquitous Turkish toweling, dampened and blotted. A drop of mineral oil, along with the trace of water remaining in the cloth, will clean and impart a fine gloss to many surfaces. One can complete the shining by rubbing down with a dry cloth such as a well-washed cotton diaper or a small hand towel. He suspects that rubbing with these traces of water and oil may reflow the surface at the molecular level. Not all surfaces respond the same. But this very old technique for cleaning and preserving was standard practice in the U.S. Army Signal Corps, where he had ample opportunity to practice on a variety of surfaces. Almost everything in the radio station was cleaned and shined in the same fashion — desks, chairs, lamps, silk-screened equipment panels, telegraph keys, microphones — wood, glass, plastic, chrome, rubber, and so on.

For a final surface that is extra hard and resistant to smudging, wipe the swatch of dampened toweling on a block of pure carnauba wax, then rub the finish in order to glaze or seal the surface with a dry-transfer technique, afterward toweling off with a soft cloth. Explaining this procedure, Eugene says, "I am not waxing the guitar, only filling or sealing the surface of the shellac."

What can go wrong? If you are using pure shellac, with some understanding of your materials, chances are you will do fine. Here are some problems and possible causes: fisheye, or bald spots in the finish — that is, the finish doesn't take in places. You may have silicone contamination. Silicone, even in parts per million, will act as a parting agent to prevent adhesion of the shellac. If you have ever bought "fisheye killer," it is silicone oil. Throw it away. Eliminate all silicone from your shop. Don't buy anything with silicone in it or on it. Another problem, soft finish and printing, may be caused by using shellac that has been in solution too long, or it may be caused by an excess of oil in the finish from using an oil-saturated pad. Sometimes a good stiffing with a clean pad will correct it. Ropiness is the result of applying too much finish without adequate drying time between applications. The finish shifts like sand dunes under the pressure of the pad. Pimpling may result from polishing a cold surface, the chill that is typical of night polishing, perhaps aggravated by the presence of pumice.

After two days of watching, listening, and trying some of these techniques, I went home eager to apply them to a guitar. The class was inspirational, and it was a great opportunity being there to experience first hand. I hope this once-removed version of the workshop will help you in your finishing attempts, and will encourage you in your experimentation. ——

Originally published in *American Lutherie #53*, 1998

Semihemispherical Fret Ends

by Harry Fleishman

SEVERAL YEARS AGO I became frustrated with the way my fret ends, in fact all fret ends, felt and the hassles I went through to deal with them. No matter how careful I was, I always seemed to mar the fingerboard if I took the fret ends to where they felt right. Also, the string wanted to slide off the end of the taper, and my hand felt each fret end like a hurdle as I moved up or down the neck.

At some point I thought of putting a quarter-spherical shape on the fret ends, thus extending their playing range and eliminating the offending edges. Since it is clearly the tiny little fret flange that tends toward sharpness, right down at the fingerboard's edge where the crown meets the board, I decided that I should deal with that to solve the problem.

The problem was how to get rid of the sharpness without scarring the fingerboard and defeating my entire anal-retentive plan. The solution was to fit the full set of frets, shaping and rounding, *before* installing. Sounds like fun, eh? It isn't really so bad once you understand the process. I have now tried several different means to achieving this end (I know, no pun intended, no pun taken) and have reduced the fret time to under two hours, finished, buffed, and ready to string. That's not much longer, if any, than it used to take me the old way. It's not factory speed, but on a custom guitar or special refret, it is worth it. This way, once I put them in, the fret ends are done.

The procedure is relatively straightforward and only takes a few tools, none terribly specialized or expensive. You should probably have them for any decent fretwork. The only requirement is that the board must be bound. I generally don't like the look of bound fingerboards, so I use ebony or rosewood to match the rest of the board. But this technique would be fine with any style of binding, and I have used it with wood, fiber, and abalone purflings. You can fret before or after gluing the fretboard on, but I tend to fret last, after the instrument is otherwise finished, which may not be so bright.

First, design the board to accommodate the binding and slot it without the binding in place. (Duh.) Slot it to just over the tang size you will use, but do not include the barbs when measuring. You will not need to deal with them. The second step is to strip the barbs off,

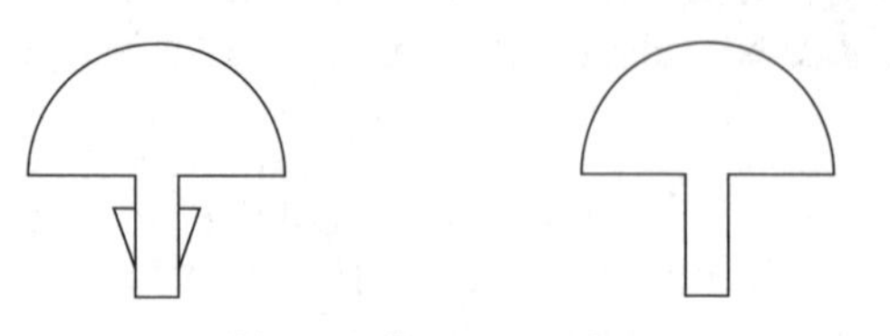

Figure 1. Fret cross sections

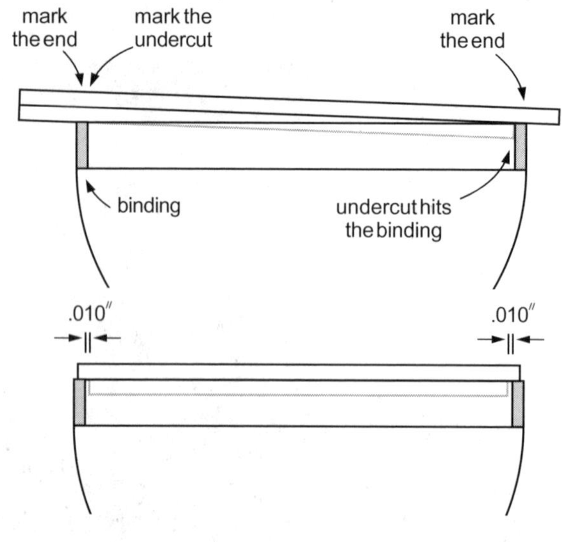

Figures 2 and 3. Fret length and undercuts

á la Erlewine in his great video, *Don't Fret.* This leaves you with several lengths of fretwire with a consistently barbless tang, as shown in **Fig. 1.** In other words, if you have a .022″ fret tang, sans barb, use a .023″ slot.

Next, bend the wire using a fretbender if you have one (and you should) to just under the radius of the board. That is, if your board has a 20″ radius, bend to a 19″ radius or so. This way the fret is going to be flush in the slot if you put slight pressure in the middle; the ends will not stick up and ruin your party.

Now for the fun part. You can either prepare all the frets at this point, or you can do two at a time, leapfrogging your way down the neck. That is now my preference, thanks to my severe aversion to repetitive tasks. Snip the end of one fret, and undercut the crown using the fret-end nipper reviewed in *American Lutherie #31* (see *Big Red Book of American Lutherie Volume Three*, p. 437), or use a file and waste a lot of time and material. The end nipper tends to put a tiny bend in the tang, which isn't a problem with conventional fretting, so make sure that it is nice and straight using the Stew-Mac fret masher. Lay this fret in the slot and up against the binding at one end of that slot. On the fret crown, mark both that edge of the fingerboard as well as the other end, as in **Fig. 2.** Then cut the fret precisely to length and undercut the second end. It should have a tang about .020″ shorter than the slot (.010″ for each end, as in **Fig. 3**) to allow for shrinkage of the board in the future.

If you have followed this at all, you should have a fret which can be pressed into the slot with its crown right out to the edges of the fingerboard. Once you get the hang of this you can actually cut the frets about .010″ short, but for now don't sweat the small stuff.

Using a diamond file (or some other really fine file, which wouldn't be nearly as easy, quick, or fun), round the ends to a sort of quarter-spherical shape, shown in **Fig. 4**. If the fret crown is .050″ tall, you will have a .025″ or so setback from the end of the fret to the crown because of the curve. This is less than a standard bevel and feels much better. Take them to the buffing wheel and buff the heck out of the ends using tripoli. This will leave them shiny and round and delightful. Do two of them if you are leapfrogging, and go back to your fingerboard. Otherwise, do them all and move on to the next step.

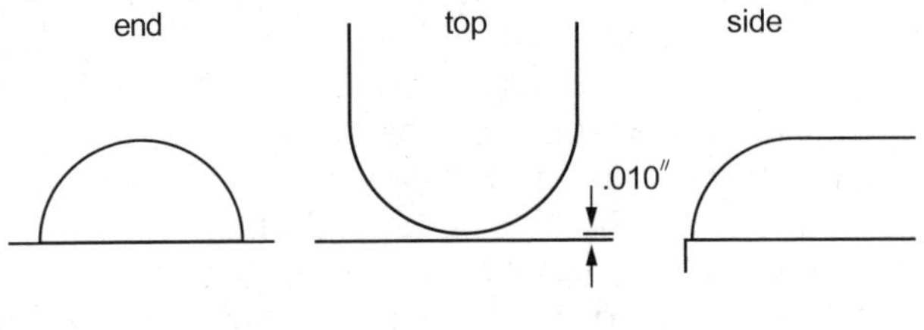

Figure 4. Fret end shape

Place the frets in the board, carefully setting each one in the right direction. Remember, you fitted it one way, not the other; it must go in the same way. Then put a drop or two of thin superglue on each side of the fret at the junction of the crown and the board, as shown in **Fig. 5**, not each end of the fret. It should wick in, under the fret and to the tang. Then put a scrap of soft wood over the two frets and clamp them down gently. You shouldn't need much pressure if you fitted them correctly and bent them just under the radius of the board. The time it takes to make the next two frets will be more than enough time for the glue to set. You can go ahead and unclamp, repeating the process until you run out of slots or it's time for lunch.

If no one has called to invite you out for a quick, two-hour coffee, now is the time to hit the frets with Uncure, a superglue remover that takes off the teensy bit of slop from glue squeeze-out or spillage from tremors. Simply polish the fret edges (not ends) and board between frets with a drop of this on a soft cloth and you're in business. Be careful! This stuff ruins lacquer.

If your board is accurately made and the frets are too, you should have little or no milling to do. I tape off and hit any high spots with a bit of sticky 320 paper on a piece of ½″ glass, giving it a light once-over, carefully avoiding the ends. Then I quickly sand with 400 and buff with tripoli. At this point I do a last dry-wheel polish, wipe it down, remove the tape, and gloat. ——

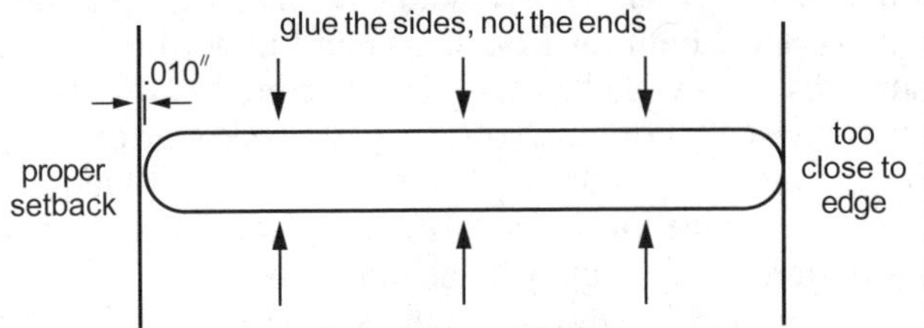

Figure 5. Gluing the fret

Originally published in *American Lutherie #49, #54 and #57*, 1997–1999

QUESTIONS

EDITED BY CYNDY BURTON

■ ***Peter Henningsen from Anne Marie, Denmark** asks:*

I recently received instrument plans from you with the string gauges given as numbers. I have found nobody around here who knows the diameter of a No. 6 musical wire, for example.

***John Calkin from Greenville, VA** responds:*

Here's an abbreviated chart from Howie Mitchell's *The Hammered Dulcimer* for spring brass and phosphor bronze wire:

Browne & Sharpe (B&S) gauge with diameter in inches

20 .0319	22 .0253	24 .0201	26 .0159
21 .0284	23 .0225	25 .0179	

Spring steel music wire
American Standard Gauge with diameter in inches

1 .010	4 .013	7 .018	10 .024
2 .011	5 .014	8 .020	11 .026
3 .012	6 .016	9 .022	12 .029

■ ***Ricardo Reyes of Williston, SC** asks:*

I need to find out what kind of clay is used in the position marker cavities of the old fretboards so I can do some restoration work on a vintage Fender. If possible I want to use the exact clay presently used by Fender.

***Tim Shaw of Fender/Nashville, TN** responds:*

I run the Guild Custom Shop. I checked with the Fender Custom Shop to get the scoop. The original clay material is unfortunately lost in antiquity. The guys in the Custom Shop do dots one of three ways:

1. Use the new production dots, which are punched out of sheet plastic. (I suspect it's ABS.)
2. Make dots out of Micarta. (Exact diameter is .250″.)
3. Use Famowood, a filler product, slightly thinned. This shrinks back like the clay did.

■ ***Stephen Bacon of Ashland, OR** comments on epoxy used as filler:*

Epoxy should not be used on old instruments. I'm working on my second Portuguese viola restoration and am appalled at early repair work, especially the layer of epoxy on the table as a leveler. Let's keep preplastic instruments plastic free, or at least reversible. I'm told by Joseph Grubaugh that there is an acrylic dissolvable by turpentine. Does anyone know where to get some?

Bradley Bischoff of Benton Harbor, MI responds:

The spirit varnish is called Soluvar and is a liquitex product made by Binney and Smith, Easton, PA. It is available in most all art supply stores in either gloss or matte. It really works great as a crack filler. ——

Originally published in *American Lutherie #54*, 1998

Meet the Maker: Joseph Curtin

by Tim Olsen

On MAIN STREET in the college town of Ann Arbor, Michigan, there is a drum shop with brightly colored signs and flashy percussion gear in the windows. Next to the drum shop is a plain green locked door. I rang the bell and was admitted to a flight of stairs leading up to an airy, well-lit space, sparely decorated with framed paintings and photos, and furnished with a simple sofa, chair, and lamp.

I was met by Joseph Curtin, a gracious, well-dressed young man who seems as pleasant and open as his surroundings. Working here with one shop assistant and one office assistant, he builds about fifteen instruments a year, mostly violins and a few violas.

Five rooms open off this central space: an office, a finish room, a tool room, a small kitchen, and a shop. The shop's neatness is almost shocking to a hippie-era guitar repairman such as myself, for whom lutherie was always inextricably associated with dust, chaos, and clutter. The focal point of this shop is a drawing board.

The tool room is very small, and the largest thing in it is an industrial-grade dust collector. Tools include a disk sander, a spindle sander, and a drill press set up with a micrometer stop. There is also a bandsaw which is surprisingly large to be in such a small room, a large router with a 1″ round-nose bit used freehand for hogging out plates, and an overhead router for establishing accurate thicknesses on plate edges.

ALL BY TIM OLSEN EXCEPT AS NOTED

The frontmost room has a large window overlooking the street. A prefab slab of kitchen counter top is set before the window, and the scores of little jars, bottles, mixing trays, and brushes that are the tools of traditional varnish application are spread across it and on the adjacent shelves. The room contains little else besides a chair and a drying box fitted with UV fluorescent tubes.

I spoke a while with Joseph Curtin about his early training, his interest in violin tradition, research, and innovation, and his association with other makers and researchers. I made some notes, and we fleshed out the interview later by e-mail.

How did you get started in lutherie?

In the late seventies I was studying viola in Toronto with Rivka Golani, who was then married to the violin maker Otto Erdesz. I had become discouraged with my playing — there was nothing I wanted to do more than play well, but I was a late starter and it began to seem impossible that I would ever be really good. I still wonder how far I might have gone if I had kept at it, though I have absolutely no regrets about going into making. I had tried to make a violin when I was fourteen and newly in love with the instrument, but did not get far. However, when the time came that I felt I needed a profession away from performing, the idea resurfaced, undoubtedly inspired by seeing Otto at his bench. At first the notion seemed a dull one — to be shut up in a room full of sawdust by myself all day. In fact I quickly found I loved it, I suppose because the aptitudes it required — a sense of line and confidence in one's hands — were ones I was comfortable with. I spent much of my childhood drawing, designing, and building things. I was twenty-three when Otto offered to teach me. I watched him working for a year, then he set up a bench for me in his studio, and I built my first instrument under his supervision, a viola based on his asymmetrical "cut-away" design. I quit my job as a pizza waiter after buying my tools, and set up on my own, going to him for frequent advice for the next several years. I have been more or less earning my living at it ever since.

After several years under Otto's supervision, I decided to move to Europe. This was not for professional reasons, but more from a sense of wanting to live there. I went to Cremona, had fun working with Gregg Alf for a month, but found the place rather depressing. The standards of making seemed low, and it was not at all like Paris, where I wanted to live. For a few years I went back and forth between the two places, and a lot of others. I was completely out of violin making circles in Paris, but learned a lot in Cremona while working with Gregg, and we decided to set up a business together in America. After Otto, the most profound education I got was from trying to make exact copies of old instruments with Gregg. I eventually felt I'd had enough of this kind of work, but for a long time it seemed an exciting thing to do — like taking master classes with Guarneri and Stradivari themselves. I'd recommend it to any young maker.

Facing page: Joseph Curtin shows off his latest instrument.
Above: Shop assistant Sharon Que at her bench.
Below: Joseph's tidy workbench.

Do you repair and deal in violins?

I decided from the outset to devote myself exclusively to making new instruments. This was partly a matter of pride and it might have seemed a bold decision, but I had seen Otto doing well at it, and thought, "Why not." I have little aptitude for either restoration or dealing, so there was really no conflict, though I must say I sometimes wish I could blame someone else, such as a long-dead maker, when an instrument does not work out!

I understand that you and Gregg Alf are no longer working together as Curtin & Alf.

Gregg and I worked together for twelve years, and we both learned a huge amount in doing so. I think we were both ready for something different. It had become a complex and exhausting enterprise, and we thought life might be simpler if we divided it in two. We work independently now, though we remain on good terms, and collaborate occasionally on projects of mutual interest.

The first time I heard your name was during Geary Baese's lecture at our 1988 convention in Vermillion, South Dakota. What do you think of his work on Classical-era varnish formulation?

I met Geary in Cremona in the mid-'80s. He was completing research for his varnish book and I was passionately curious about old varnishes. After he told me some of his findings, I couldn't sleep for several nights. I was tremendously excited that someone seemed to have worked out the old formulas, and simultaneously a little annoyed that it hadn't been me, and very eager to try working with the stuff. I was using seedlac varnishes at the time, and felt I'd gone as far as I could with them. Oil varnish offered all sorts of new possibilities, though it took a while to learn to use it well. I have subsequently used Geary's varnishes extensively, and find them to be wonderful. They were used on all the replicas I did with Gregg. Of course, like any art material, the end result depends on your eye — the look you are trying to get and your ability to manipulate the medium successfully to get it. Having a good varnish formula, I quickly learned, is no guarantee you'll get a good-looking violin. But it's a great place to start, and I'll always be grateful for Geary's work.

You are interested in scientific analysis of the violin. How fruitful has this been for your work?

I met Carleen Hutchins at a Viola Congress in Boston. I think it was in 1986. She was the first one to wake me up to the fact that a violin functions not by a succession of miracles, but within the framework of natural law. At first I was resistant to this point of view, as I think a lot of makers are, but very soon I became committed to trying to understand as much as I could. I feel very fortunate to live in the same town as Gabriel Weinreich, one of the outstanding figures in the field of

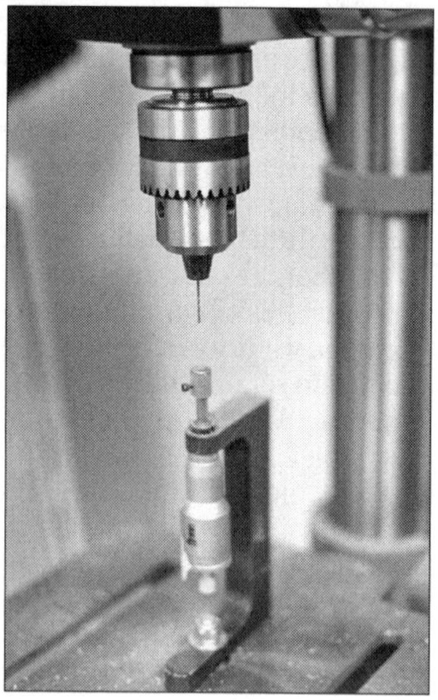

musical acoustics, and even more fortunate for his patience in answering my questions and helping clarify many physical concepts that seemed at first utterly opaque. Over the years I have collaborated with him on several projects, the Reciprocal Bow being one, and I cannot emphasize enough how important this relationship has been to me. The violin is a complex thing. Almost every "intuitive" notion I had of how it works proved, in fact, to be wrong. Of course, this is normal; our naïve ideas are gradually refined by re-examining them against the evidence. But unless you are a trained scientist, you do need help in making sense of things, and Gabi provided that help generously. I am also indebted to Oliver Rogers, French physicist Xavier Boutillon, whom I met through Gabi, and more recently, Charles Besnainou, a research scientist and instrument maker who has pioneered the use of carbon-fiber composites in concert instruments. We are working together on a project I find terrifically exciting — the use of composites for top-end violins. So yes, the scientific perspective has been very fruitful for my work — I mean directly so — influencing everything from choice of materials to setup and evaluation.

I will say at the same time that violin making has an artistic component that is in no way incompatible with a scientific approach. That, for me, is the miracle of the violin; it engages these two sides of our nature with equal force.

Anyone whose shop centers on a drafting board must have some new design ideas.

I'm currently engaged in "Project Evia" — Evia standing for experimental viola. I'm trying to take a fresh look at the instrument from all points of view — aesthetic, ergonomic, and acoustical, plus the choice of materials. Version One looks back to the viola da gamba for its shape, though I've changed the proportions and many details. The sloping shoulders allow the player lots of room, and the simplified corners and *f*-holes have a contemporary look to me. To go along with this I made a single-turn scroll, which I love. The neck is held in place with a single small bolt through the upper block, and the neck height is readily adjustable. The first prototype is made with traditional high-quality woods. Then I will try plates using carbon fiber and wood composites, and then, well, I'll see where it leads. I have a whole series of ideas to try. It is wonderful to feel you are making up the rules as you go along, trying to base your decisions on a sense of beauty and musical function rather than tradition.

How do you feel about violin-making competitions?

I've been to most of the meetings of the Violin Society of America over the past two decades. I've always — except in my very earliest years — exhibited my work rather than entering the competitions, probably because I never had a "competition style" and didn't find the spirit of competition brought out the best in my making. So I have no awards of any sort, not even a college degree for that matter. But I'm glad they have the competitions and think they've done the profession a lot of good. The VSA is wonderful. It has given me a substantial portion of my education as a maker — through the lectures and the people I meet at conferences, and more recently, through the lectures I've given, which have forced me to clarify my thinking on many issues. I like the fact that, unlike some of the other organizations, it is wide open. Anyone can join. Although this means there are some very silly conversations going on, the fact is that many of the researchers who have most influenced me would not be allowed into the strictly professional societies.

Where do your instruments go?

They go to college students, professional orchestral players, chamber musicians, soloists — Yehudi Menuhin, Erick Friedman, Csaba Erdelyi, and of course Ruggiero Ricci, Elmar Oliveira, and Donald McInnes from Curtin & Alf days. Most recently two members of the Hagen Quartet from Austria purchased a violin and a viola.

I've got clients in many orchestras, including the Berlin Philharmonic, London Philharmonia, Cleveland Orchestra, and Seattle Symphony, including a number of concertmasters and other principal players. Most of my clients are in America now, some are in Canada, and a good many in Europe and even further afield. Of course it's always exciting when a great player takes an interest, but it's also really gratifying when a talented student who has never had a good instrument buys one, and you feel you've helped them find their voice, which I suppose is what the profession is really about.

What woods do you like? Being here in Michigan, I wonder if you have looked at any of that fabled century-old Lake Superior wood?

I use more American wood than European these days, though I have a good stock of each. Some of my best instruments have been made with red maple from northern Michigan and Engelmann spruce from the West Coast. There is good wood from all over. The most important thing is knowing what properties you are looking for. The Lake Superior wood has a good story, but so far they've found mostly hard maple, which is too dense for me. It is in beautiful condition, though, and it's wonderful that they are recovering it. One is reminded of how rich we were in forests and how quickly they were squandered.

The thing that gets me angry is going to a tonewood dealer and finding all the spruce is sawn, so at least fifty percent is useless due to runout. Many dealers do this, saying they get a better yield. In any real sense the yield is much lower. What they mean is they can sell it anyway to unwitting makers; it is often difficult to see runout in sawn wood. I'd love to see makers get together on this and put pressure on dealers to do better. I salute Bruce Harvie of Orcas Island Tonewoods as a dealer I love to work with — he's concerned about forests, knows wood, keeps prices down, and splits his spruce.

Yes, Bruce is a fine musician, a guy with a great sense of humor, and handsome as the very devil!
Tell me about the people who work with you.

Sharon Que has worked with me for nine years, first at Curtin & Alf, and now at my new studio. She's a mixed-media artist who used to work at GM as a wood model maker. Her art career is flourishing, and she spends four days a week helping me. A superb craftsperson, highly creative, utterly reliable — I always feel a moment of panic when she talks about going on vacation. The same with Nancy Skinner-Oclander, my business manager. She's been with me for three years, and when she's not — these two weeks for example — things descend gradually into chaos. Sharon and I agree she's the perfect balance for us — outgoing where we tend to be introverted. Nancy has a rare combination of business talent and love for the arts. I feel enormously lucky to work with such people, and hope they stay around for a very long time!

You keep a pretty high profile in the fiddle magazines. I assume you find that advertising to be cost effective.

I don't suppose there's a need for it if you live in New York or a major center where there is a constant stream of musicians dropping by. But I do most of my business by FedEx and telephone, and the ads keep the phones ringing. Besides, I think it's good when makers get the word out about their work — not to go against each other, but to let musicians know there are alternatives to antique instruments.

What are your goals in violin making?

I'll continue to refine my work — the look, the sound. I want to understand better how violins work — that seems vital. And more and more I want to work with innovation: new aesthetics, new materials, new designs. I'm convinced that big changes are ahead, and I can't think of anything more fun than being in on them. The profession tends to have something of an overdeveloped immune system when it comes to new ideas. But that is changing rapidly. A good number of highly qualified makers are trying new things. I believe it will catch on. Look at how well bow makers are doing with composites. Musicians are open to it. I can't imagine a better time in history to be a violin maker!

Besides violins?

My wife Jesse Richards and I go for Japanese food and a movie almost every Friday night. We love this ritual. She's a performance artist, composer, choreographer, jeweler, and a passionate advocate for animals, which she adores. We live out of town on a river, and our black lab takes me out daily. My avocation is sitting in a cafe with my laptop and writing fiction. If I don't get my writing time in, I start to get cranky. One day I want to write a manual for violin makers. I suppose that will have to be nonfiction! ——

SHARON QUE

Facing page, left: Joseph Curtin's finishing room enjoys natural lighting and a bird's-eye view of Main Street. Right: This micrometer mounted to a drill press makes a very accurate depth guide for graduating violin plates. Above: Business manager Nancy Skinner-Oclander.

Originally published in *American Lutherie #54*, 1998

It's Called a What?
Some Thoughts on the Irish Bouzouki
by Graham McDonald

THE DOUBLE-STRUNG IRISH BOUZOUKI has become very popular as it has evolved over the last twenty-five years, especially in the Celtic music community; but little has been written about the instrument, its origins, or the way in which it is built.

The Irish bouzouki (or octave mandolin or cittern) is a hybrid instrument. The precise history of the instrument is somewhat lost in folklore, but sometime in the late '60s some Irish musicians ended up with a Greek bouzouki, and found that it sounded rather good as a backing instrument for their songs and dance music. The Greek bouzouki is tuned CFAD, two semitones below the top four strings of a guitar, with octave strings on the 3rd and 4th courses. The Irish players evolved a GDAD tuning an octave lower than the mandolin with the top strings tuned down to D and unison strings for the bottom two courses. Since Irish music is mostly in the keys of G and D, this tuning meant that both the 1st and 4th strings could be played open as drones, and allowed chords and melody to be played around them.

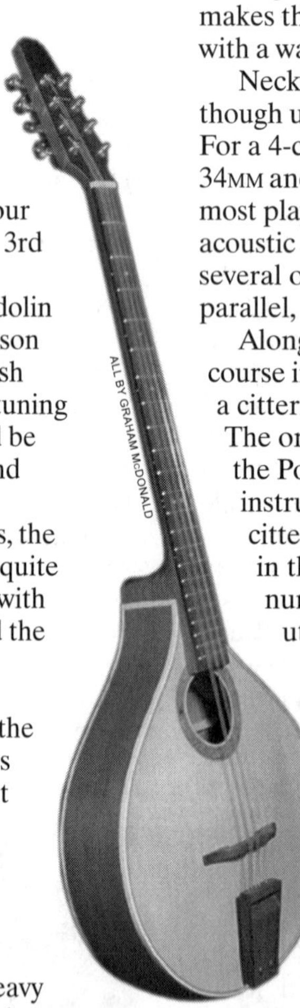

ALL BY GRAHAM McDONALD

As anyone who has ever played one knows, the bowl back of the Greek instrument makes it quite hard to play standing up. Someone came up with the idea of building them with flat backs, and the Irish bouzouki was born.

The Greek instrument commonly has a 660mm (26″) or so scale length, and many of the builders of the new flat-back variety kept this scale length along with a flat soundboard that utilized a low floating bridge, and a mandolin-style tailpiece. The 660mm scale is the usual maximum, but builders normally offer a variety of string lengths, down to around 510mm (21″), which is about the shortest you can go with a GDAD tuning without really heavy strings. Longer strings seem to give more richness and texture to the tone, to my ears at least. The bottom of the fingerboard is usually in the same plane as the top between the neck/body joint and the bridge, or kicked back only slightly. This makes the bridge quite low, usually 10mm–15mm, and the break angle over the bridge rather shallow. The top bracing is variable, from a couple of simple transverse braces to a guitar-style X.

Bodies are usually a teardrop shape of one sort or another, often scaled-up mandolin shapes. Mine are 400mm long, 350mm wide, and 90mm–100mm deep, which for a 660mm scale means a body join at the 17th fret. I use a 75mm diameter soundhole for no real reason other than it looks right with that size body. There is a lot of variety in body shape and size, and mine have certainly grown in size over the years. The teardrop shape is the most common, but there is no reason why any shape cannot be used. I have built quite a few with a small guitar-type body which, having a waist, has the advantage of being much easier to rest on the leg. Having a long neck and eight to ten machine heads makes these instruments neck heavy, so a longer body with a waist is of some advantage.

Neck profiles are similar to a steel string guitar, though usually narrower, and an adjustable rod is usual. For a 4-course instrument my neck width at the nut is 34mm and 44mm at the 12th fret, which seems to suit most players. This is about the same flare as a standard acoustic guitar. For reasons I have never understood, several of the Irish builders keep the strings almost parallel, but I think it looks strange.

Alongside the 4-course bouzouki has evolved a 5-course instrument which luthier Stephan Sobell dubbed a cittern, after a 16th-century wire-strung instrument. The original idea for these instruments owes a lot to the Portuguese guittara, a short-scale 6-course instrument with a floating bridge. The modern citterns are usually a shorter scale than bouzoukis, in the range of 510mm–610mm (21″–24″), and a number of tunings are commonly used, usually utilizing fifths between the courses. There is ongoing discussion about what to call this family of instruments, but there now seems to be a slowly forming consensus that long-scale 4-course instruments are bouzoukis, shorter-scale 5-course instruments are citterns, and anything else gets called whatever the maker wants to call it.

While the Greek bouzouki uses octave strings on the lower two courses, the Irish bouzouki usually is strung with unison strings. On my standard 26″ 4-course GDAD bouzouki (if in fact there is a standard anything in this family of instruments) I suggest .010″, .017″p, .030″, .040″ strings, but I know of others who use a .012″, .020″w, .032″, .042″ set, or some similar mix of stringing. I worked out the gauges for the first set mentioned above using graphs I drew up and that were published in *American Lutherie #2*. (See *Big Red Book of American Lutherie Volume One*, p. 78.) These enable you to work out tensions for strings of various gauges and pitches, though there is now a nifty bit of computer software available on the Internet for doing this. It is for PCs only, which is annoying for Mac users. For shorter scale instruments, the strings will obviously need to be heavier, and for a 22″ 4-course, the top string would be .012″–.013″, and the bottom G string would be around a .045″–047″. Once you get into 5-course instruments, with at least four or five common tunings used, it is a matter of going back to the calculator to work it out.

I'm the first to admit that my understanding of the various resonance modes of soundboards is imperfect, and while there has been lots of work done with guitars and violins, I don't know of any experimental work done with bouzoukis and citterns. These instruments are somewhere between guitars and violins in size and tuning, so I figured that if at least the basic air and top resonances were somewhere between fiddle and guitar resonances, I might be on the right track. One reason for using a guitar-shaped body for a bouzouki was the idea that I wanted an instrument that had the same sort of resonance and string-to-string balance as a guitar. The bottom string on a bouzouki is usually tuned to the same G as the 3rd fret on the bottom string of a guitar, so it seemed reasonable to use a body much the same size and air volume as a guitar to get some more bottom-end grunt. Good guitars usually have their basic soundboard resonance around G# on the bottom string, so it seemed reasonable that a guitar-bodied bouzouki should work with its resonance in the same relative position, four frets up on the bottom string. So I aim for a resonance around B–C on the bottom G string on a guitar-bodied bouzouki, with the air resonance a little below that. The smaller body of the teardrop-shaped instruments I look at differently. They are going to have a thinner, brighter sound, without as much richness in the bottom string. This is often the sound people want because it allows the bouzouki to be played along side a guitar without the instruments muddying each other. For example, listen to the Bothy Band recordings from the late '70s. However, others want more of a well-rounded solo instrument. The teardrop instruments seem to work best with a resonance between C# and E (somewhere around the open D string), again with the air resonance a little lower. What I don't know is what is happening with the higher vibrational modes of the soundboard. Have a look at Graham Caldersmith's articles in back issues of *American Lutherie* for the most understandable explanation of this.

Noted Irish musician Donal Lunny mentioned to me that just about all the teardrop-shaped instruments he has played over the years have a resonance peak around 220Hz. This would be the second top resonance mode, I suppose, with undoubtedly lots of others at higher frequencies.

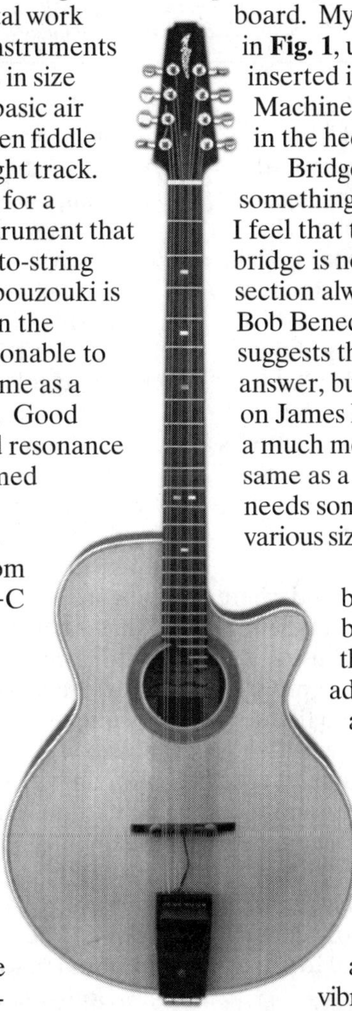

The teardrop-shaped bouzouki (opposite) has become somewhat traditional, and its thinner tone can offer it a timbral advantage in a band setting. The guitar-shaped model (above) offers better physical balance and increased bass response, making it a better choice for solo work.

Necks are attached in the same multitude of ways that people put necks on guitars. I like the idea of the neck/fretboard built as a separate unit to the body, preferably with the neck extending the full length of the board. My current method of attaching necks, shown in **Fig. 1**, uses a mortise and tenon with barrel nuts inserted into horizontally drilled holes in the tenon. Machine bolts are inserted through matching holes in the heel block.

Bridge design for archtop instruments is something for which no one has a definitive answer. I feel that the standard two-footed Gibson-style bridge is not very efficient acoustically, and the top section always seems to eventually sag in the middle. Bob Benedetto, in *Making an Archtop Guitar,* suggests that a light violin-type bridge might be the answer, but an article in *AL#37* (see *BRBAL4*, p. 2) on James D'Aquisto's instruments showed him using a much more massive bridge with a footprint much the same as a flattop bridge. It is one of those areas that needs some scientific analysis of what bridges of various size and materials do to the sound. One day....

I use a two-footed bridge with top and bottom sections, the top part located by two brass pins but otherwise fully in contact with the bottom part. If the height needs to be adjusted it can be shimmed or planed down, and it is also then practical to use an undersaddle pickup (one of the full-width sensing ones) by routing a slot in the upper section of the bridge and fitting a bone saddle. The output lead of the pickup can then run out of a curved slot in the bottom part.

Tailpieces should be massive enough so as not to absorb too much of the string vibration. Most makers use either a metal mandolin or wooden archtop guitar-style tailpiece. The main problem I see with the mandolin-style tailpiece is that they tend to take only loop-end strings,

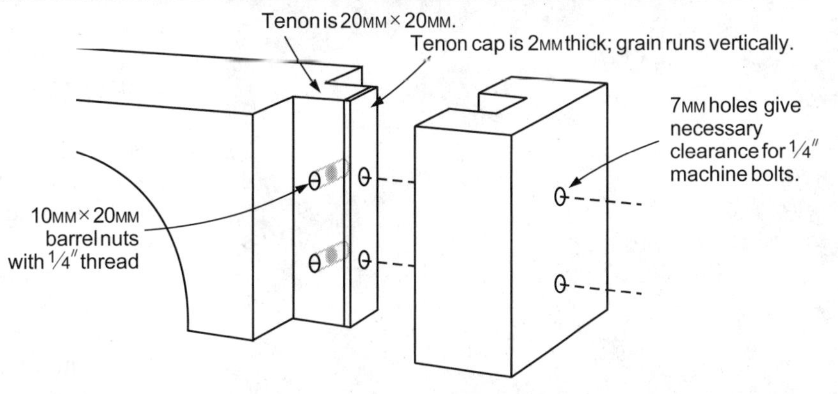

***Figure 1.** The author's bouzouki necks bolt on, and feature barrel nuts mounted in the tenon.*

and it is much easier to find ball-end single strings than loop-ends. Bouzoukis and citterns need sets of strings that have to be made out of the singles box in the music shop. I make my tailpieces from rosewood or ebony, and attach them to the instrument with stainless-steel hinges obtained from ships' chandlers. They are about 2MM thick and as solid as you want.

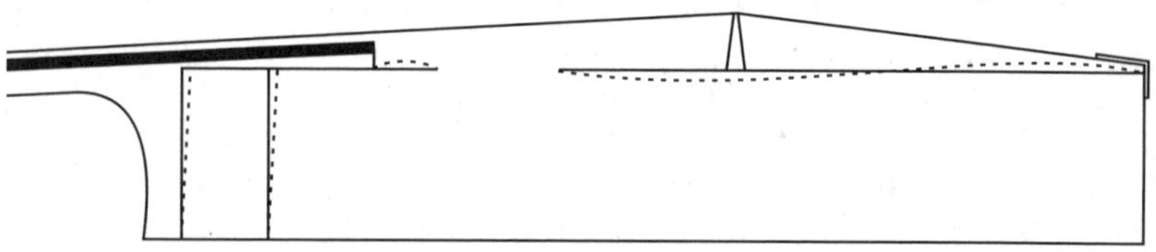

Figure 2. A flattop Irish bouzouki distorts in the manner of the dotted line. McDonald decided that there was no easy solution to this design problem, and abandoned it.

Over the years there have developed two main approaches to the way in which Irish bouzoukis and citterns are built. The first is with a flat soundboard, usually somewhat curved laterally through bracing, and a fairly low floating bridge as mentioned above. The second method uses a carved, arched soundboard, again with a floating bridge but of a height of approximately 25MM, similar to a Gibson mandolin bridge.

There are also a couple other ways of going about it. One approach is to build the instrument with a flat top and a pin bridge, like ⅔ of a 12-string guitar. The English company Fylde has built bouzoukis and citterns like this for many years, and it does make putting them together a lot easier (especially if you have built guitars), and the sound is not very different from a floating bridge.

There is also the bent- or cranked-top method where a transverse bend is put in the soundboard just behind the bridge as is usual with Neapolitan mandolins. I built a few of these some years back, routing a groove on the inside of the assembled soundboard and then bending it over a hot pipe. Transverse braces with a reasonable arch were then glued on, and the top attached to the sides with tentellones. Getting the sides and top lined up was a bit tricky, but that's why they invented bindings. The main reason I experimented with the cranked top was for strength. Putting that bend in the soundboard adds a great deal of strength to offset both the downward and longitudinal compressional forces at work.

As an aside, I was interested to note that in Robert Lundberg's article on Neapolitan mandolins in *AL#46*

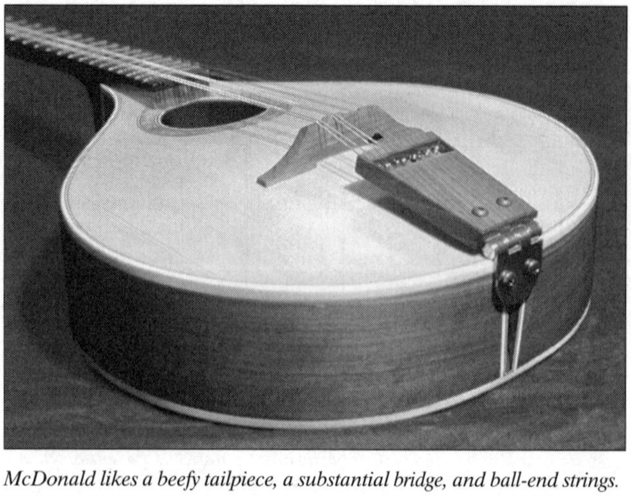

McDonald likes a beefy tailpiece, a substantial bridge, and ball-end strings.

(see *BRBAL4*, p. 316), he says that the old makers would bend each half of the soundboard separately and then glue them together. The only excuse I can offer for bending the whole soundboard at one time is that I didn't know any better.

There are a couple of inherent structural problems with the common flattop bouzouki. The stresses on the body are quite different from a guitar. There are two main stresses at work, the pressure from the tailpiece trying to collapse the body longitudinally, or at least pull the tailpiece up and over toward the machine heads, and the downbearing from the bridge trying to cave the soundboard in. Often the soundboard distorts into an S, with a hump just in front of the tailpiece, a dip underneath the bridge, and a bulge above the soundhole caused by the rotation of the heel block. The last feature also lifts the angle of the neck. **Fig. 2** shows what is happening. When building them with the neck in the same plane as the top (or kicked back only a degree or two) and using a tailpiece, the bridge must necessarily be quite low, and the break angle over the bridge quite shallow. This will mean that the down pressure on the soundboard is minimized and the soundboard isn't driven as hard as it might be, so volume often suffers. The loudness of the instrument is an important consideration for players, especially of Irish music, because they often spend a good amount of their playing time at sessions trying to hear themselves over the button accordion and bodhran player on either side of them.

Both archtop guitar and violin builders work on a 15° break angle over the bridge. This puts too much downward pressure on a flattop instrument, and some degree of structural deformation seems inescapable. Over several years of building flattop bouzoukis I tried all manner of approaches to this problem of compressional forces. I played around with the neck angle and bridge height to see what would happen. I took up Greg Smallman's idea of a plywood rim to replace the usual linings, and various sorts of flying braces from the tailpiece forward to stiffen the instrument. I finally decided that a flat top, at least with a floating bridge and tailpiece, was not the way to go.

The answer to all these structural problems seemed to be carving the tops. After all, archtop guitars, mandolins, and violins don't have anything like these structural weaknesses. But the cost of blocks of spruce big enough for bouzouki tops was pretty scary. I didn't have anything in the way of the necessary gouges and carving chisels, let alone those nifty little violin maker's planes (which I've since bought and consider the most wonderful tools I have ever spent money on). Then I came across an article in the English magazine *Early Music*, describing the restoration of a 16th-century viol, and the repairer's discovery that the soundboard appeared to have been bent and then coopered together in four sections, rather like staves of a barrel. He found what looked like scorch marks on the inside where the most radical bends had been made.

The idea of bending the soundboards into an arch was appealing for a couple of reasons. Using timber 6MM thick rather than 18MM–20MM was an obvious cost saving, to say nothing of a more efficient use of resources, and the fact that the wood fibers would run the full length of the soundboard's arch seemed structurally stronger. It might then be possible to achieve the same structural strength and stiffness with less weight, and so more efficiency in the way the instrument works. If a string has to move less mass to convert mechanical energy into acoustic energy, then more of that energy can be turned into sound. This is one of the ideas behind Greg Smallman's very light but stiff classical guitar soundboards.

I made a couple attempts at building these coopered soundboards, but it was quite tricky getting wood that was around 6MM thick to bend over a hot pipe in the complicated three-dimensional manner that was required, and the shapes were never quite right. This technique was put into the "interesting, but too hard" basket, and I continued to ponder on ways to form 6MM plates of spruce into arched soundboards.

The two forces used to bend timber are heat and moisture. I couldn't think of an easy way to heat up my soundboards while keeping them wet, but I could certainly keep them wet in a large fiberglass tray that I had in the workshop. I soaked soundboard halves for a couple days and clamped them down on a piece of plywood with an 18MM plywood hump in the middle, using a plywood caul in the shape of the body outline and extending about 20MM inside the body shape almost to the edge of the hump. After letting it dry for a few days I took the clamps off, and the arched shape remained, although the spruce sprung back so there was only a 8MM–10MM internal arch instead of 18MM.

There were still lots of problems to solve, like joining the two halves. I also discovered that it was a good idea to plane the inside surfaces before bending. I still wanted to get more arch in the tops, somewhere between a guitar and a mandolin I figured, so longer soaking periods were tried, a double soaking and clamping, and a higher hump to bend the wood over. The springback was still there, and trying to bend over the higher hump caused some noticeable compression marks in the spruce at the inside edge of the clamping caul where the upward curve started.

Heat was what we wanted as well as the moisture, and I eventually thought of Glad brand oven bags. They are made of a stiff clear plastic and are used to cook things like chickens and turkeys in the oven to keep them from drying out as they cook. The bags are good to 200°C (just under 400°F), which seemed fine for steaming wood. The small problem was that even the biggest ones were not big enough for a bouzouki soundboard, but they could be cut and opened up into sheets and then taped together quite nicely. The size problem was sorted out when I rang the manufacturer, and their PR man said I could have the end of a roll of the material they make the bags out of. The roll was about 400MM wide and doubled over, so a soundboard half fit in just right. When the plastic was cut of to a length 100MM or so longer than the soundboard half, there was plenty to fold over and seal with the masking tape.

The oven in the kitchen was just big enough to hold the wet bits of spruce in the their bags, so I fired it up to around 150°C (300°F) and left them for 20–30 minutes, until I could feel them getting flexible, then onto the mold and under the clamps with them. And it worked even better. There was still some springback, but it was considerably less. This is the way this technique has been evolving over the past couple of years.

The mold is a piece of 18MM plywood cut 50MM larger than the body shape. The hump starts 25MM inside the body outline (for a bouzouki; for a mandolin this would be closer to the body outline) and is shaped in a smooth curve flattening out on the top. Height at the center should be around 18MM with the bridge position somewhere around the middle of that area. The finished arch won't be quite that high because of springback, but I aim for around a 15MM inside arch when finished.

My current mold is made of strips of 12MM×25MM pine, the curves of which where worked out by drawing the longitudinal curve on cardboard and working out cross-section curves using a flexible rubber contour gauge and transferring the shape to the pine strips. These were then glued to the ply base and sanded so the humped shape was smooth. A solid hump is probably a better way to go, whether carved from a chunk of timber or built up from strips in this way. Having separate pieces of timber about their own width apart has meant some marking on the inside of the soundboard from the pressure used to clamp everything together. A solid hump could be carved by making up templates in the same way that I calculated the shape of the strips. Draw a visible centerline on the mold, as this is useful when aligning the two soundboard halves.

The clamping caul is also made from 18MM ply, and faced with cork. It is 40MM wide, half outside and half inside the body outline, and this gives a little room on the inside before the spruce is forced into the curve. I used offcuts from cork floor tiles about 6MM thick for the facing. This lessens the chance of crushing the spruce, especially at the initial bend point into the arch. The caul should also have a centerline marked on it.

Another curved caul is useful to clamp over the length of the center joint. I made this from a piece of 50MM×50MM wood, a little shorter than the length of the hump, cut to the longitudinal curve of the hump and again faced with cork. This keeps the timber from "lipping up" as it dries.

The soundboard must be of relatively thick pieces of spruce; 6MM would be minimal, 7MM or a little more would be best. The inside surfaces should be planed smooth, as this will save a lot of messing around later. Trim what will be the center joint so that the grain runs as parallel as possible to what will be the jointed edges. Leave the halves rectangular as this makes joining them easier. A couple of big pencil marks across the outside faces will assist in aligning the halves at the clamping stage as well as another pencil mark to show where the soundboard should be in relation to the end of the mold.

Soak both halves in water for at least twenty-four hours. If you have some way of getting them into continuously hot or boiling water this time could probably be reduced, but the cold water seems to work fine. After soaking, seal each piece into an oven bag with a little extra water. Ordinary masking tape will seal the bags effectively enough, and you want the bags fairly tight around the wood. The bags must be well sealed so that the oven doesn't boil the moisture out of the wood, since it isn't nearly as flexible when that happens. Place the two bags in the oven on its lowest setting, usually about 150°C (300°F), and leave for about twenty minutes or until the bags have swollen up from the steam, and the wood feels flexible. Gloves are useful at this stage.

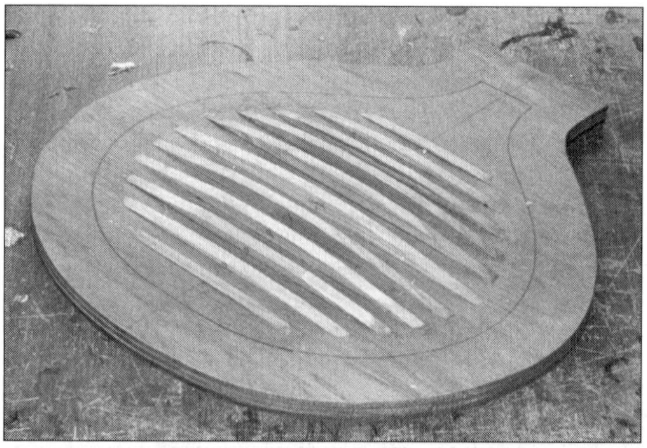

Ease of construction dictated that the arching mold be made in strips.

Have the mold, the caul, and eight or ten big clamps ready on the bench next to the oven. Some domestic negotiation may be necessary at this point. Remove the two pieces of wood from the oven, still in their bags, and align them on the centerline of the mold so they butt together, making sure that the pencil marks on the outside surface of the boards also line up. Place the outline caul on top and clamp at the ends on the centerline, then place more clamps around the caul to clamp it firmly down to the mold all the way around. This all has to be done fairly quickly while the wood is still flexible from the heat. At this point you can cut as much of the bags away as is feasible without disturbing the caul, then clamp the longitudinal caul over the centerline.

Let the whole assembly dry for at least four or five days in a warm spot. After three days or so it can be disassembled, the remnants of the bags removed, then reclamped until fully dry. The spruce will shrink appreciably across its width, with a gap of 2MM–3MM at each end and more in the center. When finally disassembled there is always some springback, but you should hope for close to 15MM of inside arch.

I use a normal shooting board and a long jack plane to joint the edges. It would be easier to have another shooting board set up the other way around as well. The soundboard halves have to be placed arch side up to joint the edges, and if the grain isn't running exactly along the proposed center joint, shooting in one direction or the other becomes a little tricky. Hopefully when the wood comes off the mold what you have are flat sections on each end. I clamp these down to the shooting board to make sure everything will be lined up at the gluing stage. A really straight cutting edge on the plane blade is important as different areas of the blade will be cutting the jointed edge because of the arch. More will have to be taken off each end to get a straight joint because the arching process leaves a curved edge to the wood. Jim Williams' method of using an aluminum level with sandpaper glued on one side is a good way of finishing off the joint. (See Jim's book *A Guitar Maker's Manual* from Mel Bay Publications. All the hands you see in the book are mine!)

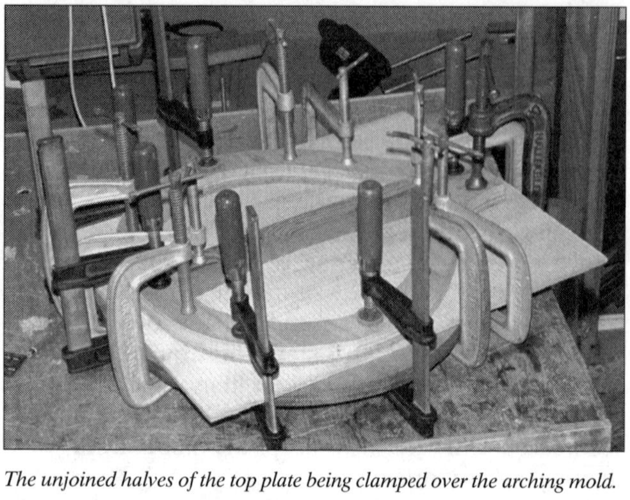

The unjoined halves of the top plate being clamped over the arching mold.

Abrasive glued to the carpenter's level dresses the plates for joining.

To glue the halves together I use the traditional Spanish method of 50MM×25MM timber bars, rope, and wedges (again as per Jim Williams). Leave off the top bar in the center and use the center wedge to just push the center of the joint together if required. After gluing, roping, and wedging, make sure that the inside edges of the soundboard are as aligned as possible, pushing them into place as necessary.

After letting the center joint dry as usual, cut out the shape of the soundboard leaving 3MM or so outside the body outline. The difference between this method and the usual carving from a solid piece of timber is that in this case the inside arch is already established, and little should need to be done with it. For my Irish bouzoukis I graduate the thickness in much the same way as an archtop guitar or mandolin, but somewhere between the two. I usually end up with 5MM or a little more in the center, down to 2.5MM–3MM in the channel 15MM in from the edge. The edges are left about 4MM–4.5MM thick. This graduating can be done quite quickly by depth drilling in concentric circles (turning a little eggshaped towards the neck) to mark the thickness at appropriate points and then carving and planing away the excess. I start by establishing the edge thickness and removing most of the wood with a large gouge, then use the two largest Ibex thumb planes for most of the rest of it. I leave finishing the outside inch or so until after the top is glued to the sides so the concavity around the edges can be smooth up to the rim.

I then glue on 8MM-wide X braces, cut to the inside curve of the arch with a height of 15MM at the crossing point, curving down to 3MM at the ends. Start with brace stock 20MM×8MM to allow for trimming and fitting. I end them 40MM from the soundboard edges which is in proportion to an archtop guitar X brace as described in Bob Benedetto's book. I use a round soundhole 75MM in diameter, but there should be no reason why *f*-holes wouldn't work. I just haven't got around to trying them yet, and I think bouzoukis look right with a round soundhole.

Teardrop bouzoukis/citterns seem to work well with a resonance about D–E as mentioned before, with the guitar-shaped instruments having a resonance around B–C. Once the spruce has been graduated to the thickness outlined above, most of them have a tap tone pretty close to these notes, but it is a matter of feel and listening, deciding when the soundboard has the right flexibility and when the tap tone develops what I can only describe as a clarity at the right point of the graduation process.

This method of bending an arch into a soundboard is decidedly low-tech and cheap, but it works. I'm waiting for someone to tell me that it doesn't work, and why, but in the meantime I'll keep doing it. I'm sure, however, that it is a method which can be improved upon, refined, and made more efficient. I have thought that a cast-aluminum mold which could be heated from below would get rid of the oven-bag idea. Vacuum forming would give a more even pressure to the process, but these are ideas that I hope someone else might have a go at. I've never tried this for an *f*-hole guitar (mainly because no one has ever asked me to), but I would be delighted to hear from anyone who tries it, or for that matter, anyone who has some thoughts on the ideas in this article. ——

The arched plate is joined using the "rope and wedges" trick.

The bending form and construction mold McDonald uses to build teardrop-shaped Irish bouzoukis.

Originally published in *American Lutherie #54*, 1998

Meet the Maker: Judy Threet

by Cyndy Burton

Judy, I've been admiring your lovely inlay work. Is this a special interest of yours?

Yes. You could say it's one of the reasons I was drawn into guitar making. I was teaching philosophy at the university and...

It sounds the beginning of an unlikely tale.

I guess it is. I should back up. My original career choice was to be a philosophy professor, to which end I went to Stanford and got my Ph.D. While in Palo Alto I met all the Gryphon-ites and started taking guitar lessons from Carol McComb and Ed Johnson. After I graduated and got a teaching job at the University of Calgary, I continued doing music. I started playing in a local swing band — playing my little Martin 0-18, of all things. I was beating it to a pulp. Another band member was Michael Heiden, who was (and is) a magnificent luthier. He talked me into getting an archtop made by him.

CYNDY BURTON

Judy Threet at the 1997 Healdsburg Guitar Festival.

This was all very exciting to me, so I started showing up at his shop with my camera and taking photos of every little thing. One day he mentioned that he hated doing inlays. My undergraduate minor was in fine arts, in print making, which is a very finicky thing, so I said to him, "I'd like to learn about inlays."

He called my bluff. He said, "I've got to do this custom inlay, and this guy knows what he wants. You redesign it so it will work as an inlay." I did that, and I chose the materials as well. Michael cut it out and inlaid it. Then he taught me how to do that part, and so for a year and a half I did the inlays on his instruments. I was still teaching at the time. He wasn't paying me anything for doing this. I was doing it because it was enjoyable and I liked hanging around the shop, and he was a good friend. Then I got caught in the "publish-or-perish" thing at Calgary and didn't get hired on as a tenured person, so I taught at the community college for a year. Six months into that I was so fed up that I approached Michael to ask if he would apprentice me. And because I'd been doing the inlay work for him and he knew my work habits, he said OK. He was thinking about taking on an apprentice anyway. I was supposed to start in September of that year, but in late August he told me he was going to have to move to B.C. because his mother wasn't well. But he'd still be around until January. I was disappointed; I'd already left my position at the community college. So I said, "OK, Michael, just so I don't end up with bad feelings about this, can I spend the next four months building a guitar in your shop?" And that's what we agreed to do. He was building two and I built one. I used his molds, his wood, and his tools. This was supposed to be a consolation prize. But halfway through I thought, "I want to do this!"

All the while I was making lists of tools I had been using, and I was taking copious notes. He was wonderful for answering in-depth any question that I had. His only rule was not to ask him the same question twice.

When he left I bought a bunch of wood from him that he didn't want to haul, and I hung out my shingle. I actually used his old shop space. We talked about how to handle this with customers. We both decided that since I didn't know my ass from my elbow there was no way in the world that he should be giving me his stamp of approval. When he left I said to him, "The only thing I know how to do is build one guitar. How am I going to learn to do repairs?" He said, "Learn the same way I did — read a lot of books."

I tried to make a policy to never take on a repair unless I could figure out in advance how I was going to do it. I wasn't going to be experimenting on other people's instruments. For the first year and a half I did only repairs, and not a whole lot of them. I lived on money I'd saved from when I had a "real" job.

Then I started designing my own guitar shape, my own headstock shape, and all that kind of stuff. Fortunately, at the time I was sharing shop space with Al Williams of Calton Cases. Michael gave me a start, and then Al was always there like a big dog watching and asking me what I was doing and why. That made me think. Al is a renaissance kind of guy. He's extremely interested in anything mechanical and has a wonderful way of coming up with jigs (though I don't use many). He was also really supportive of what I was doing.

In June of last year when I moved into this wonderful new shop space that's almost impossible to find, I thought it was the time to try to wean myself away from repairs, especially repairs on junk, and concentrate on building. But I still end up doing some repairs just to keep the money coming in. Then it was pointed out to me that the bulk of guitar sales that I'd made had been to people who had come in with a piece of junk for me to fix. So now what am I going to do?

I think that's really common. You establish a relationship with a repair customer, and they're very likely to buy from you.

Initially I thought I'd sell to someone who owned a Martin or a Larrivée or something like that. But then it was pointed out to me that, no, I had sold a guitar to someone who originally owned an Echo. And it's actually easier to sell a guitar to someone who originally owned an Echo. *(laughs)*

That's true, but I think the relationship is important. You've got to reach your clientele, and one of the ways is by having a repair business. They'll keep coming back to you. Maybe they'll have a Threet guitar, maybe they'll have a couple other good guitars, and they'll want to bring all those guitars to you when they need work. Are you going to turn them down?

No. It's also nice to build for somebody that you know, and you know what kind of music they play. You're not going to know somebody who just comes in cold off the street. You have a much better chance of knowing them if you've been working on their other guitars.

It's a very natural connection. Also I think repair work helps you become more efficient, and that really helps your building.

I guess. I certainly have to do something to become more efficient. I spend a lot of time sort of staring at the walls thinking about how to do something, rather than jumping in and doing it. I finished off a batch of four in June, and it took me forever to get started again. I think that there's so much mental and emotional energy that goes into making a guitar that you kind of need a chance to become revitalized before you jump into it again.

ALL BY RHETT DEMETRICK EXCEPT AS NOTED

"Loon," one of Judy's many artistic peghead inlays.

That's where repairs can come in, too. If you choose to do repairs between building...

It's really hard to juggle the two at the same time.

Yes, but if you do repairs for awhile between guitars, then you're refreshed again when you get back to building.

Or while waiting for the nitrocellulose lacquer to cure, preferably for three weeks, I could be starting another set, so there's never this abrupt end to a run. They just roll into each other.

That makes sense. Have you tried other finishes?

I'm extremely conservative about what I'm willing to try. I learned to spray nitrocellulose from Michael, so that's what I use. I'm amazed when I wander around the show here and I hear people say, "I tried this and I tried that." There's no way in the world you're going to catch me experimenting like that. I put too much work into an instrument to risk it.

What are you after in a guitar?

I'm after a nice clean-sounding guitar that's suitable for fingerstyle. That's the guitar style that I have some sensitivity for. I don't play bluegrass. I don't even know what a proper bluegrass guitar is supposed to sound like, so it would be a very difficult thing for me to build one. My guitars tend to have a lot of sustain and a lot of projection. They're loud, which is good if you want to be loud, but they're good for playing soft as well.

What woods are you using?

My all-time favorite wood for backs and sides is mahogany. I *love* mahogany back and sides. It's great for fingerstyle. Mahogany has this nice sharp attack and has the good grace to get out of the way of the next note. Rosewood doesn't do that. It has less of an attack, then it hangs around. So mahogany is best for the fingerstyle playing that I do. But I've heard other people doing slow, quiet fingerstyle airs on my guitars, and they sound way better on my rosewood model. Mahogany sounds wimpy on music like that. I've also tried koa, but not enough to have any real sense of precisely what it does to an instrument's sound.

I love Sitka spruce for the tops, regardless of the back and side woods. I've only done one Engelmann and I think I thinned it too much. It's my guitar. I needed to try it. I've never tried cedar. I find that with Sitka the trebles just sparkle, and I like that sound. Some people don't. I do, so that's what I use.

What's the effect of your being female in this mostly male business? I mean, what has your experience been?

Being female in a predominantly male world has done good things for me. It's easier for people to remember who I am. They'll find me in a crowd and say, "Oh, you're one of the five female luthiers at this gathering." The men don't have it so easy. Because there are so many of them, it's easy for them to get lost in the crowd. It's odd, really. If the world were constructed slightly differently, it might be that all the redheads in the room would be the novelty. I think it's just a matter of luck, and good luck actually, that not many women are guitar makers, and that I'm one of the women who is. And I've never had anybody say anything to me like, "Oh, you shouldn't be doing this," or, "You're taking work away from men," or anything stupid like that. If I've had any comments at all they've been supportive, like, "I'm glad to see a woman doing this," and I've had customers tell me that they're happier bringing their repair work to a female. I never feel out of place. This is the most accepting environment that I've ever run into.

Certainly a lot of makers are very open to it, or, I dare say, none of the women exhibiting would be here.

Yes, they're so encouraging. The makers are great. My customers are great. Every once in a while someone will call and say, "Can I talk to the guy who does repairs?" I say, "You're talking to him," and then they laugh and everything is fine. I don't make a big deal of it, so other people end up not making a big deal of it around me. Certainly I can't say enough about how supportive all the other luthiers are.

A Threet Model C custom. It sports koa back and sides, a bearclaw Sitka top, and a "Late Fall" peghead-inlay design reminiscent of maple leaves in drifts of snow.

And there is so much competition out there now, not just from other hand builders, but all these small and not-so-small production shops.

Right. The big problem that everyone will have to deal with is what to do with all the cheap, good guitars on the market. As a classical builder you probably don't run into that. Classical players have been trained, as have violin players and everybody involved in "real" music as opposed to folk music, to pay top dollar for their instruments. Because steel string guitar is primarily a folk instrument it should in some sense be readily accessible to the general public, and that means low prices. The prices keep going lower and lower on instruments now made in the United States. I think Taylor's prices are going lower, and now there's Tacoma that sells some marvelous guitars for under $1000. The big challenge for us independent hand builders — especially the steel string builders — is going to be to figure out some way to say, "Well, I know you can get a pretty darn nice guitar for under $1000, but really you should be buying mine for $5000." That's going to take quite a sales job, and I'm not quite sure how we're going to do that. One thing I have to offer as a hand builder is custom hand-carved necks and custom inlay. Whatever size neck you want, I'll do it. Whatever inlay you want, I'll do it. They can't get that from the factory. But as the prices on the factory instruments fall, it's going to be harder and harder to get people interested in hand-built instruments.

People with money know they could buy an off-the-rack Taylor or whatever and be somewhat satisfied, but when they go to a luthier they like the idea that they're buying something from the person *who made it, not a CNC machine, and I think that's great. I also believe there are more differences than just custom neck carving and inlay. As good as any factory can be, and I don't question that they are turning out very good instruments, they are not putting the care, and even love, into each instrument. If you're conscious of what sound you're trying to achieve as you handle, select, and work each piece of wood, don't you think the end product will be different for that? Those who can afford it and who understand the difference are partners with us in keeping alive a very long tradition, pre-Industrial Revolution, to say the least.*

And I think that that's a worthy tradition to keep alive. Why, I'm not sure. After all, not all traditions are worth hanging onto. (Women kept at home, barefoot, pregnant, and so on springs to mind.) But what's so great — even different — about my hand guiding a chisel to carve a brace, as opposed to my hand operating the CNC that carves it? An obvious difference is touch. When I'm guiding the chisel, I feel the wood, its resistance, the runout, and so on. This is a very intimate sort of contact. I *feel* it. The CNC operator doesn't have this contact. So? What's so great about that sort of intimate contact? Maybe nothing; not in and of itself. But if I'm *aware* of it, if I notice the resistance, the runout, I can begin to *learn* from it. If I carve enough braces — and pay attention — I can learn a lot. Actually "learn" probably isn't the right term. It's more like theorizing, but in a really vague way. What I can do, what we often do, is develop intuitions: "I should likely treat the wood this way..." "Gosh, this wood isn't behaving the way I thought it would," and so on. I think that's the big difference between hand builders and CNC operators. We tend to develop intuitions and to *rely* on them to guide us. I'm not saying that CNC operators can't develop these intuitions. I'm saying that they needn't. Intuition does not — cannot — guide the CNC. Only a program can do that.

Still, what's the big deal? Why value a brace carved by intuition more highly than one carved by a program? Maybe it's fear! Likely not, but maybe. Maybe we humans are afraid that machines will make us redundant, so we value those things that are uniquely ours (like intuition). We value them — quite literally — out of *self*-preservation. Frankly, I don't think it's as simple as that. After all, hatred is uniquely human too, and very few would argue for its value! (Geez. You can take the girl out of philosophy, but...)

For whatever reason, I'm interested in hand building. I don't want to automate. I don't want to build thirty guitars at a time. I want to have my hand — and my hand alone — in every single instrument that comes out of my shop. I want to understand its personality before I release it to the world. And you can't do that if you've got thirty on the go. You can't keep track of them. To me they're all still my children, and I want to have twins and triplets. I don't want to have a litter of guitars. But that's me, that's the way I think.

Also, I'm still learning. I mean, everybody is still learning, but I really still think of myself as a novice. And that's why it's useful for me to build in batches of three. With three I can keep very close track of what's happening to the top as I'm thinning the braces. I write down copious notes and information about how much the sound changes and how much the tap tone lowers if I scallop out another $\frac{1}{32}''$, stuff like that. And I love inlaying. There's no way in the world I'm going to give that up, to farm it out to some machine. And I really enjoy carving necks. It takes me forever, but I really enjoy it because it's so drastic! You start with a big hunk of wood and end with this elegant sweeping form. It's so cool. When it comes to a finished state and it feels great, I think, "By God, I did that!"

Exactly. But can you say how all this affects the end product? Do you make the argument that hand-built guitars are superior to factory-made guitars?

Gosh, I'd better say so! Seriously, let's take a practical look at the human vs. machine problem, and let's talk about sound, or tone. I'm not about to claim that any hand-built guitar sounds better than any

Judy's beautiful new shop space is off the beaten path so she can get more building done.

factory-built guitar. I won't even claim that my guitars sound better than most factory-made guitars. (Sure, they sound better to *me*; but just because *I* prefer that sound doesn't mean that *you* will. It's all so subjective.) What I will claim is that most hand builders achieve a *consistency* in their sound that a factory cannot achieve. Hand builders achieve this by having a goal in mind, working slowly, listening, and making adjustments; in short, by treating every piece of wood differently. Factories can't do this. Machines, in order to be cost effective, must treat every piece of wood the same. The better the factory, the better they'll figure out how *most* of their wood likes to be treated. Think of a bell curve. And, to simplify things, let's talk about price rather than sound. Arbitrarily, let's pick a price of $2000. The good (successful) factories will set up their machines so that the bulk of their $2000 guitars will easily *sell* for $2000, that is, the paying public sees them as worth that. But, as with any bell curve, despite their $2000 price tag, some will really be worth less (will sound comparable to an instrument which typically sells for $1500) and some will be worth more (could compete with instruments of twice the price). Within any price range, there are some real dogs, some real deals, and many instruments that are actually worth the price. And, sure, hand builts fall within a similar curve. It's just that the curve is usually steeper and narrower. Your chances of "getting what you pay for" are higher.

But now look at what I've done. I've all but said that a *great* factory-built guitar can sound every bit as good as anything a hand builder can provide. If someone has the time and patience to play many factory builts, to find the "real deal," why buy a hand built instead? Well, there's always that anti-machine, self-preservation stuff to fall back on. But there's something else, too, that we tend to forget.

I like to think that what I do is create playable sculpture. Hand-built guitars are not just instruments, *they are works of art.* We who make them know that. Our biggest problem is that we don't scream it from the rooftops. The general public still wants to compare what we do to what factories churn out. *Ve must stop zem!* Seriously, we have to be clearer about what we do, and for whom. We don't, we can't, compete with factories. We must compete with other artists. People who wouldn't blink at plunking down a couple thousand dollars for a print to hang over their sofa, stand aghast when they hear the price of your guitar. Why is that? It's because they *don't know* what they're looking at. They see a guitar, not a work of art. And they won't see it as any more than a guitar unless we, the builders, ask them to. I think we've got to do that. Especially those of us who build steel string guitars (you know, the folk instruments). We've got to stop apologizing for our prices (which are ridiculously low), and learn to explain to our potential clients that what they're getting is a work of art — and for the time it's taken to create it, the knowledge and skill that it involves, the care and love that's gone into it, it's one of the best buys in the world. It's a bargain — and would still be at twice the price! ——

Originally published in *American Lutherie #54 and #55*, 1998

QUESTIONS

EDITED BY CYNDY BURTON

■ ***Ethan Deutsch of Seattle, WA** asks:*

Would someone please explain what advantages there are to a classical or flamenco guitar neck that leans forward instead of being in line with the plane of the soundboard? It seems to me that any effect on the action could be achieved more easily by tapering the fingerboard thickness and/or adjusting the saddle height. The tilt is so slight (often 3MM over the length of the first twelve frets) that I can't imagine it helping a guitarist to see both hands at once. And tilting the neck complicates joining the soundboard to the heel block, the sides to the neck, and the fingerboard to the neck and soundboard. Also, it seems to me that if the neck is tilted forward, then it is more apt to warp when strung.

***Tom Blackshear of San Antonio, TX** responds:*

For years now I've made my fingerboards a constant thickness (about $\frac{1}{4}''$), set the neck slightly forward, lowered the upper edge of the soundhole about $\frac{1}{2}$MM so it is completely level with the plane of the neck, and relieved the sides slightly in the upper bout (at the top-to-side junction). The reason is to accommodate players who find it much easier to play above the 12th fret if the fingerboard is thicker (than it would be if you tapered it to achieve a good playing height at the bridge). I arrived at this by studying Miguel Rodríguez guitars.

■ ***Greg Brouelette of Santee, CA** asks:*

I'm building my first guitar. In several books, the authors recommend you build the entire guitar with the exception of gluing on the bridge, then apply the finish. Why wouldn't you simply attach the bridge before you apply the finish? Is there something inherently bad about applying a finish to the bridge? If so then wouldn't it be possible to simply mask the bridge?

***Cyndy Burton of Portland, OR** responds:*

Most classical guitars have finish on the bridge; most steel strings do not. It is customary to glue on the bridge after finish is done on the guitar because it's far easier to do a clean job. If you finish the guitar and bridge at the same time with a sprayed finish, it's difficult to maintain clean edges between the bridge and the top. This is also true if you mask the bridge. It's also much more difficult to rub out a finish on a top with the bridge already glued on. It's easier to scape a place for it after the rubout, then glue it on.

However, it is not untraditional according to Eugene Clark for French polishers to polish with the bridge on and to put finish on the bridge at the same time. (See p. 182.) He showed us his technique at the 1998 GAL Convention in Tacoma. It's tricky. ——

Originally published in *American Lutherie #55*, 1998

The Frame Guitar

by Sam Littlepage

ONE PROBLEM with the guitar in its current state of development is insufficient structural integrity of the body in regard to string tension. After all, the neck is a lever as long as the body, so we shouldn't be amazed that many guitars eventually break down under the torque generated by the tension of the strings. Conventionally constructed guitars tend to cave in around the soundhole, since this unbolstered portion of the top provides the weak link in body design. Traditional kerfed lining simply provides an extended glue joint between the sides and the top, and does little to stiffen the assembly. The top bracing must leave the plate free to speak, a factor which is defeated if the braces are made industrial strength to fight off string tension.

My goal was to reinforce the body in such a way that its sound production was left unencumbered. The design I came up with (**Photo 1**), in fact, improves the sustain of the guitar and brightens the whole tone spectrum. I have replaced the conventional kerfed linings with very stiff and stable laminated hardwood linings, which I have called *loop liners*, in conjunction with an elaborate neck block, which I have renamed the *neck hard point*. A new set of braces extend from the neck hard point to the loop liners at the waist. These braces, called *frame braces*, support the soundhole area of the top, but free the rest of the top and the back.

When I began to develop the frame guitar I applied it to conventional classical guitar design. After attending Richard Schneider's school at Lost Mountain (1995) I switched to the Kasha design but kept the frame concept. I have noticed no conflict.

After some experimentation I've settled upon red oak for the loop liners, which seems to increase sustain and makes a brighter sounding instrument. Twelve pieces are needed for each guitar, each piece measuring a bit longer than the guitar side, ¾″ wide, and 3MM thick. Some manner of bending form or machine is a huge aid toward accurate bending of the sides and the loop liner pieces, which must fit together as exactly as possible. I use the Universal Side Bender designed by Charles Fox, the hardware for which can be had in kit form from Luthiers Mercantile International. Once the sides are bent, the loop liner pieces are placed in the machine side by side and bent in the same manner. I bend six pieces at a time, which gives me enough laminations for one loop liner, two loop liners being necessary for each guitar.

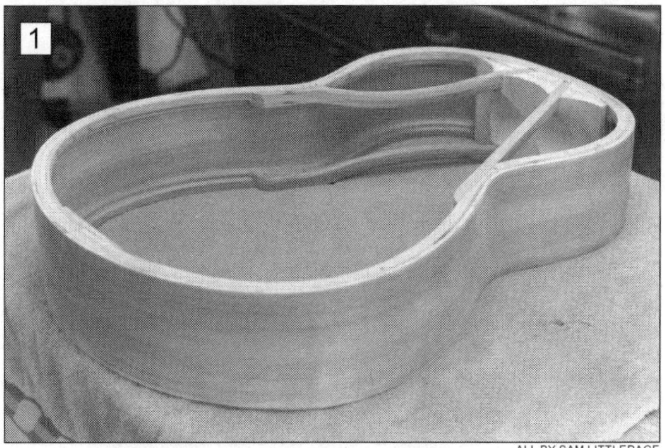

ALL BY SAM LITTLEPAGE

A frame guitar carcass with completed loop liners and neck hard point.

A mold must be made in which to lay up the loop liners. This mold looks like half of a normal guitar mold, with two important differences. The thickness of the sides must be taken into account, so the loop liner mold should follow the outline of the inside of the guitar. Also, each end of the mold should extend a bit beyond the centerline of the guitar. By doing this the trimmed ends of the loop-liner halves will have a proper curve through the butt-joint area. The loop-liners pieces are glued and clamped in the mold in a sandwich three plies thick (**Photo 2**), after which the edges are planed clean to leave the liners an even 15MM tall. I normally do this operation with a thickness sander (**Photo 3**).

Loop liner pieces are glued together after being bent in the Fox bender.

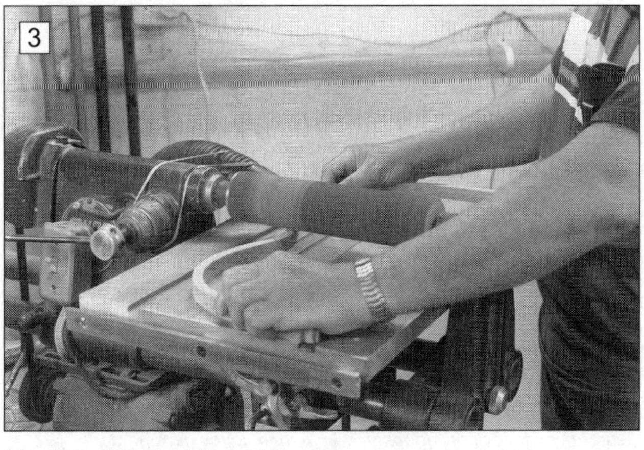

Liners are dimensionally sanded to 15MM.

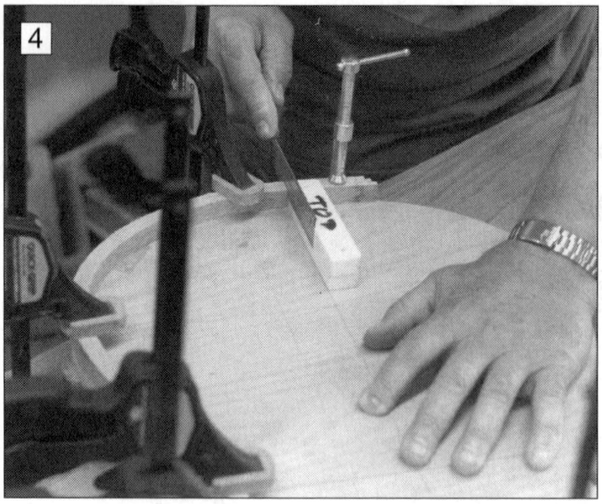

Ends of the loop liner halves are cut to the correct length.

A flat cut on the loop liner halves will receive the scab strip.

Loop liner halves are glued together with a scab strip.

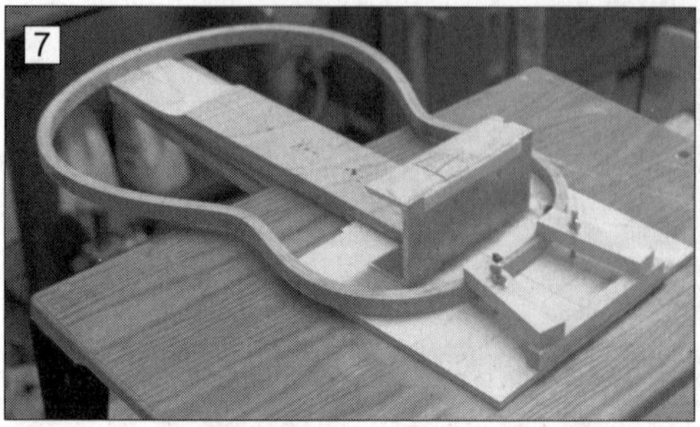

Using a pivoting jig on a table router, a 180MM radius is milled on the inside surface of the loop liners to fit them to the neck hard point.

A guitar-shaped workboard must be made that conforms to the dimensions of the loop-liner mold. In other words, the workboard would be a perfect drop fit into an imaginary guitar body. Make this workboard out of ¾″ plywood. Draw in the centerline plus a set of lines that cross the centerline at the waist and the widest points of the upper and lower bouts. Clamp a loop liner half to the workboard, arranging it to fit to the edges as perfectly as possible. The ends of the loop liner halves will be overly long and should be trimmed to form a good butt joint at the centerline (**Photo 4**).

A flat surface is cut perpendicular to the butt joints (**Photo 5**), and scab strips that bridge the joints are glued to the flats. To make this joint I clamp the liner halves securely to the workboard and draw a line that will locate the position of the flat surface. Then I remove the loop-liner halves from the workboard and trim to the line with a bandsaw and disk sander. The loop-liner halves are returned to the workboard, and the scab strips are glued in place (**Photo 6**). When the glue has cured, the outside edges of the scab strips are trimmed to conform to the outline of the workboard, again using the disk sander.

In a normal guitar, the lining ends at the neck block and tail block. On a frame guitar the lining makes a complete loop of the guitar (thus the name loop liners), and the end blocks are rabbeted to fit the loop liners. The inside surface of the ends of the loop liners are cut to a 180MM radius (**Photo 7**) to receive the neck hard point and the tail block. The center of this radius is on the centerline of the guitar and will cut about one-third the way through the loop liners.

This loop liner is now completely assembled. Make the second loop liner in exactly the same manner. When both loop liners are constructed, mark them carefully at the centerline, waist, and bouts, just as the workboard was marked. The loop liners should also be marked top and back, and which side of each loop liner faces the top of the guitar.

The loop liners must now be held in place while the guitar body is built around them. This is done with the aid of a device I call a *beetle* (**Photo 8 and Fig. 1**). You may think of the beetle as a three-dimensional workboard, or even a mold, though it looks nothing like a conventional instrument mold. It must hold the loop liners securely in the proper relationship to each other, while still giving plenty of access for gluing the tail block and neck hard point to the loop liners, and for gluing the sides to this skeleton. As you now realize, it is critical that all parts be made to fit together as

The frame will be assembled on a form called a beetle.

accurately as possible. Any misfitting of the parts will affect the strength of the glue joints, seriously weakening that portion of the structure and thus negating the reason all this work was begun in the first place.

The heart of the beetle is a piece of $\frac{3}{4}''$ plywood at least the size of the loop liner workboard. We'll call this the beetle's *central board*. Using the loop liner workboard, lay out the dimensions of the guitar's interior on the central board, again marking the centerline and the perpendicular lines denoting the waist and the widest points of the bouts. Do this on both sides of the central board. Along the centerline on each side of the central board glue a piece of straight wood to help in centering the tail block and the neck hard point. The dimensions of these parts are not critical, and $\frac{1}{8}'' \times 1'' \times 12''$ are useful guides.

Holes for $1''$ dowels must be drilled in the central board on the lines marking the waist and the widest points of the bouts. The holes should be tangent to the guitar sides but must leave room for the loop liners plus a little more. It's imperative that the holes be drilled perpendicular to the central board with a drill press. Using a hand-held drill is simply asking for grief.

The central board can now be cut to its final shape, which only vaguely resembles the outline of the guitar. A single line that runs roughly through the center of all the dowel holes will give you what you need. Such a shape will lend maximum stiffness to the bouts and the waist, yet leave plenty of access to the head and tail areas of the body.

The dowels are cut to length in pairs. The length of the dowels will determine the depth of the guitar body. Don't mix the pairs. The dowels are glued and screwed to the holes in the central board. Make sure that equal amounts of the dowels protrude from the central board on the top side. Make doubly sure that the dowel pairs are matched for length.

Cross members are now made to span between the ends of each pair of dowels. They could be made of wood, though I use polycarbonate. The cross members run across the beetle at the waist and bout points, and are secured to the ends of the dowels with screws. Make sure the cross members are accurately centered on the dowels. The beetle is now assembled, but not quite finished. Lay the beetle on the loop liner workboard and mark and trim the ends of the cross members to match the edges of the workboard. Then flip over the beetle and trim the opposite set of cross members. Again, I do this with the disk sander. Mark the bout and waist lines on the cross members.

The loop liners can now be screwed on the central board side of the cross members (**Photo 9**), using the waist and bout lines to carefully position them. I use $\#4 \times \frac{3}{4}''$ flat-head

Figure 1. The beetle

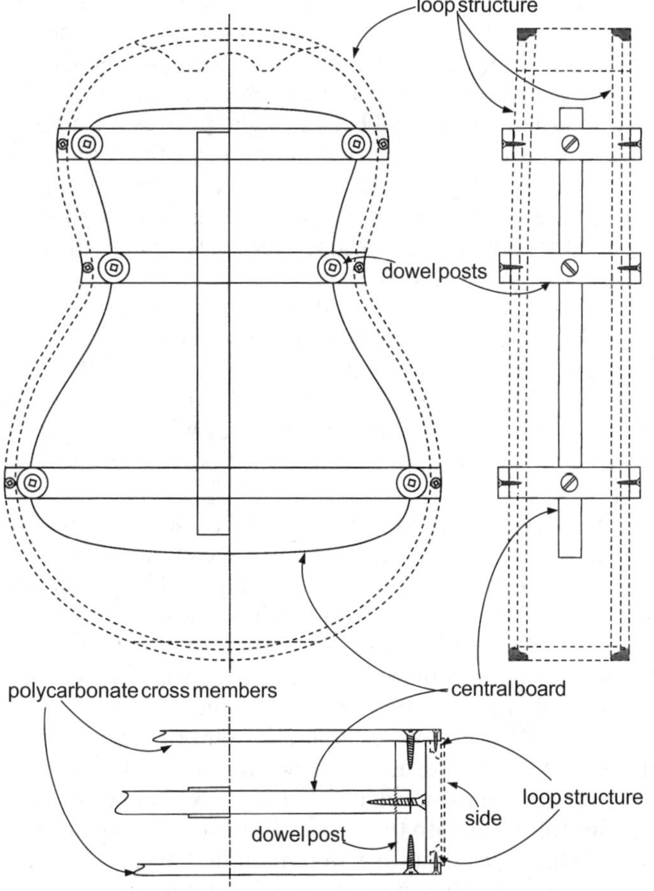

screws to secure them to the cross members. The outside edges of the loops should be trimmed until they are perpendicular to the top of the guitar. There is normally very little of this to do, and I accomplish this task at the disk sander, and the oscillating spindle sander.

The neck hard point is made of three layers, the core of which is $\frac{1}{4}''$ aircraft-grade laminated hardwood. I got my supply of this material from Woodcraft, a mail-order outfit. If it is good enough for the aircraft industry, it's probably better than any laminate I could make myself. The tail block is two layers with a $\frac{1}{8}''$ laminated layer. The other layers can be a lighter filler wood like basswood.

9

Loop liners are screwed to the beetle. In this picture the scab pieces which join the loop-liner halves have not yet been trimmed.

The end blocks must be cut with a curved rabbet to accommodate the loop liners (**Photos 10 and 11, and Fig. 2**). The height of these blocks will also fix the height of the guitar body at the ends. On my classical guitars I make the tail block 100MM tall and the neck hard point 94MM. In addition to the curved rabbets, straight grooves must be cut in the hard point which will later receive the frame braces (**Photo 12**). I do this on the table saw with a 3/8″ dado blade. The inside of the hard point is now contoured around the loop liner and frame brace groove joint areas with an oscillating spindle sander.

The four frame braces will need to be made. They are oak, 15MM × 3/8″. Depending on your soundboard configuration (acoustic struts, placement of soundhole), the frame braces could be straight, bent from front to back, or bent from side to side, but they will always run from the neck hard point to the waist portion of the loop liners.

I remove liners from the beetle and cut a decorative S-shaped cross section on the inside edge of the loop liners. I do this with a Roman ogee shaper. These shaped sections are between the sections where the end blocks and the frame braces attach. Be extra careful to keep them in proper orientation as you do this. In other words, don't accidentally create two top loop liners, or two bottoms. A little effort spent at this point to make them distinctive, attractive, and clean will hardly add to the construction time but will make your work shine when curious folk peek into the guitar. Return the loop liners to the beetle exactly as they were mounted previously.

The neck hard point and the tail block can now be glued to the loop liners. After the end blocks are trimmed to the outline of the loop liners, move on to attaching the sides. Work with one side at a time, starting at the waist and working to each end. Use spring clamps. Clamping the entire top edge before starting the bottom edge may lead to twisting the side, so I normally put a clamp or two on the top, then an equal number on the bottom.

Remove the guitar from the beetle and attach the frame braces to the neck hard point and the loop liners (**Photo 13**).

From here on, construction proceeds in whatever manner you have already established. It's a lot of work, but you can rest confident that your guitar will be built around an ultra-rigid and sound-sustaining framework, with more than sufficient structural integrity and an improved tonal spectrum. ——

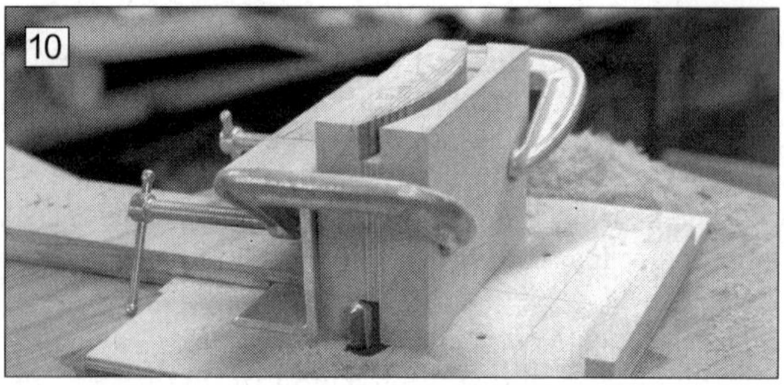

A 180MM radius is milled in the outside surface on the neck hard point to receive the neck end of the loop liners, using the same jig which was used to mill the loop liners.

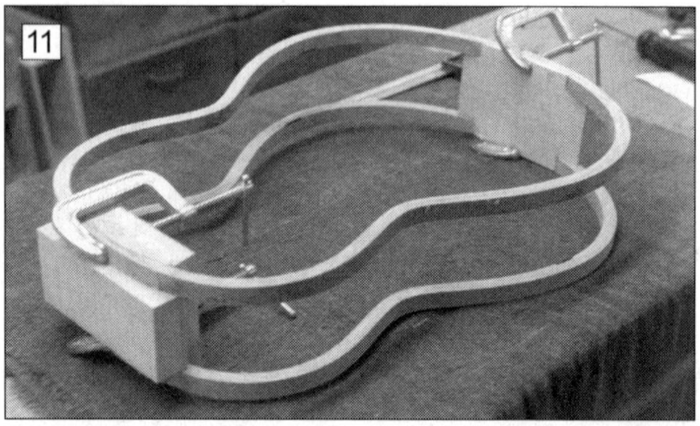

Checking the loops and blocks for fit.

Frame braces are fitted to the neck hard point but not glued in. This will happen after the sides are attached.

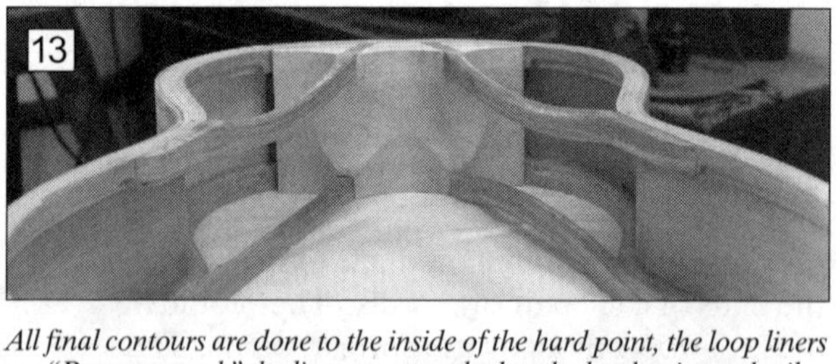

All final contours are done to the inside of the hard point, the loop liners are "Roman-ogeed," the liners are attached to the hard point and tail block, the sides are attached, and the frame braces are attached. This is a back view of the assembled carcass. This carcass is for a steel string application and has Osage orange sides.

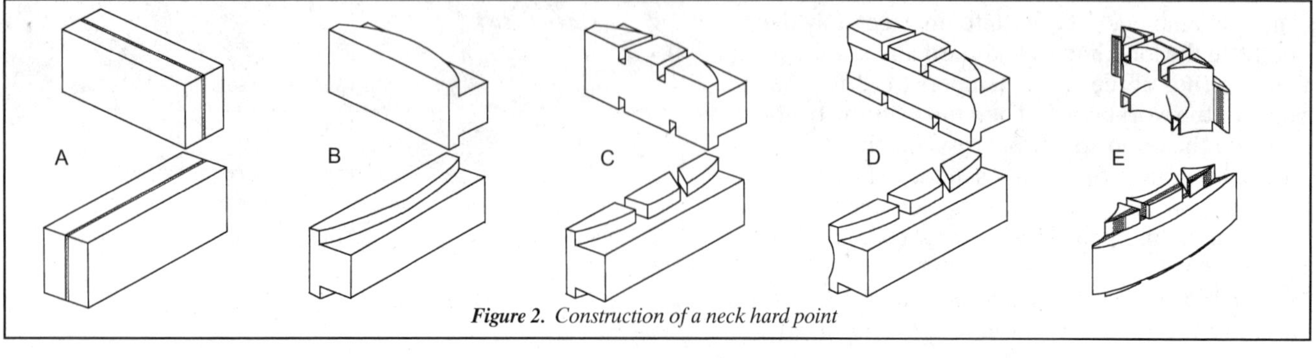

Figure 2. *Construction of a neck hard point*

IN MEMORIAM

Originally published in *American Lutherie #55*, 1998

Irving Sloane

April 27, 1925 – June 21, 1998

Irving Sloane, noted author on the art of lutherie, passed away on June 21, 1998 following a three-year battle with renal cell cancer. He is survived by his wife, Zelda Sloane, his children Roy, Linda, and David, and four grandchildren. I had the pleasure to know Irving for fifteen years and would like to share some of those memories.

I first discovered *Classical Guitar Construction* by Irving Sloane in the *Whole Earth Catalog* back in 1971. I was a graduate student in psychobiology and my interest in guitars was beginning to exceed my interest in graduate school. I remember the page in the *Whole Earth Catalog* that contained information on Irving's book, H.L. Wild on East 11th Street in Manhattan as a source for guitar woods, and a section on Gurian Guitars who's label read "Built on the third planet from the sun." I can remember reading and rereading that page in the catalog at every free moment I had.

COURTESY OF ROGER SADOWSKY

Reading *Classical Guitar Construction* was like entering a new world for me. I can vividly recall the pictures of Irving planing his wood to thickness, boiling his sides in a galvanized pan and bending them over his bending form, joining the top and back, etc., etc. I read the book over and over until every detail and specification was committed to memory, including his list of sources at the back. This book was soon followed by *Guitar Repair* which transported me to the repair department at the Martin factory and unlocked many "trade secrets." Next came *Steel String Guitar Construction* which, in spite of a rather bizarre neck joint, still provided a virtual gold mine of information and provided one of the few documented visits to Jimmy D'Aquisto's shop.

These three books provided me with all of the published information available on guitar making and guitar repair to be had at the time. They were the "Rosetta stones" of guitar making — the only key to unlock the mystery of a craft on which almost no printed information existed. The knowledge extracted from these volumes launched me on what is now a twenty-six-year career.

In 1981, I met my wife, Robin Phillips. On one of her earliest visits to my shop, she spied Irving's books on my shelf and said, "I know him — he was my neighbor when I grew up in Ridgewood, New Jersey." She told me stories of watching Irving build his guitars in the basement and of Irving serenading her on the front porch. Robin's mother Zelda worked at the Ridgewood Public Library and Irving paid a visit to his hometown around 1983 and dropped in to say hello (he was living in Brussels at the time). She told Irving that Robin had married a guitar maker, and Irv called us up and met us one day in Manhattan. It was a pleasure to meet him and he autographed my copy of *Classical Guitar Construction.*

We heard from Irving the following year. He was moving back to the States and was going to live full-time in a small country house he always had in Millerton, NY. He had designed a new premium-quality tuning machine for classical guitar and had patented the design. He was hand making them for a small number of builders and hoped to increase production as his primary source of income. The gears had the smoothest and most positive mechanism I had ever felt and were much less expensive than Rodgers, the only other quality gear available.

Irving had invited Robin and me to come up to the country for a weekend and we had a very nice visit with him. He told wonderful stories of the guitar makers and musicians he had known but his closest relationship was with Bouchet during the years he lived in Brussels. He was also very good

*(See **Sloane** on page 216)*

Originally published in *American Lutherie #55,* 1998

Meet the Maker: Paul McGill

by Mark Bass

IN 1976, at the age of eighteen, Paul McGill hitchhiked from Georgia to Vermont to begin learning the craft of repairing and building acoustic guitars with Charles Fox at The Earthworks. With little more than youthful enthusiasm and a desire to contribute to an emerging global culture dedicated to the guitar as a means of self-expression, he soon learned that there were similar enclaves of dedicated craftspeople all over the country.

After his six weeks of training in Vermont, Paul returned to Georgia for a time. At the age of twenty he moved to Madison, Wisconsin where for nearly eight years he made and repaired guitars, before moving to Nashville in 1985 to take a job with George Gruhn doing repairs and restoration work. The team of talented luthiers working there at the time made each day a learning experience. Paul recalls, "Kim Walker, who ran the shop, is a great talent. He's now building his own instruments after years of working for Gruhn, and Guild. Matthew Klein, who now runs the CNC shop for Gibson, was there, and a lot of other notable makers went through that shop including John Greven, Mark Lacey, Randy Wood, and Stephen Gilchrist, just to name a few. There was a healthy competition to impress each other, and it drove all of us to be better. Working there could sometimes be brutal to your ego, but you knew you were always taking things to the limit."

While still employed at Gruhn's, Paul started building classical guitars in his apartment, including the guitar Earl Klugh used on his album *Solo*. He also developed conviction about his motivations and building philosophy. "Most novice builders spend way too much time on the bracing pattern of the guitar, and not enough on the overall geometry," he asserts. "Just look at all of the different successful bracing patterns used on the classical guitar historically. All you're really doing is loading controlled stress into the top so that it's taut but still free to vibrate. The way to learn about a bracing pattern is to build it and experiment with it. I think experimentation and deep study are important." Paul's experience has convinced him that creating a great instrument depends foremost on starting with a great design and understanding how its elements interact. All of the other elements necessary to this process — including the materials and workmanship, as well as the talent, ambition, luck, and knowledge of the builder — are of secondary importance. "Innovations will always come along to drive designs forward, and concepts will emerge that lead us in different directions, but it is what goes on between the maker's mind and hands that will always make this an art form."

His reverence for the traditional Spanish approach to building is evident in his past use of a V joint between the head and neck stocks. He uses several Fleta-style design elements, including a bell-shaped heel block, which allows the back to vibrate more freely than does a long foot, and a dovetail joint to attach the neck to the body. "I believe that the dovetail joint is the most accurate way to customize the alignment of the neck. It also requires the most skill to set," he says. Fleta's sequence of attaching the back to the sides before attaching the top is also utilized so that the visible details of interior finishing can be dealt with more easily. This eliminates the possibility of an imperfect marriage between braces and lining, or a bead of glue squeeze-out marring the impression of masterful craftsmanship created by the exterior of the guitar.

While Paul avoids crediting any single construction detail with being the reason for the success of his instruments, he explains that there are guidelines he uses in all of them. "The weight of the top makes a huge difference in the sound. A light top creates a perception of more power and more volume, but a lot of what many players perceive as volume is really an overbearing bass. I much prefer to hear the sound open in the middle with a full, clear D and G. An open midrange will improve both the high and low frequencies, and provide a sweet, well-balanced responsiveness, without muddying up the bass."

The choice of which glue to use is another consideration in the quest for tone. "I don't want to shock anybody," he says, "but I consider Titebond to be one step above a hot-glue gun when it comes to guitar work. That's because it creeps with temperature and humidity changes, which allows the glued parts to slide. It also seems to have adhesion problems over long periods of time. I've seen a lot of joint failures with aliphatic resin, including V joints that come loose, headstock veneer and all, without a shred of torn fiber. I've used it on large wood structures I have assembled for machines in my shop, and have seen them come apart under vibration and stress. A glue that dries hard and crystallizes, like hide glue, doesn't move at all. I always use it on wood bindings. I'd rather use epoxy or white glue on top braces than use an aliphatic-resin glue. For bridges and cross-grain braces, I've used a true PVA like Elmer's white glue for years without any problems. This glue has very good adhesion and allows for some slippage when backs and tops expand across the grain, limiting the tendency for loose cross-grain braces."

Finally, Paul stresses the importance of the aging of top wood in preparing the wood for construction. "Especially with spruce, I would like to have wood aged at least ten years before using it. The effects of age on spruce are obvious. If the wood is to respond well, the gummy substances held within it must have time to crystallize."

ALL COURTESY OF PAUL McGILL

A McGill "Foldaway" resophonic guitar with a sloped-shoulder design to improve upper fingerboard access.

In 1993, with his reputation as a builder of classical guitars firmly established, he embarked on a project to develop and perfect a resophonic guitar design. Paul says he has always believed in being receptive to all areas of musical expression, but even he was surprised when Earl Klugh asked him to build a resonator guitar. Apart from knowing that the unique sound of both wood- and metal-bodied National and Dobro guitars was being used by very gifted players in every musical style imaginable, he knew nothing about the process of building a guitar with a laminated top using an aluminum cone inside the body to project the sound. "Chet Atkins happened to show Earl a 1960s-era Brazilian-made DelVecchio resonator guitar that he has used on countless recordings, and Earl was just amazed by its sound. This is a very rare and special instrument, and Chet seldom takes it out of the case unless he's recording," Paul said, remembering the events behind one of the most unexpected turns in his career. "Chet kindly offered to loan me a DelVecchio to examine, and I held onto it for about six months while I planned how to build one." Paul decided to increase the scale length slightly, from Chet's 57CM DelVecchio to 60CM, to improve intonation, and began spinning resonator cones on a lathe.

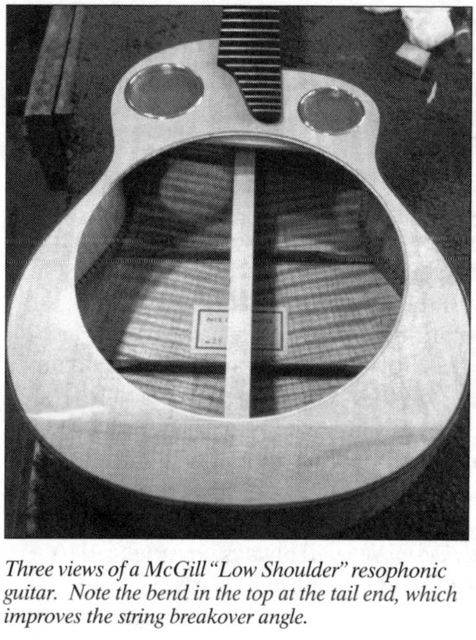

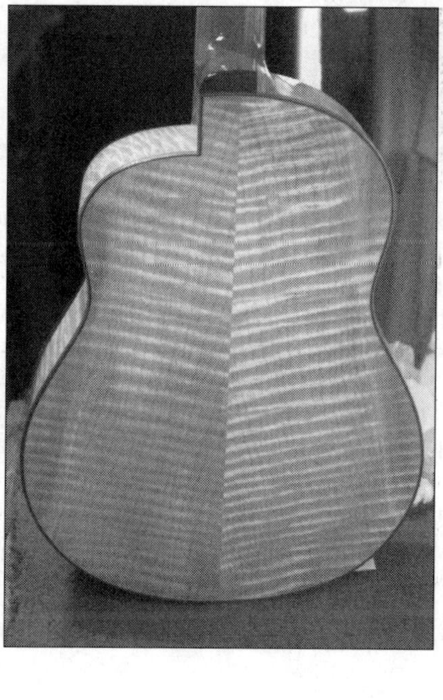

Three views of a McGill "Low Shoulder" resophonic guitar. Note the bend in the top at the tail end, which improves the string breakover angle.

What began as nothing more than an interesting project and a favor to an old friend gained a momentum of its own. Over the course of a full-scale three-year development project, he did extensive research on the effect of changing the dimensions and materials of the cylinder on which the cone rests. A unique feature of the McGill resonator guitar is a patent-pending interchangeable cylinder design which enables players to completely change the sound of the guitar at will.

With assurance from Earl Klugh and Chet Atkins that the McGill resophonic was an exceptional guitar, he began devoting more time to building them for other players, including John Schroeder (owner of *Fingerstyle Guitar* magazine), Nashville session artist Don Potter, Phil Keaggy, and Nato Lima of Los Indios Trabajaras, Steve Earl, and Branson showman and guitarist Jim Stafford. "Jim is a great guitar player. He's made two CDs that really show off exactly what the guitar can do."

Classical guitar by Paul McGill

"Building resonator guitars is really as much work as building an archtop," Paul laughs. "By the time you work your way through all the action adjustments, take the guitar apart and put it back together a few times in search of the adjustments that will bring out the best sound, you've seen a day go by." In addition to the new instrument, he continues to concentrate on building the superb classical guitars that first brought him national recognition, including a Muriel Anderson Model.

When asked what advice he would give to someone who wants to build guitars, the forty-year-old builder was characteristically philosophical. "We have to be willing to fall on our faces. It's much better to use your hands and ears and commit yourself to learning by doing, rather than getting wrapped up in a lot of theories. I'd have to agree with my legendary Indian friend Nato Lima who once said, "I'd rather be the first to do it badly than the last to do it perfectly." ——

---

*(**Sloane** from page 213)*

friends with the Assad brothers. I also learned a lot about his past. He grew up an orphan on the Lower East Side (10th St.). He spent many years and traveled the world in the Merchant Marines. His primary occupation was as a designer and he worked in the advertising industry, designing product packaging and record album covers. He taught himself metalworking and jewelry making. He designed and made woodworking tools, especially planes, which he sold under the IBEX brand. He was a writer, and in addition to his lutherie books, he had written and published a children's book titled *The Silver Cart.*

Robin and I encouraged Irving to take her mom Zelda out to dinner. They fell in love like a couple of teenagers and married the next year. There was an incredible amount of "small world" coincidence to realize I had as a father-in-law the man who was responsible for my career path.

Irving was a true renaissance man. There seemed to be no limit to the things he could do. He made magnificent fish prints on exquisite paper, did his own catalog-quality photography of his tools, made beautiful jewelry, built a new deck for his home, and played guitar and piano. But perhaps his best skill was his ability to make molds. He was self-taught in this art, but it was the mold making that permitted him to make his fine planes, tools, and the beautiful plates for the classical guitar tuning machines.

After failing to find competent workers to produce the tuning gears in his local area, he licensed the gears to Stewart-MacDonald, who now manufacture them at their Waverly shop in Montana. Irving travelled to Bozeman to set up the assembly and train the workers. Waverly then began to produce a variety of steel string guitar tuning gears utilizing Irving's patented design. Irving had also designed the finest gear available for upright bass. David Gage, ace acoustic-bass guru of New York City, has taken over the assembly and distribution of the bass gear. Most of the other tools are distributed by Bob Juzak of Metropolitan Music in Vermont. Some of his best-known tools are his violin finger planes, bridge clamp, fretting rule, bending iron, rosette cutter, thickness gauge, and crack-splicing set.

We are now in the golden age of guitar making. All of us who are in our forties or fifties have been perfecting our craft for the last twenty or thirty years and are just starting to get pretty good at what we do. As I look back over the last twenty years or so, it seems to me that every interview I have read with any guitar maker or repair person contains a line something like "The first book I ever read was Irving Sloane's *Classical Guitar Construction.*" We will always be indebted to Irving Sloane for changing our lives forever.

—— *Roger Sadowsky*

Originally published in *American Lutherie #55,* 1998

ALL COURTESY OF R.E. BRUNE

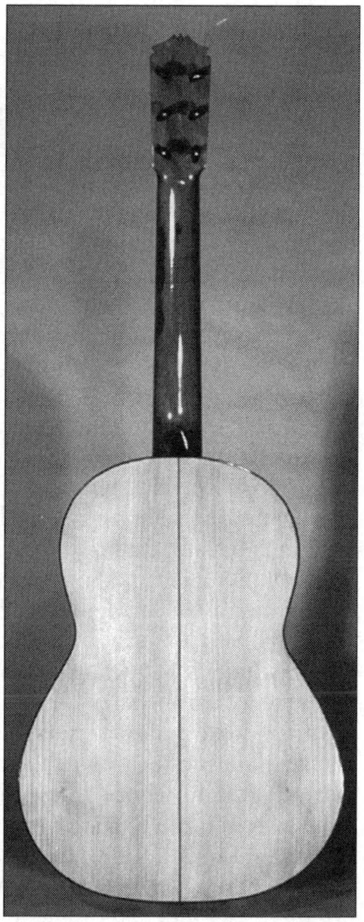

Sabicas' 1951 Marcelo Barbero

By R.E. Bruné

Two views of the 1951 Marcelo Barbero flamenco guitar, Ex. Fidel Zabal, Ex. Sabicas, Ex. Carlos Montoya, after restoration by R.E. Bruné.

WHILE IN NEW YORK CITY during the Spanish Guitar Exhibition mounted by the Metropolitan Museum of Art in the fall of 1991, I gave a lecture entitled "Andalucia and the Evolution of the Modern Guitar" at the American Institute of Guitar on West 54th St. After the lecture I had the privilege of meeting Dr. Robert Schultz, who introduced himself and mentioned that he had a Marcelo Barbero guitar which needed some repairs. Ordinarily, I am too swamped with work to take in outside repairs, but I have a tremendous love of Marcelo Barbero's guitars, as I consider him to be one of the greatest makers of the 20th century, and so I agreed to "have a look."

Some months later, Dr. Schultz had occasion to visit Chicago on business, and he brought the guitar with him to my shop so I could evaluate what it needed. When he opened the case I had the strange sensation that somehow I knew this guitar, that I had seen it before, which I mentioned to Dr. Schultz. He thought that was impossible, since it had been in his possession for almost forty years. Still, the feeling persisted. So I inquired where he had found the instrument, and he mentioned he had obtained it from his teacher Fidel Zabal in 1953, just before he went away to medical school. Still, the guitar looked very familiar.

Fidel Zabal was a gypsy from Spain whose mother preferred that he not become involved with the guitar. She had sent him to the priests in their village for his education, where he not only learned to play piano, but to read and write music. Despite his mother's best efforts, he was lured to the flamenco guitar, which he learned on his own. However, he had resented the priest's control of information, because as official village scribes, they were privy to all the gossip and private information of everyone's personal lives. Consequently, he emigrated to America, where he made a living playing flamenco engagements with his wife who was a flamenco dancer. However, her loss of hearing curtailed his performing activities, and eventually, Fidel gave up show business to work for the telephone company, and teach a few students, including Dr. Schultz.

I asked Dr. Schultz if he knew where Fidel had obtained the guitar. He told me that Fidel was given the guitar by the legendary flamenco master Sabicas in

---

Top center: Barbero used at least four different labels over the course of his career. Of the two he used towards the end of his career, this version is nearly identical to one used by Santos Hernández. He sometimes signed his labels, but not consistently. Presence or absence of a signature on the label is of no particular significance in relation to the quality of the instrument, nor is the use of one or the other label significant. Usually he also used an oval stamp across the lower left corner of his labels, but in this case he omitted it. This type of inconsistent labeling/stamping/signing is why I say you should never rely on labels, stamps, or signatures to identify an instrument's author.

appreciation of Fidel's writing down of Sabicas' creations (Sabicas did not know how to read nor write music). Suddenly the bell went off in my head, and I went to my cabinet and pulled out my copies of *Flamenco Puro,* the landmark album recorded by Sabicas and released here on the Columbia label and in Spain on the Hispavox label. On both albums, clear as the nose on my face, was Dr. Schultz' Barbero! I showed him the albums which clearly showed Sabicas with this very guitar in hands, much to his shock!

The story of Dr. Schultz' acquisition of this guitar is a fascinating one, and illustrates well the luck of the draw when it comes to finding a great instrument. In those days, Dr. Schultz was one of Fidel's best students, and when Fidel was offered an opportunity to play for a touring flamenco company, he had to decline, as he didn't want to create a hardship for his family by leaving on tour. He suggested that Dr. Schultz, his student, go instead, and since he would need a good guitar, Fidel Zabal had offered to sell Dr. Schultz either an older Santos Hernández or this 1951 Marcelo Barbero, which was practically new, yet had a beautiful sound. Dr. Schultz thought about it for a week, and when he went for his lesson, he told Fidel he wanted the Santos, whose guitars were considerably more well known than Barbero's. In the meantime, Fidel had second thoughts about selling the Santos, and only offered to sell the Barbero, which Dr. Schultz bought. However, Dr. Schultz was accepted into medical school, so he never ended up touring with the flamenco company as Fidel had originally planned; yet the guitar became his lifelong companion.

I grew up listening to *Flamenco Puro* along with Sabicas' other great recordings on Elektra, Volume 1, 2, and 3, which in the '60s were the cutting edge of flamenco guitar playing. I met Sabicas in 1976 when he played in Chicago and spent time with him. He told me that when he arrived in New York in the early '50s, he had gone into the Elektra recording studio and spent about a week recording various cuts, which he refused to accept royalties for, insisting on getting paid $1,000 for the week's work. He didn't care what they did with the recordings after that. He simply didn't trust them to monitor record sales, so he took the money and left the master tapes. Later, some of the material was sold to different record companies, such as Columbia and Hispavox, and over the years they took various cuts and assembled them into albums which were released beginning in the mid- to late-1950s.* According to the late Ivor Mairants (England's dean of the guitar) Elektra Vol. 1 and 2 (EKL 117 and EKL 121) were released in England in 1952. If my memory serves me correctly, *Flamenco Puro* came out in this country around 1957. They were all mastered in this one

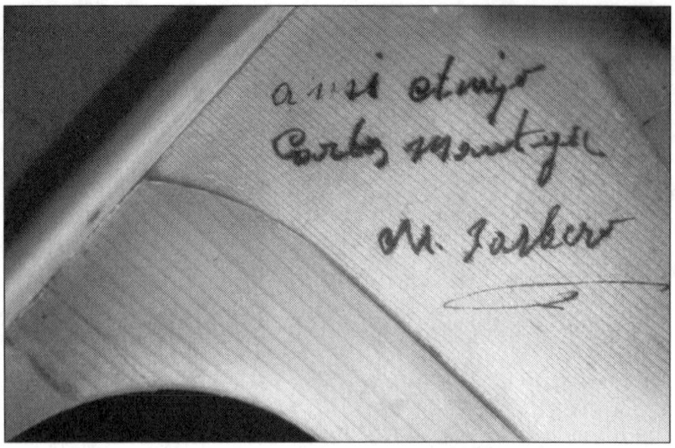

The dedication to Carlos Montoya written inside the bass side of the top by the soundhole. It reads: "A mi Amigo Carlos Montoya, M. Barbero." *(To my Friend Carlos Montoya, M. Barbero.)*

Closeup of the cover photo of the Hispavox version of Flamenco Puro *(130 076) which was copyrighted 1961. This version was released in Spain and caused quite a sensation with aficionados there, because Sabicas had left Spain in 1936 when the Spanish Civil War broke out, and he was not as well known in Spain as he was in America.*

Closeup of the American Columbia release of Flamenco Puro *(WL 154) which was released in this country around 1957. Though not as clear of a shot, it is the same guitar. Several photos were shot of Sabicas with this guitar, including the famous black and white version which was used for many years by LaBella with their "Flamenco" strings. I have a prized copy of this photo which Sabicas dedicated to me,* "Para el gran 'luthier' R. E. Bruné, Sinceramente, Sabicas" *which hangs in my shop. According to this photo, it was taken by James J. Kriegsmann of New York City, so I assume the other record jacket photos were also from his studio. Mr. Kriegsmann died in 1994 and his work was sold to the Michael Ochs Archives.*

* *I had thought this arrangement more legend than fact, but in a recent conversation with Irving Sloane, who was a friend of Jack Holzman, who owned Electra Records, this $1,000 fee was confirmed. Mr. Sloane also indicated that in those days Sabicas was earning the princely sum of $500 per week playing at La Zambra, the leading flamenco tablao in New York, which was owned by Carlos Montoya!*

1951 Marcelo Barbero Flamenco Guitar

GAL Instrument Plan #42

by R.E. Bruné

This instrument plan is available as a full-size blueprint from the GAL.

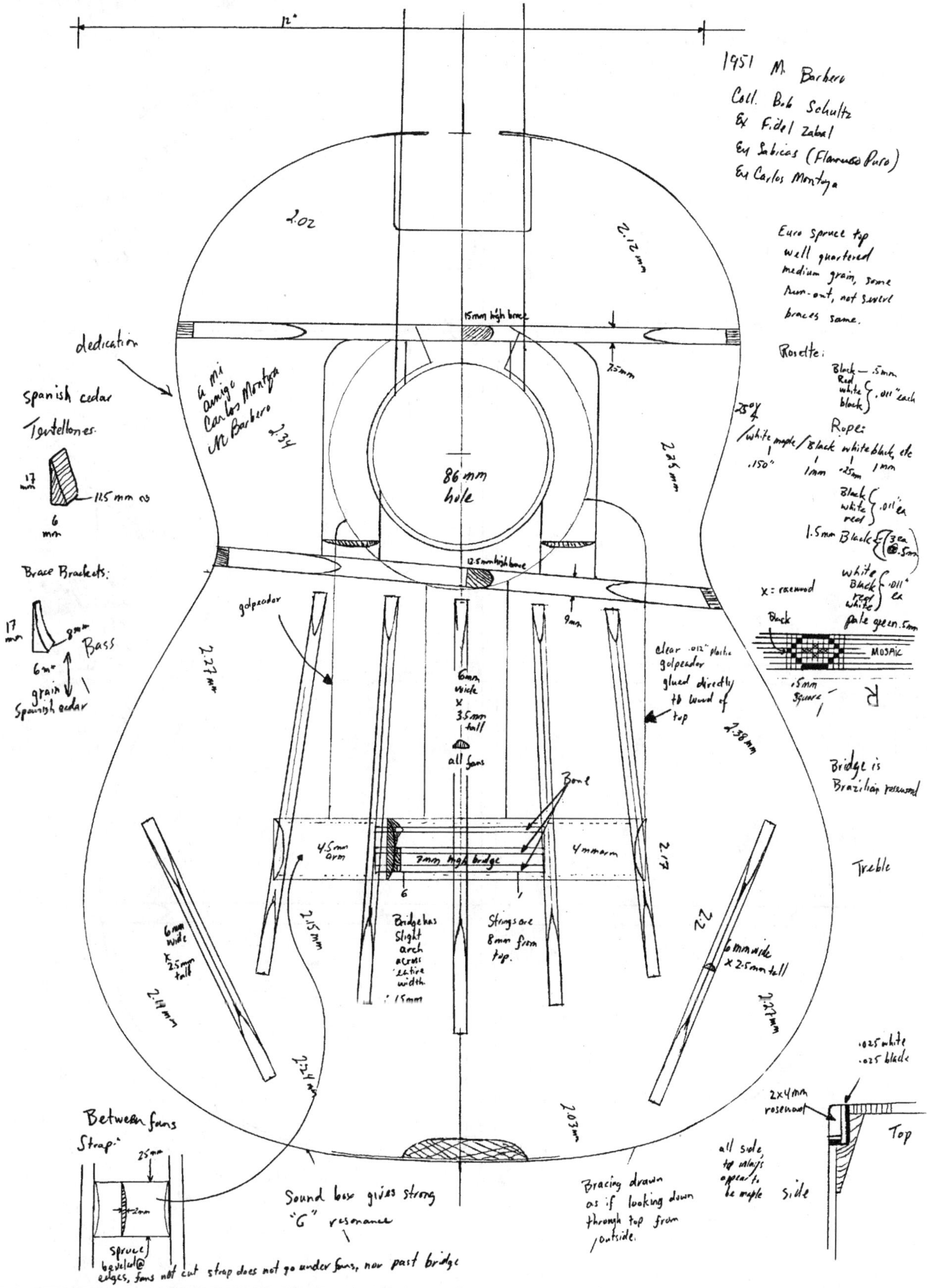

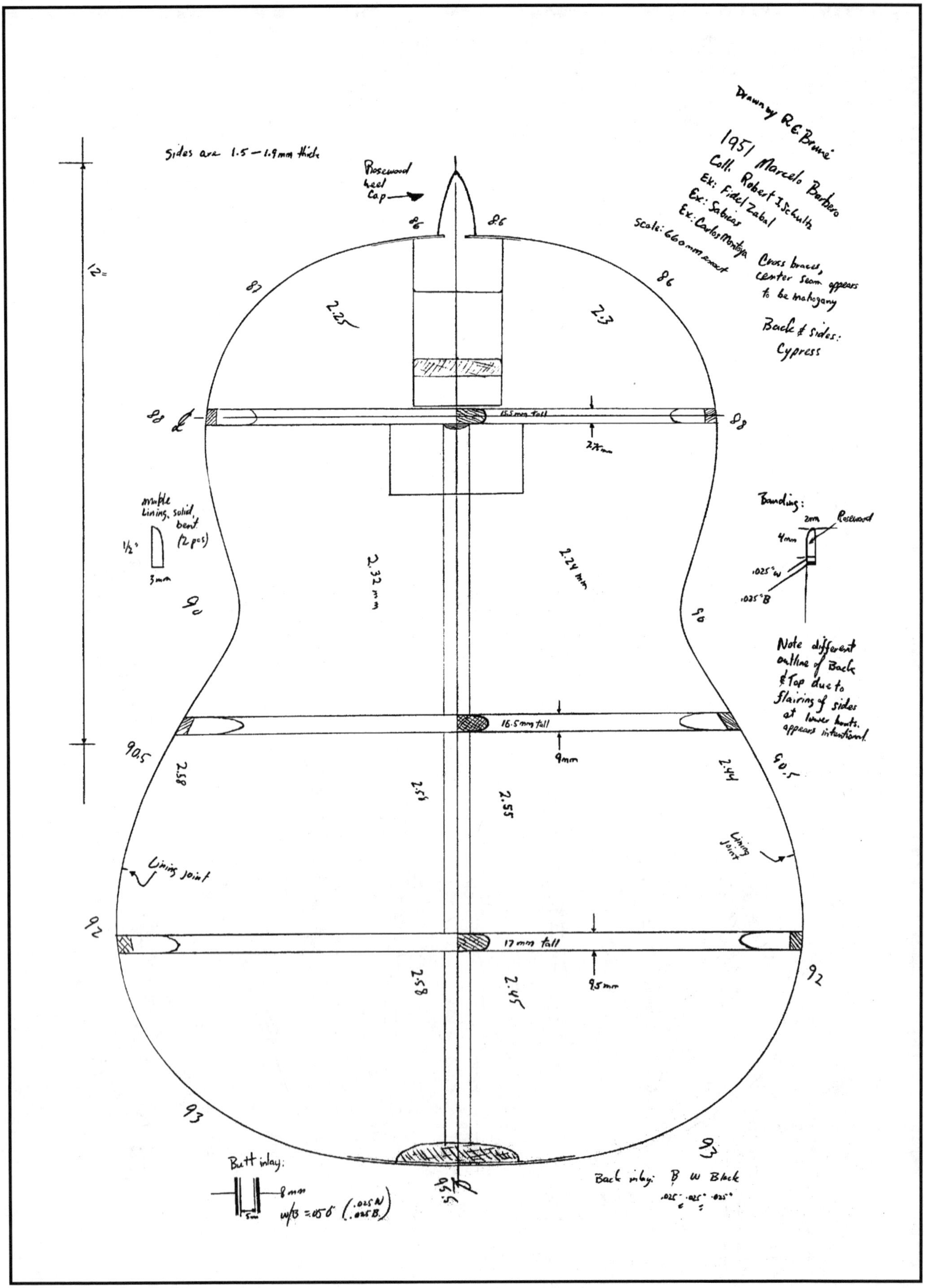

Drawn by R.E. Bruné
1951 Marcelo Barbero
Coll. Robert I. Schultz
Ex: Fidel Zabal
Ex: Sabicas
Ex: Carlos Montoya
Scale: 660mm exact
Cross braces, center seam appears to be mahogany
Back & sides: Cypress
Sides are 1.5 — 1.9mm thick
Rosewood heel cap
12"
86
86
87
86
2.25
2.3
88
88
15.5mm tall
2.75mm
maple Lining, solid, bent (2 pcs)
1/2"
3mm
2.32mm
2.24mm
90
90
Banding:
2mm
Rosewood
4mm
.025" W
.025" B
Note different outline of Back & Top due to flairing of sides at lower bouts. appears intentional.
16.5mm tall
9mm
90.5
90.5
2.58
2.56
2.55
2.44
Lining joint
Lining joint
92
92
17mm tall
9.5mm
2.58
2.45
93
93
93.5
Butt inlay:
8mm
5mm
W/B = .050" (.025W .025B)
Back inlay: B W Black
.025" .025" .025"

recording session using this 1951 Marcelo Barbero guitar.

The plot thickens. Before deciding what work to undertake, I thought it prudent to have a look at the inside, and much to our mutual surprise, there was a dedication written by Barbero inside the top to none other than Carlos Montoya! In the obituary notice for Marcelo Barbero that appeared in the March 25, 1956 issue of the *Supleménto de España,* Barbero's student Arcángel Fernández specifically mentions Montoya as one of Barbero's more well-known clients. It is likely that when Sabicas arrived in New York where Montoya was already a resident, he obtained the guitar from Montoya, who, being such a good friend of Barbero, knew he could always get another. Sabicas now had a first-rate guitar to take to the recording studio. Afterward, he gave it to Fidel, in appreciation for his written transcriptions. That's how Gypsies are.

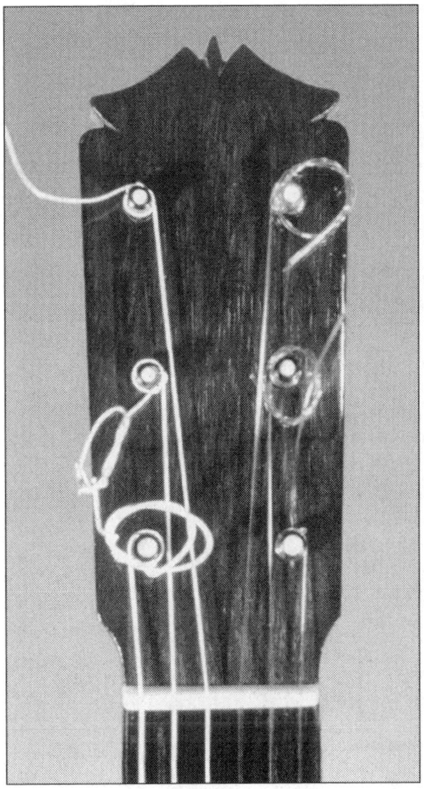

The classic Barbero headstock, which was cut free form. No two were exactly *alike.*

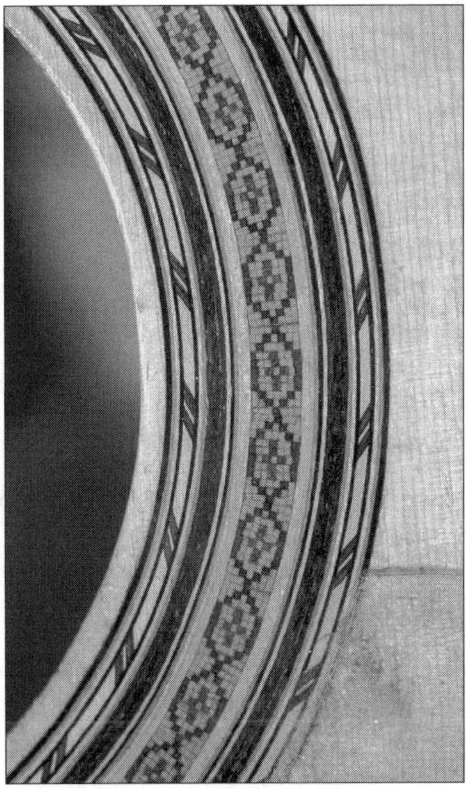

Barbero was very creative with his rosettes and made many different patterns. This mosaic is similar to designs I've seen in Santos, Esteso, and even Velázquez guitars.

Interior view of the fan braces and bridge strap on the bass side of the top under the bridge.

Marcelo Barbero was one of the most extraordinary guitar makers of this century. Born in Madrid around 1904 to an impoverished family, he was orphaned as a boy. He began in the shop of José Ramírez I and later worked for his son, José II. At various times in his life he also was a professional boxer and racing cyclist. He also supplemented his income singing flamenco in the *tablaos*, but his first love was guitar making. Curiously, he did not play the guitar, but relied on his experience and frequent feedback from other players to evolve his pattern over the years.

During the Spanish Civil War he was called into service, and saw heavy fighting around the university city of Madrid. Of his company of 150, only 23 survived.

After the death of Santos Hernández in 1943, he was hired by Santos' widow to complete the instruments left unfinished by Santos when he died, which took three years. Marcelo then began working entirely on his own from his apartment at Ministriles 6, where he had been living with his family for some time. As his fame grew, he was able to relocate his family to nicer quarters, but he kept the original apartment as his workshop.

Around 1952 or so he took on an apprentice, Arcángel Fernández who had been a cabinet maker and one-time flamenco guitarist. It is odd that Barbero did not usually finish his own guitars, but would hire a varnisher who would come to the shop to varnish the completed instrument. According to firsthand accounts, it normally took ten days to two weeks for Marcelo to complete a guitar, and the most expensive item on the instrument was the ebony fingerboard. I have spoken to several original owners who remember paying about $25 for their Barbero guitars! Ah, to have

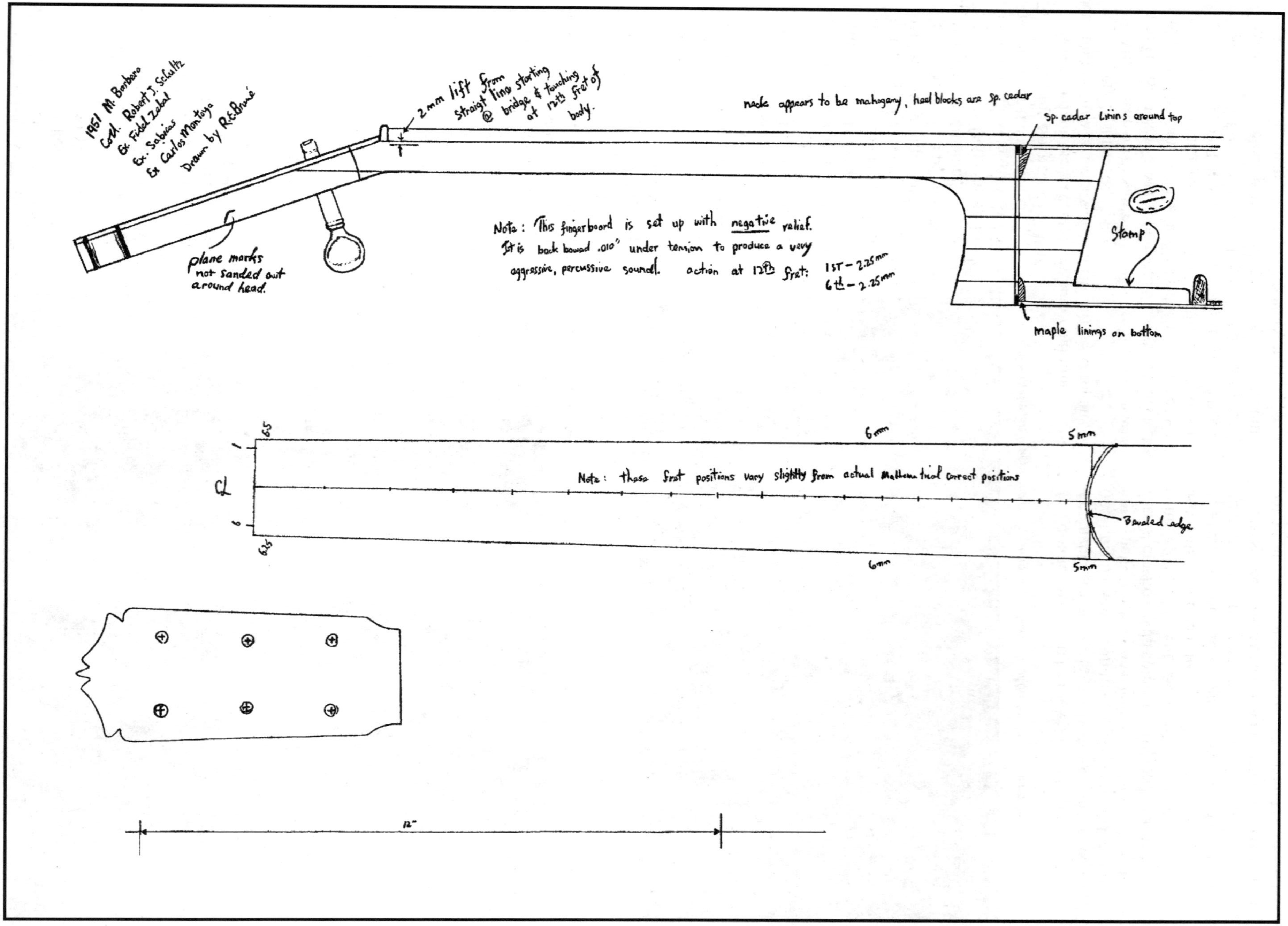
1951 M. Barbero
Coll. Robert J. Schultz
Ex. Fidel Zabal
Ex. Sabicas
Ex Carlos Montoya
Drawn by R.E.Bruné
2mm lift from straight line starting @ bridge & touching at 12th fret of body.
neck appears to be mahogany, heel blocks are Sp. cedar
Sp. cedar Linins around top
plane marks not sanded out around head.
Note: This fingerboard is set up with negative relief. It is back bowed .010" under tension to produce a very aggressive, percussive sound. action at 12th fret: 1ST – 2.25mm 6th – 2.25mm
Stamp
maple linings on bottom
6.5
6.25
CL
6mm
5mm
Note: these fret positions vary slightly from actual mathematical correct positions
Beveled edge
12"

a time machine. Marcelo died tragically on March 6, 1956 after apparently hemorrhaging for four days from an undiagnosed stomach ulcer. The Spanish press hailed him as the "Stradivarius of Lavapies" referring to the section of Madrid where his shop was located. His son, Marcelo Barbero II, currently works in the shop of his teacher, Arcángel Fernández. (Note: Marcelo Barbero hijo died in January 2005.)

There are several features on this particular instrument which merit attention. The first is the curious detail of the outline, which does not match between front and back at all, the back being nearly 5MM wider at the lower bout. I believe this to be the result of the pieced lower linings, which caused the back to spring out when they were installed. Also notable is the mahogany neck, as this makes for a heavier instrument than Spanish cedar. Barbero is reported to have bought old furniture from flea markets to cut up for materials. Judging by the random grain selection of heel and head laminations, I suspect he threw away very little wood.

The thickness of the top and back are also notable, being much beefier than a typical Santos. The back is quite massive for a flamenco guitar. The bridge is also fairly stiff, with almost no undercutting of the valley below the grade of the arms. However, it is set to carry the strings low to the top, and as a result, the instrument has fared extremely well. The fingerboard with its slight negative relief produces that aggressive, percussive sound so admired by Montoya, and allows an action that is astoundingly easy to handle. The trade-off is a slight buzzing, which is controllable with the right-hand technique.

1951 Marcelo Barbero after restoration by R. E. Bruné. Several cracks were re-repaired on the top, and the bridge was reglued. The original golpeadores *were replaced with exact copies, and the original French polish was touched up in places that were worn away. It was remarkably well preserved for a flamenco guitar of this age.*

Finally, the strap under the bridge (bridge patch) is unique, even for Barbero guitars, being wider than his typical straps, which were usually about 10MM–12MM wide. It is interrupted by the fan braces which remain glued to the top their entire length, rather than being notched for the strap. Also, the bridge strap does not extend past the two outermost fans by the ends of the bridge arms. One almost has the impression that the bridge strap was added as an afterthought after the top was braced, though this is definitely not the case. In terms of the usual reasons for having a bridge strap (stiffen the bridge area, provide a counter surface to aid in gluing the bridge, and so on) this one is nearly useless, though apparently harmless.

What about the sound? Fortunately, unlike Segovia's two guitars at the Metropolitan Museum, I was able to play this guitar extensively after its repair. I was amazed at the fidelity to the sound in Sabicas' recordings, and I had no problems achieving a credible imitation of his sound. Others who have played the guitar have also commented on the perfect "flamenco" quality of sound. I consider this guitar to be the defining flamenco guitar of the 20th century, an icon which served as the inspiration of an entire generation of flamenco guitarists through the numerous recordings Sabicas made on this guitar. As a model for a great flamenco guitar, one should look no further.

My thanks to Dr. Robert Schultz for allowing access to this instrument. ——

Originally published in *American Lutherie #55*, 1998

Meet the Maker: David Gusset

by Jonathon Peterson

Tell me about growing up. Where did you live, and where did your interest in the arts come from?

I was born in San Francisco, and grew up down the peninsula. There was a lot of art and craft around the home. My mother is an amateur artist and always had some painting, art, or garden project in the works. Her father was a professional carpenter, and I often got to watch him do carpentry around our house. He made me a pair of kid-size sawhorses which I used for making my own creations, mostly scooters and coasters. Although my other grandparents had made luggage by hand for a living in New York City, my father chose to work at a desk job, but he found a hobby in rock hounding and lapidary work. On family camping trips my mother sketched landscapes while my father hunted for rocks. My dad's '55 Oldsmobile was practically scraping the ground heading home from those trips loaded down with rocks. He used the facilities at the evening school to cut and polish rocks. My sister and I got to go along and grind and polish rocks, too. My older sister, Diane, was always very talented in everything from drawing, painting, ceramics, and print making to set design for all her high school's plays. She's now a very fine professional artist.

JENNIFER GUSSET (ALL VIOLIN PHOTOS BY DAVID GUSSET)

David Gusset at his shop in Eugene, Oregon.

What mediums do your sister and mother work in?

My sister still does everything from book illustration to large museum dioramas and displays. Of all my mother's works, my favorites are her brilliant oil pastels and her bonsai.

What led you to a career in the arts?

There are a number of factors. I've always been a very hands-on person. If some project involving art, building, or handwork needed to be done for school, I just did it and enjoyed it. I never got discouragement from my parents, or thought of any project as being too difficult. In high school and college I studied drawing, ceramics, and glass blowing. My first summer out of high school I rented a small storefront in the mountain resort town of Twain-Harte, California and made custom leather sandals, a skill my sister and I had taught ourselves by making sandals for all our high school friends. Another big influence was the two years of traveling I did when I was nineteen and twenty years old, visiting South American peoples and experiencing their traditional arts, crafts, and culture.

What was your first exposure to the violin?

I started playing the violin when I was about six years old in group lessons. Every year we gave recitals, sharing the stage with kids learning the electric Hawaiian guitar. Later I took private lessons until I was maybe twelve or so. I also studied piano, guitar, and saxophone. When I was sixteen or seventeen, an interest in folk music led me to old-time fiddle music, so I picked up the violin again.

When did you decide to become a violin maker?

According to my mother, it was when I was first learning to play that I told her about wanting to make a violin someday. My earliest memory of wanting to make violins comes from my last year of high school. The whole violin-shop thing was kind of alluring, being surrounded by all those instruments, tools, bottles, and varnish smells. I had dropped off my violin and bow at a repair shop in San Francisco, and when I returned a few days later to pick them up, I worked up the courage to tell the repairman about my aspirations to learn violin making. He put a damper on my ambitions by suggesting I buy a particular book which would tell me everything I would ever need to know about making violins. It was one of those "You can make a Stradivarius Violin" books for hobbyists, probably published by *Popular Mechanics*.

I spent the next five years doing other things. I went to college for a year and studied art, traveled in South America, went to college for another year, and then got hired for seasonal work with the Forest Service.

What were you doing for the Forest Service? Planting trees or trail maintenance?

Well, actually I did tree planting before I worked for the Forest Service. During my last year of college, besides art studies, I took classes in forestry, natural resource management, forest ecology, and forest surveying. I applied for a summer employment with the Forest Service, naïvely thinking I could get a job as a naturalist doing field studies of Native American archeological sites or illustrating pamphlets. Instead, I got picked for my surveying experience. I've always been opposed to the government's timber sale policies and practices, so surveying for logging roads wasn't an ideal job, although it got me by for a couple of summers.

I was still very interested in violin making. I went to an old-time fiddling competition late that summer and I happened to meet a young fiddler named Amos Hargrave. He told me about a new school for violin making in Salt Lake City where he had been accepted to begin in the fall. So I wrote a letter to the school expressing my interest in learning violin making and requesting literature about the school and information about any other violin-making programs. About a month later I received a reply saying that one of the students had left the program, there was an opening, and if I sent a $200 deposit, I would be accepted. It sounded a little bit suspicious to me at the time.

No exam, just send money.

No exam, no interview, I'd never even mentioned anything about my background, yet I was being offered the chance to attend. I've always wondered about that. The director of the school Peter Prier later told me that he liked my letter. Of course, in the very early days of the school there probably wasn't an abundance of applicants. Another factor might have been that I was from out of state. Can you imagine all your former pupils one day setting up shop across the street?

But really, I had little to lose. I decided to work into the fall, and then go to Salt Lake. I entered the school in November 1974, two months after my other class mates, but I managed to catch up by the end of the school year in May. Although it was a three- to four-year course, my eagerness to move on helped me finish in a record two and a half years.

Who were your instructors, and who else was in your class?

Peter was the director and head instructor, but Paul Hart was in charge of the workshop on my side of the school. Paul is an incredibly talented and prolific maker of violin family instruments, gambas, and lutes. I learned a lot just watching him work.

Violin by David Gusset, 1989. Copy of the 1700 Heberlein Strad.

The school was founded in 1972, so I was among the earliest students. The first graduates all finished within about a year beginning in late 1976. The first graduates were Kevin Smith, Chris DeGroot, and Bill Wolf. The next spring Amos Hargrave, Jim McKean, and I finished the course, and later that same year, Morgan Andersen, Guy Rabut, and Art Toman graduated. Kevin is now working in the San Diego area. Chris is, I believe, now a professor of psychiatry somewhere in the Midwest. Bill's father insisted Bill get a real education after finishing violin-making school so he sent him off to Reed College. Bill's love for jazz guitar music brought him back to the music biz in Salt Lake. Jim, Amos, Art, and Guy all went off to New York to work in the big shops, and Jim and Guy now have their own shops there. Jim is current president of the American Federation of Violin Bow Makers. Amos is working in Kansas. Art is in Boston. Morgan established his name as a bow maker and is living on Lopez Island in Washington State.

Where did you go after you finished school?

I returned to San Francisco to work in the shop of violin dealer Frank Passa. Frank had worked in the repair shop at Rembert Wurlitzer's in New York under the supervision of Maestro Simone Sacconi, and had come out to San Francisco to open his own shop in the late '50s. In its day, Wurlitzer's may have been the most important violin shop in America. Most of the Strads, Guarneris, Amatis, and Guadagninis went through Wurlitzer's shop, either for sale or for restoration. Sacconi was their head restorer. He was responsible for some major advancements in the art of violin restoration in this century.

How long was Sacconi there?

More than fifty years in New York. I believe Emil Herrmann brought him over from Italy in the early 1930s. When Herrmann retired, Sacconi went over to Wurlitzer's. Most of Sacconi's pupils and associates eventually spread out across the country and opened their own shops.

I worked in Frank's shop learning repair and restoration. A lot of nice instruments came and went through his shop as well. One of my projects was a Strad restoration, which seemed to go on forever. We would do a little bit of work on it, and then it would go back in the safe for days and weeks at a time. Actually, we were getting down to the final retouching about the time I left. The job involved correcting arches, fitting some

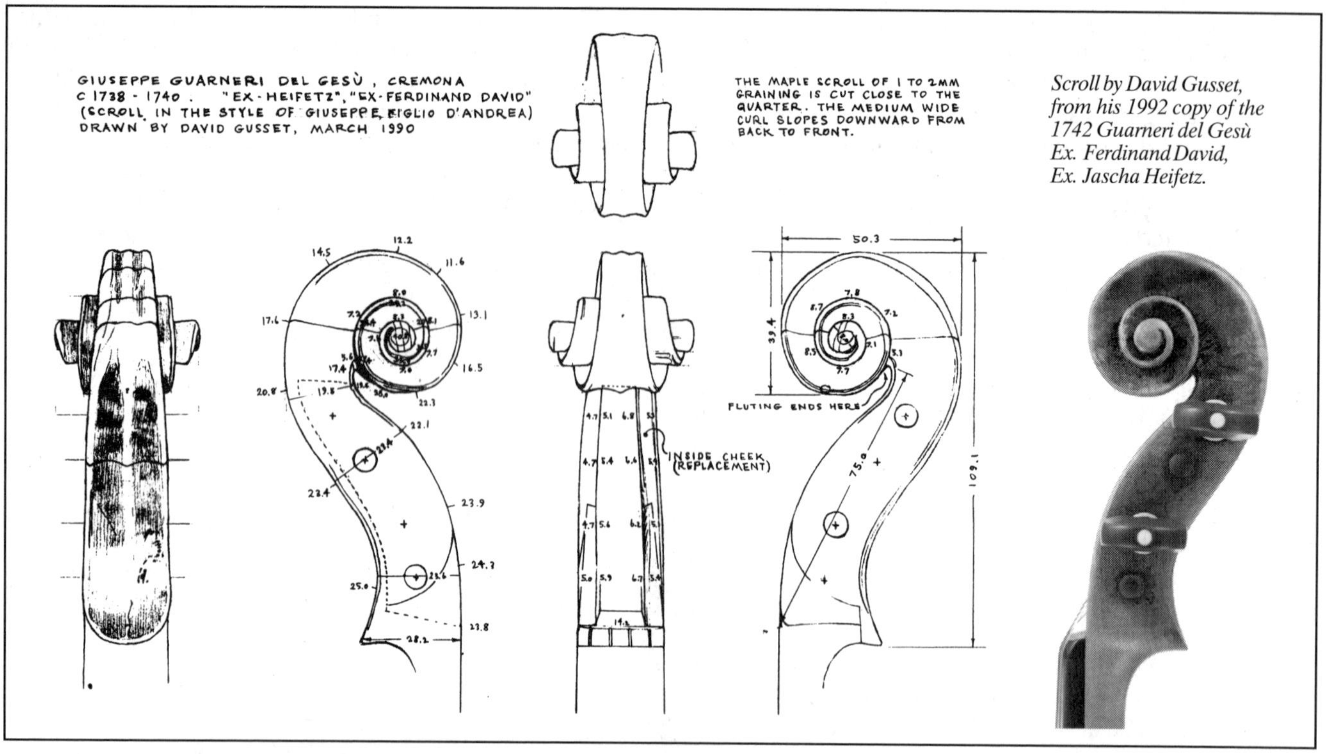

Scroll by David Gusset, from his 1992 copy of the 1742 Guarneri del Gesù Ex. Ferdinand David, Ex. Jascha Heifetz.

fairly major patches, and trying to undo a lot of unsuccessful repair work done by others. At one time I counted about fifty cracks in the top. By the time I left, they were all but invisible.

Were you doing any building of your own at that time?

Shortly after leaving Frank's shop in late 1978, I made a violin for the Violin Society of America's 2nd violin-making competition. Up until then I had never entered a competition, and most of the eleven instruments I had made were ones made while I was still in school. The model I chose to make was a Stradivari, somewhat inspired by my recollections of the Strad I had spent so many months working on. Nevertheless, it was entirely my own creation. Quite unexpectedly, I received a gold medal for workmanship. That was sort of a beginning for me, and I soon felt more confident about what I was doing.

In 1979 I took a couple of months to travel and to view and study instrument collections in Europe. The next VSA competition happened in New York in 1980, and I submitted two instruments for that, a violin and a viola, and they both received gold medals.

So you're on a roll.

Yes, I guess you could say that, but later the VSA began to realize that the same makers were winning every competition, so they decided to exclude from future competitions anyone who had previously won three or more gold medals.

What about other competitions?

There was one in Germany where I won a prize for workmanship, and there was the 1991 City of Paris Competition, for which I got the Bronze. My biggest honor was in Italy, at the 1985 Antonio Stradivari International Triennial Competition in Cremona. Most makers consider the Triennial to be the most international, and the most prestigious of all the competitions. After all, Cremona was the birthplace of the violin as we know it. The Amati, Guarneri, and Stradivari families worked there.

The Triennial's theme that year was honoring the work of Maestro Simone F. Sacconi, whom I was telling you about earlier. Sacconi died in 1975. The 1985 Triennial had a special exhibit of his work honoring his contributions to the field. He was also responsible for reviving the art of violin making in Cremona through his work with the new violin-making school there in its early days.

Had the violin-making tradition in Cremona pretty much been broken off at that time?

That's right. What little was left was largely influenced by French and German traditions. Cremonese violin making had receded into the dark ages, for the most part, when Sacconi came along. He helped some of the modern Cremonese makers to rediscover their roots. So, for the 1985 Triennial, the City of Cremona mounted an exhibit of Sacconi's work, several instruments he had made in Italy and America. A number of his associates and former pupils like Charles Beare, René Morel, and Luiz Bellini were invited to speak at a public event.

I've heard the Cremona competition maintains very rigorous rules.

That's true. The instruments, judged by an international panel of experts and players, must possess a combination of exceptional workmanship and sound, and be set up to professional standards. No artificially aged instruments are accepted. The challenge is to make a beautiful work of art without resorting to artificially aging or "antiquing" the work. Antiquing techniques (whether done well or not) are often aimed at appeasing an insecure musician. Faking up instruments may fool some people, but it was never part of the early Italian tradition, and does not demonstrate that a maker really knows his art. After all, the great Cremonese masters made "new" violins. In some of the American competitions, a whole gambit of different styles is allowed, which makes judging very difficult. Does one judge an instrument by how well a maker understands, carries on, and interprets traditional elements of the art, or by how well the fake job is done?

How large of a competition was the 1985 Triennial, and how did your instrument do?

There were 339 instruments in the competition. My violin competed among 212 violins from 31 countries, and was given the gold medal for combined workmanship and tone. It also received a special award which was given that year in honor of Maestro Sacconi. It was awarded to the instrument that in the judges' opinion best represented the ideals of the Classical Period of the Italian school of violin making of the 16th, 17th, and 18th centuries.

What was it like when you found out about your awards?

I wasn't expecting anything, and had almost forgotten about it. Then I received a telegram saying that I had won and inviting me over for the ceremony. I had about three or four days notice, and little money. A generous patron of mine bought tickets for my wife, myself, and my seven-month-old son, and we were off. I was totally unprepared. I probably needed a haircut.

So you weren't even there for the show? You just sent them your instrument?

You have to send your instruments about a month in advance, and all the judging is done before the exhibit is open to the public.

During the celebration, I was asked to give a short talk on Sacconi. I never met him, but having heard so much about him from his pupils and associates, and having benefited so much from his legacy, I told how much he was an inspiration for a lot of modern makers.

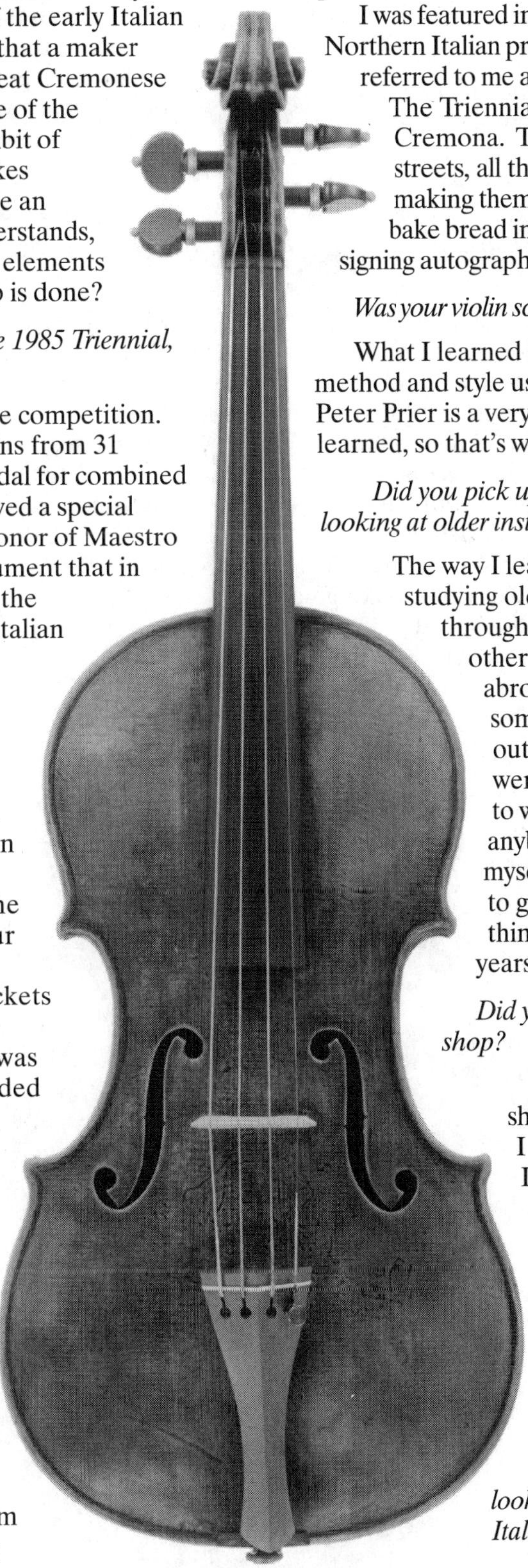

Violin by David Gusset, 1992.
Copy of the 1742 Guarneri del Gesù
Ex. Ferdinand David, Ex. Jascha Heifetz.

Could you speak Italian?

I gave my lecture in Italian, but it wasn't impromptu. Having taken a couple of semesters of Italian, I was able to write my speech and translate it, but I had someone proofread it for me. It was brief, so I read it.

I was featured in about every newspaper in the Northern Italian province of Lombardy. The media referred to me as "Lo Stradivari di San Francisco." The Triennial is a really important event in Cremona. There are huge banners across streets, all the businesses have some violin-making theme in their show windows, bakeries bake bread in the shape of violins. I spent hours signing autographs for bus loads of school children.

Was your violin schooling mostly in the Italian style?

What I learned in school was basically the method and style used in Mittenwald, Germany. Peter Prier is a very good maker, and that's where he learned, so that's what he taught at that time.

Did you pick up your Italian chops just from looking at older instruments?

The way I learn is not only by working on and studying old Italian instruments, but also through professional affiliations with other makers and shops here and abroad. Initially Frank Passa had some influence. He was able to point out certain aspects of my work that were Germanic, and once I caught on to what to look for, I didn't need anybody else's help. I could see for myself. Some makers are never able to get beyond habits or rigid ways of thinking solidified in their earliest years of violin making.

Did you make instruments at Passa's shop?

We didn't make instruments in his shop; we did repair and restoration. I made instruments at home. When I had questions about what I was making at home, I could always examine instruments from Frank's safe or instruments I was repairing at the time. I could study how other makers had handled whatever particular aspect of building I was currently working on.

What kinds of things would you be looking for? What sets the finest old Italian violins apart?

It's design, styling, varnish, graduations, and architecture. The area where many violin makers fail is the arching. It's difficult for them to perceive an instrument in three dimensions. They can take a two dimensional pattern of an outline, lay it on a piece of wood, trace it, and cut it out, which is fine. But when they get to the architecture (sculpting the convex and concave archings of the top and back plates) of the instrument, they don't have a clue.

The tools and methods that one uses — for instance the way top and back outlines are traced in the French style — can dictate aspects of styling in a way, because there's a connection between the methods you use and the end result. If you are studying old Italian instruments, you are looking at the end product. How do you pick up the other end of it, the method?

You're right. You have to understand the tools and the method to interpret the instrument. In the 19th century, French makers began to excel. To me, however, much of their work has a strong two dimensionality. Every outline of every instrument they made was exactly the same. There was no variation, because they were tracing the outline from the same pattern with every instrument. It allowed for mass production, but took all the spontaneity out of the process. The French method of violin making is similar to guitar making in that the outside form is used for building the rib structure. With the outside form, the ribs come out exactly the same every time. They could trace a template onto the top and back plates and trim to the finished edges of the plates without even having to match or compare them to the rib structures. Many of those makers were copyists. Each generation copied what their teachers did, and with each generation they got that much farther from the original idea.

Like the old game where somebody says something in someone's ear, and they pass it on to another person, who passes it on....

Exactly, and by the time it gets to the end of the line the original statement has been changed beyond recognition. People always wonder why French instruments are larger. It has been suggested that each generation of makers made their patterns by tracing their teacher's patterns.

So they keep getting the thickness of a pencil line bigger every generation?

That's one theory. My own theory is that they misunderstood the architecture of the early Italian instruments. On the French arching, the longitudinal arch of the table is usually parabolic. The Italian longitudinal arching is flatter, and is sometimes referred to as a saddle arch. It's straight along the middle of the length of the plate, which really frees up that area to vibrate. The French makers must have looked at the Italian archings and thought them weak, and that the archings had settled due to the pressure of the bridge. The French probably found it difficult to get their tops with a parabolic longitudinal arch to vibrate, so they made bigger instruments to try to get them to sound better.

You're saying the Italian arch comes up more quickly and is flatter for most of the length of the top?

I guess you could describe it that way. The longitudinal arch is straighter, flatter down the middle. In the case of spruce, a saddle arch is actually stronger and more efficient than a parabola. Because the wood fibers are longer it's stronger lengthwise, but it's not as stiff, so it's freer to vibrate. That's essentially how an engineer might look at one of these instruments. You have an area in the middle of the table between the *f*s that I call the platform, that rocks back and forth laterally.

The bridge kind of pivots off the top of the soundpost, doesn't it?

Well, the soundpost is actually positioned two or three millimeters behind the bridge foot to allow some spring and independence to the vibrations of the top and back plates. Otherwise, vibrations from the back would be bouncing back to interfere with the initial vibrations of the strings and bridge. Rosined bow hair grabs and releases the string many times a second (a violin A string cycles 440 times per second). The side-to-side movements of the strings are converted by the bridge into alternating up-and-down movements of the two bridge feet. At the instant the treble foot is up, the bass foot is down, and vice versa. The central platform of the top rocks and moves with the bridge feet.

The bridge itself must be designed and cut to have the proper amount of spring. Picture the front or back side of a violin bridge and you will see there is no place where you can draw a straight line from top to bottom without passing through a cutout area — the design is such that there is spring built into it. There must be the proper amount of give side to side to enable

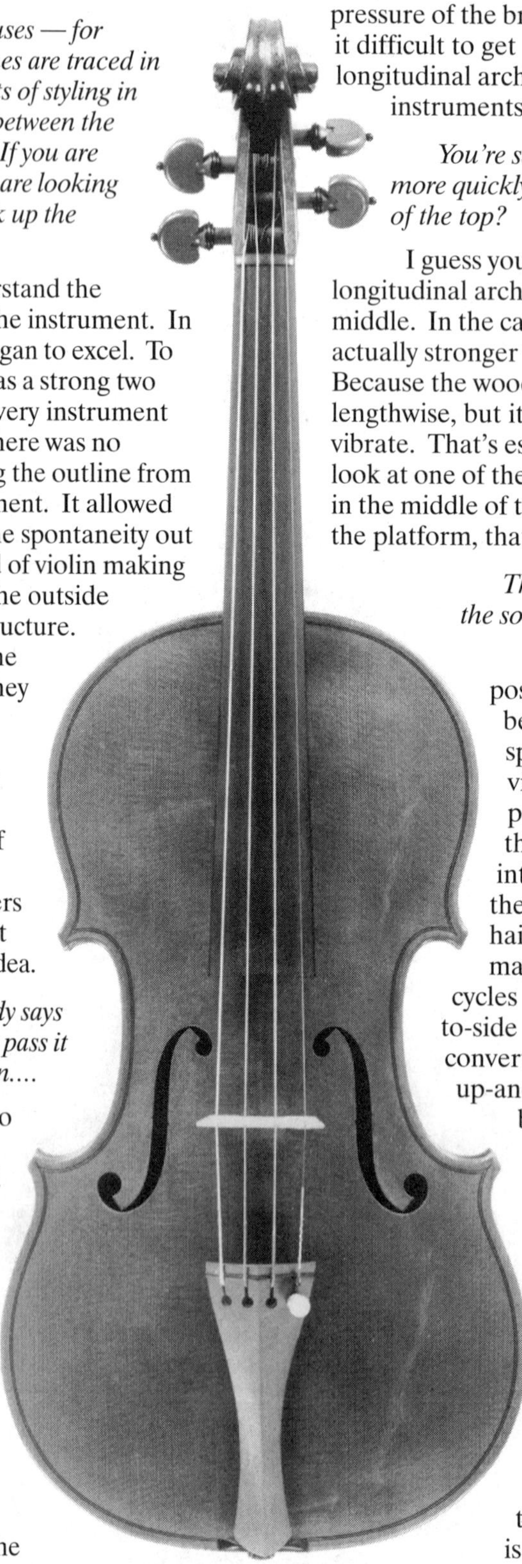

Stradivari model violin by David Gusset, made for the 1991 Paris International Competition.

the bridge to bend at its waist and thighs and then quickly recover.

The purpose of the *f*-holes is not only to let the air in and out, but to free up the platform between the *f*s to vibrate. You want that area around the bridge to vibrate freely to get the vibrations out to the larger areas of the top, the upper and lower bouts, as fast as possible. After all, those larger areas have the greatest capacity for exciting air molecules and thereby transmitting sound. Sound that reaches our ears is caused by the agitation of the molecules in the air, molecules bouncing off each other through space.

Despite the fact that a violin is a relatively small and fragile instrument, the efficiency of its archings allows for a rich complexity of overtones, which is what gives the violin its carrying power, filling a symphony hall or opera house with sound.

Another aspect of arching that many makers miss is in how the arch approaches the edge. An arch is not just a lump which starts at the purfling and ends at the purfling on the other side. If an arch is totally convex, it has the ability to flex outward, but resists flexing inward.

In that case you have an arch under compression, and if the flexibility around the perimeter is too limited the whole thing would be too stiff to vibrate efficiently.

Exactly, so you need that concavity, or reverse arch, near the edges to give the plate the ability to flex inward as well. The vibrations have to complete a full cycle. When graduating the plates, it's important to leave the area of the top and back plates around the linings and blocks very full, almost flat. For one thing, you gain a lot of spring from that, and that's important for the sound. It's also important structurally. Repairs often require that tops or backs be removed. Violins are built to be taken apart, but if you don't have enough wood backing up the edge, the edge will be very weak. I've seen what I call "bathtub graduation" on a lot of amateur instruments, where the graduation comes up steeply to the blocks and linings. That weakens the wood of the plate near the joint, and it makes the top easy to damage during removal, especially if it was put on using thick, full-strength glue, which is a common mistake that is potentially damaging. The Italians left their edges very full on the insides, almost flat as the graduation approaches the blocks and linings. So the fullness of the inside arching and graduation near the edges prescribes the concavity of the corresponding outside arch.

Is the bass bar a brace?

The function of a bass bar is not so much to support the top, but to mute longitudinal vibrations and facilitate lateral vibrations, effectively transmitting the lateral vibrations from the center platform to the upper and lower bouts. In the construction of a flattop guitar, the final curvature or tension will be built into the plates using bracing and tapering ribs. Most guitars are made starting from flat, thin tops and backs with bracing. A violin has no bracing and relies entirely on carved tops and backs to support the weight and tension of the strings.

Do you build tension into your bass bar?

Yes, but not for strength. The tension of the bar must approximate whatever tension will be built into the top as it bends over the tapered rib structure.

It really impresses me that an American who has trained in German-style building can end up being acknowledged as having the ability to make very exceptional Italian-style instruments without ever having trained under anyone specifically in Italian-style workmanship.

Thank you for saying so. Actually, there are a lot of fine contemporary makers, sort of a late 20th-century neoclassic revival of instrument making. Most of those makers have

(See **Meet Gusset** on page 239)

1687 Antonio Stradivari violin, Ex. Ole Bull.

Originally published in *American Lutherie #56*, 1998

Shaping the Sound:

A Personal Approach to Making Classical Guitars

from his 1997 American School of Lutherie lecture

by Jeffrey R. Elliott

THIS IS THE FIRST TIME I have talked about my process of building in front of a group, and I have to confess I have an ulterior motive. Many good builders are making good guitars today, but a lot of those good guitars are lacking an important quality — *allure*. That quality is often the difference between a good guitar and a potentially sensational instrument. It can sometimes be present in a guitar that is not sensational, but it is always present in a guitar that is. Allure is not something that can be measured. It is something that strikes people emotionally. So my ulterior motive is to use this opportunity to express a very strong bias toward a certain kind of classical guitar, which I feel offers that quality. And it's the kind of guitar that I strive to make. These guitars are in the Torres/Hauser tradition. They are solid, balanced, and versatile, and can have a certain personality of great appeal.

José Romanillos has written a wonderful, scholarly book on Torres (*Antonio de Torres, Guitar Maker — His Life & Work*). I'd like to quote from Julian Bream's foreword to the book, because he eloquently expresses my own feelings and biases and provides us with a historical context:

"In reading José Romanillos' book one is made manifestly aware of the most vital phase of the instrument's history, namely the transition of the early classical 19th-century guitar design in which Pages, Panormo, and Lacôte, were particularly distinguished makers to the warm, romantic guitar that was eventually to emerge from the Iberian Peninsula, largely through the intuitive gifts of a skilled carpenter — Antonio de Torres....

"The man who finally brought the guitar into the Romantic era was unquestionably Francisco Tárrega (1852–1909), the remarkable pedagogue and quite considerable artist whose new and revolutionary principles of technique were to play a vital role in the instrument's development — even to this day, and it is by no means idle speculation to suggest that without the characteristic proportions and design of the Torres guitar, Tárrega's vital contribution to guitar would have been minimal.

"Torres was to become the major influence in guitar construction right through the middle years of this century. Within the last twenty-five years the guitar as a solo recital instrument has witnessed a renaissance of a magnitude quite unknown before in its long history. A corpus of new literature has been forged for the instrument by some of the most gifted and discerning composers of our time. Some of this new music makes demands on the instrument's resources that stretch it to the point of vulnerability.

"This inherent vulnerability has been a major concern of guitar makers and indeed guitarists, and technical innovations have been introduced in an effort to create an instrument of more equal response and greater sonority. It is not my intention to argue here about the merits or demerits of recent developments in the art of guitar construction, but I would like to add that it is, in my considered opinion, *a debatable virtue to search for greater volume of sound at the expense of sound quality.* (The emphasis is mine.)

"The guitar has won the hearts of its many admirers through its unique ability to evoke a musical ambiance which is both magical and intensely personal. It is the character and quality of its musical voice that touches the heartstrings...."

Ten years later, the renaissance continues resulting in a plethora of players. Competition is high among these guitarists for the venues, and the venues tend to be enormous halls. Because these artists feel they have to fill a huge hall, many play for loudness. They feel they have to be louder than the next player. So they have made the assumption, and so have some makers, that you need a bigger instrument with a longer scale to be heard in a large concert hall. But the problem has not been solved by making longer scales and larger boxes. Those instruments may seem louder to the performer, but their lack of clarity and balance preclude their being heard in the back of the hall. And it has not yet been solved by making a guitar which is indeed a little louder, because it still can't fill most 3,000-seat halls, or most 1,000-seat halls for that matter. Some makers have made louder guitars that can be heard better in the hall, but at a great sacrifice, as Julian Bream says. The sacrifice is in tone quality and tonal palette, the very thing that drew most of us to the classical guitar in the first place. A guitar with a short scale and small body, in the tradition of Torres and Hauser, has the tone quality and can be heard as well as any in the back rows. Clarity is what projects and allows an instrument to be heard. But we still haven't solved the problem arising from the venues' being too big and the guitar's sound, even the loudest and purest, from being too small. I have experienced only one large hall in which a good guitar can be heard well, unamplified. I know there are others, but damn few. The solution from my perspective is for guitarists to use more intimate venues, since I don't expect architects to design the acoustics of a hall for the classical guitar's relatively small voice.

I would like you to consider these aspects in your own building. I'd like to see the direction of guitar making come back a little bit from going for volume at the expense of the sonority and the quality of allure. Allure is what keeps the audience engaged, it is what sells recordings, and it will keep people buying your guitars. It will keep you happy as a builder, because it is at the heart of your endeavor.

I still love what I do, and the seeds of it were planted many years ago when I was sixteen and a friend taught me three chords on his guitar. I immediately fell in love with the sound of the nylon string guitar. He introduced me to the recordings of Bream, Segovia, and Sabicas and a number of folk instrumentalists and singers, many of whom used nylon string guitars back then. I really loved playing and spent a great deal of time immersed in that wonderful sound. Later, paying gigs would help finance a lot of my college expenses, but the real reason I did it was because I loved that sound.

When I was twenty this friend decided to commission a handmade guitar, and I accompanied him to Richard Schneider's shop in Detroit, Michigan. I wasn't in that shop more than five minutes before I knew something really significant was happening. I had to make guitars. After that I visited Richard from time to time, hanging around his shop and playing for him while he worked. He understood my desire, but it wasn't until two years later that he asked me if I still wanted to apprentice with him. I began immediately and remained with him for six years. I hadn't any prior woodworking experience, but I have always liked a variety of art, especially sculpture. Richard taught me the traditional hand tool method he'd learned in Mexico under Juan Pimental, fundamentally the Spanish method.

I made my first guitar for myself and I still own and play it. Every guitar I've made since then has been a commission for someone in particular. From the beginning of my career I was drawn to what I thought made the difference for each individual and what my sphere of influence might be. I realized that I stood to learn a whole lot more on each instrument by trying to tailor each guitar, and it was also more exciting and fun because each one was different. I also realized that of all the many skills required, the most vital to successfully tailoring and realizing the potential of each instrument are intuition and sensitivity to the materials.

How do you "develop" intuition? Actually I think we are all born with it; it is part of our inner selves. Maybe all we need to do is learn to pay more attention to it. It reflects who we are, and we are all different. The voices of our guitars differ in part because we are unique individuals with our own intuitive sensibilities. It is difficult to know when it is working for you, but you know when you experience it, because it just feels right. This realm of guitar making can make the difference between a good guitar and one that is truly outstanding. When fully there, all the potential of the materials and design is realized, and your intention is fully expressed.

Before I make each instrument, I try to prepare myself to be in a peak intuitive state. It really begins with understanding what the customer is asking for. This is crucial because it points you in the right direction, and it helps you to hear the sound in your mind's ear. Then you can begin to conceptualize the instrument architecturally, select the materials, and visualize its aesthetics. In a very basic way, the combination of design, woods, and intent will make up that sound.

Once this concept is clear, I choose the materials. The choice of materials is crucial. You have to be aware of not only the responsiveness of the materials but also

WOODLEY WHITE

have some sense of the inherent tonal properties of each of these tonewoods. All of us may perceive these things differently, but it is how we relate to them that is important. Sensitivity to the materials is the easy part, really. It is just a matter of having some experience.

I am building for individuals, and each guitar is different, so I am starting over every time in order to be 100% focused on that person's expectations. I may need to redesign the instrument in some way to help encourage the responses in the desired direction. And, of course, how I surface the top and work the bracing is also fundamental (I'll talk much more specifically on this later). All these considerations are just about as important as choosing the right materials in the first place, and the coordination of them is partly an intuitive process.

To determine the design, materials, and aesthetics, I make a full-size drawing to help visualize a three-dimensional understanding of every detail. I want to have this digested consciously. I am absorbing the concept, the information. I don't want to have to think about this stuff while I am building the guitar. I try to be completely familiar with all of the details before I actually put the chisel to the wood. Obviously it's not necessary to do a full-scale drawing to reconceptualize every guitar. I do it when I am making an instrument that is enough different or when something is unfamiliar, and I feel the need. Once I have decided on all of these things, I try to remain open to change but not to compromise the goals that we set at the beginning.

When I begin building I try to work at a pace that permits a flow and momentum but without stress for a timetable's sake. I stay in touch with the sensory aspects of the tonewoods throughout all the phases of construction. When I am at key points of surfacing the top and shaping the braces, for example, I really go with my first sense about it. I don't try to second guess myself. It is possible to try too hard. If you are thinking about achieving an intuitive state while you are trying to achieve it, it is not happening.

It is important to establish your criteria of sound in order to establish a standard to work from. Ever since I discovered this sound, I have had a particular standard in my head. Although it has evolved over time, its core elements have always been the same. This is my central building concept. If someone asks me to build a guitar and doesn't ask specifically for anything, this is what I do. If they know exactly what they want, I still work off this basis in order to tailor it for the individual.

How do I know that my idea of what the player wants is the same as theirs? I might make a perfectly good guitar that I am happy with but it may not suit their purposes. In order for me to thoroughly understand what they want, we have to be speaking the same language when we describe the sound. The words we use to describe sound are often metaphorical in nature and don't necessarily evoke the same responses in each of us. We all have a somewhat different perception of sound, just as it is possible that each of us perceives the same color in a somewhat different way.

Sound Criteria

- sufficient power, volume, and projection for the concert hall
- a broad spectrum of dynamic responses, with a variety of colors, tones, and textures
- crystalline clarity with good sustain
- evenness and balance throughout
- good, clear separation string to string
- allure

In order to establish a common perception, I sit down with the person to try to understand the words that they are using. A guitarist uses certain words to describe tone color, for example. I recommend the book, *The Natural Classical Guitar* by Lee F. Ryan, which was written for players. I think as makers, if we want to custom build for people, it's good to know where the players are coming from. This book is one way to familiarize ourselves with their language and concepts.

Quoting from Mr. Ryan: "Most guitarists are familiar with the different tone colors produced by striking the strings closer to or farther away from the bridge. There are also color variations that can be produced by playing the same passage on different strings. Some of the colors obtainable just by moving the right hand are: a nasal oboe sound, close to the bridge; a brass sound midway between the bridge and soundhole; what Segovia calls the full 'natural voice' or normal sonority of the guitar at the edge of the soundhole nearest the bridge; and a very mellow harplike tone at the edge of the soundhole nearest the fingerboard. Not everyone will agree with Segovia's idea of the normal sonority of the guitar, but it is something that the guitarist should think about. In any case, remember that if you want true color variations, you must have a normal color from which you can occasionally deviate so there will be meaningful contrast." (p. 126)

Sounds to me like pretty good advice for anyone who plays the guitar. Relative to our purpose here, if you are aware of some of the guitarist's perceptions, it will be helpful in developing a common language. Then, you listen to them play and/or listen to recordings together. You talk about the tone and the color and whatever else. Then you try to describe and arrive at some common understanding of what that is.

Sometimes a player will describe as "warm" a tone that I would consider "bright." But if we have just heard a sound, and both have it in our minds, that is what is important, not whether we agree on the term to describe it. As long as I understand the sound that they want, whatever they call it, I hear it. This is a really important point.

So far I've spent a lot of time on my preparation, what I do so that I don't have to bother with minutia when I am actually building the instrument. It helps me focus on the intent that I have in my mind, the purpose for each guitar. Now let's get down to some of the nitty-gritty aspects of building.

Woods. Choice of wood is a matter of personal preference. To develop your own criteria, you need to familiarize yourself with the tonal responses present in each species. I like everything I've tried, and that includes the usual woods for backs and sides — Indian rosewood, Brazilian rosewood, mahogany, and European maple — and others such as purpleheart, koa, and African blackwood. For classical guitars I prefer the rosewoods, including African blackwood, *Dalbergia melanoxylon.* (See "Further Reading" for more information on African blackwood and other tonewoods.) My favorite wood for tops is European spruce, but I believe great guitars can be made from other spruces, especially Engelmann, and from cedar and redwood. I also pay attention to the tonal quality of the wood used for barring. For example, I favor European spruce for the fans and like to use Sitka spruce for important structural components, where its strength is required and its acoustical impact is minimal.

Wood treatment — harvesting, cutting, storing, and aging — is very important. I'll give you a quick overview of my process. In Oregon where I live, many of the tonewoods practically grow in your backyard, and if I get billets that are still damp or cool to the touch, I'll leave them outside or in the garage, where they are sheltered from the weather, but where the air can get around them and they can gradually acclimate, losing their extra humidity and becoming dimensionally stable. After a year or more, I will take them in and resaw them. Or I will leave them in billet form for another year or more. Then I'll resaw and sticker them. It's important not to shock or stress the wood by drying it too rapidly, and I also think it is helpful for the woods to go through natural, regular seasonal changes for several years before they are used, as they'll be better able to handle environmental swings as finished instruments.

My woods are stored in the basement, which is below the frostline. If we have a quick freeze, they will be all right. I've made a little room out of a 2×2 framework and stapled .010″ plastic around it. I installed an old screen door on it and put plastic on that. I have shelves in there and the wood is all stickered. It is all very low tech. I leave a 250w heat lamp on all the time. It provides a warmer, drier atmosphere for these woods and it is constant. This allows the woods to season at a steady rate in what I consider a proper climate.

I season the wood a minimum of ten years. I have a stash of probably twice what I will use. That gives me the option of choice while I rotate the stock. After two to three years in my wood room, I find the woods are dimensionally stable, and I *could* build with them without worrying about the instrument breaking up. But I prefer to age my wood for ten years, because I feel that the resins continue to harden and it becomes more responsive. It gets lighter. If you weigh a fresh, dry top when you put it in your stash and then again a few years later, it will weigh less. It will also be stiffer and more responsive to tapping and touch. I think as a starting place for a new instrument, having that extra aging going for it will make a big difference in how mature it is both right away and after just a few years.

I live in Portland, where it rains quite a bit. I try to build in 45% to 55% relative humidity. When I am doing gluings and assembly, I try to hug the drier side of this range, mid-40s. I want to give the guitar an edge against dryness, the real culprit. A guitar can handle a little excess humidity much more readily than it can handle dryness.

I require tops to be quartered most of their width. I don't mind if a top goes off quarter towards the periphery a little bit, since I like my tops to be a little more flexible towards the outside, anyway. You can achieve this in other ways, by thinning the top or shaving the bracings. But, if it is naturally there, you can work with that, too. If it is good wood and it speaks to you, then it is worth using.

My own preference for tops is pretty straight grain, but it can be wavy. I like figure, although I think it's possible to have too much. A lot of runout is not desirable. My preference is for no runout, but you seldom see this, except with cedar and redwood and sometimes Engelmann. If you get a good tree that grew straight, you can split it all in one plane and then resaw parallel to that and adjust for quartering and you will get wood that has very little runout.

Aircraft-grade lumber has specifications for runout, and different components of the aircraft must meet different specs. Runout specs are stated as a range. A government handbook I have gives it as 1″ in 12″ (minimum) to 1″ in 30″. In a 1″ thick piece, the grain would go through, from front to back, in 12″ to 30″, respectively. A guitar top is roughly 20″ long. If you work out the math, a top (1/8″ thick) with 1″ in 20″ runout, would run out in 2½″. That is, the grain would run from front to back in 2½″. You will see a reflection difference between the two halves of the top with that amount of runout. I think that's a good minimal strength standard, especially for cedar, redwood, and Engelmann. I am not a stickler if runout doesn't run to full length, and I don't mind a little color differential. If the halves are well matched, you can flip one half so that the grain direction is the same on both halves and avoid the color differential. If a top has 1″ in 20″ runout, feels good, sounds good, and seems strong and stiff in both directions, I'll use it. If it's stiffer along one edge, I'll put that at the center. I use a higher standard for brace wood — very little to no runout.

Design Considerations. First, I take into account the instrument as a whole, the relationship of the major components to one another as they affect the guitar's responses. Structural stability accounts for the consistency of responses as well as the guitar's longevity. It's easy to make a guitar that's too light. (I know; I've done it.) The result is a temperamental instrument that fluctuates greatly as the humidity changes, and one that will have a relatively short life span. Too heavy is deadening. It may last forever, but it's unlikely to be responsive enough for anyone to care. There is a really fine balance between maximum responsiveness and structural stability. I often remind myself that I am making an instrument that weighs only 3 lbs. to 3¼ lbs. and is supposed to function precisely under 75 lbs. to 95 lbs. of string tension for a couple of human lifetimes. If it is well made and well cared for, it will last and function for that long and beyond.

My partner Cyndy Burton and I recently had the good fortune to examine a 1856 Torres guitar (FE 03 in Romanillos' book) in Pepe Romero's collection. This instrument not only reinforced some of the beliefs I've been sharing with you regarding guitars in the Torres/Hauser tradition, it challenged us not to get too set in our beliefs. First of all, this guitar, almost 150 years old, sounds marvelous. The sound meets all my criteria — and is most alluring.

Although we didn't hear it in an auditorium, it seemed like it would compare well with currently made guitars, and Pepe confirmed that. Second, the back and sides are maple, *not* one of our preferred rosewoods. Third, the top is thought to be a pine native to Spain, *not* spruce. Fourth, it has a three-piece top and a five-piece back. Fifth, it has a relatively small body shape. And lastly, it has a 66CM scale, a little longer than I typically build. (Incidentally, of the eighty-eight Torres guitars documented in Romanillos' book, only one other has as long a scale, which Romanillos attributes to its having been completed by a different builder, Moya Redondo. Most are 65CM or under.) However, it is a great example of what's possible. So a guitar can remain functional for 150 years and retain all of the warmth and maturity that it has acquired over those years. But it requires consistent maintenance and more than a little luck, I suspect. If you're curious about this guitar, you can see a photo of it and basic specifications in Romanillos' book, pp. 228–229. (If you want to hear it on a recording, see "Recommended Recordings" at the end of this article.)

The 1856 Torres guitar also had a wonderful sense of proportion. By proportion I mean upper and lower bout widths plus thickness and weight relative to string scale, neck mass, depth of body — even the length of the head and the weight of the gears. It is a very light instrument, probably weighing less than 3 lbs. When you hold such an instrument, when you first pick it up, you know that you have something special in your hands. You can sense it; it feels almost weightless. If you run across an instrument like that, take a good look at it. This can expedite your own development of a sense of proportion. The more you expose yourself to great works of art from the past (or present, for that matter), the more your own sense of proportion will be developed. And the more you build, the more you'll find a way to express your own sense of it. It's interesting to note that 1856 was early in Torres' professional career, which Romanillos dates from 1850.

I have witnessed the use of the basic Torres design or Hauser design (*GAL Instrument Plans #12, 30, 33, 38*) by many people. Very many builders, even those who have had a lot of experience, tell me that they have just made their best guitar yet after using the GAL plans. The design can be modified according to the sound you hear or whatever specifications you want. You can use it for flamenco guitars. It's really versatile.

Structural/Construction Considerations. I'd like you to consider the neck/body-joint relationship for a moment. In general, I feel the neck should be less bulky than I often see, especially on novice and most mass-produced guitars. In the Torres/Hauser tradition, the Spanish heel and the neck are one component, both inside and outside the guitar. I prefer to build with a Spanish heel, because I believe the integral heel enhances the kind of interaction between the box and neck that I'm after and helps to stabilize a rather vulnerable area right in the middle of the string length. I also don't like the idea of bolts or glue and laminations in that area as they may restrict or interfere with the transfer of energy and vibrations between the neck and body. The string tension causes compression at this juncture, and when the string is in motion, it also expands and contracts along its length. When contracted, the top and the neck are pulled towards one another. When expanded, the string relaxes and the top and neck go back the other way. The heel is glued to the back so the back moves with the heel. When the top goes up, the neck goes up, and the back goes back. There is a certain amount of life in that activity, rather like breathing. The whole instrument pulsates and every guitar has a different feel and sound in part because of this. So, for all its mass, the neck/body juncture is a delicate thing and can greatly affect the instrument's sensitivity and responsiveness.

The major structural components of the top are the transverse or harmonic bars, fan braces, bridge, and

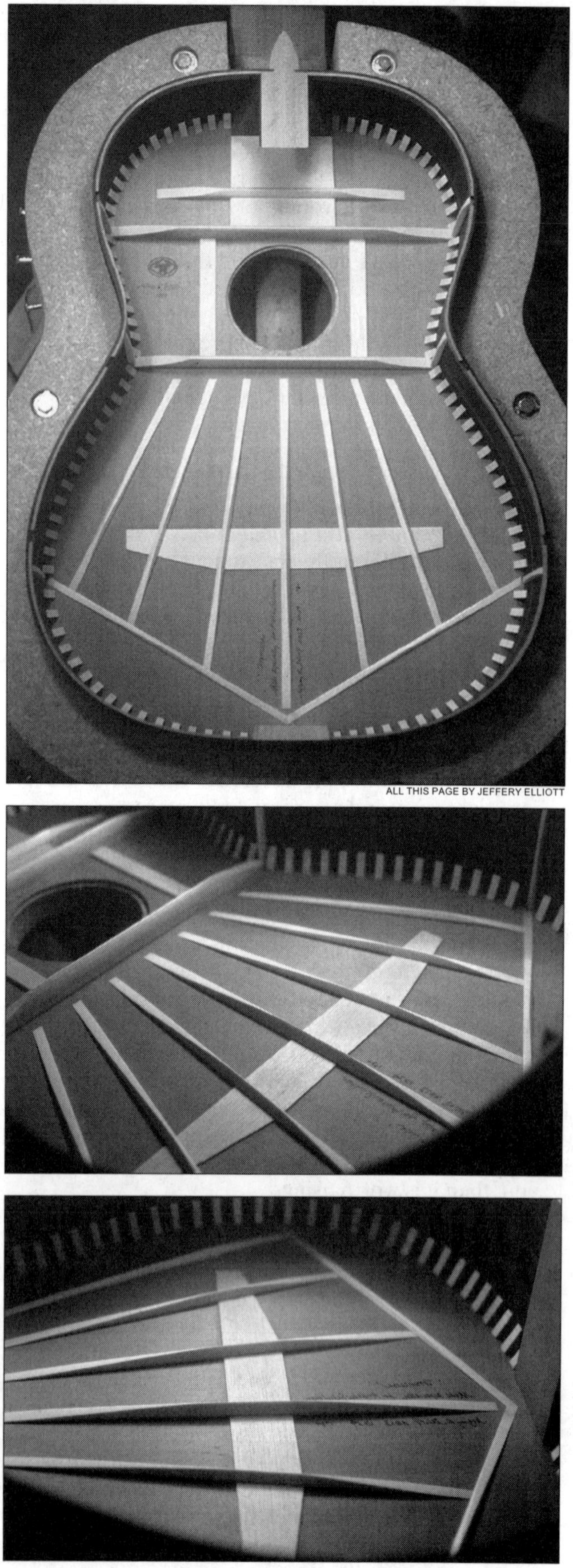

ALL THIS PAGE BY JEFFERY ELLIOTT

Interior of Elliott cedar top 8-string guitar with Torres/Hauser bracing pattern. The top and European spruce barring are about 10% heavier to offset the increase in tension of two additional strings.

fingerboard from the 12th fret to the soundhole. I locate all three harmonic bars at or very near points (nodes) on the string length where clear harmonics can be obtained: the 16th fret (a fifth harmonic); between the 18th and 19th frets (a third harmonic); and just below the soundhole (a fifth harmonic). I think this may be important. I have moved those bars in some guitars, but I think they interfere less with the guitar's natural responses without overemphasizing any particular response if they are located at these harmonic points. My 1st and 2nd transverse bars are both flat. The bar in the lower bout has a slight arch, probably about .5MM. I arch my tops 1MM–1.5MM with the peak of the dome in the middle of the lower bout radiating in all directions. I achieve this by using a slightly hollowed workboard in combination with the natural tendency of the top and its barring to curve.

Because the soundhole causes a major weakened area, the support around it is particularly important. Too little support can result in a flutter action that distorts the sound. I want this area to be fairly rigid (see photo p. 237). On most guitars the support ring has the same grain direction as the top; on some it's perpendicular. It depends on the flexibility of the top. Obviously if I want to add to the stiffness of the top, I place it cross grain to the top.

I use an under-fingerboard patch, slightly wider than the fingerboard. Typically the grain is parallel to the top. I've repaired too many of other people's guitars with cracks along the edge of the fingerboard not to use them on my own. On the '43 Hauser design they're ±2.0MM, but on my open design I use a 2.5MM thickness for both soundhole and under-fingerboard reinforcements.

The bridge stiffens the top across the grain, and it has to be a certain height to accommodate the saddle and the strings at the proper height, and in relation to the plane of the fingerboard. This is structural, acoustical, and affects playability. If you change one of these variables, it affects the others. This is where your full-scale drawings of the side view will help determine the realities of the clearances for string height that you want. The bridge generally weighs between 15G and 20G including the saddle, which usually is bone and weighs about 2G.

I try to build so that the string height is more or less a centimeter off the top. It can lower a millimeter or so from bass to treble. A range 8MM to 11MM is my comfort zone. More flexible tops usually require a string height at the lower end of this range. Within the bridge, my rule of thumb is that the amount of bone above the wood should not exceed the amount of bone supported in the wood. I like to see 1.5MM–3MM above the wood, in order to provide a decent breaking angle for the strings into the tieblock and to facilitate the rocking motion of the bridge. On a more malleable top, especially if a low bridge is required, I might choose a particularly stiff bridge blank. In this way I have some control over cross-grain stiffening as well as maintaining the wood-to-bone proportion I want.

In my experience, that 8MM–11MM range on this design of instrument provides a good loud, crisp, clear sound that is neither harsh nor weak. Within that range, you can find the string tension and height that bring out the best responses in that guitar. This may change over time as the guitar matures. If the guitarist is a hard player and requires a high action, then I design the instrument and choose the woods accordingly. If the top is arched, that height must be taken into account when you join the neck to the body. This is another reason for a good side-view drawing. You have another chance for correction or modification when you plane the fingerboard, if you start with a thick board. By knowing the fret height plus the string heights at the 1st and the 12th frets together with the string height at the bridge, you can contour your fingerboard accordingly. All you need to do is to determine those parameters ahead of time.

The bridge patch has a cross-grain stiffening effect and a really great influence proportionate to its dimension. It doesn't have to be very thick. Mine is between .5MM and 1MM, and its grain is oriented perpendicular to the top. I think it should be well quartered, straight grained, with little or no runout. I believe it gives the top a more homogenous and even response throughout its entire response range. Without it, in my experience, there is more of a deviation in character from string to string across the fingerboard. It also allows me to then lighten up in other areas because I know that it is going to have this stabilizing effect across the grain. I prefer to use a piece from the same top material in order to help unify the top. I prefer the fan bracing for each guitar to come from a single piece of stock for the same reason. This gives me more control over how I vary things, because my sphere of influence is choice of wood and dimensioning.

Top Sequence. I have three, sister cut, European spruce tops with me. I've been storing them in my wood room since 1973. You'll see when I pass these around that each one is just a little more off quarter than the previous one and each is accordingly more flexible across the grain. I am drawn to a piece of wood by its appearance first. Then I run my hand across it and listen to the sound it makes. I feel for the stiffness across the grain. I listen to its readiness to respond, how quick it is, responding to a light touch. I look for an even stiffness or a graduation of stiffness. I check for runout. All three of these tops have almost no runout. You can assess for runout by looking at the surface and adjacent side of the plate. The more you can feel the grain direction, the more runout there is. If it is rough and fuzzy, there is probably more runout. Also, if you have enough material, you can run a knife along the top and peel it, start a split, and the knife will follow the runout.

Then I tap on it. I suspend it by holding it at about one-fourth to one-fifth of its length and locate and tap the sweet spot about midway along the remainder. First I listen to the lower frequencies, then I listen to the highs. I'm also listening for sustain and for richness and complexity. I want to hear a diverse response. I want it to be focused, but I am not listening for a specific pitch. If it has a rich spectrum of response, then the instrument will have a great chance of having that quality. If the fundamental tap tone is lower, the guitar is going to have a lower voice. If it is stiffer, it will be brighter and higher. If someone wants a guitar that has darker qualities, I'll use a piece of wood that has a lower inherent fundamental tap tone. In general, these would be the softer tops, more flexible across the grain. There is a broad range in balancing these factors, especially when tailoring for individuals.

BOTH BY WOODLEY WHITE

The author demonstrates tapping a soundboard held at the sweet spot.

I like building with a symmetrical bracing pattern. It helps me produce a predictable instrument. I use European spruce for the fan braces and handle and listen to them just like I do the top. I'm listening for a certain musical quality, brightness, clarity, a ring, and sustain. I don't measure deflection. I have done that a few times mainly to confirm what I have directly observed by simply using my hands and senses to determine stiffness. For example, when I'm selecting my fan barring, I go through all the fans repeatedly, until I am satisfied that I have them lined up from most stiff to most flexible. At this point they're dimensioned the same, probably around 6MM square; otherwise comparisons would be meaningless. Then I take the stiffest one for my center fan, the next stiffest becomes the adjacent fan on the treble side, the next stiffest on the bass side and so on. Now I've stiffened the top more in the middle and less on the periphery, and I haven't changed a dimension. I still have a great sphere of influence through further dimensioning before I glue them on and through shaping their profiles afterwards.

I join and assemble the top on a slightly hollowed workboard. I glue on the bridge patch first. Then I notch the fan braces to fit over the bridge patch and glue them on. You could glue segments of bridge patch between the braces instead. I have done that on a couple guitars originally made without patches by going in through the soundhole. It's a fairly good way of finding out exactly what effect the bridge patch has. I prefer, however, for the patch to be continuous and I like the fan bars to be continuous also. It is less of a compromise to notch the bars.

This top is being made for an individual who wants a guitar that is bright but not too bright, with a rich, lush low end and a nice full midrange. A medium-stiff top has the best chance of achieving that. *(Holds up cut-out top with rosette in it.)* It is about 2.7MM in the middle and about 2.3MM at the edges for its full length. I am not so concerned with the tap tones at this point, but I am observing how it is changing through the construction process. I think that it is important to get a sense of this at several stages so that you can get an idea of the degree of change that you might expect by the time you get to final surfacings. At this point, I want to have a sense of its resilience, its willingness to spring back when I let up. You will notice that it is stiffer in the middle. It was that way before I graded it. Then I do some more tapping and listening, very much like before when I selected it. As you work the material, the pitches go down. As soon as you start bracing, they start going back up. What the pitch is doesn't really matter to me, as long as I am convinced that it has a musical quality, and it falls where I'm aiming along the lightness-to-darkness range, as well as having the right sense of stiffness and resilience. As with the bracing dimensions, there is a thickness range that I work within. This top is in the middle of my range at this stage.

The transverse bars are made from Sitka because it is stronger. I consider it a waste to use good European spruce for the transverse bars. Their main function is support, and their tonal effect is not great except, perhaps, by virtue of their location. Sitka is strong stuff and allows a broad dimensional range without sacrificing stability.

I use the 1943 Hauser plan as a basis for my bracing pattern. I like to choose materials that pretty much allow me to use the same fan splay every time, but of course, you can alter it, allowing even more control of cross-grain stiffness. If you want more flexibility, you can grade the barring, dimensioning their heights and widths from the center outward, giving the entire top greater amplitude. Or you can simply lessen the splay; make the bars more parallel. If you want more flexibility longitudinally, taper them more. If you want even more flexibility, triangulate them rather than doming their tops. The splay and shape of the cutoff bars also affect cross-grain flexibility.

For the past eight years I have opened the harmonic bars on either side of about the center third of the width of the top. This is not a new idea. Torres and Hauser both did it on some guitars, and the famous 1973 Romanillos (*GAL Plan #30*), which was based on a 1930 Hauser, also has open harmonic bars. The

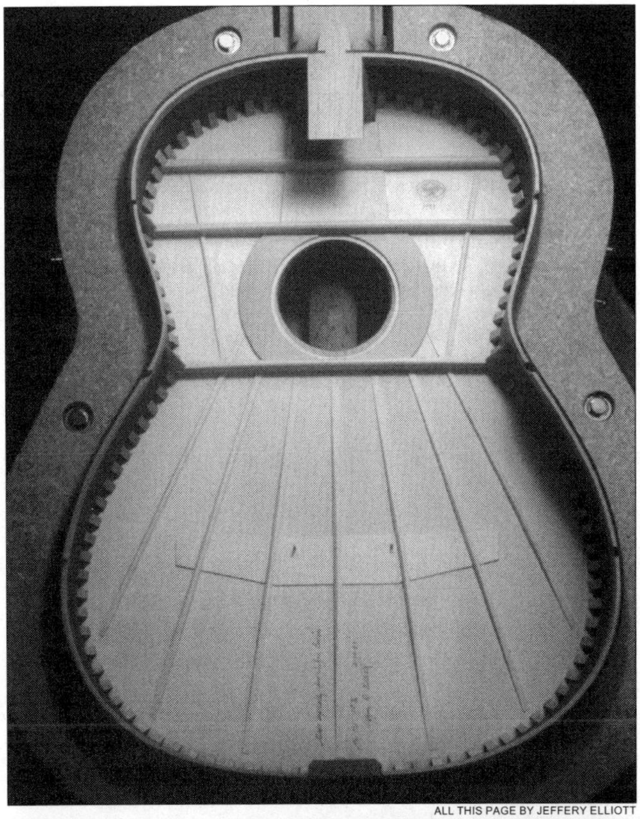

ALL THIS PAGE BY JEFFERY ELLIOTT

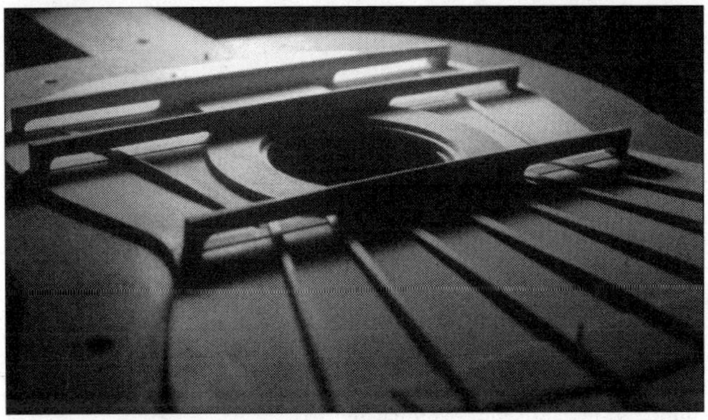

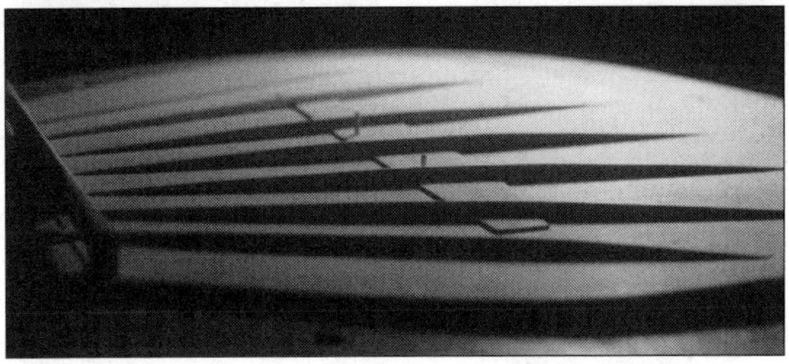

The author's version of the Torres/Hauser bracing design with open harmonic bars.

reason for opening the harmonic bars is to get more of the top's waist and upper bout surface area working in concert with the primary area below the soundhole. But it's a risky thing to do. I have seen many guitars with open harmonic bars, particularly those constructed of cedar or redwood with obvious distortions or splits in the unsupported areas. I reinforce the cutout areas with a .5mm thin slip of wood under each opening, which is let into the harmonic bar. I additionally have one diagonal support strut that runs from the outside fan to the first harmonic bar on each side. The first time I tried the open design, I didn't use those diagonals, and I noticed increased responses, but the sound was busier than my previous guitars, in fact a little busier than I wanted. Just by perverse luck, that guitar was returned to me one year later for a back replacement due to gross overuse of the dampit. I thought it would be a good opportunity to learn their effect, so before I put the new back on I put the two small diagonal braces in the upper bout. This brought it into focus. I have done it this way ever since. I try to provide a network of support for the top but in a way that doesn't inhibit it. The challenge is to control it so that it is not so busy that it clouds the fundamental response, provides enough structure to keep it from cracking, distorting, or collapsing, and not so much that you cancel or mute the increase in responses gained by the open design.

In addition to the effects of barring on the voicing of the top, I use the three main surfacings to influence the outcome. The first surfacing is just before barring. I grade the top a little bit then, leaving it .3mm or .4mm thinner at the edges. After assembly but before binding, I surface again. At that point I want to get the top to within .2mm of the final dimension. After the bindings and purflings are on, the final surfacing will prepare the instrument for finish. What I hope to end up with in a box ready for finish, is a tap tone that has a great musical quality. I want the upper bout to be responsive as well. There should be freedom in the tap tone, a readiness, a clarity, and sustain. I pay a lot of attention to the springback of the top. I want to feel its willingness to be depressed with a moderate amount of pressure. I use my finger tips around the periphery and then all over it. Then I use the palm of my hand. I feel its resistance, how quickly it wants to go down and how quickly it wants to come back. I think that this springiness is essential. It is part of the life force in the instrument. I do this on the top and on the back. It is your last major chance to influence things before fingerboard, finish, and bridge. This is the only time I really care what the pitch is. I want it to be a half or whole step on our scale, not something in-between. I don't always get this because of structural considerations, so I rely heavily on intuition here. I prefer a higher pitch on the back than on the top, which is typical because the back is a harder material. What I don't want is for them to be the same, in order to avoid possible wolf notes, although sometimes I have been fooled. I once built a steel string guitar that had an F back, an F top, and an F cavity resonance. I was really concerned, but it was far enough along that there wasn't much I could do about it. At very worst, I figured I'd learn something. It turned out fine, with no wolf, and very balanced. So, it isn't a given, it's just a theory. I trusted my instincts and it turned out to be right, even though the logical aspects were scary.

I think the back has an influence on tone which is minor compared with the top. I deal with my backs almost exactly the same as far as how I choose them, tapping on them at various stages, and so on. I use three cross braces, usually Spanish cedar, sometimes mahogany, and as per the description in the 1943 Hauser plan (*GAL Plan #12*). Because the back's pitch is usually higher than the top, it tends to support the higher frequencies, although it reinforces the entire range. Indian rosewood, in my opinion, tends to emphasize a richer, more bassy response than Brazilian, which tends to be brighter, although there's a lot of overlap between those two rosewoods and African blackwood, depending on their hardness and density. Again, I urge you to handle and try a variety of woods.

My guitars are finished in shellac. They are French polished by my partner, Cyndy Burton. I believe shellac is the best finish for not inhibiting responses and it may very well enhance some of them. That's been my experience. I learned to use shellac first in Schneider's shop during my apprenticeship. Then I sprayed lacquer until about 1980 when I switched back to shellac. The guitars pre-1980 that I've had refinished have been improved by the change, as well as several guitars from 1980–1981 that went from having only a couple seal coats of shellac to a full French polish. The difference convinced me unequivocally of the importance of a full finish as well as the superiority of shellac.

In conclusion, I urge you in your experimentation, with whatever design you use, to establish the parameters of stiffness in the woods that you choose and to try to get in touch with the different tonal properties that seem to be inherent in these woods. Above all listen for the life and the singing quality in the wood and keep in touch with that throughout the building process to ensure its ending up in the instrument. The guitar will reflect this. If you pay attention to all these details and trust your intuition, your work will become more consistent, a whole lot more of your own personality will become a part of the instrument, and you will end up with a guitar that has "your" sound. If you want to be happy with your work, enjoy it and be comfortable with the process, and if you want to end up with a guitar that has allure, then you have to pay this kind of attention to the details. Go for that sound in your head. ——

References

Articles from **American Lutherie** *(in chronological order)*

Caldersmith, Graham. "Radiation from Lower Guitar Modes." *American Lutherie#2. (*See *Big Red Book of American Lutherie Volume One*, p. 68.)

Elliott, Jeffrey R. "An Overview of the Hauser Tradition." *AL#8.* Also, "1943 Hauser Classic Guitar Plan. (See *BRBAL1*, p. 274.) Full-scale plan (*GAL Instrument Plan #12*) is available from GAL.

Jovicic, J. and O. "The Effect of Bracing on Guitar Resonance." *AL#10 and AL#12. (*See *BRBAL1*, p. 402.)

Bacon, Joseph . "An Interview with Jeffrey Elliott." *AL#12. (*See *BRBAL1*, p. 454.)

Banks, Phil . "Finite Element Simulation of Guitar Top Vibration." *AL#18.*

Elliott, Jeffrey and Burton, Cyndy. "Reflections on Segovia's Guitars at the Metropolitan Museum of Art." *AL#21. (*See *BRBAL2*, p. 358.)

Aram, Kevin. "Julian Bream's 1973 Romanillos." *AL#25.* Also, "1973 J.L. Romanillos Classic Guitar." *(*See *BRBAL3*, pp. 2, 12.) Full-scale plan (*GAL Plan #30*) is available from the GAL.

Carruth, Alan. "Free Plate Tuning, Part Three: Guitars." *AL#30. (*See *BRBAL3*, p. 136.)

Bruné, Richard. "Segovia's 1937 Hauser Revisited." *AL#31. (*See *BRBAL3*, p. 212.) Full-scale plan (*GAL Plan #33*) is available from the GAL.

Elliott, Jeffrey R. "A Timely Top Replacement." *AL#34. (*See *BRBAL3*, p. 316.)

Bruné, Richard. "Segovia's 1937 Hauser: Top and Back Thicknesses." *AL#38. (*See *BRBAL4*, p. 34.)

Bruné, Richard. "Segovia's 1912 Manuel Ramírez." *AL#40. (*See *BRBAL4*, p. 96.) Full-scale plan (*GAL Plan #38*) is available from the GAL.

Hill, Kenny. "A Walk in the Suburban Woods." *AL#42. (*See *BRBAL4*, p. 184.)

Ruck, Robert. "An Approach to Tailoring Sound in Classical Guitars." *AL#42. (*See *BRBAL4*, p. 174.)

Robison, Nicholas Von. "Ebony and African Blackwood: Rare Gifts of Nature." *AL#43. (*See *BRBAL4*, p. 198.)

Note: *Find additional readings of interest by searching the abstracts at the GAL website: www.luth.org.*

Books

Evans, Tom and Mary Anne.
Guitars, from the Renaissance to Rock.
New York and London: Paddington Press Ltd., 1977.
See especially an article by José Romanillos, one of the world's great intuitive builders, pp. 88–100, which describes his take on the intuitive process.

Guild of American Luthiers.
Lutherie Woods and Steel String Guitars, GAL Resource Book Two.
Tacoma, WA: GAL, 1997.

Luthiers Mercantile International, Inc.
Handbook–Catalog for Stringed Instrument Builders.
Healdsburg, CA: LMII, 1996.
See especially the woods sections and FAQs section, where different makers including myself talk about the qualities of different woods.

Romanillos, José L.
Antonio de Torres, Guitar Maker — His Life & Work.
Great Britain: Element Books Ltd., 1987, first edition. (Revised edition published by The Bold Strummer, 1997)

Ryan, Lee F.
The Natural Classical Guitar, The Principles of Effortless Playing.
Englewood Cliffs, NJ: Prentice-Hall, Inc., 1984.

Recommended Recordings

Bream, Julian: most guitar recordings from 1974 through the '80s, using his '73 European spruce top J. Romanillos.

Romero, Pepe: *Noches de España*. Philips, 1994, using a '70s cedar top M. Rodríguez. Also, if you can find it, a 1983 Philips recording (410 396-1) using his 1856 A. Torres.

Segovia, Andrés: recordings from 1937 to mid-'50s, especially *A Bach Recital* for the *Chaconne,* played on his famous '37 European spruce top H. Hauser, Sr.

Williams, John : recordings using his '60s cedar-top I. Fleta, especially *John Williams Plays Ponce.*

*(**Meet Gusset** from page 229)*

discovered that you have to study the great masters, and to do that, you first have to learn to see things, not just outlines of plates, *f*-holes, or scroll. You have to use both eyes and look from all directions, look at shadows formed by contours. You have to feel with your eyes and your hands, and you have to constantly question everything.

I remember seeing a PBS show about a famous Japanese chef whose advice to students, when asked what they could do to become better chefs, was to study art. That has always stuck with me. I have the feeling you might have an interesting viewpoint on this. Do you feel your background in art has helped you to develop an educated eye?

Yes. There are a couple of enlightening exercises we used to do in life-drawing class. The first involves feeling contours with the eye, not just drawing outlines of the model like a cartoon, but moving the brush or pen on paper and describing contours as if tracing cross sections of the model, letting the eyes feel how those contour lines wrap around the visual edge of the model. This exercise can help you begin to see depth and form beyond the flat outlined shapes. In the second exercise you are not allowed to look at your paper while drawing. It's a perfect exercise for short circuiting the eye-to-brain-to-hand path, or simply bypassing that part of the brain that interprets every image in the same old habitual ways.

I can tell a lot about the level of competency of a maker simply by watching the way he or she looks at or studies an instrument. A novice's eye goes straight to the purfling and the bee-stings. That's one of the last things I look at. When I pick up an instrument for study or appraisal, I first try to get an overall impression. A violin has to be seen as a whole, one entire composition from one maker's hand. A well-made violin is beautiful from any angle. Your eye wanders easily from one aspect to another. I get a feel for the choice of wood, the model, the varnish, the styling, and the maker's working habits. I look at the architecture and the edge work, I look at the back, the outline, the top, the *f*-holes, and the scroll. Probably, the last things that I look at are the purflings, or maybe the label. When I study the graduations, I'm looking at the graduations in relation to the archings, and in relation to the edges. For some instruments I will make detailed drawings and study the geometry of the acoustic design. Fine violin making goes many levels beyond flat templates or uniform outlines and bee-stings.

You must have had opportunities to look at a lot of historical instruments.

I haven't had as much opportunity to travel or see a lot of fine instruments since I left San Francisco for Eugene, Oregon in 1990. I saw a lot more instruments in my San Francisco shop. Back then I made second instruments for owners of valuable old instruments who felt uncomfortable traveling with their old instruments, or they wanted an instrument that could be played in outdoor symphony concerts. Some collectors like having copies of their old instruments made as well.

I've done studies of historic instruments for the Smithsonian Institution in Washington, D.C. and for the Fine Arts Museums of San Francisco, documenting instruments in their collections. The Smithsonian gave me a grant to document a quartet of decorated Strads that were on loan to them. They wanted illustrations and photographs. The original plan was for me to document the whole quartet in a week, but I ended up spending most of my time with the 1687 *Ole Bull* Strad, which is the most exceptional instrument of the quartet, and just photographing the rest. It has a fancy intarsia of alternating dot-and-diamond motif inlaid between two sets of purfling near the edges. The dots are shell. Fish bones were cut diagonally to create the diamond shapes. The ribs and scroll have intaglio Baroque ornamentation of black mastic fill.

When the Fine Arts Museum of San Francisco acquired Jascha Heifetz's 1742 *Ex. Ferdinand David* Guarneri del Gesù violin, I was contacted to document that instrument, as well. The museum had no idea that Heifetz's instrument was being willed to them. When the news got out, the museum began receiving phone calls from people around the world who wanted to study, handle, and play the instrument. Most of them claimed to be experts. The instrument was far too valuable to be handled by anyone and everyone. Heifetz, during his ownership, had rarely let anyone even touch his Guarneri. The museum needed accurate, full-size, dimensional drawings which they could reproduce and offer to the public.

Are those drawings currently available from the museum?

I can't say for sure. I did that work ten years ago. I do know my drawings of the *Ole Bull* Strad are still available from the Smithsonian. (Write: Division of Cultural History, NMAH 4127 MRC 616, Smithsonian Institution, Washington, D.C. 20560.)

If you ever come to my shop you will see I have drawers full of drawings, notes, studies, and photographs of historic instruments, and I use those for my models. When I have a good instrument in my shop I'll make illustrations of it, and at the same time I'll photograph it. Then I'll have the photographs reproduced to the same size as my drawings, so they're very accurate in dimension.

Do you have an interest in publishing any of that material?

What I have in mind is doing is a book on classical instrument design. I've studied a lot of different makers and different schools, Italian schools. It's information that should be of interest to somebody, but writing takes so much time. Maybe I'll write it when I retire, but being a violin maker I may never retire. ——

Originally published in *American Lutherie #56*, 1998

Martin Tenor Ukulele

by Pete Hurney

AS A UKULELE BUILDER in Hawaii, I'm becoming increasingly aware that an interest in and appreciation of these instruments exists outside the islands. Not having seen a tenor-size ukulele plan available elsewhere, I have drawn this plan of a Martin instrument that I had in the house for awhile. I'm pretty sure it was of the '50s vintage. I'd like to present these plans, not as a drawing of a specific Martin, but as a starting point for one to build a tenor ukulele modeled on a fine instrument. Martin used a variety of materials and a range of measurements, so I've hobnobbed with fellow island ukulele builders on the details. I hereby state a disclaimer to all Martin gurus: any errors you find here are probably what the other guys told me!

Tops, backs, and sides are mahogany or koa, about .070″–.085″ thick. Soundboard bracing is mahogany or spruce about .200″–.250″ wide and about 1/4″–5/16″ tall. Fan braces are ramp cut with the highest part at the transverse brace below the soundhole and tapering down toward the tail block. A thin mahogany bridge patch is used. The kerfed lining is of mahogany or Spanish cedar. Necks are usually one-piece Honduras mahogany. Neck joints are dovetailed. Fretboards are about .170″ thick and are usually Brazilian rosewood, which is also used for the pin bridges. Nuts and saddles are usually ebony. Bridge saddle compensation is about 5/32″. Backs are slightly arched, to somewhere around a 30′ radius. The back center-seam cross-grain strip is made of spruce or mahogany with the Martin logo burnt in, just like on their guitars but miniature.

Binding on the mahogany instruments is tortoiseshell plastic, and on the koa instruments is white plastic. Purfling and rosettes are thin bands of BWB or WBW plastic. The fancier models have a little ivoroid shield on the lower center edge of the soundboard. Fretboards have a single MOP or ivoroid dot at the 5th fret, a double at the 7th, and one more at the 10th. Use small guitar fretwire.

The Martin tenors are overbuilt instruments but age has mellowed them. They generally sound very good now. A 17″ scale length is used with the neck joining at the 12th fret. Most contemporary builders on the islands make tenors with a neck joining at the 14th fret and either move the bridge up higher, modify the body shape, or lengthen the scale. But the string tension is already a little high using a 17″ scale and a standard string set such as Martin, GHS, or Hilo, so I wouldn't recommend increasing string length by more than 1/4″.

PHOTOS BY JOHN CALKIN   INSTRUMENTS FROM THE COLLECTION OF WARREN DOVEL

Martin Tenor Uke

If you chose to build a 6- or 8-string variation of the instrument, brace the belly a little heavier in the lower bout, especially between the soundhole and bridge. On 8-strings I will use a five-brace fan very similar to a classic guitar, and on the 6-strings I use either the same 5-brace fan worked a little lighter, or use the normal bracing pattern for a 4-string but with heavier braces. The extra stiffness doesn't noticeably hamper the sound.

Standard tuning, the same for the soprano, concert, and tenor ukulele, is "my dog has fleas": g' c' e' a'.

Tuning for a 6-string ukulele is as follows:
g' c''/c' e' a'/a'.

And for an 8-string:
g'/g c''/c' e'/e' a'/a'.

The string spacing of the pairs is similar to that found in mandolins, about .075″ at the nut and .120″ at the bridge.

Tuning pegs on Martins varied quite a bit over the years. Good currently available choices include the Grover 4Bs and Grover 85Bs. ——

Martin Concert Uke

Martin Soprano Uke

Martin Tenor Ukulele with Soprano and Concert Ukulele Outlines

GAL Instrument Plan #43

by Pete Hurney

This instrument plan is available as a full-size blueprint from the GAL.

Tenor Ukulele Dimensions

scale	17″
body length	12 1/8″
lower bout	9 1/8″
upper bout	6 7/8″
body depth, heel	2 3/8″
body depth, tail	2 7/8″
soundhole	2 5/8″
shoulder to hole center	4 1/4″
bridge length	4″
bridge width	15/16″
bridge height, center	9/32″
bridge height, wings	.090″
peghead thickness	15/32″
neck width at nut	1 3/8″
neck width at 12th	1 3/4″
neck only depth at nut	1/2″
neck only depth at 9th	5/8″

Originally published in *American Lutherie #55,* 1998

Meet the Maker: Paul Jacobson

by Cyndy Burton

I'm wondering what first drew you to classical guitar making?

I like classical guitar music better than any other guitar music. After I got divorced in 1974 I decided to get serious about playing classical guitar, not realizing I was too old to become really proficient. In the course of pursuing that interest I met a man who made classical guitars, Macario Breseño, and I bought one from him. One day it dawned on me that I'd like to try to work with him and make my own guitar. He said OK, and I worked with him full time for approximately one year.

When I was a kid I made models constantly: boats, planes, and all kinds of little things. And when I made my first guitar there was a feeling of coming home to something that I'd left behind a long time ago.

How were you making your living when you made this discovery?

I was working on the railroad; I was a switchman. In the morning I'd work on my guitars, doing little, tiny, fine things and in the afternoon I'd go down and smash 100-ton boxcars together and throw switches. At some point the cognitive dissonance became overwhelming. I was paying more and more attention to guitar making, and it was paying off for me. I had four kids so I couldn't ignore that, either. It got so I wasn't paying so much attention at the railroad, and people started noticing, and I began thinking about the prospect of being sliced in half by a rolling boxcar. It became evident to me that I was going to have to give up my railroad job.

You're located in Cleveland, Missouri, not a central location for selling guitars I would think.

Right; it's about thirty miles south of Kansas City. I had to seek customers. I had to learn to use a computer, which made more difference than anything else. I developed a database to send out promotional materials. I attended guitar festivals — Guitar Foundation of America (GFA), American String Teachers Association (ASTA), and so on. I went to the customers and met lots of people. As a result, the circle of people I know may well be wider than other makers who haven't had to do that because they had folks closer at hand.

I heard your presentation on intonation at the 1997 Healdsburg Festival. Is this a special interest of yours?

ALL COURTESY OF PAUL JACOBSON

Paul Jacobson at the bench, preparing a back to accept cross bracing.

Yes. And I've worked on lots of other people's guitars as well as dealing with my own. I'm doing less of the upgrading or retrofitting than I used to, but I don't turn the business away, because people need their guitars to play in tune. I don't go out looking for that kind of work; it comes to me usually because someone knows someone else whose guitar I've worked on.

I understand when you intonate a classical guitar you compensate at the nut as well as at the saddle. I know John Gilbert does that as well, and in American Lutherie *#47, Greg Byers gave us an in-depth treatise on his approach (complete with very technical math). (See* Big Red Book of American Lutherie Volume Four, *p. 368.) Could you tell us what you do and how it compares to John's or Greg's adjustments?*

What I do in the way of nut compensation is more similar to Greg's approach than to John's. In fact, some of my compensation values are borrowed directly from Greg's article and rounded a little to account for the practical difficulty of getting accurate break-off points on the nut.

However, I'm not sure my reasoning is quite the same as Greg's. I'll let Greg's article stand for itself on this, but my rationale is based on the fact that string stretch when fretting consists of two components, which I refer to as travel stretch and fretting stretch. To quote from an article I wrote on this subject: "The correct place to compensate for fretting stretch is at the nut, by setting the string break-off point forward, which reduces the distance to the fret and thereby takes away sharpness caused by stretching. The reason for this has to do with the relationship between the ratio of fretting stretch to total stretch and the ratio of nut compensation to inactive string length. As notes are fretted higher on the fingerboard, the ratio of fretting stretch to total stretch decreases because of the fingerboard slope. At the same time, however, the ratio of nut compensation to inactive string length is decreasing proportionally." Anyone who would like to learn more about my theory of intonation can find the complete article on my website. There are other substantive articles at my site, too.

For years I used compensation at the saddle only. I am very much indebted to Greg's article for challenging me to rethink the whole compensation issue at a theoretical level. The important thing, though, is whether an intellectual theory, whether mathematical or verbal/logical, works in practice. I have tested my compensation values at the nut and saddle on a strobe fairly extensively on several guitars, and the values do in fact work on my guitars after taking into account the vagaries of nylon strings.

Are there other things about classical guitars that you've set out to change, to make right, to make your mark or your sound?

The answer to all those questions is no, and no, and no. I'm really not an iconoclast. I thought I was going to be at one time. I thought I had some brilliant ideas about how to change the classical guitar in a major way. I discovered that the ideas really weren't very good and made a personal decision that I was going to focus on improving what was, rather than attempting to completely change the art.

I was thinking more along the lines of evolution. What is your sound like, what are you striving for?

What I seek is what they want. I have my own opinions about what sounds good, and I know that these play a role. But my primary motivating principle is what other people want. I don't think it's the correct role of the luthier to arbitrate what constitutes good guitar sound. I feel it's my role as a maker to provide what good players want, because the whole object is to make beautiful music, and we luthiers play a support role in that. It's not anything bigger than that.

Has it been your experience that really good players know what they want?

Very definitely. And it's my conviction that you can not do anything to persuade them that what you have is what they want. So my practice has been to wait for people to come to me, but that doesn't mean I'm passive about it. I do make an effort to present what I'm doing to people who I think would be attracted to it. But I never twist anybody's arm. I try to cultivate important players. There's a dollars-and-cents reason for that, to help sell guitars; but there's also a philosophical reason. I consider myself a support player in the creation of beautiful music.

Do people come to you and say, "I want a guitar just like the one you made for so-and-so."

Yes. It's very often the case. One guitar sells another.

I know you sell through dealers as well. How does that work out?

At this point in my career I'm making twenty-plus guitars a year, and that's a lot of hard work. It requires enormous discipline in how I use my time, and freedom from distraction. I've decided I just don't like retailing; I don't want to be heavily involved with that end of the business anymore. At this point my guitars are expensive enough that there's room for an adequate commission. I sell through a local dealer here, a dealer in Los Angeles, another in Detroit, and each year about a dozen guitars go to a dealer in Japan. The remaining five or six I retail myself. So it's a little more like having a paycheck.

If you're not selling much directly, how do you continue to evolve your sound?

First of all, people who buy from dealers frequently contact me for all kinds of reasons. They may just want some reassurance that I'm really here, that what the dealer has said about me appears to be true. He or she may have a special request for some option or other. I don't have that kind of contact with my Japanese distributor, but even there, I have some. I really don't want to detach myself completely from that kind of personal contact, which is why I continue to hold several instruments each year for retail sales, instruments that

I've been working on the railroad. Paul quit his job as a switchman in July 1984 to devote his energies to lutherie. This picture was taken his last day on the job.

I have discretion over who gets them. But I like having a regular income, too. So I weigh one need and desire against another and come up with something that will keep my younger two children at the university. I've dealt with some child-rearing burdens in my time, including the period of my life when I've been a luthier, and I've had to make a living at it.

Making twenty-plus guitars a year, you must have a lot of jigs.

Yes. And I'm always thinking of ways to make routine tasks more efficient. I do a lot of things with a production setup. It takes me about an hour and a half to make a whole neck. I'm always looking for ways to be more efficient. Right now each guitar takes me 69.5 hours. That allows me to predict very accurately when each instrument will be completed.

I keep track of all scheduling of my production on my computer. For every guitar I have a task list. I know how long each task takes based on previous time studies. When I start a batch of three or four instruments, the first thing I do is set up my task list for each of them. Every morning I plan my day. All this is on the same spreadsheet. I start plucking tasks off the list. I know I've got four hours in the morning, two in the afternoon, then a little break and a little nap, then I've got two more hours. I figure in times for the glue to dry, and whatever delays there might be. But my day is very carefully mapped out. I have a very rigid starting time, which is 8:00 AM. I've got time planned for getting some exercise in the morning, which is necessary, before 8:00 AM. What do I get from all this? My day is really heavily structured. It gets really wearying sometimes. That's OK. I don't plan to do it this way forever. I need to do that to produce twenty-plus guitars a year.

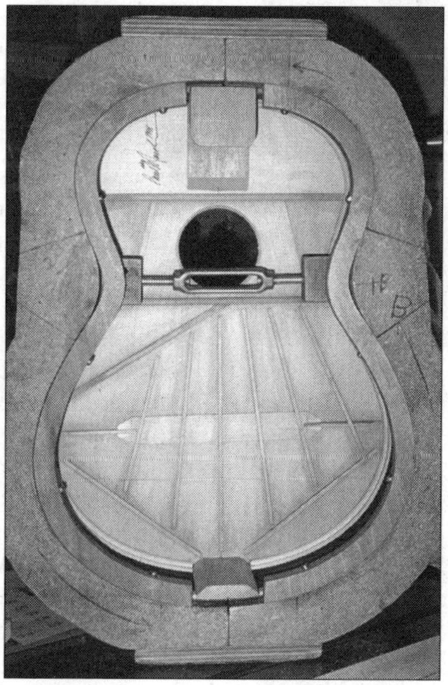

Top left and center: Two views of the jig Paul uses to slot pegheads and drill for tuning machines. Right: Paul demonstrates drilling, using drill-guide inserts with the jig.
Above: Paul's bracing pattern is seen in this view of a classical guitar it its mold. Note the faux-Spanish-heel neck block.

How did you become that disciplined?

It doesn't come naturally to anybody. You have to want to do that. The alternative is to be starting your workday at 8:00 in the morning and ending it at 10:00 at night. I don't want to do that. I don't have the energy to do that. Typically my workday ends at 6:00 PM. I may have other things to do during the day, too: for example, letters to answer, computer forms to work out for documentation for a guitar, stuff like that which doesn't pay anything. This may sound very money grubbing, but, darn it, we all have to make a living.

We are self-employed without employees, which seems like an ideal situation in many ways. Isn't there is a danger (granted not one that most of us are threatened with) of turning into the worst boss anyone ever had?

There's a limit to how much rigor any person can take before you step back from that and just relax. Part of my plan for life is to make sure I provide opportunities to get away completely. And I also want to enjoy it to a certain extent. But to me, work is work. And work is not always enjoyable. Some people talk about how they just love every minute of being on their jobs. I don't love every minute of being a luthier. There are some things we have to do that are boring. Some things are even physically exhausting. Sometimes when it's really exasperating, it just makes me mad as the dickens. I don't enjoy that. I don't especially enjoy sanding finish, processing finish. It's a necessary task; it's one that must be done carefully and with good mental focus. But it's boring. I try to focus at times like that on the outcome. I know from experience that the outcome will probably be gratifying.

It seems to me that it's important to enjoy what you're doing, otherwise you'll just burn out.

That depends on what you mean by "enjoy." If you mean doing what's fun, what's mentally stimulating, everybody would like that all the time. If we expect to be having fun all the time as luthiers we will probably end up mostly futzing and not getting much productive work done. If we're honest, we only get to have fun a little bit of the time. So what gets me through the boredom, the exasperation, the physical rigor of lutherie? I lean heavily on my Christian faith for that. I start each morning with Bible reading and prayer, in which I dedicate my day's work to the Lord. The main thing is to glorify Him, not to gratify myself. This changes my whole attitude when times are tough. It changes the meaning of the word "enjoy." When a guitar is done, I put a label inside it like most luthiers. The label has my signature. Above the signature are the letters "sdg" which stands for the Latin "soli deo gloria," the glory is God's alone.

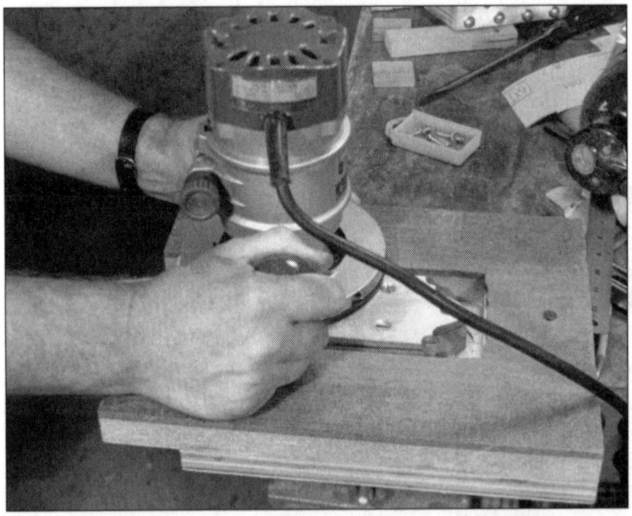

Top and above: Using this workboard and template, Paul shapes his headstocks with a router and an edge-following bit.
Below: Most of the neck shaping is done by hand.

What do you really like doing as a luthier?

I like to start guitars. I really dread completing them. The reason is I have so much invested in them at that point, and they become more and more fragile as they grow, especially once you get finish on them, and the finish is soft, and you have to be so careful with them. Once I've checked them out to be sure they're OK, I let them hang on the wall. I don't spend a lot of time picking them up and fiddling around with them. I especially like inventing tools and new ways of doing things. I like trying new guitar design variations. These activities are mentally stimulating

You mentioned that you're not an iconoclast. I'm wondering which makers have influenced your building?

My building has been influenced by exposure to certain guitars, mostly Spanish. I was exposed to several Rodríguez guitars at a time when I was avidly examining other people's guitars to find out what they knew. At a very early point in my career I paid attention to Ramírez guitars. I've relied a lot on other people's guitars to figure out how to make mine better. I picked out the ones that sounded best to me, but more particularly, those being played by good guitarists. For example, I examined a Daniel Friederich in great detail at one time because Scott Tennant was playing that guitar, and Scott is a person I respect very highly. If he says it's a good guitar, it probably is a pretty good guitar to a lot of other people, too. That's not just because people follow him because of who he is, but because his taste is good. I've done that lots of times with outstanding instruments. John Gilbert is another maker who's work I admire, and I've been influenced by it. His bridge structure is very interesting. I haven't tried to imitate it, but I paid close attention to it. I tried to estimate the weight of it and looked at how its design affected the overall properties of the soundboard. I don't want to clone them, or anybody else's guitars for that matter.

How experimental are you?

I have a high regard for empirical evidence when it comes to knowing what causes guitars to sound the way they do. When I experiment I try to structure it in such a way that I can get good information. In spite of the

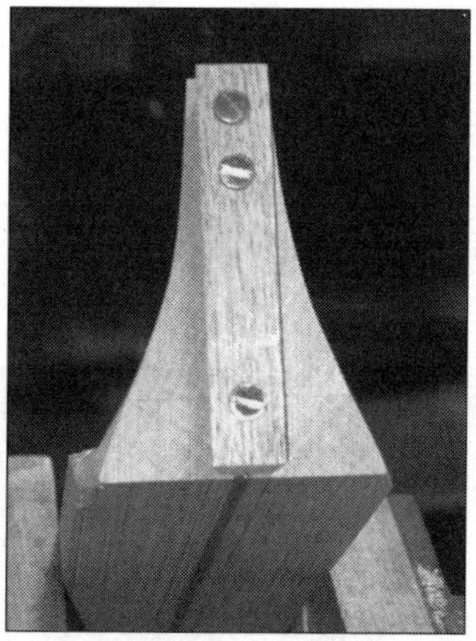

Top left: Paul's dovetail tenons are made separately from the necks, and attached after the contacting surface of the heel is table sanded for the correct neck elevation.
Top right: This table-router setup is used to cut the binding rebates.
Middle: Paul pads tung oil varnish onto a neck.
Bottom: Three bodies being bound. Note the straight dovetail slots for neck attachment, and the back extensions which will cover the end of the heel, completing the illusion of a Spanish heel neck-to-body joint.

fact that luthiers are always tempted to try to manipulate more than one variable at a time, I try to resist that. For example, recently I tried to determine if Indian rosewood makes a different sounding guitar than Brazilian. I dislike Brazilian rosewood because it's so hard to deal with. It tends to crack *after* the finish is on and settled. Indian rosewood by contrast, is a piece of cake. It seldom cracks if you're maintaining good humidity controls in your workshop.

I saw an opportunity to determine empirically if there is a sound difference between the two woods. I'd been telling people for years that if the density was the same, the sound would be the same, but I wasn't really sure of that. I used tops from the same billet and kept everything else as similar as possible. I wish I could report to you some really definitive information, but I can't. There were differences, but no clear-cut evidence trail that the determining factor was the different back and side woods. So now I tell people there's a difference, I think, but I'm not sure exactly what it is or what causes it. Indian rosewood's a lot cheaper. If you want market value, Brazilian rosewood has a certain amount of that. If you're looking for resale in the future, maybe you ought to get Brazilian. If you're looking for other things, like the guitar's not cracking, maybe Indian should be your choice. But what I'm operating on is about as sound a body of evidence as you can gather on this issue. It's not just an empty claim on my part. I try not to make any claims I can't substantiate with empirical evidence. I've experimented with bridge weight as well, and in that instance the evidence was more compelling. I came to the conclusion in comparing bridge weights between 14G and 16G that the heavier bridge probably contributed to a little more sustain in the guitar, but the guitar was a little less loud. But I'm being really guarded about it.

I view guitar making as the writing of sonnets. A sonnet is a form which is pretty structured: the expression of "a single complete thought, idea, or sentiment," having a certain number of lines, usually fourteen, of a certain length, and with certain rhyming schemes. But within that form is some of the greatest poetry that's ever been written, like Shakespeare's sonnets. Every guitar I make is a sonnet, so there are limitations to what I permit myself to do. ——

Originally published in *American Lutherie #56,* 1998

The Modern Mandolin

from his 1995 GAL Convention lecture

by Lawrence Smart

TODAY luthiers are responding to the evolving needs of musicians by departing from making direct copies of the great Gibson mandolin-family instruments of the 1920s. Small (and sometimes not so small) variations in design can provide differences in tone and playability.

An ongoing source of inspiration for me has been the concept of matched sets of instruments, especially in the violin family. Historically, a "test" of a violin maker's ability has been to produce a quartet of instruments as one unit, where all four work together in artistic design as well as tone. I had wanted for years to build such a quartet in the mandolin family, and I was finally given that opportunity with the help of a generous grant from the Idaho Commission of the Arts.

Most of the design factors in mandolins, and archtop instruments in general, are interrelated. Some of them affect each other in very significant ways, and others are more independent. I want to emphasize that all these considerations need to be balanced together with your own style of building, and this balance can only come with experience. It's important to experiment, to consider new ideas and not be afraid to try new things. It is probably most important, though, to have an idea of where you want to end up. Listen in your "mind's ear" to what you consider the ultimate mandolin sound. A clear idea of what inspires you musically is an important place to begin, whether you are building an instrument for Irish/Celtic music, bluegrass, Dawg music, jazz, or blues. Even small variations in design can provide the subtle tonal differences that musicians look for when defining their own playing styles.

One of the first things to consider in a new design is scale length, since it's going to have repercussions on the rest of your instrument, such as body shape and size, string tension, and playability, all of which are important. This is especially important on mandolin-family instruments other than the mandolin, since the mandolin's scale length has come to be more standardized. Scale length in conjunction with where the fingerboard is joined to the body will determine where the bridge is positioned on the body. A longer scale length than standard may require a longer body as well, so the bridge can be positioned to drive the top in the most effective way. Different styles of playing may require different scale lengths to achieve a desired result. For instance, Celtic musicians often enjoy a slightly longer scale length, which lets them use lighter gauge strings, which in turn provides them with the desired "string noise" effect typical of that style. In the larger mandolin-family instruments a longer scale length may serve someone who plays mostly rhythm, while a shorter scale length may be desirable for a person

EARL BROCKMAN

Lawrence Smart's mandolin family, left to right: mandolin, mandocello, F-style mandola. On its side at the bottom is an A-style mandolin. Dimensions for these instruments are in the facing page sidebar.

who mostly plays melody, since he or she will be more physically able to use the fingerboard in the way needed.

Since scale length will play a role in so many aspects of the instrument, it needs to be carefully thought out in relation to the instrument that you hear in your head. Standard mandolin scale length has come to be set at 13⅞″. This is the scale I use most, but I have built a few instruments at 14⅜″. This longer scale works well and provides the benefits associated with a bit higher string tension when using standard gauge strings, such as feel, volume, added projection, and quickness of response. Both of the mandolins in my matched quartet have a 13⅞″ scale length, but since I wanted them to do different jobs in the ensemble I altered other design aspects to achieve this.

The scale length used on Gibson mandolas is 15¾″. I've used mostly a 16″ scale length for mandolas, although I've heard of people using 17″ and even 19″. A 19″ scale length seems a bit long for the mandola, but I've had requests for instruments that can be tuned either as an octave mando or a mandola. A 19″ scale length may be appropriate for this use.

Gibson mandocello scale length is $24\frac{3}{4}''$. When I designed the mandocello in my quartet I settled on a scale length of 25″. This gave me a body size (with the bridge sitting near the middle of the top) that seemed manageable and playable, but large enough to produce the desired low-end response. I know of a few mandocellos with a 27″ scale which seem to work well, and since the cello will probably be mostly playing bass lines, 27″ is likely not too cumbersome.

Relative newcomers to the mandolin family are instruments called octave mandolins, bouzoukis, and citterns. The use of these different names probably implies the different styles of playing and music for which they will be used. I believe that Flat Iron and Stephan Sobell instruments have scales around 24″. I've used scale lengths of $19\frac{3}{4}''$ and $20\frac{1}{2}''$, which are short enough so that with a little stretching they can be played with similar fingering as the mandolin and mandola. The tradeoff is that the shorter scale lengths require heavier strings which can be very cumbersome to play, while longer scale lengths with their lighter gauge strings require more of a stretch.

I believe that everyone who builds these instruments finds with experience which woods work the best for them with their own building style. A well-known wood supplier has told me for years that he doesn't think Engelmann spruce is a good choice for mandolins, but it works well for me. For top wood I've also used Sitka spruce and Adirondack red spruce with good, yet different, results. There are generalizations that can be made about these different woods, but they are just that, generalizations. There is so much variation within the same species in terms of weight, stiffness, and so on that one needs to look at each chunk of wood as an individual. After all that, here is a generalization: Engelmann spruce is generally less dense than the other commonly used spruces, so I generally treat it as such by leaving the top thicker than I might with Sitka or red spruce.

For brace wood, I use either red spruce or Sitka spruce. Both of these are generally stronger than Engelmann, with red spruce usually being my first choice, although it seems more difficult to find red spruce with the nice tight grain that I like to see in brace wood.

I've used koa and a few different species of maple for backs and sides, again with good, yet different, results. I have a good supply of western bigleaf maple, so that is what I usually use. European maple is something I've used and really liked, and I've recently been achieving excellent results with sugar or rock maple. I think koa also works well for mandolins but is different in tone than the maples; perhaps more sweet and bell-like, but lacking the power and push of most maples. I believe that the cut of the wood for the back of a mandolin can play a role in tone color as well. Slab cut wood, being generally less stiff than quartersawn, can help the sound be "softer and warmer" while quartered wood can help provide more of that mandolin "bite."

Again, I think it is important to find the wood that works the best for your own style of building and that matches with what you want your mandolin to sound like. As you tap and scratch on the wood when you select it, listen to tonal qualities in the wood and hear in your mind's ear the mandolin you want to make.

Since the soundboard of an archtop instrument is driven by downward pressure on the bridge, we need to consider just how the breakover angle is going to effect volume, response, and sustain. Simply put, the greater (more acute) the string angle over the bridge, the greater the downward force and the greater the volume and quicker the response of the top. Less (more obtuse) breakover angle creates more sustain since less of the

Smart Mandolin Family

Mandolins
scale length: $13\frac{7}{8}''$
width of nut: $1\frac{5}{32}''$
width at 12th fret: $1\frac{15}{32}''$
strings, outside to outside,
at bridge: $1\frac{19}{32}''$
highest fret: 21
depth of neck at 1st fret: $\frac{13}{16}''$
depth of neck at 8th fret: $\frac{15}{16}''$
length of peghead: $7\frac{1}{2}''$
depth of sides only: $1\frac{9}{16}''$
width of lower bout: $10\frac{1}{32}''$
length of body: almost 14″ with scroll
max height of arch, top: usually 15MM
height of bridge: $\frac{13}{16}$
max height of arch, back:
usually 17MM
soundhole dimensions: $4\frac{9}{16}''$ long
hypothetical bridge point to tail: $6\frac{3}{8}''$

Mandolas
scale length:
$15\frac{15}{16}''$ A-style, $16\frac{3}{8}''$ F-style
width of nut: $1\frac{9}{32}''$
width at 12th fret: $1\frac{23}{32}''$
strings, outsides, at bridge: $1\frac{7}{8}''$
highest fret: 21
depth of neck at 1st fret: $\frac{7}{8}''$
depth of neck at 8th fret: $\frac{15}{16}''$
length of peghead: $7\frac{9}{16}''$
depth of sides only: $1\frac{25}{32}''$
width of lower bout:
$11\frac{1}{4}''$ A-style, $11\frac{3}{8}''$ F-style
length of body:
$14\frac{1}{4}''$ A-style,
$15\frac{3}{8}''$ F-style with scroll
max height of arch, top: 17MM
height of bridge: $\frac{15}{16}''$
max height of arch, back: 19MM
soundhole dimensions: $4\frac{3}{4}''$ long
hypothetical bridge point to tail:
$6\frac{11}{16}''$ A-style, $7\frac{3}{8}''$ F-style

Mandocello, F-style
scale length: 25″
width of nut: $1\frac{17}{32}''$
width at 12th fret: $1\frac{31}{32}''$
highest fret: 24
depth of neck at 1st fret: $\frac{7}{8}''$
depth of neck at 8th fret: 1″
length of peghead: $7\frac{15}{16}''$
depth of sides only: $2\frac{15}{16}''$
width of lower bout: $14\frac{3}{4}''$
length of body: 19″
max height of arch, top: 24MM
height of bridge: 1″
max height of arch, back: 26MM–28MM
soundhole dimensions:
oval, $2\frac{13}{16}'' \times 4\frac{13}{16}''$
hypothetical bridge point to tail: $7\frac{3}{4}''$

string's energy is lost driving the top. A greater angle will produce a more percussive tone, while less angle will produce more overtones and "warm up" the tone a bit. A greater break angle will also create more string tension, which may or may not be desirable for a particular player.

The pitch of the neck and arch of the top are the determining factors in the break angle. Since a bridge wants to be within a certain height range, all three of these factors need to be considered together. If I want to build an instrument with the greatest sustain I can achieve, I might reduce the neck angle, which by itself would make the bridge too low. This can be adjusted by lengthening the heel of the neck, thus increasing the height of the fingerboard above the top, and giving more space between the top and the raised fingerboard.

LAWRENCE SMART

Lawrence's setup for roughing out mandolin plates. The plates are secured to the bottom of the shallow box with vacuum pressure, and a router, fixed to a plexiglass sled which rides on the sides of the box, removes waste material in successive steps.

The tailpiece angle is another, more changeable way to affect string angle over the bridge. The stamped metal tailpieces common to Gibson and most other commercial mandolins don't really have the ability to adjust their angle. Cast or stiff fabricated tailpieces can be mounted up or down or the angle built into the tailpiece itself can be changed to create more or less downward force on the bridge. An adjustable-height tailpiece would be a very interesting addition to the mandolin. It would provide a nearly immediate comparison of greater or lesser string angle over the bridge. Since the mandolin has such high string tension, I think that a truly workable adjustable tailpiece may be difficult to come up with, but I hope someone does it in the near future.

As with any stringed instrument, the greater the air volume of a mandolin, the lower the basic fundamental it will produce; the lower notes of the instrument will be augmented and response time will lengthen. Decrease the air volume and you enhance the treble and quicken the attack of the instrument. Since the mandolin is an upper-register instrument by nature, the treble is innately present and it may not be necessary to overemphasize these traits.

One obvious way to increase air volume might be to simply design a larger outline. This would involve redesigning many aspects of the instrument including where the neck joins the body, scale length, and *f*-hole placement. An easier way that works within the evolved mandolin tradition is to change the depth of the sides. Gibson Loar mandolins have a side depth (not including top and back thickness) of 1½″. I have generally gone to a side depth of 1⁹⁄₁₆″ since I'm interested in enhancing the bass response of the instrument. This depth is not a rule, though. I will vary this according to what I want to build or what the customer wants.

Another obvious way to deal with air volume is with the arching. The higher the arch, the greater the internal volume of the instrument. As the arch of the top is raised, however, issues associated with string angle and bridge height come into play. Raising the arch of the top also has other tonal repercussions which will be discussed below. The arching of the back can more easily be raised to increase air volume without affecting the playability or other aspects of the instrument.

The most common way to make plates is to carve the outside first. With a carefully shaped and modeled outside, one has better control over arch height and shape, and final graduations. For people attempting their first mandolin, it probably would be best to pick up a good plan (Stewart-MacDonald's F-5, or *GAL Plan #26*, Lloyd Loar mandolin drawn by Ted Davis) and copy that arching until comfortable with making some alterations. It should be noted here that most plans I've seen seem to have a few glitches, so it's important to check things carefully before taking them as gospel.

Here is how I go about carving the outside of the top and back plates. There is no way that I could fit a pantographic router in my current shop, and I really don't want to do all the rough carving of plates by hand anymore. This system is a quick way to rough carve with a fairly high degree of accuracy and with a reduced amount of knuckle skinning. The joined top or back plate is laid out in a topographic map fashion representing the arch you want to accomplish. For a top my topo lines are typically marked at 5MM, 8MM, 11MM, 14MM, 15MM, and 16MM. To accomplish this I use a posterboard template with the topographic map of my top or back and holes punched every few inches along each topo line. This template is then laid over the wood and the pattern transferred to the wood by sharp pencil or pen through the punched holes. Then it's a matter of connecting the dots to complete the layout on the wood that is to be carved. The scroll is not marked at all other than the lines that blend into it, and is hand carved later. In the past I removed excess wood on my drill press using a 1″ Forstner bit with the center spur ground flat. This drill-press method is definitely faster than hand carving, but is slower than my new method.

John Anderson from Portland, Oregon described to me his router jig for rough plate carving at the 1995 GAL Convention. I liked it and later modified it for my own use. My jig is simply a shallow box constructed of ¾″ MDF with side rails of a consistent height, and a hole in the center of the bottom surrounded by a mandolin-shaped gasket which secures the plate to the bottom of the box with vacuum pressure. A router is attached to a "sled" which is long enough to allow the router bit to cut around the perimeter of the plate without falling off the side rails of the shallow box. I built my router sled out of ¾″ plexiglas, which works well as it is very stiff and allows me to see the work. The router bit itself is indexed off the bottom of the box to cut the appropriate height. The first cut is made so that the bit leaves 5MM of wood around the outside of the plate. This ends up being the deepest cut made and also the cut which removes the greatest area of wood. Care should be taken to make certain that the plate is securely held down in the box and that the router bit is both cutting in the appropriate direction and not allowed to dive too far into the side of the cut. After completing all cutting at a certain height, the bit is successively raised to make all the different cuts. I use a 1″ diameter straight bit with a ½″ shank which is beefy enough to reduce vibration, and is less likely to break while in use.

This whole process leaves me with a plate with topographic "steps" which need to be faired in to each other and smoothed to the finished outside arch. On the top these steps are easily worked with just a gouge, finger planes, and scrapers. Since the back is of harder wood, I like a little help with removing the bulk of the steps, so I use an angle grinder fitted with a carbide cutter. It's a rather unconventional approach, I know, but it has saved quite a lot skin on my knuckles.

In *American Lutherie #37*, Jimmy D'Aquisto talked about lowering the arch of the top, but retaining the internal volume by increasing the arch of the back. (See *Big Red Book of American Lutherie Volume Four*, p. 6.) This is something that I generally do, with my tops usually ending up 15MM high from the underside of the plate to the highest point on the outside of the plate. My backs, measured in the same way, are generally 17MM–18MM high. The lower top arch has a warming effect on the tone, which is a tonal aspect that I want in my instruments. A higher top arch will give a quicker response and a more percussive tone, which is desirable for some people.

Graduating the plate thickness is probably something of a mystery for many people. An important first consideration is the wood you are planning to build the instrument of. Is it a dense or a lightweight piece of spruce or maple? How stiff? I think it's obvious that stiffer, stronger wood should be thinned a bit more than something like Engelmann spruce, which is generally softer, lighter, and less stiff than either Sitka or red spruce. One of the reasons I like Engelmann spruce is that it generally requires a bit thicker graduation, which at first glance seems strange, but I feel that the more material I can leave on the top, the meatier the tone is going to be. I noticed on one of the D'Aquisto guitars on display at the '95 GAL Convention that the wood was very thick around the edges and soundhole area. It must have been upwards of .180″ thick, which seems kind of extreme. When I gently rubbed the inside of the soundhole, I could tell that the wood was so alive and lightweight that it needed to be that thick. It is important to pay close attention to the wood's characteristics and then use intuition. According to some of my old notes, Engelmann tops on my mandolins have ranged from .240″–.180″ in the center of the plate, to .135″–.090″ at the edges. A few red spruce tops have been somewhat thinner, with Sitka instruments somewhere in the middle.

In general, the heavier the wood, the less resonant it will be and the fewer overtones it will produce, which is very desirable for some styles of music. A thinner, lighter weight top, on the other hand, is able to resonate more freely and will develop more complex overtones as a result. A top should not be made so thin that it won't support the great amount of string tension that a mandolin produces. The trick is to balance out the need for thick and thin wood to make an instrument that will speak with the voice we want to hear while still being strong enough to help support the bridge. The top plates of my mandolins are the thinnest about ¾″ from the edge. They are generally about 40% thinner in this area than at the maximum thickness in the center of the top. I say generally because I work by intuition and feel — flexing the top, tapping, and scratching it. Scratching the wood with my fingernails allows me to hear the high end or treble response of the top or back, while tapping gives me an impression of the low end response of the wood. Based on this formula, if my top is .200″ thick in the center, I can guess that it will end up being around .120″ thick around the edge.

LAWRENCE SMART

A step-routed back, a top whose steps have been removed, and their rib set. After step-routing, tops are carved with hand tools, while backs, because of their hardness, are given their preliminary shape using an angle grinder with a carbide cutter.

The ratio for my backs is a bit higher, 40%–50% thinner around the edges. My backs are thinner in general than the tops, largely because the wood is more dense and hard, and thinning is required to coax resonance out of them.

According to the GAL Gibson Lloyd Loar plan, the top of this mandolin ranged between 4.2mm– 4.5mm thick in the center and between 3.5mm– 2.5mm thick around the edge. The back ranged between 9mm thick near the neck end of the instrument to 3.8mm in the center and 2.1mm– 3.0mm thick around the edges. I don't really know just how consistent these dimensions were to the Loar-era mandolins, but I suspect that there was a fair degree of variation based on the factors discussed above.

Like all other stringed instruments, the bracing in mandolin family instruments serves a couple of purposes. It provides structural integrity to counteract downward string pressure while providing a path for string driven vibrations to radiate to the outer edges of the top. Archtop instruments with *f*-holes have historically been braced with tone bars **(Fig. 1)**. Tone bars are associated with certain tonal characteristics: a quick response time, good volume, a very strong high end, good projection, and lack of overtones.

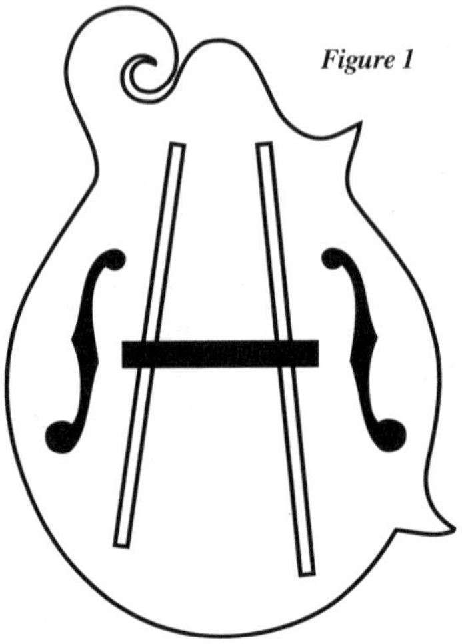

Figure 1

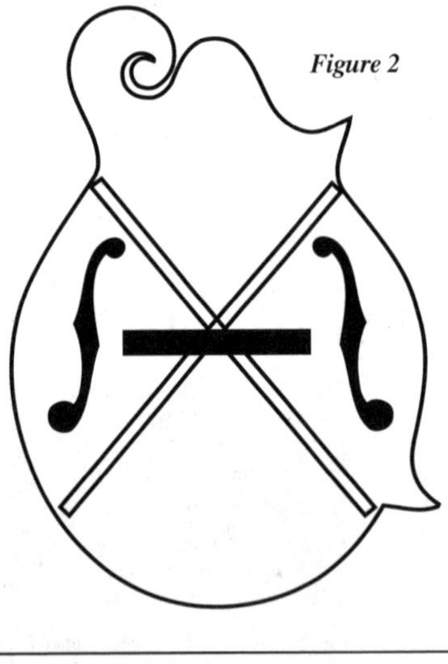

Figure 2

Builders of archtop guitars discovered some time ago that they could maintain many of the characteristics of tone bars while increasing the overtones of the instrument, thereby "warming up" the tone by using some sort of X brace. There are obviously different ways to configure the X brace and these definitely have different tonal effects. Where does the X actually cross? At what angle should the X radiate? On instruments built by Australian luthier Steve Gilchrist and later copied by Flatiron, the X crosses right under the bridge **(Fig. 2)**. I can't venture to explain in detail why this bracing system works so well on these instruments, but it seems to me that this setup will allow the bridge extra side-to-side movement, a "rocking" motion, while still providing the overall dome of the top the structural reinforcement needed. I don't know if these instruments use a different graduation in conjunction with this bracing. On most of the mandolins that I build, the X crosses at a point just forward of the bridge **(Fig. 3)** with the braces themselves passing directly under the feet of the bridge. This system, I believe, provides the strength of tone bars, with the bridge being directly supported, while also radiating vibrations quickly to the outer edges of the top. As a general rule, the more open the X in this style of bracing the warmer the resulting tone. This is a variable that I use to help tailor the tone of a mandolin for customer requests. I am limited in the angle at which the braces radiate by the *f*-hole position and my desire to run the bracing underneath the feet of the bridge.

In my mandolin quartet project, I wanted the instrument which was to play the first violin part to have a very strong and present high-end response with no sacrifice to the overtone-rich low end that I want all my mandolins to have. After a fair bit of head scratching I determined that I would use essentially a tone bar under the treble bridge foot while under the bass bridge foot I would use my standard X-brace configuration with as acute of an angle as I could get away with **(Fig. 4)**. This bracing system works well and accomplishes the job as intended. The high end is a very present, clear voice and the low end speaks with warmth and richness.

There are many other bracing options for mandolin family instruments. Gibson A- and early F-style instruments with oval soundholes used one transverse brace under the bridge area. This bracing scheme has its own unique voice that is much sought after by some players, and I think is still valid today. There are, however, a lot of these instruments with sunken tops, so it seems that care should be taken when utilizing this system.

I think that there is general agreement that A-style and F-style mandolins have their own distinct tonal characteristics. The A-style is usually associated with warmth, sweetness, and a warm rich bass response. The F-style, on the other hand, is associated with a harder, more percussive tone, longer sustain, and a greater dynamic range. These tonal differences tell us that different body styles do play a role in tone production, leading us to the conclusion that the scroll on an F-style is more than just a $2,000 strap hanger.

I think that the scroll on a mandolin acts as a lever, and its position adjacent to the neck serves to stiffen the plates in that area. This stiffening allows less string energy to be lost to the neck, thus resulting in greater sustain and a greater range to which the instrument can be pushed in terms of volume and tone production. I also view the ridge that extends in a curve from the center of the scroll and blends into the top as a sort of external brace which serves to further strengthen the top and back in this area. So as I carve the scroll area on my mandolins I try to keep in mind the structural role that the scroll plays; the little ridge might extend just a bit further than a Gibson's. This is important on the back of an instrument as well. The back is subjected to stress as the strung-to-pitch mandolin tries to pull itself apart at the same time it tries to fold the top in on itself.

Soundholes as a part of the body style play a major role in tone production. Oval holes produce a rich, warm, complex low end, but high end and sustain seem to be a little bit compromised. I haven't used oval holes much, so I can't comment on how bracing or other factors may influence the lack of high-end presence. In fact, most of my listening to oval-holed instruments has been older Gibson models with a single transverse brace. Instruments built with *f*-holes tend to have greater projection, volume, and a very present high end.

Figure 3

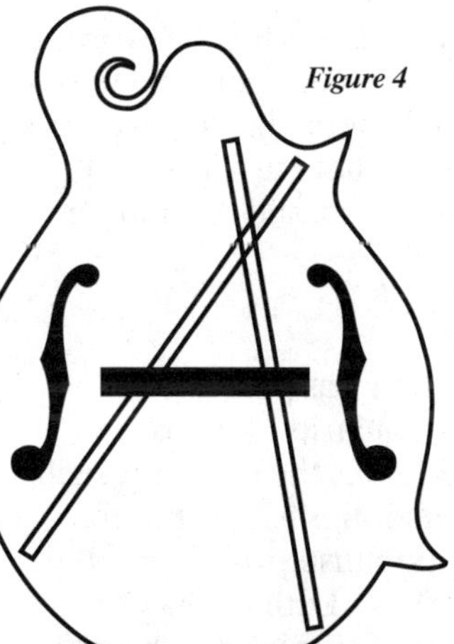

Figure 4

Although it's been written about in this magazine before, it should be noted that soundhole placement is important in pushing toward different voices. Smaller and further apart *f*-holes will augment the bass response while the treble will be enhanced by enlarging the holes and moving them closer together. This is easily observable by placing a hand or piece of cardboard over an *f*-hole while tapping on the top. You should be able to hear the fundamental resonance lower as the hole is closed up. I believe that since the mandolin is a high-voiced instrument, a strong high end is one quality that players seek out in a mandolin. If a strong and present high end can be incorporated with a warm, rich low end, I think players will be happy to have the best of both worlds.

The setup of a mandolin is the last important step in taking advantage of all the design issues that we have utilized so far. It seems that each player has their own ideas regarding how they want their instrument to feel, and I believe that it is important to listen to players and try to deliver what they want.

Many aspects of setup are completely subjective, such as fretwire size, fingerboard arching, string action, string spacing, and string type. Other aspects of setup are more involved in tone production. Nuts and bridges made of harder materials such as mother-of-pearl, or perhaps carbon fiber, can help to quicken the response and articulate tone. Tailpiece choices have increased of late to include heavier cast and fabricated brass and steel models such as the elegant Monteleone style from Saga or Randy Allen, and Gary Price's popular mandolin tailpiece. These heavier tailpieces seem to increase sustain with a stronger, more massive anchor point, but also can increase ambient string noise between the bridge and tailpiece. This can be easily solved by dampening that section of string with leather or something soft placed in the strings. Many people believe that the Gibson-style stamped tailpieces are a good choice in that their lighter weight helps produce a warmer tone quality.

I've heard many great players argue that larger fretwire enhances sustain and makes faster playing possible. I've heard others talk about smaller fretwire providing more accurate intonation. I think all those beliefs have validity and the only real impression I have is that larger wire lasts longer between refrets, and mandolins seem to eat fretwire with wild abandon.

It seems that most players today want some degree of arching on the fingerboard. Arching on the board helps players use movable chord forms and lessens hand fatigue. I do think, however, that too radical of arching can inhibit right-hand technique. The taper of the fingerboard requires that radiused boards have a compound radius with less of a curve toward the bridge. In my setups I generally match the radius at the bridge to the radius at the 12th fret. This seems to be a happy compromise to accommodate both left- and right- hand technique. The extremes that I've seen for curved boards range from about a 4″–12″ radius at the nut. What feels right to me is about 8″–9″ at the nut fading to 11″–12″ at the 12th fret.

Fingerboard width and string spacing are other aspects of setup where players have individual needs. A player with larger hands may prefer a wider fingerboard and a player with smaller hands may prefer a narrower one. This is not always the case, however, as individual technique really determines what is most appropriate. What is generally important, though, is that the individual strings of each pair be close enough together at the nut as to not be pushed out of tune when fretted, and close enough at the bridge as to allow rapid pick movement over the strings, but not so close at either end as to buzz against one another. As for string spacing between the courses, I like to have equal space between each course at both the nut and bridge. Since the wound strings are thicker, this means that the strings are not laid out symmetrically with the centerline, but more in relation to the position of the outside strings.

A variety of strings is available for the mandolin, and the make and gauge becomes a matter of the player's choice. Those who choose to play the other members of the mando family aren't so lucky. To my knowledge, only D'Addario makes string sets for the mandola and mandocello, and they only come in one set of gauges each. Mandola strings run .015″, .025″W, .035″, and .052″, high to low. Mandocello sets are very heavy, running .022″W, .034″, .048″, and .074″. String sets must be made up for the octave mandolin, and depending on the scale length, you may or may not like my choices. Most recent orders have been for instruments that incorporate octave strings for the basses, and those sets look like this: .015″/.015″, .024″W/.024″W, .016″/.033″, and .030″/.053″. Trial and error may be the best way to establish the exact string diameters for your needs. Some of the heavy, newer tailpieces will accept ball-end strings, which will really open the field for you. I've found that if wire cutters are applied to the ball perpendicular to the loop, the balls can be nibbled off the strings and the loops will seldom be damaged. If the cutters are held along side the loop, the ball can be cut off in one shot, but the chance of nipping the loop is greater.

Action at the nut is like any stringed instrument. The instrument will feel best when the strings are as low at the nut as they can be without buzzing. At the bridge, again, each player has his or her own preferences. The tradeoff in this area is volume (helped by higher action) versus playing speed (aided by lower action).

The mandolin-family instruments in general have fairly high string tension, so it is very important to pay close attention to bridge compensation. It is unlikely that a commercially available bridge is going to intonate all the strings accurately without some modification. Also, as is the case with all archtop instruments, carefully fitted bridge feet play an important role in drawing the most potential tone out of a mandolin.

These thoughts, then, are my take on design factors for the evolving modern mandolin. I really want to emphasize that each person needs to work in their own style and if these thoughts can help, that's great. As a lover of the mandolin-family sound, I have hope that musicians will continue to evolve the styles and use of the mandolin, and that luthiers will continue to respond to their evolving needs. ——

Update

In the eleven plus years since this information was presented, mandolins have experienced a huge surge in popularity. I'm just kidding when I say that I'm sure that this article was the cause for such an increase. The number of folks building mandolins has surged too and with it have come higher standards of workmanship and a greater vocabulary of tonal requirements from musicians. Luthiers have responded well and I believe that the mandolins being built today are allowing musicians to stretch their own artistic boundaries.

Obviously in the past years my own woodworking techniques and ability to "hear" have evolved, but much of the information here should still be helpful as a starting point. By the time this article originally came to press, for instance, I had already started rough carving on a pantograph, but the rough carving method described here should still work in a small shop. Whatever the woodworking technique, there is still no substitution for experience in our quest to create better tools for musicians.

It is interesting to note that the quartet of instruments presented with this material eleven years ago was one of my first attempts to match instruments. In the intervening years, I have been able to complete many pairs of matching instruments, but it is as I write this that I am in the middle of working on a commissioned mandolin quartet.

—— *Lawrence Smart (2006)*

Gibson Mandolin Family

Mandolin, 1988 F-5L (1923 F-5?)
scale length: 13 7⁄8″
width of nut: 1 15⁄128″
width at 12th fret: 1 15⁄32″
strings, outsides, at bridge: 1 31⁄64″
highest fret: 29 with extension
depth of neck at 1st fret: .930″
depth of neck at 8th fret : 1″
length of peghead: 7 5⁄16″
depth of sides only: 1.372″
width of lower bout: 9 15⁄16″
length of body: 13 5⁄8″ with scroll
max height of arch, top: 3⁄8″
max height of arch, back: 1⁄2″
soundhole dimensions: 4 9⁄16″ long
hypothetical bridge point to tail: 6 1⁄8″

Mandola, circa 1912 H-4
scale length: 15 27⁄32″
width of nut: 1.337″
width at 12th fret: 1 3⁄4″
strings, outside to outside, at bridge: 1.580″
highest fret: 21 frets w/ extension
depth of neck at 1st fret: 7⁄8″
depth of neck at 6th fret: 1″ plus
length of peghead: 7 1⁄8″
depth of sides only: 1 3⁄4″
width of lower bout: 11″
length of body: 15 5⁄8″ w/ scroll
max height of arch, top: 3⁄8″
max height of arch, back: 3⁄8″
soundhole dimensions: 2.75×1.625″ oval
hypothetical bridge point to tail: 5 3⁄4″

Mandocello, 1914 K-4
scale length: 24 3⁄4″
width of nut: 1 19⁄32″
width at 12th fret: 2″
strings, outsides, at bridge: 1 63⁄64″
highest fret: 24 frets w/ extension
depth of neck at 1st fret: 7⁄8″
depth of neck at 8th fret: 1 3⁄8″
length of peghead: 7 3⁄8″
depth of sides only: 3″
width of lower bout: 14 1⁄4″
length of body: 19 1⁄4″ with scroll
max height of arch, top: 3⁄8″
max height of arch, back: 1⁄2″
soundhole dimensions: 2 1⁄2″×3 3⁄4″ oval
hypothetical bridge point to tail: 6 3⁄4″

Gibson Mandolin Family Instruments

We thank the following for their assistance in compiling information on these instruments:
Warren Dovel, John Calkin,
John Monteleone, Robert Steinegger,
and Steven Andersen.

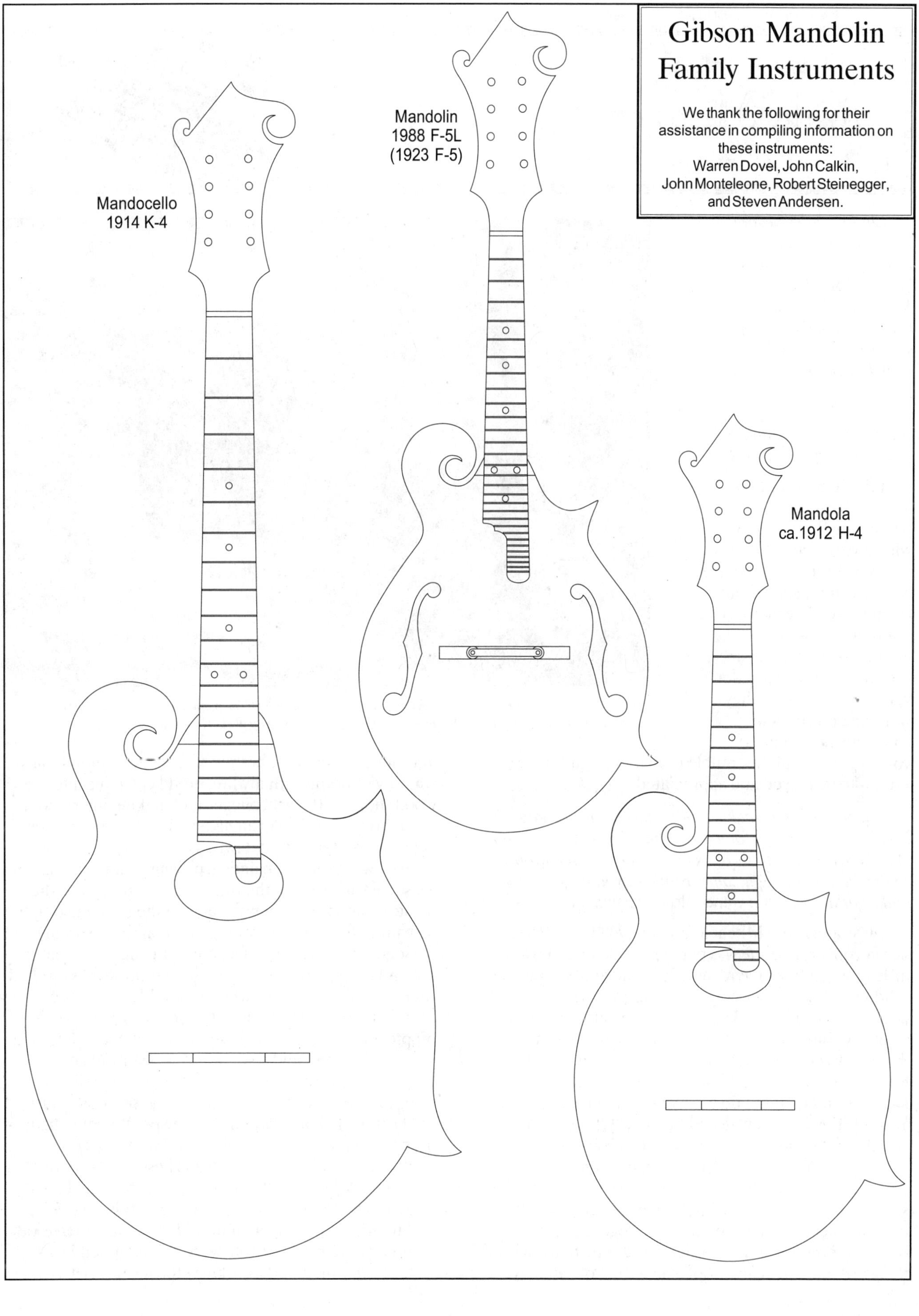

Originally published in *American Lutherie #56*, 1998

Meet the Maker: Linda Manzer

by Cyndy Burton

TONY DUGGAN-SMITH

Linda in her Toronto, Ontario shop carving an archtop soundboard. The plane she is using is a copy of D'Angelico's, made by her part-time helper Tony Duggan-Smith, who also took this picture.

Linda, you've become very well known in the guitar world, partly because you have famous clients, like Pat Metheny. Lots of beginning builders think they've got to do something to get attention, then their careers will blossom accordingly. Some think giving a guitar to a high-profile player will do that. Have you ever given a guitar away?

I don't give guitars away. I figure the professionals are the ones who have the money anyway. Besides, I think that people who *buy* them appreciate them more. I've heard so many stories about endorsers having guitars they don't play. They don't value them because they were just given them in some business deal. If you've gone to all the trouble of making a guitar, you want it to be played and appreciated.

When you started making guitars there were substantially fewer women doing it for a living than there are now. (Not that there are very many of us now, either.) I'm curious: where did that thought come from that you might want *to make guitars and that you* could *make guitars?*

I was a big Joni Mitchell fan. In 1968 I went to see her in concert and she was playing a dulcimer. I was a little teenage folksinger, and a bad one at that. Luckily I didn't follow that career. After her performance I wanted a dulcimer, so I went to the Toronto Folklore Centre to buy one. It was $160, and I had no money. When I was just about to leave, the guy said, "Well, we have these kits for $75." He said, "You could do it," and I said, "Oh, I couldn't do it." We sat on the steps of the Toronto Folklore Centre and he said, "Oh, yes you could," and I said, "No, I couldn't. I couldn't do it."

He talked me into it. I took it home, and in my spare time I assembled it. The magic of when I put the strings on it and heard its first notes — and I had made it — the bug bit. I went on to art college, but in the background I made three other weird little dulcimer-like things. After two years I took some time off, then went another two years at another art college. I didn't know what I was doing with my life, but I kept going into the wood shops at the art colleges and making instruments, even though I wasn't even involved in the woodworking department. One day it dawned on me that of all the things I was doing — painting, playing guitar, and making these instruments — the thing that I actually felt the most passionate about was being in the shop making the instruments. It was very tangible; it agreed with my personality; it wasn't as conceptual as painting, in that at the end of the day, I had something solid. So I searched for a teacher, and that's when I found Jean Larrivée.

His shop was very tiny. He had four employees — hippie guys. Hey, it was 1974! It was above a plumbing place in Toronto, and there was this beautiful golden light coming through the dusty windows. He didn't want to hire me at the beginning because I was "a girl." I kept calling him anyway, and at one point I could hear his wife laughing in the background while he told me that he was a male chauvinist pig. Those were his words, not mine. I thought, "If she's laughing, he can't be half as bad as he thinks he is." Remember, this was 1974, and feminism was in its infancy. It was misunderstood and therefore made people wary. He assumed I was "one" even though I barely knew the term. As it turned out, I would indeed spend the years dealing with the fact I was the only female in my line of work (only female until I met you!) and because of this I would have a different experience at times than my male counterparts. Perhaps it even focused me more. And having grown up with two older brothers, I was used to being a bit scrappy in order to be included in "boy only" events, so this was a natural progression for me. But as time has marched on, it has become less and less of an issue. Thankfully, we have all evolved.

I kept bugging him and he hired me. I got along really well with Wendy, his wife. She was great, and it was nice to have other female company the occasional time she was there. I worked really hard just to prove I could do it. I was trying to be a model apprentice. He kept me on even when he fired a few others. It was great, a fabulous apprenticeship. I got to do everything because it was a small and intimate shop.

And when he moved to the West Coast, to Victoria, B.C. you went with him?

I did go with him for one year, and things changed. He decided to become a factory. I got caught in that transition, and I didn't want to make the change. I didn't want to.

When did you realize that you wanted to make your own guitars?

I knew it was inevitable, although it was very comfortable working with him, and it was very hard to leave. At the three-and-a-half year mark he sort of gave me a little nudge out of the nest. I left and I didn't look back. I returned to Toronto where I had a support system. To be honest, I knew that if I stayed on the West Coast I wouldn't work hard. I'd get distracted by how beautiful it was. I knew I would be struggling with a new environment and community, that I'd be on my own, and it would be very difficult. So I went back to Toronto where I knew I could just work and concentrate on guitars. I think that was smart because I might not have been able to focus at the time when it was necessary to work ridiculous hours.

I shared a shop with a lute maker named Michael Schreiner for about a year and a half. From Larrivée I was totally spoiled by all the power tools, and when I went with Michael Schreiner, I think I brought in the table saw. We did everything by hand. He taught me how to use hand tools.

A sort of second apprenticeship.

Yes, but very informal. We were both making no money and on diets. Sometimes I'd come in and find he hadn't eaten for a couple of days. I remember him scraping together money to buy *one* bottle of beer for New Year's Eve. I'm sure most people struggle at the beginning, and you don't care about the money because you're enjoying what you're doing so much.

How do you feel about that issue now? Do you still feel that building guitars is way more important than the money in the end?

Yes. I'm in the lucky position that I can command a good price for my guitars. When I started, I was working for nothing. I'm still making a lot less than most of the people that I hang around with. But I'm making OK money now. I pay my bills. It was only about four years ago that I started being able to pay my rent without worrying about having the money each month. Even with all the endorsements I have.

If your prices are fair and you're getting a lot of publicity, I should think you'd be overwhelmed with work.

Except that with publicity comes phone calls, letters, and inquiries, and all that takes time. I still make only twelve to eighteen guitars a year. In fact I'm getting slower, because I have more things I focus on. I still like to work by hand. The process of doing the whole thing by hand is what I enjoy, so I'm not mechanized. I'm not a jig freak, although after hearing Jim Olson's talk at the 1997 Healdsburg Guitar Festival, I'm sure everybody including myself was a little tempted to jig up, just to have an extra hour a day to...

What would you do with that extra hour?

Work!

Exactly. Work, of course!

I mean, having endorsements and publicity doesn't necessarily translate into money. Once Pat Metheny buys a guitar from me at the same price everybody else pays, he doesn't keep sending me checks for fun. I'm not complaining at all. I'm getting the price I want for my guitars, but I work as hard as everybody else does to earn that money. My flattops start at $5000, which includes everything unless they want more strings or

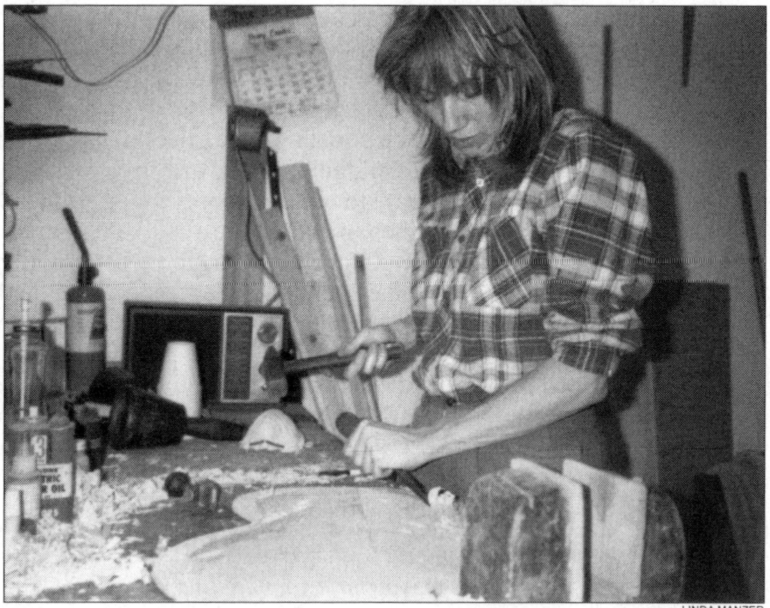

LINDA MANZER

Linda Manzer working in Jimmy D'Aquisto's shop, at D'Angelico's workbench, in 1983.

something very unusual. My basic $5000 model is exactly the guitar that Pat Metheny has, which is the one most people order. Archtops start at $8000 and go up to $14,000 or $15,000. They take twice as long to build, and they're all done by hand. I don't dupli-carve at this point, but I may do something soon to hog out the rough stuff because my arms are getting tired.

Some people seem more interested in building jigs than in building guitars. It seems as if what started as a passion to build instruments has become a passion to see how many they can build in the shortest possible time. I know both efficiency and consistency are served, but there is a risk of losing touch, quite literally.

I've thought about that, and I think they are just exploratory people. Larrivée loved doing the machinery; he became interested in the process. I know that I feel the best when I'm doing the guitar. I'm a little interested in the jigs, I must admit. It's fascinating to be able to make ten pieces in a hurry rather than standing there bandsawing and sanding. But I think they get interested in the process and the challenge of making a gizmo that does this or that.

That's different from just wanting the money at the end, which is at least part of the motivation for many to jig up.

I remember when I thought self-righteously that some people were selling their guitars for too much money. But now, twenty-four years later, I've been doing this my whole adult life, and I think I'm pretty good at it. I still think I have lots to learn, but it's OK for me to *not* have to struggle with the money part of it anymore. I've already gone hungry and been skinny, and I'm very comfortable with not having to worry about that anymore. I don't feel guilty about charging what I want for the guitars. If I was making violins this is nothing.

The question would not arise.

Exactly. About a year and a half ago, when I had a really long waiting list, I raised my prices from $3500 to $5000. I decided it was a way to slow down the orders so I could have some space. I don't want a five-year waiting list. When I studied with D'Aquisto over the course of one winter, I witnessed his dealing with a five-year waiting list. He was very frustrated by it, because he was building stuff he didn't want to build, something that he'd gone past. He had all these new ideas he wanted to try. (It was nice to see at the end of his life that he was able to finally find someone, namely Scott Chinery, to finance him to do what he needed and wanted to do.) So I watched him deal with that and I thought, "I don't ever want to get like that." I've lived by the skin of my teeth for so long that I don't need that security. A year is fine, or a year and a half is totally fine. And then I'm not locked in. I really like changing the designs if I need to or want to.

How about the customer interaction part? Is that something good? Bad? How do you limit your contact so that you can get some work done?

I guess I've gotten good at it over the years. I don't need to nurse people quite as much; I usually try to get to the point. With certain people I can have very minimal conversations and understand. Like, Pat Metheny is someone I have extremely limited interaction with. I think I know what he wants with few words spoken. On the other hand, Bruce Cockburn and I spent hours going through all the details. It was fun; I like the interaction. For the first five years of my career I sold my guitars through a store, and I missed the interaction and feedback, which is really important. I want to interact with people; I enjoy it. I have this three-month or one-year friendship with a person where we're going through building and designing this little thing. Then I make the guitar. They get it. There's a little moment where we're still interacting, then it kind of dies off and then the next person comes in. With some people, when I finish the guitar I'm almost sad, because I know that the interaction will end. I think a couple of people have actually reordered from me just because they like that interaction and the fun of it. That's half of the guitar.

Do you have lots of women customers?

I don't have more women customers because I'm a woman builder. Women guitarists don't suddenly go, "Oh, great, a woman builder!" Look at all the well-known women performers — none of them are playing guitars made by women. There's no reason why they should either. I'd say that 99% of my customers are men. However, having said that, I secretly like building for women because in the music industry we are still a pretty rare breed, and I like to see them do well. I enjoy being part of and supportive of their careers. It's a girl thing.

You've designed a lot of instruments. Most of us have seen pictures of the Pikasso guitar. You've made a lot of one-offs or, in effect, prototypes. Is that something you particularly like to do?

I love it. I do have standard models that I make. But when somebody comes in, I work with them. They'll give me more or less guidance. It's like a little adventure and I learn a lot on each one. Usually my guitars are within a certain ballpark. Some people think I'm a wild builder, but in some ways I consider myself extremely conservative compared with a lot of other people, because I'm very rigid on what I believe. For example I like to use certain woods. I'm having a hard time giving up European spruce.

Do you need to?

I don't think I need to. I've recently found out that the wood I get from Europe is sustainably harvested. That's very important to me. I like European spruce, but it's expensive. I don't think it is necessarily a better wood, I'm just used to working with it. I quite love it. It works with me and my entire guitar design, whatever I've come up with. It may not work for anybody else in the same way.

BRIAN PICKELL

Baritone guitar of German spruce and koa, 73.5CM scale length. Strung B to B or A to A, the usual string gauges are: .018″ (plain), .024″, .036″, .046″, .056″, .070″.

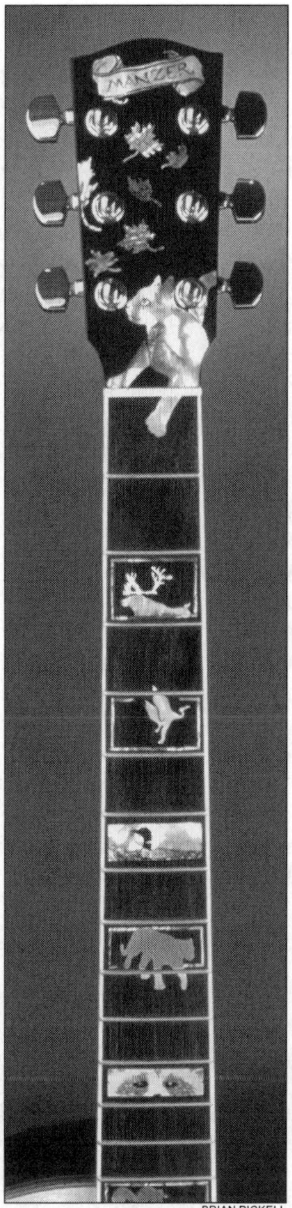

BRIAN PICKELL

Neck inlays on the prototype of Linda's The Manzer model flattop steel string.

MARK BRICKELL

Commissioned by the Canadian Museum of Civilization, this 1990 Endangered Species model archtop features a 17″ lower bout and neck inlays of endangered species.

What about back and side woods?

I'm more open minded about that, though I've stuck pretty closely to Indian rosewood back and sides. Brazilian I'm not crazy about because of the price, the inconsistency of quality, and the instability. I love how beautiful it is, and I love the way it smells. It has great built-in trebles and clarity compared to Indian rosewood, but you have to ensure that your construction methods favor a bass end that is rich and full and accounted for. And I'm mostly a steel string builder, though I do build more classicals than I used to. I stick to ebony for fingerboards and bridges, and mahogany for necks.

For my archtops I prefer maple for the backs, sides, and necks. I'll use big leaf, eastern, European, all three. A maple tree came down in my neighborhood that's brown, soft, and really curly. I'm saving it for a little series of guitars I'm planning to make at some point. Although it's quite soft, I think I can work with that. I made an archtop bass with soft, local, white curly maple. In Ontario you can get some really fabulous curly white maple. The European is sort of the next grade up in hardness. I have to admit that I prefer working with European maple, because it's like butter. It's beautiful to work with. When I finally allowed myself the pleasure of paying the exorbitant price for it and I made a guitar with it, I understood why people pay that price. I was sad that I now had to start paying that sort of money to get that kind of wood pleasure. I'm hooked!

I understand you're involved with local government over wood harvesting and forestry practices in Ontario.

Last fall (1997) I was encouraged by friends to speak at a public inquiry into the future of Ontario's forest. The Ontario government was pretending to listen to public input about the future of the public lands in this province. It's ingeniously called "Lands for Life." The area involved is *half* this province (about the size of the state of California). There are many old-growth forests that are in danger of being clear-cut soon. Most of the people in this province still don't know about "Lands For Life" because the government doesn't really want public input as they've been working out back-room deals with lumber companies.

I was motivated to become involved in forestry issues after I saw a very slick TV ad by a multinational lumber company in Canada. The company claimed to "supply Canadian guitar makers with sustainably harvested woods." I was infuriated because I knew it was a lie and that this particular company has a terrible forest management record and the rotation cycle for cutting their replanted trees is about forty to sixty years. They may supply ukulele builders with wood, but certainly not guitar makers. This coupled with being told by numerous wood suppliers that the supply of wood in North America for musical instrument makers will be gone in about thirty years (if that) has motivated me to speak out.

I have helped to organize and spoke at a rally/concert in Toronto to inform people about the "Lands for Life" issue which included video feed from Bruce Cockburn, Liona Boyd, Betty White, Ed Asner, Ed Begley Jr., and Martin Short! Currently I am helping to organize a rally that will surround our Parliament buildings with several hundred canoes, "Portage for Wilderness." That'll be a sight.

I realize it's an extremely complicated issue, but *the lumber companies should not be the sole managers of the public forest*. It's like letting the fox guard the hen house. As it stands it looks like the Ontario government is about to hand over management of upwards of 94% of the public lands to lumber companies in the form of ninety-plus year leases. It will mean the end of real wilderness in this province.

If any one wants to know more about this issue they can read about it on the Internet, and it would be a great help if they would write a letter to the Ontario Government in support of protecting more wilderness.

You are very successful. It's been a long, hard struggle but you've kind of arrived, and you still love what you're doing. What advice do you have for a woman or man starting out?

The best thing is to find your niche. There are so many books and videos and instruction courses, the stuff you and I didn't have when we started, that you don't have to be an apprentice. And the Internet, even, is great as long as you use common sense and are careful in taking the information. It's not backed up sometimes; it's just someone who's unskilled giving their opinion. There are many good, young builders out there as a result of all of this available instruction, and

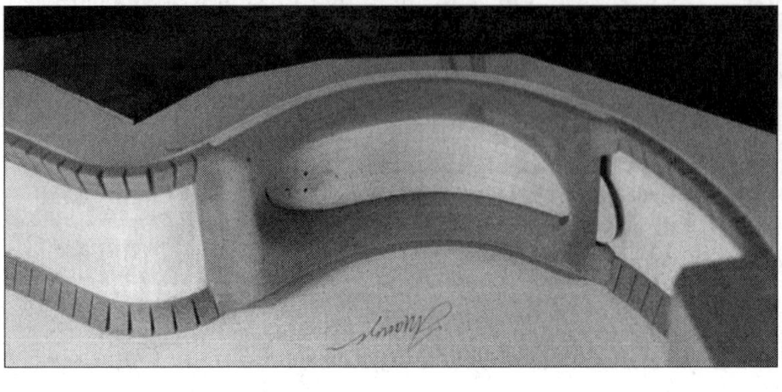

ALL THIS PAGE BY LINDA MANZER

Three views of the auxiliary soundport in Linda's Blue Absynthe archtop, built for Scott Chinery's Blue Guitar collection. The sliding panel is made from maple and ebony veneers. Leather gaskets in the door pocket guard against vibration rattles.

C. BENEDETTO

Linda and Tom Ribbecke touring the Taylor Guitar factory.
Tom: "I like the part where they thin the tops with a lawnmower!"

also because of the kind of money that's commanded. People think they can make money, which is quite a different attitude than we started with. This concept of making money is mind boggling for most of the people in our generation. You're not going to have to be the starving artist necessarily. Financial success may come early. But with so many potential competitors, I'd advise people to find their particular niche, and if there's some part of it that they're passionate about, follow that. And the other thing is not to be intimidated by the fact that there are so many people, and so many people at such high skill level with tools. There was a guy sitting behind me at Jim Olson's slide show who just wanted to throw his hands up and quit because he was thinking, "How can I compete with this?" It looks so effortless for Jim Olson. All I can say is, you need to trust your own intuition. It's the hardest thing to do, but that's the best tool you have. The best skill you can have as a luthier is developing communication with that part of yourself who knows what's right and wrong with a piece of wood when you're tapping it. If it looks like it's a great top, and it feels like it's a great top, but, if when you're tapping it there's something about it that you can't connect with, then it's not a good top for you. And that's the main thing for people to be in touch with. The computer that stores all the information in your brain is much more sophisticated than any computer program or book that you're going to read.

It's real easy not to trust that stuff, but the longer I build, the more I believe in it. In Indonesia, the gamelan orchestras are said to contain a spirit. You're not supposed to step over those instruments because you'll disturb the spirit. A friend told me he worked as the curator of a museum where there was a gamelan orchestra upstairs. He was working alone in the basement on a stormy, cold, and windy night. He heard people dancing above him, so he went upstairs, but nobody was there, just the room filled with the gamelan orchestra. I just think there's something else happening with instruments, and if you trust the force to be with you *(spoken dramatically)* I think that's the best tool that you have. Having said that, it's also really important to do your homework and read as much as you can about every technical aspect you can about wood, construction methods, and about art. It all becomes the smorgasbord that is *your* guitar.

I understand you're in the process of creating a new shop. What inspired you to do this?

I bought the house I'd been renting for fifteen years. It's a three-storey Victorian house in downtown Toronto. I bought the dump, so now I have to fix it up. *(laughs)*

One of the things I've been trying to do is industrial spy work, just going around and seeing what everybody else has in the way of shops. I've spied on Benedetto and I found the real secret to his success is that he has everything on wheels! (Don't tell anyone!) And John Monteleone has a wonderful shop that has a baby grand smack dab in the middle. What a luxury.

The back two-thirds of the first floor is my shop. The front is the office. Living quarters are above. It's great and I'm really enjoying it. When I started peeling back the walls I found three fireplaces I didn't know were there. So I guess I have somewhere to burn my scraps, right? ——

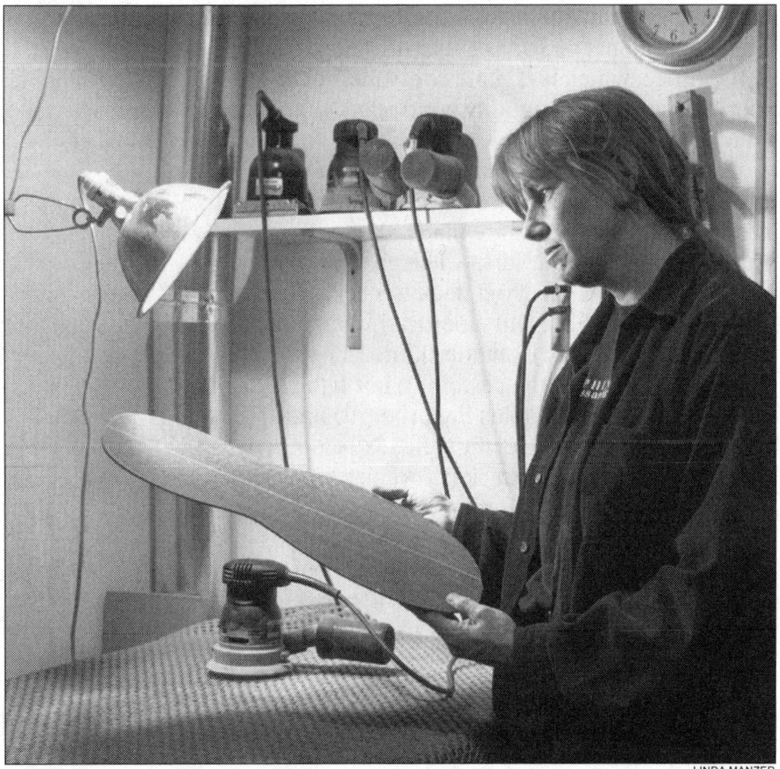

LINDA MANZER

Linda inspecting a rosewood back at her sanding table. A vacuum pulls dust through the mesh so that none leaves the work area.

Originally published in *American Lutherie #56,57, and 58,* 1998

The Chainsaw Lutherie of Tom Ribbecke

by Jay Hargreaves

TOM RIBBECKE has been playing, repairing, and building guitars for over twenty-five years. He's best known for his archtop guitars, and for several years he opened his shop to a few students who wanted to learn the Ribbecke archtop building techniques. This article is the result of attending one of Tom's week-long seminars. The classes are not a hands-on process for students, but rather a grueling schedule of ten-hour days during which the students observe the creation of an archtop guitar, complete with all the hints and tricks that Tom can throw their way.

The Ribbecke shop churns out twenty to twenty-four guitars per year. Most are built around his 17″ body and a 25.1″ scale length. Maple is the wood of choice due to its long association with the archtop. The tone character and internal dampening properties of the wood have become basic to the instrument. European maple and American big-leaf maple are similar in weight and density, and the way they transmit tone has become the chief factor in their use for archtop instruments of all kinds. Such maple adds very little tone color of its own to the sound and often lacks a bit in sustain, but it aids the notes of a closely stacked chord to be heard individually, rather than in one muddy field of noise. This is an important criterion when judging the quality of a contemporary jazz guitar. The components of Tom's guitars-in-progress are kept in the office, which is climate controlled. Though the shop proper is not humidity controlled, this is rarely an issue in Sonoma County, California.

Necks are most often made of hard maple from the eastern US. Tom likes bird's-eye maple best. Enough necks to last six months are made at one clip, usually a batch of sixteen or eighteen. The goal is to be as consistent as possible from neck to neck. Thickness at the nut will run .625″ and taper to .750″ where the heel begins to curve away from the shaft. Finished necks are dimensioned to suit the customer, but typically run .590″ thick at the nut (plus fingerboard) and .700″ at the 12th fret. The angle of the headstock is set at 15°. The headstock is .375″ thick before the laminations are added and .625″ thick after laminating.

Neck blanks are laid up from maple boards in order to make the headstock and heel integral parts of the neck. Boards are flat sawn so that after being laminated into a blank the necks are effectively quartersawn. Planks 4″×27″–30″×1.25″–1.375″ are glued together with a sheet of black veneer between them to act as a center stripe. Titebond is applied to all four sides of contact for better adhesion **(Photo 1)**. By careful cutting on the bandsaw two necks will be taken from each blank, as well as the fingerboard extensions

ALL BY JAY HARGREAVES EXCEPT AS NOTED

Photo 1. *Tom applies Titebond glue to both sides of the black veneer strip and both of the maple boards that make up the neck stock. Two necks, the fingerboard extensions, and peghead wings will come from each blank. Flatsawn maple boards will create quartersawn necks.*

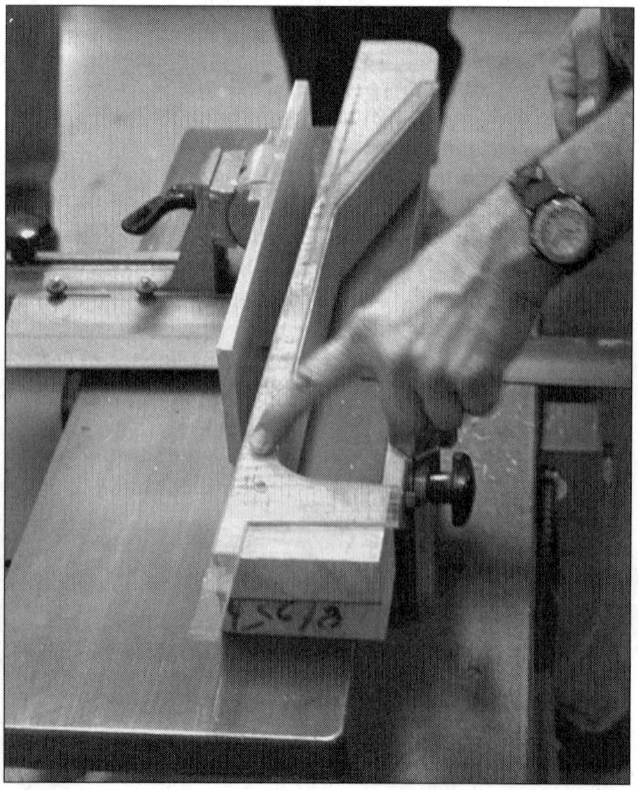

Photo 2. *The fingerboard surfaces are jointed before the stock is bandsawn into neck blanks. The next step is to sand the headstock clean and true to the fingerboard surface.*

and headstock wings. Colored pencils or crayons can be used to color code the parts until they are assembled.

Figured wood will fare better during machining if the surfaces to be cut are sprayed with Swann Glycerin Emollient, a drugstore item, mixed ¼ oz. to a pint of water. The glycerin drastically reduces tearout. (When wet wood is placed on a machine with a steel bed it often turns blue very quickly. All of Tom's machines have aluminum beds.) The edges to be glued to the fingerboard are jointed before the necks are cut from the blank. A 10° back bevel on the jointer blades will reduce the tearout on figured wood.

It's important that boards of equal width be used to form the neck blanks. The necks will be reinforced with a centrally located adjustable truss rod as well as an insert of carbon fiber on either side of the rod. The slots are cut on a table-mounted router. If the black veneer isn't located dead in the middle of the blank, different adjustments will have to be made for cuts on each side of the centerline, a needless waste of time. However, this step comes later.

Once the two necks are free of the block **(Photo 2)**, the headstocks are leveled on an 80-grit belt sander. Any waste at the heel end of the neck is cut off, then the surface that will become the dovetail is trued on the belt sander. The neck profile is formed using a jig and a tool called the Robo-Sander, which is a sanding drum with a flush-trim bearing mounted beneath it, much like a flush-trim router bit. The bearing reads the jig while the sanding drum cuts the neck to conform to it **(Photo 3)**.

The neck extension and headstock wings are given the water and glycerin treatment before they are run through the thickness planer. Tom uses a Ryobi APP12, a portable 12″ unit. Canting the stock at a 60° angle to the blades will help prevent tearout. The neck extension is planed to .625″ thick. The headstock wings are planed to .40″, which leaves just a skosh to dress down to the .375″ dimension of the headstock.

Tom's guitar necks employ the TRST truss rod from LMI, which is a double-action (two rods), one-way rod. The reinforcement system also incorporates two 18″ × ¼″ × 3⁄16″ carbon-fiber rods which extend into the neck extension in order to better align the parts during glue-up. All slotting is done on a router table **(Photo 4)**. The truss rod requires a 7⁄32″ bit set to a depth of .420″. Use at least three stepped passes to cut the slot in order to prevent breaking the bit or ruining the neck blank. No adjustment is made to the router table fence before machining the slots for the carbon-fiber rods. Rather, the bit is exchanged for one measuring ¼″, and a plexiglas spacer measuring ⅜″ is placed between the neck and the fence. The bit is set to cut to a depth of .280″. After the first slot for the carbon-fiber rod is completed, the neck is reversed and the second one is cut. This creates a truss-rod slot dead on the centerline, and a carbon-fiber rod slot equally spaced on either side of the truss rod with a wall of wood ⅛″ between them. The carbon-fiber slots are overly deep to permit a filler of wood to be glued between the rods and the fingerboard. Wood glue does not stick to carbon fiber. Once the neck extension is glued in place, the rods, which are used to index the parts, can be removed until it is time to permanently install them. The neck extension should be slotted at the same time as the neck. Care must be taken not to run the slots the full length of the extension, but only the length of the rods.

Photo 3. *The neck blank is clamped in a jig and its profile is established using the Robo-Sander, a sanding drum that has a bearing guide bolted below it. The bearing reads the jig while the drum shapes the neck.*

Photo 4. *The truss-rod slot is cut on the router table. The cutting must be done in several passes. Then a ⅜″ spacer is placed against the fence, the bit depth is readjusted, and slots are cut on either side of the truss rod for the graphite reinforcement rods.*

Photo 5. A neck blank is clamped in the dovetail jig. The entire unit is sitting on a bench top. When mounted for use, the neck will stand vertically and the dovetail area will be flush with the jig table. The dovetail is routed through the window in the jig table.

Photo 6. The router rides on the plexiglas frame mounted around the window in the table. The dovetail template slides between guides on the table and is screwed to the face of the dovetail. This adjustment permits the use of the same jig on guitars that have sides of different depths.

Photo 7. The dovetail jig in use. Note that a clamp has been added to support the dovetail template.

The neck-to-body angle of Tom's guitars is 4°. The neck should be carefully marked at the nut, the 14th fret, and where the neck extension will sit. To cut the dovetail the neck is held vertically, heel up, beneath a special router table that Tom built **(Photo 5)**. Note that in the photo, the jig is sitting on a bench top and is not mounted for routing yet. The table and the fixture that holds the neck in alignment are part of the same jig. Phenolic pins in the fixture fit into the truss rod slot, holding the neck perpendicular to the router table. A window in the table allows the heel end of the neck to sit flush with the table top. The window is surrounded by a frame of plexiglas which acts as a bed for the router

Photo 8. A step is routed in the neck to accept the fingerboard extension. The neck is clamped beneath the table. The edge of the table acts as a router guide. Pins in the bottom of the table fit into the truss rod slot to hold the neck square to the table.

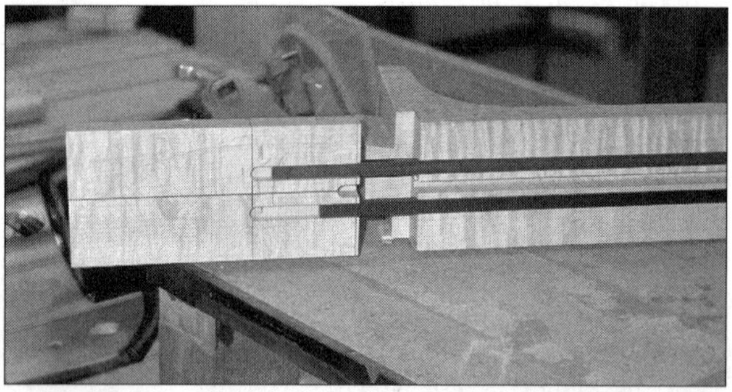

Photo 9. Carbon-fiber rods are used to hold the fingerboard extension in alignment with the neck during glue-up. The same rods will later be epoxied in place to stabilize the neck and aid the truss rod.

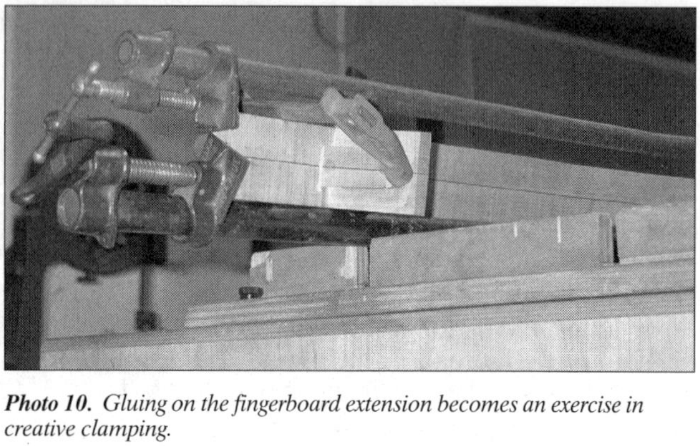

Photo 10. Gluing on the fingerboard extension becomes an exercise in creative clamping.

base. There is a slot in this frame directly above the dovetail, and a plexiglas template of the dovetail extends through this slot and onto the heel **(Photo 6)**. This template is adjustable for depth to accommodate guitars with different depths in the sides. A screw fixes the template solidly to the dovetail area of the neck. The dovetail is cut in one pass using a Porter Cable Type 5 router with an American Eagle dovetail bit, which has a ½″ shaft and a 7° taper on the dovetail **(Photo 7)**.

A step or shelf is routed into the top of the dovetail and ⅜″ of the neck to accept the fingerboard extension. This is done using a simple jig which amounts to little more than a small piece of MDF on legs **(Photo 8)**. Pins which fit the truss rod slot keep the neck at a right angle to the working edge of the jig. The neck is clamped to the bottom of the MDF and the router rides on the top surface. The cut for the shelf is ⅝″ deep. To prevent chipping as the router exits the wood, a filler strip is inserted in the truss rod slot and a piece of scrap is spot glued to the off-side edge of the heel. After the work is cleaned up, carbon-fiber rods are placed in the neck to index the neck extension, and the extension is glued in place with Titebond **(Photo 9)**. Some ingenuity may be required to come up with a satisfactory clamping arrangement **(Photo 10)**.

Wings for the headstock were cut from the same block of wood from which the necks were taken. This assures a good color match in the wood. They are glued to the headstock with Titebond. Strapping tape is used to keep the pieces from sliding under pressure **(Photo 11)**, then clamps are applied. The wings are just barely over the correct .375″ thickness, and in other dimensions might as well be way oversize for the headstock design that is used. There's no sense in getting too cute when dealing with what is essentially waste stock. When dry, the headstock is sanded and scraped to an even ⅜″, making sure that the transition of the back of the headstock to the neck shaft is even and pretty. The veneers that will be glued to the back of the headstock are usually of black, maple, black, and then a slightly thicker plate of figured maple. Index pins measuring 3⁄64″ are used in a waste area of the headstock to keep the veneers from slipping beneath the clamps. The clamping caul has an extra thick rubber pad in the curved transition area. The caul is rounded to suit the shape of this area of the headstock, and the rounded portion is hinged and held with springs **(Photo 12)**. A veneer press is used to apply pressure to this portion of the caul **(Photo 13)**. The headstock sits flat under the press. An angled block provides support for the neck shaft. Pins in the block fit into the truss-rod slot. The shoe of the press is drilled to accept pins that protrude from the top of the caul. This may seem like an elaborate setup just to glue a thin stack of veneers, but the further along the neck is taken, the more important it becomes that the work is done correctly. The flat areas are simply clamped with C clamps. The faceplate veneer is glued at another time.

Photo 11. *Fiberglass strapping tape is used to align the wings on the headstock before clamps are applied. The tape also prevents slipping of the joint.*

Photo 12. *A special caul is used to glue the veneers to the back of the peghead. The caul is indexed by pins that pierce the veneers and waste stock of the peghead. The curved portion of the caul is hinged for a better fit of the contour.*

Photo 13. *This press is used to clamp the rear headstock veneers. The small ramp supports and guides the neck. The screw applies pressure to the curved portion of the caul. Several other clamps are added to complete the operation.*

Photo 14. *Gluing the carbon-fiber rods in place. The peghead end of the rods have been trimmed to the angle of the headstock using a cutoff wheel in a Moto-Tool. Rosewood filler strips will cover the rods. The rods and rosewood are epoxied in place. The fingerboard will be glued on with Titebond, which wouldn't stick to the rods if they were left exposed.*

Photo 16. *The fingerboard stop is covered by the ebony headstock cap. Its ends will support binding, so the piece will be invisible on the finished guitar. Its function is to support the lines of purfling that flow from the neck to the headstock.*

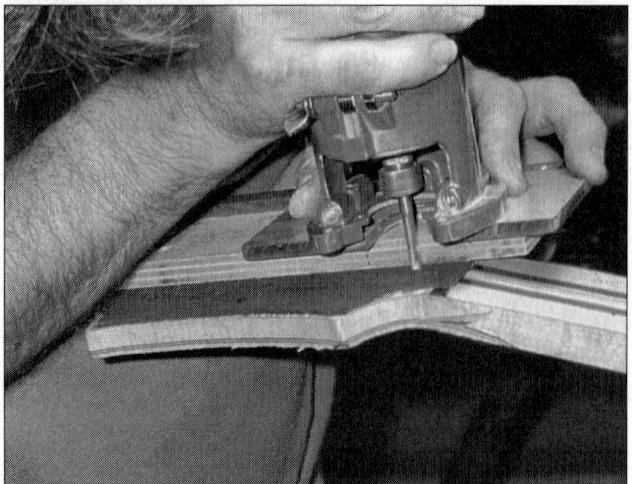

Photo 18. *A simple jig is used to open the truss-rod adjustment slot in the headstock. The jig is held to the headstock with double-sided tape.*

Photo 15. *The fingerboard stop sits beneath the nut. It will be dressed to the angle of the headstock.*

Photo 17. *The ebony peghead cap is glued in place. Pins through the center of two machine-head holes keep the parts from slipping.*

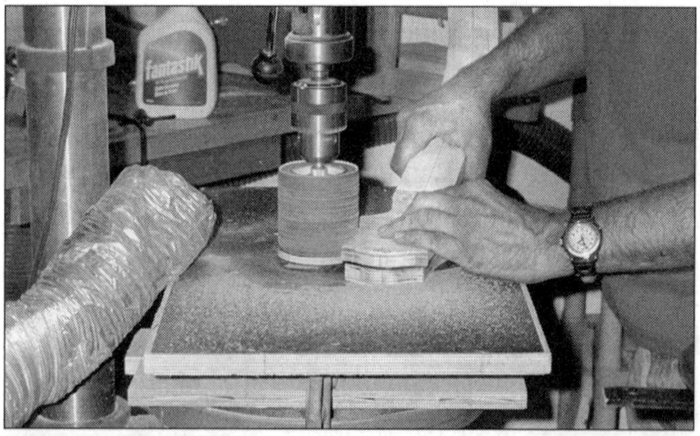

Photo 19. *The Robo-Sander is used to dress the edges of the headstock. Tape wrapped around the bearing leaves the headstock a shade oversize.*

Photo 20. *The headstock is brought to final dimensions on the router table, which leaves a crisper surface than the sanding drum.*

The ends of the carbon fiber rods extend into the headstock and they must be cut to the same 15° angle as the face of the peghead. Tom does this with an abrasive cutoff wheel mounted in a Dremel tool, trying to capture as much of the dust created as is possible. A polluted shop is an unhappy shop.

The carbon-fiber rods are wiped with acetone. The truss-rod slot is taped over, then the rods are glued in place **(Photo 14)** using Smith & Co. Tropical Hardwood Epoxy Adhesive (from LMI) followed by rosewood filler strips. The rosewood sits proud of the slots and is leveled after the epoxy has set. A straight board is used as the initial clamping caul to seat the rods and the rosewood, after which the board is removed, the squeeze-out is cleaned away, and the neck is reclamped with a metal plate for a caul. Setting time for the epoxy is twenty-four hours.

The face of the headstock is lightly trued on the belt sander. This also cleans the ends of the carbon fiber rods and the rosewood filler strips. Then the length of the filler strips is taken down with a small Stanley plane, followed by a light sanding with 80-grit paper mounted on a glass-bottom sanding block.

A small wooden item called the fingerboard stop is glued across the neck where the nut will sit **(Photo 15)**. Its purpose is purely cosmetic, even though it will be invisible once the instrument is finished. The neck and headstock binding includes a black and white purfling which must not be interrupted by the presence of the nut. The ends of the fingerboard stop support the continuous binding strip. Later the stop and the binding that contacts it will be cut down to the purfling lines to make room for the nut. The fingerboard stop is dressed to the same angle as the headstock, after which the headstock capping is glued over top of it **(Photo 16)**.

A plate of ebony .10″ thick will face the headstock. The ebony is cut roughly to the shape of the headstock, then 2mm index holes are drilled where the top two holes for the tuning machines will be. Similar holes are drilled through the headstock. The headstock is also rough shaped, then the ebony capping is glued in place **(Photo 17)**. The truss-rod slot must be extended into the capping and enlarged for wrench movement. A simple guide is fixed to the headstock with a clamp and double-stick tape and the slot is cut with a router **(Photo 18)**.

The shape of the headstock is cleaned up using the Robo-Sander with wraps of tape around the bearing to leave the peghead oversize **(Photo 19)**. Final shaping is done on the router table using a template and a CNT spiral cutter bit **(Photo 20)**. A light sanding with 180 grit will leave the headstock ready to bind. The binding slot is cut with a Ryobi laminate trimmer fitted with a bearing guide **(Photo 21)**.

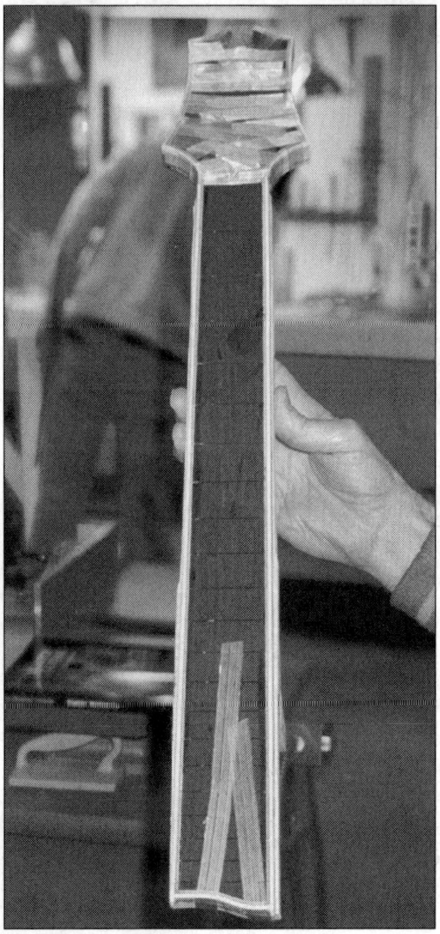

***Photo 21.** A laminate trimmer is used to rout the slots for the headstock binding.*
***Photo 22.** The binding on the end of the fingerboard is prebent using hot air, then taped in place while the glue dries. The straight binding is held by the tack of the glue.*

Fingerboards start out .280″ thick and are finished to .230″. Slotting is done on the table saw using the LMI fret-cutting system. On necks reinforced with carbon fiber the slots are cut deeper, to .140″, to permit a bit of flex. After rough shaping on the bandsaw, a template is fixed to the fingerboard with double-stick tape and the router table is used to cut the taper and the end of the board, which on Tom's guitars is not a straight line.

Headstock purfling and binding must be prebent before it is glued. Superglue is used on the purfling and IPS WELD-ON glue is used on the binding. It's held in place with strapping tape. The peghead binding is leveled with a Swedish cabinet-maker's file (crosscut/clearing).

Fingerboard purfling is .060″ wide, and the binding is .090″. Use WELD-ON 1802 cement for plastic. For prebending the curves hot air is better than hot water, since the water may cause the binding to cup. The purfling at the lower end of the board is mitered but the binding is lapped to help resist wear. Fret slots are extended through the purfling before the binding is glued in place. Curved binding can be held with strapping tape, but the straight binding needs none since the glue kicks off rapidly enough to hold it **(Photo 22)**.

Strapping tape is wrapped around the truss rod to prevent rattling. The fingerboard is indexed on the neck with four 3/64″ pins inserted through fret slots. The joint is made with Titebond and one long caul. Over-tightening the clamps can induce warping, so care must be taken at this stage.

The neck is rough shaped before the fingerboard is arched and leveled, since the removal of some maple may relieve some stress and allow the neck to move. Shaping begins with 40-grit paper mounted on the belt sander. The neck is held square to the belt and facets are ground in the maple. Much of the initial sanding is done on the heel and neck extension areas **(Photo 23)**. Tom kneels at the sander to better see the results **(Photo 24)**. The machine is activated with a foot switch, which he can hit with a knee. The belt carries dust away from his face. It's imperative to use a good dust collection system. Some practice on a mock neck is a good idea. Care must be taken at all transitional areas, such as the heel and headstock, and around binding **(Photo 25)**. Once the facets have been ground into the neck it can be rolled on the belt to achieve a final shape **(Photo 26)**. The Swedish file is used to clean up around the binding. A pattern-maker's rasp can be used to blend in the transitional areas. A scraper may be used to finalize the lines of the neck. The underside of the neck extension is shaped on the belt sander **(Photo 27)**. Once sanded clean this area is sealed with shellac before the neck is glued to the body. The neck might also be clamped onto a carving jig, then shaped with a drum sander mounted in a flexible shaft **(Photo 28)**. To remove any small flats the neck is shoeshined with a sheet of 150-grit paper made by Siares JJO.

Tom has his MOP logos and the pocket they are inlaid into cut on a CNC machine. Custom inlay is done in the normal fashion by hand. The inlays are cut with a jeweler's saw, then cleaned up with Chinese needle files. The inlays are scribed onto the ebony, chalk is put in the scribe lines, then a Dremel tool is used to cut the waste away. Finish work may be done with a knife and chisel, after which the inlays are installed with superglue.

The fingerboard is leveled with 80-grit abrasive mounted on a glass bottom block, sanding only in one direction. As it comes true, the truss rod is tightened slightly and the fingerboard is leveled again. This introduces the possibility of adjusting the neck in either direction once the instrument is strung up. The board is then rounded with a sanding block with a 15′ radius in its sole, again using 80-grit paper **(Photo 29)**. Then it's back to the glass block using 120 grit, then 320 grit.

A rectangular needle file, held edge down, is used to make a slight bevel on the fret slots, then the slots are carefully cleaned.

Fretwire should be cleaned with acetone to remove manufacturing oils. The individual frets

Photo 23. *Rough shaping of the neck begins with a 40-grit belt and a lot of care. Tom can completely shape a neck on the belt sander right to the point of final sanding.*

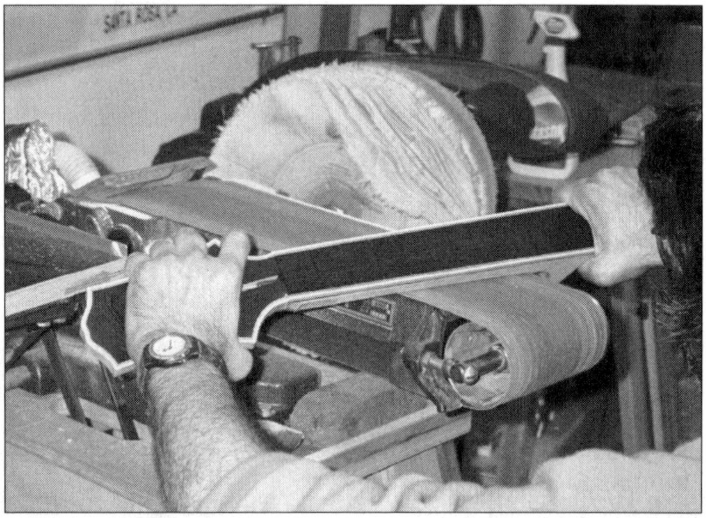

Photo 24. *Tom kneels while he grinds facets on the neck, part of the early shaping process.*

Photo 25. *Even the details are finished on the belt sander. Here Tom works around the headstock. It becomes clear how much the stack of veneers will dress up the guitar.*

are cut to overhang the binding using flush-cut nippers from Stewart-MacDonald, after which the last vestige of the tang is filed away. Fret ends are driven in first, then the middle. The hammer should not be allowed to bounce on the frets since this encourages them to spring back out. The fret ends are cut flush with end nippers, then filed to a 60° angle. The fret tops are colored with a felt-tipped marker, then leveling is done with 320-grit paper and the glass-bottom block. Scratches are removed from the fret tops with an extra-fine diamond plate rubbed across the length of the frets and over the edge of the fingerboard. The fingerboard and binding are taped off, leaving only the frets exposed. They are crowned using a three-square chainsaw file, leaving a flat of 1⁄32″. Each fret end is also lightly rounded with two quick passes of the file. Tom starts sanding the frets with 360-grit paper, then moves to 400- and 600-grit. He switches to Micro-mesh and sands in series. Oil-free steel wool is used after 8000 Micro-mesh rubbed the length of the frets, then the job is finished with 12,000 grit Micro-mesh on the rubber block that comes with the kit.

Holes for the machine heads are drilled with 2MM pilot holes all the way through the headstock. A 3⁄8″ brad-point bit will then follow the pilot hole accurately, working from both sides of the headstock. At this point the neck is complete.

As in virtually any other stringed instrument, the top plate is the heart and soul of an archtop guitar's musical being. Most Ribbecke archtops are made with a top of Sitka spruce. Fine quartersawn blanks with clear grain and eight to twelve lines per inch can retail for $200. European

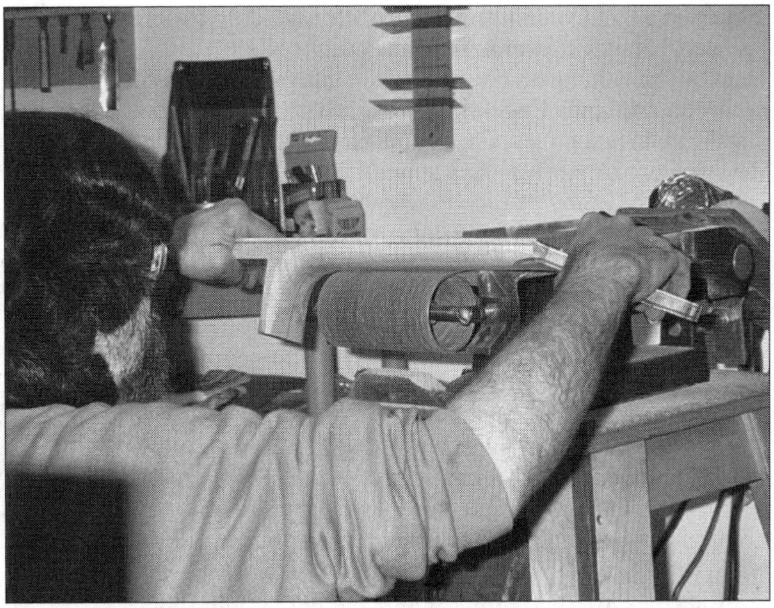

Photo 26. *The neck is rolled on the sander to eliminate the facets and bring it to final shape.*

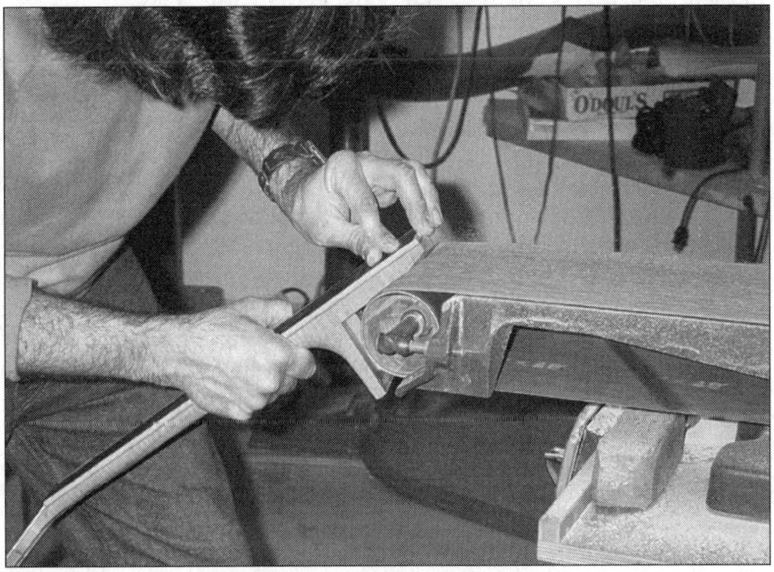

Photo 27. *Shaping the fingerboard extension.*

Photo 28. *Alternatively, the neck could be shaped by sanding drums mounted in a flexible shaft.*

Photo 29. *Shaping may relieve stresses in the neck, which is why leveling the fingerboard is left until the final stages. Tom brings it true with 80-grit abrasive and a glass-bottom block.*

spruce of a size for archtops is normally milled up for cellos and may retail for several times the cost of Sitka. Engelmann spruce has become a desirable tonewood for archtops, and since Engelmann trees are normally much smaller than Sitka trees, Engelmann blanks of equal quality may be more expensive. As a general rule, Tom will match softer, more flexible spruce to a body of stiffer maple, perhaps Eastern rock maple or European maple. Conversely, stiffer spruce is often mated to a softer maple such as big leaf, though many of the Eastern species are also soft, figured, and harvested. As always, each piece of wood must be judged on its own merits. The archtop guitar initially evolved in the hands of American luthiers and companies east of the Mississippi who had access to local spruce and maple that were very stiff. Such wood combined to create the traditional jazz guitars of the Big Band era. Those guitars are of limited versatility, and contemporary archtop makers have learned to choose combinations of wood that offer the player a much wider palette of tone colors.

Tops may arrive as dimensioned lumber or split billets. For the Ribbecke style of carving, it's vital that the bottom of the joined plates creates a flat plane **(Photo 30)**. The bottom surfaces are jointed flat and may be trued with hand planes, after which the edges to be joined are jointed square to the bottom. Titebond is Tom's glue of choice. The glue is permitted to take a light set before the clamps are applied. Again, be certain that the clamps don't distort the flat bottom of the plates **(Photo 31)**.

Master patterns are made of 3⁄8″ Lexan **(Photo 32)**. Good quality plywood is also suitable. The master patterns are created from a half-pattern to maintain symmetry, though obviously a cutaway model must have a different pattern for each side. The Lexan master patterns are used to trace the body shape onto top and back, though they are also pinned to the centerlines of the stock with 1⁄16″ index pins. The plates are roughed out on the bandsaw, then dressed to final shape on the drill press using the Robo-Sander **(Photo 33)**.

All plate carving can be accomplished with hand tools. Tom still does all the finesse work by hand on a carving form that anyone can build **(Photo 34)**. It's little more than an MDF workboard built up with a 1″ deep outline of the guitar made of the same material. The outline is 1⁄2″ smaller than the outline of the guitar body, which permits the arch of the plate to sit inside the carving form while the inside is doctored. Extensions of the outline at the head and tail act as clamping points. Plywood disks are screwed to the form to capture the plate. A steel post is mounted to the bottom of the workboard. The post slides into a pipe clamp bolted firmly to the workbench, which allows the form and plate to be turned while carving proceeds. The top of the form is covered with cork to protect soft tonewood while it is being worked.

Health precautions have forced Tom to develop some unique work habits. Years of hand carving resulted in a case of tendinitis, and a lifetime of exposure to wood dust and lacquer fumes created allergies that forced him out of the business for several years. Because of this, Tom has cut the handwork of carving to a minimum, and maintains that his shop is the cleanest portion of his life. "I feel very grateful to have a second chance in this business, so I try to run a very clean ship," he said. "I have to, I have no choice. It's cleaner than any other aspect of my life. My workshop is my cathedral." Tom's example should sound an alarm to those of us who are still healthy.

Photo 30. This is a joined top from a split billet. A straightedge is resting on the underside of the top. It's vital that this surface be true no matter how the straightedge is placed upon it.

Photo 31. The top is carefully clamped to maintain a flat bottom surface. The pipe clamps close the joint while the screw clamps keep the wood from jumping off the pipes. Tops of dimensioned lumber don't present this problem.

JONATHON PETERSON

Photo 32. Tom's master pattern is of 3⁄8″ Lexan. This and other photos were taken at Tom's 1995 GAL lecture. Most pictures, however, were taken by the author in Tom's shop during a one-week seminar.

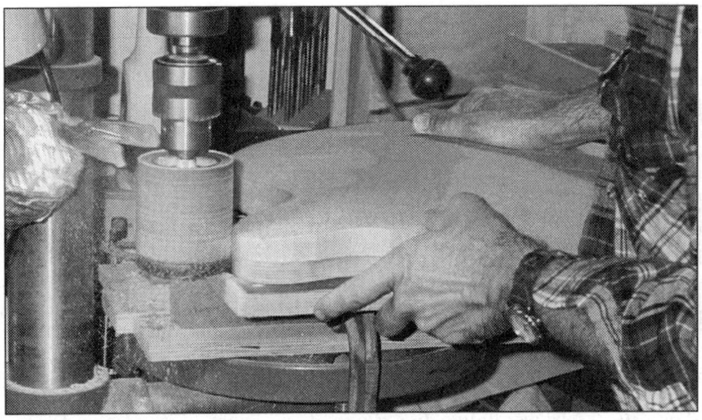

Photo 33. The bearing guide on this drum sander is run against the master pattern to bring the perimeter of the top to final dimensions. The Robo-Sander drum is available in many tool catalogs.

Tom does all his power carving inside a small booth that he calls a hood, or sometimes a cage **(Photo 35)**. It's a plywood box with an open front. The interior is large enough for a guitar body and the router system used to cut the ledge around the outside of the plate. All routing for binding is also done in the hood. A face shield of plexiglas allows the operator to see in and keeps chips from hitting his face. A strong vacuum system draws dust through holes in the back of the hood. A second vacuum system draws from the floor and serves a dual purpose. It removes dust, but it also sucks the plate to the floor, eliminating the need for clamps while power carving and sanding. The degree of vacuum clamping can be controlled by the number of holes the plate is placed over.

The outside arch is shaped in a series of steps using a router on a shop-made base **(Photo 36)**. The base bolts to the floor of the hood and suspends the router bit in space. A series of holes for guide pins is drilled in the floor. A 1¼″ straight-flute bit is chucked in the router and passes of that width are made around the plate until the rim is ¼″ thick. Then the bit is raised ¼″ and another step 1¼″ wide is created. This process is continued until the top plate is ⅞″ thick and stepped in ¼″ increments, after which the next plate is carved or the router is removed from the hood **(Photo 37)**.

Photo 34. Tom's carving form is made from three layers of MDF. The top two layers are trimmed to support only the rim of the plates, allowing inverted tops and backs to nest into the form while their innards are carved. The plate is held to the form by plywood disks screwed into the form at the head and tail regions. One form is used in the carving hood. Another, for hand carving, is mounted to a workbench by a pipe fitted underneath the form.

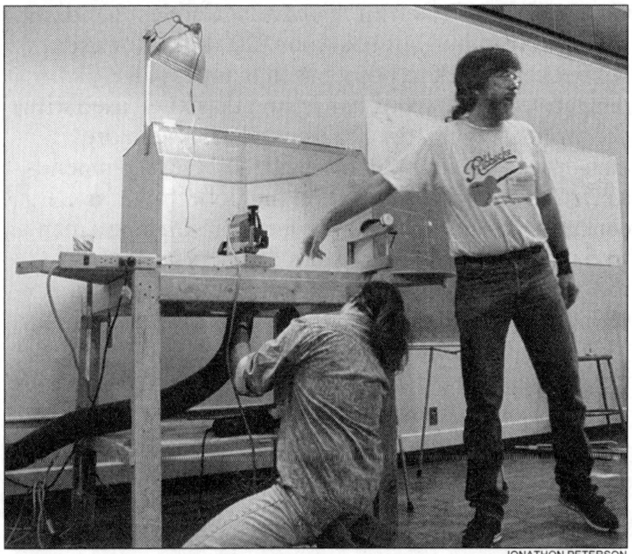

JONATHON PETERSON

Photo 35. Ribbecke's carving hood, or cage, is an open-front plywood box with two vacuum systems attached to it. A plexiglas guard protects his face while allowing a view of the interior. Big chips may escape the hood, but the clouds of dust created are captured, keeping Tom safe from allergies that once drove him from the business.

Photo 36. This router base is screwed to the floor of the carving hood. Pins in the floor allow the plates to be step carved in ¼″ increments the width of the cutter, which is 1¼″.

Photo 37. A top in the process of being step routed. The main vacuum draws through holes in the back wall of the hood. The second system draws from holes in the floor, removing dust and at the same time sucking the plate to the floor firmly enough to keep it from jumping under the router.

JONATHON PETERSON

Photo 38. Tom models the chainsaw wheel mounted in a Makita grinder. With this tool most of the excess wood is removed from the plate in a few minutes. The proper stroke is one that Tom calls "petting the doberman." The surface left by the chainsaw wheel is surprisingly clean.

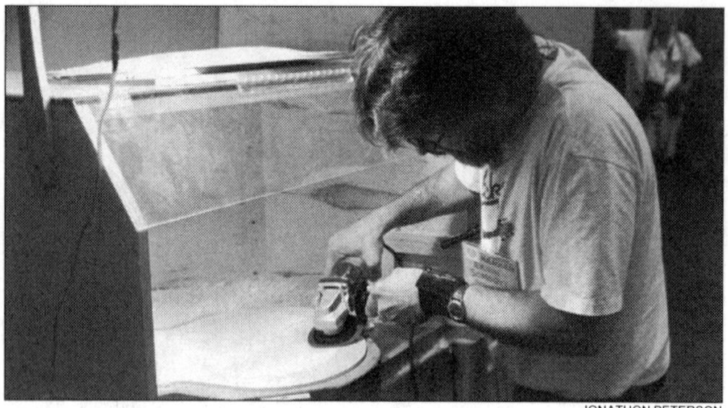

JONATHON PETERSON

Photo 39. A flexible sanding disk mounted in a Ryobi die grinder conforms to the arch of the top. Tom might start with 24 grit, "like rocks glued to sandpaper," and work his way down to 120 grit. This machine is carving wood, not just smoothing the surface.

Now is the time for the chainsaw guitar making for which Tom has become notorious. A Makita N9514B 4″ disk grinder is fitted with a Lance-a-Lot 22-tooth chainsaw wheel made by King Arthur Tools **(Photo 38)**. Care must be taken with this cutter. Careless handling can rend your body or ruin your $200 top. However, Ribbecke is quick to point out that any tool is dangerous in the wrong hands, and that when used with the proper respect, the chainsaw wheel is no more dangerous than any other machine tool. He recommends a stroke that he calls "petting the doberman," a concept that came to him while he was instructing a man who didn't have the touch for machinery and was in danger of tearing up his top. The man was quick to grasp the concept and quickly mastered the chainsaw wheel.

The longitudinal arch is established first. Enough wood should be cut away in front of the fingerboard area to provide clearance for a floating pickup (at least 80% of Tom's guitars are electrified). The shape of the arch is a large control factor in the character of the finished guitar. A tall arch that sweeps quickly to the ledge will have more of a traditional jazz guitar response, though the thickness of the top leaves room for compromise. But generally speaking, a top with a strong bell-style curve will have a quicker response, less sustain, and more cut. A flatter arch with a softer transition to the ledge will contribute to a guitar with more bass, more sustain, and a tone that more approximates a flattop guitar.

The chainsaw wheel leaves a surprisingly smooth surface, but it is not a subtle tool. Once the steps are hogged away and the longitudinal arch is established, the wheel is replaced with abrasive disks on a 4″ Ryobi die grinder that cranks out 20,000 rpm **(Photo 39).** Tom likes the Ryobi for its light weight. "We've ground down a little hub that sits in here and polished it so it doesn't do any harm to the instruments. It's great. It's amazing the surface you can leave with this, even on a spruce top."

Various grits are used to fair out the top, even starting with 24 grit upon occasion. "It's like stones stuck to a piece of sandpaper," said Tom. Typically, though, he finds that 36 or 60 grit is plenty aggressive enough to finesse the surface left by the chainsaw wheel, and he'll work down to 120 in the die grinder before switching to hand scraping. The rubber disk distorts enough to follow the shape of the arch. "You can develop a delicate touch. Make sure the wheel is balanced. We all work with sanding drums. When the drum reaches a certain speed it becomes harmonically balanced and its efficiency increases at least 15%–20% and you'll have greater control. The same thing is true with all these sanding and abrasive processes."

Tom finds that the longitudinal arch is the key to the shape of the entire plate. Once that arch is set it's just a matter of fairing the wood down to the uniformly carved ledge. It's a process that makes sense to the eye and to the hand. Though Tom depends on long experience to guide him, he recommends that first-timers get a full-size plan, cut it up, and make cross-sectional templates of the arches at different points. When Tom put an old template on a top he carved by eye, it was right on the money.

"You want to work delicately and not bear down. You can see that the marks that remain are easily removed with a scraper. We're not talking about the finished shape of the guitar by any means. We're going to get close to the outside shape and hollow the inside, then we're going to finish this with hand scrapers and some planing in small areas. This way of machine carving is really quite accessible to anyone. My first carving hood, many years ago, was a garbage can with a hole cut in the end of it hooked up to a Sears vacuum."

Photo 40. A top mounted in the hand carving form. A straightedge throws a shadow across the arch, making any inconsistency apparent to the eye.

For those who don't want to splurge on a carving hood, there's still a way to get a foot into the door of machine carving. A rotary safety planer can be used to uniformly cut the ledge of a plate to a given thickness (typically ¼″). Safety planers don't do quite as nice a job as a firmly mounted router, but the results are entirely acceptable and much easier to achieve than hand planing. Safety planers are made for both drill presses and radial arm saws, though since the machines run in opposite directions they don't interchange.

The plate is scraped to finished dimensions (on the outside) at the bench using the carving form. Most scraping is done at 60° to the grain. A straightedge can be used to cast a shadow across the top to check for smoothness of the curve (**Photo 40**). An orbital sander is used to finish the surface at this point.

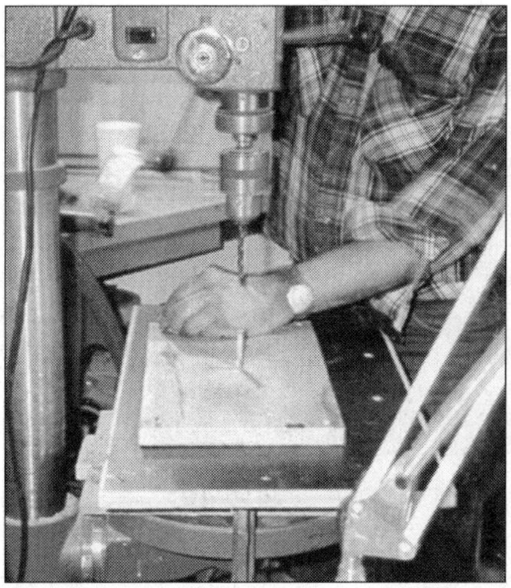

Photo 41. This simple jig is used to drill dozens of holes on the inside of the plates after the outer arch is established. The gap between the jig post and the fully extended bit should be ¼″ over most of the top. The holes act as a depth guide while the plate is carved.

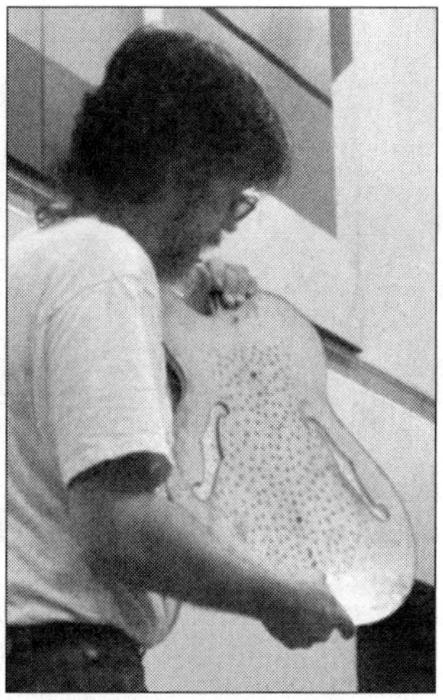

Photo 42. The object of all the holes is not to remove wood, but to act as a depth guide while carving. Tom shows off a typical drilling pattern.

The chainsaw wheel can also be used to hog out the interior of a plate. First, though, a jig for marking and drilling the inside of the top is mounted to the drill-press table. It's nothing more than a board with a hefty dowel protruding under the chuck. A spruce cap is added to the dowel to prevent damaging the spruce. The table is adjusted to leave a ¼″ gap between the dowel cap and deepest throw of the bit (**Photo 41**). Mechanical depth stops can shift during the drilling of so many holes, possibly ruining an expensive piece of wood. A tight pattern of marker holes is drilled (**Photo 42**). The plates are left full thickness over the end blocks, and ⅜″ thick where the wood approaches the blocks. Then the plate is positioned upside down in the carving form. Material is ground away until all but the tips of the holes are gone. At this point carving ceases temporarily while the *f*-holes are cut. A wash of water and glycerin will raise the dimples left by the jig post on the outside of the top. The dimples should be sanded away, lest they show up during the finish process.

There are several reasons for cutting the *f*-holes before the top is thinned to final dimensions. Any splintering that may result will be cleaned up when the top is thinned. Thicker spruce is less likely to chatter under the influence of high-speed cutters. The unfinished top will provide a wider, stronger surface for the *f*-hole binding process, which may involve a surprising amount of stress on the soundhole area. Finally, the *f* holes offer a visual cue to the maker as the top is thinned to finished specs. The binding itself helps protect and stiffen the soundholes. Weak *f*-holes can contribute to a fuzzy tone.

Tom's Lexan template for routing the *f*-holes is pinned to the inside top and held in place by double-sided tape. The show side of the top is protected from tearout by a layer of 2″ masking tape and a wash coat of shellac that protects the spruce from the tape, after which the top is clamped template side up in the carving form (**Photo 43**). Initial cuts are made with a Porter-Cable 6902 plunge router and a ¼″ Bosch spiral cutter intended for cutting plexiglas. Successive passes are made until the bit penetrates the top. This setup leaves the holes 1⁄16″ undersize. They are brought to full spec with a Ryobi router equipped with a ½″ flush-trim bit. This may sound like technological overkill, but as Tom says, "I've never ruined an *f*-hole since going to this system. The results are impeccable. It's important that the edges of the *f*-holes be 90° to the plane of the back of the guitar or they will look very sloppy, especially after they are bound. If that is accurate, the rest of it is just hard work, and knowing what to do, and staring at it. When I check out someone's guitar the first thing I look at is the *f*-holes. They are very hard to get right." Luthiers have cut *f*-holes by hand for centuries; it's a time-honored method of working and requires a minimum investment in tools, but the walls must still end up true and parallel to the ribs of the guitar. Any raggedness in the *f*-hole walls will later be filled with melted plastic from the binding and cement, so the soundholes must be scrupulously clean.

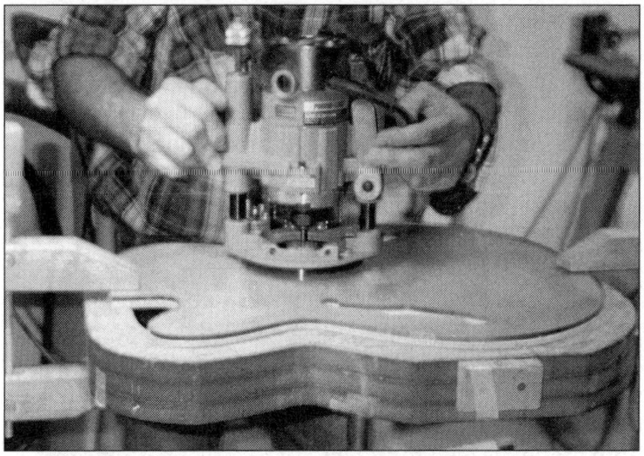

Photo 43. The f-hole pattern is pinned precisely to the inside of the top and held there by double-sided tape. The holes in the pattern act as a router guide. Initial cuts are made with a spiral bit which leaves 1⁄16″ of excess wood. The holes are then cleaned with a flush-trim bit.

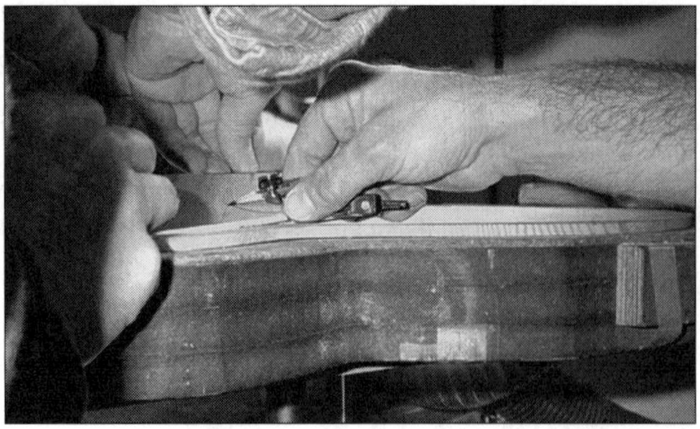

Photo 44. Dividers are used to mark the contours of the inside of the top on each side of the X braces, which are then roughed out on the bandsaw. One leg of the divider rides the top while a pencil held in the other leg marks the brace.

Ribbecke guitars will end up 3⁄16″ thick at the *f*-holes, though the full-blown electric version might be left 1⁄4″. Tom doesn't believe that small aesthetic changes in the shape of the hole have much impact on the tone of the guitar. He may occasionally make the holes smaller by adding additional layers of binding, thus raising the resonant frequency of the body. Moving the holes toward the perimeter of the guitar will increase the bass response, and moving them toward the bridge may increase the cut of the instrument, but Tom is not inclined to move them around much. "I have a consistent base-line sound that I like." In other words, each maker's guitars should sound like their own works. Presumably, customers will pay big bucks for a guitar because of the way it sounds, and asking a luthier to make big changes in that sound is asking him/her to walk on foreign ground, a trip that may end up pleasing no one.

Multiline purfling and .090″ ivoroid binding are prebent to shape by heating it with a heat gun. Dipping the pieces in boiling water will also work, but may cause the plastic to cup. Eight pieces are needed per *f*-hole. The purfling is installed with superglue and all corners are mitered. The ivoroid is glued in using IPS WELD-ON 1802 cement, and the ends are lapped for strength. Packing tape is used to pull the binding tight. The binding should be allowed to sit for a couple days, and longer is better.

The top was initially ground to be an even 1⁄4″ all over. Now the sanding disks are used to grind the spruce closer to its finished dimension of .200″ under the bridge. At the recurve area toward the ledge, the top will be faired to .100″–.125″ when finished and will flare again at the rim. By the time he reaches a dimension .020″ oversize Tom wants to be grinding with 120-grit paper. A support block should be placed inside the carving form to support the bridge area of the top. The last .020″ will be removed with a hand scraper. A cello maker's caliper can be purchased for $200, but Tom made his own for a tenth of that using scraps of wood and a Chinese dial indicator. The caliper is mounted permanently next to his carving hood. A light fixture with a 150w–200w bulb will shine through the spruce at this point, and the color of the wood can be used as a check for thickness consistency, though a change in the density of the wood may be misread as an error in carving. Again, experience counts for a lot.

Most contemporary archtop guitars are X braced, and this is certainly true of Ribbecke guitars. Tom's braces begin as quartersawn stock .875″–1.0″ tall and .375″–.400″ wide. The position of the bridge feet is marked on the inside of the top. The first brace to be marked runs from the center of the cutaway and to the foot on the opposite side of the centerline. The second brace runs under the other foot, but is offset from the centerline 1⁄8″–3⁄16″. A wider, more open X will produce a stronger bass response. A more closed X will contribute to a brighter guitar.

The braces are held in position inside the top while a pencil-equipped divider is used to trace the contour of the top on each side of each brace **(Photo 44)**. The braces are roughed out on the bandsaw (don't touch any pencil lines!), then placed in a vise where they are trimmed to the lines using a spokeshave and files.

Tom made a jig to hold the braces in position on the top. An exact fit is created by running sandpaper between the top and the brace, first using 80 grit, then 120 grit **(Photo 45)**. The glue surface is then cleaned with a razor blade used as a scraper. Then the braces are joined into an X. If a dry fit of the braces looks good, a set of guide blocks is held to the top with double-sided tape and Titebond is used to permanently mount the braces. The first clamp should be applied to the center of the X, and successive clamps should pin down the legs.

The center of the X is ground to a height of 3⁄4″ using the belt sander, after which the braces are hand carved to their final shape. The ground spot provides a relief that prevents an intentional split from unintentionally running into the opposite leg of the brace. The lower bass-side brace is scalloped from the X. The lower treble-side brace is left taller, but mass is removed from its sides. The uppers are left beefy. The braces should taper sharply to the edge of the guitar **(Photos 46 and 47)**.

Photo 45. A jig is used to hold the parts of the X brace in precise alignment during final fitting to the top and while they are fitted and joined to each other. In this picture, sandpaper is being used to transfer the contour of the top to the brace.

At this point the top is complete until it is time to assemble the box.

Backs are carved much like the tops. Tom's backs often have more arch than his tops. He treats the back as a secondary soundboard, thinning it to be responsive to the top. A flatter back will contribute to a bassier guitar that more approximates the tone of a flattop. A taller arch will be brighter with more punch.

As a final note, Tom warns that big leaf maple is often kiln dried to control a gray stain that quickly invades freshly harvested wood. Kiln-dried big leaf is prone to honeycomb checking inside the board. Tonewood is often carefully air dried to avoid both the stain and the checking. Big leaf from a lumberyard may be a lot cheaper, but it may be found to be unusable when cut open.

The default body depth of Ribbecke archtops is 3¼″. To achieve this the sides are taped together and milled to a height of 2⅞″, and there is no taper. The sides are taped together while they are jointed to maintain uniformity. After jointing they are thickness sanded to .080″. The sides are bent in a Fox Universal Sidebender **(Photo 48)** to which two important changes have been made. A Watco heat blanket supplies the heat rather than light bulbs. The blanket is nestled between the steel slats with the wood, and provides a more even heat than the bulbs. Also, the bending forms are made of Medite because it doesn't burn out like plywood often does. Maple can take a fatal blue stain from a chemical reaction between water and stainless steel. To avoid this some luthiers use denatured alcohol to wet the sides, but Tom chooses to use distilled water and glycerin (mixed ½ oz. of glycerin to a pint of water) and then wraps the wood in foil to keep it from contacting the slats.

The cutaway itself is bent by hand, an operation that takes 3–4 minutes. Ribbecke isn't eager for a machine that could release him from the hand bending chores, feeling that in a modern shop the bending of sides is one of the few old-time luthierly activities left. A standard bending iron **(Photo 49)** is used in conjunction with a large soldering iron **(Photo 50)**. Tom describes the iron as "a surplus Ma Bell iron roughly 2″in diameter, perhaps once used for soldering streetlights together."

Photos 46 and 47. *Two views of the finished braces. At this point the top is put aside until it's time to assemble the body of the guitar.*

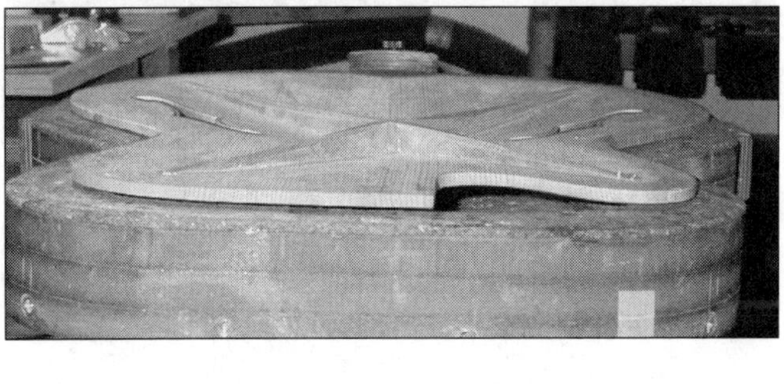

Photo 48. *Tom at work at the Fox side bender. Tom bends a side-and-a-half per guitar here. The cutaways are bent by hand.*

Photo 49. *The horn of the cutaway is bent on a commercial bending iron.*

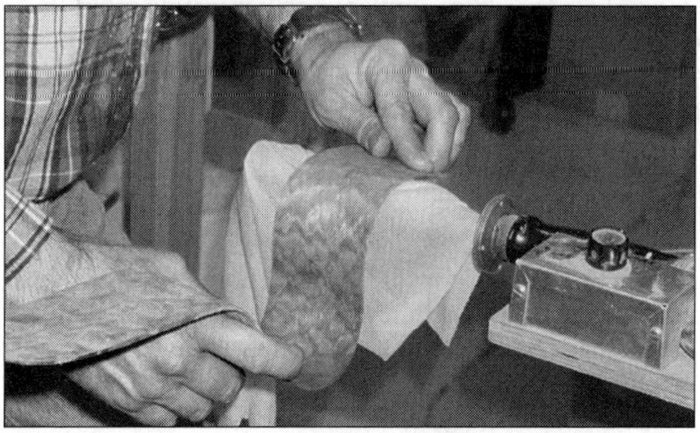

Photo 50. *A large soldering iron is used to bend the tight inside curve of the cutaway. Wet cloth provides steam and prevents the wood from scorching.*

He has fitted the shaft with extra aluminum tubes that can be slid into place to bend different radii, and even the ½″ tip can be used for some really tight bends. He has also hooked the iron to a rheostat.

Tom finds that darker, redder maples bend more easily, but that in the fanciest grades that go into his archtops, any maple can be a trick to bend. Occasionally the cutaway portion of the side must be thinned to facilitate bending. The cutaway end of the side can be repeatedly dunked in a bucket as bending progresses, and a wet terry cloth draped over the iron will help inject steam into the wood and keep it from drying out too much. It's important to feel the wood flex and give as pressure is applied. Listen to the sizzle and watch the evaporation of the moisture. Start with a rocking motion while coaxing the wood to bend, and support the off side with a block of wood to help prevent blowout. If a crack develops, repair it with superglue and keep bending. The side is frequently checked for fit in the mold, and Tom might even hold the side in the mold to help the precision part of the bending (**Photo 51**). The inside bend that leads to the heel block is the tightest, and is accomplished with the soldering iron draped with a wet towel. Strive for a perfect fit in the mold (**Photo 52**).

Photo 51*. Tom will occasionally use the side form to aid in the cutaway bending process.*

Photo 52*. The goal is a side that fits perfectly in the mold without clamps.*

The blocks are made of mahogany with a horizontal grain orientation. The heel block is a simple block of wood 3¼″×2⅞″×1¾″. The inside corners are beveled ¼″ on the cutaway side and ½″ on the driver's side. The tail block (4¹⁄₁₆″× 2⅞″×⅞″) must be rounded to fit the outline of the body. It is cut to square dimensions, then placed in a disk-sander jig to accurately grind the round portion that is glued to the sides (**Photo 53**), after which the inside corners are rounded on the belt sander.

Photo 53*. The jig sitting on the mold is used to shape the glue surface of the tail block. The jig is used with a disk sander and a table fixture that prevents the jig itself from touching the disk.*

The outside of Tom's construction molds are cut with flats to facilitate clamping the sides tightly in place (see **Photo 52,** though no clamps are in place). Note the notch where the cutaway is tucked into the mold. This bit of side wood will later be trimmed away, but for now it holds the rib securely in place and prevents damage to the corner. The noncutaway rib should be trimmed to butt cleanly against the cutaway rib at the heel block. The tail joint should also be carefully marked while the ribs are clamped in the mold. Tom uses a jig to hold the sides one at a time while the tail

Photo 54*. This jig is used to rout the rib ends for a good fit in the mold.*

Photo 55*. A laminate trimmer squares the rib ends for a tight butt joint.*

Photo 56. The fitted tail seam is taped tightly and returned to the mold to receive the tail block. The floor of the mold holds the assembly square, and the small blocks attached to the floor prevent the block from sliding.

joint is cut with a laminate trimmer **(Photos 54 and 55)**. The joint at the tail is given so much emphasis because traditionally archtops receive no butt graft as is usually found on a steel string guitar, so the exposed joint must be as perfect as possible. To this end, Ribbecke inlays the end block regions of his molds with a red, hard rubber gasket material found in hardware stores. The material is perhaps .030″ thick, and it is inlaid to stand about .005″ proud of the mold. When clamps are applied to the blocks the rubber compresses into the mold and provides the maximum amount of clamping uniformity to the joint. Also, Titebond will not stick to the rubber and bond the ribs to the mold.

The mold has a bottom platform, or floor, that is bolted on while the end blocks are glued in place. The platform assures that the ribs are sitting on a true plane in the mold. The ribs are taped together on the outside of the tail seam before they are placed in the mold. Studs mounted on the floor of the mold keep the tail block from sliding sideways when glued **(Photo 56)**. The fit of the heel block is as important as that of the tail block, since it will anchor all of the main components of the guitar. Every three or four months the interiors of the molds are covered in a mold release agent made by the Bates company, which prevents any white glue from sticking to the wood.

Ribbecke archtops are lined with basswood on the top and mahogany on the bottom. At one time he used solid rosewood linings to create the stiffest sides possible, but after awhile it occurred to Tom that the thinning of the plate rims during voicing might be partially nullified by the extreme stiffening created by the lining. Returning to a kerfed lining improved the sound of his guitars, and switching to basswood was an extension of the whole concept of freeing the top plate to vibrate. It is also thought by some that basswood acts as an acoustic dam that prevents the energy of the top from transferring to the sides. The back is lined in mahogany because it adds such a rich appearance when viewed through the soundholes, and it's also traditional. The linings come

(continued on following page)

Originally published in *American Lutherie #55*, 1998

QUESTIONS

EDITED BY CYNDY BURTON

■ ***Dennis Russell of Yuma, AZ** asks:*

Directions for building the Universal Side Bender by Charles Fox suggest using .020″ stainless steel. This will bend readily but won't go back to its flat form if it's a dead steel. Repeated bending will cause it to work harden and become brittle, and eventually break.

Where can I obtain some tempered steel for this? In my town it would be necessary to buy a large sheet and have it cut down, and that's very expensive.

***Todd Taggart, of Healdsburg, CA,** who sells the plans and kits at Luthiers Mercantile responds:*

I've never heard of anyone breaking any of the standard stainless slats that we provide. These tend to take the shape of the guitar, but not to the extent that you can't use the same set of slats for a "standard" classical shape and a dreadnought shape. It should also be understood that with spring steel, trying to get the bent sides out of the form works against the bend you just made, and makes the removal process a little unwieldy. Charles Fox (in his own production shop) uses our regular stainless steel slats. However, we will be offering spring steel for our cutaway kit.

Here are a few more suggestions for the form: Charles now uses only four ½″ bars to span the half patterns, and these are not tangential to the edge. The steel slats support the sides just fine. Some are using three half-patterns spaced evenly across the 6″ width, supported with three or four bars. They then use heating blankets, instead of light bulbs.

*Another answer, this one from **Peter Dyer of Davis, CA:***

Mr. Russell may be using the terms "stainless steel" and "steel" as if they were interchangeable. They are not. They are two distinct classes of ferrous alloys which have significantly different properties.

Mr. Russell says he tried a "dead" steel. His use of this descriptive term suggests to me that he was not using stainless, since, in general, stainless alloys are more elastic than alloys of carbon steel. I suggest he make sure he's using actual stainless steel, as Charles Fox recommends. Not only is stainless (again, in general) more elastic than steel, it won't rust. Of course, this makes a big difference in any side bending process which uses moisture. And in my nineteen years as a machinist I can't remember coming across any alloy of stainless I would describe as "dead."

McMaster-Carr (www.mcmaster.com) carries two different alloys of stainless steel for sale in relatively small sheets. The alloys are 304 and 316, and I believe either one will do. (Stainless alloys in the 400 series

*(See **Questions** page 291)*

from Thomas Peterson, who Ribbecke likes to call the King of Kerfing. ("Even the gap in his front teeth looks like a kerf," he jokes.) Lining is normally about ⅝″ wide, but since the lip of the plates is already .200″ thick Tom trims the lining to less than ½″ wide, taking the difference off the thin end of the wedge.

Photo 57. The completed side assembly. Note the rosewood side stays and the expander bars that hold the ribs tight to the mold during sanding and the gluing of the top.

Photo 58. The lining, end blocks, and ribs are leveled with a long sanding board. Only one end of the board is covered with abrasive.

Photo 59. The go-bar deck is used to glue the top to the ribs. The loaded mold is placed in the deck, then the top is carefully positioned with pins and tape to prevent skidding.

Brazilian rosewood side braces, or stiffeners, are glued between the linings. If they extended all the way to the top and back edges, the differing expansion ratios of the various woods might cause a separation of the bindings. The stays are equally spaced around the ribs to reinforce the sides and prevent cupping and splitting. They are particularly necessary in the flatter curves where the sides are more flexible. The completed rib assembly can be seen in **Photo 57**. Note the expanders that hold the ribs firmly against the mold.

The rib assembly must be sanded true to receive the plates. This is done with a plank that is covered with abrasive on one end **(Photo 58)**. The clean end of the plank is held as a pivot point while the abrasive end is swung over the ribs. Different areas are worked until the blocks and the linings are true to the sides.

With the sides in the mold and expander bars in place, the top is placed in position and pinned at the heel block by two pins made from ³⁄₆₄″ drill blanks. A wash coat of shellac is applied to the outer surface of the top to add an extra bit of protection from clamping mishaps. The mold/sides are then slid into the go-bar deck, Titebond is spread on the end blocks and linings, and the top is once again pinned in place **(Photo 59)**. Several pieces of strapping tape at the tail block keep the plate from skidding sideways as the clamps are applied, and a towel spread over the top protects it from wayward clamps that may spring loose. Note that Tom uses the go-bar clamps liberally, and positions a caul between each clamping bar and the soft spruce of the top plate **(Photo 60)**.

After the glue has dried the assembly is removed from the mold, the pins pulled, and the tape stripped off. The body is placed face down in the carving form and a wash coat of shellac is applied to the inside of the top and the end blocks, but not the sides since the rosewood is likely to bleed onto the maple. The inside of the back is also coated, and care is taken to avoid any areas to be glued.

Titebond is spread on the ribs, and then the back is aligned properly and tacked with several strips of

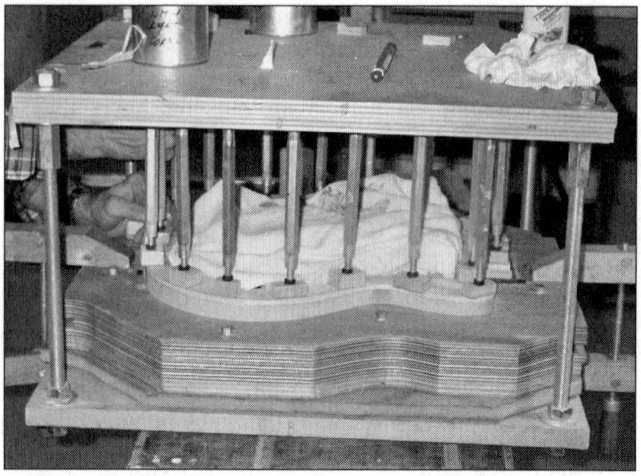

Photo 60. The top is fully clamped in position. Note the cauls used to protect the top from the clamps. The towel protects the top from accidents such as falling clamp bars.

strapping tape. The actual clamping is accomplished using as many spool clamps as will fit around the guitar. Tom's spool clamps are made from aluminum gutter spikes **(Photo 61)**.

Any of the plate material that overhangs the ribs must be trimmed away, and the sides must be dressed clean and level. Rough dressing is done on the belt sander **(Photo 62)**, and care must be taken not to sand through the sides or let the box be ripped from your hands.

The body is then mounted in the body-holding fixture of the binding machine and final dressing of the plate edges is done with the Robo-Sander mounted in the drill press

Photo 61. *The back is taped to the ribs to establish its position, then spool clamps are used to close the box.*

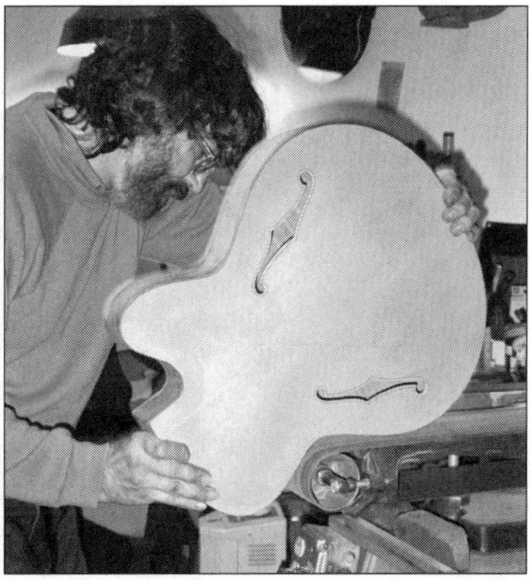

Photo 62. *Excess plate material is quickly roughed off on the belt sander. Not a job for the timid.*

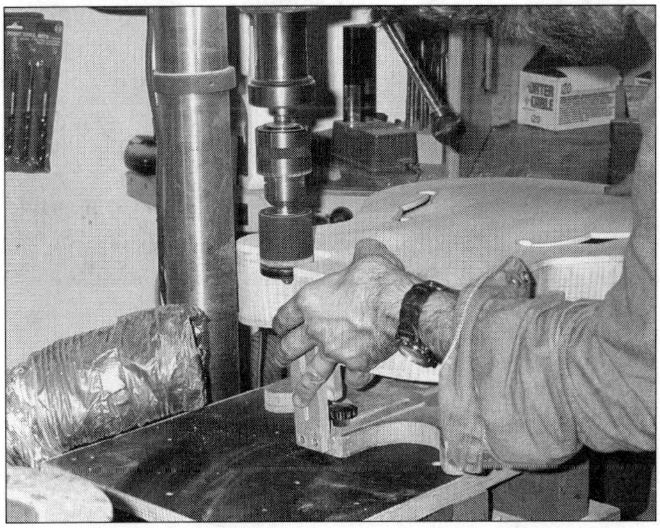

Photo 63. *The plates are sanded true to the ribs with a Robo-Sander chucked in the drill press. The box has been mounted in a fixture which holds it level.*

Photo 64. *Plate overhang in the cutaway region is removed with a drum sander mounted in a flexible-shaft tool chucked in the drill press.*

(Photo 63), one plate at a time. An Arco flex-shaft sander chucked into the drill press is used to level the overhangs in the cutaway **(Photo 64)**. A careful block sanding which dresses the entire face of the sides to 120 grit **(Photo 65)** follows power sanding.

Tom designed the rig he uses to cut binding slots, and it is available as a kit from LMI. The body is held parallel to the bench top in an adjustable jig. On a separate fixture **(Photo 66)** a Ryobi TR-30U laminate trimmer slides on a vertical column. The router foot rests only on a small portion of the edge of the guitar, nullifying the effect that the carved plates would have if a normal router were used

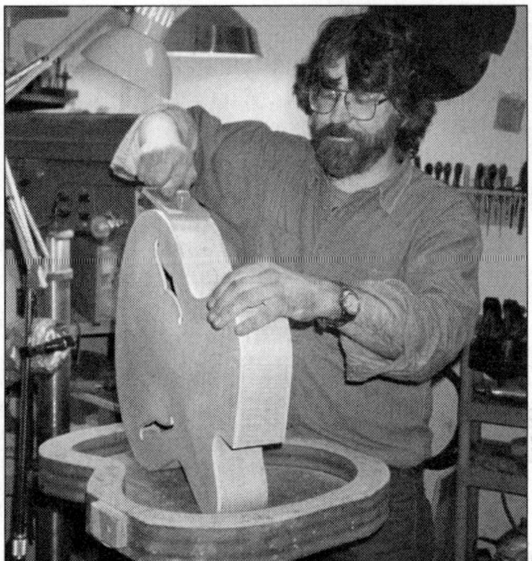

Photo 65. *Finally, a variety of sanding blocks are used to clean and true the ribs to 120-grit smoothness.*

Photo 66. *This router is mounted on a tower, or column, and is used to cut the slots for the binding and purfling.*

*Photo 67. The body is held parallel to the table top in the same fixture used with the Robo-Sander in **Photo 63** while the binding slots are cut. The router foot rests on the edge of the box and is not disturbed by the contours of the plates. This rig is available as a kit from LMI.*

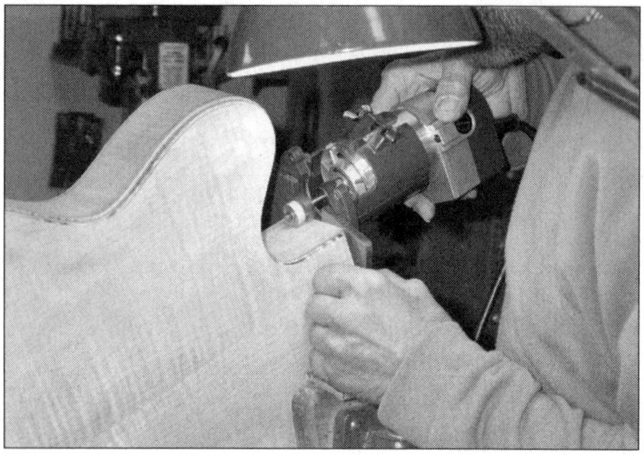

***Photo 68**. The corner of the cutaway receives a strip of binding but no purfling. The binding cleans and hides the rib joint at this point.*

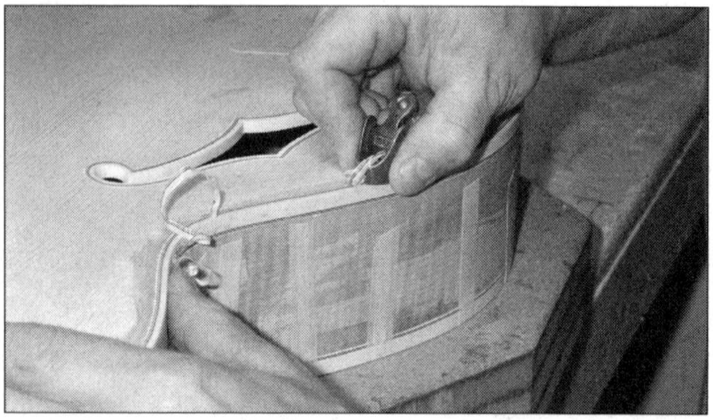

***Photo 69**. The binding/purfling is taped tightly in place until the glue dries. Here the tape has been removed and the plastic is being dressed to the level of the spruce top.*

to cut the slots **(Photo 67).** The binding slots are cut in two passes. The purfling cut measures .130″ deep by .150″ wide. The back is done first, and a climb cut is used where necessary to prevent tearout. The channel for the binding measures .310″ deep and .090″ wide. A short length of binding is also inlaId into the corner of the cutaway where the ribs meet to clean up the joint. No purfling is used here. The body is held in a universal bench vise (available from Trend-lines) and the cut is made with a different laminate trimmer **(Photo 68)**. The router is stopped short of a complete pass because it might tear out rib material as it exits. This bit of work is tidied up with a chisel.

Plastic binding is traditional on archtop guitars. IPS WELD-ON 1802 cement is used to secure the binding/purfling and filament tape is used to pull the plastic tightly into place. The .090″ binding is stiff enough to require a bit of heat to bend it around the horn and into the cutaway. A careful hand with a heat gun is the ticket. On the driver's side, the top binding can start anywhere under the neck, while the binding on the cutaway side must begin exactly in the corner of the cutaway. A different heel design on the neck might require that the binding be mitered at the corner, though it's unlikely that the driver's side purfling will show in the corner. On the back, however, it's important that the binding/purfling of the two sides meet in a clean miter at the corner of the cutaway. The binding of both plates should meet at the tail seam in a clean butt joint. A finger plane is used to dress the binding level with the plates **(Photo 69)**.

Before the dovetail slot can be cut, a ¼″ hole must be drilled dead center on the tail seam. This hole provides one of the holding points of the jig used to cut the slot. The site of the dovetail slot is accurately

***Photo 70**. This is the jig that holds the body while the dovetail slot is routed. The body is held in the jig at three adjustable points, and the entire unit is mounted vertically during routing.*

***Photo 71**. The jig and body are ready for the router. A kit of parts for this unit is available from LMI.*

***Photo 72**. The finished dovetail slot. The slot must be cut in one pass to produce a clean result.*

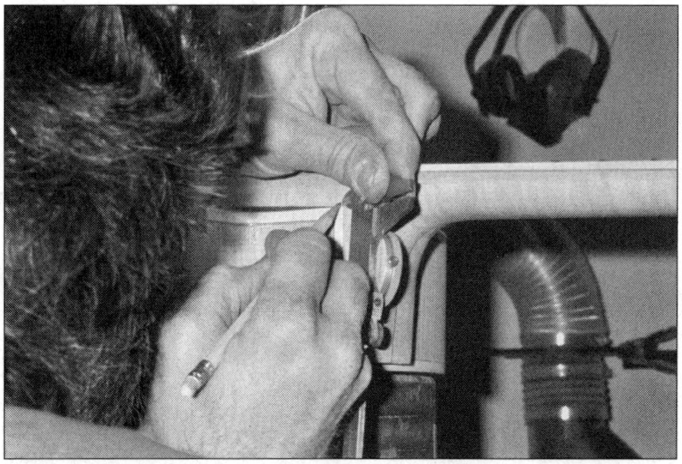

***Photo 73**. The fingerboard extension must be mated perfectly to the top as the neck is fitted to full depth in its slot. Here Tom marks wood to be removed.*

marked at the heel block region, and then the body is loaded into the slotting jig (**Photos 70 and 71**). Note that the body is loaded while the jig is held horizontally, then the jig is mounted vertically to make the cut.

The slot is routed to a depth of .520″ in one pass using a Porter Cable router in a jig which is available as a kit from LMI for those wishing to duplicate Tom's setup.

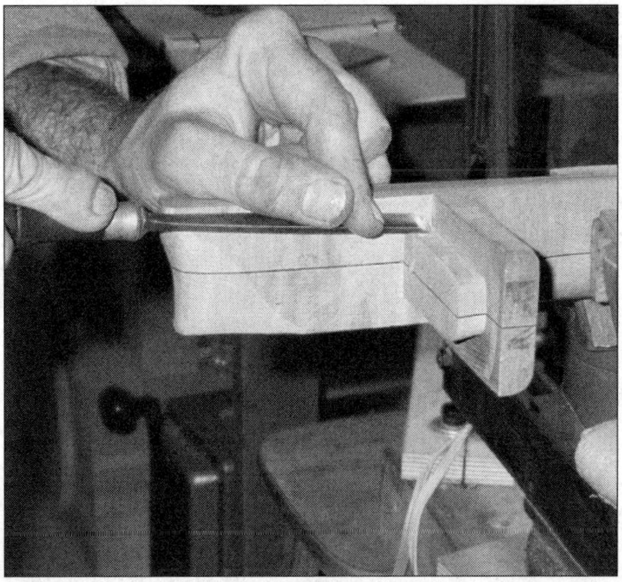

***Photo 74**. Excess wood is chiseled away as the fit is perfected.*

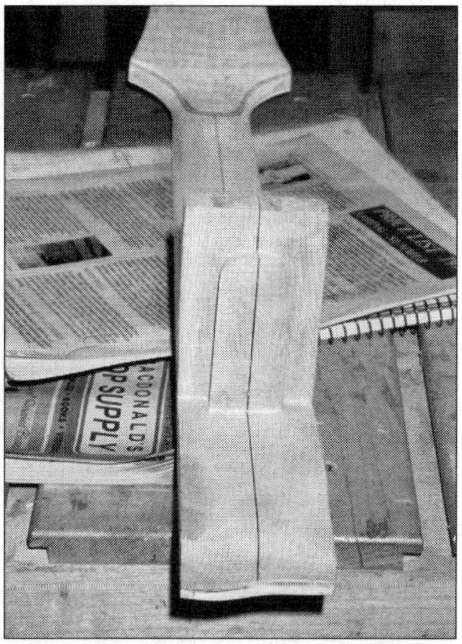

***Photo 75**. Finished dovetail and neck extension.*

Before fitting the neck, the portion of the top that will sit beneath the fingerboard extension must be made flat, true, and sanded to 220 grit. Material must be removed from the fingerboard extension until it sits flat upon the top. A first guess can be made with the neck in place as shown in **Photo 73**, but wood must be removed carefully until a good fit is accomplished (**Photos 74 and 75**). If your jigs are well engineered the dovetail joint should lock tight just when the fingerboard extension mates with the top, and the neck angle should be right on the money. A straightedge is used to check the pitch of the neck by measuring the height of the bridge (**Photo 76**). A height of 1″ will produce more of a jazz tonality, while a height of 3/4″ will lend itself to more of a flattop sound. Tom normally splits the difference with a bridge height of 7/8″. It's possible to doctor the fit of the dovetail and

***Photo 76**. Tom checks the pitch of the neck with a straightedge to assure that everything is going according to plan. He shoots for a bridge height of 7/8″.*

Photo 77. The magic moment arrives when the neck can be glued to the box.

Photo 78. The bridge blanks have been fitted with the adjustment posts and the wheels that do the adjusting.

the pitch of the neck at this point, but it's a tedious operation that can be avoided by careful jig making. A joint that's too tight may lock up before the dovetail is fully seated from swelling caused by the glue. Before the neck is glued to the body, an ebony heel cap that is the thickness of the binding is superglued in place. The neck is attached with FG glue from LMI, which is chemically much like Titebond but has a lower release temperature. Two clamps are all that's needed to glue on the neck, one over the fingerboard (**Photo 77**), and one from the heel to the butt seam of the body.

Ribbecke archtops utilize the standard two-piece floating bridge that adjusts for height using two knurled wheels mounted on threaded posts. Tom makes them from quartered ebony. The dimensions of the base blanks are 6³⁄₁₆″×.70″×.50″. The saddle blanks are 3.75″×.70″×.620″. The pieces are tacked together with superglue before the post holes are drilled with a ⅛″ brad-point bit. The holes are 3″ apart and centered both ways on the blanks. After the pieces are separated the holes in the base are tapped with 8×32 threads. The holes in the saddle are drilled out to ⁵⁄₃₂″ and elongated side to side to account for the tilt of the saddle as it is adjusted (**Photo 78**).

The bridge position is drawn on the top plate and a compass is set to the approximate arch of the top. A piece of balsa the size of the bridge base blank is marked with the arch of the top and bandsawn. A piece of 120-grit abrasive is stuck to the top and the balsa template is sanded neck-to-tail until its fit to the top is perfect, after which the fitted surface is saturated with superglue to temper it and make it wear resistant. The template is attached to a larger base equipped with toggle clamps. An ebony base blank is clamped over the template and the arch of the top is table routed (**Photo 79**). Excess ebony is bandsawn from the wings of the base and its final contours are established on the belt sander and perfected with the spindle sander.

The ends of the saddle blank are sanded to shape on the belt sander. A top view would show the ends to be half-round with the post holes centered. The top edge of the saddle is cut to the 15″ radius of the fingerboard,

Photo 79. The base of the bridge is routed to the approximate arch of the top plate.

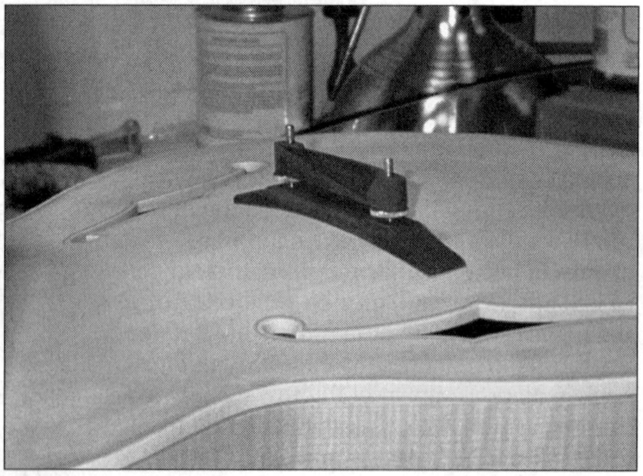

Photo 80. The finished bridge should sit perfectly in place before string tension is applied.

though during final setup the strings will be individually adjusted for height and the saddle will be reshaped to accommodate the string slots. Ultimately the post holes in the saddle will be enlarged and fitted with brass tubes to prevent metal-to-wood friction on the adjustment screws. The compensation angle and final finishing is done with files, scrapers, and sandpaper. The finished pieces are assembled into a complete bridge unit which

COURTESY OF TOM RIBBECKE

is sanded on the guitar top just as the balsa template was, using short neck-to-tail strokes until the bridge is perfectly mated to the top **(Photo 80)**.

The length of the tailpiece on an archtop guitar will affect the way the guitar feels to the player, though for the same gauge strings the actual tension will not change. A short tailpiece necessitates more string behind the bridge, and the added stretch of this string makes the action feel softer, or looser. Conversely, a long tailpiece replaces much of the string behind the bridge with ebony which has no stretch whatever, so the action feels tighter, or firmer.

Ribbecke tailpieces are laminated of ebony and a bit of carbon fiber to improve the strength and the ease of manufacture. The tailpiece proper starts as an ebony blank .30″ thick. The finished shape is drawn on it and rough-cut on the bandsaw. It is then held to a template with double-stick tape and the edges cleaned up using a table router and a pattern-maker's bit, which has the guide bearing on the bit shaft. The template is removed, and then the cutout area is made with a jigsaw. Small holes drilled in the corners allow the blade to turn around. Then the blank is stuck once again on the template and cleanup cuts are made to this area. The tailpiece is now flat and the edges are milled at 90°.

The strings pass through 1/8″ OD brass tubes, which must be laminated into the tailpiece using a special jig. Six 1/8″ round-bottom slots are routed to a depth of .270″ using a Bosch laminate trimmer. If the lines for the slots were drawn on they would converge 3″–4″ behind the tailpiece. Lengths of ebony 1/8″ wide and concave on the bottom have to be made. Six slightly long brass tubes are epoxied to the bottom of the slots. Ebony strips are glued on top of the tubes to fill the slots. After the epoxy has set, the tubes and the fillers are sanded flush with the face of the tailpiece and the filler strips are sanded flush with the top of the tailpiece. The unit appears to be a solid chunk of ebony with brass tubes set into it from the front, but it would be impossible to drill into the end grain as cleanly as the router can cut the slots. A cap of .20″ ebony is glued cross grain on the top front of the tailpiece and over the area that will become the hinge, bringing the thickness of these areas to 1/2″. The hinge slots are cut with a 60-tooth blade using a sliding table. The slots are 5/16″ wide and .6″ deep. A layer of carbon fiber glued cross grain to the front of the tailpiece finishes the construction of this part. Years ago Tom made his tailpieces freehand on the bandsaw and finished them with files. It's a slow process, but anyone with patience can still make a tailpiece without extensive jigging up.

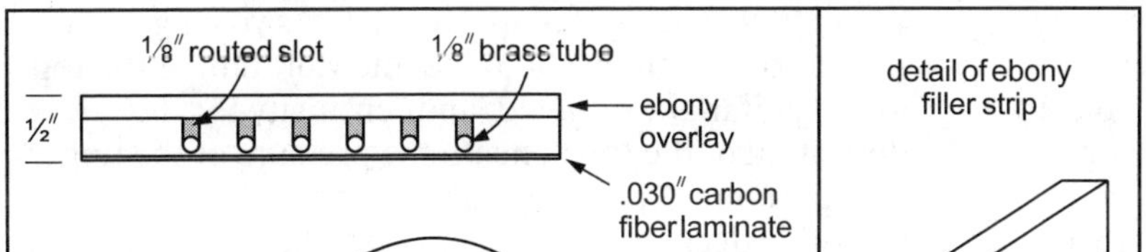

The second part of the tailpiece begins as .30″ thick ebony with a .20″ patch glued cross grain over the hinge portion. Fingers that fit into the slots of the first piece are cut on the sliding table. When the two parts of the tailpiece are assembled, a slice of paper should fit between the fingers to allow for expansion of the wood. Tack glue the two parts together at a 14° angle using water-soluble white glue. Mark the fingers for the hinge pin and drill from both sides using a 5⁄32″ brad-point bit. Drill slowly and use paraffin as a lubricant, then drill all the way through from one direction using an electrician's bit. After separating the parts, superglue is used to install 5⁄32″ brass tubes in the holes. The waste is removed with a razor saw and files. A pin of 1⁄8″ solid brass is used to hold the hinge together. Check for free movement, and use the paper trick to test the gaps between the hinge fingers. Disassemble and deepen the hinge slots in the first piece enough to allow 4°–6° of movement. A layer of .030″ carbon fiber is also glued to the back of the second part at this time. A tungsten carbide burr should be used to clean up the edges of all carbon fiber, and the weapon of your choice is used to contour the ebony to a pleasant shape.

The guitar is strung up to pitch during the voicing process. Voicing may take up to two weeks of subtle scraping. It's better to leave the plates a tad thick rather than venture too far in the voicing process and spoil the guitar. The box may not collapse but the voice will lose its focus.

To Tom, the voicing process is the most fascinating part of building archtops, and the ability to control and contribute to the final voice of the instrument in a real way is what led him to archtops in the first place. Any defects on the top and back of the guitar should be dressed away before the final voicing is begun. Voicing consists of scraping the outer third of the plates until their greatest potential to sing is released. The process is carried out in short sessions since the sensitivity of the ear lasts only a short time before tiring. Because of this factor, voicing may be stretched over a two-week period when time permits.

A bone nut is made and the guitar is fitted with the same tailpiece Tom uses to voice all his guitars. Phosphor bronze strings are used for voicing. All voicing is done while the guitar is strung to pitch. An archtop's initial voice is likely to resemble a banjo. After sitting overnight it may sound like a slightly better banjo. The voicing process rounds out the frequency response. Getting a good bass out of the instrument is the most difficult part. Unfortunately, intuition and experience are the most important tools in voicing any stringed instrument.

Thinning and perfecting the recurves with a curved scraper begins the process. Care must be taken not to disturb the clean lines of the binding. It's better the err on the thick side when voicing, since thinning taken too far can cause the sound of the guitar to lose its focus, and the guitar may instantly become a failure. Altering the lower bout on the treble side of the top has the most dramatic effect. However, Ribbecke considers the back to be a secondary soundboard, and it's important to spend time voicing this area as well. As voicing proceeds, it's important to feel the vibration of the top as the guitar is strummed, and sensitivity for the deflection of the top beneath the pressure of the fingers is important. A properly voiced top will have a smoothly decreasing thickness from the top of the arch to the thinnest part of the recurve, with no sudden jumps or inconsistencies.

Ribbecke guitars are finished with McFadden nitrocellulose lacquer. MEK dyes are used to tint the colors. All sanding during the finishing process must be accomplished by hand, since machine sanders can't follow the topography of an archtop instrument. Finish work is largely a study of its own, and is not a part of the normal seminar.

Tom is collaborating with Linda Manzer on a book about archtop guitar construction in which they hope to explore the Zen of lutherie as much as the real woodworking, and since their opinions differ in some areas, the book should be as interesting as it is informative. They also intend to include the opinions and designs of other current archtop makers. It should be a book worth waiting for. ——

Originally published in *American Lutherie #56*, 1998

Meet the Maker: David "Kawika" Hurd

by John Calkin

DAVID "KAWIKA" HURD is a guitar and ukulele maker residing in Hilo, Hawaii. Anyone who has surfed through his website (www.ukuleles.com) or consulted his advice on www.mimf.com knows that he is a thinking man's luthier who believes that the intellect should be an equal partner (at least!) to a builder's intuition, and that, in any case, science is simply too fascinating to ignore. David displayed his work at the 1998 GAL Convention, where his nylon-string guitar drew high praise during the listening sessions. I interviewed him at the PLU student center, an appropriate place to speak with an ex-teacher.

You're a staunch proponent of left-brain lutherie. Is the uke family complex enough to absorb that energy from you?

I think you mean do I apply science and engineering to making ukuleles?

I'd say that you obviously would. But unless you're using a recipe that I'm not familiar with, the ukulele is very simple compared to, say, a classical guitar, in terms of internal structure.

You're correct, but there are four different sizes of ukuleles. Typically, the very smallest size, which would be the standard or soprano size, is so small that just the top with a small bridge plate is sufficient for the instrument to sound the way people have a vision for that instrument. It's a sweet sound with not necessarily a lot of sustain. It should be clear, though. Some just bark at you. It has its own special "ka-plink, ka-plink" sound. But the point where you go to the next size, the concert size with about a 15″ scale, the instrument is large enough that you can really tune the top, the air resonance, and the back resonance. I put five fan braces on the top of a concert ukulele. They're light, but let's just say that I've never thought of the ukulele as a toy. There's a lot more that you can get out of it in terms of clarity, sustain, and projection. I've tried to make them like little classic guitars. I try to have an asymmetrical mode 3 so that there really is a difference in left and right vibrational modes. I try to couple the top resonance and the air resonance in a way that's suggested by Jurgen Myer in *The Journal of Guitar Acoustics* and by Graham Caldersmith and Al Carruth in articles in *The Journal of the Catgut Acoustical Society* and *American Lutherie.* I try to couple the back with the front. And it really works. You get a very different instrument.

But I have to say, also, that one of the reasons that I've tried to maximize the tonal quality of the ukulele is that I'm very lucky to have a kind of patron, a wonderful person named Doug Tolentino. He has a special kind of fingerstyle melody/chord way of playing which requires clear note separation. He's bought one of our guitars and eight of our ukuleles, mostly tenors and baritones, but I make a 5-string concert-size that he likes very much. He's the kind of musician who can't get enough different instruments because he sees possibility in every instrument. So if he's going to one gig he'll take a particular instrument, but at the next gig he may need to play louder or be part of a particular instrumental group. He's really quite remarkable. He's stuck with me over the last six or seven years, and my instruments have evolved to support his playing style.

I've made 400 instruments in batches of 6, and every single batch has been different. So when I began making guitars I already had a trend of 15″ (concert), 17″ (tenor), and 20″ (baritone) scale-length instruments behind me, and I had tried things from classical guitars that worked on those smaller instruments. It was a matter of scaling up my ukes to make a nylon-string guitar. But it's still very difficult to make a proper guitar with no flat spots and such.

So the uke is complex enough to absorb all your science.

Yes, easily. You don't have to make it complex, but the instruments have enough size that depending on the player's demands, you can make a wonderful instrument

COURTESY OF DAVID HURD

Kawika with grandson Kai

out of the ukulele. At the same time, though, it's supposed to be a sort of "people's instrument." It's fun, it's nonthreatening. You can learn a few chords a day for a week or two, and most sing-along songs only require three chords. It's a kind of beat guitar, a rhythm instrument in most people's hands. There are a few good players on the mainland, but if you went to Hawaii you'd find a very large number of fingerstyle ukulele players. It's really great. There are a lot of different styles of Hawaiian music.

It's not all Don Ho.

Gosh, no. Ukists play a large variety of contemporary music that leave one amazed that the instrument they're hearing is a ukulele. Brian Tolentino is a sort of a cousin to my patron Doug and is one of the most remarkable ukulele players I've ever heard.

Do Hawaiians play the vaudeville chord/melody style ?

Many entertainers play what the tourists are most comfortable with. This music is often a mixture of what people call "Boat Songs," the old cruise-ship melodies. They're called *hapa-haole,* or part-Caucasian. They're mostly English with a few Hawaiian words thrown in, and they're mostly comic songs. It used to be that there was always a Hawaiian group that met the boats as they were coming in. These songs have been around in different variations since at least 1900.

As I understand it, music in Hawaii always lags somewhat behind whatever is popular on the mainland. As the popularity of blues, ragtime, and jazz cycled through the states, the cycles reach Hawaii a year or more later. Contemporary music in Hawaii is just about everything imaginable. Some contemporary groups play a lot of Boat Songs, and they would be closest to the old vaudeville songs. But a lot of groups play only Hawaiian language songs, native material. Some play only modern songs of their own making. Or they'll play raggae, or Ja'waiian, which is strange rap-oriented half-English/half-Hawaiian stuff.

The Hawaiian sovereignty movement has had a large impact in the last five or ten years. First it was canoe paddling, then hula, and now music of all kinds centered around the guitar and ukulele. So there's a tremendous number of new ukulele makers in Hawaii. In many respects it's like the early 1920s. After the 1915 Pan Pacific Exposition in San Francisco, which featured a large Hawaiian Pavilion, Hawaiian music and the popularity of the ukulele began to spread. There was a burgeoning of uke makers both on the mainland and in Hawaii. We're in a similar period now. It's really neat that now in Hawaii kids are once again playing ukuleles in their garages and on week nights, just hanging out and singing the Hawaiian songs. I can't describe how great it is. It's really swell.

So Hawaii is consuming the bulk of the uke production?

Well, you need to know that nearly all the elementary school kids in Hawaii take ukulele lessons in the 5th or 6th grade and they all need instruments. So right there is a fairly hefty demand.

That's wonderful.

But at the same time, there's probably as many Hawaiian-born people on the West Coast as in Hawaii, so there's a demand for ukes along the West Coast as well, especially California and Las Vegas, because there's all sorts of hula schools associated with the Hawaiian music all throughout California and Nevada. We belonged to a Hawaiian club in Houston when we lived there, and clubs are scattered up and down the East Coast as well.

Most people who've only seen toy ukes don't realize the cultural impact that the ukulele has had over the years.

The ukulele has a period of popularity every twenty or twenty-five years. The first time was in the '20s.

Then Arthur Godfrey.

Yes, the '50s with Arthur Godfrey. Maccaferri sold ten million plastic ukes during that period. It wasn't a bad instrument, either, although his plastic guitar was much better. There was a smaller rise in interest in the '70s, but now in the '90s it's beginning to peak again. You can see it in the number of makers and the interest in old ukuleles of all kinds. You can see it on the Internet. My website garners about 1200 hits per month, which isn't bad for a uke site.

Your nylon-string guitar reaped a lot of praise at the listening session today, but when you said that your guitar was just a big ukulele the joke was actually on the audience, since you have developed your ukes to such an extent.

Yes, I didn't simplify the guitar, I made the ukulele more complex. But you see, one of my heroes is Graham Caldersmith. He a scientist/luthier who has a larger vision, a kind of continuum of instruments. That's the way I look at the ukulele family of instruments. If you scale it properly you can go from the guitar down through the ukulele family, or you can begin with the small ukes and scale your way right up through the classical guitar. What I'm trying to do is develop a general model for building all those instruments that will show their communality. That's the way Graham has done it for the classical guitar family.

In that case, the left-brain approach is certainly going to pay off ahead of everyone who is using intuition and shooting in the dark.

I've had a number of wonderful talks about this subject with others at this convention, and I admit to being a left-brain luthier and making no apologies for it. But having said that, I don't think that science is the "silver bullet." There are a lot of first-order corrections and manipulations that you can do by making some simple physical measurements that will prevent you from making some very stupid mistakes. For example, I have a spreadsheet on my website that allows a builder to calculate the effect of string tension, neck cross-section, fretboard thickness, and graphite-epoxy composite insert on neck deformation. But beyond that you really have to use your own senses and some sort of judgmental database to make great instruments. So there's no chance for the left-brain guys to put the right-brain guys out of business, or for either group to be a threat to the other one. It's just not so. My vision is that we should be complementing each other and trying to speak something closer to the same language.

Do you deal in pineapple shapes and dolphin soundholes and such?

In most respects I'm quite a traditionalist. So, no, I tend to avoid such playfulness.

I'd think they'd make the instrument harder to quantify.

Horrible. There's a funny story to the pineapple shape. I made one for a person, not as a joke but just as a cute idea. I made it of spalted koa; there's a picture of it on my website. It's very pretty, but I had no intention of making any quantity of them. Mostly to hold back the number of orders, I decided to charge $1,000 for them because I thought that nobody would want to pay that price. But I've already got three orders.

My gosh!

I know! *(laughs)*

So you're stuck with making them.

Yes! Why didn't I choose to charge $1500? *(laughs)*

That in itself says something about the seriousness with which people are treating the uke.

Well, people order them as collectibles. I'm only going to make two or three a year, and I'll probably never make more than fifteen or twenty. That's it. The wood is very unusual. They're going to sound great, there's no question about that, but if someone has a collection of beautiful instruments which will never be available in any quantity, the spalted pineapples might be a natural.

Is there an availability of spalted koa?

I was lucky enough to lay in a small supply. It's difficult to treat. If I make a larger instrument out of it, I have to charge a couple hundred dollars extra. We'll take thin-viscosity superglue and flood the inside surfaces. Then I'll actually coat the entire outside with boat-building epoxy, warm it with a hair drier to thin the viscosity, and spend twenty minutes rubbing it into the pores. The excess goop is scraped from the wood with my abandoned platinum credit card. The wood is wiped with paper towels and allowed to stand overnight to harden. Then it's sanded and sprayed with vinyl sealer and finished as usual.

JOHN CALKIN

David Hurd displays his guitars and ukuleles at the 1998 GAL Convention.

Spalted woods are a nightmare to finish.

Yes, but this process really works. I would never use spalted wood for a top, though. But for backs and sides it's really swell.

Does it bend okay?

If it's not too far gone. It's a bit floppier than sound koa. If it hurt the quality of the instrument I'd never use it. If there is spalting on the sides I like to get it on one edge where I can merge it into the spalted edge of the back.

When Martin was gearing up to make ukes during WWI they decided that softwood didn't provide the tone they were after, and all their ukes had mahogany or koa tops. Have you found that to be the case?

I've found that most Martin ukes are overbuilt, which is why so many of them are still around. And the ones that are still around are played in after thirty or forty years, and they sound wonderful. But they're basically overbuilt. I build mostly with koa, because it's what I have and what most Hawaiian people want. It's an OK tonewood. You can make a pretty nice sounding ukulele with a koa top. But I really prefer cedar and redwood, or even Douglas fir. Doug fir makes a very bright-sounding instrument. Six-string tenors are wonderful when topped with Douglas fir.

Doug fir is halfway to a hardwood anyhow.

Oh, yeah. Young's Modulus of Doug fir is like 2–3 million PSI. It's really stiff stuff. It's what I use for all my brace stock. This is heresy, but I just go down to the hardware store and pick out the quartersawn redwood for $3 per board foot, and that's what I use for my tops. Doug fir, same thing. I prefer to buy wood that I can see. If you hold 2×8 boards about a quarter of the way from the top and tap them on the concrete some of them just ring like a bell. That's the stuff! It makes beautiful top wood. It's all sawn and not split, so there may be some runout. I usually mark the direction of brace runout with a little arrow, just in case I have to get in there and plane the bracing after construction. The guitar that was played at the listening session was braced with Douglas fir. It has a cedar top that I was lucky enough to buy from Larry Stamm.

It's a great sounding guitar.

It's also extremely light. I followed Graham Caldersmith's advice in terms of trying to make the back a semitone different from the top and trying to relate the top to the Helmholtz resonance. And when you do all that you end up with a light instrument because the back has to be flexible enough to be in the right resonance range. People tend to boost it over their head when they first pick it up because it's much lighter than many guitars. It was my intention to make a parlor guitar and the feedback I received from the classical guitar players involved in the "winetasting" was that I had succeeded. Frankly, I was overjoyed.

Have you used other Hawaiian woods?

I've used a wood called milo (pronounced mee-lo). It's in the hibiscus family. It made the most lush-sounding tenor ukulele I've ever built. It was really remarkable. The hibiscus family tends to have soft, punky wood, but milo is quite different and is actually a very nice tonewood. The drawback is that it's quite scarce and the dust is extraordinarily toxic. I have to wear full-face protection the whole time that I'm working with it. So I haven't made many pieces from milo. It also has the other interesting property that when you've lacquered it, it suddenly looks like it's fifty or seventy-five years old. It's a beautiful blend of blacks and chocolates and oranges and reds. There's even purple. It's very pretty.

Is it rare, or are most of the trees normally too small to harvest?

Milo likes to grow near the ocean, so it has always been accessible. Much of it has been cut. But I've heard that it grows on other islands of the South Pacific, unlike koa which is isolated to Hawaii.

Have you used mango?

Mango is an interesting wood. Most mango looks kind of like margarine to me. But it can be curly and very pretty. I like the mango that runs to grays and chocolates.

That's what I've heard of, chocolate-heart mango.

Yes, but try to get it! The problem is that the big trees tend to grow in the city. And if it's a city tree, the wood is full of concrete and beer bottles and nails. Milling city wood is a crazy occupation. A metal detector is a necessity. Mango is normally \$3–\$4 a board foot in 4/4 and 8/4.

That's cheap.

Yes. Winkler sells it occasionally, but you have to be patient.

What does Kawika mean?

Ka-wi-ka? There's only thirteen letters in the Hawaiian alphabet. If you try to change "David" into Hawaiian, the D becomes a K and the V becomes a W. And no Hawaiian word ends in a consonant, so a vowel has to be added. So David becomes Kawika. It might also become Davita or Tavita if you go further south to Tahiti or New Zealand. "Ukuleles by Kawika" sounds a little better than "Dave's Ukes," especially if you're from Hawaii.

How long have you been in Hawaii?

I first went there in 1964 to attend graduate school in oceanography. I stayed until 1979, though there was a one-year excursion to Japan thrown in. We stayed on the mainland until 1991, then moved back to the islands. I'd been repairing and building instruments for a hobby for about eight years before I went back.

Lutherie is an interesting change from oceanography.

Well... I have a voice like a frog. We belonged to an Hawaiian club and I wanted to be more of a participant. A lot of the members had broken instruments, and fixing them seemed like something I could do. I had some nice factory ukuleles of my own until some druggies broke into our home and stole everything.

Ouch! Where was that?

Houston. Gotta love it, huh? I'd been trying to make instruments but the theft really spurred me on. Maybe they could steal my stuff, but they couldn't steal what I know and what I can do. I made some really ugly ukuleles back then. Really terrible. But gradually things got better. They're not bad now. They'll be better, but they're not bad. Any good builder feels the same way.

Was it hard to find an economic niche in Hawaii?

My business in Hawaii has been really episodic. When I first started seven years ago, Kamaka was basically the only one producing large numbers of instruments every year. They'd been around since 1916. Bob Gleason and David Gomes were both making very nice guitars and ukuleles in modest numbers on the Big Island. But Kamaka could only fill a third of the demand for entry-level ukes. It was a wonderful time to transition from a hobbyist maker turning out five or ten pieces a year, to a full-time maker producing thirty, forty, or fifty ukuleles a year. Whatever you made, people bought. It put me on a tremendous learning curve. At the end of two years I looked back at the previous eight years' production and decided that I'd only really learned a little bit about lutherie. And seven years later I look at those first two full-time production years and I think, "Those weren't very good either compared with what I'm doing now." I think I'm about half or two-thirds toward where I want to be. But I think that every year, so it's kind of a moving target.

In Hawaii you can learn to build ukes in night classes or at the community college. But those classes are taught by people who never had to make instruments for a living. So there's an enormous number of people out there making all kinds of ukuleles. They give them to family and friends, then set up little garage shops like mine, and might even sell them full-time. But most of these folks have never done any reading about instrument making. And they don't intend to. So when they make an especially good sounding ukulele they fall into the "what did I do right?" syndrome, and they'll never find out.

Are there enough of them to hurt the market?

Oh yeah. I went through a period where I didn't sell an instrument for six or eight months.

Wow!

Yeah, I was grumpy. But I've put about 300 instruments into the uke community in the last seven years, so my name is out there. I've also worked on my website for about a year and a half, and that's finally beginning to kick in. I get a couple serious inquiries a week from it, and I'd guess I've sold fifty or twenty instruments through the Internet up to this point. I work with three different groups of Internet people. The first send a check or Visa number from the mainland, I make the instrument, ship it out, and they never see what I look like. Often, though, they contact me to say how happy they are with the instrument. The second group sees the Internet, we do a little e-mail exchange and so forth, then they come to Hawaii on vacation and stop by the shop. They want to validate that we're for real. They either buy something that I have on hand or I take their order. The third group consists of local people who are online. They come to the Big Island to visit family or whatever, and they drop by while they're there.

How many ukes are you able to keep on hand?

Now I have none. From a totally full wall I went to zero. The latest batch of five guitars took me almost three months. So the chance of supplying a walk-in sale is totally random at this point. Right now I'm making two 8-string tenors, a 6-string tenor, and three baritones, of which one 6-string tenor, one 8-string tenor, and one baritone are sold. The next batch will be six 4-string tenors, and all of those are sold already. We'll just see what happens next. I really only need one sale a week to keep going.

The problem is that by the time I finish a batch all I can see in them is the mistakes. Fortunately, most of my sales are direct, the people love the instruments, and they never notice the mistakes. That fact gives me the upkick that lets me get on to the next batch.

Any good luthier looks at his work ten times harder than anyone else ever will.

Yes, but that's necessary if we're going to improve. I know when my work sounds good. But everyone can remember an instrument that they thought was a real dog. Right? You just kind of put it over to the side and try to ignore it. Then someone comes in and "discovers" it, tries it, and loves it at first meeting. There are so many visions out there about what comprises a great instrument that you have to be careful about not forcing your opinions on someone. And never point out your mistakes! People love what they love. It's a hard lesson to keep in mind, though.

Also, the Tao is benevolent, and given the opportunity, will give us a break. How do you join your necks? Does it vary from one size uke to another?

People are going to love me or hate me for this, but I'm a David Russell Young fan. I use a simple butt joint. I use the trick that Richard Bruné brought back from Japan. I put a 2″ sanding belt in my bandsaw, then sand the neck against the body until the fit is perfect. It makes an unbelievably tight joint. The caveat is that you must install registration pins between the parts before glue up. I use epoxy. A ½″ wide, 7″ long rubber band is used to clamp the parts together. Four hundred instruments later I've never had a problem. I've gone to using a graphite bar in the necks of tenors and baritones for double security, and I have full confidence in the procedure. The bar also does amazing things for the sustain and clarity of the notes. I also use a zero fret, which means that all the strings are fretted all the time. The timbre of the open strings and the fretted strings is always the same. I like that, and it automatically sets the action at the top end of the fretboard at the same time.

How much does the structure of the baritone uke approach the classical guitar? Or does it?

I use a 5-fan asymmetrical brace pattern in mine. And I put a graphite-epoxy patch beneath the bridge to make the footprint a little bigger. Tuning the bodies of each batch takes me about a week, and recording the data has to be added to that. It's all part of trying to make a generalized model and validating the approach.

So you're constantly trying to be as scientific as possible. Does that come from being an oceanographer?

I'm a left-brain person, that's all. I'm also a teacher. I taught high school science for four years. My website is simply another way to try to share information. My book, which tries to tie everything together, is about four years off. When it comes out, we'll see if my vision is valid. ——

Update

David Hurd's book *Left-Brain Lutherie* was published in 2004. See his website for details: www.ukuleles.com.

(2007)

JOHN CALKIN

Kawika consults with fellow classic guitar makers John Dick (center) and Eugene Clark at the 1998 GAL Convention in Tacoma.

Originally published in *American Lutherie #56*, 1998

Clearly Protective

Installing a Clear Plastic Pickguard on an Acoustic Guitar

by Kent Everett

AT LEAST ONCE A MONTH I get a phone call from someone having a problem installing or having installed a clear pickguard on one of my guitars. It is a little bit tricky to do a clean job, so I thought I'd take a moment to pass along the technique that I use.

I like to use clear laminate stock that you can find at an office supply store. My favorite is W.T. Rodgers Plain View (4″×5″, .005″ thick).

First, clean the area where the pickguard will be applied with naphtha. If there are any pick scratches or divots in the finish they will leave air bubbles, so if the area is badly beat don't bother. On new guitars you can usually get a clear pickguard to go down smoothly.

After cleaning the area, take a scrap of the clear laminate, peel off the backing, and stick it down and pull it up repeatedly in the pickguard area. "Masking" the area like this really helps get the laminate to go down without bubbles. I started doing this because I found that often on the second try I was able to get a better job. So instead of wasting time and material, I use a scrap of material to emulate the same effect.

Trim the pickguard material to shape, all except the soundhole part. Leave that corner so that it extends out over the soundhole. Before peeling the backing off, clean yourself and your work area really well. Peeling off the backing creates a bit of static electricity that will draw dust and lint. Every little dust speck leaves a blemish, so turn off any air movement, too.

OK, here we go. Before peeling off the backing align one of the pickguard edges on the top. I'll use little scraps of masking tape to spot where this edge is to go (**Photo 1**).

Then, starting with the corner that hangs over the soundhole, slowly peel off the backing. I hold the

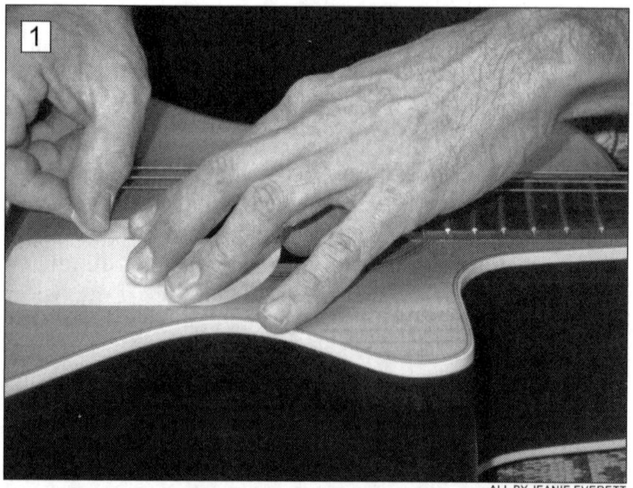

ALL BY JEANIE EVERETT

Positioning the pickguard using a piece of masking tape for alignment.

Holding the pickguard and beginning to pull off the backing.

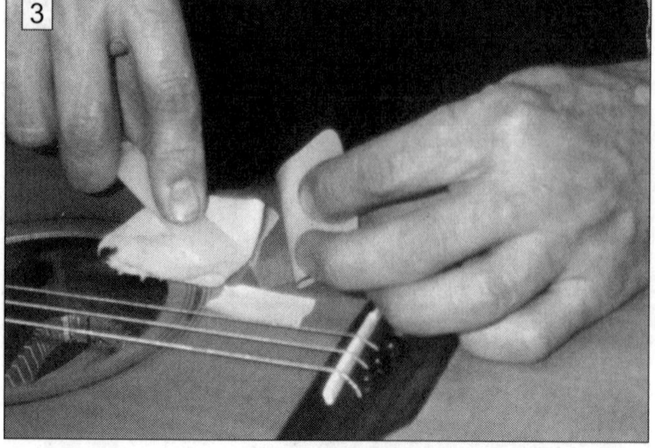

Rolling off approximately 1/3 of the backing, and pressing out the air pockets with a spatula. A cloth pad helps distribute the pressure and protects the plastic from getting damaged.

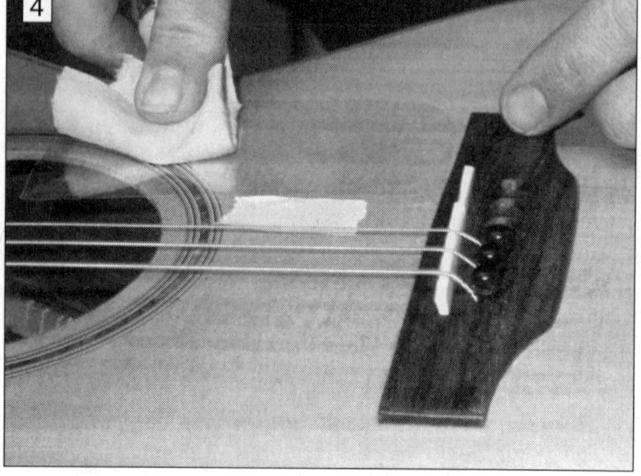

Final burnishing of pickguard, smoothing out the adhesive.

pickguard in this area, thereby leaving my fingerprint on that part of the pickguard (**Photo 2**).

As the backing is slowly peeled back, I roll down the pickguard using a small, stiff plastic spatula to push out the air bubbles and smooth out the adhesive, using a small cotton cloth between the spatula and the pickguard to keep from scoring the plastic (**Photo 3**). Do not try to do this all at once. While rolling down the pickguard, it is important not to pull it back up to correct a spot. This will crease the plastic, and you cannot rub that crease out. So move slowly, and if you blow it, do it again. This material is not very expensive, but the guitars are.

When the last of the backing has been removed and the laminate is down, the whole thing is given a final burnishing with the spatula and cloth (**Photo 4**).

Last I trim off the excess material that hangs over the soundhole, and with it my fingerprint. I use a razor blade for this, and angle it so that I slice off the excess material without touching the top (**Photo 5**).

Who would have thought that such a seemingly simple task would be so tricky, but there it is. If you are careful it is possible to install a nearly invisible clear pickguard (**Photo 6**). ——

Trimming off excess pickguard material over the soundhole.

The finished product.

Originally published in *American Lutherie #55, #56 and #58*, 1998–1999

QUESTIONS

EDITED BY CYNDY BURTON

(***Questions** from page 277)*

are generally harder and somewhat more elastic. If you can find this in small quantities, perhaps from another industrial supply place, so much the better). The thinnest sheet is .024″ (probably close enough to .020″), and it comes in various dimensions. The most convenient size available for the side bending machine is probably the 24″× 30″, at $30. They will send it immediately and it usually gets there by the next day.

*And another answer from **Dennis Abbl of Wasilla, AK:***

You can get .020″ stainless steel in shim stock (tempered steel) from bearing supply houses which is 6″ or 12″ wide and in rolls 50″ long. It can also be ordered from MSC (www1.mscdirect.com).

***Peter Dyer of Winters, CA** has the last word:*

The Metals Handbook, Desk Edition, published by the American Society for Metals (6th printing, 1991) says, "In atmospheres free from chloride contamination, stainless steels have excellent corrosion resistance. Types 430, 302, 304, and 316 normally do not show even superficial rust. Some rusting may occur in marine atmospheres or in industrial exposure where surfaces become contaminated with chloride salts."

So, if you're building guitars and using 302 or 304 stainless on the Universal Side Bender, absent the conditions described above, don't worry about rust.
I hope that this resolves any confusion generated by the seemingly contradictory statements earlier.

■ ***John Calkin of Greenville, VA** asks:*

If a luthier creates an original metal tailpiece, who can cast them in quantities that a small business can afford? If I make my own metal tailpieces just a couple at a time, who will plate them for me? I've seen do-it-yourself plating kits. Are they any good and will they plate nickel?

***Harrell Sellers of Westville, OK** responds:*

Many small businesses have custom castings manufactured. Look in the Yellow Pages of any medium-sized city under "foundries and castings." You can usually save some money if you can make or provide a complete geometry to be copied, that is, make one out of wood, clay, or plaster.

As far as plating goes, the EPA could get involved if you try to set up a home commercial plating shop. Check the Yellow Pages for "electroplaters." They plate all types of metals. Ask for one who services aircraft subcontractors. Consider electroless nickel from such a plating shop. ——

Originally published in *American Lutherie #57*, 1999

Binding Guitars

by Jeff Huss and Mark Dalton

OUR SYSTEM for machining binding and purfling slots may represent an exorbitant investment for some shops and certainly doesn't qualify as the last word in the process. We didn't even invent it, though we think we improved upon the design. However, we do have some binding tips to offer that might make more sense in the context of how we do things.

Necks are easy to explain. All our fingerboards are ebony and all fingerboards are bound. Many are bound in ebony just to hide the fret slot ends. It's a simple matter to substitute maple or ivoroid when the situation calls for it. A fixture is used to locate two steel index pins in the bottom of the fingerboard. The board is then pinned to a form that is the exact size of the finished fretboard minus the binding. A flush-trim bit in a table-mounted router brings the board to size. A climb cut is your best bet to prevent tearout. The board is next pinned to a form that is the size of the fretboard after binding. Waxed paper separates the board from the form while thick superglue is used to adhere the binding of choice to the edges of the board. A few lengths of glass fiber tape are enough to secure the joint, but full-length strips of Teflon are taped against the bottom of the binding to keep it from tipping inward. Another important part of the recipe is to use a number of clamps to keep the board sitting firmly against the fixture as any warping will disrupt the fit you've worked so hard to achieve (**Photos 1 and 2**). Once the glue has set, the binding is scraped to fit the arch of the fretboard. The steel pins stay in the fingerboard while it is glued to the neck with epoxy.

Headstocks are bound using a Dremel Moto Tool with a router base. The binding is mitered at the corners, and it's a big help to have an extra set of hands when wood binding is installed, even when the binding is prebent. The binding is forced in place while the helper squirts it with superglue and zaps it with accelerator.

We try to limit our production to standard models, but occasionally we get talked into a one-off project for which our production binding setup isn't designed. We resort to a laminate trimmer with a wooden base that includes a set of bearings that roll on the side of the guitar (**Photo 3**). The bottom of the base is cut at an angle to approximate the spherical arch of the plates. As long as the arch of the base is a bit greater than that of the plates everything will work fine. If the bearings are constantly held against the sides, the base will read the very edge of the plates, and an accurate route will be made. A vacuum clamp holds the guitar body to the bench top to permit unencumbered access to whichever plate is placed up (**Photo 4**). As with nearly all operations in guitar making, there is no

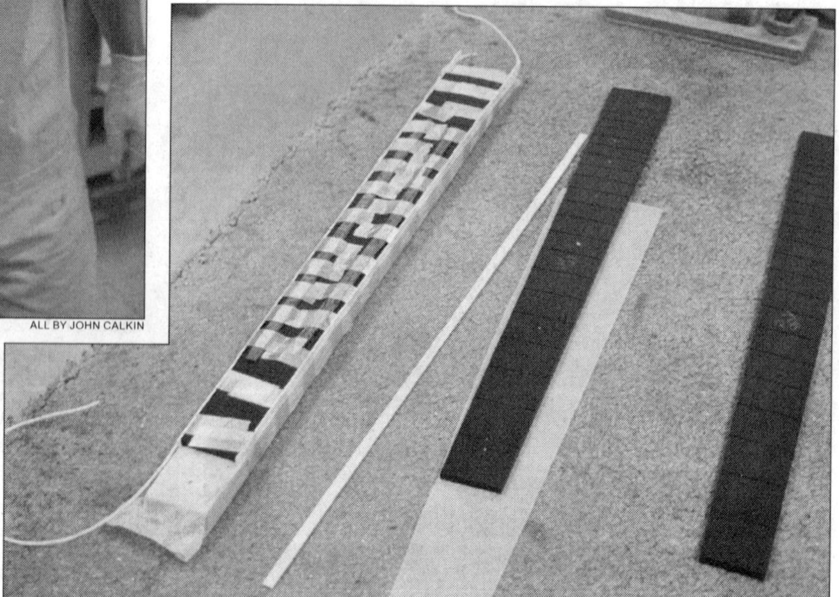

ALL BY JOHN CALKIN

***Photo 1** (above). Jeff Huss superglues binding to a fingerboard. The board is clamped to a workboard exactly as wide as the bound board. A few pieces of filament tape will hold the binding in place until dry. The fret slots will later be cleaned out with a tiny router bit.*

***Photo 2** (right). An ebony board bound with maple drying on the binding form. The "string" is actually teflon. The binding is substantially taller than the board, and the teflon strip prevents the binding from tipping beneath the pressure of the tape.*

substitute for accurate work. Test router cuts are made on a block of wood and measured with a dial caliper. Fitting the binding with the laminate trimmer is probably a shade more accurate than our production system but it takes many times longer to complete. The difference in accuracy never shows on the finished guitars.

Precision binding begins with prepping the body for routing, and this might begin even before the body is constructed. If the sides aren't flat across their width after bending they must be made so. In some cases touching them to the belt sander will suffice, but in extreme cases of warping they must be coerced into a flat position. If the sides are removed from the bender while still hot and flexible they can be clamped into the mold and will likely remain flat. Some varieties of wood tend not to cooperate, however. We consistently have trouble with figured meranti and sapele. Warpy areas of the sides are treated with heat, moisture, and reverse clamping. The ribs will eventually be treated with cross-grain braces but it's not safe to depend on them to hold warped sides flat.

When the body is handed to the binding man the excess top and back material is immediately routed away with a flush-trim bit. About half of the binding channel is then hogged out on the binding router. We have separate routers for binding and purfling. Both are mounted horizontally (**Photo 5**). We had a machine shop make aluminum bases for them to which are attached a set of bearing rollers. The axis of the bearings is carefully set on the exact center of the router collet, and although the position of the router and the bearings are both adjustable, the idea is to never have to adjust them. Auxiliary bases of aluminum screw to the main base to control the width of the slot. For instance, even though all our bindings are of the same dimensions, a D-45 treatment with abalone side trim will require a wider slot than binding that is merely purfled with veneer trim. By changing the diameter of the bearings, we control the thickness of the cut (**Photo 6**). The depth of cut on the purfling router is never changed, but different bearings are required to change from (for instance) .045″ black/white/black to herringbone. Since cosmetic changes can require that new parts be machined we don't make changes in our models lightly.

So the auxiliary base for hogging is the thickest and the hogging bearings are the widest, and only half the channel is removed. Cutting the channel in stages reduces the chance of brittle woods splintering, but the real reason at this point is to give the binder a chance to see what he's dealing with. Sides with thin spots have to be dressed

Photo 3 *(left). This shop-made base on a laminate trimmer is used to rout guitar bodies for trim configurations outside those used on standard models. The ramp provides clearance for the bit, and is not rested on the top or back.*
Photo 4 *(right). Jeff routing a meranti body for custom binding. The bearings of the router base are held firm against the guitar ribs, and only a tiny portion of the base rides the top of the guitar. The body is held to the bench by a vacuum clamp.*

Photo 5 *(right). The binding router is held horizontally to an aluminum base made by a machine shop. The bearings sit on the exact axis of the router bit. The sides of the guitar body are rolled over them. Interchangeable foot plates (above the router) are used to cut the .210″ width of the binding, which is done in three steps. Changing the diameter of the bearings controls the thickness to be cut. Though all our binding is .065″ thick, the channel is cut in two stages.*
Photo 6 *(below). These are different bearing sets for the binding and purfling routers. All H&D bindings are .065″ thick, but various kinds of trim are used on different models.*

using scrapers and sanding blocks. Otherwise, the ribs are marked in white pencil and sanded on a 60-grit belt until the pencil marks are gone (**Photo 7**). The waist must be dressed on the idler roller, but most of the rib area can reach the platen. It's a strange phenomenon that although the roller is slightly convex to improve the tracking of the belt, the waist normally is sanded flat. Soft wood like sapele or some mahoganies can sand so fast that an 80-grit belt may be safer. A very heavy wood such as Honduras rosewood may require that more rib material be removed just to keep the weight of the guitar under control. By constantly feeling the hogging slot, it's possible to know when you're getting too thin. Most of the risk is removed from the sanding process if the ribs are carefully flattened after bending. It's important that ribs only be power sanded using a new or nearly new belt. If the belt is worn, the tendency is to push the body onto the platen. This makes the belt curl at the edges, and the ribs will end up convex. This kind of power sanding requires a firm hand but a sensitive touch. It's not difficult to learn, just a bit hairy the first time out.

Tight waists and cutaways must be scraped and sanded by hand until the ribs are flat. The heel-block area must never be power sanded. It is dressed flat with a large sanding board, making sure at all times that it remains square to the centerline of the top.

Butt wedges, or end grafts, are made in bulk on a table-saw jig. Whether maple, ebony, or ivoroid, they are all the same thickness and size. The graft slot is routed using a simple jig that clamps to the body. Wooden wedges are mated with BWB purfling. Ivoroid wedges are teamed with black/ivoroid trim. Regardless of material, the wedges are glued with superglue. We used to use Titebond for wood and a plastic cement for ivoroid, but they can shrink a great deal and leave the wedge unsupported in the slot. Unsupported wedges tend to tear out when they are routed to length, meaning that the whole process must be done over. The wedges are edge-sanded on a board until they are a tight fit in the slot. Wedges and trim pieces are pushed in tight, then pulled back out just enough to permit thin superglue to seep into the joints. Use a liberal dose, then dose again with thicker C/A just to fill any unseen gaps. Quickly push the wedge home and squeeze out as much glue as possible with a piece of scrap wood, then shoot everything with accelerator. Trim off the ends of the wedge with a razor saw. Dress the wedge flat on the belt sander. Ivoroid is especially susceptible to damage at this point. If the belt is worn, the ivoroid can be turned to slag by the friction instead of being cut away.

All our guitars with wood binding also have mitered purfling. All that means at this stage is that the end graft must be left higher than the binding slot by the thickness of the purfling. The binding bearings are mounted on the router in order to cut the slot to full thickness, and the wedge plate is screwed to the main base. This will leave the ends of the wedge and its purfling .045″ taller than the finished slot will be (since most of our guitars use .045″-wide side purfling). The body is routed all the way around again. The final auxiliary plate is then mounted on the main base and the slots are finished off, being careful not to touch the wedge or its purfling. Since the router bit can't be seen during routing, it helps to wrap a tab of masking tape from the ends of the wedge onto the top and back plates to act as a guide. The slots adjoining the wedge are finished by hand, then the miters are cut on the purfling.

(There is a simpler way to do all this that we just couldn't make work. A full-size binding slot can be cut, after which the wedge is installed. When the wedge is routed to length there is no need to hand fit the slots, just chisel the miters and be done. But in practice the unsupported purfling on the off-side of the router cut often tore out, leaving the whole job to be done over.)

Photo 7. *After any overhanging plate material is routed off with a flush-trim bit, the sides are marked in white pencil and dressed flat on the belt sander. A "hogging" channel has already been routed on the edges, and by feeling this as work progresses, the thickness of the sides is kept safe. The binding will later be dressed in the same manner.*

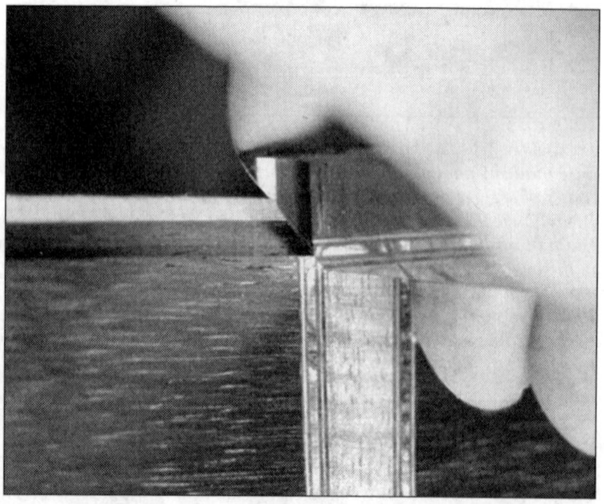

Photo 8. *This is the mirror trick. The back of the chisel is polished bright. When placed on the purfling it throws back an image that can be used to judge the angle of the cut. In this case the angle should be 90°, but you can see that it's a bit off on this abalone-trimmed butt graft. When the angle is correct the chop is made.*

There is a mitering technique handed down to us from European furniture makers called the mirror trick. The back of the chisel is polished to a mirror sheen. When placed upon the purfling, the angle of the cut can be seen perfectly in the reflection in the chisel (**Photo 8**). In this way you can also check the accuracy of the width of the slot. If the chisel blade is placed precisely in the corner of the purfling, and if the angle is carefully held at 90°, the purfling must automatically be cut to the proper dimension. If the slot doesn't meet the purfling at its bottom corner the slot must be adjusted with the chisel.

To this point we still haven't routed the body for top or back purfling. We switch to the purfling router and mount the proper bearings, that's all there is to it. Many of our models use a .060″ purfling for the top and .045″-wide purfling for the back. We feel that the top dressing should look more dramatic than the back. Herringbone or abalone trim require their own bearings. The top purfling is cut all the way around, but the back purfling must stop short of the center strip. Our zipper strip is dressed with the same .045″ purfling, and the slots must be finished by hand and the purflings carefully mitered.

It's worth mentioning that each change of the router setup is given at least two passes to ensure a clean cut, since the actual work is done blind. It's then inspected by eye and perhaps routed again. It's much easier to fix any mishaps now than when the binding is half glued in place. Routing the slots in this fashion (blind) can induce a form of disorientation that makes you doubt that the body is sitting on both bearings. Closing your eyes can help. When in doubt, pull the body away from the cutter, rock it on the bearings until your sense of touch returns, then proceed. Rolling the body smoothly over the bearings is a kind of dance with the guitar, and the object is to be as graceful as possible.

If the purfling cutter tears out any spruce — it happens all the time with Engelmann — you must sand out the tears and recut all your slots. Bummer. Using a climb cut may reduce the tearout.

OK, all the routing is done and any hand fitting is complete. Hopefully you've planned ahead and the binding is already bent. Binding can be taped together in sets of four strips, then four sets can be taped into a sheet and all of them bent at once on the Fox side bender (**Photos 9 and 10**). It pays to make a storage form that will keep wood bindings from relaxing out of shape, and this is essential with ebony bindings that are bent for cutaways (**Photo 11**). Once the ebony relaxes it's very hard to coerce into the shape you want. Maple, on the other hand, is very forgiving.

We've not mentioned plastic binding. With the exception of ivoroid, we don't use it. In fact, we try to obtain ebony bindings that are streaked with gray, just so it won't look like black plastic when finished. When we want to give our binding man a treat, we

Photo 9. *Mark Dalton is about to bend enough purfled maple trim for two guitars. Actually, since this will be a cutaway body, this batch of binding will yield four half-sets. Maple only requires a light spritzing of water before bending. Ebony, on the other hand, prefers to be soaked in warm water for about ten minutes before bending into a cutaway shape.*

Photo 10. *Here Mark is adding the last bit of squeeze to the cutaway portion of the binding. The clamps have yet to be set on the rear bout. A silicon blanket is used in conjunction with the heat provided by the light bulbs in the Fox side bender. Mark considers the bender a work-in-progress, and looks forward to the day he either perfects it or throws it out the back door in favor of a better device.*

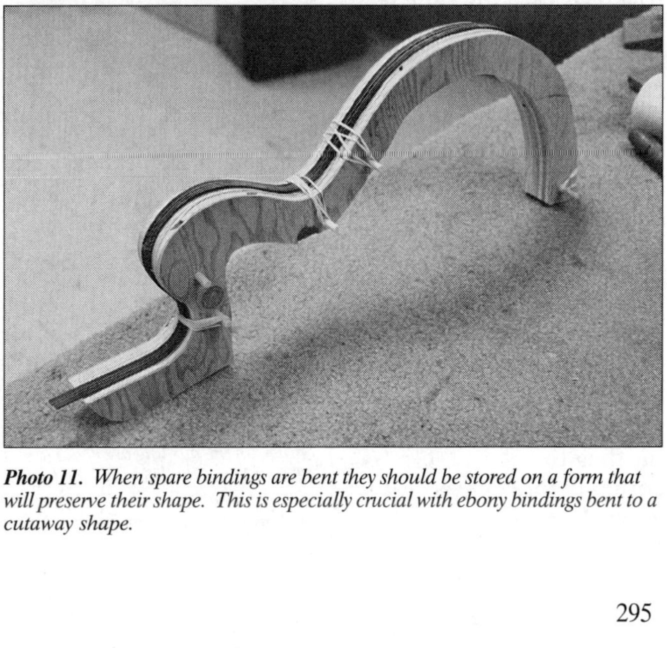

Photo 11. *When spare bindings are bent they should be stored on a form that will preserve their shape. This is especially crucial with ebony bindings bent to a cutaway shape.*

throw him an ivoroid job. None of the purfling gets mitered, and of course the flexibility of plastic makes installation easy (though it certainly could be mitered, but we're after a vintage Martin-look when we use plastic). We buy ivoroid in large sheets and saw it into binding strips. Black/ivoroid purfling comes the same way. The bottom edge of the binding is dressed flat on the belt sander, then joined to the purfling with plastic cement. The next day the back edge of the purfling is sanded even with the binding, and excess glue is sanded and scraped away. Glue must also be removed from the bottom of the purfling. It's easier to maintain flat surfaces if the glue is draw filed away rather than scraped. The inside corner of the purfling should also be beveled with a scraper. Square the strips on one end, and you're ready to bind.

The prebent wooden strips aren't ready, though. Fit them to the body until you find the sweet spot where they sit the best. Mark the binding at the center of the end graft and at the inside of the wedge purfling strip. Clip the binding to length, then chisel away the binding purfling over the wedge. You'll almost automatically leave the binding too long, but do a careful job of dressing the purfling to length. Miter the purfling using the mirror trick. The binding should sit on the wedge with no gaps and the lines of the purfling should come together in unbroken angles **(Photo 12)**. Chisel, file, or sand the ends of adjoining binding strips until they butt together with no gaps and the miters are tight (perhaps we should mention that we buy our binding strips with the purfling already glued to the bottom. Top and back purflings are laid in as separate pieces). Use the mirror trick to miter the back purfling. If this is the first time you've tried to miter binding you might want to take a coffee break at this point. You deserve it. If you muff the miters, and if you are using a simple guitar shape such as a dreadnought, you can clip off the boogered binding and start over. The binding may no longer sit in the sweet spot but it will bend into place. Binding intended for a cutaway probably won't cooperate if you try this trick. Discard the ruined binding and start fresh.

Cutaway bodies require an extra piece of purfling on the back that is mitered into the center strip and the square corner of the cutaway **(Photo 13)**. This piece is barely over an inch long, and we normally fit it in place with superglue before the rest of the back trim is begun. Cut and miter a length of scrap purfling to test fit the corner before glue is applied.

Fiddle makers lick or otherwise wet small pieces of maple before trimming with a blade to makes them more cooperative. Remember that if you use maple binding.

If you are purfling a cutaway with herringbone or other trick trim you may need to prebend it. Wet it under hot tap water for a few seconds, let the water soak in, then force it into a form until dry. Our form is a sheet of masonite with a guitar-shaped groove routed into it to accept the trim. Be prepared to lose a few pieces. In fact, it's pretty arrogant not to bend extra wood bindings before starting a job. They may not break in the bending, but you're bound to screw one up sooner or later. Not having extra pieces ready just gives you an excuse to let a sloppy job slide by.

Titebond is used for all binding, even ivoroid. Maybe it's the 60-grit scratches that make it stick, but we seldom have trouble with it. If a section comes loose during scraping, just superglue it and keep going.

There are no real tricks to installing binding. We only use filament tape, not masking tape. It costs more, but it does a far better job. Double check your miters and joints at the butt, then spread glue on two or three inches in both directions. Tape down one strip and its purfling, then start the job in the other direction. If you're right handed finish the left-side binding first. Tape down the loose ends of the right-side binding/ purfling to keep it out of the way. Keep pressing in the purfling as you work your way around. If you get enough squeeze-out you won't be able to tell how it looks, but that's OK. Lots of glue is messy, but it helps prevent gaps as the glue shrinks. Your finish person will be a much happier camper. If the binding won't sit tight at the waist take a scrap piece of maple binding, dip it in water to make it pliable, then tape it in place as a clamping caul. Use several pieces of tape if necessary. Herringbone can be bent around the guitar while it's cold and dry if you're not building a cutaway.

*(See **Binding** on page 299)*

***Photo 12** (left). Here is a tidy job of mitered purfling. The ebony end graft meets tightly with the ebony binding, and the corners of the purfling are clean and tight. The body wood is meranti, a wonderfully figured Philippine mahogany.*
***Photo 13** (right). The tiny length of BWB purfling extending from the center strip to the corner of the cutaway must be fitted separately, usually before any other back trim is glued in place. The fit is tested with a mitered scrap of purfling before supergluing the piece in place. This guitar is bound in maple.*

Originally published in *American Lutherie #57*, 1999

More Binding Tools and Tips

by John Calkin

WOOD BINDING has become a mark of an elegant guitar, and it's fun to use woods that aren't normally offered by tonewood suppliers. Bandsawn binding stock can be thinned easily with a sanding drum mounted in a drill press and a make-shift fence, then cut to width on the table saw using an MDF fence and a pair of small feather boards. The MDF has a runner that sits in the left table slot, and a featherboard attached to it applies downward pressure on the binding. Another MDF runner is jam fit into the right table slot, and to this an adjustable feather board is bolted which keeps the binding stock pressed against the fence. A Stewart-MacDonald fret-slotting blade is used to keep stock loss to a minimum (**Photo 1**).

An alternate method is to joint the edge of a board or billet, then cut off a slice as tall as you wish your binding to be. Then joint the billet again and cut off another slice. Purfling material can be glued to the full width of the jointed edge (if you can find it that wide), then purfled binding strips can be bandsawn from the slices.

At Huss & Dalton it's one of my jobs to dress the rib material for bending. When the width of the stock permits, I joint one edge of the ribs and saw off strips for future use as binding. I made a fence that slides into the miter slot of the saw table that is permanently set to make a $\frac{1}{4}''$ cut, so reclaiming a bit of wood that would otherwise be waste takes hardly any time at all. The binding strips can be sanded down to .065$''$ when needed.

In past articles I've made no bones about disliking the entire binding process, so it's ironic that H&D hired me specifically to relieve Jeff of the binding chores. That was 80-some guitars ago, and I have to say that I've come to enjoy the job. On my first day Jeff set the tone at H&D when he whipped out a tape dispenser for me from scrap particleboard, an 8-penny nail, and a bit of hacksaw blade. It was a 10-minute trick that told me I was free to invent whatever it took to do a good job. Since then I've assembled a kit of tools that I could hardly do without. Some are used to fit and install the binding (**Photo 2**), and some are used afterwards to dress the rough work to a presentable condition (**Photo 3**).

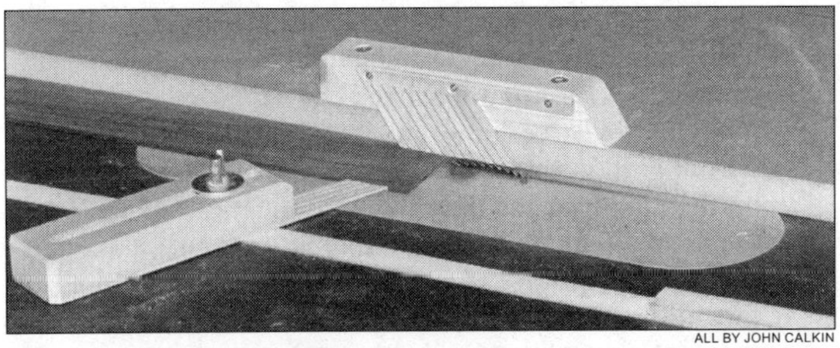

ALL BY JOHN CALKIN

***Photo 1**. This jig is used to cut binding from thin stock. A fret-slotting blade is used to preserve material. The fence and the off-side feather board both mount in miter slots, though the off-side feather board must be adjusted after each cut.*

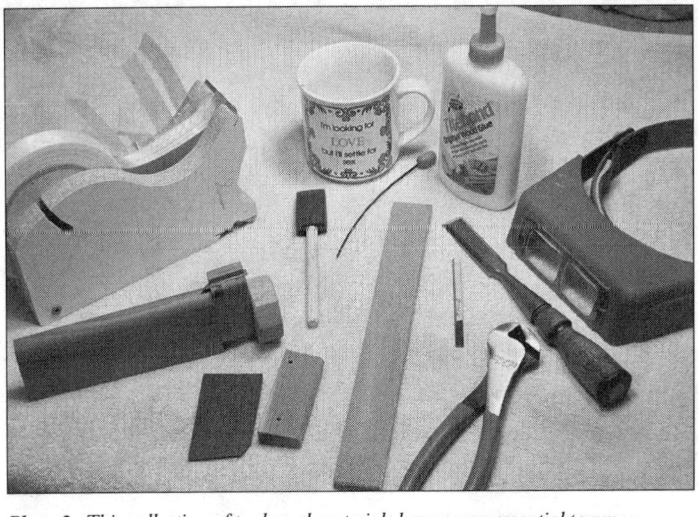

***Photo 2**. This collection of tools and materials has proven essential to my binding work. Some are standard items on every luthier's workbench. Half of them were made on the spur of the moment from scrap wood. This batch is used to install the binding and purfling. See the text for details.*

***Photo 3**. This little batch of tools is used for finishing the work. The $4'' \times 11.5''$ sanding board is used with adhesive Stikit paper, usually 80 grit. The spindle-sander drum is used with the same paper to clean up tight waists and cutaways. The jigsaw blade mounted in a handle cleans out the channel for abalone trim, and the screw driver prods the abalone into place.*

Some of these tools are obvious. The Titebond, chisel, and end nippers in **Photo 2** are part of every luthier's tool collection. My old eyes have grown dependent on the optical visor, and I could hardly work without it these days. I feel that it gives me an edge, too. If a job looks good to me at 2× it's going to look fine to *anyone's* normal vision. The skinny curved thingy is merely a few inches of BW plastic purfling set into a wooden knob. I painted the knob red with magic marker and sealed it with superglue to keep the color from running. I use it to spread glue back under the binding as work progresses. It lives in the coffee cup full of water, which also serves to help thin down the semi-dried glue on my fingers so I can wipe it off more easily. The foam brush is used to moisten the ends of binding to make them easier to chop with the chisel. The block of walnut in front of the foamy is used to force purfling into its slot, and the bit of rosewood to its left is used for chopping purfling on top of the guitar when the job is coming to a close. The bit of binding next to the chisel has its purfling mitered, and I use it to prepare the end graft to accept the real stuff. After this piece broke I cut another with the purfling cut back from both ends, and one end of the purfling is square and the other mitered. It works much better. The big rectangle is a 2″×11½″ piece of ¼″ plywood that I made into an orange stick by rubber cementing 120-grit paper to one side and 80-grit to the other. It's used for fitting purfling and binding when the chisel would be too risky, and also for sanding my nails when they get abused on the belt sander (nearly a daily occurrence). Jeff's tape dispenser is one of my favorite tools. In front of it is a marker that I made after we added a jumbo guitar to our line. I found that I couldn't confidently chisel clean channels on the round outline of the body, so the marker became necessary. Now I use it for every wood-bound guitar. Purfling cutters normally cost $30 or more, but this one took about twenty minutes to make from scrap walnut. See **Photo 4** for a better picture.

The #11 X-acto blade is superglued into a slot in the wood. I thought I'd remove it with a soldering iron when it got dull, but a bit of 600-grit paper glued to a stick sharpens it quite nicely. The head of a ¼″ bolt is buried in the knob, and a nut is sunk into the body of the tool. The adjustable section was slotted on the bandsaw, then a chunk of walnut was used to close the back end of the slot.

The second batch of tools **(Photo 3)** is much easier to describe. The sanding board is 4″×12″ and uses Stikit adhesive paper, usually 80 grit. It's wonderful for dressing all flat surfaces. When things get tight I snitch the 2″ drum from the spindle sander and use it with the same paper. The cabinet scraper is the same as everyone else's, and I find that I use it less and less. On figured maple binding it's just too dangerous. It does fine on plastic or ebony, but dried squeeze-out kills the edge. By the time I could resharpen it I can have the job done with the sanding board. The small flat-blade screw driver is used for setting abalone trim in place, and the mahogany-handled jigsaw blade is used to clean out the channels before the abalone is ready to go in.

A few random tips is all I have left to offer. Make sure the corners of the binding channels are square by scraping them with the corner of the chisel. If nothing else, this will force you to take a good look at the channels before the glue begins to flow.

All purflings and bindings have to butt together cleanly, but that doesn't apply to the Teflon strip when doing an abalone job. Leave a little tail of Teflon sticking out for the opposite set of trim to nest around. Your lines will meet more cleanly **(Photo 5)**.

On guitars with a round butt, it's difficult to tape binding in place and have the ends meet cleanly, so I made up a long C clamp out of mahogany and a ¼″ bolt. A shaped plexiglas caul completes the rig. Both sides of the binding are started at the butt and taped in place, then the clamp is applied **(Photo 6)**. Work one side until the clamp begins to interfere, then switch to the

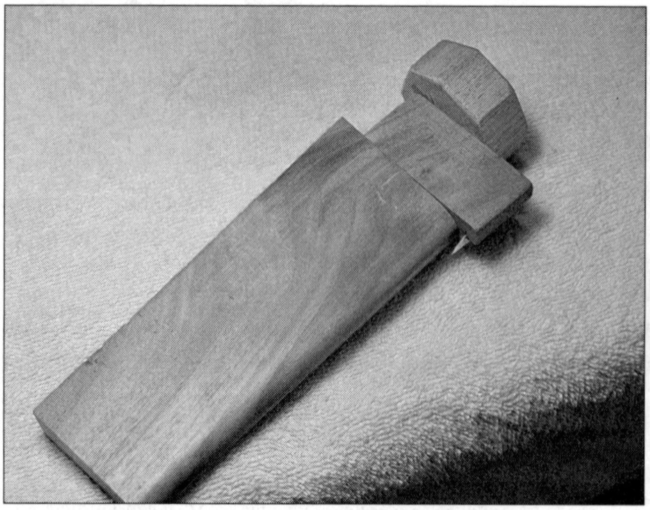

***Photo 4**. This purfling cutter was tossed together in a few minutes when the need arose. It doesn't actually remove any wood, but marks the channels precisely so that they can be accurately chiseled.*

***Photo 5**. When Teflon filler strips are used to lay up a purfling channel for abalone trim, a little tail of Teflon can be left protruding to help the opposite set of purflings line up with precision. Lines don't have to miss each other by much to catch the eye.*

other. Remove the clamp as soon as no more work can be completed with it in position.

Jeff has an electric whet stone for hollow-grinding tools, but I find that for maintaining my chisels after grinding, nothing works better than 600-grit paper taped to a flat surface. A strop of shoe leather glued to a board and charged with fine buffing compound finishes off an edge that will easily shave hair and keeps the chisel polished like a mirror at the same time.

All the little tools I've made have red knobs or handles. I can find them no matter where they land on the workbench.

A miter or butt joint in the purfling that's chopped too short should be shortened another 2″–3″. A fresh piece a shade oversize should be mitered into the original joint, then carefully fitted upstream with the orange stick. Such a patch is normally invisible. At the very least the muff will be moved away from the miter to a spot that doesn't automatically draw the eye.

This is gospel: make all initial router cuts for binding and purfling downhill to the grain of the top. That is, start each cut at the widest part of each bout and cut to the waist or the end joints of the sides. This will drastically reduce tearout of the top wood.

Hardly anything is as disgusting as a dried glue rag. I keep a damp rag handy and rinse it out three or four times a day. And my hands and the work come out in much cleaner condition.

Don't be impatient with yourself or the work. It took me dozens of guitars to feel comfortable with binding and to achieve a level of craftsmanship that I was happy with. One day I realized that things were beginning to go my way without any special effort, and now even the bitchy jobs usually turn out fine.

Oh yeah — a finisher who can ink in those muffed lines is a lifesaver, especially when you're just getting started in binding. ——

Photo 6. This clamp was made up to force a large stack of purflings and bindings into position on a round guitar body. A plexiglas caul is used to prevent sticking.

*(**Binding** from page 296)*

Wood binding grabs to the slot very quickly, but plastic tends to tip inward if the ivoroid is much taller than the slot. This causes fish mouths, or wide gaps between the rib and the plastic. Your finish person may beat you over the head for leaving this condition. Defeat it by using a length of Teflon or other nonstick substance as a clamping caul all the way around the body. Keep the Teflon low on the binding and the tape will automatically force the binding to stand straight. Now and then the Teflon can be tossed into the sink to soak off any glue that was stubborn enough to stick to it.

If you like, both free ends of the binding can be left loose to be mated at the neck end at same time. The purfling must be mitered to the back strip. A scrap of rosewood rib material can be used as a chopping block, and the work can be done right on the guitar back over the heel block. If necessary, chop it a shade long and fit it with an orange stick. With some experience you'll get it right with the chisel. Do a good job of fitting the trim that will be covered by the fingerboard, too. It's good practice.

Teflon is a lifesaver if you're installing abalone top trim. The Teflon strips are glued in where the abalone will go. When the binding has set the Teflon can be pulled out and the abalone dropped in. The Teflon strips are sometimes square and sometimes taller than wide. However, you can't pull them out until the trim is scraped flush with the top, and it's inevitable that some of the Teflon will be scraped also. After a couple of jobs it's hard to tell which dimension is the one you want. At that point it pays to measure the whole strip with a dial caliper and mark the surface that goes up. Retire the Teflon after four or five jobs. After the Teflon is removed there may still be a substantial amount of dried Titebond to remove from the slots. The best tool for this is simply a coarse jig saw blade, perhaps mounted in a wooden handle to protect your fingers. It yanks that crud right out of there.

If you've done your job right, there should be very little binding material standing proud of the ribs. Dress it off on the belt sander, then scrape any tight spots. If the binding is too tall a block plane can dress it down to the plates, though a scraper is safer and almost as fast. Dried glue is tough on scraper blades, and you may find that you need to finish with a sanding block to achieve an even surface. Figured maple binding may want to tear out no matter which direction you scrape. A few strokes in each direction will usually keep it compliant enough to get it close enough for a sanding block to finish the job. Recently we've discovered that a huge sanding block, say 4″×12″ and covered with 80-grit Stikit paper, will cut down the binding as quickly as a scraper and is much safer on figured wood.

We've made a special Dremel base for routing down abalone and the superglue it's held in with. It's fast, but it leaves a very irregular surface. A coarse sanding block will do the job if you're careful not to remove too much top material at the same time. Rough sanding the body will clean up any remaining glitches in the binding. ——

Originally published in *American Lutherie #57*, 1999

Meet the Maker: Joshia de Jonge

by Cyndy Burton

AT THE 1998 GAL CONVENTION I spoke with Joshia and Alan de Jonge, two young members of a guitar-making family from just outside Toronto, Canada. Joshia, age nineteen and her brother, age eleven, both exhibited their guitars.

Alan, you are by far the youngest guitar maker I've ever met. Tell me how this came about.

Alan: My dad has been making guitars for about thirty years. I just went into the shop. I was always making little things, like boxes. They're easy and fun. About two years ago I made a ukulele with eight strings for myself. Then I started the guitar with my dad. It's my first.

Who else in your family makes guitars?

Besides Joshia (she's the oldest), I have two older brothers who make guitars and one younger brother. He's only five, but he likes to sand things.

I really like the idea that your whole family is involved. What about your mother?

Joshia: She wants to, but she cooks for everyone. There are seven in our family plus the students taking dad's course. So she doesn't really have time. Our dad operates a guitar-making school, and the students often board with us. The school is set up to run nine weeks at a time, three times a year. Students have the option of room and board.

ALL COURTESY OF THE DE JONGE FAMILY

The guitar-making de Jonges, clockwise from upper left: Sagen (17), Sergei, Joshia (19), Alan (11), and Rubin (14).

Let's talk for a moment about the school. How many students are there? What kinds of guitars are made?

Joshia: My dad teaches either steel string or classical, whichever the students want. They get enough materials to make two guitars and he prefers to teach only two or three students each class, so they get a lot of individual attention. My dad's first love is classical guitar, but the students often want steel string, so that's what he teaches them. Anyone who wants to know more about the school can find us online (www.dejongelutherie.com).

Joshia, I understand you were born in Holland.

Joshia: Dad's originally from Holland, although he has lived most of his life in Canada and is a Canadian citizen. I was born in Amsterdam where my parents were living for one year. My brothers were all born in Canada.

Alan: I was born on the highway, actually.

You were what?

Joshia: He was born in the car. Our mom was on the way back from the dentist.

Alan: My dad was driving.

Joshia: She wasn't due for two weeks, but her water broke on the way home. They thought they still had time to get home. (My mom's had all of us at home.) My mom said, "Sergei, pull over." So he did, and out came Alan. The whole labor was fifteen minutes or so. He was put on her lap and they drove home.

That's a great story. What do your friends think of your guitar making, Alan?

Alan: They think it's pretty interesting. They like it. One of my friends would like me to make him one. I might do it if he pays me, or my dad.

Joshia, how young were you when you started making guitars?

Joshia: I was thirteen, but that first guitar took me three years. I worked on it once a week or so, an hour here, an hour there. It was a hobby. I started my second guitar when I was sixteen. I took the course my dad teaches along with the other students. For the past three years I've been building pretty steadily, although I travel for a couple months every year.

Are you still in school?

I stopped at grade eleven, and I've been doing guitars ever since except when I'm traveling. I went to Europe for two months this year, mainly for fun. I visited family we still have there. My dad and I went to a guitar festival; that was the excuse to go. He stayed for two weeks, and I stayed on six weeks longer.

I saw one of your guitars in Healdsburg last summer, which I understand you sold. What are your guitars like?

It's my own shape, which I think is more rounded and Spanish looking than my dad's, which is more Germanic looking. My dad learned from Jean Larrivée, who at the time was making only classical guitars. (My dad was his first apprentice.) Larrivée was taught by Edgar Mönch, who lived in Toronto but was originally from Germany. Larrivée now has a factory in Vancouver, which I worked at a couple of years ago for six weeks learning and doing inlay. My dad doesn't do much inlay these days, so I wanted to go somewhere else to learn it. It was a lot of fun, and it's something I would like to do more of in the future.

Joshia at work in her father's shop.

Are there any makers, besides your father, whose guitars you particularly admire? What kind of sound are you after?

I want my guitars to be loud, clear, and crisp. As for makers: Friederich in France; Jeff Elliott in the US; and a German guitar maker I met in Holland this summer, Sasha Novek. He's very traditional, uses only hot hide glue.

My dad's work is better than mine, but it's his design I'm using, except for the shape, so they sound pretty similar. My dad, brothers, and I all sort of work together on the bracing pattern. The classical guitar I brought to the convention, the one you heard in the listening session yesterday, is lattice braced. My brother Sagen (he's seventeen) got that going again. My dad also apprenticed with Patt Lister, who was working on a lattice at that time. We've been experimenting with variations on the lattice, which we make out of Sitka or Engelmann (not graphite-epoxy), on Engelmann, Sitka, cedar, or European spruce tops; even redwood now and then. I like the sound we've achieved with the lattice, and there's no distortion in the top the way there usually is with fan bracing.

I liked the sound of that guitar yesterday, and it was clearly appreciated by others, too. What woods do you like?

I like Engelmann and Sitka a lot. For back and sides, I have used Indian, mostly. The guitar you heard has ziricote back and sides and a Engelmann spruce top. I like Brazilian and maple, too. The steel string I have here is made from Canadian maple; it's pretty soft. I like the harder, denser maples, too. We've also used cocobolo, walnut, pau ferro, ebony, and padauk. One of the best guitars from our shop lately was one of my brother's, which was made of bocote (Mexican rosewood). I'd really like to try African blackwood.

Have you any special projects going right now?

Yes, I'm building a small Torres-shaped guitar, and I'm really enjoying it. I love all the woodworking at the beginning of the guitar, the bracing, bending, and so on. I don't like routers at all. And once it gets into lacquer, all the sanding and the finish work gets tedious, but I like all the hand work. We use nitrocellulose lacquer, but I'd like to learn to French polish.

How much are you selling your guitars for, and do you work through dealers?

They sell in the US for $3,600 for Indian/Engelmann; $800 to $900 more for Brazilian, and I sell through dealers, mostly.

Thanks for taking the time to talk with me. I'm looking forward to meeting the rest of your family one day. (Note: About an hour after the interview, Joshia tapped on my shoulder and announced with a big grin that she'd just sold her classical guitar, and not to a dealer, either.) ——

This photo of one of Sergei's guitars shows the bracing pattern that Joshia used on the classical guitar she brought to the 1998 GAL Convention.

Originally published in *American Lutherie #57,* 1999

Stick with Hide Glue

from their 1998 GAL Convention workshop

by Frank Ford and Don MacRostie

Frank: Don and I are going to tell you in our long-winded way that we think hide glue is the ideal wood adhesive, better than anything else in the world. But there's one small problem. It's kind of difficult to work with.

Everyone in this room has eaten hide glue. In our business we often deal with toxic materials, but there are two materials that we deal with that are approved by the FDA as food: hide glue and shellac. Hide glue is used on envelopes and stamps, where you lick it and eat it. Shellac is used on the outside of M&Ms to keep them from sticking to your hands.

Hide glue is simply gelatin, derived from the collagen of animal skins. They boil the skins in a lye solution to extract the protein. In this country, hide glue is generally made from beef skins and the gelatin that we eat is made from pork skins. You can get it in the supermarket as Knox unflavored gelatin.

Hide glue can come from rabbit skins and sturgeon swim bladders and other things in its more exotic forms, but the beef hide glue that we're using here is the common stuff. It has a lot of current industrial uses. They put cardboard boxes together with it, and certain kinds of plywood are still made with the stuff. It's what sticks the sand on the nonwaterproof garnet sandpaper. It's used a lot in book binding. We see it in instrument cases because in industrial quantities it's still about the cheapest glue you can buy. For putting the linings in cases they use the cheapest grade, which is the smelliest. It smells so bad that Harptone dumps in a bunch of oil of peppermint to cover up the stink. Gelatin is also used as the emulsion on photographic film. Eastman Kodak has their own plant making the stuff.

Hide glue has many attractive qualities. The clear grade of hide glue does not stain wood at all. It's transparent on wood, and you can even use it for sizing the wood before finishing. When it's hot it has a low viscosity, so it runs into cracks pretty well. If it's too strong or too thick you can dilute it and you don't necessarily lose all the strength. It's extremely brittle and won't slide under any circumstance, even in high heat. It cleans up instantly with water — it's great for clean up. And it is the traditional stuff instruments are made with so it is the stuff that people are likely to encounter if they're repairing instruments.

On the negative side, hide glue is the most temperamental of all the glues we deal with. It's water soluble, and that can sometimes be a problem. In warm, wet climates it is attractive to animals such as bacteria. It has poor gap-filling qualities, so parts have to fit right. You have to deal with preparing it every day. It has to be clamped immediately before it gets cool or you're dead. And it tends to swell the parts.

Hide glue also comes in a crummy commercial grade that looks like brown gravy. That's the color I always thought hide glue was. Be sure to get the good, clear stuff.

There's only one manufacturer left in North America where they actually render the skins for hide glue. It's a place called Milligan & Higgins, in Johnstown, NY. They have been in business there since 1868. They don't make an edible gelatin, although their glue tech said that their better grade of industrial hide glue probably tastes better than much of the gelatin sold for food. I don't know if you have ever cooked up Knox unflavored gelatin or tasted it, but it's pretty foul stuff.

There was another manufacturer called Peter Cooper years ago that you may think of as the classic glue manufacturer. They're out of business now. An article appeared in *Fine Woodworking* years ago that showed them using bulldozers to move the hides around in the warehouse. They were a big industrial operation.

A curious fact is that the adhesive strength of hide glue is actually measured in terms of its firmness as gelatin. They make up the desired solution, which happens to be 12½% solid protein material, let it gel, and cool it to 10°C. Then they press a ½″ diameter plunger into the jelly and measure how much force it takes to push the plunger down 4MM. That force in grams is known as the gram strength of glue.

Hide glue is available in different gram strengths. You can buy it as very strong glue at 512G, and you can buy it as very weak glue at 80G. Woodworking glues are somewhere in the range of 135G–280G. The most commonly used glue in the woodworking industry has a rating of 192. Why would you buy one strength or another? The higher the gram strength the faster it sets up and the higher the temperature at which it starts to gel, so you get less working time with the high-strength glue. In fact there's so little working time that you must heat the parts and work in a hot environment as well. It's considered too "strong" for woodworking, meaning that it gels too fast at room temperature to be clamped before it loses its ability to adhere. The weakest hide glue is incredibly strong stuff and well beyond our needs. That's why I've chosen the 192G for my use: it gives the longest working time for a reasonable glue and it also happens to be one of the strengths that's available in the absolutely transparent form.

Good quality glue is currently available from Stewart-MacDonald as Behlen's dry hide glue. This is 251 strength, by the way. You can buy it directly from Milligan & Higgins but you have to buy a 50 lb. sack. That's not a big deal, because it doesn't cost much. That's what I've done and what a lot of violin guys do. Buy a 50 lb. sack of granular hide glue, put it into little baggies, and store them in your attic or someplace dry. It has an unlimited shelf life as long as it's kept dry. Once you learn to use this particular batch of glue you'll have a lifetime supply.

This stuff is not user friendly. You don't just squirt it out of a squeeze bottle and clamp it up. First you have to weigh it out and mix it by weight with water so that you get a consistent mixture each time. You can't measure it by volume because all the fine stuff jiggles to the bottom. The bottom becomes more dense than the top and the mixture would be a different consistency. It's not like life or death, but it's easiest to get used to laying this stuff if the solution is the same each time.

Mix the granules with a little less than two times their weight in cold water. They soak up the water in an hour or two, depending on how coarse the granules are. It will be a weird jelly consistency, sort of like tapioca. It has no sticky texture to it at all. OK, maybe a little.

Now we must heat it to a usable consistency and stir it up. This is sometimes known as cooking the glue. This is a semantic problem, because "cooking" the glue can also mean overheating. When the dry glue has soaked up all the water, heat it to about 145°F, but no hotter. Stir it into a nice smooth consistency and let it cool. You'll get something very much like Jell-O.

Hide glue has to be used while it's hot in liquid form. We have to heat this Jell-O stuff up to a temperature of around 120°F–145°F, in a dry glue pot like Don's going to show us later, or some other mechanism. Some people will use a glue pot sitting there in a little cauldron of hot water, always nice and warm with a brush ready to slop on the glue when you need it. Some people will mix it and heat it at the last minute as they need it. The important thing is to not overheat the glue for a long period of time because eventually it breaks down the quality of the long-chain molecules and it loses its strength.

Hot hide glue has a fast grab. It has a better fast grab, I think, than Titebond. As you press the two pieces together, the liquid glue squeezes out between the pieces and starts to grab a little bit. At that point you put on the final clamping pressure before it turns to jelly which doesn't stick very well and can't be clamped. If you're clamping up hide glue and it turns a little gelatinous on you, you're just simply dead and the only alternative you have is either to reheat the whole piece to the point where the glue flows again or you take it apart and wash off the glue and start over.

I talked to some guys at the Martin factory who were working during the years they used hide glue, and they said "we used to swear a lot at the people who would open the door and let the cold wind in because it would blow across our work piece and we'd be washing off the glue." Their glue-up room, by the way, was steam heated year 'round to about 95°F. That was typical of manufacturing places where they wanted to keep the glue in a workable consistency and still have a little bit of open time while working. Even then, they would put the part to be glued over on the steam radiator for a little while to give it a little extra warmth, and then go back to glue it up. When I'm gluing a bridge on a guitar, I use a microwave and zap it for a few seconds to get the bridge up to 150°F–180°F so that when I walk over to the bench to clamp it down the bridge acts as a secondary heating device to make sure that my glue stays warm while I'm clamping it. Some parts you can do that with and some you can't.

Hide glue dries entirely by evaporation. There is no chemical change in the glue whatsoever as it dries. This means it has no resistance to water; water simply dissolves it. That's not a problem, because our instruments will not be soaked in water, we hope. But it also means that if you take apart a hide-glued joint, you can slap on some more warm liquid glue and it will reactivate the old glue. It can often be reclamped without cleaning the joint, which could be helpful in regluing braces.

Prepared hide glue is ⅓ glue and ⅔ water. That means as it dries, ⅔ of it is going to go away in the form of shrinkage. You have to be aware of that so you don't get a sinkhole in that area when you sand it and level. In the case of a center seam you want to make sure that it dries thoroughly way down inside, so you want that joint to stay clamped long enough to be set hard.

Like many glues, hide glue sticks by electrochemical adhesion; it makes a molecular bond to the wood itself. It does not depend on little fingers that reach up and grip into the pores. So it doesn't do a damn bit of good to rough up the surfaces, in fact it probably does a little harm. Hide glue doesn't form a good bond unless the two parts fit together tight. If they don't, you're counting on the cohesive strength of the glue. Guess what? It just doesn't have it. Hide glue has very little cohesive strength, so a thick glue joint is going to fail. Epoxy, in contrast, is a glue with a very high cohesive strength and it does get those little fingers that reach up inside the pores. Epoxy will fill a gap of any size.

For electrochemical adhesion to work, the joint needs to be very clean. I learned about this the hard way by putting a new bridge plate overlay on a Martin rosewood bridge plate using hide glue. As I was drilling the hole for a bridge pin, the overlay just fell off. I had an abject and complete glue failure. I didn't clean the surface of the rosewood first, and the heavily oxidized surface just wasn't going to accept the glue. As a result I had no adhesion at all.

By the way, "liquid hide glue" in a bottle is the same stuff as hide glue, but with the addition of chemicals known as gel extenders, urea being the chief one. With these additives, the glue doesn't gel at room temperature and so it has a very long open time. These additives also give liquid hide glue a short shelf life. But the most significant problem is that it doesn't have the one characteristic that we especially prize in hide glue, the resistance to creeping. Liquid hide glue may creep a bit under tension, especially at high temperatures. That to me is an extremely important thing for guitar bridges and any joints that are under stress, particularly when it gets warm.

Anybody who thinks guitars don't get warm is denying the reality of automobile travel. I'm not saying

ALL THIS PAGE BY FRANK FORD

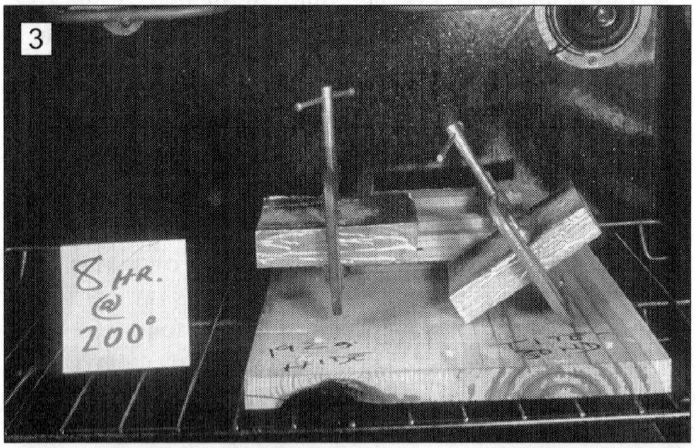

that every new Martin guitar is going to fall apart because it's put together with white glue, but I am saying that the guitars they made with hide glue in the '40s don't have the problems that the current ones do in high heat stress. With hide glue we see no tendency for bridges to slide forward, no tendency for top joints to slide, no tendency for fingerboards to slip and allow neck curvature. We do see those things with the modern Titebond.

Photo 1 shows a little rig I put together to heat test some glue. It consists of two sets of two pieces of redwood about ½″ square which overlap about ¾″. One overlap is glued with Titebond and the other with hide glue. Each of the first legs is screwed to a board, such that the joint is cantilevered out over the board and supporting a 3 lb. lead weight. The C clamps are there just to hold the weights on. I'm stressing the hell out of these little joints. If I put two of these 3 lb. weights on, it breaks the joint. That's a wood failure, not a glue failure. So I figure I'm stressing the joint to about ½ of what it can handle. I put this rig in my oven. **Photo 2** shows that after seven minutes at 200°F, the Titebond joint failed completely and the lead dropped right off. Seven minutes at 200°F was all it took. The full heat didn't penetrate the joint by any means. I'll do more heat testing later on, but this happens to be the lowest temperature that my oven can be controlled at.

Check out **Photo 3.** It's been eight hours at 200°F, and the hide glue is still doing its job. From this test, repeated several times, I concluded that hide glue is far more resistant to heat stress than Titebond. By the way, I started raising the temperature in the oven just to see what would happen and I got to the point where my smoke detector went off. *(laughter)* The wood charred at 350°F and the glue was still holding. This explains how we can see old instruments that have been in a fire with their joints still amazingly intact.

Photo 4 shows how the joints looked after failure. Titebond just completely let go. The hide glue started to let go after I stressed extra hard and broke the wood itself. This is a classic failure of white glue, which by the way is still aliphatic resin similar to Titebond.

This is a Martin guitar in **Photo 5.** You may not know it, but Martin has a policy of salvaging what they consider to be a nearly perfect guitar top. If it's in production and they find a little flaw in the wood, before it's joined to be a guitar top they'll introduce it to Mr. Table Saw and slice that piece out and convert it to a four-piece guitar top. So this is a factory glue joint that failed. You can see that it slid forward under the stress, and now it has a bad neck angle. Both braces under there are intact and still glued down, indicating that the glue slid over them and resolidified. All of this happened in a hot car. That's one reason I'm a crusader about heat stress and glue.

Don: The nonslipping characteristic of hide glue is important to me for structural reasons as well as for tonal transmission. I build instruments and I want them to sound good. It seems to me that a glue that is really a soft plastic is more of an absorber of vibrations than a transmitter. Hide glue is hard and crystalline when cured, and therefore is desirable for the following joints: tone bars and braces, top and back center seams, gluing tops and backs onto rims, neck joints, and attaching fingerboards. As you gathered from what Frank said, the only reason that all of us aren't using it is the difficulty in preparing and handling it. I'm going to describe how I have overcome these problems in my work.

Some people heat glue in a bath of hot water. I get kind of clumsy when I'm working fast, so I built this dry pot several years ago (**Fig. 1** and **Photo 6**). Now I don't risk knocking over a pot of water. This pot is just a lamp inside a couple coffee cans. The space between the cans is insulated, and there's a household dimmer so I can dial in the amount of power that goes to the light. As the light gets brighter, it produces more heat. The lid holds a little jar for my glue. I can heat very small amounts or quite a bit in there. I've got a small, inexpensive thermometer and this cover which slows down heat loss from the jar. Using the dimmer and watching the thermometer, I can control the glue temperature.

The HoldHeet glue pot, which is available through several woodworking catalogs as well as Stew-Mac, can also be adapted for smaller amounts of glue (**Fig. 2**). Make a lid to hold your glue jar. I'm using a tapered jar with a nice-fitting, bayonet-style lid, just a grocery store item. This happens to be Cheez Whiz, but you can get jam and other things in a jar like this. *(laughter)* This is a good alternative if you don't want to make a glue pot out of coffee cans. You could probably adapt a crock pot, although I have never done that.

I have a hot pot that I use for warm water, and I keep my glue brushes in it. The hot water is also good for cleaning glue squeeze.

I prepare the glue just as I need it, which would be the day before. That seems to be the most successful for me. Soak the dry glue in cool water (see **Grading Chart** for recommended mix). Let the glue granules soak up all the water and swell. This will take at least an hour or two. Heat this to 145°F, let it melt into a uniform syrup, then let it cool and gel. Sometimes I'll make up a large batch, let it cool, and cut it into chunks which I store in the refrigerator. I can throw a chunk into the glue pot and soon I'm ready to glue. I can sweeten up the glue pot when it gets low by throwing in another piece.

I've kept the gelled glue for more than a month in the fridge. If it starts to look wet, if it starts to separate, or if it gets moldy at all, throw it out. But as long as it stays dry and fresh looking, it's OK.

The difficulty is in spreading the glue and clamping quickly enough. The glue will just sit there all day in the pot ready to use, but as soon as you remove some from the pot and start using it, it's going to begin cooling and drying. And as soon as it returns to the gel state, it is no longer usable. So you will need to be prepared to work fast.

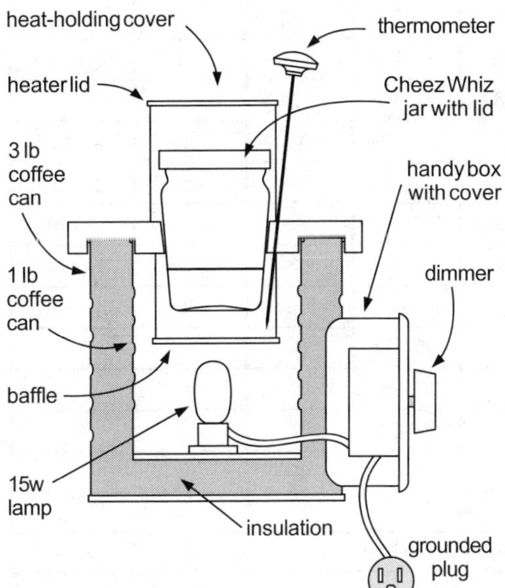

Figure 1. Don's dry glue pot

DON MACROSTIE

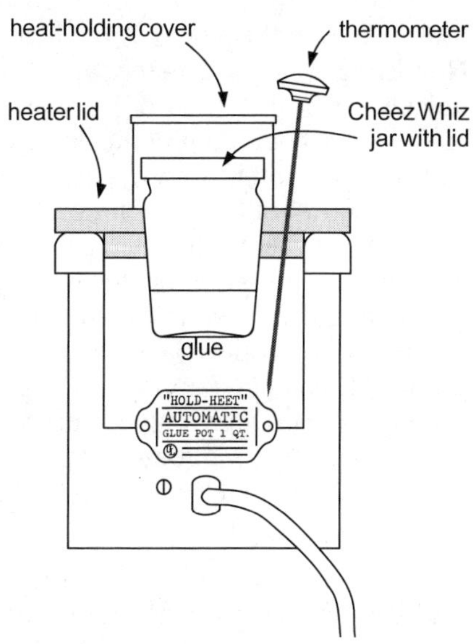

Figure 2. Modified "HoldHeet" glue pot

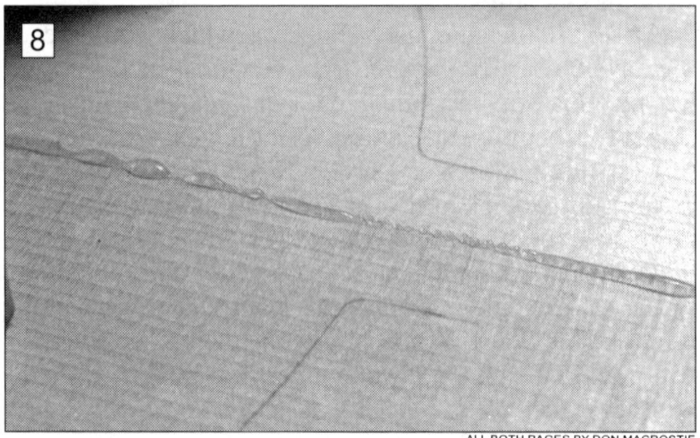

ALL BOTH PAGES BY DON MACROSTIE

I do mostly building, so I'll discuss my approach to handling hot hide glue from that point of view. One of the first things I do is glue up center seams (**Photos 7 and 8**). I get all set up, and when I'm ready to glue I use a heat gun on the parts. You want to get the surface of the wood up above 85°F–95°F, the point where the glue gels. With clamps ready to go, quickly apply a generous amount of the hot glue to the warm parts. At this point if I need any additional heat, I use a heat lamp so that I am not driving moisture from the glue with the heat gun. Now bring the parts together and clamp quickly.

The glue comes out of the pot at about 140°F–145°F and if the parts are heated to around 100°F you've got a minute or two of working time before the glue gels. If you're working in a cold room, in the winter, or if the room is drafty, your working time will be shortened. I only coat one surface, but it's heavily coated. I apply a lot of glue so it will maintain enough temperature and the proper viscosity to squeeze out well. If I were to use this much Titebond I would have a lot of squeeze-out.

Frank: The more glue you use, the longer it's likely to stay warm. A lot of squeeze-out is sometimes a good thing.

Don: There are two problems to watch for with hide glue. First is the starved joint, which you can get by over clamping or using glue that's mixed too thin. The second is a cold joint, which is caused by not working fast enough or working in too cold a room. In a cold joint the glue gels before the clamping pressure is applied. Both conditions result in joint failures.

When bracing a top I use a go-bar deck (**Photo 9**). Go-bars are very quick to set, and I use positioning jigs so I don't waste time getting parts in alignment. This tone bar gluing setup is a plaster mold of the outside of my carved top. I position my top in this mold with positioning pins. This gives perfect backup for the pressure of clamping. With this setup I am able to get tone bars glued up under any room conditions.

You're looking for some squeeze-out when you clamp. You want to see a nice clear liquid freely squeezing out. If you see thick, cloudy glue coming out, you've probably got a cold joint. It may look like it's sticking but any kind of stress will pop it.

I glue tops on in the go-bar deck also (**Photo 10**). Again with a mold to hold the rim in position, and pins to locate the top, I can focus all my efforts on quickly spreading glue, putting the top in position, and clamping. For this setup I use a heat lamp to keep the area warm. I'll spread the glue right under the heat lamp and its warmth retards the glue's tendency to cool and gel. As I spread it around, the wood will soak up

Hide Glue Grading Chart					average mix ratio water to glue by weight	
NAGM grade[1]	Peter Cooper grade[2]	midpoint grade[3]	gram strength	viscosity millipoise	porous woods	nonporous woods
18	5A Extra	512	496-529	191		
17	4A Extra	477	461-494	175		
16	3A Extra	444	428-460	157		
15	2A Extra	411	395-427	145		
14	A Extra	379	363-394	131	3 to 1	3¼ to 1
13	1 Extra	347	331-362	121	2¾ to 1	3 to 1
12	1 Extra Spec	315	299-330	111	2½ to 1	2¾ to 1
11	No. 1	283	267-298	101	2¼ to 1	2½ to 1
10	1 XM	251	237-266	92	2¼ to 1	2½ to 1
9	1 X	222	207-236	82	2 to 1	2¼ to 1
8	1¼	192	178-206	72	1¾ to 1	2 to 1
7	1⅜	164	150-177	63	1½ to 1	1¾ to 1
6	1½	135	122-149	58	1¼ to 1	1½ to 1
5	1⅝	108	95-121	53		
4	1¾	85	70-94	44		
	1⅞	58	47-69	34		
	No. 2	32	10-46	30		

[1] National Association of Glue Manufacturers

[2] Peter Cooper Co. 1827 to 1984 (first grading system)

[3] Milligan and Higgins Inc. current grade specification

the glue pretty quickly on the first application. I put it on fairly thin at first, then I go back around with a heavier coat. Because wood is like a sponge, it's going to want to suck the moisture right out of the glue.

For gluing on the back, I use spring clamps (**Photo 11**). These are real fast and I haven't yet figured out how to hold the complicated shape of an F-style body in the go-bar deck. I might wind up going to it some day, but right now, I use spring clamps. Again, quick clamping, efficient positioning, and supplemental warmth from the heat lamp are all needed.

I've used hide glue on some binding, especially on a repair where I didn't want glue solvents getting onto the finish, and it has worked well. I don't use it for attaching plastic binding to new instruments, but I think it would be ideal if you are using wood bindings. I have also glued plastic pickguards onto finished tops with hide glue and they have stayed on well. I got that idea when I found out that one of the traditional uses for hide glue is glass chipping. Professional office doors have this nice chip-textured glass. That's done with hide glue. They mix up a low-strength hide glue, lay it on the glass in a fairly thick layer, and as it dries it adheres to the glass, shrinks, and pulls little chips out of the glass. Now that's adhesion!

Audience: *Do you have a problem with people peering around in your instruments to see if there are little blobs of glue coming out from under the lining?*

Don: You can see that, but I don't mind. If you get the right amount of glue on, you'll get just enough squeeze-out. Now, this may not be the case for all instruments, but as a mandolin builder I'm a little proud of it. *(laughter)*

Frank: Mandolin players are just as big weenies as guitar players, but they're looking at different things. *(laughter)* So they are typically not criticizing a little glue squeeze-out the way you hear guitar players looking inside the guitars, trying to judge whether it looks like an old Harmony or an old Martin.

My shop is generally rather cool. Am I going to have a problem using hide glue?

Don: Either you're going to have to work extremely fast or raise your room temperature. Many of us work in small shops, and we can't devote a room to a 90°F area. I've thought about a shower curtain or something like that in one corner of my shop. I could close it off, put in a little quartz heater, and that would be my glue area. I may do that one of these days.

Frank: Violin makers often have to work on cellos, which are even nastier than guitars when it comes to how fast you can put them together. Their typical technique is to put the glue on with a thin palette knife and work a 6″ or 8″ section at a time, poking and clamping all around the edge. It works very efficiently. You can glue when the parts are very close together, you just open them up and stick the glue in and slam them shut.

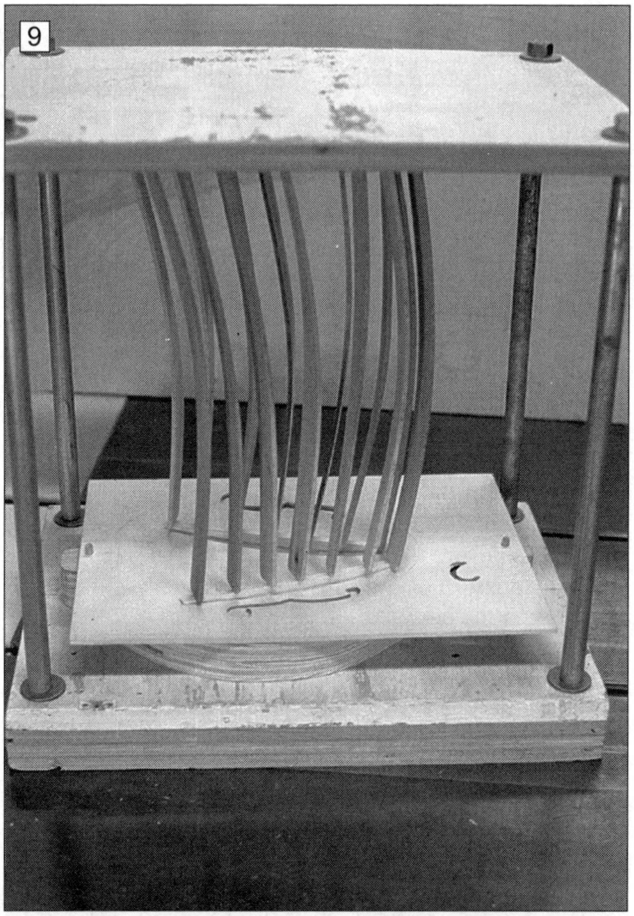
9

10

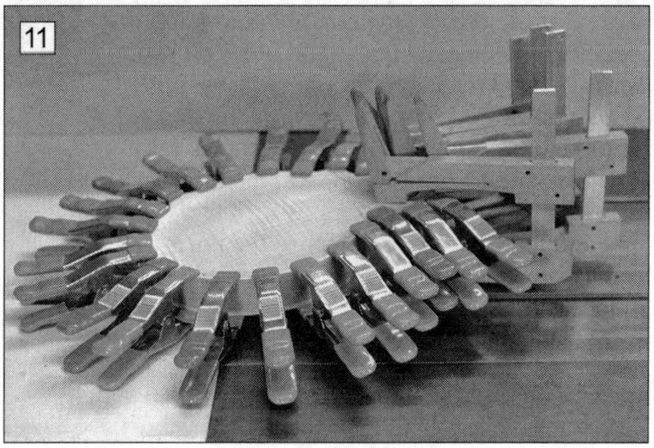
11

Wouldn't it make sense to moisten the edge of your top so that slows down the gelling process?

Frank: No, because it would dilute the glue too much.

Don: It might result in a starved joint. Too much of the glue would squeeze out.

Now we've got the body done. The next thing is to glue the neck and fingerboard. The extender joint, when it's fit well, will not need to be clamped (**Photos 12 and 13**). It has a lot of gluing surface, and is not prone to moving around. I just press it on. It's essentially a rub joint. The dovetail joint is also a good candidate for hide glue. It is quick to assemble and clamp, and I think the crystalline nature of hide glue allows for the full transmission of sound vibrations from the neck to the body.

12

13

ALL THIS PAGE BY DON MACROSTIE

In preparation for attaching the fingerboard, I put the mandolin in this setup that holds the body and supports the neck in a couple of spots (**Photo 14**). I use long rubber bands to quickly wrap and bring clamping pressure on the fingerboard. With enough wraps, you get quite a lot of pressure. This method naturally centers the fingerboard and gives it pressure at the edges where you most need it. That's been my solution to using hide glue to put fingerboards on.

I'm gluing fretted fingerboards which are backbowed. In order to keep the backbow from bowing the neck I've set this center support down about .007″–.010″, and I pull the neck down onto it with the rubber band as I am clamping the fretboard. When it dries, it springs back up, but now it's springing back to straight. It takes a little experience to figure out just how much it will spring up, but I can hit it real close.

Frank: When Don is gluing his fingerboard on he's introducing a lot of water to the top side of the neck. That's going to cause a backbow. That's the other reason for him putting that center support down a little bit lower; you can actually clamp a slight sag into it so that it springs out straight.

Any water-based glue will swell the wood. A lot of the industrial people are switching away from waterborne glues or water-soluble glues to avoid having necks and other parts change shape from moisture absorption. When I build banjo necks, they're long and skinny and extremely flexible and they'll take a reverse curve about $^{1}/_{8}$″ high in the center. If I clamp it to that exact opposite, it springs up completely straight. Because the joint can't slip and it's under tension, the neck is incredibly stiff.

How about the preparations when you glue on a bridge? Do you ever scratch it with a knife?

Frank: No, I think the best literature and the best indications are that scratching it doesn't help at all. It might hurt a little bit. Smooth is better, except that some people think that the scratches make it easier to position it and hold it in place. But I think that scratching the bottom of the bridge is a piece of older technology that's not being used much. Most of us think that just flat and clean is best. Smoothing it with a scraper is ideal.

Don: Just remember how well hide glue sticks to glass.

How long do you leave it clamped?

Don: Most joints I'll leave three or four hours, and then I won't stress or work the parts for twenty-four hours. I leave the fingerboard clamped for twelve hours. It's under stress already, so I like giving it the extra time. I've heard as little as ten minutes for some people. The rub joints certainly show that is possible.

Frank: The classic way to clamp hide glue in the old-time tradition is with no clamps at all. In fact it's simply by mashing the two pieces together by hand.

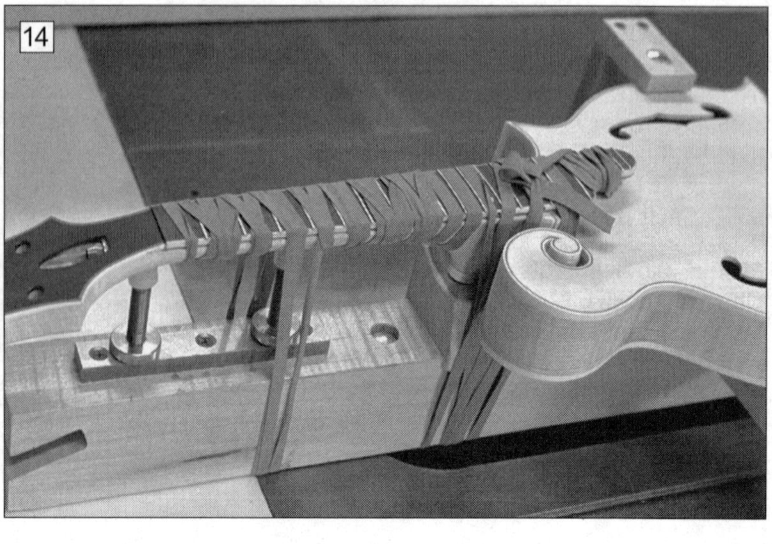
14

Eugene Clark is one of our favorite classical guitar makers and he says that he's used this style of bridge attachment for his entire career and never had any problems with it. It's what's known as a rub joint and it's the Spanish way, I understand. You have your guitar top prepared smooth and clean, and your bridge prepared smooth and clean. You slap on the glue, plop the bridge down, shove it into position very hard, and hold it. And that's it. Hold it until it gels. As it gels, the two parts are held together tight enough to hold together and if you don't disturb them they tend to suck together tighter as the glue shrinks and dries.

One of my interests in using this is to be able to remove a top. Would you briefly describe the process of taking a top off of one of these instruments after it's hide glued?

Don: I don't think hide glue makes it any easier to separate cured joints. In fact I think I can release Titebond easier using heat. Hide glue requires both heat and moisture. So I wouldn't use standard mix hide glue with the idea that you want to be able to take the joint apart. Now, if it comes apart on its own, it's easier to fix. Hide glue can be weakened by mixing it with more water. Violin builders do this with tops and backs for safe removal.

Frank: Taking a top off of one of these instruments is pure misery with lots of splinters and chips, if you're prying it off.

Are there ever any situations when you do coat two surfaces?

Frank: I always coat both surfaces. Partly because I want to have a real lake of glue there for the extra heat and partly because I can be extra sloppy since I'm doing repair work and I usually have extra time to play with. So when I mash a bridge down on a guitar and I get a bunch of squeeze-out, I let it gel and just roll it up and throw it away. Don's concerned, I think, with too much squeeze-out looking ugly inside the instrument.

What do you advise for cleaning up hide glue? Is it risky to use water while the glue is still wet?

Frank: I find water is not a problem for me. And I use the warm water that surrounds the glue in the glue pot if I happen to be using the glue pot. Dip a rag in there and then just wipe it right down.

Don: As soon as I get it clamped, I start cleaning up. A rag dampened with warm water will remove excess glue without harming the curing joint.

Have you tried gluing braces with hide glue in a vacuum clamp? Does it dry faster or create any problems?

Don: Vacuum clamping shouldn't create a problem. The vacuum draws moisture out and that's the way hide glue dries. I think it would do fine in a vacuum clamp. Temperature and speed is the name of the game. If you can keep the parts warm and get good squeeze-out, you should be OK. ——

Originally published in *American Lutherie #56*, 1998

QUESTIONS

EDITED BY CYNDY BURTON

■ ***Woody Vernice of Oshkosh, WI** asks:*

Assume that scale length and string gauge don't change. How can the break angle of the headstock, height of the bridge (assuming the same action setup), or length of a tailpiece have any affect on playability? For the feel to change, wouldn't the string tension have to change?

***Tim Olsen** answers:*

Imagine two guitars with the same scale length, string gauge, fret size, and action height. One is a shred Strat with a locking nut and bridge. The other is a jazz guitar with a long peghead and lots of string between the bridge and tailpiece. It takes exactly the same pull to bring a string up to pitch on each guitar — pitch is a function of a string's density, tension, and vibrating length, not total length — yet the two guitars will have a different playing feel. Why? Because strings are stretchy. If they weren't, they would just break and never come up to pitch. When the string is pushed to the fret, it has to stretch a little bit. The resistance you feel when fretting the Strat will be a function of the stretchiness of the vibrating length of the string. On the jazz guitar, it will be a function of the stretchiness of the vibrating length, plus the string between the nut and the tuning gear, plus the string between the bridge and tailpiece. Those areas of the string outside the playing length form a sort of spring with extra stretchiness that makes the string feel less tight, so a heavier string can be used without the feel of the action becoming too stiff.

I asked Jimmy D'Aquisto about this in 1992. He said that many makers, including his teacher John D'Angelico, had it all wrong when they made tailpieces which had the bass strings much longer than the trebles behind the bridge. Jimmy went to a straight-across tailpiece early in his career, and finally settled on a V-shaped arrangement where the E strings were the shortest. I asked him if this was not backward, considering the extra lengths at the peghead. He said no, the small wound G string should have the greatest total extra length.

*And **Jeff Elliott of Portland, OR** adds:*

The feeling of string tension is also affected by the interaction between the neck and the body when the strings are in motion. The more lightly the instrument is built, the greater the interaction. I have made two classical guitars as identical as possible in every way, and yet the "feel" was different. I attribute this to the way the instrument interacts with itself, that is, the interaction between the neck and the body. If the instrument was made of some basically immutable material, like concrete, I have no doubt that the feel would be identical. I discuss this in greater depth in my article (see p. 230). ——

Originally published in *American Lutherie #57,* 1999

Estimating an Initial Soundboard Thickness
for Various Wood Types Using Physical Properties Data
by David C. Hurd

IT IS SAID by some luthiers that since every piece of wood is different, we can't hope to develop an orderly rationale for voicing an instrument. Each piece must be flexed and tapped, and as a result of the cumulative experience of making a hundred or more instruments, one will develop a "feel" for what's right. In that many luthiers follow this approach, it must surely be valid for a portion of the lutherie community.

However, as a former research scientist, I have difficulty applying this approach to my work. I learned the hard way that my senses of touch and hearing vary from any one time period to the next. Thus I have tried to formalize the measurement process by investing in balances for measuring mass; micrometers to measure thickness of tops, backs, and braces; frequency generators for accurate tone generation; and a computer and software for doing calculations and obtaining acoustical data.

I am not alone in my interest for such techniques. Scientists and engineers have been quantifying wood properties for more than a hundred years and many of the techniques are well described. Articles in this journal and others have begun the process whereby we as a community can gather information in a more quantitative way to help those interested in such approaches.

We can measure the properties of an untried piece of wood, compare the results with other woods which have worked well for instrument making, and make a more a rational decision regarding the utility of the untried piece. Knowing the properties of a given plate or batch of brace wood also allows you to begin the voicing process from a consistent starting place. Then, if an extraordinary instrument results, you will be much closer to answering one of lutherie's most frustrating questions: "What did I do right?"

What properties can the average builder collect routinely which will yield a useful long-term data resource? Much depends on the maker's commitment and willingness to invest in time and equipment. This article will describe the simplest measurements to make, and then suggest a simplified mathematical approach for using this information to compare wood samples of varying density and stiffness for use as instrument tops.

Types of Wood Properties Data to be Collected

I think that it is safe to say that builders and players alike would agree that the stiffness of the materials used for making an instrument is of primary importance in determining its sound quality. The actual stiffness of a given piece of wood is determined by its length, width, and depth. In order to predict the stiffness of the same piece of wood for a different set of measurements, we need to determine the inherent stiffness coefficients of that piece of wood both parallel with, and perpendicular to the grain. The stiffness coefficients (Young's moduli) may be measured statically (by deformation under load) and dynamically (by frequency). From my measurements, I have found that these two approaches are comparable within 10%–15% of each other. The static approach is outlined by Hoadley (1980) and the dynamic approach by Caldersmith (1984). I do dynamic measurements on all of the brace, top, and back materials for my instruments and sometimes static measurements on brace material. I also maintain a database of these measurements for different wood types.

Static Young's modulus. From Hoadley (1980) we can see how to determine the static Young's modulus for a center-loaded beam or plate. The appropriate equation is:

Static Young's modulus along the grain

$$\textbf{(1)}\qquad E_X = \frac{K\ P\ L_X^3}{y\ L_y\ h^3}$$

where

- K is a constant dependent on the geometry of the system (for a center-loaded beam or plate, K = .25)
- P is the applied force
- y is the deflection of the beam or plate under force P
- L_X is the length (parallel to grain)
- L_y is the width (perpendicular to grain)
- h is the beam or plate thickness

In practice, h is the most difficult measurement to make accurately for plates. Measurements should be taken from a number of places around the plate and averaged.

If length and width are in inches and mass in lbs., Young's moduli will be in PSI, and usually in the range of 1–2 million PSI. For comparison, graphite/epoxy rods from Moses, Inc. are about 10 million PSI. Conversion to metric units of Newtons per square meter (N/M^2) or $KG/M/sec^2$ requires multiplying by 6897.

The parallel-to-grain stiffness will change, but in a predictable manner according to the above equation: for a constant value of E_X, if the plate or beam *length* becomes *smaller,* then stiffness *increases* and deflection *decreases*. If plate or beam *thickness* and/or *width* becomes *smaller,* stiffness *decreases* and deflection *increases*.

Dynamic Young's modulus. As explained by Caldersmith (1984), the basic data for the dynamic study of a flat sheet of wood's stiffness characteristics are the following:

- L_x is its length (parallel to grain)
- L_y is its width (perpendicular to grain)
- h is its thickness
- M is its mass
- f_x is the first natural mode parallel to grain
- f_y is the first mode perpendicular to grain
- $f_{x,y}$ is the torsional, or twisting mode

Using these data, first the density D and then the dynamic Young's moduli or elasticity coefficients E for the plate are calculated.

(2) Density

$$D = \frac{M}{L_x\ L_y\ h}$$

(3) Dynamic Young's modulus along grain

$$E_x = \frac{D\ L_x^4\ f_x^2}{1.05\ h^2}$$

(4) Dynamic Young's modulus across grain

$$E_y = \frac{D\ L_y^4\ f_y^2}{1.05\ h^2}$$

(5) Dynamic Young's twisting modulus

$$E_{x,y} = \frac{2.43\ D\ L_x^2\ L_y^2\ f_{x,y}^2}{h^2}$$

If lengths and widths are in meters and mass in KG, Young's moduli are in N/M^2 or KG/sec^2/M, and usually in the range 7–14 billion N/M^2. Equivalent English units are in millions of PSI and, as explained above, are obtained by dividing the metric units by 6897.

If the material is uniform in its properties, then reducing the width, length, or thickness will not alter the density or Young's moduli. These measurements are intensive properties (they don't depend on how much of the material is present). The various natural mode frequencies will change, but in a predictable manner according to the above equations: if plate *length* or *width* becomes *smaller*, frequency *increases*. If plate *thickness* becomes *smaller*, frequency *decreases*. This predictability of frequency is a useful concept, to which we will return later.

For both hardwoods and softwoods, there is a remarkably linear relationship between density and Young's modulus parallel to grain. **Fig. 1** shows such a plot using data from the USDA Forest Products Laboratory for North American trees (1974). **Fig. 2** shows analogous data for South and Central American trees from Yale University's Tropical Wood journal (1949, 1950, 1952, 1954, 1955). These trends provide a rough measure of Young's modulus for a given piece of wood if only density data are present,

Figure 1. *Specific Gravity vs. Young's Modulus*
USDA Forest Products Laboratory

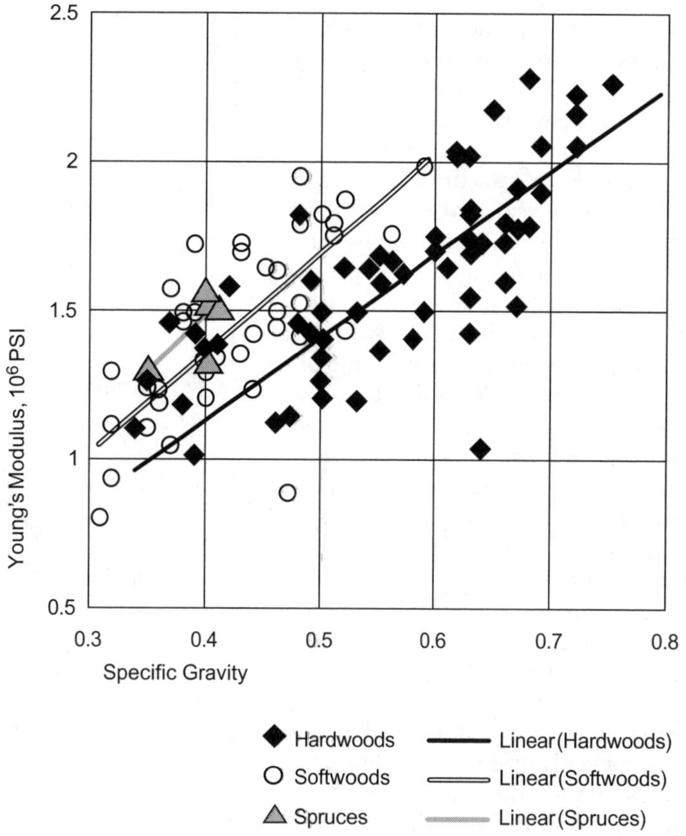

Figure 2. *Specific Gravity vs. Young's Modulus*
Yale University "Tropical Woods"

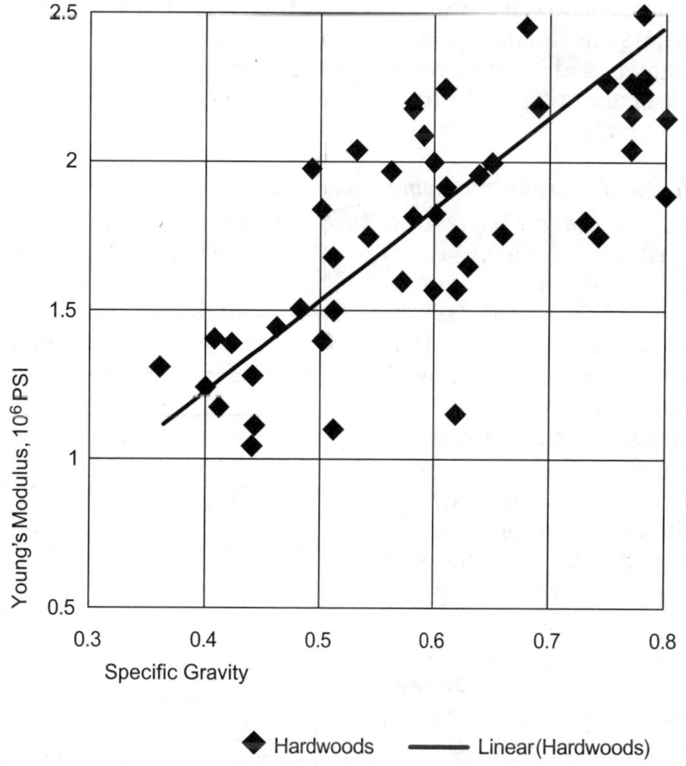

providing that the sample is quartersawn and runout is minimal.

It is important to understand that changes in runout and deviation from the quartersawn condition can greatly affect stiffness without changing the density of the wood as much. Interpretation of the data will be simpler and more accurate if straight-grained, quartersawn woods with little or no runout are chosen initially, but greater understanding of wood property variability will ensue if less standard grain patterns are eventually studied as well. **Fig. 3** shows data from some of my own wood samples. Note that although the units are in metric rather than English format, the trends and values (when converted) remain the same. The open squares, circles, and triangles represent wood with little runout or deviation from being quartersawn. In comparison, the filled diamonds have severe runout and are highly figured as well; the stiffness of these samples is only ½–⅓ of comparable density samples which are more correctly oriented. Additional discussion regarding runout by Al Carruth is included as a sidebar.

There will be a natural variability for density and Young's moduli among samples of the same species of wood depending generally on the volumetric ratio of springwood to summerwood (annual ring frequency). As noted in Hoadley (1980), a greater proportion of summerwood in softwoods makes the overall piece denser and stiffer. The opposite relation obtains in hardwoods.

Figure 3. *Density vs. Young's Modulus Author's Personal Data*

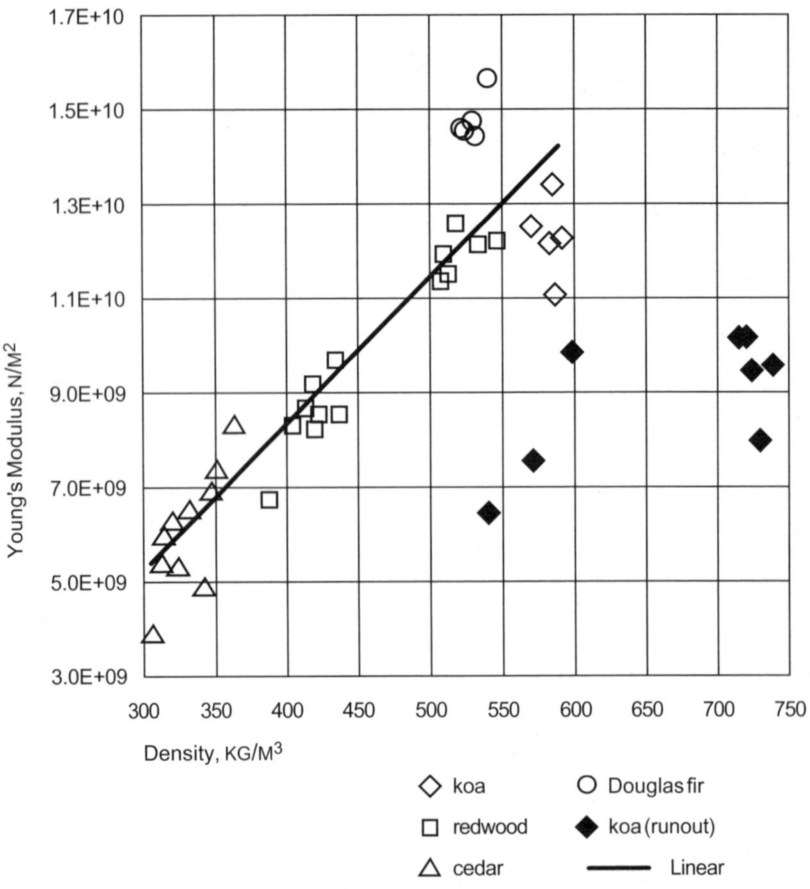

Measuring Dynamic Young's Modulus by Plate Mode Frequencies: Two Methods

Glitter. This approach is the one most commonly described in the literature, such as Caldersmith (1984) and references therein. The plate is excited directly by a loudspeaker or a "stinger" using tones from a frequency generator. Support the plate on foam blocks, sprinkle glitter or other fine dust on the plate, and excite the plate with a speaker beginning with a frequency of about 20Hz–30Hz. Slowly increase the frequency until a pair of glitter or dust lines appear parallel or perpendicular to the grain. Sweep past the point at which the lines begin to break up. Reduce frequency again and try to obtain the frequency where the lines are most well defined. Record the frequency and continue on to the next set of lines. Lines perpendicular to grain give the lengthwise flexing frequency, f_x. Those parallel to grain give the crosswise frequency, f_y.

Computer. Today the technology to record and analyze a tap tone is within easy reach, requiring only a personal computer, sound card, input microphone, and shareware. I use a program called *Cool Edit* available

Table 1. *Typical Wood Properties for Lutherie*

	measured						calculated				
Sample Name	Wt KG	L_x M	L_y M	h MM	f_x Hz	f_y Hz	D KG/M³	E_x N/M²	E_x PSI	E_y N/M²	E_y PSI
Eur. spruce	.32	.56	.41	3.0	56	23	465	15	2.2	.76	.11
Sitka spruce	.32	.56	.41	3.0	52	25	465	13	1.9	.89	.13
Red spruce	.345	.56	.41	3.0	52	23	501	14	2.0	.79	.11
White spruce	.31	.56	.41	3.0	55	29	450	14	2.0	1.1	.16
W. red cedar	.27	.56	.41	3.0	49	22	392	9.8	1.4	.56	.081
Douglas fir	.27	.56	.41	3.0	50	33	392	10	1.4	1.3	.19
Redwood	.26	.56	.41	3.0	49	29	377	9.5	1.4	.96	.14

on the Internet at www.syntrillium.com which allows the collection and analysis of sound files among other things. So I can tap on a board, save the tap sound in a file, run the sound through a fast Fourier transformation algorithm and obtain a frequency vs. loudness distribution curve showing the predominant frequencies within the tap. If I've held the plate in the right place, and tapped it in the right place, the appropriate frequency should predominate.

A Slight Digression on Tap Tones. The tap tone of a plate is a function of the plate thickness, density, length, and width. What predominant note is heard depends on where the plate is held and where it is struck. For example, if you had a rectangular plate and held it in a spot ¼ of its length and ½ of its width and struck it in the center, you would have held it on one of the lengthwise zones of least motion (a node) and struck it on a zone of greatest motion (a mode or antinode). Although many notes would be produced, the loudest should represent the first fundamental vibration of lengthwise flexing. This concept is discussed at length in Benade (1990). Turning the board 90° and repeating the experiment will yield a different set of notes which is representative of the first fundamental of widthwise bending. The duration of the notes is a function of how exactly you are placing your fingers relative to the node location, how much energy your fingers are absorbing, what type of tapping device you use, the size of the board, and the rate of internal energy loss in the wood. Sounds such as *"dunk!"* are considered less desirable than *"tuuunnnnnnnngggggg!"* or some such.

Starting Top Thicknesses for Different Woods

Let's first begin with the case of the builder with some experience. Suppose that you generally use a certain type of wood such as Engelmann spruce for your tops, but now wish to experiment with other varieties of woods such as redwood, western red cedar, or Douglas fir. In the approach first described here, it is necessary to have a set of reference values from a type of wood that you have used successfully in the past. That is, you know that for the wood you use, a certain thickness is generally a good starting point for attaching braces and beginning the voicing process. If you don't have any idea what thickness to use, later I'll give some examples using measurements from well-known makers along with some of my own data.

- Make L_x and L_y the same for all of the different wood tops, allowing plenty of room for final trimming to top shape.
- Thickness-sand or plane the tops to a thickness larger than the final thickness, for example .150″ (3.8MM). It is not critical that every piece have exactly the same thickness, but it is important to have the thickness of each plate be as uniform as possible for measurement purposes.
- Using the above dynamic procedure, collect sets of values for L_x, L_y, h, f_x, and f_y and calculate E_x, E_y, and D for one of your "typical" tops (the wood type with which you are familiar). Then collect similar information for the other tops of varying wood types that you wish to experiment with.

Table 1 shows one of my data collection and calculation formats using a portion of the data from Haines (1979). Inclusion of numbers for specific woods does not imply that these numbers will hold for all examples of each type of wood. You must measure the properties to be sure. This table is well suited for spreadsheet calculations. Metric expressions for E are in billions of N/M^2, while English units are in millions of PSI; in the first row 15 billion N/M^2 = 2.2 million PSI (rounded off to two significant figures).

Now that we have some data, let's work through the math.

Derivation of Comparison Formulae

Where are we going with this? We want a set of equations which will allow us to predict the thickness of an untried piece of top wood using measurements on both a "known properties" piece of top wood and the new piece. We know what starting thickness we usually use for our usual top wood, but how do we predict the starting thickness of the new piece? The following derivations will help us make the predictions.

In order to end up with as simple a set of comparison formulae as we can, we'll make some simplifying assumptions as we go along that will make things easier when we come to getting the answer. So let's begin with **Equation 3** as a reminder:

(3) Dynamic Young's modulus along the grain

$$E_x = \frac{D\ L_x^4\ f_x^2}{1.05\ h^2}$$

Since we have made L_x, the length of the top plate, the same for all boards, we rearrange **Equation 3** to solve for L_x, and then set the equations for the two different boards equal to each other. Note that board 1 is our reference board made of the material we use most frequently, and board 2, the one we wish to make the same stiffness by adjusting its thickness:

$$\textbf{(6)}\quad \frac{E_{x1}\ 1.05\ h_1^2}{D_1\ f_{x1}^2} = \frac{E_{x2}\ 1.05\ h_2^2}{D_2\ f_{x2}^2}$$

The constant value of 1.05 on both sides of the equation cancels. Also we have already calculated the values of E_{x1}, E_{x2}, D_1, and D_2 from our measurements of each plate so we know what these numbers are and can combine them:

$$\textbf{(7)}\quad \frac{E_{x1}\ D_2}{E_{x2}\ D_1} = \frac{h_1^2\ /\ f_{x1}^2}{h_2^2\ /\ f_{x2}^2}$$

Now, taking the square root of both sides,

$$\textbf{(8)}\quad \left(\frac{E_{x1}\ D_2}{E_{x2}\ D_1}\right)^{1/2} = \frac{h_1\ /\ f_{x1}}{h_2\ /\ f_{x2}}$$

Originally published in *American Lutherie #57*, 1999

Runout and its Effect on Wood Properties

by Al Carruth

The structure of wood is roughly like a bundle of microscopic soda straws that have been glued together with a somewhat yielding resin. These straws have two functions: to hold the tree up, and to conduct fluids to where they are needed. Generally speaking, most of the cells/straws run up and down along the axis of the tree, although there are small bundles (the medullary rays) that run out along the radius. The strength and stiffness of the wood pretty much follows the direction of the cells; that is, it is greatest along the axis of the tree, and least tangential to the circumference, with the radial direction being in between, but closer to the tangential. That is one reason we tend to cut top wood along the radius of the tree; to take advantage of the "free" stiffness conferred by the rays.

For various reasons the cells do not always align exactly with the axis of the tree's growth. The cells of the trunk, for example, have to turn aside to go around knots. Frequently a tree will grow with a twist, so that the cells run around the trunk like stripes on a barber pole (although usually not at so great an angle). This twist will usually be a certain number of degrees per meter of height. As the tree gets bigger the displacement gets larger because the circumference is increasing.

If you try to saw a top out of a twisted tree by cutting along the radius of the trunk and following the long axis of the tree, you will actually be cutting at an angle to the fibers as they twist around, and the angle will be greater as you get toward the outside of the trunk. Cutting off-axis on a tree that grew straight has the same result, but the angle doesn't change across the piece. This is "runout." It causes a number of problems, both structural and acoustic.

Acoustically, the runout decreases the stiffness of the top along the grain, and this means that you will have to leave it a bit thicker than you usually would to get the tap tones up. The extra mass cuts down on the volume of sound, all else being equal. Wood with runout also has a higher damping factor; it absorbs more sound, particularly at high frequencies.

Structurally, wood with runout is not as strong, and does not glue as well. A split on a runout top will tend to follow the grain, and this is a real problem when the bridge comes unglued. The runout changes direction across the centerline, so on one side the bridge will peel up easily, and on the other it will split into the top.

It is fairly easy to see runout under finish, as the wood reflects differently on either side of the glue line. It is harder to see it in the raw wood, particularly when it has been sanded to remove the saw marks.

Most top wood is obtained from split billets; the trees are felled, bucked to length, and split into pieces that can be handled easily. The billets are then sawn into thin pieces for tops. Since the split lines follow the grain (if the splitting is done right) there should be no runout in wood that comes from split billets, unless the tree grew twisted. A billet split from a twisted tree will, of course, have a twisted face — a dead giveaway. ——

Now we need to make judgements about thickness, h, and along-grain frequency, f_x. If the properties of the wood you are dealing with are very uniform, then the constant thickness approach, based on your experience for the sound you want is quite valid. So now take the starting top thickness you normally use, h_1, and calculate a new frequency, fx1 for your reference board using **Equation 3** rearranged to solve for f_{x1}. That is,

(9) 1st modal frequency along grain

$$f_x = \left(\frac{E_{x1}\ 1.05\ h^2}{D\ L_x^4} \right)^{1/2}$$

This would be the parallel-to-grain, first fundamental bending frequency that you would normally head toward during your initial thicknessing procedure.

If you want to begin the bracing and brace voicing process with the new board at the same starting point as the reference board, you must set the new board's frequency f_{x2} equal to the reference board's frequency f_{x1}. With that done the equations simplify to:

$$\textbf{(10)}\quad h_2 = \left(\frac{E_{x1}\ D_2}{E_{x2}\ D_1} \right)^{1/2} \times h_1$$

or

$$\textbf{(11)}\quad h_2 = \left(\frac{E_{x1} / D_1}{E_{x2} / D_2} \right)^{1/2} \times h_1$$

So the new board thickness is equal to the reference thickness times the square root of a ratio of reference and new values of E_x and D. The correctness of this may be judged by comparing f_{x2} with f_{x1} as the value of h_2 is approached. Predicting thickness for the new piece is useful when you're sending a number of tops through the sander and don't want to run back to the signal generator every time you make a pass. Of course, as the estimated new thickness is approached, comparison with the reference piece by frequency measurement, flexing, and traditional approaches is recommended rather than just blindly going to the predicted thickness. The function of these equations is to act as a general guide, not an absolute reference.

Let's now compare our earlier formula for the mechanical deformation of the plate and repeat the same exercise as above.

Static Young's modulus along the grain

$$\textbf{(1)}\quad E_x = \frac{K\ P\ L_x^3}{y\ L_y\ h^3}$$

In this case we will set y, the amount of static deformation (how much the plate flexes under the same mass of P), to be the same in both cases. So,

$$(12)\quad \frac{K\ P\ L_{x1}^3}{E_{x1}\ L_{y1}\ h_1^3} = \frac{K\ P\ L_{x2}^3}{E_{x2}\ L_{y2}\ h_2^3}$$

But, as before, we can eliminate values which are the same on both sides of the equation, so K and P cancel; and if we have made the lengths and widths the same then L_x and L_y will cancel as well. So after rearranging we're left with

$$(13)\quad E_{x1}\ h_1^3 = E_{x2}\ h_2^3$$

or,

$$(14)\quad h_2 = \left(\frac{E_{x1}}{E_{x2}}\right)^{1/3} \times h_1$$

which is somewhat different from our previous answer from dynamic measurements.

$$(11)\quad h_2 = \left(\frac{E_{x1}/D_1}{E_{x2}/D_2}\right)^{1/2} \times h_1$$

The difference in the form of the equations lies in the measurement of static versus dynamic Young's moduli. Dynamic measurements of Young's moduli must take the mass per unit volume into account because the inertia of the mass of the material under study will have an effect on how readily the material will respond to an imposed frequency.

How comparable are **Equations 11** and **14**? Let's use the differences in **Table 1** between one sample of European spruce (E_x = 1.5 billion N/M^2, D = 465 KG/M^3) and another of Douglas fir (E_x = 1.0 billion N/M^2, D = 392 KG/M^3) as an example and use the European spruce as our reference material. The right-hand ratio by which to factor our reference wood thickness from **Equation 11** is 1.12:

$$h_2 = \left(\frac{15\text{ billion}/465}{10\text{ billion}/392}\right)^{1/2} \times h_1 = 1.12 \times h_1$$

while the analogous factor from **Equation 14** is 1.14:

$$h_2 = \left(\frac{15\text{ billion}}{10\text{ billion}}\right)^{1/3} \times h_1 = 1.14 \times h_1$$

nearly identical for our purposes. Since we are dealing with ratios and the units will cancel, it doesn't matter whether metric or English units are used in the equations. To continue, if our reference thickness for European spruce is 2.2MM, then this particular piece of Douglas fir should be about 2.5MM in order to have the same frequency and stiffness.

Extending the Equations. Although we've also included equations which use the measured cross-grain stiffness coefficient, no mention has been made of it in the above derivations. This stiffness is also important in determining the sound qualities of a given top. Brian Burns (1997) likes to use the product of both E_x and E_y divided by the measured density D to obtain a greater overall sense of the stiffness of a particular top. With that in mind we can alter **Equations 11** and **14** to include cross-grain stiffness:

For dynamic measurements:

$$(15)\quad h_2 = \left(\frac{(E_{x1}\ E_{y1})/D_1}{(E_{x2}\ E_{y2})/D_2}\right)^{1/2} \times h_1$$

For static measurements:

$$(16)\quad h_2 = \left(\frac{(E_{x1}\ E_{y1})}{(E_{x2}\ E_{y2})}\right)^{1/3} \times h_1$$

How much would this approach change our top thickness ratio factors? Since Ex is poorly correlated with Ey (there is no simple, predictable relationship between along- and cross-grain stiffness coefficients), there could be a much greater difference from piece to piece in comparisons. So for the dynamic approach **Equation 15**:

$$h_2 = \left(\frac{(15\text{ billion}\times .76\text{ billion})/465}{(10\text{ billion}\times 1.3\text{ billion})/392}\right)^{1/2} \times h_1 = .86\times h_1$$

and the static approach:

$$h_2 = \left(\frac{15\text{ billion}\times .76\text{ billion}}{10\text{ billion}\times 1.3\text{ billion}}\right)^{1/3} \times h_1 = .96\times h_1$$

These are very different results from using just the along-grain stiffness coefficients, E_x. It would now appear that the overall stiffness of the Douglas fir sample is somewhat greater than that of the European spruce sample and that the Douglas fir sample should be thinner rather than thicker at the starting point! For arguments sake, let's do the same sort of calculations for all the samples in **Table 1**. **Table 2** shows the results of such calculations.

The results are quite interesting. With the exception of western red cedar, a comparison of similar equations (static vs. static, dynamic vs. dynamic) shows two

Table 2. Comparison of Ratio Calculations

	using only E_x		using E_x and E_y	
Sample Name	Static E_x	Dynamic E_x	Static E_x E_y	Dynamic E_x E_y
Eur. spruce	1	1	1	1
Sitka spruce	1.05	1.07	1.00	.99
Red spruce	1.02	1.07	1.01	1.05
White spruce	1.02	1.02	.91	.85
W. red cedar	1.15	1.14	1.28	1.32
Douglas fir	1.14	1.13	.96	.86
Redwood	1.16	1.13	1.08	1.01

things: calculations which include both E_x and E_y have lower ratios than using E_x alone; more of the samples (Sitka spruce, red spruce, redwood) appear to be more similar to this particular European spruce reference sample than before; that is, the final thickness is now estimated as nearly the same. Some samples (white spruce, Douglas fir) actually appear much more stiff overall than before.

I suggest that **Table 2** simply points out the importance of looking at both E_x and E_y when making measurements. The European spruce data should not be regarded as an icon for absolute comparisons, but rather one good sample of this frequently used wood. There is no doubt in my mind that experienced intuitive makers take both E_x and E_y into account (and many other wood qualities) simply by flexing and tapping prospective top material and mentally comparing with earlier experiences. My intention with this paper is to allow those of us with a little more technical bent (and considerably less experience) to choose better wood for instrument making according to a flexible measurement plan.

Suggestions for Initial Wood Thicknesses. If you're not sure where to begin for a top thickness for a classical guitar, Roy Courtnall's (1993) book notes the following guitar top thicknesses used by well-known makers for some of their guitars:

- Daniel Friederich, European spruce, 2.2MM
- Robert Bouchet, European spruce, 2.0MM–2.1MM
- Ignacio Fleta, western red çedar, 2.6MM

It appears that the two different wood types used by these master makers might be similar in properties to those measured by Haines, since the thickness differences parallel our calculations using the along-grain and cross-grain stiffness coefficients E_x and E_y. Of course this conclusion also assumes that these makers intuitively agree on a beginning feel for top thicknesses even before braces are applied.

For builders of smaller nylon stringed instruments, I recommend the following top thicknesses using redwood or koa:

- 4-string soprano ukulele: .070″, ≈1.8MM
- 4–5-string concert ukulele: .075″, ≈1.9MM
- tenor ukulele: .080″–.085″, ≈2.0MM–2.1MM (depending on 4, 6, or 8 strings)
- 4-string baritone ukulele, 0.085″ (~2.1MM

Tops of less stiff material (western red cedar) should be thicker; those of more stiff material (Douglas fir, spruces) slightly thinner according to the formulae above and common sense.

Acknowledgements

Constructive criticism by David Cohen and Ben Furman on earlier versions of this paper was very helpful. A last-minute read-through by Jon Sevy was helpful and appreciated. Calculation errors and possible turbidity of writing style are of course the responsibility of the author. ——

References

Benade, Arthur H.
Fundamentals of Musical Acoustics.
2nd rev. ed. New York: Dover Publications, Inc., 1990.

Burns, Brian.
"Notes on Stiffness, Density, and Q Testing of Tonewoods."
Healdsburg Guitar Festival, August 1997. Photocopied.

Caldersmith, Graham.
"Testing Tonewood Samples."
Guild of American Luthiers Data Sheet #271, 1984.
(See *Big Red Book of American Lutherie Volume Two*, 2001, p. 400.)

——— "Physics at the Workbench of the Luthier."
Catgut Acoustical Society #35, May 1981, pp. 15–18.

——— "Vibration Theory and Wood Properties – I."
Catgut Acoustical Society #42 , November 1984, pp. 4–11.

——— "Vibration Theory and Wood Properties – II."
Catgut Acoustical Society #1.2, November 1988, pp. 7–10.

Carruth, Al.
"Free Plate Tuning , Part I — Theory."
American Lutherie #28, Winter 1991, pp. 18–31.
(See *Big Red Book of American Lutherie Volume Three*, 2004, p. 136.)

Courtnall, Roy.
Making Master Guitars.
London: Robert Hale Ltd., 1993.

Dickenson, Fred E., Hess, Robert W., and Wangaard, Frederick F.
"Properties and Uses of Tropical Woods, I."
Tropical Woods #95, Yale Univ. School of Forestry, June 1, 1949.

Haines, Daniel W.
"On Musical Instrument Wood — I."
Catgut Acoustical Society #31, 1979, pp. 23–32.

Hess, Robert W., Wangaard, Frederick F., and Dickenson, Fred E.
"Properties and Uses of Tropical Woods, II."
Tropical Woods #97, Yale Univ. School of Forestry, Nov. 1, 1950.

Hoadley, R. Bruce.
Understanding Wood – A Craftsman's Guide to Wood Technology.
Newtown, CT: Taunton Press, 1980.

U.S. Forest Products Laboratory.
Wood Handbook: Wood as an Engineering Material.
rev. ed., USDA Agr. Handbook 72, 1974.

Wangaard, Frederick F. and Munschler, Arthur F.
"Properties and Uses of Tropical Woods, III."
Tropical Woods # 98, Yale Univ. School of Forestry, June 1, 1952.

Wangaard, Frederick F., Koehler, Arthur, and Munschler, Arthur F.
"Properties and Uses of Tropical Woods, IV."
Tropical Woods # 99, Yale Univ. School of Forestry, April 1, 1954.

Wangaard, Frederick F., Stern, William L., and Goodrich, Stanley L.
"Properties and Uses of Tropical Woods, V."
Tropical Woods # 103, Yale Univ. School of Forestry, Dec. 15, 1955.

Originally published in *American Lutherie #57*, 1999

Tales of True Companionship

by John Calkin

THE IDEA of building a mini-acoustic guitar was an attractive one, but a little guitar seemed just as time consuming to build as a large one. Then Martin introduced their Backpacker. I had heard of the McNalley family of simple string instruments, but never took a serious look until Martin adopted the Backpacker. If such a goofy shape could fly commercially, then maybe anything I came up with had a chance. Ease of manufacture became my primary goal. I also wanted more volume than the Backpacker had, even at the expense of a slightly larger size. A couple snazzy details wouldn't hurt, just in case my version was ever hung next to Martin's in a music shop.

I settled on 23¼″ for the scale length because I had already used it on acoustic and electric guitars and knew that it functioned all right with normal gauge strings. A bolt on neck was an automatic choice. The Martin square-tube truss was chosen because it's cheap and easy to install, though heavy. Another obvious choice was a maple fingerboard, because if left natural it would ring a bell with Fender owners and it took stain well if a dark board was desired. Maple was also cheap yet long-wearing. I decided on a flat fretboard because it saved time both in fretboard manufacture and in fretting. The rest of the neck had to be walnut, because I had a lot of it and I got it for free. When I ran out of walnut I could reconsider.

ALL BY JOHN CALKIN

Two versions of the True Companion travel guitar. The headless one is marginally shorter and balances better on a strap, but the more conventional design is easier on some eyes and may be easier to build. The tone of these instruments is reasonably good, and no airline should balk at your desire to stash one in an overhead luggage compartment. Finding a gig bag may be the greatest challenge of this project.

I wasn't afraid to put some weight in the body as long as it didn't kill the top vibration. I wanted to achieve a better balance than the Backpacker, even though a degree of neck heaviness was inevitable. The body was to be trapezoidal. The ends were to be walnut, to echo the color of the neck. The sides could match the wood used on the back, whatever it was. One of the prototypes was made of curly maple. It took me hours to sand it clean, and I knew I had to use a softer wood or give up the project. I settled on butternut, though I had never used it before. Sometimes called white walnut, it is soft, easily worked, contrasts well with walnut, is very pretty in a sedate sort of way, and was easily available, though not cheap. The top had to be spruce, since something about the instrument had to look guitarish. However, once I got into production I used spruce, cedar, and Douglas fir, pretty much whatever I could get my hands on. The quality of the spruce I considered unimportant as long as it was quartersawn, since I didn't expect to win any awards for tone and I had to keep expenses down. For a heel block I chose poplar. Poplar is about as inexpensive as hardwood gets and it's normally available in 2″ boards if you buy it rough, and since part of it would be exposed, I welcomed the color contrast. The bridge would be walnut, just to complete the color scheme, and as uncomplicated in construction as I could make it.

The first five instruments were 8″ wide and 3″ deep, and proved to be awkward to hold and to play. I changed to a design 11″ wide and 2″ deep. Everything about the instrument improved, including its tone and volume. In an elemental manner, the new guitar struck me as pretty. I came up with the name True Companion and printed up some labels using my computer.

Construction couldn't be easier. Anyone familiar with mountain dulcimer literature will recognize the method of side construction. The walnut ends are ⅜″ thick. Slots for the sides are cut in the walnut at a 15° angle. Just spread glue in the slots and slide in the ribs, no clamps necessary. The walnut that sticks out from the sides stays in place until after the plates are glued on, since it's a perfect place to tack them to prevent glue slippage. I made a jig for cutting the poplar heel blocks on the tablesaw. The heel block has to be large enough to permit the routing of a pocket for the neck to sit in. On normal electric guitars the pocket accepts 3″ of the neck, so that's what I used for the True Companion. It

Construction methods peculiar to the True Companion can be seen here. The light-colored sides are let into slots in the walnut end pieces. The solid walnut linings will be exposed after construction by a wide chamfer. The poplar neck block will also be partially exposed when a cutaway is sawn into the completed body. The "ears" of the end pieces will also be trimmed away at that time.

This jig is simply a piece of scrap plywood with a shelf cut into it to guide the creation of heel blocks for the TC. It holds the block while it's cut to fit against the side that will have a cutaway added to it after the body is completed.

Simplicity is often the name of the game at this level of production. Most of my TCs use Grover Sta-Tite tuners. This little gauge helps mark the proper spacing of the tuner holes in the headstock. Just one less item to think about while the chips are flying.

This template is really *basic. It locates the output jack for TCs that have piezo pickups. Guitar shop staffers look for such uniformity in production instruments, and they pass on their expectations to potential customers. Don't overlook such uniformity in any production project.*

turned out that this left a bit more than fourteen frets clear of the body. The heel block is glued to the top walnut end piece and one side, and the fit has to be pretty good. Once the body is completed and the neck is fitted, I saw into the end piece/side/heel block to form a small cutaway. It adds a bit of playability and improves the TC's appearance measurably.

You don't have to, but I use solid lengths of walnut for lining. I jigged a table for my belt sander to grind the lining ends at the proper miter and strive for a perfect fit of the linings inside the body. After the plates have been glued to the sides I run a router around all the edges using a chamfering bit, which creates a large, comfortable bevel and reveals a bit of the walnut lining, adding a touch of color contrast again.

After the sides, heel block, and lining have been assembled I true up the unit for adding the plates by sanding it on 80-grit paper glued to a $19'' \times 30''$ sheet of MDF. That's a mighty big sanding board, but once I had it, I found a ton of uses for it. Just make sure that it really is flat. Regular sandpaper tacked on with rubber cement will do fine. When you get flush you can cut up cloth sanding belts for the abrasive, and it will probably last for years, though you may have to reglue some edges from time to time. If you know of a better temporary glue please let me know.

Join the plates in your usual manner. The back plate gets two braces, the top gets two cross braces and a bridge plate. Nothing fancy or trick here. The braces run up to the lining but don't nest into it.

Once I decided to make these creatures I decided I might have to make hundreds of them. Do all luthiers torture themselves that way? Unless you're Bob McNalley it's not likely to happen, but I wanted to be ready for it. I made jigs and gauges for as many operations and machine setups as I could. There are little notes scribbled on my sample pieces and templates. For instance, all my bridges are made with a Robo-Sander sanding drum in the drill press using the same set of jigs, so they are all identical in every meaningful way. If the front edge of the bridge is placed $22\frac{7}{8}''$ from the face of the nut, the intonation will come out correctly, no muss, no fuss. With the neck mounted on the body, I drop a piece of masking tape across that measurement, then all I have to do is slide a bridge across the tape edge until the bridge-pin holes line up correctly with the edges of the fretboard, then push home the index pins mounted in the saddle slot.

Most neck dimensions are also fixed with the Robo-Sander. I still shape the necks by hand, but it's fun and it only takes 20 minutes or so in walnut. Once the fretboard is glued in place, true it dead flat. The square truss rod will bow just enough to offer the proper amount of neck relief. To make an angled headstock I use a standard electric guitar trick: cut off the headstock at a 15° angle, flip it over, then glue it back where it came from.

Fingerboards are slotted on the table saw using Stew-Mac's 24½″ scale length template. In this instance the 1st fret slot of the template is used as the nut position and the 2nd fret slot of the template cuts the 1st fret slot on the fingerboard. The TC has nineteen frets.

I finish my TCs in lacquer, but it's a much-abbreviated process. Sand to 220 grit and whisker with a damp rag, then sand off the whiskers with the same grit. Stain the maple fretboard if you like. I usually do.

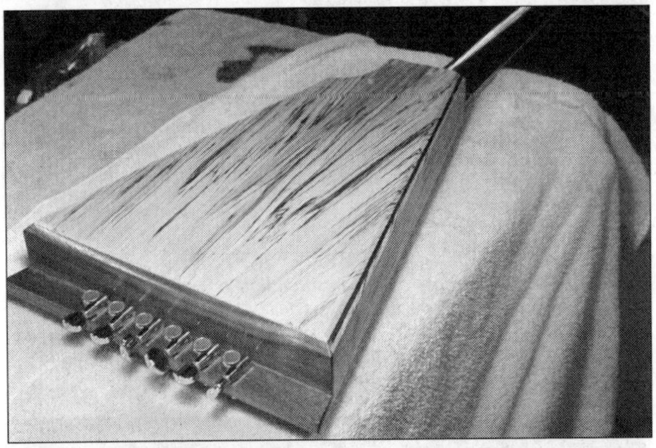

Five views of a headless version of John Calkin's True Companion.

Dark brown or black looks nice. I leave the maple edges unstained, and they end up looking like binding. It's an especially nice touch if the maple is figured. Butternut is a very fuzzy wood, so the first coat of lacquer will no doubt raise the grain again. I shoot two coats to lock the grain, then after a few hours I rub the surface gently with 320 grit wet or dry (used dry) to smooth out the surface. Two more coats and it's done. I finish right over the fingerboard, frets, and bridge, normally giving the fingerboard a couple extra coats. In a day or two the dust nibs can be knocked off with 600 grit used wet, then a light gloss is restored with a rub of Novus #2 polish. I'm more interested in the creamy texture the polish leaves than a gloss. If the guitar is pleasant to hold, the eyes will get used to the way it looks, even on something as bizarre as the True Companion.

Choose the lightest set of machine heads you can stand. The lightest sets are usually pretty junky, and there's no sense in improving the balance at the expense of tuneability.

I've mounted Fishman transducers in a few TCs. Plugging them in is like kissing the frog — they turn into big, pretty-sounding guitars. One of the first TCs was built for a fine guitarist who was about to spend a year teaching in Taiwan, where his quarters would amount to little more than a cubicle. A full-size guitar was out of the question, but he expected to find access to an amp when he got there. The True Companion was exactly what he needed.

The headless variant of the TC has a ½″ thick shelf that is 1″ wide glued to the top of the rear end piece. The top is glued over the shelf, then machine heads are mounted through the shelf/top. The saddle must be notched to space the strings, and due to the wide fan of the strings, a hold-down is necessary to keep the strings in the slots. I used a length of ¼″ birch dowel stained brown and mounted with the screws used for mounting humbucker pickup rings. When I get some walnut doweling, I'll abandon the birch to get a proper color match. Because of the shelf and the protrusion of the machine heads, the variant is nearly as long as the standard TC. Rear-mounting the ball ends of the strings, rather than positioning them through the end of the sawn-off headstock, and the use of banjo tuners would allow the instrument to be shortened another 2″ or so. The variant is more likely to slide off your lap than the conventional version because of the way it balances, but it hangs quite naturally from a strap. Just for the hell of it I added a rosette to the variant, as well as a 16″ radius to the fingerboard. The flat board and the 16″ board feel so much alike to me that the extra work is not justified. The variant is made from spalted buttonwood, creating a subspecies that I dubbed "White Tigers."

I've included some photos of a jig and some layout fixtures I use to simplify the production of TCs. If you plan to make multiple reproductions of the same instrument, it's important that they look alike, even if they all go to just one store. The time saved by such doodads may not be important to you if you only plan to make a couple pieces, but anytime you can eliminate the tedium of production work you should go for it. You may find these ideas are useful for any other project you hope to knock out in a small production setting.

I decided I had to get $175 per True Companion, wholesale, without a pickup. The retail was set at $250. That's more than the Martin once it's marked to retail, but the TC is more guitar. I'm confident that I could make five a week if it came to a crunch. For awhile I was hooked up to a national retail outlet, but before anything got going, the introduction of the Baby Taylor killed the deal, even though they were enthusiastic about the TC.

When the TC is strung with light-gauge strings it feels much like a lightly strung electric guitar. Two-fret bends on the plain strings are ridiculously easy. If you wish to simulate the tension of a full-size guitar you could use medium gauge strings, or tune the TC up until the E strings are an F#, which should approximate the tension of a normal-size acoustic with a 24⅝″ scale length. I choose to leave my TCs tuned to concert pitch and spare them the added tension, but as I mentioned, I'm relatively immune to guitar-to-guitar changes.

Try one out — you'll be surprised how musical it is. Don't be afraid to adopt any decorative or finishing options that may occur to you. I find that my True Companion gets played far more than all my conventional guitars put together, just because it's always sitting next to my easy chair waiting for me. 'See you around the campfire. ——

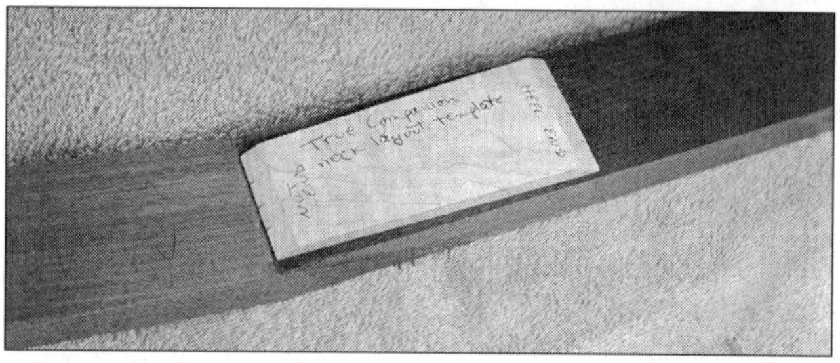

This template is normally used on a neck that's already profiled. The narrow end of the template is slid along the neck until the neck matches its width, at which point the centerline and carving layout lines are marked. Then the wide end is slid up the neck until it matches the neck in width, and another set of marks are made. I use the facet carving technique as described in American Lutherie #33. *(See* Big Red Book of American Lutherie Volume Three, *p. 306.) The marks are connected by pencil and carving commences.*

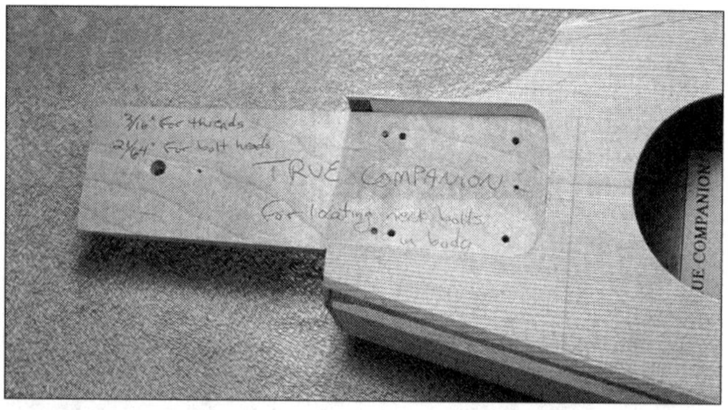

The job of this template is to mark the position for the neck bolts. Having all necks be interchangable is an aid to production manufacturing. There is a false set of holes in this template that's been filled in with dowels.

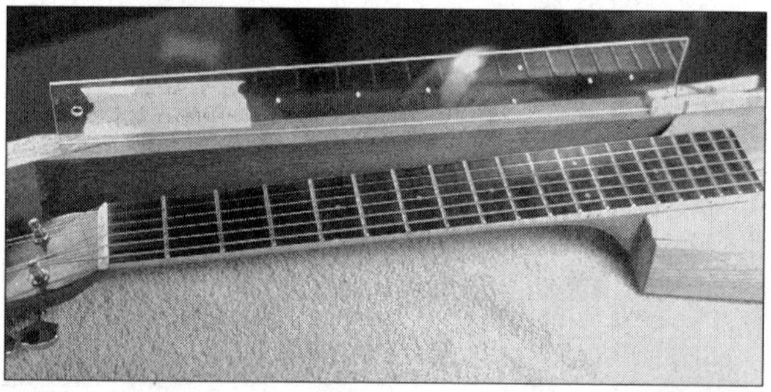

This plexiglas template lays out the position dots on the fingerboard. Holes in the plexiglas show up as white dots. The template is placed on the unfinished fretboard and an awl makes the positions through the template holes. Most of my TCs have markers or ⅛″ Delrin rod, which refuses to accept the stain used to darken the boards.

The sides of the TC fit into the end pieces at a 15° angle. This simple template is used to set the table saw blade to that angle. Once the template is made up it doesn't matter if it's exactly 15°. The sides will fit into the end pieces and each instrument will look the same.

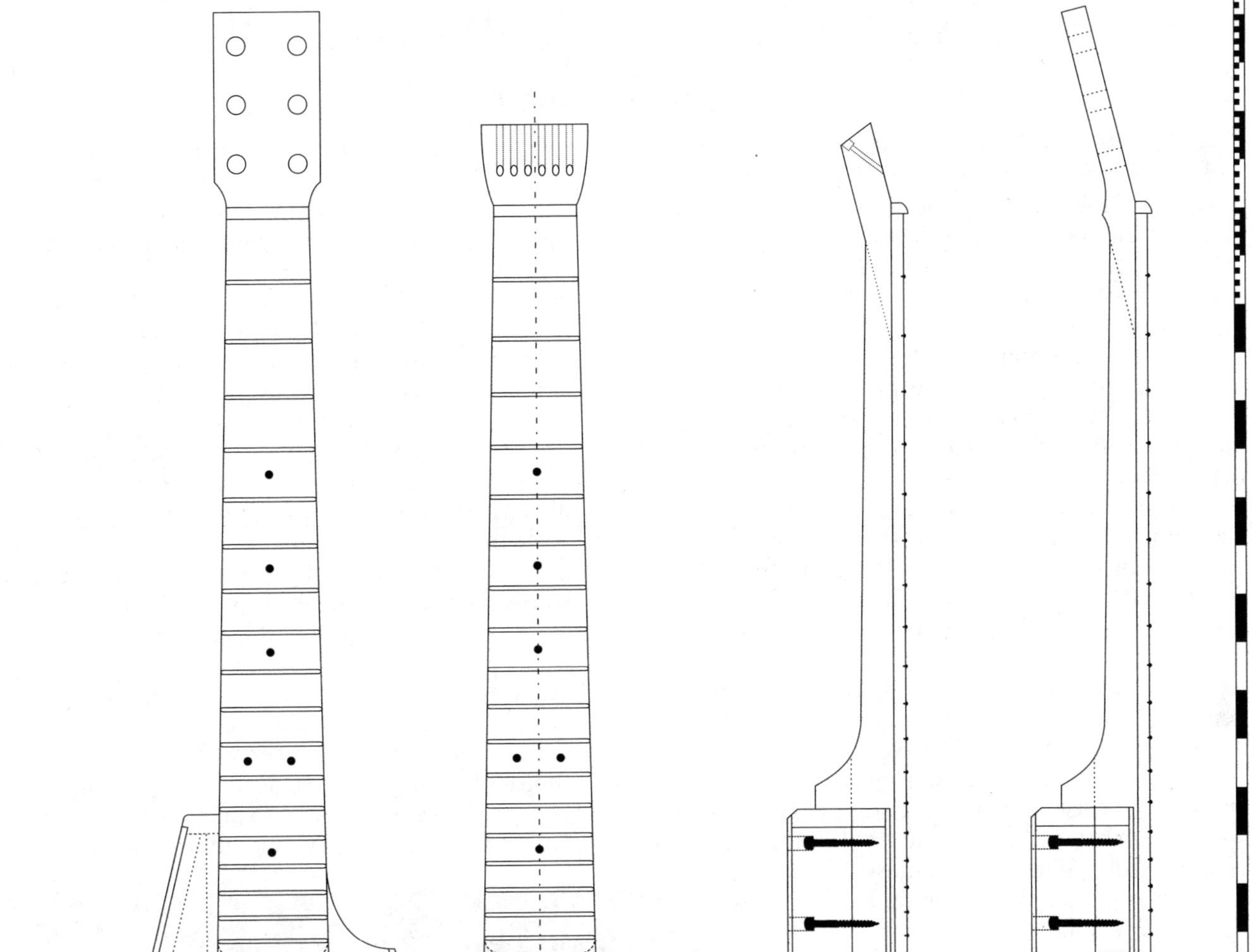

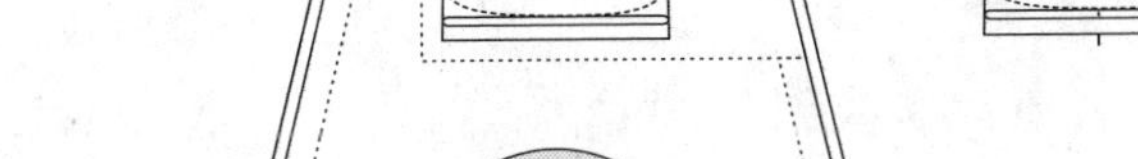

True Companion Travel Guitar

GAL Instrument Plan #44

by John Calkin

Drawn by John Calkin and David Goen.

This instrument plan is available as a full-size blueprint from the GAL.

Originally published in *American Lutherie #57*, 1999

A Few Realities about Runout

by Don Musser

THERE IS A COMMON BELIEF among many contemporary instrument builders and wood suppliers that a spruce top resawn from a split billet will be free from or have minimum runout, and will be a superior top as a result. My experience with processing spruce logs for tops has shown me that there are a few problems with that notion.

First, the important variables to consider when evaluating a spruce log are size, grain spacing, color, number of limbs, and lack of twist. Each of these factors is worthy of an in-depth discussion, but for now our focus is on twist and runout.

To evaluate twist when looking at a log, I first just sight along the length. A straight twist-free tree will have a straight look about it. Next, I check for end cracks, at the butt and at the upper end, which will show me how the split line runs in relation to the lay of the log. Finally, I'll pull off some bark midway along the length to look for any indications of spiraling grain. Any tree that shows a moderate deviation from being straight and twist free, I will avoid.

Ideally, every tree that a tonewood producer selects will have no twist, and therefore will yield perfectly true split billets that will saw up into flawless tops with zero runout. Wow! What a nice fantasy!

It is more often the case to find logs that give every indication of being straight, perfect splitters that will yield a percentage of split billets with a slight degree of twist. The reason for this is that the early growth of the tree involved some degree of spiral, and it was only as the tree aged that it grew straight. The basic fact is that very few trees grow with a uniform straight, twist-free grain from year one all the way to the outside edge of the mature tree. The bottom line is that perfectly straight-splitting trees are the exception instead of the rule, even when careful attention is given to selection for straightness and lack of twist.

What most tonewood producers will therefore be starting with is a split billet with a little bit of twist. That split billet will be quartered on the end from which the original split was made, but because of the slight twist, on the other end it will be slightly off quarter.

At this point one is faced with the problem of how to true up the billet prior to resaw in such a way as to maintain the split face to minimize runout, and to true the face to establish and maintain quarter at both ends. You've probably guessed by now — it is impossible to obtain perfection on both counts. The two things are mutually exclusive. If you true the billet to achieve minimal runout along the outside edge of the tree (the fine-grain joining edge for a guitar top) you will have one end slightly off quarter as well as an enhancement of the runout along the opposite edge (the coarse-grain edge from the tree's center). If you trim the billet to ensure perfect quarter at both ends you will effectively be maximizing runout and violating the split faces.

A few things need to be understood about stiffness in a top along and across the grain. Runout primarily diminishes stiffness along the grain. The degree to which a piece of spruce is quartered primarily affects stiffness across the grain: perfectly quartered tops are stiffer across the grain, off-quarter tops are floppy across the grain. Along the length of the grain the stiffness is typically fifteen, twenty, even thirty times greater than the stiffness across the grain. Hence, the weakest link in a guitar top is the stiffness across the grain.

Every tonewood producer, when faced with the choice of truing a billet so as to establish quartered grain at both ends, or so as to minimize runout, makes the obvious choice: to enhance the quarter and give the

ALL BY DON MUSSER

Flat, perfect-split billet

Slightly twisted billet

stiffest top across the grain. But that choice is made at the expense of maximizing, not minimizing, the runout. That is the reality of the physical limitations in the relationship between the two variables of runout and quartered grain.

Oh, those evil top wood producers who sell wood with that awful runout! How dare they do such a thing when everybody in this enlightened Golden Age of Lutherie knows that all you have to do is split your billets and your tops will have hardly any runout at all! Off with their heads! And use a froe to do it! That will teach them.

Well, the truth is they have no choice. Perfect-splitting trees are few and far between. The compromises involved in producing the highest-quality top wood from less-than-perfectly-split twist-free billets demand giving priority to quartersawn grain at the expense of a greater degree of runout.

The smaller size of the white spruce trees — like European, Engelmann, red, white, and blue spruces — does not allow much flexibility when making the adjustment between runout and quartersawn grain. If too much priority is given to minimizing runout, guitar tops get off quarter and very floppy across the grain. That is why it is common to see the two-tone top effect on many classic guitars built with European spruce. Priority was given to quartered grain at the expense of increased runout.

The larger Sitka spruce trees, though still problematic in their own way when it comes to twist, have an advantage when the adjustment for runout and quartered grain is made.

During a visit to Pacific Rim Tonewoods in July of 1998, Steve McMinn showed me some of his big Sitka logs and explained how they typically grow without twist when young and then grow with more twist the older they become — just the opposite of how Engelmann commonly behaves. Because he splits off the Sitka sapwood (the outer edge of the tree with the most twist), he can tolerate a log that shows a minor degree of spiral on the outer edge. The larger size of the Sitka logs also allows priority to be given to minimizing runout at the fine-grain/joining edge of a guitar top, at the expense of a loss of quartered grain and an enhancement of runout at the opposite edge of the top. Sitka tops just don't get as floppy across the grain as quickly as do the other spruces when they are slightly off-quarter.

There are perfectly splitting, true trees that yield twist-free billets that saw into runout-free tops. I estimate that from one or two in every five, to one in ten of the logs I select is a perfect splitter. Other tonewood suppliers I've talked to have had similar experiences regarding these ratios. There are also nearly perfectly true billets in the less-than-perfectly-splitting trees. Lower down in the log on one side they typically split out fairly flat.

The "perfect splitters" are a real pleasure to work with. They just pop apart when split, and when I flip the billet over to check the quarter, it is right on. The yield is about 10%–25% above the yield of an average tree with a little twist. Maybe there should be a whole new grade of perfect-splitting top wood: PS grade master and PS grade AAAs.

In conclusion: Perfectly quartersawn tops (with perfectly quartered grain showing at *both* ends) from anything less than a perfect-splitting tree *must* have *maximum* not *minimum* runout, regardless of whether or not you started with a split billet. Any soundboard producer or seller who claims that their wood has minimal runout because it is from split billets is not being entirely accurate. Even when careful attention is given to selecting trees that are straight and apparently twist free, there will most often be something less than perfection, and that requires a compromise. ——

Left: Twisted billet, original split end, showing quartered grain. Right: Twisted billet, end opposite original split, showing off- quarter grain. The dotted line shows necessary correction prior to resawing.

Originally published in *American Lutherie #57*, 1999

Domestic Tranquility

Quietly Containing and Controlling Dust and Fumes in a Home-Shop Environment

by Paul McGill

ALL COURTESY OF PAUL MCGILL

A FEW YEARS AGO, I bought a house and started the renovations required to install my shop in the basement. The house is built into a hillside and has a walkout basement with lots of light from windows in the back of the building. It's a wonderful situation for a shop. After doing extensive drainage work to completely dry out the space for guitar making, and doing a complete renovation of the interior of the basement, the next problem was controlling dust.

In my previous shop I had a 2 h.p. Grizzly bag collector in a garage outside the work space. The piping was plastic PVC, and the system worked OK for that space. However, I was sucking the air out of the building every time I turned it on, which I'm sure cost a considerable amount over the years I used it. The system, as purchased, moved about 550 CFM. It got me by, and was an improvement over my pre-dust-collector situation, but the garage was always a mess because the filter bags let the small particles get through. On occasion the collection bag would fill up and pull loose from its retainer hoop creating a cloud that was very unpleasant and a major hassle to clean up.

Having a shop at home is a bigger challenge. You can't have dust getting in the environment and spreading all over the building through the ventilation system. It is also cheaper in the long run not to exhaust the air from the dust collector to the outdoors. I needed a dust collector with complete containment. I also needed the system to be almost completely quiet so as not to disturb people upstairs.

I contacted Oneida Air Systems (www.oneida-air.com) and began studying their products to build my system. Most of the products they offer are designed for larger spaces than my small shop, but they do have upgrade parts designed to fit onto and improve the performance of my 2 h.p. Grizzly blower. I ordered a high-performance 12″ aluminum fan wheel to increase air speed and static pressure, and an 8″ intake flange to increase the air volume from the original 550 CFM to 950 CFM. When the day comes that I burn up my Grizzly motor, I plan to replace it with a 3 h.p. motor, and thus increase my air flow to 1350 CFM.

I also ordered their C-950 cyclone separator, which separates the smallest dust particles from the larger ones so that they can be filtered more efficiently, and a Fernbrook remote switching system, which I will describe later.

Top: Dust is collected at various work stations and piped into the main exhaust duct running along the ceiling. Visible stations include a belt sander, a polishing station, and a down-draft table.
Bottom: The collector of Paul's system, a diagram of which is shown on the facing page.

The system cleans the air in two stages. First, the air is drawn through the cyclone before it reaches the blower. The cyclone swirls the air around inside its drum and separates 99% of the particles using centrifugal force and gravity. Anything smaller than 220-grit dust goes through the blower and is exhausted into a secondary filtration system consisting of tubes made of polyester felt rated at 1-micron containment.

The rule for having efficient waste flow is to maintain 3500 linear feet per minute of air flow through the ducts to keep the debris moving so it doesn't settle and clog up the ducts. To calculate the speed of air flow, determine the area of the cross section of the pipe by using the area equation πr^2, and multiplying the area by 12 to determine the linear foot volume. Then divide the CFM of your blower by the linear foot volume of the duct to determine if it is sufficient to maintain the necessary air speed. There is a limit to the amount of volume that a duct of a given size will handle, no matter how much blower volume you have. A 4″ pipe has a maximum of 350 CFM, a 5″ pipe has around 550 CFM maximum, and a 6″ pipe approximately 750 CFM maximum. If you buy the Oneida parts they are happy to do the calculations for you and will provide a graph on which you can draw your shop layout for them to examine.

The increased air flow creates a new problem that is not as severe with slower air speeds: an increase in static electricity. You must have proper grounding for static electricity with this increased capacity. The PVC pipe I used in my previous system would create a serious fire hazard with this amount of air flow, so I needed to get some metal ducting. If you use snap-lock pipe, it needs to be at least 24 gauge. I opted for spiral pipe to insure the ducts would not collapse if I increased the pressure on the system. Local wholesale cost was $1.15/ft.–$2.50/ft. With all the elbows, Ts, and blast gates, the bill for the ducting came to $385.

The next question is back pressure on the exhaust system. Filtration slows down the rate at which air can escape the system, so there is an optimum ratio of filter surface area to moving air volume. In my case there is also a baffle box to quiet the system, which I estimate lowers the output by at least 100 CFM. Oneida recommends a 10:1 ratio of CFM to square feet of filter medium, but I went 6:1. At 950 CFM blower output I provided 150 sq. ft. of singed-one-side polyester felt filter medium. That's overkill, but if I ever increase my air speed by increasing the power of the blower, I will still have better than a 10:1 ratio, so my existing filtration will be sufficient.

I bought twelve filter tubes from MEC Filtration (www.merionpump.com/mec_manu.htm) for about $80. These are 7½′ long 1-micron tubes, and came sewn and ready to install. The material they stock is 24″ wide, which sews perfectly into a 7″ diameter tube. The singed side goes inside to prevent the dust from sticking to the felt. A few quick knocks loosen the dust from the surface if it clogs.

That covers the basics. Now for constructing the system. Ducting was run to thirteen collection points in the shop: a downdraft work table for routing and sanding, a polishing station, a belt sander, a lathe, a miter saw, two bandsaws, a router table, a drum sander, and four vacuum ports. Each work station has its own blast gate so that the air flow can be isolated and optimized. The ducting for each work station feeds into a main exhaust duct which goes to the collector, as shown in the diagram. The installation of the duct work was a bear because you need a torch to cut the spiral pipe efficiently.

I consider space to be very expensive, so I decided to build as much of the collector under the staircase to the upstairs as I could. I was able to design it so that it occupied only the space under the stairs plus a 36″×27″ adjoining area.

I constructed a two-chambered box to house the blower and a set of baffles to quiet the exhaust. The chamber which houses the blower is a 2′×4′ enclosure covered inside and out with ½″ thick black insulation

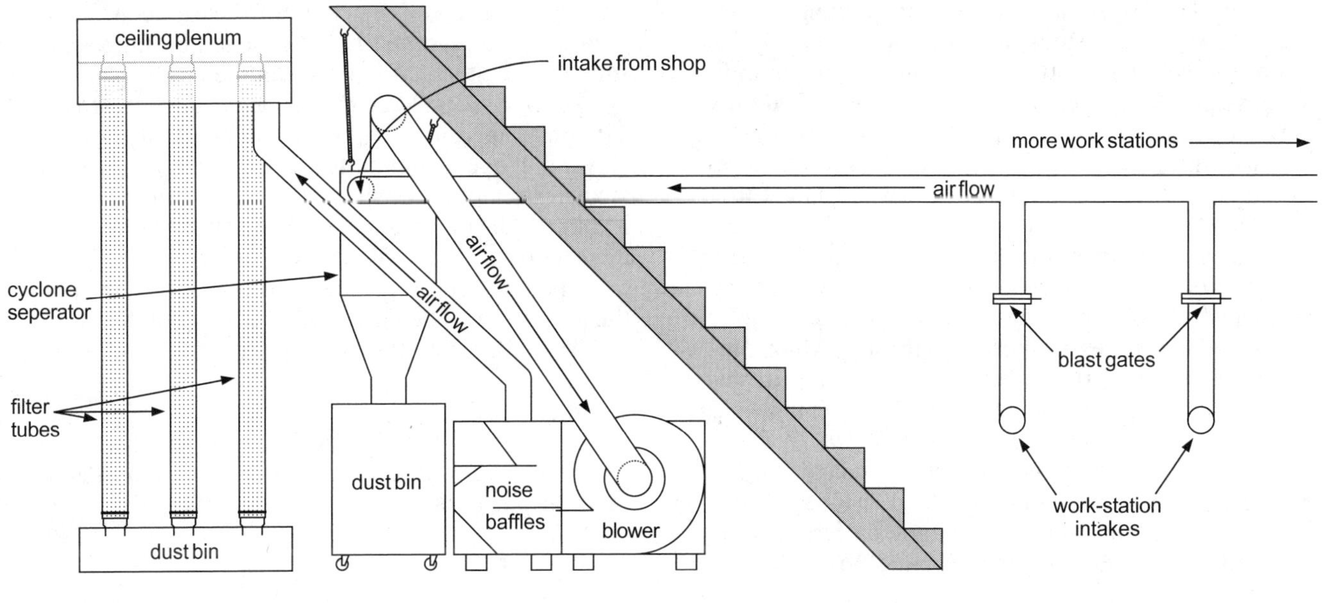

Paul McGill in his shop in Nashville, Tennessee.

board and sheetrock, and filled with pink insulation. The center divider of the box holds the blower exhaust housing which directs the exhaust through the second chamber which contains a series of baffles made of black insulation board and carpet felt. I spent considerable time redoing the baffles until I got the desired result. It's so quiet that I can stand right next to it and talk on the phone while it's running.

The main exhaust duct from the shop is connected to the intake of the cyclone separator. As the vacuum from the blower sucks particles through the cyclone, a pressure drop created by the volume of the cyclone's drum slows the air down. Heavier dust particles swirl and fall into a waste bin below the drum, while the finer dust particles are pulled up and out of the separator into the duct which feeds into the blower.

The waste bin for the cyclone is a simple plywood box, 36″×24″×20″. I installed a piece of U-channel rubber stripping over the lip of the box to seal the dust in, and used drywall screws to attach the lid. I attached the cyclone flange permanently to the lid of the box and sealed it. The upper half of the cyclone is bungied to the underside of the steps, and I remove the box by removing the retainer strap connecting the upper and lower stages of the cyclone. It doesn't seal well, and I always duct tape it after reattachment. Once separated, the box, which is on wheels, rolls outside where I empty the contents for composting. I only have to empty the waste bin twice a year.

The air flow carries the dust particles which get past the cyclone through the blower and baffles, and into a duct which leads to a ceiling plenum. The plenum is connected to a series of filter tubes through which the air passes back into the shop environment. The dust is trapped by the filters, and falls into a floor plenum which serves as a dust collector. I constructed 36″×27″×6″ plenum boxes for the floor and ceiling, and cut 12 6¾″ circles in each box for mounting the filter tubes. Each hole is centered in a square of a 9″ grid pattern, and the grid patterns are centered on the boxes. To create flanges for attaching the filter tubes, I used 6″×7″ duct reducers. I installed them with drywall screws and sealed them with construction adhesive. The upper plenum has a 7″ intake port. The lid for the lower box is held on by drywall screws which can be removed to empty the dust. I hung the upper plenum to the ceiling using heavy bungee straps to reduce the transfer of vibration to the floor upstairs.

The wiring of the switching system was another concern. I wanted to be able to turn the system on at will to insure I always used it. The answer was a Fernbrook remote device sold by Oneida. The system uses radio signals and existing shop wiring. There is a module to engage the current at the blower's plug, and a transceiver plugged into a wall outlet picks up signals from the four remote switches that are stationed around the shop. This was a slam-dunk decision. The system cost about $80. It would have cost way more to buy and hard wire a relay and four switches.

When I built this system I was only thinking of the dust contamination of the building. After working around it I will never be without this technology again. Sometimes I just leave it on to pick up ambient dust floating in the air. I never get residue on objects in the shop. I don't get affected by the dust physically. I have a downdraft table where I do most messy work, and I sometimes wonder if I'm getting anything done due to the lack of mess. The table has a 6″ intake and moves all the air in the room in just a few minutes. To further facilitate cleanliness, I designed my work area with cantilevered benches to make vacuuming the floor easier. When you have a system like this you start to see your shop as a wood removal system.

The most difficult issue to control is finish fumes. I am lucky in that the finishing area of my business is located beneath an elevated garage structure and has concrete walls and ceiling so smells from there don't get loose easily into the rest of the building. In addition I installed a great air purifier made by Alpine Industries that kills the smell of finishes, thinners, and aromatic wood dust. It works by generating negative ions and ozone. You can circulate the ozone through the ventilation system of the house to neutralize odors. It needs no filters. You just clean the electroplates every few weeks to keep the ozone production efficient. This unit has been a big improvement around here. Now I don't get complaints every time I open a can of lacquer thinner in the shop. With this device in place I have the dust-and-smell problems of my home workshop nearly completely contained.

I spent around $1600 building the system, including the air purifier. The Grizzly blower was purchased years ago for $325. It's been worth every cent. ——

Update

In 2001, Alpine Industries received a hefty fine in federal court for making unsubstantiated claims about their air purifiers.

(2007)

Originally published in *American Lutherie #57,* 1999

Meet the Maker: Steve Kinnaird

by John Calkin

I ONLY GET TO SEE Steve Kinnaird and his lovely wife Billie at GAL conventions, but we've been pen pals and friends for years. Steve enjoys fine guitars, Piedmont blues, and good humor. Other things, too, 'cause he's a deep guy, but that's mostly where our interests cross. He's so modest that I had to twist his arm repeatedly to do this interview. His beautiful spruce/koa flattop won accolades at the '98 convention listening session. Whenever the Texas weather gets unbearable he threatens to return to the Southeastern forests that he loves. I wish he would. I'd get to see him more often.

You were an organ major in college?

Yes, one of the last at my college. They dismantled the organ to redesign the facility, construction was delayed, and while the organ was in storage termites ate the wooden parts. Now the whole department is dismantled. Too bad, too, they had a great instructor. Organ music will come back; it runs in cycles. I was delighted to hear the new Fritts organ in Tacoma during the convention. Anyway, I had a sense that I was never going to set the world on fire with my playing. I went straight from my senior recital to being a carpenter, and I built houses for three years — cabinets and trim. As rough as a lot of the woodwork was, in the end it gave me the confidence to tackle something as demanding as a guitar. I'd built dulcimers, but they didn't really set me on the road to guitars. The standards that dulcimer players and guitar players set for their instruments are altogether different. Guitar players are much more critical. My emotional investment in my instruments is so high that I couldn't stand to build a wonderful-sounding guitar that was rejected for the way it looked, so for a long while I was apprehensive about approaching them.

JOHN CALKIN

Bob Tucker listens appreciatively as Steve Kinnaird picks and grins at the 1998 GAL Convention. This guitar was made by John Calkin.

How did you find yourself in the ministry?

I was in church one day and I got the call. Not to do anything in particular, but to serve somehow. I didn't know what to do. I talked to my pastor and he didn't know what I should do, so I just kept building houses. A few months later a good friend asked if I'd like to co-pastor a church in Dallas with him and be the music minister. It was a very small church with just the two of us tending the congregation, and it was there that I took my first two orders for guitars. Eventually I went to seminary. We moved back to Nacogdoches, Texas so I could pastor a little nondenominational church of my own. That was sixteen years ago, and they haven't thrown me out yet. The church is so small that I have no office there; I use the study in my house. So I can go from studying to gluing on braces smoothly. Somehow I hope it's all God's work.

So how did you start your lutherie career?

My brother John lives in Atlanta. While on a visit in the early '70s we went to see a guitar builder named J. Rhyne. He had previously been a machinist, and he took all that precision know-how and tooled up a shop like you wouldn't believe. He had automated scrapers that would cut the arch in the fretboard. He was using spherically dished workboards before anyone else was even talking about them. It was a three- or four-man shop. It struck my brother and me that here was a guy who was building our favorite instrument. We come from a long line of do-it-yourselfers, so we immediately thought, "Hey, we can do that!" We competed to see who could build the first guitar, and he got the jump on me. He's older and had a bit more experience with using his hands. I ended up building dulcimers and doing repair work, and I eased into it that way.

Was your family still in Tennessee at that point?

No, my father worked for Humble Oil, which in 1971 changed its name to Exxon. During the company shakeup he was transferred to Houston. I was just out of high school. A year or two after that is when John and I visited the shop in Atlanta, so I was already in Texas going to college at the time. I started repairing my dorm buddies' instruments, that kind of thing. After moving to Dallas, a fellow church-goer saw a couple of my dulcimers and commissioned a guitar, even though I'd never made one.

Wow, that demonstrates a lot of trust on his part. You must have made nice dulcimers.

But part of the frustration of building my first guitar was that the guy was a lefty, so when it was done I couldn't even play it. Had I been able to play it, guitar making might have become an addiction right away. Shortly afterward another member of the church ordered a guitar. He was right handed, and that's the guitar that really got me going. Somewhere in there we moved back to Nacogdoches, and I've been there ever since.

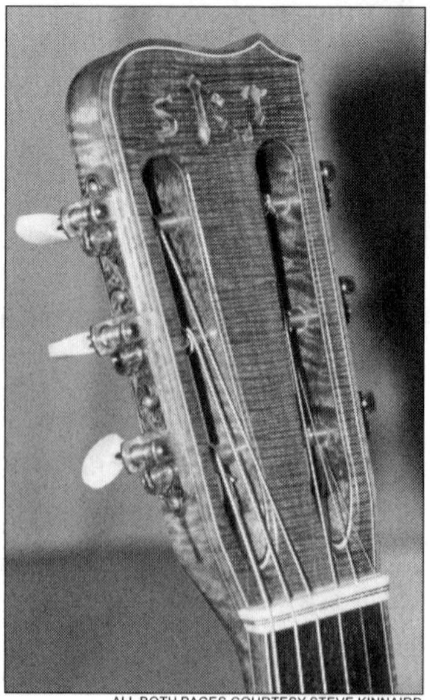

ALL BOTH PAGES COURTESY STEVE KINNAIRD

What is your lutherie situation now?

My church in Nacogdoches is so small that it doesn't make tremendous demands on my time on a daily basis, so I can devote the odd afternoon to guitar making. I also work at a local music store one day a week doing their repairs. My lutherie heart is more into building, but I probably put in more time with repairs, so it's not everything I could wish for. But it works out. I've gotten a couple orders from musicians who just came in to have repair work done.

You've told me your repair bench is a public place.

It certainly is, right in the front window. It was the owner's idea. If they could see me working it might generate business. And it works. It makes people remember about their broken instruments, and they bring them in when they might otherwise not.

How do you like it?

I'm over there right by the amps, and every Death Metal freak that comes in just drives me crazy. They insist on playing so loud. That's the only bad part. But I'm about to get moved to the back of the store, and that's great for me. Being on display isn't always a charmed situation.

Were you pleased with your guitars right from the first?

The first one, the lefty, no. I followed the plans in Irving Sloane's steel string guitar book, flipping them around for the left-handed guitar. His X pattern is slightly different than, say, a Martin, and the bridge plate is larger. Also, the top was a piece of spruce that a friend had sent me from Alaska, and it was cut pretty far off the quarter. It made a nice guitar but it was mellower than what I was looking for. On my second I went with a more traditional bracing pattern and it came out a lot better.

After that I got hold of the Martin herringbone pattern — that plan with the scalloped braces and such — and I started getting noticeable results. At the same time I threw a little Don Musser into the mix. The first time I scalloped my braces they looked so weak that I added a little brace behind the bridge patch like he does. I was real pleased with the sound. I also began to shape my tone bars as he recommended. The last big evolutionary step happened by accident. The router bit slipped out as I was cutting the binding channels, so I cut them deeper all the way around. I also had a set of binding that I just *had* to use. To make up the difference I had to thin the top pretty drastically right at the edge, and that one became my first killer guitar. I've been judiciously thinning the tops ever since. Someone once compared the action of the top to ripples caused by a stone tossed into water, and it seems to me that if you decrease the resistance at the perimeter you'll get more movement out of the whole top.

How many guitars ago was that?

That was #5. I'm lacquering #11 right now *(as of July 1998–JC)* so my output certainly hasn't been prodigious. I've got a lot of things fighting against my time. I've been building my house for years now, and for awhile it took every bit of my spare time. I try to be philosophic about it. There are luthiers who build a lot of guitars who hope one day to have a nice house. I've just gone about it backwards.

Probably makes a lot more sense your way.

It keeps the wife happier.

Whew! A very important aspect.

You betcha, buddy. If I build a thousand fewer guitars but keep my wife happy, life will have been well spent.

You've tried a variety of wood for your instruments.

I guess. The first one was made of kokko. I got it from a wood collector, but Gilmer in Portland, Oregon occasionally stocks it. My brother and I also got some padauk, purpleheart, and Santo Domingo mahogany from an Atlanta furniture maker. I made a padauk guitar and used the purpleheart for trim. I've

Two detail shots of a koa and spruce beauty that Steve showed at last summer's GAL convention.

tried maple, East Indian rosewood, mahogany, a smattering of stuff.

One of the guitars you had at the convention was made of killer koa.

Oh yeah, I've used as much koa as anything else. I can't escape it. I'm about to finish #12, which is koa, and I've got orders for four more. It just sells itself. People see the wood and it just knocks their lights out. But I'd just as soon work with Indian rosewood. I have an order for a classical in African blackwood, but I can't find a set. I keep bugging LMI, but the trees are small and the quality often poor.

Any last thoughts?

Sure. At the '98 convention I reunited with a man I first met at the '92 convention in Vermillion. He still hasn't made his first instrument. I think there are a lot of enthusiasts like that, and I think I understand. On that guitar you're planning in your mind, there's not one mistake. It sounds beautiful. It's the most beautiful guitar ever built. And as long as it stays there in your mind, you're happy. It's not until you put the steel to the wood, make the shavings fly, that you risk running into disappointment. The fear of disappointment may be what keeps a lot of wannabe luthiers from getting started. I'd like to urge them to get started anyway. Even if they don't manage to make the perfect guitar, there are a lot of tradeoffs toward the good that make the effort worthwhile, things they haven't even thought about yet.

The first time you string up your guitar and hear its voice, wow! There are few things that can equal that. And the first time you open the case for the customer and they get the first look at their new guitar, that's sweet, too, those stars in their eyes. ——

Update

Steve is happy to report that the church *still* hasn't thrown him out, his guitar count is considerably higher now, the house is virtually finished, and his wife is, basically, happy.

(2006)

Originally published in *American Lutherie #57*, 1999

QUESTIONS

EDITED BY CYNDY BURTON

■ ***Wes Brandt of Portland, OR** asks:*

I'm doing some restoration on an old Martin. I need to bend a piece of replacement ivory binding. What's the best way to bend ivory?

***Wes** called later with an answer to his own question:*

First I tried heat, which worked on little pieces, but I needed something more. I remembered the effects of vinegar on bones from way back, probably grade school. I soaked the ivory six to eight hours in white vinegar (full strength) to achieve sufficient flexibility. Then I soaked it in water for two hours before bending it. The vinegar made it somewhat translucent, but once it was dry, it became opaque again and rehardened. I left some in vinegar for sixteen hours and it shrank and stayed translucent after drying.

■ ***A Guild member** asks:*

I've been making my first steel string guitar, and as I was enthusiastically carving the neck, I exposed the edges of the truss rod. Is there an inconspicuous way to fix it?

***Jeffrey Elliott of Portland, OR,** responds:*

You are not alone. I have done the same thing and so have a lot of other builders. The most inconspicuous way to fix it is to create a flat which extends from the head joint to the heel joint and laminate on a piece of matching mahogany. It's best if it's from the same piece as the neck, of course. The cross-grain glue lines at the head and heel fall on existing joint lines, so they are unremarkable, and the long glue lines of the patch tend to blend in if they follow the grain.

If you wish to do a shorter patch, which is easier, the cross-grain lines are more apt to show, but there are ways to distract the eye away from them. You can create figure, that is *faux* figure. The cross-grain nature of pronounced figure can work perfectly to your benefit. I recommend practicing on scrap mahogany until you're very certain you've got the "figure" looking like the real thing under finish. A rounded metal piece, like the domed side of fretwire can be used to distress the neck shaft at somewhat regular intervals that include the patch glue lines, which are then filled and finished over.

Another solution is to stain or paint the neck so that the patch is invisible. A black peghead with the black extending part way down the neck could work if the patch is near the head. Or a sunburst effect could be created.

Another way to fool the eye is to inlay, woodburn (which is filled), or simply paint a pattern on the back of the neck that has enough complexity to incorporate the glue lines of the patch so that they become invisible or are replaced. A sort of tree-of-life viney pattern often seen on the surface of fretboards is well suited. ——

Originally published in *American Lutherie #57,* 1999

Adjustable Dished Workboard

by Kevin Rielly

BUILDING A UNIFORM ARCH into the top and back plates of my guitars has always been difficult for me. The problem seemed more daunting given the need for a different arch for each plate. The commercially available, rigid hollow forms seemed to be a viable solution; however, I would still need to purchase or construct two forms, one for each plate. I believe I have a simple solution to this problem with my variable-radius hollow-form design.

The form utilizes a flexible disk that is attached to a rigid base by a countersunk center adjusting screw, as shown in **Photo 1**. The edges of the flexible disk are supported around its circumference so that the center of the disk becomes concave as the screw is tightened down. I used masonite for the flexible disk since it seemed the most uniform material available, without any noticeable grain. The flat-head screw is countersunk so that it is flush with the surface of the disk. A reinforcement on the reverse side of the disk keeps the screw from breaking through the masonite.

I constructed my form by cutting two 23″ diameter disks of ¾″ medium-density particleboard and screwing them together to form a 1½″-thick disk. Two 23″ disks were cut from ¼″ masonite. The rim disk, also visible in **Photo 1**, was constructed by cutting a 19″-diameter circle from the center of one masonite disk leaving a 2″-wide rim with a 23″ outer diameter and 19″ inner diameter. The rim disk was attached to the particleboard base using several wire brads, allowing future removal if necessary. The size of the disk is based more on the availability of materials than a particular formula. Pieces of particleboard and masonite 2′×4′ yield all that is needed to construct the form. The 19″ inner diameter of the rim disk was likewise arbitrary but was selected to exceed the width of the lower bout of any guitar produced on the form.

Using a 1½″ hole saw, I cut a circle in a scrap of masonite and used the inner piece for the screw reinforcement. The center hole of this small disk was enlarged to ⅜″. A ⅜″ hole was drilled in the center of the large masonite disk. The holes in the small and large disks were aligned and the small disk was glued to the larger with epoxy. Once dry, the top of the hole was countersunk to allow the adjusting screw to lie flush with the surface of the top disk. Using the hole saw and router, I cut a recess in the center of the particleboard base on both sides. Each recess needed to be at least ¼″ deep to allow space for the reinforcement to fit into the base as the top disk is drawn down by the adjusting screw. The bottom recess was fitted with a T nut to accept the adjusting screw. The screw I used extended beyond the bottom of the base. Instead of mounting feet on the bottom of the base, I simply propped it up on some blocks of scrap particleboard to allow clearance for the screw. The only trouble I've had was when I overtightened the form and had to reglue the reinforcement to the underside of the top disk.

I set the arch in the form by using a straightedge extending edge-to-edge over the center of the disk and tightening the screw, as shown in **Photo 2**. I determine the arch by measuring from the bottom of the straightedge to the concave surface of the masonite. The maximum depth of the arch is determined by the thickness of the rim. My form was able to produce an arch up to a depth of ¼″ when measured this way. Using a formula supplied to me by Maryann Faller, a math professor at Adirondack Community College, I determined that the radius of this arch should be about 22′. A depth of ⅛″ should give a radius of about 44′.

ALL BY KEVIN RIELLY

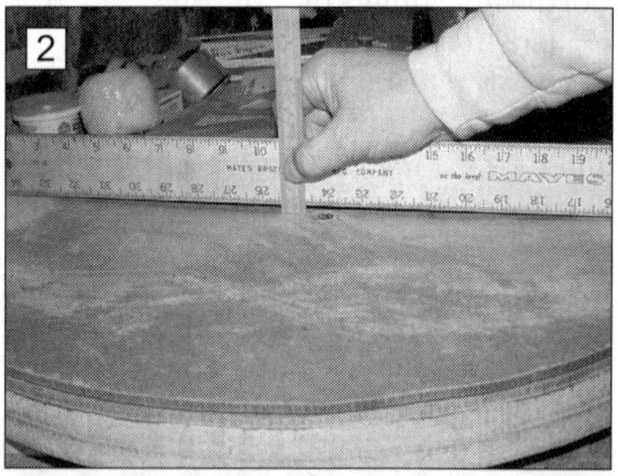

The form is cheap to make, so I drew my bracing patterns on the top disk (**Photo 3**). If the masonite gets too worn, I will make a new top disk. The form was used just as if it were a solid form. I don't glue sandpaper to the form, I just hold a sheet on the form with one hand while I move the brace with the other (**Photo 4**). Once the braces were sanded on the form, the back plate was positioned on the form and the braces glued in place (**Photos 5 and 6**). The clamp shown in the photos used a piece of ¼″ aluminum bar, which proved to be too flexible. I eventually switched to a go-bar deck. The arch was changed for the top plate and the braces were sanded and glued in a similar fashion. I even shaped the sides and glued the top to the sides on the form. The masonite has some spring to it and provides some resistance when work is clamped upon it.

I noticed that the top disk retained a slightly concave shape after the screw was released. To store the form, I reversed the top disk and replaced the screw. A scrap piece of ¼″ masonite between the top disk and base keeps the disk from being tightened down in storage. If the top disk isn't straight by the next time I use it, I'll discard it and make a new top disk. I may also consider producing a shorter radius by increasing the height of the rim or making a smaller diameter form. ——

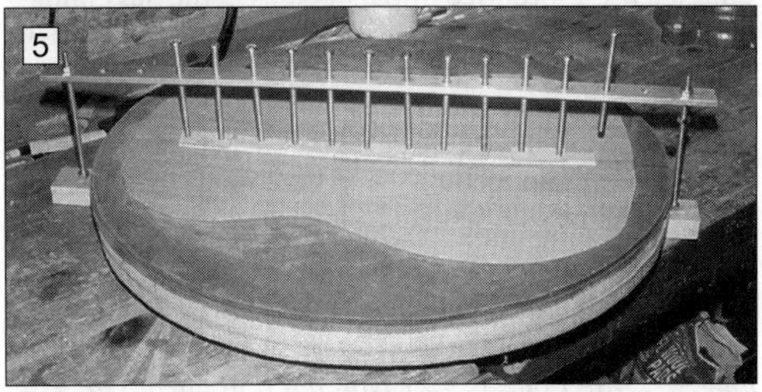

Originally published in *American Lutherie #57,* 1999

Whence the Dish?

by John Calkin

By now the spherically dished workboard has become a standard lutherie item, so it's easy to overlook the fact that it's a relatively new idea. I've always thought of it as a West Coast innovation, but after a little research I'm not so sure.

Californian David Russell Young seems to have been the first to admonish us to arch the tops of our guitars as well as the backs. His book, *The Steel String Guitar,* appeared in 1975. However, the book contains no elaborate jigs or fixtures for creating the arched braces or plates. It seems, though, that Young may have used dished workboards in his own shop at that time. He certainly had them before 1984, the year that Don Musser contributed an article to the Luthier's Mercantile catalog about making dished workboards with a router and an arched tray. By 1989 or so LMI had made the workboards a catalog item.

Kevin Rielly was aware of LMI's workboards, but found the price prohibitive and Musser's instructions for making them too messy. The workboard he came up with was easy to make and cheap (really cheap considering that only one form was necessary to make both the back and top plates). He had no way to test his forms to check for a true spherical shape, but used the shadow cast by a straightedge to look for flat spots. The form seemed to have a fair curve, so he put it into service. Kevin is quick to admit that his form isn't as rigid as a solid workboard, but the quality of his guitars indicates that it is rigid enough.

A Guild member with a good memory may recall a 1984 article by Peter Estes which detailed a dished workboard that looks very much like the Rielly form, but is not adjustable. When I talked to Peter recently, he mentioned that adjustability was a feature included in his workboard but not, for some reason, in the data sheet. He attended the 1979 GAL Convention in Boston and overheard a conversation about using an arched gluing fixture in the shape of a cross to brace the plates. The idea was attractive but the jig seemed clumsy to him, and he came up with a dished, circular workboard as a substitute. Peter mentioned that he's not as active in lutherie as he once was, but that he still uses his original workboard.

It's a good guess that in 1978 the notion of arched plates came from Young's book, which sort of completes the loop. However, Texas luthier Stephen Kinnaird told me that he saw dished workboards in an Atlanta guitar shop in 1972, three years before the book came out. So it seems that the same lightning has struck all over the place. Gibson also claims that it made guitars with radiused tops in the vintage days. All of this just demonstrates that with over five billion people on the planet, it's pretty hard to have an original idea. Whoever thought it up, though, it looks like the dished workboard is here to stay. ——

Originally published in *American Lutherie #58 and #59*, 1999

Kasha Collaboration

George Majkowski and Boaz Elkayam join forces to build ten Kasha/Schneider-design guitars to honor the memory of their late teacher, and to help keep his work alive.

by Jonathon Peterson

BOAZ ELKAYAM AND GEORGE MAJKOWSKI are as unlikely a pair of lutherie partners as you are likely to meet. The footloose, flamboyant, hand-tool-oriented Israeli, who once built a guitar on a cafe table with a Swiss Army knife just to prove it could be done; and the meticulous European-born retired engineer, who is as careful with his words as he is with his excellent tool and work-flow design, are a striking contrast. The thread that brought them together was their association with Richard Schneider; and the catalyst for their joint project, the building of ten Kasha/Schneider-design classical guitars, was Richard's untimely death.

Richard was a dear friend of mine, and I believed in his work. He was a romantic, an idealist, and a shameless proselytizer for the vision he had of a modern guitar. In a way, he was more of an R&D man than a working luthier. For most of the Kasha period of his career, his design was undergoing constant metamorphosis. When an instrument was finished he would evaluate it, have consultations with Dr. Kasha, and go back to the drawing board. The next instrument would often have dozens of changes, each based on a logical and scientifically supportable view of what was happening physically and acoustically, each executed with superb craftsmanship and attention to detail. But although the instruments changed, the vision remained constant. Richard maintained faith in his vision for years in the face of broad criticism.

The last time I spoke with Richard, in Healdsburg in 1996, he said he'd finally arrived at a design he felt good about reproducing without additional tinkering, and that if enough of these instruments got out there they would sell themselves. But, he said, he was getting too old to do that work himself. Others would have to take up the cause. He was finally being taken seriously, but no one was making the instruments in any real numbers, not even Richard.

Though Richard could not have foreseen the circumstances, Boaz and "Uncle George" (a nickname given to George by a former student) stepped forward to begin doing what he had said needed to be done — getting those instruments out there. It is my hope that the following coverage of their project will in some way help to keep Richard's work alive and growing into the future.

ALL COURTESY GEORGE MAJKOWSKI AND BOAZ ELKAYAM EXCEPT AS NOTED

From left to right, Boaz Elkayam, Dr. Michael Kasha, and George Majkowski. This picture was taken during a visit Dr. Kasha paid to the two luthiers to consult with them on their project of building ten Kasha/ Schneider-design guitars similar to the one George is holding. Richard Schneider called this design the Recording model, and considered it the most successful of his lutherie career. It was the culmination of three decades of collaboration with Dr. Kasha, who is a renowned scientist. The instrument Boaz is holding is an earlier Kasha/Schneider design which Richard called the Standard. Both of the pictured guitars were built by George Majkowski. Luthiers Mercantile International (www.lmii.com) carries plans for both designs.

Boaz: In the beginning I would like to thank Beverly Maher of the Guitar Salon in New York for supporting us financially and allowing this project to continue; Anna Majkowski who gave us her home to live and work in; Jay Hargreaves who helped us many ways; Jason Ontake, my apprentice who helped us in the beginning of the project; André who helped us; Jonathon Peterson for coming here and keeping track of our progress; and Uncle George who gave me this unbelievable opportunity. It's once in a lifetime that you come across such an opportunity, and I grabbed it. And Richard Schneider, God bless him.

Boaz, I know that you grew up in an instrument-making environment, and that you have been building guitars for most of your life. (See our Meet the Maker *interview with Boaz, p. 92.) How did your interest in working with the Kasha design ideas come about?*

Boaz: I met Richard at the Healdsburg Guitar Festival in 1996. After his lecture, I told him that what he said about the instrument just sounds right to me, and I want to take his course to learn about these ideas, but I don't have the money. He saw my instruments, and said, "Did you make these?" They were the Baroque guitar and the flamenco that you put pictures of in the GAL journal. I said, "Yes." He said, "Can you give me five minutes?" When he came back he said, "I'll give you a scholarship." I don't know where he went or who he talked to, but that's how it started.

I admired his work, and Richard loved that I also was interested in improving the acoustical function of the guitar. He stayed at my home when he was in Los Angeles, and we talked for hours about the Kasha design.

I know that he spoke very highly of your abilities and your understanding of what he was trying to accomplish. What was Richard's seminar like?

Richard really didn't give the course. It was more Uncle George and Jay Hargreaves. I got very close to Uncle George. I admire his skills, his knowledge, and his life experience. I saw like a spring of water where I can get endless information; not just someone to talk to, but someone who can also do the work.

What was your background before lutherie, George?

George: I grew up in France, and there weren't the same types of unions that we have over here. Certain specialists were allowed to cross the borders and be trained to do various things. I was a specialist that took care of the automation of systems for the production of electronics. As a result I had access to shop facilities, and I became quite proficient in using metal- and woodworking equipment to make tools. When I came to the United States, I was hired by IBM to install large computer systems. I didn't need all the skills that I acquired in my previous job.

Had you been a guitar player?

George: Yes, even when I was in France, I was playing guitar. When I came to the United States I was playing with a flamenco troupe. I was filling in with them professionally as time permitted, because I was more formally employed.

When I retired I needed something to occupy my time. I had an interest in woodworking, but building furniture was not sufficient. I wanted something more challenging. I decided it would be interesting to build a guitar, so I got Sloane's book and I built a guitar. Well, I put it together. All the pieces were in the right place. It was not the best one, you know?

Then I got a flyer announcing the Guild's 1990 convention. I had time on my hands, so I jumped in my car and drove from the Bay Area to Tacoma, and started mingling with guitar makers. I was overwhelmed. I asked myself, "What am I doing here?" Then I saw Richard's display, and I played his guitars. I was completely taken by the complexity of the stuff. It was beautiful — all these braces that were so unusual. I was very curious. He had a sign-up sheet at his table, so I put my name on it.

Soon I got a letter from Richard saying he had a seminar coming up, so again I jumped in my car and drove to Sequim, Washington. I was completely ignored by Richard. He told me later that at the time he thought, "Who is this old fart? He's just wasting my time." But he was kind enough. I went through the course, then I went home and built a Kasha guitar.

A few months later Richard was in the Bay Area and gave me a call, so I met him at Luthier's Mercantile and showed him my instrument. He was very pleased with it. Actually, he said that he was a little surprised. He said of all the students that he didn't think would do anything, I was the one who came up with a guitar.

At that time I was looking for a quieter and less expensive place to live. On the advice of a friend in Tacoma, I came up here and found a place in Gig Harbor. This was not to get closer to Richard, it was just a normal decision. Then I realized that I wasn't very far from him, so I again jumped in the car. I would go once a week and spend a couple of days with him, and we started working together. Slowly he recognized that I wasn't going to destroy anything that he was doing, so he started to trust me with work. After a couple years he had complete confidence in my abilities, and he would let me do anything I wanted in the shop. We developed a friendship, and he was quite receptive to some of my ideas. We had a lot of arguments and good times. I also helped him with his seminars and other activities. He was particularly interested in the fact that I was able to build jigs, and I helped him design fixtures. We worked together on his last series of guitars. I built some jigs for him, and I was able to build two guitars of my own. Two guitars in five years is not a big record, but we had a good time.

Before his death, I began to get frustrated. I was trying to understand what he was doing, but most of the information I needed I had to get piecemeal, just by being around and asking questions. The seminar he gave once a year was very limited. Practically all the information for building one of these guitars was just in Richard's head. He was generous with information, but you had to ask. He would not know ahead of time exactly what to tell you or not to tell you. One day I said, "Listen, you should write it all down so people can have some source of information." My idea was only to write a small shop manual, something that you could use with your blueprint. Well, he started writing, and writing, and pretty soon he had hundreds and hundreds of pages. I was delighted!

Working in France, and later for IBM, I had developed a logical approach to things, so he would have me read what he had written. If it was ambiguous I would ask "What do you mean by this?" and he would rewrite it.

We agreed that he would do the prose, and I would do the drawings, but without the text it's kind of difficult to figure out what drawings are necessary. I was waiting for him to give me text with indications for sketches, and meanwhile I was doing sketches of my own for things that I thought were needed.

Part of the tragedy of his death is that the book didn't get finished. Another part is that Richard didn't make that many instruments — very few of what was his current model at the time of his death — and after his death they became unavailable for all practical purposes. The ones that weren't already sold became the property of the family, and I understand that they are not for sale. If anyone wanted to see and touch an instrument, it would be difficult to arrange. I was afraid that in time a lack of these instruments would slowly kill the Kasha project, and the interest in building or playing this type of instrument would dwindle. So I came up with a scheme to build a series of instruments that would kind of fill the void.

It has always been surprising to me that with as many people as Richard taught, the number that actually went out and built Kasha instruments was so small. You like to show people how to build Kasha instruments, but it's frustrating to spend all the time to transfer the knowledge, knowing very well that the person is not going to use it. It bothered me, and I know that it bothered Richard. I love to talk to people about Kasha guitars, but it feels like I'm wasting my time if they go home and do nothing.

So I got together with Boaz, who was our last student. He was already a fine guitar builder when we met him, and he was absolutely intrigued by the Kasha design. We came up with a scheme that maybe by joining forces we would be able to produce a series of instruments that would commemorate Richard's work, and at the same time be available to players and builders to help keep this work alive. During the time that I was with Richard I was also able to put together a reasonably well-equipped shop, so we could start working right away.

What is your focus on this project, Boaz?

Boaz: I am focusing on the future. We made these instruments so that people can play them, people can look at the design and hear how it works. Then maybe players will ask builders to make them. We want people to be inspired by these ideas and carry on this work.

My experience is that Kasha people talk and not work. What we are trying now is to take a new direction, which means that Kasha people do more work and less talk. That's it. Do the work.

Also, to help keep this work alive, 5% of the profits from the sale of these guitars we will donate to help finish Richard's book.

George, you told me that a lot of the jigs that you're using for this series are the same ones that Richard used on his instruments, so it's not like you are just copying his final instruments — they are actually coming off of the same patterns and fixtures.

George: Every time we had to improve a fixture, I was the one who would build it, and since we were working together we were both using it. Just prior to Richard's death a lot of fixtures were becoming obsolete because of the changes he had made in developing his last design, so I made new versions. After he died all the new versions ended up in my shop since I built them.

They are not as pretty as the jigs Richard made. When he made a fixture he wanted it to look good, so he would stain it or paint it to make it look pretty. I didn't have time for that. I just wanted a jig that does the job. Eventually I would like to redo them and follow Richard's example.

Richard once said to me that the structural and acoustic efficiency of the Kasha design not only make it possible to build exemplary guitars with the materials that are available today, but that the merits of the design will become even more important as we deal with the scarcity of traditional materials in the future. A perfect example of what he was talking about is the softwood back and its bracing, which he said was a huge factor in the success of this design.

George: I think it's obvious that an excellent instrument requires excellent materials and excellent workmanship, but the structure and the bracing of this design act as an equalizer. The traditional builder often has one instrument that is excellent, but the next is not so good. There will naturally be differences between your instruments, but there will be less difference if you carefully follow this design. It is perhaps even harder to build a truly exceptional instrument with this design because of the complexity, but the design gives you better control, which should make it possible for you to build better instruments in the end.

Boaz: In my opinion, building Kashas is like building traditional guitars. You take the chances of making it good or making it bad. The difference is that you have a slightly better chance to make it good because you understand the acoustic concept. But basically, it's still you making individual guitars, and you still depend on the tips of your fingers and your heart. Dr. Michael Kasha said that in this house at this kitchen table. So that means that not every Kasha builder can create a good Kasha just by using the design. Uncle George doesn't agree.

George: No, it's just that there's a difference between saying that somebody will build a good guitar, or saying they will not build a bad one. If you follow the process carefully and stick with the design and the measurements, it's difficult to make a bad one. It's also very difficult to make an outstanding one. But if you have basic skills and a basic understanding of the concept, you have a better chance of building an acceptable instrument.

Boaz: Yes, I agree.

George: The reason, in my opinion, that there is such a variety of results in traditional guitars is that traditional construction doesn't pay enough attention to the specifics of sound production. The bracing is not controlling the instrument as much as the bracing in the Kasha does. By controlling where the sound is being produced you are going to equalize to some extent the production of the sound. That's why I believe that Kasha construction produces more consistent results. That doesn't mean all the Kashas are going to be good, because there are different builders, and different woods, and differences in bracing. But for one builder working with this design, the variation — the range from best to worst — should be narrower. If you really pay attention to the right things, chances are the instrument is going to be definitely acceptable. I believe that the bracing equalizes the efficiency of the material.

I'd like you to comment on the tooling that you use. That is obviously a big part why they are so consistent.

George: It plays a big role, absolutely. If you have proper tooling, chances are greater that every piece is going to be very nearly identical to the next, and close tolerances narrow down the possible results.

To be honest, I like to work with part-specific jigs mostly because it takes much more work to make parts exactly identical by hand. If I use a fixture, it's much easier for me to make something that will be exactly the same shape and size every time. So when I build a fixture it is not necessarily because I want to spend all this time and energy on details. It's more or less a desire not to do so much work.

Boaz: I agree with Uncle George. His fixtures are superior to any I've seen. For instance, at one point I told Uncle George I had some problems doing the holes in the bridge, and he sent me a beautiful jig. He understood my handwork process, so it wasn't a jig to attach to a pin router or something. It was made for how I work.

Most of this brace work is done by hand — planed by hand and measured. The very first braces were made with fixtures, but it did not work for me. I was more comfortable using the hand plane. I get the result I want quicker, so I continue doing the braces by hand. But the rest of the building is done with fixtures, and it is much easier that way — less guess work and better results. That's why the instruments are all so similar.

George: I shape the braces mostly with sandpaper. I do a rough shaping with the chisel and finish with sandpaper. How you do it really doesn't matter.

Boaz: As long as you stay on the measurements, that's the results you get. Now, if you want to build more freely with this design, like I did with Clarita Negra, the baritone guitar I made during this project, you will have a wonderful experience and a wonderful surprise. I consulted with acoustical engineer Bob Foster, and we applied some ideas that seem to improve acoustical efficiency. So Richard's Kasha design still has an open place for experiments.

George: Absolutely. Everything that we're doing is basically from Richard's design and measurements, but as you work with it you might see things that you want to change. I see absolutely nothing wrong with experimenting, but the point is to stay consistent. In other words, don't experiment for the sake of experimenting. Before you start building, make sure that you really understand what Dr. Kasha was trying to achieve. Stay consistent with the Kasha theory.

Before we begin looking at the construction of these instruments, it might be good to give a general explanation of Kasha bracing design for any of our readers who have not been introduced. I spoke with Jay Hargreaves about this, and he used the analogy of a triaxial speaker, in which different parts of the speaker are designed to produce different portions of the sound spectrum. A crossover feeds the signals for high frequencies to the tweeter, the midrange signals to the midrange, and the bass signals to the woofer. He said that in the Kasha soundboard you use perimeter bars to define response zones, tone bars to drive these zones, and an impedance-matching bridge to act as the crossover. The treble end of the bridge is narrowed to provide less resistance to motion when it vibrates at high frequencies. It drives the short bars which drive the restricted area on the treble side of the soundboard to reproduce the high frequencies. The widening center portion of the bridge drives the lengthening bars in the middle of the soundboard for midrange response. The bass end of the bridge is widest to more efficiently transfer the slower, longer wavelength vibrations of the lower frequencies to the long bass bars. The bass bars extend past the perimeter bars to drive the largest area, which is most of the top, producing the bass response.

Moving the soundhole away from the middle of the top has made the soundboard stronger, so a waist bar is no longer necessary. This allows the whole top to vibrate more freely, and longer tone bars can be used to get more of the top involved, resulting in an improved midrange.

Do you want to add anything to that, George?

George: Only one of the soundboard braces is continuous across the bridge area. That is the TT bar, which extends most of the width of the guitar along the bridge's rotational axis. The main tone bars only overlap the bridge's perimeter at their ends. This leaves the bridge free to move, but in a controlled way. All of the tone bars have a theoretically ideal shape which is intended to efficiently distribute the vibration generated at the bridge throughout the soundboard. They are larger and stiffer on the end which overlaps the bridge's perimeter, and they decrease in size and weight, and increase in flexibility, as they radiate outwards. The heights and positions of their crests, the tapers of their ends, and so forth are adjusted to match the rigidity of the soundboard so that their combined stiffness provides the action. The character of the sound can be somewhat controlled by adjusting the dimensions of the tone bars and their amount of overlap with the bridge outline. For instance, moving the crests of the tone bars closer to the saddle will produce a faster attack. Making the tone bars thinner in the middle will decrease the instrument's sustain.

There are a lot of components in a Kasha guitar, and there are definite close relationships between the various parts of the instrument. If an element's function is mainly structural, it is designed to improve the functioning of the acoustic elements rather than impeding them. The neck reinforcement and the floating braces are cases in point.

It would take more space than we have here to explore all of the aspects of Kasha design. I sincerely hope that Richard's book will eventually be published, as it will cover all aspects of design and construction in detail.

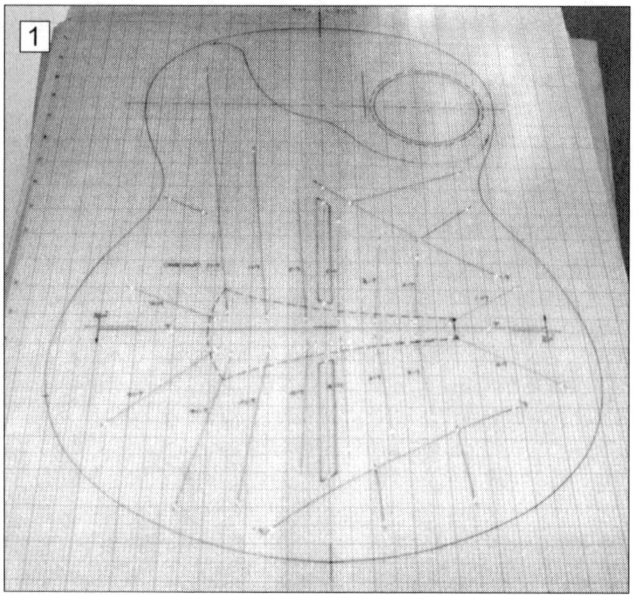
1

2

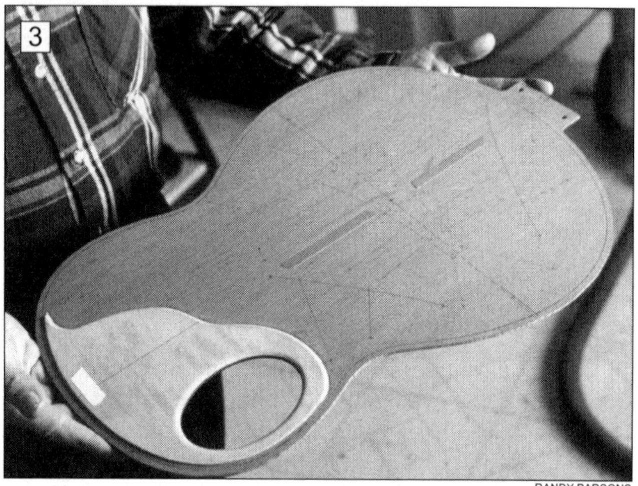
3

RANDY PARSONS

What's your take on all of this, Boaz?

Boaz: I think there is the Kasha theory, but there is also the mythology associated with the Kasha theory. The reason I say there is mythology is because I have seen and heard instruments which use these ideas that do not give noticeably improved sustain or response over traditional classical guitar designs. Results from testing two or three instruments a year do not constitute proof that these theories work. You must back up your theories, not with one or two instruments, but with many. I don't think anyone can call these theories conclusive because we are still scratching the surface. I think that the Kasha principles are an improvement to our previous understanding, but we still need a vision. There is a *much* better theory which has yet to be developed, a much better understanding, and we must keep searching until we find it.

Also, even when you are successful in making the improvements that you set out to make, it can take some time for the public's ear to evolve. The piano was not accepted over the harpsichord right away — it took time. The cello was not initially accepted over the viola da gamba. Perhaps the improvements that the Kasha design have brought are only marginal, but just wait. They laughed at the Wright brothers, and we've already been to the moon!

Since Uncle George mentioned his seminar, I would like to say that I also will be conducting seminars in the US and Europe early next year, focusing on modern acoustical concepts being applied to the construction of classical and steel string guitars. There will be a limit of four students at a time so that we can really focus on quality. (More information about Boaz, his work, and his seminars can be found on the web at: www.boazguitars.com.)

Let's begin looking at the process the two of you went through to produce your series of ten Recording-model Kasha/Schneider-design guitars.

Boaz: That's the layout of the soundboard on a semi-clear plastic sheet **(Photo 1)**. Lines show the position of each brace. At the end of each line is a hole so you can put a pen through to make a mark on the soundboard.

The first soundboard we thicknessed by hand. You use a small plane and cross plane till you get the depth you want **(Photo 2)**, and then you take a big plane and you work all over until you reach the depth you established with the small one. But we thought it was going to take forever, so you introduced us to your friend Ken Warmoth at Warmoth Guitars in Puyallup, and he used his sanding machine to thickness them. He did a beautiful job. The soundboards are giant sequoia, thirty years air dried.

George: This shows what the soundboard looks like after brace positions have been marked, the outline has been cut, and the soundhole and center-seam reinforcements have been glued in place **(Photo 3)**.

Boaz: The spruce braces are all split **(Photo 4)** to a tolerance of 2MM, and then we work them to the final shape. We have a way we treat the braces, and then we cook them for over two weeks in the oven. If they aren't truly quarter cut, after cooking they will bend. From a couple hundred braces we made, only one changed shape after cooking, which means they all have been perfectly quarter cut.

The tone bars need to be shaped to specific dimensions **(Photos 5 and 6)** before they are glued to the soundboard, and for ten guitars there are hundreds of them. It took a long time just to make all the braces.

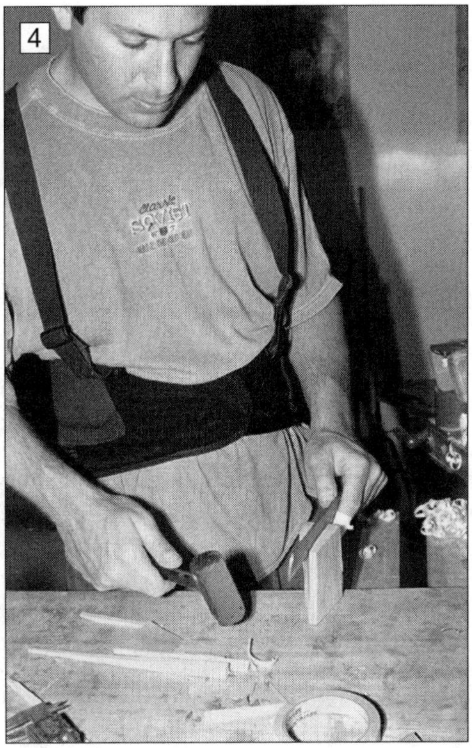

4

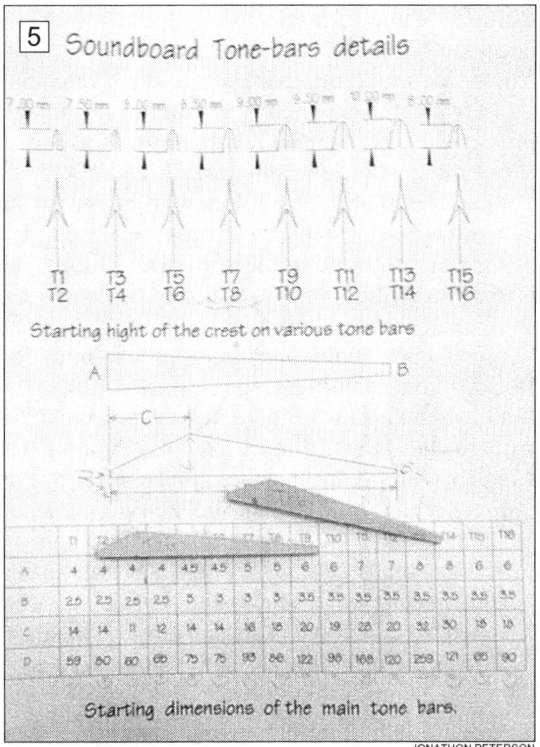

5

JONATHON PETERSON

How many braces are there on one soundboard?

Boaz: Seventeen vocal ones — sixteen tone bars plus the bar which goes across the top underneath the saddle. Then there are six other braces that make up the perimeter structures on the treble side of the top. So that's two hundred thirty top braces for the ten guitars, plus twenty-three more for my baritone guitar. There are also six on each back, not including the laminated ones, so that's sisty-six more.

How is the preliminary shaping accomplished?

George: I have a jig that goes on my bandsaw which establishes the taper on the sides of the braces when the brace blanks are cut from the split pieces. The tapers on the top are then established by hand.

Boaz: As long as you get a result it doesn't matter how you do it. I find it easiest to shape them by hand, like you see in the picture **(Photo 7)**, or sometimes I clamp my plane upside-down in the vise, so instead of moving the plane to cut, I can move the brace across the plane.

You can see the tip of the knife going into this piece of wood to make a simple marking gauge. I use that to mark exact measures for widths.

What were the tolerances for the preliminary shaping?

Boaz: Before final shaping they are within .003″–.005″. I Remember Uncle George checking them and saying, "This is unbelievable! They are within .001″!" But he only measured a few from a couple hundred.

George: Because the braces are preshaped before gluing they are already quite thin. It is difficult to guarantee correct and uniform glue joints when trying to glue so many thin strips using conventional clamping, so we use a vacuum clamp. I designed my vacuum clamp with a hinged wall mount and a hinged leg assembly so that it can fold flat against the wall when it is not in use. It has

6

JONATHON PETERSON

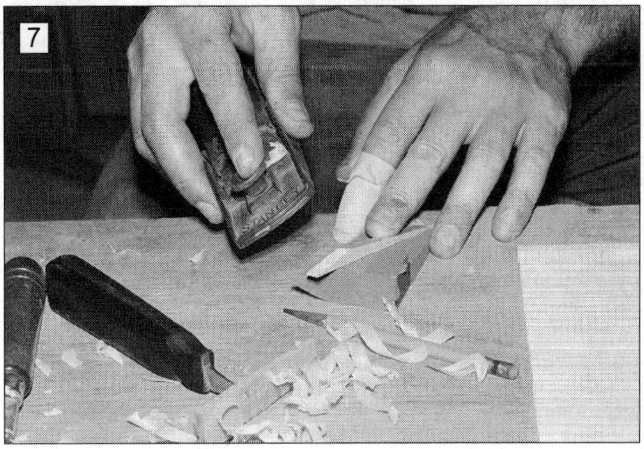

7

a hinged frame with an air seal around its underside, and a rubber membrane across the top. An air hose from a vacuum pump connects to the frame, and as the air is evacuated the membrane applies uniform pressure over the entire length of the braces **(Photo 8)** resulting in superior glue joints.

The clamp utilizes a dished workboard surface. The vacuum applies totally even pressure, which pushes all of the parts into the shape of the workboard. The result is that the soundboards are automatically domed when the braces are attached.

Here I am cleaning up glue squeeze-out **(Photo 9)**. Because the vacuum clamp encloses your work you do not have the opportunity to wipe away excess glue while you are clamping. Instead, the soundboard is removed from the clamp after a short time — after the braces are secure, but before the squeeze-out has time to fully harden — so the glue can be cleaned up. The soundboard is then returned to the clamp until the glue has fully set.

Richard developed a special curved chisel for clearing glue from braces. They are really nice tools that are useful for many other jobs as well.

Here we are beginning to shape the tone bars to make them conform to their theoretically ideal shape **(Photo 10)**. The majority of this shaping is done before the perimeter structures are glued in place so that they won't get in the way.

Boaz: Here I am flexing a soundboard to test its stiffness **(Photo 11)**. I measure with the thumb. I hold it like you hold a spongy ball and squeeze it to see if it flexes to my requirements.

George: This is a preliminary check, because in Kasha design you have a chance to voice it through the end panel after it's been completely assembled.

Boaz: You have two chances to, as you say, voice the guitar. I don't like the word "voicing." You are just measuring and adjusting flexibility. You adjust the flexibility by removing wood from the braces. What is right is up to the builder.

8

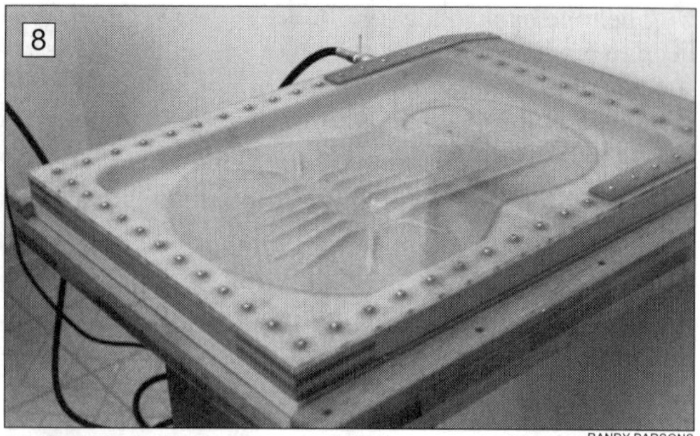

RANDY PARSONS

9

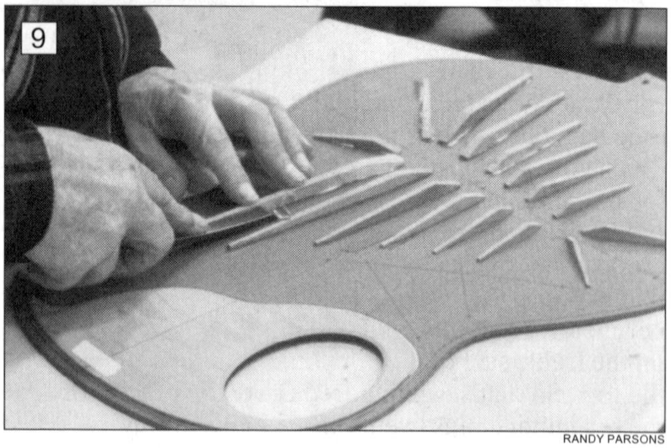

RANDY PARSONS

I use thinner soundboards than Richard. These soundboards are 3MM. We do not touch the thickness of the soundboard, just the braces.

George: You have to balance the stiffness of the soundboard with the stiffness of the braces. A very flexible top needs stiffer braces. A soundboard which is very stiff calls for thinner bracing in order to reach that balance. You also need to make sure that the braces are proportional to each other.

Boaz: That's what I'm doing here **(Photo 12)**. I use a sanding block across several braces to achieve an even register. After that is done we round off the tops of the braces with sandpaper.

10

RANDY PARSONS

11

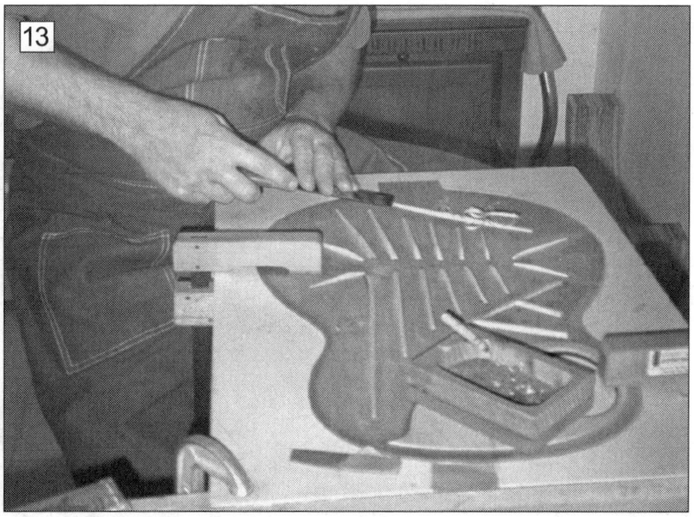

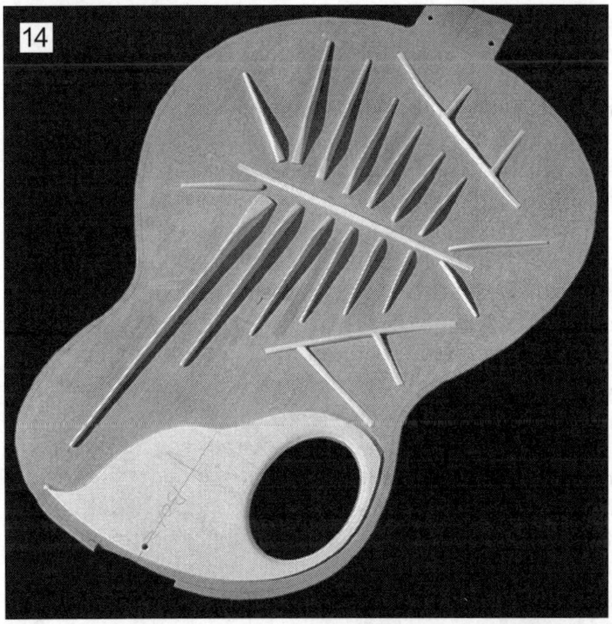

After we have finished shaping the tone bars we glue on the perimeter bars, and carve and sand them (**Photo 13**). The last soundboard brace we install is the TT bar, which is the transverse bar that crosses under the bridge. It gets glued on in the vacuum clamp, then shaped, and sanded. At this point the soundboard is complete (**Photo 14**), although, as we said, you can easily make adjustments to the brace dimensions after the instrument has been assembled if you decide it is necessary.

Here we begin to assemble the backs by gluing ebony for a decorative center stripe to one edge of half of the back. This is a traditional way of clamping center seams (**Photo 15**). The sticks hold the pieces from folding under the pressure of the rubber strip, which is wound around to provide the clamping pressure. Using this kind of clamping setup you can edge-glue plates with odd shapes. Here we are also using cam clamps to assist in alignment, but you don't need them.

When the glue is dry the excess ebony is trimmed away with a saw, then a hand plane is used to prepare the sawn edge for gluing to the other half of the back. I use fingerboards for the tapered center stripes. Each fingerboard gives me about six. You can see triangles for other backs marked on the ebony (**Photo 16**).

I used tapered stripes like this on the back of my Baroque guitar, by the way, but there were eighty of them in alternating colors, and they formed the whole back. We decided to use one tapered stripe in the middle of each of the redwood backs as a signature decoration on this series of guitars.

George: We wanted these instruments to be as authentic as possible to Richard's last instruments. However, Richard had his own signature decorations and designs which we had no right to copy, so we developed our own.

Boaz: Here we are gluing the second half using the same clamping method, but using rope to apply the clamping pressure **(Photo 17)**.

George: We use a lot of laminated bars and plates in Kasha construction for structural elements requiring strength and stability. These work to free up the tone-producing elements of the guitar by relieving them of some of their load-bearing responsibilities. In most cases, layers of rotary-cut maple veneer and epoxy are laid up on specially shaped molds to produce the blanks for these parts. The blanks are then given their final shape by some combination of machine and hand work.

Here we are getting ready to laminate the back braces by spreading epoxy on maple veneers with a credit card **(Photo 18)**. These veneers are wide enough so that we can cut four brace blanks out of each laminated piece. There are two different laminated X braces on the back — one in the upper bout, and one in the lower bout. The X in the lower bout is actually a structure comprised of two laminated Xs. A flat two-ply X is preassembled and glued to the back as a unit, and an arched X is attached to it.

These are the bars for the X brace that goes in the upper bout of the back before they have been carved **(Photo 19)**. After we take the laminated piece from the mold, we saw it into brace blanks. The blanks are then paired up and taped together at their ends so that they can be carved in pairs. This helps to insure that the two parts of the X will match.

The arms of this upper-back X that will be nearest the waist have arches laminated into them to accommodate braces which will run underneath them. The arms that will extend into the upper bout are straight and will be glued to the back and to the heel of the neck. This reinforces the joint between the neck and the body, which helps to maintain the accuracy of the string action.

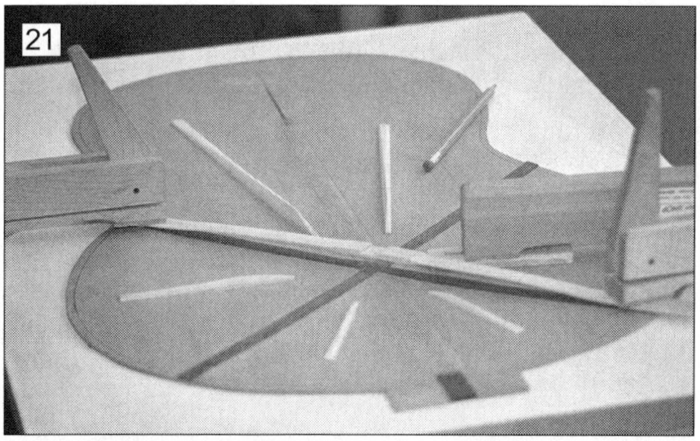

Boaz: This shows part of the shaping of the laminated braces **(Photo 20)**. Here we are filing the X braces for the lower bout of the back in pairs so they will be equal.

After the back has been thicknessed and the outline has been cut, the center-reinforcement strip is glued on. Then radial bars and the flat X are glued to the back in the vacuum clamp. When those are cleaned up and shaped the other laminated X braces can be positioned and fit. We do that on a dished workboard **(Photo 21)**. Clamps hold the brace ends in place. Another clamp presses the back into the workboard to hold it to the proper radius while the lap joints are fit.

George: Here I am marking for the lap joint in the floating X **(Photo 22)**. The floating X arches about ½″ above the back at its center, and is joined to the low, flat X at the perimeter of the plate.

Boaz: Here we are cutting the slot for the lap joint in the floating braces **(Photo 23)**.

George: This is how the X braces are attached **(Photo 24)**. The back is being pressed down into the concave curvature of the workboard while the glue sets.

The combination of the floating X and the low, flat X forms a sort of truss structure.

George: Yes. This bracing creates a very structurally sound back, yet leaves it free to move in response to the air pressure created by the vibrating soundboard. It's very light, yet it's very strong.

Here is a completed back **(Photo 25)**. This is one of my own backs, but the bracing structure is identical to

RANDY PARSONS

the ones that Boaz and I made. The end result is a back which acts like a second soundboard and greatly improves the response of the instrument. Here's a back and soundboard together (**Photo 26**).

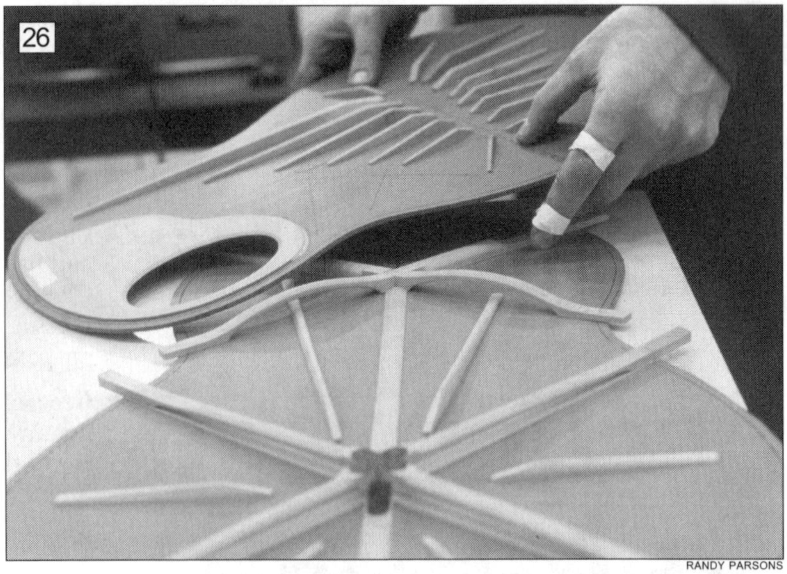

RANDY PARSONS

Let's talk about the construction of the necks. Are these necks one piece, or did you laminate the heads and stack the heels?

Boaz: They are not one piece, but we took great care to match the grain direction when we laminated the headstocks and the heels. We did not buy the mahogany for the necks in boards. We bought logs so that we would have more control. Every piece of wood for the necks was first split and then cut, so the wood is perfectly quartered. The quartered grain matches so well that you can't see the glue lines when they are finished.

Run me through the shaping process.

Boaz: After the heels and the headstocks have been laminated, the slots where the sides will fit into the heel are cut on their marks by hand (**Photo 27**).

We cut the waste from the inside heel of the neck on the bandsaw (**Photo 28**). You can see the shape of this cut on the neck in **Photo 27**.

The heel shaping is all done by hand. We start by cutting the leftovers from the sides of the heel with a hand saw (**Photo 29**).

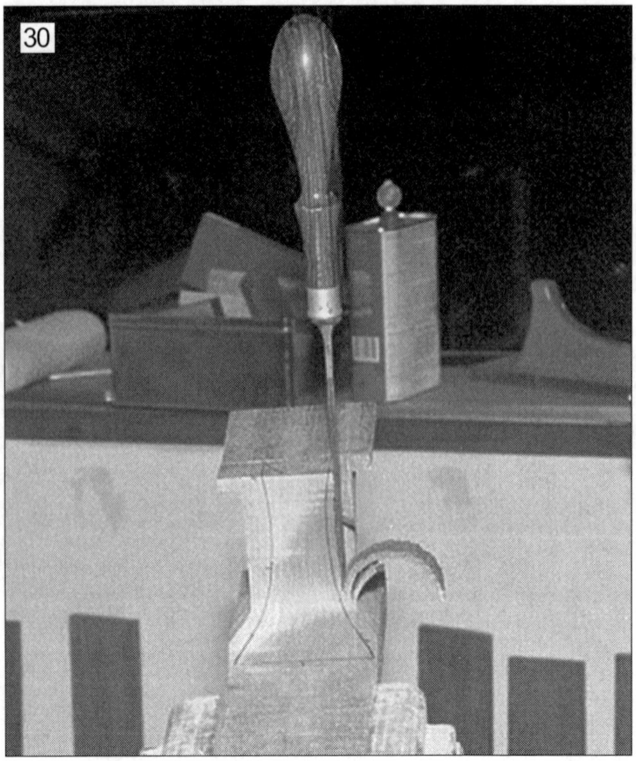

Next, we use a half-template on the centerline to establish the profile of the heel. Once it's marked you follow the lines on both sides to get the shape symmetrical, which is the hardest part. This shows how easy the quartered wood is to carve (**Photo 30**).

I used a Paracho-style knife for much of the heel carving (**Photo 31**). This shows me finishing the initial carving of the outside part of the heel (**Photo 32**). You can see how invisible the laminations are because of the care we took in matching the pieces. It looks like it has been carved from one piece.

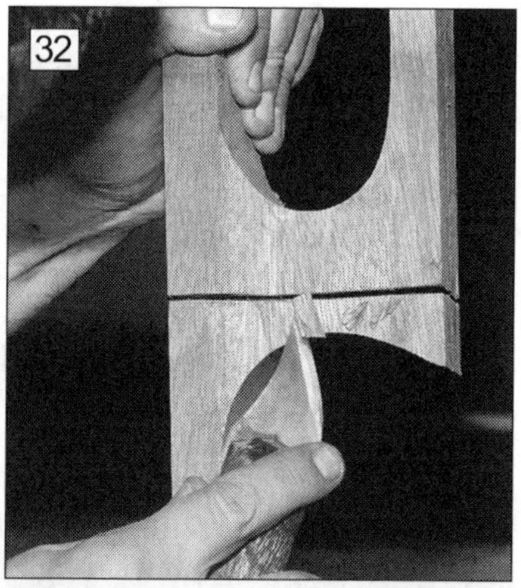

Once the profile is established, I saw off the corners of the heel to give it the rough shape (**Photo 33**). This is Uncle George's saw. I was very happy to see it. It reminds me of the good old days in my father's shop.

George: It's a miniature European bow saw. It has a narrow blade which can be turned with the handles. A coping saw would also work, as long as you can turn the blade. This is very primitive, but it shows that in spite of all the new technology we are still using basic tools.

Boaz: After the rough cuts have been made the rest can be filed, chiseled, or knifed, and then sanded. Here I use a sanding tool I made to refine the shape of the heel (**Photo 34**). I showed it to the people at Luthier's Mercantile, and they might carry it in the future if there is enough interest. They call it a *Bow-Az* bow sander. It's a nice tool. It uses sanding-belt material, and you can adjust the belt tension either by how you attach it or with your fingers as you are working. It cuts really quickly and leaves things amazingly symmetrical. Here is one side of the heel after just a few seconds of work with it (**Photo 35**). You can see the side I have sanded is already very near the final shape.

George: This is the final sanding of the heel (**Photo 36**). We finish shaping the head and the heel before assembly. The middle of the neck is left square until near the very end so that you can clamp it easily.

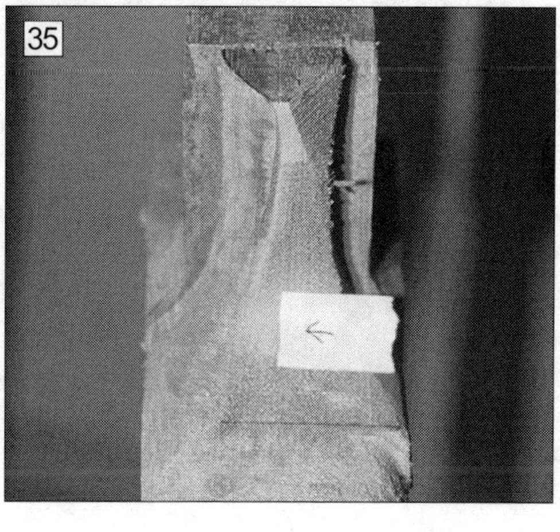

George: We groove the necks to install a $\frac{1}{2}'' \times \frac{3}{16}''$ steel reinforcement bar (**Photo 37**). It extends from the peghead all of the way into the upper fingerboard support. This adds additional rigidity to the neck. It also adds mass, which counteracts the neck's tendency to vibrate with the strings. The less energy absorbed by the neck, the more energy will be directed to the bridge. We use a green aerospace epoxy (available from Luthier's Mercantile) to install the reinforcement, and we rough up the surface of the metal and dimple it on the drill press so that the epoxy will have a better mechanical hold.

Boaz: Since we strengthen the neck with a steel bar there is extra tension at the heel. There is a bolt welded perpendicular to the bar, and this bolt goes down inside a hole drilled in the heel (**Photo 37**). The epoxy gets into the threads to hold it in place. This bolt strengthens the heel, so there is significantly less loss of energy at that point, and since the strength is down inside, I can shape the heel as small as I wish. That is what allows us to have a small heel on the outside.

George: The bolt stops about $\frac{1}{4}''$ short of the bottom of the heel. The peghead end of the reinforcement bar stops just short of the surface of the peghead. You put it in place, mark it, and then cut the angle on the end.

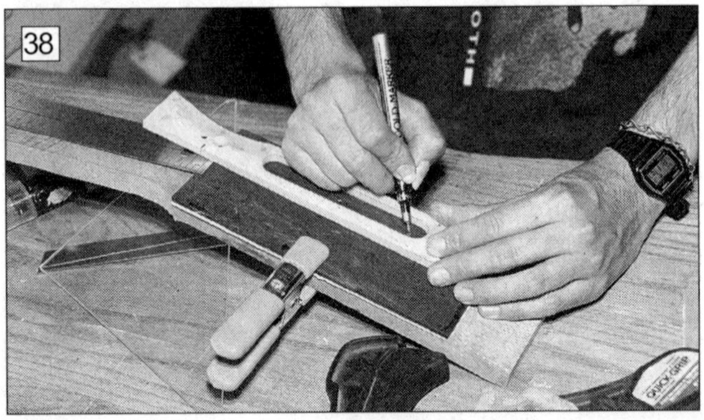

Boaz: The neck reinforcement can't be set more than 1MM below the fingerboard gluing surface because the truss rod is $\frac{1}{2}''$ tall, and the mahogany of the neck is only a few millimeters more than that after it is carved.

George: These necks are 22MM thick with the fingerboard, which is within the range of what we consider standard.

Boaz: Here we are positioning the headstock veneers (**Photo 38**). We use a half-template positioned on the centerline to mark where the slots will be cut out.

George: The cutting of the slots is done with a fixture on the pin router, so these lines are not needed for that. We use plastic pins to hold the veneers in place when we glue them, and these are just guidelines so that we can be sure that the positioning pins for the veneers will be put in a waste area.

Boaz: We drill the holes for the positioning pins on the drill press (**Photo 39**), and then we install the pins (**Photo 40**). Careful positioning of the veneer assures that the nut will fit against the head veneer exactly.

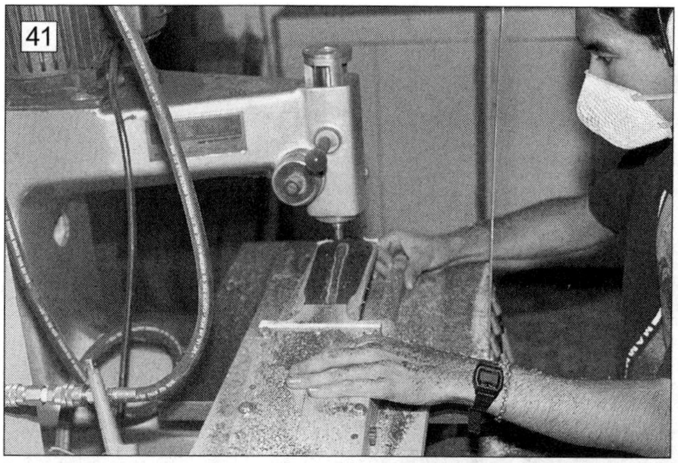

41

42

43

JONATHON PETERSON

Why is the position of the veneer so important at this point?

George: The nut edge of the veneer is shaped to the finished angle before the veneer is glued on, and this is the time we establish the position of that edge. The pins prevent the veneers from shifting when gluing.

After the veneers have been glued to the head we cut the outside shape and the slots on the pin router (**Photo 41**). This guarantees that every headpiece will be identical on every neck. Some of the final carving is done by hand. Here (**Photo 42**) Boaz is chiseling out the string ramps. On the right you can see the shape of the finished peghead.

Do you drill the holes for the tuning-machine rollers before or after cutting the slots?

George: That's done after the slots are cut. If you drill the holes before you finish shaping the head you can end up with the rollers being a little too deep or a little too shallow instead of being properly centered. Before we drill for the rollers we put a plug into the slot to guarantee that there's no split-out where the drill emerges, and to keep the sides from flexing.

Let's move on to fretboards. I think our readers will find Richard's fretting system very interesting.

Boaz: We use 1/8″ diameter rod stock for the frets. They are glued into 1/8″ wide slots which are routed into the fretboard. With this fretting system you have many more options for fret material. For instance, on these ten guitars we used beryllium-copper rod stock, but on my baritone guitar I used black Delrin plastic. It is easier on the strings, produces less noise, and it matched the color of the fingerboard, the bridge, and the headstock veneer.

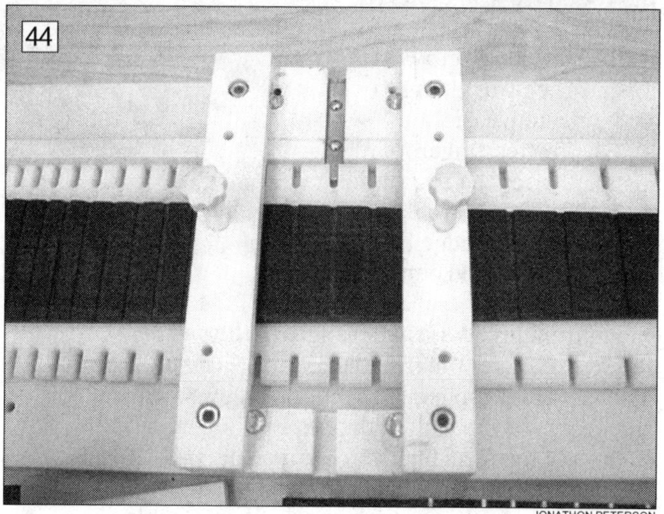

44

JONATHON PETERSON

George: A special jig built out of Corian guarantees accuracy in cutting the fret slots (**Photos 43 and 44**). The fretboard is mounted on positioning pins on a special base. The sides of the base have notches which correspond to fret positions for the scale lengths we use. The notches fit onto an indexing pin on the jig, and a dedicated router with a 1/8″ flat-bottomed bit is

45
RANDY PARSONS

46
RANDY PARSONS

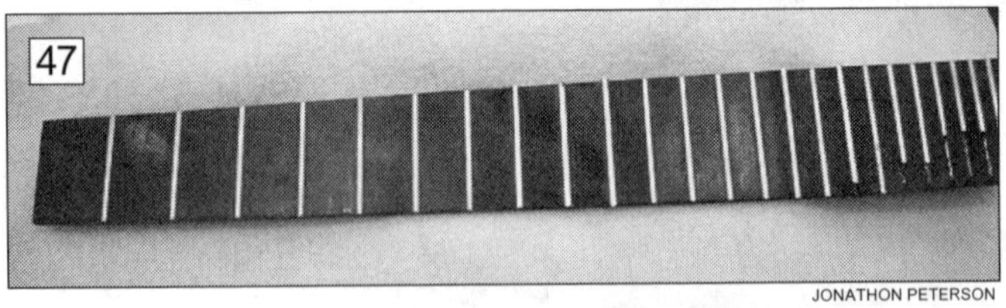
47
JONATHON PETERSON

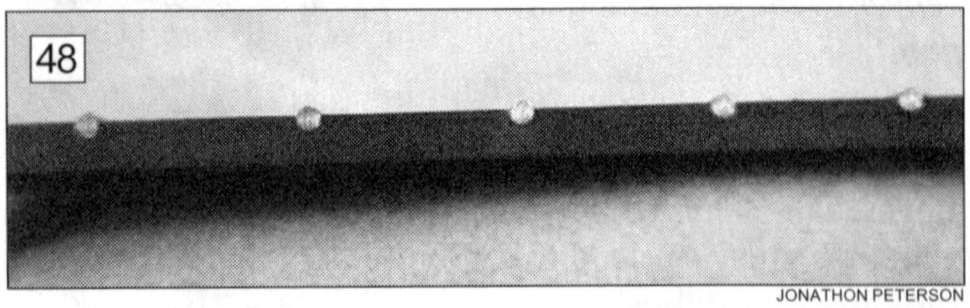
48
JONATHON PETERSON

mounted on a base which slides between fixed rails to cut the slots.

Frets are installed before the fretboard is attached to the neck (**Photos 45–48**). The frets are glued in place using a black epoxy which fills the gaps between the flat-bottomed fret slots and the round frets, and blends with the color of the fretboard. The fretboard is taped off before gluing to make cleanup easier.

49
JONATHON PETERSON

The fretted fingerboard is installed after the rest of the guitar has been assembled, but before the bridge has been glued on, and before the final carving of the neck (**Photo 49**). The steel bar is a vacuum clamp. We seal the edges of the gap between the steel bar and the fretboard with a caulking material. The suction is applied between the fingerboard and the steel bar, and the tops of the frets are aligned to the bottom of the steel bar, which is machined flat. The steel bar provides the clamping weight for the joint between the fretboard to the neck. We use a black epoxy which is thick enough to fill any imperfections in the joint. The soundboard gets masked off to make the glue cleanup easier, and we also mask the area where the nut will go. The sides of the neck are going to get carved away later, so we don't worry so much about them. (*Note: **Photo 49** shows a mock-up of the gluing operation on a finished instrument.*)

I assume that the location of the fretboard is established with positioning pins?

George: Exactly. Before we glue it we drill two holes for pins. When the fretboard goes on, the pins align it properly. The fretboard is completely finished before we glue it on. The only thing that is left is to finish the carving of the shape of the neck.

That is extremely interesting.

George: It gives us the ability to guarantee the flatness of the fretboard regardless of the imperfections of the neck because the epoxy fills in any gaps, and the tops of the frets are perfectly aligned, so except for rounding their ends, they don't have to be filed.

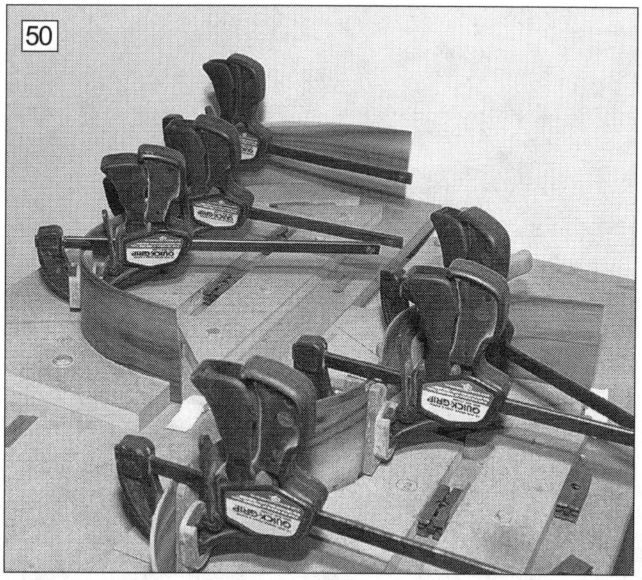

50

Boaz: We used a Fox side bender to bend all of the sides and linings. Richard used one, too. After the sides are bent we glue in the side supports (**Photo 50**).

The linings get soaked in water before they are bent because they're very thick. After they are bent they have to be notched to fit over the side supports. That is what we are doing here (**Photo 51**). The side supports are rounded, so the reliefs are shaped like half moons. You hold the lining in place, mark it, make the cut, check it, correct it, do the next one, and over, and over. That's 12 notches per guitar times 10 guitars, or 120 notches.

George: The reliefs don't extend all the way across the linings. The side support just tucks underneath. We want to make sure that the supports do not touch the soundboard or the back. If the side shrinks over a period of time, that could cause cracks.

This is a fixture for gluing the lining to the sides (**Photo 52**). We also use them to hold the sides in their proper shape when we are gluing in the side supports (**Photo 50**). An outside half-mold and a fence are fixed to a workboard, and four moveable shaped sections press the lining and side into the half-mold. The clamping pressure is provided by expanding clamps between the fence and the moveable sections.

53

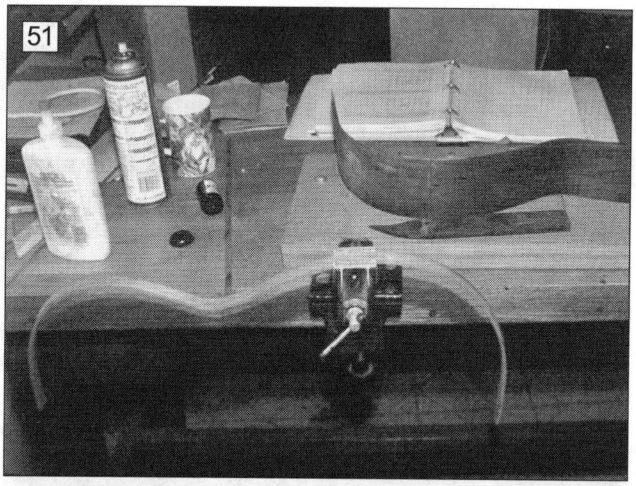

51

52

I recognize those clamps. Richard used them in a lot of fixtures. They were designed for setting type on old printing presses that used moveable metal type.

Boaz: These are sides with the supports and the linings glued in (**Photo 53**). I put them in this frame to force the ends to keep their shape.

That's my apprentice Jason shaping the linings (**Photo 54**). He's using a knife that I made for Uncle George. The blade is yellow carbide, and the handle is ebony with an inlaid decoration that I use on my traditional guitar bridges.

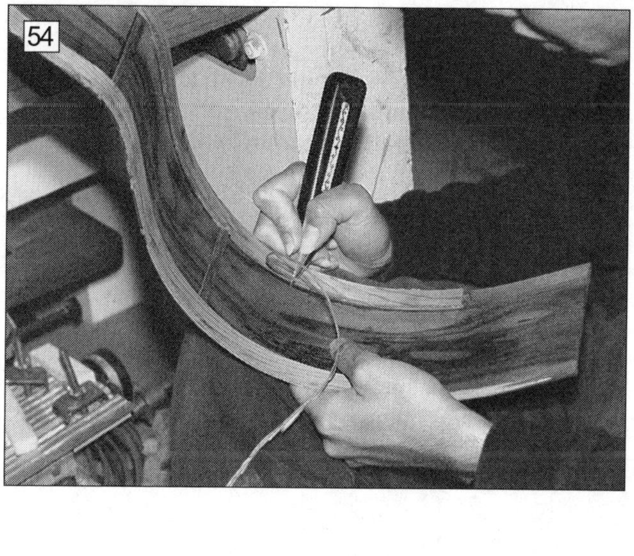

54

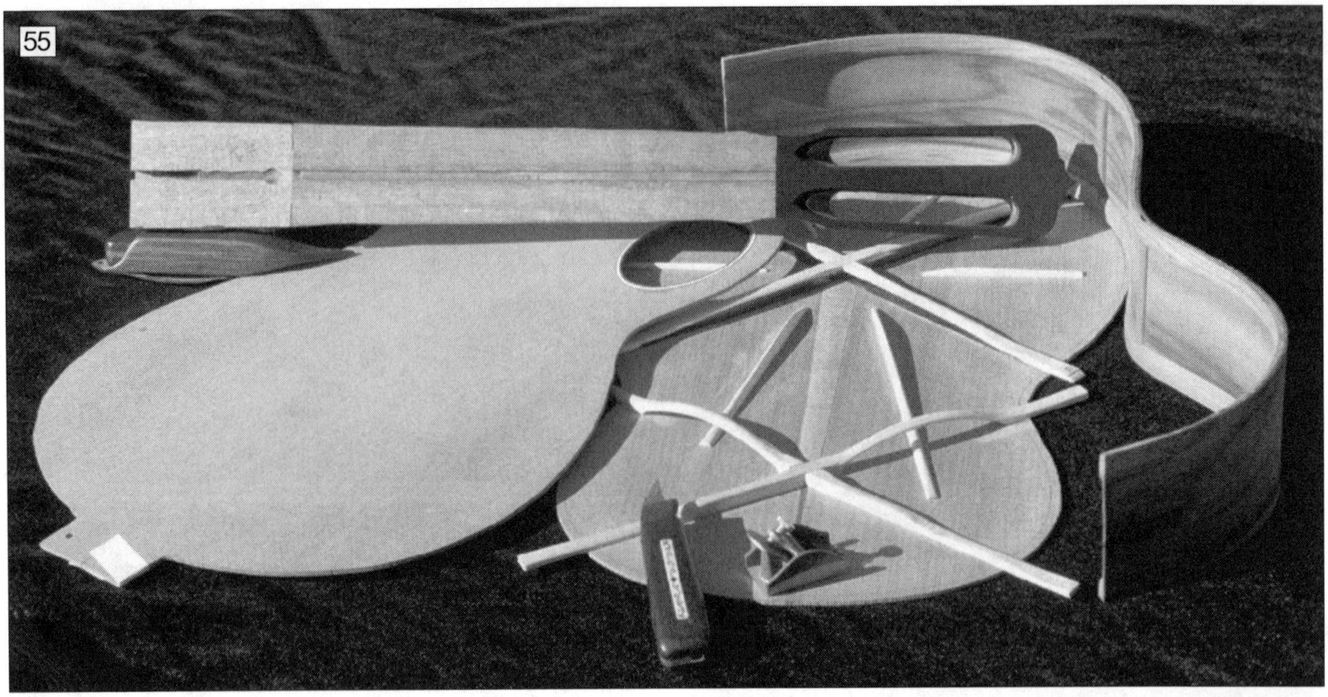

RANDY PARSONS

George: Here you can see the neck, the soundboard, the back, and the sides ready for assembly (**Photo 55**).

The frame for the end panel, which takes the place of the traditional end block, is made from epoxy-laminated veneers which are laid up in a form and then shaped on the pin router. This is what it looks like when it comes off of the pin router (**Photo 56**).

This shows the components for the end-panel door in various stages of completion (**Photo 57**). The disks are used for constructing locking mechanisms. We put ebony only in the area that will be visible, and we add maple to establish the final thickness. The maple has a slightly smaller diameter, which creates a step. Each disk is large enough to serve as a base for mounting an internal microphone, if that's what the player wants. The ebony is dimpled with a ball-end mill on the drill press to give you finger holds. The disk rotates 45° and latches the door plate to the frame at the top and bottom to lock it in place. The edges of the door plate are tapered so the door will get progressively tighter as it goes in.

Richard used screws at the corners, which required that every instrument be supplied with a tool, plus some spare screws, which usually got lost, so I decided to create a door that would not require metal hardware or tools.

We don't have many photographs of the final assembly of the guitars. Could you briefly describe that process?

George: The final assembly is done using a modified free-form method. We like this method because it gives us access to all parts of the instrument during all phases of final assembly, and facilitates the inspection of the proper alignment of all parts before final gluing.

The neck is clamped fretboard-side-down to an assembly board which is about the same width of the neck. The flat upper surface of the workboard provides the main reference. The soundboard is attached to the neck after it has been aligned using spacers to provide the correct registration relative to desired string action and the height of the bridge saddle. The sides are then clamped to the soundboard using a series of modified spool clamps. The position of the soundboard is checked again for proper alignment relative to the neck, and any final adjustments are performed. With the sides, neck, and soundboard correctly located and clamped in position, a bead of epoxy mixed with microballoon powder, which increases the glue's viscosity, is spread in the corner joint between the soundboard and the sides. This replaces the traditional tentelones and frees up the edge of the plate a little. After the final internal work is completed, the back is fit and attached. Binding and related artwork is done in the traditional way.

These are the laminated counterbalance reinforcement braces for the upper bout of the top (**Photo 58**). The soundhole reinforcement plate is only on the treble side of the soundboard, so the strength of the soundboard in the upper bout isn't balanced. We put one of these flying braces on the bass side to compensate for that.

Here you can see this counterbalance brace in position (**Photo 59**). It balances the pressure that string tension exercises on the upper bout, but leaves the bass side of the soundboard open to vibrate.

I can see something at the bridge ends of the soundboard braces. What is that, epoxy?

George: Yes, there is a bead of epoxy on the leading edges of the bracing because that's where the torsion of the bridge exerts the greatest pressure. It's a stress point, so we put a bead of epoxy around it to guarantee that those edges are going to stay solid.

You can also see the reinforcement plate for the strings. The strings are strung from inside of the instrument, with knots in their ends to keep them from pulling through. We glue in a reinforcement plate made of layers of veneer and fiberglass so that the knots won't damage the soundboard.

Boaz: Here we are trimming the sides to fit the back (**Photo 60**). The spoke shave is being used to shape the edges of the sides to accommodate the curvature of the back.

How do you establish the line to trim the sides to? Do you use a jig or a template?

George: We know what curvature the back is going to have, so we know how much to remove from the edges. We put tape around the edges, make measurements at various points, and mark where we need to cut to. Then we check our cut with the back and fine tune it.

Boaz: We fine tune the edge with a block that has sandpaper glued to a surface which has the same curvature as the back (**Photo 61**). The heel and the door frame are also shaped to match the back.

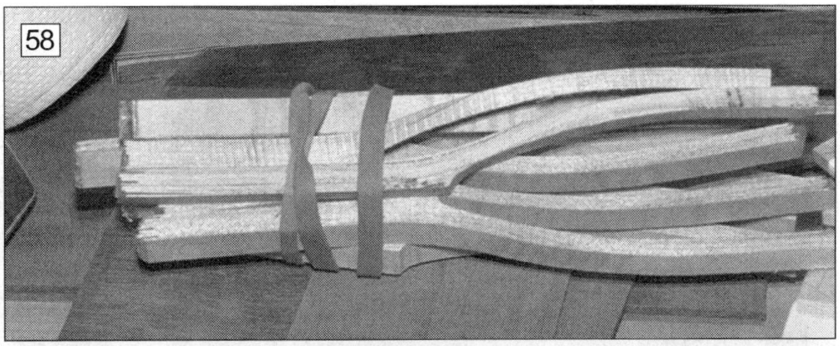
58

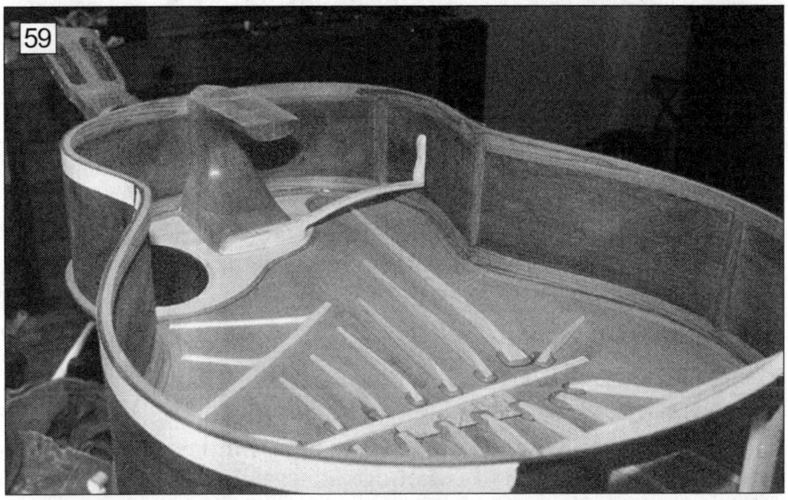
59

60

61

RANDY PARSONS

RANDY PARSONS

George: After the back is glued on, the body can be bound. We install the binding one half at a time (**Photos 62 and 63**). Glue is spread, prebent binding strips are taped in place, and a rubber strip is used to provide clamping pressure. It is wrapped in the traditional way. After the bindings are in place, the body can be prepared to receive the finish.

I see that the necks have not been carved at this point. When does that happen?

Boaz: After the tops are finished. We use the same finishing sequence that Richard did. The top is finished first, before the fingerboard and bridge are installed, and before the neck is carved. The fingerboard is glued on next, as we have already described, and then the top is masked off. Then the neck is carved, sanded, and stained with potassium dichromate, which is a chemical stain that reacts with the acid in the mahogany to darken it. Then we finish the back, sides, and neck. The bridge is glued on last, after all of the finish has been applied and rubbed out.

We haven't talked about the bridges yet. Could you describe how they are made?

RANDY PARSONS

George: This shows the laminated base for the bridge (**Photo 64**). The lamination is done in a gluing caul with the same curvature as the dished form in which the top braces were glued, so the curvature of the bridge base is identical to the curvature of the top.

We use this work block for holding the bridge when we are doing the hand shaping (**Photo 65**). The block has the same curvature as the soundboard. The bridge is held in place with location pins which are positioned where the saddle slot will be. The slot is ⅛″ wide and the pins are $3/64''$ in diameter. The location pins are very critical because they guarantee that we can continue the various operations on various fixtures without losing accuracy. Cutting the outline of the bridge base, cutting recesses for the saddle riser and the fiber inlay, and shaping the saddle riser are all done on the pin router with fixtures that use the same pin locations, and the same pin positions are used to hold the bridge in place when it is being glued to the soundboard, so there's a continuity through the whole assembly process.

This shows a bridge after we have glued in the ebony saddle riser (**Photo 66**). You can also see the fiber reinforcement which we inlay in the area where the holes for the strings will be, to prevent splitting. The saddle riser and the reinforcement go all the way to the bottom veneer of the bridge base.

You can see the pattern which is created as the veneers in the base are cut away during the hand-shaping process. We alternate walnut and maple so that we have a visual index which helps us to carve the bridge symmetrically.

67

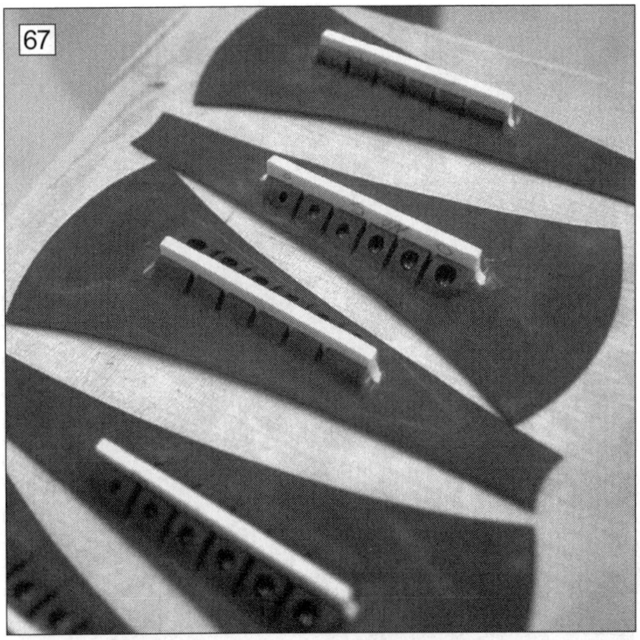

68

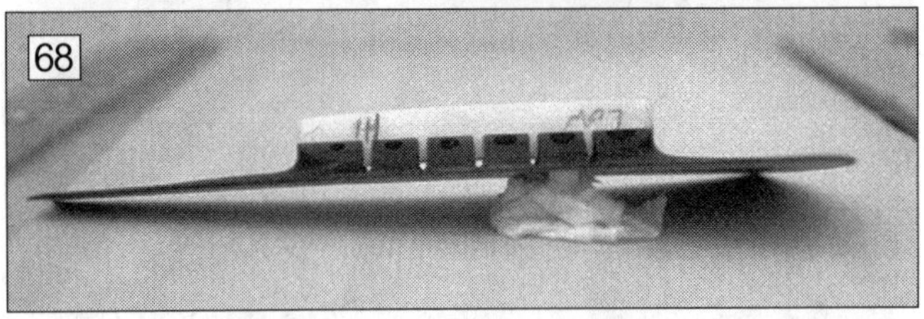

69

70

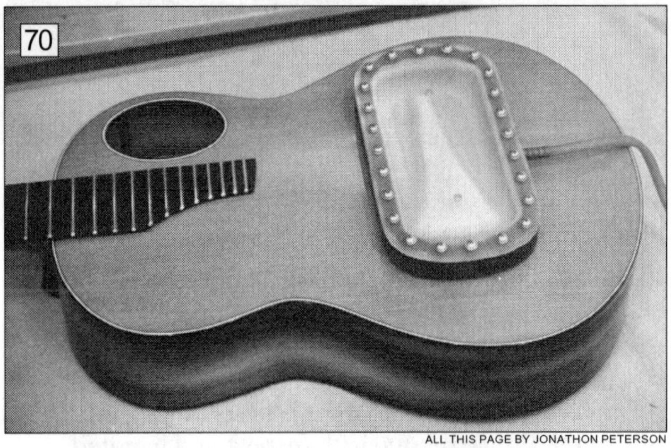

ALL THIS PAGE BY JONATHON PETERSON

The saddle riser gets its final shape on the pin router after the guitar has been assembled, because we need to make sure that the height of the bridge corresponds to our intended string action. We position the bridge on the guitar, put a straightedge on the frets, and take measurements where it intersects the saddle position. We then attach the bridge to a pin-router fixture, and do the shaping after making any necessary adjustments according to our measurements.

After the bridge has received its final shape we stain it black (**Photos 67 and 68**). To apply the stain I simply attach the bridge to a piece of wood with double-stick tape so I can hold it, and I spray the stain. After the stain dries the bridge gets finished.

Vacuum pressure is used in gluing the bridge. This method is especially useful because the soundhole is located too far from the bridge to allow the use of conventional clamps.

It is very important to make sure that equal pressure is applied to all areas of the bridge while the glue sets. Vacuum clamping does this extremely well, but the bridge has a shape which tends to distribute the tension of the vacuum fixture's membrane unequally. To compensate for this, a foam caul is constructed which fits the upper surface of the bridge exactly, and which presents a smooth surface with gently rounded corners to the membrane. This ensures uniform pressure over the bridge, resulting in a superior glue joint.

The gluing caul is made by making an impression of the bridge in expanding foam. The bridge is put in the bottom of a box-shaped form, and is covered with plastic wrap. Two-part expanding foam is mixed and poured into the form. When the foam is set it is removed from the form and trimmed back to the edge of the impression left by the bridge. The upper surface of the caul is then smoothed, and the upper corners rounded.

71

What is the gluing procedure?

George: First glue is spread, and the bridge is positioned with locating pins (**Photo 69**). The caul is put in place, and the vacuum clamp is applied (**Photo 70**). As when using the vacuum clamp for bracing tops and backs, the bridge clamp must be removed after a short time so that glue squeeze-out can be cleaned away. It is then replaced until the glue has completely set (**Photo 71**).

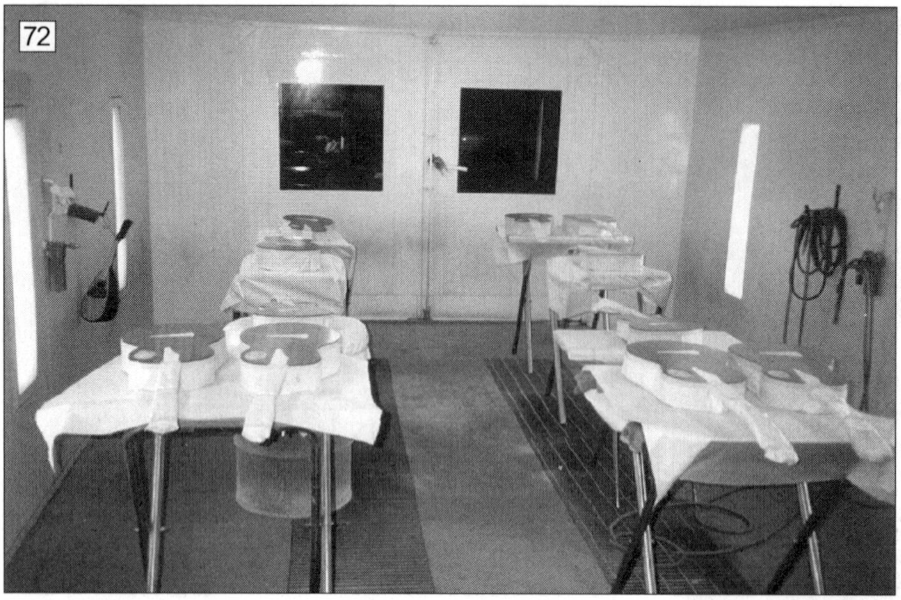

JONATHON PETERSON

What sort of finish material did you use, and what was your finishing procedure?

Boaz: We used a nitrocellulose lacquer. In some states you cannot buy this material because of environmental regulations. I am the most politically correct person when it comes to the environment, but on my guitars I do not compromise. I do what is best for the guitar, and the materials are treated with respect and handled properly.

Before the lacquer goes on, the pores must be filled and the surface leveled. I start by sanding with 100 grit, and then I put on sanding sealer. In this first coat only the sealer contains a stain so that the scratches become visible. I always sand both cross grain and with the grain, with a flat block of wood backing the sandpaper to produce a very flat surface, which is the foundation for a mirror finish. The next step is 150 grit, then sealer, but this time without the stain, then 220, sealer, 320, sealer, and finally 400, no sealer. By this time the stained scratches are all gone, the pores are filled, and we can begin applying the lacquer. This sanding process alone took two weeks, but the results were worth the effort.

For applying the lacquer we went to where Jay Hargreaves works, where they have an environmentally safe room for painting cars (**Photo 72**). Jay did a wonderful job of spraying the lacquer. He started by applying a thin wash coat to soften the surface of the sanding sealer and improve adhesion. Then three or four coats of lacquer thinned about 50% were applied, and the guitars were hung overnight. The next day they were sanded and given three or four more coats. We then took them back to the workshop and hung them to dry for a week. They were then sanded, and the process was repeated three times, until all of the surfaces were totally level and there was enough finish to polish.

Photo 73 shows the guitars hanging in a room Uncle George built which maintains constant temperature and humidity. We used this room throughout the project for storing woods, guitar parts, and guitars in-process. To level the finish we used Micro-mesh® with soap and water to avoid clogging (**Photo 74**). Then came buffing.

JONATHON PETERSON

After the bridges were glued on, we fit the nuts and saddles so that they were snug in their grooves. Then we took a piece of tape with the string spacing marked on it, and we transferred the marks directly onto the nuts with a small saw (**Photo 75**).

To establish the height of the saddle we made spacers that fit over the 1st and the 12th frets (**Photo 76**) that were the same height we wanted the strings to be at those points. Then we took a straightedge and taped an X-acto blade to the bottom of one end. On the inside face of the saddle we put a piece of tape, so that when we ran the straightedge across the tops of the spacers, the blade cut the tape at the height the saddle needed to be (**Photos 77 and 78**). This is a very old method used to set up cellos and contra basses. They used a pencil in the old days, but Uncle George is always finding an amazing new way to improve a system.

After the nuts and saddles were shaped, polished, and installed, all that was left to do was to install the tuners and string them up.

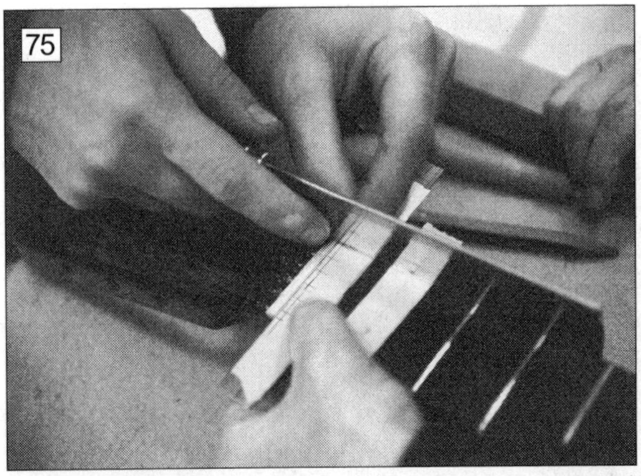

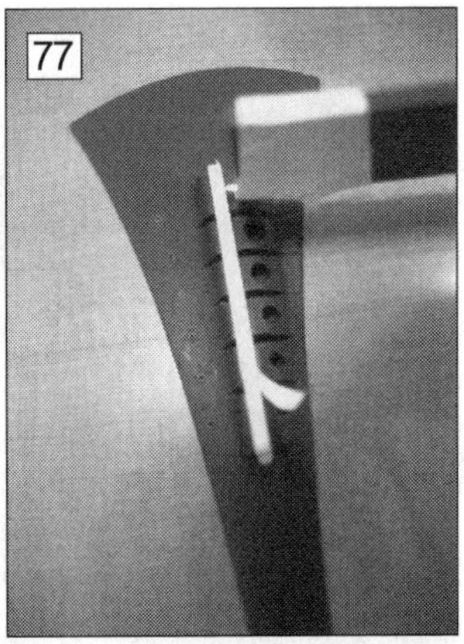

ALL THIS PAGE BY JONATHON PETERSON

How did you feel when they were finally done?

Boaz: I don't really remember what my first feelings were at that point, because George and I were totally exhausted and a little drunk from celebrating. We drank a bottle of whisky that Richard Schneider brought Uncle George from England.

When I came back to L.A., I took my motorcycle and went on a two-month vacation in Mexico. More important than how the guitars sounded was putting my life back in balance again.

I was there the evening after they were strung up, and I was amazed how identically they all sounded. Have you gotten any feedback from players or done any testing?

Boaz: Kurt Rodamer and Leona Boyd were the first to play the guitars, and they each ordered one, which speaks for itself. They sounded beautiful! We took the guitars to an echoless chamber for testing, and they showed a better bass response than the last Schneider guitar tested there. Richard's high end was better, but I'm confident that our highs will open up and improve with time.

Where did they all end up?

Boaz: One was sent to the Guitar Salon in New York, one to an agent in Austria, one to an agent in Germany, one to a wonderful player in Hawaii, and one to Kentucky. One went to the Guitar Society in Detroit, which Richard strongly supported — Detroit was his home for many years. Uncle George kept one, and I am keeping one. Although I do not collect guitars, this instrument is a reminder of a beautiful journey that I took with Uncle George, and a tribute to Richard Schneider's dream.

Where has this journey taken you? What are you up to now that this project is over?

Boaz: Clarita Negra, the baritone guitar which is my own interpretation of the Kasha concept, showed results that were so stunning that Dr. Kasha made me an advisor to the Acoustical Research Laboratory of the University of Florida at Tallahassee. I have just finished three more Clarita Negras, with some major improvements. They are the finest guitars I have ever built, and the response to them has been amazing. There is much work still ahead for me. I am always looking for ways to improve my guitars. With every instrument I am getting closer and closer to the perfect classical guitar, and to Richard's dream.

I'd like to thank both of you for taking on this work, and for allowing me to have some small part in it. Do you have any closing comments?

Boaz: I would like to thank Uncle George for his vision, and for the inspiration he has given me. I will carry his knowledge with me forever, and remember him always as the best mentor I ever had. I am proud that we have produced these amazing-quality guitars which stand up proudly to even the best Spanish classical guitars.

I would also like to thank my girlfriend, Lisa, for patiently accepting my sometimes psychotic

JONATHON PETERSON

relationship with my dream. Sometimes she only saw me for fifteen minutes a day, and while I was building these instruments she didn't see me for almost eight months.

How about you, George? Now that the instruments have been shipped, how do you feel about the results?

George: When a project comes to completion there is always a feeling of relief, but this project has exceeded all of my expectations and given me a great deal of satisfaction. It started as a tribute to Richard Schneider, but in the end I think that we have demonstrated the viability of the Kasha design. We have shown that the Kasha construction process is every bit as practical to undertake as that of any other guitar design. Eleven instruments in eight months is, in my opinion, quite acceptable.

We are grateful for the encouragement and help we received along the way, especially to Dr. Kasha for guidance and technical assistance. We hope that the results have met with his approval.

Finally, I hope that this project will foster interest in Kasha design. This would be the best tribute to the memory of Richard Schneider. ——

JONATHON PETERSON

JONATHON PETERSON

RANDY PARSONS

***Photo 79**. Boaz, and George — excited, satisfied, and relieved on the evening of the day the instruments were finally strung. Richard Schneider would have been proud.*

***Photos 80–82**. Various views of the guitars. The instrument with the soundhole in the side is Boaz' baritone guitar, Clarita Negra.*

Originally published in *American Lutherie #58,* 1999

Calculating Arc Parameters

by Jon Sevy

THE EDITOR OF THIS JOURNAL recently discovered that I'm a mathematician, and asked me to write a short sidebar incorporating and extending information about circular arcs provided in several articles which have appeared in *American Lutherie.* The central question he asked me to address was: if I know the width of my workboard (or brace or top plate) and I know how much higher the edges are than the middle, what is the radius of that arc? I'll give formulas that answer that question and several other related ones. In fact, we'll find a general relationship between three quantities: the span of an arc, the center deflection of the arc, and its radius. Then, given any two of these quantities, we'll be able to find the third.

Our basic approach will be an analytical one, using the Pythagorean Theorem to develop an algebraic equation which relates the three quantities. Then we'll solve for each quantity in turn, producing three formulas which will allow us to find each of the quantities if we know the other two. This approach is similar to that used by Chris Foss in *American Lutherie #9* (see *Big Red Book of American Lutherie Volume One*, p. 321) and described by Phil Kearny in a communication to the GAL. Maryann Faller of Adirondack Community College suggested an elegant geometric method using similar triangles. In mathematics, there are often many different ways to saw the same log — that's what makes it so interesting (or frustrating, depending on your particular taste). I'll illustrate each formula with a sample lutherie application.

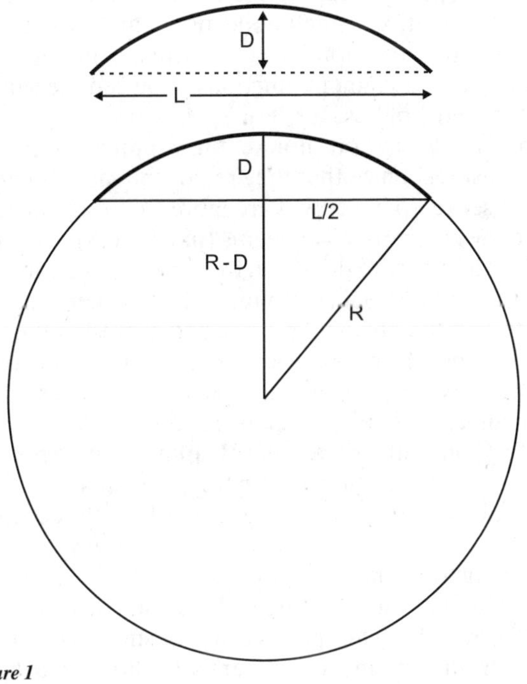

Figure 1

Formulae

In **Fig. 1**, L represents the span of the arc, D represents its center deflection, and R represents its radius. The fundamental relationship between these comes from applying the Pythagorean Theorem to the right triangle in the figure; this gives

$$(R - D)^2 + (L/2)^2 = R^2$$

This is the fundamental relationship between the span, deflection, and radius. Now all we have to do is use some algebra to solve for each variable in terms of the other two. (Derivations of the resulting formulas are given in the appendix.)

Solving for R in terms of D and L:

Result: $R = \dfrac{D^2 + (L/2)^2}{2D}$

Application: In their book *Guitarmaking, Tradition and Technology,* Cumpiano and Natelson specify that the arching for the back braces for the steel string guitar being built should have a ¼″ center deflection (they call it an offset) in a 16″ span (p. 150); the radius that this corresponds to can be calculated using the above formula. Here, D = .25″ and L = 16″, giving L/2 = 8″ and thus

$$R = \frac{(.25)^2+(8)^2}{2(.25)} = \frac{.0625 + 64}{.5} = \frac{64.0625}{.5} = 128.125''$$

or the radius is R = 10′ 8″ (ignoring the last .125″).

Note: If the center deflection D is much smaller than the span L, the D^2 term in the formula above will be insignificant compared to the $(L/2)^2$ term, and can be neglected. This leads to a simplified version of the formula: if L is at least 20 times as large as D, then the radius is given approximately by

$$R = \frac{L^2}{8D}$$

and the approximation will be good to within 1% of the true radius. If we use this simpler formula on the above example, it gives

$$R = \frac{(16)^2}{2D} = \frac{256}{2} = 128''$$

compared to the actual 128.125″ found above.

Solving for D in terms of R and L:

Result: $D = R - \sqrt{R^2 - (L/2)^2}$

Application: In his book *The Steel String Guitar: Construction and Repair,* David Russell Young specifies that the braces for the top of the guitar be arched with a 25′ radius. Suppose we want to make a template to use to check the arching of the top and scribe the arch onto the sides of the braces; if the template will be 24″ long, how much higher should the center be than the ends?

Here, we know the radius $R = 25 \times 12 = 300''$, and the span is $L = 24''$; note that it's important to use the same units for all of the quantities in the formula (don't mix inches and feet, or centimeters and meters). Then the above formula will give us the needed deflection D:

$$D = 300 - \sqrt{(300)^2 - (24/2)^2} = 300 - \sqrt{(300)^2 - (12)^2}$$

$$= 300 - \sqrt{90000 - 144} \qquad = 300 - \sqrt{89856}$$

$$= 300 - 299.7599$$

or $D = .24''$. Thus the deflection would be very nearly ¼″ for this span of 24″.

Solving for L in terms of R and D:

Result: $L = 2\sqrt{2RD - D^2}$

Application: I made a fingerboard radius sanding block to put a 10″-radius crown on my fretboards by spreading glue on the mating faces of several layers of thin plywood, and then clamping them into the appropriate arch until the glue dried. To get the correct arch, I placed two ¼″ dowels on my workbench, several inches apart and parallel, laid the plywood-glue sandwich on top, and then clamped the plies down to the workbench surface with a caul halfway between the two support dowels, as in **Fig. 2**. Thus the plies took on an arch that had a center deflection of ¼″; but I needed to know how far apart the dowels on the workbench should be placed to get the desired 10″ radius. This amounted to solving for the span L in an arc when the deflection and radius were known. Thus I knew $R = 10''$ and $D = .25''$; the formula above gave me the span L:

$$L = 2\sqrt{2(10)(.25) - (.25)^2} = 2\sqrt{5 - .0625}$$

$$= 2\sqrt{4.9375} \qquad = 2(2.222) \qquad = 4.444$$

or $L = 4.44''$. I placed the dowels 4½″ apart on the workbench. I just wanted a radius of approximately 10″, so I didn't worry about the difference between 4.44″ and 4.5″. The previous formulas indicate that if the span is 4.5″ and the center deflection is .25″, then the actual

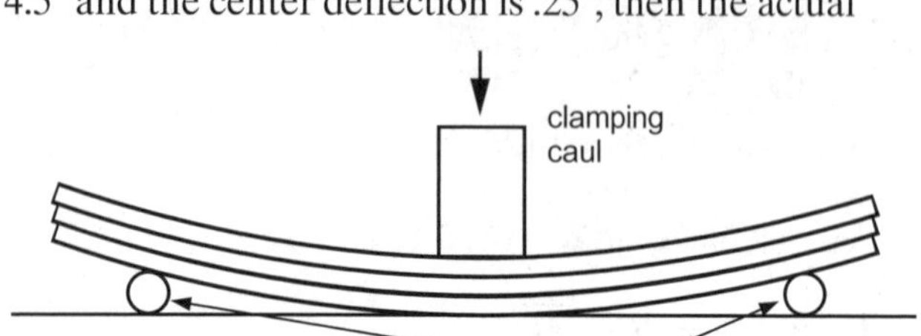

Figure 2

radius comes out to be 10.25″, which was close enough for me. In fact, this gives the radius of the *outside* of the sanding block (the convex surface); I'd be using the *inside* (concave) face to crown the fretboard. Since the thickness of the block was ¾″, the actual crown radius I obtained was $10.25'' - .75'' = 9.5''$; again, this was fine for me.

Sketching Arcs

A convenient and easily made device for sketching an arc with a large radius, which incidentally uses the span and center deflection of the arc, is the "long compass." For a description of a similar device, the curve-cutting bandsaw fence, see the GAL's *Lutherie Tools* (p. 90).

Other Curves in Lutherie

The above gives us tools to calculate the parameters of any desired circular arc. However, other curves arise naturally that can also be very useful in lutherie. First, while the "long compass" mentioned above is a great tool for sketching an arc of a circle with large radius, it requires hammering a couple of brads into the piece being marked for the compass to ride on. This suggests an even easier method for sketching the arc: put a thin, narrow piece of wood against the brads, flex it so it passes through the desired center point of the arc, and run a pencil along it to sketch a smooth curve that passes through all three points. This method has in fact been used for centuries; the thin piece of wood used is called a draftsman's spline, and the resulting smooth curve is called a spline curve. In fact, by placing a number of brads at desired spots, this method can create smooth serpentine curves that pass through any specified number of points. So why not use the spline to sketch our circular arc? Well, the problem is that pieces of wood (and other materials) don't bend in circular arcs when they're deflected: the curve sketched will be slightly "peaked" in the center when compared with a circular arc drawn with the long compass. Try it and see. Mathematically, these spline curves (for relatively small deflections) are parametric piecewise-cubic polynomial curves with maximum continuity at the segment junctions. You can see why they're called "splines" for short.

This isn't to say you shouldn't use splines instead of circles; just recognize that they're not the same thing! In some sense, spline curves are more "natural," since they're the shape physical beams (like braces) naturally take on when they're deflected by some applied force. A discussion of this can be found in books on mechanics of materials, like the one by Gere and Timoshenko. Also, the smooth curves produced in most drawing or drafting software packages are splines (sometimes called Bezier curves or B-splines), or an extension called NURBs (non-uniform rational B-splines). In these applications, rather than specifying points that the curve passes through, the designer works with "control points" that pull the curve toward (but not through) them, in the way that magnets would pull a steel guitar string. I use such software when I'm designing a new guitar body style. The splines produce smooth curves which permit very fine adjustment and allow a great number of body shapes to be explored. The only thing that's a bit unusual about working with splines from the lutherie perspective is that the curves smoothly blend from sharp turns (say at the waist of a guitar body) to broad turns (at the lower bout); there's no single place where the radius of the curve suddenly changes from one value to another, as would be the case if the body shape were designed with circular arcs. Thus hot-pipe bending the sides of a spline-designed body shape requires a little getting used to, since the radius of the curve is continually changing. But then again, this makes for smoother transitions along the body outline. ——

References

Cumpiano, William and Natelson, Jonathan.
Guitarmaking Tradition and Technology.
Rosewood Press, Amherst, MA, 1987.

Young, David Russell.
The Steel String Guitar: Construction and Repair.
The Bold Strummer, Ltd., Westport, CT, 1987.

Olsen, Tim and Burton, Cyndy, eds.
Lutherie Tools.
Guild of American Luthiers, Tacoma, WA, 1990.

J. Gere, S. Timoshenko.
Mechanics of Materials.
PWS Publishing Co., 4th edition, 1997.

Appendix: Derivations of Formulas

1. Solving for R in terms of D and L:

Result: $R = \frac{D^2 + (L/2)^2}{2D}$

Derivation:

$(R - D)^2 + (L/2)^2 = R^2$

expand the $(R - D)^2$ term (using FOIL — bring back bad memories?) to get

$R^2 - 2RD + D^2 + (L/2)^2 = R^2$,

subtract R^2 from both sides to get

$-2RD + D^2 + (L/2)^2 = 0$,

add 2RD to both sides to get this term on the right,

$D^2 + (L/2)^2 = 2RD$,

then divide both sides by 2D to isolate the R on the right, giving our result:

$\frac{D^2 + (L/2)^2}{2D} = R$.

2. Solving for D in terms of R and L:

Result: $D = R - \sqrt{R^2 - (L/2)^2}$

Derivation:

$(R - D)^2 + (L/2)^2 = R^2$

subtract $(L/2)^2$ from both sides, giving

$(R - D)^2 = R^2 - (L/2)^2$.

Then take the square root of both sides to get

$R - D = \sqrt{R^2 - (L/2)^2}$.

Finally, subtract R from both sides to isolate the D,

$-D = -R + \sqrt{R^2 - (L/2)^2}$,

then negate both sides to get rid of the negative sign in front of D, giving

$D = R - \sqrt{R^2 - (L/2)^2}$.

3. Solving for L in terms of R and D:

Result: $L = 2\sqrt{2RD - D^2}$

Derivation:

$(R - D)^2 + (L/2)^2 = R^2$.

Subtract $(R - D)^2$ from both sides to get

$(L/2)^2 = R^2 - (R - D)^2$.

Expanding the $(R - D)^2$ term on the right gives

$(L/2)^2 = R^2 - (R^2 - 2RD + D^2)$,

and simplifying the right leaves

$(L/2)^2 = 2RD - D^2$.

Now take the square root of both sides to get

$L/2 = \sqrt{2RD - D^2}$;

then multiplying by 2 gives the desired result:

$L = 2\sqrt{2RD - D^2}$.

Note: Arc-calculation spreadsheets are available for downloading on the world wide web: http://gicl.cs.drexel.edu/people/sevy/luthierie/luthierie.html

Originally published in *American Lutherie #58*, 1999

Meet the Maker: Bonnie Carol

by John Calkin

WHEN I GOT SERIOUS about mountain dulcimers in the '70s, Bonnie Carol was already showing up in song books, general dulcimer books, and in how-to-build books. Her dulcimers combined contemporary gracefulness with beautiful American hardwoods. They married a lack of ostentation with instant recognizability, a very rare trait. Bonnie became a recording artist, and has now completed her fifth solo album as well as dozens of other studio projects. By 1976 her touring schedule had taken a big bite out of her building time. She also authored one of the better mountain dulcimer tutors to ever see print, *Dust Off that Dulcimer and Dance!* (available at Bonnie's website www.bonniecarol.com). However, unable to resist the lure of the wood shop, she now builds about ten dulcimers each year while managing her little empire of book, CD, and tape sales along with a busy performance schedule. She lives near Boulder, Colorado.

How did you find yourself in lutherie?

I met Max Krimmel, who was building guitars at the time. We were both in our mid-twenties.

There's a strong GAL connection right there.

Exactly. I was fascinated that someone could go to the lumberyard, buy some wood, and convert it into guitars. I'd never met anyone who made a living at any kind of craft or art. I'd never even met anyone who was self-employed. The closest thing to it that I knew about was sewing. He let me hang out at his shop, though creation and self-sufficiency was so second nature to him that he couldn't understand my fascination. We became friends, and eventually he made me a dulcimer for Christmas. It was a beautiful piece of art, although it didn't amount to much more than a weekend project for him. I was working in mental health at the time, doing psychiatric counseling, but I lost my job due to funding cutbacks in the counseling field. I was searching for a job, which I hate doing, and Max said, "Well, I could teach you how to make dulcimers." Max and I were living together by then. So I made dulcimers for a couple of years, and it was great fun.

What time period was this?

This was 1971. But by 1973 I thought, "Well, this is fun, but it isn't a living." I'd been putting off things

ALL PHOTOS BY MAX KRIMMEL

like new cars and dental work. It was time to get a real job. My last fling before diving back into the real world was a trip to the first Kindred Gathering, a dulcimer festival near Seattle. It blew me away. I was completely taken by the whole dulcimer scene. I came back with renewed vigor and a determination to stay with the dulcimer. I've never made as much money as I did in the psychiatric world, but I'm not starving and my teeth are fixed, so it must be working.

I'd say your longevity speaks for itself at this point.

Sure. But the Kindred Gathering was the turning point. I realized that if I wanted to stay in the scene I'd have to work much harder.

You had a lot of exposure early on. There were several photos of you and your dulcimers in The Dulcimer Songbook, *and you were heavily featured in Roger Harris' construction book.*

I met Roger while touring. I had contributed to a record called *The Pacific Rim Dulcimer Project.* At that time if you made a record people thought you had real credentials as a musician. Today it's so easy to turn out a CD that it's questionable. After the record came out people asked me to come and play, and since I've always loved to travel I couldn't resist the opportunity.

So touring was never your target in the beginning?

Not at all. I can't remember exactly how I met Roger, but we connected through the scene somehow and he explained that he was writing a dulcimer construction book. It sounded like great fun, so we collaborated. The original galleys were lost, but I still have the photos and the material. I've thought of reissuing it. It's a matter of scanning in the stuff, which I know how to do, so maybe someday I'll do it.

I wish you would. It's a great little book.

Maybe I will.

I was on the sidelines at the time, but it seemed to me that the '70s were a time of real energy and excitement in the dulcimer scene. I wasn't deluded, was I?

Not at all. Before that the dulcimer had been sort of a quaint, regionalized phenomenon — an Appalachian musical oddity. Jean Ritchie began its renaissance in the '50s. As virtuoso players appeared, new demands were made on the dulcimer to play in tune and at greater volume. The dulcimer suddenly joined the 20th century. Crowds turned out to hear the new professionals, and many more people took up the instrument. It was an exciting scene. The change actually began in the '60s and exploded in the '70s.

Howie Mitchell's book and records must have set the pace early on.

Yes, Max originally built with Howie's ideas and he taught me that way. Lynn McSpadden had an early impact, too. He made a lot of instruments and they were very good quality. In those years he set the standard. Suddenly dulcimers had to have functional tuners and the frets had to be in the right place. Players weren't inclined to stick with instruments that were made with a disregard for precision. They weren't as forgiving simply because the dulcimer had a folksy upbringing. Howie Mitchell brought science and experimentation to the dulcimer, and McSpadden was a master of execution. He made it into a real instrument.

How did you end up moving to the hammered dulcimer?

Again, I was touring, and I stayed with Dana Hamilton and his family in Arlington, Texas. He offered to swap one of his hammered dulcimers for one of my mountain dulcimers, and I accepted. I had to go home eventually to build his piece, but he sent me away with a hammered dulcimer. The first time I tried to tune it I decided the instrument was not for me, so I shipped it home with the intention of selling it. But in the quieter atmosphere of the Colorado Rockies I managed to get it in tune and found that I took to it quite easily. For the next year I did little else but play the hammered dulcimer. I went to New York City and played on the streets, and I found that I could make money while I played the few tunes that I knew over and over until my chops came up. Then I returned to Colorado and kept after it. At the end of that year I won the National Hammered Dulcimer Contest at Winfield, Kansas.

Wow! Congratulations. Did you decide to build hammered dulcimers?

I've built three, and I don't play one that I've built so that should tell you something.

Do you still play your original hammered dulcimer?

No. That one weighed 47 pounds, which is a little less than half of what I weigh. When I became acquainted with newer, lighter instruments I was quick to switch. I played a lighter Dana Hamilton for awhile, then a Dusty Strings followed by a Master Works. Currently I play a Lee Spears. I still have them all except my original Hamilton. I gave it back to Dana when his personal dulcimer was stolen. He's a big, burly guy so he can deal with the weight.

Has the mountain dulcimer evolved much in the last thirty years?

Not in any extraordinary way. They are made with more precision now. Hardly anyone has to suffer along with a dulcimer that can't play in tune or that has tuners that work poorly. One emphasis in the last ten years or so has been on getting the action down. Dulcimer setup seems to have become as sophisticated as guitar setup. The artistic aspect of the dulcimer seems to have

Bonnie's shop, located in Nederland, Colorado.

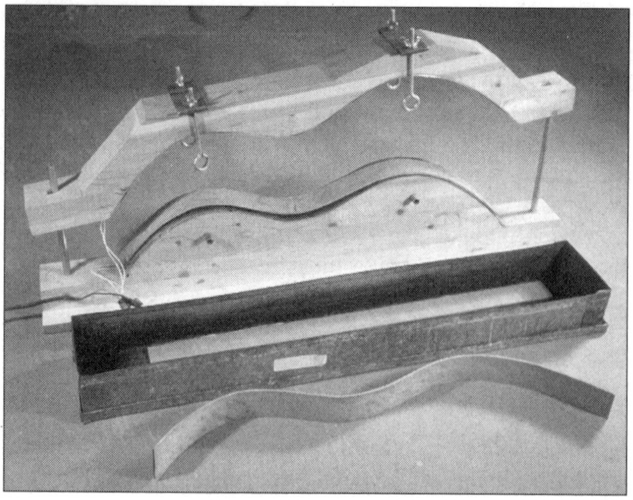

The bending form uses silicone blankets on the top and bottom.

blossomed in interesting directions, also. The dulcimer has never been standardized as has the violin, or even as much as the guitar. Joellen Lapidus sort of set the trend in individual design. Janita Baker has done some wonderful inlay work in a style that doesn't recall the traditions of other instruments. I took a cue from Joellen and began working in wood inlay rather than shell. The other major direction the dulcimer has taken is toward producing more sound, and this is the reason for the larger box I use as well as the lighter fingerboard.

How many dulcimers have you made?

Oh, 307, 308, something like that.

Do you have any construction tips you'd like to share?

Sure. Most people seem convinced that the wood is the main factor. They say, "My McSpadden dulcimer is

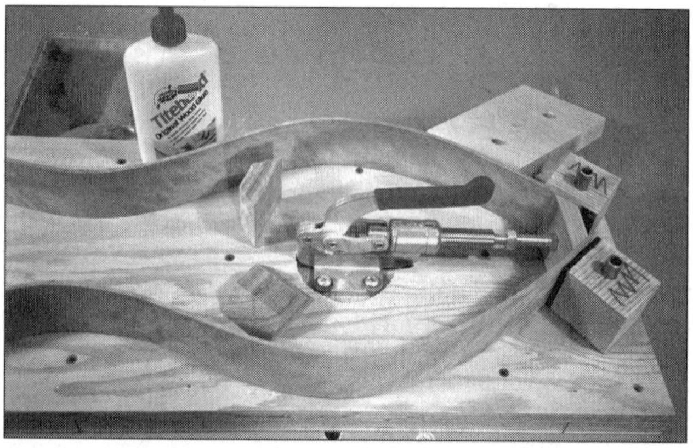

Bonnie's jig for installing end blocks.

Using a table router with an edge-following bearing to trim the top.

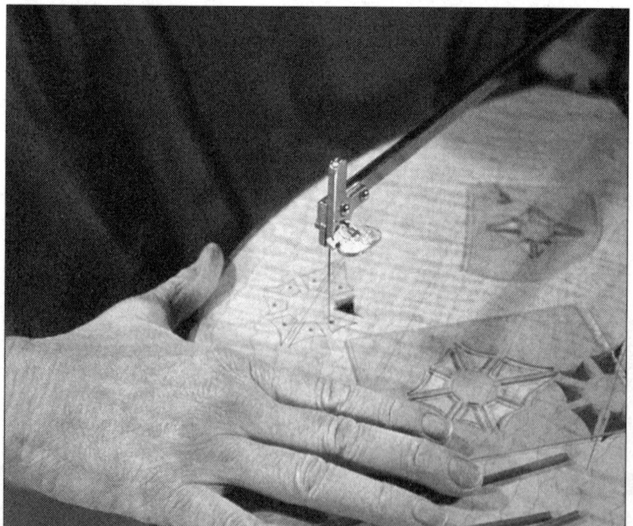

Cutting soundholes.

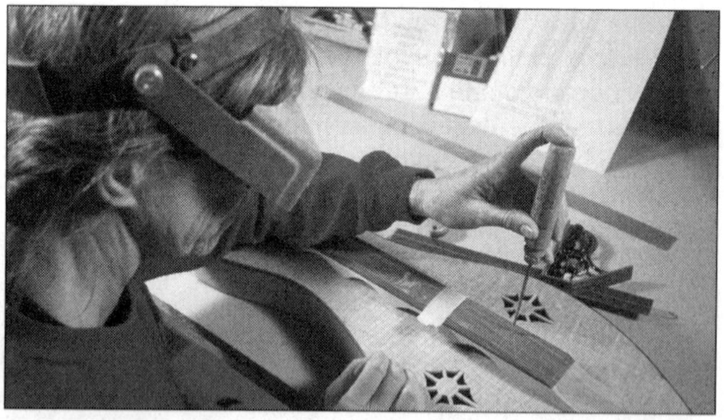

Marking fret positions.

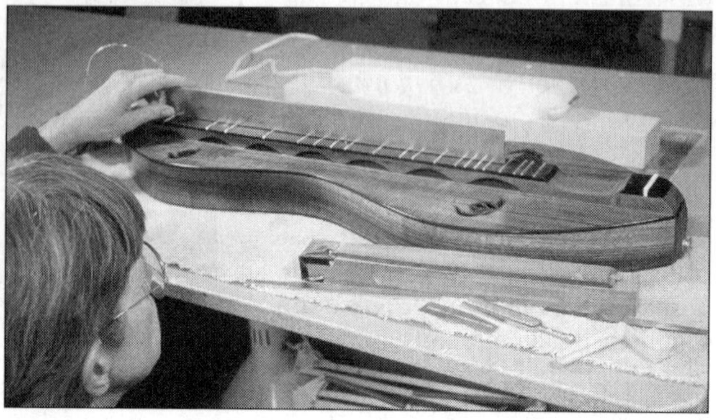

Checking the action during setup.

Bonnie Carol and Max Krimmel. Max served on the GAL Board of Directors in the early '80s. In the fifteen years since he reached the height of his guitar building phase, he has gone to art school, spent a couple of years painting and drawing, spent a decade building a house for himself and Bonnie on eleven acres in the Rockies above Boulder, and now turns alabaster vessels which he sells through galleries nationwide.

made of walnut and it sounds really great, so I'd like my Carol dulcimer made of walnut." Well, the wood is certainly a factor, but there are many other ways the builder can control the final sound. The fingerboard design is crucial. When you get down to it the fingerboard is just a big brace that runs the length of the top. It could be a solid board, a hollow board, or a board with arches cut into the edge that contacts the top, which is what I use.

Do you still hollow the board after cutting the arches?

No, I only did that for a short time. I felt that it might have hurt the stability of the fingerboard. And not only is the internal volume of the dulcimer a control factor, but the relationship of the width of the top to the depth of the sides is important. Joellen Lapidus built dulcimers that were very wide but perhaps only an inch deep, and they were very bright and had a lot of punch. Other dulcimers of a more average width but very deep sides sound muddy to me. I prefer hardwood tops, too. I do build dulcimers with spruce tops, but I've never been moved to keep one of them for my own use. Other builders use a bridge that sits directly on the top of the dulcimer in the middle of the lower bout, *à la* Kurt Simmerman, or use the suspended fingerboard as Howie Mitchell and Keith Young did. Design changes intended to increase volume often change the tone in a way that may or may not be desirable. New builders should be aware that the dulcimer world is larger than they might imagine. ——

Originally published in *American Lutherie #58*, 1999

QUESTIONS

EDITED BY CYNDY BURTON

■ ***Eddie DeWeese from cyberspace** writes:*

Do you have any publications on identifying Ramírez guitars by serial number? I have a 1988 model 1a which I would like to find more about.

***Richard Bruné of Evanston, IL** responds:*

Much information about Ramírez and his guitars can be found in his self-published book, *Things About the Guitar*, which for all its funky presentation is a pretty unfiltered representation of Jose Ramírez III and his opinions about the guitar. As for the serial numbers, this is an interesting subject, as they are opus numbers which have no relation to actual opus numbers.

Prior to 1967, no Ramírez guitars were serial numbered and no accounting was ever made within the shop to determine how many had actually been made. Due to pressure from the government tax people, Ramírez began using serial numbers in 1967, beginning arbitrarily with #1000, and letting them run sequentially. By the early '90s the numbers reached into the 25,000 range, an obscenely large production which prompted the shop to begin using different serial number sequences for each model actually made in the Ramírez shop (1a, Elite, and so on). Adding a slight monkey wrench to the situation, in 1973 an infamous Chicago dealer began sending inferior wood to Ramírez who agreed to make the instruments but on the condition that they were sold as seconds or 2a's and these were given a different serial number sequence, also beginning with #1000 (preceded by the letter "R" which stood for rojo, the Spanish word for red which was the color of the border around the labels of these 2a's). The 2a's were made as such until 1976 and the numbers went up to the low 1800s.

Today, the same 2a label (minus the lower part containing the signature/serial number) is used on the "R" series which are not made in the Ramírez shop, but bought elsewhere and sold by the Ramírez family. These are not to be confused with their other, E series, which are also not made in the Ramírez shop, but elsewhere. The bottom line is that the only useful information to be gleaned from Ramírez serial numbers is to confirm whether an instrument being offered sight unseen by a seller is either a 1a or a 2a according to Ramírez' own designation. ——

Originally published in *American Lutherie #58,* 1999

Reconciling Structural and Acoustic Design in Violin Making

from his 1998 GAL Convention lecture

by Graham Caldersmith

EVERY VIOLIN MAKER, repairer, and restorer regularly deals with problems arising from the deformation of violin-family bodies under string tension. Violins with thicker plates deform less than violins with thinner plates, but it usually turns out that good-sounding violins need to be made thin enough to exhibit some deformation under string tension. The purpose of this paper is to suggest body design factors that will minimize body deformations and optimize acoustic performance, in an attempt to reconcile inevitable but acceptable deformations with a favorable sound quality.

Deformation Listing

Fig. 1 shows the string tension forces imposed on the violin and the consequent strains. We can list the deformations accordingly.

1) Neck root rotation. The "give" (strain) in the neck root causes the fingerboard to drop. Many makers set the fingerboard projection onto the bridge plane at 28MM instead of 27MM to anticipate some droppage. Others leave a step at the pegbox/fingerboard junction for tilting the fingerboard up after initial droppage. There has been some experimentation with dowels set in the neck root to counter rotation. Degree of rotation is much dependant on wood properties. I have suggested heating neck wood to 50°C for two hours to "cure" it, i.e., to fuse cross fibers.

2) Soundpost fulcrum. The bridge bears down through the treble foot in front of the soundpost support. This depresses the *f*-hole wing and raises the *f*-hole flank. Most makers set the soundpost length to support the treble region of the belly so the *f*-hole wing is level with the belly when the strings are tensioned. But the flank remains raised, sometimes dramatically in flat-centered or thin-centered bellies.

3) Belly compression. The belly tries to bulge up under compression, but the bridge pushes the center down. The higher the belly, the greater the uplift. To that extent, the belly is in some structural equilibrium.

If the longitudinal belly curvature predominates in the ends of the plate, as in Stainer and some Amati designs, the ends may bulge up (center joints open) and the middle sags. At the same time the front and rear ribs are sprung outward and pop off the belly.

4) Back stretching. The button is pulled forward and the tail block twisted so that the back is stretched, though with smaller forces than belly compression. But the soundpost thrusts the center of the back outward, compounding the stretching effect in the front and rear bouts of the plate and reducing the curvature there. This stretching may be further augmented by the long-term shrinking of the maple, apparently both along and across the grain, since many old violins need rib perimeter reduction, and they exhibit body convexity.

5) Bass bar depression. The bass bar is thrust down by the bass foot of the bridge while belly compression springs the belly up where the longitudinal curvature is greatest. The result is depressions in the belly around the ends of the bass bar and/or general sinking along the length of the bar. These depressions are broader in bellies with less longitudinal curvature in the ends of the plate. They are evident in some French violins and flat-arched cellos.

Combinations of belly compression, back stretching, and bass bar depression produce some curious body deformations and usually contribute to fingerboard drop and even body concavity. However, strong back shrinkage may produce body convexity which elevates the fingerboard.

Since all these deformations become evident to some extent in wooden instruments within months of stringing up, it is relevant to consider the long-term effects of string tension deformation on vintage instruments. Many, if not most, have had plate curvatures "corrected" in molds adjusted to counter deformations. While experienced restorers reverse

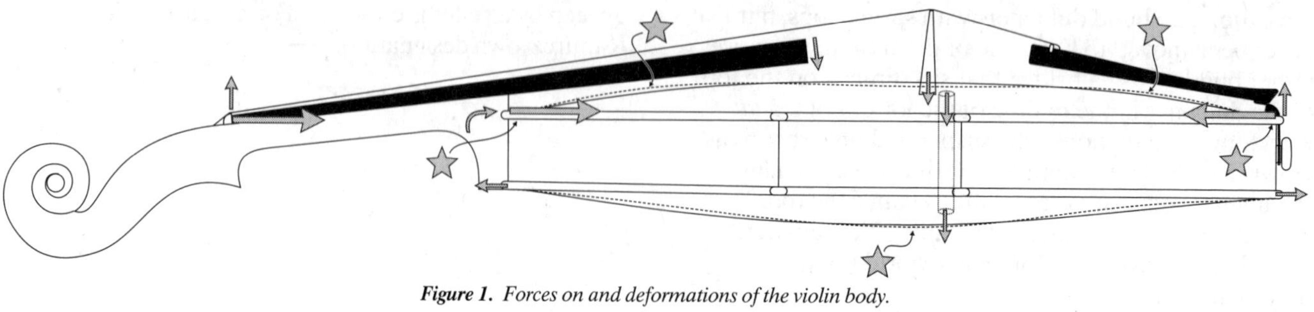

Figure 1. Forces on and deformations of the violin body.

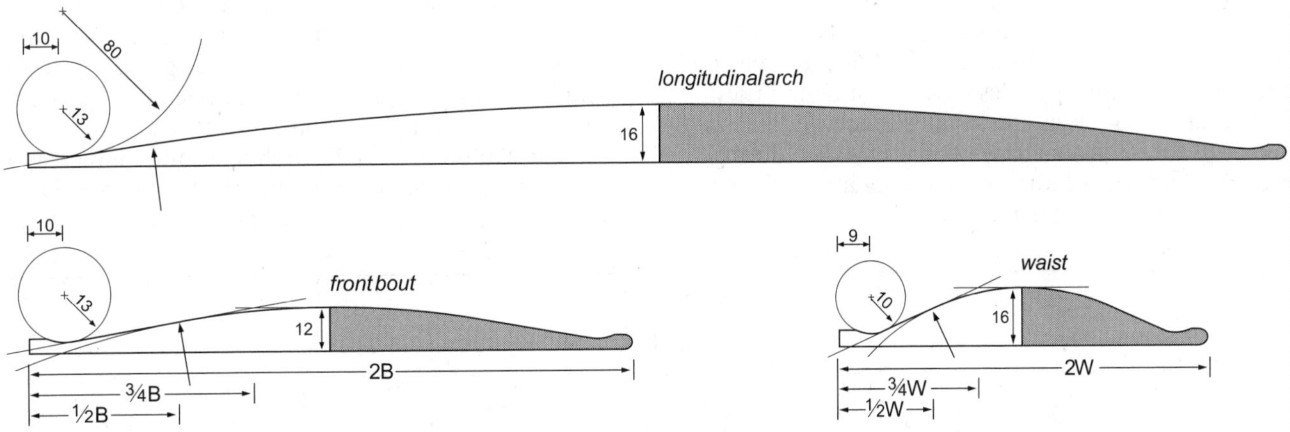

Figure 2a. *Arching profiles for minimal deformation.*

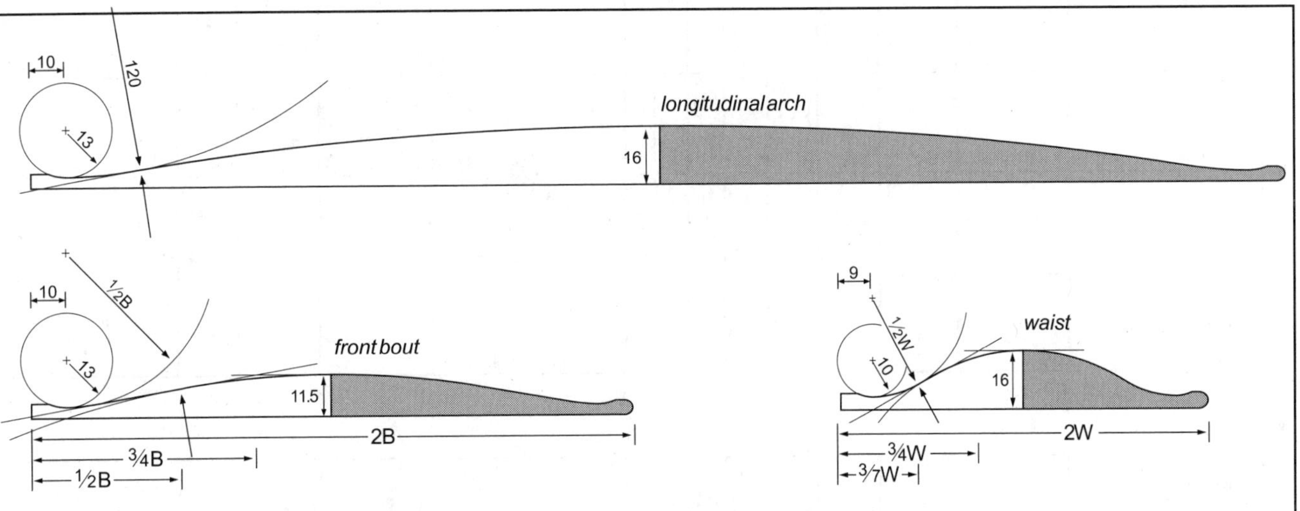

Figure 2b. *Scooped arching profiles for minimal deformation.*

local deformations and asymmetries in the plates, the original overall arching profiles must remain uncertain in plates subject to centuries of string tension deformation and wood shrinkage.

Sacconi states that the different belly and back profiles and contours given in his *"Secrets" of Stradivari* (pp. 63–77) have allowed for bulging under the fingerboard and bridge depression. He does not mention back deformation. He refers to the six arching templates (five cross arching and one long arching) but they do not appear in the catalog of the Stradivarian relics at the end of his book. We do not have any direct information on the undeformed arching profiles of the Cremonese makers.

It is worth contemplating the hypothesis that if the founding makers had used identical arching profiles for backs and bellies, the deformations described as 3 and 4 above would change those identical archings toward the flatter-centered bellies and the rounder-centered backs we regard as standard profiles today. Perhaps within less than a century, makers emulating the Cremonese masters were adopting modestly deformed bellies and backs as sacred lore. However, perusals of side elevations in violin catalogs and *Strad* posters does indicate some great makers conceived belly and back archings differently.

Bellies with arching curvature focused in the ends of the plate are pushed up by compression, but those with flatter ends and curvature focused in the middle of the plate are depressed by the bridge's down bearing. Bellies may go up or down. Both types will show bass-bar depression, the flatter-ended plates more broadly.

The 17th- and 18th-century violin makers had latitude in varying arching profiles because the lower string tensions of that era did not cause plate deformations to anything like the extent that modern string tensions do. Modern makers must shape plates and fit bars for both structural and acoustical integrity. **Fig. 2** shows longitudinal and cross arching designs for a belly of any height that in my experience minimizes deformation and allows plate graduation for acoustic performance. However, this arching prescription* limits the range of violin timbre or "voice" available in modern violins, consideration of which is the second part of this argument.

* The radius of the gutters may be varied for aesthetic and/or timbre preferences.

Violin Timbre and Frequency Response

Conventional violin wisdom has it that the earlier Amati and Stainer violins with their "chicken-breasted" and "barrel" arching profiles produced a clear, bright timbre suited to salons and smaller concert halls. As demands for stronger-voiced violins emerged during the 18th century, Stradivari and the Guarneri Family developed the powerful and projecting smoothly arched violins that have become definitive models for most current violin makers. The profiles given in **Fig. 2** are marginally smoother than the profiles given by Sacconi and I have suggested that the difference may be due to plate deformation and wood contraction.

The evolution of violin arching profiles indicates an important relation between timbre and arching. Of course, graduation and wood properties are the other

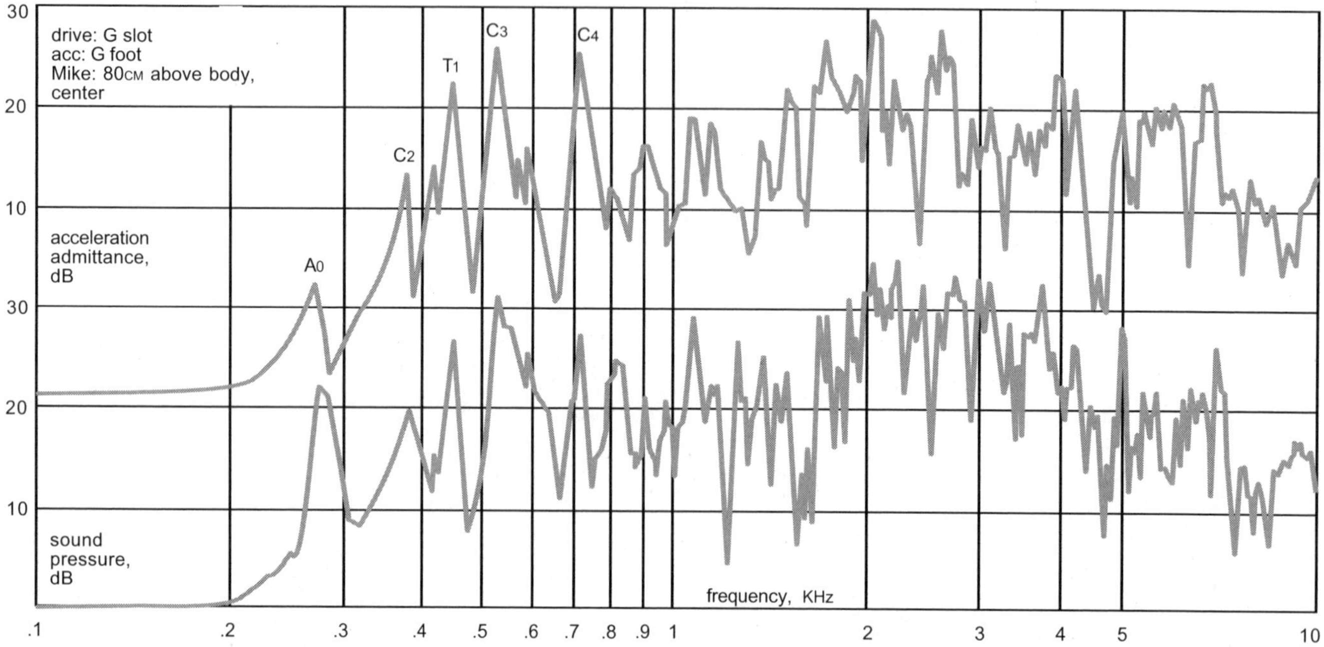

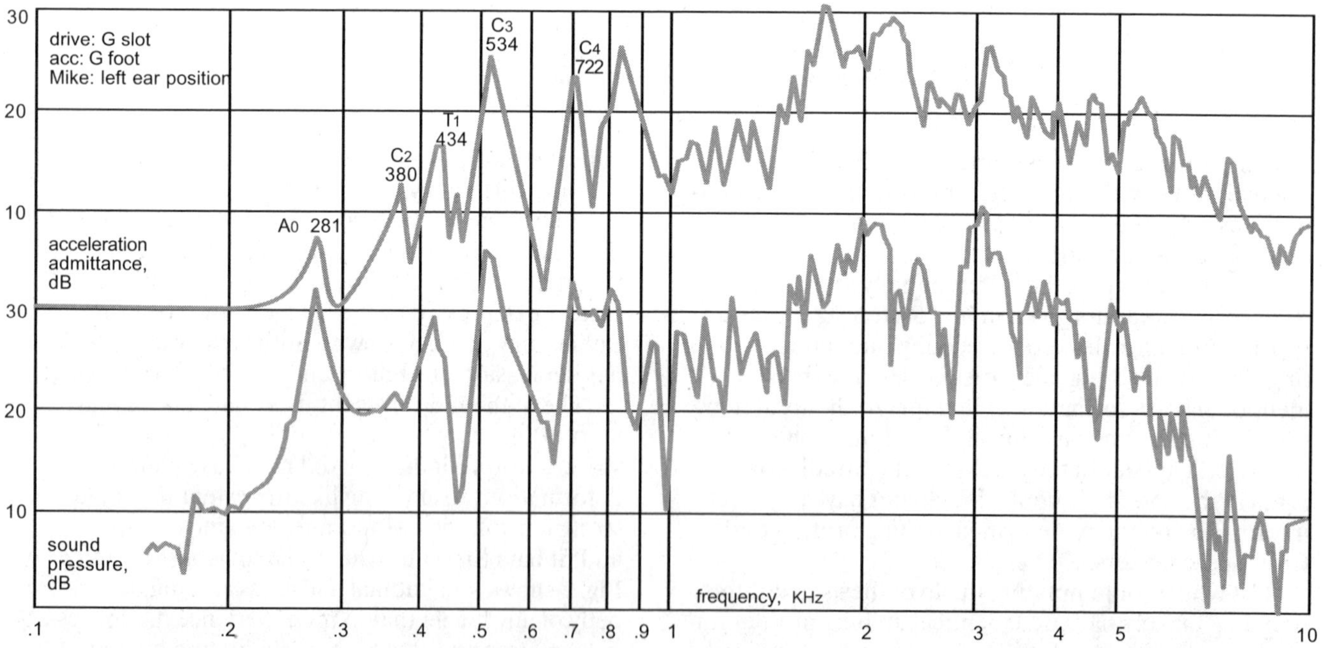

***Figure 3a** (top). Violin frequency response, Collin-Mezzine, 1900, France.* ***Figure 3b** (bottom). Violin frequency response, Caldersmith violin #86, King William pine and Australian blackwood. The peaks labeled A_0, C_2, T_1, C_3, and C_4 in the frequency responses occur when the violin body resonates at low frequencies (below 1KHz) in natural modes of vibration. A_0 is the "air resonance" where the "air pistons" in the f-holes are activated through the internal air volume by the pumping motion of the plates. C_2 is a body ("corpus") mode where the violin body flexes as a whole but produces little sound. T_1 is a "pumping" mode activated by the bass foot of the bridge and C_3 is a "corpus" mode activated by the bass foot of the bridge. Both T_1 and C_3 are efficient sound generators. C_4 is activated by both feet of the bridge and is a fairly efficient sound generator. The frequency of A_0 depends mainly on the volume of enclosed air. The frequencies of T_1–C_4 depend on the frequencies of free plate modes in* ***Fig. 5** and on plate edge thicknesses. The amplitude geometries of these modes A_0–C_4 are illustrated in many articles published in the* Catgut Acoustical Society Journal.

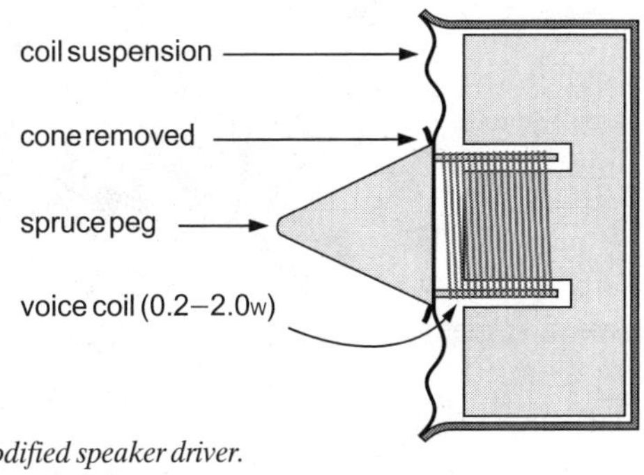

Figure 4. *Modified speaker driver.*

two factors influencing timbre (which is regulated by bass bar, bridge, soundpost setting, and strings). We seek a coherence between the structural integrity of the violin and its acoustic performance.

While the ultimate test of a violin is its ease of response, timbre, and projection in the concert hall, a useful measure of its musical quality is its frequency response. The violin frequency response **(Fig. 3)** is a trace plotted out on a chart which records amplitude vs. frequency. On the vertical axis, the strength of the violin's vibration amplitude in decibels (dB) at the bridge and/or the sound produced (sound pressure) is shown in response to a pure-tone, constant-amplitude driving force applied to the bridge and swept over an appropriate frequency range along the horizontal axis. The bridge or bridge-foot vibration amplitude (acceleration in **Fig. 3** but often velocity) is detected with a .8g accelerometer, and the sound produced is detected with a microphone placed at a selected location near the violin. Sometimes several microphones are used to average out spatial variations in the sound radiated.

The driving force is applied directly to a peg glued to the voice coil of a minispeaker with its cone removed, forming a modified speaker driver **(Fig. 4)**. The peg and voice coil together weigh .8g. Other methods of driving have been used, and new computers can extract a frequency response from the accelerometer and microphone signals produced by tapping the bridge.

The well-defined peaks below 1kHz indicate the violin's response to the driving force in its lower natural modes of vibration. These modes continue to be the subject of intensive research. Above 1kHz the resonance peaks merge into a continuum, the average profile of which reflects the timbre of the violin. The relative strengths of the 1kHz–2kHz band and the 2kHz–5kHz band is a prime factor in the timbre and power of the violin.

Violins with strong resonances (high peaks) below 1kHz may sound full or rich in the low strings, but are often perceived as "tubby" or "boomy" and are subject to wolf notes.

All good violins have strong response in the 2kHz–5kHz range (augmented by a well-selected and well-cut bridge). This band imparts the clarity and sweetness of the violin tone and coincides with the optimal sensitivity of human hearing. Muting the violin suppresses the 2kHz–5kHz response with well-known results. Violins with strong response above 5kHz are shrill and scratchy.

Violins with low response in the 1kHz–2kHz band are sweet and clear but not powerful. There is evidence that highly arched Amati- and Stainer-type violins have lower response in this band.

Violins with the 1kHz–2kHz response level closer to the 2kHz–5kHz level are rich, dark-toned, and powerful, lending toward the nasal timbre. They say "oo" and "er" rather than "eh" and "ee" in the low strings. This is characteristic of smoothly arched violins with arching height usually less than 16mm. If bass bars are not too stiff, smoothly arched violins have a stronger response below 1kHz as well, hence their greater power.

But whatever the arching profiles, violins with thicker plates have individual peaks and resonance bands at higher frequencies than violins with thinner plates. Most makers agree that thick violins are shallow and shrill, and that thin violins are at best mellow and sweet, or often muted and nasal, and subject to plate deformations. That is to say, the whole resonance profile may be shifted up in frequency for thick plates and down in frequency for thin plates except for the air resonance, which is mainly set in frequency by air volume and *f*-hole size.

Many violins have a strong band around 1kHz, and for thick plates this band is pushed up toward 1.5kHz producing a nasal quality. At the same time the strong 2kHz–5kHz band is raised in frequency, adding a shrill and scratchy quality to the sound. Some violins with normal thicknesses have a strong peak around 1.5kHz due to unusual archings and sound nasal.

With thin plates the 2kHz–5kHz band drops toward 1.5kHz and the higher frequency response is reduced. The result is a violin which is nasal and muted, often full and rich in the low strings, but lacking articulation and sparkle in the top strings. It would probably lack projection too, although I have no evidence for the projection argument.

Obviously we aim to make our plates not too thick and not too thin. We allow for stiffer and less-stiff woods with one or two tenths of a millimeter less or more than the standard thicknesses given by Sacconi and others. However, my experience in common with other contemporary makers indicates that bellies must be more than 3.0mm thick in the middle to avert soundpost deformations. Sacconi reports Stradivari's maximum thickness of 2.8mm around the *f*-holes, but I suggest this is inadequate for modern string tensions and find even 3.5mm in the soundpost region is advisable for most tonewoods. In my experience, backs with 4.5mm centers and 2.5mm–2.2mm crescents are structurally sufficient.

Plate Tuning

The final question, then, linking structural integrity with acoustic balance reflected in a frequency response profile which is not dislocated too far up or down in frequency is: are tap tones or free-plate mode frequencies and nodal geometries useful guides to setting both the lower mode set of the complete violin A_0, T_1, C_3, and C_4 at desirable frequencies and the 1kHz–5kHz response profile so the violin speaks clearly and sweetly?

*(See **Violin Design** on page 373)*

Originally published in *American Lutherie #58,* 1999

Meet the Maker: Gary Southwell

by Cyndy Burton

You arrived here last night, all the way from Nottingham, England, just in time to hear James Kline in concert on an 11-string arch guitar you made. What are your first impressions?

It's been a whirlwind, but everyone's been really friendly and helpful. The number of people with questions is incredible, and I really like the mix of fine leading makers with beginners and people who are doing it for a hobby. There's no sense of, "I'm a really top maker and you're not." I've been knocked back by the number of people who've come up to me and said what a wonderful guitar James played on. It's very refreshing when makers feel comfortable acknowledging another's work.

I heard a lot of people talking about James' guitar. What is an arch guitar and how is it braced?

It's a hybrid. James had in mind the music he wanted to play and knew how many strings and what sort of tuning would be required. He wanted it to be somewhere between a lute and a guitar, but neither of those. The name 11-string arch guitar is a made-up name that's a reflection of its taking its pedigree from guitars and the Baroque arch lute, which also has floating bass strings. Basically he said, "This is what I want the instrument to do, what do you think will work well?" To get some of that lute- and early guitar-type quality, I've kept the body very small, which also helps balance the instrument. Quite often on guitars with added bass strings, the bass becomes overpowering. Having a small body tends to accentuate the high, sweeter notes, keeps the bass under control, plus it helps focus the sound as well. It becomes very clear and nothing really dominates. The head and the bridge mimic a Baroque guitar style, so there are aesthetic references to the Baroque, also. The scale is only 63CM, partly for ease of reaches and also to keep the instrument on the sweet side, not having too many bass overtones. The barring is very simple transverse bars above and below the soundhole, as per the normal guitar, then a slanted bar close to the bridge on the treble side, and I think there's also a smaller bar just behind the bridge. It's quite a standard, early 19th-century, French style of bracing, like René Lacôte. The back and sides are bird's-eye maple, a wood very commonly used by French makers back then.

HAP NEWSOM

Where did you get the bird's-eye?

From America — the same place I believe those 19th-century makers did. I think it's the only place it grows.

How did you become involved in guitar making?

As a boy I was quite a keen classical guitarist, to what we call A-levels in school — what you do before you get your degree. I was also good at crafts and art. I was studying art, particularly pottery, which I even won some awards for. My father was a cabinet maker and had a home workshop. I was used to being around it. Although I didn't really take to woodworking as such, I did mess about and make things. And when I started playing a lot we did knock up some dulcimer-type instruments. Then I was looking for a direction of study

JONATHON PETERSON

James Kline plays his Southwell 11-string arch guitar during a concert at the 1998 GAL Convention.

and just happened to see this course at the London College of Furniture on guitar making and thought it would be a good way to combine my interests. I studied there for three years. I was about twenty-one when I left. My teachers were very encouraging and I was young and didn't have responsibilities, so I set up my own workshop.

I didn't specialize at first; I was just making standard modern guitars. But I very quickly got interested in some historical guitars and a friend of mine, Stephen Barber, a lute maker, helped me with those first early guitars. He sort of gave me the sensibilities of a lute maker, which enabled me to make the instruments much lighter than I might otherwise have done. Modern guitar makers tend to overbuild early guitars when they're first starting. He helped me get over that hurdle quite quickly.

ANDREW DALEY

Southwell A-Series guitar, a modern guitar based on a Viennese rather than Spanish tradition.

I saw the duo of Leif Christensen and Maria Kämmerling give a concert on original, period guitars, and it really brought that music to life for me. I got very interested in the guitars that they were playing, a Panormo and a Lacôte. I made some copies of Panormo guitars first and then went on to make some Lacôte copies. At the time no one else was doing that seriously and the few players who were playing on these instruments quickly heard about my copies, and Leif and Maria and Nigel North, a very good early guitar player, all ordered guitars from me. So within a couple years of starting in business, I already had some really big names in that field using my guitars. They encouraged me to look at more and more unusual 19th-century guitars and discover more about different makers of the period. I spent a lot of time researching guitars, going through private collections in Europe and amassing a lot of information on them, and importantly, handling these instruments, doing restoration work on them, and really just getting a thorough knowledge of them. Because of the well-known players who were using my guitars, the word spread, and most of my business for about eight years was restoring and building copies of 19th-century guitars.

For no apparent reason, I got a desire to make a modern classical guitar again. I used some of the ideas I'd learned from the 19th century, like using just transverse barring and stylistic touches, like bridge designs with very tapered ends, which were more early guitar than modern guitar. Because I had so much early guitar work, it really didn't matter so much if people accepted or rejected those instruments. I could just design them how I wanted, and if people liked them fine, and if they didn't, they didn't.

A big change in my career happened when David Starobin ordered a 19th-century guitar from me. I made him a copy of a Stauffer, a Viennese guitar. David is mainly known for his modern guitar playing. On the Stauffer, he focused on 19th-century music. I'm not sure to what extent having the Stauffer copy encouraged his love for this music. In any case, he was so taken with the guitar he asked me if I would make a modern guitar for him with similar qualities, but would have the big sound he wanted for modern music, that he could play aggressively as well. That really interested me as a project. I tried to come up with a modern guitar which was based on that Viennese tradition rather than the Spanish style. One of the prominent features of that is the adjustable neck with a floating fingerboard, which was a feature he was particularly taken by. And again it relied on transverse bars; I've actually blended the two together. There's some fan strutting in there, but only a very few light fan struts. The waist is more tightly curved (narrower) than a Spanish instrument, the lower bout is wider, but in length, it's shorter. It took quite a few years to refine this design. I call this my A-series guitar.

The adjustable neck — does David adjust it to raise the action, say when the humidity changes? Or to play different music?

For both of those reasons, really. If you're playing chamber music, for instance, you may want the action high so you can play aggressively. It takes only seconds to adjust with a key and you don't have to detune. If you want to play very gently again you can lower the action and play with a very soft touch. And if the action changes due to differing humidity conditions, you can just adjust it. It puts the player in control. As a maker there's nothing more frustrating than a player saying, "Can you take the action down just a touch?" Then, "It's buzzing a bit now. Can you raise it a touch?" This just does away with that completely. Like so many good ideas, it's an old one. Stauffer invented it back in the early 1800s, and I've refined it slightly, but not in any major way.

That design took a while to get right and David showed a lot of faith in me for four or five years. Only last year he finally said, "This is it. This is what I've been looking for." He's now got a pair of them and used them on his new recording, *Newdance*. It's a really exciting recording of new music on this guitar.

Another feature of this guitar is that it has built-in pickups and microphone and everything for amplification, again because David does a lot of work with other musicians including orchestras. He really wanted one guitar that does everything, and he feels that this does. A reality that a lot of classical players are starting to face is how to amplify. I've started making quite a few with built-in amplification; David Tanenbaum has one as well.

Are they playing the full repertoire on them?

Yes. They are mainly playing modern music on it. It is in no way an early guitar. It's a modern guitar with the aesthetic based on a Viennese rather than a Spanish tradition.

I know you've been working with Julian Bream on quite a different sort of instrument. How's that been?

It's quite a contrast. He has a great love of the Hauser guitar, for him the ultimate guitar. He has on loan a very nice Hauser guitar that belongs to Rose Augustine. I think what he was looking for from me was a reproduction of that guitar, so he could rest it or give it back to Rose. It's Indian rosewood and very lightly built, compared to Segovia's '37 for example, which is Brazilian rosewood and has thicker woods throughout, I believe. Of course, it's very difficult to make a guitar that he will feel the same about. Impossible, really. He's a player with tremendous insight into instruments, and he's one of those rare guitarists who can not only give you a good and honest, sometimes difficult-to-take critique of your guitar, he can also point you in directions to try to improve. Undoubtedly, over the past few years of working with him, my work has improved immensely. He's incredibly critical and incredibly demanding. I've made quite a few guitars in the Hauser style now, and he's said good things about them, so other good players have started to buy them.

ANDREW DALEY

Gary's shop in Nottingham, England. Stop in on your way to the leather-underwear store!

You're building a great variety of instruments — 19th century copies, modern guitars with some features of Stauffer guitars like adjustable necks, and guitars in the style of Hermann Hauser I. Is there a commonality that runs through them all, a Gary Southwell sound?

I think it's bizarre that you can make such widely different instruments and yet there will be a certain quality of sound that runs through them all. It's hard to describe in words, but there is something. Other people have said that they are very focused, clear, and balanced. The Hauser-style instruments also have very rich overtones, very different from the Stauffer guitar which is sweet and intimate, but quite a punchy sound as well.

Tell me about your workshop. Is it at your home?

No, I've never worked from home. My workshop is part of a communal group of workshops in a nice old Victorian building in Nottingham, which actually used to be a hospital. I'm sure there are some ghosts afloat about that place at night. *(laughter)* There's a weird mixture of people — from those making suits of armor and swords for films through to people making erotic leather wear. Quite a mixture. It's nice having a community around you so you can talk to people if you want to, but most of the time you're just in your own small room in your own small world working. I have my wife Sarah, new baby daughter Maria, and three-year-old Emily at home. It's quite nice to be able to shut up the workshop at the end of the day, put that to one side and go home and be with my family and enjoy that life. My wife isn't a guitarist or maker, so she hasn't a particular interest in guitars, and I feel it might intrude on our home life if my shop was at home. There would always be the temptation to go and do a bit. The other good thing about it is that I go to the workshop and it's an intense thing. I'm there for a number of hours each day and I can give myself completely over to that with no distractions. Then I can just go away and leave it. I've learned that it's quite a good thing to do yet sometimes very difficult: if you have a problem, leave it. Go home; forget about it and have a nice evening out or whatever. Go back and sort it out the next day when you're fresh and not all worked up about it. That can be very positive. I tend to work regular hours, 9–5 or 9–6. I might work there twenty hours nonstop if I'm under the pressure of a tight deadline or really involved in a project. It's not a rigid thing, but I try to do a fairly standard forty-hour week.

Since you build a variety of instruments, how is your workshop set up?

I was taught in a very traditional manner, so I still make things predominantly with hand tools. I spent probably the first half of my professional career doing almost everything by hand. I have made things more efficient now by having a certain amount of machinery. I usually make two instruments at a time, for example, one close to being finished and one near the beginning. Two is the maximum; I might be making an A-series guitar with a little Panormo guitar. I don't use a lot of jigs, but I do use molds. Each one is so different, that I don't think it's effective use of my time to jig up and make a lot of pegboxes, for example. Everything is done at the time, and each part is created afresh. It gives me a lot of flexibility, for instance, to change the shape of the instrument slightly if I want to. I like that. For the same reason, I bend by hand. It's a process I enjoy doing anyway. Those little irregularities you get there with hand bending are natural; they add to the character. But again, it also means that I can bend a set of sides for a Hauser and a set for a Lacôte on the same day if I want to. Making very different instruments keeps me fresh. I don't get stuck in any routines. I just made a pair of A-series guitars and enjoyed that, and now I have a little 19th-century guitar to make. That will be a nice change. If I had another A-series to make, maybe I would start to get a bit tired of it and not give quite as much of myself, which I think you need to do when you're making very fine instruments.

I have a small number of tools and few jigs. I have about three hand planes, two of which I like using, about six chisels, a couple of knives, a bending iron, a few files and rasps, and that's really about it. On the machine

JONATHON PETERSON

Gary speaks with Swedish luthier Michael Sandén after a lecture at the 1998 GAL Convention, while Cyndy Burton and Mike Doolin listen in.

GARY SOUTHWELL

Gary, his wife Sarah, three year-old Emily, and baby Maria.

side, I have a small bandsaw, a pillar drill for accurate drilling (I think you call that a drill press), and a hand-held router. My latest acquisition is a sanding thicknesser which I use to rough thickness, but I still like to do the last millimeter or half by plane and scraper. I feel sometimes with machines that things happen too quickly. With a plane you can only take one shaving at a time in one area, and it's very rare that you suddenly overdo it, because it's much more gradual and there's more control. It's what I'm used to, so I feel comfortable with it. I really love that feeling when you've just sharpened your plane and it's razor sharp. You get a piece of wood, and the shavings you get off of it — those beautiful, curling, silkly shavings, and the sound of the plane as it whistles. I could just stand there all day just making shavings. I think when you're doing it for a living, the moments like that become fewer, you just have to get on and make a living in a sense. But if you can't still enjoy the odd moment like that, it would be a sad day, because that's the empathy with the natural material, just working that material. So I really enjoy bending sides and planing. And I really enjoy putting the strings on it and giving it to a player when it's all done. *(laughter)*

And getting paid, I hope.

Yes, but you don't go into instrument making for the money; let's face it. If you're not enjoying it, then there's no real reason to be doing a job like ours. When you're making instruments for a lot of demanding professional players, there's a great deal of stress involved. They're demanding a lot from you, and they can sometimes be very difficult people to work for. So if you can't get some pleasure from working with the materials and shaping those materials, I couldn't see a purpose of doing it. It would mean nothing to me. ———

Originally published in *American Lutherie #58,* 1999

About the Cello Tailpiece

by Eric Fouilhé

MANY OF THE VENERABLE 200-year-old cellos circulating in the auction sales have attracted my attention. Looking at them, I get a feeling of incongruity, like looking at a beautiful piece of furniture with a wood-grained Formica top. It's that shiny plastic tailpiece. I was upset to see that this "string-kini" eyesore was hiding the instrument! Something had to be done about this, at least for aesthetic reasons.

I am a maker of fittings and my knowledge of the setup and adjustment of instruments is limited. However, some questions arise regarding the evolution of the fittings of the instruments of the classical quartet.

The bridge, positioned right in the middle of the instrument, is the center of acoustical gravity. It produces the sound, so it is normal that violin makers pay a lot of attention both to the conception and practical realization of the bridge. The cutting of the bridge, repeated over and over again, opens the way to a process of experimentation and, over the years, violin makers have developed some personal recipes. A bridge carries the maker's individual touch, and the sense of his or her craft, in an attempt to bring the instrument to the best of its possibilities. But such attention to the bridge can lead to neglect of some other important parts, such as the fittings.

We are far away from the times of Stradivari, when the master designed everything including beautiful iron hinges for his violin cases. Our present-day industrialization has divided the tasks, and the violin maker has stopped making tailpieces, pegs, or chin rests, and so can no longer influence their evolution.

Who would imagine that the violin fittings, including the fingerboard, represent a quarter of its weight? I myself wonder why those accessories, honest components of a beautiful object — this fine tool called "a violin" — have evolved so much. The chin rest is five times larger than a hundred years ago, the cello end pin has increased three times in length over the same period, but the instruments themselves have evolved little. Why?

ALL COURTESY OF ERIC FOUILHE

The staff of Bois d'Harmonie, left to right: Eric Fouilhé, his wife Françoise ("queen of the managment"), finish specialist Miquette, and Dominique. Two others, Michel and Patrick, work from their homes.

The fittings, which act as an interface or connection point with the musician, were the first to answer the technical modifications required by musical and cultural changes. Have these modifications of the accessories respected the instrument? Do they enhance all of the its capacities as an acoustical tool?

Acoustically and mechanically speaking, it is obvious that a good tailpiece will not perform miracles — on a Strad or a cheap fiddle — but in some cases it can help. This subject has interested few violin makers, maybe because the tailpiece, being machine made, is a contribution which is external to the workshop. It is often put on "as is" and the violin maker has to "make up for it" by working on other parameters to influence the sound.

In the last hundred years, the evolution of the tailpiece does not seem linked to the acoustical, mechanical, or aesthetic needs of the instrument. Here are some examples:

- There was a notable reduction in the width of the string end of the ebony tailpieces made in Mirecourt at the beginning of the century, maybe to save wood.
- The ebony blank of the post-Baroque tailpiece became thicker, thus becoming heavier. The ebony selected for industrial fabrication was more or less porous, and it was necessary to increase the size to avoid the risk of breaking **(Fig. 1)**.
- The German "tulip" shape was introduced. The two corners were rounded off, making the tailpiece easier to machine produce, and preventing tangling with clothes or hair. All this resulted in an unfortunate aesthetic modification **(Fig. 2)**.
- When "fine tuners" were requested by musicians, the industry quickly and solidly integrated them into the tailpieces — and when I say solid I mean solid! Two of these fine tuners weigh as much as a Mirecourt ebony tailpiece.
- The adjustable nylon screw loop was substituted for the catgut string that seemed more interesting acoustically.
- For a century, the German industry of instrument accessories has furnished and is still furnishing the whole world, due to the fact that the manufacturers standardized the fittings: strong and not expensive.
- The French and English makers, known since the 19th century, disappeared in the '50s. I am thinking about Mr. Ruer in Mirecourt or the Hills in London.

Let's take a look at the tailpiece models available on the market today:

Pusch: With its numerous metallic parts, it is not so efficient in the sound setup. The only advantage is that it is made of wood.

Akusticus: Made of plastic, it works well and is not expensive. I am not fond of its aesthetics, and surprisingly, it weighs the same as a traditional ebony tailpiece.

Wittner: This model is commonly used, as it is more aesthetically pleasing and works well. The aluminum alloy used for its fabrication makes it 50% heavier than ebony.

The question of weight has been at the center of my studies. Weight does not seem to be a single criterion; the material used is also important. Both Akusticus and Wittner are successful, though one is very light and soft and the other heavy and sturdy. The distribution of weight along the tailpiece seems important. Tailpieces fitted with integrated metallic fine tuners carry most of their weight at the tip, a few centimeters away from the bridge. Could this create a muting effect?

The importance of the bridge's oscillation from one foot to the other seems basic to me, so I tried an experiment. While a friend was playing his cello, I fixed some 40G clamps on various points of the tailpiece. The balance of the four strings was immediately modified. The most critical point was at the string end. With extra weight there, the sound was irregular and weak, and the response was slow. The excessive weight of the fine tuners acts as a mute. This brought me to the design of a new tailpiece, the "Harmonie" series, featuring light composite fine tuners incorporated into an equally light wooden tailpiece of ebony or boxwood.

The rigidity, or acoustic conduction, of the tailpiece material seems less important. However, tests comparing a tailpiece made out of heavy ebony or "grenadille," and a light tailpiece in pernambuco seem significant. To evaluate the acoustical contribution of a tailpiece is difficult, especially when the instrument has new fittings or has only recently been set up. Nevertheless, the "grenadille" tailpieces seemed to give a large, acute, and well-detached sound, where the pernambuco gave a brilliant, compact and fast sound. If we compare these sounds to the guitar, ebony is like the classical guitar and pernambuco the flamenco guitar. Pernambuco was used to make tailpieces in Mirecourt during the Second World War, when ebony was rare. At the time, nobody noticed anything particular regarding the sound.

Lastly I considered the tail gut and its elasticity. Unfortunately, the traditional gut string is seldom used anymore. The use of threaded nylon has quickly become popular to facilitate the adjustment of the string afterlength between the bridge and tailpiece, without taking the time to compare the respective qualities of nylon and gut. It seems to me that a soft material like nylon is more apt to absorb the vibrations of the tailpiece.

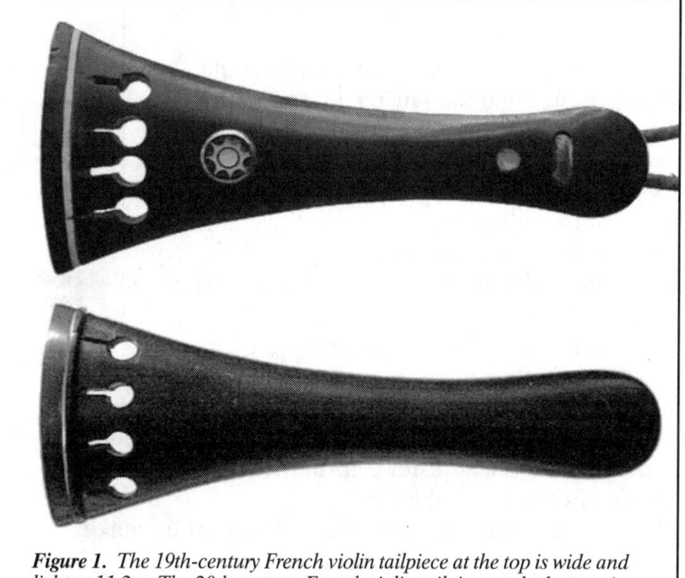

Figure 1. *The 19th-century French violin tailpiece at the top is wide and light at 11.2G. The 20th-century French violin tailpiece at the bottom is tight, thick, and heavier at 13.8G.*

As an experiment, I tried lightly fixing the foot of the tailpiece with two small pieces on the edge of the instrument top. The sound lost some of its strength. The study of sonograms shows an important reduction of the acoustical energy below 1000Hz. This is the same situation as with the viola da gamba, where the foot of the tailpiece is fixed.

The way the ends of the tail gut are tied balances the strings acoustically. To me, the sound quality seems undoubtedly dependent on whether the tailpiece can rotate **(Fig. 3)**.

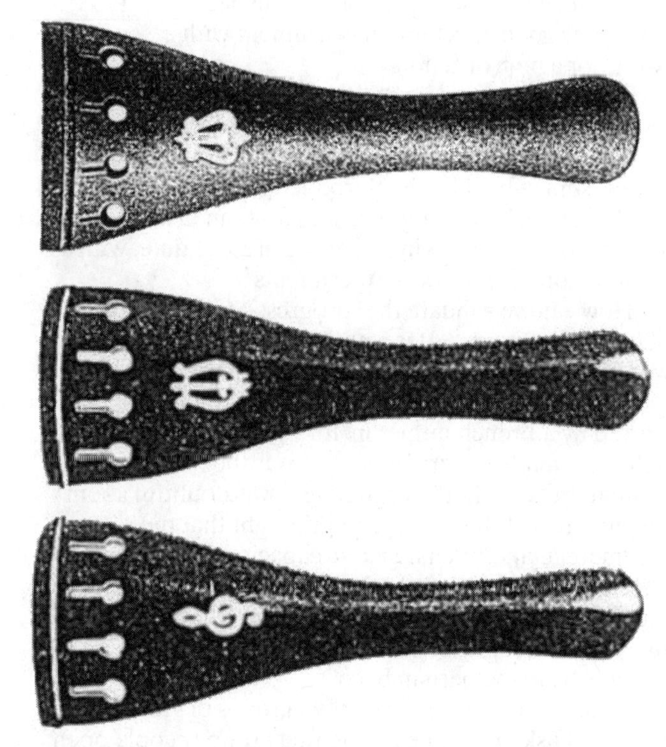

Figure 2. *Industrial evolution and automatic woodworking improvement: A 1928 German tailpiece from Markneunkirchen (at top) and two 1980 German tailpieces from Mittenwald.*

The use of a steel adjuster seems to please violin makers acoustically, if not aesthetically. I don't know the reason, but steel is more rigid than nylon, and two strands of the adjuster in this kind of attachment are often closer together. So trying to make the tailpiece vibrate more easily at the tail gut seems interesting. Some experiments could be done:

- ▸ Lengthening the tail gut by using a shorter tailpiece.
- ▸ Trying other materials that have an elasticity coefficient closer to that of the gut.
- ▸ Making the attachment *"a la baroque,"* or *"cavalier."* This will let the tailpiece be less fixed than the modern system where the adjuster exits in the middle of the tailpiece's thickness **(Fig. 4)**.
- ▸ Using a single strand attachment, like violin maker Roger Lanne in Paris is doing at present.

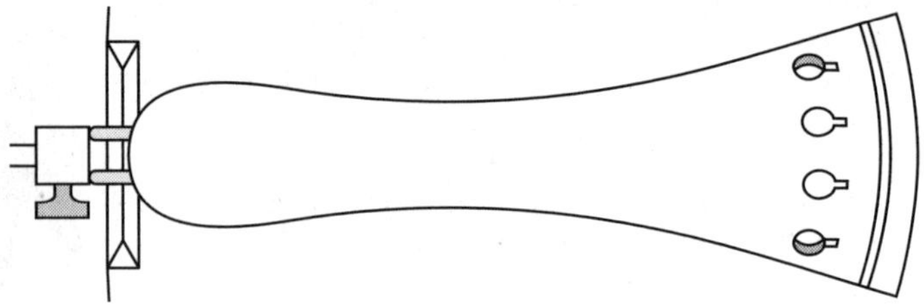

Figure 3. *The length and gap of the two ends of the tail gut control the freedom of the tailpiece to rotate.*

Many other experiments need to be done regarding tailpieces. The gap between the strands of tail gut as they come out of the tailpiece could be modified. This could influence the bridge's freedom of movement. Various weights and various woods could be tried. Each tailpiece has a particular resonant frequency, and its material has an acoustical transmission speed (I am referring to Lucchi's tester used by many bow makers). Is the sound frequency of the part itself important? Does a tailpiece need to be tuned? Could it be tuned like a xylophone key, to get a particular note, often from G to E? Could the tuning of a tailpiece have some good effect for an instrument with a "wolf," or a hole on a note?

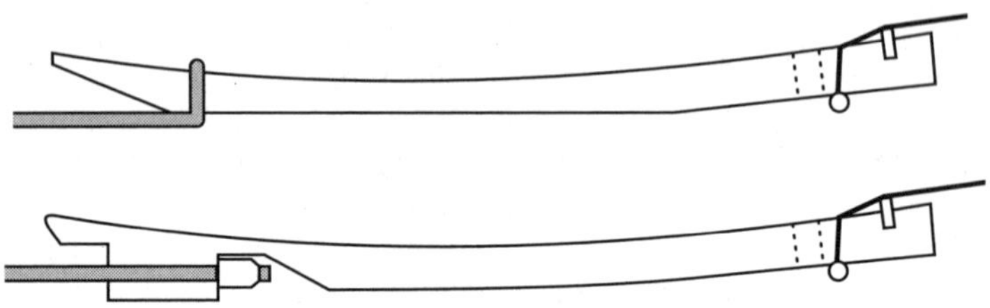

Figure 4. *Top: Baroque tail gut attached "en cavalier." The tailpiece is less fixed. Bottom: Modern tail gut attachment.*

The breakover angle of the string at the bridge is also interesting. The French tailpieces are rounded to match the shape of the bridge. The Hill tailpieces are flatter, somewhat like the Baroque tailpieces, and the breakover angle of A and C is weaker than D and G. This is what I am working on at the present time, with a commission of acoustical experiments.

How can we validate the "progress" or the "results" of our experiments? It is a problem for me. Now I would like to tell you the pernambuco story.

Three years ago, an experiment on fittings was started by a French luthier in Tokyo; specifically, on tailpieces made in pernambuco. I was the maker of those tailpieces. In the beginning, I was doubtful about the qualities of this wood, and I thought that the commercial and/or charismatic capacities of this luthier were conditioning the trend. According to the musicians, the results were miraculous. But where did these results come from? From their imagination, or actually from the pernambuco?

I tried an experiment with two groups of violin makers: I asked the ones in the first group (people open to new experiments) to try this new extraordinary tailpiece. A second group, selected from violin makers who were more doubtful, was also asked to try this tailpiece. The results from both groups were perfectly identical: six out of ten found some improvement: fast and better sound emission, opening up of the instrument and, sometimes, reduction of certain unwanted noises.

The conclusion is that in this situation, the product spoke for itself without too much — or in spite of — human interferences; the experiment can be considered valid. I have doubts about the validity of experimental methods, as I know that an instrument will never be set up or played twice in the same way. The results, even if they are real, will not be applicable to your neighbor's instrument.

As I indicated, the evolution of the tailpiece in the last century caused it to become a "foreign" part of the instrument. Its modifications were due to the violin-making industry, which neglected to take into account the role of acoustical transmission played by the tailpiece (as well as the importance of using good wood), and also by the musicians, who required fine tuners for a comfort rather normal nowadays. The results were an addition of weight detrimental to the sound quality.

Both the violin maker and the musician often neglect the fittings and consider them only for their mechanical function; they seem almost invisible as long as they function. You are more likely to notice your car or your telephone when they are out of order! So, perhaps it is natural to see a shiny plastic tailpiece on a Strad at Sotheby's. The tailpiece is "transparent!" ——

Update

The latest innovation from Bois d'Harmonie is a tail gut made of high-tech multifiber braided cord which is nine times as strong as steel wire and does not stretch.

(2006)

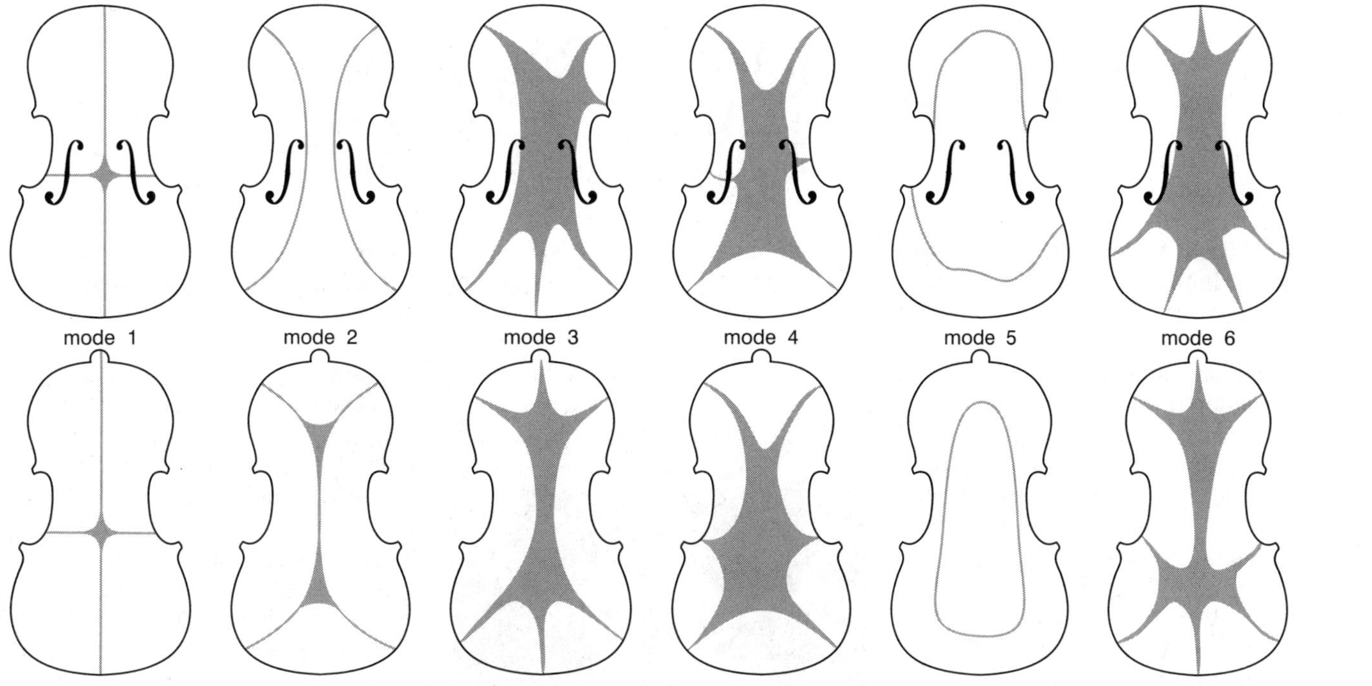

Figure 5. *The first six free-plate modes of the violin.*

(***Violin Design*** *from page 365)*

The musical quality assigned to a violin is always subject to the complexities of tone perception, the environment (social, climatic, and acoustic) in which it is played, and the preferences and experience of the player and listeners. I have found indications of different preferences between nationalities and schools of violin teaching.

The free-plate tuning scheme setting modes 5, 2, and 1 in the belly at 360Hz, 180Hz, and 90Hz and in the back at 360Hz, 180Hz, and 110Hz is called the bi-tri-octave scheme and is recommended for "concert" violins. Schemes for violas, cellos, and basses relate free-mode frequencies to internal air mode frequencies, which depend on body dimensions. It would be useful to compare these schemes with plate mode frequencies from instruments favored by seasoned musicians, both old and new. The first six violin modes are illustrated in **Fig. 5**.

While placement of the A_0 and T_1 modes on the frequencies of the two middle strings of violins (and the same fifth interval for violas somewhat above the two middle strings) is recommended, my own research indicates that the scheme with modes at 360Hz results in A_0 just below D and T_1 just above A440. However, the consensus of opinion on my own instruments is that the best balance across the lower notes is achieved with A_0 on $C^\#$ and T_1 just below A440. To achieve this placement with the archings described, I find the belly mode #5 needs to be at 330Hz or just lower and the bass bar maximum height at 10mm or 11mm. A bi-tri-octave relationship relative to a 330Hz mode #5 may be attempted, but my experience suggests that matching belly and back mode #2 at 150Hz–160Hz after ground coating is sufficient to produce an instrument well-balanced and sweet enough to be optimized by bridge, soundpost, and stringing adjustments.

This scheme also averts the tendency of C_3 to be an octave above A_0 (at around 550Hz) which produces a strong, even wolfy tone on $C^\#$–D. At the same time, C_4 falls on or near E660, the first of a band of resonances activated by the treble foot of the bridge and yielding a good fundamental content to all notes on the E string. Then the rise toward 2Hz–5kHz from the 1.5kHz valley provides the basis for a clear, sweet tonality to be honed by bridge selection and cutting.

Conclusion

Body deformations manifest in violins graduated to achieve a balanced and appealing sound may be minimized by arching design.

A flexible scheme of free-plate tuning is a guide to graduating so that the lower mode set and resonance continuums excited by both bridge feet result in the balance and timbre intended by the maker. ——

HAP NEWSOM

Graham Caldersmith (right) and Fred Sandoval at the '98 GAL Convention.

Originally published in *American Lutherie #59,* 1999

The Squishy Subject of Restoration Ethics

from his 1998 GAL Convention lecture

by Frank Ford

I'M REALLY NOT HERE to answer a lot of questions. I think I'm here more to ask questions than to answer them. I want to talk about ethics, which is kind of a squishy subject to get your hands around. And when I state something as a fact, it's more likely to be an opinion than anything else.

Here's a quick definition: I see ethics as being very much a matter of conforming to the standards of the community, and in our case, it's a community of musicians, instrument restorers, collectors, and dealers. These are the people who care about the instruments we work with.

JOHN CALKIN

Frank's looking sharp at the '98 Convention.

All of us have an ethical responsibility to share what we know, and that's what I'm here to do. I don't think that if I tell everybody exactly how I do something, down to the smallest detail, that I'm generating extra competition that will cut into my business. I'm showing what I do, nothing more or less than that, the same as surgeons share techniques in the medical journals. We raise the standards of the industry, our community, and ourselves by doing that. Sharing information raises our stature as a community of restorers. Holding secrets only keeps you from being able to learn from the others and share. It's important for me to share information, and it's important for me to remember that my competitor isn't going to have an easy job of it just because he knows my techniques. It's difficult work to do. No matter how many times I tell somebody how to do something, in order to compete with me they're still going to have to work as hard as I do, and I don't think that there are too many people willing to do that. So I don't worry about adding to the competition. I think that all I do is make sure that the standards of the craft are increased.

In addition to keeping up with others in the craft and sharing what I know, I have a responsibility to keep up with the instrument market. I know what instruments are worth, in a general sense. I don't need to know specifically how much a 1939 D-28 sold for last month in Nashville. I just need to know the general value of an instrument so I can advise the client — my customer, the musician, or the collector — how it fits into the scheme of things, and how restoration then fits in with the value of the instrument and his or her financial situation.

It's paramount to keep the customer's best interest at the top of the list at all times. I need to make sure that the customer knows what it is that I want to do to the instrument and why. I like to lead the owner by the hand through the diagnosis process. They can discover, as we're talking, what needs to be done and why, rather than saying, "It needs a neck reset; that's $350." Nobody wants to hear that. They want to hear in very gentle terms how it got to the point where it needs to have its neck reset. From there we can discuss what repair work is in order, and what it's likely to cost. This process eases the burden on customers who are about to get sticker shocked. It also helps them understand if the renewed health of the instrument is in their best interest.

One of the things we have to do is be very careful not to generate unnecessary work. There's any number of people around doing unethical things, and I like to help people avoid those folks. But you can't simply tell your customers that so-and-so down the road runs a chop shop that's going to butcher their instruments, because that only puts a bad smell on you. If you knock the competition and call them a bunch of hacks, all that does is eat away at your own credibility. It doesn't do much in the way of convincing a customer that they shouldn't be doing business with the other shop. You should simply talk about what should be done with the instrument.

We had a shop around us that was a rough place to take an instrument. In fact, they were hard on us, specifically, because they'd take in an instrument and do some pretty nasty things to it, then tell their customer that we'd give them the best price for it. As an example, about twenty years ago a woman took them the family's Gibson L-4, which she described as a guitar that had a few scratches on it. At the time it was probably worth about $600. The shop owner looked at the instrument and said, "Oh, hey, this is a valuable old guitar, and those guys up in Palo Alto would pay you $1500 for it. But before you present it to them you really ought to have it refinished so it looks its best." At that point she paid $300–$400 to strip the finish, run the orbital sander over it, and spray it with clear lacquer. She came to us saying, "Well here I am, I'm ready for my $1500." And all we could do was very gently try to explain to her why

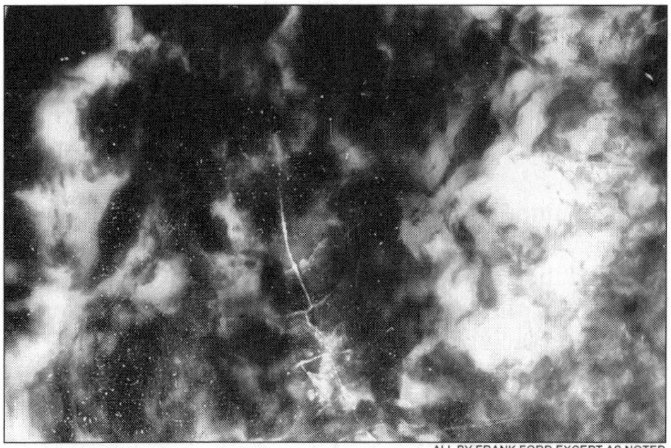

ALL BY FRANK FORD EXCEPT AS NOTED

Photo 1 (above). Some materials incorporated into instruments have a finite lifespan. This celluloid pickguard has begun to rot. Choices made in dealing with older materials can present the repairman with ethical decisions. ***Photo 2*** *(below). Celluloid rot in a more dramatic form.*

her instrument wasn't worth a lot of money and others were. At that point it was up to her to realize those guys had done something bad. We didn't start by saying, "Those guys did something bad to your instrument." It's important, as much as possible, for people to make that discovery themselves. We need to be gentle with the folks out there. These instruments mean a lot to them. They are an important part of their lives.

It's important to keep in mind that we really can't take responsibility for the future actions of the owner of an instrument we've worked on. Our customers may resell something that we just fixed, and we could unknowingly participate in a scam on the person who buys it later on.

The period we're in now is one that I didn't expect would come to pass. We're in such a conservative mode that everybody is just nuts about restoration and originality. The first question on everyone's mind is "What's this piece going to be worth to collectors in five years?" It doesn't even matter that the item you're talking about hasn't a ghost of a chance of collectibility, they're still being talked about that way. I recently had a guy in the shop with a Yamaha guitar that had a tuning machine problem, and he literally refused to put new tuners on it for fear of spoiling its originality. This was just a production instrument, and not even a fancy model. It's something he's been taught by the community, and something that we need to be aware of.

The question I have first off, from a restorer's standpoint, is how the hell long are these things supposed to last, anyway? How long is a guitar suppose to last? Are we stretching some of these instruments past their logical lifetime? Past their productive lifetime? Should we be doing this? That to me is a very interesting question. From a dollars-and-cents standpoint, we know that we should be doing it. If a prewar D-28 is worth $40,000, and you just paid that amount of money for it, you want it to be worth as much money as possible when you decide to sell it, rather than say, "Well, next year it's going to be used up." If it was a computer or a car, you'd use it up and throw it away. But instruments, we presume for some reason, are going to be timeless. And we *act* as though they are going to be timeless items. By default, every repairman becomes a restorationist, like it or not.

In the photos that follow, I'd like to point out many commonly encountered repair problems. Every problem begs the answer to any number of ethical questions. I intend to pose a few of the questions. The stringed-instrument community at large may have to answer them, and I'm very curious what the answers will be.

We build instruments out of volatile materials, and one of my very favorite volatile materials is celluloid. **Photo 1** is an old celluloid pickguard.

Photo 2 is a even better example. You can see what happens to celluloid with age. It just rots away.

The corner of the F-5 mandolin in **Photo 3** has been damaged by the celluloid binding. The binding has shrunk so much that it's caused the body point to kind of peel away from the body. We see that crack quite often, and we need to know how to deal with that kind of problem. Years ago my friend Jon Lundberg said, "You know, the irony of this stuff is that these damned instruments are going to be so valuable in the future. Because of the volatility of fake ivory, we may be replacing fake ivory with real ivory." And by the way, we would expect that it probably would make the instrument worth less money. Kind of a weird one.

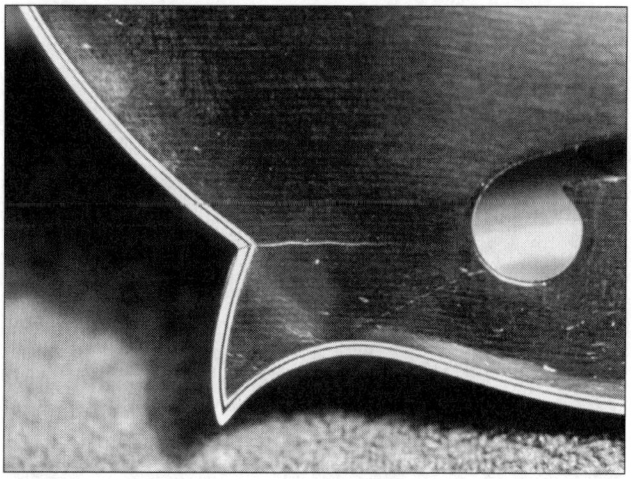

Photo 3*. As the binding on this mandolin shrinks it is tearing the body point off the instrument. No one realized that this booby trap was being built into the instrument, but it is a common problem for today's repairmen.*

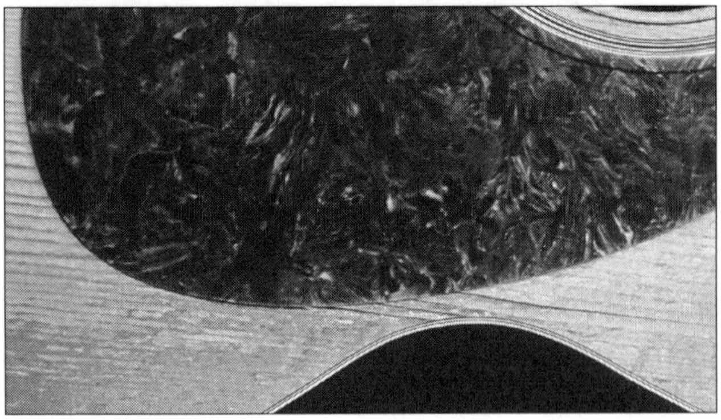

Photo 4. Martin knew long ago that gluing celluloid pickguards directly onto their guitar tops caused the tops to split as the pickguard shrank, yet the practice went on. Tradition is often more important than reason where instruments are concerned.

Photo 5. All of us have seen shrunken, crumbling tuner buttons. Saving the originals is often not an option.

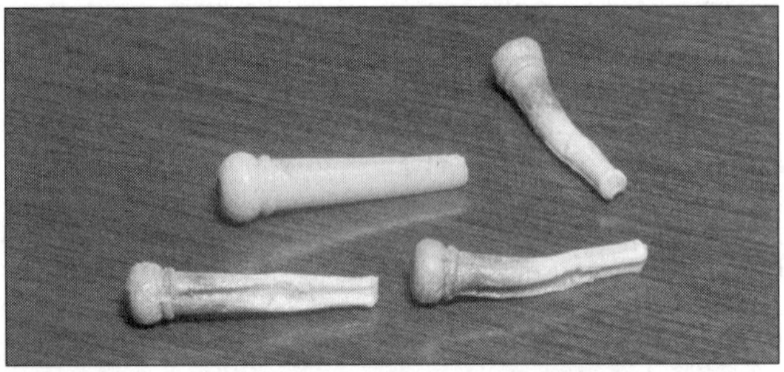

Photo 6. Plastic bridge pins are cheap but short lived. No one tries to save them.

Photo 7. The plastic face of this headstock has shrunk as its volatile elements evaporate, yet this material is still being used today.

Photo 4 is of a tortoise-shell-colored pickguard on a Martin guitar. Martin never used real tortoise shell on their instruments. But they often used tortoise-shell-colored celluloid, and you can see the cracks that are occurring as a result of the tension buildup as the stuff shrinks.

The tuner button in **Photo 5** is decomposing with time. All the tuners that were made by Kluson in the '40s and the early '50s seem to have incorporated some kind of volatile plastic. So we're pulling those babies off and replacing them with new ones.

Photo 6 demonstrates why saving original plastic bridge pins is never a big issue. Everyone accepts that they have a limited life span.

People are still making instruments today with celluloid glued on a face surface, yet **Photo 7** shows what happens to it essentially 100% of the time. Given enough time or exposure to heat, it starts to separate and shrinks away.

The celluloid fingerboard in **Photo 8** has self-destructed. You can see the way the celluloid has scalloped up around the frets. There's no hope of refretting this instrument without replacing its fingerboard as well. At that point the celluloid goes away, and this celluloid happens to be a unique pattern that isn't made anymore. Then we start to ask ourselves those questions about volatility and collectibility and so on.

The classic binding problem is gaps that show up on the inside curves of the instrument (**Photo 9**). We see celluloid binding constantly pulling away on instruments with time. So how long are they suppose to last, and what do we do about celluloid? Do we just keep replacing the celluloid on the instrument? Isn't it kind of abusive to do that? I think it is. But we don't have much choice.

Well, maybe there are better materials than celluloid, but the question for the restorer is, "How about those instruments that already exist that incorporate celluloid?" We still need to deal with them. But certainly the number of instruments being made today that incorporate celluloid would indicate that we're expecting them to kind of die and go away.

How about modern glues? Or some of the adhesives that are in composites that are being used right now? We don't really know about the life span of these materials. It's not impossible that we are adopting materials into our instruments that will come back to

Photo 8. This celluloid fingerboard has self-destructed, begging the question, "Shall we make it playable or leave it collectable?"

bite us the same way some of the dyed veneers did at the turn of the century. Necks were laminated vertically using a core of dyed veneers that failed the test of time, and those necks split in half as the veneers failed.

The light sensitivity of stains varies, leading colors to fade and sunbursts to disappear. Are we to live with the consequences of our materials choices, or will the colors be restored after failure? Should we be searching for finishes that offer a longer life span? The '40s vintage Gibson in **Photo 10** is a perfect example of a finish with a short lifespan. Lacquer is clearly is not going to last as long as the old varnishes have. If you look at the Stradivari violins of 300 years back, or other instruments of that period, their natural varnishes are intact, or potentially intact.

Yet it appears that the nitrocellulose lacquer that we've been using for the last couple of generations is all just sort of evaporating away. And given some UV exposure, like this old Gibson, it eventually turns to a flaky weird surface that may not stay with us for very long. So when we encounter an instrument that exhibits the finish cracking that leads to decomposure, do we preserve the instrument's originality by not touching it? Or do we try to add solvents to reamalgamate the lacquer, and then draw the slings and arrows of the angry collectors who say, "Eew! You oversprayed it!" Tricky question.

Electronics are currently being built into tons of acoustic instruments. One thing we know is that pickups and other electronic products will either become obsolete or nonfunctional, given enough time. Yet the instruments they are stuck in, we are to presume, are timeless artifacts **(Photo 11)**. How are we supposed to deal with them?

Clearly, restoration always affects the originality and the value of an instrument. An instrument only has one chance at originality, and sometimes it's not even possible to say whether it was or was not worked on. **Photos 12 and 13** illustrate a case in point. If you look closely at this Gibson mandolin you'll see that there's a network of extremely fine crazing in it. I don't think that there is anybody on the planet who would know that this was refinished. I happen to know it was, because I know the guy who sent it back to the factory in 1923 and had it done. At that time, the instrument

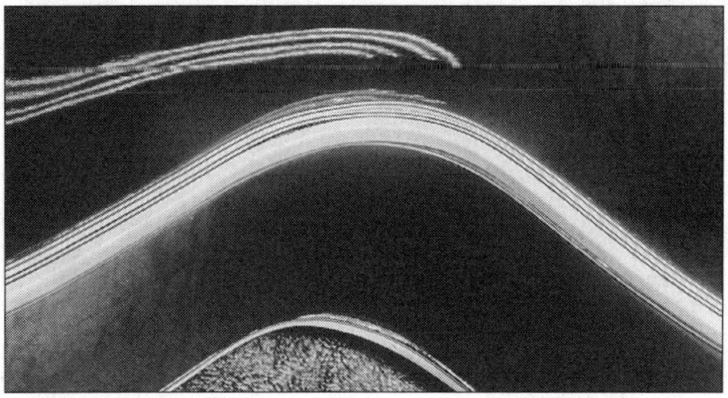

***Photo 9**. Here's one of the most common examples of celluloid deterioration: binding that has pulled itself free of its original position due to shrinkage.*

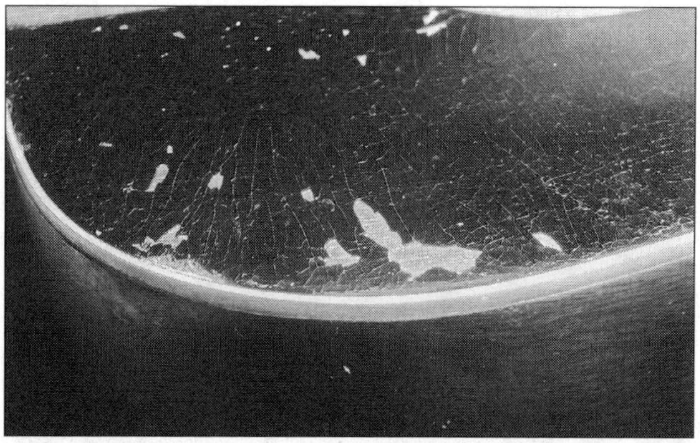

***Photo 10**. The lacquer on this '40s Gibson has begun to deteriorate and flake off. Is this charming, or should the guitar be restored?*

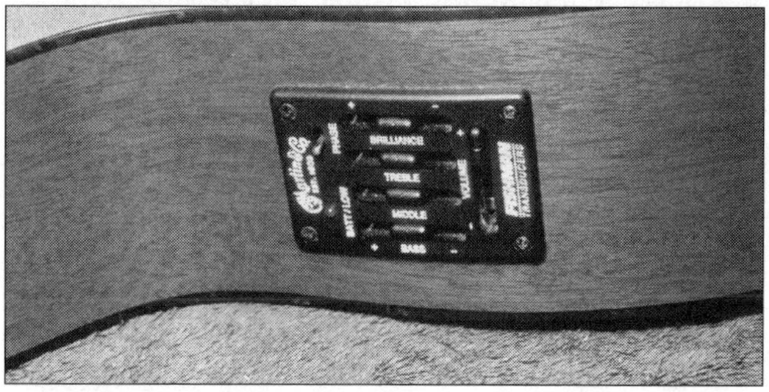

***Photo 11**. Electronic components placed into instruments as original equipment will eventually become obsolete. The repairmen and collectors of the future will have to decide on the value of these instruments and whether or not to modernize them.*

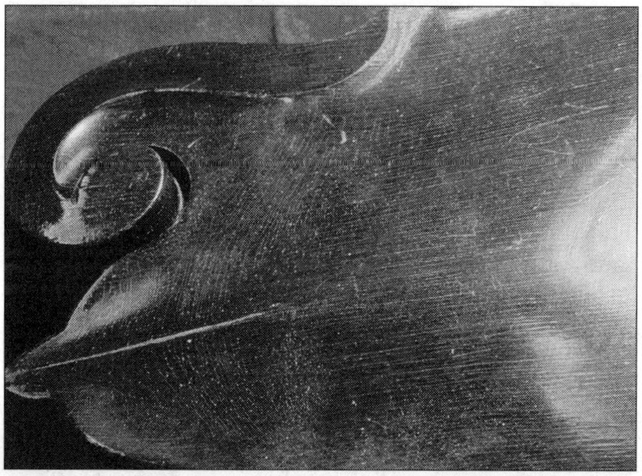

***Photos 12 and 13**. This Gibson mandolin was refinished by the factory in 1923, but anyone not privy to that information would never know it had been refinished. Do we tell and lose value on the instrument?*

***Photo 14** (left). Over-spraying this guitar top to protect the autograph may ruin its value to instrument collectors, but inhance its value to autograph collectors. Who should we try to please?*

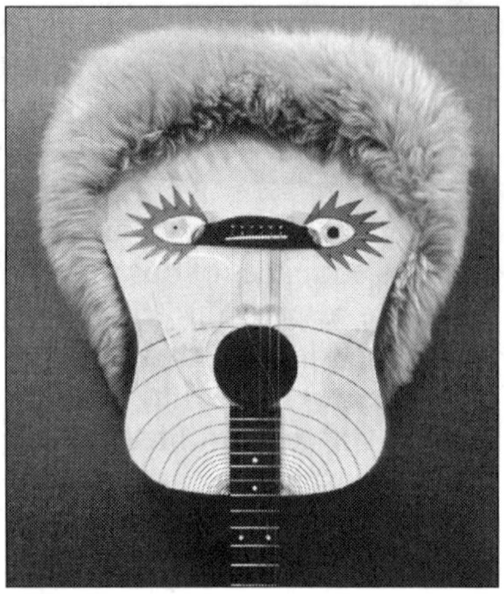

***Photo 15** (right). Can a modification actually enhance the value of an instrument? This guitar has become a piece of folk art that is more interesting, and perhaps more valuable, than the guitar underneath it. It may only be our vision of the guitar as an American icon that interferes with more creativity of this sort.*

was only about eleven years old. It is a refinished instrument. At some point, some of the refinishing work we do may become so old that it won't be possible to tell that it was done. Another question, then, for the ethicist: Do you tell people that it was refinished if there is no possibility that anyone can tell the difference?

Sometimes celebrity instruments that have been modified can be worth more money than original ones that weren't. **Photo 14** shows the autographed top of a modern Gibson guitar. My job was to overspray the top of the guitar. I even know some collector types who would get upset about that because I added extra finish to it, but the signature may be worth more than the guitar.

The guitar in **Photo 15** has become a wonderful piece of folk art. To me, in this particular instance it's the piece of folk art that should be preserved, not the instrument that's under it. I think it's extremely cool. The kid that created it brought it into the shop to have a little bit of intonation work done. He was very sheepish about taking it out of its case, because he was so ashamed of having butchered up his guitar. We looked at it and said, "Man, you are the coolest dude!" He just about died, especially when I asked if I could take a picture of it.

The banjo in **Photo 16** is about 100 years old. Here's a restoration job of sorts from about 75 years ago. Look closely and you'll see that the little leaves are made of snail pearl, except for about half of them that are multicolored celluloid. Grandpa did this. It was the original banjo in the family, it belonged to the customer's Grandpa, and Grandpa did this inlay job on it. His inlays are made out of old straightened-out thumbpicks that he jammed in there, and they are not even sanded off level. In fact, one of them interferes with the playing of the instrument because it stands up higher than the frets. Our job was to put it back together without doing anything to disturb the butchery that Grandpa did to it, because all she had to remember her grandfather by was his old banjo, and she remembers it as he had it. Its sentimental value outweighed any other consideration. She said, "By all means, let's get it back together, and I can play it a little bit. I'm not going to play it a lot because it's my grandfather's artifact. But I want to remember him with it." So we stuck it back together and it looks wonderfully funky, actually.

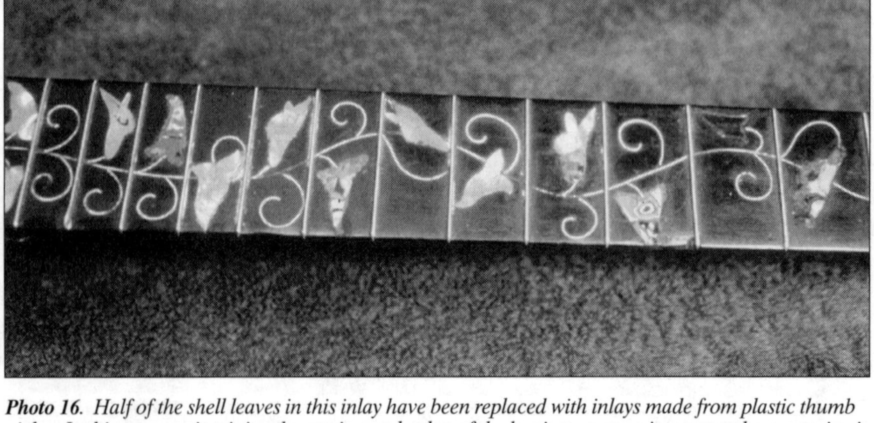

***Photo 16**. Half of the shell leaves in this inlay have been replaced with inlays made from plastic thumb picks. In this case, maintaining the sentimental value of the banjo was more important than restoring it to full potential as a collectible.*

In the past we used a lot of materials that are now considered endangered. What happens when we're confronted with an instrument that's made of materials that we can't get anymore, or not supposed to get anymore? How do you reconcile the ethics of restoring an instrument with the fact that you're not supposed to use the materials that are necessary to do the job?

Here's a mandolin from the turn of the century. The back of the neck and the front of the peghead and the pickguard are real tortoise shell. Our job on this instrument was to replace the face of the peghead **(Photos 17 and 18)**. These photos were taken after the restoration. The face of the peghead was mostly missing. How did we deal with that? Twenty years ago we declined to sell tortoise-shell flatpicks because it was politically incorrect. We just didn't think it was appropriate to sell tortoise-shell picks when celluloid and nylon do the job pretty well. Publicly, we have no tortoise shell in the shop whatsoever. But we did have a piece stashed in the back room, and when this mandolin came in we decided to use it. And that's kind of the way we work things in our shop. Sometimes it's necessary to make a judgement call. Is the instrument worthy? Does the customer understand the situation?

The mandolin in **Photo 19** also has a fancy peghead and a fancy pickguard. But what's interesting about it to me is that the pickguard is actually celluloid inlaid with real pearl, yet the peghead is real tortoise shell inlaid with real pearl. Now if that one needed work on the peghead, my inclination would be to say, "You can't get the shell anymore, so let's just piece in a little hunk of celluloid. The instrument already has a combination of materials in it from its original state." But it's an interesting kind of judgement call to have to make.

We make the same judgement call where ivory is concerned. Officially, we don't have any in the shop. But if a worthy instrument requires ivory for a restoration, we have some. **Photos 20 and 21** show two old Martins that proudly display an original ivory bridge and ivory friction pegs. These parts should only be restored with original materials in the event of damage. Should either one require a new nut, we will certainly use ivory. It's as simple as that. But if you come in with a D-35 that needs a new nut, we don't have ivory.

I think the person with a contemporary guitar who wants an ivory nut only wants what he's been told he can't have. That's not a good enough reason. If you think about Brazilian rosewood for very long, you'll probably end up with the same conclusion I have.

Photos 17 and 18. *This mandolin is covered in real tortoise shell. The author believed it was important enough to use real tortoise shell in the restoration, his ethical leanings not withstanding.*

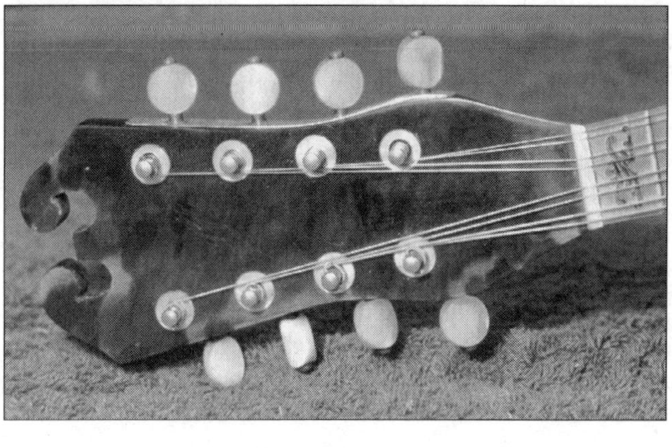

Mostly, people want it because they've been told they can't have it.

Most things wear out with use. Instruments wear out as they're being played. They also suffer abuse, neglect, and accidents. And certainly we all agree that if something gets broken it needs to be fixed. But what about good, honest wear? What about if it's just starting to wear out a little bit? On instruments the first thing to experience wear is the finish, and that's the area in which we are hearing an awful lot of talk from collectors and restorers these days. Original finish is so precious to the collector's value of the instrument that we have to ask some questions about refinishing instruments if we're going to talk about restoration at all.

Photo 19. *This headstock is capped with tortoise shell, but since the original pickguard is partially celluloid, Ford would feel justified in patching the tortoise shell with properly colored celluloid.*

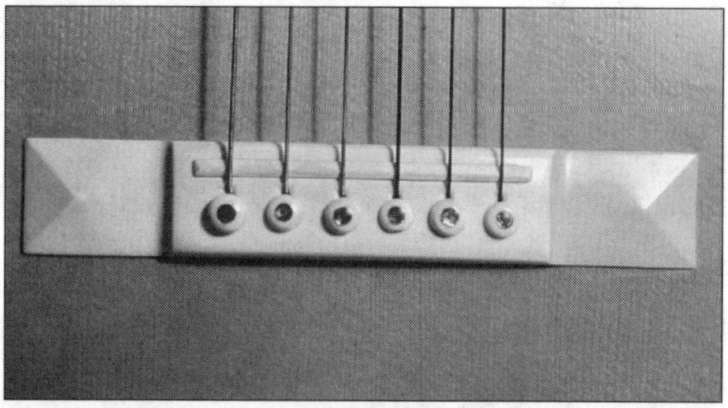

Photos 20 and 21. *These old Martins sport their original ivory parts, but should replacements be needed, they should only be made of ivory. The importance of the instruments warrants it.*

Photos 22, 23, and 24. These Gibson Loar mandolins all exhibit different degrees of wear. Is the mark of time honorable or ugly?

Photo 25. Ford thinks the wear on the ridge line of this scroll is unattractive. Others may think of it as the charming sign of a long life.

Some people think that a certain amount of honest wear just adds to the charm of an instrument. Other people think that the tiniest little scratch makes it look uglier. We have an interesting balance to make because everybody's style of playing is different; everybody's sense of aesthetics is different. And different groups of people seem to like their instruments to look different. For instance, the tenor banjo community likes their instruments to be nice, shiny, and bright. The bluegrass community, however, will stand a very worn-out guitar before they would consider refinishing it. The aesthetic sense is different. It's not a matter of one idea being better than the other, they're just different.

I don't believe that refinishing has much affect on the tone of the instrument if it's done properly; that is, if you haven't hurt the instrument when taking the old finish off, or sanded it too much, and if the new finish is basically the same as the original finish. It does have a nasty affect on celluloid, though. Refinishing a guitar that has celluloid on it seems to cause an extremely rapid deterioration of the celluloid. So then we ask the question, "If you're going to refinish the guitar, do you need to put all new celluloid on it too? Pickguard? Binding? Soundhole rings?" Tricky stuff, because some of that can really make a mess of things.

Refinishing reduces the collector's value, but it protects the stuff underneath which also might have collector's value. **Photos 22, 23, and 24** are all of necks on 1923 and 1924 Gibson Lloyd Loar F-5 mandolins. The first one **(Photo 22)** is an example of a really fine, all original instrument in which there is just a little wear starting to show at the thumb position. You can see that there is just a little color missing. Everything else is completely sound, solid, and original. Its owner brought it into the shop when he first got it. "I just got this instrument," he said. "What do you think I should do to it?" I said, "You should start scratching your head and think real hard about the neck on that. Because as you play it the finish is going to wear off and it's going to wear off fast. It's not going to be long before you have a look sort of like this one" **(Photo 23)**. As it happens, this one was in the shop at the same time, and it has no finish left on the neck at all. Plays fine, and it feels fine. But there is none of the coloring left at all. Some collectors and some players would look at the worn-out one and say, "Yuck, that looks awful." But the owner of the instrument said, "That's the way they get when you use them. I'll let mine get that way."

Other people don't make the same choice. The mando in **Photo 23** is a fairly high mileage instrument. It's about ready for the last few notes to be played on it before it has to have frets. It never had any abuse; it's only had wear. But the mandolin in **Photo 24** is the same age and it's had the same amount of playing on it. It's one that I've been maintaining for the last twenty-five years because I didn't want the finish to wear through. I didn't want to lose the color. I made the choice to keep adding a little bit of French polish as the finish wore thinner to avoid losing the color. Because, to me, what's really nice about the neck on this instrument is the way it looks. The color is great. I showed it to a dealer of this style of instrument and he wrinkled up his nose and he said, "I don't know how to break it to you, but there's been finish work done on this thing." And I said, "Well, yeah, by me." And then he got to feeling kind of like he maybe stepped on my toes. And I said, "No, no, that's OK. I'm not selling it to you, this is just the way I like it." And he said, "Oh well, in that case, do what you want."

Photo 25 is the back of that same worn mandolin. The scroll looks pretty worn-out and kind yucky to me. To some players, that's the sign of use and that's the way an instrument should start to look. All I can say is heaven help the guy who wants to make the color come back without refinishing the whole back.

The 1973 D-28 in **Photo 26** seems to have had some temperature abuse. Most of us agree that, since Martin finishes don't check unless they're subjected to extreme cold, this sort of checking is not attractive. Refinishing may be in order. I don't know too many people who would say, "What a shame to refinish this guitar and ruin its collectibility." It's a 1973 guitar, and we can put on a new finish that doesn't look too bad. In fact, it'll look just like the original, and in a few years it won't be distinguishable.

Here's one of those bluegrass guitars (**Photo 27**). Most of the people who encounter this 1953 D-28 think it would be a tragedy to touch it up. It has the right look. The guitar in **Photo 26** looks a little like temperature abuse, but this one looks like it's been playing shit-kicking music for years, and it's just the right sort of look for a vintage cowboy guitar.

The guitar in **Photo 28** has a nasty cross-grain scratch. It's not the kind of scratch a guitar gets in normal use. In fact, it's a pretty ugly scar. There's also a nasty crack along the grain, from dryness, perhaps, with lots of dirt rubbed into it. But it's not nearly as ugly in most people's minds as the dirty cross-grain scar. Do we slowly pick out all the dirt and make that look like a touched-up scratch? Or just leave it as an old war wound? No answers, really, but these are questions we have to ask.

The 1940s-vintage Martin D-18 in **Photo 29** has another common problem caused by abuse. The little white areas where the finish is no longer adhering are the result of wounds that it took. As a result of the scratches, and the nicks in the peghead, it looks a little tattered. Do we restore the finish before it gets any worse? Or leave it alone, saying that's a part of the aging process?

Photo 26*. Few people would find the cold checking on this Martin to be charming. Since it's only a 1973, refinishing may enhance its value, and in a few years will be indistinguishable from its original finish.*

Photo 27*. This 1953 D-28 shows the marks of hard playing that bluegrassers admire so much. To them, touching up this guitar would be unthinkable.*

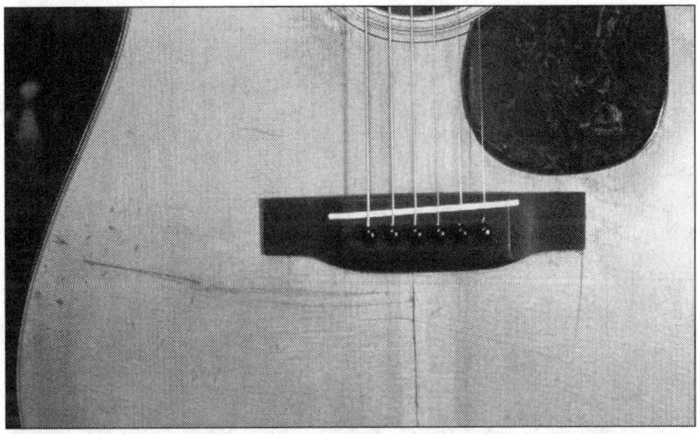

Photo 28*. To most people the cross-grain scar on this guitar is much uglier than the dirty, open center seam. Should we attempt to fix it and have an obvious repair, or leave it as a war wound?*

Photo 29*. We can restore the finish on this '40s D-18, but should we? Touch-up work is seldom invisible. But the real question is: are we trying to hide some sort of essential truth about the instrument?*

The tenor guitar in **Photos 30, 31, and 32** is an example where I felt that restoration was justified. The finish was so loose along the grain that a fingernail could flake it off. The first two photos show the guitar as it came to me. The finish was so far gone and so close to jumping off the instrument that we had one last-ditch chance to save it. We soaked it with a spray of Cellosolve to amalgamate the finish. Then it was sanded lightly and given a skin of new finish over the top. The result is an instrument that looks refinished but wasn't. Still, there's no sign of the original cracked finish. All the color is still there, and so is the original

Photo 30. The streaks on the headstock of this tenor guitar are cracks in the finish. The lacquer is so flaky that it's not long for this world.

Photo 31. This is the top of the same headstock. The finish on the entire guitar looked like this.

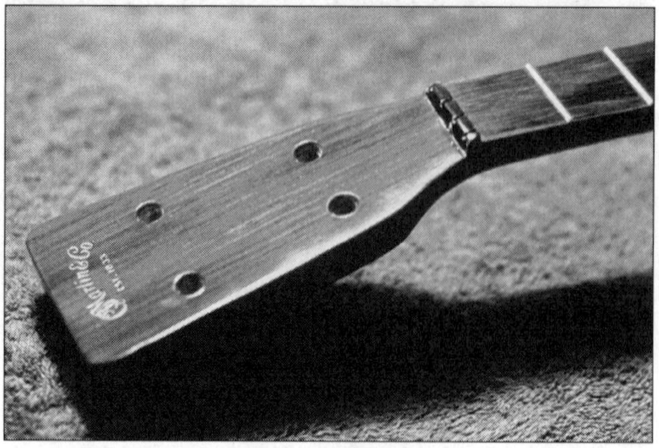

Photo 32. This is the guitar after treatment. Cellosolve was used to reamalgamate the lacquer, after which the guitar was oversprayed. The difference is obvious.

decal. We saved something by sort of encapsulating it, but then we have an altered guitar as a result. I think most of us will agree that in this case the logic was compelling.

We can often alter the playability of an instrument for the better, but can we afford to do that anymore? Shortening the nut end of a Martin fingerboard by .020″–.030″ will make the entire guitar play in tune better. A wider nut then has to be made to make up the difference. In our shop, we decided that we don't want to be known as the guys who cut the ends off of precious Martin fingerboards, even if it improves the intonation of the guitar. If the wider nut didn't give away, the fact that the guitar has been doctored I'd see no problem with the alteration. On a contemporary guitar I'd see no problem. But vintage guitars have reached the point where cash value has surpassed the importance of playability.

Or consider the '30s Martin in **Photo 33**. It plays 20 cents sharp on the low E string, and this is perfectly common on vintage Martins. If you spend some time doing the math, 20 cents works out to a lot of correction, something on the order of 3/16″ or 1/4″, enough to land the saddle right in the middle of the bridge pin hole. It's not possible to put a compensated saddle on this particular guitar without making a serious change. We didn't take this job. This guitar was in such perfect condition that we felt that playing out of tune was a small price to pay to keep it original.

Somebody else worked on the guitar in **Photo 34,** and they made the opposite choice. They decided to make the thing work correctly. But by doing that they had to put all the bridge pins in at an angled aspect, and it really chews away at the original look of the bridge. And as a result, everybody looks at it and says, "That's been altered!" It plays perfectly in tune, but in this case perfect work may actually have harmed the luthier's reputation. Doing no work at all might have been the smarter choice.

We can sometimes improve the playability of instruments by making them a little more modern. Cutting a neck thinner and adding a truss rod, for instance, can make an old instrument more playable. We're not doing much of that anymore. We did that in the '60s, but the holy collector value of even the clunky vintage guitars prevents it now.

The mandolin in **Photo 35** is a wonderful Gibson F-2. It's like right out of a time machine, there isn't a scratch on it. It looks like a little jewel. Its owner said, "It doesn't play well for me. I want a new fingerboard with a real steep radius and fat frets, so it'll play like a modern instrument." I looked at it for awhile and hemmed and hawed, then finally said, "You know, I think that's not the thing to do to this instrument." After a half an hour of conversation I convinced him to sell this instrument and get a modern one that plays well, that it would actually be cheaper to do that. He had simply presumed that it would be cheaper to fix the one he had, which he wasn't really attached to. So a lot of times a little consultation and time will really pay off.

Photo 35. This F-2 Gibson mandolin came into the author's shop for extensive alteration. Ford convinced the owner that it would be cheaper to sell his vintage piece and buy a modern mandolin that would suit his needs as a player. In the process, a wonderful instrument was preserved.

The instrument in **Photo 36** involved a bunch of consultation. The other guys in the shop and I don't necessarily agree on what we did to it, but I was the one talking to the owner and we went ahead with the job. This is a turn-of-the-century August Pohlman mandolin banjo. It's a pretty rare one, a mandola body on a 5-string banjo neck, and a very cool old timer. It's especially appealing to anybody who plays banjo who'd like a little different sound. It had the original friction pegs, and the guy said it didn't tune easily. We went through the effort of tuning it up and showing him how you can actually sort of make them work. Then he struggled with them and proved to us that they didn't work that well. We said, "If it was ours, we'd leave it alone and just consider it a novelty instrument." But he was insistent. He wanted to play the damn thing! We told him that if we redrilled the peghead and put in tuners it would be a one way street and he'd never be able to go back. He looked me square in the eyes and said, "This instrument has sat around in mint condition for 100 years looking pretty because nobody could play it."

Guess what? That little kick in the butt was what it took. I said, "You're right. Let's get out that drill bit."

In this particular case we had to countersink the nuts into the top of the peghead, because the peghead was too thick for any modern tuners. We had to do some fairly serious surgery to it. But it came out looking pretty good, and now it can used for its original intent.

This brings us back to our original conflict. Are the old instruments more important as cultural artifacts or as musical tools? Today we're clearly making instruments to be collected, and you have to remember that the old-timers did, too. The fanciest presentation instruments were not necessarily sold to people who played music on them. And they weren't presumed to be the regular workhorse instruments that just happened to be fancy.

The Martin guitar back in **Photo 20** had the same problem. Because of the ivory friction pegs, it doesn't tune very well. Adding mechanical tuners would almost be a desecration. The thing has survived as a cultural icon. It's also in mint condition, and it's just such a beautiful old instrument. We would just say, "Instead of putting modern tuners and steel strings on it, it should be fitted with the gut strings it was made for. Then the friction pegs will work fine." And as it happens, that's what the owner of this guitar is interested in doing.

How about a strap button on that vintage Martin? I don't think so. There are new guitars as valuable as the vintage guy. Is it wrong to add a strap button to them? The new ones are going to be a 100 years old some day. Will we be sorry we personalized them? I don't know. I kind of doubt it, but we have to make that cut.

Some instruments are just too cool because they are what they are, like Grandpa's banjo that I mentioned earlier. Some instruments, like Bill Monroe's mandolin

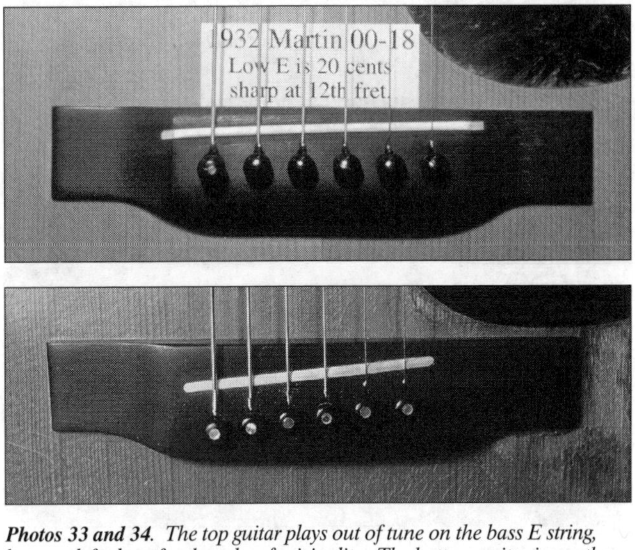

***Photos 33 and 34.** The top guitar plays out of tune on the bass E string, but was left alone for the sake of originality. The bottom guitar is another '30s Martin on which the intonation has been corrected. Which luthier made the right decision?*

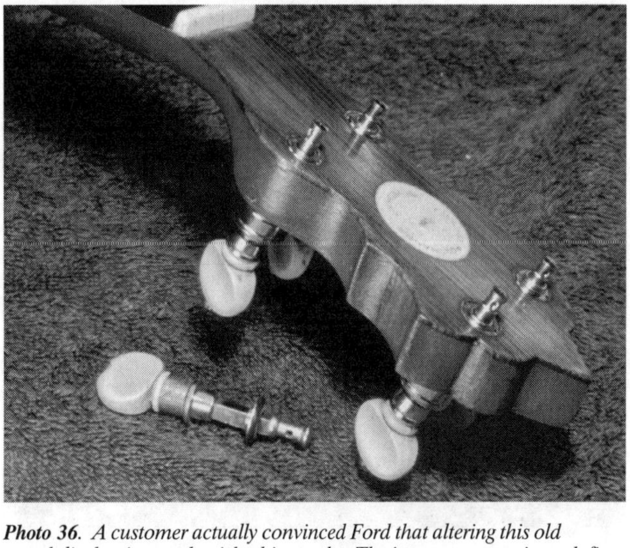

***Photo 36.** A customer actually convinced Ford that altering this old mandolin-banjo was the right thing to do. The instrument was in such fine condition because the original friction pegs had prevented anyone from ever playing it. Ford drilled it out for geared pegs.*

or Willie Nelson's guitar, are rather beat up. Would you fix them? No, you wouldn't. Their value is no longer based on their stature as musical tools. In fact, I don't think that such instruments should have a next generation of players own them. They've reached such a cultural status that once the owner passes on, the instrument ought to go into kind of a suspended animation as a reminder of their lives.

Some instruments are simply not useful for much. Some of the rickety old autoharps and patent instruments that nobody can play anymore don't fill a musical need and aren't worth a lot of money, but might still be worth restoring because they're representative of an age or a time in our history. And history is a cool thing.

Back to the real business of real restoration, though. One of the most important things that we have to consider while we're working with instruments is what is best called the principle of reversibility. That is to say, we can do something to an instrument to correct a problem and/or restore it *if* what we do can always be undone. We don't really know what life is going to be like, either for that instrument, for us, or for the craft in general. So it's important to keep a sense of making reversible changes. For instance, if you have a guitar that plays drastically out of tune you can fill the saddle slot, and put the saddle in a new place. Now you have a guitar that plays more accurately in tune, but you may have really injured the bridge. Still, all you have to do to have a perfect restoration on that guitar later is to replace the bridge. By and large, a bridge is replaceable on a guitar and it can be replaced perfectly without a problem.

However, in the example where the bridge pin holes were moved (**Photo 34**), you have not just a bridge to replace, but the bridge plate underneath that's been destroyed by the new holes. There's an extra set of holes in the guitar top, too. Some things become difficult to approach when it comes time to restore them more fully later on. The question becomes, how will posterity look upon us and the work we did?

Some useful operations can be thought of as temporary. One of my favorite temporary jobs is the bridge plate overlay. The bridge saddle in **Photo 37** has been relocated by moving the bass end closer to the pins, but beyond that it looks pretty healthy. However, the double wrapped lengths of the strings are coming right up over the top of the saddle, and we all know that's not good for sound.

Photo 37. Moving the bass end of this bridge saddle closer to the pins to correct intonation has allowed the double-wrapped lengths of the strings to pass over the saddle, which is a detriment to tone.

The bridge plate of this guitar is in pretty good shape (**Photo 38**). However, the combination of the bridge, bridge plate, and top are too thin to take up the length of the double-wrapping on the strings. My fix for this guitar was to add to the thickness of the bridge plate with a little maple overlay about $3/32''$ thick, and that will draw the strings down farther into the pin holes (**Photo 39**). The firmer anchoring of the balls might contribute to better tone. It will certainly allow the regular wound area of the strings to lie on top of the saddle, which will definitely improve the tone of the guitar.

If, in the future, someone decides to reset the neck and put on a taller bridge and saddle, they can reach in and take off that overlay section of the bridge plate. It may not be the easiest thing to take off, but it's certainly possible to do safely. So it's kind of a temporary job.

This overlay is also my favorite thing to do to bridge plates that have been chewed up by the string balls. This condition weakens the plate along the line of the holes. It can easily bend or even crack and take with it the bridge on top. A little bridge plate overlay can add a lot of stability to the bridge area. Then, if somewhere down the line

Photo 38. This is the bridge plate of the guitar in Photo 37. String balls have chewed up the plate around the holes.

Photo 39. Placing a thin maple overlay on the bridge plate is a reversible way to add support for the string balls and prevent the double-wrap of the strings from reaching over the saddle. Holes have yet to be drilled.

somebody says, "No, we're not doing that anymore. This is 2010, and that's what we did back in the '90s," the bridge plate could as easily be replaced then as it could be now.

We've passed the point of altering instruments just to please a customer. We know now, as perhaps earlier generations of luthiers didn't, that we are responsible to the future, and that responsibility is more important than simply pleasing a customer to pay the bills.

Keeping up with new techniques is vital to restorers. There may be discoveries made about materials, techniques, ways of imitating age, ways of restoring old finishes, getting things apart, putting things together, straightening wood, or whatever. These little techniques are still coming up all the time by guys who work on antique artifacts. So keeping up with what's going on is really crucial, yet that's something that the guitar-making community is just nosing into. Some of the other crafts have been at it a long time and they've been sharing knowledge much more effectively than we have. But I don't think that I've ever met anybody who held on to trade secrets who, in fact, actually knew something worth keeping as a secret. I've met some guys with some really terrific talent, and to a person they're willing to tell you exactly what they know. They know the real secret is that nobody is willing to work as hard as they are. And that's how the job gets done.

As much as possible, using ancient techniques on ancient instruments is a good idea. If the thing was made with hide glue in the first place, epoxy might not be the best idea to pop into your head. It may be that the only way to fix an antique is to use modern materials, but if there is a chance to do it with the original stuff, that ought to be the first choice. This may mean broadening your own abilities. Just as easily it could mean knowing when to refer a piece of work to someone who is more tuned in than you are. It's not necessarily a matter of competence. Each of us can only reach so far.

The best example, for me, is the violin family of instruments. I think I'm about as good a woodworker as most of the violin guys I know, but I don't know their ethics, their style, or their materials. So if a sensitive violin job comes along, I'm not going to jump into the wrong end of the swimming pool and paddle around with the big boys. I'll suggest that my customer take it to a regular violin craftsman and see what he or she has to say about it. That will be a lot safer for me. It's a better service to the instrument and my customer, too.

In addition to sending people away because they have something that's out of my league, I think it's also important to send some people away because I just don't want to do the job. There's a whole category of people I don't want to work for, most of whom I actually do end up working for, but there is a certain group that scares me. Now that we're seeing instruments that are worth $150,000 in our field, we start to ask some liability questions. What if the quality of your work is not up to the expectations of the customer? Someone who's got a lot of money, namely a heavyweight collector, could say, "What are you going to do to make me happy? Would you like to be sued?"

As restorers, we can always mark our work if we want to. And I think it's a choice that more of us should take. I'm starting to do it a bit more than I used to. It doesn't take very long, and you can always put some kind of little disclaimer on a instrument. If you're refinishing a vintage Fender guitar, there's a neck pocket or pickup cavity in which you can put a little note saying it was refinished, along with the date. And if you've got the guts, you'll put your name on there, too. This marks the instrument so it doesn't accidentally get out into the world and get sold as an original item that was never touched. Believe me, that stuff happens a lot these days. I've seen lots of instruments that are forgeries to varying degrees. It's not illegal or immoral if it isn't intentional, but it would be better if somebody would put a little label in there, and it would save a tremendous amount of work.

Photo 40 shows the sort of label I use in my repair work. It says, "I fixed it." If somebody wanted to take it out all they would have to do is put a damp sponge on it and the glue will release itself and be washed off completely without a trace. It's not possible for anybody to say that you've hurt the instrument in any way by doing it. All you do is make up a really weak solution of hide glue, three or four parts water to one part of your glue mix. Dunk in the label and pretend it's a decal. Just soak it until it uncurls, then paste it on. Dab it with a dry cloth and you've got a label perfectly pasted in place with a glue that doesn't cost any money or grief.

The last little item I wanted to mention is the past. We have a lot of rocks to throw at guys that have hurt instruments in the name of restoration, but the one thing we can't do is judge the past by present knowledge. Yet it's something of which many of us are guilty. People bring instruments to me and say, "Can you imagine why anybody ever did this?" It's perfectly reasonable that some instruments were worked on at a time when they were considered to be of little value. If they weren't butchered back into usefulness they would've simply been thrown away. What would your choice be? Better not to judge the past to harshly. ——

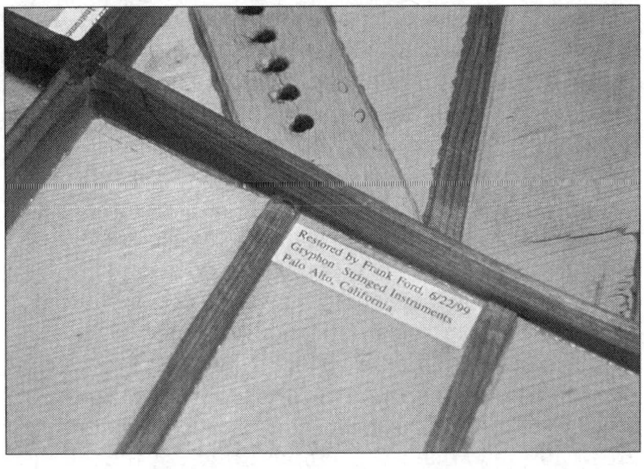

***Photo 40**. A small, removable label placed inside a repair or restoration may prevent many misunderstandings in the future. If the owner elects to remove it, the fate of the instrument falls on his conscience, not the luthier's.*

Originally published in *American Lutherie #59*, 1999

Meet the Maker: Steve Kauffman

by David Melly

I FIRST MET STEVE KAUFFMAN at a Northern California Association of Luthiers (NCAL) meeting in 1993. The next year an NCAL meeting was held at his beautiful shop in Lafayette, California. Steve had built the shop adjacent to his house on a wooded slope with a wonderful view. At the meeting, he and Steve Klein presented to other NCAL members the prototypes of the Taylor bass. Since then I have been inspired by Steve and his impeccable craftsmanship. I value him as a kindred spirit and respect him for his integrity.

When did lutherie come into your life?

I've always worked with wood. My Mom tells me that my first toys were tools, and I can't remember ever not being passionate about woodworking. Other kids were talking about being doctors and firemen when they grew up, and I always wanted to work with wood. It was around age eighteen when I realized that guitars were actually made of wood and maybe it was possible for something other than a factory to create one of these things. I grew up in San Francisco in the '60s and that was at a pretty eventful time and place to find one's self. There was a lot of music going on and a lot of change. I was there kind of in the midst of it and it had a big impact on how I feel about music and its importance in my life. I started playing guitar pretty young. All my idols were musicians.

Did you go to see a lot of gigs and stuff?

I lived adjacent to Speedway Meadow in Golden Gate Park, a prime location for the so-called "Happenings." All the great bands played Golden Gate Park. The concerts were free, and there was even free food. You've seen the '60s photos of people running around naked with flowers in their hair. That was at Speedway Meadow. To me it was kind of a spiritual movement. Music seemed like such an important part in the inspiration of that evolution that it's at the very core of my being. I think that's why I make music and why the greatest satisfaction to me is when I create an instrument.

Dad wasn't an accomplished woodworker, but to his credit, he was someone who would do it himself. He never called a plumber or an electrician that I can recall. He would do work around the house. So I was exposed, if not to the specifics, at least to the concept that things are doable, and that's very empowering. By the time I was ten or so I had my own workbench and my own tools in the garage workshop. My ultimate paradise would be living in a place that allowed me to do everything that needed to be done. To create the plates from which I eat, and grow the food, raise the trees that I cut down to turn into furniture to sit on, and so on.

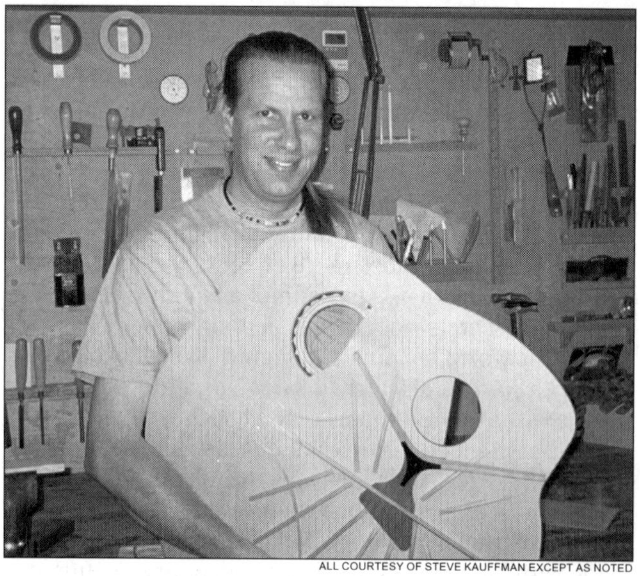

ALL COURTESY OF STEVE KAUFFMAN EXCEPT AS NOTED

Am I right that you built this house? Or just the shop?

I built the shop. The house is sort of rebuilt. When I say that I built the shop I don't mean that I drove every nail, but I picked the fun jobs for myself. I built the doors. I did a lot of the design and detail.

I started building guitars about 1975. I was about nineteen years old, and the first one took a year to make. My goal at that time was to be a guitar builder; that's what I wanted my life to consist of. Steel string guitars were my passion.

I supplemented my lutherie income by whoring myself out as a carpenter, but I got to do a lot of fun woodwork along the way. I got to build a lot of interesting structures, and furniture, and fireplace mantels — anything that can be made out of wood. By the time I was twenty-five things were looking a little meager in the music business. At that time I had an experience that made me realize that my goals in life extended beyond lutherie and might also include a home and a family. So I undertook what I thought of as the five-year plan, the concept of which was that I was going to continue to live at a low level of consumption while doing a lot of work and earning a lot of money. I would use the money to create a house and property and a nice place; build a workshop and stock it full of all the most fun tools with a stash of exotic wood; and live out my days building beautiful guitars.

Didn't you feel there were other options open to you?

I was never very interested in repairs. Repairs required other skills than those I had developed in my building. What was available was a lot of cabinet and furniture work. The first big job that I undertook was all the fixtures for a store that was opening up in the local mall. I made more money in the space of a month than I made in the previous two years building guitars. The writing was clearly on the wall.

A lot of the luthiers of the '70s had great visions of new and interesting instruments, of excellence, and of making the ultimate guitar without any thought to marketing. And that's really reverse marketing, creating a product and then looking for a market for it, hoping that somebody will buy this wonderful thing you've created. Forward-thinking marketing consists of looking at the market first, deciding where the needs are, and fulfilling those needs while creating a company image that will be attractive to the people who need those products. If any of the individual luthiers of the time thought that way they never mentioned it to me. When luthiers got together they talked about better ways of doing things. We argued over the effects of what we did, of what might make the instrument sound better.

How did you start with Steve Klein?

I met Steve in Boston at the 1979 GAL Convention. I'd heard of him, of course, and I'd seen some pictures of the interior of his guitar. He had the good fortune of being in a family that Dr. Kasha was friends with, and so he got his inspiration from Kasha very early on. And to my knowledge he never built the traditional instrument. I started out building traditional guitars according to the designs that were available and I almost immediately started experimenting. Moving braces around, trying different woods and different combinations, trying to make a better instrument, trying to make something that was unique and different. What I saw was that the steel string guitar had evolved, for the most part, in the hands of big guitar factories, and what I suspected was that they had compromised in some aspects of the design in order to make things more manufacturable. I had the idea that if I developed the design without economic restriction, I could make something really great. I think a lot of people felt that way at the time; that seemed to be the energy behind what we were all doing.

Was Steve famous then?

He'd just completed the Joni Mitchell guitar when we met. So in my mind he was already a famous luthier. I was very honored to meet him, and it took a lot for me to work up the courage to ask him if he would take me on as an apprentice. It's funny that we lived so close, yet we met in Boston.

TIM OLSEN

Steve and his dreadnought at the 1979 GAL Convention, where he met Steve Klein. Facing page: Steve Kauffman in his shop, where he builds both Kauffman and Klein guitars. He's holding a couple of Klein guitar tops. Below: Steve "Sticks" Kauffman, age eleven.

Famous or not, I thought he had done an amazing thing. I don't like to take credit for ideas because I think that most ideas are a combination of information that people have gathered from different sources. The thing that's unique is the way in which individuals put those components together. But there are a few original things in the world and the Klein guitar is really one of them. It was a radical departure. Steve changed everything at once. He changed the structural stuff, he changed the tone bar stuff, he changed the shape, he changed the neck attachment, he changed a lot of the methods and materials by which the things were put together. And he did that all at once. It's really quite remarkable.

My apprenticeship with Steve was established as a two-day-a-week affair so that I could continue to build my own guitars. Certain things I never did on Steve's guitars, but eventually I got to the point where I had made all the parts for the guitar and it was suggested that I start making Klein guitars in his shop and we could sort of collaborate.

How long did that last? What years were they?

This evolved over a long period of time, so it's difficult to pin down a time. I was twenty-five when I undertook my five-year plan, which took almost exactly ten years to complete. By that time I had actually completed a Klein guitar. It's a good story. Steve showed this guitar that he and I built together to a lot of people because he didn't have any other finished acoustic guitars to show around. The intention was that this would become my personal instrument sort of in payment for the work that I had done with Steve. But people were trying to buy this guitar from Steve and he called me up and said, basically, "What do you think we ought to do?" And my response was, "Are you crazy? Sell the damn thing! Let's make more of them and sell more."

It looked like we had the possibility of a great partnership there. Steve's a creative genius and a very divergent thinker. He's always seeking out a new and exciting project. He loves a new challenge. Although he's an incredible craftsman, he's not good at doing the same thing over and over. My love is starting with a great design and evolving it, shaping it into its ultimate form, molding it and nurturing it along. I like attending to details. Steve brushes in the broad strokes, and my role is more in long-term refinement, though I don't by any stretch want to imply that I'm taking credit for the evolution of the design of a Klein guitar. Perhaps I've been an influence, but it's really Steve's creation, and the design was pretty well established by the point that we suggested a partnership. What really kicked off our partnership, though, was Steve's ideas about how to build an acoustic bass. He approached Bob Taylor about the addition of an acoustic bass to the Taylor line. Bob had been receptive to the concept, but nothing more had been done about it. So I stepped in and, with Steve's permission, wrote a proposal to Taylor that we would build some prototype instruments and we would receive some royalties. Then I undertook to build the four prototype guitars in my own workshop. Once the proposal was written the whole project went into high gear immediately. That was the thing that motivated me to give up my woodworking business which was pretty well established over ten years.

I continued to go the NAMM shows with Steve. He kept generating orders for acoustic guitars, yet at the same time he was involved in a lot of other projects.

The electrics and such?

Yeah, things that were very interesting to him from a design standpoint. He had orders for acoustic guitars which he hadn't worked on for years. He had taken deposits for these instruments and wasn't even promising anything in the way of a deadline, and remarkably he was getting more orders. He needed to do something about it. There I was standing there with my hand up and having proven that I was capable of building these things under his supervision, and it was suggested that I might now be able to take over a large part of the woodwork on the Klein guitars. Initially I did some of the work in Steve's shop and some of the work in my own shop, but I got tired of commuting to Sonoma, which is about an hour's drive from here. So as quickly as possible I replicated all the dedicated setups and jigs and fixtures and so on — the tooling as it existed in Sonoma — in my own shop. One by one my needs for making the commute dropped away until finally the only reason I'd drive there was to deliver the finished instruments. Steve still does all the fretting and setup on the instruments. He initially did the lacquer, but we now have Fred Latta do that. I think Steve masks the area under the bridge and does the fretting. Then the instrument comes back to Steve and he makes the saddles and does the setup. Our capacity right now is about sixteen instruments per year. That's a lot of Klein guitars to build in a year. They're very labor-intensive. I make parts in big batches. Where machine work is involved I like to do that in as big a number as I can tolerate. For easier parts I might make a five-year supply, difficult parts I might only make a six-month supply. That's because I can only tolerate a certain duration of production work.

The instruments are literally built one at a time. I start one guitar and take it through to completion. I'll do stuff like make rosettes perhaps ten at a time. So it's neither really one instrument at a time, nor is it manufacturing. It's the middle path, and that's a nice compromise between production work and individual hand work. It allows each instrument to still evolve individually and with the instantaneous benefit of the knowledge gained from the previous instrument finished. There's pretty fast feedback that way.

A lot of luthiers are switching over to that now, if they didn't start that way. You make a lot more.

The emphasis now seems to be more on marketing and production than I've ever seen in the past. I think a lot of builders, and rightfully so, hope and expect to be able to make a living wage from building guitars. That's wonderful. From my perspective it seems that a lot of them are doing it in a way that would diminish the quality of lifestyle that I have now.

Unhappily, diving into the production of a proven design in order to make a living doesn't allow a luthier the luxury of trying ideas that might fail. Fortunately, the creation of furniture and such subsidized my guitar making at first and I didn't have to worry about selling them. I only made a couple guitars per year, but I was able to experiment a lot. I made some really miserable failures, but I made some pretty neat guitars, too. I satisfied myself that a pretty nice guitar can be made out of a variety of materials, some of which are very plentiful and beautiful. Unfortunately the market place hasn't quite gotten around to realizing that those

Interior and exterior views of a current Kauffman guitar

instruments have equal value to the Brazilian rosewood/German spruce guitars.

I've seen your guitars in a lot of different woods. Honduras rosewood, walnut....

Yeah, I've done a lot of really bizarre, exotic woods. I built an imbuia guitar years and years ago. It just recently came to be a commercially harvested hardwood from Brazil. The prototype basses were imbuia. Actually imbuia is a variety of walnut to my understanding. So Bob selected imbuia for the basses because it could be had for a lot less money in the master quality. It's a beautiful wood.

What other woods have you used?

Zebrawood. I've got some gorgeous cherry, which makes wonderful guitars. I've got some terrific sets of a wood called ziricote, which is just heart-stoppingly beautiful.

You've been using these mostly on Kauffman guitars?

Exclusively on Kauffman guitars. I haven't been able to talk Steve into using any of these woods yet, although Steve was initially open to alternative woods and was a pioneer of alternative woods in my mind. As far as I can see he was the first person to ever use figured walnut on a guitar. But he has established his market place, too, and his customers basically want a walnut guitar or a Brazilian rosewood guitar. With the exception of two recent Guatemalan rosewood guitars, that's all we've done with Kleins. The ratio is maybe 70/30 in favor of Brazilian.

Steve, his wife Susan, and daughter Jenna.

We've talked about the bass, which has been pretty much handed off to Taylor, and Klein guitars. What's in the future for your own guitars?

My original vision of what I wanted to do with the Kauffman guitar was sort of an evolutionary instrument, rather than a revolutionary one. I wanted to try a lot of new ideas but I wanted the instrument to feel rooted in what had gone before. So I favor a body shape that's a little more of a takeoff on a traditional instrument. In fact, the body shape of the Kauffman guitar is based on the Gibson J-200 although it's been manipulated a little bit. I never really wanted to do an asymmetrical bridge or a displaced soundhole because I like the traditional look. But that didn't stop me from messing with the guts of the thing. I put braces just about every place you can imagine, and tried different kinds of structural systems to hold the thing together without inhibiting it. The final evolution of that will probably been seen as the next model of the Klein guitar. In fact, you see a little of that in the Taylor bass as well.

One reason I wanted to do this interview was that you provide a good role model. You don't have to do it on your own or in a big factory. It's a good example.

It's another example of the middle ground. Originally I had a lot of ego invested in the concept of the Kauffman label being a well-known brand. But when I really took a good hard look at my life and how I want to spend my time — my life consists of what I do and how I feel about that from moment to moment — where I really want to be is at my workbench. When I saw an opportunity to make a living at my workbench, doing the work I most love, and not having to convince the world to buy my products, it was very easy for me to let go of my need to have my name become a household word among musicians. It was very easy. My first loyalty is to Klein Guitars. As long as Steve can generate enough orders to keep me busy that's what I'll do. Since the Klein guitars are in such a high price range I can envision the possibility of my production capabilities exceeding the demand. In which case I'll probably seek to fill the gaps with Kauffman guitars. What I appreciate about my existence is that its not about manufacturing a trainload of guitars. It's not about making a lot of money. It's about having a certain validity and quality to my life. It's a lifestyle thing. It's all part of the same package, that who I am is who I always am. I don't come down here and put on my luthier hat, though it looks that way. While I'm down here I'm still accessible as Daddy, and I'm still husband to my wife and accessible as that. And when I'm in my home my workshop is still very accessible, so if I have a stroke of what I perceive is brilliance in the middle of the night, I can come down here and hack it out on my workbench. It's all very blended.

Your family seems to be taking a lot of your energy right now.

My family gives me far more energy than it demands. I'm a father, and a husband, and a luthier, and so on — I'm really all of those things at once and I'm also this evolving being. The other thing I want to express is that a really big part of my life is my partner, Susan, and how supportive that relationship is. She keeps me focused on the importance of my work. It's so easy to get diverted into thinking that I'm making a product, a mere thing. I look at the work that she does — she's a healer — and how important her work is. Down here in this isolated environment it's easy to lose sight of the importance of my work. Susan keeps me reminded. I tend to look at musicians and how important their work is, but it's easy to lose sight of the importance of our work. ——

Originally published in *American Lutherie #59*, 1999

A New Look at the Chromatic Dulcimer

by Merv Rowley

PERHAPS THE STRONGEST appeal of the Appalachian mountain dulcimer for the past century or more has been its simplicity. New players are attracted by its ease of tuning, its uncomplicated diatonic fretboard for playing melodies, and its drone accompaniment system which minimizes left-hand fingering requirements. Simple tablature arrangements are readily available to players who cannot read musical notation.

These features encourage many players to adopt the mountain dulcimer as their first musical instrument. Eventually, however, the limitations imposed by the dulcimer's diatonic scale cause many to yearn for more frets to facilitate key changes without retuning. In fact, one or two additional frets have been inserted into the diatonic fretboard in recent years, more or less at the urging of the more experienced, progressive-minded players who want to extend the envelope of the instrument. We might think that this group would be asking for a fully chromatic fretboard, yet this is not the case. There are a couple of reasons for this.

- As with any new instrument, a player usually requires some basic instruction in how to tune the strings and where to locate individual notes and chords. Even more helpful is music which is specifically arranged to be played on the instrument. For the traditional dulcimer player, this means suitable tablature arrangements.
- Most of us are taught to play the dulcimer in a downhand position while watching the left hand and the fretboard. The gaps between the diatonic frets act as position markers as the melody strings are fretted. When these gaps are filled to produce a chromatic scale, the player is confused when trying to select fret positions, even from tablature.

References describing the mountain dulcimer verify that numerous chromatic instruments have been made from time to time, but there is virtually no information about how or if they were played. Perhaps these were experimental curiosities which were eventually abandoned because of the reasons just described. On the assumption that such is the case, I began a project in 1995 to develop a user-friendly chromatic dulcimer which satisfies the needs of existing dulcimer players.

Traditional diatonic dulcimers were often built using some of the older, untempered musical scales, or even scales of unknown nature which had been copied from earlier instruments. Needless to say, the chromatic scale of today must be based on the system of equal temperament in order to allow transposition of keys without dissonance.

Although scale length and total number of frets selected for the chromatic dulcimer are optional, I chose a nominal length of 28½″, provided with twenty-four frets (full two octaves). Fretboard width is also optional, but should be chosen so as to allow ease of chording in the downhand position. The instrument described here has a fretboard 1½″ wide fitted with full-width frets. This is about the maximum width accommodated by dulcimer capos currently available.

Schematic views of the diatonic and chromatic fretboards are illustrated in **Fig. 1a** and **Fig. 1b**, respectively. Note that the chromatic frets can be thought of as being inserted into the diatonic fretboard, with tablature number designations +, 1+, 3+, 4+, 6+, and so on. This maintains the fret numbering system already familiar to dulcimer players.

The instrument described here was intended to be as simple as possible in order to make it attractive to new users. For this reason it was designed to be played using only three strings. This proved to be more than adequate for ease in playing, even in the chord/melody style. All other design features of the instrument were unchanged from those of the regular diatonic variety.

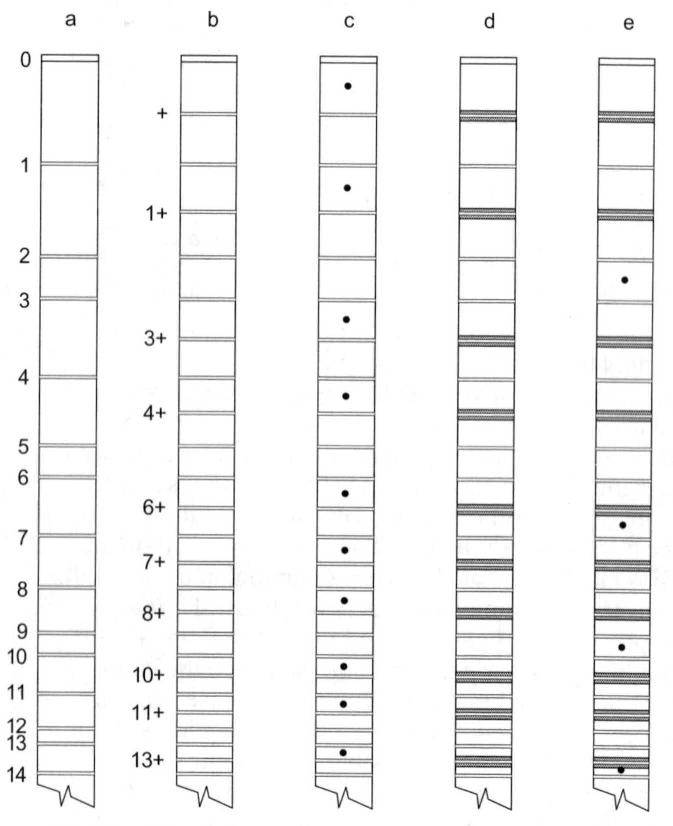

***Figure 1.** Alternative fret marking systems for chromatic fretboards.*

The main purpose of a fret-position marking system is to assist the player in moving from one note or chord to another when changing left-hand finger positions. Mention has already been made that the gaps in the diatonic fret pattern serve this purpose very nicely for the dulcimer player. It therefore seems logical that a fret position marking system for the chromatic dulcimer should be one which identifies the original locations of these diatonic frets, surrounded by the new chromatic frets. The terms diatonic and chromatic, when applied to frets, may seem incongruous to many readers but seem to make sense to dulcimer players. Without more precise vocabulary, we may say that the black and white keys of the piano keyboard are analogous to the chromatic and diatonic frets, respectively.

Fig. 1 shows a few optional approaches:

▸ Insert a series of fret position markers to the left of each new (chromatic) fret, as shown in **Fig. 1c**.

▸ Isolate and identify each new fret with a color stripe placed on either side of the fret as in **Fig. 1d**.

▸ Apply both color stripes and position markers to show octave positions of both the Ionian and Myxolydian scales, shown in **Fig. 1e**.

▸ One further option is to mark all frets in contrasting colors, black and white, perhaps.

Players' needs for detailed fret position marking may differ initially, and may diminish or disappear after playing experience is gained. It is suggested that temporary marking be chosen so that changes can be made easily. The color striping may be done by using the narrow, self-adhesive pinstriping tape available at any automotive supply store.

One of the more challenging problems was that of selecting a versatile tuning system. Many tunings were tried, primarily to note how easily melodies could be played, how many chords were available at each fret position, and how easily they could be reached and played by the left hand. Space prevents detailed discussion here, except to say that several tuning schemes were found to have possibilities. The most versatile tuning, however, was what dulcimer folks call the 1-5-5 tuning, such as D-A-A (low to high). For the diatonic fretboard, this tuning places the keynote on the 3rd fret of the melody string and enables us to play the Ionian modal scale. In today's English, this means we are in a major tuning, so it is not surprising that we find a great abundance of chord possibilities. With this tuning, in fact, each fret position on the melody string enables us to play no less than thirteen separate and distinct chords: three majors, three minors, three dominant sevenths, two diminished, one augmented, and one flatted fifth.

It is important to use full-width frets, rather than partial ones. The availability of chromatic notes on the bass string not only adds a new source of melody notes, but also adds numerous new chords which could not otherwise be played. This is a strong argument against choosing to use only partial frets extending under the melody and/or middle strings.

An additional advantage of a 1-5-5 tuning is that it is one of the modal tunings used with the diatonic dulcimer, and thus permits us to play the instrument in the conventional manner (with drones) if desired. This means that we have an instrument, which can play both modally and as a contemporary chromatic instrument without retuning!

Having solved the problems of fret position marking, tuning, and note-mapping of the chromatic fretboard, we still face a necessity for customized tablature arrangements to simplify the playability of the instrument. I have prepared more than twenty such chromatic tablatures, some more complicated than others. Abbreviated examples of these appear in **Fig. 2**.

Using these tablatures, I have thoroughly investigated and tested the feasibility of this chromatic dulcimer system, and I have discovered that the material presented here enables the dulcimer player of average ability and experience to play both folk music and contemporary melodies without difficulty. Better yet, no new skills are required! Suddenly, the charming dulcimer we knew takes on a fresh personality and lends its unique voice to melodies of the 20th century.

Builders and players alike will be interested to know that I have placed all this information in public domain for free and unrestricted use. This brief report is based upon a lengthy, unpublished document which covers details not included here. Copies of this full document, as well as sample tablatures, can be made available to those interested. ——

Update

A number prominent builders have reported increases in orders for chromatic instruments from players who also play another chromatic instrument, such as the guitar. The interest in special position marking of the fretboard has been minimal, and no fixed tuning systems seem to predominate.

Interest has also stimulated renewed discovery of the fact that open tunings (three strings tuned to a major triad) can provide a full array of chromatic notes on a diatonic instrument. See an in-depth summary at: www.mountaindulcimer-1-3-5.com.

—— *Merv Rowley (2006)*

Figure 2. *Chromatic dulcimer tablature example.*

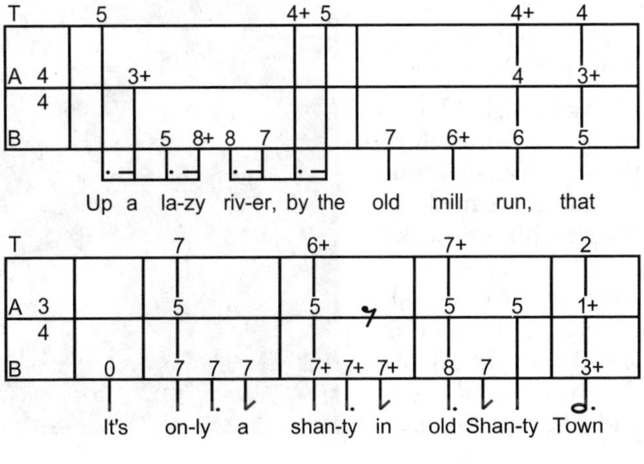

Originally published in *American Lutherie #59*, 1999

Gene Rhinehart: Northwest Resophonic Connection

by Jonathon Peterson

GENE RHINEHART has been a fixture at the Portland Handmade Musical Instrument Exhibit for years. I cornered him at the show and we talked about his resonator guitars.

Tell me about this drawing.

This is the pattern of the first resonator guitars that I made in about 1986. It's just a guitar-shaped box, really. The resonator produces all of the sound, so the body doesn't have to be very responsive. The plates are flat, thick, and heavily braced. The only really critical dimensions have to do with the hole for the cone. The hole has to fit the cone properly, and since the position of the hole determines the position of the bridge, you have to plot it out carefully.

I've got a '30s Regal, and the body is all 3-ply maple. What body woods are you using?

Dobro, Regal, Hollywood — all the early wooden resonator guitars were made out of laminated wood. In fact, I think that the only solid-wood model that Dobro has ever made is their Jerry Douglas model, which used mahogany for the top, sides, back, and neck. I've made a couple of laminated mahogany boxes, but most of mine are laminated walnut. I bought some sheets of it surplus, but it's the kind of material you can get from cabinet-supply shops or catalogs. The laminated material is stiffer, stronger, and more stable than solid wood.

How difficult is it bending laminated woods?

It's not hard. You have to bend it slowly. Back when I started, I just heated the wood over an electrical element and bent it over a stovepipe. Now I use a heating blanket and a mold, and I'm getting much more accurate results.

Are you're using laminates for tops too?

You can, but I'm using solid spruce for the tops, usually about ⅛″ thick. I've made a couple with 3⁄32″ thick tops, but I think the weight is the only real difference. Either one is stiff enough. All of the stress is end-to-end, like on a violin, a banjo, or an archtop guitar, so the top isn't being torqued at the bridge the way a regular steel string guitar top is. The only place on the top that's really stressed is at the upper end of the fretboard. String tension makes the neck want to pull up, which pushes the upper end of the fretboard down, so the top has a tendency to push in there. That makes the action a little higher, which is not a big deal on a slide guitar, but it's not really desirable, either. To prevent that, I glue a plate that is at least ⅛″ thick to the inside of the top between the neck block and the top brace to stiffen up that area.

What do you like to use for neck material?

I like mahogany because it's a stable wood, but I have made some out of black walnut. Black walnut is a lot heavier than mahogany.

How are you attaching your necks?

I'm bolting them on. I install two ¼″×20tpi inserts in the face of the heel to receive the neck bolts. I seat the inserts with superglue. It hardens the wood and improves the bite of the threads. I've used epoxy to seat them, but superglue is easier. The inserts are recessed a little when they are installed. That way, if you have to sand off a little bit of the contacting surface of the heel when you are fitting the neck, you can do it without hitting the inserts.

Before you fit the neck you should relieve most of the face of the heel so that just the outside edges contact the body. When you are trying to perfect the fit with sandpaper, it's easier to take a little off the edges than a whole lot off the entire surface.

ALL BY JONATHON PETERSON

1986 Rhinehart Resononator Guitar

Neck Dimensions:	
scale length	25″
number of frets	19
width at nut	2″
width at 12th fret	2¼″
thickness at nut	¾″
thickness at 7th fret	⅞″
nut dimensions	2″ × 3/16″ × ⅝″
neck angle	-2½°

Body Dimensions:	
top thickness	1/8″
side thickness	3/32″
back thickness	1/8″
width of upper bout	10¾″
width at waist	9 1/16″
width of lower bout	14⅜″
body depth	3¾″

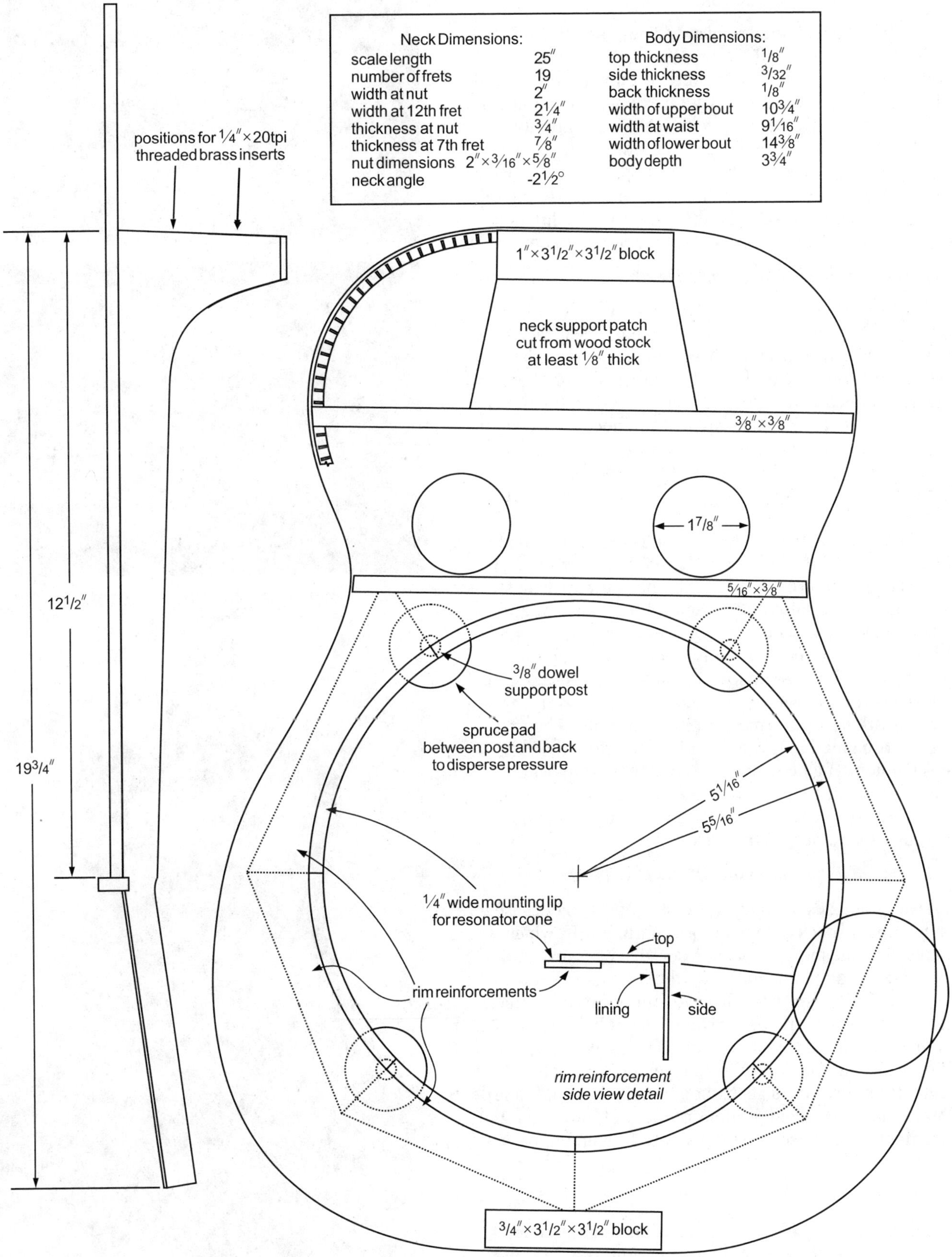

I'm working on a '30s National Style O, and it has posts which support the rim of the hole for the cone. I've also worked on Dobros that use cylindrical wells to support the rim. How do you support the rim?

I've built them all kinds of ways. There are different ways you can make a well. Dobro uses a continuous ring of wood with holes about 2″ in diameter evenly spaced around it. I've done that. Another way I have done it is to make the well in pieces, so it's more like baffles than a continuous wall. For that I use leftovers from the sides, bend them to the proper curve, and glue them in with spaces about 2″ wide between them. In either case the well is attached to the top with the same kind of kerfed lining I use for attaching the top and back to the sides, usually spruce or mahogany.

How do you go about installing a well?

I begin by gluing some lining around the underside of the hole in the top. It is positioned so that the surface that the well will be glued to is flush with the edge of the hole. That way the top edge of the well becomes the rim that the cone will sit on, and the glue seam is exposed on the top, which makes it easier to take apart if you need to do repair work later on. I used to glue lining for the well to the back too, but now I just let the bottom edge of the well sit free on the back. I learned the hard way not to make it too hard to remove.

If I'm not going to use a well, I reinforce the underside of the top around the hole with 4½″–5″ long segments of wood. Their ends are angled so that they butt up against one another. They also butt up against the waist bar and the tail block. I use scraps of whatever body material I'm working with for that. The reinforcements overlap the edge of the hole by about ¼″ to form a rim for the cone to sit on. I line the surface of the rim with cork. The rim is tied to the back with four posts made from ⅜″ dowels. The tops of the posts are glued to the underside of the rim reinforcement. I glue spruce pads on the bottoms of the posts to spread the contact over a larger area of the back, and glue the pads to the back. If you don't use pads the posts can cause cracks in the back.

How much difference in sound does a well make?

A well stabilizes the body more than posts do because it ties the top and back together more continuously, which isolates the cone more. The back doesn't get as involved in the sound, so you're depending on the cone itself to do all the work. With posts you only have four points of contact. The back pumps a little better when it's not held so solidly, and that gives it a little bit different sound. Which is better just depends on what kind of sound you're looking for. I like the freer sound you get without a well. It sounds a little fuller to me. I've pulled portions of the wells out of a lot of instruments — even some Dobros — to free up the back a little bit.

Are you using a solid or a slotted peghead?

I use a solid peghead with Grovers most of the time. Both Dobro and National built a lot of guitars with slotted heads so they could mount the tuners with the handles sticking up from the front of the peghead to make them easier to get at from on top, but that seems backwards to me. It makes it so the handles turn the wrong way. To get them to turn the right way you have to mount the gears upside down *and* backwards. If you are going to mount them conventionally with the handles on the back of the peghead you might as well save yourself the trouble of cutting slots. That gives you a stronger head and makes changing strings easier, too.

Where do you get your cones?

I spin them myself. The cone in this guitar is based on Dobro's 1929 cone, the John Quarterman cone. John worked for Dobro when they first started, and he ended up owning their original '29 cone mandrel, which he said is just like their '28 mandrel. The mandrel is the form that the cone is shaped against. According to John, Dobro needed to have the '29 mandrel resurfaced because it had gotten chipped up from use, but it cost more to have it resurfaced than to have a new one made. So they replaced it, and he talked them out of the old one and payed for resurfacing it himself.

Describe the process of spinning a cone.

The mandrel is attached to a faceplate on the lathe, and an aluminum disk is attached to the center of the mandrel with a small pin. You turn on the lathe, and while it's spinning, you use a tool to press the aluminum into the contours of the mandrel. I start at the outer edge so I can get the rim formed around the edge, which locks the aluminum in place on the mandrel. Once that's done you speed it up to 2,000 rpm–3,000 rpm and finish the shaping. I've got a 1″ diameter steel rod with a rounded end that's been hardened and polished for shaping the disk. A wax is used to lubricate the tool to keep it from grabbing and to keep it cool. If you try to shape the cone without lubrication it will end up with a hole in it.

Where do you get your other hardware?

I get the screens and tailpieces from Stew-Mac. I get a little discount by buying them twenty to thirty at a time, and I resell them. In fact, I sell cones, covers, spiders, and most everything you need to build these guitars. I have my own strings made, too, especially for acoustic lap steel.

Do you always set these up for slide, or do you sometimes make round necks and set them up for playing bottleneck?

I usually set them up for slide, although I have built a couple with round necks. I use a 12-fret neck in either case. With a bottleneck on the end of your finger you can reach up high on the fretboard pretty easily, so you don't need fourteen frets clear of the body or a cutaway. The action is usually set a little bit higher for bottleneck than it is for fingerpicking, but not as high as for slide.

With a round neck I would advise you to put in a truss rod. The one in the drawing and the photographs is set up for slide, and there is enough material in the neck that you don't need a truss rod. People call them square necks, but I put a little bit of angle on the sides of the neck, and the thickness of the neck tapers down towards the peghead.

You don't show any frets in your drawing. How do you handle that?

If you are building a guitar for playing bottleneck, of course you just fret it normally. If you are building a slide guitar you can put in regular frets, or you can paint them on, or you can inlay a contrasting wood to mark the fret positions. Most of my fingerboards are black walnut, so maple works real well for fret markers. You never touch the fretboard when you play slide, so it doesn't really matter what you use so long as the frets or fret markers are placed accurately. The frets just give you an indication of where you should put your bar. Most of the bars these days are wide enough that you can't see the contact point, so you have to use your ear.

Do you get out to play much?

Yeah. We've got a bluegrass group called the Puddletown Ramblers. There's two guitars, a banjo, resonator guitar, bass, and fiddle. We get together to practice pretty regularly. We go out and play at the local lodge halls and bluegrass venues, and we get to some of the bluegrass festivals. It's a lot of fun, and that's the reason I got involved with these things in the first place. ——

Originally published in *American Lutherie #59,* 1999

Making Compensated Saddles

by Jeff Huss and Mark Dalton

COMPENSATED GUITAR SADDLES seem to be a relative newcomer to our technology. Even Martin didn't slant its saddles to compensate the bass strings until they went to the belly bridge in the late 1920s, though they had been making steel string instruments for decades. Perhaps a change in string manufacturing instigated the slanted saddle, but it's just as likely that guitarists were used to the sound of a straight saddle and never complained about their instruments playing out of tune. There are various explanations for string compensation, some of them firmly embedded in guitar mythology. String compensation will no doubt one day receive a technical explanation that satisfies everyone, but most builders will likely continue to deal with compensation in a practical manner that simplifies saddle production as much as possible while still meeting the demands of musicians.

Various saddle designs have appeared, especially from small shops where such innovations often begin these days. However, probably 99% of the builders and players of steel string flattops find that an accurately placed slanted saddle is still sufficient for most musical needs. We want Huss & Dalton guitars to fall firmly within the tradition, so giving up the one-piece slanted saddle was never an option. Still, we decided on an ⅛″ wide saddle rather than 3⁄32″, to leave room for adequate correction, and we decided to carve each saddle in a manner that compensated each string individually. It is the creation of such saddles that we want to talk about.

Methods of making a precisely intonated saddle to accommodate a particular guitar and set of strings, or even a particular tuning, already exist. We recommend Don Teeter's first volume of *The Acoustic Guitar*. But that's not what we're talking about here. We make models that we think of as flatpick guitars, which we ship with medium-gauge strings installed, and models that seem to us to fall into the fingerstyle tradition, which are shipped with light-gauge strings. They are all made with similar saddles simply because we have no control over what strings the musician will want to use. We've also learned that, for reasons of their own, many dealers restring our guitars before putting them out, so we have sought a middle-of-the-road intonation correction that (we hope) indicates to guitarists that we are doing our best without making any particular strings unusable on our instruments. So far no one has complained. The refinement of instruments often comes in small increments, and truer compensation is something we may address in the future as the need arises.

In the meantime, here's how we make saddles. We use bone exclusively, though for chronic string breakers we have supplied a Tusq™ or even a graphite saddle. Bone blanks come .140″–.150″ thick, and the first step is to reduce them to .130″. For this we use a 120-grit belt sander. The blank is flipped and turned frequently to keep it coming down evenly, and measured on both ends and the middle as sanding progresses. It's then thinned to .124″ on a 220-grit sanding board, still turning and flipping it. A snug fit that requires no tools to pull the saddle back out is just right. It's worth noting that if a worn router bit is used to cut the slot, the result is often a slot that is wider than normal, not narrower. This is because a worn bit is more inclined to chatter. If you rough out bridges in batches, it pays to keep track of the slot dimensions, or your perfectly made .124″ saddles may end up rattling around in a .130″ slot.

Blanks come in various lengths. We offer guitars that incorporate a through-saddle, as in older Martins, and blanks for such a saddle run about 4″ long. Since Jeff makes all the bridges, he carves these saddles as part of the process. But by far, most of our guitars use a saddle that drops into a blind slot. Regardless of type, all saddles are intonated in the same manner. Blanks intended for a slot bridge are bandsawn to 3.125″ long. All further machining is done using a spindle sander, though a drum sander mounted in a drill press could do just as well.

The first jig is used to cleanly square the ends of the blank and bring it down to about 3.010″ long (**Photo 1**). The exact dimension isn't critical, since our saddle slots run about 2.996″. A sample bridge is kept at hand to test each blank. We don't want it to be a jam fit in the slot in either length or thickness.

The next step is to arch the saddle to match the fingerboard, and another simple jig serves that purpose (**Photo 2**). All saddles are left too high, then cut down to suit a particular guitar as they reach the setup room. At this point, while the arched edge is still flat, the saddle could be fitted to proper action height and the intonation cut for a particular set of strings, but we don't do that.

Jeff roughs out bridges in batches of ten to twenty-five. When a batch of bound bodies comes to him he draws an equal number of bridges from his stash and gives them numbers that correspond to the guitars' numbers. The bridges are then passed to the saddle man, who draws arched blanks from his supply. If need be, the saddles are thinned to fit the slots using the 220 sanding board. We like them tight, but not so tight that tools are needed to remove them. The blanks are sanded to exact length, then rounded, using an 80-grit sanding stick. A 220-grit sanding stick is then used to clean the ends and prevent a jam fit. The saddles are numbered to match the bridges.

ALL BY JOHN CALKIN

Photo 1. *This simple jig sets the length of the saddle before hand-fitting.*

Photo 2. *The second jig is used to grind the proper arch on the top edge of the saddle blank. The arch should match the arch of the fingerboard.*

The string positions are marked on the saddles (**Photo 3**), after which a cross mark is made to indicate the intonation points of all strings. A simple formula is used for this. The high E is left in the middle of the saddle, the B at the rear edge (that is, closest to the bridge pins), the G in the middle of the saddle, the D at the front edge, and the A and low E strings at the rear edge (**Photo 4**). At this point the bridges are returned to Jeff for finishing.

To visualize the next step it helps to draw a snaky line that smoothly connects all the intonation points (**Photo 5**). The top edges of the saddle must be ground away until only the pencil line is left. The angle of the grind and the width of the bone line that actually bears the strings is open to some individual interpretation. If the blank is held at too acute an angle to the sanding drum, the grind will extend below the bridge slot, which is ugly and robs the saddle of support. If the angle is too obtuse, it robs the saddle of grace. If the saddle is made too pointy, it will tend to break strings and wear out faster. If it is left too round, much of the intonation correction is lost. We made a fixture that holds the saddle to the sander to establish the angle (**Photo 6**), but the cut is made by eye. A jig that controlled the depth of the grind would certainly be a step in the right direction, but hand-grinding is so fast that we haven't bothered yet. A last gentle pass is made on each side of the saddle to smooth the new contours.

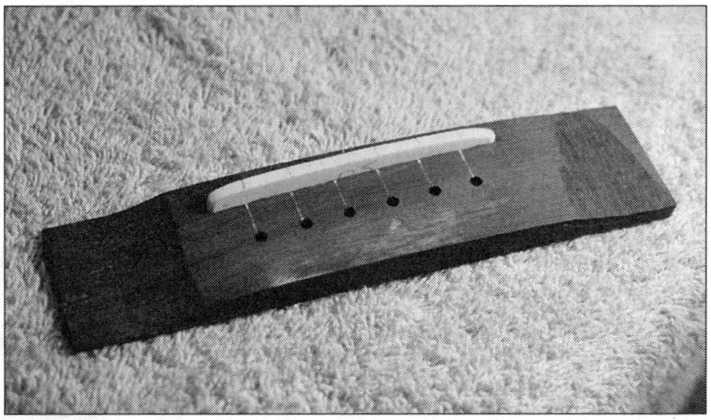

Photo 3. *This test bridge is used to set the string spacing on the profiled saddle, though it could as easily be done with the finished bridge by using the pin holes as a guide.*

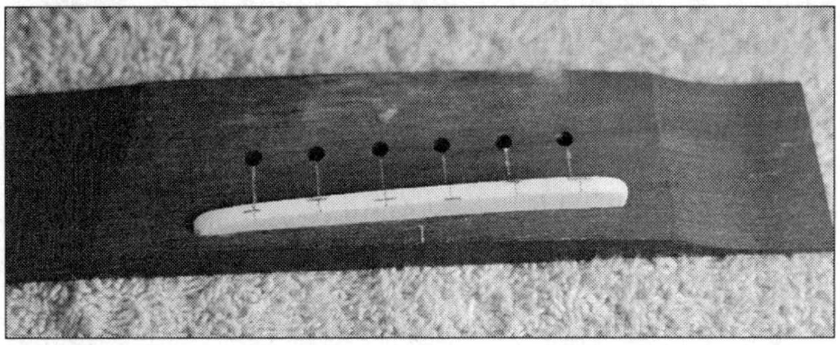

Photo 4. *The intonation points are marked according to a simple formula. The high E is marked in the middle of the saddle, the B at the back edge, the G in the middle, the D at the front edge, and the A and low E at the rear edge.*

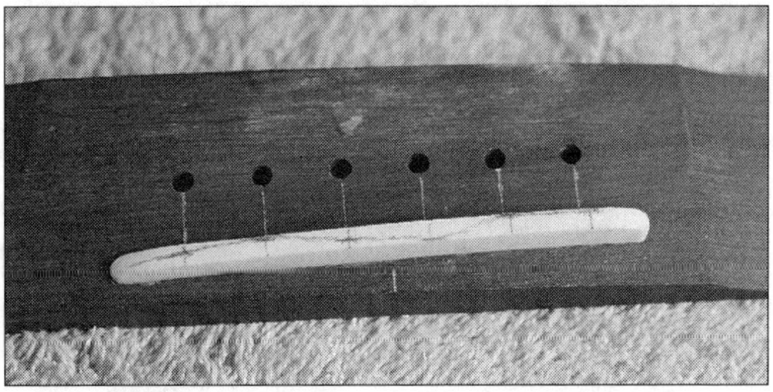

Photo 5. *At first it may be easiest to connect the intonation points in a snaky line before grinding them. The top edge is ground until only the pencil line is left, plus a bit of bone on each side of the line.*

Photo 6. *Though free-hand grinding can be done successfully, we use this jig to keep our work consistent. The exact angle of the grind is not critical, but the range is fairly small. Too acute and the saddle will be ground below the bridge line; too obtuse and the top will be too round to be usefully intonated.*

From here it's a simple matter to sand the ground portion of each blank with 120 grit to erase any machine marks and blend the harsh lines, taking every effort to stay off the sides that have already been sanded to 220. Successively finer grits are used to smooth the bone and refine the top of the saddle, running through 220, 400, and 600 grits, after which they are power buffed and the saddle man is done with them. The finished saddles are racked in the setup room until Mark needs them.

The entire shaping process takes between thirty to forty minutes per saddle. We've made a clamp for holding each saddle during hand sanding, the idea for which was taken from a blacksmith's vise (**Photo 7**). It's taken a lot of the torment out of the saddle maker's life.

The finished saddle isn't extreme enough in shape to immediately draw the eye, but it's a fine and graceful detail that (we hope) confidently informs the musician that we are on his side in the quest for truer pitch and prettier music. ——

Photo 7. *This clamp was made up to hold the saddles while they were sanded. The idea was taken from the upright of a blacksmith's vise.*

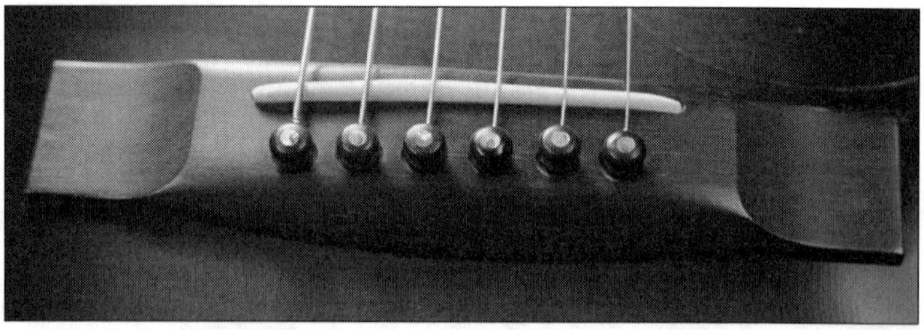

Photo 8. *The finished saddle has a subtle sculptured look that adds a handsome detail to the guitar as it enhances the musical quality of the instrument.*

Originally published in *American Lutherie #60*, 1999

QUESTIONS

EDITED BY CYNDY BURTON

■ ***Janna MacAuslan of Portland, OR*** *asks:*

I recently acquired an older model Kohno guitar. I was told the finish is "pecan oil varnish." I'd like to refinish at least the top. Does anyone know what this varnish is and a source for it?

Kirk Sand of Laguna Beach, CA *answers:*

In my experience, Kohno finishes of that vintage were catalytic, similar to the Ramírez epoxy-like finishes from the '70s on. Many years ago when I requested some original Kohno finish to touch them up, I was sent a two-part (catalytic) finish; one can was labeled "cashew." I'm not sure any nut, cashew, pecan, or other ever came near that finish. (Anyone speak Japanese?) I believe the finish used on Ramírez guitars is no longer sold in this country for environmental reasons. Because Kohnos are not rare from a collector's point of view, changing the finish should not devalue the instrument. I recommend using the finish of your choice.

■ ***Brian Daves of Minneapolis, MN*** *asks:*

While attending a class at the American School of Lutherie, I heard of a local builder who was sent to the hospital due to cyanoacrylate (CA) glue exposure. My question has to do with safety issues in using these glues. A recent Stew-Mac catalog article gives the impression that although the fumes are noxious, the glues and accelerators pose no serious safely concerns. Given my own experience and those of others, exposure to the glue and its fumes seems more than "noxious." I am interested in any feedback and information that others might have to share.

Mike Wilson of Detroit, MI *responds:*

To comply with OSHA's Hazard Communication Standard, Material Safety Data Sheets (MSDS) should be available for cyanoacrylates and all other chemical products. An MSDS can be obtained directly from a manufacturer or supplier and can often be viewed on a company's website. If you are concerned about the health hazards of any product, this can be a good place to start.

Cyndy Burton of Portland, OR *adds:*

Here's what I found when I checked out one such website. Under Section VI, Health Hazard Data, "Signs and Symptoms of Exposure: Vapor is irritating to eyes and mucous membranes above TLV (Threshold Limit Value). Prolonged and repeated overexposure to vapors may produce allergic reactions with asthma-like symptoms in sensitive individuals." And "Precautions to Be taken in Handling and Storage: Store below 75°F to maximize shelf life; avoid contact with skin and eyes; avoid breathing vapors." Although this is helpful, it hardly seems like the whole story. ——

Originally published in *American Lutherie #60,* 1999

Arching and Voicing in Violin Plates

by Graham Caldersmith

BELOW 800Hz, violins produce sound from the activation of a set of natural modes which usually includes A_0, T_1, C_3, and C_4. Other modes C_1 and C_2 are also activated but do not produce much sound. The air inside the violin is activated by coupling with T_1, C_3, and C_4 to generate A_0, A_1, and so on.

Above 800Hz the violin modes begin to overlap into a resonance continuum. When plotted against frequency, the decibel (dB) strength of this continuum has an average profile, the shape of which reflects the timbre or voice of a particular violin.

All good, clear-speaking violins have strong response (and sound production) in the 2kHz–5kHz band and lesser response in the 1kHz–2kHz band. If the violin plates, which are the sound producers, are graduated so that the lower mode set A_0–C_4 occurs at recommended frequencies, then the 1kHz–5kHz response profile is influenced by the shape of the plates. Hence it is valid to say that in arching

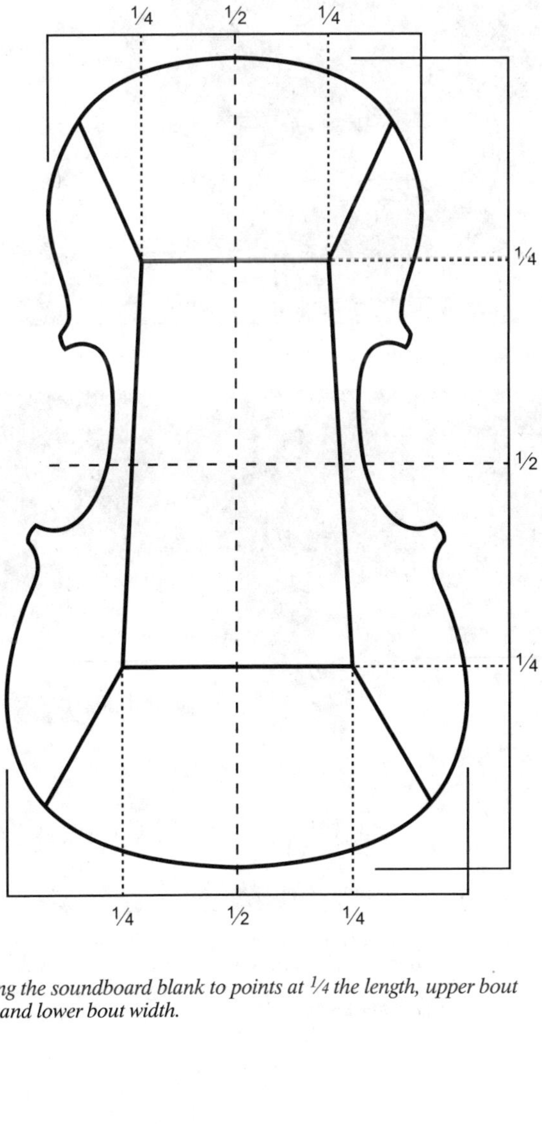

Faceting the soundboard blank to points at ¼ the length, upper bout width, and lower bout width.

the plates, the maker voices the violin. Of course, if the plates are too thick or too thin and the bass bar too stiff or too flexible, then the whole response profile is dislocated and the above description does not apply.

There is evidence that plates with peaked arching have a lesser response in the 1kHz–2kHz band than smoothly arched plates. The archetype of the peaked plate is the Amati arching, and of the smooth plate is the Guarneri del Gesù. Stradivari's movement from Amati archings to his own smoother profiles after 1700 is well documented.

The lesser 1kHz–2kHz response in peaked plates is due to the lower amplitude of the 1kHz–2kHz modes in the center of the belly where the bridge feet excite them: the antinodal zones are more confined to the ends of the plates than in smooth plates where the antinodes spread into the center region and are more strongly excited. One can hear the greater content of the fundamental on notes played above the E octave (1320kHz) on the top string of a smoothly arched violin.

The timbre of the lower notes is also a good indicator of the strength of the 1kHz–2kHz resonance band. The stronger 1kHz–2kHz content of lower notes in peaked violins gives a "clear, sweet" tone, but not as powerful. This "lighter" characteristic is compounded by a generally lesser excitation and radiation from the lower mode set in peaked violins.

My article "Reconciling Structural and Acoustic Design in Violin Making" in *American Lutherie #58* (p. 362) includes geometrical construction of arching profiles for minimum deformation under string tension. The "normal" and "scooped" profiles are examples of the types of archings one can draw with the method proposed. Such variations, it is argued, influence the voice character of the violin due to the effects described above for the "smooth" and "peaked" models. The various violin making traditions have incorporated arching design as one element in the evolving sound character of their violins. The sound character of violas and cellos cannot be explained in the same way since their sound radiation envelopes do not relate to the ear/brain hearing function as violins do.

The purpose of this article is to offer modern makers a link between the shape of their violin plates and the "shape" of the sound of the completed instrument: its voice. The emphasis on resistance to deformation is to ensure the violins will stay in shape long enough to be appreciated; that is, for decades.

The method of carving archings illustrated in the following steps is a flexible, spontaneous, but systematic procedure which requires aesthetic judgement rather than adherence to standard templates. It promotes evolution of the maker's arching designs rather than reproduction of established models. If variations in wood properties, graduation, and bass bar dimensions are "normalized" by means explained in *AL#58,* then the maker can legitimately develop arching profiles as a method of voicing violins. ——

Update

I now use King William pine arching heights of 17mm rather than 18mm. This is to smooth the profiles marginally, and I believe this increases the 1kHz–2kHz responses similiarly.

—— *Graham Caldersmith (2006)*

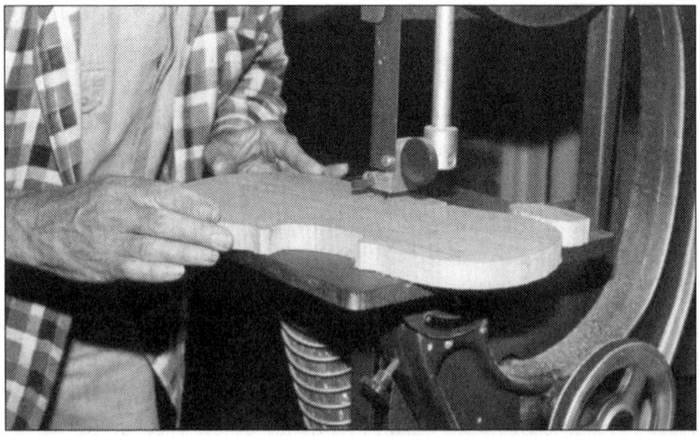

Photo 2. *The marked outline is sawn about 1mm from the line.*

Photo 3. *The belly blank is planed to the chosen arching height. Spruce bellies are usually arched to 15mm–16mm, but in this case, using King William pine, which is not as stiff along the grain as spruce, the arching height is 18mm to compensate for the lower stiffness.*

Photo 5. *The blank is faceted to about 1/4 of the length and bout widths just clearing the edge depth scribed with a marking gauge: 4.0mm bouts, 4.5mm C bouts. I use a power planer, but hand planing is fast enough, too.*

ALL COURTESY OF GRAHAM CALDERSMITH

Photo 1. *The outline of the belly is marked from the rib cage onto the underside of the belly blank. The sharp pencil is planed on one edge so it marks the outline at 3.0mm from the ribs, the standard overhang.*

Photo 4. *Checking the arching height. It's close at 18.3mm.*

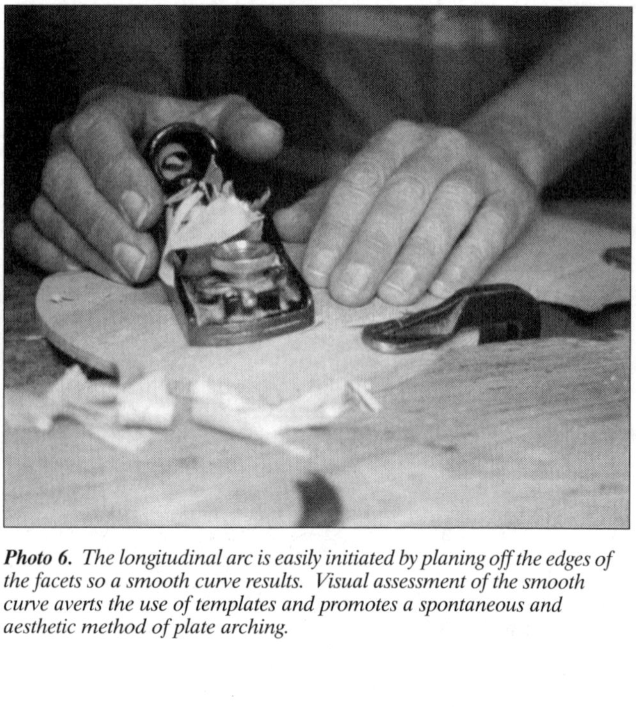

Photo 6. *The longitudinal arc is easily initiated by planing off the edges of the facets so a smooth curve results. Visual assessment of the smooth curve averts the use of templates and promotes a spontaneous and aesthetic method of plate arching.*

Photo 7. *The arching gouge quickly roughs out the curves joining the "coastline" at the edge thickness mark to the "plateau" at maximum belly height.*

Photo 8. *Thumb planes with their domed soles blend the "coastline" to the "plateau." The width of the flat "coastal plain" from the edge will set the degree of "edge scoop" in the archings described geometrically in* AL#58 *(p. 362). Sighting the belly from the ends reveals the degree of scoop emerging and the symmetry and evenness of the arch across the bouts. Use of the left hand as a clamp in the split bench top allows the belly to be quickly oriented for efficient planing.*

Photo 9. *Oblique natural or artificial lighting reveals the evenness and symmetry of the arching along and across the plate as planing proceeds. Visual assessment allows the maker to carve quickly and spontaneously, and to vary the arching geometry with accruing experience.*

Photo 10. *Scraping the belly removes plane strokes and finalizes the profiles. The scraper is ground to curves just sharper than belly curves.*

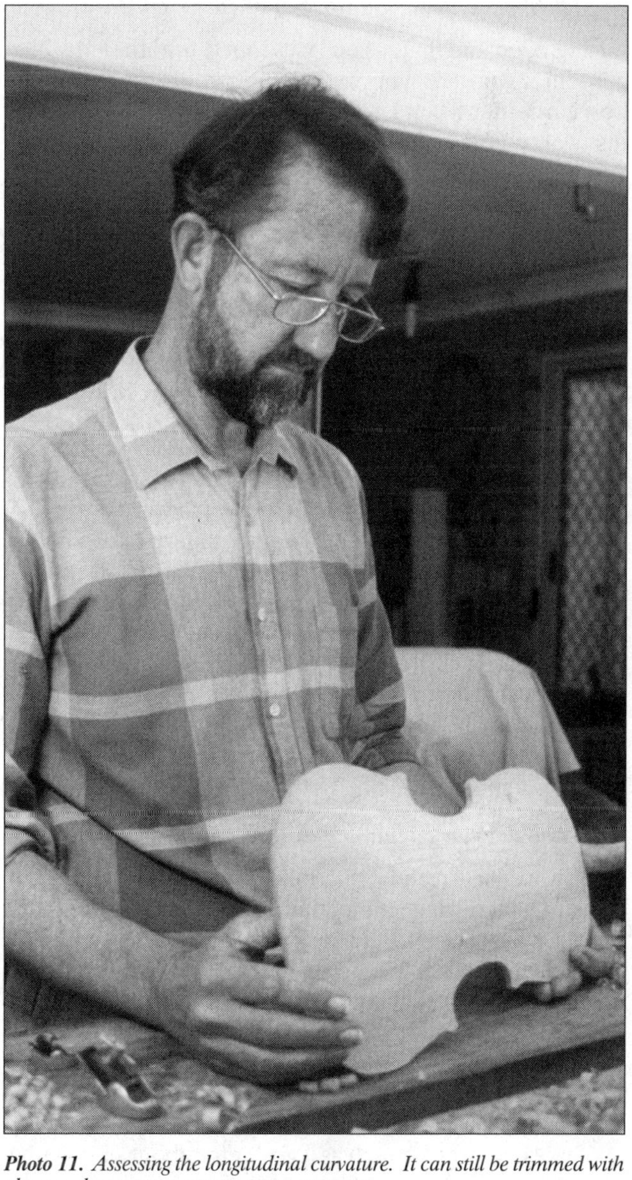

Photo 11. *Assessing the longitudinal curvature. It can still be trimmed with plane and or scraper, as can cross curvatures.*

Originally published in *American Lutherie #59,* 1999

Meet the Maker: Grit Laskin

by Gordon Gray

TORONTO-BASED luthier William "Grit" Laskin was recently a featured speaker at the Canadian Craft Museum in Vancouver, British Columbia. Entitled "Give Me Wood and I'll Make It Sing For You," Grit's presentation included an extensive slide portfolio of his incredible inlay work, and an overview of the art and craft of lutherie from his nearly three decades at the bench. Grit was interviewed the evening following his presentation.

Which came first, your love of music or craft?

I've been told that, when I was four, I told the carpenter who was working on our carport that I would be a carpenter when I grew up. It could have been that I just wanted play with his stuff, but I've always liked tools and wood, natural wood.

When I was nine years old, my father asked me if I wanted to learn to play the guitar. He probably wanted to learn when he was a kid and his father wouldn't bother to teach him. Like many parents, he wanted to give his children things he never had. I said "Sure," and he bought me a little Harmony guitar, which I still have somewhere.

Were you serious about music from the start?

Yes. Through teenage years most people seem to need something to stay sane. I took a few lessons from the Mel Bay guitar-method books, which were boring, but then a friend showed me how to fingerpick, and I got excited again. He was a very good musician and helped me to train my ear — how to learn things from records, how to find chords on the neck, how the formation of a chord will sound in different positions compared to the root position — it's all ear training. This was very helpful. He was very gifted musically, and could have followed that, but he went into law and he's now a judge.

When did you get into building?

It was just after my 18th birthday. I really wanted to work in a recording studio, but no one had told me that there were college-level courses to learn studio engineering. I didn't even know it was possible, or I would have gone that route. So, during Christmas holidays, when my parents were away, I hitchhiked to Toronto, went into Eastern Sound — I knew the name from the back of a Bruce Cockburn album — and got a job. Then I came back home and quit school.

I worked pretty much as a go-fer for about six months until the business side of it and all the ad executives just

GRIT LASKIN

turned me off. I was there just for music, but this was how they made most of their money. I was doing some basic low-level engineering by the time I left.

I played music for a summer, and then I met Jean Larrivée. I had seen his guitars at the Toronto Folklore Centre, and for the first time it struck me that instruments were made by human beings. I recall looking at where the peghead veneer joined the headstock, seeing ebony going into mahogany, and seeing nothing in-between. The ebony ended and the mahogany began with no visible glue line. I had no concept of how real people, real hands, did that, and it fascinated me.

Jean had been building for less than three years and still worked in his basement. On a whim, I asked if he would be willing to take me on. He said we'd try it out for a few months. I started when he started building again in the fall. This was before the days of climate control, so in humid weather you didn't do any building.

There were two other people who started to work with Jean around that time. One was Sergei de Jonge, who is still making guitars, but for most of the next two years, it was just Jean and I. Jean was sleeping on a piece of plywood on the third floor of the Folklore Centre, and I was renting a room — just a teenager, no cares, no car, no expenses, no nothing. It was great! I just worked all the time unless I was away for the weekend doing a gig or something. That was my life.

And that was when?

It was from the fall of 1971 to the fall of 1973. In the second year I was with Jean, he and I each did about half the work on the guitars. Jean was quite generous. He said I really should be signing the labels too, but only twelve of the sixty guitars we built that year have my signature in them as well as his, mostly because we'd forget. We'd glue the label over the reinforcing strip, so it was hard to sign properly. During that same year in my spare time, I built and sold three of my own guitars.

After that second year I decided to go out on my own. People knew I was leaving and saw the work I was doing, so I had orders even before I went down to the hardware store and bought a saw.

I'm pretty spoiled. I've always had orders. That doesn't mean I haven't also sold through stores, and gone all around the world to get my guitars where I wanted them to be. But I had some security when I started. And I was selling them for peanuts!

Have you ever come across any of those early guitars?

Sure, those that are alive. Sometimes they impress me, and sometimes I'd like to burn them. There were some I built when it was a little too humid, and they dried out. I've replaced a couple of tops, and in one case I replaced a whole guitar. But I occasionally see some from the early days that are surprisingly good, and those were guitars that I might have sold for $300.

When you did go on your own, did you have a clear idea of the styles of instruments you wanted to build?

Well, I was still pretty much a greenhorn, but I had thought about it. I had designed my own shapes, my peghead shapes, my rosettes, my mosaics.

You perhaps are best known for your inlay art. How did that develop?

It was a slow build through the years. It wasn't even that conscious. As inlay work came in, I was somehow prepared to be a little more adventurous in how I depicted things. I began pushing the boundaries. I recall one time doing an inlay where I had a character walking onto the peghead, and it suddenly occurred to me that I didn't have to show the whole scene. I could do something a bit more playful, more fun. I started teaching myself how to engrave in 1975. I still remember my first hesitant scratches with the graver on an instrument I was making for myself. I just bought the tool and figured out how to use it, or a way that worked for me — slowly learning how to make a bold line, a line that looked confident rather than a thin shaky line, and how to accent lines with the graver, and how to use different gravers, and how to engrave various materials. It just slowly evolved.

Are you also self-taught in the life drawing you use in designing your inlay?

Yes. I never went to Art 101, although I will say that everyone in my family — I have three natural sisters and a stepfamily — they all have some artistic ability, so I probably have some instincts too, but they weren't developed, weren't honed. That just came slowly and painfully. I'd need to draw a hand, and I'd stand there in front of the mirror, my arm twisted in a certain way, and think, "OK, is that how it looks?" Or I'd go to the dentist next door and I'd ask the nurse, "Could you just look downward and slightly to the left? I've got to see what an eye does." I'd do research in libraries. You can get your images there without having to buy books or hire models. That's how I did it.

At one point I hit on a book called *Drawing on the Right Side of the Brain.* It had some wonderful exercises which wake up the way you really look at things as an artist, and that makes all the difference, especially when it comes to making something realistic. I've been at symposiums and get-togethers with phenomenal guitar makers, very talented people, and I've seen them stand in front of my guitars and say, "The faces; how do you do the faces?" There's no magic. You just look at it the way an artist would, and use the medium as an art medium instead of thinking of it as inlay decoration on a guitar. Think of it as a medium of expression that emerged out of a tradition of musical instruments.

You mentioned last night your idea of the guitar as functional art.

Yes, that's how my customers tend to see it, but the instrument has to be a musical tool first and foremost. It's a failure if it looks stunning but doesn't play well. Inlay is a purely decorative process which has nothing to do with the success or failure of the guitar as an instrument. But here I have my canvas, and I'm getting paid to have fun on something that also has other layers of creativity. The guitar has many artistic dimensions. Besides the design of the instrument, there's the construction, and the creativity of pulling the music out of it, and the artist being creative in performance. On top of that you have the visual art aspect which adds an additional dimension to something that's already complex and multidimensional. It's just richer because of it.

What instruments are you currently building?

I build what I call the flattops, even though we know they're not flat — steel strings, classicals, and flamencos. Obviously, I don't do a lot of inlay on classical or flamenco guitars.

But it's interesting to think of a classical guitarist at Carnegie Hall in formal attire, playing a guitar with wild inlay on it.

Well, I've had a few classical players say, "You know, I might be ready to do that. I'd be kind of noticed." It'd be fine with me! I've done a little, but most people are very afraid to buck tradition if they're working on their career. That's the prejudice of the moment coming out of the modern aesthetic of the classical world, and that's perfectly fine because I still get the pleasure of the woodworking and the acoustics, and the satisfaction of getting a flamenco action just right so that a player falls in love with it. Those are wonderful creative highs, and it gives my inlay juices a bit of a break.

Does a client come to you with an idea for an instrument and an idea for the inlay?

If a steel string player comes to me they are usually thinking they will get some kind of inlay because they know about what I do, however they generally don't yet know what it will be, or they have a few vague ideas. After we finish discussing all the other aspects that need to be resolved I get to inlay, and that's often the toughest issue for them because it's not a black-and-white decision. It's not like needing the neck wider or thinner, or building it for medium gauge strings, or wanting Brazilian rosewood. Those are easy decisions — this or that. It's more like I'm saying, "I'll do a painting for you. What do you want it to be about?" I try to get them thinking about ideas that mean something to them, and I ask a lot of questions. I listen for clues that might lead me to a subject, and I listen for the adjectives that tell me what kind of interpretation they're after. I keep going until I feel confident that I can deliver the kind of thing they're after. I need to get a sense of who they are and what they want so that I don't disappoint them, because in the end they're going to leave it up to me and trust me.

Luckily, as the years have gone by, more and more of my inlays have been seen by more and more people, so when someone comes to me they usually have a sense of what's possible, where in the early days they didn't. But even though they have some ideas, and they've seen some instruments, it's still not such a popular art form that they're familiar with all the parameters of what can be achieved, and that works to my advantage. I generally supercede their ideas about how the subject will be depicted. It's usually more impressive in the dimensions, in the realism of it, in the medium — it's beyond what they're used to seeing, even if they've seen a few things of mine. I'm confident I can ask them to trust me not to do anything distasteful.

So you start with research, which leads to models, which leads to sketches, which leads to the inlay itself?

I use live models when it's people, other forms of models when the subject is plants or animals. I need to find out what things really look like. Sometimes someone will send me a picture and ask me to do a version of it. Just like any artist I do the research and rough sketches to come up with a finished sketch, which is always a pencil sketch on tracing paper. Once the finished sketch is done I photocopy it so that I can glue patterns to the various materials.

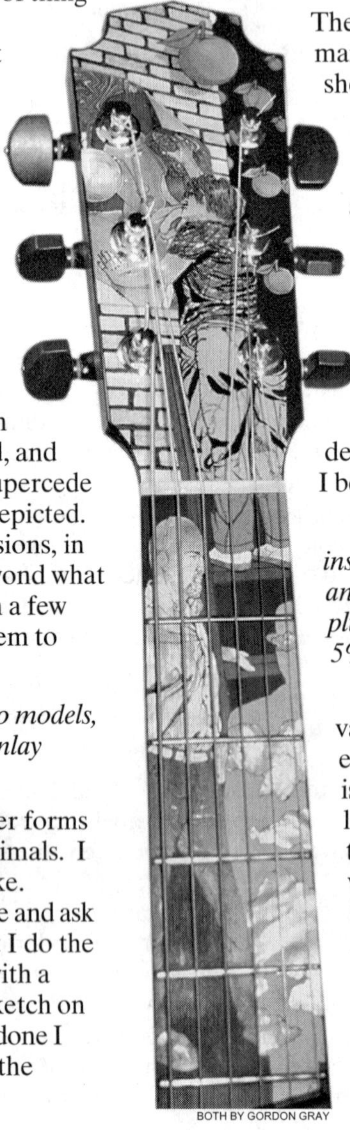

BOTH BY GORDON GRAY

Deciding the mix of materials, the colors and sheens and how they are juxtaposed to each other, can be a slow process. I'll lay the materials out, change my mind five times, and sometimes even cut a piece and then look at it and think, "No, no! I shouldn't have done that." Choosing the exact piece of each material is another very slow stage. It can get a bit esoteric looking at the reflective angles of the shell, the graining of the shell, taking into account not only what it looks like on the surface, but also what it will look when you sand away a third of it. Paying attention to those aspects of the raw materials can be the difference between the final result just being good and it being excellent, because they add to the total effect you are trying to create, in addition to your engraving and the shape of the materials.

In addition to pearl, shell, and metal, you've recently starting using reconstructed stone.

Yes. It's doubled my palette overnight. The stone offers me rich primary colors, and many more shades and textures. It still has the sheen of a hard material, which I love, as opposed to using stained woods to get reds, greens, or blues.

Recon Stone, which is what it's called, is actual stone that's been pulverized and then reassembled in a vacuum with a resin, so it ends up with a looser molecular structure. You can cut it, file it, and sand it. It works somewhat like ivory, but it's a little more brittle and tricky in some ways. I was turned on to it by Larry Sifel, who had seen it in knife maker's catalogs. They use it for decorating knife handles and things like that. I believe it was originally developed for carvers.

You were saying last night that the job of the instrument maker is to maximize frequencies, and that 95% of the energy generated from a plucked string dissipates as heat energy, and only 5% goes into producing sound.

That's an unfortunate truth. Those values are approximations, of course, but the energy is largely lost, and that small amount is what's left to work with. I was talking to a lay audience last night and trying to give them a sense of how the instrument maker views the instrument. A lot to musical-instrument building is strictly intuitive. All intuition, all gut feeling, is really the subconscious sifting data outside of your awareness and giving you signals. You might feel uneasy about doing something and not know exactly why, but there's a real process going on. A good maker with experience under his or her belt will have a lot of data they've absorbed, even at a subconscious level — tactile things, sensation of how something vibrates, memories of how it worked with something else, information that isn't in your immediate recall, but it's there. And the more you have, the more you bring to bear on every decision you make. The brain sifts all this data, and the hand-maker will make decisions, maybe even somewhat outside of conscious awareness. This intuitive level aids you in producing instruments which bring out the very best subtleties of music.

One example which demonstrates the importance of this level of decision making is Stradivarius. There were two family members who worked with him who became violin makers. They never made violins as good as he, even though they were right there, doing what he did, watching what he did, being told what to do. There were some things that Stradivarius would himself do that were so unconscious that he wouldn't think to convey them by instruction or by verbal explanation. He would just be doing these things automatically, things that resulted in better instruments. Even though these other people made good instruments that are considered valuable, they were never as good as Stradivarius.

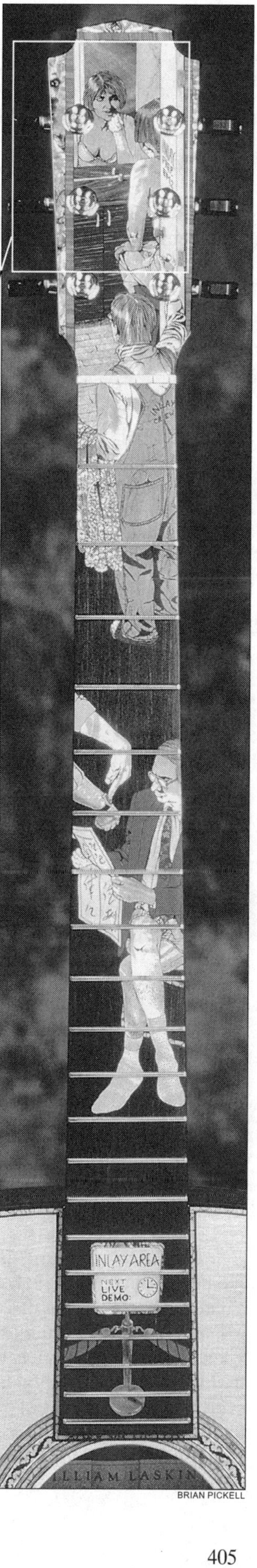

BRIAN PICKELL

You've maintained your performance side, both personally and professionally, ever since you started building. What does that add to your lutherie, or vice versa?

Well, it sure don't hurt! Being at a folk festival as a performer and being backstage with sixty other performers, somebody's going to say, "Hey, your guitar sounded great. You made that? Hey, I've heard of you. Can I try it?" It sure helps to get you customers, and it gives them confidence that you're someone who performs and has the same concerns as they do, and they know those concerns will get dealt with, without ever having to bring them up.

You received the Bronfman Award for 1997. You're in pretty "tall timber" with past winners like Bill Reid. That must be very gratifying. But since it's a Canadian award, I'm not certain how many people will know about it.

It is extremely gratifying. The Bronfman is sort of the granddaddy of the Canadian national craft awards. I was the twenty-first recipient. A jury judges submissions from all craft disciplines across all of Canada, so there's a lot of potential people there. To win this award, you have to not only have been in your craft for a while, and show excellence of work and innovative thinking, but you also have to have done a lot to increase public awareness of craft — given back to the community — and that aspect has to be just as strong as your work. Winning the award means that your own community has noticed what you've been up to, and that makes it doubly satisfying. I was the first instrument maker to receive it.

What is the award?

It's actually quite nice. You get $20,000. Also, our main museum, the Museum of Civilization in Ottawa, which is the Canadian equivalent of the Smithsonian Institution, commissions a piece of your work, and a video is made documenting your work for posterity. There's a public presentation, and you get a little brass thing for the mantelpiece! It's really, really nice, and it's a real high.

You spoke last night about instrument collectors, and one of the points you brought up was that you feel uncomfortable with people buying your instruments simply to collect them. Could you talk a bit about that?

Like many makers, I've watched the vintage scene wake up, and guitars becoming collectible, like violins and other high-priced items. That's wonderful, and it adds to the scene, but the down side is collectors who just want things to buy and sell. Many of them are players, too — I must say that — but just being collected, and not being played regularly, is not what the instruments are really for, and it makes me a little uncomfortable. People tell me all the time I could double my prices with no problem and still have a long waiting list, but it would mean far fewer working musicians would be able to afford my instruments. I like musicians to be able to have my instruments. If they are $15,000–$20,000 instruments, how many musicians do you know who could afford them? They'll just go into collections, and that doesn't appeal to me as something I want to do with my life.

I've seen it happen. I'll build a guitar, and I'll have a lot of conversations with the buyer. It's very personal. You're thinking about them and their wants and needs all through the building process. Sometimes when I'm doing something that's boring or tedious I'll think, "Well, it means something to them," so I'll do it. And then, a year or two later, a Mandolin Brothers catalog comes to my door, and there's the guitar on which I worked so hard doing things that didn't appeal to me, but I thought it was important to them, and there it is for sale. I know, and my customer knows, that they were going to turn it around in a short time and sell it for twice what they paid me. That rankles a bit, but what can you do? Generally, I'm pretty spoiled. I have a lot of very appreciative customers, and I really have no complaints.

BOTH PAGES BY BRIAN PICKELL

You mentioned that, during the last recession, you felt that the market dropped for custom guitars sold through stores, but that there was no drop in the number of individual buyers coming directly to makers.

Well, I was talking about crafts in general, and some crafts more than others. The point I was making was that there's a growing personal satisfaction in doing a transaction directly with the person who built the thing, whatever it is, making a personal connection. I think that's tremendously important, and I think that's part of what's fueled the current market, which has legitimately been called the Golden Age of Guitars. Players are buying instruments from local makers whom they've gotten to know, instruments which have been especially tailored for them. So there's lots of demand, and lots of work for everybody. There's lots of different guitars out there, and lots of different makers, and there's room for everybody because more and more musicians are trusting them, as opposed to only looking to the big manufacturers.

You've created guitars with built-in arm rests and rib rests. Did that first come from one of these connections?

Yes, a classical player asked if I could round off the purfling where his arm came around. It bothered him. I asked him how much I should round it, and he said, "Whatever you want, whatever you think you can do." I thought that as long as I was going to do it, I should really think about it — what's really needed, what's logical. So how it looks and what it does was just the result of this guy wanting it a little more rounded. My design has a copyright *(laughs)*, but lots of individual makers have used it. Happily, most of them have asked my permission. I always give it, but it gives me a chance to ask for a photo when it's done, and to ask them to please give credit where due, where the idea first came from.

I'm certain you've been asked by people about apprenticeships. Have you ever considered it?

I do get asked all the time, as do most makers, but I haven't taken anybody on. I like working alone. I like to be able to just do my work when I'm in the shop and not have to worry about anybody else. My days can be erratically scheduled because I do so many other things. I like it that way, but it would make having an apprentice difficult. At some point I will want to pass on what I know. If I start to feel arthritis in the joints I might take on an apprentice.

But you are doing a master class in inlay for the American School of Lutherie this fall.

Yes, Todd Taggart at Luthier's Mercantile is getting that going, and I was really happy to see it get started. What a neat thing it is to bring all the best people from all over to give master classes, workshops, and seminars in one place. I was very pleased to be asked. I'll be going down in October for five days.

How is your workshop going to be organized?

I'm going to split it into two parts, and I think that people can sign up for either or both. One will be a three-day intensive seminar on inlay, focused mainly on design and engraving, which are the two most difficult parts. You will really need to have done some inlay already or you'll be lost. I won't have time to deal with the basics. The other two days I've summed up as, "How You Go About Delivering the Guitar the Customer Wants." It will deal with all the things you explore with the customer — the physicalities of the instrument, the acoustics, the playing needs, the aesthetics, materials, and so forth. So there'll be lots of tangents to instrument making under that topic.

How many instruments do you build in an average year?

About twelve to fourteen, depending on the complexities. I've had some inlays that took 150 hours, so there goes building another basic guitar. You get paid for it, of course, but the sheer numbers go down. And I customize them in many other ways also.

Three years ago I also started a record company in partnership with other people, a folk music label, something that Canada didn't have. I put in at least fifteen hours a week on that, but it will be a labor of love for years yet.

And you're also a writer.

Yes, in a couple of ways, I guess. I write books, or have. I have one novel published out of three I've written, and a nonfiction book about the instrument makers of Toronto called *The World of Musical Instrument Makers — A Guided Tour.* I actually was starting research for another novel when the record company thing got started, so that's been put aside for a few years. But I'll get back to it. I really enjoy fiction. And then there's songwriting, which I've been doing since my early teens.

This experimental design attempts to incorporate the steep soundboard angle of the classical harp into a guitar. A hinged trap door in the end block allows knotted strings to be run through holes in the bridge, as in a harp. Norbert Kraft played it for three months, and while the instrument was physically awkward, he described the sound as "orchestral" in its fullness. A revised design was drawn but never built. This instrument is now in The Museum Of Civilization in Ottawa.

How do you balance instrument making with all the other things?

Instrument making pays the bills, so the work's gotta get done! If I'm not away performing — I try to limit that to a couple of weekends a month — I'm in the shop six days a week. I take Saturdays off. If I have to spend the morning on the phone for Borealis Records, I just work late. My hobby is the record company, so sometimes I do my hobby in the morning, instead of the evening. My typical day, including paperwork, is about fourteen hours, but I'm doing stuff I like. I'm excited by it all and it's all a challenge. I honestly believe that nothing's worth doing if it's too easy, but it's all the more satisfying when you achieve something. I make a decent living as a guitar maker. I'm not getting rich, and I never will, but I don't care.

Earlier you mentioned guitar making's Golden Age. Maybe a good way to wrap up is to ask where you think we are, and where the instrument maker goes from here.

I think it was Bill Cumpiano who summed that up in an article a few years back. Because there are many of us who have been at it for two, three, and more decades, there are just more of us who've gotten good at it. That, and the fact that the guitar is such a popular instrument, in all its forms, all around the planet. And there are so many more players ready to try handmade guitars than there were before. It's just fueled the whole thing. There are more and more makers, more suppliers of tools. We're just getting such a high quantity of good and innovative work. It's exciting to be a part of it.

Who knows how long it will go? I don't think you can really predict it. The guitar is such a popular instrument because, like a piano, it's got both the bass and treble register. You can do more with it than a single line instrument, and it's portable. Those things will always be there to help maintain its popularity.

Where are we going? I guess I hope that we have wooden guitars for a long time yet. They're not going to be made with rosewood and ebony for too much longer, but it may not matter. I believe that as long as the memory is there for the sound you get out of wood vibrating, people will want guitars. We'll use different woods, and we may lose the collective memory of how good certain instruments made with certain woods may have sounded a long time ago. But, to tell you the truth, the quality of the wood you can get is still outstanding. It's been that way for awhile, partially because there's so much demand that people are cutting well, which is tremendous. Now that Brazilian rosewood is an endangered species, the woods that are coming out in its place are better stuff than you've seen for a long time because it's worth people's time and effort to sell it now.

Personally, I hope to make guitars until I drop. Even if other things take over more of my life, I can't see myself giving up guitar making. It's an endless challenge. You've never done quite as well as you'd like to. You're always striving for a bit more. The carrot's always hanging there, and there are so many satisfactions. No matter how long you're in it, it's always a treat to get that joint nice and clean with one chisel stroke. It's still a high. When you get that, and then the sound, and the action just falls into place, and the player loves it, and you hear it played — and then I get into the inlay... I'm just spoiled, you know? I need a high level of creative satisfaction, and if I don't get it, just give me the razor blade now and I'll get it over with!

Grit, thank you.

You're very welcome. ——

Originally published in *American Lutherie #60*, 1999

The Maalaea Special

by Rich Mermer

I HAVE ALWAYS LOVED David Lindley's music, particularly his work on acoustic steel guitar. He has been a major proponent of the Weissenborn style of instrument. It didn't take much to push me over the edge, and after reading Ben Elder's article, " 'Born Again" (*Acoustic Guitar* #37, January 1996) I jumped in with heart and soul. The article contained a few bare dimensions of both Weissenborn and Kona instruments. Having not ever seen an original instrument, other than in photographs, I thought of the sound I was hoping to capture and drew up plans for a sort of hybrid instrument. It wasn't until after my first acoustic steel was completed and out the door that I was lucky enough to acquire a beautiful blueprint of a Weissenborn Style 1 (circa 1927) drawing by the gifted Flip van Domburg Scipio (thanks Flip!). I must admit to being surprised at how close my original design was to the instrument drawn by Flip.

I've put together a variety of in-progress photos of one of my lap-steel designs that I call the Maalaea Special. Maalaea is a bay on Maui where a couple of times a year, when conditions are just right, swells break from out of the south to create probably the fastest rideable waves in the world. I've been a surf rat ever since I was a kid, so Maalaea seemed like a natural when I was looking for a name.

Photo 1 shows a figured koa back that has the mahogany back braces and spruce center strip. The gluing surface of the back braces are contoured in a 15′-radius sanding dish. Once the braces are glued in place I use a finger plane and chisel to shape their profile before sanding.

Photo 2 shows a braced back lying on a flat surface (the underside of a dished workboard) so that you can see the brace profiles and the arching of the back.

The label is attached prior to gluing the back to the rim/top assembly (**Photo 3**). I generate the label on my computer. Note that I apply a thin wash coat of shellac to the instrument's interior surface in order to retard the wood's shrinking and expansion as a result of humidity

1

ALL COURTESY OF RICH MERMER

2

3

4

5
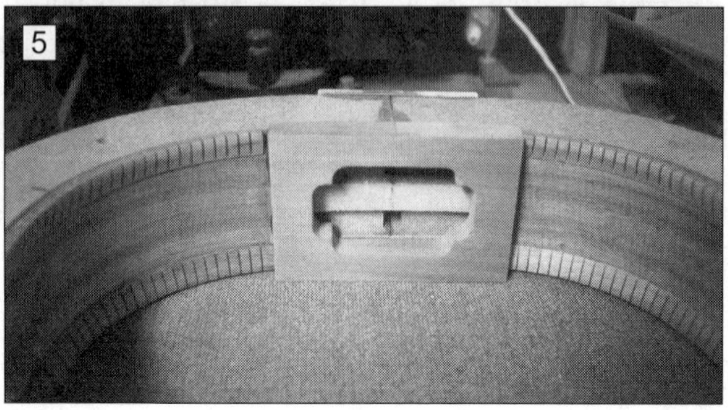

changes. I try to keep my shop at 45%–50% relative humidity and 75°F–80°F. I live near the central Florida coast, and this means that my dehumidifier and my air conditioning unit are in nearly constant use. I try to keep in the middle of the range because the instruments are getting shipped all over the place.

Photo 4 shows the liner strips being glued to the sides. I use small binder clips for this operation. These can be found in most office-supply stores. Small C clamps are used in the waist, where the curve of the sides is the tightest. This photograph also gives you an exterior view of the roughed-out trapdoor opening. I make the tail block with its cavity separately, and mark and cut most of the waste material away from the sides where the hole will be before the sides are glued to the block. After the glue has set, the edges of the hole are cleaned up with the use of a flexible straightedge and a sharp knife. **Photo 5** shows an interior view of the rim assembly and the tail block.

I shape the peghead/block assembly and glue a koa overlay on the face of the peghead prior to gluing the sides to the block. The block extends into the hollow neck chamber to a point about equal distance between the 1st and 2nd frets, just enough to give the sides and the back an adequate gluing surface. **Photo 6** shows the peghead/block assembly as it fits to the sides.

After the peghead/block assembly has been attached to the rim, I glue a koa veneer over the back of the peghead and the curved surface of the block. This is done prior to gluing on the instrument's back plate. This picture (**Photo 7**) was taken before the veneer was attached, but you can see the surface which will be cleaned up to accept it. When the instrument is complete, the only mahogany of the peghead/block assembly which will be visible will be on the edges of the peghead.

Photo 8 shows a top, back, and a rim prior to final assembly. The top gluing surface of the rim assembly is profiled with a 25′-radius sanding dish, as are the gluing surfaces of the braces for the top plate. The back gluing surface of the rim assembly is profiled with the aforementioned 15′-radius sanding dish.

Photo 9 shows the rim assembly with the top attached. Both this and the previous photograph were taken before the brace over the center seam between the two X-brace junctions was installed. Also, the bridge patch is smaller than the one in the drawing. Use your judgement.

I build instruments with either a traditionally placed soundhole, a single offset soundhole in the upper bout, or double offset soundholes in the upper bout (one on each side of the fretboard). This instrument features a single offset soundhole. I got the idea of using offset soundholes from Richard Schneider. In March of '88 or '89 I was visiting some friends from

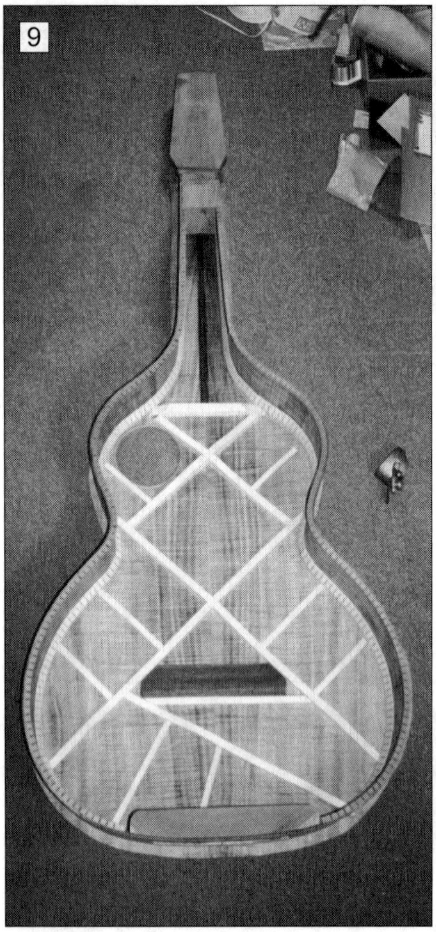

9

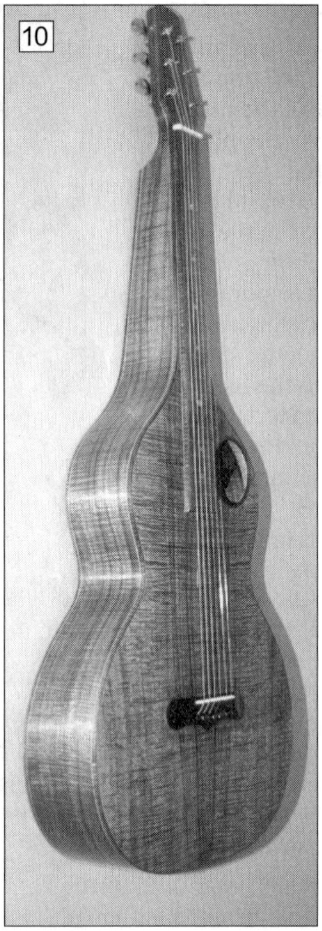

10

12

college who were living on the Olympic Peninsula, in Washington State. One of them had studied with Richard, so I had the pleasure of visiting his shop and seeing some of his work. Since then I have seen offset soundholes on instruments by Mark Wescott, Steve Grimes, and a variety of other builders. It is a design option which is becoming more popular all the time for a variety of reasons.

I like the idea of a single offset soundhole as it gives me an additional 25%–30% of the top plate's surface to manipulate and utilize for sound production. To accommodate this arrangement I glue a second X brace in the upper bout, which supports the top plate under the fingerboard. This replaces the multiple transverse braces which are commonly used in this region in conjunction with a traditionally placed soundhole. I am currently using variations of this double-X pattern on all my steel string instruments, whether lap-style or Spanish-style (minus the graphite fingerboard support and the single transverse brace in the upper bout). If the client desires a traditionally placed soundhole, it will easily fit between the junction of the upper and lower X braces. It will also accommodate dual-offset soundholes in the upper bout.

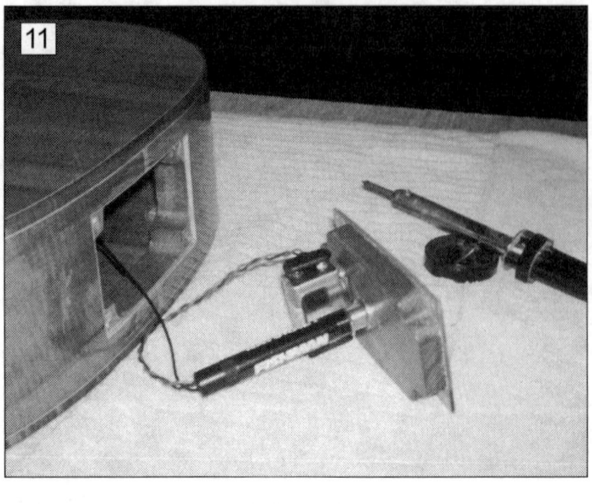

11

Photo 10 shows a completed instrument. It is equipped with an internal microphone and a piezo pickup.

Photo 11 shows a completed trapdoor assembly. This is another idea I got from Richard Schneider's work. The door allows for easy access to the interior of the instrument, and is a great platform for the mounting of electronics packages. My doors are held in place by four small bolts that screw into metal inserts which are countersunk in the tail block.

Photo 12 is a partial view of a fully bound variation of the Maalaea Special which I call the Artist Series. All other things being equal, the addition of a second soundhole enhances the treble frequencies of the aural spectrum.

This instrument belongs to Bob Taylor of Taylor Guitars. He contacted me last December, saying how he loved Lindley's music also, and that he had a hankering to learn to play. I was happy to build it for him, and at last check he was settling in with some instructional videos and enjoying himself. ——

Mermer Acoustic Steel Guitar: Maalaea Special

drawn by Rich Mermer

Top, back, and sides of highly figured koa; binding of maple and figured koa; figured koa peghead veneers front and back; rosewood fingerboard with maple fret lines and pearl dot inlays; rosewood bridge; rosewood bridge pins with pearl dots; Schaller tuners with pearloid knobs; bone nut and saddle; mahogany back braces; Sitka spruce top braces; Sitka spruce center-seam reinforcements; kerfed linings of mahogany on all-koa instruments, cedar or spruce if the top plate is of that material; mahogany peghead/block assembly and tail block.

Dimensions

scale length	25.50″
fingerboard width at nut	1.85″
fingerboard width at 19th fret	2.38″
body width at nut	2.00″
body width at 12th fret	5.50″
width at upper bout	10.25″
width at waist	8.40″
width at lower bout	15.25″
body depth at 1st fret	2.00″
body depth at 12th fret	3.40″
body depth at tail block	3.90″
total length	38.44″
top thickness	.093″
back thickness	.093″
side thickness	.085″
fingerboard thickness	.25″
string spacing at saddle	2.375″
string height at 1st fret	.25″
string height at 19th fret	.32″
nut height	.30″
saddle height	.1875″
bridge height	.375″

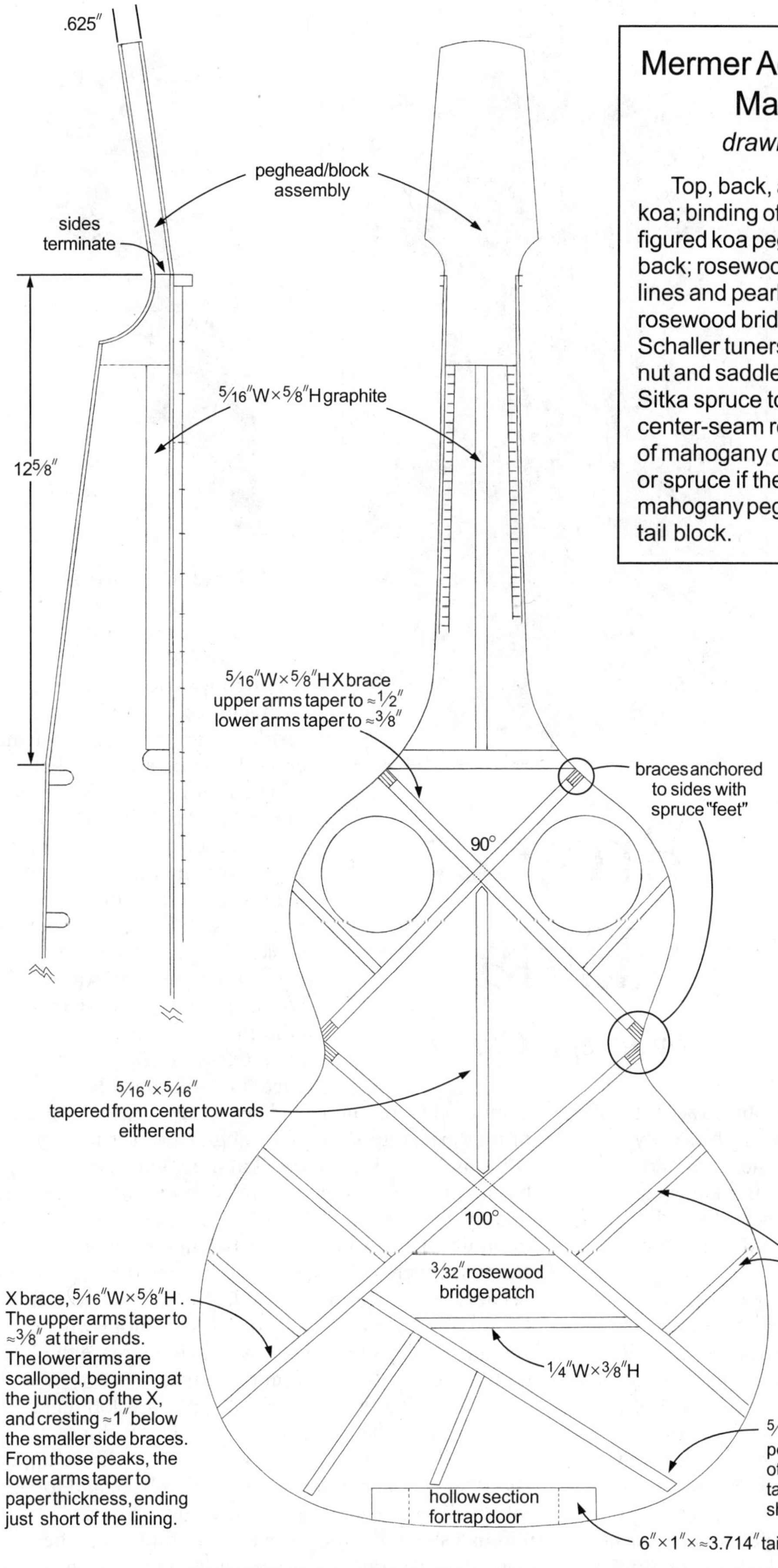

Originally published in *American Lutherie #60,* 1999

2

1

3

ALL BY JOSEPH CURTIN

Project Evia

by Joseph Curtin

THE LAST HALF of the 20th century has seen rapid development in the creation and use of new materials — and in our understanding of violin acoustics. The scarcity of good old stringed instruments is opening up the market for good new ones, and a number of makers and researchers have experimented with non-traditional designs and materials. Such violin makers as Guy Rabut, Roger Lanne, and Christophe Landon concentrated on aesthetic innovation, while researchers Hutchins and Haines, Charles Besnainou, and Leonard K. John have developed instruments using alternative materials. At the same time, the reluctance of classical musicians to accept nontraditional designs and materials may be slowly giving way. Bow makers such as Michael Duff and Benoît Rolland, using graphite fiber (also known as carbon fiber) and other synthetics, have achieved considerable commercial success — and made some very good bows.

For my part, after twenty years as a traditional violin maker, I have started taking time to look for new directions. This article gives an overview of "Project Evia" ("Evia" for **e**xperimental **via**ola) — my attempt to redesign, using new materials, the least-standardized instrument of the violin family. I decided to build a wooden prototype, which might then be progressively rebuilt using graphite-fiber/wood composites. My hope was to come up with a design that answered the ergonomic and tonal needs of the professional musician, my own sense of line and form, and the laws of nature. I did not want to worry about the sometimes stifling traditions of classical violin making.

Acknowledging that most useful innovation — aesthetic as much as structural — is the result of a great deal of trial and error, I wanted a design that allowed for rapid replacement of parts that didn't work. This seemed especially important when experimenting with new materials and unfamiliar processes. After many months of sketching ideas, I came up with something I felt was worth building. The overall shape (**Photo 1**), with its sloping shoulders and simplified corners, looks back to the gamba, while retaining, at least to my eye, some sense of modern simplicity. The single-turn scroll (**Photos 2 and 3**) reads well at a distance and to me has a sense of the architectural about it, rather than the merely decorative. The *f*-holes were designed to minimize the resistance to air flowing through them. Because much of the damping to the main air resonance occurs at the edges of the *f*-hole, the shorter overall length of edge produced by this design, along with a slight rounding of the edges, serves to increase the amplitude of this important resonance.

The sloping shoulders give the player's left hand easy access to the higher positions. This is done without decrease in internal vibrating length; the upper shoulder region of a traditional viola's back and top is left thick, and further immobilized by the block. **Photo 4** shows the linings, which continue over the corner blocks, rather than being set into them as is usually done. I should point out that most of the above elements have shown up in instruments of the past, though not all at once or in quite this arrangement.

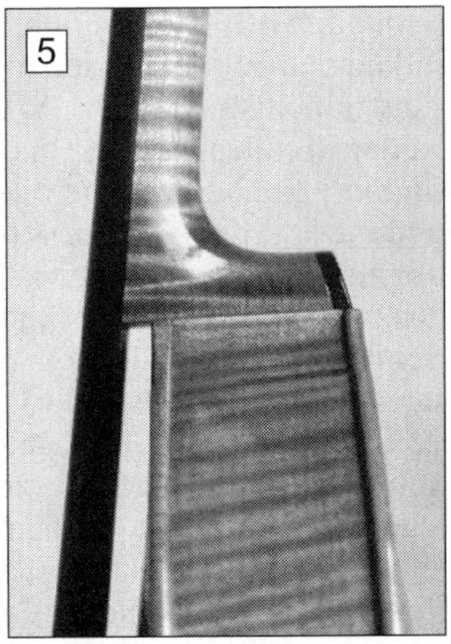

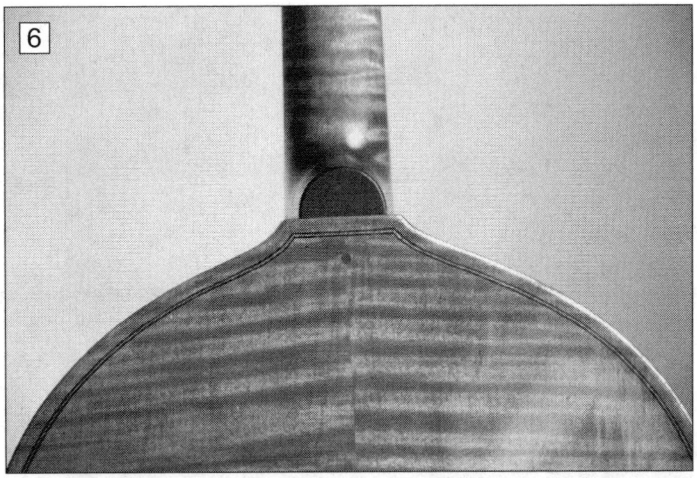

Photos 5 and 6 show the neck as it meets the body of the Evia. Traditionally, the neck is mortised into the end block, making it difficult to reset when the neck needs raising or replacing. The Evia's neck is held in place with a single bolt through the upper block. The simple slide mechanism (**Photos 7 and 8**) allows quick changes in the overstand (and thus the fingerboard height) to accommodate the seasonal changes a wooden top undergoes, and to allow new tops with different arching heights to be tried. An extended Allen key is inserted through the end pin hole in order loosen and tighten the bolt. The bolt itself (**Photo 9**) passes through the block into a threaded hole in a rod set into the neck stock. The design has the advantage of allowing the top and back to be removed easily. The button is not attached to the back, and the neck only minimally interrupts the top.

If one looks at the traditional viola from the vantage point of several centuries of repair and restoration, the vulnerabilities of its structure become clear. The soundpost, critical to the performance of the instrument, is often the locus of serious damage. A crack in the soundpost area will devalue the instrument (even when well repaired), and normal wear and tear often results in dents to the inner surface of the top. This makes soundpost adjustment difficult, and predisposes the wood to cracking.

In order to prevent such damage, we (I work with an assistant, Sharon Que, a superb craftsperson and artist in her own right) tried installing a veneer of maple about .25MM thick in

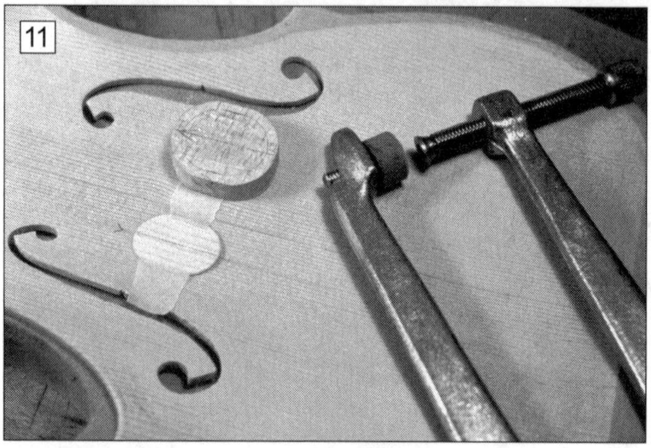

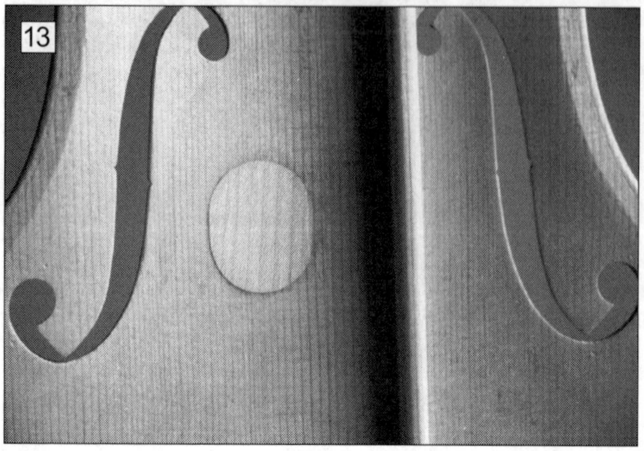

the soundpost area of a violin. It worked so well that we installed one on the wooden top for the Evia, and on all my instruments since then. While developing the idea, I talked with colleagues who had been putting traditional soundpost patches into their new instruments. They found the additional stiffness helped the sound. For those not familiar with the violin world, a soundpost patch is a small oval of spruce set into the top in order to reinforce a repaired crack. If the grain of the patch is rotated a little with respect to that of the top, the top becomes somewhat stiffer across the grain in that area. If you use slightly denser wood, it resists damage better. Because a fair amount of original wood is removed, the operation is nonreversible.

It seemed reasonable, when trying to prevent damage to a new top, to simply glue a veneer on the inner surface. I considered using laminated spruce, parchment, and graphite fiber. In the end I decided on maple. It is denser and harder than spruce and so the post isn't likely to dig in. Unlike graphite fiber, it has about the same rates of expansion/contraction as spruce. We make a veneer of quarter-cut plain maple and trim it to the oval shape traditionally used for soundpost patches, about 23MM by 28MM.

Two methods for installing a soundpost veneer have been used. The first was developed by Sharon Que. **Photo 10** shows a small counterform being fitted to the top using Bondo, a fast-hardening compound used for car body repair. A thin layer of tin foil, held to the top with a little spray-on adhesive, stops the Bondo from adhering to the top. The counterform is simply a piece of ½″ thick maple cut to the same oval shape as the veneer. The bottom surface is scored to hold the Bondo better. The Bondo is mixed and spread onto the counterform, then placed lightly on the top. It spreads easily and makes a very nice cast of that area of the top, drying in about 30 minutes. In **Photo 11**, the veneer has been taped in place (hide glue already applied) and is ready for clamping (**Photo 12**). We found that a counterform was needed only on the inner surface of the top, as long as the other side was adequately padded. Once the glue is dry, the veneer is taken down to a thickness of about .25MM at the center, feathering down to about .1MM at the edges. **Photo 13** shows the finished soundpost veneer, the grain of wood rotated slightly with respect to that of the spruce.

We recently adopted a quicker method for installation, using a vacuum bag. Hot glue is applied to the veneer, which is then lightly taped in place (as in **Photo 11**). The top is put in a thin plastic bag, which is sealed and then evacuated with a vacuum pump. The force of the vacuum produces a very even clamping pressure, with no tendency to distort the top. (More on vacuum clamping later.) Because the pump tends to pull out any moisture along with the air, a clamping time of one hour seems entirely adequate.

I was, for a long time, reluctant to try soundpost veneers because the soundpost area is such a sensitive one acoustically. But the veneer seems to work extremely well from every point of view: soundpost

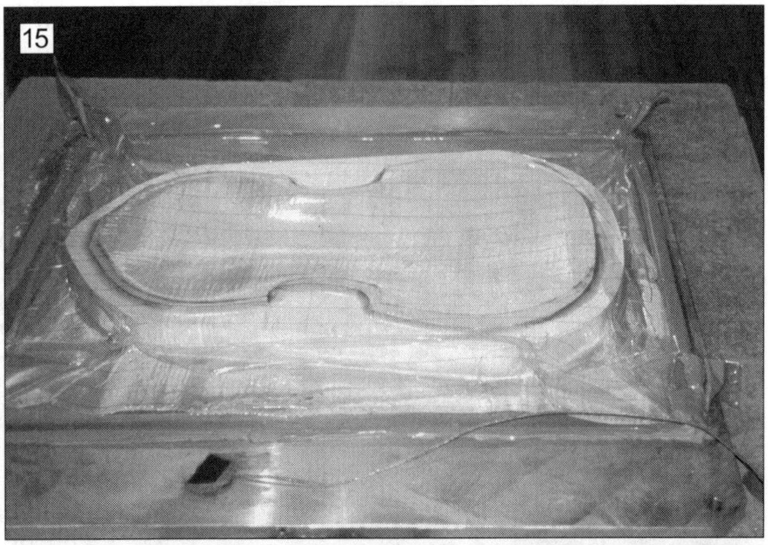

adjustments become easier, wear is reduced, and the acoustical effects seem, if anything, beneficial. And because the veneer can easily be removed, the process is completely reversible.

A number of individuals and companies have experimented in the past two decades with the use of graphite composites for musical instruments. My own experience in the area comes from working with Charles Besnainou, a research scientist and luthier at the *Laboratoire d'Acoustique Musicale* in Paris. In 1985, he began building guitars and lutes using wood veneer, graphite fiber, and acrylic foam. He soon teamed up with violin maker Stephane Vaiedelich to develop composite violin-family instruments. Although Besnainou's methods have been licensed to several large firms intent on mass production, they have the advantage of being well suited to individual craftspersons. The equipment needed can be put together for several thousand dollars, is easy to use, and fits comfortably in a small shop.

Besnainou's system is based on unidirectional graphite fiber, preimpregnated with epoxy resin. It comes in sheets, with a layer of paper on either side of the graphite, making it relatively safe and easy to handle. It can be cut to shape with ordinary scissors (which are gradually ruined in the process!). The paper is peeled off and the graphite, along with layers of acrylic foam and wood veneer (**Photo 14**) is set in a plaster mold. This is placed in a vacuum bag and the air drawn out, forcing the materials to conform to the mold with great precision (**Photo 15**). The whole assembly is then heated to about 280°F for a number of hours. The heat is provided, at least on my setup, by silicone rubber heaters stuck to the underside of a ¾″ thick aluminum plate (**Photo 16**). These heaters came from a science supply catalog and cost about $70 each. They provide extremely even heat distribution, are easy to mount using silicone cement, and four of them cover the 2′-square plate nicely. Together they give 2000w of power, which is about right for a plate that size. (It is important, for proper curing, to be able to bring the mold up to temperature within half an hour.) The heaters can be controlled by a simple thermostat, though I used an electronic temperature controller and a solid-state relay, which does the job more efficiently and accurately (**Photo 17**).

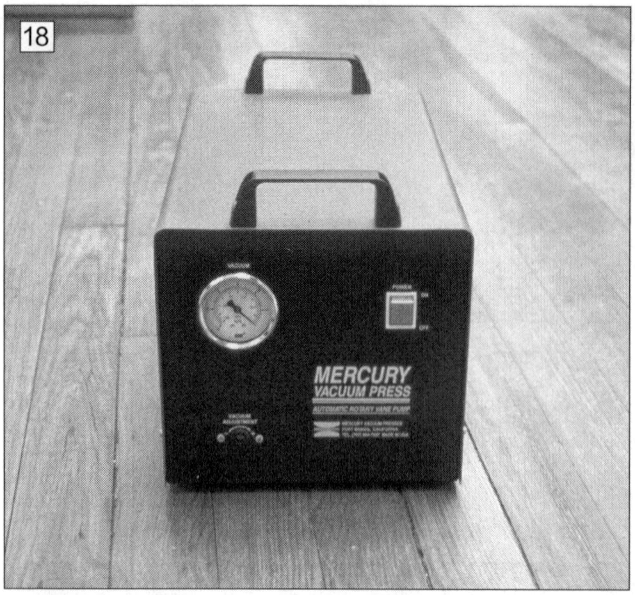

18

Photo 18 shows our vacuum pump, a Mercury model rated at 5 CFM. It has an automatic switch which cycles the pump on and off as needed, maintaining the vacuum at a set level (adjustable with a small screw). For a fuller understanding of the scope of vacuum clamping techniques, there are several good books devoted to their use in veneering furniture.

There are people who worry about the aesthetics of graphite fiber. I don't have any qualms in this regard. It can be covered with wood veneer or some other material. Left exposed, the black contrasts beautifully with wood when the two are used side by side, as in **Photo 19**, a wooden lute by Charles Besnainou with a graphite top. Black also ties in with the violin's frequent accompanist, the piano, and of course the black clothing favored by classical musicians for concert wear.

But why use composites in the first place? There are several advantages and some disadvantages. Graphite is extremely stable in the face of changing humidity, a quality wood can hardly claim. This creates a problem when using it together with wood; the difference in expansion rates, when not accounted for, can create instability. Graphite fiber has an extremely high tensile strength (resistance to stretching), and by sandwiching it over a light core material, stiffness-to-weight ratios not achievable with spruce (the stiffest wood for its weight) are possible. This can be very beneficial for the power and response of the instrument. Tone quality is greatly influenced by the damping of the materials used. Graphite is less damped than maple or spruce (i.e., it will ring longer when tapped), and so optimal damping must be achieved by combining it with core materials that counterbalance it. This is too complex a matter to go into here, but I believe it represents one of the central challenges to be faced in creating first class bowed-string instruments using alternative materials.

I should add that graphite fiber is not cheap. It is difficult to buy in small quantities and costs more than first-class spruce. Furthermore, it has a shelf life — though this can be extended by keeping it in a freezer. But vacuum forming a plate is considerably faster than carving one, and the material's consistency is attractive beside the unpredictability of wood. Many of the characteristics of composites make them suitable for mass production. This, however, is an area with its own set of problems, and not one I am much interested in.

Project Evia is an ongoing one. The wooden prototype, as expected, sounded much like my other violas. I now have a number of composite backs and tops waiting on my bench for trial. Given the limited amount of time I have to devote to such things, I imagine it will take several years before anything resembling a marketable instrument is developed.

There is a saying among material engineers that something rebuilt using composites is badly designed if it ends up looking the same as the original. Every material creates its own design problems and opportunities. The traditional violin evolved closely around the properties of the woods used. It is therefore inevitable, I think, that the adoption of new materials will send instrument design off in new directions. I find this very exciting, and feel fairly sure that successful composite instruments will begin showing up in concert halls within the next decade. I would love to have my label in some of them! ——

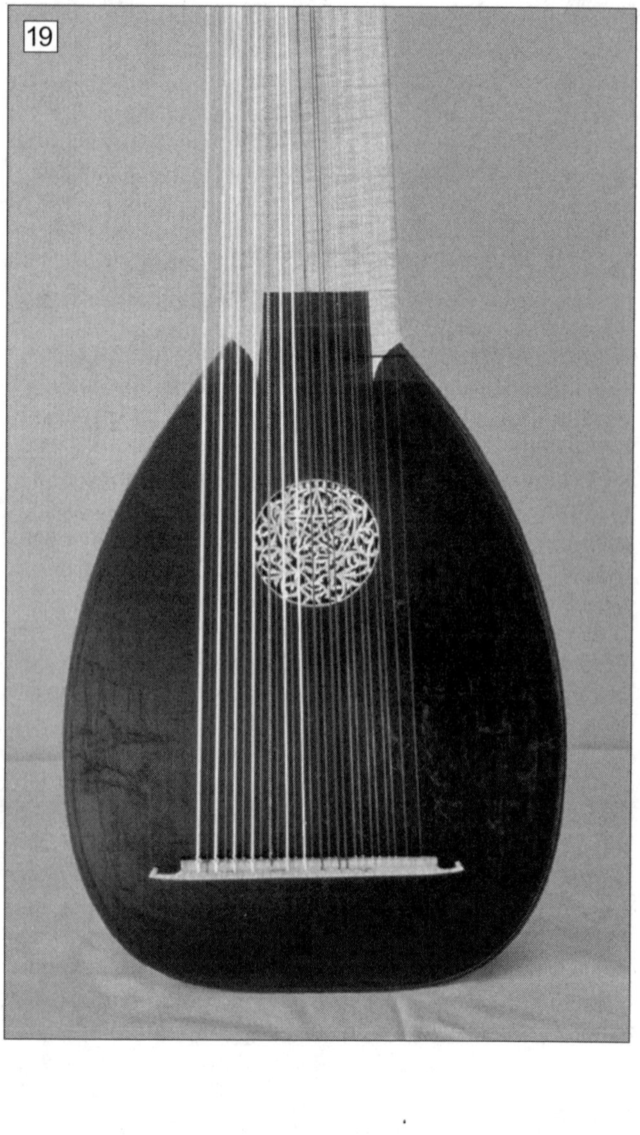

19

Originally published in *American Lutherie #60,* 1999

On the Selection and Treatment of Bracewoods

By Ervin Somogyi

SOME YEARS AGO I got into a discussion with John Gilbert about his method for stiffness testing his bracing woods. Up until then I'd been careful only to use vertically grained material. That was, after all, what everyone had always told me to do, since the very beginning. But I'd not done anything to determine whether any selections of vertically grained woods really were the stiffest. I did know, from previous experience of overbuilding, that you could make things *too* stiff. And, likewise, too loose. So where to draw the line?

I'd had two prior pieces of information about brace wood selection which differed from the imperative to vertical graining that I followed. The first came from a workshop I took in the mid-1970s from Nico Van Der Waals, a highly prominent Dutch luthier who specializes in building and restoring lutes and other early musical instruments. He told us about an interesting learning experience he'd had, in which a client had commissioned him to restore a lute which had been badly damaged. In fact, it was handed to Van Der Waals in the form of the proverbial bagful of broken pieces of wood. In due time, Van Der Waals put the pieces together and handed his client back an instrument which had a lovely and mature sound in spite of the fact that it had been literally broken to pieces for many years and, obviously, not played. Van Der Waals had noticed in the course of this reconstruction that the lute's "J-bar," normally made of vertically cut wood, was in this case perfectly slab cut. This was unusual. And to this factor Van Der Waals attributed a more flexible bass response in the restored instrument than he had thought could be gotten from a lute of that type and size. He said that he was glad he'd paid attention to this detail, because it enabled him to be a more skilled luthier after that. I filed this piece of information away and forgot about it.

The second piece of counter-vertical-grain information came from a *Frets* magazine R&D article by Roger Siminoff, published sometime around 1980. Siminoff had cut brace wood into square stock which was perfectly quartered or slabbed depending on how you oriented it, and subjected these strips to deflection tests. He reported that the slab cut wood was stiffer than the vertically cut wood. I ignored this, and for many years continued to use vertically grained braces.

Anyway, the conversation with John Gilbert started me thinking about the benefits of paying closer attention to one's choices of bracing wood. At the time, I was using brace wood cut from appropriately sized blanks or cutoffs from top wood billets, just as we all do. I dimly knew that some of my braces were from denser, heavier stock than others, and that some were made of tightly grained wood and some weren't, but I wasn't systematic about my bracewood selection or treatment in any way other than to ensure that the braces were vertically grained, period. So here, I thought, was a chance to use wood in a more controlled and intelligent way: selecting on the basis of *stiffness per weight* in addition to orientation of grain.

ALL BY ERVIN SOMOGYI

Ervin Somogi's brace-stiffness tester is made from scraps of MDF, some 1/4″ pins, and a dial-gauge caliper.

John's brace-stiffness tester was simple and ingenious: it made possible a consistent and easy method for assigning numbers to bracing blanks based on their resistance to bending under a weight. Grain count and orientation can be had by simply looking, of course, and density is obtained by dividing the weight by the volume. I made myself a brace tester with some scraps of MDF, some 1/4″ pins, and a dial-gauge caliper. My weight was a metal clamp, as shown in the photo. My method was to place a precisely sized brace into my jig and set my measuring caliper to it to establish the "zero" setting. Then I'd hang the weight on the brace at a set distance from the holding axis and measure the resulting bend in it in thousandths of an inch (rounded off to the nearest .005″). Any child with a post-baccalaureate degree in physics can do this.

As for the woods I was going to test, I picked three blocks of Sitka spruce which are representative of the spectrum of woods I've used for bracing: one was average in mass, one was quite heavy in comparison, and one was quite light. I'm sure you've all had such woods in your hands. Grain count was comparable in each. I wanted to find out how the density, aside from grain orientation, affected stiffness. I still have samples of the original chunks, and I use them as teaching devices when I give workshops. I'm not reporting actual densities of these samples in terms of comparative pounds per cubic foot (or grams per cubic inch, or whatever) numbers. I want to present this experiment in the same hands-on way in which I operate normally, and I consider informal labeling such as "heavy," "average," or "light" to be meaningful if other factors are equal or similar.

I cut a number of bracing samples from each dense, medium, and light plank to as close to .500″ × .250″ as I could. I did the final dimensioning with a Wagner Safe-T-Planer on my drill press: it's a nicely accurate device, and variation was no more than .005″ as measured by dial gauge caliper. I cut braces from each plank into four grain orientations: (A) perfectly vertical, (B) perfectly flat or slab cut, (C) off vertical by 30°, and (D) off vertical by 60°.

I used the woods as they came from the lumberyard. That is, all samples were cut from the plank as purchased, without splitting it or other treatment. No consideration was made for the effect of any runout, other than to note that no sample seemed to have a significant amount of it as determined by a visual check. (As runout would have been present as a constant factor in each block I cut up into braces, and would affect stiffness in a constant way, I believed that I could rule it out as a factor to worry about.) However, because much spruce does have pockets of wider grain right next to areas of closer grain, and because my "average" plank had pronounced examples of this, I did cut wood for columns 2Ba and 2Bb (see below) out of such contrasting pockets, just to get additional data. Otherwise, I made the assumption that the physical properties of the woods tested would hold up and carry over in actual bracing applications regardless of how braces are shaped, scalloped, or tapered. Lastly, all wood samples were free of knots, cracks, conspicuous areas of grain irregularity, or other obvious flaws.

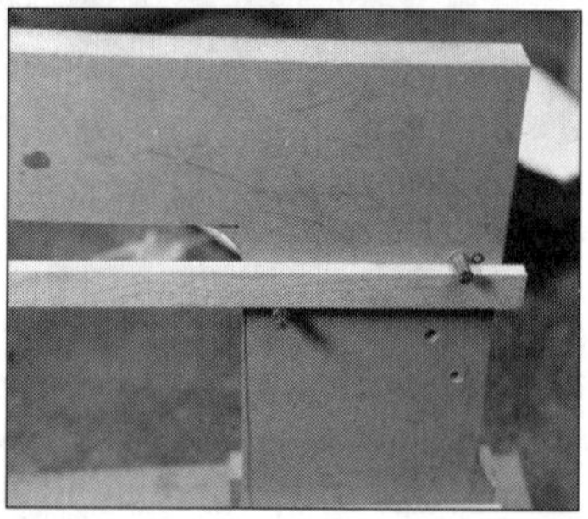

Below are the raw data I collected. The numbers represent deflection measurements in .005″ increments, when the standard weight was placed on the bracing stock and it sagged under the load.

What do these data mean? For one thing, the numbers in each category are consistent with one another to a few thousandths of an inch, so one would think this is a method that does have consistency going for it. The largest spread of readings is on the order of .015″ as seen in columns 1D, 2C, 3A, and 3B. Braces in column 3C were out of consistency by an uncommonly large factor (.035″) compared to other braces, and your guess is as good as mine as to why.

densest wood				medium wood					lightest wood			
1A	1B	1C	1D	2A	2Ba	2Bb	2C	2D	3A	3B	3C	3D
150	150	150	140	180	155	180	150	160	250	230	230	250
155	150	155	150	185	165	170	155	165	260	250	235	250
150	155	145	155	180	165	160	160	155	260	240	235	245
155	155	155	150	190	160	170	150	160	260	240	260	245
150	155		155	190	160	175	155	160	265	245	245	
							170	160	265	230	265	

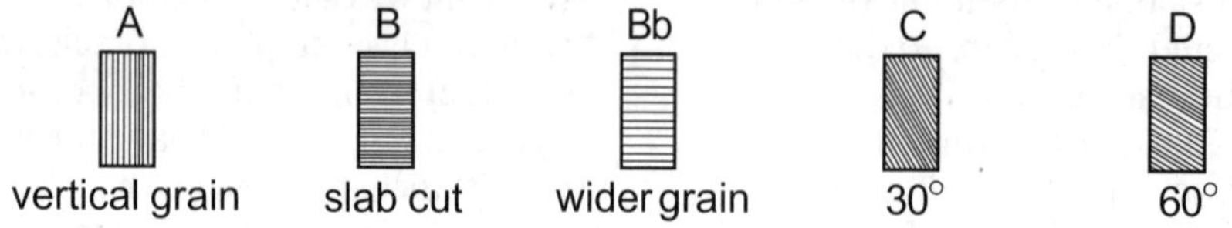

Deflection measurements in .005″ increments. Bracing samples .500″×.250″ in cross section.

The measurements are the distance moved from horizontal resting position under the weight load, and the larger the number, the greater the deflection. That is, the larger the number, the weaker the wood; the lower the number, the stiffer the brace would be.

Measured stiffness in *dense* spruces seems independent of grain orientation, period. *Densest* woods are stiffer than *lightest* woods regardless of grain orientation, evidently in proportion (although I don't know whether in direct proportion) to the difference in densities. I assume this reflects the effect on stiffness of sheer amount of cellulose/structure (as opposed to air) in the wood: the more cellulose the greater both the weight and the stiffness and the more the capacity to resist force.

Measured stiffness in *medium-weight* spruces seems affected by grain orientation. Vertically grained wood seems the least stiff, contrary to popular belief. Density/consistency of grain count in bracewood seems a significant factor, as is proven by the readings in columns 2Ba and 2Bb. The 2Ba braces were cut from a section of that wood in which the grain density was representative of most of that same wood; the 2Bb braces were cut from a wide-grained pocket of that wood. Here, again, I assume that the presence or absence of a threshold amount of wood cellulose is an important factor in determining a wood's ability to resist force.

Grain orientation is a factor in stiffness in the *least dense* woods, also in a manner at variance with traditional wisdom. Here, nonvertical grain has about a 10% greater stiffness than vertical grain, and the more vertical the grain in the brace sample, the less stiff it got.

As these results are surprising, I'd suggest others try this test and double-check my results, and write to this publication about their findings. I have no reason to think my findings were aberrant, although my friends who know my work and methods have all assured me that they wouldn't be surprised by anything I came up with. Still, I feel I was careful in my methodology and measurements, and will stand behind these numbers.

I want to close by saying the obvious: These data are simply a gateway to a way of brace wood selection, not a map as to how to do or use bracing. Since it is actually the *stiffness-to-weight ratio* of a wood (Young's Modulus of Elasticity) which is important, and not simply the weight or stiffness in themselves, one can appreciate that a heavy, stiff wood might have the same modulus/ratio as a lighter, weaker one. Which choice is better? Are small-but-heavy braces better to use than bigger, lighter ones? The answer to this question would take us into areas far afield from the subject of this report and toward, probably, a subsequent article. You might want to corner me at the next convention to have a discussion of the effect of the overall mass of a tone producing system on its behavior, or, in other words, the effect of weight on an ideal of tone. Until then, I leave you to ponder this related question: How heavy is the best woman? ——

Originally published in *American Lutherie #58*, 1999

QUESTIONS

EDITED BY CYNDY BURTON

■ ***Roy Barger of Dayton, TN** asks:*

I'd like to build a vihuela. Do you know where I could obtain a plan?

***Bob Lundberg of Portland, Oregon** answers:*

I do not know of any plan you can order. The one extant vihuela in the Jacquemart André Museum in Paris is not typical of most vihuelas built in the 16th century. Raphael Weisman described it in detail for the *Galpin Society Journal*, Vol. 35 (March 1982) in an article called "The Paris Vihuela Reconstructed." No plan was made available.

You'll find a comprehensive article on the vihuela by John Rollins in American Lutherie #10. *(See* Big Red Book of American Lutherie Volume One, *p. 362.)*

■ ***Sheldon Urlik of Los Angeles, CA** asks:*

In *AL#58 (see p. 366)* Gary Southwell mentions that bird's-eye maple always comes from America, even though one often sees it on very old European-made instruments. Torres used it in several extant guitars, including two in my collection (First Epoch, #24, 1867 and Second Epoch, #129, 1889). Could it be that there are other maples, perhaps ones grown in Europe, which exhibit the bird's-eye figure when slab cut?

***Bruce Harvie of Olga, WA** responds:*

I have not had actual personal experience with harvesting European bird's-eye maple, but I do know that it exists. There are two major species of European maple that are cut for musical instruments, the so-called sycamore (*Acer pseudoplatanus*) which grows all over England and the Continent, and the Balkan maple (*Acer hyrcanum*) which only grows on the Balkan peninsula. I've looked at thousands of pieces of the former and have never once seen bird's-eye characteristics. This leaves the latter species, in which I've seen numerous pieces. I have no idea how common or uncommon it is, but I assume it's as rare as American bird's-eye, which is quite sought after.

American bird's-eye maple occurs in Eastern sugar maple (*Acer saccharum*) only, and is displayed when cut on the slab. For violin making, the general consensus is that bird's-eye maple cut from American trees is too dense and therefore too heavy for violin making. There have been fine instruments made from American bird's-eye, but the general feeling is that it's too heavy. European bird's-eye, on the other hand, is lighter and more in the ball park weight-wise for violin making. In guitar and mandolin making, the issue of weight does not seem to come into play quite as much, so American bird's-eye is heavily valued, and rightfully so. ——

Originally published in *American Lutherie #60*, 1999

Meet the Maker: Bob Gernandt

by John Calkin

I FIRST MET BOB GERNANDT at Merlefest '98, a large folk festival held each year in Wilkesboro, North Carolina, in honor of Merle Watson. The craft fair is a large part of Merlefest, and Bob's booth was a busy one. The crowd can reach near-stampede proportions, with people pointing and grabbing, but Bob stayed cool as he talked to folks, demoed his instruments, and guarded his clutch of creations from harm. Patience like that shouldn't go to waste, so it was only natural he became a luthier. This phone chat followed Merlefest '99.

Where is your hometown of Bryson City?

It's almost at the western edge of North Carolina, near the Great Smokey Mountains. Near Cherokee.

How did you get into lutherie?

My Dad had a dulcimer. I didn't play it much, but when I came down here to work for the Outdoor Center I had an opportunity to buy a kit. I had no information on fret scales or any of that, so a kit seemed like the best introduction to the craft. When I started there was almost no information whatsoever.

When was this?

In 1977. I didn't come across any good information until the mid-'80s. By the time the kit was finished I realized that it wasn't an especially well-made item, that I could do better on my own. My second dulcimer was a copy of the kit, but after that I began changing things around. I made a bunch of them as gifts, then the word got around and I began to sell them. I made dulcimers until a friend requested a guitar, again in the mid-'80s.

That's a pretty good leap.

Yeah. It came out pretty good for a first attempt. It had some problems, but it sounded good and it's still holding up. But I began to change gears when I was introduced to a mystery instrument by the Celtic musicians I was hanging out with. They all played dulcimers, but on their records I began to hear a unique sound made by, as I finally discovered, a bouzouki. Sobel was the only bouzouki builder that I knew of back then, and his instruments were pretty high dollar. I figured that if I couldn't afford to buy one I'd have to learn to make one.

Do you still have it?

ALL JOHN CALKIN

No, I sold it pretty quickly. As soon as the first one was finished I started another for myself, this time an archtop, so the first one became expendable. Number two was the first carved instrument I attempted.

It's unusual to make a bouzouki as your first carved-top instrument.

Again, that was the Stefan Sobel influence. He was my idol. I got hold of the GAL flattop bouzouki plan that Westerman drew and used that for the rough dimensions, then added a carved top and back. I also changed the neck joint. I made a couple more for friends, then began to modify the construction. I was actually more pleased with the sound of the flattop bouzoukis, so I returned to that form of construction. But carving introduced me to mandolin making, and I've carved so many mandolins now that I'm sure I could carve a bouzouki and come up with the sound I want. I love to carve. It's a much slower form of production, but the work is a pleasure. My first mandolin was an F-model, which I still have. I bring it to the festivals, but I've decided not to sell it.

How many instruments do you build per year?

I'd say between eighteen and twenty-five, depending on the mix. More dulcimers means a larger total. More mandolins and the number drops.

At this festival you've got flattop guitars, A- and F-style mandolins, dulcimers, Irish bouzoukis, and citterns (a 5-course bouzouki). How do you decide what to build next?

Up until now I've just been following the sales trail. But the response here at Merlefest has been a slap in the face. I believe I'll stop speculating on dulcimers and only build to order. People like my guitars, but sales have been slow. I'm going to build more mandolins; they've all sold quickly. Mostly, though, I'm going to concentrate on citterns and bouzoukis. That seems to be the most successful niche for me. Darrell Scott plays one of my bouzoukis and is talking about a cittern as soon as we home in on the tone he wants. He's pretty high profile, and he's tried to talk Tim O'Brien into a bouzouki. Al Pettaway is a terrific guitarist who bought both a mandolin and bouzouki from me. I've also hooked up with a store in Washington, D.C. called the House of Musical Traditions, and they said they'll take everything I send them. I couldn't keep a cittern or bouzouki in the place at first.

You use a lot of cedar tops. Do you favor nonspruces?

I actually enjoy redwood as much as anything. The bouzoukis I had at the show in '99 all had cedar tops. The citterns both had redwood. The cedar seems to have a darker, warmer, mysterious element to its tone that sets it apart from other instruments in a band. The citterns are more easily confused with 12-string guitars or even dulcimers. I don't think it's the redwood's fault, though. The citterns are often tuned to an open chord and played with a lot of drones. Players think of them differently than they do bouzoukis.

I love red spruce, too. In Bryson City was a ninety-year-old building made with red spruce beams that were cut out of the national park before it was a park. When the building was demolished the beams were going to be torched, so I asked to have them. Recycling wood isn't very efficient unless the wood is free and you have a lot of time on your hands. There was a lot of loss, but I ended up with plenty of wonderful mandolin tops.

You use a lot of walnut, too.

I love it, but it's more a function of where I live. I can get walnut, maple, and cherry trees for free. I take them to the mill and help the guy saw them up. Only the primo stuff goes into my instruments, but I must have at least a twenty-year supply. Walnut is a wonderful tonewood. And I've got some curly cherry I've been saving — dramatically beautiful stuff. But, you know, people have their minds set. They may rave about the tone of your guitars, but if they aren't made of mahogany or rosewood they'll buy someone else's.

I think it's herd mentality.

I think it's just a fact of life. There's no sense in trying to buck such a strong trend and then getting upset when folks won't buy your goods. It's not a big deal. I only have to keep enough people happy to keep me in business. ——

Facing page: Bob Gernandt talks shop while holding one of his citterns at Merlefest '98.
Left: A Gernandt flattop guitar shares the rack with a cittern and an Irish bouzouki.
Above: Bob holds court during a quiet moment at Merlefest.

Originally published in *American Lutherie #60*, 1999

JOHN CALKIN

TIM OLSEN

Expanding Steel String Design

JOHN CALKIN

JONATHON PETERSON

from their 1998 GAL Convention panel discussion

by Harry Fleishman, Fred Carlson, William Eaton, and Saul Koll

Harry: When asked to assemble this panel, I started looking around for people who I thought would have an interesting variety of views on designing. And designing is not necessarily how things look, designing encompasses many aspects in the same way that guitars have many faces. It's something that evolves. I think that if the guitar came to a point of perfection, it would be very uninteresting at that point for me. I just don't think I'd bother. I believe that if I live a long, healthy life I won't run out of guitar, I won't run out of the impulse to design guitars.

With that in mind, I'll introduce the panel and we'll talk about what drives design and aspects of design. We design what we design for various reasons. We're all very different, and it's fun to see the incredible variety of directions that people take. Some of them are very obvious, some very weird looking, some very conventional looking but with really interesting voices. We'll try and hit on those things.

Saul Koll currently plays in a tribute band to the group Blondie, called Baldie, led by the singer Harry Debbie. The instruments he creates cover the gamut from retro to shocking.

Fred Carlson is known for many interesting instruments including the Sympitar, which is a guitar with sympathetic strings. And sometimes it's great at the end of the day to go into the shop and have the strings understand how things have been.

William Eaton is a founding father of the Roberto-Venn School. William is in the lucky position of having a patron; he has been working for the last ten years for one customer. And that customer is sometimes satisfied and sometimes not, but always loves him. He has built the last ten years' instruments for himself.

William: A cheap but compassionate benefactor.

Harry: This was my first guitar **(Photo 1,** left), and I put this up as an example of what I would call bad design. To me it's not integrated well. This was before I had started thinking in terms of the guitar as a whole, the entire unit. I liked the bridge; I thought it was cool looking and I liked the rosette; I thought it was cool

HARRY FLEISHMAN

HARRY FLEISHMAN

***Photo 1.** Harry Fleishman feels that this guitar from 1974 (left) lacks the design cohesion that he has been striving for in his work. The photo on the right shows how much his thinking had changed by 1992. This design was derived from measurements taken by the customer from ten guitars he liked or disliked. The size and shape then followed from his needs. Designed around a circle, it ended up looking like a Klein with failure-to-thrive syndrome.*

looking. Later on I decided that the shoulders were pretty squared, had a kind of Joan Crawford look. I realized that I was not seeing beyond the guitar as the sum of its parts.

I started looking outside of guitars. Every man-made object suffers or rejoices in its design. Design is unavoidable. One of the things that happens, particularly in a place such as the GAL Convention, is we see a variety of instruments, some of which are fetishly finished. Every little thing, it's all the little details that we're after. I think that some of those details are incredibly interesting and fun. And there's also a place in guitar design for very funky, loose pieces. We may see some of those today and sometimes we'll dismiss them, thinking, "Oh, this person hasn't got their craft together yet." I have a friend who makes really fun instruments whereon the craft is really not particularly together at all. And sometimes I'll ask him about it and he says, "Well, that really isn't what interests me, that's not where I want to be. I'd rather make a whole bunch of things and hear them and play them and just have fun with them." And so some people look at his stuff and they don't get it at all, some other people look at his stuff and they go, "Oh, that's really cool, that's really fun."

And some people are really concerned about modernity, about defining something for the future. Maybe some of the things we think are wacky today will be the things that define the norm in the future. And maybe some of the things that are the norm today will be the things that we look back at as charmingly weird. What will happen when we look back at a Micro-frets, a Teisco, a Regal, or a KayKraft? Those are wacky-ass things, and they're really cool. But what will the future think of them, and what will the future think of our guitars?

Take it away, Fred.

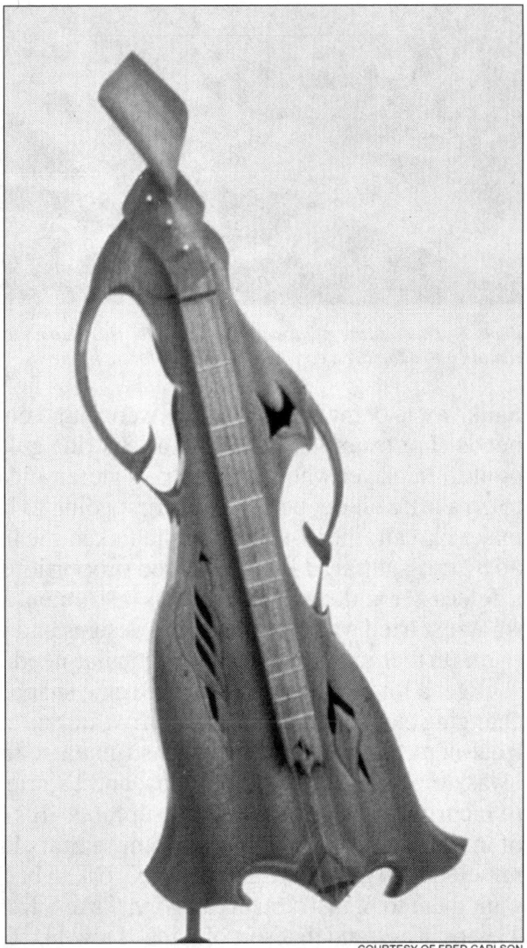

COURTESY OF FRED CARLSON

Photo 2. It ain't square! This dulcimer designed by Ken Riportella is an example of the design style to which Carlson was first exposed.

Fred: My earliest influence was a wild young artist named Ken Riportella, who is not building anymore as far as I know. Ken summed up his design philosophy in four words, "Why make it square?" And my interpretation of that is if you're going to invest a large amount of your person, time, and energy in the creation of something, why not start out with an open mind and consider all the possibilities available to you and be conscious of the choices you make. This doesn't necessarily mean doing something weird or nontraditional; and having an open mind doesn't necessarily mean that your brain has fallen out. Be aware of the choices you make and the limitations they impose on you. I think the essence of any design project could be looked at as choices and limitations.

Photo 2 is of one of Ken's Appalachian dulcimer sculptures from the early 1980s, and it's a really good example of the treatment of the entire instrument as a piece of sculpture. Everything in that is part of the visual sculpture and the tactile sculpture.

How did it sound? It sounded good. You can do an awful lot to an Appalachian dulcimer and still have it sound good. And he made up all sorts of wonderful strange stuff about the acoustics of it. I'm not sure if he believed it or not, but it was wonderful stuff that he came up with.

From Ken I got this sense, this wonderful permission to free myself from some of the limits set by tradition, and to make my own choices using my creative intuition as it developed. And later, while studying guitar building with Charles Fox, I learned very simple, elegant techniques for designing a guitar from scratch and making it work. Over the years I've taken numerous side trips, little journeys off the guitar building highway into all sorts of wonderful bizarre things. Viola da gambas, marimbas, a bunch of very strange xylophones, Javanese gamelon instruments, thumb pianos, flutes, whistles, percussion, all sorts of things. Sometimes instruments were instigated by commission. I would build a viola da gamba for somebody for $200 or $300, or whatever it was. And learned how to do it. And all these things, all these excursions deepened my knowledge and experience in ways that I now find just incredibly useful in building. What I do now, mostly, is build custom instruments for very brave people who come to me with some kind of vision of what they'd like created. Recently though, I've found myself wanting to get back to a place where I could spend more of my time making instruments purely of my own envisioning. I have all that accumulated experience to draw from, but I also have a waiting list of commissions to build for people, so I have to content myself with the challenge of making my customer's visions into designs that work for me as well.

ALL THIS PAGE BY SAUL KOLL

Photo 3. This 8-string guitar based on the Telecaster shape was Koll's first venture into adapting a conventional design to suit his needs.

Saul: Some of my earliest designs were based on players' needs. For example, **Photo 3** is an 8-string guitar that I built for a player who had a 7-string guitar and wanted to go a little bit deeper. He was first going to have me make him another 7-string, but he talked me into trying an 8-string guitar. I kind of moved proportions around a Telecaster and came up with this instrument. But what it started was taking existing designs and pushing them further in order to suit a particular need.

I get a lot of mileage out of the same shape. By changing elements such as pickguards and surface treatment I create entirely new instruments. In college I was doing sculpture and painting, and I started trying to incorporate sounds into my sculptures. It's all kind of intertwined at this point. With my guitars I give myself a very narrow framework to work in because I want them to fit in a certain category. I like Silvertones, Tiescos, Kays, and that sort of thing. I also like Gibsons and Gretschs. I want my guitars to fit in that same realm. I want people who play vintage guitars to buy my instruments as well. I like vintage instruments, but often they're old and have problems, so I create a new instrument that looks and feels like an old instrument. A player who feels more comfortable playing an older instrument can have a brand new instrument that will hang in there for him. I feel more comfortable getting out my deeper thoughts and looser feelings through my painting and sculpture. I try to do them at the same time. I find it much easier to sell my guitars than my art. The art is a part of me that I haven't really brought to my guitar making. There's a little bit of humor in my guitar designs, but I haven't turned myself loose. I don't know what I'll be doing in five years, but I assume I'll be getting the art and the instruments closer and closer.

Photo 4 is a guitar that I've been working on lately. A player came to me who wanted a 7-string Klein guitar. He knew I made 7-string guitars and he wanted a Klein design. He liked the way the Klein sat on his leg and the angle of the neck and how that fit in his hand. But he couldn't find a 7-string version of that, and the bridge was a tremolo he didn't need. He wanted more of a jazz guitar. He normally plays a big archtop guitar. So I thought, "Well, I can make a 7-string Klein guitar. Sure I can try that." But then I got to designing this thing and thinking about how it would just look wrong on this guy, and I decided to incorporate some of the archtop thing to it, with the *f*-hole and that. So I've been trying to put these two things together, and maybe this shows the marriage of those two aspects of my life, the very conservative traditional guitar shape combined with looser organic shapes. It's a growth process. I've made eight or nine of these, and all are a little bit different. I refine this and I refine that.

I typically don't really care for the super-fancy exotic wood. I think it's beautiful, but in my designs I tend to use more of the plain woods. I will usually paint my guitars. I color them; I seriously alter the wood so it doesn't matter how much figure is in it. I tend to use figure in the same way that Ford would use chrome or something like that, where it's just kind of an embellishment. Although on this particular instrument **(Photo 5)**, I had such nice wood that I decided to orient it in a slightly different way. I split matched it rather than bookmatched it, so the flare goes out to kind of make it look like a fan. But this is not very typical of what I do. I tend to like to control every aspect and be real tight with my surface treatment. I just feel more comfortable being able to manipulate every aspect. I don't like people to recognize what it was I started with. I think wood is beautiful but I don't like to have to rely on that. I like to be able to buy another piece of plain mahogany or maple and be able to finish it and put my colors on it and so forth.

Photo 4. This guitar is Koll's cross between a Klein solidbody and a conventional 7-string archtop jazz guitar.

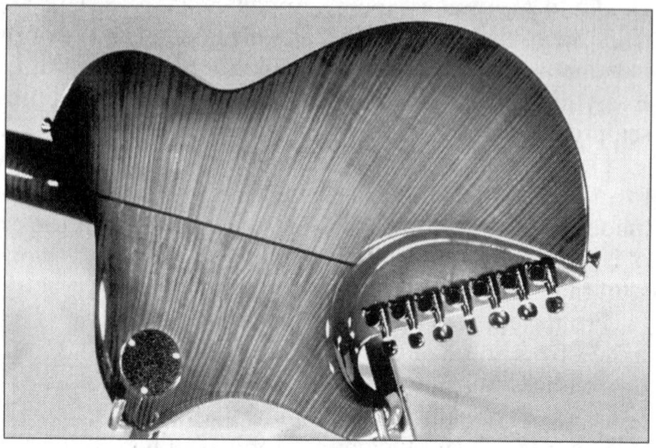

Photo 5. Koll elected to arrange the grain structure of this guitar back in a dramatic fashion that didn't involve bookmatching.

ALL THIS PAGE BY WILLIAM EATON

Photo 6. John Roberts, Eaton's first teacher, holding a double neck he built in 1980. All woods and stone inlays used are symmetrically bookmatched. Eaton considers this to be a model of fine design.

William: For me design is a way of life. It's an art, a mystery, an unending mystery. Each moment reveals some part of the mystery and it just continues on and on, a sequence of nows. The act of awareness itself is part of the design process. I should add that the people on this panel are influences, just as many of you sitting here today are inspirations to what goes into the work that I do. Just coming to an event like this, you gather up so many ideas. The students and faculty at Roberto-Venn are the people with whom I collaborate and work every day — all of whom inspire my work. There are lots of people from the past who have inspired me as well.

Here is a double-neck acoustic steel string guitar (6- and 12-string) that John Roberts built (**Photo 6**). To me this instrument is the epitome of symmetry and figured-wood selection. All of the wood used, including quilted mahogany back and sides, Nicaraguan rosewood sculptural overlays, flamed redwood top, mahogany necks, and ebony fingerboards are bookmatched. All of the stone inlay (turquoise, verasite, azurite) used on the fingerboard and the half-circles (turquoise) surrounding the body of the guitar are bookmatched pieces as well.

I have designed instruments to suit my own needs as a musician. This is a 16-string burl-maple lyre. The bridge is placed at $\frac{2}{3}$ of the string length, allowing octave pitches on each side of the bridge (**Photo 7**).

Photo 8 is the instrument I call a Spiral Clef. The geometry expressed within the circle (between bridge and fingerboard) was partially serendipitous. The

Photo 7. Eaton's 16-string lyre can be played above and below the bridge. Small triangle wedges at the base are moved to adjust intonation.

Photo 8. Eaton's Spiral Clef design evolved from sketching variations on a treble (G) clef.

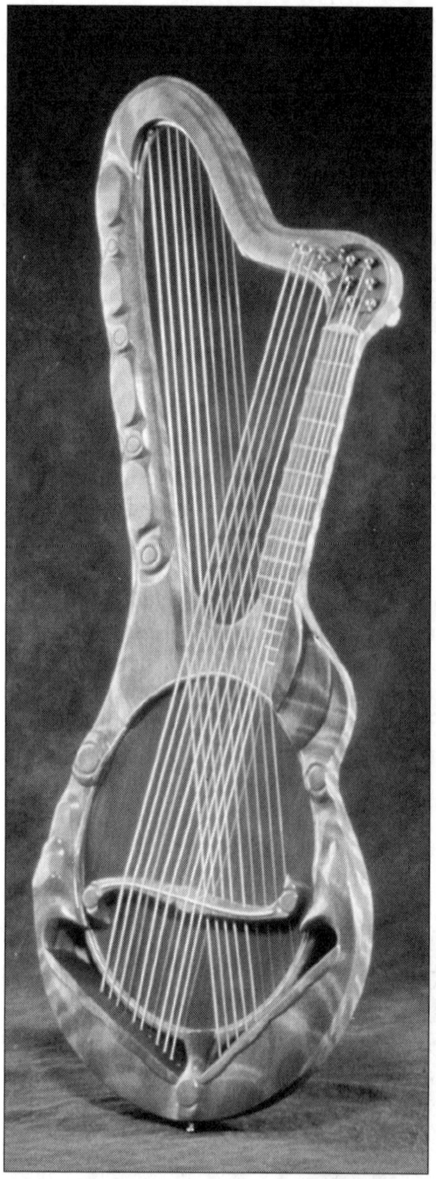

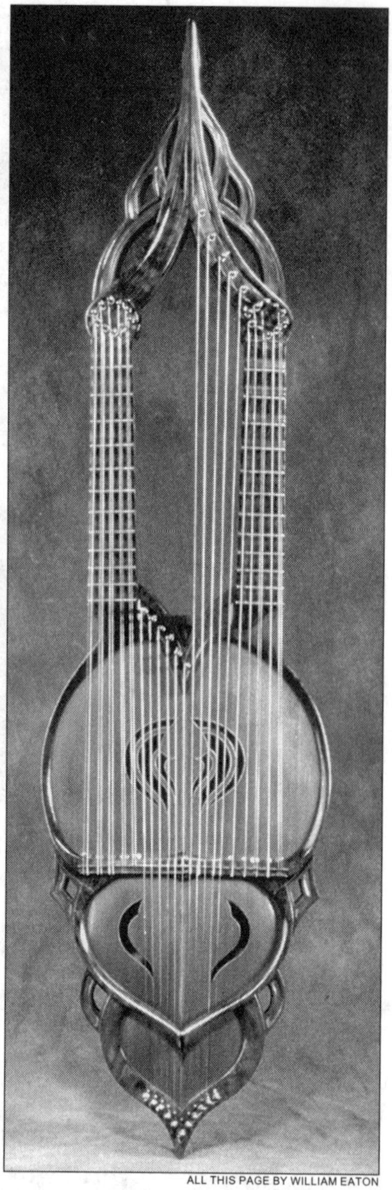

Photo 9 (left). This instrument of quilted birch was Eaton's first harp guitar.
***Photo 10** . The 26-string guitar has a 12-string guitar neck with unison courses (higher octave). Two additional sets of 7 strings attach to the body.*
***Photo 11** (right). An O'ele'n Strings.*

ALL THIS PAGE BY WILLIAM EATON

triangle, diamond, and star shapes were created by joining the lines made from iron-load pickup bars (placed under each set of strings) with ⅛″ brass stock. The four pickups are hand wound using an old sewing machine motor that Bob Venn rigged up. The overall design began as a treble-clef symbol, which was then modified by sketching through a number of variations.

This is my first harp guitar **(Photo 9)**. The strings are actual folk and concert harp strings. The frets, bridge saddle, and nut are made from elk antler that I found in the Rocky Mountains of Colorado.

Photo 10 is my first multistring instrument, a 26-string guitar that I call an Elysian Harmonium. I was studying Sufi mysticism and Eastern Indian mythologies when I designed and built it. This instrument is a variation on themes of the lotus petal or tear-drop-shaped forms in the Taj Mahal and other Indian art and architecture. You can see variations in the body design, head stock, oval soundhole, bridge, and tailpiece that reflect this shape. The additional soundholes to the left and right of the oval soundhole are symbolic shapes representing the principle masculine and feminine dualities. Their placement on the soundboard allows them to witness the sound and vibration that emanate from the body cavity or symbolically, the "void from within and without."

I've named this double-neck instrument an O'ele'n Strings (pronounced oh-aye-len) **(Photo 11).** The name derives from two words: octave and eleven. Octave in that it was the eighth instrument I've built, and eleven, a recurring number in the dimensions of the instrument (i.e., 22″ scale length — 11″ to the 12th fret, 11″ body width, eleven panels make up the sculpted back of the instrument, eleven courses of strings on each symmetrical side of the center of the instrument, and so on). The shapes found in this instrument reflect the mathematical expression of how plant leaves grow in logarithmic growth spurts. These same mathematical parallels are found in most organic growth patterns. The design for the O'ele'n Strings began by observing a shape/symbol on an armoire. This shape was traced onto paper and variations evolved from the original circle-and-arches

WILLIAM EATON

Photo 12. Eaton's lyraharp guitar was initially inspired by the bow harp, a smaller version of the musical hunting bow that evolved into the berimbeau and other related stringed instruments that use attached cavities made of gourds, coconuts, and other natural materials. The four instruments on these two pages are shown in proper size relationship to each other.

symbol. The strings above and below the bridge are playable. The fretboards are scalloped to make it easier to bend string pitches, similar to the Indian sitar.

The design of the lyraharp **(Photo 12)** began with the simple bow harp or shaman's bow.

Harry: The driving forces behind design can be aesthetic, a personal goal for an instrument, a spiritual goal, or a need of a customer. It's interesting to see how on the one end Saul's taking a kind of post-modern approach of combining ideas but he's doing it in a specific, defined framework so as to be able to reach a certain kind of an audience or to be able to please or satisfy certain needs of certain musicians. If you are your only customer, you can take a different route. If your purpose is to come up with sight gags then you can design guitars around humorous elements like dovetails. If your customers come to you with weird needs that you've never satisfied, then your design elements can lead you to learning something new in order to satisfy what they need.

***Dan Auerbach:** I've been overwhelmed by some of Fred's incredible creations, but I'd like to hear from all of you your thoughts on integrating your artistic view with considerations of acoustics.*

Fred: It depends on what it is you're trying to do acoustically, obviously. And that depends on the reason that you're building the instrument. Are you building the instrument for yourself? Are you building it to sell to a market? Are you building it for a specific customer? I often start very visually and then reconcile the acoustics to what I want to do visually. That's a broad generalization. I always know, in the back of my mind, what it is that the particular project needs acoustically, and so that's there kind of feeding the visual stuff. You start out with choices and limitations, like I said earlier. So I have some ideas, I figure out what the limitations are, and I go with that. The acoustics are affected by so many different factors. I'm limited in what I can do visually or artistically by acoustic considerations, no question about that.

Harry: If I'm working for a customer, I'm really trying to learn what that customer needs musically for the way they play and the voice that they are imagining. Most of you have probably gone through that process and know that it's very, very difficult to get inside somebody else's head and hear, to visualize or auralize what it is that they're hearing. But over time I've found that it has gotten easier. I have a very specific voice that I'm after and so that drives everything I'm trying to do, and if a customer comes to me for a guitar that I can't satisfy with the voice that I find interesting, I'll send them to someone else. I may do less of that; if I run out of orders I'll start taking everything.

The visual aspects always follow, for me, after I've come up with what the voice is that I'm interested in. My asymmetric guitars **(Photo 13)** to me are very logical because I was trying to keep a very even response from string to string but increase the depth of the bass response. Not make a louder bass, make a deeper bass. The thinking behind it was to expand the bass side, compress the treble side, loosen it up in areas where I could loosen it, and tighten it up where I could tighten it to keep the same basic voicing that I had, but to kind of slightly tilt the contour a little bit; but it's the voice that drives the design.

That's a mixture of redwood and spruce and people ask about it. It's a very subtle tone control element; it's not a big thing. You can do the same thing with two different

HARRY FLEISHMAN

Photo 13. After a five-year retirement, Fleishman's design was more playful, better integrated, and more personal. This asymmetrical style of work is representative of Fleishman's current work.

pieces of spruce that have different tonal characteristics or any things you chose that appeal to you timberally. Aesthetically, people find it kind of striking, which is good if you want people to remember you, but if it were two different pieces of spruce that I really liked and they had the qualities I was after, I would choose them. And it's not a matter of bass/treble, I want to make that clear. It's not a left/right stereo thing. You could probably put them in stripes even; the effect would be different. So if you start doing that and you have a reason for doing it, call me and let me know how it sounds.

William: It is helpful to learn about the traditional evolution of guitar making and how the integration of art and acoustic theory have influenced that evolution. This helps to form a foundation for understanding contemporary design and serves as a point of departure for innovation. This study includes becoming aware of what is available in the marketplace, the sound and aesthetic characteristics incorporated into various designs, and what people's expectations are: kind of a collective consciousness of the contemporary guitar sound and structure.

When designing instruments I intend to play myself, it starts with sound. The form and aesthetics grow organically from this sound contemplation. It is an intuitive approach. When I imagine achieving an audibly definable acoustic sound, certain shapes, cavity volumes, materials, string lengths, and other factors present themselves. I would say that this intuition comes directly out of an experiential base gathered by examining and playing all sorts of different stringed instruments. I would also say that this process for me is very much a boundary-dissolving activity. It's a meditation. Designing and building become a vehicle for me to express the art in life.

Saul: Yeah, what he said!

About 95% of my work is commissioned. Customers generally have very specific ideas of what they want. They play a certain kind of music, and they expect a certain kind of sound. If I go outside of that sound then I'm not going to sell that instrument; they're not going to be happy with it. I'm trying to make guitars within that framework. Some of my favorite times are on those other instruments that are not commissioned, that I'm just doing purely for the fun of it and for my own pleasure. I'm manipulating the wood, choosing this wood instead of this wood. And bracing it this way instead of that. And having the thing around my shop for awhile. That's what I enjoy, but with my commissioned solidbody and semi-solidbodies and that kind of stuff, the customer is pretty much buying the shape and a kind of traditional sound. I'm pretty conservative when it comes down to the design, and I'm trying to break out of that.

***Audience:** When you're designing string lengths, is that intuitive or are you calculating the tuning that you're going to have ahead of time, and calculating the compensation and clang tones and that kind of thing? What's the balance there? Or is it random, sometimes intuitive and sometimes calculated?*

William: I know all of us have worked with different string lengths. The vibrating string length informs all elements of the design process. It is possible to calculate string tensions and get an idea of pitch and tone information from quantifiable methods. I have relied more on

BOTH THIS PAGE BY SAUL KOLL

These photos show Koll's willingness to work within popular styles.

intuitive direction. Early on, I started playing a lot of different instruments with different kinds of strings and string lengths. Also, I've invested some time in studying the evolution of strings and the various materials used in strings. This has given me some background for what kind of pitches will result and what kind of tone and sound characteristics result from the use of different materials, gauges, and string lengths. Of course, strings cannot be studied in a void. It's all interdependent upon structural materials, cavity dimensions, soundboards, bracing, and so on. When I begin to imagine a new instrument, all of these elements come into view simultaneously, rather than designing string lengths in isolation, for example. I usually don't have a particular tuning scheme in mind, but I do envision the string lengths that will allow the pitch ranges I'm after. I have used this envisioning process for all of the multistringed instruments I've built.

Fred: I've learned a lot in the last couple years working with string makers. I've had to work through the whole process of having custom strings made because I built an instrument thinking one thing was going to work and then it absolutely didn't. We had to start all over again and start with what's going to work for this string for the sound the customer wants. The customer got the instrument and whoa! What do you do with a 6-string, nylon-string bass? A new instrument can inspire new musical ideas, so a customer may not even know what he wants to play on a double-neck guitar (for instance) until he's had it awhile. When he figures that out, it may require different strings than you initially designed for. And then he begins to figure out what the kind of sound balance could be, and you start all over again.

You start out with some ideas, and certainly you have to start out with the string length, and you try to approximate what the tension is going to be, what kind of strings you're going to use so you know how to brace appropriately. Everything is based on that. In fact, the beginning of any of my designs is a straight line down the middle of a piece of paper with the string length marked on it. They pretty much all start that way. So the string length is very important.

***G.D. Armstrong:** Are your designs taken all the way on paper and then built that way or do they change in the building process from what you've come up with originally on the paper?*

BOTH THIS PAGE BY FRED CARLSON

With Carlson's Pinwheel guitar (left and above), the upper-bout shoulder and cutaway as well as the soundhole and fingerboard inlay motifs are based on sections of the same circle. This device helps to add visual cohesiveness. The Pinwheel features a unique "layered" top-bracing design in which radial struts are glued to the soundboard; a second, transverse layer of braces is glued to the backs of the radial struts; and longitudinal struts are glued to the backs of the transverse layer.

Saul: On custom instruments, I do everything I can on paper first. I'll start with a centerline and fingerboard templates that I've made out of acrylic, so it goes rather quickly. I can lay out on paper what I think I'm going to make, then cut out the paper and show it to the customer. If he's interested in it on paper, I have a start. But it changes incredibly when it's in 3D, when it's off the paper and not flat anymore. If it's something I really like I'll make a new template from it. Sometimes it's easier to sand a fair curve than it is to cut or draw one.

Fred: I'm very good at three-dimensional visualization, so I will often see something in my head very completely, certainly before I build it. But I pretty much always have every element of it designed and on paper to get all the possible problems worked out. I never do, but I try and anticipate as much as I can. There are some little carvings or inlay things that may be added later.

My partner Suzy Norris, who makes wonderful, unusual sympathetic-string violins, works completely differently. She actually makes a mold. I don't usually work with a mold, so that's different. But she's very free form about it, she doesn't like to draw everything out. She has a basic drawing that she starts with, but then it just all kind of develops. It works that way, too.

Harry: I'll build a new instrument in my head and play it for awhile to try and figure out what's working and what's not. Then I'll draw it. If it's for a customer, I'll send a blueprint. If it's for me, I'll usually just dive in; it will evolve as I'm going. But if it's for someone else, I think they have to have a say about it. I'll sometimes call them up and tell them, "It's not going to be what I told you. Here's what it's going to be instead," and see if they buy into that. I'm real manipulative.

William: Visualization is my primary tool. It almost always precedes the drafting process. I really appreciate what Harry said about building and playing the instrument in your head. Audio images are important to the visualization experience. I go through the process of imagining everything three dimensionally, miniaturizing myself, and going all the way around the work, checking out the angles, all the planes, all the sculptural details. In order to examine alternative possibilities, I find myself going through morphing exercises, similar to what's available on computer animation software. Imagine, for example, a dreadnought shape morphing into a jumbo shape, through a multiplicity of forms. My designs usually evolve in this fashion. Beginning with one form I'll imagine all kinds of permutations that become choices for the selection of the final form.

At some point sketching becomes an integral part of the process. Sometimes sketching or doodling is the catalyst for getting into an initial idea. I usually begin with smaller sketches. I might make twenty or thirty of those to flesh out the ideas I'm visualizing. Then I go to full-scale drawings, and I might go through three to six of those before I come to a final drawing. The last one has erasing all over it from moving and morphing the lines. From the final drawing I create any templates, molds, or jigs I will need. Once the building process begins, there may be additional design changes to make.

Whether it's designing a headstock or a bridge or an entire instrument, I try to imagine every construction process that will follow, the sequential nature of how these materials are going to be put together, what carving or sculpting I will do, and what kind of lamination or joinery techniques to use. However, when I begin to work with the actual materials I often confront something I haven't considered or visualized. One piece of wood may inspire a whole new shape or design direction, right from that point. One small change can affect everything. It's kind of like a chess game where you have to imagine how one play will affect everything else in the whole spectrum of moves, or in this case, construction processes. So it continues, this process of looping and revising. I guess time is the real determining factor in finalizing the decision-making process. ——

FRED CARLSON

Carlson's 30-string "Guitarangi da Gamba" was designed to meet a customer's request for an instrument that could be plucked or bowed, combining aspects of Sympitar, viola da gamba, and East Indian sarangi.

Originally published in *American Lutherie #60*, 1999

Meet the Maker: David Santo

by Todd Novak

DAVID SANTO, like John Henry, was born with a hammer in his hand. Descended from a long line of furniture makers, watchmakers, and craftsmen in Budapest and Prague, he prides himself in the Old World craftsmanship he has been taught since boyhood. Following in his family's tradition, Dave believes that tremendous skill and a strive for perfection are necessities in the lutherie trade.

In the '60s, Dave first applied his inherited skills to finishing instruments for guitar shops in Greenwich Village in New York City. He worked for repairmen and builders such as Matt Umanov and Michael Gurian, eventually becoming a builder himself. In time, Santo and Gurian became partners and formed Gurian Guitars. Some of their first guitars built went to customers such as John Sebastian, Richie Havens, and Bob Dylan. During this time, Dave also worked for Bill Lawrence manufacturing pickups, and he also helped design the prototype for Dan Armstrong's clear-plastic guitar. Eventually Gurian and Santo parted ways, dissolving their partnership but remaining friends.

Dave then set out on a nomadic life that led him to Hawaii and to Southern California. There he worked for Earthwood helping to develop the first acoustic bass guitar, and was a consultant and builder for many of the major guitar companies of that era. He also experimented with ideas such as Teflon coated guitar strings and truss rods. Dave then began building guitars under his own name, which, keeping true to his high standards, were designed to stand the test of time. Finally settling in Costa Mesa, California, he opened his own guitar repair shop where he developed innovative guitar designs such as the Ionic Microtonal Guitar with forty-four frets.

After many successful years, Dave disappeared from the world of lutherie and returned to his native New York State. He now owns and runs a successful dock-building business and has a plumbing invention on the market. He lives in an idyllic lake-side community in the Hudson Valley with his wife Jackie, an architect, and his two sons, Jacob and Julian.

I first met Dave when he came in to my friend Vic Schwarz's guitar shop in Cold Spring, New York. His knowledge of instruments, combined with his metaphysical and cerebral comments made him a fascinating character. I was surprised when Vic told me later that day that Dave was one of the most respected luthiers in the business some years back. I had been studying lutherie in my spare time when I came across a Bay State Ditson parlor guitar (actually owned by Artie Traum). It needed a neck reset and other repairs that I absolutely would not attempt myself. I called Dave, who, out of respect and love for the workmanship of 19th century parlor guitars, agreed to do the work. It was the beginning of our friendship, and of my lutherie training. Dave is an incredible teacher, a perfectionist, a mystic, or, as I call him, my "Guitar Yoda."

TODD NOVAK

David Santo playing one of his own guitars.

Recently, my wife Jasmine got accepted to U. C. Berkeley, and we moved from New York to California. Dave helped me land a job working for his longtime friend Marc Silber in Berkeley. It's a gas working for Marc and we often talk (and laugh) about our friend Dave, and hope he returns to California someday. I can no longer drive through the mountains to Dave's for lutherie sessions, a quick swim, or to play a little guitar, but my friendship and schooling with Dave is ongoing. I now get my lutherie questions answered by telephone or via the Internet.

Les Paul once said that no matter how old you are or how long you live, there's always something slightly out of reach that you strive for. When I get frustrated, I try to remember those words. And then I call Dave. ——

Originally published in *American Lutherie #60,* 1999

Refret with David Santo

by Todd Novak

DAVE SANTO agreed to go through a refret with me on a Style-0 Favilla from the '50s. This guitar had no binding and close to no frets left at all. After checking for structural problems, we were on our way.

Before we started, I copied a few refretting jigs that Dave had made in the '60s so that I could proceed from my home shop. Included were a neck jig with Dunlop capos and a wing-nut attachment for swinging the guitar out for access from every angle (**Photo 1**) and a screw-in body rest (on the right in **Photo 2**). Dave stressed the importance of keeping tools sharp, clean, and square. Well-cared-for tools can last a long time. Dave's fret files have been used on hundreds of guitars.

He started by demonstrating fret filing on the old beat frets, using a guard over the body of the guitar (**Photo 3**). He has an old metal guard with felt on the underside. I use plexiglas.

With the guitar in the neck jig and at a comfortable height, Dave started removing frets. He held the removal tool firmly against the fretboard to prevent the fingerboard from chipping as each fret's tang was pulled out of its slot (**Photo 4**). Using this "squeeze method," he took one half-inch bite at a time. He explained that starting the end nippers under the end of a fret was the hardest part of the routine, and that one should take an even smaller bite there, holding the tool perfectly flat. I then removed the rest of the frets. Dave's sense of humor and knowledge of all aspects of building and repair were very inspiring.

Dave pointed out that the fret slots were very shallow. He measured them with standard automotive feeler gauges. The neck was pitted from being played with very worn frets (**Photo 5**). Dave suggested that we should get rid of the zero fret and make a new nut.

Putting on our dust masks, Dave showed me how to straighten out the fingerboard using a flat stone and sandpaper, while still leaving a little radius. He then explained how to repair minor fingerboard damage by mixing a little ebony or rosewood dust with glue or epoxy, and then filling the scars and cavities in the fingerboard with this mixture. Dave also explained how to lightly sand the patched areas level to match the rest of the fingerboard.

ALL BY TODD NOVAK

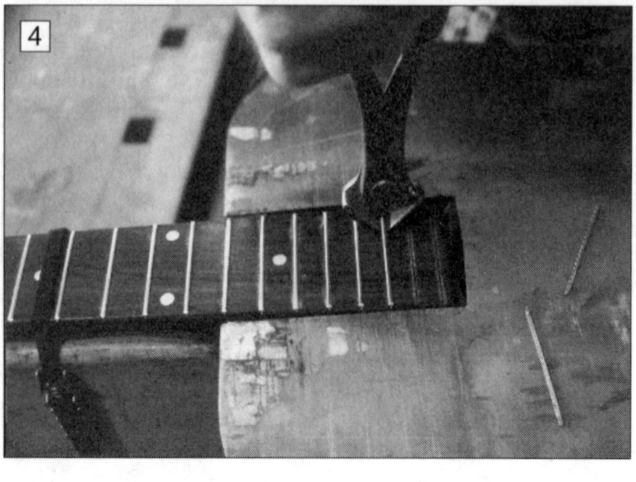

5

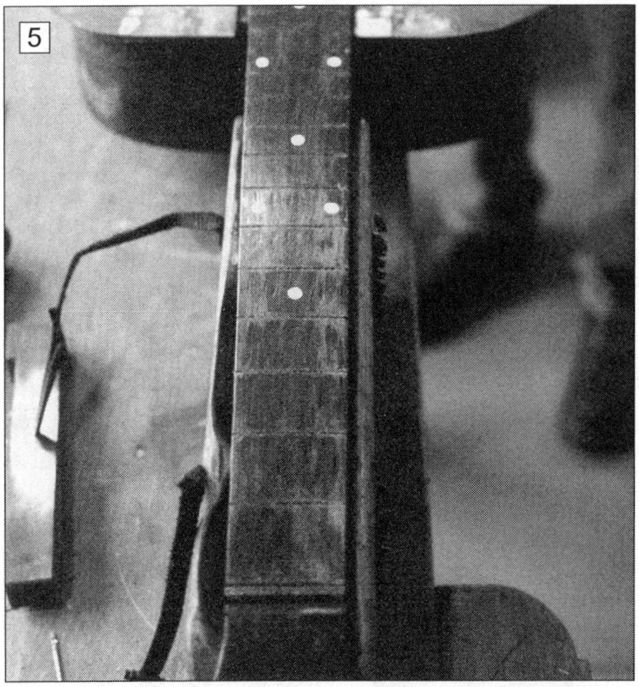

6

7

We popped out the nut and zero fret (**Photo 6**) and continued flattening the neck surface using 80-grit sandpaper and an oilstone (**Photo 7**). The neck had a small bump in the middle and no truss rod, so we took it down by hand. We then used a straightedge to check the neck from the nut area to the 12th fret (**Photo 8**). Dave explained, "If it had a truss rod, we'd loosen it and spring the neck, then retighten it just so the fretboard had a tiny high spot in the middle."

We continued flattening the fingerboard, keeping a slight radius and checking for relief with the straightedge. We then switched from the stone and 80-grit paper to a cabinet scraper to remove a little isolated mass from a small high spot. "OK, we're getting close," Dave advised. "Just a little more with 100-grit and the stone." Riding the straightedge over the crest of the radius, we noticed there was still a slight bump. A little more 100-grit sandpaper and we had it (**Photo 9**). It was time to approach the actual fretting. By my request, we decided to do it the old fashioned way, with a tried-and-true hammer.

8

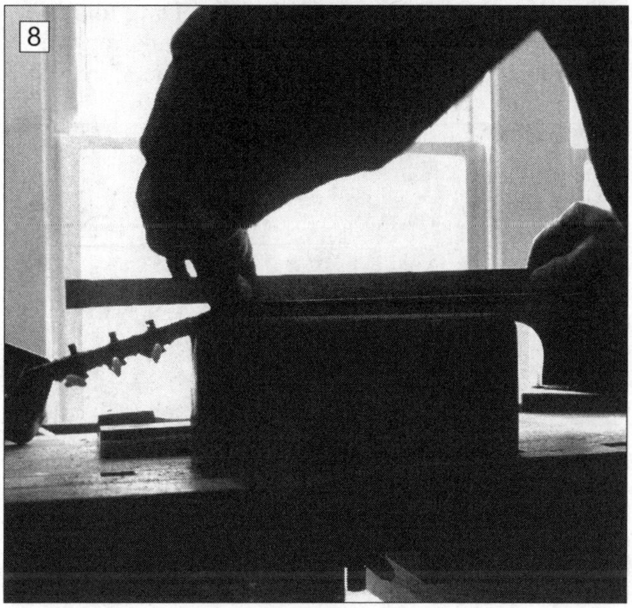

9

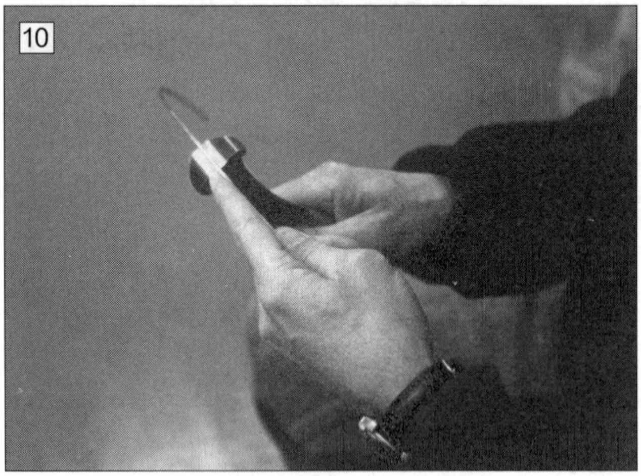

Dave first used feeler gauges to check the fret-slot dimensions. We cleaned up the fingerboard a little more while discussing the *chi*. The chi embodies Dave's tooling approach, which applies the Eastern philosophy of using positive energy to create smooth and natural movements in these procedures. Dave explained how his Japanese planes, and other tools that work on the pull, rather than the push stroke, coincide with the chi, and this philosophy. He criticized Western luthiers for watching too many John Wayne movies and applying a brute approach to their building techniques (although I've seen Dave use a lot of force when necessary for a given procedure). Watching him work, I realized it was time to slow down myself and use a gentler approach. Sorry Duke!

Next, using finisher's felt as a sanding pad, we worked the fingerboard with finer, and then still-finer-grit paper, then cleared the fret slots. Dave likes to use finisher's felt, a sanding pad sold through Mohawk, for the latter stages in the sanding procedure. We then moved up to 400-grit wet/dry carbide paper and then on to steel wool.

For old-Martin-style refrets, Dave likes to use Jim Dunlop High/Narrow fretwire, which he says most resembles original square Martin frets. Dave told me that his friend Eddie Diehl used to pull bulk fretwire through a drilled hole in a piece of sheet metal to acquire the proper radius for fretting. A lot of Dave's techniques were taught to him by Eddie in the '60s. Eddie taught Dave the old technique of adding barbs to fretwire by hitting a fret's tang with the sharp edge of a tack hammer. Dave passed the technique on to me, which I now use for seating loose fret ends. Since this interview I've gone to several of Eddie Diehl's gigs and picked his brain a little too. Eddie, like Dave, is very reclusive, and equally passionate about lutherie. He now teaches fretwork in New England (and is also one of the finest jazz guitarists you'll ever hear).

Next we needed to bend the fretwire, and Dave demonstrated how it's done. He held one end of the fretwire with the end nippers and pulled it down into a curve. He then moved the nippers closer to his hand, bending the wire further (**Photo 10**). He continued this process along the wire until a desired radius had been reached (**Photo 11**). I watched him closely to pick up on the technique. We then precut some of the frets and put them in a series of drilled holes in a board for safekeeping. Dave (who, as you may recall, was born with a hammer in his hand) told me I had to find a hammer that was right for me, whether ball peen, cobbler's, mason's, or standard carpenter's. I chose the ball peen that Dave uses.

Working with four frets at a time, we prepped the slots with brown carpenter's glue before hammering the

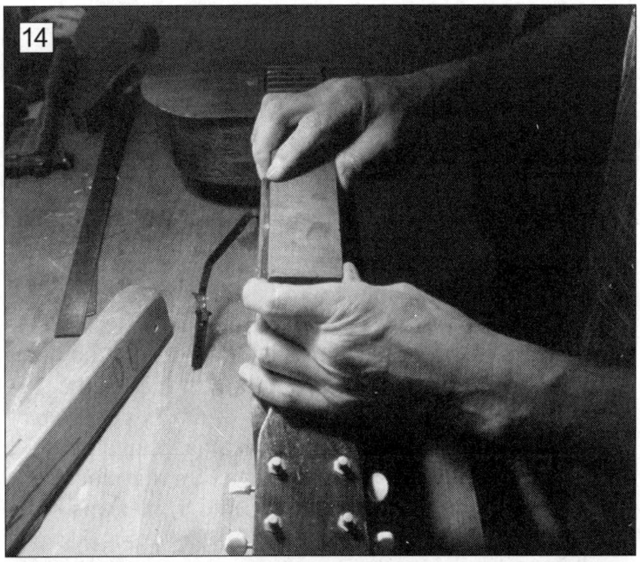

frets in. Dave had a little cup of water for immediate cleanup of glue squeeze-out. Dave's father was an upholsterer and taught him the feel and balance of a "dead blow" that he now applies to his own craft. He explained, "Let the hammer fall so it won't buck or bounce." He also stressed to not hit the fret again if it's already seated. Dave had me hammer in the rest of the frets, with the exception of those over the fingerboard extension. He told me to choke up a little on the hammer so that I could feel the proper impact.

For the frets over the fingerboard extension, we used a small steel fret buck measuring 4″×1½″×⅜″, held underneath the soundboard. For the last fret I held the fret buck by its narrow end and placed it next to the brace above the soundhole. After all the frets were in, we let them sit overnight.

In our next session we cut the fret ends flush to the side of the fingerboard (**Photo 12**). Dave taught me to place the flattened end of the end nippers against the fingerboard edge, as in the photo, and then cut. We then used his fret file as shown (**Photos 13**) to first flush and then bevel the fret ends. Dave told us that when he worked for Steinberger they had an inspection for every fret installation and tried to maintain "military tolerance," to which my response was, "Sir, yes sir!"

Next Dave gently knocked the tops off of the frets using his level sharpening stone (**Photo 14**) and then a mill file (**Photo 15**). He then used a stone that had radius from a lot of use in fretwork to match the fret tops to the radius of the fingerboard, saddle, and bridge. We continued to work the tops of the frets, examining them periodically with a straightedge.

Dave began the fret rounding process using rounding files (**Photo 16**), and finished them off using the handle end of a needle file wrapped with a small amount of fine sandpaper (**Photo 17**). He demonstrated this gentle process of applying pressure to the side of the frets, and not to the fingerboard. Dave discussed different fret end dressings used by various companies and individuals throughout the years. He then demonstrated a Martin fret-end taper, using my Gurian fret file. Awesome. While he was working, Dave mentioned that Michael Gurian had never met anyone that owned one of his tools, but he sure did sell a lot of them. So I made sure to tell Michael, when I met him at the Healdsburg Guitar Festival this year, that I owned one of his fret files.

For the final polishing, we moved from 600-grit paper to 1000-grit wet/dry paper, and then to fine steel wool. I took the instrument home and used a little buffing compound on the fingerboard and frets. ——

Originally published in *American Lutherie #49–#54 & #56*, 1997–1998

PRODUCT REVIEWS
by Harry Fleishman

"This column reflects my opinions based on my experience. It does not necessarily reflect the views of the Guild or its members. If you have had different results from the same product, please tell me so that we can all profit from the ensuing dialog."

Moto-Tool Bases; Neck-Making Tools; JAWS
Stewart-MacDonald www.stewmac.com
Luthier's Mercatile www.lmii.com

Since I often receive tools for review, it is often like Christmas here at Fleishman Instruments, with the accompanying joy and occasional disappointment. I find myself in the position of a kid who, after opening all of his presents, finds that each is very close to what he was hoping for, but some also miss the mark by a fraction. I remember receiving a sweater the wrong color or a toy car of the wrong model. I appreciated the attempt, the thought that counted, but still longed for the Porsche Speedster instead of the Ford Mustang, the forest green cotton rather than the red wool.

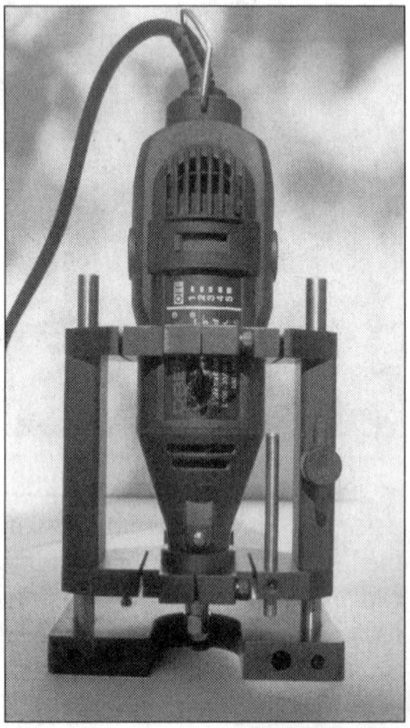

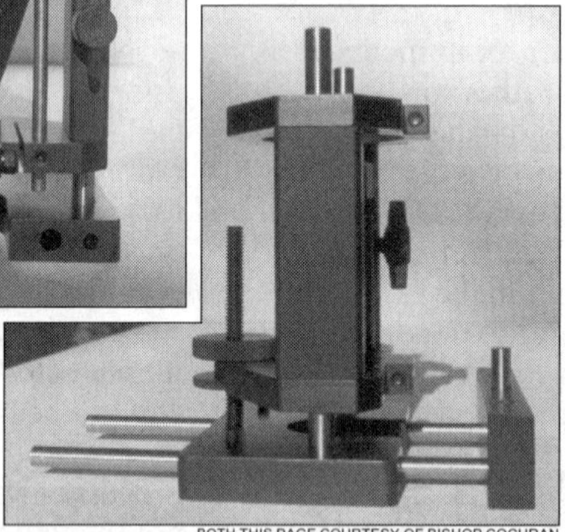

BOTH THIS PAGE COURTESY OF BISHOP COCHRAN

As at the end of an orgy of gift opening, I find that some of the offerings, at first passed over, are just exactly what I had hoped for. Like books that seemed no fun to a kid expecting a game, but give years of true joy, some tools that looked pedestrian are giving me the most use and pleasure, improving and easing my work. Perhaps the hardest part of my job, like sending thank-you notes after the holidays, is writing up the mixed responses I have to some of the tools I have tested.

After years of suffering through the exasperating shortcomings of the Dremel tools and accessories, and after finding the "improved" Model 5 tool not so improved as we might like, I awaited the new Moto-Tool bases from Stewart-MacDonald and Luthiers Mercantile International with great excitement. They each strive in different ways to replace the old, rickety, chintzy, plastic, POS tool base with an easily adjustable, metal base of higher quality. While this column is definitely not a shootout between the two tools, it is inevitable that comparisons and contrasts will be drawn. They are actually quite different. One is small, simple, light, and relatively inexpensive; the other big, complex, heavy and somewhat costly. Each offers a vast improvement over the old base, but also leaves something to be desired.

Luthiers Mercantile International is selling the base designed by Bishop Cochran, a luthier in the Pacific Northwest. (See *American Lutherie #48, Big Red Book of American Lutherie Volume 4.*) He has spent a good deal of time and money developing a tool that does many things very well. Where the old Dremel was lightweight plastic, the LMI tool ($147.50) is massive machined aluminum. It is not only heavy, but solid. Increasing mass translates directly into less chatter. The Dremel still lacks the bearing precision it needs, but the LMI base tames it. Depth adjustment of the LMI base is similar to the Dremel, a thumbwheel setup, but it works without tilting the tool and it is predictable. Unlike the Dremel, the LMI base moves straight up and down when you move the adjustment wheel — hence the name "plunge router base." To truly plunge, this base would need some sort of springloaded, lockable device. (What do you think, Bishop?) There is a nifty presetting rod that lets you set the depth of the tool before starting and then adjust to it as you work. For instance, you could place a piece of pearl under the rod, tighten the set screw, remove the pearl, and lower the cutter, knowing that at the depth stop the cut would be exactly the depth of the pearl's thickness. Not bad.

The LMI base also has a nicely machined fence that, flipped over, doubles as a circle attachment. I really liked the way I could dial the radius in precisely. This base has also been designed to work with old Dremel base attachments by screwing them into the threaded holes in its underside.

The only problem I have with this tool is that it interferes with visibility in many cases. I simply cannot see clearly to the sides and back of the bits while working, and this leaves me guessing at times when I really want to know precisely where the bit starts and ends. The lines of my rosettes seldom continue unbroken around the soundhole, leaving me with the need to start and stop the cut as I go. While the mass of the tool makes the cut smoother, the impaired visibility makes it hard to know exactly where to begin and end the slot.

I would like to see a couple of slight changes that would make the tool more flexible without adding much extra work or cost to their production. By drilling and tapping one more hole, or centering the existing one, the circle adjust could also allow dial-in adjustment of the fence. Relieving the area around the cutter could maintain strength while increasing visibility.

ALL THIS PAGE COURTESY OF STEWART-MACDONALD

Bishop Cochran has been very responsive to input from luthiers and is already making minor changes to improve the tool. He switched from standard to rolled stainless for the circle adjusting screw, and changed a set screw or two. The side locking screws are now color coded to make it easier to reassemble after removing the fence.

Stew-Mac has also brought out their Dremel base replacement recently. At about $40, it is less costly than the LMI base. It is also much smaller, lighter, and less ambitious. Consisting of an aluminum base around ⅛″ thick and two adjustable posts, this jig simply screws onto the Dremel like the old Dremel collar would. It is then quite securely held. Adjustment is via the two posts. At first I found it tricky to get the depth right. A little practice, and I do it almost without thinking (that's right, the way I do my writing; I can hear you out there). In keeping with their pricing policy, Stew-Mac has seen fit for this thing to adjust .035″ per rotation of the post. Not 1⁄32″, not 1MM; .035″. Truth is, I do it by eye. I will probably add a feature like the Bishop Cochran depth stop to my Stew-Mac.

The Stew-Mac base has very good visibility. I can see around the bit with no obstructions. This really helps in tricky setups or tight spaces. It does not have a fence or circle attachment, however. It will work with the circle jig offered by Stew-Mac; that's good. A fence would take a bit of conjuring. Also, it only works with recent Dremels.

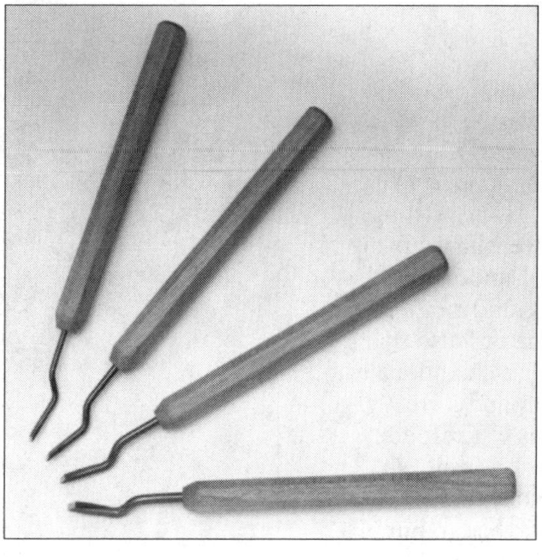

The LMI base is super stable, massive, and flexible; the Stew-Mac is simple, light, and cheap. Both offer good, usable improvements over the old, cheesy original.

There wasn't room in my last column (about neck-making tools) to include a couple of my favorite new tools, so here they are. First a few tiny, lovely chisels. The dog-leg micro chisels (Stew-Mac #1628 at $24.98) are just great for getting down into the nut slot to clear that last bit of glue or wood burr, squaring up an inlay pocket, and making infinitesimal adjustments to any small job. At 5½″ long they are small, light, and well made. The set of four includes 2MM, 2.4MM, 2.75MM, and 3.25MM. They come well sharpened and seem to be very nice steel, holding a good edge even under abusive use like hardened glue clearing. Now that I have them I find that they are among of the first tools I grab for. They are tiny but tough and at about $6 each, a good deal, if you aren't buying them by the pound. I use them with greater precision and safety instead of X-acto #11s and in place of too-large chisels.

Last, but certainly *not* least, is JAWS, the new, but long-anticipated, fret-pressing tool from Stew-Mac's Dan Erlewine (with an assist, I presume, from Don MacRostie). This is a big ol' tool. Larger than most locking-jaw pliers, JAWS takes a little practice to get used to. First of all, it feels upside down, with the moving lever on the top. I suppose you could turn the guitar over and it would all feel just fine, but then you'd need an antigravity device to keep the frets in place until you were ready to squeeze them. And squeeze them this thing does. You can quite easily press the frets practically through the neck if you aren't careful. You can readily feel them press in, however, if you pay even reasonable attention.

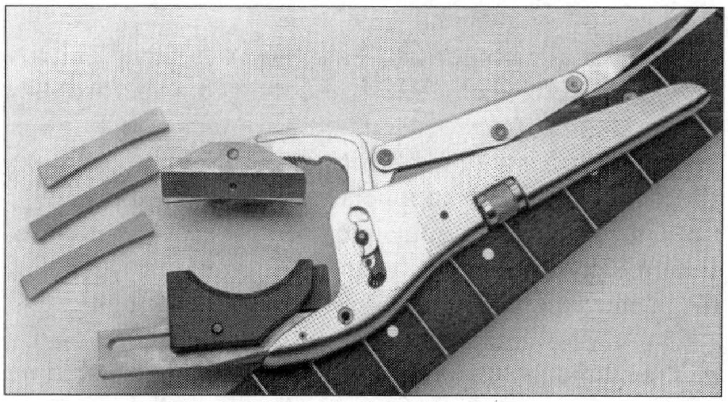

JAWS comes in two offerings. First, #4381 at $129.75 (from Stew-Mac) gets you the JAWS portable fret press and four cauls. For $113.75 you get #4380, the press only, letting you choose cauls separately at $3.99 each. The cauls are available in radii from 6″ to 20″, as well as flat. You could make cauls in other radii pretty easily from flat brass stock if needed, but these are well-crafted and reasonably priced.

So why bother with another fretting tool after buying every hammer and glue on the market? First of all, this thing presses the frets in with *no* spring back from their proper curve. If you prep the frets right, they go right in, no fuss, no muss. If you like to wick in superglue, this is your baby. Simply press in the fret and hold it as the glue sets. I like to wipe accelerator on the tang and wick in one or two drops per fret. The glue sets right up and since the fret is already dead tight, it never moves until I heat it up to remove it. You need very little pressure to press in a fret. Unlike with hammered frets, the fret is not hardened and tempted to lift at the ends. I will go into my far-too-involved method of fretting in a future writing, but until then let me simply say that this thing makes life easier.

JAWS does have limitations, sadly. It doesn't work past the heel on an acoustic guitar. It won't reach all the way across a wide 6-string bass fretboard. It doesn't do windows (or Windows). However, in spite of those minor shortcomings, I recommend it, especially for bolt-on builders. JAWS is solidly made and the back of the press is nicely protective of the neck. I tried to make one after seeing Dan's prototype; I couldn't. Stew-Mac did their homework and I hope they reap their reward on this one.

Speaking of homework: these guys actually spend a lot of time testing and improving their tools before they hit the stands, so to speak. I am in contact with many people who design tools, selling them independently or through the lutherie suppliers, and they all put much time, thought, and money into their tools. Occasionally I see tools, in one form or another, before they reach the public, and it is fun to see the changes wrought by the input of luthiers around the country and the world. A screw here rather than there, plexi or aluminum, large instead of small, each part is weighed for effectiveness and affordability.

I have designed tools myself, as most of you have, and we know how hard it is taking the time and effort away from lutherie that is needed to make a good tool great. My gosh, I can feel the tears welling up in my eyes, so I better stop right here and get a tissue.

(1997)

Fret Tang Pliers
Stewart-MacDonald www.stewmac.com

Bridge-Slotting Jig
Luthier's Mercatile www.lmii.com

Fret work will take as many or as few tools as we are willing and able to use. I've done frets with nothing more than a piece of wood and a little sandpaper; I've used $1000 worth of specialized tools. At this writing, I think I'm finding a happy medium. Over the years my frets have improved in two ways. First, I understand the process more. For this I thank the Guild members who have shared their experience and ideas; I also thank Dan Erlewine for his great video *Don't Fret.* Additionally, I now have the means to do them carefully and correctly. Tools and materials really do help in this last respect.

Fret work can be used to adjust a neck as well as adjust the way it feels and plays. In the days before Martin started using adjustable necks, we had to put in oversized tangs to push back an upbowed neck. Conversely, undersized tangs let in a bit of relief when needed. Martin only made one crown, though, and if you didn't like or want it, tough. When a good variety of frets came on the scene, it meant keeping a huge inventory of sizes to meet any eventuality. Still, if you wanted jumbos on a Strat, and the tangs were wrong, you were out of luck. No longer.

Stew-Mac's tool guru Don MacRostie has developed a pair of tools that I find really help me with odd-sized fret slots and with fret-related fingerboard adjustments. They look like pliers or end nippers, but the jaw faces are machined and designed for serious business. One tool has flat, hardened-steel faces on its jaws. The other has hardened matching serrations, sort of like a really macho steel pie-crust crimper. If a fret is too tight, the flat-faced tool works quickly and easily to press the barbs down reducing the pressure on the fret slot. It will actually squeeze the tang a bit narrower if you're pretty strong. A loose fret tang can be widened by crimping with the serrated jaw. This widened tang will then put more pressure on the fret slot, forcing the fingerboard to arch back slightly. The serrated tool leaves the barbs, unless you really bear down oppressively. With these pliers, you have the equivalent of an unlimited number of fret tang/barb sizes.

Using these two tools (fret tang mashing pliers, as they call them, are $24.65; fret tang crimping pliers are $36.45; the set is $55.95), a neck can be manipulated to where you want it, even if it's an old Martin with no rod. Of course, it takes a lot of practice to understand the mechanics and application of fret work as a neck adjusting method; but it can often mean the difference between saving a bad neck and having to do major reconstruction.

Another similar use is refretting a previously glued fret set. Like many other luthiers, I used to epoxy my frets in an oversized slot. I'm not as keen on that as I used to be, although I still think it can be a good method in the right hands. (Don Teeter isn't left handed is he?) I had to refret one like that a couple of years ago, and it meant filling in the slots and recutting them. Now, using these new tools, I reshape the barbs using the

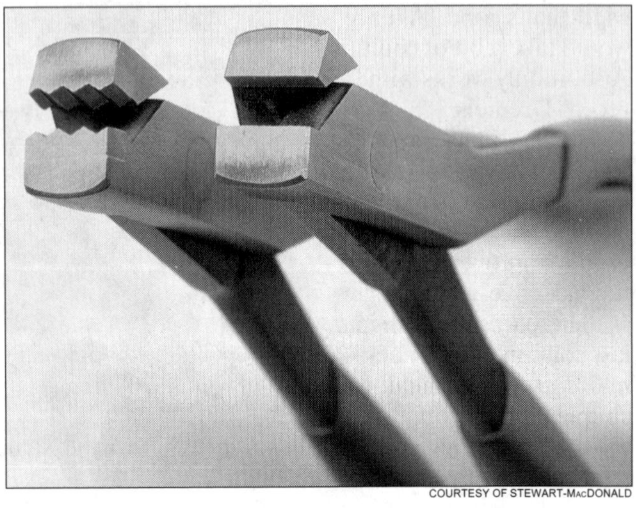
COURTESY OF STEWART-MACDONALD

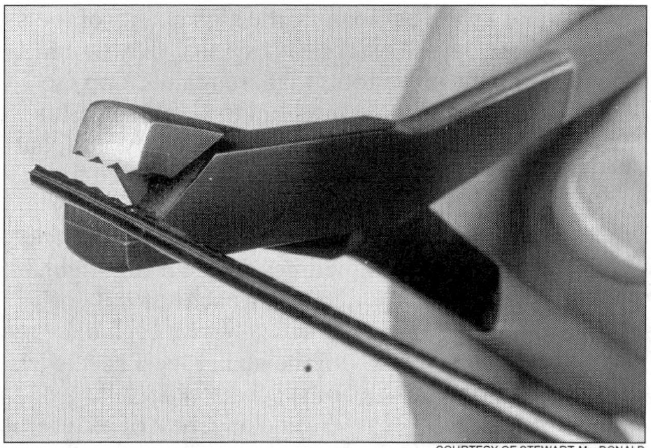

COURTESY OF STEWART-MACDONALD

serrated plier and fit them in snugly to the oversized slot. In the same way, the flat-jawed plier can be used to fit a new fret into a smaller slot. I recently replaced a few frets on an old Gibson banjo. Only five were worn, so I searched my materials for a length of fret with the right crown. Rather than try to find the right tang and barb combination, on top of the right height and width (underneath actually, but that sounds wrong, somehow), I matched the playing size of the fret and compressed the barbs to fit. One drop of superglue, wicked in, and the fret was ready for dressing. Yum.

These are very nicely made tools, designed for a lifetime of use. It would be tough to make these things, although those of us with too much time and money on our hands might try. My only complaint is that they are blue. If they were purple or forest green I wouldn't mix them up with my fret cutters. As it is, all my fret tools are color coordinated. Never mind; moving right along — along the guitar from the neck to the bridge, that is.

I often slot my bridges once the guitar is completed. If I am installing a pickup, such as the Highlander, it ensures that the slot has a perfectly flat bottom. Also, it allows perfect intonation. For this job I used to rely mostly on makeshift setups; then I started using the routing jig offered by Stew-Mac and reviewed in *AL#43.* (See *BRBAL4.*) I really like that jig and find that it works well for many guitars. However, it won't work on my new guitars. I have been using either one soundhole on the treble side of the neck, or two different-sized soundholes, one on each side of the fingerboard. I will write further on the theory behind this change in a future article. For now let me just say that it hasn't made my life any easier.

As if on cue, along comes a new jig from Luthiers Mercantile International that fits my new guitars. Drew Gallahar has designed a bridge-slotting jig that fits across the entire face of the guitar, spanning the bridge and allowing safe, easy slotting for the saddle or pickup. This is a new incarnation of an existing jig, with an important difference: the old jig was shorter and did not reach the guitar's rims. I felt that this could be dangerous on a fragile, or possibly already damaged, guitar. Also, I don't like to clamp to a guitar's face or back, preferring always to clamp anything at the sides for extra support. While talking to Drew I suggested that I needed a longer jig and, *voilà!*, he supplied it and redesigned the future jigs to the new size. Talk about responsive to luthier's suggestions.

The new jig (available in the wonderful new LMI catalog as part #SPBSRJ, at $90), sits nicely across the guitar, safely cushioned by 3⁄16″ closed-cell foam rails. These rails are fully adjustable to both width and angle, so they should fit just about anything. (They fit my large asymmetric guitar and that's saying something.) The dimensions of Drew's jig are 16″×7½″. The base of the jig is 3⁄8″ thick and doesn't deflect unless you bear down harder than you should. Back off and you'll be OK. The rail supports on either end are 5⁄16″ thick and it should clear virtually any bridge. In the event you need greater clearance, this style of foam is readily available in other thicknesses.

The jig will cut a slot of up to 4½″, but it could easily be made to cut a longer slot, for a through-slot 6-string bass, for instance. In other words, it's long enough, I'd guess. Also, there is room for 3⁄8″ slot-width adjustment. This means you can make a wide slot by cutting one pass and then moving the guides a set amount without moving the whole jig. Everything is snugged down with nice little brass thumb screws, so no tools are needed. My saddles are generally about 3⁄8″ wide at the bass end and taper to 3⁄16″ at the treble. This jig lets me cut the front edge, move the rear guide where I want it, then adjust the front guide to match. If you want to widen the entire slot an even couple of thousandths, all you would do is put in a shim on the side you wish to enlarge and snug it up, then pull out the shim, bring the other guide to it, and it's set. Pretty easy.

I've been frustrated lately by the lack of interchangeability between many of the "dremelesque" jigs. Happily, Drew's jig works with the new Dremel stuff and includes a base to screw on most of the Dremels from over the years. It also should be easy to fit a laminate trimmer to this thing if that's your pleasure. I appreciate the openness and responsiveness that tool designers are showing. Every time I talk to Todd at LMI, or Jay and Dan at Stew-Mac, they seem to be working on something new in response to a luthier's

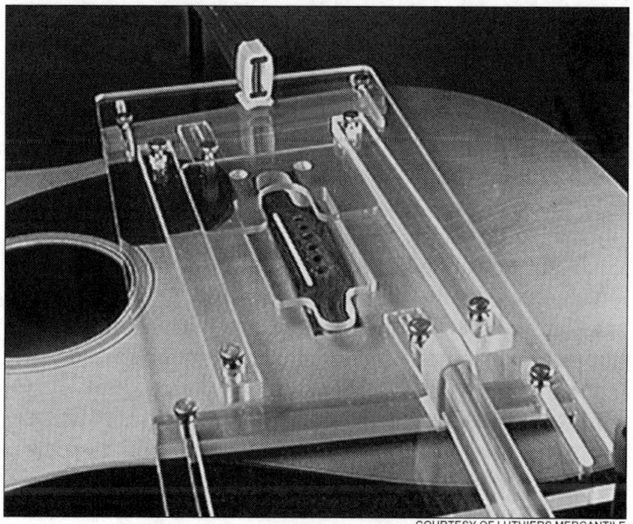

COURTESY OF LUTHIERS MERCANTILE

request. It makes our wallets lighter, but our jobs easier.

I'd like to leave you with a little trick I found for lining things up. Take a piece of thin plastic (I keep some .020″ clear polycarbonate around for just such uses), tape it to the base of your tool so it doesn't move. Drill through both the thin sheet and the base with a bit that matches a tiny brad, so that the brad is not in your way. Then, put the brads in and with the Dremel bit moving, lower the cutter through the thin sheet, establishing an exact mark of where the cutter will cut. It is then a simple matter of lining up this little sheet whenever you wish to cut a slot. After it is lined up, pull off the sheet, and you know exactly where your slot will start, end, and line up. You could make one in about two minutes for each cutter you might use.

(1997)

Crack Repair Set
Stewart-MacDonald
www.stewmac.com

Those of you who have begun the art and craft of lutherie relatively recently, say in the last ten years, can't fully appreciate just how much our field has changed. Not only did most luthiers of the past walk to work and back through deep snow, uphill in both directions, they also made most of their own tools. Most of us still make many of our own tools, even with the proliferation of excellent suppliers. There is a special satisfaction that comes with making a tool that doubles as an object of desire, a thing beautiful in itself, more than just a means to an end. It is probably a good thing that we have access to so many lovely tools; however, I still suggest making tools as a separate and valuable endeavor. I don't know if I would have been a better guitar maker, sooner, with more readily available specialized tools. I certainly don't assume that you will somehow be less of a luthier with so many to choose from. I guess I'm simply interested in the symbiotic relationship between luthiers and suppliers.

ALL THIS PAGE COURTESY OF STEWART-MACDONALD

Both Stewart-MacDonald and Luthiers Mercantile International, our largest lutherie suppliers, as well as smaller, independent tool and supply people, have become increasingly responsive to our needs as luthiers. They work with successful repair people and builders to find what works and what doesn't. The idea for the fret crimping and mashing pliers came from Frank Ford, a fine repairer who is capable of refretting anything, including household pets. Stew-Macs' Jay Hostetler and I were bemoaning the high quality of tools these days. I was suggesting that they should send me some tools that are really crappy so I could have something bad to review. I wish I could warn people away from shoddy stuff, but most tools have been well tested before they hit the street. "We reject a lot of stuff," Jay told me. "We put eight months of R&D into a tool and then sometimes decide it isn't right."

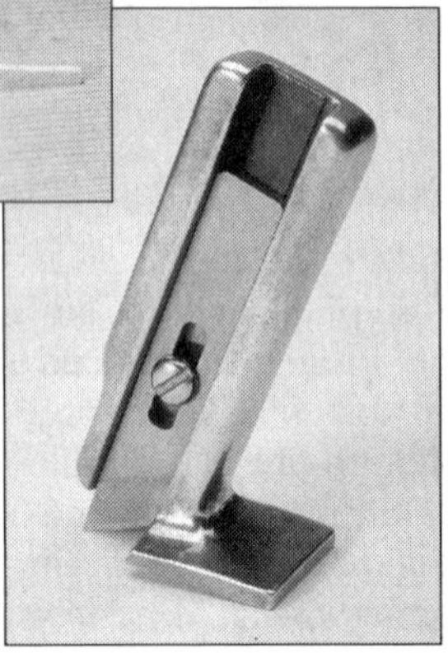

With each new catalog, practically with each delivery of the mail, I see a new batch of specialized, artfully crafted and, best of all, useful tools. Sometimes the catalogs themselves transcend their catalogetude and become both objects of desire and the means to acquire more objects.

The Sloane crack repair set includes two of the most beautiful tools I've ever seen. These babies are so pretty I'm sure that nonluthiers will be buying them and displaying them as objets d'art, thus forcing the price up. The set, available from Stewart-MacDonald as #4482 for $76.36, consists of a Crack Repair Knife (#4480 at $36) and a Splint Shaping Jig (4481 at $48). Each of the tools is beautifully machined from bronze and finished like jewelry. You'll want to lean on guitars and crack 'em, just to get the chance to use these puppies. In Colorado we get more than our share of top cracks, so I didn't even have to break anything to try these things out. ("Things" was all I could come up with after "babies" and "puppies.")

The Splint Shaping Jig has been nicely designed to thin wood slivers for repairing cracks. The description in the Stew-Mac catalog suggests this jig will thin slices to from .040″ up to .375″. Wow! Imagine making a teensy-weensy little ⅜″ sliver to fix a crack! I haven't seen that big a fissure since the LA earthquake. If you ever had to fix a crack that big, though, with this tool you'd be ready. And seriously, it will do much better than .040″. I took a piece of spruce down in my Performax sander to .022″ and then using the Sloane jig pared it to a perfect .010″. That's about the size crack I like to deal with. Making a nice, even, slightly tapered .010″ sliver is no mean feat, as I'm sure you know; I usually break at least a half-dozen trying to get a good, long one. The ability to adjust not only the width but the taper is extremely helpful. In this case, I was fitting a tiny sliver for a long, thin crack from the bridge to the end block of a midsized guitar. I didn't want to open the nice, clean crack any larger than it was, so I went for the slimmest fillet I could make, allowing for the slight wandering of the grain line. I believe this tool allowed me to make the nicest crack fillet of my long, unillustrious career.

The Crack Repair Knife is equally well made, but didn't suit my needs as well as the Splint Shaping Jig. I think it would make a nice clean opening for a larger splint, say around .040″ or larger (that number keeps coming up), but a .010″ slot is really tricky. With practice, perhaps, I could do it. I did find it very useful for a slight cleanup of an existing slot, however, by using it backwards, on the push stroke like a tiny scraper (I canna' get enough power Cap'n Kirk; I'll have to reverse polarity. Ahhhg!). It worked very well for cleaning the slot walls and preparing them for the tiny splint I had made. The use of it as a push tool is tricky and I'll make a slightly different blade for that purpose; but what I liked is the way it left a tapered slot that perfectly matched the tapered splint. It meant a repair that was nearly invisible and maintained the integrity of the instrument as fully as possible.

(1997)

Sewing Shop Finds; Cutting Burrs; Spring Clamps
Woodcraft www.woodcraft.com

Of course, the first place any luthier would look for fine new tools is the local sewing shop. I'm no different. Checking out Elfriede's Fine Fabrics here in Boulder, as well as my local So-Fro, I found a couple of things no serious luthier should be without. At the latter I located a bin of discounted aprons, sized from petite to diminutive. The petite was a tad small for me, more suitable for a person of about five feet tall. The larger sizes, however, were just right. I found a few that fit. This column was originally planned as an apron shootout between LMI, Stew-Mac, and So-Fro, but that will have to wait. As I searched the store for more lutherie tools, I congratulated myself on finding aprons without pockets. I've decided that no shop apron should have pockets; I'll tell you the sad tale that brought me to this decision.

I had just finished a guitar of which I was extremely proud and called my family in to show off. As my wife and kids came into the shop, my son handed me a tuning fork he had retrieved from the floor. I thanked him, put it in the pocket of my old apron, and bent to open the case of my newest guitar. This instrument is the second I've built from a fifty-year-old Brazilian rosewood table I purchased from an old woodworker friend. The top was inlaid with a Celtic lute rose surrounded by a Brazilian and abalone rosette. I felt that this guitar was the prettiest and best sounding I had made. As I leaned over and reached to take the guitar from its case, the fork fell from my apron pocket and bounced gleefully around the top, redesigning both the redwood bass-side and the treble spruce with further carvings. At that moment I swore off of apron pockets and began the laborious process of repairing my customer's new guitar.

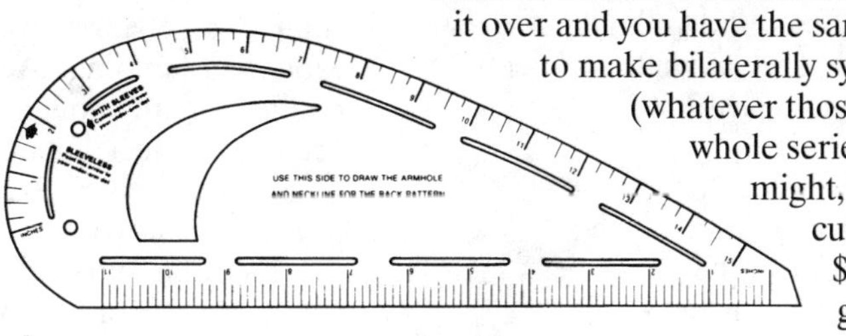

Made of medium-weight canvas, So-Fro's aprons do a very nice job of protecting your T-shirts from glue and dust. The slightly rough fabric grabs glue well, leaving your fingers clean and dry to handle guitars. Since they were only $2.50 each, I decided to spring for a batch, and headed toward the bias tapes. I don't know if all So-Fros carry a ready stock of aprons; you might call before making a special trip.

Bias tape is expensive but works great for tying on binding, as well as for putting on tops and backs. The only problem (besides the cost of about $.50 per foot) is that as you install it, the tape acquires a half twist each wrap. You must then remove it carefully to simultaneously remove the twist. The nice thing about bias tape versus ropes is that it doesn't put pressure in such a tiny spot, instead spreading it over about a 3⁄8″ area. I use a box with a hole in its top for dispensing the tape. When I'm done, I open the box and let the tape lay in as it wants, leaving it ready for the next use. While bias tape is a lovely thing, I was after bigger game.

Heading to Elfriede's Fine Fabric, I thought perhaps I might even check out cooking shops next. Elfriede's sells a long, curved, plastic ruler that I now find indispensable for designing guitars. One of my pet peeves is guitars with clunky curves, and long straight lines, looking like they were drawn by eye, or enlarged from an etch-a-sketch. I don't mean long graceful, original lines; I mean clunky. I understand — not everyone has a natural sense of line (although it is probably like a sense of humor: everyone thinks they have one). Elfriede's sells a dressmaker's rule made by the Dritz company of Spartanburg, South Carolina. It is like a large French curve with a wonderful addition: not only is it scaled for drawing guitar-sized curves, it also has markings for inches, in eighths, from its curved end towards the straighter end. The Dritz Styling Curve ($6.95 at sewing shops everywhere) is about 13″ long and shaped like half a heart. It is very flexible and marked on both sides and both edges. Draw a line; flip it over and you have the same markings, allowing you to make bilaterally symmetric guitar drawings (whatever those are). I wish they made a whole series of these rules (and they might, for all I know) in different curves. I'd buy them all. At $6.95, they are one of life's great deals. I would be lost without mine. I also have another sewing curve, made by the Fairgate company, of Cold Spring, New York, that I've used for about twenty years. Made of aluminum and 24″ long, the Fairgate Vary Form Curve Rule has a long gradual curve ending in about 9″ of straight section. It is wonderful, too; however, I can't find a place that sells them, so I don't know where to send you. If anyone knows where to obtain the Fairgate, please let us all know.

In addition to at least a basic design class, I recommend the Dritz Styling Curve for improving the lines of most luthiers' guitars. Together with a few large French curves, the Styling Curve will make designing easier and the designs more fluid.

I'm afraid the cooking shop only had a couple of nice spatulas, which might have been used for pulling bridges in a pinch, and a big salmon-poaching trough, which Wolfgang Puck might use for steaming mandola sides before bending, if he were a luthier. On to the catalog that arrived in today's mail, so much like the catalogs that show up virtually every day.

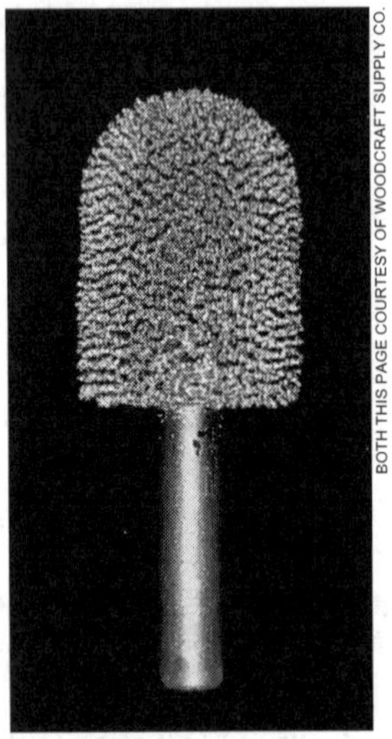

BOTH THIS PAGE COURTESY OF WOODCRAFT SUPPLY CO.

The Woodcraft catalog carries a plethora of tools for woodworkers, among whom guitar makers often count themselves. I sometimes think I'm a woodworker by default. I either do the woodworking, or I don't make guitars. I got to woodworking as a means to an end. Sometimes I want to get to that end quickly and I look to a strong abrasive or a big cutter. The Woodcraft people sell some big carbide burrs that fall somewhere between those two. The one I tested is 7/8″ in diameter and nearly 1 1/4″ long, studded with chunks of carbide. This thing is aggressive. With its bullnose shape, cylindrical and half-spherical on its end (unlike a bull's nose, from my limited experience with bulls) it will cut quickly without digging a sharp edge into your work. I made quick work of hollowing out the fingerboard end for a 6-string electric upright bass. The board was over 5″ wide and over 1″thick, solid ebony, and needed to be contoured on its underside. I would have spent a full day with a gouge, my tendons screaming in overcooked agony. The tungsten carbide burr ($15.99, part #18N1-E) in a power drill took about fifteen minutes, leaving me ready for sanding or scraping. Woodcraft offers these carbide burrs in ten shapes, all 1/4″ shank, ranging from long and thin to wide and fat, as well as a 1″ sphere and a teardrop. A set of all nine is $62.50.

A similar twelve-piece set is available in 1/8″ shank, which would work in Dremels. I used the 1/4″ burr in my electric drill, locking the trigger in the "on" position, with good results. An air-drive tool or an in-line electric grinder would probably be even better.

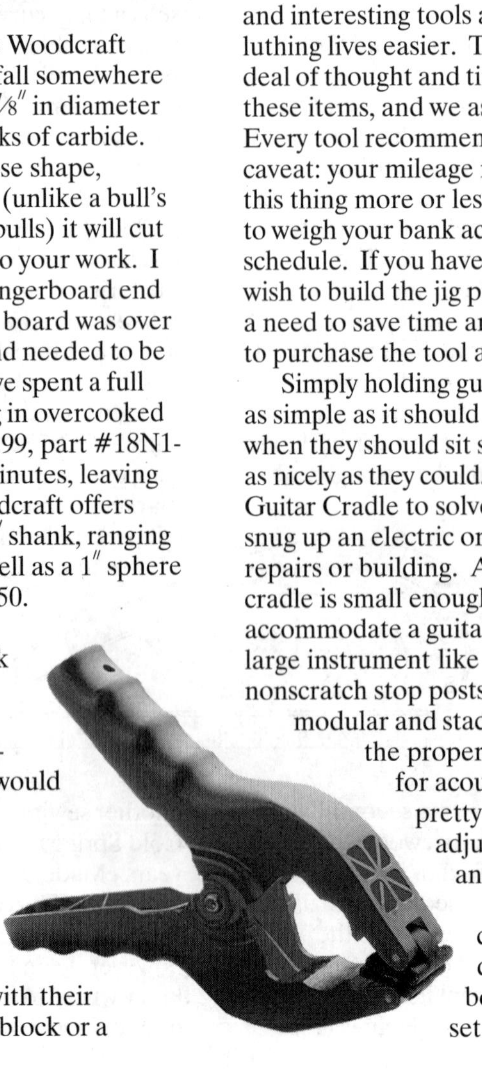

The last tool I tested, also from Woodcraft, was a variation on a familiar theme: the humble spring clamp. I use spring clamps for lots of little holding operations in the shop. Most of these clamps mar the surface with their metal jaw, necessitating an extra clamp block or a veneer. If they have a coated jaw, it wears off easily and soon. The clamps I tested, however, are molded plastic, a polycarbonate I suspect, and tipped with a pivoting molded-silicone piece. The combination of pivot and slightly conforming material adds up to a vastly superior clamp. First, no marring. Second, they don't tend to slip around. Third, they hold uneven and angled parts, up to a point. Fourth, these things are *powerful.* The one downside is that I must use both hands to apply them. I have tendonitis and these things are simply stronger than I am. They are available in 1″, 2″, and 3″ openings, as well as a set of two each. The cost is, respectively, $1.50, $2.50, and $3.50, or $13.50 for the set. (There is a small discount for 3 or more.) I have a lot of other spring clamps around the shop, but they'll go at the next garage sale.

(1997)

Guitar Cradle; Mirror; Fret Tools; Go-Bars; Guitar Neck Removal Jig
Stewart-MacDonald www.stewmac.com

Pro 7a Mike
AudioTechnica www.audio-technica.com

The newest Stew-Mac catalog contains many new and interesting tools and jigs designed to make our luthing lives easier. The crew at Stew-Mac put a great deal of thought and time into designing and producing these items, and we as luthiers spend a lot buying them. Every tool recommendation I make comes with a simple caveat: your mileage may vary. That is, you may like this thing more or less than I did. Also, it is important to weigh your bank account and compare it to your schedule. If you have more time than money, you may wish to build the jig pictured in the catalog. If you have a need to save time and work efficiently, you may wish to purchase the tool and get right to work with it.

Simply holding guitars while working on them is not as simple as it should be. They slide around, move when they should sit still, and generally don't cooperate as nicely as they could. Stew-Mac offers their Bench Guitar Cradle to solve this problem. It allows you to snug up an electric or acoustic guitar and stabilize it for repairs or building. At 14″ wide and 36 3/4″ long, the cradle is small enough to fit any bench that will accommodate a guitar, yet large enough to hold even a large instrument like a bass guitar. By adjusting the nonscratch stop posts (short enough for electrics, modular and stackable for acoustics) and choosing the proper neck rest (short for electric, tall for acoustic), you should be able to hold pretty much anything. There is plenty of adjustment for both length and height, and nothing I tried refused to fit.

I set up a Strat, just like in the catalog picture, to test the downward pressure on the neck and body. Since we might use this jig to set intonation, I figured we should know how much it could affect our measurements. I had to really tighten the hold-downs to force the guitar to go flat even 3 cents; in normal use the guitar stayed right in tune. Moving the neck support as close to the body as is practical would alleviate much of that. There's really no reason to tighten things down too much; the posts are silicone wrapped and the tail block holder is covered in rubberized cork. The instrument stays put.

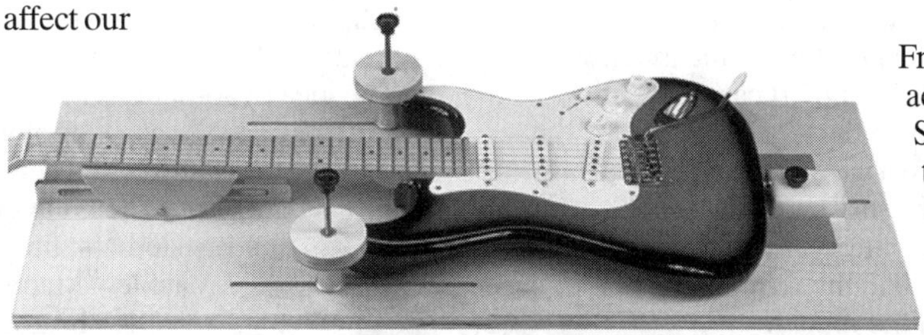

ALL THIS PAGE COURTESY OF STEWART-MACDONALD

I like the way the neck supports pivot to hold the neck solidly. Also, they are scooped under the neck to allow capoing of strings when working on the bridge. However, I found that the end block got in the way of drilling and reaming the end pin during pickup installations. I had to move the guitar back and remove the rear push block to get at things. I have no solution for this other than to do the rest of the work, move the block, drill and ream, and then replace the block. It's not too big a deal.

I really like this jig for the rest of the pickup installation. It lets you hold everything steady while routing and wiring. For many repairs and for setup, this jig will make life easier. Several years ago I reviewed the "Apprentice," a far more versatile jig offered by Bill Schmidt. This Stew-Mac jig ($145. — I had to look twice at the weirdly even price) is more solid, since it clamps to the bench, but far less flexible in terms of tricky holding situations. It's not very good at holding a guitar face-down, for instance, though it can do it in a pinch. As is often the case, I see this jig as a mixed bag — what it does, it does well; it doesn't do it all. I'm going to mount this jig to my bench with a recessed ¼×20 flat-head bolt and a T-nut, and it can swivel around to let me get at different angles. When it's not in use, it can hang on the wall next to my bench where I can find it.

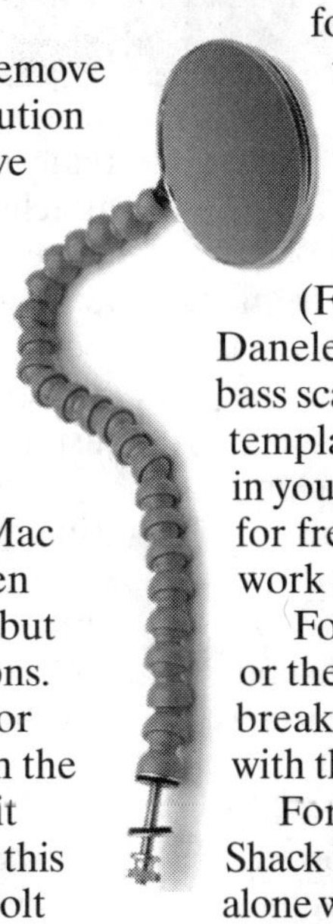

The modestly named Ultimate Guitar Mirror is designed to mount into the guitar's end pin hole, allowing "hands-free" repairs inside an instrument. Modestly priced at "only" $29.95, it is an expensive way to see into a guitar. That said, however, I must admit the way it flexes to go where you want it and then stays there is pretty neat. You could coil the arm like a cobra to act as a stand if needed. One side is a 3″ diameter flat mirror for normal viewing. The other side is convex and allows a sort of fisheye or wide-angle view. The wide angle is great for checking inside your guitar before pulling out into traffic. It won't work if you have an end-pin jack, and it won't work in *f*-hole guitars or my multisoundhole guitars. Oh well, you weren't going to build that sort of thing anyway, and no one brings those in for repairs anymore.

Stew-Mac is offering a Fret Slotting Miter Box and accompanying Dual Fret Scale Templates. Although the miter box (#4730, $59.50) is designed to use Stew-Mac's #660 saw, it will work fine with other similar backsaws. You may have one you are happy with already. It will probably fit. Made of aluminum and brass, the miter box is easily and fully adjustable for various saw widths and for fingerboards up to 3″ wide. It will accommodate wide guitar boards and most bass fingerboards, but not some 5- and 6-string basses. Setup is easy. The rails set the blade width; the brass stops set the depth of cut. That's all there is to it. An included 1⁄16″ pin locates the template for slotting and ensures precision. You can use this tool with your own fingerboard templates or purchase a selection from Stew-Mac. The Stew-Mac Dual Fret Scale Templates really are a bargain at $19.50, and they offer dual scale templates of 24.9″/25.4″ for Martin scales; 25.5″ (Fender)/25″ (Paul Reed Smith, Dobro, Danelectro); 24.75″/25.25″ (both Gibsons); and 30″/34″ bass scales. For other scales, you could make your own templates by sawing a 1⁄16″ notch at each fret position in your own material. Should you set up a table saw for fretslotting in the future, these templates will work equally well with that machine.

For the last two tools, do you want the good news or the bad news first? The bad news; OK. After a break to look at a nice inexpensive mike, we'll be back with the bad news.

For a few years I've recommended a cheap Radio Shack lavalier mike for its price-to-sound ratio. Price alone would not have been enough, but the sound was pretty good, better than anything else I had reviewed. At some time a year or so ago, I noticed a change in their mikes but tried to continue using them anyway, with less enthusiastic results. I have recently found a very good mike in the same price range, but with significantly better sound.

Audio Technica makes their Pro 7a especially for guitars, which suggested to me that it might be a good one to try. The only problems were the attached power supply, the balancing module, and the $144 retail price. Even with a dealer net of $72, it was relatively pricey.

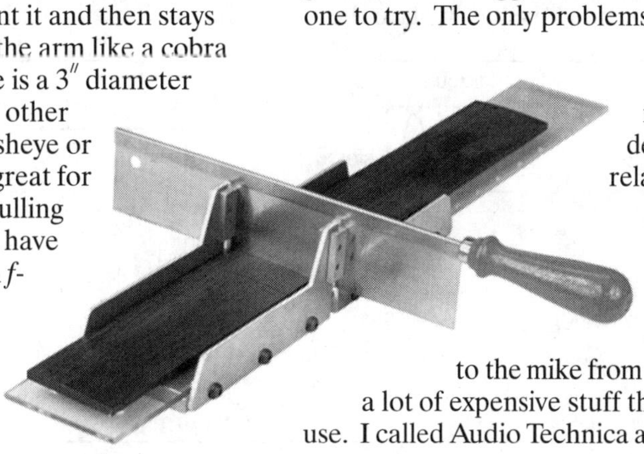

To use this mike with the Highlander IP-2, as I generally do, I needed to cut away the unneeded parts, reduce the voltage to the mike from 9v to 1.5v, and throw away a lot of expensive stuff that I paid for but couldn't use. I called Audio Technica and they were very helpful.

I now purchase just the mike capsule and a windscreen, $30 and $6, respectively. Much better for me and my customers. Solder one end of a .047µf capacitor and one end of an 18KΩ resistor to the red wire. Solder the other end of the capacitor to a wire going to the output, and also the other end of the resistor going to the 9v supply positive (or a battery if you are using this setup alone). Tie the other three wires that come from the mike to the shield. Bob Wolstein at Highlander suggested this setup for the RS and it works even better for the AT.

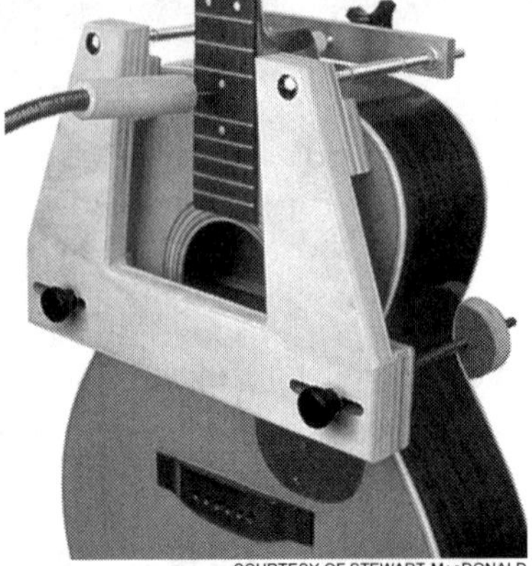
COURTESY OF STEWART-MACDONALD

The mike operates very well at this reduced voltage and sounds great mounted near the neck block, not too close to the soundhole or too near a corner or side. I advise angling it toward the treble side. The tone of this mike is clear and well detailed, with very good feedback resistance. I compared the mike in several installations to the previous mike and the AT far outperformed the RS. The AT also balanced well with the level of the Highlander IP-2 output. And now, the bad news.

The bad news is the Stew-Mac go-bars. Made from fiberglass and measuring 24″ long × .166″ × .500″, these go-bars are just the right strength for pushing the braces right through the top of your newest creation. They are perfect for those times a part just won't clamp up with C clamps, you've tried the pipe clamps, and you've bent your Pony clamps for lack of clamping strength. You could back your panel truck over the brace or you could pull out your Stew-Mac go-bars and they'll be powerful enough. In other words, these things are too strong!

I tested several braces, from classical to steel string, on spruce, redwood, and cedar. I deliberately allowed the go-bar to push off the brace and hit the top, as they occasionally do. The results were sobering, to say the least. As it slipped off the brace onto the spruce top, the go-bar left a .035″–.045″ dent, over .125″ wide and nearly ½″ long. Onto redwood, the bar dented in only about .030″. Perhaps I could turn this into a top tuning device after all. Into (and nearly through) the cedar top, the go-bars dinged a whopping .075″. That would be through the edge of some guitars! With glue applied, I carefully go-barred a brace and as I propped the bar in place the glue slipped and I shot the brace across the room. I could have put my little brother's eye out!

The idea of go-bars, as I understand it, is to put many light pressure-producing bars along a brace, rather than a few very strong clamps. You get better, more even pressure. These guys just don't do it. I have suggested 3⁄16″ fiberglass kite spars to both Jay at Stew-Mac and Todd at LMI.

OK, the good news. The new Stew-Mac Guitar Neck Removal Jig is a simple, honest beauty. It has pads where you need them, adjustment, and plenty of it, where you need it, and a price you'll more than recoup the first time you put it into service. Of course, you could make one. But could you make it as nicely, as efficiently, and as user-friendly as this one? I think not. Pulling a dovetailed neck off any guitar, much less a priceless vintage masterpiece, is scary enough. This jig really makes it doable. I'd spring for the steam attachment and hook it to the pressure cooker or espresso machine, if I were you. The hefty thumbscrew lets you put gradual pressure on the heel as the steam loosens the glue joint. However, I'd put a bit of rubberized cork or leather between the pad and the heel just to be safe.

Stew-Mac made this jig a little larger than you'll usually need. This gives more clearance to see what you're doing and to hold things. This jig belongs in every serious repair shop. It's well made, affordable, and simple to use. At $54.90, it will pay for itself the first time you set it up.

(1998)

Wood Thickness Indicator
Ove Veggerby, Bainbridge Island, WA

Nut Files; Fret Slot Cleaning Tool
Stewart-MacDonald www.stewmac.com

As a guitar maker, I have little connection to violin building other than an openness to ideas that cross over from one discipline to the other. When I was starting out, I thought that if I could fix a guitar, I could fix a fiddle. I no longer believe that is always true. However,

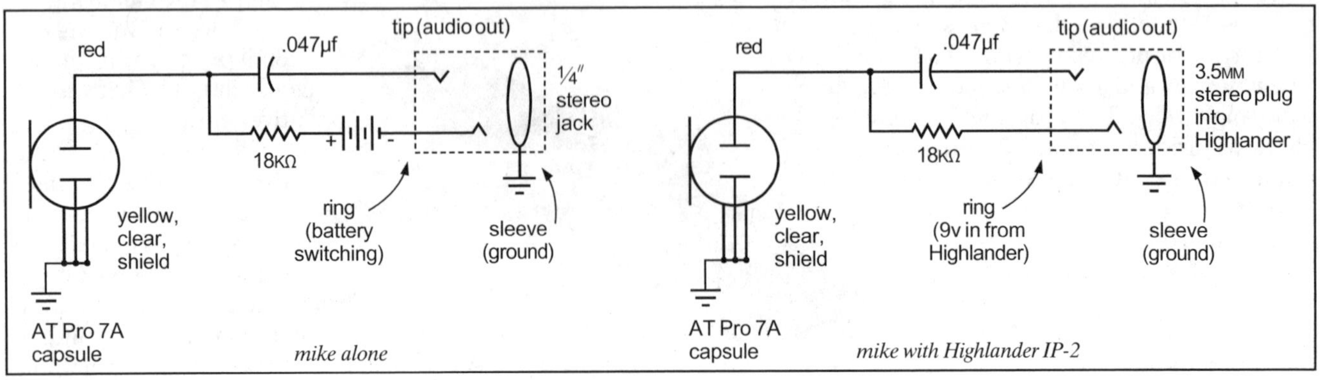

my understanding of the guitar making process allows me to extrapolate what might work in the violin field. Ove Veggerby, a luthier and tool maker in the Pacific Northwest, sent me a tool with which to determine the thickness for carving violin tops. Using an old idea and updating it in a new tool, Veggerby's Bjørndahl-Linton Wood Thickness Indicator lets you use "puncture points" to mark the depth for your carving. Rather than carve a little, measure a little, carve some more, measure some more, with Veggerby's tool you can make a series of tiny holes in the wood to which you then plane. With care, you are assured of a uniform thickness.

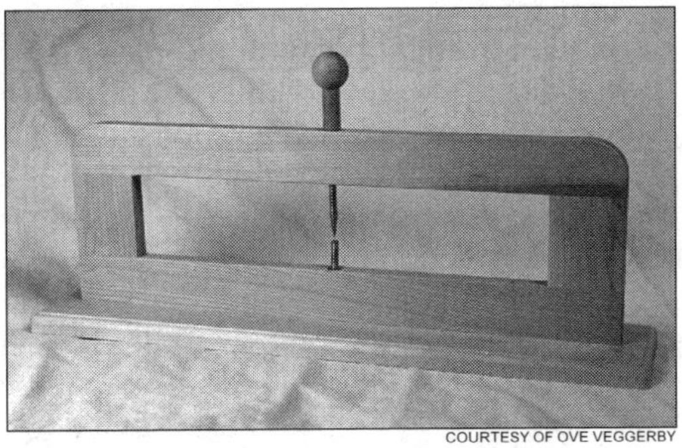

COURTESY OF OVE VEGGERBY

Somewhat misnamed, the Bjørndahl-Linton Wood Thickness Indicator, is less an indicator than a marker. Consisting of a wood frame and moving point, it is a simple machine. Very nicely made from hard maple, this tool is stiff and solidly constructed. The point, which punctures the wood to a predetermined depth, is steel and the bushings for both the point and the adjustable steel foot are phenolic. There is a hard rubber washer under the handle where it hits the top of the crossbar to absorb a bit of shock. It is hard enough that it does not seem to deform. The depth, therefore, remains pretty constant.

Designed for the violin, viola, and mandolin, the tool I tested is, of course, too small for a guitar. Veggerby tells me he makes a similar larger tool, by special order, for puncture-point marking archtops and cellos. Since I am not building any violins, I instead tested the Wood Thickness Indicator on a guitar top, puncture-point marking it and then planing to the bottom of the holes to see how effective a method it is. For hand planing a top, or back for that matter, this tool is very useful. Instead of measuring and planing, hoping not to go too far, using Veggerby's tool you can set the hole depth to whatever you wish and then plane until you reach the bottom of the holes. If you wish to plane one area to a different thickness than its neighbor, simply mark the thick areas first, then remark the deeper cuts, or mark both and cut to the different dimensions.

The Wood Thickness Indicator ($125, from P.O. Box 4580, Bainbridge Island, WA 98110; 206-842-0309) comes with a nifty gauge for setting the thickness. Made of nylon, the gauge is a long, tapered wedge marked at millimeter and half-millimeter increments. Simply slide the gauge to the depth you want and adjust the foot to touch. Puncture and plane your way to the thickness you have set.

The Wood Thickness Indicator is a simple but well-made tool that does its one job nicely. My only suggestion for a small improvement would be to put a low-tension spring around the shaft above the crossbar to lift the punch about 1/4″. Then one would only have to tap the punch down while moving the top around. The punch would automatically lift between holes. Such a spring is available from McMaster-Carr company (9434K139, $1.80, P.O. Box 4355, Chicago, IL 60680-4355; 630-833-0300).

McMaster-Carr is an excellent source for all sorts of stuff, by the way, from nuts and bolts, to thin latex for vacuum clamping. McMaster-Carr sells many good files, but no nut files, I'm afraid. I have purchased many nut files since I started, always looking for something both more accurate and more comfortable. My first files were from Germany, designed for violin work, I suspect. It was the early seventies, and I waited about six months to receive them after faithfully sending my money, converted to Deutschemarks. They cost about $10 each, quite a sum in those days. I used them for a decade or so, as they became duller and duller. I tried sharpening them using acid, but they just turned weird colors, ran around the shop, and started screaming at me in Basque.

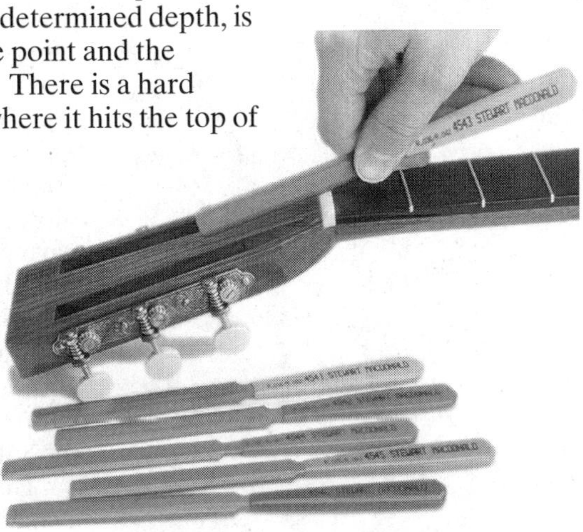

COURTESY OF STEWART-MACDONALD

I still have those German files, though I doubt I'll use them again. More recently I made nut files from needle files, grinding their width to the size I wanted, or from ignition point files, in the rare instances when I could find them with cut on the edges. Neither of these methods made a very accurate slot. Neither was very comfortable. I kept looking.

The new Double-edge Nut Files from Stew-Mac are quite a bit different from most files I've used. They feel different, and work better than most I've tried. I think they may be just the files I've been looking for.

Six files are available, as well as a set of the six that saves you some money over buying them one at a time.

#4541 has .016″ on one side and .022″ on the other
#4542 has .026″ and .032″
#4543 has .036″ and .042″
#4544 has .050″ and .060″
#4545 has .075″ and .090″
#4546 has .105″ and .120″

Of course, you can approximate the in-between sizes by rocking the file as you move it back and forth. The cutting length of each file is about 3 3/8″, as listed in the catalog. Some are as much as 1/8″ longer.

The first thing I noticed when I started to test these files, besides their colors, was their comfortable size and shape. They have rubber-coated handles that you can actually get a good grip on. The files are color-coded to make choosing the correct one simpler. However, the colors are in no particular order. I would have liked them to run in rainbow order to indicate that the next logical color was the next logical size, but the size and number of each is clearly marked on the side of the file. Again, a small improvement might have been to have either an arrow pointing to the side indicated by the specific size, or to always have the smaller, or larger, of the two on top when reading the number. Stew-Mac's Jay Hostetler told me that he tried to get the factory to do this, but that they couldn't or wouldn't. Mike Lindskold, who has written some really nifty electronics columns in the Stew-Mac catalog, suggested simply marking them myself! Next he'll be expecting us to grind the little teeth on the edges ourselves. I'm getting too lazy and picky as Stew-Mac offers too many tools.

I tested the files on some scraps before moving on to a couple of guitars I was building. I liked the feel of these files far better than any others I've used. They have a feeling of solidity which comes directly from their different design. Instead of carrying the slotting width all the way back from the edge (i.e., a .016″ file would be .016″ wide and therefore pretty flimsy), these files are thick through their midsection, making them stiffer and more massive. I immediately felt more control when filing with them. Although some of these files look a bit wavy on the edge, I didn't find it to be a problem. And though they are a relatively coarse cut, they seem to do a pretty smooth job. I haven't had any problem with strings hanging up in the groove. (Note: you're probably already putting #2 pencil lead in the nut grooves, so I won't suggest it.) The biggest difference, a direct result of their design, is that the slot wall is slightly angled outward (a V-shape with a round bottom, rather than a U), toward the top. I didn't find this to be a problem at all. I generally keep the string slot depth to half the diameter of the string, so the angle doesn't even show up on the nut. If you make it deeper, the angle should be above the point that could cause buzzing. In other words, it isn't an issue.

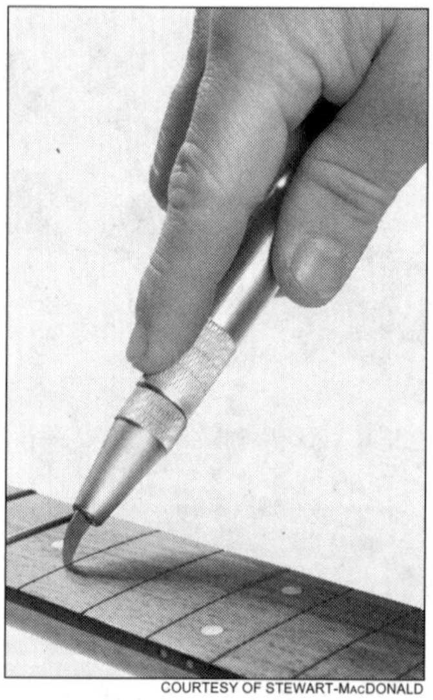
COURTESY OF STEWART-MACDONALD

I like that Stew-Mac included files large enough to do 5-string basses. The .120″ is great for low Bs. There still isn't a perfect way to do the first string on an electric guitar, with a .008″ or .009″; but you can grind the edge of a small file to a sharp profile and it works pretty well. If I really had my way, I'd like diamond-coated files, which would be great for graphite and mother-of-pearl nuts. Until I run the world, however, I'll leave my other files on the shelf and use these new ones from Stew-Mac.

Some of the tools I review in these pages are pretty expensive. The renaissance in lutherie that has occurred over the past few decades is bearing enough fruit for enough luthiers that a market for high-ticket tools has emerged. Hundred-dollar sets of files, hundred-plus-dollar routing jigs abound. For those luthiers with long waiting lists or working spouses (How do you get a luthier off your porch? Pay for the pizza.), these tools save time and earn their keep. However, lutherie isn't always lucrative and many fine builders and repairpeople can't afford expensive, specialized tools. For many years, most of my career, most luthiers built the tools and jigs they needed, time being far more bountiful than money. For many luthiers, this led to deep-seated feelings of guilt, perhaps even a painful empathy with the owners and families of Stew-Mac. No more guilt!

Stew-Mac now offers tools for even the poorest luthier. If you own an X-acto knife handle, you can be part of the lutherie-tool buying frenzy. The new Fret Slot Cleaning Tool (#4853, $.48) is a beautifully conceived and manufactured tool. At a mere .015″ thick, this tool gets into the corners of fret slots to remove glue, caked sawdust, filings, or any other little bits of gradoo that might accumulate. The catalog lists it as .016″, so you're not getting your full 48¢ worth, but remember, the files are ⅛″ longer than advertised and therefore worth more than you're paying. If I can stop complaining, so can you. Jay tells me that Stew-Mac is planning a line of these tools in other thicknesses for .022″ slots, .030″ slots, and so on. If they do, I'll devote an entire column to them. I'll buy every size they offer and so should you.

The Fret Slot Cleaning Tool is available with a heavy-duty handle (two cleaning tools with a handle, #4851, $12.50), and as a complete set (two cleaning tools, the handle, and ten each of three different super-sharp surgical-steel blades, #4852, $23.90). The blades are really sharp; the handle is really heavy duty. In fact, the handle is the biggest, heaviest-duty X-acto-style knife handle I've ever seen. Even *I* feel manly using it. Made of machined aluminum and brass, this handle means business. If you own a few handles already, you probably don't need it, but if your self-esteem is weak, or bullies have been kicking sand in your face, it's a small price to pay. The Fret Slot Cleaning Tool works very well to get the tiny scabs of glue residue from the slot when fretting a bound fingerboard. It allows a better fit for the fret and a more reliable glue job also. Perhaps, like me, you've been feeling bad that you didn't buy the Taylor Fret Buck (#4092, $229). Don't worry. At 48¢, we can all afford to do our part for the lutherie-based economy. ——

(1998)

Originally published in *American Lutherie #57–#60*, 1999

PRODUCT REVIEWS

by Fred Carlson

I hereby guarantee that nobody else works exactly the same way I do, or has exactly the same tastes as me, or has exactly any of my other problems. Therefore, it's pretty likely that what I write here doesn't exactly represent anyone but me. Take it with a grain of salt, and if your opinions or experiences are different, let us know. Learning from each other is what this is all about!

Turbo Carver

UltraSpeed Products www.turbocarver.com

Instruments have been my livelihood and much of my artistic output for over twenty-five years. For most of that time I've used the same set of simple hand tools I started with, augmented by a few commonplace machines. On the other hand, I've been an experimenter with materials since day one. Perhaps I'm less open minded toward new tools than alternative woods, but I'm willing to give my opinions on just about anything to do with lutherie. Heck, why not?

This first tool I'll be reviewing is intended for much wider craft and hobby application than just lutherie, but it has its roots in dentistry, as do certain other tools now common to aspects of instrument construction and ornamentation. I'll admit that part of my long-standing dislike of Dremels comes from association with dental experiences, mainly that familiar sound. When I started building guitars I got a Moto-Tool, mostly for routing binding channels. I burnt out the motor of that first one in about three guitars, then switched to a real router for bindings. I kept a Moto-Tool around for things like inlay, but since I didn't have a concept of the need for a good base to help guide the tool and give a consistent depth of cut, I never developed inlay skills with it. I was working freehand, which was the intuitive approach for me, but the results were disastrous. I learned to do inlay with knives and chisels, and saved the Dremel for sanding small parts, occasional root canals on my dog, and so on.

COURTESY OF ULTRA SPEED

So it was with a mixture of trepidation and curiosity that I agreed to review the **Turbo Carver**, made by Ultra Speed Products, Inc. This is essentially a really-o truly-o dental drill, optimized for use as a carving and etching tool. Available directly from Ultra Speed for $171 delivered, the Turbo Carver comes with a video that is well crafted and lays out the basic operation of the tool clearly. It features some peppy background music and a friendly guy in a suit who seems to *really like* the Turbo Carver. The best thing about the video is the demonstration of carving an ostrich egg. This may have limited use for your run-of-the-mill luthier, but if, like some of us, you have excess ostrich eggs around the shop (and a *lot* of spare time) this is a very cool project.

I was wondering about this tool's usefulness in regards to instrument building. I was also a bit concerned about the extensive warnings, in the video and manual, referring to the importance of lubricating the bearings every fifteen minutes(!). The Turbo-Carver handpiece (as they call it) is powered by compressed air; if you don't have a compressor you can rent a CO_2 tank from a welding supplier, but this can get pricey. I spray with a compressor, but don't have a lot of other experience with air tools, and was a bit concerned about setting it up. Happily, getting up and running with the Turbo Carver was easier than I'd feared.

Before testing, I gave some thought to the areas of lutherie in which the tool might be most useful. The major thrust of Ultra Speed's promotional materials is the use of the handpiece in doing relief carving in wood or other materials, and etching in glass, metal, and shell. They also promote an inlay technique that involves carving out a relief in wood and filling it with colored casting resin. They supply very clear instruction on this technique, both in the video and on their extensive website. It is difficult to get a consistent depth of cut working freehand; the use of casting resin in place of a solid piece allows for a recess that has uneven depth. It also allows for very intricate detail work, more along the lines of etching, but I think most builders would find this a bit far afield from what they think of as traditional inlay. Experimenter that I am, I could see great possibilities in the casting technique. I decided not to try it, mostly because of health problems that require me to minimize my exposure to toxic materials like epoxy casting resin. Truthfully, my initial guess was that the Turbo Carver would have limited use as an inlay tool when working with typical marquetry-type inlay. Rather, I expected it to shine as a tool for etching inlaid materials, like shell and metal. In my own work, I've always enjoyed doing relief carving on pegheads or scrolls, on necks, and around soundholes. Some traditional styles of ornamentation make use of floral relief carvings, such as those found on some banjo necks/heels and viola da gamba scrolls. I also sensed potential for the Turbo-Carver to be useful in those kinds of jobs.

I scrounged up a piece of spruce, a scrap of ebony, and a couple bits of abalone shell plate to play around with. After adjusting the regulator on the compressor to run the handpiece at optimum speed (a whopping 400,000 rpm!) and spritzing the bearings with the included can of spray lubricant, I was ready to play dentist. The dog ran when he saw me coming, so I started operating on the piece of spruce instead. The Turbo Carver handpiece is wonderfully light, about half an ounce by itself. It's about 4″ long, and the air feed that powers it is very flexible rubber (plastic?) tubing, about 1⁄8″ in diameter and also very light. Operating this tool really is a lot like wielding a pen or pencil; similar feel and something of that degree of control. It's activated (on/off; speed) by a simple and effective foot valve patched into the air line. The unit I tried came set up with 6′ of tubing from foot-valve to handpiece; more than enough for comfortable working. I found the whole setup to work very intuitively, for a power tool, and I was rather charmed by it (despite memories of staring up into a bright light with the evil dentist's silhouette hovering above me).

I began by writing my name in the spruce, like my school teachers always had me do on my homework. Suddenly, I felt a strange tingling sensation in the top of my scalp, and before I knew it I was channeling the energies of famous luthiers of the past! I began to carve, and soon there emerged two faces, in relief, obviously the channeled work of the great Stradivarius (who, in fact, worked as a dental assistant in San Jose before moving to Cremona to become a legendary violin builder). As can be seen from the picture, one of the carvings is clearly a depiction of the previous author of this column, which can be determined without question, despite the fact that Strad spelled Harry's last name wrong.

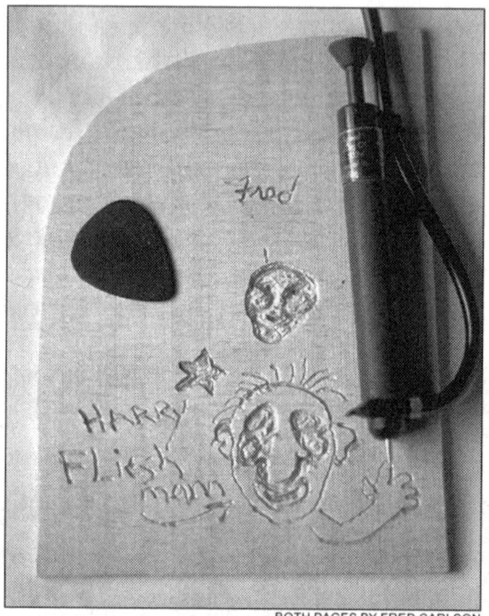

BOTH PAGES BY FRED CARLSON

Carving done with the Turbo-Carver, by the author, while channeling the spirit of Stradivarius.

In any case, I found it quite easy to carve the spruce (though Strad and I could do with a bit more practice!). The incredibly fast rotation fairly well eliminated the tendency for the bit to "grab." Next I tried the ebony, and found it nearly as easy to work, though I had to be more cautious about pushing it too hard. I had recently done an intricate, small inlay in a custom fretboard, with some sections less than 1⁄16″ in width. Working with knives and chisels this small recess took me several hours to complete, and came out very well, although it was hard to get a consistent depth. After a bit of playing around, I ascertained that I could get an accurate enough depth in small areas with the Turbo Carver, and I probably could have done that same recess in about fifteen minutes, with comparable accuracy.

I then tried engraving a piece of abalone, and was as pleased as I'd expected. I've never gotten good at using hand engraving tools, and the Turbo Carver felt a lot like drawing with a pen. Since I had a piece of shell in my hand, it occurred to me to cut out a shape, which I would ordinarily do with a jeweler's saw and needle files, although some use a Dremel for this part of inlaying, as well. I was amazed at the ease with which the tool slid through the .050″ abalone; the degree of control and smoothness of cut were wonderful. The best part was being able to hold the abalone in one hand while cutting with the other; no vise or cutting board. This meant being able to rotate the piece as needed, freely. The rotary cutting action seemed much less likely to break the shell than the push/pull of a saw. The small size of the tool made visibility great. There is an obvious dust problem when cutting shell this way, and though I didn't try any underwater cutting, that is the way to go with any quantity of work, and in fact the instruction video recommends and describes just that technique.

I was pleasantly surprised by the Turbo Carver, but I wanted to compare it to a similar tool. There are two popular "handpiece" type tools that I'm aware of; Dremel's flexible-shaft attachment, or the heavier-duty tool made by Foredom. You can get a Dremel Multi-Pro Flex-Shaft Kit, which comes with a variety of bits and accessories, for about $90; the Foredom lists for over $200. If you have a recent Moto-Tool or Multi-Pro you can get just the Flex-Shaft attachment for about $35. I decided to try the Dremel attachment. Since I already have a Moto-Tool, setting it up was simple, and I got a 1⁄16″ collet so I could use the same, tiny dentist burrs that the Turbo Carver uses. I immediately noticed how clunky the Dremel unit is; the handpiece itself weighs around 2.5 oz., or more than four times that of the Turbo Carver. The flexible shaft is stiff and noticeably harder to hold up and move around than the light tubing of the Turbo Carver. For optimal use, you need to hang the Moto-Tool that powers the handpiece somewhere above and near your work. The shaft is only 3′ long, and can't tolerate bends tighter than a 6″ radius without excessive heating up. I found that the shaft tended to heat up a bit anyway. Besides the relative discomfort of the heavier tool, I really noticed that the slower cutting speed (30,000 maximum rpm) made for a less smooth, easy cut. However, I did find that I was basically able to do the same tasks; the relief carving was rougher, the engraving seemed to work well, and cutting shell seemed slower and took more effort, but the results seemed nearly as good.

Clearly, for ease of use and general function in the areas I performed my limited tests in, the Turbo Carver won out. In addition to features I've mentioned, it is also very quick and easy to change bits, as they just press-fit into the handpiece. The lubrication was not as big a hassle as I'd thought it might be, though every 15 minutes is pretty often (I notice the Dremel's

Flex-Shaft requires greasing, but only after 25–30 hours of operation). I did have a problem with the Turbo Carver spraying oil on my work piece after I lubed it. I called up Bill Vogel at Ultra Speed, to ask him about that, as well as to find out more about the life expectancy of the tool. He told me it was necessary to run the handpiece for a moment, away from your workpiece, immediately after lubricating, to clear excess oil. The Turbo Carver comes with a three-month warranty on the bearings, which, he said, need to be taken care of to last. There's really not much else in that tiny handpiece. The problem comes when you introduce dust or grit into the bearings, either when you insert a new bit, or when you spray in the lubrication. Apparently, with most air-powered handpieces of this type, the likeliest time for dirt to get into the bearings is just after you shut off the air, to stop the tool. At that moment a vacuum is created which can draw dirt particles in through the lubrication opening. Ultra Speed's design features a closed lubrication tube; you pinch it open to insert a tube from the spray can to lube it. This feature helps keep dirt out of those precious bearings, which, according to Bill, can extend the life of a Turbo Carver well beyond the industry's average life expectancy of about 200 hours for this kind of tool. I pressed for a bit more definite sense of how long a Turbo Carver might last. Bill responded that it will vary greatly, depending on how the tool is used and cared for. He points out, for instance, that besides dust, it's important to be sensitive to the heating up of the incoming air tube and the bearings; ideally you match the air pressure from the compressor to the carving load on the tool, and no excess heat is generated (less air pressure for delicate work, more when you're hogging off a lot of material). Although he suggests that about one year of "average use" can be expected (typically more than 200 hours), he claims instances of Turbo Carvers lasting five years. Although 200-plus hours doesn't sound like much, in my own work I can't imagine putting that much use on one in a year's time. And then, I wonder how many hours one can expect from a Dremel Moto-Tool?

A Dremel does have its advantages: it's relatively cheap, you can use it with a base (without the flexible shaft attachment) for consistent depth of cut, and there is a much wider variety of bits and attachments available for tasks as varied as grinding, cutting, and routing. There are also now a large number of neat Dremel-based jigs and tools, specifically designed for luthiers' needs. The Turbo Carver has, in comparison, very specific and limited use.

If you do a lot of inlay and engraving, and you have an air compressor, the Turbo Carver may be a real godsend for you. If you are new to inlaying and relief carving, the accompanying video describes a method of using stencils to transfer a design and guide your work, to help get you started. For the occasional inlay artist on a limited budget, it's certainly not a must-have tool. I don't think I'll get one right away; I already have a Dremel, and I like working with quiet, slow-moving tools too much to feel compelled to part with the money for another dentist drill. But I do think it's a lovely tool, and some of you may soon find it to be indispensable, if you decide to get one.

(1999)

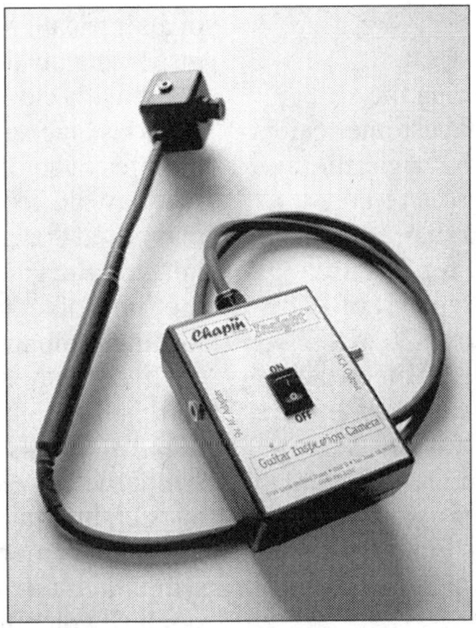

Chapin Insight *Guitar Inspection Camera*

Chapin Guitars
www.chapinguitars.com/insight.html

Toward the end of last year, a mysterious box appeared at my door. I love getting packages, especially unexpected ones, and I opened it eagerly. Inside were several unusual apparatuses that had a distinctly luthierly look to them, but no written instructions or other indication of possible use. I received around the same time a brief, cryptic email message from the Fleishmeister concerning this box and its contents, which apparently were products intended for review in future columns. Harry refers to one of the items as the "luthier's proctoscope." That being the only scrap of information I possessed, I figured it as good a place to start as any.

Having only a vague, foreboding sense of the meaning of "proctoscope," I consulted my trusty 1944 Webster's. The definition I found there made me begin to feel a bit uneasy about conducting testing of this tool. However, a remarkable stroke of good fortune came upon this humble reviewer when, in a sudden feat of unprecedented journalistic observation, I read the label on the product in question.

It turns out that what I held in my hands, and what I review for you here today, good luthiers, is none other than the **Chapin *Insight* Guitar Inspection Camera,** made by luthier Bill Chapin of Chapin Guitars. It also turns out that I had seen Bill Chapin himself demonstrate one of these things at a meeting of the Northern California Association of Luthiers, so I even sort of knew what it did.

To make sure I had all the info right, I called the number listed and eventually got hold of Bill Chapin on his cellular phone (am I the only living luthier without a cell phone?). Bill assured me that the label was correct, that I did in fact have one of his guitar inspection cameras. He'd been wondering what happened to it. Bill also steered me to his website for more info on the camera.

So, what this thing is, is a "low light, miniature video surveillance camera" on a stick. The "stick" is a flexible neck that allows for positioning of the tiny lens-and-circuit-board camera, which is housed in an approximately 1⅜″ diameter cube-shaped enclosure. Through the flexible neck run the wires that send video signals out and power in. These attach to a simple connection box sporting an on/off switch, a place for a 9v battery to power the unit, an input for an AC adapter to run the thing on household (shop) current and an RCA output which you connect to the line-in/video-in on your TV with a standard RCA cord.

So what use would a luthier have for a tiny video camera? Lots, according to its creator. Chapin recommends the Insight for tasks like:

- authentication: finding and reading/photographing internal dates and signatures
- locating cracks, loose braces, loose kerfing/linings, and so on
- being able to see what you're doing inside a guitar when you have your arm in the soundhole (might be just the thing for reshaping bracing)
- placing internal pickups

He got especially enthusiastic about using the camera to "sell" a repair job: if a potential customer can see the internal damage with their own eyes, right there on the screen, Bill says they always go for the repair.

This would seem to indicate that the tool presents its greatest value to repair shops. In fact, repair guru Frank Ford ("the Ben Franklin of guitar repair") of Gryphon Stringed Instruments in Palo Alto, CA is a major fan of the guitar inspection camera. (You owe it to yourself to check out Frank's amazing website at www.frets.com, where you will not only find a special section on the Insight with lots of cool pictures taken inside guitars, but also vast amounts of info on repair, lutherie, instruments, and so on. Thanks, Frank!!) I contacted Frank to get his comments on, and uses for, the inspection camera. Here's what he said.

"This little camera is just the thing for demonstrating work inside guitars when I'm lecturing or teaching. I've gotten so used to working blind inside that sometimes I forget to use the camera when I could. It's great for the website because I can show some stuff that most folks haven't seen.

"There are some crack repairs I've been able to pull off easily because I could see exactly what I was doing inside, even when my arm filled up the soundhole; precise alignment of [crack reinforcing] cleats in impossible places, for example. I did a pickup installation that had two jacks side by side with interior nuts to tighten, and was able to see what I was doing with a crow's-foot wrench.

"On occasion I'll use the camera to illustrate a crack, damaged bridge plate, or loose brace to a customer. I'd use it more often that way, except we can't afford the real estate to keep the monitor on the counter."

Bill Chapin also mentions a use for it not necessarily specific to repair work: as a magnifying device for inspecting or working on very small areas, external or internal. He finds it useful, for instance, in the inspection of fret ends. I find myself doing a lot of work with a big magnifying lamp, and could see the benefits of instead having something I could manipulate easily, and approach any part of the work from any angle, as would be the case with this tiny camera.

One thing I brilliantly surmised early on is that you need a TV (or other monitor) on or near your workbench for optimum usefulness of a tool like this. That could be a drawback, especially if you have an already small workspace. To test the camera I had to use my partner Suzy's mom's TV; this meant setting up a guitar on the dining room table, amidst a jumble of newspapers, mail, books, cats, and so on (at least it was cleaner than my workbench!). I slid the combo TV/VCR unit close enough to plug the RCA cord into the video-in. Even for a stone-age luthier like me, it was easy to get the TV to display the signal from the camera (a minor miracle, considering that I can *never* figure out how to play a video on the thing!)

In very short order, I found myself deeply engrossed in an intricate and important lutherie project: inspecting my dental work. And whoa!! Have you ever-looked at a closeup of your own tongue, writhing in glorious black and white on a 21″ screen? After ten minutes or so of inner mouth movies, I moved on to my two-day-old growth of chin hair. From ½″ away, magnified dozens of times (or a lot, anyway), I could imagine the giant redwood stumps of my stubble to be the ruins of an old-growth forest, clear-cut by some evil logging company.

Eventually, since Suzy and her Mom were watching all this, I felt obligated to actually look at a guitar's innards. I had a Sympitar (one of my guitars with sympathetic strings inside the neck and body) ready to inspect, but quickly ran into a problem when I tried to insert the camera through the soundhole: the dang sympathetic strings blocked most of the already smallish hole; the camera wouldn't fit. This would indeed even be a problem for less weird guitars, if they

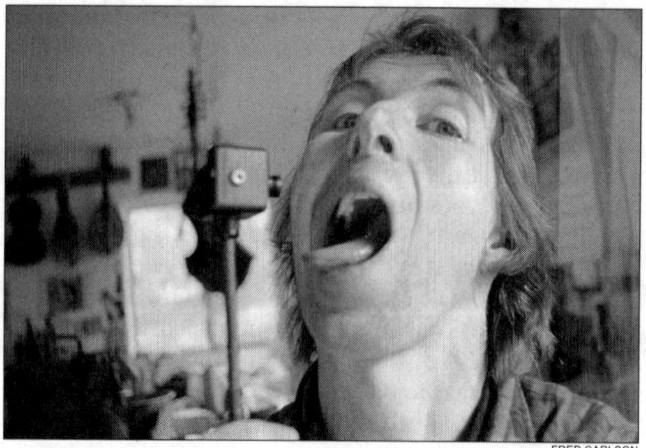

FRED CARLSON

This is what you would see if you were inside the TV screen as our new Product Reviews *columninst Fred Carlson inspects his dental work with a* Chapin Insight *Guitar Inspection Camera.*

happened to be *f*-hole archtops, to say nothing of mandolins and fiddles. Chapin is currently working on a model for archtop guitar-size holes, but so far has found nothing small enough to work with a violin *f*-hole.

I was stumped, until I remembered that I build trap doors into the backs of Sympitars (good thing I was around to think of this!), and that would make a perfect access point. Camera inside, I looked around at weird braces, lots of dust, cobwebs, a half-eaten bagel with peanut butter, several dozen guitar picks, and so on. I could even make out a signature on the underside of the top; on closer inspection it turned out to be mine, or a plausible forgery.

Two marvelous features of this camera are its depth of focus (you can focus on something less than ½″ away, or clear across a room), and its ability to function well in low light conditions. This latter feature means that to get a clear view of your guitar's insides you merely need to have an external light shining down on the guitar top. With most top woods, plenty of light will penetrate through the thin wood to illuminate the picture (this process is called "candling" the top). This won't work with hardwood tops (mahogany, koa) or guitars covered with opaque paint or old, dried-up pizza toppings.

Since I'm not doing much repair work these days, this tool might not get a lot of use in my shop. One thing I would use it for would be to take cool pictures of the insides of my guitars, to put on my website and show to customers. You can set up a personal computer to "capture" video frames, which you can then edit and use like any digital photograph. I'd also love to make movies using a guitar insides as the set.

In fact I can think of tons of fun stuff to do with this camera. Unfortunately, the amount of practical use I'd make of it might not justify my spending the $349 (plus shipping) it would take to get me one from Chapin Guitars. On the other hand, if I was running a lutherie school, this could be a really important addition to teaching capabilities. If I was doing lots of repairs, it would be a great help in some situations. Bill Chapin has done a good job of assembling a good tool, and the price seems reasonable for what you get.

ALL THIS PAGE BY FRANK FORD

Frank Ford took these three photos with a Chapin Insight *Guitar Inspection Camera. The images were then captured and put on his website (www.frets.com), from which we downloaded them with his permission. From top: Collings OM-2H; signature inside a 1900 Martin 00-28; two sets of top lining mortises in a Selmer Maccaferri guitar.*

I should point out, however, that for the adventurous do-it-yourselfer, or a starving luthier-type who can't live without a tiny video camera like this, there are alternatives (and not just the tried-and-true automotive inspection mirror). A friend of mine fluent in high-tech stuff decided he'd like to try putting together his own inspection camera. He brought what he'd come up with over to my shop, so I could compare it with Chapin's. The main differences are a slightly larger camera enclosure (but still easily fitting through a standard, round soundhole), and no flexible neck, just a little black box with a lens, and a wire coming out of it. It also doesn't have the connection box with the battery compartment. Instead, the wire coming out of the camera terminates in two jacks: one accepts an RCA cord and plugs into the TV, the other plugs into a standard power supply. The camera itself seemed to have similar characteristics to the unit Chapin uses; it works just fine. It wouldn't be too hard to rig up some kind of a flexible neck, and voila!, you'd have virtually the same setup. The components for the one I checked out, that is camera, enclosure (box/case/housing) and power supply ended up costing my friend around $75. The same supplier also sells battery enclosures and a whole range of different miniature cameras with differing sizes, specs, and prices, both B&W and color (Chapin's unit is B&W; color is definitely costlier, and probably not needed for most uses). I noticed a slightly smaller camera with perhaps slightly better features for around $100 (camera and housing only), listed in the catalog my friend ordered from. This catalog, from the company "Supercircuits," will, if nothing else, give you an education about miniature video stuff. They have a website (www.supercircuits.com). If you want to play around with this kind of stuff on your own, I recommend getting their catalog.

If you've got the money and want something that works great with out any fuss, get a Chapin *Insight* Guitar Inspection Camera. Bill's a luthier like the rest of us; it's sort of like keeping the money in the family. You can order one from Chapin Guitars, or from Luthier's Mercantile International (www.lmii.com) for the same $349 (plus shipping).

So do it, and start making those "X-(brace) Rated" movies today!

(1999)

Iboney
Pete's Music Center www.petesmusic.net

Hey, kids! Welcome to another exciting column of product reviews! In an effort to continually outdo myself with entertaining, informative (and modest) articles about what's late and great in the world of lutherie "stuff," I am about to institute what may be the first Singing Product Review in the history of the GAL. Actually, you will have to do the singing (and make up the tune), but I did write the words to a song about one of this issue's featured products. It's a bone nut and saddle material called "Iboney," and I got so excited by it (bone products can do this to a luthier) that this burst from me spontaneously:

The Iboney Song
I put I-bo-ney on my I-ba-nez
And it sounded so good
I could eat my fez.
If I et my hat, I'd be still hun-gry
for the soulful sound
of that I-bo-ney!

Iboney is, like I said, a bone product. Pete Van Alstyne (Pete's Music Center) takes bovine front femur bones (I think that's sorta like cow's leg bones) and slices them up into blanks for nuts and saddles. Somewhere along the way, he treats the bone in some way that he calls "refining and tempering," with the goal of getting a harder, more consistent product without the chalkiness of some bone. Although he's not divulging the actual process, Pete says that the hardness also in part comes from the exclusive use of the front femur, which he feels contains the hardest bone. Typical bone available for nuts and saddles has been bleached and may have had acids or other chemicals used in the cutting process that contribute to a chalky quality of texture. Iboney is treated only with hydrogen peroxide and Pete's special recipe.

My tests of Iboney seemed to confirm Pete's contentions. I recently strung up a new guitar for which I made two saddles, one of Iboney and one of the standard bleached bone pieces that I get from a prominent lutherie supply house. I made notes along the way, comparing workability, hardness, appearance, and tone. The Iboney seemed to actually cut easier (I roughed the blanks out with a jeweler's saw), and it may have been my imagination, but it seemed a bit easier to machine-sand as well. That being the case, I was surprised at how the sanded blanks felt: the Iboney was hard and slippery under my thumbnail; the bleached bone had a definite chalky feel. Holding the now virtually identically sized blanks up to a light, I noted that the bleached bone was very consistent in its translucency, whereas the Iboney had a lot of variation, dark and light areas. I wondered if it was the bleaching that created the consistency of light permeation, or if inconsistencies in the Iboney, or something in Pete's treatment, made that material more variable. In any case, I never noticed any problem that could be related to this. The Iboney polished up to a creamy, natural bone yellow, with color variations and occasional dark flecks (kind of like my teeth). The bleached bone polished up snowy white. I find both attractive in their own way. As I sort of expected, after switching back and forth between the two saddle materials on the instrument several times, I couldn't make any definitive judgment about tone differences. The Iboney definitely didn't sound significantly different from the bleached bone; both had that nice, crisp bone sound that I like. When I inspected the wear on the two saddles with a magnifying lens, after testing them on the instrument, the Iboney saddle was definitely slightly less cut into by the strings. All this seems to indicate a very favorable comparison in function, so what about price? Pete will supply Iboney in "planks" big enough for two saddles or three nuts, at a cost of $4 a plank (plus shipping). These will be cut thick and will require quite a bit more machining than a prethicknessed bone nut or saddle. However, that can be an advantage — I often end up with bone blanks that are warped, and the presized saddles don't have a lot of extra thickness to sand away to flatten them. In comparison to the Iboney cost, I've been spending $4.44 per nut and $5.77 per saddle for blanks of standard, bleached, roughly presized bone.

My conclusion from this limited testing: if you don't mind doing a bit more grinding of bone, Iboney has the sound of a good deal.

(1999)

Routing Jig; Router Base for Moto Tool; Fingerboard/Bridge Heating Iron
Stewart-MacDonald www.stewmac.com

Stewart-MacDonald's Guitar Shop Supply has been valiantly churning out tools and jigs designed for use with the Dremel Moto Tool, or its current "professional" version, the "MultiPro." They've come up with a wonderfully simple, solid, no-nonsense design for a jig that helps in the task of routing purfling channels in violin top and back plates. This job is usually undertaken when the plates have their outline shape and outside arching completed, but before the plates are graduated and glued to the ribs. Traditionally, the purfling channel is marked with a double-bladed marking tool and cut by hand with a knife. The Stew-Mac jig is of solid machined aluminum in two parts; an upper bar that the MultiPro screws directly into is attached to a lower section that bears against the edge of the violin plate, acting as a guide. My older #395, type 4 Moto-Tool fits just fine. Pretty basic, but it works.

The distance in from the edge that the cut is made can be adjusted by loosening a knurled nut with your fingers, and sliding the bar (and Dremel) in the appropriate direction. You put a bit of the correct width for your purfling channel into the Dremel, set the depth of cut by how much the bit protrudes out of the chuck, and off you go. You have to be careful to keep the tool's axis perpendicular to the part being routed. The violin plate is held or clamped on a (hopefully) nice, flat surface, and you basically just slide the tool around it, maintaining that perpendicularity. Problems? Well, my first impression was that the jig, with the Dremel attached, is rather tippy. The design would benefit from a wider foot or base. Also, having to adjust the depth of cut by loosening the Dremel Tool's chuck and sliding the bit in or out takes some trial and error to get the setting right; the addition of some kind of integrated fine adjustment mechanism would be great. I found that the tool guided the cutting quite nicely in my test, and wasn't hard to control; however, it won't replace my usual method of doing this task. I fit my Moto-Tool into a Dremel "drill press" (a commonly available Dremel accessory), which I have mounted over a table sporting an adjustable guide, and I use it as an overhead router, sliding the plate along against the guide instead of moving the tool. The really nice thing about that is you can set the depth stop on the drill press, and it's really easy to raise and lower the bit when starting, stopping and going around the corners. Still, Stew-Mac's jig is way easier than using a knife, and at $36.96 plus shipping, certainly affordable. Another suggested use of it is for cutting purfling channels around guitar soundholes. I don't think I'd be likely to do that job with this tool, at least not on a round soundhole. It's easy to make a jig (for Moto-Tool or router) to cut concentric circles and to cut such a channel before the soundhole is cut. I could imagine, however, Stew-Mac's Purfling Channel Routing Jig working great for a channel around a nonround soundhole, assuming the hole is big enough for the tool's footprint.

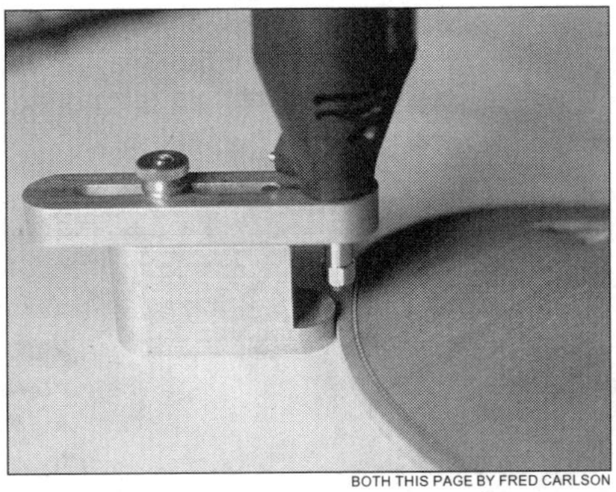

BOTH THIS PAGE BY FRED CARLSON

Another tool to be used with your Dremel is a cute little brass gizmo that screws onto Stew-Mac's Precision Router Base for MultiPro/Moto-Tool, and is an edge guide for routing binding channels for "bindings of any thickness up to ⅜″." It attaches neatly to the two holes in the foot of the router base. A third screw loosens the sliding arm that has a roller guide on one end, for adjustment of distance from guide to cutter. Depth is adjusted on the router base. This accessory is a great addition to the router base. My only thought is that I would prefer that the screws supplied for attachment and adjusting be Phillips head, instead of ones that require a little Allen wrench. I'm always losing those dang little hex wrenches! Stew-Mac sells the edge guide for $25.90 (plus shipping).

I should point out that the fine quality of the above-described tools does not make up for variations in the quality of the Moto-Tool or MultiPro's construction. Jay Hostetler at Stewart-MacDonald says that the newer MultiPro model is greatly improved. My experience with the earlier Moto-Tools is that there is a certain degree of "wiggle" to the chuck that varies from tool to tool and can translate into some sloppiness of cut. Jay suggested, and I concur, that a review/comparison of the current MultiPro and similar tools would make a good future column.

Luthier's Waffle Iron? And finally, a tool I had to guess about. This thing is a rectangular hunk of metal, about 2″×3″ and 1″ thick, with a wooden handle coming off it at an angle. One surface has five parallel grooves in it and a concave radius. My first guess was some kind of waffle iron, or something for branding fret markings into the tops of breads or muffins. To find out, I called the American Instant Biscuit-Mix Company's Consumer Hotline (1-800-Eat-Starch). And to my surprise, I didn't have to wait to talk to a representative. Unfortunately, I didn't get far into my question about Luthier's Waffle Irons before the tech-support guy terminated the connection, rather abruptly. Luckily, I came across the tool soon afterward, pictured in (once again) the Stew-Mac catalog. Turns out it's a Fingerboard/Bridge Heating Iron. The solid aluminum block is meant to be heated up and put on the area of a guitar fingerboard that extends over the body, to heat and loosen the glue joint prior to removal. The block's radiused and grooved surface is meant to contact the fingerboard, the grooves accommodating the frets and allowing the heated metal to sit directly on the wood. The end of the tool opposite the handle is also slightly radiused, and is intended for similarly heating up a guitar bridge to facilitate removing it. They say it is "designed to be heated on your hot plate to 250°F" and they also sell a surface thermometer to help avoid that "Louisiana-style" pan-blackened cooking effect.

This is a very nicely designed tool in terms of shape and size. The handle is positioned perfectly; the thing has a very nice heft to it, and in my limited testing I successfully used it to remove a fretboard extension. I heated it up on an old electric clothes iron (the tool I usually use for removing fretboard ends), and set it to work on the 'board. I found that it didn't hold its heat quite long enough to soften the Titebond in the glue joint on the first application; it seemed like two or three heatings were necessary (while the tool was being reheated, the joint was cooling a bit). I suspect the heat might be channeled more efficiently to the glue joint if the tool is rested on top of the frets, rather than directly on the wood. Because the radiused surface of the block will not be a perfect match for every fretboard (it was certainly quite different from that of my test guitar), only the edges of the block will contact the wood in many cases. If the tool rested directly on the metal frets, the heat would be conducted more quickly into a larger area of the fingerboard, and closer to the glue joint as well. In response to this idea, Jay at Stew-Mac comments that the tool was designed to "stay away from the frets" as much as possible. He contends that heating the frets directly may be more likely to cause them to move or loosen, especially in the case of frets that are glued in place. His point is well taken. However, if the fingerboard gets hot enough to loosen its joint with the top, it seems that it would also get hot enough to affect glue in fret slots. In my experience, the act of removing and replacing a fretboard extension necessitates a certain amount of fretwork. As a matter of course, I usually end up doing at least a partial level-and-dress of the frets as part of such a job.

Ultimately, this tool did help me in removing the fretboard end, and I suspect it would be useful in heating up bridges for removal as well, although its design makes it more appropriate for bridges with a shape and profile more similar to those on Martin guitars than the ones I make. Stew-Mac's Fingerboard/ Bridge Heating Iron sells for $59.50 (plus shipping). I've been using an old clothes iron (that cost me zero) for removing fretboard ends for years. It works, but it's also not perfect. I've been meaning to look for a little travel iron; that might be about right. What I'd really like is a tool about the size and shape of Stew-Mac's, but with a heating element in it, and a control for the amount of heat. And, if the fret grooves were instead ridges, I could make grooves in the tops of my Luthier's Waffles, to hold the butter and syrup!

Start with a Song, End with a Song. When I talked to Jay at Stewart-MacDonald to get his comments on the above review, I could tell (using my finely-honed Luthier's Intuition) that he was really deeply disappointed that I hadn't written a song about any of his company's products. He didn't actually say anything, in fact he did a very good job of concealing it, but I could tell by the way he couldn't bring himself to say how much he liked *The Iboney Song* that there was a lingering sadness that might affect our relationship in the future, if I didn't rectify it somehow. Well, that was all it took to get inspiration flowing. So here it is, for Jay and all the good folks at Stew-Mac, what you've all been waiting for:

FRED CARLSON

The Luthier's Waffle Iron Song

Well, me and my apprentice, Byron,
sure love our Luthier's Waffle Iron.
In the evening when we start a-tirin'
after a long hard day of pickup wirin'
we get the ol' hot plate a-firin'
and heat up that Luthier's Waffle Iron.
Then, when we're stuffed, we tune up the lyre an'
sing songs until we hear the siren.
The cops say we're disturbing the peaceful environ
but me and my apprentice, Byron,
sure love our Luthier's Waffle Iron!

(1999)

Custom Cases

Calton Cases www.caltoncases.ab.ca
Hi-Tone Cases
Mark Leaf Cases

There is one issue every instrument builder confronts at some point in the process of bringing a new musical tool/artwork into the world: whether it's an instrument for yourself, your granddaughter, a customer, or "the marketplace," the thing will need to be stored and transported in some kind of case.

Case History. When, as a teenager, I built myself a little plywood banjo, I sewed a case for it out of an old rummage-sale raincoat. Back in those days before home computers and multiple nose rings, when I built my first guitar at Charles Fox's little school in rural Vermont (GRD), I suddenly had a need for a more substantial kind of case. The school offered to place a bulk order — if each of the six students got a case, we could get a price of $35 apiece. These were pretty generic cases, typical examples of those reasonably good hardshell black boxes that we are all familiar with. For me, an unemployed, nineteen-year-old aspiring luthier living by the good graces of the communal homestead where I shared income, $35 was a small fortune; I had to call home from the school to make sure it was OK to spend the money.

For my next guitar, the first I made on my own, I was determined not to waste all that cash when I could certainly make a fine case myself. In fact, since I had neither the dealer connections, bulk purchasing power, or really any idea where to get a case except at a retail music store, it would have cost me considerably more than the previous one.

But I really was sure I could make a case. Having little understanding of the materials and their possible interactions with each other, I went to the hardware store and got some one-inch styrofoam ("bead-board") insulation, a can of fiberglass resin, some fiberglass fabric, and some bright red colorant. I made a trapezoidal box with the styrofoam, covered it with cloth and the red goop, and sat back to watch as the styrofoam proceeded to melt into something that probably would have qualified me to receive federal funds for toxic waste cleanup. Magically, the catalyst kicked in before the thing had completely liquefied, and it hardened up into a, well, a sort of amorphous, lumpy red coffin. Having thus perfected the technique, I went on to make a cover, reinforcing the edges of the lid and the top edge of the open coffin with wood strips. Somehow I got hinges attached, and a leather strap for a handle. I lined the inside with a soft foam covered with some cheap, silvery-white velvet-like stuff (which I thought, at the time, was *really* fancy and beautiful), and I had my completed case. In fact, this case was possibly the most hideously ugly object ever created, and featured the added attraction of giving off really vile, toxic smells for its entire life. I actually sold the instrument that lived in it, and was glad to see the case go too; unfortunately for me, the first thing the customer did was to buy a case from a local music store, and generously return the red coffin to me. My feelings were a little hurt, though eventually I threw the thing out.

After that experience, I started buying cases for my guitars. In fact, as my penchant for designing unusual instruments continued to develop, I had a rule that any guitar I built had to fit into a commercially available case. However, I was also building other instruments that definitely didn't fit into guitar cases, and often I wouldn't have the money to spring for a commercial case. In these instances I took to making boxes out of 1⁄8″ "doorskin" plywood, which I reinforced and lined with foam and velvet. For guitar-sized instruments, these boxes tended to be huge and unwieldy. One customer complained that the bass viola da gamba case I made was too big to fit into his car! So, as the years went by, I tended more and more towards designing instruments to fit in available cases (what a radical concept, huh?), and as I became more commercially successful as a luthier, I located sources for such cases, and could even afford them.

Boxed In by Case Designs. Then, a couple of things changed in my thinking about cases: first, I began to dislike the fact that I was allowing my instrument designs to be constricted by those mass-produced cases. I mean, I'm an artist, dang it all, why should my creativity be limited by the shape of a guitar case? And second, I began to find the cases I was using to be rather ugly. I'm selling an instrument that's hopefully a beautiful work of art, and the case is part of the package. Shouldn't it be beautiful as well? I thought about trying to make my own cases again; I really could make a beautiful case if I wanted to. But I just don't want to. So I started looking into what was available.

I ended up trying out Mark Leaf Cases, largely because their construction process seems to allow the potential of extensive customization of shape and size (they made me an awesome double-neck guitar case!). I've been very happy with the cases I've gotten from them, but their exterior look is a little "industrial," and they tend to be a bit bulky in size. I've had this desire for something a bit more aesthetically refined, so I keep looking. One I've looked into but haven't tried yet is Calton Cases. They seem really well made and durable, but aren't as flexible in custom shape options. Actually, when I talked to them a couple of years ago, they were very willing to take on custom work, but said I would need to supply a wooden form if the exterior shape differed from the ones they offer. I'd consider that readily if I was going to reproduce a particular shape, but with one-of-a-kind instruments I'd be spending a lot of time making forms for cases, which is part of what I want to avoid.

BOTH THIS PAGE COURTESY OF HI-TONE

I use Mark Leaf and Calton cases for some comparisons later in this review, largely because they are in the appropriate general ballpark of quality and pricing. I have some degree of familiarity with them, and suspect that many readers will as well. There is no intention on my part to slight the many other manufacturers of cases.

At a festival a year or so ago, I had the opportunity to meet Sam Mancuso, who builds Hi-Tone guitar cases. I was immediately attracted to the sleek aesthetics of his design, and he expressed a willingness to take on unusual custom jobs, so I decided to give Hi-Tone a try.

Top and above: Hi-Tone guitar cases

Sam Mancuso calls his cases "Handcrafted Works of Art," and steadfastly proclaims that his "goal is to produce the best instrument case available on this planet." High claims and lofty goals for a guy who admits that it's been only three years since he built his first case that didn't end up in the dumpster. But his current work seems to show a real commitment to those good intentions.

The Case for Hi-Tone. Hi-Tone currently offers two basic styles of guitar case, in three standard sizes. Called Classic, Dreadnought, and Archtop, the standard sizes come in either the BC Model with flat top and back construction and generally simpler detailing, or the KW Original, which has a 6-ply hardwood-laminate arched top and flat 3-ply back. Both models are available with a covering of heavy-duty padded vinyl, or pigskin leather. A more expensive version, the CC (Creme de la Creme) model comes covered in cowhide and isn't included on the price list because it "scares people away" (personally, I'm pretty scared by pigskin). The Hi-Tone standard shape is a kind of "Coke-bottle" outline, somewhere in between the straight-sided, round-ended trapezoid of the Mark Leaf and a more tightly-wasted guitar shape like the Calton. The KW Original, especially, has some unique features to its construction — most notably the perimeter of the top and back have a "binding" of high impact rubbery material that is actually inlaid like the binding around a guitar body. This inlaid "bumper" absorbs knocks and bumps occurring to those edges. A little wood inlay detailing at the seam of the covering material on the sides adds a classy touch. Standard exterior colors are — in vinyl: black, "variegated black," or brown; in pigskin: black or brown; cowhide: black, brown, hunter green, or burgundy. Interiors are lined and custom fitted to support your instrument with a high density polyfoam that claims a ninety-pound crush resistance (this foam feels really great, like nothing I've encountered in a case before). Hi-Tone provides a kit containing materials and instructions to help accurately trace and measure an instrument for custom fitting. The crushed velvet interior lining comes in four standard colors: green, dark blue, bright red, and wine red. Because of the rather wide neck area of the case design, the interior accessory compartment is big and roomy. The compartment's lid is shaped to cradle the neck of the instrument, and is designed to have an upright position that will support the guitar leaning on it, which raises the peghead up to position that is supposed to make it possible change strings with the instrument in the case (frankly, it scares me to leave an instrument in a case in that position). A two-piece mating rubber valence lines the joining edges of case lid and case body.

As I said earlier, one thing that interested me in Hi-Tone cases was Sam's willingness to do custom work. I've recently gotten two custom Sympitar cases from Hi-Tone, both with the KW Original appointments. I wasn't particularly interested in a case covered with expensive dead animal parts (all right, so the leather *is* beautiful — just not my thing), but I did want different colors of vinyl covering than his standard offerings. I just don't go for the idea of a dark colored case — I mean, you don't have to be a rocket scientist to know that dark colors absorb more heat if your case is in the sun. My ideal case is bright white. Sam tried to discourage me from this, saying it would show every bit of dirt it ever touched. I had had pretty good luck with white cases from Mark Leaf, so I went for an only slightly subdued white for the first case from Hi-Tone. Sam was right on the dirt issue — that case looked filthy after six months of use. The thing is that the lovely padded vinyl material has a matte finish that seems to really pick up the grime. The Mark Leaf exterior is a hard, somewhat glossy surface, much less likely to grab the dirt, and easier to wipe off if it does. The second case I got from Hi-Tone, we went with a light gray/tan color that is much more practical and still light enough to reflect a lot of heat. In both instances there was a small extra charge for the custom colors (in one I got a custom brown interior that my customer requested), and Sam was happy to accommodate me with these changes. There was also a charge for the larger length required by the Sympitar; again this seemed very reasonable. I gave Sam several months notice in both instances, and he supplied both cases by the times I needed them.

Structurally, the arched top KW Original case seems very strong; I felt like I could have jumped on the top of it with an instrument safely inside (in fact, Sam claims it tests fine against 200 lbs. of pressure; I weigh a whopping 115 in my clothes, which I tend to leave on so I don't get swept away by the breezes). The flat plywood back is surprisingly strong as well, though not like the top. I would prefer having the security of an arched back. Nevertheless, this is a case I feel as safe about having a precious instrument in as any, in terms of impact protection. The owner of the Sympitar housed in the first Hi-Tone case I got proclaimed it to be successful protection after he took a cross-country airline trip, checking the instrument as baggage (all I could think was, "You did what?! With my baby?" Of course it was his by then). When he got the instrument off the baggage conveyor at the end of his journey, it wasn't even out of tune! The question of "What do I do about airline travel?" is one Sam Mancuso says they get asked a lot at Hi-Tone. His first response, like mine, is, "You're going to take *my* case on an airplane?" What he always recommends is a case cover. Hi-Tone offers a cover that is custom made by Small Dog (a company specializing in case covers) that fits their standard models, for $140. Probably a good investment to consider for the frequent traveller.

In Any Case, Life Is Never Perfect. I have had one significant criticism of both cases I got from Hi-Tone, regarding the valence that ostensibly seals out the outside world when you close the lid. My criticism in two words is "it doesn't." With the first case, although the valence contact seemed passable (not perfect), there was an area near one hinge where it was twisted, and seemed to get caught and pulled out of place when the lid was closed. This problem has gotten worse, and I tried a couple of different adhesives (one that Hi-Tone sent me) to get it stuck back in place, with no luck. The owner of that case acknowledged that it "wouldn't keep out water" but simply said he wouldn't take it out in the rain. I made sure Sam addressed that problem on the second case I got, and this time there was no twisting or separating of the valence in that problematic area near the hinge. Unfortunately, the valence on that case didn't make as tight a seal as I would have liked. I deemed it not quite bad enough to warrant returning the case, but not really up to my standards. To Sam's' credit, he has listened to this criticism and has been working to correct the problem with the valence. He writes:

"We will probably keep the bottom valence as it is. The top piece is the issue. Right now we have about twelve quotes from companies that can make the new upper valence... It will probably be PVC, which is very rigid and glues on better. Once we choose a company and pay the tooling costs samples will begin to arrive...." He expects the bugs to be worked out, and the new valence to be on the cases by January 2000. Sam also mentions that they've solved the problem of valence buckling around the hinge, and says that once they're on line with the new upper valence, they will offer to replace the valence on any of their older cases at no charge (except shipping). He is "certain the result will be a better closure, but don't toss the case into a lake to test it."

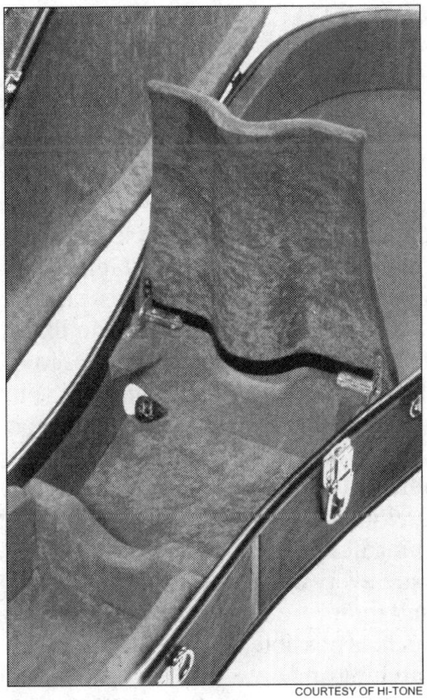
COURTESY OF HI-TONE

Hi-Tone guitar cases feature spacious compartments.

The Hi-Tone case is pretty heavy (about 14.5 lbs. for the Dreadnought size); with a Sympitar in it, it's quite a project to haul around. But compared to other cases that offer similar protection, it's really not out of line. Calton weighs in at around 14 lbs. (they offer a heavy duty version that adds 2 lbs.– 4 lbs.); Mark Leaf's standard Dreadnought case is 16 lbs.– 18 lbs. Sam says he is always thinking about how to build a lighter case, and Hi-Tone has tried a lot of things but is unwilling to compromise protection and overall quality of construction. The Hi-Tone case is very well balanced, and the leather handle is comfortable, both of which help with ease of transport.

A Case of Cost. Current prices for the standard Hi-Tone models, despite the classy touches and Sam's obvious attention to detail, seem very reasonable. The Classic, Dreadnought, and Archtop sizes of the KW Original model, with vinyl covering, have suggested list prices of $350, $400, and $425 respectively (pigskin adds about $50). Sam says they have orders stacked up through the end of 1999, at which time they will be implementing a variety of improvements, including the discussed valence, and list prices will be rising somewhat. Obviously, for custom work there will be additional charges. For comparison, standard Mark Leaf and Calton (Dreadnought size) cases currently carry suggested retail prices of $595 and $575–$625 respectively. Regarding prices, discounts vary, but a professional luthier can hope to purchase directly from the company at significantly less than the suggested list price.

To Sum Up the Case. While I won't claim that Hi-Tone has achieved "best case available on this planet" status yet, it seems headed in the right direction. I do think it's a contender for the handsomest case out there, and it is very solidly built. Although it may seem a minor point to some, one of my very favorite things about the Hi-Tone case is its smell, or rather lack thereof. Most new guitar cases reek inside — a toxic, solvent sort of stink that I always assumed comes from the contact adhesive used to adhere the lining materials to the case and each other. This stench can take months or years to disappear, and, for us sensitive type,s can negatively affect the experience of playing guitar. The interior of a Hi-Tone case has a mild, almost pleasant smell, and Sam tells me they have found a better glue that smells even less.

In summing up, I'd say I think the Hi-Tone is a good deal in a truly elegant looking case, with the valence problem being the main thing that keeps me from calling it the best deal. Sam Mancuso has so far proven himself, in my dealings with him, to be a craftsman of integrity with a real intention to make a superior product. Hi-Tone is actively expanding and improving their line of cases. Sam says they have forms for banjo and mandolin cases now in the works, again hoping to be on line by the start of the new century.

Once it has a valence that consistently creates a good seal, this will be a great case. I would encourage Hi-Tone to offer a model with an arched back (as well as top), and to adopt some lighter colors for standard exterior choices.

And I would encourage other luthiers to check Hi-Tone Cases out. Hi-Tone has a great website that will give anyone interested a good look at what they make: www.hi-tone.com

Meanwhile, I don't think I'll go back to making my own cases out of fiberglass and styrofoam anytime soon. ——

Originally published in *American Lutherie #49–#57*, 1997–1999

Violin Q&A

by Michael Darnton

■ ***What in general are the effects of arching style on tone, power, and responsiveness? The number of great instruments that I have seen seems to indicate that there is no "right" arching style, but there must be some rules to follow. Is there a source for reliable arching templates, or better yet, for actual three-dimensional molds (impressions) of high-quality instrument plates?***

What is the effect of pattern on tone? I have always been drawn to the Amati family styles, even those of Andrea Amati. Are these patterns too narrow to yield good results or can they make a nice instrument, presuming the arching and thicknesses used are more modern?

These questions go well together. The central question is what makes a good violin, and I think the right answer is all of the above, and then some. My experience indicates that everything matters — for instance, (in no particular order): wood, outline, arching, graduation, varnish, setup, and age. Certainly (starting at the initial concept — the shape of the violin) the model is important, and the history of violin making up to Stradivari and Guarneri del Gesu is the history of models more than anything else.

I guess you could use the Amati family patterns if you wanted, but that would be abandoning the last hundred years or more of the development of the violin. My attitude about this is that as modern violin makers, with apparently no hope of making anything like Stradivari or his best contemporaries made every day, we need all of the help that we can get, and therefore should follow only the best models as much as possible.

I do not believe that "more modern" arching and thickness (by which I assume you mean "of later Classical Period") can rescue you from the problems of working with a less-than-optimal outline, especially if that pattern is a narrow one. No matter how good a job you do, you will still have a small violin, and these days small violins don't sell. Mostly, that's because they sound small, and I don't believe you will reliably be able to overcome that. If, however, you are not looking to make a good violin by the prevailing standards you can try whatever you want. Also, there's always a chance that things will work out like you want, and you will like the results — you never can tell!

I really do think that you should think in terms of optimizing your design by choosing a model which has proven itself as a whole package over time. This is why most (not all) makers at least nominally make only Stradivari and Guarneri models.

Your first question was on the effect of arching. I think that if you look at good old violins you will see consistencies, rules, as you suggested, and that it is very important to bring these consistencies into your own making as much as you can. In the best old violins the arch of the top usually comes up very fast at each end, and the length between can be very, but not quite, flat. Across the middle, from side to side, can be very scooped at the edges, and round in cross section, however. Modern violins often reverse this to a greater or lesser degree, the top arch looking relatively round or pointed when viewed from the side, with the cross arch in the middle being as broad as possible. The back of an old violin is more like everyone makes it today, except most older violins are arched with a definite scoop around the waist, making the arch, even as it rises from the purfling, concave for almost an inch, just as on the top. A convex arch all the way to the purfling is not a traditional thing, statistically speaking, though it can be seen on some Classical Period violins.

Generally a good arch is smooth, but exactly what that is varies from maker to maker. The early Amatis that you like so much often have a sort of figure-8 bulginess to them caused by fatness in the extreme edges of the upper and lower bouts. A really nice middle-period del Gesu can almost look like the arch is constantly dropping from the bridge outward, as much like an egg contour as he could make it without having an egg outline, and this can get pretty tricky in the extreme areas of the bouts. A Strad can approach what is often called a "barrel arch," but in his best period it somehow remains fat all the way to those same extremes, without the figure-8 look. This also is a neat trick, and almost impossible to execute.

Graduation is another issue. I think you cannot do better than to use the numbers provided by Sacconi in *The 'Secrets' of Stradivari,* with the reservation that Sacconi was being conservative: most Strad tops that I have measured are thinner than the figures he gives — sometimes a lot thinner!

In passing I will mention plate tuning: there is no possibility that any original plate tuning remains in Classical Period instruments, therefore I believe this technique is not necessary, and might even be counterproductive.

Because each maker did something slightly different, I think it is best to try to work in the style of a particular maker and not mix types. Of course, violin makers in the mass have been ignoring this advice for centuries, with negative results. Everyone wants to believe that he is better than Stradivari and can improve the model, reinventing the violin. Nevertheless, those who have done the closest copies of the original models are consistently in the greatest demand (I think that Lupot and Lott are wonderful examples of this), and those who went with their own ideas have been mostly rejected from serious contention (Dieudonne comes to mind).

The really nasty part of this is that nothing quite looks the same after the instrument is varnished and set up, so learning what to do really is a matter of experience — quantities of completed violins, that is. Working from plaster casts or real violins as models can be helpful, but not in a precise way, since unless you're making bench copies (scratch-for-scratch duplicates) you will want to correct for age-induced distortions, bringing the problem back from one of templates to one of eyes. Additionally, templates really help only to a certain extent: the last few tenths of a millimeter are what make the difference between right and wrong. Therefore, most of the violin makers I know do not use templates, but do all the arching by eye and concept. Certain aspects of the arch — around the *f*-holes — really have to be attacked in stages, and I don't think this is an area where templates help get the job right.

If you could obtain molds to help your eye work (rather than to use as templates) I think that would be the second best way to work. My first choice would to be able to have samples of real first-class violins present. I do not know of a commercial source for impressions of valuable instruments, but they do at least exist in fairly large numbers in restorers' closets.

I haven't tried at all to answer your question about what accounts for certain tonal characteristics. What I am doing is to suggest that you find a maker whose tonal results consistently please you and then try to make violins as much like that maker would have made as you can. Eventually you may learn enough of the characteristics to approximate his model. If you make enough that are close enough to that concept you will eventually make something you like. Whether we like the idea or not, violin making is more copying than creating, and the sooner you resign yourself to that idea the better your instruments will be.

If you cannot connect with good violins on a regular basis, you will have problems keeping your senses sharp. Historically the best violins have come from locations where the best examples lived and the makers had exposure to them regularly. This is the main reason for the high number of really good violin makers in this country today, many of whom have worked in restoration in good shops, surrounded by fine instruments.

Of course I know there are makers and players out there who will say I'm being narrow minded, but it is worth repeating: through the centuries many people have come up with new designs for violins that they thought were better, but those "improvements" have been repeatedly rejected in the marketplace as not doing the job — not by snobs like me and collector-connoisseurs, but by players who have voted with their wallets. Stradivari and Guarneri violins, and those most closely modeled on them, have consistently won.

■ ***I've seen bridges raised higher by pieces of wood added onto the bottoms of the feet. What's this all about?***

I'm familiar with this method to avoid cutting a new, higher bridge for an instrument. The additions sometimes are called "shoes" and are added by makers and restorers with the idea that if an instrument is working well with a certain bridge it might be a good idea to keep using that bridge. I can't remember having seen this on anything other than a cello, and that makes sense, since cello bridges can move up and down quite a bit with the seasons.

I've never done this myself, and it's a bit cheesy looking, but the idea seems fine. It might also be a good way to avoid cutting a new bridge for a cheaper instrument, if the only problem is that the present bridge is too low.

The feet that I have seen all seem to be in the neighborhood of 1MM thick. One person I spoke with who does this on cellos said that he does not touch the top of the bridge nor the original bottoms of the feet so that he can peel the shoes off if he needs to when the season changes.

I've seen and heard lots of before-and-after examples of this procedure and, regardless of what you might think, it doesn't seem to have a significant effect on the tone of an instrument if it's well done.

■ ***When I fit new pegs they wear in quite a bit in the first few months and soon the ends stick out too much. Can I prevent this somehow? Also, my pegs either slip or stick — I can't get them to work just right for very long. Do you have any tip that will help?***

Ideally the small ends of the pegs should be flush with the outside wall of the pegbox and stay that way forever. If they start to stick out at all, the tidy look of nicely set pegs is lost very quickly! A friend gave me a great tip for keeping this relationship: he once worked for someone who decided he'd give the pegs their first year of wear in five minutes by doping them up really well and spinning them in place under fairly high pressure (not enough to crack the pegbox, though) for several minutes instead of the usual few seconds. I thought it was a stupid idea until I tried it. Yes, it does work! The pegs and holes can compress quite a bit, and spinning the pegs in takes care of this compression right away. Additionally, all of the final reaming in of the pegs should be done with the reamer turning backwards. This helps compress the peg holes even more.

As for getting pegs to work right, what I do is first use lots of dope of the dark stick type, such as the Hill or Sacconi brands. Really pile it on and spin it in, then keep putting on more. Now the pegs will probably slip too much. Next I dip the peg in pumice and spin it just once or twice in its hole, then remove the peg and wipe the extra pumice off.

Pumice disintegrates with use and therefore will not wear out the peg holes, but it does make the peg sticky enough to work nicely until the dope starts to dry up some. Do realize that no treatment is permanent, but that the more dope you pile on the longer the peg will stay functional. The insides of the peg holes should be thoroughly black. A discreet and genteel amount of dope will last about two days, with luck, so don't be afraid to really pile it on.

■ ***How can I detect a loose bass bar?***

Players seem to have zeroed in on this as the main problem that causes instruments to rattle. I don't know how many times I've heard that the bass bar must be loose, but actually, I've only seen one loose bar in sixteen years. It was a cello, and it sounded fine. The arch looked completely desperate, however.

My usual reaction to this statement, therefore, is to politely say, "I'll look," take a mirror, look, not find anything, and then find the real problem (usually a loose seam somewhere).

If the bass bar really is loose the only way to diagnose it is to look inside with a mirror and a light, and the only right way to fix it is by taking the top off.

■ ***I dressed a fingerboard, and it came out with tan streaks and spots. Why is this happening and how can I stain it? I tried wood dyes and they didn't work.***

Good dense and jet-black ebony is hard to find and a thing of the past. Today different sources and lower qualities are used, leading to this kind of problem. Usually an old fingerboard looks all right, since it has been stained and darkened by use, but cutting through this reveals the horrible truth underneath.

The last step in dressing a board is usually to "wet" sand with oil. If the fingerboard isn't dark enough skip this step, wet sand through the finer grades of paper with water, then wash over the board with a coat of India (drafting) ink. If you haven't already oiled the wood the ink will make it look great. Don't worry — the color won't come off on the player's fingers, since there is a small bit of varnish in the ink to make it permanent.

As a bonus, with your bare hand you can polish the surface of the board up to a pretty nice shine. This looks great if you've been very careful, but otherwise it reveals all the flaws in your planing and sanding.

■ ***Someone mentioned to me a "Russian" string setup for violin. What was he talking about?***

Some players like to play with different string combinations with the idea that they can find a magical set which works better than a standard set designed to work together. Usually on violins I think this is a waste of time and is the violinist's version of the search for Stradivari varnish, but on cellos it is the norm to see different strings at the A and D positions from those of the G and C.

There is one set which I keep seeing and didn't make much sense of until I saw it on one of my own violins and had a chance to really try it out. This is a normal unwound steel E string (with a fine tuner), a wound steel A (I haven't figured out which brand yet, with a fine tuner), a wound gut D (Pirastro Olive, for instance — my violin came back with a Dominant D, which I think is actually a better choice), and a wound gut G.

This looked pretty stupid (especially since the tuners are usually different types) until I played it, and now I think I understand it. The steel A makes a pretty good transition from the bright tightness of the E to the relatively normal D string, and the gut G continues the transition into warmth beyond what the Dominant G string would give.

Viola players are always talking about wanting their high strings to sound like a violin and the low, especially the C, like a cello (I never understood what was wrong with a viola sounding like a viola, myself) but usually can't manage to achieve the transition smoothly. This violin stringing seems to do the violin equivalent: spread the tonality of the instrument across a wider range, but it does it smoothly, without any particularly disturbing jumps. I suspect that many players used to more normal string groups might have a hard time getting used to this set, but it does have its good side, especially with the Dominant D string to smooth the transition.

■ ***Why is quartersawn wood used for violin necks, with the quarter on the side of the neck? I thought of using flatsawn wood, but don't want to be sadly surprised later.***

I made a violin with a slabbed neck once, and the pegbox split almost immediately after I fit the pegs. I've since noticed more broken peg holes on the very few instruments of other makers with slabbed scrolls, though not every slabbed scroll I've seen has been broken. For the most part only very early violins have slabbed scrolls. I think the early makers caught on quickly.

I believe, but can't prove, that the cross figure (rays) of quartered maple play an important part in keeping the pegbox from exploding. Quartered wood also does not move as much with weather change, which I imagine could contribute to scroll cracking in slabbed scrolls as the pegs become trapped in contracting wood. By the way, slab backs on ancient instruments, as attractive as they are, are often shredded with cracks at the ends of the plates, from the same causes, I would think.

Whatever the contributing causes, I'd stay away from making slab-cut scrolls if I were you. If I did make one I might make the walls of the pegbox a bit thicker, just in case.

■ ***I need a safe way to thicken an alcohol varnish solution. What's best?***

I can think of three reasons to want to safely boil off alcohol. Some oil varnish recipes call for the addition of colored extracts in an alcohol solution. After the varnish and color are mixed it is necessary to get rid of the alcohol. Sometimes we just make a mistake, and add too much alcohol to a spirit varnish and want to thicken it as the question above requires. Last, some oil varnish resins with a high content of wax and other trash can be purified by first dissolving them in alcohol, then boiling off the alcohol to get a pure resin which can be used for oil varnish.

Boiling alcohol is strange stuff — it wants to take off furiously if disturbed. This means one has to be very careful to keep the temperature low enough that stirring to check for thickness doesn't cause the pot to boil over. Also, the method of heating should be as safe as it can be. For this reason I use a water bath in my glue pot (a thermostatically-controlled West Bend dorm-room coffee-heating pot, by the way), not a stove, and especially not a gas stove.

I put the varnish in a deep stainless-steel martini jigger and gradually move the temperature up to the boiling temperature of the alcohol, then back off a bit. The alcohol does not have to actually boil to boil off, and I feel safer if it doesn't. I just let it sit on the corner of my workbench for a day or two, steaming away — no rush. Since breathing alcohol (especially of the denatured variety) can be harmful, you might want to think about ventilation, or doing this in the back yard, but definitely not out of sight inside. If something goes wrong (and it can in a flash, so to speak) you will want to be there to stop it.

■ ***Can you state the making of lake pigments in a way that I can understand?***

First, pigments are solids, like pieces of colored rock, as opposed to stains, like tea and analine dyes, which are actually dissolved in a solvent.

The lake pigment is made by combining two water-soluble chemicals — lye and alum (aluminum potassium sulfate) or something similar — in water solutions. This causes a third, insoluble, rock-like substance — aluminum oxide, more or less — to precipitate out. It is rock-like when dry, that is. It is mush-like when first formed. If one of the water solutions used for this process is stained, then the precipitate picks up that color and is itself stained.

In a day or so this precipitate sinks to the bottom of the container in which the reaction occurs and the extra water is poured off. Then the precipitate is washed several times with clean water (water is added, allowed to settle, and is poured off) then filtered out (I use a big paper coffee filter), dried, and ground to a fine pigment.

All this is the simple explanation, of course, and probably not exactly accurate chemically, but you get the idea. Using the right quantities of each component is important, as are the exact chemicals used, which has an effect on the precise color which develops. It's not incredibly complicated or difficult. Such pigments have been made for hundreds of years.

Lake pigments are usually cited for adding permanence to colors, but notoriously unstable colors (like annatto) remain notoriously unstable in lakes, and I doubt that permanence alone is much of a reason to use lakes. The greater advantage is in the variety of colors which can be obtained with the same sources, and the ability to experiment with colors which are not available on the market. Additionally, colors which will not go into oil varnish any other way can be brought in as lakes.

The requirements for a painting pigment are not the same as for varnish makers, and this limits varnishers to the colors painters like if pigments are purchased rather than made. For instance, most red painters' pigments are pink when used weakly, and become opaque medium-colored paint when thick, but it seems apparent (to me, at least) that Classical Period varnishes start out yellow when thin, turn orange, then red, then purple-black and black the thicker they are used. No modern pigment or pigment combination will do this. If you believe that a pigment is the source of this wonderful variety of colors, then you're going to have to make your own.

Additionally, modern pigments as used in painting are extremely finely ground, and some sources indicate that coarser pigments are more transparent. If true, this would be a distinct advantage to making one's own, especially since grinding down past a certain point is a real pain and very time-consuming.

Originally lakes were developed to convert organic sources to pigments. The first lake was red and came from lac, as in shellac, which is why the name "lake" conventionally refers to red pigments generically. Shellac red is no longer used, and the common modern lakes are the madder and alizarin (natural and synthetic, respectively) reds. Other sources are possible, including strongly colored dye woods such as pernambuco, and plant sources, among which madder root is exemplary and annatto is not. Probably you could even make a pigment from strong tea, but I have no idea what it would look like.

I could probably come up with recipes to make lakes, but right now you know about as much as I knew when I started making them. Completely covering the details of making lakes would need a few more pages and more experience than I have. Remember, lye is dangerous and you should wear goggles when using it. Work with small quantities of all of the materials (except for water — use lots of water), and stir everything a lot every time you are adding or mixing things. Don't be afraid to make mistakes. Good luck.

■ ***I have a cello in my shop which has something strange happening over the post on the top. It isn't a post crack — it almost looks like the grain lines are pushing up through the varnish, but only in this one area. Do I need to put in a patch?***

Cello wood usually has wider, softer grain than violin wood, but sometimes the tops are not a whole lot thicker. What you are seeing is the post pushing on the hard lines of the grain inside the instrument and displacing them outwards through the top. You are right: in a way they are being pushed up through the varnish. This usually happens on instruments which have been sanded inside rather than scraped, for reasons which become clearer below.

I haven't ever seen serious damage from this, but it sure looks scary! Eventually, of course, the varnish will wear differently in this area, and not to good effect. If you have the top off the instrument at some time you can take a very dull scraper and scrape the top inside at the post. The dull scraper will push the soft wood between the grain lines down and cut the stiffer hard grains, which will leave a corduroy texture on the top where the post presses, unlike sanding, which leaves everything level. This extra, soft padding will take the force which previously all went to the hard grains, pushing them through.

Of course, I know that you won't do this to a fine old instrument — only to one that is not incredibly valuable, and you won't do more scraping than described above as necessary to correct the problem.

■ ***My varnish jobs never look as clear as I would like them to be. What can I do to make the varnish clearer?***

If you want some idea of how the very best varnish looks, soak a piece of curly maple with turpentine. When you have compounded a varnish which looks this good and has color, and will stay this way when completely dry (how it looks just after you've painted it on doesn't count!), you will have a good start.

First, your problem is probably not in the varnish, though that can be a cause if you use pigments for color or have an unusually poor recipe. Most varnishes are not too bad themselves — remember that looking through two inches of something in a bottle is not going to be the same as seeing a few thousandths on a violin. More likely causes are poor wood treatment or sealer, poor choice of colors, and too much isolation of the color layers from the wood.

Whatever you are putting on the wood first affects everything afterwards. After the first layer of varnish reveals how your sealer has done, each subsequent step obscures the wood more, so things can only get worse and worse from that point, never better! The sealer must enhance the transparency and luster of the wood, and increase those qualities as much as possible. The great thing about some old Cremonese varnish jobs is not the varnish, it's what's under it. Restorers know that if the original undercoat is intact then the retouching can end up looking as good as the rest of the violin. On these old instruments even the worst types and cuts of wood look wonderful, so don't try blaming your wood.

As a sealer, hide glue (the old German sealer) is mostly neutral, but egg can definitely be negative. Some resin combinations (spirit varnish sealers, a traditional French approach) can be positive. Linseed oil (taught by modern German-founded schools) is a sealer used by some. It has the reputation — earned or not — for looking good, especially when old and yellowed, and also for damaging the tone. I suspect the tonal problem might be better attributed to the construction under the oil.

Some makers simply start with a clear version of their usual varnish and switch to color when they are sure the wood is sealed and won't stain. The ultimate sealer has yet to be found by most of us when we compare our work to great 17th- or 18th-century Cremonese varnishes, though there are some notable exceptions to this rule (Carl Becker of Chicago and Alfred Smith of Australia, for instance). Every type of sealer has its proponents and detractors. Obviously this issue is far from being decided!

The other two things I mentioned were pigment type and placement. Though I have always used tube oil colors in the past, I have recently come to believe that neither they nor commercial dry pigments can approach the transparency of homemade and hand-ground pigments. Commercial pigments are sometimes treated to make them opaque (good for painters; bad for violin makers) and some sources indicate they may have been ground too finely for optimum transparency.

Additionally, it seems very important to put the pigments (if you use them) as close to the wood as possible, which means keeping the sealer layers thin and forgetting the one or two clear varnish coats some makers start with. Seal well and go right to color. This was originally pointed out (by David Brownell, I think) in the Michigan Violin Makers Association Newsletter, where the comparison was made with the proper use of nonglare glass in picture framing (right against the picture, if you expect to see anything through it).

If you're using an oil varnish, you can take a small comfort in knowing that it gets clearer as it dries through the years (the progress in the first year is particularly encouraging), but never enough to bail you out.

■ ***I want to make a small violin. Any advice on developing a model?***

Sure. The first thing to do is go to the copy shop, taking with you tracings of all of your various templates and a ruler. The "official" size factor is about 92.5%. A ¾ violin is that much smaller that a full sized one. The same relationship follows all the way down, ¾ to ½, ½ to ¼, ¼ to ⅛, and so on. These numbers will need to be adjusted a bit as you go, since the copier percentages are inaccurate, and the proper sizes are close, but not necessarily exact. Also, there are several size standards. That's the concept, however, and one trip will give you all the drawings you'll ever need. If you work from photos, as I often do, take them along and size them down too.

These percentages work for every part, even the graduations, except for rib thickness, which I might cut a bit, but not much, and rib heights, which benefit from some additional height.

For tone you can hardly make the top and back too thin in the smaller sizes, but the results will, of course, be more fragile. I use red cedar to great advantage for smaller violins (it's awful for full-sized ones!), but it is very soft, so I increase the top thickness to compensate.

Also, when the neck is set, the pitch should be set as high as the bridge blank allows. Players report to me that if the tension of the setup is increased in this way the violin sounds much better, and can in some cases use full-sized strings instead of the dead ropes sold for small violins.

When you get back to your shop, superglue the copies, except for the *f*-hole, on formica, which is a great material for violin templates. Superglue will not cause the paper to distort. Saw, sand, or file out your templates, and you're on your way!

■ ***I have a hearing problem which makes me hypersensitive to the sound of my violin. Not only is the sound of it too loud in my ear, but when I use earplugs to lower the volume, the sound transmitted by bone conduction through my jaw is still too much to bear. Can you suggest some way to cut the volume of my violin without changing the tonal quality of it?***

Any normal modification of the instrument which would cut volume also would affect the tone greatly. You don't say if the earplugs were a step in the right direction, but if they were, the next thing I would try is a sponge cushion on the chin rest, to isolate it from your jaw. One such device is the Strad-Pad, and there are other brands of the same thing, which is essentially thin, dense foam with adhesive on the back. If one layer didn't do the job perhaps two might.

The common methods I alluded to at the beginning are mutes, especially heavy brass practice mutes, and mute violins, which are "practice violins," with all the right string stuff, but only a hollow framework for a body. One German company manufactures these for a fairly reasonable price. This would surely solve the problem, but wouldn't work in a group, nor be very satisfying, I imagine.

■ ***I think that many A strings are defective. Often on violins I set up, the A string sounds like a duck. Can you suggest a good and consistent brand?***

For some reason, the position that everyone has decided on as standard for the soundpost often yields this result. The solution lies not with strings but in the post: move it a bit to the north and I'm sure that the problem will go away.

I use as my guide that the post should be as far south of the bridge as the top is thick, rather than using a definite number for this distance. I suspect a rather distant post works better on cheap student violins with thick tops than it does on better ones with thin tops. The rule giving a definite, measured distance may have originated in shops setting up a lot of cheap instruments to a compromise standard.

■ ***I have been making guitars for three years now, and this year I will build my first violin, for my daughter. The only claim to uniqueness my guitars have is in my high-gloss oil finish. Yes, I said "high-gloss" and "oil" in the same breath. Properly applied, twelve to fifteen coats of gunstock oil will buff to a high gloss... after a while. The finish is beautiful, feels like silk, and is remarkably easy to repair, so I thought I would finish this violin the same way.***

My Dad was horrified when I mentioned the idea. He's sure that the conventional "hard" finish on a violin has a considerable impact on its voice, and that if I use oil, the instrument will have little or no voice at all. I must admit that my oil finishes, though they wear well, cannot, by any stretch of the imagination, be considered a "hard" finish. How important is it to have a conventional finish on a violin, and if I use oil, will the thing need a transducer and amp just to be heard at all?

After first confessing that I don't know the product you are using, I will say that it sounds like what you actually have is an oil varnish, not oil alone as you believe. In my experience, at least, you can get a gloss finish from oil as easily as you can a gravel road: it just won't happen alone without adding something, like tar. Or resin, in the case of varnish.

In the last few years many products have been brought out along the lines of the "Danish oil" concept: some quick-drying oil like tung oil, with a resin added to build thickness rapidly. These wipe on like oil, dry quickly, and build to form a layer which can be polished. Strictly speaking I think they would be called "long oil" varnishes.

If we can agree that it's an oil varnish you are using, then the usual concepts for violin varnishing apply, whatever your philosophy on that topic is. I believe that you should try to keep the stuff out of the wood. Since you're probably not after exotic results I'd suggest that before you start with your gunstock oil you should paint on two coats of hide glue or unflavored gelatin diluted about 1:10 with water (hot to dissolve the stuff, then allowed to cool). This will seal the wood enough, and your favorite treatment should build up faster as well.

You haven't mentioned color, so I should add that unlike guitars, violins are always colored rather than left white, and that the color is always in the varnish, not the wood. Therefore, if there's a colored version of your favorite oil that pleases you, I would use it.

You will understand (as will others reading this) that I'm not advocating you use the finish you have suggested, but that if that's the plan then the above ideas can help make the results more like a traditional violin paint job. Tonally the finish is very important, but the worst negative effects should be minimized if you seal the wood first. In short, you do run the risk of killing the violin if you permit the wood to become saturated with an unproven foreign substance, but a bad surface varnish will do less harm.

Of course you didn't ask, but I can't resist saying that the best of all possible varnishes for a violin is probably a traditional type of violin varnish, so it doesn't make a whole lot of sense to use something else if you want the best results. I can't imagine why you would want to intentionally stack the deck against yourself!

■ ***One of my customers put a big nick on his violin. What's the accepted way to deal with this?***

There are several common ways to cover up a scratch. If the scratch is in an area covered by colored varnish you might think the proper repair would be to match the varnish and fill the hole with it. That can look fine for a while or even forever, but if the original varnish is soft and prone to wear and yours isn't, then the result in a few years can be a bare-wood area with your bright little piece of work standing inexplicably firm against the elements.

Another common way to fix the spot is to quickly color the bare area and then add some varnish on top to cover and level the repair. This is even worse! When the original varnish and the little island of repair varnish have finally both worn away there will be a little red measle in the wood itself to remind everyone what you did. If you did a lot of this work all over the violin it really will look like a case of measles. This can happen pretty fast — sometimes even before you have retired, and then it will be your problem to deal with, not the next guy's.

The third method can be less pleasing to the customer, but better in the long run. You really should explain what you are going to do and how it will look first, so the customer doesn't expect something else. The offensive thing about that scratch is not that it is there, but that it is new. So make it old. First seal the bare wood with a touch of very soft French polish used as a retouch varnish into the scratch — not painted on around it! A little dirt or neutral color pigment chosen to match the dirt in other old scratches can be painted into the scratch next (but use very little — just enough to pull the newness off the scratch), then a little very soft French polish is painted (again, only into the scratch, not anywhere around it) to seal the color. A very light polishing finishes the job by smoothing your soft and fresh new work without dissolving and changing any of the surrounding area. When finished the scratch won't be invisible or flush, but will hopefully look like the other scratches on the violin and won't call attention to itself.

By the way, that point about explaining the results to the customer before the repair is a good idea all of the time. Many problems are avoided when a customer knows what will be done, why, how it will be done, how it will look when finished, and of course how much it will cost. If the repair will affect the tone of an instrument (or could possibly change it) the customer should always understand this and consent in advance, even if you think he or she will be happily surprised if you don't tell first.

Violin Views

The Value of Violins

Despite what you might think, the pricing of violins is logical and well-established, not at the whim of dealers. The most important factor in pricing is demand.

Three years ago I switched from strictly being a violin maker to being more involved with sales. It was an unexpected change, but has been very enlightening. Many issues which were never much on my mind have become very important. One of the most interesting has been the very wide price range of the instruments available for purchase, and the variation in fiscal attitudes players bring to choosing an instrument.

Violins can be bought for from about one hundred dollars up to several million. Many players have a hard time accepting that fact. Maybe the situation could be better expressed that at some point along that price line many players start believing that high prices are all the fault of "those greedy dealers."

Many people don't understand the interactions of supply and demand, and the effect that having tens of thousands of people trying to acquire any commodity which is in relatively short supply can have on prices, with or without the presence of dealers: witness Beanie Babies! Historically, the relative values of the works of violin makers is the result of many years of sorting out of the relative desirability of the average quality of a maker's body of work. The overall levels of prices are the result of hundreds of years' market forces combined with inflation. This force is clearest with regard to professional quality instruments of known make, and that is the category which I will be speaking of here. Strads and Guarneri del Gesùs are as expensive as they are not because of what I might ask for one, but what a long string of buyers has been willing to pay relative to the prices of other instruments.

For instance, when players don't want additional Strads, Strad prices don't move, and sales don't occur. When demand is high, prices rise until the number of purchasers willing to pay the price equals the number of available violins. If owners choose to ask too much, buyers don't buy until either the owners lower what they ask or inflation catches up. You may have seen this at work in your own shop. Do you have a violin which has gone out on approval countless times, only to come back unsold having lost out to some violin from another dealer? That doesn't mean yours is a bad violin. Once or three times might be coincidence, but if this happens over and over it simply means that the violin is priced too high compared to other similar ones. As the price of that item is lowered, sooner or later it will get to the point where it will be a fair match to others at that price and will get sold. Contrary to what many violinists think, customers ultimately control the market, since in the end it is their choice to buy or not to buy, and their behavior dictates pricing.

Therefore, if someone buys an instrument which some people feel was overpriced, that indicates nothing more sinister than that those critics were wrong — each individual unique item needs to find only one buyer to validate its price. A free market is very much like an auction in that if two people are still willing to buy one unique item, then the price is still too low!

Notice I didn't say prices fall when demand is low. The nature of the rare violin market is such that owners will hold onto their instruments rather than sell them when demand is low. As with stocks, if one waits long enough prices will eventually go up, and the only people who sell when their blue chips are low are the ones who are momentarily desperate for money.

Notice also that there's no process for deciding who gets instruments based on merit — money and how much you have of it determines who buys what in general. Some players seem to seriously resent this when violins are the issue. Many musicians think it unfair that they cannot have whatever instrument they want. That's life, but it often affects the attitude a player takes when faced with searching for an instrument.

I've used Stradivari violins as examples above, but every price range is affected by the same forces, both regarding pricing and price inflation. I think we will be seeing some interesting movement in the lowest price ranges, for instance, with the increasing sophistication of Asian violin factories. While the quality of German student instruments has been slipping since about the 1930s to the point where many of those instruments are embarrassing examples of craftsmanship, Asian makers have become increasingly savvy. For some time now even their lowest-priced instruments have been nicely crafted, and recently they are starting to sound good, too, correcting the one defect that has been permitting the Germans to hold the student-violin market. What the German manufacturers do to counter this situation will be interesting to watch.

The situation has changed in the individual-maker market as well. Thirteen years ago, when $400,000 was considered a ridiculous price for a Strad, I thought that $3,000 would be a pretty good price for an established maker's new instruments. Now, when Stradiculous is more like $5,000,000, most established professional makers can get at least $9,000 for their violins. In that respect, the market has acted like a Slinky™ — when one pulls it up by the top, the highest coils rise and separate a lot, and moving down toward the bottom they still separate, but less so; thus, when the very most expensive instruments go up in price, almost everything else of professional quality is dragged upward as if by suction from above, but at differing rates.

All that said, is the situation hopeless for players who are not wealthy? I don't think so. There's a definite relationship between price and quality, but one of the things I have learned is how many good violins there are in virtually every price range. Each additional small increment in quality comes at an increasingly higher cost. That is, a $3.6 million violin is not 400 times better than a $9,000 one, so musicians shouldn't despair. And while many can, large numbers of violinists can't perceive the difference between a good instrument and a great one. Personal taste often confuses the issue. The business is filled with stories of amateurs being casually handed really great instruments (unidentified) and immediately declaring their dislike. Once as an experiment I handed a hard-to-please young violinist a spectacular old Italian violin which had been owned by two of the greatest violinists of this century and after playing two or three measures she proclaimed it "not good enough."

Additionally, several criteria used by musicians in choosing a violin really don't relate to quality as perceived by an audience, and that's good news, especially for strong players. For example, one attribute of a violin that is not apparent to an audience and yet most obvious (and, unfortunately, potentially more irritating) to less-skilled players is how easy or difficult it is to play. If the violinist can get beyond this subjective issue — and, ironically, skilled professional players with better incomes and the ability to buy the expensive instruments often can and do — there are many more choices of good instruments in all ranges.

Within the various price ranges there are spots where one can get the most for one's money, and the educated player will look for those instruments. For instance, some of the best things to become available within the last ten to fifteen years are new instruments by well-informed makers. For $10,000 to $15,000, one can find a new violin which is easily better sounding than an old one costing $20,000 to $30,000. This is due to the premium traditionally placed on old instruments, which places some bad older instruments at roughly the same price as better new ones. A musician looking for a tool which costs about the same as a car but won't depreciate will consider a new violin, and many do, accounting for the resurgence in modern making. In general, in today's market one must invest $30,000 or more in order to reap the benefits of having a fine older violin. What is gained by the player who buys an old violin is the investment value, which probably will continue to rise faster than that of new ones.

All in all, I think money spent by musicians for violins has historically been proven to be money well spent, as one can see by querying violinists who have bought wisely and held their instruments for long periods. In every range, professional-quality violins are a better investment than comparably priced consumer goods, so the money has been spent, but it has not been wasted!

Issues of Preservation and Restoration

In the last twenty years or so the technology and standards of violin repair and restoration have changed a lot. There have been great repairers for well over a century, but with the massive increases in the value of violins in recent years, there is more incentive than in the past to be doing a better job. Additionally, an "organic" concept of quality has emerged which demands more adherence to the original state of the instrument and is less tolerant of alterations to conform to contemporary aesthetics.

Our standards of restoration have been shaped by the sometimes-conflicting interests of many different parties, and therefore "proper" restoration is defined in a variety of different ways. At one extreme, museum specialists hardly accept the commercial restorer's concept at all, and customers sometimes don't ever realize there's an issue — equating "condition" with "visibility of damage." In reality the issue has become very complex, as the different interests are balanced.

In the museum field, one idea of restoration is a minimal concept, involving stabilization of change and the removal of the accrued missteps of everyone who has touched the art since its origin. The most hard-line stance does not accept the cover-up of previous damage, and even regards repairs of existing damage as being a possibly deleterious act. This is a "pure" concept, but has received a lot of criticism because it leaves the least attractive result. Hard liners also require that any repairs be marked so they can be discounted. Few of us would accept a violin where every crack is marked with a blue line and any retouching or unoriginal parts are marked with blue crosshatching to make them obvious.

The treatment received by violins at the hands of curators is mixed. A large museum once took the controversial step of "reverting" several Classical Period instruments to Baroque specifications — hardly a conservative act, especially given that some schools of thought believe that every change which has happened (that is, had previously happened to these particular instruments, for instance) to a piece is historically important, as a part of that piece's past.

On the other hand, another institution apparently refused to repair an ever-enlarging crack in an important instrument, possibly on the grounds that it would be interfering with the current state of the instrument. At the same time they required researchers to check their metal rules at the door and wear cotton gloves while handling the instruments, in what would seem to be a very inconsistent attitude about the preservation of items in their care. "Our abuse is acceptable — yours is not."

This kind of inconsistency appears in the commercial world as well, ranging from "restorers" who will do anything they are paid to do to with no qualms, to those who try to do their jobs with minimum interference with original material. But within the commercial world, the one common standard of the best work is to hide any damage as much as possible — something which is contrary to the attitude of some museum restorers.

With this wide range of apparent acceptability there will not be total agreement about what is proper, but there are certain things which are clearly wrong or clearly right. At a minimum, most commercial restorers believe in preventing damage from spreading. This means fixing open cracks and keeping seams and other glued pieces glued. It also means repairing worn areas — not only for cosmetic reasons, but to re-establish a buffering wear zone.

For instance, once a corner has worn to a certain point the purfling begins to be attacked. Given that such wear will continue to occur, most restorers will choose to rebuild the corner before the damage spreads to the next defining feature of the instrument in that area, the purfling. Half-edging a top (or a back) is very invasive, but if it is not done at some point the whole edge will begin to crumble when the bridge of wood beneath the purfling has worn away to leave the edge outside the purfling completely unsupported. Other areas are treated similarly. At a certain point the balance tips and simple wear undermines structure, causing further damage, and must be halted, but only at the latest possible time. For instance, varnish overcoating is controversial, but when original patina no longer exists for some reason then overcoating can prevent the further wear of what remains of the original coat. Once an instrument has been overcoated, however, it is never really possible to revert to the previous state completely successfully.

Another concept is that the repair, once decided on, should be undertaken in the least invasive manner. For example, in almost every instance it is not necessary to remove original varnish. Glued cracks can be filled and retouched without feathering out the varnish at the edges of the repair, and having to do so should really be regarded as a weakness of technique, as is sanding glued cracks level. Varnish additions should be formulated so as to be completely and easily removable. Cleaning is a delicate operation which should be undertaken only by someone who is certain not to remove any original varnish in the process. Original wood should not be removed merely as a convenience to facilitate another process; original varnish or wood should not be brutalized in repair by sanding out or having permanent additions made, such as stain or punched holes. I have heard the technique of using wood filler in tearouts on the underedges of tops criticized by repairmen who would rather plane away 20% of the thickness of that entire edge to accomplish the same surface. Getting beyond the visceral dislike of plastic wood held by most craftsmen, one procedure results in the loss of absolutely no original material while the other removes substantial amounts of original wood. Small pieces fitted and glued to fill holes is time-consuming, but also conservative. These are basic processes — the everyday work of violin repair — which the commercial restorer should master, or have the sense not to attempt.

Beyond this are the more unusual procedures, exotic or major repairs, and complex restoration for mainly visual purposes. For almost every significant repair, a noninvasive procedure has been developed by someone, somewhere. A worker who doesn't already know a good method will develop one which does no damage, replaces no original wood, and harms no varnish. Or do nothing.

Wholesale replacement of wood for merely cosmetic reasons is a thing of the past in the best shops. At the turn of the century it was common to replace entire pegboxes because of a few simple cracks. One respected contemporary book advocates the replacement of the entire sides of a scroll to hide a few unsightly, but small, holes. This kind of "repair" is irresponsible and unnecessary, but the drift away from this type of work has been very gradual, as the value of old instruments has risen, and their treatment become more conscientious. Wholesale overcoating and polishing of an instrument for no reason other than to satisfy a customer's (or, for that matter, a dealer's) demand for a good shine is another example falling into this category of unnecessary damage which has nevertheless been slow to disappear.

Well, this is fine for great instruments, but what about the more normal ones? Looking at examples of violin prices in the past makes one lesson clear: you can't predict the future. At one time lesser Italian maker's violins weren't all that important. Previous to World War I they sold for about the same price as a new violin, and replacing "inferior quality" blocks and linings was a normal restoration procedure in some of the best shops of the time. Other parts weren't all that sacred, either, such as those pegboxes which were easier to replace than fix.

Now we know that those repairs were the wrong thing to do, but such intrusive damage is impossible to undo. If a cheap German violin worth a few hundred dollars now lasts three or four hundred years longer it's not going to be cheap anymore, I suspect, and someone might be judging our quick-and-easy repairs rather harshly. Even if we don't feel the pressure of preserving our future reputations, these instruments do give an opportunity for us to try our best, and hone our methods, gaining good experience where it matters less. After all, doing second-rate work is only practice for doing more second-rate work. It's not the path to being a first-rate restorer!

Evaluating Condition for Acquisition and Repair

Evaluating the condition of an instrument is one of the most important day-to-day tasks in a shop. Whether you're buying, selling, or estimating a repair, you need to know everything about the condition of the instrument under consideration. Here are some of the things to look at.

Originality. Is the instrument complete? What has been replaced? Some things don't matter at all, like strings, pegs, and other fittings. Some people have gotten the idea that replaced necks indicate something important, but that really isn't true. It might indicate the instrument is pre-1800, as some people want to believe, but it also might mean the instrument is two weeks old and the original neck broke last week and was replaced, or it might mean some faker made it that way originally to mislead you, or simply to complete the effect of an old instrument on a newly made one. Sometimes players like to believe that if a neck has been grafted that the instrument must be worth something to deserve the work, and I've even heard it said that the existence of a graft adds $100 to the value. (We're not talking about important instruments here, obviously!) No matter what, it doesn't matter.

The major parts to be concerned with are the scroll, all of the ribs, and the top and back. Any violin of "a certain age" will probably have had the fittings replaced several times in its life. Though it's always a pleasure to see original fittings, that's interesting but not valuable unless the instrument is particularly old, in which case the matter would be of great interest to a small part of the market and an possible impediment for a sale to some other parts. That is to say, at the extreme, that an instrument from 1750 with all its original parts is exceedingly interesting to me, but very hard to sell to a modern player! There are, by the way, only three known Cremonese instruments from the Classical Period of violin making which have their original necks, fittings, and setup.

At any rate, the best situation is to have the four major components named above all there, and the rest might well be counted as a bonus.

How can you tell if parts are original? Well, this is one of the finer points of making an appraisal, but even if you aren't an expert there are a few things you can see. Does the varnish match all over the instrument? Usually scrolls will look a bit drier than the rest, but should have essentially the same color and consistency as the rest of the instrument, and the same type of wear. Though it's possible to match ribs really well, sometimes a quick turn around the perimeter will reveal something strange. The top is another often-replaced part. On old violins, a top was often taken from another old violin and modified to fit. This will be seen in unmatched purfling and outline, with perhaps traces of the old purfling being visible if the new top has been cut, repurfled, and re-edged to fit. Completely new tops are harder to spot because the maker will probably have made a careful attempt to match the rest.

Repairs. Exactly what has been fixed, and (a very important issue) how well? Some kinds of damage detract relatively little from the value, and some can destroy a significant proportion. Usually the worst of all the possible kinds of damage is a soundpost crack in the back. This can remove 50% of an instrument's value, while at the same time making it nearly impossible to sell. Even if it has been invisibly repaired (yes, this is... well, nearly possible to do) it is still there. Other kinds of back cracks are much less important, but can make an instrument more difficult to sell because of the prejudices of players.

Top cracks (and rib cracks as well) are important in proportion to the age of an instrument. A soundpost crack, which is unsightly in a new instrument, is a much more normal occurrence as time passes, and almost to be expected in a violin made previous to 1800. Wing cracks in *f*-holes are common at almost any age, as are top cracks running down from the bottoms of the *f*s. These certainly aren't fatal problems, and if and how they affect the value of the victim is very much tied up with how well they have been repaired. Scroll cracks (especially ones at the A-string peg) are undesirable, but sometimes just unavoidable. Again, age matters. Repaired bass-bar cracks seem to be of concern at the lower price levels (more due to the alarm of inexperienced customers that any real threat to the integrity of the instrument).

In fact, in most cases, the worries of the customer are greater problems than the repairs themselves, if they have been correctly executed; thus, in all types of repairs the quality of the repair matters. Players will almost always be worried about cracks and other repairs in proportion to their visibility. This isn't rational, since ugly repairs can and do hold for years, but there is more to the desirability of a violin than just how it sounds and holds together, and it really has to look nice to be nice. Good shops regularly make a lot of money by buying ugly instruments and making them pretty — in fact, the majority of the work in the best shops is the redoing of bad old work, not the fixing of new damage. In the same sense, a bad repair (whether you are the one who did it, or the one buying or selling it) does actually devalue an instrument in a very real way. The appearance aspect of repair work is almost always the most difficult and expensive part, and the part most liable to be botched.

How do you spot repairs? Your best tools are a strong desk light and a dental mirror with a long thin handle. Look carefully at every point, inside and out, and pay special attention to potential trouble spots, such as around the soundpost on both the top and the back. Invisible repairs can often be revealed by placing the light as closely as possible in line with your eye (this means directly over your shoulder, or even between you and the violin) and looking at the top or back from a very low angle (from the ends). It is possible to almost hide any repair, and the repairman works for the best effect from a normal viewing angle. A low approach with the light in line with your eye is the very hardest angle to make perfect. Also, by turning the instrument while looking at an area, you can sometimes see repairs pop up and disappear as the angle of the lighting changes. Wood and varnish reflect light differently from different angles and repairs rarely are uniformly perfect in that respect. You will have heard of the use of UV light to reveal repairs, but this is not as useful as it might seem, since it doesn't look through varnish, polish and dirt, but rather reveals them, making it of most use for varnish cleaning and repair.

Damage. How are things holding together? In the same vein as the above, current damage affects everyone's perception of an instrument. However, the repairperson's perception depends on what he or she will be able to do about it. In short, can you handle the job? If you can't, it's better to turn it down. Especially with new damage you often get only one chance to do a repair so that it can disappear. After that first time, everything gets harder. So if you're not the one for the job, admit it.

Any unrepaired damage does detract from the value of an instrument, and generally a good shop will want the stuff it sells to be in tip-top condition. Given this, what you decide to do with what you have is a delicate balancing act among your standards, your abilities, the expectations of your customers, and the future of the instrument. Let's be honest: some things aren't worth fixing. Nevertheless, those things have some value, even if it's small, to someone. There's a fine balance between all the things that can happen to a violin, its value, and the work needed to get it going and out the door again. Being able to assess this is one of the most valuable skills for running a shop.

Setup. Last of all, and most likely to need attention, is the setup: pegs, nut, fingerboard, bridge, soundpost, tailpiece, saddle, end button, and the set of the neck. These are the things which affect the player's relationship with the violin and maximize its tonal potential. Virtually every violin will benefit from work in this area. This is a complex and subtle topic, but most repair people will be able to find something to improve here, even if it is only lubing the pegs and putting on a new set of strings (my number one favorite "adjustment" by the way!)

Expertise

The violin market is one of the few areas of commerce where uncertainty can exist as regards what is really being bought and sold. The values of fine instruments are so high that assurances from recognized experts, in the form of certificates, arose as a device for establishing the maker of an instrument. This would be a simple issue if different makers' instruments were radically different, clearly marked, recent, and registered, as cars are. Instead, purchasers rely on the keen skills of relatively few experts, who are themselves of uneven reputation.

As the status and the quality of the instruments in a shop rises, it becomes more and more important that a shop be absolutely certain that the items it sells are what they are purported to be. Customers should and do have a right to know that what they have bought is indeed as described, and a shop incurs greater and greater financial liability as the class of its merchandise rises. It is a very different thing to stand behind a $1,000 instrument than to support the sale of a $3,000,000 one.

Shops take various strategies towards this. At the most basic and lowest dollar-value level, instruments are sold on their utility value — no authenticity is implied or needed. When a shop specializing in utilitarian instruments does sell a higher-priced one, it may do so from the naïve position that it's not necessary to doubt or prove the label in an instrument, and sell to an equally naïve customer who doesn't doubt the qualifications of the dealer to specify what has been sold. At its most ridiculous, there's a whole undercurrent of instruments being sold as Stradivaris and Guarneris, for values in the hundreds of dollars, by people who seem to think Stradivari was a long-lived company, like General Motors. They see no inconsistency in these instruments bearing labels reading "Made in Germany," and I've even had people tell me he must have made it "on vacation in Germany." (You think I'm joking, but I'm not!) One might call this "the level of no expertise." Many of these folks must have some inkling of where they're at, since when they have something which in their mind might be really good, they tend to fabulously overprice it.

Sooner or later, however, a shop acquires something of possible real value, and does need written backup. At the most basic this usually takes the form of old certificates (more on these later), often combined with a certain amount of what might be called "gossip," along the line of "(insert the name of a locally known 'expert,' who may or may not be legitimate, or just as easily, a violin teacher who knows virtually nothing about instruments) saw it and thinks it's fine!" This type of selling usually intentionally avoids getting any help from a qualified expert, for two reasons: first, fear of the wrath of the competition (which is the natural relationship of any two people in the same business), and second, the nagging suspicion that something really is wrong. At this level, remaining ignorant is sometimes more financially rewarding for the dealer, since this is also the level where the most questionable objects find themselves being sold.

This kind of dealing is often accompanied by a fair amount of paranoia that the big guys are sticking it to the small shop not because of the quality of the specific item, but through the insatiable need to conquer. Once a shop gets beyond this level of paranoia it will discover that a very active network exists to move good instruments from shop to shop, depending on who might have the right customer, that it can be very lucrative for everyone involved, and that yes, there are a lot of fakes floating around.

At the next level, a shop may actually make an attempt to get an honest and current opinion of a real expert. This is a bigger step than one might realize, and often the first impulse is to do it through an intermediary, many of whom seem to exist. After years of watching one's own customers repeatedly defer to a larger shop (to one's own loss) it must be very difficult for the small shop owner to seek that competitor's opinion — and yet it offers real opportunities to both. Many small shops really don't have the connections necessary to sell expensive instruments, and after they work through their most likely leads, an item is essentially dead. On the other hand, bigger shops do need a constant flow of inventory, and a certain amount of that comes from smaller shops. On an even more basic level, the top-level shop does make its living selling its opinions, either in the less-obvious form of instruments or the more direct one of certificates and appraisals, and a customer is a customer, whether it be a violinist looking for a violin or a smaller shop needing an appraisal. Eventually this can lead to a long-term relationship beneficial to everyone, including both shops' retail customers.

With all this in mind, let's take a look at the expertise situation.

At the turn of the century and before, expertise was less important than it is now. Ancient minor makers' instruments didn't have the same value they have today. The price difference between them and new ones was not all that great, and consequently they were sold more on a basis of their utility. The upper levels were more important, and more attention was given to them. Initially, purchasers received a certificate stating, "The instrument is...," which court cases subsequently diluted to, "In my opinion the instrument is...," recognizing the skill of the certifier as a factor, and the certificate as a statement of opinion, not fact. For legal reasons all modern certificates take that form.

This hints, and indeed it's true, that not all certificates are created equal. The certificate is a product of the skill, exposure, experience, and especially the morals of the writer. Even within a single firm, the quality of certificates written varies greatly, depending on who is the dominant personality in the firm at that time. In the early years, one of the most important Chicago firms (now defunct as a violin dealer) had as its expert a man who reputedly had been a horse thief in the West. His certificates are not currently highly respected.

Therefore, since expertise is as much a gift as anything else, every firm with a very long history is likely to have had better and worse periods, depending on who was providing the bulk of the expertise at any given time. A cert from The Ajax Violin Co. in 1955 could be a very different animal from one dated 1965, for instance, and have nothing to do with what was being written in 1920, which might very possibly be total fantasy.

Generally, earlier certs are less to be trusted, for the reasons given earlier: really precise expertise has developed constantly for the better, and new research is revealing facts which were unknown even twenty years ago. Players like to see old certs, but many are disappearing from circulation as their absurdity is recognized. Even good instruments can have bad certs. The other common reason for the unavailability of old certs has to do with previous owners keeping them as souvenirs. Violinists always want them when they buy, but don't mind keeping them when they sell.

Modern experts can draw on many sources, but the best one is consistent and repeated exposure to great instruments. While many shops might see a really fine instrument every month or so, if then, the most respected experts have a constant flow around them of the best violins in the world. In addition, most modern shops will have some sort of photo collection of instruments which have visited or been sold by the shop, and least importantly, a complete collection of publications relating to the violin. Experts make it their life and hobby to understand as many makers' work as possible. Though they might not necessarily want you to know it, they communicate with each other, share interesting information on their primary hobby, and are constantly involved in research in their field.

Contemporary expertise centers on several concepts:

- intimate knowledge of many unquestioned instruments with original, unmoved labels;
- the ability to sort out a maker's own work from that of neighbors and imitators and a complete knowledge of those imitators' own characteristics;
- the possession of enough information to sort a maker's life and work into periods and styles;
- a great pair of eyes to realize the potential of the information at hand; and
- a track record respected by other experts.

Perhaps the most important point is the last one. Lots of people have small pockets of knowledge — some particular maker, perhaps — but a true expert needs many such areas, and most importantly, needs to know what he or she doesn't know. A good track record doesn't come from correctly identifying instruments; lots of people can do that to some extent. Rather, it comes from not ever making mistakes, so that a customer can have total confidence in that expert's opinions when they are given. The most dangerous pretenders are the ones who can do the impossible, and always come up with a name for every violin they see. This is just not a real option, no matter how good one is. ——

Originally published in *American Lutherie #49, #51–#55*, and #57–#60, 1997–1999

REVIEWS

Bow Making Course
Joseph Regh
Wappingers Falls, NY

The Art of Bow Making by Joseph Kun and Joseph Regh is not about traditional bow construction methods, but is focused on machine tools and jigs. This method seemed ideal for a builder with my background. I decided I needed a copy of my own. I telephoned Joseph Regh and while discussing the price ($250 for the library edition), he informed me he would be giving classes, limited to three students and each student would leave with a bow after two weeks. I ponied up the $1000 and made arrangements to go to Wappingers Falls, New York for a couple of weeks.

I found Joseph to be very helpful with the logistics of staying in a town without public transportation. He had negotiated a lower rate with a local motel and found me a roommate to share expenses. The room had a small refrigerator and we used it to avoid spending money at restaurants. A commuter train goes to Grand Central Station, making travel to New York City very easy.

There was one cancellation in our session, so we had only two students. Joseph was well prepared, and had prepared materials for four bow sticks and three frogs each. I was happy to find we would have some chances to make mistakes. We were allowed to keep the best bow. We talked about Joseph's method for wood selection and started work right away.

We first routed the sticks to an oversized octagon shape and rough-shaped the heads. Next we started to machine the frogs. At each step Joseph would set up the tools ahead of us and demonstrate their use, then he would watch us do our operations. There was a large emphasis on safety. The jigs and fixtures were of top quality and everything went very smoothly.

At the end of the first week the majority of machine operations were done and the hand work started. My classmate had almost no woodworking experience, and it started to show when we had to start working by hand. By the beginning of the second week, he was afraid to do any work on his best bow.

At this point the real bow making began by taking the sticks to final dimensions, shaping the heads, and fitting the silver parts and the slide. Joseph supplied all the hand tools, and they were very sharp, which facilitated the precision work required. By Tuesday of the second week, I started to feel the pressure of getting a bow done by Friday. I fitted all the parts for three frogs but abandoned all except the best when it came to final shaping. I only shaped two heads and only finish sanded the best stick. I would have liked another few days to get these fine details correct.

Joseph's help was beyond the call of duty. My classmate had broken all of his frogs trying to fit the slides and was afraid to ruin anything else. To insure he would have a bow to take home, Joseph repaired his frogs and proceeded to demonstrate the remaining operations on my classmate's best bow.

On the last day we were in pretty good shape but there was a lot to do. We had finished the sticks with shellac the night before and all we had to do was assemble the bows, but at this point the pace was too fast for me to keep up. I had done the assembly operations before and was happy to take my stick and frog as they were. Joseph and my classmate were intent on completing the bows, so Joseph machine polished the silver, wrapped the grips, and haired the bows. The work was rushed and I was a little disappointed. Machine polishing rounds the edges that we had gone to great pains to keep sharp. I left with a very nice bow, but I don't think I would fool any bow makers into thinking it was anything but my first.

Joseph was very forthcoming with his methods, ideas, and tricks. It easily saved me two years of learning on my own. His method is based on jigs and fixtures; if you prefer to work by hand, his class is too brief to offer up the lessons required to make a bow. This course was presented as bow making 101. Joseph offers private classes for anyone who has completed the two week class. It would be easy to spend another week on head shapes and yet another on stick camber and taper.

To duplicate his methods would take considerable effort and I would not recommend it unless you are very comfortable with tool making or have enough money to pay for the necessary work. If, however, you would like to get the experience of making a bow, Joseph is an excellent teacher and the class will provide you with the confidence to try it on your own. I learned enough about bow making to use either his method or hand methods to build another bow.

One of the best parts of the class was being able to look at Joseph's completed bows and examine the detail we had worked on that day. His workmanship was excellent. Joseph was also very conscious of making the class into what we wanted. If there was something we were very interested in, he would take the time to explore it.

I am very happy to have attended his class. I feel I have learned a great deal and I am much better prepared to make bows on my own. I also learned a lot about bows that will help my ongoing repair responsibilities.

—— *Colin Kaminski (1997)*

Musical Instrument Design
Bart Hopkin
See Sharp Press, 1996
ISBN 1884365086 (paper)

Musical Instrument Design isn't about building a better guitar or a better anything else. It's about starting from scratch and discovering that the earth is littered with musical instruments, and that the hardware store is chock full of them. Hopkin's goal is to give you a new set of eyes. He's also going to expand your mind, and maybe even your definition of music.

There's a lot of theory here, lots of acoustical physics of a very gentle sort. It's necessary, because Hopkin doesn't want you to make random noises and call it music. You'll need to know where to pinch a bar gong to make it play a scale. You'll have to tune your pan pipes to a given key if you want to play in the band. A little science is inescapable, but in the end it will set you free.

General principles are more important to Hopkin than specific designs. Rarely does he spend more than half a page describing one instrument. Instead, he introduces you to the principle of, say, the marimba, then offers a bunch of optional ways to construct one. Wind and percussion instruments receive the lengthiest treatment, probably because the craft involved is within the reach of most people. The chapter on string instruments is good but very general, lots of information but few specific instrument designs are offered.

Sadly, the only photos in the book are on the back cover. The shot of Hopkin playing a five-belled kelphorn makes me wish I lived on the Pacific Coast. I don't care how it sounds, I want one. There are scads of drawings, however, and they serve just fine. They are functional and humorous, and a sense of humor is mandatory if you're going to spend time with Hopkin. Some of his instruments are going to make you laugh out loud, no matter how they might sound.

I've made one of Hopkin's instruments, a solidbody guitar with a pair of styrofoam coolers as resonators. Sort of unrecycleable sitar toombas. If I live long enough I'm going to build a lot of Hopkin's beasties. Hopkin won't turn you into a Stradivarius, but I bet you'll have a lot more fun than that old Italian guy had.

—— *John Calkin (1997)*

Things about the Guitar
José Ramírez III
The Bold Strummer Ltd., 1994
ISBN 8487969402

If you make guitars, play guitars, or are interested in the history of the guitar, this book will be an important addition to your library. You will also have a blast reading it. José Ramírez III produced some of the most important guitars during the first half of the twentieth century, and he is also part of a family dynasty of makers whose name is virtually synonymous with the development of the modern classical guitar.

There is technical information about making guitars here, but this is more a book about his thoughts and observations on various subjects. The book has no particular theme and does not feel like it was written as much as it was told. One can read these articles in any order. Some chapters are purely anecdotal while others are concerned with construction techniques and aesthetics. What is important about this book is its sense of history. This is an extremely important figure in the history of the guitar talking about the guitar and its history.

There are times when his arrogance is almost unbearable. Remember that this book was written in 1990 when you read the following quote: "I am not familiar with any works (literature) on guitar construction and repair, and if there were any, I would certainly be aware of them." Incredible! I almost had to stop reading when I hit that passage, and that was in the preface. However, he goes on to talk at length about the history of the guitar and is, for the most part, exactly right. What can you do? He is important and he knows it. And he is Spanish, so he wears it with pride. I found myself entertained, educated, impressed, and often seriously amused by his stories. He shows his humility openly, talks of his failures and successes, and above all demonstrates his devotion to the guitar through his life's work.

The chapters on his relationship with Segovia I found particularly interesting and touching. I also enjoyed seeing the genealogy of his family and brief histories of each member. There was no single chapter in which I did not find something of interest. The language is both antique and translated, which gives the book a unique feel. There are also rare photographs and copies of historical documents. It is fascinating to see items like: a 1986 Segovia program; a letter from Tárrega to José Ramírez I dated November 11, 1903; a signed photograph of Agustín Barrios to José Ramírez II dated November 4, 1921; and a photo of José Ramírez III receiving the Title of Exemplary Artisan from General Francisco Franco.

Praise must also go to The Bold Strummer Ltd. for making this book widely available. If you care about the guitar, you should own this book. I guarantee you will be amused, fascinated, pissed off, entertained, educated, but never bored. I will place it on my bookshelf right next to autobiographies of Julian Bream, Andrés Segovia, and Frank Zappa.

—— *Bryan Johanson (1997)*

Woodshop Dust Control
Sandor Nagyszalanczy
The Taunton Press, 1996
ISBN 156158116X

If clouds of wood dust wafting through your shop don't bother you, just give it about fifteen years. You could join the ranks of woodworkers who are sidelined by dust-induced medical problems.

Woodshop Dust Control will give you a jump start at keeping your shop air breathable, starting with the right choice in dust masks and finishing with the proper installation of a complete central dust collection facility. And while a centralized system will certainly be out of reach for most of us (even if it would fit into your shop), there are plenty of tricks that utilize a simple shop vacuum. The step up to a basic portable dust collector is a meaningful one. And if you live in a sufficiently rural area, you can even get a lot of mileage from a set of judiciously placed portable fans that simply blow your bad air out the window.

Nagyszalanczy not only offers you options that suit your operation and your budget, he has a slew of dust collecting gadgets you can build yourself. He starts with a PVC wand and floor sweeper for your vacuum and goes on to an air filtration device, hoods for various stationary machines, and a down-draft sanding table. If you can't pick up a couple good dust collection tips on just a quick scan of the book, you're paying too much attention to the television. The more serious you are about permanent solutions to your dust headaches, the more use you'll get from the book. I had no idea there was so much engineering involved in setting up a centralized dust collection system. Nagyszalanczy's clear explanations and instructions bring the scale of the operation down to a size we can deal with ourselves.

The book introduces just a bit of science, but it's fun. How big is a micron, anyhow? How long does it take a five-micron particle to fall six feet to the floor? (Thirty minutes.) The writing is informal and chatty. At the very least, get this book from the library to see how you can control your personal dust storms right now, and what you can reasonably plan for in the future. The author is a pretty good teacher. Let's hope he lets you call him Sandor, rather than Mr. Nagyszalanczy.

—— *John Calkin (1997)*

Gibson's Fabulous Flat-top Guitars
Eldon Whitford, David Vinopal, and Dan Erlewine
Backbeat Books, 1994
ISBN 879302976 (paper)

Strum any large Gibson flattop and one of the dominant tones is that of a small person beating on a barrel with a wooden spoon. The other day I played a customer's early '50s J-45. "Hear that sort of tubby, wooden, dead quality?" I asked. He was so excited he was nearly jumping up and down. "Sure, sure. That's the Gibson sound. Great, isn't it?"

Not to me. Which is why this book took me by surprise when I checked it out from the local library. The photos knocked me out at first glimpse, and the authors' enthusiasm is almost overwhelming. This is the first collector's book I've read that made me want to own the guitars inside it, despite my low opinion of those guitars. Also included are tons of Gibson endorsements from musicians I respect. I began to doubt my own ears.

As any collector knows, the Gibson story doesn't flow. The company's course seems to have been charted wholly by outside events such as the Great Depression, market competition, wartime materials shortages, and the whims of the celebrities whose endorsements Gibson came to depend upon. Models came and went and came again, and specs changed almost randomly. On top of it all, Gibson kept such slipshod production records that some guitars are nearly impossible to nail down to a specific year, and even identifying the model can be difficult. But then, they never foresaw the vintage market looming way off in the future, nor did they guess that instruments would one day have a value far beyond what their quality should dictate.

I'm sure the authors never dreamed anyone might read their work cover to cover. It's a catalog of specs, dates, original prices, and miscellaneous information. It's a reference work, not a novel. Nevertheless, every session with the book will draw you farther in than you intended to go. This is really the tale of three likable men in love with a company.

—— *Woody Vernice (1997)*

The Ukulele, A Visual History
Jim Beloff
Miller Freeman Books, 1997
ISBN 0879304545 (paper)

It would have been pretty cool to have been there on August 23, 1879, when Joao Fernández leaped onto a Hawaiian dock and, instead of kissing the ground to give thanks for his safe arrival, played a tune on his *braguinha,* and thereby introduced the Hawaiians to what quickly became known as the ukulele. Yet despite the millions of ukes that have been manufactured since, the instrument remains a joke in the eyes of most musicians. Jim Beloff's goal is to change all that.

Although the odds are stacked against him, Beloff tries hard. He gives us a history of the instrument and a description of the great players and manufacturers, along with lots of Hawaiian ads, photos of record jackets, old sheet music, musicians, and method books. And ukes, of course. Lots of ukes, plus closeups of pegheads, soundholes, paint jobs, decals, and stencil work. Manufacturers have treated the ukulele more creatively than any other stringed instrument. Pretty amusing, these "jumping fleas." Uke folks are obviously a breed apart. I can't figure out if they're nuts or the rest of us are just boring.

—— *John Calkin (1997)*

Video: ***Guitar Electronics with Lindy Fralin***
Northwoods Video

Seems like Lindy Fralin pickups started a buzz among Nashville guitarists years before the word got out to the rest of us. Along with making vintage-quality pickups, he has developed an ace reputation for rewinding and repairing old pickups. Nevertheless, Fralin has remained something of a mystery to me, and I'm glad this video gave him the chance to step into the light.

When I first began making electric guitars I was hot to make my own pickups simply because commercial pickups seemed to cost so much. I gave up the idea as impractical, but maybe it's not. This tape is a good introduction to the factors that go into pickup design. The coil winding machine used for the demonstration should be within the reach of any clever mechanic. No sources are given for magnets, wire, or bobbins, however. The footwork is up to you.

Even if you're satisfied with the current crop of pickups, there's plenty here that every electric guitar builder ought to know. The seminar begins with a lecture about electronic theory, including definitions of terms like inductance, capacitance, resistance, and so on. It's best to bite the bullet and deal with them; it makes everything else easier. The video picks up steam when the winding begins. It really gets rolling during the segments about pickup repair, potentiometer alteration, and wiring modifications. This is stuff you can run out to the shop and try right away. Fralin even insists that pickup potting is within the reach of the average shop, an opinion not shared by everyone in the business.

After the first hour Lindy seems to relax, and the second half of the tape is the most fun. Plugging in different pickups and wiring configurations is the most dramatic event. Perhaps in future seminars a more sensitive microphone can be set up by the amp in a room where higher volumes won't disturb the other classes in progress. It would be more instructive to hear how the tones change at different amp volumes than to just talk about it.

Single-coil fanatics should appreciate the bits of Fender lore presented here. Repairmen who have avoided pickup surgery will have their eyes opened (and their incomes augmented). Anyone with pickup-making aspirations will find this a good introduction to the craft. A pretty good time will be had by all.

— *John Calkin (1997)*

Tom Ribbecke's Archtop Building Course
Healdsburg, CA

I'd always wanted to try my hand at making an archtop guitar. For me, the displays and listening sessions at the 1995 GAL Convention were the stuff dreams are made of. I built an archtop mandolin, which, although sounding not too bad, was lumpy-looking. This made me shy of trying another archtop instrument. Tom Ribbecke's 7-day demonstration course on archtop guitar building sounded like exactly what I needed. The Manitoba Arts Council awarded me a short-term study grant to help defray the costs.

After a flight delayed by the largest single snowfall in Winnipeg's history, I arrived in Healdsburg. The other two students (Ed Schaefer from Fort Worth and Craig Korth from Edmonton) were understanding and Tom would be able to spend a couple of hours with me recapping what had been covered on the previous day. A couple of factors let me catch up fairly quickly: I had seen Tom's lecture on his system of carving tops and backs at the 1995 convention in Tacoma; and I had considerably more experience in building musical instruments than the other two.

Although the work day was listed in Tom's brochure as lasting from 9:00 AM to 8:00 PM, a more typical day extended till 11:00 PM or later; and we even had a couple of work nights that extended well into the wee hours of the morning. As a result we were able to witness the production of an archtop guitar right from raw lumber to stringing up and playing in the white. During the six very long days I was there, I took some thirty pages of notes and shot nine rolls of film.

I went to this workshop mainly to learn about the techniques Tom uses for carving of the top and back of a guitar. I was able to examine Tom's modified pin-router setup that he uses for the initial rough shaping and to watch the use of an angle grinder with first a Lancelot chain-saw wheel and then sanding disks, to create the actual shape of the arch. We tried out the Lancelot (a fairly new device, which is also used by wood sculptors) on some scrap wood. I became an immediate convert.

As Tom worked, he constantly talked to us about various aspects of archtop making. We spent a lot of time discussing how the shape of the arching, relative thickness of various parts of the top, shape and position of sound holes, and variations in top bracing can affect tone.

Tom is a master at designing jigs for increasing speed, accuracy, and efficiency in producing many of the parts that comprise a guitar. His system for cutting the dovetail joint is several orders of magnitude better than the one I had been using, and I'm preparing to build my own like his. Similarly, jigs for rough-shaping the neck, making the tailpiece, shaping the headstock, and cutting the binding ledges on the body all pointed me in a new direction. Pattern-routing was a concept that I was familiar with but had not explored very much, and seeing Tom's use of the technique opened doors to a new level of work for me. I also learned more about new materials, specifically carbon-fiber reinforcement.

A word about Tom Ribbecke as a teacher and human being: during my week there, he always treated me as an equal. Even though his experience in archtop building is far beyond my own, nonetheless he accepted me as a colleague, asking my opinion about aesthetic factors and soliciting my input when one of the others had a question about flattop instruments or repair.

Naturally, there were field trips. The first was to Luthiers Mercantile, and I really did feel like a kid let loose in a toy store. It took me a lot of effort to hold back from way overspending my budget. The other trip was as exchange students, with Ed, Craig, and myself going over to Charles Fox's American School of Lutherie, while Charles' students trooped into Tom's studio. The two places are a study in contrasts: Tom's shop filled with the sort of amiable clutter seen in old woodcuts of luthiers' workshops in the 17th century, while Charles' resembles more a modern hospital. Each has his own mode of work, and for each it works. Beautiful instruments come out of both shops, but I suspect if they were forced to trade shops for a day, they'd both end up frustrated and exhausted.

This course has given me new potential for growth as a luthier. In addition to the actual technical skills

I've learned, there is also just the experience of spending time with a master of our craft, soaking in not only his ways of doing things, but the very attitudes that he brings to lutherie. Not only has my time with Tom given me the groundwork necessary for me to begin production of my own archtop guitars, but I feel that my approach to the flattop instruments I already build has profited from the experience. Thanks, Tom!

—— *Fred Casey (1997)*

The Classical Guitar: A Complete History
Edited by John Morrish
Backbeat Books, 1997
ISBN 0879305029

This a one of the most beautiful books on the history of a musical instrument I have ever seen. Layout is superb, and there are hundreds of gorgeous color photos with a dozen stunning fold-out spreads. At first glance this looks like one of those coffee-table editions, filled with beautiful photos but thin on content. Don't be fooled by its size (10″×13″) and beauty. There is real substance here that makes this a must-purchase.

This book is based on the collection of fine and rare concert guitars owned by Dallas, Texas collector Russell Cleveland. No one collector can own guitars by every maker, and there are conspicuous gaps in his collection, mostly living luthiers and pre-Torres 19th-century guitars. But what he does have is astounding. Several pre-Torres instruments are listed, but his collection, and this book, really begins with the Torres guitar. He has instruments by the Ramírez family, the Hauser family, Bouchet, Fleta, Rodríguez, Rubio, Gilbert, Romanillos, Humphrey, Ruck, and Smallman just to name a few. Each is lovingly photographed and presented so that details are clear and visible.

The book's substance is in the accompanying articles. British writer and journalist John Morrish has served as both editor and contributor and has collected essays by leading guitar authors including Colin Cooper, Tony Bacon, Brian Jeffrey, Graham Wade, Paul Fowles, and Jaap van Elk. He also received consulting help from Robert Spenser, Paul Fischer, and Raymond Ursell. This is an impressive list by any standard, and each author has provided essays in his own field of expertise.

The editorial perspective is unusual; performers and makers are considered as equal historical partners. There are wonderful biographical sketches for Tárrega and Torres, Agustín Barrios and José Ramírez, Segovia and Hauser, Bream and Romanillos, Williams and Smallman, and many others. This book makes a great case for including instrument makers as part of the general study of music history.

There are also articles on guitar methods, technique and playing styles, flamenco guitars and players, unconventional guitars, anatomy of a modern guitar, composers, even an article on the future of the guitar. Each of these articles is well written and illustrated with photos and diagrams.

For instrument makers, the attraction of this book will be the photography and specifications. Each instrument is shown with photos of the front, back, and right side. There is also a specification chart for each giving the completion date and serial number (when available), the woods, length, weight, scale length, string spacing at both the nut and saddle, neck width at the nut and 12th fret, neck depth at the 1st and 8th fret, body width, and side depth. In some cases there is information about the repair history or current physical condition, rosette design, finish and refinishing, and replacement of parts.

Most of the information on individual makers is biographical with little discussion of actual construction methodologies. Many of the makers represented here deserve independent full-length studies. One problem I had with this book is that it does not represent anything like a complete history of the classical guitar. There is very little discussion of the origin of the classical guitar, and important makers like Louis Panormo and Johann Stauffer are barely mentioned.

A large portion of the book talks about luthiers, yet none of the articles are written by one. The majority of authors are British, and the overall perspective is Anglo. If the book is meant to be a complete history of the classical guitar, the slighting of North, Central, and South American luthiers is a problem. For example, only three American instruments are shown (Robert Ruck, John Gilbert, and Thomas Humphrey), and there is no mention of the ground-breaking work of Richard Schneider. What has been included in the book is fascinating; what has been omitted is regrettable.

But the responsibility of a survey like this is to give us the main line of historical development with accurate biographical and technical information. This book delivers that in spades. It is also incredibly beautiful and will, I have no doubt, become a collectors' item. The publisher says there have been only 6000 copies printed. I would be less than responsible if I did not urge you to buy your copy immediately.

—— *Bryan Johanson (1998)*

A Collection of Fine Spanish Guitars
from Torres to the Present
by Sheldon Urlik
Sunny Knoll Publishing Company, 1997
ISBN 0966077105

The guitar's status as poor cousin to the violin is perhaps starting to change. During the latter part of 1997, two collectors published major books based on their collections of classical guitars: this book, and *The Classical Guitar, A Complete History* covering the Cleveland collection. Both books largely cover the same time period, mid-1800s to the present, and both are extravagant — wonderful indulgences of color photography, spacious layouts, and information of interest to guitar makers.

I believe the interest in older guitars that prompted these collectors to collect reflects a change in the classical guitar's lowly status. Obviously this is good news for makers. Although classical guitars rarely maintain their full musical value after twenty or thirty years of use (unlike violins), there seems to be an increasing desire to own, maintain, restore, and even play some of these instruments. The result is higher prices and increasing interest.

Sheldon Urlik, a successful businessman with a passion for classical and flamenco guitars, has amassed a collection of sixty-eight instruments which he has decided to share with the world through a very beautiful book. In his own words:

"Bringing together these fine Spanish guitars to form this collection magnifies and reinforces the importance of the craftsmanship, design development, and work that their great makers did to create them, and the collection environment also contributes to the preservation of the instruments, some of which are extremely rare.... Comparisons and contrasts that can be drawn from this representative collection make the whole greater than the sum of its parts, and also, I believe make the collection more important than the collector. That is a compelling reason to collect." (From the Preface, p. vii)

The title "Spanish Guitars" is a little misleading at first glance. Urlik uses it to cover guitars made by makers in other countries, including Hauser I, II, III, Bouchet, Friederich, Kohno, Smallman, Rubio, Gilbert, Ruck, Bruné, and Humphrey. For example, some may disagree that Hermann Hauser I made Spanish guitars (no matter how many he studied), although no one would deny him an important place in any serious collection. We can quibble over the term, "Spanish," but, in the end, every guitar in the collection has its roots back in Spain.

The collection appears, both from the photographs and from Urlik's description, to be in extraordinarily good shape. He defines the exact terms he uses for each instrument's condition, from "as new," to "excellent," to "very good," and "restored." "Restored" is, Urlik writes in his preface, "a condition where a guitar, usually a fine and important one to justify the expense, has undergone extensive rebuilding or repair. Restorations may even necessitate replacing original parts with remade ones, with the ultimate goal of returning the guitar as close as possible to its condition when new."

This goes beyond the usual standard for restoration used by museums. Robert Lundberg, no stranger to *American Lutherie* readers, tells me that museums, like the Smithsonian for whom he has done extensive restoration work, typically wants an instrument restored back to the most recent restoration and, in some cases, to be made functional as well. Very often, especially with older instruments, it is not possible to know the maker's original intent, therefore not possible to achieve it. This is where the relatively short past of the classical/flamenco guitar works in our favor. Several guitars in the collection have been restored, but more often than not, it would seem that they were purchased in very good condition. I believe all are functional musical instruments.

Each instrument is given at least two pages, and several are given three or four. For each there are color photos of the full frontal and oblique back views, and "floating" shots with the white page as background of the rosette and label. Several have other closeups of the bridge, head, purfling/binding, or some other detail as well. A written description accompanies each guitar and contains construction information, the guitar's condition, and some other details like grain spacing in the top, how well matched the back and sides are, bracing particulars — and very often information on where this guitar fits in historically, both within a given builder's life's work, and in relation to other builders and the overall history of the guitar. Extra space and longer descriptions accompany guitars of particular interest, for example the 1912 Manuel Ramírez. Because of the importance of Segovia's 1912 Manuel Ramírez, any M. Ramírez from 1912 is bound to be the focus of attention. Of course there are other good reasons to grant this guitar and maker extra space. In Urlik's words:

"Manuel Ramírez... is an essential luthier in the history of the Spanish guitar. He widened the acceptance of the Torres principles of guitar design and construction by training important craftsmen who then went on to produce some of the finest guitars ever made."

Those craftsmen are named as Santos Hernández, Domingo Esteso, and Modesto Borreguero, all of whom are well represented in the collection. In fact, there are three Hernández guitars (two classical, one flamenco), three Estesos (same), and two Borregueros (one flamenco, one classical) representing their makers.

On the same page with the color photos is a list of nineteen important dimensions, including the weight of each guitar. In addition, each has a very basic schematic drawing showing bracing placement for the top and back. The label is seen not only as a photo, but the information is printed below the photo to ensure legibility. Would you be able to build a 1912 Manuel Ramírez-like guitar from this information? Similar, no doubt. (Of course, if you had GAL *Plan #38* of Segovia's 1912 as well, you probably could make a pretty close replica.)

Useful and fascinating as this book is, readers should still not accept its contents as completely accurate. There are factual errors, which I expect will be corrected in the next edition. For example, Manuel Ramírez died in 1916, not 1920. And Marcelo Barbero died in 1956, not 1955. (Richard Bruné has a copy of his published obituary!) Apparently Harvey Turnbull's book, *The Guitar from the Renaissance to the Present Day*, is the source of some of the errors. Urlik relies on many sources, some more reliable than others. He dutifully footnotes much of the history in his descriptions and lists sources at the end of the book. *American Lutherie*, a pretty reliable one, I can't help but say, is cited quite frequently.

I would like to have seen more contemporary makers represented in this collection. There are quite a few well-known makers who are not represented. I hope this will be corrected over time as well. A time lag between when an object is made and when it is deemed collectable pretty much goes with the territory.

And this book would be even more useful if some of the extra space which was left blank were used to make the schematic drawings larger and more detailed. Perhaps there would have been room for bracing dimensions, shapes, and thicknesses of various components.

These shortcomings are minor in the larger scheme of things. If you can only purchase one of the collection books and you wonder which, maybe I can help. This book has more nuts-and-bolts lutherie than the Cleveland collection book; and this one has more than twice as many guitars. But get them both — one for your birthday, another for Christmas.

—— *Cyndy Burton (1998)*

Video: ***Easy Guitar Maintenance and Repair***
Harvey Citron
Homespun Tapes
ISBN 0634054546

Young luthiers may not know Harvey Citron, but he was among the small independents who set up limited production of high-end electric guitars and basses in the era when major manufacturers suffered a sag in quality. He made this video in 1984, which makes him one of the "old men" of video instruction. Video technology has come a long way since, but aside from his urban cowpoke shirt, this tape is surprisingly up-to-date.

Though useful to any guitar owner, the tape is electrically biased. This is more than a reflection of Citron's interests. Disco not only killed live music in general, it wiped out the acoustic landscape. Citron doctors a Strat, a Les Paul, and a few basses that include his own gorgeous creations. His whole focus rests on showing the musician how to make his ax a custom fit for his own hands and ears using only tools that come from the hardware store (except, I think, for the truss rod wrench). This is an admirable goal, even today.

The complexities of setting the action are carefully covered, then it's on to adjusting pickups and cleaning pots. Citron demonstrates how to mill frets, for those players who have enough hair to give it a try. If your fret ends are poking out the side of the fingerboard you are covered, and if your nut slots are worn too low you'll learn to fix those, too. Most players want their pickups adjusted for maximum output, but Citron would rather that they were adjusted for balance and tone preference, which is a whole other matter. Further, his instruction is to set all string heights at 1⁄16″ over the highest fret, but he's quick to mention that such buttery playing comes at the price of some rattle. Citron has his feet planted firmly in the real world, exactly where he wants everyone else to stand. However, if your guitar has a locking trem system you'll get no help here. Mr. Rose was just getting his wings when this video was made.

This tape is unpretentious and useful to those with no lutherie experience. Give this tape to your son. If he can get his guitar back together and make it playable he might be ready for bigger things. It could happen.

—— *John Calkin (1998)*

Video: ***Archtop Guitar Design & Construction***
Robert Benedetto, 1996
ISBN 0963977113

I've not seen Bob Benedetto's book about archtop construction. Though it immediately became the standard source of information about building the jazz guitar, I wanted first to investigate the video set on its own merit. It was obvious from the first minutes that the tapes were going to be a marvelous companion to a text, but I was hoping they would be detailed enough to help me build a guitar without the book. And they are, but I'd like to qualify that judgment. I'll get to that shortly.

It's easy to think that the premier guitar makers somehow coax and cajole their wood to blossom into finished instruments in the same way that gardeners create award-winning roses. Foolish, I know. But Benedetto shows a loyalty to a few choice tools, just like I do, and some of his shortcuts are crazier than anything I've tried. By the fourth or fifth hour of viewing I felt like I was watching a good friend at work. "Boy, that Benedetto and me, we're like two peas in a pod, yessir!"

Well, maybe not. But that's the kind of comfort level the videos create. I hasten to add that virtually all of the program was taped during an instruction seminar, so Benedetto is working to a live audience. The class is very small, and the camera becomes just another member of the congregation. Though this contributes to the friendly atmosphere, it's also very seldom that any special concessions are made to let the camera get the best possible view. There are intimate views of the binding of the *f*-holes, but many other operations that involve small details are watched from afar. Work done to the fingerboard stop, the tailpiece saddle, and the binding miters are viewed from a distance that will leave you scratching your head and sneaking closer to the screen if you don't already understand what is going on. So if you're truly a rookie, you'll have to pop for the book, too.

I like the way Bob debunks a lot of lutherie theory as so much mythology, but then insists that the luthier must live inside that mythology as long as his customers take it as gospel. I like the way he maintains that tap tones are meaningless in evaluating the quality of tonewood, and then demonstrates how to use the tap tone as a means of perfecting the plates. I was amazed by how fast a skilled pair of hands can carve a top. Or bend sides. Or bring the guitar to a primo gloss with only five coats of lacquer. The first time he slides a neck into its dovetail, all the angles are perfect! Of course, that's what jigs are supposed to do for you, but it still seems like a marvel.

It's also wonderful to hear tap tones while they are being explained. The sound of wood is important in many ways as it is shaped into a guitar, and video makes it obvious as no book ever has. Bob also trues the guitar ribs on a belt sander, and then dresses the binding in exactly the same way. In print this would just sound foolhardy, but on tape I stand convinced and I'm going to try it. The creation of a sunburst finish could never be as dazzling on the pages of a book, either. I'm sure that in many details the videos can't touch the book, but I'm also certain that in many ways the videos are superior to the book, and function overall as more than just a supplement to the printed word.

I'm pretty confident that an accomplished creator of other instruments could make a good archtop guitar with just these videos to guide him/her. There's just over 9½ hours of running time in this tape set, and it covers the ground pretty well and won't put you to sleep. Imagine the education to be had if you attended the whole seminar!

—— *John Calkin (1998)*

Spray Finishing
Andy Charron
The Taunton Press, 1996
ISBN 1561581146

Spray Finishing is intended for the cabinet maker, but the book should also be useful to luthiers who are about to take the plunge into finishing with air.

The book's strong suit is its explanation of spray equipment, be it guns, turbines, compressors, booths, or spray systems. There are more equipment options available today than ever before, and the first 68 pages or so of this book will help you make sense out of all those catalog pages. Charron weights his discussion in favor of HVLP systems and waterborne finishes, and I think we can take that as a sign of things to come for the small shop of the future. On the other hand, he doesn't delve into brand names or recommend specific gun types. By the end of the book you still won't know if you need a full production gun or if a smaller doorjamb gun might suit your needs. Charron is also quick to point to spray cans as the proper and cost effective method of doing touchups, and nowhere in the text does the word airbrush crop up. Perhaps there's not as much overlap between luthiers and furniture makers after all.

The rest of the text describes proper spray gun technique, methods of coloring raw wood with your gun, and applying various top coats. It's interesting reading, but not luthier specific. *American Lutherie* has more and better info about lacquering than is found here.

If you haven't purchased any equipment yet, you should get this book from the library before you do. A good salesperson could set you straight, but it will be a big help to understand painter's jive talk before you face him. If you're buying from a catalog, you better know your stuff before you write the check. This book will help. If you just want to know how to paint a guitar, get the Stewart-MacDonald finishing videos.

—— *John Calkin (1998)*

Basic Pickup Winding
and Complete Guide to Making Your Own Pickup Winder
Jason Lollar
Lollar Publishing, 1998
ISBN 0966259904

Sampling the different styles of pickups can be a daunting task: there are a great many manufacturers, each with many different designs. At $50–$150 apiece, the search for the appropriate pickup can be a very expensive proposition.

The ideal choice is to roll your own. Information on how to do this has been in fairly short supply, but this changes with Jason Lollar's book, *Basic Pickup Winding and Complete Guide to Making your Own Pickup Winder*. By building the winding machine detailed in the book and then winding pickups using the author's instructions, electric luthiers will be able to exercise far greater control over their instruments' sound.

The majority of the book is devoted to construction of the winding machine. The mechanism is complex, but building it should not pose any problems for anyone with reasonable skills and minimal tooling. Materials are readily available. The heart of the mechanism is a used variable-speed sewing machine motor. Instructions are thorough, including detailed drawings and photographs of the project.

The title is a little misleading. The book is really a guide to making a pickup winder, with only a little on pickup design. For instance, he doesn't provide templates for pickup bobbins, but simply suggests tracing a Strat pickup cover. A brief mention of general resistance ranges for "normal" (7K–9KΩ) and "hot" (9K–14KΩ) pickups is about as far as he goes towards discussing design theory. Wire and magnets are discussed and sources of supply are presented in an appendix.

This book definitely fills a gap in existing electric guitar literature. Using the winder detailed in the book and then following the author's instructions on winding will enable the electric luthier to enter the endlessly fascinating and complex world of pickup design.

—— *Bishop Cochran (1998)*

Wood: The Best of Fine Woodworking
The Taunton Press, 1995
ISBN 1561580996

I love the title of this compendium of thirty-two articles and essays from *Fine Woodworking* magazine. Wood. Simply that, for a material that is as varied and complex as a Spanish *paella*, each fraught with disaster for the neophyte indulging in experimentation without some solid underpinnings.

Newcomers as well as oldtimers will find a wealth of information on wood with scads of color photos of trees, wood, magnified end grain, and photomicrographs. I can't put this book into the category of being a serious research resource (it wasn't intended to be), but more of a discovery, or rediscovery, of local U.S. woods and backyard exotics with a nod to some imported woods like mahogany and a discussion of rainforest issues. Bruce Hoadley plays Sherlock Holmes in some wood ID adventures, eight contenders for the title of "ironwood" are considered, and there's a really good article about bird's-eye maple, to remark on a few of the more outstanding offerings.

The cutting, drying, storing, recycling, and harvesting your own timber items are well presented collectively, and it's a shame that this book was published far after Hurricane Andrew made a windfall of hundreds of species of normally unavailable tropical timbers to collectors and craftspeople. If you've lived through an El-Niño-ravaged area this year, where a lot of downed trees are free for the clean up, this book might just get you started "rolling your own."

—— *Nicholas Von Robison (1998)*

Video: ***Basic Inlay Techniques***
Video: ***Intermediate Inlay Techniques***
Larry Robinson
Robinson Custom Inlays, 1996

Only a handful of people have attempted to make a career out of inlay alone. Of these, Larry Robinson is probably the best known since the publication of his book, *The Art of Inlay*, in 1994. The techniques he has developed encourage more precision in this work than those of any other source of instruction I've seen. In this style of work, precision is the name of the game.

When Robinson says "basic" he's not talking about snowflakes and banjo curlicues, he means a butterfly of shell and silver made of fifteen or so pieces, many of which fit inside the others. *Basic Inlay Techniques* is a complete enough tutor to set you well on your way.

Robinson displays an array of inlayable stuff that you might never have thought to use. From there it's on to tools and how to use them, how to keep your health while you inlay, a bit about collecting patterns, and then down to work. Robinson is articulate and the instruction is well-filmed. There are good closeups where they need to be. The pace won't outdistance anyone. The viewer is urged to dive in. Thanks, Larry, I believe I will.

In *Intermediate Inlay Techniques*, design becomes a crucial consideration. You've seen vine-of-life inlays, but they probably don't resemble the vine Robinson conjures up. It sprouts four kinds of flowers, supports butterflies and hummingbirds, and shelters a nesting warbler. There are hundreds of pieces made of shell, metals, and wood. The inventory of shell necessary for such a project is as daunting a prospect as the work itself. The scope of the job is pretty intimidating.

The actual work is no different than that described in the beginner video. There is a quick review of sawing techniques in the second tape, but the focus is on heavier matters. The elements of design are discussed in depth. The camera dips into Larry's sketchbook for a peek at many other vines in several styles. Very little time is spent cutting shell. The routing and sanding are done in fast forward to save time, since they were explained in detail in *Basic Inlay Techniques.* The tape ends with an examination of engraving tools and the engraving and dying of the inlays.

Each video is densely packed no down time. If you hope to add this kind of work to your bag of tricks, I hardly think you'll be disappointed. A third tape on advanced inlay is anticipated. I hope it's obvious that I'm looking forward to it.

—— *John Calkin (1998)*

Video: ***Advanced Inlay Techniques***
Larry Robinson
Robinson Custom Inlays, 1998

After a book and two videos of inlay instruction you might wonder if anything is left for Larry Robinson to teach. Well, there's plenty, including some leftover stuff if Larry ever decides to make a fourth video. Robinson's book gave scant coverage to inlaying signatures, and that's where the bulk of instruction is placed in *Advanced Inlay Techniques.* The signatures start as mere pencil lines, and by the time they are reduced to fit on the fingerboard at the 12th fret, they are very thin lines indeed. On work of this delicacy he tries to talk each customer into inlays of gold or silver, rather than shell, and the signatures inlaid in the video are cut from gold sheet stock. The signature in cursive is narrower than the cuts made by the 000 jeweler's saw blades, less than .010″. Cutting such work from shell might well be left to lasers. There is also a trick method of routing for such intricate work that pretty much guarantees accurate results and prevents the tearout of ebony where only dots and bits are to be left. A side excursion is made to examine the use of computers to lay out and alter signatures and lettering, which may be eye-opening for anyone still trying to fight off computer literacy. Robinson maintains that this one program has more than paid for his computer, as well as having brought a measure of ease to his work life. The lettering segment goes on to address block lettering, shaded letters, and the use of various fonts inlaid in a variety of materials.

Another lengthy segment is dedicated to inlaying abalone pin stripes into a neck, complete with swirls and wiggles. This is over-the-top decoration that probably only hints at what's to come if this form of inlay catches on. The router base that Larry made up to get into the tightest curves may be worth the price of the tape. The same base is used later in a brief segment about inlaying the carved top of a solidbody guitar.

The tape is filled out with a discussion of 3D inlay and the use of alternative materials. Perhaps after two and a half decades of inlay work Robinson is finding traditional styles too confining. The 3D work uses elements of the inlay set at various heights above the surface of the instrument to suggest added depth and giving the guitar a tactile sensation beyond that of slick smoothness. There is even a sample of flowers that are carved in some depth and merely appliqued to the sides of an electric guitar. This segment includes no instruction, just description.

The promised video gallery of inlay work hasn't happened, but I haven't given up hope. Larry's book is very nice, but the chance to see exotic guitars in detail way beyond life size could be enough to send me on a hunt for an affordable humongous-screen TV.

—— *John Calkin (1999)*

Acoustics of Wood
Voichita Buchur
CRC Press, 1995
ISBN 0849348013

Voichita Buchur's book *Acoustics of Wood* is a synthesis of over fifty years of work by the scientific community into the physics of how this complex material responds to vibrational wave stimuli. With almost 800 references into the literature and about ten years from inception to its being published in 1995, it is a tremendous resource for the luthier's understanding of his/her main material. I don't get the feel from the text that the author is a maker herself, even though she is a member of the Catgut Acoustical Society. The book is heavily weighted towards violin family instruments, but this doesn't make the book any less valuable to guitar makers.

After a short, well written, general discussion on the anatomical structure of wood (macro, micro, and molecular), a brief outline is presented dividing the book into three major sections. Part One explores the physical phenomena associated with the effects of acoustic waves in forests (windbreaks to attenuate noise) and architectural acoustics (concert halls, office buildings, restaurants) with wood being used as a construction material and insulator in conjunction with other nonwood materials. A survey of six European concert halls and their geometrical, acoustical, and construction data is pretty interesting.

Part Two deals with the theory and material characterization of wood and wood composites. Solid wood presents an orthotropic symmetry (as opposed to plywood or composites which have transverse isotropic symmetries), where three mutually perpendicular mirror planes of symmetry exist, related to the directions of growth. The differences of ultrasonic wave transmission velocity in the longitudinal and radial/tangential planes may be as high as 15:1. The analysis of the theory (using Young's moduli, Poisson's ratios, density, tensile and shear strengths) and techniques for the measurement of the elastic and viscoelastic properties of wood is well covered starting with generalizing Hooke's law and then getting deeper and deeper into the equations. The science part of the acoustics of wood is really Buchur's metier and she describes the current state-of-the-art of nondestructive wave measuring techniques (ultrasound, laser interferometry, acoustic microscopy) in detail.

Part Three, titled "Quality Assessment," is the meat and potatoes for the luthier. Chapter Seven, "Wood Species for Musical Instruments," has the following subsections: acoustic properties of resonance wood for violins, guitars, woodwinds, percussion, and piano soundboards; relationships between elastic properties of resonance wood and its typical structural characteristics; tonal quality of musical instruments and wood properties; factors affecting acoustic properties of wood for musical instruments; influence of environmental conditions; influence of long-term loading; influence of varnishing; chemical treatments for improving the acoustic properties of common solid wood used for mass-produced instruments; composites as substitutes for resonance wood; and a small appendix of values for resonance wood of various origins.

A small sampling of the questions answered or at least discussed are: the acoustically perfect grain and increment width for violins, keyboards, and guitars; the importance of gradual earlywood to latewood transition in spruce grain; is curly maple utilized in violins solely for its beauty or does it have high acoustic properties too; the optimal storage time for wood; how do you achieve a high Q factor in guitar tops; did the Italian and German masters use sapwood in their tops; the influence of natural aging; the age in which dry storage of wood produces optimal acoustic quality; alternatives to traditional resonance woods (very meager); the best altitude to harvest resonance wood; can curly maple or wood defects in a tree be determined by nondestructive techniques; and so on. Just the sort of topics bandied about at any luthiers bull session, only here, hard scientific data backs it up.

That's enough teasing. Here's just one conclusion from the book. The hypothesis that Strad and other old Italian masters soaked their logs in water for periods of time to stimulate enzyme activity which would selectively destroy the bordered pits in spruce and result in an acoustically superior wood has been talked about for many years. In 1990, Claire Barlow and J. Woodhouse used scanning electron microscopy to examine samples of many old Italian violins and could find no evidence of bacterially degraded pits. Though there are mechanical and chemical differences between old and fresh wood, the evidence is that there are no anatomical changes, at least in the 500-year span that the researchers investigated. So, another lutherie legend is flushed down the drain.

One aspect of any reviewer's task is to recommend, or not, the work. One of the subthemes at the last convention was, "Do you take an intuitive or scientific approach to your work?" My perception (and that of others I've talked with since) is that most GAL members favor an intuitive approach, with a small, hard-core band of luthiers championing scientific lutherie. If you get faint at the sight of a mathematical equation, then this book is not for you. All in all, *Acoustics of Wood* is a remarkable book worth taking a look at, but at a buck a page ($239 + tax + S&H) it's really priced itself out of the running for the luthier's bookshelf.

—— *Nicholas Von Robison (1999)*

Tambura
Dusan Brankov
Tamburitza Association of America, 1998
ASIN B0006FDGZK

The tambura is a Yugoslavian version of the guitar featuring four courses (the first string is doubled), a Fender-style headstock, a floating bridge, and an oversize pickguard inlaid into the top. Back and top are ladder braced. This only describes the middle member of the tambura family; the smallest tambura has a body carved from a solid board and a much smaller scale, and the two largest members have cello-like scroll heads. I gather that tambura makers in eastern Europe have always taken an individual approach to the size, shape, and construction. Brankov's mission is to garner international recognition and respect for the instruments he loves, and to standardize them as much as the violin family has been standardized. He doesn't anticipate the first happening without the second. Only time will tell if he is successful.

Brankov's book is a good one. Anyone wishing to build tambura should find all the information they need here. Instruction is put forth in a formal and reasonable manner. There is a lot of math for those who wish to study it, along with a good dose of scientific theory about the way stringed instruments function. This scholarly approach is no doubt part of the quest for international status for the tambura.

Most American luthiers should need little more than a good set of plans to be about their tambura business. Compared to any guitars, tambura are easy to build. Tamburas have traditionally been fretted with steel wire which is bent into the shape of a staple, the ends of which are driven into holes in the fretboard. This is the method that Brankov uses. Do American tambura makers maintain this tradition? I don't know.

Brankov is adamant that the top plate must not be arched by its braces, since this introduces unwanted stresses, and this at a time when many Western luthiers are converting to arched top plates. This is just one area where the book and contemporary American lutherie are out of synch. There is no jig trickery, and certainly no sense of cutting-edge information. If the instruments are ever updated to include such niceties as truss rods and modern fretwire I bet that it happens outside of the tambura's homeland.

—— *John Calkin (1999)*

Ring the Banjar!
The Banjo in America from Folklore to Factory
Robert Lloyd Webb
The MIT Museum, 1984
ISBN 0917027019

In 1984 the MIT Museum sponsored an exhibition of banjos that focused on the companies that existed in and around Boston. This book is a catalog of the instruments exhibited, and the essays sort of explain why such a prestigious organization spent so much energy on such a humble instrument. Contemporary luthiers think that they are leading the way for the factories. Webb maintains the reverse, that individual builders were basically hackers who kept the instrument alive until the large factories brought it to its zenith.

The banjo began life as a stick and a gourd. It evolved rapidly into a recognizable configuration and the Victorian banjo craze that followed the Civil War made it a hot-ticket item, bringing a rush to make better and fancier models. Venues changed from parlors to large burlesque halls, and louder and gaudier banjos filled the need. The jazz age and the banjo were both put to death by the Great Depression, and Webb credits Pete Seeger and Earl Scruggs as the men who resurrected the latter. It's a thumbnail sketch, but a good one.

The second essay is by James F. Bollman, a collector who supplied many of the banjos for the exhibition. It consists of short biographies of the men who built the factories that built the banjos in the Boston area. Men are more fascinating than what they make, and that's the true message of the essay.

However, the heart of the book is the illustrations. There are plenty of old woodcuts, photos, and catalog page reproductions. The photos of the instruments in the exhibition are fine. The factories must have gone through tons of shell while making the higher-grade banjos, and they glitter and gleam from the page. This small book is a must-have for any fan of the open-back banjo.

—— *Woody Vernice (1999)*

Making and Playing Musical Instruments
Jack Botermans, Herman Dewit, and Hans Godefroy
University of Washington Press
ISBN 0295969482

This book is primarily for hobbyists. Not that one could not find buyers for the kalimbas, alpenhorns, and talharpas made from descriptions to be found in its pages, as such instruments are staples at craft fairs, weekend markets, and other venues for ethnic and folk art. But it just might be of greater use to professionals than is apparent.

The urge — or summons — to make something special for a musically inclined friend or relative will eventually strike anyone known to make instruments. Explaining the economic realities of instrument making is embarrassing at best. I have sat in the homes of luthiers in several countries and listened as they played a cheap offshore instrument. Believe me, you are not alone. This book may help provide a solution.

Ever want to do something really special for your cousin's irritating children? Make them some nice "tongue-clappers" or a cog rattle! I think this is usually called a "racket," and with good reason. Be forewarned that the introduction of such contraptions into the family must be avoided when one has children in one's own house.

The book is divided into four sections dealing with aerophones (things you blow), idiophones (things you rattle), membranophones (things you hit), and chordophones (things you should know about if you read this magazine).

Besides practical instructions and examples of traditional folk instruments, the authors have provided lots of interesting rhymes and lyrics from Northern European folklore to spice things up. Much useful historical color is included. Allow me to quote from one such passage. As concerns the "Jew's harp": "For centuries it was played by young men in love; the seductive, soft sound intended to convince the lady in question that she was the only one for him." Aside from the obvious question of whether the author has actually *heard* a mouth harp, I am very curious to know how much effort he has spent trying to impress young Jewish women. Not enough, I'll wager.

— *David Riggs (1999)*

Video: ***Violin Making — Live!***
Video: ***Watch Me Make a Cello, Step-by-Step***
Henry Strobel, 1997
ISBN 0962067385

Henry Strobel has written a fleet of books about making violins, violas, and cellos, all of which build one upon the other. To use the cello book you should have first read the violin book, and so on. This video set uses the same idea, i.e., to use it to best advantage you must have the cello book, which needs the violin book for complete understanding, and so on, all in the house that Jack built. But if you buy the video set, Strobel will sell you the cello book for $10 instead of $30, which might remove some of the sting. And if you haven't got a cello guru to run to as you tear into your first instrument, Strobel on tape may be the next best thing.

The videos are not intensely detailed or perfectly complete. Almost no operation is carried through to completion on tape. But Strobel has the capacity to make cello creation seem wonderfully doable. The first three hours of tape whiz by with so little effort that even a casual viewer might decide to buy a whacking big gouge and a fistful of teeny planes. Carving the plates often seems like the scariest part of cello making, but Strobel makes it look like fun.

The same techniques can be used to build a violin or viola, but the large scale of the cello made it easier for a novice movie maker to capture for the home audience. For make no mistake about it, these are home movies in the worst sense. Strobel had to draw upon the aid of various family members to drive the camcorder. The lighting is generally bad, the skin tones horrible, narration is clipped off, and in many cases the sound drops out altogether. The show is as rough as a cob, but as a teaching tool, it will suffice. There is a moment at the end of the tape where the cellist sits alone in a room. The camera randomly pans about as the resonant, throaty voice of the instrument seems to fill the world, and it becomes finally apparent that we are often seduced by our work until we forget that the music is the thing, not the shine on the wood. I'll say the same thing for these videos. The teaching's the thing, not the lack of gloss in the film making.

— *John Calkin (1999)*

Julian Bream, the Foundations of a Musical Career
Stuart W. Button
Scolar Press, 1997
ISBN 185928390X

This is a small book, a scant 121 pages of text, plus photos, appendices, bibliography, and index. Its cost in American dollars is great, $59.95. The contents cover the period of Julian Bream's musical life starting in 1944 and ending in 1951 with his debut at Wigmore Hall at age eighteen. The book consists of many letters (some quoted completely, others partially), most of which (forty-six) written by Henry Bream, Julian's father, to Wilfrid Appleby, a friend, amateur guitarist, and supporter of Julian's career. In addition there are nineteen other letters, concert programs, and sixteen pages of photos. The author's commentary strings these original materials together and provides a context for them. (It is based on his Ph.D. thesis and is duly, copiously footnoted.)

Anyone with an interest in Julian Bream or the classical guitar will find something to enjoy here. You will not find anything about building instruments, but the photos and text do highlight the succession of instruments Bream owned and was loaned during this time. Some historical information is given on the Panormo family of guitar makers and a whole chapter is called, "Maccaferri's 'Monstrosity'," the name given Julian's Maccaferri guitar due to the blasphemy of its having more than six strings, ten to be exact. (The photograph of a diminutive Julian playing this huge cutaway guitar is priceless.) If you're interested in learning about Julian Bream the person, you may be disappointed. This book is in no sense the sequel or prequel to *Julian Bream: A Life on the Road,* by Tony Palmer. Some care is taken to acknowledge his genius and normalcy in other areas of life, but very little space is given to any insights about character or personality. On the other hand, Bream's Foreword is a wonderful and all-too-brief statement about his life as a young guitarist and offers the best glimpse of a personal nature. In addition, the reader may infer from Henry Bream's letters and actions his own extreme dedication, determination, and persistence — all of which were required to launch Julian's career, and all of which had to be present in Julian to transcend the difficulties of building and maintaining it.

Henry Bream recognized his son's musical gifts and dedicated his short life to their fulfillment. This was no small feat. Many of the "players" in this drama were egotistical, small-minded men who were anxious to protect their own meager turf. Very much of this book is about the obstacles that had to be dealt with for Bream's extraordinary talent to reach an audience that could appreciate him. It also chronicles the generosity and support of many people who were helpful in this endeavor.

England in 1945, the time when Julian was just beginning to play guitar, was picking up the pieces from the devastation of World War II. The classical guitar had no place in the world of serious music, no audience, and little repertoire. Julian Bream writes in the book's Foreword, "as a classical instrument the guitar was held in almost total disregard by lovers of serious music. Even the great Segovia, a distinguished international artist, could not draw more than 100 people for a guitar recital in Manchester or Birmingham. What hope would there be for an obscure young Englishman.

"Although father was obviously concerned about my future, he was obsessed with the idea that England should have a world-class virtuoso guitarist, and specifically an English school of composition for the instrument."

Henry Bream died of a serious illness (not specified) in November of 1950, one year before Julian's Wigmore Hall debut, an event he worked so diligently to bring about. (The book is inconsistent about the date of Henry's death, stating 1950 in several places and 1951 in several others. It seems that 1950 is likely correct from the cited letters.)

The relationship of Segovia to the young Bream is naturally of interest. Bream writes, again from the Foreword, "his (Segovia's) concerts (1947) at Wigmore Hall were sheer magic for me. His technical accomplishment, together with the mellifluous sound of his guitar were inspirational beyond belief. It was to be Segovia who eventually convinced my father and others that I possessed the talent and promise to make some sort of career on the guitar."

The letters of Henry Bream and Button's commentary tell the story of how Segovia let the Breams down, by reneging on a promise to take Julian on the road with him in 1948 in order to personally teach him. The reasons are not entirely clear, but at least a contributing factor was gossip reaching Segovia, the gist of which was that Henry Bream had said his son could learn nothing from Segovia.

Another milestone in the young Bream's career and indirectly for the classical guitar was his acceptance at the Royal College of Music. Again, Julian writes briefly of this event in the Foreword, and we're given a more in-depth, behind-the-scenes look through Button's documentation.

Today we take for granted the classical guitar's place on the concert stage. If nothing else, this book gives us a glimpse of an earlier time when that was not so. We often credit Segovia with opening that particular door, but this little book makes more than clear the role of another great artist, Julian Bream, whose legacy is yet to be fully realized. Julian Bream will celebrate his sixty-sixth birthday on July 15. Although he has vastly reduced his concert schedule and range of travel, we hear he's still performing brilliantly.

—— *Cyndy Burton (1999)*

Acquired of the Angels
Paul William Schmidt
Scarecrow Press, 1998
ISBN 1578860024

In the fall of 1983 I had the good fortune to be invited to study in the shop of James D'Aquisto. I confess that while I knew James D'Aquisto was a respected and famous archtop builder, I didn't know the half of it when I walked through those doors the first time.

As I worked side by side with him, listening to his stories, watching him work, and watching various characters in his life come through the doors of his workshop, I realized I wasn't just at a workshop but I was witness to a very magical moment in guitar history.

The tools, the woods, the layout of the shop, the music we listened to, the stories he told, and most of all his guitars, all were another world for me. These impressions were the groundwork for my own path as an archtop builder and for many other builders. So when I learned that Paul William Schmidt had written *Acquired of the Angels: The Lives and Works of Master Guitar Makers John D'Angelico and James L. D'Aquisto* I was very curious to see how his impressions would compare with mine.

"Acquired of the Angels" is the literal translation of the combination of two mythic names in the archtop world, D'Aquisto and D'Angelico. In Schmidt's book we come closer to an understanding of how two of the archtop's most revered creators worked the magic that lives today in their inspired works. What the reader acquires in *Acquired of the Angels,* along with a number of fine photographs and D'Angelico's ledger, is an array of firsthand accounts of two men who pursued their art despite such career-stopping setbacks as loss of shop, loss of business, and ill health; and through it all developed a relationship of deep devotion akin to father and son.

The pages of *Acquired of the Angels* are filled with stories gathered from family, friends, customers, and Jimmy D'Aquisto himself. They will be of interest to both the builder and the connoisseur of the archtop as they are rare glimpses into a world beset by hardship and touched by brilliance. Such stories are to be treasured as there are few such accounts of the lives of these immensely talented builders who both died, in midcareer, at age fifty-nine.

D'Aquisto's stories are of particular interest as they provide information on both D'Angelico and himself. Because D'Angelico is one of the founding fathers of the archtop, the information on him and his techniques alone is worth the purchase price.

Schmidt's transcriptions of D'Aquisto's colorful accounts of his relationship with D'Angelico bring this rarefied world, complete with wood dust and poignancy, to the reader's senses. D'Angelico's life seems to have been both a brief and solitary one. Revealed are his charm, incredible artistry, and the perennial problems a guitar maker faces.

Of special interest is the recounting of the fateful series of events that crossed the paths of the two "D'As" (as Schmidt calls them). Invited to leave commercial art school, forced to perform in clubs to support his growing family, D'Aquisto was poised, at age seventeen, to immerse himself in the fascinating world at 37 Kenmare. When D'Angelico broke off his relationship with his apprentice Vincent DiSerio, D'Aquisto became his sole apprentice and had the energy to insist D'Angelico resurrect the business when its closure overwhelmed him.

Such firsthand accounts, while never unbiased, will be of great interest to fans of the archtop and add to the mystique that surrounds it. And if D'Angelico, now dead for forty years, remains shadowy, his artistry and legacy, as handed down to and continued by D'Aquisto, is clear. The heart of the book is a celebration of the D'A's artistry and innovative style.

This is a beautiful book. There are some superb color studio photos of D'Aquisto's works by Joshua McClure. There are also some wonderful construction shots by Tim Olsen and the author Paul Schmidt. These alone tell volumes about the way D'Angelico and D'Aquisto thought and worked with the various woods.

Acquired of the Angels also contains the complete ledger of all the instruments built by D'Aquisto and D'Angelico, minus the names of the owners. I have spoken with some of the owners of these instruments and apparently there are some errors within this list. But whether these errors exist in the ledger itself or occurred during the preparation of this book, the ledger is nonetheless an extremely interesting component.

What I would like to have seen, in addition to the wonderful stories and pictures, is a bit more information in the area of building techniques. If the reader is looking for in-depth details of the works of these great builders, they will be largely disappointed. Technical information is fairly sparse. Chronicling of specific model information is patchy, but the most significant works are profiled. Probably the most complete information on their actual building techniques comes from the various articles and interviews with D'Aquisto by Tim Olsen of the Guild of American Luthiers.

Those who knew him well knew that there were struggles within D'Aquisto. These struggles are hinted at in *Acquired of the Angels* but not explored. Jimmy himself said many times that it was important to put all of yourself into each guitar, not just your good side. Perhaps appropriately, this particular intensity and passion is not really touched on in this book. But it would have been fascinating to explore this side of D'Aquisto, as there is as much to learn from these struggles of the soul as there is from life's easier victories.

Having said that, *Acquired of the Angels* is a truly wonderful and carefully prepared book, and I highly recommend it. Paul William Schmidt did his homework. Readers are advised to put their feet up and enjoy a great slice of archtop building life. Schmidt has conjured up a fascinating story. He makes us believe in the angels that touched the fusing of tradition and innovation that the D'A's relationship symbolizes.

What comes through in the pages of *Acquired of the Angels* is the tough but rewarding life of the guitar builder. The plot twists make it read at times like a novel. The D'A's find each other at a crucial moment and build a very special relationship, and together they navigate a world of hardship and victories that ends just as D'Aquisto finally gets his stride with his own exploration of the archtop. His life ends suddenly and unexpectedly just as he has reached what many would consider the peak of his career, but not before finding that most enviable of treasures — the certainty that you are doing what you are meant to do with your life.

John D'Angelico and Jimmy D'Aquisto acquired an artistry that is an incredible legacy to every builder of the archtop today. The reader will enjoy this testimonial to the lives and the guitars of two exceptionally gifted and visionary builders.

—— *Linda Manzer (1999)*

Research Papers in Violin Acoustics 1975–1993
Carleen Maley Hutchins, Editor
Virginia Benade, Associate Editor
Acoustical Society of America,
ISBN 1563966093

It is with some trepidation that I pen this, my first book review for *American Lutherie*. As I noted to Tim Olsen, "But I've never made or even played a violin. How can I review such books and do them justice?" "Well," he replied, "most of our readers are in the same position. And, having written the review, you can keep the books." So began several months of fascinated reading of this two-volume set of violin research papers.

A little over half of the papers in this collection are from the *Journal of the Catgut Acoustical Society,* Series 1 or 2 and the Society *Newsletter.* Both the Society and the journal are still alive, well, and active in mostly violin family instrument research. The remainder of the articles come from such technical journals as: *Journal of the Acoustical Society of America, Acustica, Journal of the Acoustical Society of Japan, Journal of Audio Engineering, Journal of the Violin Society of America, Scientific American, Wood Science and Technology, Acoustics Australia, Acta Metallica, Music Perception, American Journal of Physics, Interdisciplinary Science Review, Strad,* and *Physics Today.* Papers from the proceedings of several conferences on acoustics and modal analysis are also represented.

For those not familiar with technical research papers dealing with the violin, the depth, breadth and complexity of some of the papers in these two books could be quite daunting. However, Ms. Hutchins and Ms. Benade have made a laudable effort in bringing new readers up to speed by providing perspective overviews of each collection of papers within a given subheading. No particular mathematics background is necessary for reading these overviews; anyone who enjoys reading *American Lutherie* from cover to cover will surely benefit were they only to read the overviews from these volumes. Thus I began by reading only the overviews of each chapter until I had worked my way through both volumes. These overviews alone cover more than 130 of the total 1250 pages of text and were critical in allowing an outsider such as myself to appreciate both the complexity of the instrument and the degree of progress which has occurred.

Volume 1, Part I is a 12-page, century-by-century overview of violin research from the early 16th century through the 19th century. Part II, and the subsequent 650+ pages of this volume, deal with a perspective of 20th-century work up to 1973, followed by papers dealing with: Sound Radiation; The Bowed String; The Bow; The Bridge; The Soundpost, Bassbar, and Tailpiece; The Normal Bending Modes of Unattached Violin Plates; The Modes of the Completed Violin Body; and The Violin Air Cavity Resonance Modes.

Volume 2 (an additional 650+ pages) continues with: The Interrelation of String, Wood, and Cavity Resonances of the Whole Violin; The Wood (use of pre-20th-century wood, Wood Properties, Moisture in Wood, Acoustical Properties of Wood, Effects of Wood Properties, New Materials, and New Analysis Techniques); The Varnish; Psychoacoustics Research; The Catgut Acoustical Society; Acoustic Theory and Research Techniques; and a look to The Future.

Can you leave these two volumes with a sense that the understanding of the violin from a physical, theoretical perspective is essentially finished? Can the average reasonably well-skilled artisan with technical leanings make a superior instrument by following specific recipes therein? No. (Luddites may breathe a little easier at this point.) Nor to be fair is this the purpose of these volumes, which however do show the tremendous progress made in our understanding of the physical system of the violin. Many more questions are raised than answered, which is after all the nature of science. It is clear to this reviewer that this type of research has many new directions to follow and that volumes such as this will excite a new generation of both active researchers and interested bystanders.

Are there hundreds if not thousands of ideas which will pique the interest of an open-minded person interested in expanding the left portion of their thinking with respect to violin sound quality in particular and instrument making in general? Yes. And Ms. Hutchins does everything within reason to encourage the reader to dig into what's in these two volumes and go further as well. It is difficult to judge how much of the information in these volumes would be applicable to other fields, but I would hazard a guess that somewhere between a quarter and a third of the information would be generally useful to the lutherie community outside the violin family of instruments.

Should one purchase these books? One quote comes to mind which has often swayed my thinking regarding the acquisition of literature. "Chance favors the prepared mind" (paraphrased from René Vallery-Radot in *The Life of Pasteur* [1927]). Although the articles are largely technical in nature, and many difficult to read as a result, that should not frighten us away from expanding our knowledge of this remarkable family of instruments. From a personal perspective, I routinely use information and approaches from articles in the now-defunct *Journal of Guitar Acoustics* which took me many months of re-reading to begin to comprehend. And these techniques have made all the difference in the quality and consistency of my work. We cannot know how the reading of what appears to be some arcane text will in fact trigger a new idea that will forever alter how we view our craft.

In an apparent attempt to reduce publication costs, the papers appear to have been photocopies from their original journal format, resulting in a bewildering collection of type sizes and fonts some of which were annoyingly difficult to read because of their small size.

I suggest that these volumes, although slightly pricey for an individual, would be an excellent purchase for lutherie groups with a critical mass of members and enough confidence in and respect for one another to begin an internal lending library.

—— *David Hurd (1999)*

Video: ***Shoptalk 5***
Todd Sams, Don MacRostie, Dan Erlewine
Stewart-MacDonald

At the '99 Merlefest in North Carolina I had the good fortune to find myself manning a booth next to Stew-Mac. It was a pleasure to meet Todd Sams and get to know Jay Hostetler better. It was also astonishing to hear so many self-proclaimed luthiers confess that they had never heard of Stewart-MacDonald. Where do these luthiers buy their tools?

My guess is that they aren't buying them at all, that what they can't find at Ace Hardware or cobble together in the shop they are doing without; that they don't even know about the tools that could make their work better and their lives easier.

Such blissful ignorance is no excuse for the old pros who immediately turn a cold shoulder to the new generation of more sophisticated, more expensive tools that have become available. To many, a neck jig is a funny looking, expensive contraption that they have done without for decades and, by God, they'll get along quite nicely without in the future, thank you very much!

I hope this doesn't describe you. Education is as big a key to future success as increased skills. To that end, Stew-Mac has long produced videos that showcase new tools, describe their development, and show them in action. Sure, Stew-Mac wants you to buy more stuff, but the Shoptalk videos are more educational than video catalog. Do you really need this item? Will it pay for itself? Do you have room for it? Will it give you an edge on the other guy in town? For $7.50 you can find out, and I'd call that a bargain.

Shoptalk 5 showcases neck and bridge removal tools and techniques, jigs for routing dovetailed neck joints and how to use them, and how to set up and use the new neck jig. These aren't catalog reruns, these are real luthiers doing real work with sawdust in the air and lots of noise. Dammit, this is entertaining stuff, never mind that it's educational, too. This tape can answer useful questions before you drop big bucks on new jiggery. Yes, steaming off a neck looks as scary for the guitar in the hands of Don MacRostie as it does on your own bench. No, your wife is never going to let you rout dovetail joints on her kitchen table (even if you promise her a style-45 guitar). Yes, the neck jig is going to impress your customers but, no, you shouldn't get one if you've yet to fret an instrument. Yes, this little video hopes to sell you product, but it will end up on your book shelf next to Teeter and Sloane.

—— *John Calkin (1999)*

Mandolin Magazine
www.mandolinmagazine.com

The premiere issue of *Mandolin Magazine* announces that this is a quarterly magazine for mandolin players and enthusiasts, welcome news to be sure! There has been much renewed interest in the mandolin of late, and editor Ginny Hollon has done a fine job of presenting us with this new magazine.

The magazine is full of articles that are of interest to mandolin players and builders. Luthier Ken Cartwright, whom I met at Wintergrass several years ago, writes a regular column called MandoMedic. This issue had a very informative installment on mandolin bridges.

There is a three-page feature article with GAL member Lawrence Smart. Lawrence talks about what he is looking for tonally when he is in the building process. It is exciting to see high-quality articles like this about fellow builders. We all learn from each other and articles like this draw attention to custom builders in general. I think that helps all of us. Of course any magazine that makes a regular habit of featuring small builders gets my vote for sure!

It has been said that you usually have time to build or you have time to play, but one rarely has time for both. As a builder, I work way too many hours and I play when I can. I only have time for one compulsive-behavior disorder at a time! There is much written music and tab included in the magazine. I know that this feature will be a great benefit to players at various levels. The tab is written directly under the notation so you have access to whichever works best for you.

The contributors list reads like a who's who list of the mandolin world including: Dix Bruce, Bruce Graybill, Steve Kaufman, Joe Carr, and many others. The magazine has a wide spectrum of music styles including bluegrass, jazz, Celtic, and classical, to name a few. Did you know there is even a Classical Mandolin Society? There are also mandolin orchestras, and this issue included an article on the Nashville Mandolin Ensemble with Butch Baldassari. I am really glad to see this magazine arrive on the scene and it looks like this will be a good one for builders and players alike.

—— *Randy Allen (1999)*

Video: ***Assembling a Solidbody Electric Guitar***
Dan Erlewine
Stewart-MacDonald, 1999

Though Dan Erlewine and I are contemporaries, I can't resist thinking of him as Uncle Dan. Through his writing, videos, and convention appearances he has spread his wide knowledge and undying enthusiasm for guitars across the entire population of luthiers and players, making him a sort of good uncle to our entire clan.

Assembling a Solidbody is one of Erlewine's more basic video lessons. In the first half he builds a guitar around a raw Strat-style body, and in the second, a finished Tele body hits the operating table to become a guitar. All emphasis is placed on doing clean work that anyone might be proud of, though a difference is made between how a pro might build a guitar from parts and how a kitchen-table luthier might be forced to handle the same job. Using this tape, the rookie ought to turn in as creditable a job as a seasoned guitar man. The raw body is left unfinished, as lacquer work is the subject of other Stew-Mac references. The Strat is assembled according to Fender specs, which is a useful touch, and there must be a hundred tips to help your work come out cleaner and more precise.

There's also a bit of troubleshooting involved when things don't go exactly right, but since all the parts are from Stew-Mac they *want* to go together properly. A bit more might have been done in this direction. It's much more typical for a guitarist to collect a body from one source, a neck from another, a pickguard from a third, and hardware from several sources. All companies involved might claim that their parts retrofit Fenders, but if you've been around for awhile you know the frustration of assembling mismatched parts. The solution, as Erlewine points out, is to work slowly, follow the proper steps, and be as fastidious as possible in execution. The pleasure of playing a functionally flawless guitar is worth whatever time it takes.

I've seen dozens of hacked-up parts guitars, and have made a lot of money fixing them. Every first-time assembler should make this video a part of their budget. It will be cheaper in the long run, and they'll have a lot more pride in their ax when it comes out just right.

Way to go, Uncle Dan! You might single-handedly rid the world of botched-up guitars.

—— *John Calkin (1999)*

Originally published in *American Lutherie #53*, 1998

Ten Fiddle Books
reviewed by John Calkin

I claim no violin expertise whatever, but not every tome intended for professionals is right for the beginner. I'll compare a few of the cheaper books. I'll use Strobel's *Violin Making* as a control. It's not my favorite, but it gets reasonable marks from the pros and it's only $30. I have two questions for each of the others: Could I build a fiddle from this book? Is it as good as Strobel's?

Violin Making, Step by Step
Henry A. Strobel
Self-published, 1994
ISBN 0962067369

Michael Darnton says this book is just OK. It's sad to think it may be the best book with which to begin your violin career, but the field has yet to find its Cumpiano/Natelson. To quote Darnton again, "Any of the major guitar building books I own is better than any of the violin making books." Yes, I could use it to build a fiddle. Would it make me slump over my bench in a death-simulating stupor? I'm afraid so. A high density of instruction, which is good, often makes it deadly dull, which is bad. A small display of enthusiasm would have done wonders.

There are two complete sets of plans for the mold, the instrument, and the templates. They are useful and intelligible, but you'll need to make copies since many patterns overlap others. The photos are good and they are cleanly printed, but there aren't quite enough of them to carry the story without the text. It's irritating that the reader is so frequently referred to other books in the author's series. This manual is only seventy-eight pages long, a few more paragraphs to fill it out wouldn't have broken the bank.

I fear I'm being too harsh just because he compressed the personality out of his work. If investing in Strobel's seven books turned you into a competent creator of violins, violas, and cellos, anyone would consider the $140 an amazing bargain.

Cello Making, Step by Step
Henry A. Strobel
Self-published, 1995
ISBN 0962067377

To use this one, you need his violin book; the cello book concentrates on the differences. Since plate carving is more demanding for the cello, various power tools are considered. Strobel mentions, but doesn't recommend (because of safety considerations) grinder and chainsaw carving. Perhaps it's the variety of options that makes this a more interesting book than *Violin Making*, or perhaps the author simply gave himself a license to loosen up a bit. Although Strobel's photos are just as good for this manual, the printing of them is rather poor.

The Technique of Violin Making
H. S. Wake
Self-published, 1973
ISBN 960704809

The obvious difference between Wake's book and Strobel's is the leaps that have been made in desktop publishing in twenty years. Strobel's looks pro, while Wake's looks like mimeographed typewritten sheets with line drawings (plus fold-out plans for mold, violin, and templates). The typos and strange punctuation are distracting and confusing. Wake is chattier and easy to read, but I'd rather have Strobel at the bench with me.

Wake describes how to make some tools, such as a small thickness sander, a bending iron, neat little steel clamps for joining wedge plates, and an ultraviolet drying cabinet, and a peg shaver. I'd rather he spent the time talking more about fiddles.

Wake has some strong opinions. He urges us to begin with high-quality wood because we'll be less likely to get careless and ruin it. We should mount the neck with permanent glue. He likes oscilloscopes for tap tuning, but he'd have us carve plates by eye rather than be bound to templates. He's a forward-looking old fogey.

I've never read a description of scroll making that convinced me I could do it, and Wake's is no exception. He also unintentionally suggests that if you can't find delight in concocting batches and batches of sticky liquids out of arcane substances you should be making guitars or furniture instead of violins.

For a couple decades this was the only nonerudite fiddle-making book out there. It's no longer the best in its class, but you still might like to have it.

A Luthier's Scrap Book
H. S. Wake
Self-published, 1970
ISBN 0969704825

This book contains scant information about building violins, but offers a ton of other stuff you might like to know. There are alternative mold designs, violin repair techniques and suggestions, extensive descriptions of tool creation (including the little planes that were so rudely snubbed in *Techniques*), more recipes, bow-hair bug information, and a tip or two about bow maintenance. If you already have Strobel I'd get this book next.

Making a Simple Violin and Viola
Ronald Roberts
David and Charles, Inc., 1975
ISBN 0715369644

This good little book explores the trapezoid violin created by Félix Savart in 1819. The flat plates vary in thickness across their width, but they are in no sense carved. Page-sized plans are included for ½, ¾, and full size violins, as well as two sizes of viola. Roberts saw the trapezoid violin as a wonderful introduction to the craft of lutherie and a strong first step toward the traditional violin, but he makes no apology for the playability or tone of his ugly ducklings.

To most people, if a fiddle doesn't look like a fiddle, it isn't a fiddle, no matter how it sounds. If that's you, skip this book. If you don't suffer from that brainlock you'll probably have a good time with Ronald Roberts.

The rest of these books are not dedicated to the violin, but have chapters about fiddle construction mixed with sections that concern the creation of other instruments. Don't be too quick to turn up your nose. In general these books are a good investment if your experience has given you a degree of independence.

Making Musical Instruments
Irving Sloane
E. P. Dutton, 1978
ISBN 087690293X

Sloane presents forty-nine pages about constructing a Hardanger fiddle, which he suggests can be a good starting point for the budding luthier because it removes "the perfection anxiety that goes with copying Strads." He doesn't have to justify himself to me.

The plans aren't as good as others, and they aren't as readily understood. As always, his photos are fine and his drawings first rate. He makes several guesses as to how the old Norwegian folk luthiers made their fiddles, and according to letters published in *American Lutherie,* he fell short of the mark. Sloane is better company, but in this instance Strobel is a more worthy teacher.

Making Folk Instruments in Wood
Dennis Waring
Sterling Publishing Co., 1982
ISBN 0806975407

Waring's fiddle is made of plywood, the plates are flat, and the *f*-holes are only slots. A beginner might knock out a Waring fiddle before starting a legit violin. They'll have something to play during the long process of whittling a Strad, and they might be surprised how much music is in their little toy. Make a joyous noise unto the Tao, even if it turns out to be a barbarous yawp. The fiddle chapter is only twelve pages, but that's enough, since the design avoids the need for a mold or elaborate templates. While devoid of sophistication, this book contains more raw joy than all the others combined.

The Making of Stringed Instruments
George Buchanan
B. T. Batsford, Ltd.
ISBN 0013481404

This book is built upon the theory that making a violin can prepare you for making a mandolin, and that the two together can train you to make a jazz guitar. Fortunately for the fiddle maker, the violin comes first and has the largest chapter by far at ninety-four pages.

The book contains good photos, but the copious, nicely wrought drawings sorely lack detail. They spread across two pages, which means you'll have to dissect your book to make the most use of them. Leave them where they are and buy a set of plans that are more complete, then let the book help you get on with it.

Buchanan recommends starting with common wood rather than taking a chance on botching good timber. He likes to support the plates in a bed of wood chips as he carves. The violin made for the book is of bird's-eye maple, the viola of birch, and the cello of cherry. Bravo! His segment on purfling is more extensive than either Strobel's or Wake's (Wake's is especially pathetic). Plate carving methods are hazier than Strobel's and too much is left to the artistic inclination of the beginner.

The informal nature of Buchanan's book makes it a pleasure to read, and there's a good chapter about tool creation and maintenance. I like this book especially for the mandolins, but if budding fiddle builders decide to go with Strobel's book they should at least check this one out of the library. The two together should work better than either alone.

Making Musical Instruments
Edited by Charles Ford
Pantheon, 1979
ISBN 0394735617 (paper)

This book is far too ambitious in scope, and suffers badly for it. Five authors offer building instruction on five different and complex instruments that should each have a book to themselves. The thirty-page violin chapter was written by Adam Paul. There are no illustrations other than plans. The plans aren't too bad, but I doubt that a beginner will be able to take advantage of them. Instruction is compressed to the point of near uselessness. Arch carving instruction amounts to one paragraph. I was able to muddle my way through the chapter, but at times I would have been hopelessly lost had I not read the other books first. Cross-sectional drawings and 1⅓ pages of text explain the differences between modern and Baroque violins. If fiddles are your only interest skip this book.

How to Make Your Own Violin
Leroy Geiger
Ernst Heinrich Roth Co., Inc., 1963

I've thrown this in just for collectors who want to track down all the violin books. This spiral bound booklet was $3 when I bought it in 1975, and even back then the continual references to "the hobby of violin making" grated on me. Geiger has reduced fiddle construction to a game of Simon Says. There are simple line drawings and some photos, but the book looks like a project out of a 1950s *Mechanics Illustrated*. Included are fair plans for a Stradivarius and a del Gesù (fair for beginners, not for a museum). As bad as it is, this is much better than Ford's book. ——

Originally published in *American Lutherie #49–#56 and #58–#60*, 1997–1999

IT WORKED FOR ME

■ When cutting pegheads, bridges, tops, or tailpiece shapes for guitar or violin, I use a pattern-following router bit mounted in a drill press. But there are not enough blades on a standard router bit to cut smoothly on a drill press rotating at only around 3200 rpm. To solve this problem I devised a bit which gets many more cuts per rotation, and therefore makes cleaner cuts. This bit should only be used in drill presses operating at less than 3500 rpm. Do not use it in hand-held or table-mounted routers!

The bit consists of a cutter out of a pencil sharpener, a machine screw (either a #10 or a #8, depending upon the bore in the cutter you find), a lock washer and a nut (or a locking nut), and miscellaneous washers. The bit is simple and efficient when used correctly, and it does not cost much to make two of them since there are usually two cutters in a pencil sharpener.

To construct this bit find an old hand-crank pencil sharpener at a flea market, or buy a new one at an office supply store. Dismantle it as far as you can with screwdrivers or wrenches. The cutters, which have spiral-fluted blades, are made of hardened steel, and are usually held in place with a pin each. If the cutters will not come out by disassembly you may have to put the pencil-sharpener frame (usually made out of some cheap alloy) in a vise and pry or break it until the cutters fall out. Be careful not to damage them.

The cutters will have a gear fixed to one end (**Fig. 1**) which must be removed. This can be accomplished with a hacksaw, cutting the gear off flush with the end of the cutter, or by simply pulling the gear out of the end of the bit. The second method may leave a countersunk hole in certain cutters, which you can deal with by using a machine screw with a countersunk head when assembling your router bit (**Fig. 2**, top). The method of sawing the gear off is recommended due to the greater versatility of the finished bit.

Once you cut off the gear, there should be a size 8 or 10 hole through the cutter (**Fig. 2**, bottom) Assemble the bit by inserting the proper size screw through the hole and tightening a locking nut or a nut with a lock washer on the opposite end of the cutter (make sure that the blades are pointing in the same direction your drill press will be rotating). You can adapt the bit as your equipment and the job requires by using different lengths of screws, adding washers to either end of the cutter, or adding a pattern-following bearing (**Fig. 3**).

The bit can be used as an edge-finishing tool (due to the fineness of its cut), a shaper, or a pattern-following bit, depending on how it is set up. It works especially well for trimming thin plastic and headstock veneer. Another handy feature is that the cutter can be

Figure 1
Spiral cutter from a pencil sharpener before the gear is removed.

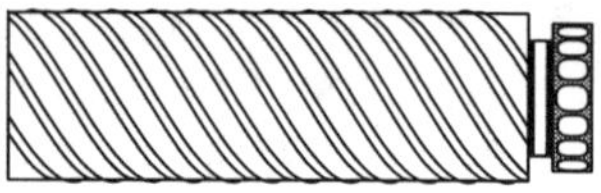

assembled with the cutter inverted to cut in the opposite direction of normal rotation.

Usually the cutters come out of the sharpener ready for use, so I do not recommend sharpening if it is not necessary. When the cutter does need sharpening it can be done on the drill press. Disassemble the bit, invert the cutter on its shaft, chuck it up, and with your drill press rotating at a low speed use oiled sharpening stones and fine honing stones to sharpen the blades.

—— *Nathan D. Missel (1997)*

Figure 2
Gear removal: Pulling out a press-fit gear may leave a countersunk hole (top), requiring that a machine screw with a tapered head (middle) be used for your shaft. Sawing the gear off flush with the end of the cutter (bottom) is recommended.

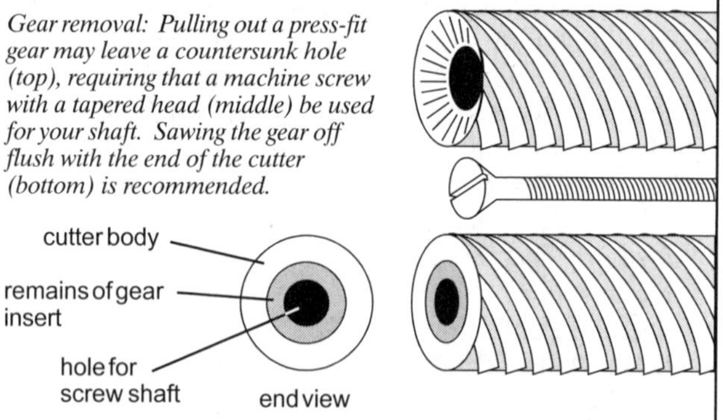

Figure 3
Two finished bits: With a pattern-following bearing (top); with countersunk screw head for general shaping (bottom).

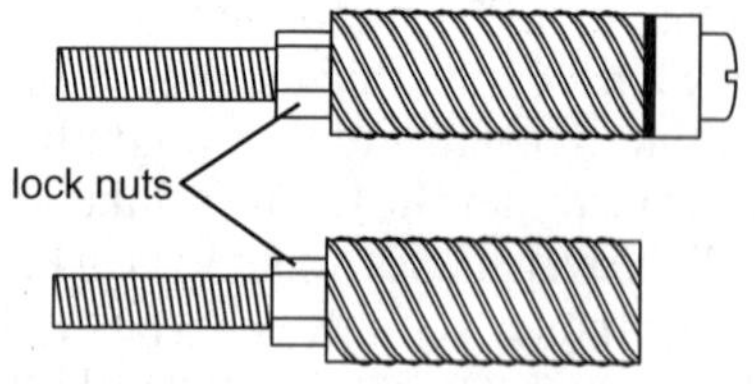

■ Small-shop luthiers who hate the smell of nitrocellulose lacquers like I do should try the ready-made shellac and/or the amber varnish (lacquer) of the AURO company. The shellac smells like their alcohol #219, which should be used for thinning, and is available in blonde #213 and orange #211. The amber lacquer #222 is actually an oil varnish which contains some lemon oil, and therefore smells like lemon. I strongly recommend you use their thinner, balsam turpentine #191, with the amber lacquer. I learned that other thinners, like turpentine substitutes, do not work properly even for cleaning the spray gun or brush. The shellac is sprayable (at least the first two coats), and the amber lacquer is fully sprayable in very thin coats. It's also a pleasure to brush with a fine quality brush.

I recently got beautiful results on a double bass by spraying the amber lacquer, two layers for sealing (their shellac could also be used for this purpose), followed by four layers tinted with a few drops red aniline dye. I used a HVLP spraying system. After wet sanding with 400/600 grit and soapy water I polished by hand with a felt pad, water, and "Wiener Kalk" (available from C.A. Götz — I believe Irving Sloane calls it powdered rottenstone). The finish needs additional drying time of at least one week after polishing.

Don't swallow it, although it smells really sweet! It's not cheap, but it goes very far, and it has a good shelf life. I've had some for two years, and it's still usable.

AURO is a German company, but the products are obtainable nearly everywhere. Exact product descriptions are on their websiste: www.auro.co.uk.

—— *Peter Schaefer (1997)*

■ I've make my buffing setup (Buffing Arbor System from Stew-Mac) extremely safe by loosening the motor's V belt sufficiently that if I push a little too hard, it stops. In other words, it can't "grab" the instrument and dump it on the floor, nor can it "burn" the finish.

—— *John Mello (1997)*

■ Many of us have tried acid for sharpening files with less than acceptable results. When I was contacted by Boggs Tool (www.boggstool.com) and told my files would be good as new, I was sceptical, to say the least.

They use a liquid honing process. Abrasive is sprayed under high pressure to grind a relief on the back side of the cutting edge, which leaves the leading edge intact. This is also the final step in making a new file.

I sent some pretty dull files as a test. The first was worn evenly by about .002″ off all the teeth. The second had some very bad damage in streaks and many missing teeth. When the files were returned the invoice was $2.40 plus shipping for two 8″ files! The first file was sharper than new. The second, much to my surprise, was repaired in about 20% of the extremely damaged areas. The rest of the damaged area was too far gone to sharpen, but they had made it into a usable file instead of one I was going to throw away. They say that a file can be sharpened a couple of times.

The customer service I received from this company was incredible. They took the time to answer all of my questions, and the turn around time was only a couple of weeks.

—— *Colin Kaminski (1997)*

■ One of my favorite tools is a body or neck rest with an interesting history. It was given to me by a seventy-two-year-old violin repairman. I went to him to buy strings for my daughter's viola, and told him that I was learning to do some repair work and starting to collect some tools. He asked what I was repairing, and I told him a banjo-mandolin that needed a new fingerboard. He reached up on the top shelf and pulled down a frame made of three pieces of wood with a leather strap fastened between the two uprights of the frame. The dust on it was a quarter-inch thick, and the leather looked at least fifty years old. He told me that this was the rest that he used when he repaired round-backed mandolins, but he hadn't seen one of those in years. The back of the mandolin sat cradled in the curve of the leather strap, perfectly stable. He said he also used it to hold guitar necks when he worked on them, but now they were "too big to bother with." When I tried to offer him some money for it, he said, "No, just use it."

The picture shows the body or neck rest, along with the Plasti-Cut combination rasp and smoothing file I wrote about in *American Lutherie #47,* (see *Big Red Book of American Lutherie Volume Four*, p. 497) which is 13.5″ long.

—— *Glenn Uhler (1997)*

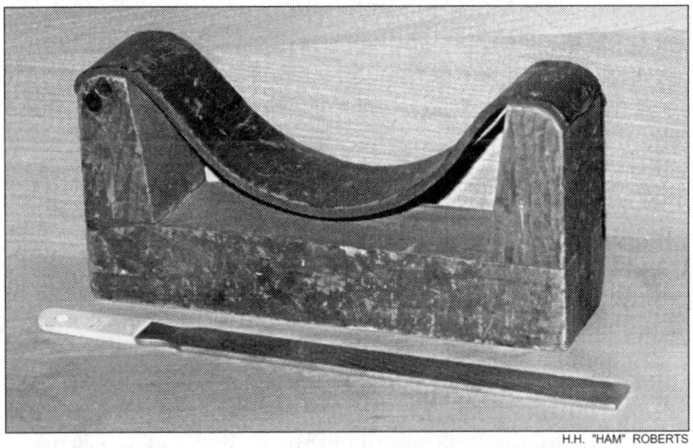

H.H. "HAM" ROBERTS

■ A couple of years ago, I discovered to my delight the Micro Plane Rasps that Harry Fleishman reviewed in *AL#48.* (See *BRBAL4*, p. 440.) These rasps work wonderfully on flamed maple necks. I especially like their half-round rasp. However, I found the hacksaw-frame handle a bit clumsy, so I invented a comfortable handle that works way better. The rasp hooks over a very short 3⁄16″ pin on each end. It's light, and you can very quickly change the rasp end for end to change from a push to a pull stroke. I put my first one together on a whim out of scraps of wood and superglue. It worked so well I'm still using it.

—— *Chuck Shifflett (1997)*

CHUCK SHIFFLETT

■ Here are four tool ideas which have worked well for me. Perhaps they will be helpful to you too.

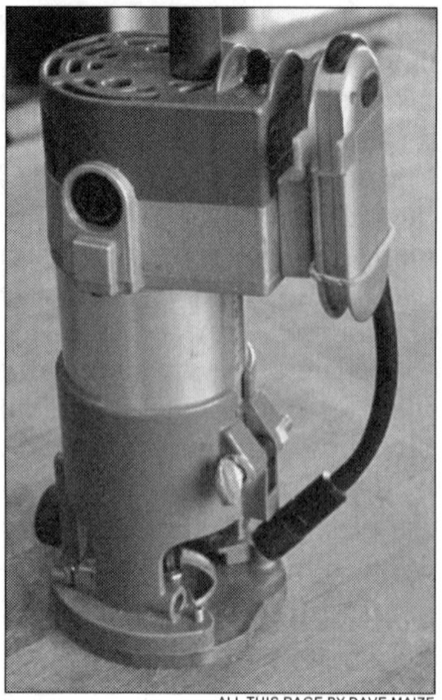

ALL THIS PAGE BY DAVE MAIZE

Before I began guitar building I had a business making entry doors and doing intricate hand-carved designs on them. I would spend hours routing away waste wood before beginning the carving itself. Trying to follow irregular line drawings with a router bit wasn't too easy, but eventually the light bulb went on (literally). I found a small battery-powered (uses 2 AAA batteries) gooseneck lamp, and figured a way to attach it to my router. The gooseneck lets me aim the light beam right where I want it. (I also replaced the black router base with a clear acrylic one to be able to see the design easier.)

The back of the lamp comes with a plastic clip to attach it to whatever. I beveled the edges of the clip, and made a corresponding wood piece in which I cut a slot with angled sides to receive the clip (sort of a sliding dovetail joint), and I bolted the wood piece onto the case of the router. Since I use more than one size of router, I attached an identical wood piece to each router so that I can easily move the lamp from one to another.

With a lot of use, the lamp sometimes blinked off and on. I traced the problem to a poor contact at the battery terminals. Light sanding of the contacts solved the problem. The lamp is made by ZELCO Industries. See their website at www.zelco.com.

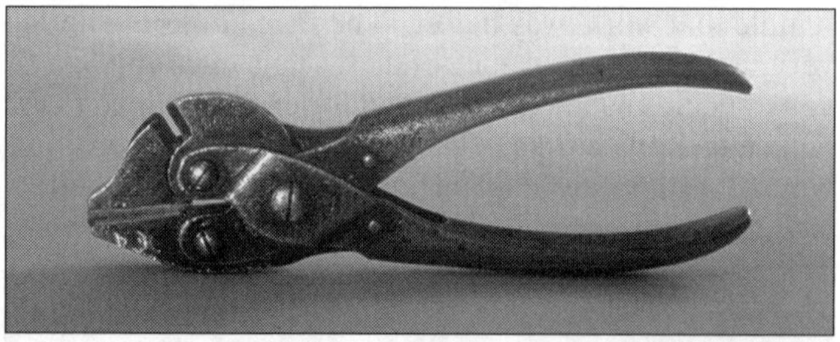

This type of pliers, called Bernards, was commonly found in toolboxes years ago. I recently discovered a great use for them. By first gluing strips of leather to the jaws to prevent marring, they are perfect for removing snug-fitting bridge saddles, nuts, and bridge pins. The nice thing about these pliers is that the jaws are always parallel no matter how wide they are opened. I don't believe Bernards are still manufactured, but they can be found at flea markets fairly often.

This next one I use practically every day. It's also my cheapest and lowest-tech tool. Maybe there's a connection there. I'm talking about bamboo shish kebab skewers. They are about $1/16''$ diameter, and have a sharp point at one end. You get 100 to a package. They are perfect for doing drop fills, glue spreading, glue cleaning around guitar bridges, or putting that micro piece of inlay in place. A package of 100 goes a long way.

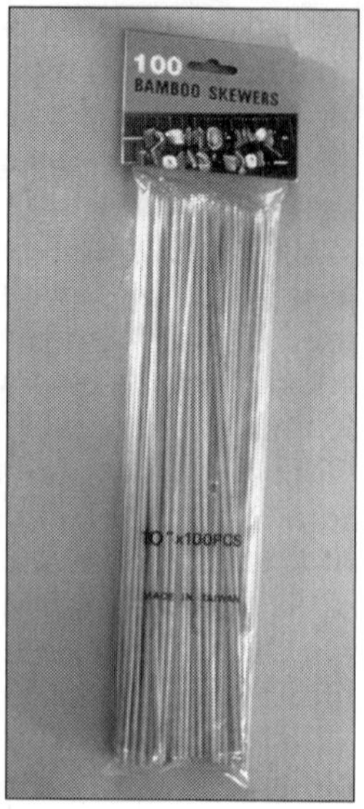

A house painter friend turned me on to this great scraper. It has a very ergonomic handle, and an efficient angle of the blade to the handle. The blade is stainless steel, and the cutting edge is ground to a very low angle (about 20°). The blade's steel is relatively soft, so I made an identically shaped one from an old circular-saw blade, which holds an edge much longer. The blade is attached with two machine screws.

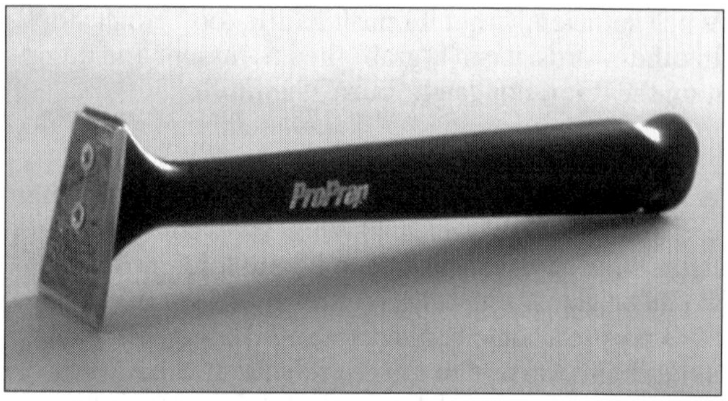

I use this scraper (usually sharpened without a burr) to clear glue along guitar braces. Its trapezoidal shape, with 80° corners, allows it to fit into weird brace intersections. It is also a great tool to scrape the finish from a guitar top where the bridge will be glued. Using it I feel like I have plenty of control during this operation. This tool is one of a line of scrapers called ProPrep. It is model #US-100, manufactured by Pacific Handy Cutter, and is available in most Sherwin-Williams paint stores for around $12.

—— *Dave Maize (1997)*

■ To speed up the sharpening of bandsaw blades, I cut a narrow slot down one side of a 5″ piece of scrap wood with a narrow-rimmed saw blade on my table saw, the same blade I use for cutting fret slots. With the bandsaw blade fit firmly in this slot, and the block held in a vise, I can file about 5″ of blade in less than a minute, and then slide the blade through the slot to sharpen the next section.

I haven't done it myself, but I have read that for some jobs even new bandsaw blades can benefit from a quick touchup — just a couple of light strokes on each tooth with a three-cornered file.

—— *James Patterson (1997)*

■ Occasionally a dulcimer comes into my shop to have more frets installed. It's usually just one, the infamous 6½ fret. Dulcimer fretboards are laid out diatonically, with the major scale beginning on the 3rd fret with its octave note on the 10th fret. All other scales are in various modes, depending on what fret you start on. The scale that begins at the nut is mixolydian, that is, it has a flatted seventh note (which is the 6th fret). The octave note of this scale falls on the 7th fret. So an extra fret is often added to offer the player a complete major scale starting at the nut: the 6½ fret. This corresponds to the 11th fret on a guitar.

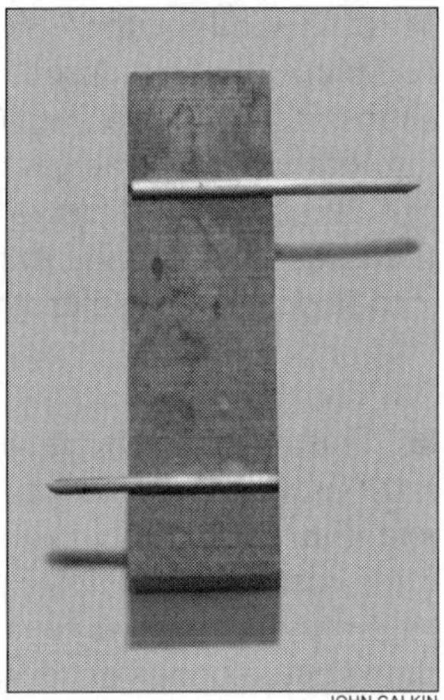

JOHN CALKIN

Dulcimers are made in many scale lengths, and sometimes they are made by folks who don't have a clear notion of where the frets should go — any of them. Rather than try to figure out the placement of the 6½ mathematically, I made a portable fret (see photo). It's nothing more than a bit of wood with a fret extending from it in a perpendicular manner. The tang of the extension is filed away, and a point is filed on the end of the fret centered as well as possible. My gizmo has two frets, one normal size and one jumbo. Tune the dulcimer and play a scale to the tuner. Are the frets in the right place? Great! Place the portable fret under the melody string(s) between the 6th and 7th frets and slide it back and forth until the tuner tells you you've found the spot. Mark the fingerboard at the point of the fret. You might want to tape off the fingerboard and try to find the location several times, just to make sure you've got the right spot. Keep checking the open string, too, just to be sure its tuning hasn't wandered. If the instrument doesn't play in tune to itself very well, you'll just have to please your own ear, or get the customer in and let it please his/her ear.

A square narrow enough laid on the fingerboard will help you cut the slot. Pounding in the fret may split the dulcimer's top. I normally grind the barbs off the tang of the fret and superglue it in place.

Other frets are sometimes added. I have a dulcimer with a 1½ fret (3rd fret on a guitar). You could make the crazy thing chromatic and confuse everyone. Have fun!

—— *John Calkin (1997)*

■ I picked up a neat trick on the folk harp mailing list recently about touching up polyurethane. Sometimes it's hard to get the new stuff to stick to the old, but if you mix in about 10% of acetone or lacquer thinner, it will bite nicely. I used it on a couple of repairs in the last few weeks, and it worked fine.

—— *Al Carruth (1997)*

■ I have used a laminated all-wood tailpiece on several of my archtop guitars. The general design and construction method were the result of trying to figure out a simple way of gaining more control over the dimensions, weight, and aesthetics of the tailpiece.

Lamination is done over a shaped caul. The bend at the back is rigid rather than hinged, so the tailpiece can be prestressed during lamination to slightly increase the downward pressure of the strings on the bridge. The amount of free string behind the bridge is completely variable. The veneers can be dyed prior to lamination to complement the purfling of the instrument. Using shortened bridge pins for string attachment makes changing strings easier.

—— *Buzz Vineyard (1997)*

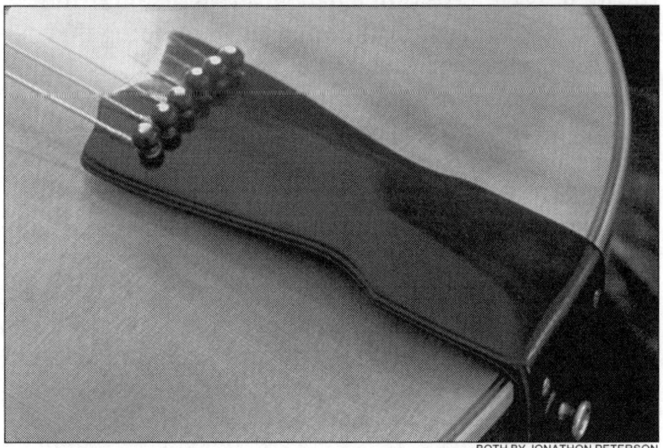

BOTH BY JONATHON PETERSON

■ A National Duolian resonator guitar may come into your shop buzz-free, only to work up a terrible clatter as soon as you get it back together. If the standard reasons for buzzing don't check out, take the resonator cover off again and reseat the cone. The ideal tool is a length of violin soundpost stock sharpened in a pencil sharpener and then sanded blunt again. Rub it around the perimeter of the cone. A lot of pressure is not required. In a pinch any piece of dowel would work, or even a dull pencil, but having an official tool for the job will amaze your customers. So far, it's worked every time.

—— *Woody Vernice (1997)*

■ Here's a dirt simple, yet incredibly effective procedure to create accurate side templates, and we don't have to boot up a CAD program. I think of the back as a dome, or a section of a sphere, and the following procedure is designed to produce side templates which conform to that shape. This is a technique that is well known to anyone who has done cabinet installation or finish carpentry, the same technique which is used to scribe a line to fit a joint or to mate a piece of wood to an irregular surface.

Materials needed:

▸ Dished form:

This should have the same radius as your back braces. I make my own dished forms, but they are available from Luthiers Mercantile.

▸ Outside mold:

To those of you building in the Spanish style, this method could very easily be adapted by using bent sides in place of the outside mold.

▸ Dividers:

These can be your top-shelf Starrett #92s, or a set you borrowed from a first graders' pencil box, as long as it holds a setting.

▸ Manila paper or any light cardboard.

▸ Double-sided tape:

I highly recommend 3M #410 double-sided tape. It will soon become one of the most useful items in your shop.

Strike an accurate centerline on your dished form. The fact of the matter is that any line that passes through its center point can be used as a centerline. I use these dishes for other phases of building that require a reference line.

Cut the manila paper into strips, the width of which matches the maximum depth of your outside mold.

Double-stick tape the paper into the mold being sure that you keep the paper flush with the guitar-top edge of mold, and that the ends of the paper strips overlap guitar's centerline by $\frac{1}{2}''$ or more. Mark the guitar's centerline onto the paper.

Mark the waist line on the paper by squaring a line down at the waist's narrowest point. Place the mold atop the dish, taking care to match up their centerlines.

Most guitars are deeper at the tail block than they are at the neck block, so you'll need to shim up the tail end of the mold to account for that discrepancy. For example, if the guitar is $3\frac{1}{2}''$ deep at the heel block end and $4\frac{1}{4}''$ deep at the tail end, you'll need to shim the tail up $\frac{3}{4}''$ so that the top of the mold is level relative to the dished form. Recheck your centerline alignment.

Set your dividers so that one of its tips makes contact with the bottom of the tail end of the mold at the centerline, while the other tip contacts the dished form's centerline. Lock that setting.

Now simply draw the dividers along the paper from the tail end to the heel block end of the mold, being sure to keep one tip in contact with the dished form and the other tip directly above the first and in contact with the paper. The dividers will transfer the curvature of the dished form onto the paper, creating a profile for a set of sides which will accept a back with the same curvature as the dished form. All that's left is to transfer a line representing the top edge of the sides onto the paper.

—— *Julius J. Borges (1997)*

■ I've found another use for a superglue debonder product called Un-cure Debonder found in hobby shops. To reamalgamate lacquer checks squirt a small amount into the crack, wait three or four days, and rub out. I recommend trying this on a test piece first. It has the effect of softening the lacquer sufficiently to allow it to flow back together, then it rehardens.

—— *John Mello (1997)*

■ This is an addendum to my *It Worked for Me* tip in *AL#43*, (see *BRBAL4*, p. 497) where I described installing two small braces between the bridge patch and waist bar of a classic guitar in an effort to correct a slight caving in. The repair worked beautifully, with the unexpected bonus of adding some kick to the trebles. I used to place those braces so that their ends stopped just short of the bridge patch and the waist bar, but they are obviously even more effective if they are notched to overlap the patch. It's kind of tough, however, to know exactly how deep to make the notch to accommodate the patch just by looking through the soundhole.

Everyone knows about Post-it notes. They stick, but just a little, and since they are made of paper they will hold a fold. I found a way to use them as depth gauges. Stick one onto the underside of the soundboard right in front of the bridge patch with the sticky strip parallel to the fan braces (**Fig. 1**), holding one side up with your index finger while rubbing it into the corner and over the bridge patch with your thumbnail. Now remove it very carefully and the creases you have made will make an excellent depth gauge for the brace notch.

I make the two little braces of cedar $\frac{3}{8}'' \times \frac{1}{8}''$ or a little thicker, preshaped as in **Fig. 2** with a somewhat parabolic shape, and I butt them right up to the waist bar, leaving them $\frac{1}{16}'' - \frac{3}{32}''$ tall at the joint. Curve the

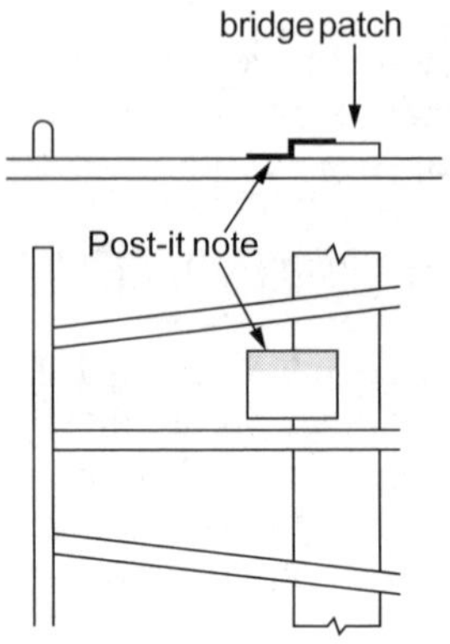

Figure 1

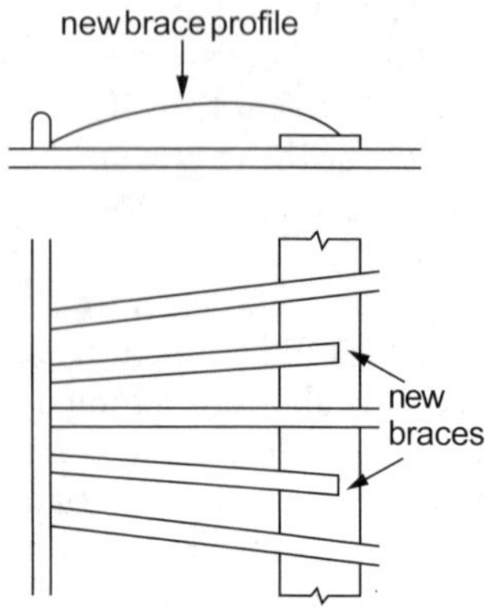

Figure 2

bottom slightly to match the arch of the soundboard, and then proceed to cut the notch with a chisel using your Post-it depth gauge and a straightedge held up against the bottom of the brace to check that the notch has a uniform depth all along its length.

Now you are ready to glue it in. Do several dry runs! I just press it in place with my fingers for 10–15 minutes and let it dry overnight before restringing the guitar.

Remember, this solution doesn't work for extreme cases of cave-in. You will almost always notice an improvement in your trebles and sustain.

—— *Filippo (Filo) Avignonesi (1997)*

■ For years I never hammered in a fret. I cut frets exactly to length with a jeweler's saw, then ground the beads off the tangs with a stone mounted in a Dremel tool while I held them with a small vise-grip. After the frets were bent to shape, they could be pressed into the slots with finger pressure, then superglued. I never had to worry about what size the fret slots might be. More importantly, I never had to alter a set of slots when refretting. The next guy to refret the instrument wouldn't find himself in a jam he hadn't anticipated because of anything I had done, as long as he used heat to pull the frets. My frets popped right out when hot, and any glue residue was normally wicked into the wood and didn't clog the slots.

The next step in the process came at a lutherie convention when another builder said, "Yeah, that's the way I do it, but I grind off the fret tang beads while the stock is still a 2′-long stick. Then I cut them to length." It was one of those moments of enlightenment that leaves one feeling completely stupid for past behavior.

Then came Dan Erlewine's file trick. Break a flat file in half and grind the edges safe. Put a shim of the proper thickness between the files (using a set of thickness gauges), mount them in a vise, then pull the tang of a stick of fretwire between the files. The tang can be adjusted to the slot width very quickly. So I'm back to hammering in my frets again, not because it does a better job, but because it's faster than clamping them in. I still use superglue for almost every fret job.

I used to use a small vise-grip to pull the fret tangs through the files, but it was never very satisfactory. Then, after reading Larry Robinson's inlay book, I bought a set of sheet-metal vise-grips, which are sort of a duckbilled locking pliers. Not only do they do a good job of holding MOP while it's filed clean, they grab a stick of fretwire by the tang without distorting it or letting go. At last, the whole process is trouble free.

—— *John Calkin (1997)*

■ I haven't needed to buy wet-or-dry sandpaper for many, many years. I keep a solution of 20 Mule Team Borax and water warm on my stove. Used wet-or-dry paper goes into the pot. The paper is unclogged and ready for more use. Used French polishing cloths also clean up beautifully, too.

—— *Eugene Clark (1997)*

■ It is inevitable that instruments with serious side dents will be brought into the luthier's shop. We have found one particular tool design which works exceedingly well in correcting this kind of damage. The simplicity and ease of construction have made this side dent puller and reshaper invaluable in the day-to-day routine of our shop.

The materials needed for this device are a block of any readily available hardwood of sufficient size for the intended repair, a guitar string, a guitar or bass tuning key with bushings, and wax paper.

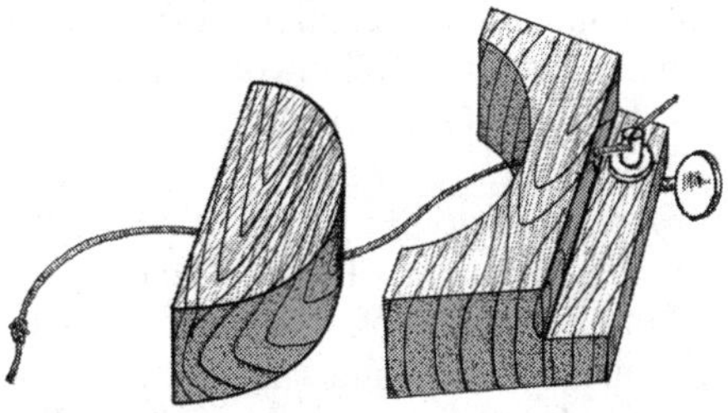

A typical dent involves some splintering and short cracks which separate pieces of wood which are held in place by loose but interlocked fibers. If, in the course of repairing the instrument, the top or back are removed, the dent can sometimes be pushed out by hand, but a controlled pressure evenly distributed over an area around and including the dent is preferable for a clean and accurate repair.

By holding a block of hardwood flush against the top or back of the instrument adjacent to the damaged area with half of the block exposed, the contour of the body can easily be traced onto the block. When the block is cut on the bandsaw following this traced line, you create two blocks which will serve as inside/outside clamping cauls for the repair of the dent. If the top or back has been removed, it is a simple matter to inject glue into the dent and clamp these blocks in place, using wax paper to prevent seizure.

However, if it is not absolutely necessary to remove a top or back it should not be done. In those cases we use our side dent puller and reshaper. It is made as follows. A hole is drilled through each block so that a guitar string can be strung through them while they retain their original orientation. On the block which is to be the outside caul, a tuning key is attached to receive the string and provide clamping pressure. A convenient way of attaching the tuning key is to cut a rabbet on the outside of the caul and drill the tuning-key hole in the rabbet's shoulder.

The repair is then carried out in the following manner. Inject glue into the breaks in the dent. Cut the ball end off of the guitar string and thread it through the center of the dent (making only a minute hole) from the outside into the body. Reach into the soundhole and pull the string within sight, being careful not to pull it completely through the dent. Place wax paper on the working surface of the inside caul, thread the string through the wax paper and through the hole in the caul, and tie a knot in the end of the string which is of sufficient size and strength to keep it from slipping back through the caul. Move the inside caul into position over the dent while pulling on the other end of the string. Make sure that it is positioned properly relative to the intended position of the outside caul. Pass the free end of the string through a piece of wax paper, through the hole in the outside caul, thread it through the tuning key, and start tightening. The pressure will force the dent to flatten out to its original shape. Allow adequate drying time. Only the small hole through which the guitar string was threaded should remain when the cauls and string are removed. This hole can easily be filled, sanded flush, and the finish touched up. We hope this serves you well in your work.

—— *Nathan Missel and Christopher Smith (1998)*

■ When my wife decided to explore life in the craft lane we bought a Delta scroll saw. She didn't take to it, but I did. I must have cut out the pieces to a hundred of her projects, all the while wondering how the new machine might be applied to lutherie work. The scroll saw is a reasonable substitute for the bandsaw when changing the bandsaw's blade would be required. For instance, a very fine-toothed blade is called for when cutting out instrument tops because the wood chips so readily, especially cedar. Coarse scroll saw blades have about 9tpi, and are still capable of leaving cedar edges really ragged. Finer blades have about 40tpi and leave a lovely clean edge on coniferous wood. Unfortunately, they don't track well in wood with alternate hard and soft grain lines, but since I cut plates oversize this is no big deal. Intermediate blades are good for cutting thin hardwood stock. I break a lot of blades, but they don't cost much. By the time I could install a superfine bandsaw blade, I'll have the job done on the scroll saw.

Cutting intricate soundholes is a job custom made for the scroll saw, though the shallow 16″ throat of my machine prevents me from getting adventurous on guitar-size instruments. Again, choosing the right blade is crucial. The coarsest blade that doesn't chip your wood is the one you want.

With the coarsest blade installed, the scroll saw will cut 1½″ stock and leave an edge so clean it'll nearly look sanded. My Delta will handle material up to 2″ thick, but it had better be fairly soft wood if you want to accomplish the cut in a timely fashion.

A professional scroll saw might work for cutting out inlays, but I've never heard of anyone doing it. The best saws cost $1000 or so. The Delta lists for about a quarter of that and can often be found on sale for a lot less. I never would have bought one just for lutherie work, but now that I've got it, I keep finding more uses for it.

—— *John Calkin (1998)*

■ Rough carving the top and back plates of archtop guitars and other archtop instruments can be a very time consuming and tedious task. One way to save time is to power carve them into rough form before beginning final graduation. There are many ways of doing this, but I have found one setup which is relatively cheap and easy to assemble and use. The concept is based on descriptions of a similar idea presented by Glenn Markel in the Guild's book *Lutherie Tools* (p. 95). His device was an archtop "carving gauge," composed of a drill press and a cone-shaped piece of wood which was used to mark a plate for planing to a uniform thickness. This description expands on that basic idea incorporating a router for carving.

To construct the carver you will need a router which is detachable from its base, a 2″×5″×12″ piece of hardwood (maple or mahogany are good), a 12″ piece of 1¼″ pipe threaded on one end, a 1¼″ threaded floor flange, four flat-head bolts approximately 3½″ long with washers and lock nuts, a hanger bolt about 2″ long, a wing nut to fit the hanger bolt, three square-head bolts approximately 5½″ long with wing nuts and washers for each, a ⅞″ diameter cove bit (with no bearing), and a 2″×2″×2″ block of hardwood. These materials will be assembled into an apparatus resembling an overhead pin router.

On a strong, stable bench or table, mount the floor flange using the flat-head bolts secured with the lock nuts. This is the foundation of the apparatus and must be secure. Screw the pipe into the floor flange tightly.

Measure the diameter of your router motor with calipers and cut a hole to match towards one end of the 2″×5″×12″ hardwood block. Cut a hole at the other end matching the diameter of the standing pipe. From each end of the board cut ¼″ wide slits into the holes with a bandsaw. Bandsaw out a "shoulder" in one corner of each end of the board into which the square-head bolts will be installed. Drill holes in each end of the board and install the square-head bolts so that they seat against the shoulders. These bolts will secure the router in the board and the board to the pipe, and will be used for depth-of-cut adjustments **(Fig. 1)**.

Slide the smaller hole in the block onto the standing pipe (this should fit snugly), and secure the block to the

Figure 1

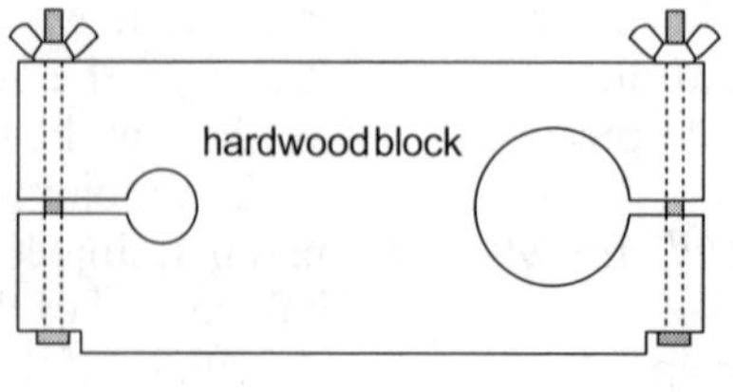

Figure 3

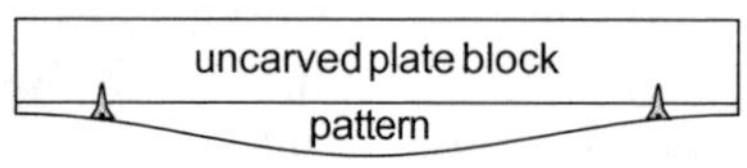

Figure 2

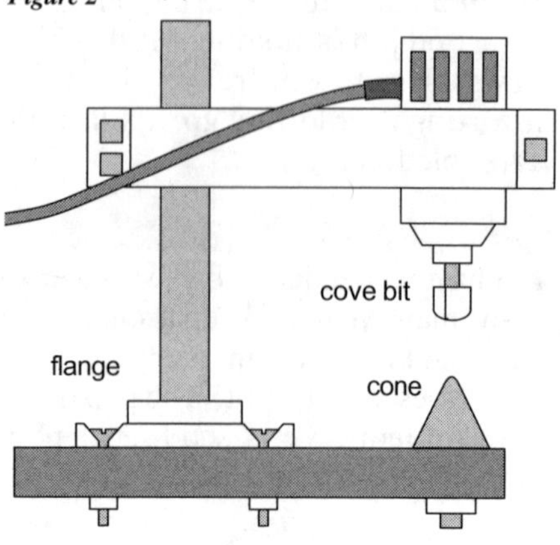

pipe by tightening the wing nut on the square-head bolt. Install the router into its hole, and tighten the square-head bolt **(Fig. 2)**.

Shape the 2″×2″×2″ block of hardwood into a symmetrical cone with a slightly rounded tip. Drill a hole in the flat face of the cone and screw in the hanger bolt. Drill a hole in the top of the bench and insert the hanger bolt. Fasten the cone in place by tightening the wing nut on the hanger bolt. The cone must be exactly under the center of the router collet, as in **Fig. 2**. Install the cove bit into the collet. The device can be adjusted by moving the block on the standing pipe or by moving the router in the block.

In order for it to function, one side of a given plate must already be carved, or a pattern must be used. This pattern consists of a plate which has been carved to the desired shape on *one* of its faces. It is secured to the stock which is to be carved. There are several ways this can be carried out. One way is to glue a small amount of paper in-between the pattern and the uncarved plate block, thus facilitating separation with relative ease. Another way is to secure the pattern onto the uncarved stock with short aluminum screws (aluminum is a safety factor in case the screws get hit by the router). The holes left by the screws will eventually be carved away **(Fig. 3)**.

This device makes rapid work of rough carving. Please use caution and eye protection with this device, and invest in high-quality bits. I am no stranger to carbide blades flying off a router bit at a high velocity. Good luck, and happy carving.

—— *Nathan Missel (1998)*

■ Welcome to another episode with the evil cave-ins. In the last two episodes (see p. 492) I talked about correcting slight cave-ins between the bridge and the waist bar. This time I'll talk about sinking soundholes, i.e., weak waist bars.

I was experimenting with how light I could go on the waist bar on my guitars, until I went too far. If a waist bar is too light, the guitar loses sustain, response, volume — everything. If it is too stiff, you will have a guitar that sounds like a stiff guitar.

Recently, I was on the phone with H. Hauser III, talking about one of his father's guitars that I saw here in Rome. It was quite collapsed, and he was telling me about a technique he had been using over the years to revive some of his family's instruments that had been built a little too lightly. His technique is very similar to the one I came up with, which I will describe here. I have since used this technique to repair and rejuvenate several guitars of different qualities, and all benefitted from this treatment. If the sinking is extreme and remains even without string tension, this technique may not be enough.

The idea is to support the waist bar in the center with a smooth arch that rests against the sides, which, because of the tight curve of the waist, are extremely rigid and have no problem withstanding the load.

I use a flat stick with some 80-grit sandpaper glued to it to create a flat area on top of the center of the waist bar. I then glue the new arched bar on this flat using three small C clamps. After the glue has dried for a few hours, I glue the two little support blocks in place by pressing them in position with my fingers. You can increase the stiffness, if you think it is necessary, by pressing them in place a little stronger and toward the soundboard, creating some spring effect on the arched bar.

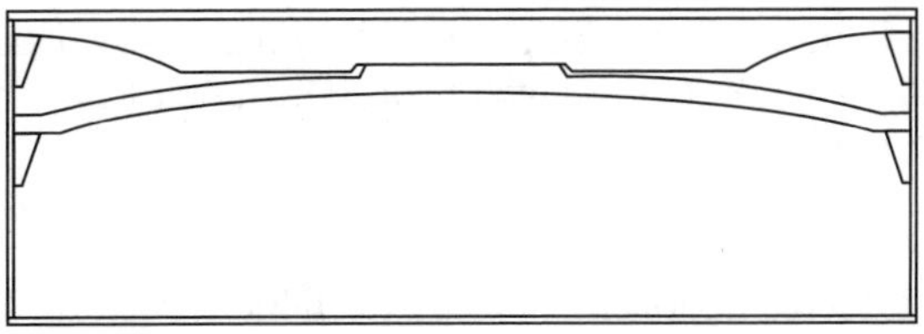

When is a waist bar too light or too stiff? Well, first determine whether the soundboard was built domed or flat. A domed soundboard shouldn't flatten out under string tension. With the guitar unstrung and face up on the bench, push down with your thumb in the center of the waist bar using fairly hard pressure — it should barely move. If it doesn't move at all, it might be too stiff. If the soundboard was built flat and is too weak, I suggest using some of that spring effect to push it outwards into a very slight dome. If once the arch is in place the waist bar has become too stiff, I will shave some wood from the arch until it feels right.

I use Canadian Engelmann spruce for this arched bar, and it is between 3⁄16″ and 1⁄4″ square in cross-section.

—— *Filippo Avignonesi (1998)*

■ Clamping loose brace ends in the nether regions of a guitar box can be effectively accomplished by wedging sticks between the brace and the opposite plate of the guitar. The guitar box becomes a go-bar deck, a tool for repairing itself! If you do a lot of repair work, take the time to cut a bunch of sticks in graduated lengths so that you will have the ones you need at the critical moment. I sometimes use blocks of wood instead of sticks to spread the pressure over a larger area. Two opposite corners are rounded so that the block provides progressively more pressure as it is rotated into position. Besides being useful for clamping, internal props can be used to support the plates in situations where clamping pressure needs to be applied to the outside of the box.

While on the subject of internal box work, I would like to thank Dale Randall for his tip on using plexiglas mirrors in *AL#20*. (See *BRBAL2*, p. 318.) It bears repeating. You can cut them any size you want, and with an inspection light and a couple of largish mirrors lying on the back inside, you can see everything! No more fussing around aiming a teeny inspection mirror, and both hands are free.

—— *Jonathon Peterson (1998)*

■ In my quest for a nonclogging applicator for superglue I tried using a 1cc syringe and loading it from the bottle. To my surprise it worked very well, and if you suck the glue out of the needle and store standing up, it is reusable for a day or two. If the manufacturers could supply superglue in a bottle similar to a medicine bottle, with a self-sealing rubber top, the shelf life would be greatly increased as very little air or moisture would ever be introduced.

For injecting glue into a crack or joint where you want to protect the adjoining area, apply masking tape and rub its edge to get good seal. I use the end of a knife handle. By rubbing carefully you get very little capillary action to damage finish. The tape idea is from the great books by Don Teeter.

—— *Dale Randall (1998)*

■ I attach a neoprene or closed-cell foam backing to Micro-mesh which makes it particularly handy for sanding the many curved surfaces of violin family instruments (or any place else you find them). The Micro-mesh is glued with a strong spray mounting glue (contact cement) to 1⁄16″ neoprene (wet suit material is just right) or a product called "Foamies" found in hobby stores. They last a very long time with frequent washing. When they're almost dead, I give them to Michael Yates, a bow maker, who finds more life in them.

—— *Guy Rabut (1997)*

■ Here's my five-minute epoxy filling method. Thoroughly seal the guitar with shellac. I usually use a pad; a brush is good in tight intersections and if bleeding is extreme. On Indian rosewood and African blackwood, both of which give up their resins readily in the presence of alcohol, it may take three or four applications over a couple days to seal properly.

Mix epoxy in very small batches, about 1⁄4″ to 1⁄2″ from each tube (I use 5-minute Devcon brand). Squeegee it into the grain, with the grain, using a single-edge razor blade scraper (as per Tim Olsen's "Razor Scraper" in *Lutherie Tools*, p. 29) with "safed" corners. A rubber squeegee or old credit card could also be used, but I've found I have greater control with the blade.

Wipe excess epoxy from the blade with alcohol-dampened paper towel as you go. Leave very little or, ideally, no epoxy on the surface. To be doubly sure, just before epoxy becomes too set up — at the 7- or 8-minute mark, I sometimes take an alcohol-dampened paper towel and wipe across the grain and then with the grain. I typically have to fill twice to get the grain full enough that the finish will complete whatever else is necessary. The second application can be done almost immediately.

Let it sit overnight or 24 hours. Sand lightly with the grain with 400 paper dry to be sure there is no extra buildup anywhere. Try not sand back to the wood. If you do sand through anywhere, it's OK, just proceed normally, reseal and apply finish.

You may notice some open grains or other little places that need filling after you've applied several applications of finish. At any time you may spot fill using epoxy using the razor blade scraper, sand lightly the next day with 400 grit or finer, and continue building up the finish.

A few precautions: fill a small amount at a time until you get the feel of it — like one-fourth of the back; keep epoxy off your skin; and use a mask that will block epoxy vapors.

—— *Cyndy Burton (1997)*

■ I've been using this jig to make joints for attaching necks to bodies for about two years now, with very good results. Both the heel and the body are slotted, and they are joined by a flat wooden spline. I know of several other people using this type of joint, but most of them slot the neck block before assembling the body. I slot it after the body is assembled, bound, and rough sanded. (Binding the body without the neck

1

2

ALL BY FILIPPO AVIGNONESI

3

4

in the way is considerably easier and faster.) The only power tool I need is a router, and the jig is easily adaptable to not only classical guitars, but also steel strings, archtops, ukuleles, and A-style mandolins. For F-style mandolins you'd probably need an extra long ¼″ router bit.

Making a splined joint is obviously much easier and faster than a making a dovetail, and it may be easier than a mortise and tenon. It is probably not as strong as a Spanish heel, as it could suffer from extreme heat like a dovetail or mortise and tenon would. Also unlike a Spanish heel, it would be difficult to extend the back over the heel, so you have to use a separate heel cap. On the other hand you could probably disassemble it like a dovetail or mortise and tenon, if needed.

I like to make my neck block with a Spanish foot so it will look just like a Spanish joint once assembled, and also so it will work like one, with the same leverage on the back. The neck blank, including the heel, is left square until it is slotted. On my classical guitars, I cut the face of the heel at 90° to the length of the neck and make adjustments with a chisel later. On steel strings I would probably cut a 1° or 2° backward angle.

To make the jig I joined two boards with a simple butt joint. The end of board A is flush with the surface of board B (**Fig. 1**). I just screwed and glued the two boards together using Titebond and four screws.

The fence against which the router will run must be perpendicular to board B. This is the only critical part

Figure 1

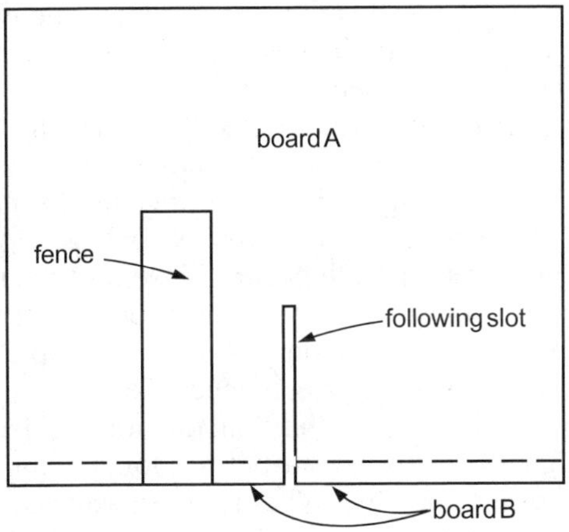

Figure 2

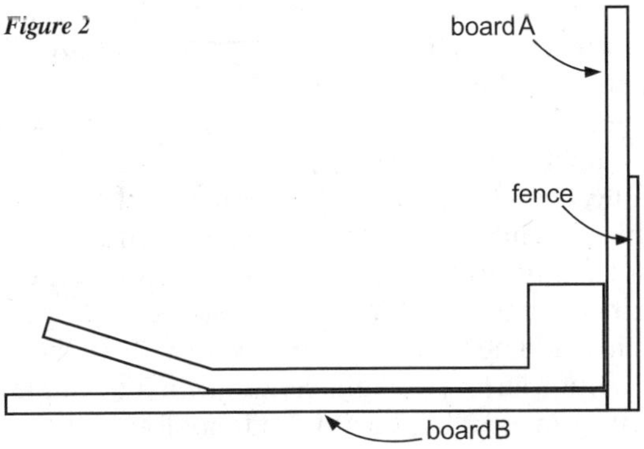

in making this jig. You can use a square to mark the position for the fence's working edge, or you can just position the fence with a square and superglue it in place.

Next, decide how long to rout the following slot. This will depend on the depth of your instrument at the heel. Remember that you don't want to rout through the back of the guitar.

I use ¼″ splines, so I routed the following slot ½″ wide to provide a little clearance in the jig. To cut the slot, I clamped the jig to a bench, ran the router against the fence using a ½″ bit, and routed the slot to the desired length. It must be deep enough to go all the way through A, and ½″–¾″ into B. Then, holding a square against A, I marked the centerline of the jig on the inside surface of B and in the slot itself. As a final touch I bandsawed a couple of reliefs on either side of B to allow for clamp clearance. We're ready to roll!

Clamp the neck to the jig (**Fig. 2**) on the centerline with a couple of cam clamps, clamp the jig to the bench (as in **Photo 1**), put a ¼″ bit in your router, and rout a slot into the heel ½″ deep, and ⅛″ shorter than the body depth.

Shape the head, glue on the fretboard, and shape the heel and the neck. Prepare a spline ¼″×1″× slot length, with the grain running parallel to the length of the neck, and glue it with Titebond (**Photo 3**). I usually use ¼″ plywood for the spline. The spline should fit snugly into the slot, but not be tight. If it is just a hair loose, try wetting the slot and the spline, and once dry try the fit again. If it is very loose, glue some veneer to the spline to make it thicker.

Clamp the body to the jig as you did the neck (**Photos 1 and 2**), using shims if necessary to adjust the angle of the body so that the fretboard gluing area of the soundboard is perpendicular to the slot length. Rout a slot into the neck block 9⁄16″ deep — you need some empty space for the glue squeeze-out.

Fit the face of the heel to the body, as you would for a dovetail or a mortise and tenon joint, with chisels and sandpaper. Trim the fretboard to length, and clamp everything together dry. Drill a couple of small holes through the 13th fret slot for brads which will help keep everything aligned during the actual glue-up. **Photo 4** is an example of a clamping setup. Glue it up. Once dry, glue the heel cap and go on as usual from there.

—— *Filippo Avignonesi (1998)*

■ I had no idea how useful a belt sander would be until I had one for a few months and became absolutely reliant on it. Someday I'll have two, one permanently horizontal and the other permanently vertical. Changing operations is a pain in the neck, especially since the vertical setup requires that the belt and table must be set at a perfect 90° angle, and my machine likes to fight about it. (It's a Shop-Tek. Don't buy one unless they've made vast improvements. Judging from the catalog, they haven't changed a thing.)

Aside from the obvious sanding chores, the belt sander makes a much better grinder than a bench grinder does. Even hollow grinding is possible right over the rollers. Belts too worn for woodwork do fine for grinding, but rather than keep an old one on hand I try to remember to grind something before changing each belt. I've seen 150-grit belts recommended for regrinding chisels, but if you are going to finish them on a bench stone, a worn 80-grit belt will work faster. The only advantage of a fine-grit belt is that it can produce a wonderful finished edge. I keep a 150-grit belt on hand, but hardly ever use it. For rougher work, such as grinding awls, center punches, diagonal cutters, and fret nippers, an 80-grit belt is fine, and always on my machine. I'm more inclined to replace drill bits than to sharpen them, since most that I use are small and cheap, but I bet the belt sander would do a fine job on them, too.

Burning an edge while grinding has never been a problem for me, except on very delicate blades. A gentle touch is generally called for, along with frequent dips in the water bucket. What I like about belt sanders is their ability to grind a surface with no facets. A good hand with a grind stone can do that, too, but prettier and sharper work is easier to get on the belt. I'm not sure there's much difference in the heat produced.

—— *John Calkin (1998)*

PAUL JACOBSON

■ I set up this router with a planer bit. The whole thing is mounted on a rigid platform which suspends it over the worktable. A clock spring under the platform holds the work against the table. This is a very accurate thicknessing tool which is an excellent low-cost substitute for a drum sander.

—— *Paul Jacobson (1998)*

■ One bit of advice for weekend luthiers like myself: since we end up clearing the bench in the middle of the project for other more pressing projects (like painting the garden bench, or making a footstool), my advice is to make or procure the instrument's case before you make the instrument. Then when you clear your bench you will have a safe place to put the instrument!

—— *Topher Gayle (1998)*

■ Sometimes a machinist can be your best friend, though they certainly don't rescue you for free. We've always held our guitar necks on with steel pins and bolts, but lining up the bolt holes in the neck block as the body was made was often a crapshoot. It may not hurt anything to enlarge the bolt hole to get a fit, but it feels bad. So we had a machine shop cut a Forstner bit from its stem and weld the stem to the cutting side of the bit. Now we drill the bolt holes from the outside, insert the altered Forstner bit stem from the inside, chuck it up in a drill set to spin in reverse, and we pull on the drill to cut the countersink for the bolt heads. It's fast, clean, and the holes are always on center.

—— *Jeff Huss and Mark Dalton (1998)*

■ I build for fun, and only make two or three instruments a year. The shop is fairly minimal with no spray booth. I "rent" the spray room of a local finishing shop for a bottle of Merlot, so I have to be spray-ready when I come through the door.

Padding lacquer is a combination of lacquer and shellac. Several companies make it, and I have been happy with Behlen's Ultra Qualasole. It goes over anything and has a slight amber tint which doesn't interfere with my color schemes.

Once I have sanded to 320 grit and wiped it down with alcohol I apply a wash coat of the lacquer. This darkens the wood and dries to the touch in a couple minutes. I look for scratches or blemishes and correct them on the spot. Then I put another heavy coat on and let it dry. Keep in mind this compound is lacquer and you need to use a mask in a well-ventilated room or suffer the consequences.

Padding lacquer raises the grain a little, so I sand it back with 400- or 600-grit nonloading paper and add another coat. Application only takes five minutes. I just smear it on as heavy as it will go without dripping, using retired underwear. It's water thin, but will build and stick quickly if you don't keep the skivvies moving. With a practiced touch you could completely finish a guitar to a satin sheen, much like French polishing.

My success with filling the pores is decidedly mixed. That's one of the reasons for doing so much handwork before spraying. Whether I use water- or solvent-based filler, I invariably have to do it again. I apply the filler as per the instructions and give it a day to cure. I then sand back, apply another coat of the padding lacquer and let it dry for an hour. Just as small scratches showed up with the first coat, unfilled grain pores are now evident. Refilling, resanding, and resmearing should remedy this. You can do this as many times as it takes to get it right — a blessing for me.

Hopefully, I now have a smooth, dull surface. I could keep rubbing in more coats for a thin, hard finish, although spiriting-off to a deep sheen has eluded me. I now sacrifice my bottle of Merlot and start shooting nitro over the padding lacquer. It sticks very well. In the past I have shot four or five light coats, given it a couple days to set up, sanded it back a little and shot four or five more. Polish it in the usual way after at least a week.

This could be tedious for someone who has a better setup, but it really doesn't take very long, and it saves a lot of trips to the booth. Nowhere in the process are you past the point of no return. It has also saved me having to look at an 80-grit scratch under a pretty finish.

One's mental discipline also helps. As I mentioned above, I am not the world's best sander, so my policy is that I never immediately apply the finish after sanding. Instead, when I am done sanding, I hang the guitar up until the next shop day and reexamine it with a patient eye. I always find something I can make a little better.

—— *Skip Helms (1998)*

■ Here is a tool that may be of use to others. I call it a fingerboard plane, but it can be used for more than that.

Most planes have the frog at 45° to the sole. Block planes have less angle, and low-angle planes less again. These planes work well on softwood and end grain.

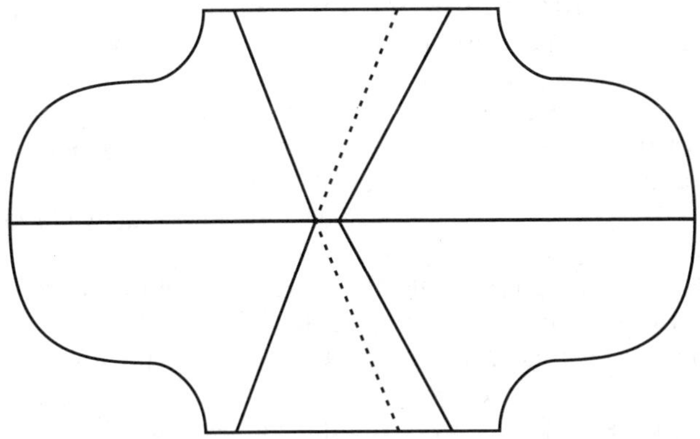

Symmetrical pattern for the layout of two halves of a plane body. This is for a plane which uses tapered recesses to hold the wedge and blade.

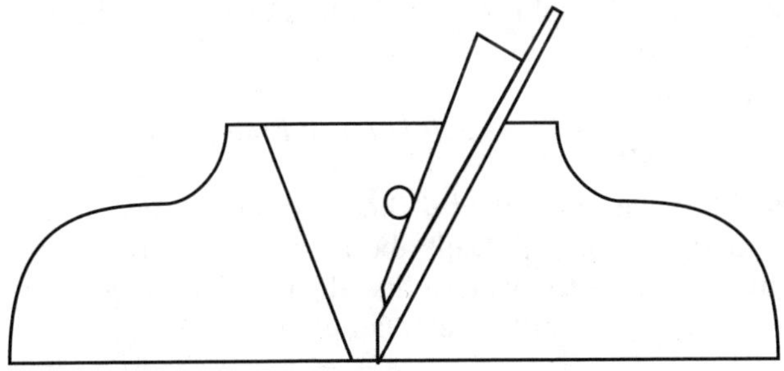

Cutaway side view of a plane which uses a metal rod instead of the tapered recesses.

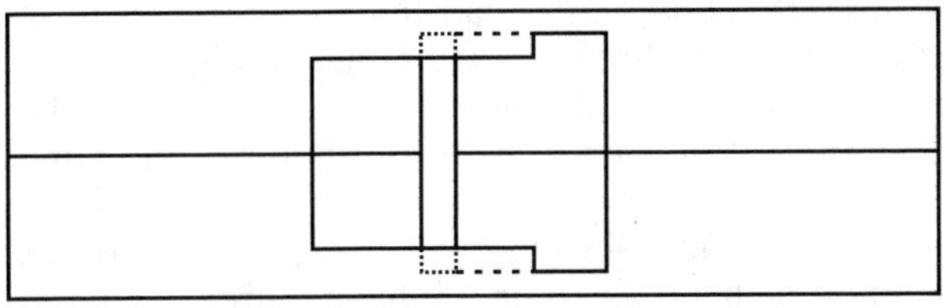

Top view of a plane body showing the tapered recesses which hold the wedge and blade.

But for hardwoods with cranky interlocked grain or fiddleback figure, tearout is more common than not, and with a slotted fretboard, chunks small and large can tear out no matter how sharp or what direction you plane. Sanding or cabinet scrapers may be the only alternative. Sanding causes dust which is a health hazard and should be minimized whenever possible.

A plane with a 60° frog overcomes these problems. With the blade turned over and sharpened at 30° it puts the cutting edge at 90°, and the plane becomes a scraper plane. It will handle slotted rosewood or ebony fingerboards without any of the problems associated with standard planes. Fiddleback timber may require that the plane be held at a slight angle to produce more of a slicing type of cut.

The easiest way to make the body of this type of plane is to make two mirror-image halves and then join them along a lengthwise center seam. Rock maple, striped ebony, or any other stable hardwood is suitable. Lay out two pieces of wood, cut the frog, and clamp them together. Next I drill for and set screws which will be used to hold the pieces in alignment while the glue dries. Take off the clamp, remove the screws, spread glue, then screw and clamp together.

A piece of metal rod can be used to hold the wedge if you don't feel like cutting a recess. For the blade, an old file can be softened, cut, and ground to shape. For wooden planes a wedge-shaped blade works best.

Never throw out old files as they can be used to make any number of tools such as chisels, draw knives, blades, and anything else that requires carbon tool steel.

To harden and temper, first heat the file until red hot, allow it to cool slowly in a safe place, and shape it to your requirements. Then reheat it to a glowing cherry red. Dip in oil or water and allow to cool. With some emery paper, clean the scale from the blade.

Now the tempering process can begin. If you used water for cooling, the metal will be harder than if you have used oil. This needs to be taken into account when tempering. With a gas torch, heat the noncutting edge of the blade, and watch the colors appear. Reduce the heat and watch the colors move toward the cutting edge. When the yellow reaches the edge, dip it in oil. If you used water you may need wait until the blue reaches the edge.

Tempering softens the metal. This process may require some practice. If the blade chips when used, the steel is too hard and the blade will need retempering. Repeat the whole process and go to the next color.

When hardening, an oxy torch, fuel stove, or a good fire can be used to heat metal to red hot. Gas is good for tempering. Tool making is an art worth learning for all woodworkers, as it enables them to make customized tools to suit special needs that may arise, or to make tools they cannot afford. For larger blades, old car springs are a good source of carbon steel. Mild steel can only be casehardened and this is a different process. Only use carbon steel for tools. Good Luck.

—— *Tim O'Dea (1998)*

■ I am not well practiced in bending frets with a pair of pliers and I did not have the money or desire to buy a variable fret bender, so I came up with this simple design which works very well for me. It cost less than $1 to make, and about a half-hour of my time from start to finish. The materials I used were a piece of ¾″×5″×8″ hardwood for a base (I picked a piece of poplar out of my scrap pile for this), two smaller blocks of maple, each about ¾″×2″×4″ (also from the scrap pile) and three ¼″×2″ flat-head bolts, washers, and nuts.

I drew the radius of the fretboard across the length of the face of one of the maple blocks, using the caul from my Stewart-MacDonald fret press to get an accurate curve. The resulting line was not centered, but its exact location is not important. Using my scroll saw, I cut the block in two using the radius line as a guide. It is important that this cut be accurate since the fretwire will be pressed against the resulting concave surface to produce the curve.

The other maple block was cut into a teardrop shape to form a cam lever. The bottom of the shape was made by drawing a circle 1¾″ in diameter. Two converging lines tangent to the side of the circle finished the shape. This shape was then cut out taking care to ensure the circular end was round with no flat spots. Then, using my Eclipse saw fitted with a .8MM blade, I cut a slot around this rounded end to receive the fret tang. The resulting slot was wide enough to allow the fret tang to slide through it freely, but narrow enough to support the fret bead. A ¼″ diameter hole was then drilled about ⅛″ off center on the circular end to accept a mounting bolt which would serve as a pivot.

KEVIN RIELLY

The cam is slotted to receive the fret tang, and the block is radiused to the desired bend. In the background is another bender he made for straightening coiled wire in preparation for final bending. It has a slotted block and an unslotted cam.

The curved block was drilled and fastened securely to the base block using two bolts. The cam block was then placed at a right angle to the curved block, with the slotted face of the cam in contact with the curved face. Then, using the hole in the cam lever as a guide, the base was drilled and the cam lever was bolted in place.

To use the fret bender, the base is secured in my bench vise and the cam lever is rotated until a space develops between the two blocks. By slowly feeding the fretwire into the slot in the cam and gently working the cam against the curve, the fretwire assumes the desired shape. If you apply too much pressure with the cam, it is possible to kink the wire, so you have to be careful. It takes about two minutes to accurately curve 4′ of fretwire.

This bender will produce only one radius, but the curved block is easily replaced, so it could be set up to bend other radii. If you used a larger base, you could cut radii on more than one side of a block and position cams accordingly to make a jig that could be used to make different bends without having to swap out blocks.

Because of the way this jig works, fretwire must start out straighter than the radius of the curved block. To straighten rolled wire I use a similar device which has a slotted straight block and an unslotted cam.

—— *Kevin Rielly (1998)*

■ Regarding reversible glue for holding abrasives to various fixtures mentioned in *AL #54* (p. 108), 3M makes a series of spray glues that serve the purpose well and are much faster than using rubber cement. Art supply stores carry everything from easy-peel, light-tack glue to permanent glue, but we usually get the heavy-duty stuff while at the auto paint store. It never lifts by itself, but a few seconds with a heat gun loosens the glue nicely with no damage to the fixtures. The abrasives peel right off. The glue is expensive, about $13 for a big can, but it lasts a good while and saves us a lot of time.

—— *Jeff Huss and Mark Dalton (1998)*

■ The inner core of a butcher-paper roll is usually a cardboard tube with walls about ½″ thick. This can be cut into pieces to make radiused pads of whatever size you need for making neck-clamping pads or neck rests.

—— *Gene Simpson (1999)*

■ Sometimes a change in the most basic procedure you can think of makes a difference in your work. I recently switched to a Benedetto glue applicator. All that really means is that I used to spread glue with my index finger, and now I use my pinky. It feels (and may look) like an effete gesture, but it instantly made a difference in the cleanliness of my work. There are almost no random glue smudges that have to be sanded clean later. The difference is most obvious in my brace work. I wouldn't mention such a trivial item if it hadn't surprised me so pleasantly.

—— *Woody Vernice (1998)*

ALL THIS PAGE BY ANDREA ANDALO

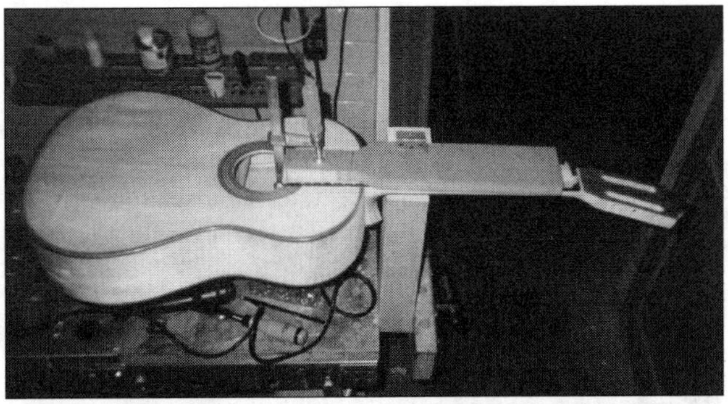

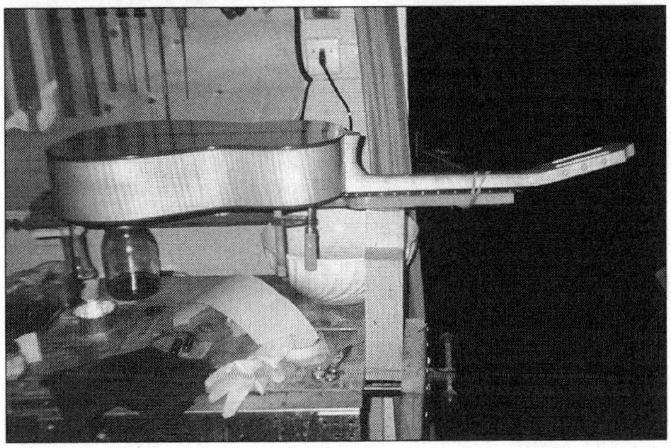

■ I use shellac varnish, and I have found it difficult holding the instrument while applying the finish. It's easy to mar the back while working on the front, and vice versa. Moreover, I work in a small space, and it is very easy to knock the instrument against something when repositioning it. I developed this simple device to hold guitars during the finishing phase. It has improved my humor, and finishing has become a breeze!

The jig consists of an upright which can be held in a vise, and a workboard to which the neck of the guitar can be secured, leaving the body, the back of the neck, and the headstock free for sanding and finishing. The workboard is hinged to the top of the upright so that the instrument can be flipped over.

My upright is spruce with a 10cm × 10cm cross section. A relief is cut into its upper end to provide clearance for the neck when the instrument is in the face-up position. The workboard is 2.5cm thick MDF, and is cut to the width of the fingerboard at the body end so that I have full access to the soundboard. The guitar is secured to the workboard with a clamp through the soundhole. A clamping caul protects the inside of the guitar. Two or three rubber bands wrapped around the neck and fixed to two screws in the workboard help to stabilize the instrument, and can be quickly removed for work on the neck.

I improved the device shown in the photos by enlarging the top of the upright and adding a second hinge, as shown in the drawing, to improve the stability.

—— *Andrea Andalò (1999)*

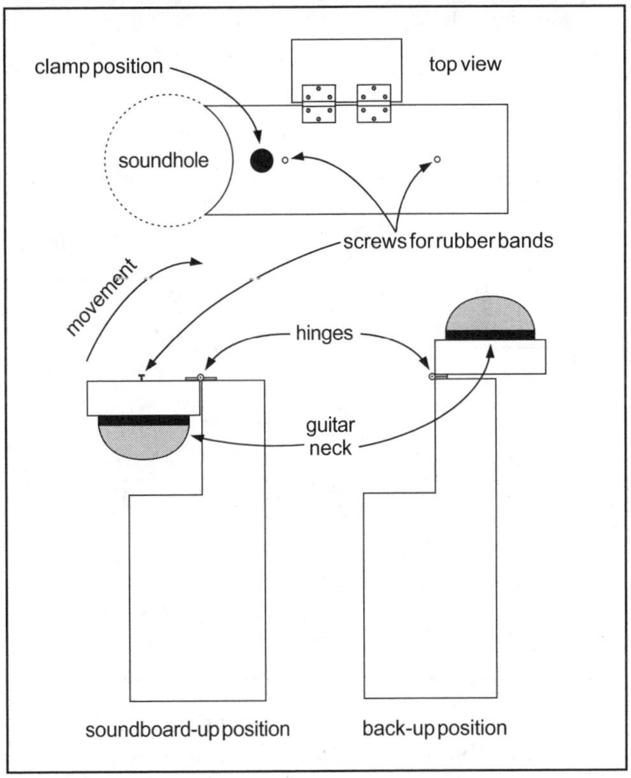

■ A good method for finding the height of mandolin-family sides is to place a violin soundpost height gauge into the lower (larger) *f*-hole eye which is closest to the outside perimeter, position it next to the lining, and open the tool up to get your measurement. This gives you the real side height; the distance between top and back. This figure can be subtracted from the overall outside measurement (inclusive of top, sides, and back) to give you the dimension of top and back together. Divide those two to give you the real dimensional thickness at the very edge.

—— *John Monteleone (1999)*

■ Recently I was asked to remove the shank of a strap-button screw from the upper horn of a Stratocaster. The head of the screw had broken off. The threads in the wood had not been stripped, and the break had occurred slightly below the surface.

My solution was to first carefully remove a little wood from around the last 2mm or 3mm of the shank with a very small Dremel bit. I then chose a brass bolt with a chunky, slotted, round head, and a threaded shank just large enough to enable me to skim off the threads, leaving a shaft slightly greater in diameter than the broken screw's shank, and just smaller than the relief I had cut around it. I counterbored the brass screw all the way through and cut it short so that it fitted closely over the broken screw, with the slotted head just proud of the guitar body. I heated the brass head with a soldering iron and attached it to the broken screw by feeding rosin-cored solder through the hole in the center of the head. I let it cool and carefully unscrewed the broken shank from the body.

To finish, I trued up the hole and widened it with a countersink drill bit to the diameter of a straight-flute reamer sized for a suitable plug cutter. I made a plug of similar wood and grain orientation, and filled the hole. A quick and easy refinish of the area with tinted cyanoacrylate glue buffed out nicely, and was in any event hidden underneath the replacement strap button. By carefully drilling a pilot hole for the replacement screw through the short plug, I was able to pick up the original screw hole.

—— *Darelle Anne Le Maitre (1997)*

■ I recently made a quick jig for cutting bridge slots and tieblock inlays for use with a plunge router. The jig is no more than a mahogany cutoff and some scraps. For steel string guitars I use a slot that is both angled back for string pressure and angled slightly along the length for string compensation. The classical bridges only have the back angle.

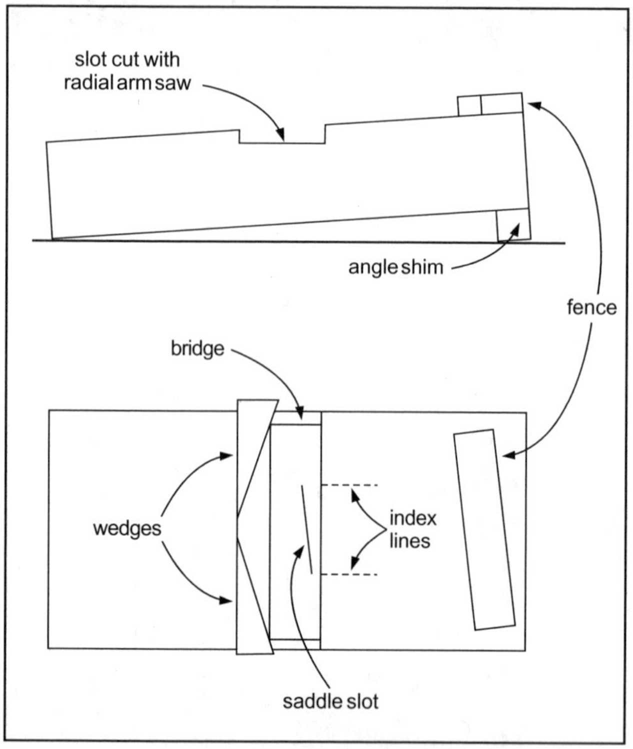

A radial saw works well for hogging waste but you could use a table saw or router. Starting with a 6/4″ block of wood 10″×10″, I glued a shim on one end so that the angle of the top surface would correspond to the back angle I wanted. Cross-cutting on the radial saw deep enough to recess the bridge at the shallow end, I hogged the waste. The slot is 2″ wide to accommodate the bridge and a couple small wedges to hold it secure against the edge nearest the fence. Smooth the bottom of the dado with a plane or chisel. I left the temporary shim on the jig to hold it steady in my bench vise. Next, attach a small fence so the router bit will travel along the desired compensation line. Since the router will travel further than the length of the slot, mark the start and end points on the jig with a felt pen.

I made separate jigs for steel strings and classicals so I don't need to adjust the fence. The classical also has a dado on the flip side that is the same size but has no string angle. This fence is setup to cut the channel in front of the tieblock. Two spacers between the router base and fence set the cut for the tieblock inlays. If you don't angle your string slot, this dado can be used for all the cuts.

That's it! You are looking at ten minutes work. I wasn't too specific about bit sizes or compensation angles since you'll have your own opinions there anyway. Good luck!

—— *Skip Helms (1999)*

■ I made the following bow-tip-gluing jig out of pure frustration. It was designed for fiddle bows, but larger ones could be made for cello or double-bass bows.

I started with two pieces of 4″×1½″×¼″ hardwood, and drilled 7/32″ holes 1″ in from each end to receive the two 3″ long 10×24 thread clamping bolts. The V-block is 1½″×⅞″×⅞″, with a tapering groove ⅜″ wide by ½″ deep. The clamping block has the curvature of the face of the bow tip filed into it, and both the V groove and the clamping block are lined with cork, felt, or leather.

To use the clamp, place the bow tip in the V block, put glue on the bow-tip plate, position the plate, and tighten the wingnuts. It's not difficult to line everything up, and it is a real headache saver.

—— *Michael Breid (1999)*

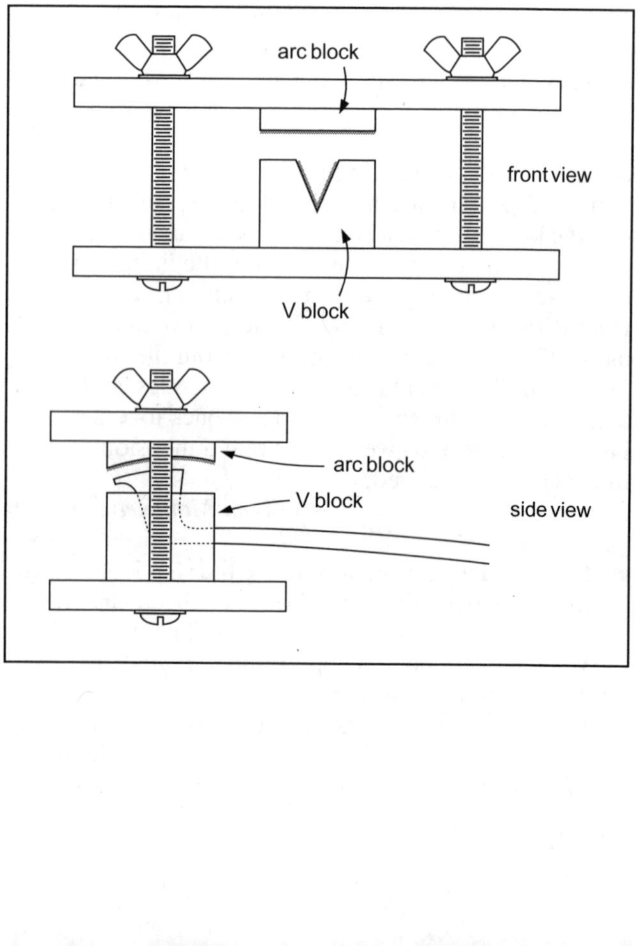

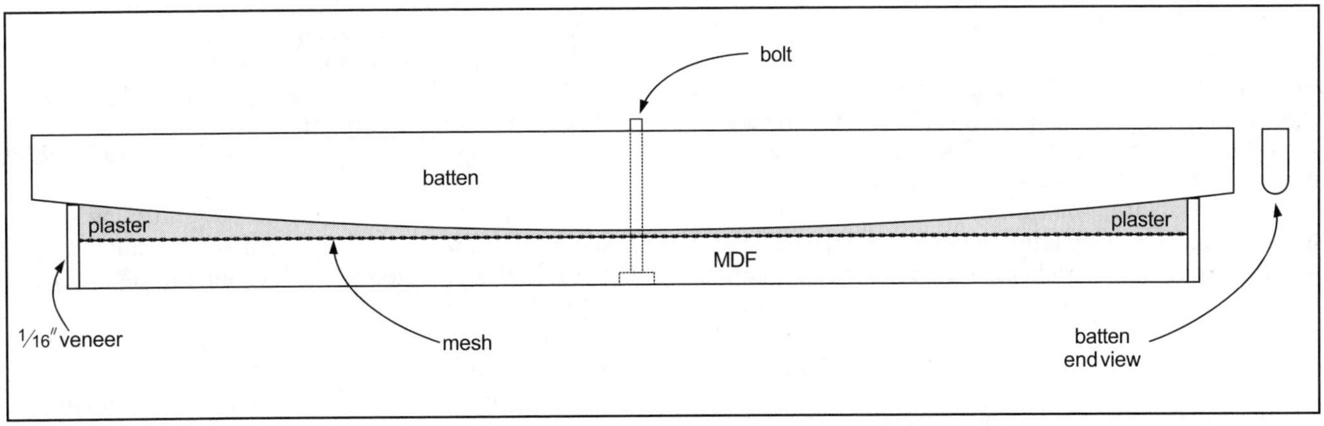

■ Here is an easy way to make dished forms using plaster to create the dished surface. First I cut a 23″ disk from a sheet of ¾″ MDF and fix a bolt at its center to act as a pivot. A strip of 1/16″-thick veneer is then attached around the edge of the disk so that it protrudes about ⅜″ above its top surface. It is important that the top edge of this rim strip be flat and uniform all of the way around. Metal mesh is then spot glued to the top surface of the disk with epoxy. This mesh will key into the plaster to make it stronger and more stable. I then prepare a batten from a piece of wood about 25″×3″×1″. A hole is drilled in the middle of the batten to receive the bolt, and a radius of, for instance, 15′ is marked and cut along one of the edges. The radiused edge is then rounded over. To cast the dish I spread a sufficient amount of hand-finishing plaster over the surface of the disk. By turning the batten on its pivot and running its ends along the rim strip, it acts as a rotating trowel. When the plaster is dry I coat its surface with a plastic resin. The resulting dished form can be used as a workboard or can be covered with 80-grit sandpaper and used for preparing guitar sides to receive tops or backs which have the same radius.

To fit the backs of my guitars, I first cut out a guitar-body-shaped piece of MDF and fix a 1″ wide strip of 1/16″ veneer around its edge to model the sides of a guitar. I also install a center block and drill a hole in it to fit the pivot bolt in the dish.

The dish is covered with 80-grit sandpaper, and the jig is rotated on the pivot to sand the edge of the veneer to match the curvature of the dish. This mimics the edge of the guitar's sides as they should be shaped to receive a back which has the same curvature as the dish. A strip of thin card stock can then be used to trace and transfer the contour to the guitar sides, referencing off a datum line on the guitar sides. After tracing the contour and planing to the line, the linings are fitted to the sides, trimmed, and finally sanded in the dish.

I make my backs with four struts and a substantive back strip, ¾″×⅛″, for extra support. The gluing edge of each strut is shaped on the sandpaper in the dish, and then notched so that it will fit over the center strip. The center strip and struts are glued to the back in a dished form using the go-bar deck.

The go-bar deck is also used to glue on the back. For this I cut two rims from ½″ MDF. One sits in the deck to support the edge of the slightly arched top, which has previously been fitted to the sides. The other rim has a series of notches corresponding to the locations of my strut ends, and acts as a clamping caul. The notches receive the first eight clamping rods, which guarantees good gluing pressure directly over the ends of each strut. Other rods are then fitted between the notches around the perimeter of the back.

—— *Peter Giolitto (1999)*

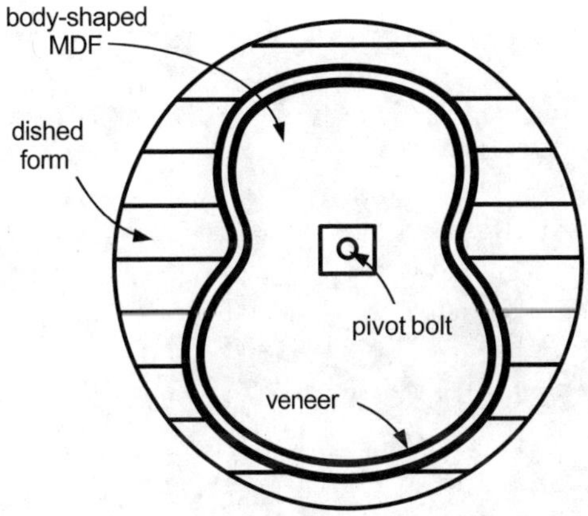

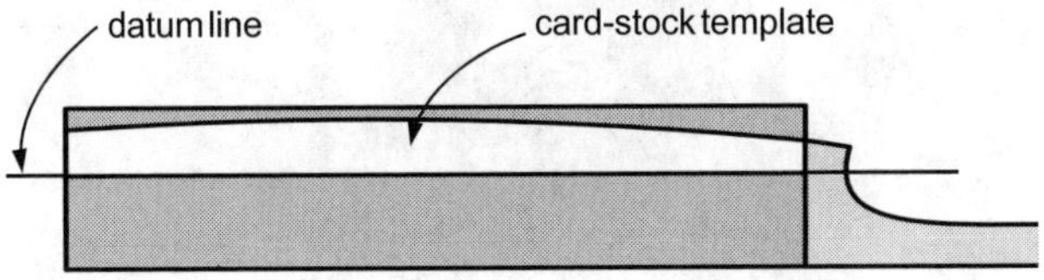

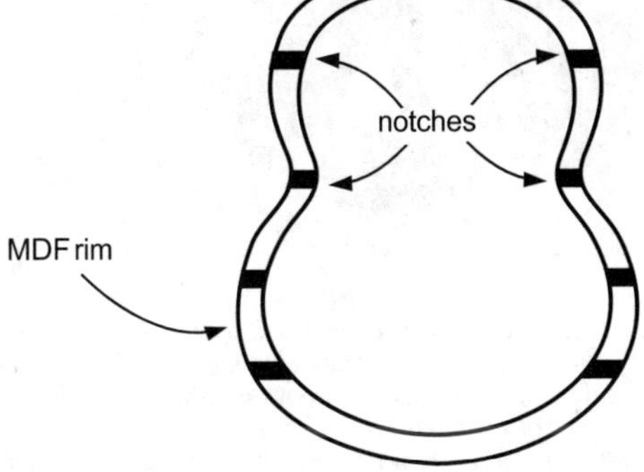

■ I thought I had found a great recycling idea, but this one *Didn't Work for Me*. After going through many gross of large rubber bands to bundle my stickered backs, sides, and tops I thought of innertubes. Yes, of course! Innertubes with holes cost nothing. Soon I was slicing hundreds of loops with my handy paper cutter which, now that I think about it, doesn't seem to cut so well anymore. But after one summer in my drying room, the loops started snapping left and right, sending stickers and rubber flying everywhere. It seems the combination of heat and tension was too much for the little buggers. Oh, well.

—— *Dave Maize (1998)*

■ Here is a photo of my modification to the Bishop Cochran plunge-router base. I read Harry Fleishman's product review of the base in *AL#49* (p. 436) a day or two after I ordered mine, and quickly noticed the obstruction of view he mentioned. This is caused by the lugs which secure the collar that the router screws into. There are different collars for various routers, but by dedicating my base to the Dremel I have, I figured I could do away with the lugs.

With the collar snug, I positioned the router in the base to my liking, with the on/off switch convenient to my right thumb. I marked the collar's orientation, disassembled the pieces, cleaned off the color coating with the Dremel wire brush, and epoxied it in with JB Weld, barely tightening the Allen screw.

The only challenge was to saw off the lugs without scratching the collar. A felt marker capped off the job, and the improvement is worth the effort.

—— *Scott van Linge (1999)*

SCOTT VAN LINGE

An LMI Dremel router base, designed by Bishop Cochran, with Scott van Linge's alteration. Originally the two lugs and bolt seen in the foreground were used to clamp the lower end of the Dremel tool into the base. They were sawn from the dark area immediately above the Dremel's collet in order to improve the line of sight to the bit. The mounting collar, which the lugs used to clamp in place, is now permanently secured with epoxy.

■ After a couple of years of collecting tools that were useful for lutherie work, I ended up with four large cigar boxes full of specialized tools. Digging through a cigar box filled with sharp tools to find the right one was often hazardous. Obviously, I needed a good tool box to hold my treasures. Commercial wooden tool boxes were too expensive, and I was afraid metal drawers would damage the tool edges. Eventually, I found a plastic toolbox made by Rubbermaid that was almost perfect.

H.H. "HAM" ROBERTS

My toolbox is a Rubbermaid Model #7714 and was priced at $17.77 at a local national home center. The color is bright yellow. The box is about 8″ wide by 20″ long and almost 10″ high. Its two stacking trays lift out together. In the photograph there is a 12″ ruler lying across one of the trays to give you an idea of the scale. There is plenty of room in the bottom for fretting hammers and larger tools. There is also a larger model, #7716, that is black in color and priced at $19.77. The box closes tightly to keep dust out, and has two large hasps and a lock ring to keep the lid shut. When I use the tools, I just unstack the trays and place them in front of the box. All my hand tools are accessible in an area that measures 19″×24″.

—— *Glenn Uhler (1997)*

■ In an attempt to come up with a good way to measure and cut accurate fret slots for odd scale lengths, the automotive person lurking in my brain shouted "micrometer!" With that in mind, I worked out a fixture to cut fret slots using an older 9″ DeWalt radial arm saw.

Fret-Slotting Jig with Micrometer Adjusting Table

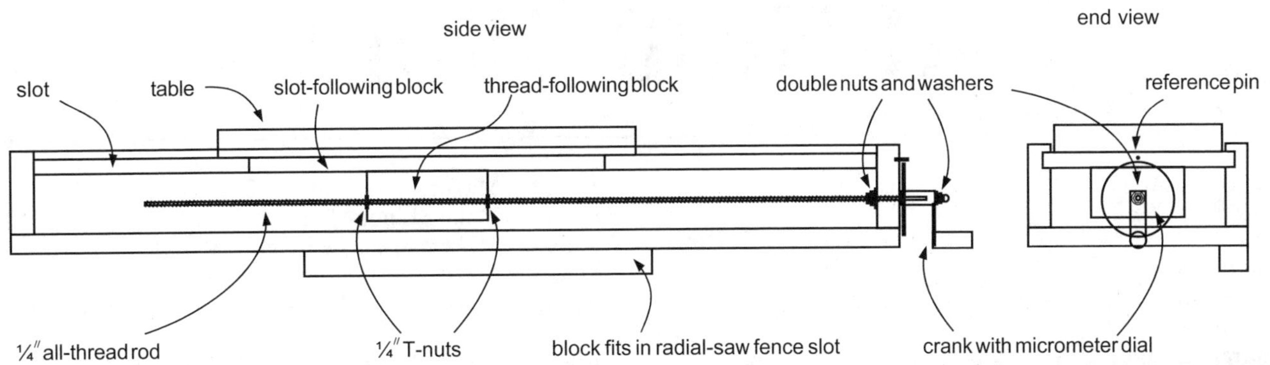

The jig consists of a long, narrow, stationary box with a traveling table which can be moved along the length of the box with measured accuracy by turning an indexed crank. The table is half the length of the box, and the box is long enough to allow the table to move the required distance. For instance, if the fixture is to be used for a bass-guitar fretboard with a 34″ scale length and twenty-four frets, the table needs to be 25½″ long (the distance from the nut to the 24th fret), and needs to be able to travel 25½″.

The table is mounted on a carriage that slides in grooves cut in the inside walls of the box. The table is moved by turning a crank which is attached to a length of ¼″×20 all-thread rod. The rod passes through a thread-following block which is attached to the underside of the table's carriage. One full turn of the rod moves the table .050″, and twenty turns moves it 1″. A dial with fifty equally-spaced marks is attached to the rod's crank, and a pin in the end of the box serves as a reference point for the dial. This allows control of the movement of the table in increments of .001″. To maintain accuracy, there must be no end play in the all-thread rod and no slop between the rod and the thread follower that drives the table. Rod end play can be controlled by using double nuts and flat washers where the rod goes through the crank and the crank end of the box. The threaded follower is made installing ¼″×20 T-nuts in opposite ends of a hole drilled through a wood block. The T-nuts are spaced to create enough interference to eliminate slop, but still allowing the rod to thread through both nuts. There must also be a good fit between the table's carriage and the slots that it slides in to keep the table from unwanted movement.

A piece of wood shaped to fit into the saw's work table in place of the fence is attached to the underside of the box. This positions the box perpendicular to the blade when the saw is in the cross-cut position. The fretboard to be slotted is attached to the table with double-stick tape. The saw blade (Stewart-MacDonald's #1557) cuts a .023″ kerf. The depth of cut is set using the radial saw's controls. A slow, steady cut makes an accurate kerf, but pulling the blade through the wood too quickly can cause the blade to distort, making the kerf a bit wide. If a wider kerf is desired for glued-in frets or for a fretwire with a wider

BOTH THIS PAGE BY SAM TUCKER

tang, the table can be stopped a few thousands of an inch short of a fret-position's centerline for one cut, and then moved an equal distance past and a second cut made. In this way the width of the kerf can be very accurately controlled.

When I first made this fixture, I set it up to use with a miter box, cutting slots by hand with a backsaw, so the micrometer-adjustment feature can be used even if you don't own a radial arm saw.

— *Stan Tucker (1999)*

AUTHOR INDEX

TOPIC INDEX

Philosophy

Physics, guitar

Physics, violin

Plans

Repair, crack

Tuners and tuning pegs

Tuning, temperament, intonation

Ukulele

Violin

Wood, selection